Dedication

This book is dedicated to all those practicing the art of hospitality — especially with travelers. Our world is a happier and more peaceful place because of their efforts and creativity.

Acknowledgements

Corinne, George, Ione, Ralph, Tommie, Bonnie and Flora for your help, love, and support—thank you.

Edited by: The Editorial Staff at LanierBB: Shannon Holl, Kelly McRae.

To my friends who were so generous with their time and skills:

Nicole Day, Courtney Keeney, Gini Rhoda, Justina Long-Am, Laurence Blanchette, Eduard Phipps-Bennett, Venetia Young, Carol McBride, Marianne Barth, Vincent Yu, Madelyn Furze, Rus Quon, Terry Lacey, John Garrett, Chris Manley, Mary Kreuger, Mr. Wiley, Adele Novelli, Mrs. Gieselman (the best English teacher ever), Mary Institute, Ingrid Head, Sumi Timberlake, Marvin Downey, Marguerite Tafoya, Peggy Dennis, Judy Jacobs, Derek Ng, Katherine Bertolucci, Margaret Callahan, Mary Ellen Callahan, Mariposa Valdés, Hal Hershey, Leslie Chan, Jane Foster, Carolyn Strange, Carrie Johnson, Sally Carpenter, Mary Flynn, Karen Aaronson, Fara Richardson, Gillian Pelham, Rachel Cullen, Byron Whitlock, Troy Arnold, Valerie O'Brien, Cliff Burdick, Chelsea Patocchi, Ruth Wilson, Janet Jenkins, Megan Cole, Miles Mattison, Stephen High, Lucius Bono, Rafe Magnuson, Staci Van Wyk, Melody Stewart, Russell Rottkamp, Steve Kelez, Molly Craig, Amber Janke, Vivian Sturdavant, Katrina Daniels, Zack Gold, and Melissa Miranda.

Special thanks to Richard Paoli and George Young.

To the great folks in the Chambers of Commerce, State and Regional Departments of Tourism, I am most grateful.

To the innkeepers themselves who are so busy, yet found the time to fill out our forms and provide us with all sorts of wonderful information, I wish you all the greatest success.

Pamela Lanier's

BED & BREAKFASTS,
INNS AND GUESTHOUSES
INTERNATIONAL

Dreams do come true at B&B's Around the World

Your gift with purchase of this
guidebook to
Bed & Breakfasts, Inns
& Guesthouses International:

This certificate entitles the bearer to a
free night, with the purchase of one or more nights,
at any one of the participating B&B inns.

Valid through May 31, 2012
Certificate must be attached to the guidebook

See page xv for complete list of participating inns.

This section must be completed by the lodging property
when the certificate is accepted and redeemed.
Innkeepers and Guests, please read the terms and conditions below.

Name of Guest:

Name of B&B Inn:

Signature of Innkeeper

Innkeepers, please mail back the redeemed certificate to Lanier Publishing. All redeemed certificates will count as one vote towards Inn of the Year for your property. Please mail to:

> Lanier Publishing
> P.O. Box 2240
> Petaluma, CA 94953
> Attn: Dreams Do Come True Awards

PARTICIPATION TERMS AND CONDITIONS

This Certificate is good for one free consecutive night with the purchase of one or more nights at the B&B's regular rate. The offer not valid at all times, so please contact the B&B in advance for availability, rate, reservations, cancellation policies and other B&B requirements, terms, and conditions. This offer is valid only at specially marked, participating B&B Inns featured. This offer is generate not valid at most B&B's during holidays and requires a minimum of a two-night stay. Reservation requirements vary from property to property, so please check with the individual inn for applicable details. Each individual certificate is valid for no more than 2 people and no more than 1 room. Other restrictions regarding occupancy may also apply. Bed tax, sales tax, and gratuities are not included. Lanier Publishing International is not responsible for any changes in B&B Inn operations or policies, each of which can change without notice. This certificate may not be reproduced and cannot be used in conjunction with any other promotional offers unless specifically authorized by the B&B itself. The certificate must be redeemed no later than May 31, 2012.

This Certificate has no cash value and is redeemable only for the offer described above.

What they're saying about

The Complete Guide to Bed & Breakfasts, Inns & Guesthouses ...

... all necessary information about facilities, prices, pets, children, amenities, credit cards and the like. Like France's Michelin ...

— New York Times

Definitive and worth the room in your reference library.

— Los Angeles Times

... innovative and useful ...

—Washington Post

A must for the adventurous ... who still like the Hobbity creature comforts.
— St. Louis Post-Dispatch

What has long been overdue: a list of the basic information of where, how much and what facilities are offered at the inns and guesthouses.
— San Francisco Examiner

Standing out from the crowd for its thoroughness and helpful cross- indexing ...
—Chicago Sun Times

A quaint, charming and economical way to travel—all in one book.
— Waldenbooks (and USA Today)

Little descriptions provide all the essentials: romance, historical landmarks, golf/fishing, gourmet food, or, just as important, low prices. Take your pick!
— National Motorist

For those travelling by car, lodging is always a main concern ... The Complete Guide to Bed & Breakfasts, Inns & Guesthouses provides listings and descriptions of more than 2,500 inns.
— Minneapolis Star & Tribune

... the most complete compilation of bed and breakfast data ever published.
—Denver Post

Unique and delightful inns ...
— Detroit Free Press

www.TravelGuideS.com has been awarded the Yahoo! Gold Star and named Best Bed and Breakfast Site on the Internet.

Come visit us for in-depth B&B information, a valuable guide to most U.S. cities, thousands of blue-ribbon inn recipes and much more. TravelGuideS.com offers you the best information on worldwide lodgings, maps, weather and reservations, all in one beautiful and fun-to-use site!

Wishing you
Sweet Dreams

THE COMPLETE GUIDE TO

BED &
BREAKFASTS,
INNS & GUESTHOUSES

IN THE UNITED STATES, CANADA, & WORLDWIDE

PAMELA LANIER

YAHOO!® **Internet Life's Gold Star Sites:** | **BEST BED & BREAKFAST GUIDE**

Pamela Lanier's **www. TravelGuideS.com**

❝Cozy and charming, a bed-and-breakfast inn can be a refreshing change of pace from staying in a hotel. Whatever your destination, Pamela Lanier's site covers small inns around the world with a personal touch. Besides searching by geography, you can specify whether you're looking for a family place or a romantic getaway, select such amenities as historic locale or vegetarian food, and even limit your choice to B&Bs that you can book online. Most inn pages feature a photo and links to a map. Some even tell you which room is the best in the house, so you know what to ask for.❞

Visit our websites: *www.LanierBB.com*
www.TravelGuideS.com
Email: *Lanier@TravelGuideS.com*

Other Books By Pamela Lanier

Bed and Breakfast, Australia's Best
All-Suite Hotel Guide
Elegant Small Hotels
Elegant Hotels—Pacific Rim
B&B Guide for Food Lovers
B&B Getaways in the South
Condo Vacations: The Complete Guide
Family Travel & Resorts
Golf Resorts: The Complete Guide
22 Days in Alaska
Cinnamon Mornings & Chocolate Dreams
Cinnamon Mornings & Savory Nights

For special editions of the Guide for your business, or any other business opportunity, contact **bizdev@travelguides.com**

For further information, please contact:

The Complete Guide to Bed & Breakfasts,
    Inns and Guesthouses
PO Box 2240
Petaluma, CA 94953

© 2011 by Lanier Publishing Int., Ltd.
All rights reserved. Published 2011
2011 edition. First printing – 1982

ISBN 978-0-9843766-8-1

Distributed to the book trade by:
    National Book Network
    15200 NBN Way, Bldg. B
    Blue Ridge Summit, PA 21264-2188
    website: nbnbooks.com   *tel.* 1-800-462-6420

Cover by Laura Lamar

Typeset by John Richards

Printed in USA

Rated #1
GUIDEBOOK
by Innkeepers
nationwide

In a nationwide survey of innkeepers conducted by *Innsider Magazine*

Contents

Inns of The Year ⤳ Honor Roll

2010	Heartstone Inn & Cottages, Eureka Spgs, AR
2009	Amid Summer's Inn B&B, Cedar City, UT
2008	Devonfield Country Inn B&B, Lee, MA
2007	Tyee Lodge Oceanfront B&B, Newport, OR
2006	The Daughter's Inn, Napa, CA
2005	Amoré by the Sea B&B, Victoria, BC
2004	Cornerstone Victorian, Warrensburg, NY
2003	The Boothby Inn, Erie, PA
2002	Rosewood Inn, Bradford, NH
2001	Candlelite Inn, Bradford, NH
2000	Albergo Allegria, Windham, NY
1999	Black Friar Inn, Bar Harbor, ME
1998	Calico Inn, Sevierville, TN
1997	Legacy, Williamsburg, VA
1996	Chicago Pike Inn, Coldwater, MI
1995	Williamsburg Sampler, Williamsburg, VA
1994	Cap. Freeman, Brewster, MA
1993	Whalewalk Inn, Eastham, MA
1992	Lamplight Inn, Lake Luzerne, NY
1991	Kedron Valley Inn, S. Woodstock, VT
1990	The Veranda, Senoia, GA
1989	Wedgwood, New Hope, PA
1988	Seacrest Manor, Rockport, MA
1987	Governor's Inn, Ludlow, VT
1986	Carter House, Eureka, CA
1985	Joshua Grindle, Mendocino, CA

2011 INN OF THE YEAR
Yelton Manor B&B &
The Manor Guest House
South Haven, Michigan

Elaine and Robert, self-described "corporate escapees," began scheming about opening a bed and breakfast in the early 80s although neither one had ever stayed in a B&B! They wanted to create a rich, warm experience, a retreat for mind, body and soul, and they believed that location and luxury were key elements. So they built two spectacular Victorian mansions, side by side, steps to the beach and loaded with unprecedented lodging pleasures.

The Manor has eleven guest rooms, each with private bath, most with Jacuzzi and fireplaces. The Manor Guest House has 6 suites complete with fireplace and Jacuzzi, some with balconies. The inn is famous for its proximity to the beach, huge library (1000s of beautiful books and movies), gorgeous décor, relaxing pleasures, fabulous food and award-winning gardens. Luxury is maintained constantly, with premium bedding, linens and personal products, plus a never-ending focus on absolute cleanliness. Both houses have large, comfortable party parlors full of amusements and cozy nooks on each floor for more private retreats.

Elaine and Robert, serving up their beautiful inn and their individual, personal service to nearly 400,000 guests over the decades, think they have the largest family imaginable!

United States/Canada 2011 Award Winners

BEST OVERALL

INN OF THE YEAR
Yelton Manor B&B & The Manor
Guest House South Haven, MI
INNKEEPERS OF THE YEAR
The Pack House Inn Edenton, NC
MOST ROMANTIC
Gables Inn B&B Hot Springs, AR
BEST AMENITIES
A.G. Thomson House Duluth, MN
MOST INTERNATIONAL
The Irish Inn Ozark, IL

FOOD

BEST OVERALL BREAKFAST
Heartstone Inn & Cottages
Eureka Springs, AR
BEST CUP OF JOE
The Mermaid & The Alligator Key West, FL
BEST COMPLIMENTARY AFTERNOON SNACK
Inn Victoria Chester, VT
BEST AFTERNOON TEA
The Edge of Thyme, A B&B Inn Candor, NY
BEST BAR/PUB
The Historic Fairfield Inn Fairfield, PA
BEST VEGETARIAN FOOD
Chestnut Street Inn Sheffield, IL
BEST CHEF
Mission Oak Inn Henry, IL
BEST SELECTION OF RECIPES
Berry Patch B&B Hershey, PA
BEST RESTAURANT
1906 Pine Crest Inn and
Restaurant Tryon, NC

AMENITIES

MOST COMFORTABLE BED
The Woodstocker Inn Woodstock, VT
BEST TURNDOWN SERVICE
10 Fitch B&B Auburn, NY
BEST ROBES
Stonehurst Place Atlanta, GA
BEST LINENS, COMFORTERS & PILLOWS
Cameron Park Inn B&B Raleigh, NC

LOCATION/ARCHITECTURE

BEST URBAN B&B
Inn on 23rd St. New York City, NY
BEST RURAL B&B
The Bike Lane Inn Templeton, CA
BEST GARDENS
Azaela Inn and Gardens Savannah, GA
BEST POOL
Casa Grandview Luxury Inn, Cottages
& Suites West Palm Beach, FL
BEST WILDLIFE
Homestays at Homestead Eagle River, AK
MOST RUSTIC
Ledford Mill Wartrace, TN
MOST UNIQUE SETTING
Steamboat Inn B&B Mystic, CT
BEST MOUNTAIN VIEW
Elkwood Manor Luxury Bed &
Breakfast Pagosa Springs, CO

BEST SEASIDE SETTING
'By the Sea' Guests B&B &
Suites Dennisport, MA
BEST SUNSET VIEW
Elk Cove Inn & Spa Elk, CA
BEST FOR OUTDOOR SETTING
A Pearson's Pond Luxury Inn &
Adventure Spa Juneau, AK
BEST ARCHITECTURE
1884 Bridgeford House Eureka Springs, AR
BEST BEACH OR SHORELINE NEARBY
Inn at the Park B&B South Haven, MI
BEST FRONT PORCH
Barclay Cottage Bed & Breakfast
Virginia Beach, VA
BEST ANTIQUES
The Rivertown Inn Stillwater, MN
BEST PERIOD RESTORATION
James Ghetty Hotel Gettysburg, PA
BEST OVERALL LOCATION
Carriage House B&B Jefferson, TX

PETS

CUTEST B&B MASCOT
Sobotta Manor B&B Mount Airy, NC
MOST PET FRIENDLY
Phineas Swann B&B Inn
Montgomery Center, VT
BEST FOR HORSE ENTHUSIASTS
The Inn at Westwynd Farm
Hummelstown, PA

ABOUT THE INN

MOST ATTENTIVE STAFF
Casa Bella Inn Pittsfield, VT
BEST FOR ANNIVERSARIES
Copperstone Inn Rockton, IL
BEST FOR WEDDINGS/REUNIONS
The Arlington Inn Arlington, VT
BEST B&B TO MEET OTHER GUESTS
Queen Anne Guest House Galena, IL
BEST FOR SPECIAL OCCASIONS
A Georgian Manner B&B Logan, OH
MOST AFFORDABLE LUXURY
Angel of the Sea Cape May, NJ
BEST FOR RELAXING/UNWINDING
Devonfield Country Inn B&B Lee, MA
BEST BUSINESS SERVICES
Fariview Inn Jackson, MS
BEST ARTWORK
The Villa BB Daytona Beach, FL
BEST GIFT SHOP
Spinnakers Brewpub & Guest
House Victoria, BC
BEST EDUCATIONAL CLASSES
Standford Inn by the Sea - Big
River Lodge Mendocino, CA
BEST FOR HANDICAPPED ACCESSIBILITY
Holden House 1902 B&B
Colorado Springs, CO
BEST SPA SERVICES
Buhl Mansion Guest House &
Spa at Tara Sharon, PA
MOST GREEN CONSCIOUS
Big Mill Bed & Breakfast Williamston, NC

BEST VALUE
Teapot Inn Chino Valley, AZ
MOST LIKELY TO VISIT AGAIN
Los Poblanos Inn Albuquerque, NM
BEST WEBSITE
The Brewster Inn Dexter, ME
BEST SPECIALS OFFERED
Adair Country Inn & Restaurant
Bethlehem, NH
MOST PRIVACY
Lynfred Winery B&B Roselle, IL
BEST THEME
Adobe & Pines Inn Taos, NM
MOST FAMILY FRIENDLY
River House B&B Getaway
Retreat Rockford, IL
BEST HISTORIC INN
Governor's House Inn Charleston, SC
BEST JACUZZI/HOT TUB
Heritage Manor Inn Fennville, MI
BEST DÉCOR
Brampton B&B Inn Chestertown, MD

OUTDOOR ACTIVITIES

BEST NEARBY ACTIVITIES
Amid Summer's Inn B&B Cedar City, UT
**BEST LOCATION FOR WALKING TO SHOPS/
DINING**
Lime Rock Inn Rockland, ME
BEST FOR NEARBY OUTLET MALLS
Through the Grapevine B&B Waterloo, NY
BEST CHANGING OF THE LEAVES
The Yellow House Waynesville, NC

BEST FOR ALL SEASONS
Brewery Gulch Inn Mendocino, CA
BEST FOR HUNTING
Pine Lakes Lodge B&B Salesville, OH
BEST FOR FISHING
Lower Lake Ranch Pine, CO
BEST FOR FARM ACTIVITIES
North End Crossing Barn and Bed Flora, OR
BEST FOR NEARBY HISTORIC SITES
Oasis Guest House Boston, MA
BEST FOR NEARBY MUSEUMS
A Painted Lady Inn Portland, OR
BEST FOR NEARBY NATIONAL PARKS
The Stovall House Country Inn
and Restaurant Sautee, GA
BEST FOR OUTDOOR SPORTS
Washington School Inn Park City, UT
BEST FOR NEARBY GOLF
McConnell Inn Green Lake, WI
BEST FOR NEARBY SPORTS ARENA
Earlystown Manor Boalsburg, PA
BEST FOR SUMMER SPORTS
The First Colony Inn Nags Head, NC
BEST FOR NEARBY WINERY
A Touch of Europe Yakima, WA
BEST FOR WINTER SPORTS
Silver Fork Lodge Salt Lake City, UT
BEST FOR NEARBY THEME PARK
Gregory Inn, LoDo Denver, CO
**BEST FOR NEARBY COLLEGES OR
UNIVERSITIES**
Lehrkind Mansion Bozeman, MT

International 2011 Award Winners

BEST OVERALL

INNKEEPERS OF THE YEAR
Amsterdam B&B Barangay
Amsterdam, Netherlands
MOST ROMANTIC
Los Altos de Eros Tamarindo, Costa Rica
BEST AMENITIES
Umaid Bhawan Jaipur, India

FOOD

BEST CUP OF JOE
Lastingham Grange Lastingham,
England, U.K.
BEST COMPLIMENTARY AFTERNOON SNACK
Picard Beach Cottages
Portsmouth, Dominica
BEST AFTERNOON TEA
Cashel House Hotel County Galway, Ireland
BEST BAR/PUB
Xtabi B&B Negril, Jamaica
BEST CHEF
Mango Beach Inn Marigot Bay, St. Lucia
BEST SELECTION OF RECIPES
Eden Park B&B Mt. Eden, New Zealand
BEST RESTAURANT
Adventure Inn Hotel San Jose, Costa Rica

AMENITIES

MOST COMFORTABLE BED
Dorian House Bath, England, U.K.

BEST TURNDOWN SERVICE
Casa de Leyendas B&B Mazatlan, Mexico
BEST ROBES
Casa Encantada Antigua, Guatemala
BEST LINENS, COMFORTERS & PILLOWS
Pencarrow Queenstown, New Zealand

LOCATION/ARCHITECTURE

BEST URBAN B&B
Tudor Court Hotel London, England, U.K.
BEST RURAL B&B
La Frateria Di Padre Eligio Cetona, Italy
BEST GARDENS
Barrowville Town House Carlow, Ireland
BEST POOL
Podere Salicotto Buonconvento, Italy
MOST RUSTIC
Castello di Ripa d'Orcia
Castiglione d'Orcia, Italy
MOST UNIQUE SETTING
Pura Vida Retreat and Spa
Alajuela, Costa Rica
BEST MOUNTAIN VIEW
La Haut Resort Soufriere, St. Lucia
BEST SEASIDE SETTING
Coral Cove Resort Little Bay, Jamaica
BEST SUNSET VIEW
Casa Amorita Puerto Vallarta, Mexico
BEST FOR OUTDOOR SETTING
Bath Paradise House Hotel
Bath, England, U.K.

BEST ARCHITECTURE
Riad Malika B&B Marrakech, Morocco
BEST BEACH OR SHORELINE NEARBY
Hibiscus Lodge Hotel Ocho Rios, Jamaica
BEST FRONT PORCH
Serenity Sands B&B Corozal, Belize
BEST ANTIQUES
Villa Magdala Bath, England, U.K.
BEST PERIOD RESTORATION
Schloss Haunsperg Oberalm
bei Hallein, Austria
BEST OVERALL LOCATION
Casa Las Piedras Troncones, Mexico

PETS

CUTEST B&B MASCOT
Ascot Parnell Fine Accommodation
Auckland, New Zealand
MOST PET FRIENDLY
The Cariari B&B Ciudad de
Cariari, Costa Rica

ABOUT THE INN

BEST FOR ANNIVERSARIES
Fort Recovery Beachfront Villa & Suites
Hotel Road Town, Tortola BVI
BEST FOR WEDDINGS/REUNIONS
Quinta Maria Cortez Puerto Vallarta, Mexico
BEST B&B TO MEET OTHER GUESTS
Castle Fragsburg Relais and
Chateaux Merano, Italy
BEST FOR SPECIAL OCCASIONS
Hotel Heritage Bruges Brugge, Belgium
MOST AFFORDABLE LUXURY
Casa De Tintori Firenze, Italy
BEST FOR RELAXING/UNWINDING
Riad Karmela Marrakech, Morocco
BEST BUSINESS SERVICES
The Great House Inn Belize City, Belize
BEST ARTWORK
Rote Rose B&B Regensberg, Switzerland
BEST GIFT SHOP
Orquideas Inn Alajuela, Costa Rica
BEST EDUCATIONAL CLASSES
Present Moment Retreat Troncones, Mexico
BEST FOR HANDICAPPED ACCESSIBILITY
Aparthotel Silver Barcelona
Barcelona, Spain
BEST SPA SERVICES
Boutique Hotel Beau-Site Fitness & Spa
B&B Adelboden, Switzerland
MOST GREEN CONSCIOUS
Casa Olea Priego de Cordoba, Spain
BEST VALUE
El Numero 8 Granada, Spain
MOST LIKELY TO VISIT AGAIN
Claridge Hotel Zurich Zurich, Switzerland

BEST WEBSITE
Le Prieuré du Chateau de
Biron Biron, France
BEST SPECIALS OFFERED
High Hope Estate St. Ann's Bay, Jamaica
MOST PRIVACY
Hotel Mocking Bird Hill Port
Antonio, Jamaica
BEST THEME
Casa Del Sol B&B Inn Ajijic, Mexico
MOST FAMILY FRIENDLY
The Barn Liverpool, England, U.K.
BEST HISTORIC INN
The Ambers Auckland, New Zealand
BEST JACUZZI/HOT TUB
Casa Estrella de la Valenciana
Guanajuato, Mexico
BEST DÉCOR
Hotel Britannique Paris, France

OUTDOOR ACTIVITIES

BEST NEARBY ACTIVITIES
Alex's Bed and Breakfast Rome Rome, Italy
**BEST LOCATION FOR WALKING TO SHOPS/
DINING**
B&B Olleros 3000 Buenos Aires, Argentina
BEST CHANGING OF THE LEAVES
Roundwood House Mountrath, Ireland
BEST FOR ALL SEASONS
Sweetfield Manor B&B St. Michael, Barbados
BEST FOR FISHING
Mata Rocks Resort San Pedro Town, Belize
BEST FOR FARM ACTIVITIES
El Moli Siurana d'Emporda, Spain
BEST FOR NEARBY HISTORIC SITES
San Felicissimo Perugia, Italy
BEST FOR NEARBY MUSEUMS
B&B Amsterdam Amsterdam, Netherlands
BEST FOR NEARBY NATIONAL PARKS
Rancho Sak Ol Libertad Puerto
Morelos, Mexico
BEST FOR OUTDOOR SPORTS
Small Hope Bay Lodge Andros, Bahamas
BEST FOR NEARBY GOLF
Casa da Pergola Cascais, Portugal
BEST FOR SUMMER SPORTS
Cerrito Tropical Panama City, Panama
BEST FOR NEARBY WINERY
L'Ancienne Boulangerie Caunes-
Minervois, France
BEST FOR WINTER SPORTS
Flueli Berne, Switzerland
**BEST FOR NEARBY COLLEGES OR
UNIVERSITIES**
Hotel Villa Mirasol San Miguel
de Allende, Mexico

Below is the list of inns that are accepting the Dreams Do Come True certificate. Please contact the B&B in advance for availability, rates, reservations, cancellation policies, and other B&B requirements, terms, and conditions.

Introduction

There was a time, and it wasn't so long ago, when bed and breakfast inns were a rarity in the United States. Travelers made do at a hotel or motel; there was no alternative. The few bed and breakfast inns were scattered across the rural areas of New England and California. They were little known to most travelers; often their only advertisement was by word of mouth.

But in a few short years that has changed, and changed in a way that could only be called dramatic. There has been an explosion in the number of bed and breakfast inns. Today, inns can be found in every state, and often in cities; they have become true alternatives to a chain motel room or the city hotel with its hundreds of cubicles.

This sudden increase in bed and breakfast inns started less than two decades ago when Americans, faced with higher costs for foreign travel, began to explore the back-roads and hidden communities of their own country.

Other factors have influenced the growth and popularity of bed and breakfast inns. Among them, the desire to get away from the daily routine and sameness of city life; the desire to be pampered for a few days; and also the desire to stay in a place with time to make new friends among the other guests.

The restored older homes that have become bed and breakfast inns answer those desires. The setting most often is rural; the innkeepers provide the service—not a staff with name tags—and the parlor is a gathering place for the handful of guests. They are a home away from home.

The proliferation of these inns as an alternative lodging has created some confusion. It's been difficult to find—in one place—up-to-date and thorough information about the great variety of inns.

An effort to collect as much information about as many inns as possible in one book has been overdue. Now that has been remedied. You hold a copy of the result in your hands.

Richard Paoli,
Travel Editor
San Francisco Examiner

How to Use This Guide

Organization

This book is organized with the United States first, alphabetically by state, and within a state, alphabetically by city. The Commonwealth of Puerto Rico and US Virgin Islands are listed within the states. After the United States, Canada is listed alphabetically by province and then city. The Worldwide listings follow, organized by country and within the country by city. Our web site www.lanierbb.com can provide nearby cities and regions.

Three Types of Accommodations

Inn: Webster's defines an inn as a "house built for the lodging and entertainment of travelers." All the inns in this book fulfill this description. Many also provide meals, at least breakfast, although a few do not. Most of these inns have under 30 guestrooms.

Bed and Breakfast: Can be anything from a home with three or more rooms to, more typically, a large house or mansion with eight or nine guest accommodations where breakfast is served in the morning.

Guest House: Private homes welcoming travelers, some of which may be contacted directly but most of which are reserved through a reservation service organization.

Breakfasts

We define a **full breakfast** as one being along English lines, including eggs and/or meat as well as the usual breads, toast, juice, and coffee.

Continental plus is a breakfast of coffee, juice, and choice of several breads and pastry and possibly more.

Continental means coffee, juice, bread or pastry.

If there is a charge for breakfast, then we note it as (fee).

Meals

Some inns serve lunch and dinner or have a restaurant on the premises. Be sure to inquire when making your reservation.

Can We Get a Drink?

Those inns without a license will generally chill your bottles and provide you with set-ups upon request.

Prices

Price range is for double room, double occupancy in U.S. dollars, Canadian dollars, Euros (e), or international currency symbol ($).

Appearing to the right of the price is a code indicating the type of food services available:

BB Breakfast included in quoted rate

EP (European Plan): No meals

MAP (Modified American Plan): Includes breakfast and dinner

AP (American Plan): Includes all three meals

All prices are subject to change. Please be sure to confirm rates and services when you make your reservations.

Payment Methods

Not all establishments accept credit cards; however, if they do, it will be noted as Visa, MC, AmEx, Disc or Most CC. Some inns do accept personal checks. Inquire about the inn's policies.

Ratings

One of the beauties of bed & breakfast travel is the individual nature of each inn, and innkeepers thrive on their independence! Some inns are members of their local, state or national inn association (most of which have membership requirements), and/or are members of or are rated by AAA, Mobil and others. Each of these rating systems relies upon different inspection protocol, membership and evaluative criteria. We use *Rated* in the listings to designate inns which have informed us that they have been rated by or are affiliated with any of these groups. If ratings are important to you, we suggest that you call and inquire of the specific inn for details. We continue to find, however, that some very good inns remain unrated, simply because of their size or idiosyncratic nature.

Reservations

Reservations are essential at most inns, particularly during busy seasons, and are appreciated at other times. When you book, feel free to discuss your requirements and confirm prices, services and other details. We have found innkeepers to be delightfully helpful. Please tell your hosts that Pamela Lanier sent you!

Visit our web site — http://www.lanierbb.com

A deposit or advance payment is required at some inns.

Children, Pets, Smoking, and Handicap Equipped

Children, pets, smoking and physical handicaps present special considerations for many inns. Be sure to inquire when you book your room. Whether or not they can be accommodated is generally noted as follows:

	Yes	Limited	No
Children	C-yes	C-ltd	
Pets	P-yes	P-ltd	P-no
Smoking	S-yes	S-ltd	S-no
Handicap Equipped	H-yes	H-ltd	H-no

Bathrooms

Though shared baths are the norm in Europe, this is sometimes a touchy subject in the U.S.A. We list the number of private baths available directly next to the number of rooms. Bear in mind that those inns with shared baths generally have more than one.

When in accommodations with shared baths, be sure to straighten the bathroom as a courtesy to your fellow guests. If you come in late, please do so on tiptoe, mindful of the other patrons visiting the inn for a little R&R.

Manners

Please keep in mind when you go to an inn that innkeeping is a very hard job. It is amazing that innkeepers manage to maintain such a thoroughly cheerful and delightful presence despite long hours. Do feel free to ask your innkeepers for help or suggestions, but please don't expect them to be your personal servant. You may have to carry your own bags.

Sample Bed & Breakfast Listing

Name of inn
Street address and zip code
Phone numbers
Name of innkeeper

Price and included meals
Numbers of rooms and private baths
Payments accepted
Travel agent commission •
Limitations:
   Children (C), Pets (P)
   Smoking (S), Handicap Equipped (H)
Foreign languages spoken
Open all year unless noted

Name of city or town

Private bath

Extra charge for breakfast

ANYPLACE

Any Bed & Breakfast
Any Street, ZIP code
800-222-2222
Fax: 444-444-4444
555-555-5555
Tom & Jane Innkeeper

75-95 B&B
8 rooms, 6 pb
Visa, MC •
C-yes/S-ltd/P-no/H-ltd
French, Spanish
Closed Feb–Apr

Full breakfast (fee)
Lunch, dinner
sitting room
library, bicycles
antiques

Redeem Certificate: Anytime. Room Upgrade.

Large Victorian country house in historic village. Hiking, swimming and golf nearby. Old-fashioned comfort with modern conveniences.
✉ innkeeper@anyb&b.com 🌐 www.anyb&b.com

Description given by the innkeeper
  about the original characteristics of his
  establishment

Meals and drinks
Amenities

Addresses for e-mail and
web site

Inns that accept the Dreams Do
Come True certificate are shown
in this section

Note about International Phone Numbers: When dialing an international number the + sign indicates that you must dial 011 then the number listed. International properties that have a United States phone number will be displayed as 10 digit numbers and you will only need to enter 1 before calling.

Alabama

ALEXANDER CITY

Mistletoe Bough
497 Hillabee St 35010
256-329-3717
JoAnn & Jesse Frazier

85-120 $US BB
5 rooms, 5 pb
Most CC, Cash
C-yes/S-ltd/P-no/H-no

Full breakfast
Ice tea, hot tea, or lemonade, is
offered. Also, join us for ice cream
sundaes served every night
Air-conditioning, alarm clock, bath
robes, desk, high speed Internet,
radio, and television.

Step back in time to a genteel atmosphere. The Mistletoe Bough Bed & Breakfast is a perfect place to relax and unwind. Walk in the beautiful gardens, sit and relax on the patio, or simply rock on one of the spacious porches.

 mistletoebough@charter.net ❍ www.mistletoebough.com

ASHVILLE

Roses & Lace Bed and Breakfast
20 Rose Lane 35953
205-594-4366
Jim and Suzanne

119-175 $US BB
3 rooms, 3 pb
Visa, MC, Disc
C-ltd/S-ltd/P-no/H-no

Full breakfast
Free WiFi, business services,
weddings and reception services,
beautiful gardens, privacy

Lace at the windows, original stained glass, woodwork and heart pine floors, a wide verandah overlooking the Rose Garden—the Elisha Robinson House combines the exquisite beauty of Queen Anne architecture with the warm hospitality of the old South.

 suzanne@20roselane.com ❍ www.20roselane.com

ATMORE

Royal Oaks B&B
5415 Hwy 21 36502
251-368-8722
Foster Kizer

95 $US BB
3 rooms, 3 pb
Most CC, Cash, Checks
C-yes/S-no/P-yes/H-ltd

Full breakfast
Soft Drinks, Snacks
A/C, WiFi, pool, satellite TV, screened
porches

A French country home that's perfect for a relaxing stay. Settled in a beautiful, southern Alabama town, Royal Oaks offers 2-person apartments with private baths, surrounded by gardens full of flowers and greenery which attracts birds and other wildlife.

 roexit57@aol.com ❍ www.royaloaksbandb.com

FAIRHOPE

Emma's Bay House
202 S Mobile St 36532
251-990-0187
Betty Rejczyk

260-320 $US BB
4 rooms, 4 pb
Most CC
C-ltd/S-no/P-no/H-yes

Full breakfast
High speed Internet, fresh cut flowers,
balconies, seating areas, executive
workspace, coffee, A/C

Experience the relaxing atmosphere and superb amenities that set Emma's apart from other B&Bs. With its spectacular views and beautiful surroundings, Emma's is perfect for romantic getaways, corporate travel, special events and weddings.

 emmasbayhou1458@bellsouth.net ❍ www.emmasbayhouse.com

LEESBURG

The Secret Bed and Breakfast Lodge
2356 AL Highway 68
W 35983
256-523-3825
Diann & Carl Cruickshank

95-165 $US BB
8 rooms, 8 pb
Visa, MC, AmEx,
Rated
S-no/P-no/H-no

Full breakfast
A hearty breakfast is served daily at
9:00 a.m.
Sitting room, Jacuzzis, pool, fireplace,
VCR, private balconies, views

Perched atop Lookout Mountain lies the secret Bed & Breakfast Lodge – the best kept (secret) in the south! Scenic mountain top lodge overlooks beautiful Weiss Lake and two states. Spectacular view by day, enchanting view by night.

 secret@tds.net ❍ www.bbonline.com/al/thesecret

MONTGOMERY ─────────────────────────────────────

Red Bluff Cottage	110-155 $US BB	Full breakfast
551 Clay St 36104	4 rooms, 4 pb	Wireless Internet, plush towels &
888-551-2529 334-264-0056	Most CC, *Rated*	robes, flowers, iron, lighted parking,
Barry & Bonnie Ponstein	C-yes/S-no/P-no/H-no	porches, gardens, gazebo

Award-winning B&B in the oldest historic neighborhood in Montgomery's Cottage Hill District. This two-story raised cottage offers panoramic views of the river plain and state capitol.

✉ info@redbluffcottage.com ◐ www.redbluffcottage.com

TALLADEGA ─────────────────────────────────────

River Rest, A Bed,	145-250 $US BB	Full breakfast
Breakfast and Beyond	5 rooms, 5 pb	HD-TV, whirlpool tubs, WiFi, fire pit,
3883 Griffitt Bend	Visa, MC, Disc	hammock, boat rides, golf cart
Road 35160	S-no/P-no/H-ltd	
866-670-7378 256-268-0101		
Richard & Ellen Mixon		

On Lake Logan Martin, white sandy beach, 6 decks, king beds, HD-TV in all rooms, 2 mile view of lake and hills. Boat rides, golf carts, spacious and private, most rooms with view, owners are very personable & great food! Y'all Come Back Now!

✉ richard@riverrestbedandbreakfast.com ◐ www.riverrestbedandbreakfast.com

Alaska

ANCHORAGE

Anchorage Jewel Lake B&B
8125 Jewel Lake Rd 99502
877-245-7321 907-245-7321
Troy Roberts

99-250 $US BB
5 rooms, 5 pb
Most CC, •
C-yes/S-no/P-no/H-no

Full or continental breakfast
Teas, wines, snacks & other munchies
Large deck, fireplace, sitting room,
guest kitchen, laundry facility

A wonderful alternative to a busy hotel. We are 3 miles from the Anchorage International Airport. Airline schedules to Anchorage usually mean late night arrivals and early departures, so take advantage of the extra sleep you will gain staying with us!

✉ info@jewellakebandb.com 🌐 www.jewellakebandb.com

Anchorage Walkabout Town
1610 E St 99501
866-279-7808 907-279-7808
Sandra J. Stimson

95-115 $US BB
3 rooms, 2 pb
Most CC, *Rated*, •
C-yes/S-no/P-no/H-no
April-October

Full breakfast
Deck, cable TV, freezer, free laundry,
parking, 4 in a room

Downtown convenience with beautiful park and coastal trail access. Hearty Alaskan breakfast of sourdough waffles and reindeer sausage. Family friendly.

✉ reservations@anchoragewalkabout.com 🌐 www.anchoragewalkabout.com

---

Big Bear Bed & Breakfast
3401 Richmond Ave 99508
907-277-8189
Carol Ross

85-125 $US BB
4 rooms, 4 pb
Visa, MC, Disc, •
C-yes/S-no/P-no/H-no

Full breakfast
Variety of complimentary sodas,
coffees, hot chocolates & teas
Log home, antiques, Alaska art, Native
crafts, private bathrooms, flower
garden w/waterfall & pond.

Log home with unique antiques, Alaska Native art & exceptional breakfasts. Enjoy a taste of the real Alaska with food, surroundings, and old fashioned Alaska hospitality hosted by lifelong Alaskan and retired home economics teacher, Carol Ross.

✉ bigbearbb@alaska.net 🌐 www.alaskabigbearbb.com

Glacier Bear
4814 Malibu Rd 99517
907-243-8818
Cleveland & Belinda Zackery

70-120 $US BB
3 rooms, 3 pb
Visa, MC, *Rated*, •
C-ltd/S-ltd/P-no/H-no

Continental plus breakfast
Complimentary snacks & beverages
Hiking & biking trails, restaurants
nearby, sitting room, 8 person spa

First class accommodations at reasonable rates. Luxurious contemporary home 1.2 miles from the airport & 3 miles to downtown. The rooms of this beautiful inn are decorated with a mix of Oriental and Victorian pieces.

✉ gbearak@gci.com 🌐 www.glacierbearbb.com

BIG LAKE

Alaska Sunset View Resort
5322 S Big Lake Rd 99652
877-892-8885 907-892-8885
Kathy & Newell Glines

150-350 $US BB
11 rooms, 11 pb
Most CC, Cash,
Checks, •
C-yes/S-no/P-no/H-ltd

Full breakfast
Afternoon tea, snacks
Sitting room, Jacuzzis, suites,
fireplaces, TV, washer, dryer, iron,
computer, gym, weddings

Come visit our lakefront resort between Anchorage and Denali National Park, and you may wish you could stay forever. Everything you want is right here with your choice of lodging in either vacation homes or our Bed and Breakfast, the ultimate in luxury.

 stay@alaskasunsetviewresort.com   alaskasunsetviewresort.com

COOPER LANDING

Kenai River Drifters Lodge	145-375 $US BB	Continental breakfast, High Season
Mile 48.3 Sterling Hwy 99572	12 rooms, 7 pb	Fresh baked goods, croissants, fresh
866-595-5959 907-595-5555	Visa, MC, Disc,	fruit, bagels, cereal, juices, brownies,
Bob Rima, Frank Williams	*Rated*, •	restaurants nearby
	C-yes/S-ltd/P-no/H-yes	Awesome views, sauna & nightly
	Some Spanish &	campfire at rivers edge, BBQ's, guided
	German	fishing, rafting, activities

Located at the Headwaters of the world famous Kenai River, enjoy first class riverfront cabins with incredible views of the Kenai River and Chugach Mountains. Known for the abundance of recreational opportunities, Cooper Landing is a destination for all.
✉ lodgemail@arctic.net 🌐 www.drifterslodge.com

EAGLE RIVER

Homestays at Homesteads	85-150 $US BB	Full breakfast
1711 South Creek 99503	3 rooms, 1 pb	Afternoon tea, snacks, kitchen
907-272-8644	•	privileges available by request
Sharon Kelly	C-ltd/S-no/P-ltd/H-no	Take time to enjoy the surroundings
		– on the porch, in front of the fire or
		skiing on our trails

Free Night w/Certificate: Anytime. Limits to 1 room a night or 2 guests

Surrounded by wilderness, this secluded valley is 10 miles from Anchorage and 7 miles from the highway. "Heaven Crest" accesses hiking & ski trails back valley to 2 glaciers, a year-round stream, and when visible, perfect views of Denai. ✉ aaatours@ptialaska.net

FAIRBANKS

2 Kings Country B&B	79-139 $US BB	Delicious hot breakfast
3714 Mitchell Ave 99709	4 rooms, 2 pb	Business traveler accommodations,
907-479-2570	Visa, MC, Disc,	WiFi, TV in all rooms
Sylvia King	*Rated*, •	
	C-yes/S-ltd/P-no/H-no	

Enjoy pioneer Alaskan hospitality. Experience our garden setting, the four quality, cozy and comfortable rooms and a delicious hot breakfast. A full kitchen, TV/DVD/VCR, wireless Internet, laundry facilities and private entrance all for your convenience.
✉ kingscountry@gci.net 🌐 www.kingscountrybb.net

7 Gables Inn & Suites	55-180 $US BB	Full gourmet breakfast
4312 Birch Ln 99708	30 rooms, 30 pb	Complimentary refreshments
907-479-0751	Visa, MC, AmEx,	Wireless Internet throughout; library,
Paul & Leicha Welton	*Rated*, •	cable/DVD, fireplaces, Jacuzzis,
	C-yes/S-ltd/P-ltd/H-yes	canoes
	Spanish, German	

Luxury accommodations at affordable rates. Our rooms and suites have private baths with Jacuzzi tubs, cable TV/VCRs. A full gourmet breakfast is included in the room rates.
✉ gables7@alaska.net 🌐 www.7gablesinn.com

Dale & Jo View Suites	124-189 $US BB	Full breakfast
3260 Craft ave 99709	4 rooms, 4 pb	Vegetarian options available, extensive
907-456-6838	Visa, MC	breakfast menu
Dale & Jo	C-yes/S-no/P-no/H-ltd	Suites have kitchens and dining
		rooms, in room thermostats, privacy,
		amazing views, laundry, WiFi

Located on Chena Ridge (West Fairbanks)with panoramic mountain and rivers views, Dale and Jo View Suites B&B offers you luxury accommodations chosen for comfort and pampering.
✉ daleandjo_ak@yahoo.com 🌐 www.daleandjo.com

Fox Creek B&B	68-128 $US BB	Full Alaskan-style Breakfast
1.1 Mile Elliott 99712	2 rooms, 1 pb	Historic, quiet, secluded, setting.
907-457-5494	*Rated*, •	sitting room, deck, spacious rooms,
Arna King-Fay & Jeff Fay	C-yes/S-ltd/P-yes/H-no	family friendly facility

Modern Alaskan-style home. Located in a quiet, secluded setting in historic Fox, Alaska. Just 12 miles from Fairbanks. Frequent northern lights, aurora and wildlife sightings. Lifelong Alaskan proprietors are your hosts. ✉ pam@foxcreekalaska.com 🌐 www.foxcreekalaska.com

Denali EarthSong Lodge, Healy, AK

HAINES

The Summer Inn B&B	70-130 $US BB	Full homemade breakfast
117 Second Ave 99827	5 rooms	Tea & cookies in the afternoon
907-766-2970	Visa, MC, •	Comfortable, spacious living room
Jenty Fowler & Mary Ellen	C-yes/S-no/P-no/H-no	with Alaskan book collection, porch
Summer		

Charming, historic 5 bedroom house overlooking Lynn Canal. Celebrating our 24th year of innkeeping in 2011! Walking distance to sites of Haines, Chilkat Valley Bald Eagle Preserve and Glacier Bay.

✉ innkeeper@summerinnbnb.com   🌐 www.summerinnbnb.com

HEALY

Denali Dome Home B&B	110-190 $US BB	Hardy, full Alaskan breakfasts
12 miles north of Denali	7 rooms, 7 pb	Coffees, teas, juices & homemade
National Park 99743	Visa, MC, Disc,	snacks
800-683-1239 907-683-1239	*Rated*, •	Car rental; Rock fireplace; libraries;
Ann & Terry Miller	C-yes/S-no/P-no/H-yes	decks; free, paved parking; Jacuzzi;
	Spanish, Russian,	Wifi; office; 5 acres.
	Alaskan	

Located 12 miles north of Denali National Park, Denali Dome Home is the longest established bed and breakfast in the Denali area. The Millers are keenly aware of area's best attractions and best restaurants. Their service is professional and personal.

✉ info@denalidomehome.com   🌐 www.denalidomehome.com

Denali EarthSong Lodge	155-195 $US EP	Breakfast, espresso bar, packaged
Mile 4 Stampede Rd 99743	12 rooms, 12 pb	lunches, light dinner menu, snacks,
907-683-2863	Visa, MC, *Rated*, •	drinks to purchase
Karin & Jon Nierenberg	C-yes/S-no/P-no/H-no	Staff Naturalist, Sled Dog Kennel tours,
	May through September	Coffeehouse, Diva's Gift shop, WiFi,
		sitting area with view

Denali's secluded alternative to the commercial park experience. Lovely wilderness lodge with 12 log cabins, private baths and many added amenities. Sled Dog Kennel tours, winter dog sled adventures, staff naturalist, gift shop, coffeehouse. Near Denali.

✉ info@earthsonglodge.com   🌐 www.earthsonglodge.com

HEALY

Denali Touch of	125-198 $US BB	Breakfast Bar Buffet
Wilderness B&B Inn	9 rooms, 9 pb	Complimentary hot beverages, bag
2.9 Stampede Rd 99743	Most CC, Cash,	lunches available
800-683-2459 907-683-2459	*Rated*, •	Sitting room, fireplaces, fax, WiFi,
Barbara & Daniel Claspill	C-yes/S-no/P-no/H-yes	kitchenette, snack & gift shop, hot tub

Denali Touch of Wilderness Inn invites you to experience Alaskan hospitality. Experience the comfort from your choice of 9 beautifully decorated rooms. Delicious full breakfast included.

✉ barb.denalitouchow@gmail.com   🌐 www.touchofwildernessbb.com

HOMER

Alaska Adventure Cabins	245-395 $US EP	Fully equipped kitchen with coffee for
2525 Sterling Hwy 99603	14 rooms, 14 pb	1st & 2nd morning, spices for cooking
866-287-1530 907-223-6681	Visa, MC, Disc, •	your catch
Bryan Zak	C-yes/S-no/P-no/H-ltd	Decks, greenhouse, living rooms

The privacy of your own deluxe cabin, rail car or ship with a spectacular view overlooking Homer, Alaska. Kitchens, decks, satellite TV. Glaciers, Homer Spit, Kachemak Bay, Cook Inlet.

✉ info@alaskaadventurecabins.com 🌐 www.alaskaadventurecabins.com

Alaska Beach House	99-259 $US BB	Continental breakfast
1121 Seabreeze Court 99603	5 rooms, 5 pb	Hot tub overlooking the bay, wireless
907-235-3232	Visa, MC, •	Internet, BBQ on deck, cable TV in
Doug & Sue Alaniva	C-ltd/S-no/P-no/H-no	every room
	Closed October-April	

Lodging located on the edge of the water. Beach front views, of glaciers and Homer Spit. Hot tub on the bluff and deck over the water, and beach access near. Deluxe rooms. Close to town and the Homer Spit.

✉ homerbeachhouse@gmail.com 🌐 www.homerbnb.com

Halcyon Heights	95-195 $US BB	Full hosted breakfast
1200 Mission Road 99603	5 rooms, 5 pb	Tea, Snacks,
877-376-4222 907-235-2148	Most CC, Cash,	Large decks, BBQ Stove. Wireless
	Checks, •	Internet. Hottub with glacier & bay
	C-ltd/S-no/P-no/H-no	view. Piano. Family Suite.
	Some Spanish, Chinese	

Perched on East Hill in Homer, Alaska, this proud Alaska Bed and Breakfast/Inn will thrill you with its views of the famous Homer Spit, Kachemak Bay, the Grewingk Glacier, the Kenai Mountains, Homer itself, and more! ✉ info@halcyonheightsbandb.com 🌐 www.homerbb.com

JUNEAU

A Cozy Log B&B	125-155 $US BB	Full breakfast
8668 Dudley St 99801	2 rooms	Complimentary tea, snacks & wine
907-789-2582	Visa, MC, Disc, *Rated*	Guests services include free WiFi,
Judy & Bruce Bowler	C-ltd/S-no/P-ltd/H-ltd	wood stove, cable TV/VCR/DVD, and
		local information

A top rated B&B in a civilized wilderness. Imagine yourself in a log home in Alaska, looking out on the forest, with a warm woodstove & local delights like blueberry pancakes and smoked salmon for breakfast.

✉ cozylog@alaska.net 🌐 www.cozylog.net

A Pearson's Pond Luxury	149-799 $US BB	Continental plus breakfast
Inn & Adventure Spa	8 rooms, 8 pb	Afternoon snacks/tea, hospitality
4541 Sawa Circle 99801	Most CC, Cash,	hour, packed lunch & dinner catering
888-658-6328 907-789-3772	*Rated*, •	available for add'l fee.
Maryann Ray	C-ltd/S-no/P-no/H-no	Hot tubs, sauna, fireplaces, bikes,
		BBQs, kayaks/boats, WiFi, massage,
		gym, wedding/tour planning

Free Night w/Certificate: Anytime.

Casual elegance, exciting activities & magical master-planned gardens. Perfect for adventure, honeymoon, wedding, romance & business travel. Alaska's only AAA 4-Diamond Resort. Complete Alaska Wedding & Trip Planning services. Packages available.

✉ pearsonspond@gci.net 🌐 www.pearsonspond.com

Alaska's Capital Inn	99-339 $US BB	Full breakfast
113 W 5th St 99801	7 rooms, 7 pb	Afternoon treats, bottomless cookie jar
888-588-6507 907-586-6507	Most CC, *Rated*, •	and refreshments.
Linda Wendeborn & Mark	C-ltd/S-no/P-no/H-ltd	Outdoor hot tub. Tour reservations.
Thorson		Wedding Commissioner. Planning and
		catering. Champagne/flowers.

Experience turn-of-the-century elegance with contemporary comfort when you spend the night at this award-winning hillside mansion. Located in Juneau's historic district, everything is a short walk away.

✉ innkeeper@alaskacapitalinn.com 🌐 www.alaskacapitalinn.com

KETCHIKAN

Black Bear Inn	100-225 $US BB	Continental plus breakfast
5528 North Tongass	6 rooms, 6 pb	Snacks and drinks are always
Highway 99901	Most CC, Cash, Checks,	provided in the Bed and Breakfast.
907-225-4343	*Rated*, •	Fireplaces, TV's with DVD/VCR
James & Nicole Church	C-ltd/S-ltd/P-ltd/H-ltd	players, refrigerators, cable TV &
		wireless Internet, spa, laundry.

Ketchikan's Finest Waterfront B&B and Vacation Rentals. We can accommodate our guests with anything from a one-bedroom with private bath rental to an entire house Vacation Rental. Our Elegant Rooms / Fireplaces and Covered Porches Overlooking the Ocean.

✉ blackbearalaska@aol.com   🌐 www.stayinalaska.com

Corner B&B	100-145 $US BB	Continental plus breakfast
3870 Evergreen Ave 99901	1 rooms, 1 pb	Breakfast consists of fresh baked
907-225-2655	*Rated*, •	muffins or Alaska size biscuits, fresh
Carolyn & Win Wilsie	C-yes/S-ltd/P-no/H-ltd	fruit, yogurt & juice
		Kitchen, living room, private
		bathroom, queen beds, twin roll-away
		available, two TV's, DVD/VCR

Fully equipped, one bedroom suite. Completely private. No stairs. Private phone and bath. Two TVs, DVD/VCR. Clean and comfortable. One block to bus. Friendly hosts on site.

✉ cjwilsie@KPUNET.net   🌐 www.cornerbnb.com

PALMER

Tara Dells B&B	80-100 $US BB	Full breakfast
4504 N Heaton 99645	5 rooms, 2 pb	Free Wireless Internet, Sun room,
800-745-0407 (in AK)	C-yes/S-no/P-yes/H-yes	facilities for infants, TV, VCR &
907-745-0407		telephone, laundry facilities
Andy & Donel Dowling		

Located in the Hatcher Pass area of the Matanuska-Susitna Valley just one hour from the Anchorage airport. Five wooded acres near Wasilla Creek make the perfect Alaska setting.

✉ stay@taradells.com   🌐 www.taradells.com

SELDOVIA

Seldovia Rowing Club B&B	100-135 $US BB	Full breakfast
Bay Street 99663	2 rooms, 2 pb	Lunch, dinner by request
907-234-7614	Visa, MC, •	Bicycles, boating, sea kayaks, skiffs
Susan J. Mumma	C-yes/S-no/P-ltd/H-no	
	Spanish, French	

Private unit in historic home on Old Sedovia Boardwalk overlooks waterfront, can accommodate a family. Excellent service, cuisine; close to points of interest.

✉ seldrowclub@gmail.com   🌐 seldoviarowingclub.net/rowingclub.html

SEWARD

Angels Rest on	69-259 $US EP	Kitchenette:sm fridge, toaster,
Resurrection Bay, LLC	7 rooms, 7 pb	microwave, coffee maker, BBQ grill,
13730 Beach Drive, Lowell	Visa, MC	coffee, tea, sugar, half-and-half, ice
Point 99664	C-yes/S-no/P-ltd/H-yes	FREE hi-speed WiFi on site, AK
907-491-7378 907-224-7378		reading materials, AK DVDs,
Lynda & Paul Paquette		binoculars, free parking, tour
		bookings.

This lodging is among the nicest places to stay anywhere! And the cleanest! Experience heavenly relaxation in these charming, modern cabins and view rooms, that sit on the beautiful shores of Resurrection Bay, Seward Alaska. Wildlife & scenery are amazing

✉ guest.services@angelsrest.com   🌐 www.angelsrest.com

SEWARD

Bear's Den B&B and Lodging
221 Bear Drive 99664
800- 232-7099 907-224-3788
Richard & Shareen
Adelmann & Family

85-185 $US BB
3 rooms, 3 pb
Visa, MC, •
C-yes/S-ltd/P-no/H-ltd
April to October

Hearty continental breakfast
Coffee & tea
Flat screen TV in Den, vcr, dvd,
movies, WiFi, gas grill, patio/deck,
private entries, extras,

Comfort & relaxation await you at Bear's Den B&B and lodging. With three dens to choose from, our goal is to provide the perfect lodging choice for your visit to Seward. Honeymooners, business travelers and families will find what they need at Bear's Den.

✉ innkeeper@bearsdenalaska.com ◯ www.bearsdenalaska.com

Brass Lantern B&B
331 2nd Ave 99664
907-224-3419 907-224-3419
Maureen Lemme

95-150 $US BB
1 rooms, 1 pb
Visa, MC, Disc, •
C-yes/S-no/P-no/H-ltd

Continental breakfast
Welcome basket, coffee & teas
TV, DVD, CD, radio, coffee pot,
microwave, stove, refrigerator,
propane grill, deck & patio, WiFi

Whether you're after holiday adventure or a quiet escape from the world, Brass Lantern B&B is your haven. Rest, relax and retreat. ✉ brasslanternbandb@yahoo.com ◯ www.brasslanternbandb.com

---

Harmony B&B
2411 Spruce St 99664
907-224-3661 907-224-3661
Michael & Karen Vander
Vegt

125-135 $US BB
3 rooms, 3 pb
Visa, MC, Disc
C-yes/S-no/P-no/H-no

Continental breakfast
Coffee, tea, hot chocolate, at all hours
Cable TV, WiFi , private baths, Private
entrances & decks

Harmony B&B is peacefully nestled in the Forest Acres neighborhood, located 1 mile north of the harbor. Private rooms tastefully decorated with full baths & cable TV. A generous continental breakfast will get the day started deliciously!

✉ harmonybnb@arctic.net ◯ www.harmonybedandbreakfast.com

SITKA

Alaska Ocean View Bed & Breakfast Inn
1101 Edgecumbe
Drive 99835
888-811-6870 907-747-8310
Carole & Bill Denkinger

89-199 $US BB
3 rooms, 3 pb
Most CC, *Rated*, •
C-ltd/S-no/P-no/H-ltd

Full and continental plus available
Snacks, popcorn, cookies, candy, nuts,
chocolates, mints, snack mix, herbal,
teas, coffee
Concierge, library, robes, hot tub spa,
fireplace, WiFi, free-movies, guest
computer, Wii/Fit, fax

Free Night w/Certificate: Anytime. Subject to availability during peak season.

Western red cedar executive home in scenic setting. Walk to beach, wilderness trails, shopping, attractions and historic sites. Wonderful amenities in casual, relaxed setting with king and queen size beds.

✉ info@sitka-alaska-lodging.com ◯ www.sitka-alaska-lodging.com

SOLDOTNA

Longmere Lake Lodge
35955 Ryan Ln 99669
907-262-9799
Chuck & Leora Gibbons

120-290 $US BB
6 rooms, 6 pb
Visa, MC, •
C-yes/S-no/P-no/H-no

Hearty breakfast
Sunday continental breakfast
Beautiful lakeside setting, fishing,
meetings & groups welcome, WiFi,
room with Jacuzzi

Picturesque lake setting, immaculate facilities, and warm service by born and raised Alaskan hosts have given our lodge a strong reputation. ✉ bblodge@ptialaska.net ◯ www.longmerelakelodge.com

TALKEETNA

Grace & Bill's Freedom Hills B&B
22046 S Freedom
Drive 99676
888-703-2455 907-733-2455
Bill & Grace Germain

120-140 $US BB
5 rooms, 3 pb
Visa, MC, •
C-yes/S-no/P-no/H-no
Filipino

Full & Continental
Kitchen, sun deck

Bed and breakfast in Talkeetna, AK with a great view of the Alaska range (Foraker, Hunter and Mt. McKinley). Enjoy accommodations at our B&B with spectacular view of Denali, clean and comfortable lodging, and a hearty full breakfast. ✉ gmgermain@att.net ◯ www.gbfreedomhillsbb.com

TALKEETNA

Meandering Moose Lodging
14677 E Cabin Spike Ave 99676
907-733-1000
Kathy Stoltz

60-150 $US BB
7 rooms, 5 pb
Visa, MC
C-yes/S-no/P-no/H-no

Light Continental breakfast
4 private cabins, shuttle service, free WiFi

While in Talkeetna Alaska you will find Lodging in our log cabins or B&B suites or rooms to serve as your base camp. Our accommodations will make a great jumping off point for all your memorable Alaska winter or summer vacation adventures.

✉ info@meandering-moose-lodging.com 🌐 www.talkeetna-alaska-lodging.com/index.html

Talkeetna Roadhouse
13550 E. Main Street 99676
907-733-1351
Trisha Costello

21-140 $US EP
7 rooms
Most CC, Cash,
Checks, •
C-yes/S-no/P-ltd/H-ltd

Breakfast, bakery, soups, beer & wine, pasties, cinnamon rolls, sourdough hotcakes, strong coffee
Private rooms, bunks and cabins.
Coin-op laundry & complimentary WiFi, coffee, tea & cocoa, library

The Roadhouse, built between 1914–17, is one of the oldest establishments in "Beautiful Downtown Talkeetna." Our kitchen is open to the public, we've become famous for breakfast, hearty soups, homestyle baking, genuine frontier hospitality and cozy rooms.

✉ reservations@talkeetnaroadhouse.com 🌐 www.talkeetnaroadhouse.com

VALDEZ

Downtown B&B Inn
113 Galena Dr 99686
800-478-2791 907-835-2791
Glen & Sharron Mills

55-110 $US BB
31 rooms, 21 pb
Visa, MC, Disc, •
C-yes/S-no/P-ltd/H-yes

Continental plus breakfast
Afternoon tea
Sitting room, cable TV, accommodate business travelers, free WiFi

Downtown B&B Inn offers travelers excellent accommodations year-round. Cozy and clean rooms, private bathrooms, and great continental breakfasts. Perfect location for those interested in fishing, sightseeing, and glacier tours in Prince William Sound.

✉ 1n2rs@gci.net 🌐 www.valdezdowntowninn.com

WASILLA

Alaska's Lake Lucille B&B
235 West Lakeview Ave 99765
888-353-0352 907-357-0352
Carol Smith

89-189 $US BB
5 rooms, 5 pb
Visa, MC, •
C-yes/S-no/P-no/H-no
German

Choice of Full or Continental
Coffee pot with complimentary coffee, tea & cakes; complimentary popcorn for evening snack
Sitting room, meeting room for 12, lake and mountain views, crafting retreats

Stay at home with us at Lake Lucille B & B and let us provide you with the perfect romantic getaway. You're at home with country charm and a perfect location for crafting and scrap-booking retreats. We'll do all the work for you. ✉ Stay@alaskaslakelucillebnb.com 🌐 www.alaskaslakelucillebnb.com

Pioneer Ridge B&B Inn
2221 Yukon Dr. 99654
800-478-7472 907-376-7472
Shannon & Leny Cullip

99-159 $US BB
6 rooms, 5 pb
Visa, MC, Disc,
Rated, •
C-yes/S-no/P-ltd/H-ltd
Summer

Full breakfast
Self-serve breakfast bar with fruit, cereal, etc.
Great room, 360 degree view room, sauna, WiFi, Internet

Whether you are looking for a romantic getaway, family vacation, scrapbooking retreat or business meeting, Pioneer Ridge provides guests with a home away from home in a setting of casual, Alaskan charm. ✉ info@pioneerridge.com 🌐 www.pioneerridge.com

WASILLA

Shady Acres B&B
1000 Easy St 99654
907-376-3113
Marie Lambing

130-150 $US BB
2 rooms, 2 pb
Visa, MC, AmEx, •
C-ltd/S-no/P-no/H-yes

Hot homestyle breakfast
For breakfast, enjoy fresh eggs from
our own chickens, fresh bread, fruit
and other side dishes.
Wheelchair accessible, telephones,
roll-in showers, cheerful home-style
atmosphere, smoke free

Located in Wasilla near Parks Highway and downtown. Surrounded by quiet, serene forest. Warm, cheerful, homey atmosphere, with indoor and outdoor entertainment space. Completely wheelchair-accessible.   ✉ lambing@mtaonline.net 🌐 www.shadyacresbnb.com

WILLOW

Alaskan Host B&B
27803 Old Parks
Highway 99688
907-495-6800
Kathy & Jim Huston

95-110 $US BB
4 rooms, 4 pb
Visa, MC, *Rated*, •
C-yes/S-no/P-ltd/H-ltd

Full breakfast

Alaska Host Bed and Breakfast opened its doors in 1996. Your hosts, Kathy and Jim Huston, live in a spacious home on two-hundred acres with a private lake and hiking trails. Moose and other Alaskan wildlife are frequent visitors to the peaceful estate.
✉ akhost@alaskanhost.com 🌐 www.alaskanhost.com

Gigglewood Lakeside Inn
48976 S Rainbow Ridge
Dr. 99688
800-574-2555 907-495-1014
Larry & Linda Cline

120-140 $US BB
3 rooms, 3 pb
Most CC, Cash, Checks
C-ltd/S-no/P-no/H-no

Stocked breakfast items
Rental stocked with coffee, tea, eggs,
link sausage, juice, bagels
Rentals have fully furnished
kitchenette, linens and towels, patio,
gazebo, gas grill, paddle boat

Three full-furnished vacation cabin rentals located on Upper Caswell Lake, 4.5 miles off the George Parks Highway at Mile 87.9 Just 20 minutes north of Willow and 35 minutes south of Talkeetna, Alaska and mid-way between Anchorage and Denali National Park
✉ gigglewood@mtaonline.net 🌐 www.gigglewood.com

WRANGELL-ST. ELIAS NATIONAL PARK

Kennicott Glacier Lodge
Lot 15, Millsite
Subdivision 99510
800-582-5128 907-258-2350
Rich & Jody Kirkwood

159-259 $US BB
35 rooms, 10 pb
Most CC, Cash,
Checks, •
C-yes/S-no/P-no/H-yes
May 21 – Sept 11, 2010

Continental plus breakfast
Full service restaurant, breakfast
buffet, lunch menu, family-style
dinner, beer, wine & snacks
Sitting room, library, panoramic front
porch, glacier hikes, flightseeing,
rafting, etc.

Enjoy the awesome beauty of America's largest National Park from the comfort of our first-class wilderness lodge. The Kennicott Glacier Lodge, built in the style of the ghost town, has all the conveniences of a modern hotel, with 35 rooms and restaurant.
✉ info@KennicottLodge.com 🌐 www.KennicottLodge.com

Arizona

BISBEE

Bisbee Grand Hotel
61 Main St 85603
800-421-1909 520-432-5900
Bill & Valerie Thomas

79-175 $US BB
13 rooms, 13 pb
Most CC, Cash,
Checks, •
C-ltd/S-no/P-no/H-no

European Continental Breakfast
Cafe and saloon with full service,
downstairs
Sitting room, library, TV in all rooms/
suites, saloon, pool table, cafe, located
downtown

Elegantly appointed with antiques and fine art, the Bisbee Grant Hotel is a romantic step back to the turn-of-the-century with Old West Victorian charm.

 lodging@bisbeegrandhotel.com 🌐 www.bisbeegrandhotel.com

**Calumet & Arizona Guest
House**
608 Powell St 85603
520-432-4815
Joy & John Timbers

70-110 $US BB
8 rooms, 4 pb
Visa, MC
C-yes/S-ltd/P-yes/H-ltd

Full breakfast
Guests select breakfast from our menu
and it is cooked to order; there are
many choices
Living room, music room, dining
room, patios, porches, library,
information on the area

Grand Southwest home, built in 1906. Mission revival theme throughout beautiful house and gardens. The home was originally for the Secretary Treasurer of the Calumet & Arizona Mining Company, it later became their guesthouse and is now an elegant B&B.

✉ info@calumetaz.com 🌐 www.calumetaz.com

CAMP VERDE

Luna Vista B&B
1062 E Reay Rd 86335
800-611-4788 928-567-4788
Frank & Kala

165-235 $US BB
4 rooms, 4 pb
Most CC, Checks,
Rated, •
C-ltd/S-ltd/P-ltd/H-ltd

Full breakfast & Sunday Brunch
Snacks, social hour refreshments,
dinner available on request for added
cost
Pool, spa, library/office, family room,
private & common area patios

A secluded B&B oasis with luxurious amenities including pool, spa, steam room, gardens, creeks & trails, exquisite meals, happy hour and the utmost in hospitality. Great location for weddings, reunions and retreats.

✉ info@LunaVistaBandB.com 🌐 www.lunavistabandb.com

CAVE CREEK

**The Happy Hidden Ranch
B&B**
6914 E Continental Mountain
Dr 85331
480-575-7191
Govert Shea

105-150 $US BB
4 rooms, 4 pb
Visa, MC
C-ltd/S-ltd/P-no/H-no

Full breakfast
Private patio & entry, queen beds,
satellite & flat screen TV's, private
bath with Jacuzzi

Happy Hidden Ranch is surrounded by rugged terrain, you can enjoy the peace and solitude of the Sonoran Desert. We offer a desert retreat just 30 minutes from Phoenix and Scottsdale. Wake up to the sound of the birds and the sight of abundant wildlife.

✉ doublehranch2010@live.com 🌐 www.thehappyhiddenranch.com

CHINO VALLEY

Teapot Inn
989 W Center St 86323
877-636-7721 928-636-7727
Vera & Jim French

69-109 $US BB
4 rooms, 4 pb
Visa, MC, Disc
C-yes/S-no/P-ltd/H-ltd

Full breakfast
Pillow top beds, cable TV/VCR,
wireless Internet, plush robes, library,
airport shuttle, weddings

The Teapot Inn B&B is a refreshing alternative for the business traveler, vacationer or couple. Our Gazebo Garden area is perfect for a small outdoor wedding. This is where you "Arrive as a guest and leave as a friend." Just 15 miles north of Prescott.

 info@teapotinn.com  🌐 www.teapotinn.com

CORNVILLE

J Bar T Ranch B&B
800-246-7584 928-634-4084
April & Jean Troxell

125-175 $US BB
4 rooms, 3 pb
C-yes/S-ltd/P-no/H-no

Breakfast fixings provided
Stocked refrigerators
Satellite TV, nature, beautiful views, patio, exposed-beam ceilings, Jacuzzi tubs, swimming pool

Relax in our secluded, restful and quiet atmosphere, where the air is clean, the skies are blue and the sounds of nature are not forgotten. We are on Oak Creek, just 20 minutes from Sedona, Arizona.

🌐 www.westerntravel.com/jt

ELGIN

Whispers Ranch Bed and Breakfast
1490 Hwy 83 85611
520-455-9246
Toni

80-160 $US BB
5 rooms, 4 pb
Visa, MC, Disc,
Rated, •
C-ltd/S-no/P-no/H-yes

Full breakfast
Special dietary needs accommodated — vegetarian, allergy-free & gluten-free foods available
Classroom & Conference Room, Internet Cafe, great for corporate getaways!

Close to Tucson and Sierra Vista, worlds away from fast-paced city life. A beautiful Inn with exposed wood beams, loft sitting area and a stone fireplace is a serene sanctuary. At 5,100 ft elevation and in a National Forest, the location is unique.

✉ whispersranch@gmail.com 🌐 www.whispersranch.com

FLAGSTAFF

Abineau Lodge
10155 Mountainaire
Rd 86001
888-715-6386 928-525-6212
Wendy White

129-199 $US BB
9 rooms, 9 pb
Visa, MC, Disc, •
C-ltd/S-no/P-no/H-yes

Full breakfast
Snacks including cereal bars & cookies, beverages available all day in dining room
Meeting rooms, wireless Internet, fireplaces, European sauna, concierge services, massage

You're invited to stay at the Abineau Lodge, a country inn and B&B just south of Flagstaff, Arizona. We offer you a unique experience that you won't find inside the city limits. This is what mountain living is all about. ✉ info@abineaulodge.com 🌐 www.abineaulodge.com

Fall Inn to Nature
4555 S Lake Mary Rd 86001
888-920-0237 928-714-0237
Annette & Ron Fallaha

109-170 $US BB
3 rooms, 3 pb
Visa, MC, Disc, *Rated*
C-ltd/S-no/P-no/H-no

Full sit down served breakfast
In-room full body massages, tours to Grand Canyon, flowers, WiFi, robes, small fridge

Rustic elegance with historic charm & hospitality, the "Best in the Southwest"! Get pampered in Georgette's Suite, the Southwest Room, or the Family Suite (kids 8+ welcome). Amenities include massages, balcony, fireplace and an in-room jetted tub.

✉ info@fallinntonature.com 🌐 www.fallinntonature.com

GLOBE

Noftsger Hill Inn
425 North St 85501
877-780-2479 928-425-2260
Dom & Rosalie Ayala

90-125 $US BB
6 rooms, 6 pb
Most CC, *Rated*
C-yes/S-no/P-no/H-ltd

Full breakfast
Free WiFi, complimentary bottled water & soft drinks

High above the Cobre Valley in the shadow of the Old Dominion mine, The Noftsger Hill Inn stands — a monolithic monument to miner, academic, and architect. Filled with rustic elegance and framed by mining era houses.

✉ info@noftsgerhillinn.com 🌐 www.noftsgerhillinn.com

GOLD CANYON

Sinelli's B&B
5746 & 5692 S. Estrella
Rd. 85118
480-983-3650
Carl & Patricia Sinelli

95-120 $US BB
3 rooms, 3 pb
•
C-ltd/S-ltd/P-no/H-yes

Continental breakfast
Full breakfast available by request, snacks, complimentary wine
Lunch & dinner available, sitting room

Casual Southwest living in the foothills of the Superstition Mountains. Short or long term stays available. Host able to teach popular poker games!

✉ sisu1941@msn.com

HEREFORD ──────────────────────────────

Casa de San Pedro B&B
8933 S Yell Ln 85615
888-257-2050 520-366-1300
Karl Schmitt & Patrick Dome

169-169 $US BB
10 rooms, 10 pb
Most CC, Cash, Checks,
Rated, •
C-ltd/S-no/P-no/H-yes

Full gourmet breakfast
Coffee, tea, home made pies, fresh
baked goods, refrigerator, BBQ, etc
available for your own dinner
Great room, library with PC & printer
+ WiFi, bird guides, hiking trails,
gazebo, lots of feeders

Casa de San Pedro B&B is located on 10 acres adjacent to the San Pedro Riparian Reserve and the San Pedro River. The perfect place for the eco-tourist/naturalist to explore and relax. Above all, it is quiet. 90 miles SE of Tucson, only inches from heaven.

✉ info@bedandbirds.com   🌐 www.bedandbirds.com

NOGALES ──────────────────────────────

Hacienda Corona de Guevavi
348 S River Rd 85628
520-287-6503
Phil & Wendy Stover

189-249 $US BB
8 rooms, 8 pb
Visa, MC, Disc, •
C-ltd/S-no/P-ltd/H-yes
Spanish

Full breakfast
Complimentary beverage and hors
d'oeuvres
Fireplace, patio, living room, game
room, library, gardens, pool, wireless
Internet

Corona murals, birds singing in lush gardens, a sparkling mosaic tile swimming pool and delicious breakfasts all delight guests at historic Hacienda Corona. Central location between Tubac, Patagonia and Nogales makes exploring Santa Cruz County a breeze.

✉ stover@haciendacorona.com   🌐 www.haciendacorona.com

PHOENIX ──────────────────────────────

The Honey House
5150 N 36th St 85018
602-956-5646
Jeanette Irwin

89-109 $US BB
3 rooms, 3 pb
Visa, MC, AmEx,
Rated, •
C-yes/S-no/P-yes/H-no

Full breakfast
Sitting room, library, bikes, hot tub,
conference facility, WiFi

Historic homesteaded property (1895). Lush acre has citrus grove, antique roses, and arbored gardens. Centrally located near museums, shopping and a golfer's paradise.

✉ honeyhous@aol.com   🌐 www.travelguides.com/home/honeyhouse

PINETOP - LAKESIDE ──────────────────────────────

Byrd House Inn
2911 W White Mountain
Blvd 85929
928-368-6594
Max & Rita Byrd

85-175 $US BB
4 rooms, 4 pb
Most CC, Cash
C-ltd/S-no/P-no/H-ltd

Full breakfast
Freshly baked bread & cookies
TV/VCR/CD player, common
recreational room, pool table,
fireplaces, gardens, terrace, Jacuzzis

This B&B has the kind of cozy ambience you want in a White Mountain getaway, with brick & stone fireplaces, skylights, oak floors & ceilings, and walls of knotty pine.

✉ maxbyrd@cableone.net   🌐 www.byrdhouseinn.com

PRESCOTT ──────────────────────────────

Prescott Pines Inn
901 White Spar Rd 86303
800-541-5374 928-445-7270
Tony & Janet Fenner

100-300 $US EP
12 rooms, 12 pb
Most CC, *Rated*, •
C-yes/S-no/P-no/H-ltd

Full breakfast avail. $5.00. Homemade
cookies, coffee & teas
BBQ, kitchenettes, library, heating &
A/C, games, TV/DVD library, WiFi

Rated Prescott's best B&B for five years; 11 guestrooms in 3 guesthouses, and an A-frame chalet that sleeps up to 10, all on an acre with Ponderosa pines, Deodar cedars & gardens. Some rooms with fireplaces & kitchenettes. ✉ info@prescottpinesinn.com 🌐 www.prescottpinesinn.com

The Pleasant Street Inn
142 S. Pleasant St 86303
877-226-7125 928-445-4774
Jeanne Watkins

130-185 $US BB
4 rooms, 4 pb
Visa, MC, Disc, *Rated*
C-ltd/S-no/P-no/H-ltd

Full hot gourmet breakfast
Soft drinks & bottled water are
complimentary in hall refrigerator.
Cozy living room with fireplace,
lending library, CD player, board
games & wireless Internet.

Courthouse Plaza is only three blocks from the Pleasant Street Inn. Once you're settled in, it's easy to stay or go because everything that's wonderful about Prescott is close by. Sometimes just hanging around this lovely B & B is all that's needed.

✉ info@pleasantbandb.com   🌐 www.pleasantbandb.com

SEDONA———————————————————————————————————————

A Sunset Chateau	199-389 $US BB	Gourmet Breakfast
665 S Sunset Dr 86336	23 rooms, 23 pb	Pool, Jacuzzi, kiva fireplace, patio,
888-988-3988 928-282-2644	Most CC, Cash,	garden, pond & waterfall, tennis,
Jean-Christophe Buillet	Checks, •	concierge, conference room
	C-yes/S-ltd/P-no/H-yes	
	Spanish	

A Sunset Chateau sits on a hilltop overlooking Sedona's famous red rock mountains. Spacious 600+ square foot suites start at only $199 a night. Amenities includes pool, spa, stream, conference room, fireplaces, 2 person Jacuzzi tubs, kitchens & more.
✉ information@asunsetchateau.com ◐ www.asunsetchateau.com

Briar Patch Inn	219-395 $US BB	Full breakfast buffet
3190 N. State Route	19 rooms, 19 pb	Afternoon snacks, homemade cookies,
89A 86336	Most CC, Cash,	brownies, cheese & crackers, fresh
888-809-3030 928-282-2342	Checks, •	fruit hot cider or iced tea.
Rob Olson	C-yes/S-no/P-no/H-ltd	Sitting room, library, wireless Internet
	Spanish	in lodge, fireplaces, facials, massage,
		swimming hole

One of the most beautiful spots in Arizona. Cottages nestled on 9 spectacular acres on sparkling Oak Creek. Warm, generous hospitality. A real gem!
✉ stay@briarpatchinn.com ◐ www.briarpatchinn.com

Canyon Villa B&B Inn of Sedona	159-349 $US BB	Full breakfast
	11 rooms, 11 pb	Afternoon appetizers, evening coffee,
40 Canyon Circle Dr 86351	Most CC, Cash, Checks,	tea, & fresh cookies
800-453-1166 928-284-1226	*Rated*, •	Sitting room, WiFi, library, swimming
Les & Peg Belch	C-ltd/S-no/P-no/H-ltd	pool, golf, hiking from premises, and
		full concierge service

Southwest-style inn faces the highlands desert, with unmatched bedside views of Sedona's red rocks. A luxury B&B providing exceptional guest service. All rooms have private or semi-private patios or balconies. ✉ canvilla@sedona.net ◐ www.canyonvilla.com

Casa Sedona B&B Inn	149-309 $US BB	Full Four-Course Breakfast
55 Hozoni Dr 86336	16 rooms, 16 pb	Raspberry iced tea or hot spiced
800-525-3756 928-282-2938	Most CC, *Rated*, •	cider, coyote cookies, late afternoon
Paul & Connie Schwartz	C-ltd/S-ltd/P-no/H-ltd	appetizer buffet
		Spa tubs, fireplaces, TV/VCR or
		flat screen TV/DVD, CD players,
		refrigerator, iron, ironing board

AAA 4-Diamond Inn featured on Travel Channel's "Best of the Best Hotels & Inns" series. Panoramic Red Rock views. Designed by a Frank Lloyd Wright protege. Quiet, romantic and relaxing.
✉ casa@sedona.net ◐ www.casasedona.com

El Portal Sedona	199-459 $US EP	Full breakfast option
95 Portal Lane 86336	12 rooms, 12 pb	Breakfast available daily.
800-313-0017 928-203-9405	Most CC, *Rated*, •	Spa facilities, all guestrooms include
Steve & Connie Segner	C-yes/S-no/P-yes/H-yes	TV, radio, DVD, free Internet & local
		phone calls

El Portal redefines the bed & breakfast experience. A private retreat of exceptional quality. Authentic 1910 adobe architecture, 1900–1930 furnishings, finest food and wines, and a fabulous location. A pet friendly hotel located in Sedona's Arts District.
✉ info@elportalsedona.com ◐ www.elportalsedona.com

Lantern Light Inn	129-335 $US EP	Morning goodies at your door,
3085 W Hwy 89A 86336	5 rooms, 5 pb	cookies, candy, fruit
877-275-4973 928-282-3419	•	Private baths, TV, refrigerator,
Ed & Kris Varjean	C-ltd/S-no/P-no/H-no	fireplace, recreation room

Rated one of "Arizona's 23 Best B&Bs and Homey Hideaways" by Phoenix Magazine. The New York Times recommends Lantern Light Inn as one of 3 in Sedona. Charming oasis of greenery, hidden in the trees facing Thunder Mountain in the heart of Sedona.
✉ info@lanternlightinn.com ◐ www.lanternlightinn.com

SEDONA

Rose Tree Inn
376 Cedar St 86336
888-282-2065 928-282-2065
Gary Dawson

95-145 $US EP
5 rooms, 5 pb
Visa, MC, AmEx,
Rated, •
C-ltd/S-ltd/P-no/H-no

In-room coffee & tea, kitchenettes
Patios, library, TV/VCR in rooms, free
WiFi

"Sedona's best kept secret . . ." is conveniently located near uptown Sedona. Five affordable, quiet rooms, two with fireplaces. Small, charming and cozy like a bed and breakfast, but with private kitchens. Free Internet access.

✉ info@rosetreeinn.com 🌐 www.rosetreeinn.com

Sedona Cathedral Hideaway
30 Serendipity Trail 86336
866-973-3662 928-203-4180
Kathy & Larry Jaeckel

257-340 $US BB
2 rooms, 2 pb
Visa, MC, AmEx,
Rated, •
C-ltd/S-ltd/P-no/H-ltd

Gourmet breakfast of your choosing
Afternoon or evening snack including
homemade ice cream, health drink,
gourmet menu
2 person shower, jetted tub, spa
gourmet menu, small weddings, fridge,
LCD TV/DVD, Sleep# beds, Wifi

New romantic, serene, private red-rock wooded setting on 2 acres in Sedona. Healthy gourmet menu. In Room: massage, WiFi-IPod hookup, 2 person jetted tub & huge shower room. Anti-aging spa. Near trails, golfing & wineries. Small weddings. Green.

✉ CathedralHideaway@wildblue.net 🌐 www.sedonacathedralhideaway.com/index.html

The Canyon Wren – Cabins For Two
6425 North State Route 89A 86336
800-437-9736 928-282-6900
Mike & Milena Pfeifer-Smith

155-175 $US BB
4 rooms, 4 pb
Most CC, Cash, Checks
S-no/P-no/H-ltd
Slovenian

Continental plus breakfast
Coffee, tea, hot chocolate always
available
Daily maid service in cabins, planning
activities, in room massages available,
CD & DVD library

Come and experience a different type of getaway! Fodor's "best value in Oak Creek Canyon!" In a spectacular canyon with red rock views. Cozy western cedar cabins have queen beds, full kitchens, fireplaces whirlpool tubs, decks & patios with gas grills.

✉ canyonwrencabins@gmail.com 🌐 canyonwrencabins.com

SIERRA VISTA

Birders Vista B&B
5147 S Kino Rd 85650
520-378-2493
Johnnie & Audrey Eskue

89-140 $US BB
4 rooms, 3 pb
Visa, MC, •
C-yes/S-ltd/P-no/H-ltd

Full breakfast
A vegetarian, vegan or gluten-free
menu, enjoy our home made jams,
preserves & breads
Library, garden with a pergola, large
orchard, bird watching areas, sitting
room with fireplace

Birders Vista B&B is a quiet, country retreat with wonderful views of the Huachuca and Mule mountains and a beautiful backyard garden with plenty of birds. It is a stucco home at an elevation of 4500 feet, on 4 acres, with an orchard.

✉ birdersvista@ssvecnet.com 🌐 www.birdersvista.com

ST. DAVID

Down By The River B&B
2255 Efken Pl 85630
520-720-9441
Mike & Angie Hug

85-139 $US BB
4 rooms, 4 pb
Visa, MC, AmEx
C-ltd/S-ltd/P-no/H-no

Full breakfast
We will try to provide for special
dietary restrictions. Please notify us at
the time of reservation
BBQ, telescopes, pool table, wireless
Internet, private patios, whirlpool tubs
in big rooms

Down By The River is a 15 acre property that borders the San Pedro River, within sight of the northern end of the world famous San Pedro National Riparian Area. Sit back on the porch or play pool inside in the evening and enjoy the peace & quiet.

 downbytheriverbb@hotmail.com 🌐 www.downbytheriverbandb.com

TUBAC

Artist's Suite	115-145 $US BB	Continental plus breakfast
7 Camino Otero 85646	1 rooms, 1 pb	TV, WiFi Internet, phone, fax, expert
800-255-2306 520-398-9001	Most CC, Cash,	concierge services, full kitchen
Trisha Ambrose	Checks, •	
	C-ltd/S-no/P-no/H-ltd	
	Canadian, French,	
	German and Spanish	

The Artist's Suite is located at the Quilts Ltd. Gallery in the heart of Tubac. This custom decorated 3 room suite features pieces from the owner's private art collection, designer rugs and custom furnishings.

✉ daryen@gmail.com

TUCSON

Bed and Bagels of Tucson	85-130 $US BB	Choice of familiar or exotic foods
10402 E Glenn St 85749	3 rooms, 1 pb	Beverages, snacks, hot fudge sundaes,
520-760-5595	C-yes/S-ltd/P-yes/H-ltd	baked goods
Sharon Arkin	Spanish, German,	Pool/spa, bikes, in-room phones,
	Hebrew	robes, TV/VCRs, cable, Internet, fax,
		computer, laundry available

Free Night w/Certificate: Valid except Jan. 30-Feb. 14

Casually elegant pet/child/senior-friendly mountain view home. Gourmet breakfasts, homebaked treats, laundry, cable, Internet, guest computer, pool/spa, safety fence. Birding aids. Near tennis, golf, hiking, dog park, shopping, post office & library.

✉ sharon@bedandbagels.com 🌐 www.bedandbagels.com

Casa Tierra Adobe B&B	135-285 $US BB	Full gourmet vegetarian breakfast
Inn	4 rooms, 4 pb	Guests receive a welcoming basket of
11155 W Calle Pima 85743	Most CC, Cash,	fruit & snacks, iced tea & chocolates
866-254-0006 520-578-3058	*Rated*, •	upon arrival
Dave Malmquist	C-yes/S-no/P-no/H-no	Common room with movies &
	August 15 – June 15	games, hot tub, computer, WiFi, gym,
		telescope, courtyard, private patios

This rustically elegant home, Casa Tierra (Earth House), recalls haciendas of old Mexico. The all-adobe home features over fifty arches and includes entryways with vaulted brick ceilings and beautiful interior courtyards.

✉ info@casatierratucson.com 🌐 www.casatierratucson.com

Catalina Park Inn	109-189 $US BB	Full breakfast
309 E 1st St 85705	6 rooms, 6 pb	Afternoon tea & cookies
800-792-4885 520-792-4541	Most CC, Cash, Checks,	Flat panel TV/DVD, AM/FM/CD Stereo
Mark Hall	*Rated*	with iPod dock, plush robes, iron and
	C-ltd/S-ltd/P-ltd/H-no	board, hairdryer, and Wifi

Stylish 1927 historic inn featuring six, beautifully decorated guestrooms and a full range of amenities. Enjoy our lush desert garden. 5 blocks to the University of Arizona.

✉ info@catalinaparkinn.com 🌐 www.catalinaparkinn.com

Desert Dove B&B	125-145 $US BB	Full breakfast
11707 E Old Spanish	2 rooms, 2 pb	Soft drinks, tea, coffee & afternoon
Trl 85730	Visa, MC, *Rated*	snacks
877-722-6879 520-722-6879	C-ltd/S-no/P-no/H-no	Spa (including bathrobes), phone,
Harvey & Betty Ross		common area, refrigerator &
		microwave; wireless Internet

Our territorial adobe bed & breakfast is situated on four acres nestled in the foothills of the Rincon Mountains. Private bathrooms & entrance, full breakfast, desert gardens, great views, spa and walking distance from the Saguaro National Park East.

✉ info@desertdovebb.com 🌐 www.desertdovebb.com

TUCSON ───────────────────────────────────────

El Presidio B&B
297 N Main Ave 85701
800-349-6151 520-623-6151
Patti Toci

125-155 $US BB
4 rooms, 4 pb
Visa, MC, AmEx,
Rated, •
C-ltd/S-no/P-no/H-no

Full hot country breakfast
Complimentary in room beverages
and snacks
Phones, TV, WiFi, some rooms with
kitchenettes

Step back in time and experience the Southwestern charm of a desert oasis with the romance of a country inn. El Presidio B&B is a splendid example of American Territorial, blending the rich cultural heritage of Mexican and American building.

✉ elpresidio_bb@yahoo.com

El Rancho Merlita Ranch House B&B
1924 N. Corte El Rancho
Merlita 85715
888-218-8418 520-495-0071
Pattie Bell

100-275 $US BB
4 rooms, 4 pb
Most CC, Cash
C-ltd/S-no/P-no/H-yes

Full breakfast
Afternoon treats
Labyrinth, spa, pool, library, sitting
room, luxury linens & bath amenities,
massage, yoga and more

Relax under deep shaded porches or enjoy breakfast in the spacious breezeway beneath a long mission tile roof with views of the Catalina Mountains. Stroll the paths to the large swimming pool directly from your room, soak in the whirlpool as you watch the

✉ info@ranchomerlita.com 🌐 www.bedbreakfasttucsonaz.com

Milagras Guesthouse
11185 W Calle Pima 85743
520-578-8577
Helen & Vivian

100 $US EP
1 rooms, 1 pb
Rated
C-ltd/S-ltd/P-ltd/H-ltd
Sept-May

Snacks, fresh fruit & beverages on
arrival
Hot tub, fountains, hiking, nearby
attractions

This Guest house offers 2 rooms with a private bath, 30 min west of Tucson. Romantic, private, patios, outdoor fireplace, fountains, kitchenette, Direct TV, VCR, CDs and private phone. All rural in the lush Sonoran Desert.

✉ info@milagras.com 🌐 www.milagras.com

Mountain Views
3160 N Bear Canyon
Rd 85749
520-749-1387
Roy B. Kile

100 $US BB
2 rooms, 2 pb
Visa, MC, AmEx,
Rated, •
C-ltd/S-no/P-no/H-ltd

Full breakfast
Complimentary wine
Sitting room, swimming pool, cable TV,
accommodate business travelers

Mountain Views B&B is nestled on 3.3 acres of secluded, vegetated desert on Tucson's far eastside, with beautiful panoramic mountain views. Mountain Views offers comfortable bedrooms with private baths and a delicious breakfast each morning.

✉ Rkile85749@aol.com 🌐 www.mtviewsbb.com

Sam Hughes Inn
2020 East 7th Street 85719
520-861-2191
Susan Banner

85-135 $US BB
4 rooms, 4 pb
Most CC, *Rated*, •
S-no/P-no/H-ltd

Full breakfast
Game room, WiFi, guest PC, shower
robes, refrigerators, individual heat/
cool

If you are a tourist, visiting relatives, or have other business in the Tucson area, come sample the bounty that Tucson and the Sam Hughes Inn Bed and Breakfast have to offer.

✉ innkeeper@samhughesinn.com 🌐 www.samhughesinn.com

Shoppe at Civano B&B Suites
5324 S. Civano Blvd 85747
520-207-2539
Alan Boertjens & Adele
Coronado

79-119 $US BB
5 rooms, 5 pb
Most CC, Cash, •
C-yes/S-no/P-no/H-no

Continental plus breakfast
Evening treats and gourmet coffee &
teas
Pillow-top beds, wireless Internet,
mini-fridge, pool, tennis, yoga, facials,
massage, painting

Five exquisitely decorated rooms available in the environmentally planned neighborhood of the Community of Civano. Also offering yoga & pilates classes, holistic skin care facials and waxing services, massage therapy and watercolor painting classes.

✉ shoppe.at.civano@gmail.com 🌐 www.shoppe-at-civano.com/SaC_BnB.htm

TUCSON

White Stallion Ranch	264-600 $US AP	Full breakfast
9251 W Twin Peaks Rd 85743	41 rooms, 41 pb	Buffet-style lunch and dinner.
888-977-2624 520-297-0252	Most CC, Cash,	AC, private patios, heated pool & hot
Russell True	Checks, •	tub, fitness center, horseback riding,
	C-yes/S-ltd/P-no/H-ltd	free WiFi, meeting room
	Norweigen	

This charming, informal ranch gives you a feeling of the Old West. Only here can you find 3,000 acres of wide-open space at the foot of ruggedly beautiful Tucson Mountains and Saguaro National Park.

✉ info@whitestallion.com 🌐 www.whitestallion.com

WILLIAMS

Grand Living B&B	140-290 $US BB	Full Gourmet Breakfast
701 Quarterhorse Rd 86046	6 rooms, 6 pb	Complimentary refreshments, wine or
800-210-5908 928-635-4171	Most CC, Cash, *Rated*	non-alcoholic beverages, chocolates
Bill & Gloria Job	S-no/P-no/H-ltd	& cookies
		Wireless Internet, books, DVD/VHS,
		fridge, fireplaces, HDTV, 2-person
		jetted tub, outside porch

Our large log home offers country Victorian decor and art from all over the world, spacious guestrooms with private bath & entrance, hardwood floors, wireless Internet, a big parking area and beautiful mountain scenery to view from a wrap-around porch.

✉ job@grandlivingbnb.com 🌐 www.grandlivingbnb.com

Arkansas

ARKADELPHIA

Captain Henderson House	80 $US BB	Full breakfast
B&B	7 rooms, 7 pb	Assorted snacks & drinks provided
349 N 10th St 71923	Most CC, Cash	with baked goods brought up each
866-478-4661 870-230-5544	C-ltd/S-no/P-no/H-yes	night
Vickie Jones		Dining room, conference room,
		wireless Internet, in-room phone & TV,
		Jacuzzi tubs

This large 9,000 square foot home has been delicately restored; the detailed fretwork, pocket doors & elaborate paneling evoke just some of the charm you will encounter on your journey through the house.

✉ hendersonhouse@hsu.edu 🌐 www.hsu.edu/Captain-Henderson-House

CONWAY

Ward Mansion B&B	135-175 $US BB	Full breakfast
1912 Caldwell St 72034	3 rooms, 3 pb	
501-764-0900 501-499-1400	Most CC	
Joanne Stevens	C-ltd/S-no/P-no	

The Ward Mansion is elegance and beauty at its best. Planning a wedding, reception, dinner or some other special happening? The Ward Mansion is the perfect location for an event to remember.

✉ jstevens@conwaycorp.net 🌐 www.wardmansionbandb.com

COTTER

White River Inn Luxury	175-325 $US BB	Full breakfast
B&B Lodge	5 rooms, 5 pb	Complimentary drinks in the guest
924 CR 174 72626	C-ltd/S-no/P-no/H-no	refrigerator
870-430-2233		Hot tubs, fireplaces, satellite TV,
Moose & Tina Watson		wireless Internet, Great Room, expert
		fishing guides

The White River Inn is a world class lodge for fly fishing enthusiasts, sporting fanatics, couples on a romantic holiday, vacations and travelers looking for a idyllic, quiet getaway. Guest wing with three luxury suites, all with private entrances.

✉ moose@thewhiteriverinn.com 🌐 www.thewhiteriverinn.com

EUREKA SPRINGS

11 Singleton House	95-150 $US BB	Full gourmet breakfast
11 Singleton St. 72632	5 rooms, 5 pb	Guest ice-box, microwave,
800-833-3394	Most CC, Cash, Checks,	complimentary iced+herbal teas,
Barb Gavron	*Rated*, •	lemonade, hot cocoa, snacks.
	C-yes/S-ltd/P-no/H-ltd	Vegan+Diabetic
	Some Spanish	B&B Internship Program, free parking,
		small garden weddings, early check-in.

Quiet Historic District. Breakfast balcony overlooking Award-winning garden. Some rooms with TWO beds. Suite sleeps five. Jacuzzi suite w/private balcony. Cottage at separate location. One block walk to shops or trolley. Seen on HGTV's If Walls Could Talk.

✉ info@singletonhouse.com 🌐 www.singletonhouse.com

1881 Crescent Cottage Inn	109-149 $US BB	Full breakfast
211 Spring St 72632	4 rooms, 4 pb	Complimentary soft drinks, fresh-
800-223-3246 479-253-6022	Visa, MC, Disc, *Rated*	baked cookies
Ray & Elise Dilfield	C-ltd/S-no/P-no/H-no	In-room Jacuzzis, 2 rooms w/ fireplace,
		2 large back verandas, classic English
		gardens w/ waterfall

All the charm and elegance of a National Historic Register Victorian home just a few minutes' stroll from downtown Eureka Springs' shops, galleries, restaurants, and night life.

✉ raphael@ipa.net 🌐 www.1881crescentcottageinn.com

11 Singleton House, Eureka Springs, AR

EUREKA SPRINGS

1884 Bridgeford House	95-179 $US BB	Full breakfast
263 Spring St 72632	5 rooms, 5 pb	In room treats
888-567-2422 479-253-7853	Visa, MC, Disc,	Some with fireplaces, Jacuzzis, cable
Nadara (Sam) & Jeff	*Rated*, •	TV/VCR, private entrances, decks,
Feldman	C-ltd/S-ltd/P-ltd/H-no	gardens, weddings
	Spanish	

Free Night w/Certificate: Valid Sundays-Thursday, except major holidays and festivals

Southern hospitality combined with Victorian charm await you at our beautiful Queen Anne/Eastlake "Painted Lady" home! Nestled in the very heart of Eureka Springs. Listed on the National Register of Historic Places.

✉ innkeeper@bridgefordhouse.com 🌐 www.bridgefordhouse.com

5 Ojo Inn B&B	105-189 $US BB	Full breakfast
5 Ojo St 72632	9 rooms, 9 pb	Complimentary in-room soft drinks &
800-656-6734 479-253-6734	Most CC, Cash,	snacks
Richard & Jan Grinnell	Checks, •	Hot tub, gazebo, Jacuzzis for two,
	C-ltd/S-ltd/P-ltd/H-no	fireplaces, weddings, off-street parking

Experience historic charm, exemplary Ozark hospitality and fabulous gourmet breakfasts. Situated on over an acre of wooded lot on the Historic Loop, and just a short stroll to downtown shopping, galleries and restaurants.

✉ innkeeper@5ojo.com 🌐 www.5ojo.com

Arsenic & Old Lace	145-289 $US BB	Full gourmet breakfast
60 Hillside Ave 72632	5 rooms, 5 pb	Complimentary sodas, wine,
866-350-5454 479-253-5454	Visa, MC, Disc,	homemade cookies, snacks
Beverly & Doug Breitling	*Rated*, •	LCD TV, DVD, VCR, individual
	C-ltd/S-ltd/P-ltd/H-no	thermostats, large video library,
		Jacuzzi tubs, fireplaces, spa shower

The premier Bed & Breakfast destination in Eureka Springs. Queen Anne style Victorian mansion with large wraparound veranda. Beautiful, private hillside setting in the Historic District. Escape to a time when life was slower and more romantic!

✉ ArsenicOldLaceBB@gmail.com 🌐 www.eurekaspringsromancebb.com

EUREKA SPRINGS

Cliff Cottage Inn – B&B	189-230 $US BB	Elf delivers full-gourmet breakfast
Suites & Historic Cottages	8 rooms, 8 pb	Complimentary Champagne or white
479-253-7409	Visa, MC, *Rated*, •	wine, sodas, teas, coffee, hot cocoa,
Sandra CH Smith	C-ltd/S-ltd/P-no/H-no	cookie samplers
	French, Spanish,	Free video/book library; reservations
	German, Catalan,	to Passion Play, music show, carriage
	Papiamento	rides, in-house massages

Free night in Queen Jacuzzi Suite w/Certificate: Valid Mon.-Thurs., not valid May or October, or holidays/festivals. Room Upgrade

Named one of top 6 "Most Romantic Inns in the South" by Romantic Destinations Magazine/Southern Bride. Only B&B in heart of Eureka's Historic Downtown. Off street parking. Elegant Jacuzzi suites, historic cottages. Gourmet breakfasts DELIVERED to suites.

✉ cliffcottage@sbcglobal.net   🌐 www.cliffcottage.com

Evening Shade Inn Bed	139-199 $US BB	Full Homemade Breakfast In-Room
and Breakfast	8 rooms, 8 pb	Homemade desserts in the evening
3079 E Van Buren 72632	Most CC, Cash, Checks,	Jacuzzis, fireplaces, wireless Internet,
800-992-1224 479-253-6264	*Rated*	cable TV, in-room phones, fax, gift
Clark & Donna Hinson	S-ltd/P-no/H-no	shop, weddings

Evening Shade Inn is one of Eureka Springs, AR's finest B&Bs, featuring luxury suites and private honeymoon cottages perfect for any vacation or romantic getaway. Evening Shade Inn combines luxury, privacy, seclusion and convenience.

✉ inn@eveningshade.com   🌐 www.eveningshade.com

Heart of the Hills Inn &	109-150 $US BB	Full breakfast
Cottage	4 rooms, 4 pb	Private Chef catered dinner check out
5 Summit Street 72632	Visa, MC	specials for this option.
800-253-7468 479-253-7468	C-ltd/S-ltd/P-ltd/H-no	Sitting rooms, Jacuzzis, suites,
David Mitchell		fireplaces, cable TV, wireless WiFi, see
		full list on web page.

The Inn features two three room Victorian suites, a French country cottage that sleeps four and a two story cottage called Rose Cottage that sleeps four.

✉ dmitchell@heartofthehillsinn.com   🌐 www.heartofthehillsinn.com

Heartstone Inn & Cottages	99-169 $US BB	Full gourmet breakfast
35 Kings Hwy 72632	11 rooms, 11 pb	Complimentary beverages &
800-494-4921 479-253-8916	Most CC, *Rated*, •	homemade treats
Rick & Cheri Rojek	C-ltd/S-ltd/P-no/H-no	Weddings, Jacuzzi suites, movies,
		massage therapy, golf privileges,
		gazebo, library, concierge

The Heartstone Inn & Cottages in Eureka Springs, AR, Selected as Pamela Lanier's 2010 Inn of the Year. Stay at the definitive, full-service luxury B&B, a beautifully restored estate listed on the National Register of Historic Places.

✉ info@heartstoneinn.com   🌐 www.heartstoneinn.com

Red Bud Manor	89-149 $US BB	Full breakfast
7 Kings Hwy 72632	3 rooms, 3 pb	Gourmet coffees & teas, small
866-253-9649 479-253-9649	Most CC, Cash, •	refrigerators stocked with
Deborah Stroup	C-ltd/S-no/P-no/H-ltd	complimentary beverages
		Porches, gardens, rear deck, parlor,
		antiques, TV w/DVD, flowers, coffee
		makers, Jacuzzi, weddings

Relax and pamper yourself at Red Bud Manor, one of Eureka's finest inns. Built in 1891, Red Bud Manor is conveniently located on Eureka's Historic Loop within easy walking distance to the finest shops, spas and restaurants. Gourmet Tea & gluten-free

✉ redbudmanor@cox-internet.com   🌐 www.redbudmanorinn.com

HOT SPRINGS

1890 Williams House Inn	129-299 $US BB	Full breakfast
420 Quapaw Ave 71901	9 rooms, 9 pb	Refreshment area with delicious
501.624.4275	Most CC, Cash,	homemade cookies, cocoa, cider &
Cathi	*Rated*, •	tea, in-room coffee & bottled water
	C-ltd/S-ltd/P-ltd/H-ltd	Upstairs library and two spacious
		verandas, video library, WiFi access,
		garden sitting areas

Relax in comfortable elegance at 1890 Williams House Inn. This Victorian Inn envelopes you to rejuvenate your body and soul. Located within walking distance of historic downtown Hot Springs. Intimate weddings and special events customized to your taste.

✉ info@1890williamshouse.com   🌐 www.1890williamshouse.com

Gables Inn B&B	109-159 $US BB	Full breakfast
318 Quapaw Ave 71901	4 rooms, 4 pb	In Room Coffee Service . . . We feature
800-625-7576 501-623-7576	Most CC, Cash	Wolfgang Puck Estate Grown Coffee.
David & Judy Peters	C-ltd/S-ltd/P-no/H-no	Hot Tea & Hot Chocolate.
		In Room Fridge, Microwave. 32" Flat
		Screen TV/DVD. Free DVD movie
		library for overnight guests!

Walk to most downtown attractions. Luxurious accommodations all at an affordable price, with only 4 guestrooms, this National Register Landmark makes for an intimate setting but with amenities & thoughtful features typically found in a five star hotel.

✉ stay@gablesn.com   🌐 www.gablesn.com

Lookout Point Lakeside	137-499 $US BB	Full gourmet breakfast
Inn	13 rooms, 13 pb	Complimentary Innkeepers Reception
104 Lookout Circle 71913	Most CC, Cash, •	with delectable desserts, cheese &
866-525-6155 501-525-6155	C-ltd/S-no/P-ltd/H-yes	crackers, wine & tea
Kristie & Ray Rosset	limited Spanish	Sitting room & sunroom, book & video
		library, fireplaces, cable TV, WiFi,
		canoe, labyrinth, gardens.

An exceptional experience of peace & tranquility, pampering, and luxury in Hot Springs, Arkansas. This award-winning inn, on beautiful Lake Hamilton, in the Ouachita Mountains is designed for guest comfort, relaxation, and romance. Perfect for weddings.

✉ innkeeper@lookoutpointinn.com   🌐 www.lookoutpointinn.com

MENA

Willowbrook Cottage	95-160 $US EP	Waterfall, fireplace, Jacuzzi bathtub,
1047 Polk County Rd	2 rooms, 2 pb	free wireless Internet, privacy, videos,
42 71953	Visa, MC, Disc, •	books, board games
479-883-5492	C-yes/S-no/P-ltd/H-ltd	
Dr. Thomas & Carolyn		
MacMahon		

Charming storybook, ivy-covered stone cottage with fireplace, jetted tub, waterfall, flowers, 10 acres of wooded hills in the heart of Ouachita Mts, 3 mi from scenic Mena. Other cute private cabins available. Ideal honeymoon, anniversary, or girl retreat.

✉ carolyn@willowbrookcottage.com   🌐 www.menacabins.com

California

AHWAHNEE ────────────────────────────────────

Apple Blossom Inn
44606 Silver Spur Trail 93601
888-687-4281 559-642-2001
Candy 'Apple' Arthur

110-240 $US BB
5 rooms, 4 pb
Visa, MC, AmEx, •
C-yes/S-ltd/P-ltd/H-ltd

Full breakfast
Fruit, snacks & candy apples when
the apples are ripe, picnic lunches
available on request
Sun deck & spa with gorgeous view
of the Sierras, VCR's & video library,
organic apple orchard

The Apple Blossom Inn is located in Gold Country on historic Highway 49, the front yard of Yosemite National Park. Enjoy the serenity of your stay in the midst of our organic apple farm & gardens, while visiting the many recreational spots nearby.

✉ appleblossominn@sti.net ◐ www.appleblossombb.com

──

Sierra Mountain Lodge
Bed & Breakfast
45046 Fort Nip Trail 93601
800-811-7029 559-683-7673
John & Brenda Eppler

125-175 $US BB
7 rooms, 7 pb
Visa, MC, •
C-ltd/S-ltd/P-no/H-ltd

Continental plus breakfast
Waffle or pancake bar, sausage (vege
too), fresh fruit platter, cold cereal,
coffee, tea, milk, OJ
Private kitchenettes, panoramic
mountain views, wireless Internet,
DVD & reading library, cable TV

Private 1 & 2 bedroom suites nestled in a quiet country oasis near Yosemite's Southern Entrance. Panoramic mountain views, hot continental breakfast, cable TV/DVD collection, and wireless Internet. Children 2 or older are welcome.

✉ innkeepers@sierramountainlodge.com ◐ www.sierramountainlodge.com

──

The Homestead
41110 Rd 600 93601
800-483-0495 559-683-0495
Cindy Brooks & Larry Ends

119-374 $US BB
6 rooms, 6 pb
Most CC, *Rated*, •
C-ltd/S-no/P-no/H-ltd
Spanish

Continental breakfast
Free Internet access, toiletries, daily
maid service, concierge services, in
room massages available

Romantic private cottages with fully equipped kitchens on 160 wooded acres close to Yosemite, Gold Country, golf, hiking and restaurants. Equine layover available.

✉ homesteadcottages@sti.net ◐ www.homesteadcottages.com

ALBION ──────────────────────────────────────

Albion River Inn
3790 Hwy 1 N 95410
800-479-7944 707-937-1919
Pat Turrigiano

195-325 $US BB
22 rooms, 22 pb
Most CC, *Rated*
C-ltd/S-no/P-no/H-yes

Full breakfast
Acclaimed ocean view restaurant
serves dinner nightly; full bar, award
winning wine list, music.
Wine, coffee, teas, robes, fireplaces,
decks, spa tubs, cooking classes, wine
dinners, workshops.

Called "One of the West's Best Small Inns," by Sunset Magazine, our romantic oceanfront Inn and restaurant sits on ten clifftop acres with spectacular ocean views. Enjoy luxury, privacy, comfort, acclaimed cuisine, and our award winning wine list.

✉ pat@albionriverinn.com ◐ www.albionriverinn.com

──

Fensalden Inn
33810 Navarro Ridge
Rd 95410
800-959-3850 707-937-4042
Lyn Hamby

139-253 $US BB
8 rooms, 8 pb
Visa, MC, *Rated*, •
C-ltd/S-ltd/P-ltd/H-ltd

Full three course gourmet breakfast
Wine & hors d'oeuvres at 5pm each
evening in our Great Room
Sunporch with board games & jigsaw
puzzle; office with fax, wireless
Internet, hairdryers in room

1850s Stagestop on several acres overlooking Pacific. Quiet romantic getaway, w/pampering atmosphere, antique appointed rooms w/fireplaces & private baths, gourmet breakfasts, evening hor d'oeuvres; 2 pigmy goats, 7 ducks, 2 pups & local wildlife & birds.

✉ inn@fensalden.com ◐ www.fensalden.com

24 California

APTOS

Historic Sand Rock Farm
6901 Freedom Blvd 95003
831-688-8005
Kris Sheehan

185-225 $US BB
5 rooms, 5 pb
Visa, MC
C-yes/S-no/P-no/H-ltd

Chef-prepared gourmet breakfast
Wine reception & special meals by
arrangement
Jacuzzis, down comforters, gardens,
sitting areas

Free Night w/Certificate: Anytime. Room Upgrade.

Historic, country estate featuring Jacuzzi tubs, arts, antiques, down comforters, private baths, and gracious amenities on 10 wooded acres. Secluded between Santa Cruz and Monterey.
✉ reservations@sandrockfarm.com 🌐 www.sandrockfarm.com

ARROYO GRANDE

Casitas of Arroyo Grande
2655 Lopez Dr 93420
805-473-1123
Pat & Tony Goetz

179-399 $US BB
4 rooms, 4 pb
Most CC, Cash, •
C-ltd/S-no/P-no/H-no
German

Full breakfast
In room fireplace, private deck, HDTV,
Bose radio with iPod connection,
Ralph Lauren bedding, WiFi

Situated on a 7 acre estate, The Casitas of Arroyo Grande Bed and Breakfast overlook central coast vineyards and hillside; perfectly located half way between Los Angeles and San Francisco. Come for the peace and quiet, leave with your peace of mind. ✉ tony@casitasag.com 🌐 www.casitasag.com

ATASCADERO

Oak Hill Manor
12345 Hampton Ct 93422
866-OAK-MANR 805-462-9317
Maurice & Rise Macare

179-239 $US BB
3 rooms, 3 pb
Most CC, Cash, •
C-yes/S-ltd/P-no/H-ltd

Full breakfast
Wine, hors d'oeuvres, soft drinks, tea
& cookies
Sitting room, library, pool table,
Jacuzzi, fireplace, cable TV, views

Comfortable elegance on three acres of oak-studded hills, fantastic views and sunsets and gracious hospitality. Three suites, each styled after a different European country await your visit. Fireplaces and whirlpool tubs surrounded by vineyards.
✉ macare@oakhillmanorbandb.com 🌐 www.oakhillmanorbandb.com

BALLARD

Ballard Inn & Restaurant
2436 Baseline Ave 93463
800-638-2466 805-688-7770
Christine Forsyth

245-315 $US BB
15 rooms, 15 pb
Visa, MC, AmEx,
Rated
C-ltd/S-no/P-no/H-yes

Full breakfast
Afternoon wine & hors d'oeuvres
included with stay
Turn down service with homemade
cookies

Located in the Santa Ynez Valley, about forty minutes from Santa Barbara, the Ballard Inn offers comfortably elegant accommodations in a peaceful and quiet setting.
✉ innkeeper@ballardinn.com 🌐 www.ballardinn.com

BEN LOMOND

Fairview Manor
245 Fairview Ave 95005
831-336-3355
Gael Glasson Abayon & Jack
Hazelton

149-159 $US BB
5 rooms, 5 pb
Visa, MC, Disc,
Rated, •
C-ltd/S-no/P-no/H-ltd

Full breakfast
Complimentary wine & hors
d'oeuvres
Sitting room, bordered by river,
weddings & meetings

Romantic country-style redwood home, majestic stone fireplace, 2.5 wooded acres in the Santa Cruz Mountains. Total privacy. Walk to town. A whole generation can identify with Santa Cruz, America's beach town. ✉ fairviewbandb@comcast.net 🌐 www.fairviewmanor.com

BERKELEY

Rose Garden Inn
2740 Telegraph Ave 94705
800-992-9005 510-549-2145
Kevin Allen

109-399 $US BB
40 rooms, 40 pb
Most CC, *Rated*, •
C-yes/S-ltd/P-no/H-ltd
Spanish

Full buffet breakfast
Coffee & tea available 24 hr, afternoon
cookies
Free parking on a space-available
basis, Direct TV, WiFi, fireplaces,
housekeeping, newspapers

Experience . . . the charming comfort of our 40 guestrooms surrounded by flowering gardens, some with sweeping views and soothing fountains. Walking distance from UC Berkeley and among the finest of Bay Area highlights.
✉ rosegardengm@aol.com 🌐 www.rosegardeninn.com

BERRY CREEK

Lake Oroville
240 Sunday Dr 95916
530-589-0700
Cheryl & Ronald Damberger

135-175 $US BB
6 rooms, 6 pb
Most CC, Cash, Checks,
Rated, •
C-yes/S-ltd/P-yes/H-yes

Full breakfast
Lunch & dinner available, snacks
Sitting room, game room, Jacuzzis,
fireplaces, cable TV, accommodate
business travelers

Lake views, sunsets, stargazing. Secluded country setting, covered porches with private entrances. Enjoy a evening picnic while watching the beautiful sunsets over the lake. A woodburning fireplace in the parlor, or a good book in the sunroom or library.

✉ cheryl@lakeorovillebedandbreakfast.com ◑ www.lakeorovillebedandbreakfast.com

BIG BEAR

Alpenhorn B&B
601 Knight Ave 92315
888-829-6600 909-866-5700
Timothy & Linda Carpenter

185-275 $US BB
8 rooms, 8 pb
Most CC, Cash,
Rated, •
C-ltd/S-ltd/P-no/H-yes

Full breakfast
Wine with appetizers in the evening,
after dinner liqueurs, chocolates
In-room spas for two, fireplaces, TV/
VCRs, private balconies, extensive
video library, host weddings

Free Night w/Certificate: Valid Monday-Thursday; except holidays

This beautiful bed and Breakfast in Big Bear Lake hosts garden weddings, romantic getaways, family reunions and small groups. Near the village, lake and ski resorts. Offering the finest AAA lodging and accommodations in the San Bernardino Mountains.

✉ linda@alpenhorn.com ◑ www.alpenhorn.com/welcome.html

Gold Mountain Manor
1117 Anita 92314
800-509-2604 909-585-6997
Cathy Weil

149-299 $US BB
7 rooms, 7 pb
Visa, MC, *Rated*, •
C-ltd/S-ltd/P-ltd/H-no

Full Gourmet breakfast
Gooey chocolate chip oatmeal cookies
Billiard table, parlor with
woodburning fireplace, wraparound
porch, library, concierge service

Historic log cabin B&B, secluded & romantic. Lots of special touches. Park-like setting, woodburning fireplaces, wraparound porch, candlelit breakfast, Jacuzzi tubs, spa treatments.

✉ info@goldmountainmanor.com ◑ www.goldmountainmanor.com

BIG BEAR LAKE

Eagle's Nest B&B
41675 Big Bear Blvd 92315
888-866-6465 909-866-6465
Mark & Vicki Tebo

110-165 $US BB
10 rooms, 10 pb
Most CC, *Rated*, •
C-ltd/S-ltd/P-ltd/H-no

Full breakfast
Snacks
Sitting room, spas, suites, fireplaces,
cable TV

Full log 5 room B&B nestled in Ponderosa pines, mountain lodge decor with antiques and custom furnishings, full hearty breakfast. In 2 additional buildings, 5 cottage spa units, breakfast optional.

✉ eaglesnestlodge@earthlink.net ◑ www.eaglesnestlodgebigbear.com

CALISTOGA

Aurora Park Cottages
1807 Foothill Blvd 94515
877-942-7700 707-942-6733
Joe Hensley

230-305 $US BB
6 rooms, 6 pb
Visa, MC, AmEx, •
C-yes/S-no/P-no/H-yes

Continental breakfast
Bottled water, apples, biscotti, jelly
bellies, coffee & tea
Mini-fridge, coffee makers, cable TV,
AC, plush towels, comfy robes &
private decks

Free Champagne — Mention Lanier when you make your reservation and we'll have some chilled champagne and chocolates awaiting your arrival. Aurora Park Cottages is your private vacation retreat in Napa Valley wine country.

✉ innkeeper@aurorapark.com ◑ www.aurorapark.com

Bear Flag Inn
2653 Foothill Blvd Hwy
128 94515
800-670-2860 707-942-5534
McNay Family

199-249 $US BB
5 rooms, 5 pb
Visa, MC, Disc, •
C-ltd/S-ltd/P-ltd/H-no

Full breakfast
Beverages & snacks
Parlor, pool, hot tub, hammocks, pool
table, player piano, garden, treadmill,
cable TV, WiFi

Featuring charming guestrooms, a full breakfast made with farm-fresh eggs produced here, and wine & appetizers in the afternoon, Bear Flag Inn is your home away from home in Calistoga.

✉ 2mcnays@ap.net ◑ www.bearflaginn.com

CALISTOGA

Brannan Cottage Inn
109 Wapoo Ave 94515
707-942-4200 707-942-4200
Doug & Judy Cook

155-280 $US BB
6 rooms, 6 pb
Visa, MC, AmEx,
Rated, •
C-yes/S-ltd/P-yes/H-ltd
Spanish

Full, multi-course breakfast
Friday evening wine & appetizers with
local wineries, homemade chocolate
chip cookies every night
A/C, fridge, queen bed, down
comforters, ceiling fans, fireplaces in
most rooms, WiFi, private entry

Free Night w/Certificate: Valid weekdays only Nov. 1-March 31; Sunday-thurs.

Charming 1860 cottage-style Victorian, country furnishings, lovely grounds with gardens, lawn & patios. It is walking distance to famous restaurants & spas & 25 wineries are within 3 miles. The inn is available for small meetings and special events.

✉ brannancottageinn@sbcglobal.net 🌐 www.brannancottageinn.com

---

Chelsea Garden Inn
1443 2nd St 94515
800-942-1515 707-942-0948
Dave & Susan DeVries

165-275 $US BB
5 rooms, 5 pb
Most CC, Cash, Checks,
Rated, •
C-yes/S-ltd/P-ltd/H-ltd

Full breakfast
Afternoon hors d'oeuvres, cheeses,
complimentary beverages
Spacious suites, fireplaces, WiFi, TV/
DVD, free movies, guest computer,
concierge, pool, library

Free Night w/Certificate: Valid Mon-Wed., Nov. 12-April 15. based on rooms priced $195 or higher. Room Upgrade

This charming Napa Valley B&B is conveniently located near wineries, spas, restaurants & other area activities. Spacious & private romantic suites with fireplaces, robes, cable TV w/DVD. Pool. Afternoon hors d'oeuvres, Free WiFi. AAA 3 diamonds, breakfast

✉ innkeeper@chelseagardeninn.com 🌐 www.chelseagardeninn.com

Christopher's Inn
1010 Foothill Blvd 94515
866-876-5755 707-942-5755
Christopher & Adele Layton

189-389 $US BB
23 rooms, 21 pb
Most CC, Cash,
Rated, •
C-ltd/S-no/P-no/H-ltd

Breakfast delivered to your room
Complimentary wine tasting passes,
Discounts at restaurants
wireless Internet access, a/c,
fireplaces, Jacuzzi hot tubs with robes,
Cable TV, Special spa pkg

Elegant 23-room country inn and gardens. Laura Ashley interiors, cozy wood burning fireplaces, romantic garden courtyards with fountains, in-room Jacuzzis. Christopher's Inn has been honored as a Golden Grape Award Finalist, one of three in the county.

✉ christophersinn@earthlink.net 🌐 www.christophersinn.com

Hillcrest B&B
3225 Lake Co Hwy 94515
707-942-6334
Debbie O'Gorman

69-165 $US BB
3 rooms, 3 pb
Most CC, Cash, Checks,
Rated, •
C-yes/S-ltd/P-yes/H-ltd

Continental breakfast
Sitting room, library, Jacuzzis, movie
channel, fireplaces, conference room

Secluded hilltop home with "million dollar view," furnished with antique silver, china, rugs, artwork, fireplaces, and ensuite Jacuzzis. Swimming, hiking and fishing on 36 secluded acres. Pet friendly.

🌐 www.hillcrestcountryinn.com

La chaumiere
1301 Cedar St 94515
800-474-6800 707-942-5139
Ursula

175-250 $US BB
3 rooms, 3 pb
Visa, MC, *Rated*, •
C-ltd/S-no/P-no/H-no

Full Gourmet breakfast
Afternoon wine & cheese
Living room, hot tub, courtyard,
redwood tree with tree house

Come away to Calistoga, in Napa Valley's Wine Country, where a night's stay at La chaumiere awaits. On a quiet picturesque residential street, across from city park, ½ block from downtown Calistoga.

✉ lachaumierebnb@yahoo.com 🌐 www.lachaumiere.com

CALISTOGA

Mount View Hotel & Spa
1457 Lincoln Ave 94515
800-816-6877 707-942-6877
Andrea Hoogendoorn

169-439 $US BB
31 rooms, 31 pb
Most CC, *Rated*, •
C-ltd/S-ltd/P-no/H-yes

Continental breakfast
Breakfast delivery, 2 On-site
Restaurants (JoLe & Barolo), 2 Full
Bars, Located Downtown
Garden Courtyard, Jacuzzi, Heated
Swimming Pool, Full Service Day Spa,
FREE WiFi, DVD, iPod docks

At the Mount View Hotel & Spa in Calistoga, we celebrate the Art of Relaxation. We provide the blank canvas and the resources for you to experience the perfect wine country getaway.
✉ relax@mountviewhotel.com 🌐 www.mountviewhotel.com

Scarlett's Country Inn
3918 Silverado Trail 94515
707-942-6669
Derek Dwyer

155-250 $US EP
3 rooms, 3 pb
Rated, •
C-yes/S-no/P-ltd/H-no
Spanish

Breakfast upon request
Complimentary wine & cheese,
lemonade
Sitting room, A/C, TVs, microwaves &
refrigerator, coffeemakers, pool, hot
tub, wireless Internet

A charming 1890 country farmhouse, nestled in a private canyon, with a quiet mood of green lawns and tall pines overlooking the vineyards at the edge of a forest.
✉ scarletts@aol.com 🌐 www.scarlettscountryinn.com

The Chanric Inn
1805 Foothill Blvd 94515
877-281-3671 707-942-4535
Ric Pielstick

209-349 $US BB
6 rooms, 6 pb
Most CC, *Rated*, •
C-ltd/S-no/P-ltd/H-no
Mandarin Chinese,
Some Spanish

3 Course Chef-Prepared Brunch
Select beverages provided throughout
your stay, wake-up coffee and tea
service
Pool, spa & sauna, full concierge
service, property-wide WiFi,
bathrobes, Aveda bath amenities

The Chanric Inn is an intimate, boutique inn providing luxurious amenities, a chef prepared gourmet breakfast, pool, spa & full concierge service. It is central to the finest wineries, restaurants & spas Napa Valley & Sonoma have to offer.
✉ ric@thechanric.com 🌐 www.thechanric.com

The Craftsman Inn
1213 Foothill Blvd 94515
707-341-3035
Gillian & Nick Kite

149-349 $US BB
5 rooms, 5 pb
Most CC, Cash,
Rated, •
C-ltd/S-no/P-no/H-no
French

Full gourmet champagne breakfast
Bottled water, complimentary wine,
nightcap decanter of Madeira with
homemade cookies
Flat screen TV/DVD, robes, luxury
toiletries, A/C, heat, wireless Internet
access, CD/radio alarm

Our passion is to help our guests gain as much pleasure from their visit to this wonderful valley as we do from living here. ✉ info@thecraftsmaninn.com 🌐 www.thecraftsmaninn.com

Trailside Inn
4201 Silverado Trl 94515
707-942-4106
Lani Gray

165-185 $US BB
3 rooms, 3 pb
Most CC, *Rated*, •
C-yes/S-ltd/P-yes/H-ltd

Continental plus breakfast
Complimentary wine
Mineral water, fireplace, kitchens,
library, A/C, spa, private deck, pool,
Internet access, TV

The Trailside Inn is a charming 1930s farmhouse centrally located in the beautiful Napa Valley. Antique furnishings, full private bathrooms, private entrances, heated swimming pool, TV and hi-speed Internet are prized features of our inn. Family friendly!
✉ innkeeper@trailsideinn.com 🌐 www.trailsideinn.com

Valley Oak Inn
2273 Grant St 94515
707-942-4720
Jeannette

165-295 $US BB
2 rooms, 2 pb
S-no/P-no/H-no

Continental breakfast
Use of BBQ and Outdoor Fire Pit
Solar pool, swim towels, WiFi access,
privacy

It is perfect for a romantic getaway—honeymoon, anniversary, or that special occasion. Enjoy relaxation and privacy. Our exclusive cottage or our magnificent suite await your arrival. A continental breakfast is served to you each morning on the patio.
🌐 valleyoakinn.com

Zinfandel House, Calistoga, CA

CALISTOGA

Wine Way Inn	100-225 $US BB	Full Gourmet Breakfast
1019 Foothill Blvd 94515	6 rooms, 6 pb	Afternoon wine & cheese
800-572-0679 707-942-0680	Most CC, Cash, *Rated*	Extensive decks, WiFi throughout the
Gillian & Nick Kite	C-ltd/S-no/P-no/H-no	property
	French, a little Dutch	
	and German	

Converted from a Craftsman-style family home in 1978, the Wine Way Inn is Calistoga's oldest B&B. The loving care of the previous and current owners, have preserved the best of the original while providing lodging with period charm and modern convenience.

✉ winewayinn@aol.com   🌐 www.winewayinn.com

Zinfandel House	130-155 $US BB	Full breakfast
1253 Summit Drive 94515	2 rooms, 2 pb	Complimentary wine
707-942-0733	Visa, MC, *Rated*	Library, sitting room, hot tub, goose
Bette & George Starke	C-ltd/S-no/P-no/H-no	down comforters, music room and
		deck

Beautiful home nearby to wineries, situated on wooded hillside, overlooking vineyards and mountains. Lovely full breakfast served on outside deck or in solarium.

✉ bette@zinfandelhouse.com   🌐 www.zinfandelhouse.com

CAMBRIA

J. Patrick House	175-215 $US BB	Full breakfast
2990 Burton Dr 93428	8 rooms, 8 pb	Offering evening wine & hors
800-341-5258 805-927-3812	Visa, MC, *Rated*	d'oeuveres & killer chocolate chip
Ann & John	C-ltd/S-no/P-no/H-no	cookies
		Sitting room, library, in-room
		massage, host weddings/elopements,
		complimentary concierge services

Award winning Inn on the California Central Coast. Authentic log home and carriage house nestled in the pines. Irish country comfort in accommodations with rooms uniquely appointed in "traditional" yet comfortable decor. Wood burning fireplaces.

✉ jph@jpatrickhouse.com   🌐 www.jpatrickhouse.com

CAMBRIA

Olallieberry Inn	135-225 $US BB	Full breakfast
2476 Main St 93428	9 rooms, 9 pb	Complimentary wine, hors d'oeuvres,
888-927-3222 805-927-3222	Visa, MC, AmEx,	cookies
Marjorie Ott	*Rated*, •	Gathering room, fireplaces, antiques,
	C-ltd/S-no/P-no/H-yes	special diets, massages, wireless
		Internet connection

Free Night w/Certificate: Valid Oct. 2011-Dec. 20,2011; Sunday-Thursday nights; excluding holiday periods

1873 restored Greek Revival home, warm and inviting, nestled in the heart of the enchanting village of Cambria. Walk to antique shops, art galleries, gift shops and fine restaurants.

info@olallieberry.com   www.olallieberry.com

Pelican Cove Inn	119-419 $US BB	Full breakfast
6316 Moonstone Beach	42 rooms, 42 pb	Wine and cheese tasting reception,
Dr 93428	Most CC, Cash, Checks	evening desert & coffee.
800-966-6490 805-927-1500	C-yes/S-no/P-no/H-yes	Fireplace, mini-fridge, tv, Internet,
George Marschall		microwave, on-demand movies,
		hairdryer, iron, coffee maker

A charming artists village in an idyllic setting half-way between San Francisco and Los Angeles on scenic Highway One. The Pelican Grove Inn is home to pristine beaches, wild and rugged hiking trails, quirky Nitt Witt Ridge and unique shops.

reservations@pelicancoveinncambria.com   www.pelicansuites.com

Sea Otter Inn	79-299 $US BB	Continental breakfast
6656 Moonstone Beach	25 rooms, 25 pb	Fireplace, whirlpool tubs, ocean view,
Dr 93428	Most CC, Cash, Checks	heated pool and spa
800-966-6490 805-927-5888	C-yes/S-no/P-ltd/H-yes	
George Marschall		

Welcome to Sea Otter Inn on Moonstone Beach on California's Central Coast. Our location on Moonstone Beach in Cambria, one hour north of San Luis Obispo and one half hour south of Big Sur, makes Sea Otter Inn the perfect destination for exploring California.

info@seaotterinn.com   www.seaotterinn.com

Summer Place	85-95 $US BB	Great breakfast
1416 Leonard Place 93428	1 rooms, 1 pb	Living room with large stone fireplace
805-684-5745 805-927-8145	•	available to guests for reading, movies,
Don Urbano	S-no/P-no/H-no	music or relaxing.

Charming 2 story Cape Cod home. Lovely gardens, sitting areas, home decor to match. Large stone fireplace is a favorite gathering for guests. Location is very quiet and peaceful. Queen bed private bath in room. Deck ocean view.

The Blue Whale Inn	315-470 $US BB	Full breakfast
6736 Moonstone Beach	7 rooms, 7 pb	Afternoon tea and baked goods,
Dr 93428	Most CC, Cash, Checks,	complimentary wine, hors d'oeuvres
800-753-9000 805-927-4647	*Rated*	& cheese
Marguerite & Mary	C-ltd/S-no/P-ltd/H-yes	Sitting room, library, fireplaces, cable
		TV, romantic mini suites

The Blue Whale Inn Bed and Breakfast is nestled on the green carpeted bluffs of Cambria and overlooks the Pacific Ocean. You will be welcomed with unexpected luxury and gracious hospitality in a setting beside the California Pacific ocean.

innkeeper@bluewhaleinn.com   www.bluewhaleinn.com

White Water Inn	100-280 $US BB	Continental breakfast
6790 Moonstone Beach	17 rooms, 17 pb	Fireplace, cable TV, hairdryers, iron &
Dr 93428	Visa, MC, Disc, *Rated*	board, complimentary videos, sitting
800-995-1715 805-927-1066	C-yes/S-no/P-ltd/H-ltd	room, ocean views
Cindy Taylor		

One of the few independently owned inns in Cambria opposite the ocean. A calm, 17 cottage style establishment in the Monterey Marine Wildlife Sanctuary, half way between San Francisco and Los Angeles.   innkeeper@whitewaterinn.com   www.whitewaterinn.com

CAPITOLA

Capitola Hotel
210 Esplanade 95010
877-705-7377 831-476-1278
Michael & Christine Herberg

84-275 $US BB
10 rooms, 10 pb
Visa, MC, Disc, •
C-ltd/S-no/P-no/H-yes

Voucher for local restaurant
A complimentary cup of gourmet
coffee or tea and a biscotti available in
our lobby each morning
Free Wifi, Plasma screen with HBO,
free local telephone, private bath,
ceiling fan

Steps to the beach, in the center of Capitola Village — clean comfortable upscale rooms, full breakfast, gourmet coffee, biscotti and WiFi. The beach is across the street, live music, great dining, shopping, unique events and year-round outdoor activities

✉ info@CapitolaHotel.com ◐ www.capitolahotel.com/index.html

CARDIFF BY THE SEA

Cardiff by the Sea Lodge
142 Chesterfield 92007
760-944-6474
James & Jeanette Statser

140-385 $US BB
17 rooms, 17 pb
Most CC, Cash, •
C-yes/S-no/P-no/H-ltd

Continental plus breakfast
Rooftop Garden, fireplaces, whirlpool
tubs, beach chairs, wet bars, free
wireless Internet

Steps away from the blue Pacific Ocean and beach. Minutes from all San Diego has to offer, here is a place where lush gardens bloom year-round.

✉ innkeeper@cardifflodge.com ◐ www.cardifflodge.com

CARLSBAD

Pelican Cove Inn
320 Walnut Ave 92008
888-PEL-COVE 760-434-5995
Nancy & Kris Nayudu

95-215 $US BB
10 rooms, 10 pb
Visa, MC, AmEx,
Rated, •
C-yes/S-no/P-no/H-yes

Full breakfast
Fireplaces, feather beds, business
accommodations, TV, private
entrances, Internet, beach equipment

Sun, blue skies, endless beaches, glorious sunsets, and the wide Pacific welcome you to Pelican Cove B&B Inn. We strive to make your stay memorable and enjoyable. Only steps from the ocean, fine restaurants and pleasant shops.

✉ PelicanCoveInn@pelican-cove.com ◐ www.pelican-cove.com

CARMEL

Carmel Country Inn
Dolores & 3rd Ave 93921
800-215-6343 831-625-3263
Amy Johnson

195-425 $US BB
12 rooms, 12 pb
Visa, MC, AmEx,
Rated, •
C-ltd/S-no/P-yes/H-no
Spanish

Expanded Continental Breakfast
In-room coffeemaker, complimentary
cream sherry
Fireplaces, private baths, private
entrances, off street parking, wireless
Internet, TV/DVD players

Carmel Country Inn Bed and Breakfast in Carmel, California offers a great blend of convenience, comfort, romance, and surrounding natural beauty near the beaches of beautiful Carmel by the Sea.

✉ info@carmelcountryinn.com ◐ www.carmelcountryinn.com

Edgemere Cottages
San Antonio between 13th &
Santa Lucia St 93921
866-241-4575 831-624-4501
Gretchen Siegrist-Allen

120-295 $US BB
4 rooms, 4 pb
Visa, MC, Disc, •
C-yes/S-no/P-yes/H-ltd
German, French,
Spanish, Italian, Dutch

Full, homemade breakfast
Sitting room, fireplaces, cable TV,
accommodations for business
travelers, WiFi

Edgemere features quaint private cottages, continental breakfast, beautiful gardens, and is just a one block walk to Carmel Beach. The perfect setting for a romantic escape to the Monterey Peninsula.

✉ info@edgemerecottages.com ◐ www.edgemerecottages.com

Happy Landing Inn
Monte Verde bet. 5th & 6th
Ave 93921
800-297-6250 831-624-7917
Diane & Dawn

135-235 $US BB
7 rooms, 7 pb
Most CC, Cash,
Checks, •
C-ltd/S-no/P-yes/H-no

Continental plus breakfast
Hot breakfast served to your room.
Great room, gazebo & gardens, TV,
DVD/CD players, WiFi, reading lamps,
hairdryers

Hansel & Gretel cottages in the heart of Carmel, like something from a Beatrix Potter book, one of Carmel's most romantic places to stay. All accommodations with private baths, 3 with fireplaces and 3 suites. Enjoy a warm breakfast brought to your room.

✉ info@carmelhappylanding.com ◐ www.carmelhappylanding.com

CARMEL

Lamp Lighter Inn
SE Corner of Ocean Ave &
Camino Real 93921
831-624-7372
Bobby Richards

185-475 $US BB
11 rooms, 11 pb
Visa, MC, AmEx
C-yes/S-no/P-yes/H-no

Breakfast Basket
Wine & cheese reception Thursday–
Sunday from 5–7 p.m
Fireplaces, TVs, phones, private
entrances, flat-screen TVs, on-site
parking

Charming inn with two cottages and four guestrooms, just steps to the beach. Couples, families and small groups will find accommodations at the Lamp Lighter Inn, some rooms with fireplaces, all have private baths. An enchanted setting with lush gardens.

✉ innkeeper@carmellamplighter.com 🌐 www.carmellamplighter.com

---

Monte Verde Inn & Casa de Carmel
Monte Verde St. at Ocean
Ave. 93921
800-328-7707 831-624-6046
Randal Gilbert

150-235 $US BB
17 rooms, 17 pb
Most CC, Cash, •
C-yes/S-no/P-yes/H-ltd

Continental plus breakfast
Sherry, coffeemaker, wine & cheese,
close by restaurants
TV, phone, refrigerator, hair dryers,
gardens & patios

Tucked into the famous artisan village of Carmel-by-the-Sea are two classic country-style bed and breakfast inns — Monte Verde Inn and Casa de Carmel. All rooms have a private bath, television, telephone and our signature sherry.

✉ reservations@monteverdeinn.com 🌐 www.monteverdeinn.com

Sandpiper Inn
2408 Bay View Ave 93923
800-590-6433 831-624-6433
James Hartle

109-235 $US BB
17 rooms, 17 pb
Most CC, *Rated*, •
S-no/P-no/H-no

Continental plus breakfast
Afternoon tea & cookies
Library, wireless Internet, fireside
lounge, close to tennis, golf, hiking

One-half block to Carmel Beach. European-style 1929 country inn, with some antiques and individual decor. Ocean views, gas-log fireplaces, 3 cottages, patio & garden areas. Mobil 2-star rating, 3 Diamonds AAA rating. ✉ info@sandpiper-inn.com 🌐 www.sandpiper-inn.com

---

Sea View Inn
Camino Real @ 11th &
12th 93921
831-624-8778
Marshall & Diane Hydorn

135-265 $US BB
8 rooms, 6 pb
Visa, MC, AmEx,
Rated
C-ltd/S-ltd/P-no/H-no

Continental plus breakfast
Afternoon tea & coffee
Complimentary evening wine, sitting
room, library, garden, free wireless
Internet

When you arrive at the Sea View Inn you will be greeted by a friendly and knowledgeable staff, happy to advise you about the restaurants, shops, and the scenic and historic places that make our Village such a special place. ✉ seaviewinncarmel@gmail.com 🌐 www.seaviewinncarmel.com

---

Tally Ho Inn
Monte Verde at 6th St 93921
800-652-2632 831-624-2232
John Lloyd

189-349 $US BB
12 rooms, 12 pb
Most CC, *Rated*, •
C-yes/S-no/P-no/H-yes
Spanish

Continental plus breakfast
Afternoon tea, brandy, continental
plus breakfast on Sat. & Sun.,
American buffet breakfast Mon-Fri.
Floral garden, sun deck, fireplaces,
ocean views, close to beach

The Tally Ho features 12 rooms with private decks and ocean views. Rooms have fireplaces, 55" LED TV's, Jacuzzi tubs, Bose Wave radios & refrigerators. Also featuring complimentary wireless Internet and during the week a full American breakfast buffet.

✉ jlloyd@pine-inn.com 🌐 www.tallyho-inn.com

The Colonial Terrace
San Antonio & 13th 93921
800-345-8220 831-624-2741

119-599 $US BB
26 rooms, 26 pb
Most CC, *Rated*, •
C-ltd/S-no/P-no/H-ltd
Spanish

Expanded Continental Breakfast
Afternoon tea reception offering fresh
fruit & fresh-baked cookies
All rooms have fireplaces, many with
ocean views, Jacuzzi tubs, wet bars,
some w/ kitchenettes, WiFi

Historic boutique hotel, one of Carmel's original hotels. Just steps from Carmel Beach, we offer rooms with fireplaces, ocean views, suites, and whirlpool tubs. Each room offers its own charm and personality.

✉ reservations@thecolonialterrace.com 🌐 www.thecolonialterrace.com

CARMEL

Tickle Pink Inn
155 Highland Dr. 93923
800-635-4774 831-624-1244

299-599 $US BB
35 rooms, 35 pb
Visa, MC, AmEx,
Rated, •
C-ltd/S-ltd/P-no/H-yes

Continental plus breakfast
Evening wine and cheese reception,
Limited room service and wine list
menu.
Limited room service menu, breakfast
delivered to your room, daily
newspaper, movie library, robes.

Established and operated by the Gurries family, the Tickle Pink Inn at Carmel Highlands has graced this setting since 1956. With 35 rooms and suites, the Inn is intimate and private and offers the discriminating guest a variety of personalized services.
✉ kparker@ticklepinkinn.com ◐ www.ticklepinkinn.com

Vagabond's House Inn
4th & Dolores 93921
800-262-1262 831-624-7738
Julie Campbell

155-275 $US BB
13 rooms, 13 pb
Most CC, Cash, Checks,
Rated, •
C-ltd/S-no/P-yes/H-no
French

Continental plus breakfast
Wine, snacks
Sitting room with fireplace, library,
courtyard, 2 blocks to downtown

Antique clocks and pictures, quilted bedspreads, fresh flowers, plants, shelves filled with old books. Sherry by the fireplace and breakfast served in your room.
✉ innkeeper@vagabondshouseinn.com ◐ www.vagabondshouseinn.com

CARMEL VALLEY

Country Garden Inns
102 W. Carmel Valley
Rd 93924
800-367-3336 831-659-5361
Dirk Oldenburg

119-215 $US BB
39 rooms, 39 pb
Visa, MC, AmEx, •
C-yes/S-no/P-no/H-no
German, Spanish

Buffet with waffle bar
Evening wine & cheese hour

#1 Rated B&B in Carmel Valley. Out of the reach of the coastal fog nestled in the Santa Lucia Mountains and close to Carmel-by-the-Sea. Buffet style breakfast with waffle bar included. Walk to village for wine tasting, shopping and dining.
✉ concierge@countrygardeninns.com ◐ www.countrygardeninns.com

CAYUCOS

**Cass House Inn &
Restaurant**
222 N. Ocean Ave 93430
805-995-3669
Grace Lorenzen

165-325 $US BB
5 rooms, 5 pb
Visa, MC, AmEx
C-yes/S-no/P-no/H-yes

Full breakfast
Dinner served Thursday–Monday,
reservations recommended
In-room spa treatments, wine tours
(private vineyard tours & barrel
tastings), DVD library

The Historic Cass House Inn and Restaurant, originally built in 1867, is located in Cayucos, California on the stunning Central Coast. The Cass House Inn offers guests five luxurious rooms, an elegant restaurant, a beautiful garden and ocean views.
✉ guestservices@casshouseinn.com ◐ www.casshouseinn.com

CHESTER

The Bidwell House
One Main St 96020
530-258-3338
Eva & Filip Laboda

85-175 $US BB
14 rooms, 12 pb
Visa, MC, *Rated*, •
C-ltd/S-no/P-no/H-yes

Three course gourmet breakfast
Afternoon sherry served by fireplace,
fresh fruit, giant chocolate chip
cookies
Sitting room, library, DVD library,
Jacuzzi tubs in rooms, fireplaces, WiFi

Historic Inn on the edge of Lassen National Park, beautiful Lake Almanor and next to the Feather River. Gourmet breakfast, a four-season paradise, world class dining, golfing, boating and shopping.
✉ reservation@bidwellhouse.com ◐ www.bidwellhouse.com

CHULA VISTA

**El Primero Boutique B&B
Hotel**
416 Third Ave 91910
619-425-4486
Pie & Sol Roque

90-120 $US BB
19 rooms, 19 pb
Most CC, Cash
C-yes/S-no/P-no/H-yes

Full breakfast
24 hour guest services, friendly staff,
courtyard, kiosk, cable TV, WiFi, off
street parking

El Primero is Chula Vista's best-kept hotel secret. An historic, award winning B&B where guests wake up to a sumptuous, gourmet breakfast. Recipient of the city's first Historic Preservation Award and the Mayor's 2005 Beautification Award. ✉ pie@elprimerohotel.com ◐ www.elprimerohotel.com

CORONADO

Cherokee Lodge
964 D Ave 92118
877-743-6213 619-437-1967
Ed & Mary Melvin

135-175 $US BB
12 rooms, 12 pb
Most CC, Cash,
Checks, •
C-yes/S-no/P-ltd/H-no

Continental breakfast
Breakfast vouchers for continental
breakfast at a local diner, coffee & tea
in rooms
WiFi, washer/dryer, satellite TVs,
fridge, free phone calls worldwide, AC

The Cherokee Lodge is across the bay from downtown San Diego in the heart of Coronado Island and is located one block from downtown Coronado near numerous charming bistros & restaurants, & just three blocks from the beach & the historic Hotel Del Coronado

info@cherokeelodge.com 🌐 www.CherokeeLodge.com

Coronado Village Inn
1017 Park Pl 92118
619-435-9318
Jauter & Ana Sainz

85-95 $US BB
15 rooms, 15 pb
Visa, MC, AmEx
C-yes/H-yes
Spanish

Self-serve continental breakfast
Fully-equipped kitchen available to
guests 24 hours a day
Laundry, sitting room, cable TV, maid
service

Located off Coronado's main street, Coronado Village Inn is a historic bed and breakfast decorated in old Spanish style. 1½ blocks to the ocean! 🌐 www.coronadovillageinn.com

CROWLEY LAKE

**Rainbow Tarns B&B At
Crowley Lake**
505 Rainbow Tarns Rd 93546
888-588-6269 760-935-4556
Brock & Diane Thoman

110-155 $US BB
3 rooms, 3 pb
Rated
C-ltd/S-ltd/P-no/H-yes
Closed Dec 24-25

Full country breakfast
Afternoon wine, snacks, veggie meals
by arrangement
Sitting room, library, 2 rooms with
Jacuzzis

Relax in the heart of High Sierra Mountains where the soothing sounds of flowing water and gentle breezes in the pines, the crystal clear sky and sparkling starry nights blend into an enchanting and memorable experience. Between Bishop and Mammoth Lakes.

innkeeper@rainbowtarns.com 🌐 www.rainbowtarns.com

DANA POINT

The Blue Lantern Inn
34343 Blue Lantern St 92629
800-950-1236 949-611-1304
Lin McManon

185-600 $US BB
29 rooms, 29 pb
Most CC, Cash
C-yes/S-no/P-no/H-yes

Full breakfast
Afternoon wine, tea & hors d' oeuvres,
freshly-baked cookies, drinks available
throughout the day
Meeting rooms, bikes, Jacuzzi, evening
turndown, WiFi, concierge service,
movies, books & games

Enjoy fabulous views of the Pacific from just about every window of this four diamond bed and breakfast inn – dramatically located on a bluff above the Dana Point Yacht Harbor.

bluelanterninn@foursisters.com 🌐 www.bluelanterninn.com

ELK

Elk Cove Inn & Spa
6300 S. Highway One 95432
800-275-2967 707-877-3321
Elaine Bryant

125-395 $US BB
15 rooms, 15 pb
Most CC, Cash, Checks,
Rated, •
C-ltd/S-ltd/P-no/H-ltd
Spanish

Full gourmet champagne breakfast
Direct beach access, European-style
day spa, free WiFi, guest lounge with
TV, gazebo

Situated atop a bluff in peaceful seclusion with breathtaking views this romantic Mendocino coast historic inn offers ocean and garden view rooms in the 1883 mansion, four bluff top cottage units and four luxury oceanfront suites.   innkeeper@elkcoveinn.com 🌐 www.elkcoveinn.com

---

Sandpiper House Inn
5520 S Hwy 1 95432
800-894-9016 707-877-3587
Jaci Schartz

150-275 $US BB
5 rooms, 5 pb
Most CC, *Rated*, •
C-ltd/S-no/P-no/H-no

Gourmet Breakfast
Wine & hors d'oeuvres in the evening;
complimentary wine in your room
Antiques, fresh flowers, gardens,
fireplaces, fine linens, down
comforters, feather pillows

Seaside country inn built in 1916. Rich redwood paneling in the living and dining rooms, lush perennial gardens that extend to the ocean bluff, stunning oceanviews, fireplaces in all of the rooms.

 sandpiperhouseinn@yahoo.com 🌐 www.sandpiperhouse.com

ENCINITAS

Inn at Moonlight Beach
105 N Vulcan Ave 92024
760 561 1755
Ann Dunham & Terry
Hunefeld

129-169 $US BB
4 rooms, 4 pb
Visa, MC, *Rated*
S-no/P-no/H-yes
Spanish

Continental plus breakfast
Delicious home-made, warm from
the oven breads and muffins. See our
website for photos and menus.
Our sunny breakfast room with
fireplace is yours to use 24/7. WiFi in
rooms.

Ann Dunham's Inn at Moonlight Beach has been voted San Diego's most romantic Pacific Coast Bed & Breakfast Inn featuring meditative gardens and beautiful sunsets. We overlook Moonlight Beach, the Pacific Ocean and the quaint beach-town of Encinitas.
🌐 www.innatmoonlightbeach.com

EUREKA

Carter House Inns & Restuarant 301
301 L St 95501
800-404-1390 707-444-8062
Mark & Christi Carter

155-385 $US BB
32 rooms, 32 pb
Most CC, Cash,
Checks, •
C-yes/S-no/P-yes/H-yes
Spanish, French

Full breakfast
Wine, hors d'oeuvres, cookies, tea,
chocolate truffles
Whirlpools, fireplaces, sitting rooms,
Jacuzzis, TV/VCR, CD, stereo, gardens,
bar on mezzanine level

Carter House Inns is perched alongside Humboldt Bay in Victorian Eureka with luxurious amenities, superior hospitality, spas, fireplaces, and antique furnishings. Also stop by our Restaurant 301, a Wine Spectator Grand Award winning restaurant.
✉ reserve@carterhouse.com 🌐 www.carterhouse.com

Cornelius Daly Inn
1125 H St 95501
800-321-9656 707-445-3638
Donna & Bob Gafford

130-225 $US BB
5 rooms, 4 pb
Most CC, *Rated*, •
C-yes/S-no/P-no/H-no

Full breakfast
Wine, hors d'oeuvres
Music room, library, Victorian gardens,
game room, TV room, laundry room

A beautifully restored turn-of-the-century mansion, one of Eureka's finest. The Inn is located in the historic section of Eureka a few blocks from the Pacific Ocean and a short drive to the majestic Red-woods State & National Parks. ✉ innkeeper@dalyinn.com 🌐 www.dalyinn.com

The Ship's Inn B&B
821 D St 95501
877-443-7583 707-443-7583
Genie Wood

130-175 $US BB
3 rooms, 3 pb
Most CC, Cash
C-yes/S-ltd/P-ltd/H-no

Full breakfast
Cookies & lemonade at check-in,
Brandy in the parlor
Internet access, WiFi, TV, VCR, robes,
dining room, fireside, common areas,
library

Step back in time to those seafaring days in a cozy, relaxing atmosphere befitting Eureka's Victorian Seaport. Just blocks to charming Old Town and the new boardwalk.
✉ genie@shipsinn.net 🌐 www.shipsinn.net

FELTON

Felton Crest Inn
780 El Solya Heights
Dr 95018
800-474-4011 831-335-4011
Hanna Peters

199-375 $US BB
4 rooms, 4 pb
Visa, MC, AmEx
C-ltd/S-ltd/P-no/H-ltd
German

Continental breakfast
Champagne & chocolates on arrival
Cable TV, VCR, video library,
telephone, private baths

A romantic getaway set in the majestic redwoods of the Santa Cruz Mtns. Enjoy all that the beautiful Monterey Bay and California's Central Coast have to offer. Uniquely located between San Francisco, Carmel and Pebble Beach and the Santa Clara Valley.
✉ hannapeters@comcast.net 🌐 www.feltoncrestinn.com

FERNDALE

Victorian Inn
400 Ocean Ave 95536
888-589-1808 707-786-4949
Lowell Daniels & Jenny Oaks

145-295 $US BB
13 rooms, 13 pb
Most CC, *Rated*, •
C-yes/S-no/P-no/H-ltd

Full breakfast
Lunch & dinner available, snacks,
restaurant, bar, afternoon wine &
cheese
Sitting room, suites, fireplace, cable
TV, wireless & cable Internet access

The Victorian Inn stands as a monument to luxurious comfort and exquisite craftsmanship. It embod-ies the elegance and romance of the timber boom era on the North Coast.
 innkeeper@victorianvillageinn.com 🌐 www.victorianvillageinn.com

FISH CAMP

Narrow Gauge Inn
48571 Hwy 41 93623
888-644-9050 559-683-7720
Martha Vanaman

79-195 $US BB
26 rooms, 26 pb
Visa, MC, Disc,
Rated, •
C-yes/S-ltd/P-yes/H-no

Continental breakfast
Fine dining restaurant (seasonal)
Seasonal pool & hot tub, gift shop,
nature trail

Celebrating the mountain atmosphere, the Narrow Gauge Inn is just 4 miles from Yosemite. Offering 26 charming rooms with balconies and mountain views, some pet-friendly. Seasonal restaurant. Weddings, reunions and events welcome.

✉ ngi@sti.net 🌐 www.narrowgaugeinn.com

FORESTHILL

Christmas Tree Vineyard Lodge
38400 Foresthill Road 95631
916-599-0141
Joe, Claudia and Liz

100 $US BB
6 rooms, 6 pb
Visa, MC
C-yes/S-no/P-no/H-yes

Full Breakfast
Community Kitchen use is available at
a nominal fee per day. TV, DVD player
and free WiFi.

Discover the seasons of the Sierra Nevada back country, minus the crowds! Winter, Spring, Summer or Fall . . . there are no cozier accommodations anywhere in the high country in the Sierra Nevada Mountains.

✉ loglodge1@gmail.com 🌐 www.christmastreevineyardlodge.com/index.ht

FORESTVILLE

Farmhouse Inn and Restaurant
7871 River Rd 95436
800-464-6642 707-887-3300
Catherine & Joe Bartolomei

295-695 $US BB
18 rooms, 18 pb
Most CC, Cash, *Rated*
C-ltd/S-no/P-no/H-yes

Full breakfast
4 star restaurant – Michelin & Zagat
reviewed. European style service,
superb wine list. Th-Mon
Full concierge services, heated pool,
spa services, WiFi, beverage bar, fire
pit & s'mores.

A Northern California Wine Country Inn & Restaurant. One of Travel & Leisure's Top 30 Inns, Michelin star, Zagat Best in Sonoma County, and Chronicle 100 Best Restaurants. Luxury spa on site. Romantic getaway central to Napa & Sonoma wineries.

✉ innkeep@farmhouseinn.com 🌐 www.farmhouseinn.com

FORT BRAGG

Country Inn
632 N Main St 95437
800-831-5327 707-964-3737
Bruce & Cynthia Knauss

55-145 $US BB
8 rooms, 8 pb
Most CC, Cash, Checks,
Rated, •
C-yes/S-no/P-no/H-yes

Full gourmet breakfast
Fireplaces, sun deck, parlor, hot tub,
Spa Treatments available, Skunk Train
nearby

Free Night w/Certificate: Anytime. Room Upgrade.

The Country Inn Bed and Breakfast, located in Fort Bragg surrounded by the splendor of Mendocino, invites you to "be our guest." For 30 years, the Inn has been serving country hospitality along the north coast of California.

✉ cntryinn@mcn.org 🌐 www.beourguests.com

GEORGETOWN

American River Inn
6600 Orleans St 95634
800-245-6566 530-333-4499
Will & Maria Collin

95-130 $US BB
14 rooms, 9 pb
Most CC, *Rated*, •
C-ltd/S-no/P-ltd/H-yes

Full breakfast
Complimentary evening wine & hors
d'oeuvres in the parlor
Pool, Jacuzzi, Bicycles, Bocce Ball,
Table Service

Free Night w/Certificate: Anytime. Valid Sunday-Friday and October-May.

Historic Queen Anne-style bed & breakfast inn, complete with old fashioned hospitality and turn-of-the-century antique furnishings. Refurbished Summer '07 to exceptional beauty. Fantastic featherbeds. Exotic therapeutic Jacuzzi. Table Service.

✉ visitus@americanriverinn.com 🌐 www.Americanriverinn.com

GEYSERVILLE————————————————————

Hope-Merrill/Hope-Bosworth B&B	149-289 $US BB	Full breakfast
21253 Geyserville Ave 95441	12 rooms, 12 pb	Complimentary water, 24-Hour coffee,
800-825-4233 707-857-3356	Most CC, Cash, Checks,	tea & chocolate machine, other
Cosette & Ron Scheiber	*Rated*, •	beverages available for purchase
	C-yes/S-no/P-ltd/H-ltd	Sitting room, library, Jacuzzis, suites,
	Spanish	swimming pool, fireplace, cable TV in
		some rooms

Facing each other are the Queen Anne Craftsman style Hope-Bosworth House and the strikingly re-stored Eastlake style Victorian Hope-Merrill House.
✉ moreinfo@hope-inns.com 🌐 www.hope-inns.com

GROVELAND————————————————————

Blackberry Inn B&B	150-265 $US BB	Full breakfast
7567 Hamilton Station Loop	5 rooms, 5 pb	Chocolate chip cookies, full tea
at Buck Meadows 95321	Visa, MC, AmEx,	service, lunches available upon
888-867-5001 209-962-4663	*Rated*	request
Steve McCorkle & Alexandra	C-ltd/S-no/P-no/H-yes	Wrap-around porch, hummingbirds,
North		loft, snow shoes, chocolate chip
		cookies, free wireless Internet

The Blackberry Inn, a Yosemite National Park bed and breakfast, is the quintessential American coun-try farmhouse with a lovely wraparound porch. Hundreds of hummingbirds visit this conveniently located Yosemite lodging facility on Hwy 120 closest to SFO.
✉ innkeepers@blackberry-inn.com 🌐 www.blackberry-inn.com

Groveland Hotel at	145-285 $US BB	Full, Hot Innkeeper's Breakfast
Yosemite National Park	17 rooms, 17 pb	Cellar Door Restaurant, Wine
18767 Main St 95321	Most CC, Cash,	Spectator Magazine's "Award of
800-273-3314 209-962-4000	*Rated*, •	Excellence" wine list, full service bar
Peggy & Grover Mosley	C-yes/S-no/P-yes/H-ltd	Cable TV, free WiFi, balconies, gold
		rush saloon, weddings, maps &
		guides, conferences, parties

Free Night w/Certificate: Oct 15-April 15. Excluding holidays and special events.. Room Upgrade.

Comfortable and luxurious rooms, 1849 Gold Rush hotel. 25 minutes to Yosemite. Indoor or courtyard dining, Wine Spectator Award winning wine list. Pet friendly, spa services, hiking, photography, bik-ing. Open all year. Conferences, weddings, retreat
✉ guestservices@groveland.com 🌐 www.groveland.com

Hotel Charlotte	119-159 $US BB	Buffet Sausage&Pancakes&Scrambled
18736 Main St 95321	10 rooms, 10 pb	Complimentary coffee, tea or iced tea
800-961-7799 209-962-6455	Visa, MC, AmEx, •	available almost any time, restaurant
Victor Niebylski & Lynn	C-yes/S-no/P-ltd/H-ltd	& bar on site 7 days/wk
Upthagrove	Spanish, some Italian,	Guest salon, Satellite TV, DSL Internet
	French, German	& WiFi, piano, game room, balcony,
		itinerary planning

Free Night w/Certificate: Valid Jan. 1-March 31, 2011 and Oct. 15, 2011-March 31, 2012, holiday periods excluded. Room Upgrade.

Hotel Charlotte is an historic B&B hotel on the way to Yosemite featuring a full service restaurant & bar. Yosemite National Park & Tuolumne River white water river rafting are popular local activities, as are wine tasting regions & Gold Rush towns. ✉ hotelcharlotte@aol.com 🌐 www.HotelCharlotte.com

GUERNEVILLE————————————————————

Applewood Inn	195-345 $US BB	Full breakfast
13555 Hwy 116 95446	19 rooms, 19 pb	Our Zagat rated restaurant offers
800-555-8509 707-869-9093	Most CC, Cash,	exceptional wine country fare, picnic
Sylvia & Carlos	*Rated*, •	baskets & cheese boards
	S-no/P-no/H-yes	Massage and Spa services, Pool with
	Italian and Spanish	Hot Tub.

A popular Sonoma County destination for food and wine enthusiasts seeking a getaway to Sonoma County's idyllic Russian River Valley. This historic and casually luxurious B&B is an ideal starting point for excursions. ✉ stay@applewoodinn.com 🌐 www.applewoodinn.com

GUERNEVILLE

Creekside Inn & Resort	98-270 $US BB	Full breakfast
16180 Neeley Rd 95446	28 rooms, 24 pb	Breakfast not available in cottages,
800-776-6586 707-869-3623	Visa, MC, AmEx, •	however cottages have full kitchens
Lynn & Mark Crescione	C-yes/S-ltd/P-ltd/H-yes	Library, sitting room, conference
	Spanish	facilities, direct phone, pool, WiFi,
		HBO, sun decks, picnic area

A relaxed and friendly atmosphere best describes this bed & breakfast, situated in the redwoods near the Russian River. We have a delightful bed & breakfast, an assortment of charming cottages, sunny decks, a pool, picnic areas, and affordable rates!
✉ stay@creeksideinn.com ◑ www.creeksideinn.com

Fern Grove Cottages	89-259 $US BB	Continental plus breakfast
16650 Hwy 116 95446	20 rooms, 20 pb	Sitting room, library, spa tubs, suites,
888-243-2674 707-869-8105	Most CC, Cash, *Rated*	pool, cable TV, wine tours, wireless
Mike & Margaret Kennett	C-yes/S-no/P-ltd/H-yes	Internet, bbq area

Comfortable cottages in the redwoods — many with living rooms, and fireplaces; some with spa tubs. Relax among beautiful gardens. Enjoy the pool. Easily walk to town, river, or beaches. Expect warm hospitality. Indulge with a great breakfast. ✉ innkeepers@ferngrove.com ◑ www.ferngrove.com

Sonoma Orchid Inn	149-245 $US BB	Full gourmet breakfast
12850 River Rd 95446	10 rooms, 10 pb	Homemade cookies, complimentary
888-877-4466 707-869-4466	Most CC, Cash,	water, juice, port & sherry, on-site
Brian Siewert & Dana	*Rated*, •	catering, guest kitchen
Murphy	C-yes/S-ltd/P-yes/H-ltd	Outdoor hot tub, great room w/
		fireplace, library, satellite TV/Tivo,
		cable TV, DVD/VCR, WiFi

Historic Sonoma Orchid Inn is nestled along the Russian River offering comfort & charm, in the heart of Sonoma County's Wine Country. Easy access to wineries, the coast & San Francisco.
✉ innkeeper@sonomaorchidinn.com ◑ www.sonomaorchidinn.com

HALF MOON BAY

Landis Shores Oceanfront Inn	225-345 $US BB	Full breakfast
211 Mirada Rd 94019	8 rooms, 8 pb	Appetizers, premium wines
650-726-6642	Most CC, Cash,	Whirlpool tub, fireplace, TV/DVD,
Ken & Ellen Landis	*Rated*, •	fitness room, private deck, extensive
	C-ltd/S-no/P-ltd/H-yes	wine list, Internet access
	Spanish	

Free Night w/Certificate: Valid Monday-Thursday, and November-May; Except holidays.

Elegant oceanfront accommodations, private balconies, fireplaces, whirlpool tubs, TV/VCRs and more. Enjoy a gourmet breakfast each morning and premium wines and appetizers every afternoon.
✉ luxury@landisshores.com ◑ www.landisshores.com

Old Thyme Inn	139-299 $US BB	Gourmet full breakfast
779 Main St 94019	7 rooms, 7 pb	Complementary afternoon wine &
800-720-4277 650-726-1616	Most CC, Cash, Checks,	cheese
Rick & Kathy Ellis	*Rated*, •	Library of videos and recent
	C-ltd/S-ltd/P-no/H-no	magazines, peaceful herb and flower
	French	garden

Spend enchanted nights. Herb and flower garden provides tranquil setting in coastal village, ½ hour from San Francisco and Silicon Valley. Furnished in antiques and fine art; 7 rooms each with cable TV/VCR, free WiFi, queen bed, and private bath.
✉ innkeeper@oldthymeinn.com ◑ www.oldthymeinn.com

Pacific Victorian B&B	150-195 $US BB	Full breakfast
325 Alameda Ave 94019	4 rooms, 4 pb	Parlor, dining room, down comforters,
888-929-0906 650-712-3900	Most CC	fine linens, decks, whirlpool tubs,
Jeff & Lori Matthews	C-yes/S-ltd/P-no/H-yes	movie library, WiFi

Elegantly decorated Victorian style Inn located in beautiful Miramar Beach, Half Moon Bay, California, within easy driving distance of San Francisco. The Inn is nestled in a scenic coastal setting 1.5 blocks from the beach. ✉ pacificvictorian@msn.com ◑ www.pacificvictorian.com

HALF MOON BAY

San Benito House
356 Main St 94019
650-726-3425
Cristina Carrubba

90-150 $US BB
12 rooms, 9 pb
Most CC, Cash, Checks,
Rated, •
C-yes/S-no/P-yes/H-ltd
Italian, Spanish, French,
Portuguese

Continental breakfast
delicious sandwiches made on
homemade bread, soups, pasta, salsa,
salads, muffins, cookies, brownies
Fresh flowers, sauna, redwood deck,
garden with croquet lawn and swing,
saloon, weddings, deli-cafe

Located at 356 Main St in Half Moon Bay, the San Benito House is open year round for restful bed and breakfast accommodations. 12 guestrooms, 9 with private bath. Old fashioned saloon, deli-cafe, beautiful gardens. Ideal for weddings and special events.

✉ inquiries@sanbenitohouse.com ◐ www.sanbenitohouse.com

HEALDSBURG

Camellia Inn
211 North St 95448
800-727-8182 707-433-8182
Lucy Lewand

139-329 $US BB
9 rooms, 9 pb
Most CC, Cash, Checks,
Rated, •
C-yes/S-no/P-ltd/H-ltd
Spanish

Full breakfast
Wine & cheese tasting, hot beverages
& cookies, on Wednesdays chocolate
& more chocolate
Parlor, pool, whirlpool tubs, fireplaces,
King beds, WiFi, winery passes, spa
discounts, concierge

A charming 1869 Italianate Victorian Inn set in California's Sonoma Wine Country. Surrounded by 50 varieties of its signature camellias, the Inn blends an authentic, vintage environment with modern and luxurious amenities for a memorable romantic getaway.

✉ info@camelliainn.com ◐ www.camelliainn.com

Haydon Street Inn
321 Haydon St 95448
800-528-3703 707-433-5228
John Harasty & Keren
Colsten

190-425 $US BB
9 rooms, 9 pb
Visa, MC, Disc
S-no/P-no/H-no

Full breakfast
Homemade chocolate chip cookies
in the afternoon, wine hour in the
evening
Comfortable public spaces, all king
rooms have fireplaces, Jacuzzi and
small fridge.

Historic Wine Country Queen Anne home in this friendly Sonoma County town. Walk to historic town plaza with great restaurants, antique stores and wonderful boutiques.

✉ innkeeper@haydon.com ◐ www.haydon.com

**Healdsburg Inn on the
Plaza**
112 Matheson St 95448
800-431-8663 707-433-6991
Jennifer Byrom

275-375 $US BB
12 rooms, 12 pb
Most CC, Cash, *Rated*
C-yes/S-no/P-no/H-yes

Full breakfast
Afternoon wine, tea & hors d' oeuvres,
freshly-baked cookies, drinks available
throughout the day
Evening turndown, early newspaper
delivery to your room, wireless
Internet, movies, books & games

This Four Sisters Inn blends the modern luxuries and sophisticated services of a boutique hotel with the traditional amenities and architecture of a B&B in the best location in town, right on the historic Healdsburg Plaza. ✉ healdsburginn@foursisters.com ◐ www.healdsburginn.com

Holcomb House
401 Piper St 95448
707-433-9228
Lucille

165 $US BB
2 rooms, 2 pb
Visa, MC, AmEx
C-ltd/S-no/P-no/H-yes

Self-serve Continental
Jacuzzi, fireplace, cable TV,
accommodate business travel, VCR,
DVD, high speed Internet

California Craftsman bungalow built at the turn of the century. Furnished with antiques and a quilt collection that gives character, charm and a homey atmosphere to the house.

✉ holcombh@comcast.net ◐ www.holcombhouse.com

Irish Rose Inn
3232 Dry Creek Rd 95448
707-431-2801
Chris & Lanny Matson

160-200 $US BB
3 rooms, 3 pb
Visa, MC
C-ltd/S-no/P-yes/H-no

Full breakfast

The Irish Rose is a wonderful Craftsman home built in 1912, and is located in the heart of Dry Creek Valley in Sonoma County, California.

✉ chris@theirishroseinn.com ◐ www.theirishroseinn.com

HEALDSBURG

Raford Inn of Healdsburg
10630 Wohler Rd 95448
800-887-9503 707-887-9573
Dane & Rita

155-255 $US BB
6 rooms, 6 pb
Visa, MC, AmEx,
Rated, •
C-ltd/S-no/P-no/H-ltd

Full breakfast
Complimentary evening wine & hors
d'oeuvres, tea, coffee & snacks in
dining room
Porch, vineyard views, garden, patio,
some fireplaces, roses, in-room
massage, WiFi, satellite TV

Victorian farmhouse overlooks vineyards in the heart of the Russian River Valley of Sonoma County. Beautiful country setting is just 1½ hours from San Francisco, a 15 minute drive to Healdsburg Plaza.

✉ innkeeper@rafordinn.com 🌐 www.rafordinn.com

HOMEWOOD

Rockwood Lodge
5295 West Lake Blvd 96141
800-538-2463 530-525-5273
Lou Reinkens & Connie
Stevens

100-225 $US BB
5 rooms, 5 pb
Visa, MC, *Rated*, •
C-ltd/S-no/P-ltd/H-no

Continental breakfast
Complimentary cordials
Sitting room, game room, swimming
pool, billiards

Rockwood Lodge is an "Old Tahoe" estate nestled in a pine forest on the west shore of Lake Tahoe. Many fine appointments, exquisite architecture and beautiful, natural surroundings. Breakfast on the patio in summer.

✉ lou@rockwoodlodge.com 🌐 www.rockwoodlodge.com

HOPE VALLEY

Sorensen's Resort
14255 Hwy 88 96120
800-423-9949 530-694-2203
John & Patty Brissenden

115-550 $US BB
35 rooms, 33 pb
Most CC, Checks,
Rated, •
C-yes/S-no/P-ltd/H-ltd
Some Spanish

Sorensens Country Cafe
Snacks, restaurant, wine & beer
service
Library, hot springs nearby, bikes &
skis nearby, wood burning stoves

Cozy creekside cabins nestled in the Alps of California. Close to Tahoe and Kirkwood and Hope Valley Outdoor Center. Hope Valley Resort features fly fishing, art and photo classes, and history tours.

✉ info@sorensensresort.com 🌐 www.sorensensresort.com

IDYLLWILD

Quiet Creek Inn &
Vacation Rentals
26345 Delano Dr 92549
800-450-6110 951-659-6110
Jim Newcomb & Mike Ahern

130-160 $US EP
10 rooms, 10 pb
Most CC, Cash,
Rated, •
C-yes/S-ltd/P-ltd/H-ltd

In room kitchenettes
In room gourmet coffee. Water, sodas,
Gatorade, hot teas, hot chocolate &
popcorn in the lounge
Borrow iron & ironing board,
Adventure Pass & Wilderness Trail
Map; hiking trail advice

Quiet Creek Inn offers deluxe, Sunset Magazine recommended, duplex cabins on over 6 acres along Strawberry Creek with fireplaces & private decks. Quiet Creek Vacation Rentals offer individually owned, well-appointed homes & cabins throughout town.

✉ info@quietcreekinn.com 🌐 www.quietcreekinn.com/Quiet-Creek-Inn.html

Starwberry Creek Bunk
House
25525 Hwy 243 92549
888-400-0071 951-659-2201
Rodney Williams

89-189 $US BB
18 rooms, 18 pb
Most CC, Cash
C-yes/S-no/P-yes/H-ltd

Continental breakfast
All guestrooms have private balconies,
a kitchenette, coffee maker, great
forest views.

Seated on a hillside overlooking the San Jacinto State Forest, the Strawberry Creek Bunkhouse is an affordable, eco-friendly lodge tailor-made for hikers, rock-climbers, fisherman, mountain-bikers, or travelers who want a kid or pet friendly vacation.

✉ innkeeper@strawberrycreekinn.com 🌐 strawberrycreekinn.com/index.htm

IDYLLWILD

Strawberry Creek Inn	109-239 $US BB	Full breakfast
26370 State Hwy 243 92549	10 rooms, 10 pb	Sodas, bottled water, coffee, tea,
800-262-8969 951-659-3202	Most CC, Cash, *Rated*	snacks, evening appetizers on Friday
Rodney Williams & Ian Scott	C-ltd/S-no/P-no/H-yes	& Saturday
		Library, fireplaces, refrigerators,
		hammock, wireless Internet, Aveda
		amenities, organic ingredients

Cool, clean mountain air, outdoor decks, hammocks & gardens overlooking Strawberry Creek. A member of the Green Hotels Association. Featured in "Best Places to Kiss" & "Great Towns of Southern CA." Nine inn guestrooms and one private cottage.

✉ innkeeper@strawberrycreekinn.com ❂ www.strawberrycreekinn.com

The Lodge at Pine Cove	85-105 $US BB	Full breakfast
24900 Marion Ridge	5 rooms, 5 pb	Assortment of coffee, teas, hot
Dr 92349	Visa, MC, AmEx,	chocolate
866-563-4372	*Rated*	Small refrigerator, decks, VCR & cable
951-659-4463	C-ltd/S-no/P-no/H-no	TV
Geary Boedeker		

The Lodge at Pine Cove is a 5-room B&B high in the San Jacinto Mountains at 6,200 feet, just minutes from the beautiful mountain village of Idyllwild. Romantic packages. Wonderful private getaway.

✉ innkeeper@thelodgeatpinecove.com ❂ www.thelodgeatpinecove.com

INVERNESS

Dancing Coyote Beach	175-250 $US BB	Full breakfast
800-210-1692 415-669-7200	3 rooms, 3 pb	Fully equipped kitchens in our
Janet Osborn	*Rated*	cottages for self-service dining
	C-ltd/S-ltd/P-ltd/H-no	Fireplaces, views, decks, parking,
		in-room massages, beachfront,
		outdoor BBQ, outdoor
		shower

You won't forget the time you spend at Dancing Coyote Beach. The graceful curve of the shoreline, the sheltering pines and cedars, and relaxing by a fire crackling in the fireplace will call you back again and again.

✉ Theparsonage@hotmail.com ❂ www.dancingcoyotebeach.com

Inverness Valley Inn	130-219 $US EP	Kitchenettes stocked with coffee, teas
13275 Sir Francis Drake	20 rooms, 20 pb	& spices
Blvd 94937	Most CC, Cash	Cable TV, thermostat-controlled gas
800-416-0405 415-669-7250	C-yes/S-no/P-yes/H-yes	fireplace, private patio, clock radio,
Alden & Leslie Adkins	Dutch, German, Italian,	tennis courts, pool, WiFi
	French	

Located on 15 acres of natural beauty, 1½ hours from San Francisco, our refurbished A-frame cottages each consist of four spacious units with high ceilings and plenty of light. Some rooms and suites dog-friendly. Green "eco-friendly" inn.

✉ info@Invernessvalleyinn.com ❂ www.invernessvalleyinn.com

JAMESTOWN

1859 Historic National	140-175 $US BB	Breakfast buffet
Hotel & Restaurant	9 rooms, 9 pb	Dining in our highly-acclaimed
18183 Main St 95327	Most CC, Cash,	restaurant is a gourmet's delight;
800-894-3446 209-984-3446	*Rated*, ●	full-serve saloon & espresso bar
Stephen Willey	C-ltd/S-no/P-yes/H-no	Historic saloon, concierge services,
	Spanish	patio dining, balcony & a fun staff

Free Night w/Certificate: Valid Sunday thru Thursday; holiday periods excluded; reservations only 24 hours in advance

Hotel c.1859 in the heart of Gold Rush country. Our rooms are restored to the elegance of a romantic by-gone era. Enjoy our highly acclaimed restaurant with full bar on premises. Antique shopping, live theatre, golf, hiking & wine-tasting. Near Yosemite.

✉ info@national-hotel.com ❂ www.national-hotel.com

JENNER

Jenner Inn Restaurant & Cottages
10400 Coast Hwy 1 95450
800-732-2377 707-865-2377
Richard Murphy

118-348 $US BB
21 rooms, 21 pb
Visa, MC, AmEx,
Rated, •
C-yes/S-no/P-ltd/H-yes
Spanish

Meatless breakfast
Tea & coffee, cookies
Sitting room, fireside lounge, sauna,
hot tubs & fireplaces

A unique country Inn on Sonoma's wine country coast. Panoramic waterviews from most rooms, suites and cottages. Fine dining, entertainment and many activities. Beautiful sunsets and romance abound. Whale watching in the winter months.

✉ innkeeper@jennerinn.com 🌐 www.jennerinn.com

JULIAN

Butterfield B&B
2284 Sunset Dr 92036
800-379-4262 760-765-2179
Ed & Dawn Glass

135-185 $US BB
5 rooms, 5 pb
Most CC, Cash,
Rated, •
C-ltd/S-ltd/P-no/H-ltd

Full breakfast
Complimentary coffees, tea, cider,
cocoa, popcorn & dessert in the
afternoon; guest stocked fridge
Sitting room, library, suites, fireplace,
cable TV/VCR/DVD/CD, WiFi, piano,
guitar, games

Relax on our three-acre, country garden setting in the quiet hills of Julian. Five unique rooms from country to formal decor. Famous gourmet breakfast. Just an hour from San Diego.

✉ info@butterfieldbandb.com 🌐 www.butterfieldbandb.com

Eaglenest B&B
2609 D St 92036
888-345-6378 760-765-1252
Jim & Julie Degenfelder

165-185 $US BB
4 rooms, 4 pb
Most CC
C-yes/S-ltd/P-no/H-ltd

Full breakfast
Dessert snacks are fresh baked for
your stay
Pool, spa, fireplaces, A/C/heat, hot
tubs, TV/VCR/CD

Eaglenest offers all the amenities of a four-star resort in the privacy & comfort of a beautiful home in this mountain hamlet in San Diego County. It is a one block walk to local shopping, fine dining, attractions & entertainment in historic Julian.

✉ info@eaglenestbnb.com 🌐 www.eaglenestbandb.com

Julian Gold Rush Hotel
2032 Main Street 92036
800-734-5854 760-765-0201
Steve & Gig Ballinger

135-210 $US BB
16 rooms, 16 pb
Visa, MC, AmEx,
Rated, •
C-yes/S-no/P-no/H-no

Full breakfast
Tea time-Enjoy sharing in our
afternoon tea served daily 5pm to 6pm
in the historic dining room.
Sitting room, library, wireless Internet,
parlor games, group meeting space,
AC, wake-up calls

The town's only designated landmark, capturing the charm and character of this 1800's Southern California mining town. In the heart of the Historic District, within walking distance of antique stores, gift shops, restaurants, museums and gold mines.

✉ bnb@julianhotel.com 🌐 www.julianhotel.com

Orchard Hill Country Inn
2502 Washington St 92036
800-716-7242 760-765-1700
Pat & Darrell Straube

195-450 $US BB
22 rooms, 22 pb
Visa, MC, AmEx,
Rated, •
C-yes/S-no/P-no/H-yes

Full breakfast
Complimentary afternoon hors
d'oeuvres, a four-course dinner is
served on select evenings
Masseuse available, video library,
conference facilities, weddings

Restful and romantic premier bed and breakfast with AAA Four Diamond attention to detail, caring staff and excellent dining. Gracious ambience, sweeping sunset views and seasonal gardens make us an unforgettable destination.

✉ information@orchardhill.com 🌐 www.orchardhill.com

KENWOOD

Birmingham B&B
8790 Highway 12 95452
800-819-1388   707-833-6996
Nancy & Jerry Fischman

160-295 $US BB
5 rooms, 5 pb
Visa, MC, AmEx,
Rated
C-ltd/S-no/P-ltd/H-ltd

Full breakfast
Upon request afternoon refreshments
include tea, coffee, cookies, and other
snacks
Parlor, wrap-around porch, vegetable
& flower gardens, concierge service,
free wine tasting card

*Sit on the wraparound porch of this historic home and gaze out at the beautiful vineyards and moun-
tains of Sonoma Valley. The Inn is beautifully decorated in the Arts & Craft tradition, featuring Stickley
furnishings and original works of art.*

✉ info@birminghambb.com   🌐 www.birminghambb.com

KLAMATH

Historic Requa Inn
451 Requa Rd 95548
866-800-8777   707-482-1425
Janet & Marty Wartman

89-179 $US BB
12 rooms, 12 pb
Most CC, Cash, *Rated*
C-ltd/S-ltd/P-no/H-ltd
May 1 to September 30

Full breakfast
Dinner/evening meal available.
Beverage bar, baked goodies in the
afternoon.
Spectacular riverview, fireplace in
living room, excellent library

*The most unique and historical B&B in the Redwood National Park. Offering spectacular river views
and rustic accommodations, our central location makes the us your ideal basecamp to explore where
the Redwoods meet the Sea.*

✉ reservations@requainn.com   🌐 www.requainn.com

LA JOLLA

**Bed and Breakfast Inn at
La Jolla**
7753 Draper Ave 92037
888-988-8481   858-456-2066
Margaret Fox

179-479 $US BB
15 rooms, 15 pb
Most CC, Cash, Checks,
Rated, •
C-ltd/S-no/P-ltd/H-ltd
Spanish

Full Gourmet Candlelit Breakfast
Complimentary fresh fruit, wine &
cheese, sweets, fine sherry, snacks &
tea, bottled water
Library/sitting room- complimentary
beach towels, chairs & umbrellas-
tennis rackets/balls -concierge

*Whether for business or a relaxing getaway at this historic & elegantly charming Inn, we have it all. A
block from the beach in the heart of La Jolla by the Sea. So close, yet so far from it all, where romance
makes memories & business becomes a pleasure.*

✉ bedbreakfast@innlajolla.com   🌐 www.innlajolla.com

Redwood Hollow Cottages
256 Prospect St 92037
858-459-8747
Martin Lizerbram

125-339 $US EP
8 rooms, 8 pb
Most CC, Cash,
Checks, •
C-yes/S-no/P-no/H-ltd

Kitchens stocked with oatmeal, teas,
coffee, popcorn, hot chocolate &
goodies on arrival
Free WiFi, private cottages, sleeper
sofa, living room, fireplaces, beaches,
maid service (fee)

*A registered San Diego Historic Site with cottages and duplex homes in a garden setting. Cottages are
family friendly, 4 with fireplaces, most with full kitchens. Close to everything La Jolla offers, down the
street from Whispering Sands Beach access.*

✉ lejolla@aol.com   🌐 www.redwoodhollow-lajolla.com

LA SELVA BEACH

Flora Vista Inn
1258 San Andreas Rd 95076
877-753-5672   831-724-8663
Deanna & Ed

195-240 $US BB
5 rooms, 5 pb
Most CC, Cash
C-ltd/S-no/P-no/H-ltd

Full breakfast
Complimentary wine (or tea) and
cheese in the afternoon, box lunches
available ($12 per person)
Clay tennis courts, TV, wireless
Internet, private bathrooms, two
person spa-tubs, gas fireplaces

*Located along the Pacific Coast Bike Route, between Santa Cruz and Monterey, the historic Flora
Vista Inn is nestled among lush flower and strawberry fields, a short walk from spectacular beaches.*

✉ info@floravistainn.com   🌐 www.floravistainn.com

LAGUNA BEACH

Casa Laguna Inn & Spa
2510 South Coast Hwy 92651
800-233-0449 949-494-2996
Francois Leclair, Kathryn
Mace

160-650 $US BB
22 rooms, 22 pb
Most CC, •
S-no/P-yes/H-no
Spanish

Full gourmet breakfast from menu
Gourmet wine & cheese reception
each evening.
A/C, luxurious bedding & robes, DVD
& CD players, high speed Internet

Voted Best in Orange County nine consecutive years by the OC Register, Two time Medal Winner in Inn-credible Breakfast Cook-off. Terraced on a hillside overlooking the Pacific Ocean, this historic Inn is a Sunset magazine featured Romantic Stay.
✉ innkeeper@casalaguna.com ◐ www.casalaguna.com

LAKEPORT

Lakeport English Inn
675 N Main St 95453
707-263-4317
Karan & Hugh Mackey

155-221 $US BB
10 rooms, 10 pb
Visa, MC
C-ltd/S-no/P-no

Full breakfast
High Tea served Saturday & Sunday
between 12:00 & 2:30
Evening turndown service, Italian
Frette Sheets, plush towels & robes,
spa & concierge service, WiFi

Lakeport English Inn is a delightful B&B, and no passports are needed here. Located in beautiful Lakeport, CA, with the best of Britain: scones with Devonshire cream and jam, English roses, darts, billiards, shopping and a library.
✉ lakeportenglishinn@mchsi.com ◐ www.lakeportenglishinn.com

LEMON COVE

Plantation B&B
33038 Sierra Hwy 198 93244
800-240-1466 559-597-2555
Scott & Marie Munger

149-239 $US BB
7 rooms, 7 pb
Most CC, Cash, Checks,
Rated, •
C-ltd/S-ltd/P-no/H-no

Gourmet breakfast
Complimentary beverages & snacks
Hot tub, verandas, courtyard,
swimming pool, fireplaces, landscaped
gardens

Nestled in the foothills of the Sierra Nevada Mountains, only 16 miles from Sequoia National Park. Seven romantic "Gone With The Wind" themed rooms. Full, gourmet breakfast prepared by Chef Marie. ✉ relax@plantationbnb.com ◐ www.theplantation.net

LEWISTON

The Old Lewiston Inn B&B
71 Deadwood Rd 96052
530-528-9554
J.C. Osborne

110-125 $US BB
7 rooms, 5 pb
Visa, MC
C-yes/S-no/P-yes/H-yes

Full breakfast
Each lodge room comes equipped
with a refrigerator and coffee maker.
Private entrances, private baths, air
conditioning, direct T V and decks
overlooking the river.

The Inn is located on the Trinity River and all rooms have porches or balconies over looking the river. There is fly fishing in the back yard and launching for canoes and kayaks as well.
✉ ualfox6314@clearwire.net ◐ www.theoldlewistoninn.com

LITTLE RIVER

Blanchard House B&B
8141 Coast Hwy 1 95456
707-937-1627
Melody

225 $US BB
1 rooms, 1 pb
Visa, MC
C-ltd/S-no/P-no/H-no

Full breakfast
Coffee pot & bar refrigerator in service
alcove
Cable TV with DVD & CD players

The spacious accommodations, spectacular location and superb hospitality at the Blanchard House will make this your home away from home. With only one room, it is the ultimate romantic hideaway for any couple.
✉ blanchrd@msn.org ◐ www.blanchardhouse.com

Inn at Schoolhouse Creek
7501 N Hwy 1 95456
800-731-5525 707-937-5525
Steven Musser & Maureen
Gilbert

156-399 $US BB
19 rooms, 19 pb
Most CC, •
C-yes/S-ltd/P-yes/H-yes
French

Full breakfast
Complimentary wine & hors
d'oeuvres
Oceanview hot tub, in-room spa tubs,
fireplaces, private beach access,
massage & spa services

The Inn at Schoolhouse Creek on the Mendocino Coast provides a unique experience on the Northern California Coast with cottages and rooms spread out over 9 acres of lush gardens, meadows and forested land as well as our cliff side cottages.
✉ innkeeper@schoolhousecreek.com ◐ www.schoolhousecreek.com

LITTLE RIVER

The Andiron Inn & Cabins	119-279 $US BB	Full Breakfast
6051 N Hwy One 95456	12 rooms, 12 pb	Complimentary wine
800-955-6478 707-937-1543	Most CC, Cash, Checks	Large spa, private cabins or individual
Scott Connolly & Madeline	C-yes/S-no/P-yes/H-no	rooms, private baths, Internet access
Stanionis		available

Welcome to The Andiron—Seaside Inn & Cabins, the relaxed vacation rental or overnight room along the Mendocino Coast. Our individual cabins are very private and the large spa in the forest is serene and romantic. See what awaits you.

✉ Hello@TheAndiron.com   ❍ TheAndiron.com

LOCKEFORD

Inn at Locke House	150-245 $US BB	Full breakfast
19960 Elliott Rd 95237	5 rooms, 5 pb	Varies: Confection of the day,
209-727-5715	Most CC, Cash, Checks,	California cheeses, artisan crackers,
Lani & Richard Eklund	*Rated*	local fruit,& special beverage
	C-ltd/S-ltd/P-no/H-no	Private bathrooms, fireplaces, WiFi,
		phones w/free local calls, iPod /cd/
		radios, ceiling fans, AC

Free Night w/Certificate: Valid Sunday-Thursday (except holiday and special events).

"Experience a treasure, create treasures memories." A destination in itself, The Inn at Locke House is a California Landmark and a National Register of Historic Places site. Located in the heart of the Lodi Wine Appellation.

✉ lockehouse@jps.net   ❍ www.theinnatlockehouse.com

LONG BEACH

Dockside Boat & Bed	195-325 $US BB	Continental plus breakfast
Dock 5, Rainbow	6 rooms, 6 pb	Complimentary light snacks & water
Harbor 90802	Most CC, Cash,	on-board
800-436-2574 562-436-3111	*Rated*, •	Complimentary high speed wireless
Kim Harris-Ryskamp & Kent	C-yes/S-no/P-no/H-ltd	Internet, BBQ grill, DVD library
Ryskamp		

Spend the night on a Yacht! Guests enjoy their very own private yacht at Rainbow Harbor. Beautiful views and steps away from fine dining, shopping and activities. Convenient to many major Southern California attractions.

✉ boatandbed@yahoo.com   ❍ www.boatandbed.com

LOS OSOS

Julia's B&B by the Sea	85-95 $US BB	Continental plus breakfast
2735 Nokomis Ct. 93412	1 rooms, 1 pb	Includes small fridge, range top &
805-528-1344	Most CC	microwave for guest use
Julia Wright	C-ltd/S-no/P-no/H-ltd	Spectacular view of the ocean and
	German, French,	Morro Rock Bay; large deck w/ sitting
	Spanish	area & firepit; satellite TV

B&B by the Sea in the San Luis Obispo area. Charming bed and breakfast overlooking the ocean, perfect for short vacation, weekends, romantic getaways or a retreat. Close to Avila, Cambria, Hearst Castle, Paso Robles and Morro Bay.

✉ lmjuliawright@sbcglobal.net

LOWER LAKE

Spirit Lake B&B	90-145 $US BB	Breakfast from an extensive menu
11865 Candy Ln 95457	4 rooms, 4 pb	Drinks and snacks
707-995-9090	Visa, MC	98-degree warm pool, private 4 acre
Elaine Marie	C-ltd/S-no/P-no/H-no	lake, canoes, Watsu & massage, lovely
	German	trails

Our vision as innkeepers was to create a very special place where anyone can come rest, relax and rejuvenate. The profoundly healing modalities of Watsu and Aquatic Massage are celebrated here.

✉ aquaticmassage@gmail.com   ❍ www.spiritlakebnb.com

MALIBU CANYON

The Malibu Bella Vista
25786 Piuma Rd 91302
818-645-1159 818-591-9255
Beth & Michael Kin

125-165 $US BB
2 rooms, 2 pb
Most CC, Cash, Checks,
Rated
C-yes/S-ltd/P-ltd/H-no

Full breakfast
Please let us know if you have any
special dietary needs
Wood fireplace, A/C, TV/VCR/DVD,
spa, private bath, massage, wireless
Internet

Located in Malibu Canyon, 5 miles from the Pacific Ocean. Nestled on the side of the Santa Monica Mountains with gorgeous views, thus the name Bella Vista. Children welcome. There are many amusement parks within a one hour drive.

✉ michael_kin@charter.net 🌐 www.malibubellavista.com

MAMMOTH LAKES

Cinnamon Bear Inn
113 Center St 93546
800-845-2873 760-934-2873
Russ & Mary Ann Harrison

89-198 $US BB
22 rooms, 22 pb
Most CC, Cash,
Rated, •
C-yes/S-no/P-no/H-ltd

Full breakfast
Snacks, complimentary wine
Sitting room, Jacuzzis, suites,
fireplaces, cable TV, ski packages, WiFi
in common areas

"Who needs the Ritz?" We feature friendly folks, full breakfasts, free hors d'oeuvres & fabulous ski packages. Enjoy forest view rooms with private baths.

✉ cinnabear1@aol.com 🌐 www.cinnamonbearinn.com

MARIPOSA

Restful Nest B&B
4274 Buckeye Creek
Rd 95338
800-664-7127 209-742-7127
Lois Y. Moroni

125-150 $US BB
3 rooms, 3 pb
Visa, MC, Disc,
Rated, •
C-yes/S-ltd/P-ltd/H-no
French

Full gourmet breakfast
Hot tubs, swimming pool, A/C, spa,
DVD & VCR

We offer relaxation, old California hospitality, and the flavor of Provence in the beautiful foothills of the Sierra Nevada mountains near Yosemite. Private guest cottage.

✉ restful@yosemite.net 🌐 www.restfulnest.com

MCCLOUD

McCloud River Mercantile Hotel
241 Main St 96057
530-964-2602
Kevin & Darlene Mathis

129-200 $US BB
10 rooms, 10 pb
Most CC, Cash
C-yes/S-no/P-yes/H-yes

Full breakfast
Private bathrooms, central heat/air
conditioning, spa, massage, yoga,
classes, merchandise store.

Get away from it all and spend your vacation at a McCloud hotel. The McCloud River Mercantile Hotel is in an historic setting surrounded by the beauty of tall pines and the grandeur of Mount Shasta.

✉ info@mccloudmercantile.com 🌐 www.mccloudmercantile.com

MENDOCINO

Alegria Oceanfront Inn & Cottages
44781 Main St 95460
800-780-7905 707-937-5150
Elaine Wing & Eric
Hillesland

159-299 $US BB
10 rooms, 10 pb
Visa, MC
C-yes/S-no/P-no/H-ltd

Full breakfast
Complimentary tea, coffee and hot
chocolate
Coffeemaker, refrigerator, TV/VCR,
microwave, hot tub, fireplace

Alegria is an ocean front B&B inn located in the village of Mendocino, CA. It features ocean view rooms and cottages, fireplaces, decks, a hot tub and a path to the beach. Interesting shops, galleries, fine restaurants, and the beach is just steps away.

✉ inn@oceanfrontmagic.com 🌐 www.oceanfrontmagic.com

Brewery Gulch Inn
9401 North Highway
One 95460
800-578-4454 707-937-4752
Jo Ann Stickle

210-495 $US BB
11 rooms, 11 pb
Most CC, Cash, Checks,
Rated, •
C-ltd/S-no/P-no/H-yes

Full gourmet breakfast
Wine hour with hors d'oeuvres; tea &
coffee, fine food
Robes, toiletries, hairdryers, wine
bar, concierge service, ocean views,
fireplaces, Jacuzzi tubs

Set high on a bluff among natural landscaping overlooking Mendocino's Smuggler's Cove, each of Brewery Gulch Inn's 11 spacious & luxuriously appointed guestrooms are individually designed to capture views of the ocean. ✉ manager@brewerygulchinn.com 🌐 www.brewerygulchinn.com

MENDOCINO

| **Dennen's Victorian Farmhouse**
7001 N Hwy 1 Little River 95460
800-264-4723 707-937-0697
Fred Cox & Jo Bradley | 135-270 $US BB
11 rooms, 11 pb
Visa, MC, AmEx,
Rated, •
C-ltd/S-no/P-no/H-ltd | Full breakfast delivered to room
Complimentary coffee and tea on request during the day and evening.
Spa tubs, wood fireplaces, feather beds, ocean access, in-room massage, free WiFi. Concierge Services |

Romantic Victorian home that inspired artist Thomas Kinkade. Private oceanview cottage. Featherbeds, fireplaces, spa tubs, ocean access, breakfast in bed. Free hi speed wireless Internet. AAA Three Diamond. Affordable luxury. Romance without pretense.

✉ innkeeper@victorianfarmhouse.com 🌐 www.victorianfarmhouse.com

| **Glendeven Inn**
8205 North Hwy One 95460
800-822-4536 707-937-0083
John & Mike | 135-345 $US BB
10 rooms, 10 pb
Most CC, Cash, *Rated*
S-no/P-no/H-ltd
German | Full in-room 3-course hot breakfast
Wine & hors d'oeuvres included, the Wine Bar[n] offers local fine wines, cheeses & charcuterie
Sitting room, suites, wood fireplaces, llamas & chickens, fresh eggs, wine bar, full concierge |

Free Night w/Certificate: Valid Jan.-April.

Vogue Magazine's pick for Mendocino lodging, this 8-acre, luxury farmstead offers ocean-view suites, fireplaces, private balconies, gardens, pastured llamas, farm-fresh eggs, in-room breakfasts, a wine hour in Glendeven's Wine Bar[n], and free WiFi.

✉ innkeeper@glendeven.com 🌐 www.glendeven.com

| **Headlands Inn B&B**
10453 Howard St. 95460
800-354-4431 707-937-4431
Denise & Mitch | 99-249 $US BB
7 rooms, 7 pb
Most CC, Cash, Checks,
Rated
C-ltd/S-no/P-no/H-ltd | Full breakfast served in rooms
Afternoon tea & cookies, complimentary juices, spring water & sherry always available in the parlor
Robes, hairdryer, CD am/fm clock radio, bath amenities, bedside chocolate, SF newspaper w/breakfast |

Relax on a featherbed in a romantic oceanview room, with a crackling fire and an exceptional full breakfast lovingly prepared & delivered to your room! Charming 1868 New England Victorian Salt Box located in the Historic Village of Mendocino.

✉ innkeeper@headlandsinn.com 🌐 www.headlandsinn.com

| **MacCallum House Inn & Restaurant**
45020 Albion St 95460
800-609-0492 707-937-0289
Herman Seidell, General Manager | 149-399 $US BB
30 rooms, 30 pb
Most CC, Cash, •
C-yes/S-no/P-yes/H-ltd | Full gourmet breakfast MTO
Fine dining & full bar Lighter fair in Cafe
Gourmet breakfast, bar service, spa tubs, fireplaces, cottages, ocean views, Weddings, Elopements |

An 1882 vintage Victorian with charming garden cottages, in the heart of Mendocino village. MacCallum House is a collection of the finest properties within the village of Mendocino. Each of our rooms offers a romantic and peaceful environment.

✉ info@maccallumhouse.com 🌐 www.maccallumhouse.com

| **Sea Gull Inn**
44960 Albion St 95460
888-937-5204 707-937-5204
Jim & Ayla Douglas | 75-198 $US BB
9 rooms, 8 pb
Visa, MC, AmEx
C-ltd/S-no/P-no/H-ltd
German | Organic breakfast
Choice of Coffee, tea or hot chocolate
Breakfast delivered to your room, fresh flowers, garden and ocean views, suites, wireless Internet |

Sea Gull Inn is one of Mendocino's first bed and breakfast inns — located in the heart of town, the Sea Gull Inn is best known for its ocean views, garden setting, distinctive guestrooms, and organic breakfast fare.

✉ seagull@mcn.org 🌐 www.seagullbb.com

MENDOCINO

Seafoam Lodge
6751 N Coast Hwy
One 95460
800-606-1827 707-937-1827
Kathy Smith

110-265 $US BB
24 rooms, 24 pb
Most CC, Cash
C-yes/S-no/P-yes/H-ltd

Continental breakfast
Ocean views, TV, VCR, refrigerators,
microwaves, enclosed hot tub, decks

The Seafoam Lodge is located on a sweeping hillside, overlooking the Pacific Ocean. Panoramic ocean views and breathtaking sunsets await our guests from every room. Our comfortable guestrooms offer an affordable getaway you may wish to visit many times.

✉ info@seafoamlodge.com 🌐 www.seafoamlodge.com

Stanford Inn by the Sea-
Big River Lodge
Hwy 1, Comptche-Ukiah
Rd 95460
800-331-8884 707-937-5615
Joan & Jeff Stanford

195-470 $US BB
41 rooms, 41 pb
Most CC, *Rated*, •
C-yes/S-yes/P-yes/H-yes
French, Spanish

Full breakfast
Afternoon hors d'oeuvres, wine,
organic vegetables, vegetarian cuisine,
full bar and dinner service
Indoor pool, hot tub, decks, nurseries,
llamas, bicycles, canoe rentals, high
speed Internet, spa

Welcome to Mendocino's most celebrated Resort Lodge – a bed and breakfast hotel on the Mendocino Coast. A truly elegant country inn in a pastoral setting. All accommodations with ocean views, fireplaces, decks, antiques, four posters and TVs.

✉ stanford@stanfordinn.com 🌐 www.stanfordinn.com

MIDDLETOWN

Backyard Garden Oasis
24019 Hilderbrand Dr 95461
888-987-0505 707-987-0505
Greta Zeit

95-184 $US BB
4 rooms, 4 pb
Most CC, Cash,
Rated, •
C-ltd/S-ltd/P-no/H-yes
Spanish

Full Country Breakfast
Coffee & tea in your own Cottage
Hot tub, king bed, fireplace, A/C,
fridge, skylight, wireless Internet, TV/
VCR, phone, cottages

Just 20 minutes from Calistoga, on the quiet side of the wine country, a AAA three Diamonds cottage in the mountains. Hot tub under the stars! King beds! Skylight! Great Breakfasts! Therapeutic Massage! Near Langtry Estate Winery and Harbin Hot Springs.

✉ greta@backyardgardenoasis.com 🌐 www.backyardgardenoasis.com

MILL CREEK

St. Bernard Lodge
44801 Hwy 36 E 96061
530-258-3382
Jim Vondracek & Sharon
Roberts

89-149 $US BB
7 rooms
Most CC, Cash, Checks
C-yes/S-no/P-no/H-no

Full breakfast
Full restaurant and bar service.
Afternoon wine and hors d'oeuvres.
Deck, stocked trout pond, Outdoor Hot
Tub, indoor and outdoor games, robes
and slippers, ice,

Historical lodge with restaurant and seven rooms upstairs. Each room paneled with rustic knotty pine. Rooms overlook a broad meadow ringed with pine trees. Horse boarding available. Tavern area downstairs with pool table and T.V.

✉ stbernardlodge@citlink.net 🌐 www.stbernardlodge.com

MILL VALLEY

Mill Valley Inn
165 Throckmorton
Ave 94941
800-595-2100 415-389-6608
Justin Flake

159-419 $US BB
25 rooms, 25 pb
Most CC, *Rated*, •
C-yes/S-no/P-no/H-yes
French, Spanish

Continental breakfast
All day tea service with choice of
herbal, green and black teas, evening
wine reception
Fireplaces, cable TV, parking, voice
mail, CD players, robes, Sun Terrace
Lounge, business services

This intimate hotel in Mill Valley California is tucked away in a redwood grove at the foot of majestic Mt. Tamalpais, just steps away from the bustling town plaza, where galleries, fine restaurants, boutiques and theaters abound.

✉ millvalleyinn@jdvhospitality.com 🌐 www.marinhotels.com/mill.html

Jabberwock B&B, Monterey, CA

MONTARA

Goose & Turrets B&B
835 George St 94037
650-728-5451
Raymond & Emily Hoche-Mong

145-190 $US BB
5 rooms, 5 pb
Most CC, Cash, Checks,
Rated, •
C-ltd/S-no/P-no/H-ltd
French

Four-Course Delicious Breakfast
Complimentary afternoon tea and
treats available
Free WiFi, sitting room with wood
stove, books, music; fireplaces, quiet
garden

A historic, classic B&B focusing on both B's: comfortable beds and four-course breakfasts. A slow-lane haven pampering fast-lane folks. Set in an acre of gardens.

✉ goosenturretsbnb@gmail.com 🌐 goose.montara.com

MONTE RIO

Rio Villa Beach Resort
20292 Hwy 116 95446
877-746-8455 707-865-1143
Ron Moore & Bruce Behrens

110-199 $US BB
11 rooms, 11 pb
Most CC
C-yes/S-ltd/P-no/H-ltd

Continental breakfast
Decks, gardens, river, fireplace

A cluster of green & white villa suites & studios surrounded by spacious decks, abundant gardens & lush lawns, sheltered by the redwoods. Located on the Russian River.

✉ innkeepers@riovilla.com 🌐 www.riovilla.com

MONTEREY

Jabberwock B&B
598 Laine St 93940
888-428-7253 831-372-4777
John Hickey & Dawn Perez

169-299 $US BB
7 rooms, 7 pb
Visa, MC, *Rated*, •
C-ltd/S-no/P-no/H-no

Full breakfast
5:00 hors d'oeuvres, sherry, wine &
other beverages, fresh baked cookies
Sitting room, sun porch, 3 rooms
with Jacuzzis, suite, massage by
arrangement, bocce ball court

Once a convent, this charming Arts & Crafts style home sits just 4 blocks above Cannery Row & the Monterey Bay Aquarium. From the sunporch, overlook our gardens and enjoy fine Monterey Bay views. 3 rooms have Jacuzzis for two & 4 have fireplaces.

✉ innkeeper@jabberwockinn.com 🌐 www.jabberwockinn.com

MONTEREY

Old Monterey Inn
500 Martin St 93940
800-350-2344 831-375-8284
Patti Valletta

269-449 $US BB
10 rooms, 10 pb
Visa, MC, *Rated*
C-ltd/S-no/P-ltd/H-ltd
Spanish

Full gourmet breakfast
Tea, evening hors d'oeuvres, wine,
breakfast in bed
All rooms have fireplace, 5 whirlpool
tubs for 2, robes, hairdryers,
weddings, gardens, spa

Classic English-style Tudor amid lush gardens. Exceptionally romantic. Service oriented inn with privacy valued. Breakfasts in bed are not to be missed.

✉ omi@oldmontereyinn.com   🌐 www.oldmontereyinn.com

MOSS BEACH

Seal Cove Inn
221 Cypress Ave 94038
800-995-9987 650-728-4114
Dana Kelley

215-350 $US BB
10 rooms, 10 pb
Most CC, Cash
C-yes/S-no/P-no/H-yes

Full breakfast
Afternoon wine, tea & hors d' oeuvres,
freshly-baked cookies, drinks available
throughout the day
Executive board room for small
meetings up to 14, daily housekeeping,
robes, fireplaces

Just 24 miles south of San Francisco, this serene hideaway is spectacularly set amongst a meadow of wildflowers and bordered by towering cypress trees. Enjoy secluded beaches, watch frolicking seals, and the beautiful ocean bluffs of Half Moon Bay.

✉ sealcoveinn@foursisters.com   🌐 www.sealcoveinn.com

MOSS LANDING

Captain's Inn at Moss Landing
8122 Moss Landing Rd 95039
831-633-5550
Capt. Yohn & Melanie Gideon

145-275 $US BB
10 rooms, 10 pb
Visa, MC, *Rated*
C-ltd/S-no/P-no/H-yes

Full breakfast
Fresh evening cookies, snacks on
Fri and Sat., Early bird brown bag
breakfasts for early starters
High speed Internet, Fresh flowers,
fireplaces, cozy robes, phone w/voice
mail, TV, feather pillows

Waterfront views with plush top beds, soaking tubs or romance showers, spa bath soaps, fresh flowers & glowing fireplaces. Snuggle & cuddle under comforters & quilts with feather pillows.

✉ res@captainsinn.com   🌐 www.captainsinn.com

MT. SHASTA

Mount Shasta Ranch B&B
1008 WA Barr Rd 96067
877-926-3870 530-926-3870
Mary & Bill Larsen

70-180 $US BB
12 rooms, 5 pb
Most CC, Checks,
Rated, •
C-yes/S-no/P-yes/H-no

Full breakfast
Afternoon tea, wine, snacks
Sitting room, library, ping-pong, pool
tables, TV & phone in room

This Northern California, 2-story ranch house offers affordable elegance in a historical setting. Present-day guests can still enjoy the unique atmosphere and mood of those early years which are reflected in the Mt. Shasta Ranch Bed & Breakfast.

✉ mbenton1@snowcrest.net   🌐 www.stayinshasta.com

MURPHYS

Dunbar House, 1880
271 Jones St 95247
209-728-2897
Arline & Richard Taborek

200-300 $US BB
5 rooms, 5 pb
Most CC, *Rated*
S-no/P-no/H-no

Full country breakfast
Fresh baked cookies, comp. appetizer
plate & local bottle of wine, port,
sherry & chocolates
Lovely gardens, sitting rooms, library,
gas-burning stoves, clawfoot tubs, TVs,
DVD.

Intimate and authentically historic Italianate style bed & breakfast inn that offers guests a refreshing sense of ease, personal comfort, fine accommodations, hospitality, and unforgettable country cuisine. Walking distance to Main Street.

✉ innkeep@dunbarhouse.com   🌐 www.dunbarhouse.com

MURPHYS

The Victoria Inn
402 Main St H 95247
209-728-8933
Michael Ninos

128-385 $US BB
17 rooms, 17 pb
Most CC, Cash
C-ltd/S-no/P-no/H-yes

Continental plus breakfast
Fireplaces, woodstoves, clawfoot tubs
or spas

Charming inn on historic Main Street in Murphys, CA. In the heart of Gold Country, Calaveras County. Fireplaces and wood stoves, clawfoot tubs or spas, eclectic furnishings. 3 large suites, 10 guestrooms, 4 vacation rentals.

✉ victoria_inn@sbcglobal.net ◔ www.victoriainn-murphys.com

NAPA

Arbor Guest House
1436 G St 94559
866-627-2262 707-252-8144
Dan & Candy Cocilova

159-259 $US BB
5 rooms, 5 pb
Most CC, Cash, *Rated*
C-ltd/S-no/P-no/H-yes
All year (12/24 & 25 no)

Full breakfast
Complimentary afternoon tea and
snacks available
Fireplaces, spa tubs, bedside
chocolates, fine garden, TV's wireless
Internet, gourmet breakfast

A Napa Valley Bed and Breakfast inn is the best way to enjoy the Napa Valley and Wine Country. This dazzling getaway includes elegant rooms, private baths, fireplaces, and hearty, gourmet breakfasts await guests looking for a special place to stay.

✉ innkeeper@arborguesthouse.com ◔ www.arborguesthouse.com

Beazley House
1910 1st Street 94559
800-559-1649 707-257-1649
Carol & Jim Beazley

150-340 $US BB
11 rooms, 11 pb
Visa, MC, *Rated*, •
C-ltd/S-ltd/P-yes/H-ltd
Spanish

Full gourmet breakfast
Complimentary sherry & fresh baked
Chocolate Chip Cookies daily, Daily
Wine & Cheese Hour.
HDTVs, fireplaces, garden, in-room
whirlpool tubs, wireless Internet,
Concierge, Dog friendly

Beazley House is a beautifully kept 1902 masterpiece! Elegant guestrooms have private baths and garden views. This Napa Valley Bed and Breakfast includes in-room whirlpool tubs, spa services, free wireless high speed Internet, fireplaces & lush gardens.

✉ innkeeper@beazleyhouse.com ◔ www.beazleyhouse.com

Bel Abri
837 California Blvd 94559
877-561-6000 707-226-5825
Mary Alice Bashford

139-309 $US BB
15 rooms, 15 pb
Most CC, Cash
C-ltd/S-no/P-no/H-yes

Full breakfast
For a late night snack, we have a mini
refrigerator and honor basket, evening
wine & cheese
Egyptian cotton linens, vanities, plush
robes, CD/clock radio, cable TV, wine
tasting accommodations

Welcome to the Bel Abri, French for Beautiful Shelter. This 15-room French Country Inn is located just off I-29 and First St in the revitalized town of Napa, nestled in the heart of the famous Napa Valley.

✉ info@belabri.net ◔ www.belabri.net

Blackbird Inn
1755 First St 94559
888-567-9811 707-226-2450
Emily Deeter

160-285 $US BB
8 rooms, 8 pb
Most CC, Cash
C-yes/S-no/P-ltd/H-yes

Full breakfast
Afternoon wine, tea & hors d' oeuvres,
freshly-baked cookies, drinks available
throughout the day
Porch, fireplace, downtown, jet tubs,
daily housekeeping, private patio,
evening turndown, concierge

Blackbird Inn offers the intimacy of a vintage hideaway, yet is an easy walk to many shops and restaurants. With its spacious front porch, huge stone fireplace and liberal use of fine woods, Blackbird Inn creates a warm, welcoming atmosphere.

✉ blackbirdinn@foursisters.com ◔ www.blackbirdinnnapa.com

NAPA

Cedar Gables Inn
486 Coombs St 94559
800-309-7969 707-224-7969
Ken & Susie Pope

199-359 $US BB
9 rooms, 9 pb
Most CC, Cash,
Rated, •
C-ltd/S-ltd/P-no/H-no

3 Course Gourmet Breakfast
Chocolate chip cookies, evening wine
& cheese in the Tavern, fruits, sodas &
teas all day
Jacuzzi tubs, bath bombs, port,
chocolates, robes, blow dryer, WiFi,
concierge, large screen TV

Built in 1892, this 10,000 square foot Shakespearean mansion contains many intriguing rooms, winding staircases, an Old English Tavern and of course secret passageways. There are full bathrooms in all 9 rooms. Cooking classes are paired with Napa wines.
✉ info@cedargablesinn.com ❂ www.cedargablesinn.com

Churchill Manor
485 Brown St 94559
800-799-7733 707-253-7733
Joanna Guidotti & Brian
Jensen

165-345 $US BB
10 rooms, 10 pb
Most CC, Cash,
Checks, •
C-ltd/S-no/P-no/H-ltd
Spanish

Full gourmet breakfast
Evening wine reception, tea and coffee
service, afternoon sweets
Gardens, veranda, fireplaces, 2-person
tubs, 2-person showers, WiFi, croquet,
tandem bikes, TV/DVD's

Located on an acre of perfectly-landscaped gardens in the City of Napa, Churchill Manor is well located for your Wine Country getaway. Beautifully restored 1889 mansion, the first Napa residence to be listed on the National Register of Historic Places.
✉ Be@churchillmanor.com ❂ www.churchillmanor.com

Hennessey House B&B
1727 Main St 94559
707-226-3774
Kevin & Lorri Walsh

129-329 $US BB
10 rooms, 10 pb
Most CC, •
C-ltd/S-no/P-no/H-no
Spanish

Full scrumptious breakfast
Complimentary wine & cheese,
afternoon tea
Patio & garden, parlor with flat panel
TV, WiFi, sauna, whirlpool tubs &
fireplaces in some rooms

Napa's 1889 Queen Anne Victorian B&B. "A Great Place to Relax." Walk to restaurants and shops. Share wine and conversation by the garden fountain.
✉ inn@hennesseyhouse.com ❂ www.hennesseyhouse.com

Hillview Country Inn
1205 Hillview Ln 94558
707-224-5004
Al & Susie Hasenpusch

175-275 $US BB
4 rooms, 4 pb
Most CC, Cash, *Rated*
C-ltd/S-ltd/P-no/H-no

Full breakfast
Cookies, candy, wine, bottled water,
soda, coffee
Living room, deck & lawn area, cable
TV

Spectacular 100-year-old estate. Each guest suite is distinctively decorated, with queen size bed, private bath, fruit and wine upon arrival, and a sweeping view of Napa Valley.
✉ info@hillviewinnnapa.com ❂ www.hillviewinnnapa.com

Inn on Randolph
411 Randolph St 94559
800-670-6886 707-257-2886
Deborah Coffee

149-349 $US BB
10 rooms, 10 pb
Most CC
C-ltd/S-ltd/P-no/H-yes

Full breakfast
Sweet treats, coffee, tea
Parlor, library, game room, grand
piano, gardens with patio, sundeck,
gazebo, fireplace, spa

Situated on one-half acre of landscaped grounds in historic "Old Town" Napa, you'll enjoy the serenity of a quiet residential neighborhood within walking distance of popular restaurants, tasting salons and entertainment venues. ✉ innonrandolph@aol.com ❂ www.innonrandolph.com

McClelland-Priest B&B Inn
569 Randolph St 94559
800-290-6881 707-224-6875
Celeste Carducci

159-269 $US BB
6 rooms, 6 pb
Most CC, •
C-ltd/S-no/P-ltd/H-no

Gourmet breakfast
Evening hors d'oeuvres, wine
receptions
Spa, en-suite Jacuzzis & fireplaces,
evening receptions, self-guided winery
tours, concierge service

Experience the Napa Valley from the stately elegance of the McClelland Priest B&B Inn. Originally built in 1879 with a stained glass entry, ornate ceilings, spacious rooms, European ambience, modern comforts & luxury that sets this B&B apart from others.
✉ celeste@mcclellandpriest.com ❂ www.mcclellandpriest.com

NAPA

Oak Knoll Inn
2200 E Oak Knoll Ave 94558
707-255-2200
Barbara Passino & John
Kuhlmann

350-750 $US BB
4 rooms, 4 pb
Visa, MC, *Rated*, •
C-ltd/S-ltd/P-no/H-ltd
Spanish

Full multi-course breakfast
Substantial evening wine hour & hors
d'oeuvres, usually with small winery
representative, AM coffee
Complimentary wine, in-room spa
services, swimming pool, free use of
nearby gym, concierge

Romantic, elegant stone country inn surrounded by vineyards and panoramic views in the Napa Valley. Spacious rooms with woodburning fireplaces. Napa's top rated inn has an exceptional concierge service, nearby gym, great rooms, views and food.

 oakknollinn@aol.com   www.oakknollinn.com

---

Stahlecker House
1042 Easum Dr 94558
800-799-1588 707-257-1588
Ron & Ethel Stahlecker

112-349 $US BB
5 rooms, 5 pb
Most CC, Cash,
Rated, •
C-yes/S-ltd/P-no/H-ltd
Spanish

Full Candlelight Breakfast
Coffee, sodas, lemonade, tea,
chocolate chip cookies, brownies,
cakes.
Gardens, Creek setting, Sun deck, free
WiFi, sitting room, spas in suites, free
off street parking

Stahlecker House, a secluded, quiet, charming Bed and Breakfast located on 1.5 acres of lush manicured lawns and flowering gardens. Close to the Napa Valley Wine Train, it is a nostalgic gem of the Napa Valley. Three Course Breakfast. Fireplaces and HDTV.

stahlbnb@aol.com   www.stahleckerhouse.com

The Inn on First
1938 First St 94559
866-253-1331 707-253-1331
Jim Gunther & Jamie Cherry

205-385 $US BB
10 rooms, 10 pb
Most CC, Cash,
Rated, •
S-no/P-ltd/H-ltd
Limited Spanish
Mem.D-10/31, 11/
1-Mem.D

Full Gourmet Breakfast
Sparkling wine, truffles, specialty
refreshments & baked goods are
waiting for you upon arrival
Whirlpool tubs, fireplaces in all rooms,
private bathrooms, concierge service,
free WiFi

The Inn On First is the premier Napa Valley Bed and Breakfast experience for foodies. A unique breakfast awaits you with every visit.

innkeeper@theinnonfirst.com   www.theinnonfirst.com

NEVADA CITY

Emma Nevada House
528 E Broad St 95959
800-916-EMMA 530-265-4415
Andrew & Susan Howard

169-249 $US BB
6 rooms, 6 pb
Most CC, *Rated*
C-yes/S-no/P-no/H-ltd

Full breakfast
Afternoon tea, dessert, non-alcoholic
beverage, or a favorite made-to-order
espresso drink
A/C, bath robes, fireplace, whirlpool
tub, cable TV, business facilities,
library, laundry, weddings

This charming home has been carefully restored and sparkles like a jewel from an abundance of antique windows, one of many marvelous architectural details. For the ultimate in gracious living and relaxation plan your next getaway at The Emma Nevada House.

emmanevada@comcast.net   www.emmanevadahouse.com

Parsonage B&B
427 Broad St. 95959
530-265-9478
Patti Woomer

90-195 $US BB
6 rooms, 6 pb
Visa, MC, AmEx
C-ltd/S-no/P-no/H-ltd

Full Breakfast

The Parsonage Bed & Breakfast, located in Historic downtown Nevada City, is one of the best and most convenient bed and breakfast locations in the area. This B&B is full of history dating back to the mid-1800s.

captcshea@yahoo.com   www.theparsonage.net

NEWPORT BEACH

Little Inn by the Bay
2627 Newport Blvd 92663
800-438-4466 949-673-8800
Gita, Rahul & Viru

100-300 $US BB
18 rooms, 18 pb
Most CC, Cash,
Rated, •
C-yes/S-no/P-no/H-ltd
Spanish, Gujarati &
Hindi
May to September

Continental breakfast
Beach equipment, bicycles, chairs,
boogie board etc., WiFi, MP3 line-in,
HDTV & luxurious rooms

Thanks to its abundance of sun, surf, sand and shopping, everything you need for the perfect Newport Beach vacation can be found at the Little Inn By the Bay, one of the best Newport Beach hotels!

✉ reservations@littleinnbythebay.com 🌐 www.littleinnbythebay.com

NIPTON

Hotel Nipton
107355 Nipton Rd 92364
760-856-2335
Jerry & Roxanne Freeman

79 $US BB
5 rooms
Visa, MC, Disc
C-yes/S-no/P-no/H-ltd

Continental breakfast
Restaurant also serves delicious lunch
& dinner, catering for groups also
available
Outdoor hot tubs, seclusion, mountain
biking, parlor

Hotel Nipton, a romantic adobe inn, was a favorite of 1920's silent film star Clara Bow. Located in Mojave National Preserve.

✉ hotel@nipton.com 🌐 www.nipton.com

OAKHURST

Hounds Tooth Inn
42071 Hwy 41 93644
888-642-6610 559-642-6600
Williams – Kiehlmeier

95-225 $US BB
12 rooms, 12 pb
Most CC, *Rated*, •
C-ltd/S-no/P-no/H-yes

Full breakfast
Afternoon wine, tea and coffee
Library, Jacuzzis and mini suites
available, rooms with fireplaces, cable
TV, sitting room

12 room Victorian style inn located 12 miles from Yosemite's Southern entrance in Oakhurst, 6 miles from Bass Lake. One luxury cottage available.

✉ robray@sti.net 🌐 www.houndstoothinn.com

Pine Rose Inn
41703 Rd 222 93644
866-642-2800 559-642-2800
Anita & Greg Griffin

79-179 $US BB
9 rooms, 9 pb
Visa, MC, *Rated*, •
C-yes/S-ltd/P-yes/H-no

Hot country breakfast
Complimentary wine, tea, coffee
Rose gardens, weddings, Jacuzzis, in-
room spas, kitchens, fireplaces

This quaint 9 room Inn, nestled within the Sierra Mountains, offers the peace and tranquility of the surrounding national forest. We also have vacation houses.

✉ pineroseinn@sti.net 🌐 www.pineroseinn.com

OCCIDENTAL

Inn at Occidental
3657 Church St 95465
800-522-6324 707-874-1047
Jerry & Tina Wolsborn

199-339 $US BB
18 rooms, 18 pb
Visa, MC, AmEx,
Rated, •
C-ltd/S-no/P-yes/H-yes

Full breakfast
Coffee, tea, cocoa, sweet treats, wine
& cheese
Private bath/spa tub, WiFi, phone,
radio/CD player, fireplace, A/C,
hairdryer, bathrobe, computer

A gem nestled among giant redwoods, near vineyards and wineries, orchards, the Russian River and the ocean. Antiques and comfortable furnishings offer charm and elegance exceeded only by hospitality and a gracious staff.

✉ innkeeper@innatoccidental.com 🌐 www.innatoccidental.com

OJAI

Emerald Iguana Inn
110 Pauline St 93023
805-646-5277
Julia Whitman

169-389 $US BB
12 rooms, 12 pb
Most CC, Cash
S-ltd/P-no/H-ltd
Spanish

Continental breakfast
Snacks
Jacuzzis, swimming pool, suites,
clawfoot tub, fireplace, cable TV

This property perfectly exemplifies the charm of the Ojai Valley. Exquisitely designed and decorated cottages and rooms in an extraordinarily beautiful and serene setting.

✉ innkeeper@iguanainnsofojai.com 🌐 www.iguanainnsofojai.com

OJAI

Lavender Inn
210 E Matilija St 93023
877-646-6635 805-646-6635
Kathy Hartley

115-300 $US BB
8 rooms, 6 pb
Most CC, Cash, •
C-yes/S-no/P-yes/H-no
Sign language, Spanish

Full fresh breakfast
Wine & cheese & hors d'oeuvres,
cooking classes
Events & garden weddings, cooking
classes, on-site day spa, cancer retreat,
romantic, Jacuzzi

Leave it all behind at Ojai's most sophisticated, boutique hotel The Lavender Inn. A charming 1874 historic inn with private, enchanting gardens located in Ojai Village, with across from shops, galleries and restaurants. The gardens are breathtaking!
✉ innkeeper@lavenderinn.com   🌐 www.lavenderinn.com

The Blue Iguana Inn
11794 N Ventura Ave 93023
805-646-5277
Julia Whitman

119-299 $US BB
12 rooms, 12 pb
Most CC, *Rated*, •
C-yes/S-ltd/P-yes/H-yes
Indonesian, Dutch,
French, Spanish

Continental breakfast
Snacks
Jacuzzis, swimming pool, cable TV,
single guestrooms

Called "Hip & Stylish" by Sunset Magazine, the Blue Iguana is uniquely decorated, with one-of-a-kind furnishings from Mexico & throughout the world & original artwork from local artists.
✉ innkeeper@blueiguanainn.com   🌐 www.blueiguanainn.com

The Ojai Retreat
160 Besant Road 93023
805-646-2536
Ulrich, Clare & Teresa

79-249 $US BB
12 rooms, 10 pb
Visa, MC
C-ltd/S-no/P-no
German, French and
Swiss

European Style Buffet
free WiFi, 5 acres of gardens, small
library, living & meeting room, yoga
classes, massage

With spectacular views from all guestrooms, the Ojai Retreat is a haven of beauty and tranquility. Nestled on a five-acre hilltop with lush gardens and walkways, the Ojai Retreat offers twelve completely renovated guestrooms.   ✉ info@ojairetreat.com   🌐 ojairetreat.org

PACIFIC GROVE

Gosby House Inn
643 Lighthouse Ave 93950
800-527-8828 831-375-1287
Sharon Carey

120-225 $US BB
22 rooms, 22 pb
Most CC, Cash,
Rated, •
C-yes/S-no/P-no/H-yes

Full breakfast
Afternoon wine, tea & hors d' oeuvres,
freshly-baked cookies, drinks available
throughout the day
Morning newspaper delivery, evening
turndown, bikes, daily housekeeping,
fireplaces, patio

Located on the Monterey Peninsula, Gosby House Inn has been welcoming guests for over 100 years. This cheerful yellow and white Victorian mansion, with its carefully tended gardens and central patio, sets the standard for gracious innkeeping.
✉ gosbyhouseinn@foursisters.com   🌐 www.gosbyhouseinn.com

Green Gables Inn
301 Ocean View Blvd 93950
800-722-1774 831-375-2095
Honey Spence

140-305 $US BB
11 rooms, 8 pb
Most CC, Cash
C-ltd/S-no/P-ltd/H-yes

Full breakfast
Afternoon wine, tea & hors d' oeuvres,
freshly-baked cookies, drinks available
throughout the day
Some with fireplaces, spa tubs; daily
housekeeping in all

Perhaps the most beautiful and famous inn located in California, the Green Gables Inn is a historic gem with panoramic views of the Monterey Bay. Every detail in this exquisite Queen Anne Victorian, built in 1888, has been meticulously restored.
✉ greengablesinn@foursisters.com   🌐 www.greengablesinnpg.com

Inn at 213 Seventeen Mile Drive
213 Seventeen Mile Dr 93950
800-526-5666 831-642-9514
Innkeeper

135-340 $US BB
16 rooms, 16 pb
Visa, MC, AmEx
C-yes/S-no/P-yes/H-yes

Full breakfast
Complimentary hors d'oeuvres, wine;
fresh-brewed coffee, light snacks
Garden, sitting & reading rooms,
fireplace, spa

Set between Pebble Beach, Carmel, Monterey and close to the Big Sur coast. The area is renowned for its natural beauty, seasonal Monarch butterflies, grazing deer . . . along with the finest beaches, world class golf courses and Cannery Row.   ✉ innkeepers@innat17.com   🌐 www.innat17.com

PACIFIC GROVE

Martine Inn
255 Oceanview Blvd 93950
800-852-5588 831-373-3388
Don Martine

169-499 $US BB
25 rooms, 25 pb
Visa, MC, Disc,
Rated, •
C-yes/S-no/P-no/H-yes
Spanish

Gourmet Breakfast
Wine, hors d'oeuvres, water, soda,
cookies, coffee, tea, cocoa, fresh fruit
Sitting rooms, Game room, Conference
room, display of six Vintage MG autos,
library, WiFi, courtyard

Steps from the sparkling blue waters of Monterey Bay, this lavish once private home, is now a meticulously restored mansion, where every fixture & furnishing is an authentic antique. Breakfast is served on silver, crystal & lace. WiFi is throughout. ✉ don@martineinn.com ◐ www.martineinn.com

Old St. Angela Inn
321 Central Ave 93950
800-748-6306 831-372-3246
Jerry & Dianne McKneely

139-285 $US BB
9 rooms, 9 pb
Visa, MC, *Rated*
C-ltd/S-no/P-no/H-ltd

Full breakfast
Complimentary wine, snacks &
cookies
Solarium, garden with waterfall and
outdoor firepit, rooms with fireplaces
& Jacuzzi tubs

Intimate Cape Cod elegance overlooking Monterey Bay. Walking distance to ocean and beaches, Monterey Bay Aquarium, Cannery Row, and restaurants. Delicious breakfast.
✉ dianne@oldstangelainn.com ◐ www.oldstangelainn.com

Pacific Grove Inn
581 Pine Ave 93950
800-732-2825 831-375-2825
Christine Weaver

115-259 $US BB
16 rooms, 16 pb
Most CC, Cash,
Rated, •
C-ltd/S-no/P-ltd/H-yes

Gourmet Breakfast served everyday
Hosted Wine reception with hors
d'oeuvres with tea & water, freshly
baked cookies at night with milk
Fireplaces, TV/VCR, video library,
phone, in-room fridge, heated towel
racks

The Pacific Grove Inn is a boutique hotel in Pacific Grove California that provides charming accommodations with the intimacy of a bed and breakfast.
✉ info@pacificgroveinn.com ◐ pacificgroveinn.com

Seven Gables Inn
555 Ocean View Blvd 93950
831-372-4341
Susan Flatley Wheelwright
and Ed Flatley

199-559 $US BB
25 rooms, 25 pb
Visa, MC, AmEx,
Rated, •
C-ltd/S-no/P-no/H-ltd
French, Spanish

Full breakfast
Complimentary Monterey County
wines & cheese served 4–6pm,
housemade cookies & milk served
8pm.
Complimentary high speed wireless,
evening turndown service, concierge
services, daily room treats.

A truly romantic inn on the very edge of Monterey Bay. All guestrooms have ocean views, private baths and are comfortably furnished with a comfortable collection of fine furnishings. Guest comfort and service is of utmost importance to us. See you soon!
✉ reservations@pginns.com ◐ thesevengablesinn.com

PALM DESERT

The Inn at Deep Canyon
74470 Abronia Trl 92260
800-253-0004 760-346-8061
Linda Carter

111-261 $US BB
32 rooms, 32 pb
Most CC, *Rated*, •
C-yes/S-yes/P-yes/H-yes

Continental plus breakfast
In room coffee and tea
Jacuzzi, pool, suites, fireplace, cable
TV, accommodate business travel,
wireless Internet

Charming hotel oasis in the desert. Quiet, secluded, heated pool, Jacuzzi and just blocks from El Paseo shopping district. ✉ innkeeper@inn-adc.com ◐ www.inn-adc.com

PALM SPRINGS

Casa Cody Country Inn
175 S Cahuilla Rd 92262
800-231-2639 760-320-9346
Therese Hayes & Frank
Tysen

79-429 $US BB
27 rooms, 27 pb
Most CC, Cash, Checks,
Rated, •
C-ltd/S-ltd/P-ltd/H-yes
French, Dutch, German,
Arabic

Continental plus breakfast
Whirlpool spa, 2 swimming pools,
cable TV, WiFi

A historic 1910 adobe two-bedroom house, once owned by Metropolitan Opera star Lawrence Tibbett and frequented by Charlie Chaplin, is now open for our guests to stay in the heart of Palm Springs Village. ✉ casacody@aol.com ◐ www.casacody.com

Inn at Deep Canyon, Palm Desert, CA

PALM SPRINGS

Orbit In	119-259 $US BB	Continental breakfast
562 W. Arenas Rd. 92262	9 rooms, 9 pb	Complimentary Cocktails, sodas &
877-996-7248 760-323-3585	Most CC, *Rated*, •	water + chips & snacks.
Kevin Miller	S-ltd/P-no/H-yes	Pool chiller, Jacuzzi, bikes, in room
		massage, record players, concierge
		service, movies & books.

Orbit In to the Palm Springs modern vibe, and leave your worries behind as you lounge in luxurious mid-century style. Breathtaking mountain views, poolside breakfast, cocktails, cruiser bikes and spa services — all served up at a small boutique hotel.

 mail@orbitin.com   www.orbitin.com

POSH Palm Springs	154-249 $US BB	3 Course Gourmet Breakfast
530 E. Mel Ave. 92262	11 rooms, 11 pb	A complimentary light lunch is
877-672-6825 760-992-5410	Most CC, Cash,	available to guests
Susan and Michael Antal	*Rated*, •	As a member of the prestigious
	S-ltd/P-no/H-yes	Diamond Collection properties, we
		provide full Concierge Ser. for our

Free Night w/Certificate: Anytime.

POSH Palm Springs Inn is Palm Spring's newest luxury boutique Inn, where the true meaning of POSH is exemplified from the moment you arrive. Experience your own POSH vacation right here in the beautiful desert where the sun shines 365 days out of the year

 info@poshpalmsprings.com   poshpalmsprings.com

Sakura Japanese Style	90-125 $US BB	Full breakfast
B&B Inn	3 rooms, 3 pb	Breakfast can be served in either
1677 N Via Miraleste 92262	Most CC, •	American or Japanese fashion,
760-327-0705	C-yes/S-ltd/P-no/H-no	afternoon tea, snacks
George Cebra	Japanese	Jacuzzis, swimming pool, cable TV,
		VCR, tennis courts within walking
		distance, golf courses

A distinct, quiet, relaxing, authentic Japanese experience, with beautiful Japanese artwork, antique kimonos, handmade futons, shiatsu massage, shoji windows, and a Japanese garden.

 george@sakurabedandbreakfast.com   www.sakurabedandbreakfast.com

PALM SPRINGS

Sea Mountain Inn, Spa & Resort
9850 Donna Ave 92262
877-928-2827 877-928-2827
Julie Dewe

199-999 $US BB
18 rooms, 18 pb
Most CC, *Rated*, •
S-yes/P-no/H-ltd
Spanish, French,
Japanese, Russian,
Italian

Full breakfast
Wine & cheese, coffee, tea, iced tea,
gourmet dining, appetizers & sweet-
rices, margaritas, lunch
Pools, sauna, spa services, 24 hr.
club, flat-screen plasma & LCD TVs,
wireless Internet access spa

An award-winning spa retreat in Southern California. Enjoy 24-hour whirlpool and contemplate the mountains above you. Relax in the sun and swim nude in the fresh pool. The curative mineral waters have been used for centuries. Clothing optional.

✉ info@seamountaininn.com 🌐 www.nudespa.com

Villa Rosa Inn
1577 S Indian Trail 92264
800-457-7605 760-327-5915
Jay

79-169 $US EP
6 rooms, 6 pb
C-ltd/S-no/P-no/H-ltd

A lovely property in Palm Springs.

✉ villarosainn@att.net 🌐 www.villarosainn.com

PASO ROBLES

Ann & George's B&B at Voladores Vineyard
1965 Niderer Road 93446
805-423-2760
Ann & George Perham

200-250 $US BB
2 rooms, 2 pb
Visa, MC, *Rated*
C-yes/S-no/P-no/H-ltd

Full Ranch Style Breakfast
A bottle of wine, a plate of fruit, cheese
& crackers are provided in your room
Coffee maker, fresh flowers in room,
hair dryers, robes, wireless Internet,
discounts for local wine

Travel down a narrow country road to our secluded property overlooking beautiful westside Paso Robles Wine Country, in Central California. Queen-sized beds in spacious private quarters overlooking Rancho de Voladores Vineyard. Enjoy the incredible views.

✉ ann@voladoresvineyard.com 🌐 www.voladoresvineyard.com/bb.htm

Asuncion Ridge Vineyards & Inn
805-461-0675
Philip Krumal

249-349 $US BB
3 rooms, 3 pb
Most CC, Cash
C-ltd/S-no/P-no/H-ltd

Full breakfast
Guests are encouraged to enjoy a glass
of locally crafted wine and cheese in
one of 3 public rooms
Elegant suites, patios, private baths
with soaking tubs, fine linens, stone
fireplace, private decks

Asuncion Ridge Vineyards & Inn rests on 320 private, oak studded acres with unobstructed ocean and forest views. Featuring luxury suites, fine linens, patios and large private baths with soaking tubs. Mouth-watering, Chef prepared gourmet breakfasts.

✉ asuncionridge@hughes.net 🌐 www.asuncionridge.com

Chanticleer Vineyard B&B
1250 Paint Horse
Place 93447
805-226-0600
Carolyn Stewart-Snow

225-275 $US BB
3 rooms, 3 pb
Visa, MC
S-no/P-no/H-yes

Full breakfast
Wine in room on arrival
Full baths, luxury robes, iPod docking
stations, fireplaces, morning kitchen,
iron & ironing boards

A romantic B&B located on 20 acres in Paso Robles. Three rooms with luxury bath, fireplace, private deck and vineyard view. Walking distance to 8 wineries. Enjoy unpretentious comfort, thoughtful attention to detail with a touch of country charm.

✉ info@chanticleervineyardbb.com 🌐 chanticleervineyardbb.com/index.php

Creekside B&B
5325 Vineyard Dr 93446
805-227-6585
Lynne & Dave Teckman

199-250 $US BB
2 rooms, 2 pb
Most CC, Cash
C-yes/S-ltd/P-ltd/H-no

Gourmet breakfast delivered to you
Complimentary local wine upon
arrival
Porch, fireplace, kitchenette

Enjoy a relaxing and luxurious get-away in the heart of Paso Robles' Wine Country. Wine tasting, gourmet breakfasts and privacy awaits. Private entrance, baths and kitchenettes. Discover for yourself the best kept secret on the Central Coast.

✉ LTeckman@percazocellars.com 🌐 www.thecreeksidebb.com

PASO ROBLES————————————————————————————

Dunning Ranch Guest Suites
1945 Niderer Rd 93446
800-893-1847
Jim & Angela Dunning

210-350 $US BB
3 rooms, 2 pb
Visa, MC, *Rated*, •
C-yes/S-no/P-ltd/H-no

Continental breakfast
Complimentary wine tasting at
neighboring Estate winery, other
winery tours by appointment
Large decks, outdoor BBQ, porches,
kitchenettes, wireless Internet, SAT
-TV, luxury bath products

Dunning Ranch Guest Suites are located on 40 acres with vineyards and an award-winning winery just steps away . . . The Inn features very luxurious, private guest suites, a 1 bedroom suite and a 2 bedroom suite. Wine tasting is included.

✉ reservations@dunningranch.com 🌐 www.dunningranch.com

High Ridge Manor
5458 High Ridge Rd 93446
805-226-2002
Cynthia Vaughn & James Roberts

235-345 $US BB
3 rooms, 3 pb
Visa, MC, *Rated*, •
S-ltd/P-no/H-no

Gourmet breakfast
Every day at 5:30pm hors d'oeuvres
and wine served in the billiard room
Billiard room, wine cellar, fireplaces,
large whirlpool tubs in room, private
entrance & patios

High Ridge Manor offers magnificent views, tastefully appointed living quarters with oversized whirlpool tubs in every room. Enjoy the best views in Paso Robles from every room! We offer gourmet meals and an elegant dining experience for all guests.

✉ highridgemanor@hotmail.com 🌐 www.highridgemanor.net

Orchard Hill Farm
5415 Vineyard Dr 93446
805-239-9680
Deborah & Doug Thomsen

230-285 $US BB
3 rooms, 3 pb
Visa, MC, AmEx
C-ltd/S-ltd/P-no/H-no

Full gourmet breakfast
Assorted beverages, local wines, fresh
fruit, homemade baked goods
Fresh flowers, robes, featherbeds,
down comforters, fireplaces, private
decks, sitting areas

Wonderful setting on 36 pristine acres in the Paso Robles Wine Region. Beautiful gardens and views. Fresh flowers, antiques, comfy seating areas, beautiful interiors, comfy seating areas with fireplaces. Gourmet breakfasts and local wines included.

✉ orchardhillfarm@aol.com 🌐 www.orchardhillbb.com

Seven Quails Vineyard
1340 Valley Quail PL 93446
805-237-2598
David & Karina Brucker

145-195 $US BB
2 rooms, 2 pb
C-yes/S-no/P-no/H-ltd

3 Course Full Breakfast
Appetizers at dusk, libations, a
vineyard tour
Vineyards, Wine tasting, comfortable
suite, unmatched amenities and
service to our guests

Welcome to Seven Quails, an intimate, luxurious two suite Paso Robles, California bed and breakfast for two to six people. Explore the lovely town of Paso Robles. Sample wine with the owner/winemaker. Our home is your home.

✉ info@sevenquails.com 🌐 sevenquails.com

Winemaker's Porch at Frances James Vineyard
4665 Linne Rd 93446
805-237-2168
Marlowe & Corinne Evenson

190-265 $US BB
3 rooms, 3 pb
Most CC, Cash, Checks
C-ltd/S-no/P-no/H-ltd

Full breakfast
Complimentary bottle of wine,
appetizers & wine tastings in barrel
room
Sitting area, soaker tub, fireplaces,
wireless Internet, views of the
vineyard

The Winemakers Porch B&B sits on top of a knoll overlooking our Bordeaux vineyards. Our guests are invited to spend time sharing in our vineyard lifestyle. Luxury accommodations, complimentary bottle of wine, wireless Internet and gourmet breakfast.

✉ FJVineyard@aol.com 🌐 www.francesjamesvineyard.com/bnb.html

PENN VALLEY

Grandma's Room
19365 John Born Rd 95946
530-432-3226
Helen Albano

75 $US EP
1 rooms, 1 pb
Most CC, Cash, Checks
C-ltd/S-no/P-ltd/H-yes

Home baked cookies upon arrival. Bottled water/cold/hot drinks/ breakfast snacks/fruit-complimentary Direct TV, DVD player, free WiFi Internet, refrigerator, coffee maker, private bathroom, front porch.

Free Night w/Certificate: Anytime.

Grandma's Room is reminiscent of a time when staying at Grandma's house meant good feelings, warm quilts, hospitality & homebaked cookies. Sit on the porch or beneath the shade trees, swim in the nearby river, watch the wildlife, and enjoy the quiet!

✉ grandmasroom@gmail.com 🌐 www.grandmasroom.info

PESCADERO

Pescadero Creek Inn Bed & Breakfast
393 Stage Rd 94060
888-307-1898 650-879-1898
Ken Donnelly

175-255 $US BB
4 rooms, 4 pb
Visa, MC, *Rated*, •
C-ltd/S-ltd/P-no/H-no

Full gourmet organic breakfast Afternoon wine & cheese from nearby Harley Farms Goat Dairy & wine we made ourselves Free WiFi, snuggly down comforters, feather mattresses, antique claw foot tubs

Offering a romantic escape on the California coast, Pescadero has secluded beaches, miles of hiking trails in redwoods and biking along farm fields. Gourmet organic breakfast and wine & Harley Farm goat cheese included. Walk to Duarte's.

✉ ken@pescaderocreekinn.com 🌐 www.pescaderocreekinn.com

PLACERVILLE

Albert Shafsky House B&B
2942 Coloma St 95667
866-385-6466 530-642-2776
Rita Timewell & Stephanie Carlson

135-185 $US BB
3 rooms, 3 pb
Most CC, *Rated*, •
C-ltd/S-ltd/P-no/H-ltd

Full hearty breakfast Wine & snacks at check-in between 4–7, cookies in the early afternoon, guest refrigerator Sitting room with library, games & satellite TV/VCR with movies, free high speed wireless Internet

Luxury in the heart of Gold Country. Queen Anne-style Victorian bed & breakfast, built in 1902, is close enough to stroll to town. Stay in Placerville & visit El Dorado wineries, Apple Hill, Coloma. 3 Diamond rated by AAA.

✉ stay@shafsky.com 🌐 www.shafsky.com

Blair Sugar Pine B&B
2985 Clay St 95667
530-626-9006
William & Kay Steffen

130-160 $US BB
3 rooms, 3 pb
Most CC
C-ltd/S-no/P-no/H-no

Full breakfast Evening refreshments, tin of chocolates upon arrival Book & video libraries, WiFi, central A/C, feather beds, private baths, sitting room, chocolates

A unique turreted 1901 Queen Anne Victorian bed and breakfast located in historic downtown Placerville, featuring hillside gardens, original woodwork and a history of romance. Walk to shops, restaurants and more.

✉ stay@blairsugarpine.com 🌐 www.blairsugarpine.com

Eden Vale Inn
1780 Springvale Rd 95667
530-621-0901
Mark Hamlin

149-349 $US BB
5 rooms, 5 pb
Most CC, Cash, Checks
C-yes/S-ltd/P-yes/H-no

Full breakfast Beverages available throughout the day DVD library, delivered newspapers, HDTV & spa tubs in some rooms

Retreat to Eden Vale Inn, a casually elegant destination in California's Gold Country near Placerville. In this superb Sierra Foothills setting, accommodations are suffused in rich natural colors reflective of the lush gardens and natural beauty.

✉ innkeeper@edenvaleinn.com 🌐 www.edenvaleinn.com

60   California

POINT REYES STATION

Marsh Cottage
415-669-7168
Wendy Schwartz

145-190 $US BB
1 rooms, 1 pb
Rated
C-yes/S-no/P-no/H-no

Full and continental plus
Complimentary coffee & tea
Kitchen, library & sitting area,
fireplace, porch, sun deck

Carefully appointed private cottage along Tomales Bay, near Inverness and Point Reyes National Seashore. Kitchen, fireplace, queen bed, deck overlooking the marsh and "Elephant" Mountain.

✉ wenpaints@gmail.com   🌐 www.marshcottage.com

QUINCY

The Feather Bed
542 Jackson St 95971
800-696-8624 530-283-0102
Bob Janowski

120-175 $US BB
7 rooms, 7 pb
Most CC, *Rated*
C-yes/S-no/P-no/H-yes

Full breakfast
Afternoon tea, cookies & fudge
Sitting room, porch, Victorian garden,
bikes, fountain, fireplaces, A/C

Relax on the porch of this country Victorian inn. Enjoy the slower pace of a small mountain town. Savor fresh berry smoothies with a delicious breakfast. Experience the warmth & personal hospitality that are a tradition in Quincy and at The Feather Bed.

✉ info@featherbed-inn.com   🌐 www.featherbed-inn.com

The Sporting Inn
505 Main Street 95971
877-710-4300 530-283-4300
Claudia & Marvin Vickers

95-160 $US BB
8 rooms, 3 pb
Most CC
C-yes/S-no/P-yes/H-no

Full Country Style Breakfast
Snacks and soft drinks
Wireless Internet access, upstairs
facility, guide service available, boat
and trailer parking.

Located in Plumas County at the top of the Feather River Canyon in historic downtown Quincy, California. Walking distance to the museum, theaters, shops, restaurants. Charming old-style hotel atmosphere, with full, country breakfast. Internet access.

✉ thesportinginn@sbcglobal.net   🌐 thesportinginn.com

REDDING

Tiffany House B&B
1510 Barbara Rd 96003
530-244-3225
Brady Stewart

125-170 $US BB
4 rooms, 4 pb
Most CC, *Rated*, •
C-yes/S-ltd/P-no/H-ltd

Full breakfast
Complimentary refreshments
Sitting room, 1 room with spa, gazebo,
swimming pool, parlor

Romantic Victorian within minutes of the Sacramento River, beautiful lakes, water sports, championship golf are all near by. Views of the Lassen mountain range. View of Calatrava Sundial Bridge from front yard.

✉ tiffanyhse@aol.com   🌐 www.tiffanyhousebb.com

REDWOOD CITY

Atherton Inn
1201 W Selby Ln 94061
800-603-8105 650-474-2777
Tricia Young

139-249 $US BB
5 rooms, 5 pb
Visa, MC, AmEx,
Rated, •
C-ltd/S-ltd/P-no/H-no
German & Spanish

Full breakfast
Cookies, cocoas, selection of teas,
freshly squeezed orange juice, large
fruit bowl
Free WiFi, TV, DVD, robes, hairdryer,
message phone, Euro down pillows,
elevator, fireplaces in room

Warmth, luxury & hospitality abound in this newly built French style chateau. Conveniently located in the heart of the San Francisco Peninsula in a quiet residential neighborhood just one block from Atherton. We pamper you.   ✉ athertoninn@gmail.com   🌐 www.athertoninn.com

SACRAMENTO

Amber House B&B
1315 22nd St 95816
800-755-6526 916-444-8085
Judith Bommer

169-279 $US BB
10 rooms, 10 pb
Most CC, *Rated*, •
C-ltd/S-no/P-no/H-no
French, German

2 course gourmet breakfast
Fresh cookies with beverage at
turndown, coffee, tea & sodas any
time
Jacuzzi tubs, fireplaces, free parking,
WiFi, am beverage tray, gourmet
breakfast, in room massages

Just 8 blocks from the State Capitol in Midtown, on a quiet street of historic homes, the Inn offers the perfect blend of elegance, comfort, and hospitality. The Inn is perfectly located, walking distance from downtown, restaurants, shops and galleries.

✉ info@amberhouse.com   🌐 www.amberhouse.com

SAN ANSELMO

San Anselmo Inn
339 San Anselmo Ave 94960
800-598-9771 415-455-5366
Peter & Julie McNair

99-199 $US BB
15 rooms, 13 pb
Most CC, Cash
C-yes/S-no/P-no/H-yes
Fluent in German &
French

Continental plus breakfast
Our Sunflower Cafe offers a full
breakfast and lunch menu
Suites, WiFi, cable TV, Irons, ironing
boards, Hair-dryers

This European style Inn provides privacy and comfort along with warm hospitality. Our B&B is the perfect base for exploring Marin County, San Francisco, the Napa, Sonoma wine countries, and Pt. Reyes National Seashore. Hosts speak fluent German & French.

✉ innkeepers@sananselmoinn.com 🌐 www.sananselmoinn.com

SAN CLEMENTE

Casa Tropicana Boutique
Beachfront Inn
610 Avenida Victoria 92672
800-492-1245 949-492-1234
Rick & Sue Anderson

225-775 $US BB
8 rooms, 8 pb
Most CC, Cash,
Rated, •
C-yes/S-no/P-no/H-ltd
Spanish and Spanglish

Extensive Buffet Breakfast
Each room has a mini-fridge stocked
with a fun assortment of snacks and
goodies — all complimentary!
fireplace, wireless, Jacuzzi tub,
flatscreen TV, gated parking, beach
bags, super comfy bed, more

Free Night w/Certificate: Valid Oct 1-April 15; holidays, special events excluded, may not be combined.

Spanish-inspired architecture, ocean views, stylish and comfortable decor, thoughtful amenities and at the pier, beach and sand in San Clemente. Casa Tropicana, not just a San Clemente address, a California state of mind.

✉ info@casatropicana.com 🌐 www.casatropicana.com

SAN DIEGO

Carole's B&B Inn
3227 Grim Ave 92104
619-280-5258
C. Dugdale & M. O'Brien

119-259 $US BB
10 rooms, 5 pb
Most CC, *Rated*, •
C-ltd/S-ltd/P-no/H-no

Continental plus breakfast
Cheese
Sitting room, conference for 10, salt
water pool, hot tub, player piano,
cable TV

Historical house built in 1904, tastefully redecorated with antiques. Centrally located near the San Diego Zoo and Balboa Park. A friendly and congenial atmosphere. New large, saltwater pool.

✉ carolesbnb@hotmail.com 🌐 www.carolesbnb.com

Jamul Haven
13518 Jamul Drive 91935
619-669-3100 619-669-3100
William Roetzheim

199-349 $US BB
4 rooms, 4 pb
Visa, MC, •
C-ltd/S-no/P-ltd/H-ltd

Full breakfast
Pool, 2 spas, water slide, waterfalls,
gym, game room, pub, disco, pool
pavilion, business center

Free Night w/Certificate: Valid Monday-Thursday; not valid with other offers or discounts, limit one free night per stay.

Fully restored 1890 Victorian mansion in the mountains 25 minutes away from downtown San Diego. The six acre compound features a health spa, game room, gym, pub, disco, spas, pool, waterfalls, and much more. ✉ info@jamulhaven.com 🌐 www.jamulhaven.com

SAN FRANCISCO

Annie's Cottage
1255 Vallejo 94109
415-923-9990
Annie Bone

160-175 $US EP
1 rooms, 1 pb
C-yes/S-no/P-no/H-no

Coffee, tea, cereal provided
Near wharf & downtown, phone &
answering machine, TV/VCR, queen
bed, wireless Internet

Guestroom with private entrance, private bath, sitting area, deck, refrigerator & microwave. A country hideaway in the middle of San Francisco. Furnished with antiques.

✉ annie@anniescottage.com 🌐 anniescottage.com

62 California

SAN FRANCISCO ————————————————————————

Castillo Inn
48 Henry St 94114
800-865-5112 415-864-5111
Mario

65-90 $US BB
4 rooms
Visa, MC, AmEx, •
S-no/P-no/H-no
Spanish

Self-serve Continental breakfast
Wireless Internet, phone, voice mail,
refrigerator, microwave, parking at
$10.00/night

Gay accommodations mostly, though all are welcome. Clean, quiet and safe. Centrally located close to Castro & Market Streets. Ask about our seasonal discounts (holidays and special events excluded).

✉ castilloinn@yahoo.com

Country Cottage
5 Dolores Ter 94110
800-452-8249 415-899-0060
Richard & Susan Kreibich

79-99 $US BB
4 rooms
Visa, MC, AmEx,
Rated
C-ltd/S-ltd/P-no/H-no
Czech

Full breakfast
Two sitting rooms, quiet garden patio,
free WiFi Internet in every room,
parking available

The Country Cottage B&B is a cozy country-style B&B in the heart of San Francisco. Four guestrooms are comfortably furnished with American country antiques and brass beds. It is a short walk to park, tennis courts, cafes, restaurants & bars. Free WiFi.

✉ reservations@bbsf.com

Inn on Castro
321 Castro St 94114
415-861-0321
Jan de Gier

125-195 $US BB
8 rooms, 7 pb
Most CC
C-yes/S-no/P-no/H-yes

Full breakfast
Complimentary brandy
Living room, contemporary
furnishings, fresh flowers throughout
the inn, fireplace, library

An incomparable way to experience San Francisco's charm and hospitality from the heart of the City's gay and lesbian community. The Castro. The Inn on Castro is at Castro and Market on the residential side with views over the city and the Bay.

✉ Innkeeper@innoncastro.com �','www.innoncastro.com

Monte Cristo
600 Presidio Ave 94115
888-666-1875 415-931-1875
Jack & Carl

129-250 $US BB
14 rooms, 14 pb
Most CC, Cash
C-ltd/S-no/P-no/H-ltd

Full breakfast
Authentic antiques, Persian rugs,
hardwood floors, flat-screen cable TV,
complimentary WiFi

The Monte Cristo Inn, a San Francisco bed and breakfast hotel in the city's exclusive and popular Pacific Heights neighborhood, offers the comfort and privacy of an historic inn — European style.

✉ jack@montecristosf.com 🌍 www.BedandBreakfastSF.com

Ocean Beach B&B
611 42nd Ave 94121
415-668-0193
Joanne

125-205 $US BB
2 rooms, 2 pb
C-ltd/S-no/P-no/H-no

Continental plus breakfast
Homemade cookies always available
Board games, hairdryer, iron,
microwave, fridge, library, movies,
wireless, Internet

Distinctive B&B accommodations with views of the Pacific Ocean located in a quiet, residential neighborhood just six blocks from Ocean Beach and three blocks from Golden Gate Park in San Francisco.

✉ oceanbeachbb@aol.com 🌍 www.oceanbeachbb.com

Queen Anne Hotel
1590 Sutter St 94109
800-227-3970 415-441-2828
Michael Wade

105-199 $US BB
48 rooms, 48 pb
Most CC, Cash,
Rated, •
C-yes/S-no/P-no/H-yes
Spanish, Portuguese,
Mandarin

Continental plus breakfast
Afternoon tea & sherry with cookies
In-room massage, dry-cleaning, event
catering, complimentary limo service

The Queen Anne offers unforgettable accommodations in an unforgettable city! One-of-a-kind guestrooms & suites with luxurious private baths. Some with original marble wetbars, fireplaces or Jacuzzi tub.

✉ stay@queenanne.com 🌍 www.queenanne.com

SAN FRANCISCO

Seal Rock Inn
545 Point Lobos Ave 94121
888-732-5762 415-752-8000
Rick Landerman

114-167 $US EP
27 rooms, 27 pb
Most CC, Cash
C-yes/S-no/P-no/H-yes

Restaurant on site
Patio and pool, limited undercover
parking, free WiFi

Located far from the noisy downtown traffic and crowds, yet still in the city in a resort-like location. We are just two blocks up the hill from the historic Cliff House and Sutro Bath Ruins and four blocks north of Golden Gate Park.

✉ Reservations@SealRockInn.com 🌐 www.sealrockinn.com

The Chateau Tivoli
1057 Steiner St 94115
800-228-1647 415-776-5462
Nico Lizarraga

100-290 $US BB
9 rooms, 7 pb
Visa, MC, AmEx
C-yes/S-no/P-no/H-ltd
Spanish, Cantonese,
Mandarin

Continental plus breakfast
Continental Breakfast M–F; Weekend
Champagne Brunch, daily evening
wine & cheese
Wedding facilities, concierge, formal
parlors, American Renaissance
furniture, fireplace, suites

Welcome to the Chateau Tivoli! An opulently restored Victorian mansion, located in San Francisco's historic Alamo Square district, Chateau Tivoli is one of the city's most charming bed and breakfast inns. ✉ mail@chateautivoli.com 🌐 www.chateautivoli.com

---

The Inn San Francisco
943 South Van Ness
Ave 94110
800-359-0913 415-641-0188
Marty Neely

120-335 $US BB
21 rooms, 19 pb
Most CC, *Rated*, •
C-yes/S-no/P-no/H-no
Spanish, French,
Cantonese, Mandarin

Full buffet breakfast
Complimentary fruit, coffee, tea,
sherry
Sun deck, English garden, hot tub,
phones, TVs, parking, Whirlpool tubs,
suites, complimentary WiFi

Capturing the romantic spirit of the Victorian era, The Inn San Francisco invites you to be our guest and discover bed and breakfast comfort and hospitality with a warmth that is distinctly San Franciscan. Be welcomed as a friend. ✉ innkeeper@innsf.com 🌐 www.innsf.com

---

The Parsonage
198 Haight St 94102
415-863-3699
Joan Hull & John Phillips

180-250 $US BB
5 rooms, 5 pb
Visa, MC
C-ltd/S-no/P-no/H-ltd

Multi-course breakfast
In the evening guests are welcomed
home to a tray of chocolates and
brandy!
Marble bathrooms, fireplaces,
2 parlors, library, goose down
comforters & imported linens, WiFi

An 1883 Historical Landmark, Victorian home (formerly the McMorry-Lagan residence). The Parsonage's large, airy rooms are elegantly furnished with European & American antiques. Convenient to all San Francisco attractions. ✉ theparsonage@hotmail.com 🌐 www.theparsonage.com

---

The Studio on Sixth
1387 Sixth Ave 94122
415-504-2142

65-115 $US EP
1 rooms, 1 pb
Most CC, Checks
C-yes/S-no/P-no/H-no

Coffee houses, cafes & excellent
restaurants nearby
Garden, private entrance, fully
equipped kitchen, LCD TV, telephone
& wireless Internet

Studio apartment that opens onto an ornamental garden. Private entrance, queen-size bed, fully-equipped kitchen, separate bath and vanity, LCD TV, private phone, and wireless Internet
✉ studioonsixth@gmail.com 🌐 www.studioonsixth.com

Washington Square Inn
1660 Stockton St 94133
800-388-0220 415-981-4220
Maria & Daniel Levin

179-329 $US BB
16 rooms, 16 pb
Most CC, *Rated*
C-ltd/S-no/P-no/H-yes
Portuguese, Spanish

Continental plus breakfast
Wine & hors d'oeuvres in the evening,
tea
Self parking, lobby, antiques, fireplace,
cable TV, robes, courtyard, business
services in lobby

Delightfully situated in the very heart of San Francisco, the Washington Square Inn welcomes its guests with all the charm & comfort only a small European hotel can provide. Sixteen rooms feature European antiques, cable TV, soft robes and private baths.
✉ info@wsisf.com 🌐 www.wsisf.com

SAN FRANCISCO

White Swan Inn	129-309 $US BB	Continental Gourmet Breakfast
845 Bush St 94108	26 rooms, 26 pb	Complimentary wine & hors
800-999-9570 415-775-1755	Most CC, *Rated*, •	d'oeuvres, afternoon tea and
Eric Norman	C-yes/S-no/P-no/H-ltd	homemade cookies
		Daily laundry & valet service, fitness
		room, computer station, WiFi, meeting
		room w/ deck, concierge

With crackling fireplaces in all 26 guestrooms and suites, the White Swan Inn is a romantic and atmospheric small hotel in the Nob Hill/Union Square area.

✉ whiteswan@jdvhospitality.com ❂ www.whiteswaninnsf.com

SAN LUIS OBISPO

Bridge Creek Inn B&B	150-190 $US BB	Full breakfast
5300 Righetti Rd 93401	2 rooms, 2 pb	Light, gourmet refreshments, wine to
805-544-3003	Most CC, Cash	whet your appetite
Sally & Gene Kruger	C-ltd/S-no/P-no/H-no	Sauna, outdoor hot tub, close to
		Historic SLO, secluded, wireless
		Internet, deck, TV/DVD

Nestled near the vineyards of the Edna Valley, just ten minutes from historic San Luis Obispo, the Bridge Creek Inn offers pastoral views of the Santa Lucia Mountains and a spectacular nightly show of uncountable stars. ✉ info@bridgecreekinn.com ❂ www.bridgecreekinn.com

Petit Soleil	159-299 $US BB	Full homemade breakfast
1473 Monterey St 93401	16 rooms, 16 pb	Complimentary wine & light appetizer
800-676-1588 805-549-0321	Most CC, Cash, Checks,	in the evening
John & Dianne Conner	*Rated*	Outdoor patio, garden, getaway
	C-yes/S-no/P-yes/H-ltd	packages, wine tasting, private baths,
	Spanish	wireless Internet, telephones

Find a touch of French village life at this delightfully renovated B&B. Individually themed rooms have whimsical art, custom furnishings, and CD players. Rates include wine pairings in the early evening and gourmet breakfasts.

✉ reservations@petitsoleilslo.com ❂ www.petitsoleilslo.com

SAN MIGUEL

Work Family Guest Ranch	225 $US MAP	Full breakfast
75903 Ranchita Canyon	6 rooms, 2 pb	Dinner & complimentary wine
Rd 93451	Visa, MC	included. Lunch optional.
805-467-3233	C-yes/S-no/P-yes/H-ltd	Sitting room, library, tour of farm
George & Elaine Work		

Stay on a 5th generation working ranch. Each room has a beautiful view with full breakfast and 3 course dinner included. On the ranch there are walking trails and horseback riding is available. Golf and world class wineries are in the area. ✉ elaine@workranch.com ❂ www.workranch.com

SAN RAFAEL

Gerstle Park Inn	189-275 $US BB	Full breakfast cooked to order
34 Grove St 94901	12 rooms, 12 pb	Complimentary evening wine & all
800-726-7611 415-721-7611	Most CC, Cash,	day sodas & snacks
Jim Dowling	*Rated*, •	Main parlor with a fireplace, limited
	C-ltd/S-ltd/P-yes/H-yes	open kitchen, 2½ acres of gardens,
		woods & orchard

This romantic historic Inn is private and quiet like being in the wine country. It's rural setting in an urban environment offers tranquility yet easy access to all the Bay area. A comfortable, elegant hotel surrounded by rich fabrics and antiques.

✉ innkeeper@gerstleparkinn.com ❂ www.gerstleparkinn.com

Panama Hotel	120-195 $US BB	Continental plus breakfast
4 Bayview St 94901	10 rooms, 10 pb	Full restaurant
800-899-3993 415-457-3993	Visa, MC, AmEx	Historic dining room, tropical garden
Daniel Miller	C-yes/S-no/P-ltd/H-yes	patio, room service
	Spanish	

A landmark inn and restaurant for 60 years, between San Francisco and the Wine Country. The Panama Hotel is celebrated for its eccentric charm.

✉ info@panamahotel.com ❂ www.panamahotel.com

SANTA BARBARA ─────────────────────────────

A White Jasmine Inn
1327 Bath St 93101
805-966-0589
Marlies & John

154-309 $US BB
12 rooms, 12 pb
Most CC, Cash, Checks,
Rated, •
C-ltd/S-ltd/P-no/H-no
German, Spanish

Full, hot, in-room breakfast
Wine & hors d'oeuvres, home made
cookies, etc.
Jacuzzis & fireplaces, in-room
massages, relaxing gardens, parking,
secure WiFi throughout & more.

Charming inn in prime residential downtown area and in the vicinity of beach. Inviting facility. Delightful amenities. Lovely grounds. Cozy parlor. Accommodations range from tastefully playful to romantically elegant.

✉ stay@whitejasmineinnsantabarbara.com 🌐 www.whitejasmineinnsantabarbara.com

Bath Street Inn
1720 Bath St 93101
800-341-2284 805-682-9680
Marie Christensen &
Deborah Gentry

136-295 $US BB
12 rooms, 12 pb
Visa, MC, *Rated*, •
C-yes/S-no/P-no/H-ltd

Complete gourmet breakfast
Afternoon refreshments of home
baked cakes & cookies, tea &
lemonade, evening wine & cheese
Complimentary WiFi, video & book
library, off street parking, upstairs &
downstairs sitting rooms

Located close to the heart of old Santa Barbara, the Inn offers the traditional warmth & hospitality of a European Bed & Breakfast.

✉ innkeepers@bathstreetinn.com 🌐 www.bathstreetinn.com

Casa Del Mar Inn
18 Bath St 93101
800-433-3097 805-963-4418
Yun Kim

124-329 $US BB
21 rooms, 21 pb
Most CC, Cash,
Rated, •
C-yes/S-no/P-yes/H-yes
Spanish

Continental plus breakfast buffet
Evening wine & cheese buffet
Sitting room, hot tub, Internet access,
pet accommodations, guest kitchen,
fireplaces, TV

The Casa Del Mar Bed Breakfast Inn is the perfect accommodation destination of choice for a California beach vacation. A Mediterranean-style villa, quiet, charming and there is a Courtyard Jacuzzi. Several units with fireplaces & kitchens.

✉ yunkim@casadelmar.com 🌐 www.casadelmar.com

Cheshire Cat Inn
36 W Valerio St 93101
805-569-1610
Christine Dunstan

159-425 $US BB
18 rooms, 18 pb
Most CC, Cash,
Rated, •
C-ltd/S-no/P-ltd/H-no

Continental plus breakfast
Wine & hors d'oeuvres every
afternoon
Hot tubs, balconies, fireplaces, spa
treatments, outdoor Jacuzzi, gardens,
WiFi

Enjoy the flower-filled gardens amidst the historical ambience of our two historical Queen Ann houses built in 1894. Our romantic & cozy rooms, suites and cottages feature delightful decor and furnishings, some with in-room Jacuzzi, fireplaces & patios.

✉ cheshire@cheshirecat.com 🌐 www.cheshirecat.com

Old Yacht Club Inn
431 Corona Del Mar Dr 93103
800-676-1676 805-962-1277
Eilene Bruce & Vince Pettit

119-299 $US BB
14 rooms, 14 pb
Most CC, Cash,
Rated, •
C-yes/S-no/P-ltd/H-ltd
Spanish

Full breakfast
Afternoon wine & cheese social,
sherry in all rooms, candy &
chocolate chip cookies throughout
day.
Free bike rentals, beach chairs &
beach towels, free wireless Internet,
whirlpool tubs, free parking

Free Night w/Certificate: Anytime. Room Upgrade.

1 block from famous East Beach! Best location in the area! Complimentary home made breakfast. Free bike rentals, beach chairs and towels. Free wireless Internet & free parking. Complimentary wine & sherry. 1 block to 25 cent electric shuttle.

 info@oldyachtclubinn.com 🌐 www.oldyachtclubinn.com

SANTA BARBARA

| **Secret Garden Inn & Cottages**
1908 Bath St 93101
800-676-1622 805-687-2300
Dominique Hannaux | 121-255 $US BB
11 rooms, 11 pb
Most CC, Cash,
Checks, •
C-yes/S-no/P-yes/H-no
French-Spanish | Full gourmet breakfast
Wine & hors d'oeuvres at 5 pm
Sitting room, garden, brick patio,
bicycles, massages, weddings, private
hot tub in cottage |

Guestrooms, suites and private cottages filled with charm, in a delightfully quiet and relaxing country setting. Four rooms with private patio and outdoor hot tubs.
✉ garden@secretgarden.com 🌐 www.secretgarden.com

| **Simpson House Inn**
121 E Arrellaga 93101
800-676-1280 805-963-7067
Gillean Wilson | 255-615 $US BB
15 rooms, 15 pb
Most CC, Cash,
Rated, •
C-ltd/S-ltd/P-no/H-yes
Spanish | Gourmet vegetarian breakfast
Wine, Mediterranean hors d'oeuvres
buffet, hot/cold beverages, afternoon
tea & dessert buffet
Full concierge services, wireless
Internet, private patios & decks, in-
room massage, morning paper |

Welcome to North America's only AAA Five-Diamond B&B. This beautiful Inn is located in a prestigious historic neighborhood of downtown Santa Barbara, and secluded in an acre of English gardens.
✉ reservations@simpsonhouseinn.com 🌐 www.simpsonhouseinn.com

| **The Orchid Inn at Santa Barbara**
420 W Montecito St 93101
877-722-3657 805-965-2333
Riviera California
Investments LP | 132-259 $US BB
8 rooms, 8 pb
Visa, MC, •
C-ltd/S-no/P-no/H-ltd
Spanish, Italian, French | Full hot breakfast
Afternoon wine tasting featuring
renown Santa Barbara Winery select
wines included in are room rates
Full service spa, Jacuzzi tubs,
fireplaces, colorful decor, sitting areas,
business accommodation |

A stylish, contemporary bed and breakfast, two blocks from West Beach in Santa Barbara. The Orchid Inn offers a pleasurable escape to relax and feel at home in the charming ambience.
✉ info@orchidinnatsb.com 🌐 www.orchidinnatsb.com

| **The Upham Hotel**
1404 De La Vina St 93101
800-727-0876 805-962-0058
Jan Martin Winn | 220-450 $US BB
58 rooms, 58 pb
Most CC, Cash,
Rated, •
C-yes/S-no/P-no/H-no
Spanish/French | Continental plus breakfast
Complimentary wine, coffee, tea,
Louie's Restaurant
Garden veranda, garden, valet
laundry, phones, WiFi |

A Victorian treasure in the heart of downtown Santa Barbara. Constructed of redwood with sweeping verandas, the 1871 landmark is surrounded by an acre of gardens and combines the intimacy of a B&B with the convenience of a full-service hotel.
✉ innkeeper@uphamhotel.com 🌐 www.uphamhotel.com

| **Villa Rosa**
15 Chapala St 93101
805-966-0851
Julia Finucan | 129-339 $US BB
18 rooms, 18 pb
Most CC, Cash, •
C-yes/S-no/P-no/H-ltd
Spanish, French,
German, Scandanavian | Continental plus breakfast
Wine & hors d'oeuvres served from
5 to 7 in the evening, sherry or port
served from 9 to 10
Spa, pool, walled-in courtyard, garden,
fireplace, conference facilities, dry
cleaning, masseuse |

Let us pamper you in International style. Located just 84 steps from the beach. It exudes a warm, personal and sophisticated atmosphere. A cozy spa and pool are nestled in a walled-in courtyard for your privacy and relaxation. ✉ villarosainnsb@gmail.com 🌐 www.villarosainnsb.com/html/home.html

SANTA CRUZ

| **Adobe on Green Street**
103 Green St 95060
831-469-9866
Brion Sprinsock | 149-219 $US BB
4 rooms, 4 pb
Visa, MC, *Rated*
S-no/P-no/H-ltd | Continental plus breakfast
Sodas, bottled water, chocolates
Jacuzzi tubs, gas fireplaces, sitting
room, courtyards, gardens, DVD
library, DVD player in room |

Peace and quiet just three blocks from downtown. Private bathrooms, fireplaces, jet tubs, the most comfy beds, parking & free WiFi. Midweek rates from $149. Last Minute rates Sun-Thurs: $129.
✉ santacruzadobe@gmail.com 🌐 www.adobeongreen.com

SANTA CRUZ

Cliff Crest	95-265 $US BB	Full breakfast
407 Cliff St 95060	6 rooms, 6 pb	Happy to accommodate special
831-252-1057 831-427-2609	Most CC, •	dietary needs
Adriana & Constantin	C-yes/S-no/P-no/H-yes	Sitting room, large garden, free parking
Gehriger	Spanish, German,	
	French, Swiss German	

Built in 1887 on Beach Hill above the Santa Cruz Beach Boardwalk, this historic Queen Anne Victorian overlooks the picturesque Santa Cruz Mountains and beaches. The Inn features 6 guestrooms, each with private bath and several with fireplaces.

✉ innkpr@CliffCrestInn.com   🌐 www.CliffCrestInn.com

Pleasure Point Inn	225-295 $US BB	Expanded Continental Breakfast
2-3665 E Cliff Dr 95062	4 rooms, 4 pb	A welcome basket with goodies
877-557-2567 831-475-4657	Visa, MC, *Rated*, •	Fireplaces, whirlpool tubs, 4 suites,
Tara & Ivy	C-ltd/S-ltd/P-no/H-yes	TV, private phones, private baths,
		cable TV, iPod dock, WiFi

Pleasure Point Inn is an oceanfront B&B at the famous Pleasure Point Beach and offers spectacular views of the Pacific Ocean. The Inn has a large roof-top deck where you can soak in the hot tub.

✉ Inquiries@PleasurePointInn.com   🌐 www.PleasurePointInn.com

---

The Darling House A B&B	150-295 $US BB	Continental plus breakfast
Inn by the Sea	7 rooms, 5 pb	Complimentary beverages. Fresh
314 W Cliff Dr 95060	Most CC, *Rated*, •	baked goodies.
831-458-1958	C-ltd/S-ltd/P-no/H-ltd	Fireplaces, extra large bathtubs,
Darrell & Karen Darling		fireplaces in rooms, retreats,
		weddings, free WiFi

A 1910 oceanside architectural masterpiece designed by William Weeks. Lighted by the rising sun through beveled glass, Tiffany lamps and open hearths, and the grace of genuinely open hearts.

✉ ddarling@darlinghouse.com   🌐 www.darlinghouse.com

West Cliff Inn	185-400 $US BB	Full breakfast
174 West Cliff Drive 95060	9 rooms, 9 pb	Afternoon wine, tea & hors d'oeuvres,
800-979-0910 831-457-2200	Most CC, Cash	freshly-baked cookies, drinks available
Michael Hoppe	C-yes/S-no/P-no/H-ltd	throughout the day
		Outdoor jetted hot tub, WiFi, evening
		turndown service featuring delectable
		Le Belge chocolates

This distinctive inn is on a bluff across from Cowell's Beach and the famous Santa Cruz Beach and Boardwalk. The stately, three-story Italianate Victorian with its spacious, wraparound porch was completely renovated and features a breezy, coastal decor.

✉ westcliffinn@foursisters.com   🌐 www.westcliffinn.com

SANTA ROSA

Melitta Station Inn	159-219 $US BB	Full 3 course gourmet breakfast
5850 Melita Rd 95409	6 rooms, 6 pb	English afternoon tea, snacks, tea &
800-504-3099 707-538-7712	Most CC, Cash,	coffee, soft drinks all complimentary
Jackie & Tim Thresh	*Rated*, •	Central air, ironing board/iron, free
	C-ltd/S-ltd/P-no/H-ltd	wireless Internet, spa & massage room
	French, Dutch, Italian	with 40 jet hot tub
	(some)	

English cottage hospitality at its best. The inn is cozily furnished with the owners' European antiques, and lies opposite Annadel State Park for biking. It is central to all Sonoma and Napa wineries.

✉ info@melittastationinn.com   🌐 www.melittastationinn.com

SANTA ROSA

Vintners Inn
4350 Barnes Rd 95403
800-421-2584 707-575-7350
Percy Brandon

185-550 $US BB
44 rooms, 44 pb
Most CC, *Rated*, •
C-yes/S-no/P-no/H-yes
Spanish

Continental plus breakfast
John Ash & Co. restaurant, Front
Room Bar & Lounge, Vintners Inn
Event Center, Wedding Pavilion
Wireless Internet, bell service,
outdoor hot tub, walking trail, gym,
massage room, bocce ball court

A European-styled estate in 92-acre vineyard. All king rooms offer patio/balcony with views of vineyards, gardens or courtyard & fountain. Award-winning John Ash & Co. Restaurant. Luscious grounds and Event Center. AAA Four Diamond rating.

info@vintnersinn.com   www.vintnersinn.com

SANTA YNEZ

Santa Ynez Inn
3627 Sagunto St 93460
800-643-5774 805-688-5588
Rick Segovia

255-495 $US BB
20 rooms, 20 pb
Most CC, Cash, Checks
C-yes/S-no/P-no/H-yes

Continental plus breakfast
Enjoy wine, hors d'oeuvres, evening
desserts, a full gourmet breakfast in
the morning
Whirlpool tub, balcony or patios,
concierge service, fitness suite with
sauna, flat screen HD TV's

Discover Victorian grace and hospitality in the heart of Santa Barbara County wine country. Located just 3 miles from Los Olivos and Solvang, the Santa Ynez Inn offers lavish suites with fireplaces, Jacuzzi tubs and many amenities.

info@santaynezinn.com   www.santaynezinn.com

SEBASTOPOL

Pearlessence Vineyard Inn
4097 Hessel Rd 95472
707-823-5092
Linda and Greg Pearl

195-245 $US BB
1 rooms, 1 pb
Visa, MC
C-yes/S-ltd/P-no/H-ltd

Full breakfast
Complimentary Bottled Water and Soft
Drinks, In-Room Gourmet Coffee, Tea,
Cocoa, and Hot Cereal
New upscale furnishings, heated slate
floors, original artwork, cable TV,
plush robes, wet bar

Come enjoy the gardens, tranquil pond, and our scenic vineyard. Private enough for a romantic weekend getaway while only a short drive to the Russian River, Bodega Bay, and area wineries.

info@pearlessenceinn.com   www.pearlessenceinn.com

SHAVER LAKE

Elliott House
42062 Tollhouse Rd 93664
888-841-8601 559-841-8601
Joanne & Greg Elliott

159-219 $US BB
7 rooms, 7 pb
Most CC, Cash,
Rated, •
C-yes/S-no/P-no/H-yes

Full gourmet breakfast
Evening happy hour with California
wines, desserts, champagne breakfast
in bed, picnic baskets
Fireside room, garden, weddings and
events accommodations, intimate
sitting Area, Satellite TV, deck

Throughout the B&B, charming collectibles are mixed with stylish furniture, original watercolor paintings by local artists and fresh flowers. The array of warm, vibrant colors and soft lighting complete the design details of the B&B.

elliotthouse@psnw.com   www.elliotthousebandb.com

SOLEDAD

Inn at the Pinnacles
32025 Stonewall Canyon
Rd 93960
831-678-2400
Jon & Jan Brosseau

200-290 $US BB
6 rooms, 6 pb
Visa, MC
C-ltd/S-no/P-no/H-yes
All Year, Weekends
Only

Full breakfast
Wine & cheese
Sitting room, suites, gas fireplaces,
private patios, air-jet tubs, swimming
pool, wireless Internet

Mediterranean-style country inn with surrounding vineyard and hillside views. Romantic setting. Four miles to the Pinnacles National Monument (west entrance).

info@innatthepinnacles.com   www.innatthepinnacles.com

The Sonoma Hotel, Sonoma, CA

SONOMA

A Victorian Garden Inn	159-359 $US BB	Continental plus breakfast
316 E Napa St 95476	4 rooms, 3 pb	Breakfast served in the garden, dining
800-543-5339 707-996-5339	Visa, MC, AmEx,	room, or in your room, afternoon tea
Donna J. Lewis	*Rated*, •	or coffee & snacks
	C-ltd/S-ltd/P-no/H-no	Therapeutic hot tub, swimming
	Spanish	pool, lush gardens, on-site massage
		services, free WiFi, iPod docks

Let us spoil you at the Victorian Garden Inn. Just a short walk from Sonoma's historic town plaza, breakfast served in the garden, dining room, or in room, free WiFi, pool, and therapeutic hot tub. Everything a quintessential bed and breakfast should be.

✉ info@victoriangardeninn.com 🌐 www.victoriangardeninn.com

The Inn at Sonoma	205-300 $US BB	Full breakfast
630 Broadway 95476	19 rooms, 19 pb	Afternoon wine, tea & hors d' oeuvres,
888-568-9818 707-939-1340	Most CC, Cash	freshly-baked cookies, drinks available
Rachel Retterer	C-yes/S-no/P-no/H-yes	throughout the day
		Hot tub, bikes, fireplace, WiFi access

Fall in love with the quiet pace, beautiful vistas and fabulous food and wine of the Sonoma Valley. Conveniently located just two blocks from the historic Sonoma Plaza, the Inn at Sonoma is the perfect destination for your Wine Country visit.

✉ innatsonoma@foursisters.com 🌐 www.innatsonoma.com

The Sonoma Hotel	110-248 $US BB	Continental breakfast
110 W Spain St 95476	16 rooms, 16 pb	The Girl and The Fig Restaurant on
800-468-6016 707-996-2996	Most CC, *Rated*, •	site
Tim Farfan & Craig Miller	C-yes/S-no/P-no/H-yes	A/C, TVs, phone with data port
	Japanese, French,	
	Spanish	

A wonderful vintage hotel (circa 1880) on Sonoma's historic plaza. Modern amenities have been added, including private baths, phones, TVs and A/C. Guests can walk to shops, historic sites and wineries. ✉ sonomahotel@aol.com 🌐 www.sonomahotel.com

SOUTH LAKE TAHOE

Black Bear Inn	210-315 $US BB	Full breakfast
1202 Ski Run Blvd 96150	10 rooms, 8 pb	Evening wine & cheese
877-232-7466 530-544-4451	Visa, MC, Disc	Hot tub, fireplace, free WiFi, daily
Kevin & Jerry	C-yes/S-no/P-no/H-yes	maid service, TV/DVD.

A small luxury lodge with five guestrooms plus three cabins on a wooded acre in South Lake Tahoe. Close to the lake, restaurants, shopping, skiing, hiking, biking and boating.

✉ info@tahoeblackbear.com 🌐 www.tahoeblackbear.com

SOUTH PASADENA

Bissell House
201 Orange Grove Ave 91030
626-441-3535
Janet Hoyman

150-350 $US BB
7 rooms, 7 pb
Most CC, *Rated*
C-yes/S-no/P-no/H-ltd
French (some) Italian
(some)

Full breakfast 7 days a week
24 hour tea service. afternoon dessert.
Library, Premium cable TV/DVD (most
rooms), Pool, in room data ports,
wireless Internet access

1887 Victorian mansion beautifully appointed with antiques. 12 minutes and 100 years from down-town LA, we've received many commendations from CABBI. Members PAII, CABBI, CHLA and Pasa-dena & South Pasadena Chambers of Commerce.

✉ info@bissellhouse.com   🌐 www.bissellhouse.com

ST. HELENA

Ambrose Bierce House
1515 Main St 94574
707-963-3003
John & Lisa Runnells

159-299 $US BB
4 rooms, 4 pb
Most CC, *Rated*, •
C-ltd/S-ltd/P-no/H-no
Spanish

Full gourmet champagne breakfast
Premium wines & cheeses are served
each evening
Hot tub, Jacuzzi tubs, canopy beds,
antiques, A/C, satellite TV, WiFi, warm
hospitality

Located on Main street in Historic St. Helena, walk to fine dining and unique shopping. We invite you to experience the romantic charm of our 1872 Victorian bed and breakfast inn, right in the center of the finest wineries of Napa Valley. .

✉ ambrose@napanet.net   🌐 www.ambrosebiercehouse.com

Shady Oaks Country Inn
399 Zinfandel Ln 94574
707-963-1190
John & Lisa Runnells

189-269 $US BB
5 rooms, 5 pb
Most CC, Cash, Checks,
Rated, •
C-ltd/S-ltd/P-no/H-ltd
April 1st-November 1st

Gourmet champagne breakfast
Premium wines & cheeses are served
each evening
Fireplaces, Roman pillared patio;
innkeepers knowledgeable concierge,
private entrance, TVs, WiFi

Romantic and secluded on 2 acres, among finest wineries of Napa Valley on Zinfandel Lane. Walk to wineries. Elegant ambience, country comforts, antiques, fireplaces, port and fine linens in guest-rooms. "Warm and gracious hospitality!"

✉ shdyoaks@napanet.net   🌐 www.shadyoakscountryinn.com

The Ink House
1575 S. St Helena Hwy 94574
866-963-3890 707-963-3890
Kevin Outcalt

135-260 $US BB
6 rooms, 6 pb
Visa, MC, *Rated*, •
C-ltd/S-no/P-no/H-no

Full gourmet breakfast
Evening wine & appetizers included,
sherry & port available
Parlor, VIP Winery pass, game room,
bicycles, glass observatory, concierge
services, Internet access

Treat yourself to Victorian elegance in the Napa Valley's world famous wine growing region. Among the vineyards, and neighbors to some of the finest wineries and restaurants with a fabulous gourmet breakfast, luxurious rooms with flat screen TV & Internet

✉ inkhousebb@aol.com   🌐 www.inkhouse.com

The Wine Country Inn & Gardens
1152 Lodi Ln 94574
888-465-4608 707-963-7077
Jim Smith

215-660 $US BB
29 rooms, 29 pb
Visa, MC, *Rated*, •
C-ltd/S-no/P-no/H-ltd
Spanish

Full Buffet breakfast
Wine tasting & appetizers at afternoon
social; complimentary evening
restaurant shuttle service
Heated pool year round, balconies
or patios, fireplaces, spa or hot tubs,
daily tour to wineries

Built to resemble a converted winery, this Inn sits atop a landscaped knoll overlooking the vineyards of Napa Valley. Casual, comfortable, green luxury is the hallmark of this renowned hostelry. Family built, owned and operated for over thirty years!

✉ jim@winecountryinn.com   🌐 www.winecountryinn.com

ST. HELENA

The Zinfandel Inn
800 Zinfandel Ln 94574
707-963-3512
Jerry Payton

195-325 $US BB
3 rooms, 3 pb
Visa, MC, *Rated*, •
C-ltd/S-no/P-no/H-no

Full breakfast
Complimentary wine truffles on
arrival, world famous cookie jar
Sitting room, whirlpool tubs, suites,
fireplaces, cable TV, phones, A/C, YVI
lagoon style pool

English Tudor that looks like a castle in the vineyard. Located in the heart of Napa Valley. Two acres with a hot tub and beautiful lagoon pool. Acclaimed in Wine Spectator Magazine, Sunset Magazine, Food & Wine, and Best Places to Kiss.

❂ www.zinfandelinn.com

Wine Country Villa
2000 Howell Mtn Rd 94574
866-963-9073 707-963-9073
Bill & Diane

125-300 $US EP
2 rooms, 2 pb
Visa, MC, AmEx,
Rated, •
C-yes/S-ltd/P-yes/H-no

Self-catered
Well equipped kitchen & dining area
Great room with fireplace, pool, spa,
sauna, balconies, gardens, kitchen

Wine Country Villa is set in a secluded and beautiful area with views of wooded hillsides, mountains and vineyards. Impeccably designed and appointed, it is an ideal retreat in the heart of the Napa Valley. ✉ info@winecountryvilla.com ❂ www.winecountryvilla.com

SUTTER CREEK

Foxes Inn of Sutter Creek
77 Main St 95685
800-987-3344 209-267-5882
Monique & Morgan
Graziadei

160-325 $US BB
7 rooms, 7 pb
Most CC, *Rated*, •
C-ltd/S-no/P-no/H-ltd

Choose from numerous entrees
Coffee, tea & homemade cookies
Clawfoot tubs, library, fireplace,
TV, VCR, music systems, cathedral
ceilings, private entrances

Victorian Jewel in historic downtown Sutter Creek. Walking distance to shops, restaurants, wine tasting and theater. Select your gourmet breakfast from the menu, made-to-order and served to each room /the lush gardens. The only AAA 4-Diamond Amador Cty.

✉ innkeeper@foxesinn.com ❂ www.foxesinn.com

Sutter Creek Inn
75 Main St 95685
209-267-5606
Lindsay Way

93-195 $US BB
17 rooms, 17 pb
Visa, MC, Disc,
Rated, •
C-ltd/S-ltd/P-no/H-ltd

Full breakfast
Complimentary refreshments
Large living room, piano, library,
A/C, gardens, massage, wood-burning
fireplaces & swinging beds!

The Inn has been open and serving thousands of guests for over 35 years. Spacious grounds, patios, fireplaces, 17 rooms and cottages, and 4 of Jane Way's famous swinging beds. Eclectic style. Enjoy relaxed hospitality. ✉ info@suttercreekinn.com ❂ www.suttercreekinn.com

TAHOE CITY

Cottage Inn at Lake Tahoe, Inc.
1690 W Lake Blvd 96145
800-581-4073 530-581-4073
Susanne Muhr

158-340 $US BB
15 rooms, 15 pb
Visa, MC, *Rated*, •
C-ltd/S-no/P-no/H-ltd
German

Full breakfast
Homemade cookies and coffee bar
Private saunas, fireplaces, TVs/VCRs,
fax machine, rock Jacuzzi, private
beach, wireless Internet

The Cottage Inn, 2 miles south of Tahoe City, features original knotty pine paneling throughout, with unique themes and charming Tahoe appeal.

✉ cottage@ltol.com ❂ www.thecottageinn.com

TAHOMA

Tahoma Meadows B&B Cottages
6821 West Lake Blvd 96142
866-525-1553 530-525-1553
Dick & Ulli White

109-389 $US BB
16 rooms, 16 pb
Most CC, Cash, •
C-yes/S-no/P-yes/H-yes
German

Full Gourmet Family style breakfast
Afternoon Wine and Cheese Event
Catering brunchs, BBQ's Weddings
and Special Events
Private entrances and baths, many
with claw foot soaking tubs, fireplaces,
kitchens.

Step back in time at Lake Tahoe and visit our historic and charming little red cottages. This is what Tahoe was 50 years ago. We are located on Lake Tahoe's quiet West Shore. Away from the noise, crowds and casinos of the South and North Shores.

 info@tahomameadows.com ❂ www.tahomameadows.com

TEMPLETON ───────────────────────────

Bike Lane Inn	89-99 $US BB	Full breakfast
749 Gough Ave 93465	2 rooms, 2 pb	Wi-fi, patio, TV with DVD, CD player,
805-434-0409	Most CC, Cash	toiletries and robes for use during stay
Scott and Elaine McElmury	C-ltd/S-ltd/P-no/H-no	
	Spanish	

Comfortable, affordable and fun! Located in the heart of Templeton, a perfect starting point for bike-and motor-touring thru the rolling vineyards of Templeton and Paso Robles. Close to dozens of wineries, great restaurants, spas and salons.

✉ info@bikelaneinn.com 🌐 www.bikelaneinn.com

Carriage Vineyards B&B	140-260 $US BB	Full breakfast
4337 S El Pomar 93465	4 rooms, 4 pb	Snacks, complimentary soft drinks,
800-617-7911 805-227-6807	Visa, MC, Disc, •	estate olive oil tasting
Leigh Anne Farley	C-ltd/S-no/P-no/H-ltd	Sitting room, carriage house with
		18 carriages, vineyards and olives,
		carriage rides, vineyard tours

100-acre ranch with 28 acres of wine grapes & 850 olive trees. Lovely rooms, great hospitality & delightful breakfasts. Peaceful & quiet.

✉ Stay@CarriageVineyards.com 🌐 www.carriagevineyards.com/bbhome.html

The Hidden Hills B&B	155-325 $US BB	Continental breakfast
4490 S El Pomar 93465	4 rooms, 4 pb	Morning coffee, afternoon tea or a
805-239-3115	Visa, MC, Disc	glass of regional wine at sundown
Kris Jardine	C-ltd/S-ltd/P-no/H-ltd	Light refreshments, en suite
		bathrooms, king size beds, superior
		linens, luxurious comfort

A scenic vineyard drive leads you through glorious countryside to the serenity of Hidden Hills Bed & Breakfast. This wine country getaway is nestled amongst rolling hills and majestic oaks.

✉ info@hiddenhillsbb.com 🌐 www.hiddenhillsbb.com

The Santa Rita Inn	125-175 $US BB	Full breakfast
1215 Santa Rita Rd 93465	4 rooms, 4 pb	Fresh baked goodies
805-748-6134 805-434-1634	Visa, MC	Garden, barbecue area, picnic
Charlotte	C-ltd/S-ltd/P-yes/H-yes	area, pool, parlor, cottages include
		kitchenette & complimentary wine

Begin your journey to the Paso Robles Wine Country with a relaxing afternoon on our wrap-around porch. Sip our estate bottled wine. Stroll through our lush vineyards and enjoy the quiet beauty of the Santa Rita hills. ✉ santaritainn@yahoo.com 🌐 santaritainn.com

TIBURON ───────────────────────────

Waters Edge Hotel	169-499 $US BB	Continental breakfast
25 Main St 94920	23 rooms, 23 pb	Complimentary wine & cheese hour,
877-789-5999 415-789-5999	Most CC, *Rated*, •	fresh green apples
Catherine Nelson	C-yes/S-no/P-no/H-yes	Fireplaces, cable TV, VCR, CD
		player, spa robes, A/C, viewing deck,
		complimentary in room WiFi

Located on a historic dock along Tiburon's Main St, Waters Edge brings an added ambience of global sophistication to this unique part of Northern California. 23 guestrooms, including two Grand Suites with views of San Francisco and Angel Island.

✉ watersedgehostl@jdvhospitality.com 🌐 www.marinhotels.com/waters.html

TRINITY CENTER ───────────────────────────

Coffee Creek Guest Ranch	199-259 $US AP	Full breakfast
4940 Coffee Creek Rd 96091	15 rooms, 15 pb	All meals included, banquet services
800-624-4480 530-266-3343	Most CC, *Rated*, •	available
Ruth & Mark Hartman	C-yes/S-ltd/P-no/H-yes	Restaurant, bar, bicycles, Hot tub
	Dutch, German	spa, Heated swimming pool, suites,
	April to Thanksgiivng	fireplaces

Picture-postcard views await you on 127 acres within the Trinity Alps Wilderness of snowcapped mountains and sparkling lakes. Secluded cabins lie along Coffee Creek, meals, romantic weekends, horseback riding, and more! ✉ ccranch@tds.net 🌐 www.websiteq.com/member/coffeecreek/index.a

TWAIN HARTE

McCaffrey House
23251 Hwy 108 95383
888-586-0757 209-586-0757
Michael & Stephanie
McCaffrey

139-169 $US BB
8 rooms, 8 pb
Visa, MC, AmEx
C-yes/S-no/P-yes/H-no

Full breakfast
Complimentary wine & sparkling cider
in the early evening; tea & cookies in
the afternoon
Spa, concierge, business facilities,
black iron fire stoves, individual
thermostats, private patios

Four Diamond AAA/Select Registry B&B — Pure Elegance in a Wilderness Setting. An exquisite experience of comfort blended with fresh adventure, culinary excellence, and personal guest services.
✉ stephanie@mccaffreyhouse.com 🌐 www.mccaffreyhouse.com

UKIAH

Vichy Hot Springs Resort
2605 Vichy Springs Rd 95482
707-462-9515
Gilbert & Marjorie Ashoff

195-390 $US BB
26 rooms, 26 pb
Most CC, Cash, Checks,
Rated, •
C-yes/S-ltd/P-no/H-yes
Spanish

Full buffet breakfast
Warm carbonated Vichy mineral
baths, hot pool, Olympic size pool, hot
stone massage, facials

The best of two worlds-a hot springs resort and country inn. Rates include a full buffet breakfast, use of the naturally carbonated warm mineral baths and hot soaking pool, Olympic size pool in season and 700 private acres for walking and hiking. ✉ vichy@vichysprings.com 🌐 www.vichysprings.com

VENTURA

Bella Maggiore Inn
67 S California St 93001
800-523-8479 805-652-0277
Thomas J. Wood

75-180 $US BB
28 rooms, 28 pb
Most CC, *Rated*, •
S-no/P-no/H-yes

Full breakfast
Appetizers & beverages served
between 5pm–6pm daily
Free parking, TV, Internet, private
baths, some rooms with decks, A/C,
spas, fireplaces

The Bella Maggiore is an intimate Italian-style small hotel in the heart of downtown Ventura. Nona's Courtyard Cafe is on site. Complimentary evening appetizers and beverages and a full breakfast are included. ✉ bminn@pacbell.net

---

Victorian Rose B&B
896 E Main St 93001
Nora & Richard Bogatch

99-169 $US BB
5 rooms, 5 pb
Most CC, Cash
C-ltd/S-no/P-no/H-no

includes hot entree

The Victorian Rose is a one-of-a-kind Victorian Gothic church turned Bed & Breakfast. Appreciate 26-foot high carved beam ceilings graced by an abundance of elaborately-designed stained glass windows. ✉ victrose@pacbell.net 🌐 www.victorianroseventura.com

WEAVERVILLE

Weaverville Hotel
481 Main St 96093
800-750-8853 530-623-2222
Jeanne & Brian Muir

99-260 $US EP
7 rooms, 7 pb
Visa, MC, *Rated*, •
C-ltd/S-no/P-no/H-ltd

Daily $10 Hotel Credits for each room,
good at several nearby restaurants.
Lounge, parlor/library, porch, on-site
gift store, WiFi, use of gym across the
street.

Located in the midst of the Trinity Alps, in the historic downtown district of the old Gold Rush town of Weaverville, California. There is not a single stoplight in the entire county. This is truly God's country!
✉ stay@weavervillehotel.com 🌐 www.weavervillehotel.com

WESTPORT

Howard Creek Ranch
40501 N Hwy 1 95488
707-964-6725
Charles & Sally Grigg

75-198 $US BB
12 rooms, 12 pb
Most CC, *Rated*
C-ltd/S-ltd/P-yes/H-ltd
German, Italian, Dutch,
Spanish

Full Ranch Breakfast
Complimentary coffee, hot cocoa
& tea (garden fresh mint tea),
kitchenettes & barbecues
Piano, hot tubs, sauna, gardens,
library, solarium, swinging bridge,
massage, WiFi, hiking, beach

Historic, rural farmhouse on 60 acres filled with collectibles, antiques & memorabilia. Unique health spa with privacy & dramatic views adjoining a wide beach. Refurbished historic carriage barn from virgin redwood milled by Inn owner. Onsite trails.
✉ howardcreekranch@mcn.org 🌐 www.howardcreekranch.com

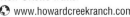

YORKVILLE ───

LindaVista Bed and Breakfast
33430 Hwy 128 95425
707-894-2591
Bob & Linda Klein

165 $US BB
2 rooms, 2 pb
C-yes/S-no/P-no/H-no

Full Breakfast
Pool, courtyard, whirlpool tubs, suites, sitting room

Visit beautiful Yorkville in Mendocino County, only eight miles from Cloverdale. Enjoy intimate lodging in large bedroom suites with queen sized beds, private baths with whirlpool bathtubs and separate showers. All rooms are suites.

✉ reservations@lindavista.com ◑ www.lindavista.com

YOUNTVILLE ───

Bordeaux House
6600 Washington St 94599
800-677-6370 707-944-2855
ext. 19
Jean

115-247 $US BB
8 rooms, 8 pb
Visa, MC
S-no/P-no/H-ltd

Full buffet breakfast
Guests may relax with a late afternoon beverage (or a glass of port, sherry, or brandy).
Contemporary decor & French antiques, gas/wood fireplaces, outdoor whirlpool, patios or decks.

The Bordeaux House, nestled in the midst of lush landscaped grounds, features a formal red brick structure with classic English and French influences. We offer everything you need for a comfortable, well appointed Napa Valley vacation.

✉ bordeauxhouse@gmail.com ◑ www.bordeauxhouse.com

Lavender B&B
2020 Webber Ave 93942
800-522-4140 707-944-1388
Gina Massolo

225-300 $US BB
8 rooms, 8 pb
Most CC, Cash, •
C-yes/S-no/P-no/H-yes
Sign language

Full breakfast
Afternoon wine, tea & hors d' oeuvres, freshly-baked cookies, drinks available throughout the day
Porch, veranda, daily housekeeping, patios, fireplaces

Intimate and luxuriously cozy, Lavender combines the warm colors of Provence with contemporary design elements to create a vibrant setting that blends old and new. A lovely heritage home is the centerpiece of the inn's four buildings.

✉ lavender@foursisters.com ◑ www.lavendernapa.com

Maison Fleurie
6529 Yount St 94599
800-788-0369 707-944-2056
Gina Massolo

130-300 $US BB
13 rooms, 13 pb
Most CC, Cash
C-yes/S-no/P-no/H-yes

Full breakfast
Afternoon wine, tea & hors d' oeuvres, freshly-baked cookies, drinks available throughout the day
Concierge services, daily housekeeping, private patio, fireplace, robes, hot tub, pool

Napa Valley's Maison Fleurie, the "flowering house," is situated on half an acre of beautifully landscaped gardens—welcoming visitors to a Napa Valley inn reminiscent of southern France.

✉ maisonfleurie@foursisters.com ◑ www.maisonfleurienapa.com

YUBA CITY ───

The Harkey House
212 C St 95991
530-674-1942
Bob & Lee Jones

125-225 $US BB
4 rooms, 4 pb
Visa, MC, AmEx,
Rated, •
C-yes/S-ltd/P-yes/H-ltd

Fresh ground coffee, scones, breads
In room coffee & teas, afternoon tea, cookies, hot chocolate
Concierge services, phones, wireless Internet, TV/CD/DVD, pool, spa, library, horse shoes, weddings

An elegant and historic inn with intricacies not to be quickly unraveled. This B&B will charm newcomers with its beauty, while still engrossing those who know it well. Voted 'The Best Inn Yuba-Sutter Area 2009'. Walking distance to restaurants & parks.

✉ lee@harkeyhouse.com ◑ www.harkeyhouse.com

Colorado

AVON

West Beaver Creek Lodge
220 W Beaver Creek
Blvd 81620
888-795-1061 970-949-9073
Theresa & Robert Borg

149-299 $US EP
9 rooms, 9 pb
Most CC, Cash, Checks,
Rated, •
C-yes/S-no/P-no/H-ltd

Catering with prior arrangement
including arrival night dinner,
rehearsal dinner, wedding cakes
Sitting room, Jacuzzis, suites, cable
TV, wireless hi-speed Internet, video
library, pool table

Free Night w/Certificate: Not valid 12/16/11-1/2/12.

If you want to ski in world class Vail and Beaver Creek, and stay in the finest accommodations without paying those high rates, then West Beaver Creek Lodge in the heart of the Vail Valley is for you. Full service wedding ceremony & reception available.

✉ info@wbclodge.com ◔ www.wbclodge.com

BOULDER

Briar Rose B&B
2151 Arapahoe Ave 80302
888-786-8440 303-442-3007
Gary Hardin & Jessika
Kimes

164-204 $US BB
10 rooms, 10 pb
Visa, MC, AmEx, •
C-ltd/S-ltd/P-no/H-no

Full, organic breakfast
Tea & cookies
A/C, fireplaces, high-speed WiFi, guest
computers

Bed and breakfast in the heart of Boulder offers organic breakfast, fine teas and ecologically conscious hospitality.

✉ info@briarrosebb.com ◔ www.briarrosebb.com

BRECKENRIDGE

Abbett Placer Inn
205 S French 80424
888-794-7750 970-453-6489
Emma & Niels Hagen

99-239 $US BB
5 rooms, 5 pb
Visa, MC
C-ltd/S-no/P-no/H-no
German, French

Full breakfast
Afternoon tea including homemade
cakes and a selection of teas
Hot tub, flat screen TVs with DVD, free
WiFi, guest computer, fireplace, deck
with view, kitchenette

Located in the heart of Breckenridge's historic downtown district, we are a fully restored and recently renovated charming Victorian home, listed on the NHRP, offering gourmet breakfasts, modern amenities and all the creature comforts of home.

✉ abbettplacerinn@comcast.net ◔ www.abbettplacer.com

Allaire Timbers Inn
9511 Hwy 9 – S Main
St 80424
800-624-4904 970-453-7530
Sue Carlson & Kendra Hall

145-390 $US BB
10 rooms, 10 pb
Visa, MC, Disc,
Rated, •
C-ltd/S-no/P-no/H-yes

Full breakfast
Snacks, tea & coffee
Great Room with fireplace, outdoor
hot tub, sunroom, free ski area shuttle,
wireless Internet

Looking for an accommodation away from the hustle and bustle? Want to find Breckenridge lodging that is romantic and intimate? You have found the most intimate way to experience Breckenridge at Allaire Timbers Inn, a distinctive B&B experience.

✉ allaire@colorado.net ◔ www.allairetimbers.com

Fireside Inn
114 N French St 80424
970-453-6456
Niki & Andy Harris

88-199 $US BB
9 rooms, 5 pb
Visa, MC
C-yes/S-no/P-no/H-no
German, French

Full breakfast
During Ski Season "tea time" included
Singles, couples and families welcome;
suites, rooms and dorm-style

Conveniently located 2 blocks from Main St in the national historic district in Breckenridge, the Fireside Inn is a 10 minute walk or a free, short ride on the shuttle bus to Breckenridge Ski Area.

 info@firesideinn.com   www.firesideinn.com

CARBONDALE

Van Horn House-Lions Ridge
0318 Lions Ridge Rd 81623
888-453-0395 970-963-3605
Susan & John Laatsch

90-110 $US BB
4 rooms, 3 pb
Visa, MC, AmEx, •
C-ltd/S-no/P-no/H-no

Full breakfast
Special dietary requests & restrictions
honored to the best of our ability
Fluffy comforters, quilts, robes,
spectacular views, hot tub & guest
lounge

Comfort of a home away from home in the heart of the Roaring Fork Valley. Easy access to Aspen, Snowmass, Glenwood Springs, Carbondale, Redstone, the hiking and biking trails, ski slopes, fishing streams and hot springs of the White River National Forest.

✉ jlaatsch@aol.com 🌐 www.vanhornhouse.com

CASCADE

America's Rocky Mountain Lodge & Cabins
4680 Hagerman Ave 80809
888-298-0348 719-684-2521
Brian & Debbie Reynolds

85-225 $US BB
8 rooms, 8 pb
Visa, MC, Disc, *Rated*
C-ltd/S-no/P-no/H-no

Gourmet 3-course breakfast
24-hour coffee, tea, cocoa & cookies
Guest fridge, microwave, outdoor hot
tub, fireplaces, tub for 2, cable TV/
DVD, wireless Internet

Nestled in the mountains at the entrance to Pikes Peak sits America's Rocky Mountain Lodge & Cabins, a rustic, elegant Colorado B&B & two private cabins with hot tubs, fireplaces & 3 course breakfasts. Romance & attractions packages. Family Reunions!

✉ info@rockymountainlodge.com 🌐 www.rockymountainlodge.com

Eastholme in the Rockies
4445 Hagerman Ave 80809
800-672-9901 719-684-9901
Deborah & Ken Rice

95-150 $US BB
8 rooms, 8 pb
Visa, MC, Disc,
Rated, •
C-yes/S-no/P-no/H-ltd

3-Course Gourmet Breakfast
Private Dinners for Two, afternoon
snacks & catering for special events
Library, Jacuzzis, suites & cottages,
cable TV/VHS/DVD, fireplaces

Our Colorado Springs bed and breakfast inn is the perfect Rocky Mountain location for intimate weddings, romantic getaways, family reunions, vacations, and business retreats. Large sunny rooms and private cottages welcome you to Eastholme in the Rockies.

✉ info@eastholme.com 🌐 www.eastholme.com

COLORADO SPRINGS

Black Forest B&B Lodge & Cabins
11170 Black Forest Rd 80908
800-809-9901 719-495-4208
Susan Redden

75-375 $US BB
7 rooms, 7 pb
Most CC, Cash, Checks,
Rated, •
C-yes/S-ltd/P-ltd/H-ltd
Some Spanish

Continental plus breakfast
Snacks, coffees, teas, cocoas
Sitting room, library, weddings,
retreats, fireplace, kitchen, reunions,
retreats

AAA-3 Diamond Lodge Log B&B on 10 acres of fragrant pines overlooking the city lights and Rocky Mountains. Minutes away yet worlds apart from all Pikes Peak area attractions and businesses and colleges.

✉ blackforestbb@msn.com 🌐 www.blackforestbb.com

Holden House 1902 Bed & Breakfast Inn
1102 W Pikes Peak
Ave 80904
888-565-3980 719-471-3980
Sallie & Welling Clark

145-160 $US BB
5 rooms, 5 pb
Most CC, *Rated*, •
S-no/P-no/H-yes

Full gourmet breakfast
Afternoon wine social & appetizers,
freshly ground coffee, tea, bottomless
cookie jar
Living room w/fireplace, verandas,
garden w/gazebo & fountains,
refrigerators, snuggly robes, TV/DVD

Award-Winning Inn voted "Best" for Honeymoon/Anniversary and nearby attractions! Romantic and historic inn w/fireplaces and "tubs-for-two" Gourmet breakfast/afternoon wine social. Leisure/business packages. Central location. AAA Inspected. WiFi/TV's/DVD.

 mail@HoldenHouse.com 🌐 www.HoldenHouse.com

Black Forest B&B Lodge & Cabins, Colorado Springs, CO

COLORADO SPRINGS

Old Town GuestHouse	99-215 $US BB	Full breakfast
115 S 26th St 80904	8 rooms, 8 pb	Afternoon wine, beer & hors
888-375-4210 719-632-9194	Most CC, Cash, *Rated*	d'oeuvres, complimentary soda, water,
Shirley & Don Wick	C-ltd/S-ltd/P-no/H-yes	coffee, tea & hot chocolate
		Elevator, private hot tubs, steam
		showers, WiFi, game room, exercise
		room, conference facility

Experience historic Old Town in urban luxury. Upscale amenities for adult leisure and business guests. Rooms have scenic views, private balconies, hot tubs or steam showers and private baths. Private conference facility with video-conferencing.

✉ Luxury@OldTown-GuestHouse.com 🌐 www.oldtown-guesthouse.com

Our Hearts Inn Old	100-165 $US BB	Continental plus breakfast
Colorado City	5 rooms, 5 pb	Coffee & tea service in each room;
2215 W Colorado Ave 80904	Most CC, Cash, Checks,	biscotti, cookies, waters & sodas
800-533-7095 719-473-8684	*Rated*, •	available
Andy & Pat Fejedelem	C-yes/S-no/P-yes/H-no	Jetted tubs for 2, fireplaces, WiFi,
	May – October, high	Queen, King, twin, full kitchens,
	seas	private balconies, cable TV

Cozy country Victorian B&B in two Colorado Springs' historic districts in the shadow of Pikes Peak Mountain; just 3 miles from Manitou Springs & 1½ hrs from Denver. Cabins, two locations, offering full kitchens, fireplaces, jetted tubs, TVs, A/C & WiFi

✉ hearts@inn-colorado-springs.com 🌐 www.inn-colorado-springs.com

Summit House Inn	95-149 $US BB	Full breakfast
1116 N. Wahsatch	3 rooms, 3 pb	Fresh morning coffee and tea, self-
Avenue 80903	Most CC, Cash, Checks	service snacks and beverages are
866-907-3255 719-635-7942	C-ltd/S-no/P-no/H-no	available throughout your stay
Carol Harper & John Donlin		Hot tube, free WiFi, cable TV, fireplace,
		library, garden. baby grand Petrof
		piano, AC, sitting room

The Summit House Inn welcomes you! This stately 1920 Colonial Revival home is a quiet retreat nestled in the historic North End of downtown Colorado Springs, where you will escape to restful days spent lodging with a view of Pikes Peak.

✉ innkeeper@summithouseinn.com 🌐 www.summithouseinn.com

CORTEZ

Kelly Place Retreat & B&B	95-190 $US BB	Full country breakfast
14663 Road G 81321	11 rooms, 11 pb	Snacks, drinks, fruit, wine & beer
800-745-4885 970-565-3125	Visa, MC, Disc, •	available, lunch/dinner for groups of
Jerene Waite & Marc Yaxley	C-yes/S-ltd/P-no/H-ltd	8+, sack lunches available
		Conference room, lounge, courtyard,
		library, fireplace, hiking trails, wireless
		Internet, sweat room

Comfortable adobe lodge & cabins on an archeological preserve near Mesa Verde National Park; bordering Canyons of Ancients National Monument, SW of Cortez. Ancient Anasazi ruins & kivas on-site. Hiking, biking, horse trips in sculpted red rock canyons.

✉ kelly@kellyplace.com 🌐 www.kellyplace.com

CRESTED BUTTE

Cristiana Guesthaus	85-125 $US BB	Home made continental plus
621 Maroon Ave 81224	21 rooms, 21 pb	Complimentary hot beverages – teas,
800-824-7899 970-349-5326	Most CC, Cash, •	coffee, hot chocolate & cider
Rosemary & Martin Catmur	C-ltd/S-no/P-ltd/H-no	Sitting area with fireplace, outdoor hot tub with views, sauna, WiFi Internet access

Built in the early 1960s, Cristiana owes its heritage to the ski lodges of Europe. A large stone fireplace in the cozy lobby invites guests to sit back, relax, and relive the day's adventures – whether on the slopes or exploring the surrounding mountain

✉ info@cristianaguesthaus.com ❂ www.cristianaguesthaus.com

Nordic Inn	85-150 $US BB	Continental breakfast
14 Treasury Rd 81224	27 rooms, 27 pb	Complimentary tea and coffee served
800-542-7669 970-349-5542	Most CC, Cash	all day.
Allen Cox	C-yes/S-no/P-no/H-yes	Ample free parking, daily housekeeping, ice machine, library, board games, and use of conference room

For your Crested Butte vacation, the Nordic Inn features comfortable accommodations and cabin rentals, with many amenities plus a convenient location in the winter or summer season.

✉ info@nordicinncb.com ❂ www.nordicinncb.com

Purple Mountain B&B and Spa	95-215 $US BB	Full breakfast
714 Gothic Ave 81224	5 rooms, 5 pb	Coffee, juice & teas
877-349-5888 970-349-5888	Visa, MC, •	Hot tub, gardens, patio, spa services
Chris Haver	C-ltd/S-ltd/P-yes/H-no	

Crested Butte's historic Bed and Breakfast. The Purple Mountain B&B and Spa is located in town within walking distance of everything. Once Crested Butte's Mining Office we now have five cozy guestrooms, private bathrooms, and an outdoor hot tub . . .

✉ mail@purplemountainlodge.com ❂ www.purplemountainlodge.com

The Ruby of Crested Butte	149-349 $US BB	Full Gourmet Organic Breakfast
624 Gothic Ave 81224	6 rooms, 6 pb	Fair trade organic coffee & espresso
800-390-1338 970-349-1338	Most CC, Cash, •	drinks, assortment of teas, homemade
Andrea & Chris Greene	C-ltd/S-no/P-ltd/H-no	cookies
		Townie bikes, HD TVs with DVD & digital music, guest robes, iPod dock, free wireless Internet.

Rated #1 Colorado Inn by TripAdvisor.com. Recommended by Sunset and Southern Living magazines! Colorful. Authentic. Connected. Truly Crested Butte! The Ruby – where affordable luxury and environmental responsibility create an exceptional guest experience!

✉ info@therubyofcrestedbutte.com ❂ www.therubyofcrestedbutte.com

CRIPPLE CREEK

Carr Manor	100-400 $US BB	gourmet breakfast
350 E Carr Ave 80813	14 rooms, 14 pb	Suites have cable TV, phone &
719-689-3709	Most CC, Cash, *Rated*	Internet access, small fitness spa, art
Gary & Wini Ledford	S-no/P-no/H-ltd	gallery and gift shop.
	All Year – check winter	

The Carr Manor, a former 1890's school house, is delightfully appointed as a boutique hotel and operated in the home style of a bed & breakfast. The resort offers first-class accommodations, a conference center, ballroom, fitness & massage facilities.

✉ reservations@carrmanor.com ❂ www.carrmanor.com

DENVER

Capitol Hill Mansion	114-219 $US BB	Full breakfast
1207 Pennsylvania St 80203	8 rooms, 8 pb	Complimentary wine, snacks,
800-839-9329 303-839-5221	Most CC, Cash, *Rated*	refrigerator
Carl S. Schmidt II	C-yes/S-no/P-no/H-ltd	Sitting room, hot tub, A/C, cable TV,
		phones, wireless Internet, fireplace,
		heirlooms, original art

Downtown, walk to convention center, museums & restaurants from this nationally listed 1891 ruby sandstone mansion. Features high turrets, balconies and soaring chimneys.
 info@capitolhillmansion.com 🜚 www.capitolhillmansion.com

Castle Marne B&B	115-270 $US BB	Full breakfast
1572 Race St 80206	9 rooms, 9 pb	Special luncheons, teas & dinners
800-92-MARNE 303-331-0621	Most CC, Cash, Checks,	Lending library, gift shop, computer,
The Peiker Family	*Rated*, •	fax, copier, WiFi, free parking, free
	C-ltd/S-no/P-no/H-no	bottled
	Spanish, Hungarian,	
	Karen (Burmese)	

Denver's premier luxury urban inn is just minutes from the convention center, business district, shopping and fine dining. A National Historic landmark, Castle Marne offers nine rooms, three with private balconies and hot tubs for two. Small weddings
 info@castlemarne.com 🜚 www.castlemarne.com

Gregory Inn, LoDo	139-219 $US BB	Full breakfast
2500 Arapahoe St 80205	9 rooms, 9 pb	Parlor, gathering room, veranda, room
800-925-6570 303-295-6570	Visa, MC, Disc	service, big-screen projection TVs,
Stephen Gregory	C-ltd/S-no/P-no/H-yes	WiFi

Superior luxury hotel accommodations in a small, elegant Inn setting. Walking distance to Coors Field, Convention Center, 16th Mall Shopping and LoDo – Denver's Lower downtown entertainment district.   info@gregoryinn.com 🜚 www.gregoryinn.com

Holiday Chalet Victorian	50-145 $US BB	Full breakfast
1820 E Colfax Ave 80218	10 rooms, 10 pb	Full service tea room we also offer
303-437-8245 303-437-8245	Most CC, Cash,	lunch and dinner selections by
Crystal Sharp	*Rated*, •	appointment
	C-yes/S-no/P-yes/H-no	Video Library, baby-sitting, pet
	Russian	friendly including doggie day care,
		beautiful courtyard, WiFi

Nestled in Denver's historic Wyman district, offering warmth and comfort to travelers for over 52 years. Our luxury B&B is ideal for business travelers, vacationers and romantics. Full kitchens in every room. Pet-friendly. High speed Internet.   holidaychalet@aol.com 🜚 www.holidaychalet.net

Queen Anne B&B Inn	115-215 $US BB	Made with local & organic foods
2147 Tremont Pl 80205	14 rooms, 14 pb	Regional wines served in the
800-432-4667 303-296-6666	Most CC, Cash,	afternoon along with appetizers
Milan Doshi	*Rated*, •	Phone, A/C, jet tubs, garden, bicycles,
	C-ltd/S-ltd/P-ltd/H-ltd	wireless Internet, free parking
	Spanish	

Award winning Victorian Inn, on National Register, faces quiet downtown park. Walk to mall, shops, museums, convention center/business district. Airport shuttle vans serve the inn. Selected for some 40 awards of excellence in its 21 years. GREEN HOTEL
 travel@queenannebnb.com 🜚 www.queenannebnb.com

DIVIDE

Stonehaven Inn	125-125 $US BB	Full breakfast
1815 Calcite Dr 80814	4 rooms, 4 pb	Homemade desserts, coffee & tea
719-686-0833	Visa, MC, Disc	Hot tub, WiFi, large porch, beautiful
Janis & Ferrel Minick	C-ltd/S-no/P-no/H-no	private room for meetings or any
		special event

Our unique B&B is built of 300 tons of Colorado river rock, and is situated on the western slope of Pikes Peak. Enjoy spectacular mountain views from our porch and listen to the sound of waterfalls or hike to a beautiful waterfall just minutes away.
 stonehaven.innkeeper@gmail.com 🜚 www.stonehaveninnbnb.com

DURANGO

**Leland House B&B Suites
& Rochester Hotel**
721 E Second Ave 81301
800-664-1920 970-385-1920
Diane Wildfang & Kirk
Komick

129-359 $US BB
25 rooms, 25 pb
Most CC, *Rated*, •
C-yes/S-no/P-ltd/H-yes
French

Full gourmet breakfast
Afternoon tea & homemade cookies
Sitting room, conference space for 75,
catering available, wireless Internet

*Located in the historic district of downtown Durango, CO. Authentically restored late-Victorian, 15
room Rochester Hotel with the charm of the Old West; 10 luxury suites offered in the Leland House.
Beautifully landscaped setting and flower-filled courtyard.*

✉ stay@rochesterhotel.com ◐ www.rochesterhotel.com

Lightner Creek Inn
999 Lightner Creek Rd, CR
207 81301
800-268-9804 970-259-1226
Charlotte & Carlos

100-219 $US BB
9 rooms, 9 pb
Visa, MC, AmEx,
Rated, •
C-yes/S-no/P-yes/H-yes
Some Spanish and
Italian

Full breakfast
Evening wine, beer, snacks
Outdoor hot tub, free WiFi, guest
computer, 120-channel TV + HBO, CD/
radio

*A beautiful turn of the century French style farm house nested in a charming and tranquil Colorado
mountain valley. Minutes away from Durango, Colorado shopping, restaurants, and the famous D&S
Railroad. We provide guests with a relaxing atmosphere!*

✉ innkeeper@lightnercreekinn.com ◐ www.lightnercreekinn.com

EMPIRE

The Peck House
83 Sunny Ave 80438
303-569-9870
Gary & Sally St. Clair

65-135 $US BB
10 rooms, 9 pb
Most CC, •
C-ltd/S-no/P-no/H-ltd
French

Continental breakfast
Restaurant, dinner available, also
Memorial Day thru Labor Day we offer
a Sunday Brunch
Bar service, sitting room, library,
Jacuzzi

Free Night w/Certificate: Valid January-May and October and November

*1862 Victorian Inn furnished in antiques. Near ski areas and historic districts. In Empire, 5 miles from
Georgetown, this historic landmark is known for excellent food and dramatic mountain scenery. Gateway to Rocky Mtn. Natl. Park and Trail Ridge Road.*

✉ thepeckhouse@yahoo.com ◐ www.thepeckhouse.com

ESTES PARK

Black Dog Inn B&B
650 S St Vrain Ave 80517
866-786-0374 970-586-0374
Carlos Albuquerque

170-250 $US BB
6 rooms, 6 pb
Most CC, Cash, Checks
C-ltd/S-ltd/P-ltd/H-no

Full breakfast
Tea, hot chocolate, ice tea, sweets
In-room massage service, weddings &
elopements, retreats, small meetings,
jetted tubs, fireplaces.

*Romantic secluded getaway in the Rocky Mountains. Beautiful rooms with two person Jacuzzi. Rated
as one of the top ten most romantic bed and breakfasts by Forbes Traveler.com 2009*

✉ carlos@blackdoginn.com ◐ www.Blackdoginn.com

**Taharaa Mountain Lodge,
Inc.**
3110 S St Vrain 80517
800-597-0098 970-577-0098
Ken & Diane Harlan

155-345 $US BB
18 rooms, 18 pb
Most CC, Cash,
Rated, •
C-ltd/S-no/P-no/H-yes
Spanish

Full gourmet breakfast
Happy hour with wine, beer & sodas
daily
Great Room, Den, Dining Room,
Meeting Room, Spa with dry sauna,
hot tub & massage room, Great Hall

*Taharaa Mountain Lodge is a luxury B&B-style lodge offering unique accommodations: nine suites
and nine lodge rooms, designed with the total comfort of our guests in mind. A Great Hall with panoramic views is available for weddings up to 200 guests.*

✉ info@taharaa.com ◐ www.taharaa.com

Black Dog Inn B&B, Estes Park, CO

ESTES PARK

Wildwood Inn
2801 Fall River Rd 80517
800-400-7804 970-586-7804
Cindy Younglund-Liddell

58-428 $US EP
33 rooms, 33 pb
Visa, MC, *Rated*
C-yes/P-no/H-yes

Coffee in room
Full service day spa, library, hot tub
room, video/DVD library, in-room WiFi

Large family vacation homes, spacious river- or mountain-side suites, private deck rooms & hot tubs. Our upscale accommodations are surrounded by mountain peaks. Views of the Rocky Mountain National Park. We offer a full service day spa on site.
✉ info@esteswildwoodinn.com 🌐 www.esteswildwoodinn.com

EVERGREEN

Bears Inn
27425 Spruce Ln 80439
800-863-1205 303-670-1205
Vicki Bock

145-220 $US BB
11 rooms, 11 pb
Most CC, Cash, Checks,
Rated, •
C-ltd/S-no/P-ltd/H-no

Full breakfast
Afternoon tea, snacks
Sitting room, wireless Internet, fax, spa

Nestled in the pine trees at 8,000 feet. Great snow-capped mountain views, 11 rooms, private baths, 1 two bedroom cabin, cable TV, outdoor spa and gas campfires.
✉ booknow@bearsinn.com 🌐 www.bearsinn.com

Highland Haven Creekside Inn
4395 Independence
Trail 80439
800-459-2406 303-674-3577
Gail Riley & Tom Statzell

150-575 $US BB
18 rooms, 18 pb
Most CC, Cash, *Rated*
C-yes/S-no/P-ltd/H-no

Full breakfast
Wireless Internet, romance trays,
private hot tubs, Jacuzzi tubs, Steam
Showers, corporate facilities

Award winning mountain hideaway with exquisite views of mountains, streams, towering pines and gardens. Stroll to quaint shops and fine dining on Main Street in Evergreen. Choose between Suites, Cottages or Guest Rooms. Full breakfast included.
✉ info@highlandhaven.com 🌐 www.highlandhaven.com

FORT COLLINS

The Edwards House B&B
402 W Mountain Ave 80521
800-281-9190 970-493-9191
Rachel Rancourt

99-175 $US BB
8 rooms, 8 pb
Most CC, Cash
C-ltd/S-no/P-no/H-no

Full Gourmet Breakfast
Evening refreshments in the parlor
Fireplaces, cable TV, exercise room,
sauna, patio, conference room,
wireless Internet, parking

This gorgeous inn is located one block from Historic Old Town Fort Collins. It is within easy walking & biking distance of many great Fort Collins attractions, including City Park, Historic Old Towns' shopping and restaurant district, & Colorado State.
✉ edshouse@edwardshouse.com 🌐 www.edwardshouse.com

FRASER

High Mountain Lodge
425 County Road 5001 80442
800-319-8006 970-726-5958
Julie & Tom Beckwith

70-199 $US BB
11 rooms, 11 pb
Visa, MC, •
C-yes/S-no/P-ltd/H-ltd
Spanish

Full breakfast
MAP in ski season. Two selections
each morning, coffee, tea, juice. Happy
Hour.
Indoor pool, hot tub, rec room, library

The High Mountain Lodge, a bed and breakfast country inn near Winter Park, Colorado, is casual, comfortable, and welcoming to singles, couples, and families alike. Dogs with well-mannered owners enjoy the friendly atmosphere, too.

✉ innkeeper@highmountainlodge.com 🌐 www.highmountainlodge.com

FRISCO

Frisco Lodge
321 Main St 80443
800-279-6000 970-668-0195
Bruce Knoepfel, Susan
Wentworth

49-169 $US BB
18 rooms, 14 pb
Most CC, Cash, Checks,
Rated, •
C-yes/S-no/P-no/H-no

Full Gourmet Breakfast
Wine & cheese, afternoon snack of
homemade bread & soup in winter
season, cookies & lemonade
Hot tub, Award winning Courtyard
and Gardens, Internet access, WiFi in
rooms, ski/bike room, phones

An historic bed and breakfast lodge built in 1885. A unique inn on Frisco's historic Main Street, featuring 1800s ambience. A distinctive mountain lodge with Victorian flair.

✉ info@friscolodge.com 🌐 www.friscolodge.com

GEORGETOWN

**Silver Queen Bed and
Breakfast**
314 Argentine Street 80444
877-569-3511 303-569-3511
Joyce Jamele

145-199 $US BB
3 rooms, 3 pb
Visa, MC, Disc
C-ltd/S-no/P-no/H-no

Full breakfast
Welcome glass of wine, afternoon
snacks, coffee and tea.
Parlor, Library, TV Room (HDTV),
Gardens, High Speed Wireless
Internet.

This elegant 1892 Second Empire Victorian, located in the heart of Georgetown's historic district, has been restored and extensively updated to provide comforts and amenities for the most discerning guests.

✉ silverqueenbnb@mac.com 🌐 www.silverqueenbandb.com

GOLDEN

The Dove Inn B&B
711 14th St 80401
303-278-2209
Annette & Bill Lyttle

90-140 $US BB
8 rooms, 8 pb
Most CC, Cash, *Rated*
C-ltd/S-no/P-no/H-no

Full breakfast
Coffee makers with coffee & tea
provided in rooms, complimentary
bottled water in rooms
Free wireless Internet access, A/C,
cable TV, DVD, clock radios, patio,
porch

Built in 1868, the inn is nestled in the West Denver foothills. Walking distance to activities and shops in downtown Golden. Denver attractions and Rocky Mountains nearby. Full cooked breakfast. Private baths in all rooms. Whirlpool tubs & fireplaces.

✉ stay@doveinn.com 🌐 www.doveinn.com

HESPERUS

Blue Lake Ranch
16000 Hwy 140 81326
888-258-3525 970-385-4537
Shirley & David Alford

135-375 $US BB
16 rooms, 16 pb
Most CC, Cash, Checks,
Rated, •
C-yes/S-no/P-no/H-yes
German, Spanish,
Nepali, Arabic

Regional gourmet breakfast
Coffee & tea facilities, refrigerators,
microwaves
Suites and Casitas feature Jacuzzi tubs,
fireplaces, private patios and more,
WiFi, movie library

Southwest Colorado's award winning country inn, just minutes from Durango, Colorado and Mesa Verde National Park. Recently featured in Travel and Leisure's "30 Great Inns."

✉ bluelake@frontier.net 🌐 www.bluelakeranch.com

MANCOS

Ruby Rose Ranch	165-300 $US BB	Full breakfast
37951 Hwy 184 81328	9 rooms, 6 pb	Coffee & tea all day, baked goods in
970-533-9083	Most CC, Cash	the afternoon
Sandy Rosen & Jim Maxwell	C-ltd/S-no/P-ltd	Hot tub, horseshoe pit, bbq, outdoor
		fireplace, WiFi, DVDs, massage, small
		weddings, events

The Ruby Rose Ranch is a B&B mountain lodge retreat located between Mesa Verde National Park and the La Plata Mountains of Durango, Colorado, with easy access to all of the wonders and activities that this amazing 4 Corners area has to offer.

✉ Sandy@RubyRoseRanch.com   🌐 www.rubyroseranch.com

MANITOU SPRINGS

Blue Skies Inn	125-240 $US BB	Full breakfast as room service
402 Manitou Ave 80829	10 rooms, 10 pb	Chocolate-dipped strawberries, snack
800-398-7949 719-685-3899	Visa, MC, Disc,	baskets, or an entire garden wedding
Sally & Mike	*Rated*, •	with a scrumptious cake
	C-yes/S-no/P-no/H-yes	Sitting rooms, private suites,
		fireplaces, cable TV/DVD, WiFi,
		Jacuzzi, A/C, hot tub under the stars

Artist painted B & B by streamside in Victorian Colorado town with Manitou mineral springs. Lush gardens, hot tub gazebo, and rushing waterfall in the Secret Garden. Pikes Peak wedding package in romantic setting; pastor, cake, bouquet & photos included.

✉ fun@blueskiesinn.com   🌐 www.blueskiesinn.com

Onaledge B&B	115-235 $US BB	Full breakfast
336 El Paso Blvd 80829	6 rooms, 6 pb	Complimentary afternoon wine, tea &
888-685-4515 719-685-4515	Visa, MC, *Rated*, •	coffee, two 4-star restaurants within
Brett Maddox	C-yes/S-no/P-no/H-no	walking distance
		WiFi, fireplace, Jetted tub, WiFi,
		outdoor spa, gardens, beautiful views,
		mountains nearby, romance

This historic Arts & Crafts Bed and Breakfast offers lodging with the warmth and charm that Manitou Springs has become known for in Colorado. A luxurious Rocky Mountain retreat, ideal for a romantic weekend getaway or extended vacation.

✉ info@redcrags.com   🌐 www.onaledge.net

Red Crags Bed & Breakfast Inn	100-235 $US BB	Full breakfast
	8 rooms, 8 pb	Afternoon coffee, tea, wine, dessert
302 El Paso Blvd 80829	Visa, MC, Disc,	King beds, fireplaces, down
800-721-2248 719-685-4515	*Rated*, •	comforters, robes, hot tub, cable TV,
Brett R. Maddox	C-ltd/S-no/P-no/H-no	wireless Internet, sitting room

Historic 1880 Victorian mansion romantic hideaway. Lose yourself "Somewhere in Time." Antiques throughout, large common rooms, herb & flower gardens. King beds, private baths, fireplaces. A favorite of Teddy Roosevelt. AAA 3 Diamond, Mobil 3 Star.

✉ info@redcrags.com   🌐 www.redcrags.com

Rockledge Country Inn	160-325 $US BB	Full breakfast
328 El Paso Blvd 80829	7 rooms, 7 pb	Afternoon coffee, tea and wine service
888-685-4515 719-685-4515	Visa, MC, Disc,	with snacks, wine & cheese on
Brett Maddox	*Rated*, •	weekends, romantic dinner
	C-ltd/S-no/P-no/H-ltd	Whirlpools, fireplaces, robes, luxury
		linens, bicycles, concierge services

Rockledge Country Inn, a Manitou Springs Bed & Breakfast, provides a private and peaceful destination for the discriminating traveler, minutes from downtown Colorado Springs, Colorado College, U.S. Air Force Academy, and the Olympic Training Center.

✉ info@redcrags.com   🌐 www.rockledgeinn.com

MANITOU SPRINGS

Two Sisters Inn
Ten Otoe Pl 80829
719-685-9684
Sharon Smith & Wendy
Goldstein

79-188 $US BB
5 rooms, 4 pb
Visa, MC, Disc,
Rated, •
C-ltd/S-no/P-no/H-no

Full 3-course gourmet breakfast
Manitou sparkling lemonade,
homemade treats (i.e. cookies
& brownies with a kick), unique
breakfasts
Itinerary planning, hiking/biking maps,
friendly hospitality, dinner/theater/
attractions reservation

Frommer's 2010 Choice for "Best Bed and Breakfast in Colorado." B&B & cozy cottage welcoming guests since 1990. Caring, fun owners prepare award-winning creative & beautifully presented gourmet breakfasts with "Best Muffin in CO,"

✉ info@twosisinn.com   ◐ www.twosisinn.com

OURAY

China Clipper Inn
525 2nd St 81427
800-315-0565 970-325-0565
Hans & Ingrid Vander Ploeg

90-230 $US BB
13 rooms, 13 pb
Most CC, Cash,
Rated, •
S-no/P-no/H-ltd
Dutch, German and
French

Delicious full breakfast
Some rooms have in-room coffee
Sitting room, library, hot tub, phones
& data ports, free wireless Internet,
TV, A/C, hairdryer

Elegant, luxurious, romantic, comfortable inn centrally located in Ouray, "Switzerland of America" in the San Juan Mountains. In-room tubs for two, fireplaces and garden hot tub. Pampering and utter relaxation guaranteed.

✉ vander.ploeg@hotmail.com   ◐ www.chinaclipperinn.com

**Wiesbaden Hot Springs
Spa & Lodgings**
625 5th St 81427
888-846-5191 970-325-4347
Linda Wright-Minter

132-349 $US EP
21 rooms, 21 pb
Most CC
C-ltd/S-no/P-no/H-ltd

Complimentary coffee & tea
Hot springs Vaporcave, outdoor pool,
private outdoor spa, massage & spa
treatments

A small, intimate natural hot springs spa and lodge known for its peaceful atmosphere, casual elegance and European flair. Located in a small mountain town; surrounded by the San Juan Mountains.

✉ wiesbadenouray@msn.com   ◐ www.wiesbadenhotsprings.com

PAGOSA SPRINGS

Be Our Guest
19 Swiss Village Dr 81147
970-264-6814
Tom & Pam Schoemig

89-124 $US BB
5 rooms, 3 pb
•
C-yes/S-ltd/P-yes/H-no

Deliciously prepared
Other meals provided with prior
arrangements
Large, comfortable common areas,
sunroom dining, deck

Come to the mountains and "Be Our Guest" at this ongoing labor of love. With Tom and Pam's care and attention, this great B&B/Guesthouse has accommodated travelers and vacationers for nearly 16 years. Choose the room that suits you and let us do the rest!

✉ beourguest@skywerx.com   ◐ www.beourguest-bnb.com

**Elkwood Manor Luxury
Bed & Breakfast**
85 Easy St 81147
970-264-9166
Darlene & Daniel Gonzales

145-169 $US BB
4 rooms, 4 pb
Most CC, Cash, Checks,
Rated
C-ltd/S-no/P-no/H-ltd

Formal 3-Course Breakfast
Comp Wine & Appetizers daily.
Romantic Dinners available. Box
lunches/picnic baskets also available.
Candlelight Dinners, Movie Library,
Massages, (Full SPA Serv Coming
Soon),Wireless Internet, Jacuzzi

Free Night w/Certificate: Anytime. Room Upgrade.

Simple Elegance with a Country Feel Captures the character of Elkwood Manor. Luxury Suites with sitting rooms, fireplaces, private patios/decks & panoramic views. Comp Wine. Jacuzzi/Sauna on site. Free Wireless Internet; Anniv, B-day Honeymoon/Wedding Pk

✉ gonzada03@yahoo.com   ◐ www.elkwoodmanor.com

Bross Hotel, Paonia, CO

PAONIA

A Simpler Time Bed and Breakfast	95-135 $US BB	Full breakfast
228 Onarga Ave. 81428	2 rooms, 2 pb	If you have special dietary needs
970-527-49999	C-ltd/S-no/P-no/H-no	please let us know
Scott & Sharon Morley		

A beautifully restored Victorian-era home providing quality lodging year round in the heart of Paonia. We serve a full breakfast featuring fresh locally grown fruits and vegetables. Weather permitting, you will be able to enjoy it in our walled gardens.

 cohair@tds.net 🌐 www.simplertimebnb.com

Bross Hotel	125-135 $US BB	Full breakfast
312 Onarga Ave 81428	10 rooms, 10 pb	Snacks, lunch & dinner for groups
970-527-6776	Visa, MC, *Rated*, •	when prearranged.
Linda Lentz	C-ltd/S-no/P-no/H-no	Sitting room, library, cable TV, Wireless Internet, meeting room, hot tub.

Free Night w/Certificate: Anytime.

The Bross Hotel is a restored 1906 hotel furnished with period antiques. It provides easy access to Colorado's finest outdoor adventuring as well as cultural events and activities.

 brosshotel@paonia.com 🌐 www.paonia-inn.com

PINE

Lower Lake Ranch	135-185 $US BB	Full breakfast
11883 S Elk Creek Rd 80470	5 rooms, 5 pb	Cool drinks in summer & hot tea &
303-838-6622	Visa, MC	coffee in winter, afternoon snacks
The Dunwody Family	C-yes/S-ltd/P-no/H-ltd	Group Gatherings, Weddings, Fly Fishing, Winter Ice Skating, or bring your horse to ride trails

Free Night w/Certificate: Anytime

Historic, Lower Lake Ranch began as a Guest Ranch in the late 1880s. Upon arrival, guests are warmly greeted and made to feel right at home. The same beauty and hospitality of years past is preserved for visitors today. Just 30 minutes SW of Denver.

information@lowerlakeranch.com 🌐 www.lowerlakeranch.com

SALIDA ──────────────────────────────────

Mountain Goat Lodge	85-158 $US BB	Full breakfast
9582 Hwy 285 81201	6 rooms, 6 pb	Afternoon refreshments and snacks,
877-495-4628 719-539-7173	Most CC, Cash, Checks,	24 hr avail. of coffee, teas, cocoas.
Gina & D'Arcy Marcell	*Rated*, •	Pet-Friendly, Great Room w/2 story
	C-yes/S-ltd/P-yes/H-yes	fireplace, Kitchen, hot tub, Decks,
	Spanish	balconies, 19 acres, WiFi

Free Night w/Certificate: Not Valid: June 15-19, Weekends June-Aug, or Dec 26-31. Room Upgrade.

Experience our cozy cabin lodge and meet the mountain goats! Each room has WiFi, Flat screen TV, HBO, Showtime, DVD, private bath, log beds, Mountain Views, Balconies. Hearty country breakfast served from 8:00–9:00am. Afternoon refreshments. Espresso.

info@mountaingoatlodge.com www.mountaingoatlodge.com

The Thomas House	85-159 $US BB	Full breakfast
307 E 1st St 81201	6 rooms, 6 pb	Snacks, kitchenette stocked with soda,
888-228-1410 719-539-7104	Most CC, *Rated*, •	coffee, tea & pretzel jar
Tammy & Steve Office	C-yes/S-no/P-no/H-ltd	Sitting room, library, Jacuzzis, suites,
		cable TV, kitchenettes

1880's railroad boarding-house decorated with family heirlooms, antiques & collectibles. Located in Salida's Historic Downtown.

office@thomashouse.com www.thomashouse.com

Tudor Rose B&B and	81-200 $US BB	Full gourmet breakfast
Chalets	11 rooms, 11 pb	Afternoon refreshments, cookies and
6720 County Rd 104 81201	Most CC, Cash, Checks,	snacks
800-379-0889 719-539-2002	*Rated*, •	Horse lodging, sitting room, library,
Jon & Terre' Terrell	C-ltd/S-no/P-ltd/H-yes	expansive deck, hot tubs, suites, free
		long distance, WiFi

Quiet privacy on a secluded 37 acre mountain paradise. Surrounded by striking mountain views but only 1½ miles to historic downtown Salida. ¾ mile hiking trail, lots of trees and wildlife. 6 room B&B as well as 5 Chalets that sleep up to 6 ea

info@thetudorrose.com www.thetudorrose.com

SOUTH FORK ──────────────────────────────

Arbor House Inn	130-165 $US BB	Full breakfast
31358 W US Hwy 160 81154	5 rooms, 5 pb	Snacks, soft drinks, coffee & tea,
888-830-4642 719-873-5012	Visa, MC, AmEx,	complimentary chocolates
Keith & Laurie Bratton	*Rated*	Hot tub, riverside deck, sitting room,
	C-ltd/S-ltd/P-no/H-ltd	fridge, satellite TV, VCR/DVD, WiFi, fire
		pit, fishing

Relax by the river in rustic mountain elegance. Five themed guestrooms. River, cliff, mountain and meadow views. Outdoor hot tub, private baths, honeymoon suite with in-room whirlpool tub and fireplace.

info@arborhouseinnco.com www.arborhouseinnco.com

STEAMBOAT SPRINGS ──────────────────────

The Alpine Rose B&B Inn	110-155 $US BB	Full breakfast
724 Grand St 80477	5 rooms, 4 pb	Snacks
888-879-1528 970-879-1528	Visa, MC, AmEx	Sitting room, library, Jacuzzi, fireplace,
Merry Jo Riley	C-ltd/S-no/P-no/H-no	cable TV, WiFi, accommodates
		business travelers

Located in historic "Olde Town" Steamboat Springs, Colorado, the Alpine Rose offers the hospitality of a family Bed and Breakfast and all the comforts and conveniences that make for a special and unique mountain vacation.

 bnb@alpinerosesteamboat.com  www.alpinerosesteamboat.com

Tudor Rose B&B and Chalets, Salida, CO

TRINIDAD

Tarabino Inn
310 E 2nd St 81082
866-846-8808 719-846-2115
Teresa Vila & Kevin Crosby

76-116 $US BB
4 rooms, 2 pb
Most CC
C-ltd/S-no/P-no/H-no
Spanish

Full breakfast
Tea, chocolates & cookies
Cotton robes & slippers, library, TV,
VCR, telephone, fine art gallery

Tarabino Inn Bed and Breakfast is one of the finest examples of the Historic Inns found in the Rocky Mountain region of Colorado. Visit Trinidad, Colorado and stay at Tarabino Inn B&B.

✉ host@tarabinoinn.com 🌐 www.tarabinoinn.com

WOODLAND PARK

Pikes Peak Paradise
236 Pinecrest Rd 80863
800-728-8282 719-687-6656
Ron & Michael

150-240 $US BB
5 rooms, 5 pb
Most CC, Cash,
Checks, •
C-yes/S-no/P-ltd/H-ltd

Full breakfast
Picnic lunches available, soft drinks,
dessert, complimentary beer & wine
Fresh flowers, beautiful views, hot
tubs & whirlpool tubs

Relaxation was never better than at Pikes Peak Paradise! There is a spectacular view of Pikes Peak, and the surrounding wildlife and birds. Fresh flowers. A breakfast buffet offered with a smile. Fireplaces and in-room hot tubs!

✉ info@pikespeakparadise.com 🌐 www.pikespeakparadise.com

Connecticut

BOZRAH

Bozrah House B&B
347 Salem Tpke Rt 82 06334
888-488-7073 860-823-1551
Ed Hadley

88-150 $US BB
3 rooms, 3 pb
Most CC, Cash
C-ltd/S-ltd/P-no/H-no

Full breakfast
Complimentary wine, tea & coffee
Sitting room, bicycles, cable TV,
accommodations for business
travelers, Internet access

Bozrah House B&B has three private accommodations. Each has a private bath and is distinctly furnished with treasures such as a pristine cherry sleigh bed. Enjoy a full candlelight breakfast.

✉ bozrahouse@aol.com 🌐 www.bozrahouse.com

Fitch Claremont Vineyard B&B
83 Fitchville Rd 06334
877-889-0266 860-889-0260
Nora & Warren Strong

149-179 $US BB
4 rooms, 4 pb
Visa, MC, *Rated*, •
C-ltd/S-no/P-no/H-no

Referred to as "the best breakfast"
A complimentary wine from our
vineyard
Fireplace, library, dining room, &
outdoor patio

A four room, 3 diamond Inn on the Old Fitch Farm Vineyard in Southeast Connecticut. Minutes away from Foxwood & Mohegan Sun Casinos and a short ride from Mystic coast and country, Mysticmore and all New England activities.

✉ innkeeper@fitchclaremonthouse.com 🌐 www.fitchclaremonthouse.com

BRISTOL

Chimney Crest Manor B&B
5 Founders Dr 06010
860-582-4219
Dan & Cynthia Cimadamore

135-195 $US BB
5 rooms, 5 pb
Visa, MC, AmEx,
Rated, •
C-ltd/S-no/P-no/H-no
Feb 12 thru December
23

Full breakfast
Tea & cookies in Sun room.
Suites with fireplace, kitchen or
thermospa, feather beds, down
comforters, private spa on premises.

Tudor mansion with an unusual castle like atmosphere. Located 100 miles from New York and Boston. In the historic Federal Hill District. Chimney Crest Manor, built in 1930 is listed on the National Historic Register. In house spa.

✉ Innkeeper@ChimneyCrestManor.com 🌐 www.chimneycrest.com

DEEP RIVER

Riverwind Inn
209 Main St 06417
860-526-2014
Elaine & Leo Klevens

128-240 $US BB
8 rooms, 8 pb
Most CC, *Rated*
C-ltd/S-no/P-no/H-no

Full breakfast
Complimentary sherry, snacks,
beverages
4 common rooms, 3 with fireplaces,
one is a 12 foot stone cooking
fireplace, WiFi

Immaculate rooms with period country antiques & reproductions. Candlelit country breakfast by the fireplace begins the day; communal or private seating. Numerous common areas to relax by the fire or enjoy a book. Wireless Internet.

✉ innkeeper@riverwindinn.com 🌐 www.riverwindinn.com

EAST HADDAM

Bishopsgate Inn
7 Norwich Rd 06423
860-873-1677
The Kagel Family

145-220 $US BB
6 rooms, 6 pb
Visa, MC, Disc, *Rated*
C-ltd/S-no/P-ltd/H-no

Full breakfast
Dinner available
Sitting room, library, fireplaces, suite
with sauna

Bishopsgate Inn is a Colonial house circa 1818, furnished with period antiques, and each floor of the Inn has a sitting area where guests often relax with a good book. Gracious hospitality and well appointed accommodations in a secluded setting.

✉ ctkagel@Bishopsgate.com 🌐 www.bishopsgate.com

GLASTONBURY

Butternut Farm	99-125 $US BB	Full breakfast
1654 Main St 06033	4 rooms, 4 pb	Complimentary wine, chocolates
860-633-7197	*Rated*	Private entrances, living room, TV/
Don Reid	C-yes/S-no/P-no/H-no	VCR, secluded patio, full kitchen,
		fireplaces, wireless Internet

Welcome to Butternut Farm Bed and Breakfast in beautiful Glastonbury, CT! This 18th-century jewel is furnished with period antiques. Attractive grounds with herb gardens and ancient trees, dairy goats and prize chickens. 10 minutes from Hartford.

 www.butternutfarmbandb.com

The Connecticut River	185-250 $US BB	Full breakfast
Valley Inn	5 rooms, 5 pb	A variety of beverages & snacks or
2195 Main St 06033	Visa, MC, AmEx	mini servings of hot or cold foods
860-633-7374	C-ltd/S-no/P-ltd/H-no	Fireplaces in every room, gathering
Wayne & Patricia Brubaker		room, 4 season south facing porch,
		beautiful grounds

Located in the geographic center of Connecticut and on the shores of the Connecticut River, this recently restored and updated historic property built in 1740 combines a historic past with the modern style & conveniences of the 21st century.

 frontdesk@ctrivervalleyinn.com   www.ctrivervalleyinn.com

GREENWICH

Homestead Inn-Thomas	350-495 $US EP	Thomas Henkelmann restaurant
Henkelmann	18 rooms, 18 pb	on site, award winning exceptional,
420 Field Point Rd 06830	Most CC, *Rated*, •	contemporary French cuisine
203-869-7500	C-ltd/S-ltd/P-no/H-yes	A/C, modem & wireless Internet, cable
Theresa & Thomas	French, German,	TV , MP3 Player, 24-hr concierge,
Henkelmann	Portuguese, Spanish,	newspapers, meeting room
	Italian	

Homestead Inn-Thomas Henkelmann is a four star luxury hotel and restaurant located in Greenwich, CT. A member of Relais and Chateaux, Grand Chef, Tradition et Qualite (Les Grandes Tables du Monde) and recipient of 4 stars from the New York Times.

 events@homesteadinn.com   www.homesteadinn.com

Stanton House Inn	149-239 $US BB	Continental plus breakfast
76 Maple Ave 06830	21 rooms, 21 pb	Common room, dining room, patio,
203-869-2110	Most CC, *Rated*	pool, garden, fireplace, balcony,
Tog & Doreen Pearson	C-ltd/S-no/P-ltd/H-ltd	whirlpool tub, A/C, hair dryers
	Spring/Summer/Fall	

In this setting of cozy old world charm, The Stanton House Inn's twenty-one individually decorated bedrooms and suites offer modern comforts and amenities presented in an unpretentious and relaxed atmosphere. We offer a home away from home environment.

 shiinn@aol.com   www.shinngreenwich.com

LAKEVILLE

Wake Robin Inn	149-329 $US BB	Continental breakfast
104-106 Rt 41 Sharon	38 rooms, 38 pb	Private pub available for private
Rd 06039	Most CC	parties & lodging guests
860-435-2000	C-yes/S-no/P-no/H-no	Multiple parlors, decks, front porches,
Michael Bryan Loftus		A/C, 24-hr guest-use PC, wireless
		Internet in main Inn

Hilltop Georgian-Colonial Inn on 11 acres. 38 rooms with private baths, A/C, TV, multiple parlors, porches, decks. Michael Bryan's on-premises is a non-public Pub available for group booking for weddings, retreats and parties.

 info@wakerobininn.com   www.wakerobininn.com

LEDYARD

Stonecroft Country Inn
515 Pumpkin Hill Rd. 06339
800-772-0774 860-572-0771
Jason Crandall

99-285 $US BB
10 rooms, 10 pb
Visa, MC, Disc, *Rated*
C-ltd/S-no/P-no/H-yes

Full Country Breakfast
We invite you to relax and experience
fine dining and creative regional
cuisine.
Fireplaces, whirlpool tubs, gardens &
pond, HDTV with DVD library. History
& Luxury.

Stonecroft Country Inn, a Mystic, Connecticut bed and breakfast, offers luxury lodging and fine dining in an atmosphere of relaxation and romance. It is our goal to make your stay here as special as possible. We look forward to meeting you at Stonecroft!

✉ stonecroftinn@comcast.net 🌐 www.stonecroft.com

LISBON

Branch Place B&B
34 Newent Rd 06351
860-376-5885
Ethel & Thomas Bosse

100-145 $US BB
2 rooms, 2 pb
Visa, MC
S-no/P-no/H-no

Full breakfast
Afternoon tea, snacks, continental
breakfast available for early risers
Sitting room, library, fireplaces,
reading room, patio

Our B&B is a beautiful historic home built by Revolutionary War Veteran, Stephen Branch around 1790. Featured on "Every Town Has a Story" on WFSB, the house has been beautifully restored to its original charm and is completely livable in the 21st century.

✉ branchplace@comcast.net 🌐 www.thebranchplace.com

MADISON

Tidewater Inn
949 Boston Post Rd 06443
800-834-8608 203-245-8457

115-245 $US BB
9 rooms, 9 pb
Most CC, Cash, *Rated*
C-ltd/S-no/P-no/H-ltd
Greek

Full breakfast
Cold drinks, snacks, hot tea & cocoa,
coffee; late afternoon wine & cheese
reception
High speed Internet, beach passes,
maps, brochures, hair dryers, irons,
ironing boards, fax, copying

Enjoy elegant, romantic, luxury accommodations in beautiful Madison, CT. Close to beaches, Yale, Chamard Vineyard, Goodspeed Opera House, Essex & Chester villages – a wonderful alternative to a hotel or motel! Rooms with canopy bed, fireplace or Jacuzzi.

✉ escape@thetidewater.com 🌐 www.TheTidewater.com

MANCHESTER

The Mansion Inn B&B
139 Hartford Rd 06040
860-646-0453
Bruce Hamstra

95-145 $US BB
5 rooms, 5 pb
Most CC, *Rated*
C-ltd/S-no/P-no/H-no

Full breakfast
Homebaked goods
Library, guest refrigerator stocked with
sodas & bottled spring water

Read in bed by the fireside, on pillows slipped in hand embroidered linens; the library's books are all yours in a silk baron's mansion home. Historic District Award. Easy Interstate highway access.

✉ mansioninnkeeper@cox.net 🌐 www.themansioninnct.com

MYSTIC

Harbour Inne & Cottage
15 Edgemont St 06355
860-572-9253
Claude Falardeau

55-300 $US BB
7 rooms, 7 pb
Rated, •
C-yes/S-ltd/P-yes/H-no
French

Continental breakfast
Kitchen privileges
Sitting room, A/C, canoe & boats,
cable TV, fireplaces, hot tub,
barbecues, picnic tables, kayak launch

Six room inn and three room cottage on Mystic River. Pets welcome. Long waterfront trails to walk your pets nearby. Bring your camera and binoculars to see wildlife. Tour the Mystic River on a coal fired steamer or classic power launch.

 harbourinne@earthlink.net 🌐 www.harbourinne-cottage.com

MYSTIC

House of 1833 B&B 72 N Stonington Rd 06355 800-FOR-1833 860-536-6325 Evan Nickles & Robert Bankel	129-295 $US BB 5 rooms, 5 pb Most CC, Cash, • C-yes/S-no/P-ltd/H-no Greek, French	5 course full gourmet breakfast Fresh baked cookies & hospitality in the parlor afternoons, sherry or sparkling cider en-suite Full size pool, clay tennis court, en- suite massage or spa services nearby, Jacuzzi tubs, HDTV

Welcome to Mystic's celebrated Greek Revival Mansion and National Landmark, House of 1833. Featuring 5 luxurious suites, 19th century furnishings, working wood-burning fireplaces, hot tubs & gourmet candlelight breakfasts. Comfort, romance & convenience.

✉ innkeeper@houseof1833.com 🌐 www.houseof1833.com

Pequot Hotel B&B 711 Cow Hill Rd 06355 860-572-0390 Nancy Mitchell	95-175 $US BB 3 rooms, 3 pb Visa, MC, *Rated*, • C-ltd/S-no/P-no/H-no	Full country breakfast Complimentary non-alcoholic beverages screened porch, 2 sitting rooms, library, A/C, whirlpool tub, fireplaces, wireless Internet access

Authentically restored 1840s stagecoach stop. Friendly, casual elegance among period antiques. Relaxing parlors and romantic fireplaces. ✉ pequothtl@aol.com 🌐 www.pequothotelbandb.com

Steamboat Inn 73 Steamboat Wharf 06355 860-536-8300 Kate Abel	135-300 $US BB 11 rooms, 11 pb Most CC, Cash, *Rated*, • C-ltd/S-no/P-no/H-ltd	Full breakfast Complimentary beverages, sherry & cookies Common Room, A/C, whirlpool tubs, fireplaces, water views

Steamboat Inn is the perfect escape for romantics. Our individually decorated and spacious guestrooms offer charming sitting areas, fireplaces, whirlpool tubs, and spectacular river views.

✉ kate@steamboatinnmystic.com 🌐 www.steamboatinnmystic.com

The Whaler's Inn 20 E Main St 06355 800-243-2588 860-536-1506 Richard Przybysz	109-259 $US BB 48 rooms, 48 pb Most CC, Cash, *Rated*, • C-yes/S-no/P-no/H-ltd	Continental plus breakfast 4 Star in-house Restaurant Bravo Bravo & Lounge Fitness Center, Bicycles, Free Parking, Sitting room

Enjoy all the charm and nearby attractions Mystic, CT offers as a guest at the Whaler's Inn. A phenomenal location, traditional architecture and decor with all the modern amenities a guest might desire.

✉ sales@whalersinnmystic.com 🌐 www.whalersinnmystic.com

NEW MILFORD

The Homestead Inn 5 Elm St 06776 860-354-4080 Bill Greenman	85-200 $US BB 15 rooms, 15 pb Most CC, Cash, *Rated*, • C-yes/S-no/P-ltd/H-ltd Tagalog	Full breakfast Sitting room, front porch, gardens, in village center, wireless Internet access

A small 150 year old country inn, The Homestead Inn is located in a picturesque New England town, next to village green, near shops, churches, restaurants, antiques, galleries, hiking and crafts.

✉ reservations@homesteadct.com 🌐 www.homesteadct.com

NIANTIC

Inn at Harbor Hill Marina 60 Grand St 06357 860-739-0331 Dave & Sue Labrie	135-265 $US BB 9 rooms, 9 pb Visa, MC, AmEx, *Rated* C-ltd/S-no/P-no/H-no	Classic Breakfast Buffet Complimentary beverages & snacks Fireplaces, water views, balconies, TVs, A/C, WiFi Internet, kayaks, beach, gardens, boat rides

Free Night w/Certificate: Nov 1-April 30; Sun-Thurs; holidays excluded.

Selected 2009–2010 "Best in New England." In Marina District, with panoramic views of the harbor, our nine room, award-winning Inn features private baths, A/C, fireplaces, WiFi, balconies and breakfast. Near Mystic, Mohegan Sun & Foxwoods.

✉ info@innharborhill.com 🌐 www.innharborhill.com

NORFOLK

Manor House
69 Maple Ave 06058
866-542-5690 860-542-5690
Michael Dinsmore & L. Keith
Mullins

130-255 $US BB
9 rooms, 9 pb
Visa, MC, •
C-ltd/S-ltd/P-no/H-no

Full breakfast
Complimentary tea, coffee, cocoa &
cookies
Whirlpools, wood & gas fireplaces,
private balconies, piano, gazebo,
gardens, luxurious spa services

Historic Victorian mansion furnished with genuine antiques, on 5 acres. Offering guests romantic and elegant rooms. Deluxe room with gas fireplace and a 2 person Jacuzzi.

✉ innkeeper@manorhouse-norfolk.com 🌐 www.manorhouse-norfolk.com

NORTH STONINGTON

Inn at Lower Farm
119 Mystic Rd 06359
866-535-9075 860-535-9075
Mary & Jon Wilska

100-175 $US BB
4 rooms, 4 pb
Visa, MC, AmEx,
Rated
C-yes/S-no/P-ltd/H-no

Full breakfast
Afternoon tea with homemade cookies
& stocked guest refrigerator
WiFi, fireplaces, porch with a swing
& rocking chair, library-sitting room,
hammock, recliner

Named a 2008 Editors' choice inn by "Yankee Magazine" and near Mystic, CT. AAA 3 diamond rated B&B near Stonington, New London, Westerly, RI, Foxwoods, and Mohegan Sun Casinos. A perfect respite in the heart of "Mystic Country". ✉ info@lowerfarm.com 🌐 www.lowerfarm.com

NORWALK

The Silvermine Tavern
194 Perry Ave 06850
203-847-4558
Frank & Marsha Whitman

125-150 $US BB
10 rooms, 10 pb
Visa, MC, AmEx, •
C-yes/S-no/P-ltd/H-no

Continental breakfast
Sitting room, weddings and
conferences

From its creaky wooden floors and venerable ancestor paintings to its traditional New England hospitality and antique canopy beds, the Silvermine Tavern is everything a country inn should be: warm, friendly, inviting and brimming with charm.

✉ innkeeper@silverminetavern.com 🌐 www.silverminetavern.com

OLD LYME

Old Lyme Inn
85 Lyme St 06371
800-434-5352 860-434-2600
Keith and Candy Green

135-185 $US BB
14 rooms, 14 pb
Visa, MC, AmEx,
Rated
C-yes/S-no/P-ltd/H-ltd

Continental breakfast
Brunch, Lunch & Dinner available,
restaurant
Sitting room, Library, TV, WiFi,
phones, clock radios, porch,
weddings, parties, corporate, catering

Elegant 1850 Victorian mansion located in Old Lyme's Historic District. 3-star restaurant (New York Times, 3 times). Empire and Victorian furnishings.

✉ innkeeper@oldlymeinn.com 🌐 www.oldlymeinn.com

OLD MYSTIC

The Old Mystic Inn
52 Main St 06372
860-572-9422
Michael S. Cardillo, Jr.

135-215 $US BB
8 rooms, 8 pb
Most CC, *Rated*
S-ltd/P-no

Full country breakfast
Afternoon tea, Specialty Dinner
packages, Special Occasion Baskets
Hammock, gazebo, library, Keeping
Room, patio, parlor, wireless Internet

Dating back to 1784, The Old Mystic Inn is located just minutes from Mystic Seaport and Aquarium. This charming Inn, formerly The Old Mystic Book Shop, has carried on that theme by naming each of the eight guestrooms after New England authors. ✉ info@oldmysticinn.com 🌐 www.oldmysticinn.com

OLD SAYBROOK

Deacon Timothy Pratt B&B
325 Main St 06475
860-395-1229
Richard Dunn

120-200 $US BB
7 rooms, 7 pb
Visa, MC, AmEx,
Rated, •
C-ltd/S-no/P-no/H-no
German and Dutch

Full wkends, expanded wkdays
Port wine, teas, coffee, hot chocolate,
cookies, spring water always available
Beach passes, maps & lots of advice
provided; in-room massage available,
picnic area, pretty grounds

Magnificent, award-winning B&B in Old Saybrook, a National Historic Register Inn. Elegant rooms with fireplaces, Jacuzzis, canopy beds. In historic district, on gas-lit Main Street. Walk to everything! Yankee Magazine's Editors Choice for 2006!

✉ stay@pratthouse.net 🌐 www.Pratthouse.net

POMFRET CENTER

Feather Hill B&B
151 Mashamoquet Rd 06259
866-963-0522 860-963-0522
Fred & Angela Spring

135-190 $US BB
5 rooms, 5 pb
Visa, MC, AmEx
C-ltd/S-no/P-no/H-no

Full breakfast
Special diets welcome
Comfortable and well appointed
rooms, scenic drives to area
attractions, cable, AC, and library!

Feather Hill Bed and Breakfast in Pomfret offers a traditional New England country inn experience, yet with modern, open, airy and spacious rooms. Welcome to the "Quiet Corner" of Northeast Connecticut!

✉ acspring@featherhillbedandbreakfast.com 🌐 www.featherhillbedandbreakfast.com

POQUETANUCK VILLAGE

Captain Grant's 1754
109 Rt 2A 06365
800-982-1772 860-887-7589
Ted & Carol

89-179 $US BB
7 rooms, 7 pb
Most CC, Cash, •
C-ltd/S-no/P-ltd/H-ltd

Full breakfast
Dessert, cookies, wine, beer & soda
complimentary all day
3 common rooms, 3 story deck, use of
kitchenette including fridge, free WiFi,
fireplaces, cable TV

Captain Grant's is a National Historic Inn located in a 1687 Colonial Village. We were featured on HGTV in 2002 and USA today in 2003. Our canopy beds and fireplaces are elegant and affordable. Let where you stay be as memorable as the places you visit.

✉ stay@captaingrants.com 🌐 www.captaingrants.com

RIDGEFIELD

West Lane Inn
22 West Ln 06877
203-438-7323
Ms. Mayer & Debbie Prieger

185-450 $US BB
18 rooms, 18 pb
Most CC, Cash,
Rated, •
C-yes/S-no/P-no/H-no

Continental breakfast
A la carte breakfast(extra cost)
e.g.,eggs, French toast. Complimentary
tea in lobby.
Wireless DSL, Satellite TV, Heated
towel rack, Refrigerator, 24 hour phone
service, DVD upon request

The West Lane Inn, built in 1849, combines the charm of an intimate country inn with the amenities of a large hotel. Located in the historic district of Ridgefield, one of New England's most scenic towns, with a beautiful Main Street and quaint downtown.

✉ west_lane_inn@sbcglobal.net 🌐 www.westlaneinn.com

SALISBURY

Barbara Ardizones B&B
62 Main St 06068
860-4353057
Barbara Ardizone

155-195 $US BB
3 rooms, 3 pb
C-ltd/S-no/P-ltd/H-no

Fresh and seasonal
Brandy, sherry, liquor available in
the library, tea, wine or mulled wine
served in the fall
Porch terrace, gardens, hammocks,
lounges, lib books, TV/VCR, AC

My property, over an acre, is just outside town. The gardens are an escape from a busy life, with lounges & hammocks. There are 3 B&B rooms, each with private bath & A/C for those warm summer months. The beds are all made up with down pillows & comforters.

✉ ardizone@sbcglobal.net 🌐 www.barbaraardizone.com/bandb.htm

Earl Grey B&B
860-435-1007
Patricia & Richard Boyle

175-195 $US BB
2 rooms, 2 pb
C-ltd/S-no/P-no/H-ltd
French, German, some
Dutch, and a little
Japanese

Full gourmet breakfast
Afternoon tea, snacks &
complimentary wine
Fireplaces, private baths, garden
terraces, libraries

1850s era house with barn on a quiet, private hill, in and overlooking Salisbury village center. Two spacious rooms to choose from and a memorable full breakfast.

✉ richard.boyle@att.net

STONINGTON

Another Second Penny Inn	129-249 $US BB	Five Course Full Breakfast
870 Pequot Trl 06378	3 rooms, 3 pb	Coffee, tea, hot chocolate, homebaked
860-535-1710	Most CC, Cash, Checks,	cookies
Jim & Sandra Wright	*Rated*, •	Library, patio, five acres of gardens,
	C-ltd/S-ltd/P-ltd/H-no	fields & forest

Consider: "If you have 2 pennies, with the first buy bread & with the second buy hyacinths for your soul." Our 1710 home offers 3 large guestrooms, private jetted baths, fireplaces, gardens, quiet country near Mystic. Voted Best Breakfast in New England.

 inn@secondpenny.com  www.secondpenny.com

Inn at Stonington	150-445 $US BB	Continental plus breakfast
60 Water St 06378	18 rooms, 18 pb	Complimentary wine & cheese hour
860-535-2000	Visa, MC, AmEx, •	Sitting room, library, bikes, suites,
William Griffin, Susan Irvine,	C-ltd/S-no/P-no/H-yes	fireplaces, cable TV, accommodations
Anne Henson		for business travelers

Elegant hotel in the heart of the historic Stonington Borough. Stay in & enjoy your Jacuzzi tub, gas fireplace, & view of the Fisher's Island Sound. 400' deep water pier for yachts.

manager@innatstonington.com www.innatstonington.com

SUFFIELD

Lily House B&B	125-160 $US BB	Full breakfast
13 Bridge St 06078	3 rooms, 3 pb	Refrigerator stocked with
860-668-7931	Most CC, Cash	complimentary soda, bottled water,
Lorraine Erickson	C-ltd/S-no/P-no/H-no	snacks and other beverages
		Common room, games, books,
		convenience area, CD players,
		wireless laptop for guest use, packages

Set in the historic district of Suffield, this rambling old Victorian home offers a lovely place to stay as you journey through a quaint New England town. Close to fine and casual dining, parks, the "Walk of Homes" as well as Suffield Academy.   lorraine@thelilyhouse.com www.thelilyhouse.com

THOMPSON

Lord Thompson Manor	135-245 $US BB	Full breakfast
Rt 200 06277	6 rooms, 3 pb	Afternoon tea, snacks, bar service
860-923-3886	Visa, MC	Sitting room, suites, fireplaces, cable
Jackie & Andrew	C-yes/S-no/P-no/H-yes	TV, accommodations for business
		travelers

The stately elegance of Lord Thompson Manor, the serenity of the manicured grounds, luxury suites and outstanding service provide guests with the ultimate getaway or Weekend Wedding.

mail@lordthompsonmanor.com www.lordthompsonmanor.com

The Cottage House	135-225 $US BB	Continental breakfast
351 Route 193 06277	7 rooms, 7 pb	Spa room, massage services,
860-923-3886	Visa, MC	fireplaces, private entrances, front
	C-yes/S-ltd/P-no/H-ltd	porch

Situated in the picturesque Quiet Corner of Connecticut, the Inn combines the grace of elegant luxury with the tranquility of beach house charm. Calming and comfortable, we're the perfect destination for a vacation retreat or a romantic getaway.

mail@LTMcottagehouse.com www.LTMcottagehouse.com

WALLINGFORD

The Wallingford Victorian B&B	159-179 $US BB	Full breakfast
245 N Main St 06492	4 rooms, 4 pb	Kitchenette, refrigerator, microwave,
203-269-4492	Most CC, Cash, Checks,	snacks, rooms equipped with coffee
Brenda Lee	*Rated*	& tea
	C-ltd/S-ltd/P-ltd/H-no	Games, movies, books, free wireless
		Internet access, large flat screen cable
		TV

Private rooms and suites in an 1891 Queen Anne Victorian offering updated amenities and personal service. Enjoy a brass bed and whirlpool tub; or fireplace and private balcony. Full breakfast served daily. Centrally located between Rt 91 & Rt 15.

innkeep@bedandbreakfastwallingford.com www.bedandbreakfastwallingford.com

Captain Stannard House, Westbrook, CT

WESTBROOK

Captain Stannard House	150-220 $US BB	Full breakfast
138 S Main St 06498	9 rooms, 9 pb	Complimentary wine, beer, soft drink
860-399-4634	Most CC	& snacks
Mary & Jim Brewster	C-ltd/S-no/P-no/H-no	Billiards table, library, sitting room, bicycles, walk to the beach, formal dining room, gardens

Connecticut Shoreline Inn offers 9 guestrooms, all with private baths and individually decorated. Large common areas. A full breakfast served at a candlelit table for two. A perfect romantic getaway.

 mary@stannardhouse.com   www.stannardhouse.com

Talcott House	175-265 $US BB	Continental breakfast
161 Seaside Ave 06498	4 rooms, 4 pb	Sitting room, fireplaces, cable TV,
860-399-5020	Visa, MC	private veranda, private bath, ocean
Lucy Bingham & James M.	C-ltd/S-no/P-no/H-yes	views, sandy beach
Fitzpatrick	Spanish	
	Mar.-Nov. but call ahead	

All rooms have beautiful ocean views! Complete with private baths, fresh flowers, a grand piano, pure elegance, sunrises over Long island Sound, antiques, and ambience, and a sandy beach right across the street!

 lucretiawb@aol.com   www.talcotthouse.com

WOODSTOCK

B&B at Taylor's Corner	100-145 $US BB	Full breakfast
880 Route 171 06281	3 rooms, 3 pb	Homemade cookies upon arrival,
888-974-0490 860-974-0490	Visa, MC, Disc, •	complimentary fruit & sodas
Brenda Van Damme	C-ltd/S-no/P-no/H-no	Wireless Internet, DirectTV, private bathrooms & fireplaces

A romantic Connecticut farmhouse (c.1795) offers 3 comfortable air-conditioned bed chambers with private baths and fireplaces. Surrounded by manicured gardens & towering trees. Listed on the National Register of Historic Places.

 info@taylorsbb.com   www.taylorsbb.com

Delaware

DOVER

State Street Inn
228 N. State St. 19901
302-734-2294
Mike & Yvonne Hall

125-135 $US BB
3 rooms, 3 pb
Visa, MC
C-ltd/S-no/P-no/H-no

Full breakfast
Whirlpool tubs, exercise room, parlor,
family living room with TV

The State Street Inn offers charming guestrooms, each with private bath (two with whirlpool tubs). All four lovely guestrooms are beautifully decorated and furnished with antiques and reproductions. In-room amenities include cable TV and A/C.

✉ info@statestreetinn.com 🌐 www.statestreetinn.com

GEORGETOWN

**The Brick Hotel On The
Circle**
Eighteen the Circle 19947
877-88-7425 302-855-5800
Lynn Lester

125-250 $US BB
14 rooms, 14 pb
Most CC, Cash, Checks
C-ltd/S-no/P-no/H-yes

Continental breakfast
Complimentary snacks & fresh ice
water
High quality linens, heated towel
racks, gardens, Rooftop Terrace, on-
site restaurant & tavern

Boutique style, 14 room Inn with an onsite restaurant and tavern. Built in 1836 and listed on National Historic Registry. A multi-million dollar renovation in 2008 restored what had been a bank for 50 years back to its original use as an Inn and tavern.

✉ relax@thebrickhotel.com 🌐 www.thebrickhotel.com

LEWES

John Penrose Virden B&B
217 Second St 19958
302-644-0217
Ruth & Jim Edwards

120-250 $US BB
3 rooms, 3 pb
C-ltd/S-no/P-no/H-ltd

Full breakfast
Afternoon snack & beverage, fresh
fruit & flowers in room
Central heat, A/C, private parking,
bikes, beach towels, chairs &
umbrellas

The Virden House is a fourteen room, 19th century Victorian located on the main street of Lewes, DE, within walking distance to many shops, fine restaurants and ½ mile to the beach.

✉ redwards@virdenhouse.com 🌐 www.virdenhouse.com

Lazy L at Willow Creek
16061 Willow Creek
Rd 19958
302-644-7220
Joanne Cassidy

125-190 $US BB
6 rooms, 6 pb
Visa, MC, Disc, *Rated*
C-ltd/S-no/P-yes/H-ltd

Full breakfast
We specialize in cooking vegetarian or
vegan breakfasts upon request. Free
Ice Cream
Heated swimming pool, hot tub, pool
table, screened porches, exercise area,
extensive outdoor space

This bed & breakfast is a great choice for a winter getaway or a summer vacation. Outside the resort town of Lewes, this 8 acre gem has it all. Very large guestrooms with large guest lounges & large game room. VERY dog friendly, off leash play area.

✉ vacation@lazyl.net 🌐 www.lazyl.net

The Inn at Canal Square
122 Market St 19958
888-644-1911 302-644-3377
Ted Becker

118-625 $US BB
24 rooms, 24 pb
Most CC, *Rated*
C-yes/S-no/P-ltd/H-yes

European-Style Breakfast
Seasonal fruit & cheese tray
Fireplace, cable TV, CD player,
refrigerator, robes, business center,
fitness center, massage studio

Nantucket style on the Delaware Coast. Located on the waterfront in the heart of historic Lewes. Large rooms with private baths, open year-round with complimentary European style breakfast. Ideal coastal escape and event destination.

✉ innatcanalsquare@verizon.net 🌐 www.theinnatcanalsquare.com

Governor's B&B, Milton, DE

MILFORD

The Towers Inn
101 NW Front St 19963
302-422-3814
Daniel & Rhonda Bond

120-160 $US BB
4 rooms, 4 pb
Visa, MC, AmEx
S-no/P-no/H-no
Russian

Full breakfast
Fruit juices & drinks, bottled water,
complimentary sherry
WiFi, A/C, off-street parking, fireplaces,
piano, garden

Located in historic Milford, Delaware, The Towers is an architectural gem waiting to be enjoyed, a luxurious, adults only bed & breakfast.

 daniellbond@gmail.com ❂ www.mispillion.com

MILTON

Governor's B&B
327 Union St 19968
866-684-4649 302-684-4649
William & Deborah Post

95-135 $US BB
3 rooms, 3 pb
Most CC
C-ltd/S-ltd/P-no/H-no

Full gourmet breakfast
Special menu by request
Sitting room, library, fireplaces, cable
TV, refrigerator/microwave, A/C

Built in 1790, the inn is situated on two landscaped acres in the Milton Historic District. It was built by John Hazzard who piloted Washington across the Delaware. It is private and secluded.

✉ wdpost@aol.com

REHOBOTH BEACH

Rehoboth Guest House
40 Maryland Ave 19971
800-564-0493 302-227-4117
Tom Napier-Collins

100-230 $US BB
14 rooms, 10 pb
Most CC, Cash
C-ltd/S-no/P-no/H-no

Continental breakfast
Complimentary wine & cheese on
Saturdays in season
Porch, sun decks, outdoor enclosed
cedar showers, wireless Internet

The Rehoboth Guest House is a charming gay owned and operated Victorian beach house located in the heart of Rehoboth Beach, Delaware, just steps from the boardwalk, beach, and the Atlantic ocean.

✉ manager@rehobothguesthouse.com ❂ www.rehobothguesthouse.com

The Royal Rose Inn B&B
41 Baltimore Ave 19971
302-226-2535
Andy Dorosky

60-185 $US BB
7 rooms, 7 pb
Visa, MC, Disc
C-ltd/S-no/P-no/H-no

Buffet style breakfast
Tea & coffee
Sitting room, porch, sundeck, wireless
Internet

Centrally located on Baltimore Avenue in the heart of Rehoboth Beach, the Inn is steps away from shops, fine boutiques and the area's best restaurants and night life.

✉ innkeeper@royalroseinn.com ❂ www.royalroseinn.com

District of Columbia

WASHINGTON

Adam's Inn
1746 Lanier Place NW 20009
800-578-6807 202-745-3600
Laurel Mawema

109-169 $US BB
26 rooms, 15 pb
Most CC, Cash
C-yes/S-no/P-ltd/H-ltd
Spanish

Continental breakfast
Tea, coffee, juice
Wireless Internet access, sitting rooms,
TV lounge, guest kitchen, laundry
facility, patio, garden

Free Night w/Certificate: Valid Jan.1-Feb 28, July1-August 31, and Nov.1-Dec. 31

Only 1 block from the Adams Morgan's restaurant district & 7 blocks from the Woodley Park Red Line Metro, the newly-renovated Adam's Inn is convenient to everything. Limited parking is available.

✉ stay@adamsinn.com 🌐 adamsinn.com

Swann House
1808 New Hampshire Ave
NW 20009
202-265-4414
Mary Ross & Rick Verkler

169-369 $US BB
12 rooms, 12 pb
Most CC, *Rated*
C-ltd/S-no/P-no/H-no

Continental plus breakfast
Afternoon refreshments & evening
cordials
Parlour, Jacuzzis, swimming pool,
suites, fireplace, cable TV, conference

Grand Richardson Romanesque mansion in Dupont Circle, D.C.'s most vibrant neighborhood. Eat at local outdoor cafes, walk to museums or relax by the pool or on our roof deck.

✉ stay@swannhouse.com 🌐 www.swannhouse.com

Florida

ALFORD

La Maison de Lucy
2388 Park Avenue 32420
850-579-0138
Michael Setboun

190-290 $US BB
12 rooms, 12 pb
Most CC, Cash, Checks
C-ltd/S-no/P-no/H-yes
French, Spanish

Full breakfast
Afternoon tea and pastries
Free WiFi High Speed Wireless
Internet, Special weekend activities,
private bath

A historic school house on the inside, beautifully appointed suites internationally themed on the inside, the contrast is astounding, a must see!

✉ lamaisondelucy@yahoo.com 🌐 www.lamaisondelucy.com

AMELIA ISLAND

Addison On Amelia
614 Ash St 32034
800-943-1604 904-277-1604
Bob & Shannon Tidball

175-280 $US BB
14 rooms, 14 pb
Visa, MC, AmEx,
Rated
C-ltd/S-no/P-no/H-ltd

Full breakfast
Happy Hour appetizers daily, baked
goods always available
WiFi, bicycles, beach equipment,
24-hour coffee, concierge services,
parlor, courtyard

The Addison on Amelia is a tranquil 14-room boutique inn seamlessly blending the elegance of a bygone era with the modern amenities and conveniences the discriminating traveler expects.

✉ info@AddisonOnAmelia.com 🌐 www.AddisonOnAmelia.com

Amelia Island Williams House
103 S 9th St 32034
800-414-9258 904-277-2328
Deborah & Byron
McCutchen

175-275 $US BB
10 rooms, 10 pb
Most CC, Cash, Checks,
Rated, •
C-ltd/S-ltd/P-no/H-yes

Full gourmet breakfast
Home Baked cookie and beverages in
room on arrival, Social hour offering
wine & appetizers
Whirlpool tubs, fireplaces, hot tub on
priv. porch, bikes, WiFi, beach towels,
flat screen cable TV

Award winning B & B on Amelia Island. Romantic getaway & spa packages, Whirlpool tubs, fireplaces, Christmas Package, Destination weddings, Vow Renewals.

✉ info@williamshouse.com 🌐 www.williamshouse.com

Elizabeth Pointe Lodge
98 S Fletcher Ave 32034
800-772-3359 904-277-4851
David & Susan Caples

225-475 $US BB
25 rooms, 25 pb
Most CC, Checks,
Rated, •
C-yes/S-no/P-no/H-yes
French

Full breakfast
Light lunch & dinner service
available, complimentary wine & hors
d'oeuvres, 24 hr room service
Newspapers at the door daily,
concierge services, complimentary
WiFi, beach equipment, bikes

The Pointe sits directly on the beach overlooking the Atlantic Ocean on the barrier island of Amelia. The Main House offers 20 different rooms, the Ocean House has 4 spacious rooms & decks, the Miller Cottage is 2B/2B with porch and entertainment area.

✉ djcaples@lodgingresources.com 🌐 www.elizabethpointelodge.com

ANNA MARIA ISLAND

An Island Getaway at Palm Tree Villas
207 66th St 34217
888-778-7256 941-778-0910
Peggy Sawe

99-235 $US EP
6 rooms, 6 pb
Most CC, Cash, Checks,
Rated, •
C-yes/S-ltd/P-no/H-ltd

Full Kitchens, BBQ
Heated pool, new full kitchens, king
size beds with pillow-top mattresses,
garden patios, WiFi

Palm Tree Villas is your answer to an enchanting island vacation. Recommended by LIFE magazine and top-rated by guests, this small piece of paradise offers all the comforts of home in newly remodeled villas in a lush tropical resort setting by the beach.

 info@palmtreevillas.com  www.palmtreevillas.com

APALACHICOLA

Bryant House B&B	87-250 $US BB	Full German breakfast
101 6th St 32320	4 rooms, 4 pb	Complimentary wine
888-554-4376 850-653-3270	Visa, MC, AmEx,	Sitting room, DSL Internet access,
Brigitte Schroeder	*Rated*, •	cable TV/VCR, rose garden, fountain,
	C-ltd/S-no/P-ltd/H-ltd	fish pond
	German	

European hospitality in a quaint Victorian setting. Each room has its own special character, designed to fit your mood. Relax in a rocker on the wraparound porch or enjoy the quiet in the patio under the 150 year old magnolia tree.

✉ ken@bryanthouse.com 🌐 www.bryanthouse.com

Coombs House Inn	119-229 $US BB	Gourmet Breakfast
80 Sixth St 32320	23 rooms, 23 pb	Fresh fruit, yogurt, baked goods,
888-244-8320 850-653-9199	Visa, MC, Disc,	gourmet coffee
Lynn Spohrer	*Rated*, •	Beach chairs, towels, umbrellas &
	C-yes/S-ltd/P-ltd/H-yes	bicycles; weddings, meetings, family
		reunions, anniversaries

The Inn consists of The Mansion, Veranda Suites and The Villa, welcoming special guests who appreciate the charm and historical authenticity of another era, in an intimate atmosphere.

✉ info@coombshouseinn.com 🌐 www.CoombsHouseInn.com

BIG PINE KEY

Barnacle B&B	125-195 $US BB	Full breakfast
1557 Long Beach Dr 33043	4 rooms, 4 pb	Hot tub, bicycles, refrigerators, A/C,
800-465-9100 305-872-3298	Visa, MC, Disc, •	weddings & receptions, bbq grill,
Tim & Jane Marquis	C-ltd/S-ltd/P-no/H-ltd	private beach, WiFi

Our intriguing Caribbean-style home "that nature designed." The Barnacle is located on the lush tropical island of Big Pine Key, FL, where peace, quiet and leisurely breezes prevail.

✉ barnacleb@bellsouth.net 🌐 www.thebarnacle.net

BOKEELIA

Bokeelia Tarpon Inn	159-325 $US BB	Full breakfast
8241 Main St 33922	5 rooms, 5 pb	Appetizers with wine, snacks & cold
866-827-7662 239-283-8961	Most CC, Cash, Checks,	beverages are available in the kitchen
Cynthia Welch	*Rated*	at any time
	S-ltd/P-no/H-yes	Concierge services for tours &
		activities

Steal away to this romantic Fort Meyers area bed and breakfast inn — an exquisite Pine Island Florida waterfront lodging near Sanibel and Boca Grande in charming Bokeelia. The Bokeelia Tarpon Inn is perfect for vacations and special occasions.

✉ info@tarponinn.com 🌐 www.tarponinn.com

BRADENTON

The Londoner B&B	120-180 $US BB	Full breakfast
304 15h Street West 34205	6 rooms, 6 pb	Tea Room open Monday – Saturday
866-472-8283 941-794-4657	Visa, MC	11:30 to 3:00, complimentary snacks &
Jennifer Taylor	C-yes/S-no/P-ltd/H-ltd	soft drinks
		WiFi, flat screen TV, robes, quality
		linens & toiletries, carriage house,
		special events

The Londoner B&B is centrally located near historic downtown, offers excellent accommodations and delightful tea room tastings.

✉ innkeeper@thelondonerinn.com 🌐 www.thelondonerinn.com/index.html

CAPE CORAL-PINE ISLAND

Inn on the Bay	109-199 $US BB	Continental plus breakfast
12251 Shoreview Dr 33993	4 rooms, 4 pb	TV, A/C, refrigerator, views, porches,
239-283-7510	•	free use of canoes, free local calls
Tell us Lanier sent you	C-ltd/S-ltd/P-ltd/H-ltd	
	Matlacha	

Tropical island waterfront B&B, view manatee and dolphins from your porch, fantastic sunsets, free use of canoe, two 90' docks. Near Sanibel-JN Ding Darling Preserve.

✉ cmanatee2@gmail.com 🌐 webbwiz.com/inn

CAPTIVA ISLAND

Captiva Island Inn
11509 Andy Rosse Ln 33924
800-454-9898 239-395-0882
Sandra Stilwell

99-400 $US BB
18 rooms, 18 pb
Most CC, Cash,
Rated, •
C-yes/S-no/P-no/H-ltd

Full breakfast
Lunch & dinner available, restaurant
Bicycles, suites, cable TV, beach
chairs, accommodate business
travelers, daily housekeeping, pool

Stay in the main inn or the surrounding cottages. Some have full kitchens and separate bedrooms. Our new 5-bedroom house is perfect for weddings. Pool and spa with gazebo on site.

✉ Reservations@captivaislandinn.com ☋ www.captivaislandinn.com

DAYTONA BEACH

River Lily Inn
558 Riverside Drive 32117
386-253-5002
Art & Polly Cappuccio

135-220 $US BB
7 rooms, 7 pb
Visa, MC, Disc
C-ltd/S-ltd/P-no/H-no

Full breakfast
Private baths, fine linens & towels,
flat-screen TVs, cable TV, DVD player,
high speed WiFi

The River Lily Inn B&B is located on one and a half acres overlooking the Intracoastal Halifax River, five minutes from the famous Daytona Beaches. Our majestic 1904 riverfront Inn stands five stories tall with the cupola proudly gracing the top.

✉ riverlilyinn@cfl.rr.com ☋ www.riverlilyinnbedandbreakfast.com

The Villa B&B
801 N Peninsula Dr 32118
888-248-7060 386-248-2020
Jim Camp

130-250 $US BB
5 rooms, 5 pb
Visa, MC, AmEx
C-ltd/S-ltd/P-ltd/H-no

Continental plus breakfast
Color remote TVs, DVD/VCRs, CD
player/clock radio, tub w/ shower,
wireless, air conditioning & heat

Enjoy elegant accommodations in a Historic Spanish Mansion, located on over 1 ¼ acres of land in the heart of Daytona Beach, and is listed on the National Register of Historic Places.

✉ thevillabb@aol.com ☋ www.thevillabb.com

FLAGLER BEACH

**Island Cottage Oceanfront
Villa Inn, Café and Spa**
2316 S Oceanshore
Blvd 32136
87-ROMANCE-2 386-439-0092
Toni & Mark Treworgy

239-399 $US BB
8 rooms, 8 pb
Visa, MC, Disc,
Rated, •
C-ltd/S-no/P-ltd/H-ltd
Feb – Aug 14 & Nov
1-Jan

Full breakfast
Afternoon Tea, Home Baked
Cookies & Snacks each day, plus
Complimentary in-room coffee & tea.
Heated pool, Gourmet breakfast each
day plus in-room menu for afternoon
and evening room service.

One of Florida's top honeymoon, anniversary, romantic getaway and elopement destinations. Fire-places, Jacuzzis for 2, king canopy beds, private decks, patios, heated swimming pool and private beachfront. Includes hot gourmet breakfast each morning. ☋ www.islandcottagevillas.com

FORT LAUDERDALE

Granada Inn
3011 Granada St 33304
866-463-4900 954-463-2032

90-225 $US BB
12 rooms, 12 pb
Most CC, *Rated*, •
C-yes/S-no/P-ltd/H-no

Continental breakfast
Outdoor swimming pool, ceiling fans,
stereo CD system, A/C, fridge, phone

Free Night w/Certificate: Anytime. Room Upgrade.

Just a few short steps to the beach and ocean . . . .Relax as you enter your private oasis, nestled around a lush tropical courtyard & swimming pool. Experience our warm hospitality & personalized service that make guests return time after time.

✉ thegranadainn@bellsouth.net ☋ www.granadainn.net

La Casa Del Mar
3003 Granada St 33304
866 4672037 954-467-2037
Ohad Soberano

95-242 $US BB
13 rooms, 13 pb
Most CC, Cash,
Rated, •
S-no/P-no/H-no

Continental breakfast
Kitchenette with each room.
Garden, swimming pool, cable TV,
Internet cafe, gazebo, rental movie
library

Free Night w/Certificate: Anytime. Room Upgrade.

Welcome to La Casa Del Mar! Located just a stone's throw from the beach in sunny Fort Lauderdale, the "Venice of America," where you can enjoy the sub-tropical climate, ocean, beach, sun and fun!

 lacasadelmarbnb@hotmail.com ☋ www.lacasadelmar.com

FORT MYERS BEACH

Manatee Bay Inn
932 Third St 33931
239-463-6906
Connie & Axel Schulz

78-198 $US BB
6 rooms, 6 pb
Most CC, Cash
C-ltd/S-ltd/P-no/H-yes
German

Continental plus breakfast
Boat docks, BBQ grill, heated pool,
daily maid service (except Sundays),
bikes, private balconies

A tropical oasis in a quiet, prime location right next to Old San Carlos Blvd. shopping district and colorful Times Square in the heart of Fort Myers Beach. Just 1/5 blocks to the beautiful white gulf beaches.　✉ info@manateebayinn.com　◐ www.manateebayinn.com

GAINESVILLE

Magnolia Plantation
309 SE 7th St 32601
800-201-2379 352-375-6653
Joe & Cindy Montalto

135-350 $US BB
14 rooms, 14 pb
Most CC, Cash, Checks
C-ltd/S-no/P-ltd/H-no

Full breakfast
Complementary snacks & beverages
throughout day, evening social hour
with wine & snacks
Library, sitting room, bicycles, 60-foot
pond, gazebo, wireless Internet

Restored 1885 Victorian in downtown. Two miles from University of Florida. Beautifully landscaped gardens, pond, waterfalls and gazebo. 1, 2 and 3 bedroom cottages available.

✉ info@magnoliabnb.com　◐ www.magnoliabnb.com

Sweetwater Branch Inn
625 E University Ave 32601
800-595-7760 352-373-6760
Cornelia Holbrook

90-245 $US BB
18 rooms, 18 pb
Visa, MC, AmEx,
Rated
C-yes/S-no/P-ltd/H-ltd
Spanish, Italian

Full breakfast
Wine and Cheese hour, snacks. Dinner
available upon request.
Sitting rooms, wireless Internet,
airport/univ. transport, on-site bike
rentals, group venue.

The Sweetwater Branch Inn Bed & Breakfast, in historic downtown Gainesville, is part of a Victorian complex which offers all the amenities you'd expect in a world-class bed & breakfast and much more.

✉ reserve@sweetwaterinn.com　◐ www.sweetwaterinn.com

GULFPORT

Sea Breeze Manor B&B Inn
5701 Shore Blvd 33707
888-343-4445 727-343-4445
Lori Rosso

155-180 $US BB
7 rooms, 7 pb
Most CC, Cash, Checks,
Rated
C-ltd/S-yes/P-ltd/H-yes

Full breakfast
Beverages, snacks, wine & cheese,
sherry, port
Private balconies, bicycles, lounge
chairs, beach towels, in room TV/
VCR/CD

Waterfront B&B in charming artsy community. Private balconies and sitting areas in each suite give you a private resort feel. Park your car and walk to over 30 restaurants and shops on the waterfront. Indulge!　✉ rsvp@seabreezemanor.com　◐ www.seabreezemanor.com

The Peninsula Inn & Spa
2937 Beach Blvd S 33707
888-9000-INN 727-346-9800
Jim and Alexandra Kingzett

100-200 $US BB
11 rooms, 11 pb
Most CC, Cash,
Rated, •
C-yes/S-no/P-ltd/H-yes

Continental breakfast
Fine dining restaurant, bar, spa
services on-site
Massage, facials, spa treatments on-
site; pool, tennis, golf at nearby club

Elegant historic inn/spa, fine dining, cocktails. Perfect for short getaways, extended stays, business travel, intimate weddings, social/corporate events. Minutes from Tampa & St. Pete airports.

✉ inn_spa@yahoo.com　◐ www.innspa.net

HIGH SPRINGS

**Grady House Historic Bed
& Breakfast**
420 NW 1st Avenue 32655
386-454-2206
Paul & Lucie Regensdorf

115-280 $US BB
5 rooms, 5 pb
Most CC, Cash
C-ltd/S-no/P-no/H-no

Full breakfast
Complimentary beverages, coffee, tea,
soft drinks & home baked treats
Wireless Internet and computer for
guest's use, daily maid service, self-
contained cottage available

Grady House will provide the setting for an idyllic retreat, complete with a perfect night's sleep and a memorable meal. We offer the warm hospitality and special touches to our guests that are too often forgotten in today's fast-paced world.

✉ lucie@gradyhouse.com　◐ gradyhouse.com

INDIALANTIC

Windemere Inn by the Sea	160-440 $US BB	Full gourmet breakfast
815 S.Miramar Ave	9 rooms, 9 pb	Guests enjoy "tea" with homemade
(A1A) 32903	Visa, MC, *Rated*	pastries, tea and sherry. Daily comp.
800-224-6853 321-728-9334	C-ltd/S-no/P-no/H-ltd	beverages and home made snack
Beth Fisher		Concierge services for dining &
		recreation, cable TV, wireless Internet,
		special events & weddings

Windemere is a luxury ocean front B&B, east of Melbourne on the beach, catering to both leisure & business travelers. Rooms are finely appointed with crisp linens, antiques & contemporary furnishings. TV available on request, wireless Internet access.

✉ stay@windemereinn.com 🌐 www.windemereinn.com

ISLAMORADA

Casa Thorn	79-239 $US BB	Full breakfast
114 Palm Ln 33036	5 rooms, 3 pb	Pool, wireless DSL, color TV, VCR,
305-852-3996	Visa, MC	movies, CDs, bathrobes, hairdryer,
Thorn Trainer	S-ltd/P-yes/H-yes	iron, refrigerators, etc.

A charming, one-of-a-kind Islamorada hotel, Casa Thorn offers five beautifully decorated rooms nestled in a lush and secluded tropical setting.

✉ casathorn@webtv.net 🌐 www.casathorn.com

JACKSONVILLE

House on Cherry Street	89-115 $US BB	Continental Plus breakfast
1844 Cherry St 32205	4 rooms, 4 pb	Afternoon tea
904-384-1999	Visa, MC, AmEx,	Sitting room, color TV, A/C, river
Victoria & Robert Freeman	*Rated*	porch, dock, fax, organic garden,
	C-ltd/S-no/P-no/H-no	extensive collection FL art
	Oct. 1st – March 30th	

The House on Cherry Street is nestled in Jacksonville's historic Riverside Avondale area along the St. Johns River. It offers a quiet, relaxing atmosphere, perfect for weekend getaways, business travelers, or anyone attending special events

✉ houseoncherry@bellsouth.net 🌐 www.geocities.com/houseoncherryst/index.htm

Riverdale Inn	110-220 $US BB	Full breakfast
1521 Riverside Ave 32204	10 rooms, 10 pb	Full service Pub available for guests
866-808-3400 904-354-5080	Most CC, Cash, •	with hors d'oeuvres prepared by our
Daniel Waln	C-ltd/S-ltd/P-ltd/H-ltd	chef.
		Free wireless Internet, local phone
		service, on-site parking; Jacuzzi in
		some rooms

The Riverdale Inn is a turn-of-the-century mansion located in the historic Five Points area of Riverside. A full service pub is on the premises along with private guest only dinner service.

✉ info@riverdaleinn.com 🌐 www.riverdaleinn.com

JACKSONVILLE BEACH

Fig Tree Inn	99-185 $US BB	Full weekend/ Continental weekdays
185 4th Ave S 32250	6 rooms, 6 pb	Tea, wine, beer, water, soda, snacks
877-217-9830 904-246-8855	Most CC, Cash, *Rated*	Library, TV/VCR/DVD, movies,
Dawn & Kevin Eggleston	C-ltd/S-ltd/P-ltd/H-ltd	wireless high speed Internet, robes,
		fireplace, local gym

Originally built in 1915 as a summer beach home for the Arnot family, Fig Tree Inn is a lovely old cedar shake shingle cottage just one half block from the beach. Wonderful times can be shared with family and friends for any occasion.

✉ egghouse@comcast.net 🌐 www.figtreeinn.com

JACKONVILLE BEACH

Pelican Path B&B by the Sea 11 N 19th Ave 32250 888-749-1177 904-249-1177 Tom & Joan Hubbard	140-205 $US BB 4 rooms, 4 pb Visa, MC, Disc, *Rated*, • S-no/P-no/H-no 6 months	Full breakfast Beverages placed in guest refrigerator daily: bottled water, soft drinks, fruit juice Sitting room, bikes, cable, Jacuzzis, phones, TV/VCR, refrigerators, spa tubs

"Lieu de Loisir (A Place of Leisure)." Pelican Path enjoys a superb location—an oceanfront, residential neighborhood with easy access to the beach, stores & restaurants.

✉ info@pelicanpath.com ◐ www.pelicanpath.com

KEY WEST

Albury Court 1030 Eaton St 33040 877-299-9870 305-294-9870 Julie Fondriest	109-349 $US BB 38 rooms, 38 pb Most CC, *Rated* C-yes/S-no/P-no/H-yes	Continental breakfast Flat LCD TVs, fireplaces, waterfall splash pool, wireless Internet, Jacuzzi, all rooms non-smoking

Albury Court is a small compound of 5 historic buildings, in the Old Town area of Key West & two blocks from the harbor. Tailored for those looking for a peaceful & romantic setting, in easy reach of Key West's best restaurants, nightlife & waterfront.

✉ albury@historickeywestinns.com ◐ www.historickeywestinns.com/properties/albu

Andrews Inn & Garden Cottages 223 Eanes Lane 33040 888-263-7393 305-294-7730 Tom & Nancy Coward	130-369 $US BB 10 rooms, 10 pb Most CC, Cash, *Rated*, • C-ltd/S-ltd/P-ltd/H-no Some French	Champagne Continental Breakfast Complimentary afternoon happy hour Swimming pool, tropical gardens, bikes, vaulted ceilings, private baths, A/C, Jacuzzis, WiFi, boat

Stroll down a shady lane off of Duval St., and you will find a lush tropical courtyard with a pool at its center and five charming rooms with private baths awaiting your arrival. We also have 3 cottage suites complete with their own Jacuzzis.

✉ info@andrewsinn.com ◐ www.andrewsinn.com

Center Court Historic Inn & Cottages 1075 Duval St, C19 33040 800-797-8787 305-296-9292 Naomi Van Steelandt	118-1,158 $US EP 85 rooms, 85 pb Visa, MC, Disc, *Rated*, • C-yes/S-ltd/P-yes/H-yes	Great restaurants all around us! Full Concierge services including bikes/mopeds delivered to your unit, inroom massage, water sports.

Comfortable, luxurious, affordable and just steps from Duval Street, we offer lodging in many settings: guesthouses, historic inn rooms, villas, cottages and houses, all offering romantic Key West hideaways with private Jacuzzis, some with private pools.

✉ reservations@vacationrentalskeywest.com ◐ www.vacationrentalskeywest.com

Chelsea House Pool & Gardens 709 Truman Ave 33040 800-845-8859 305-296-2211 Julie Fondriest	119-259 $US BB 33 rooms, 33 pb Most CC, *Rated*, • C-yes/S-no/P-ltd/H-yes	Continental breakfast Cable TV, off-street parking, bath amenities, hair dryer, phone, room safes, all rooms non-smoking

Beautiful Historic Inn in the heart of Old Town Key West within walking distance to everything. Large, sunny pool with lush tropical gardens. Private off-street parking. Choose from 33 unique rooms, intimate to grand, all with private baths.

✉ chelsea@historickeywestinns.com ◐ www.historickeywestinns.com/properties/chel

Conch House Heritage Inn 625 Truman Ave 33040 800-207-5806 305-293-0020 Sam Holland	108-248 $US BB 10 rooms, 10 pb Most CC, *Rated*, • C-ltd/S-ltd/P-no/H-yes Spanish	Continental plus breakfast Swimming pool, phone, TV, A/C, parking, bikes, refrigerators, gardens, wireless Internet

The Conch House offers charming and romantic accommodations with traditional antique furnishings or tropical poolside cottages. Every luxurious amenity including breakfast and parking.

✉ info@conchhouse.com ◐ www.conchhouse.com

KEY WEST——

Curry Mansion Inn
511 Caroline St 33040
800-253-3466 305-294-5349
Edith Amsterdam

195-365 $US BB
28 rooms, 28 pb
Most CC, Cash, Checks,
Rated, •
C-yes/S-no/P-ltd/H-yes
French, Spanish,
German, Italian

Full breakfast with omelets
Open bar cocktail party with snacks
and live music
Heated pool, hot tub, Internet access,
parking

The Curry Mansion Inn . . . where the elegance of Key West's past is equaled only by the elegance of its presence.

 frontdesk@currymansion.com ○ www.currymansion.com

——

Cypress House
601 Caroline St 33040
800-525-2488 305-294-6969
Dave Taylor

169-475 $US BB
22 rooms, 16 pb
Most CC, Cash,
Rated, •
S-ltd/P-yes/H-ltd
Spanish, Russian, Polish

Continental plus breakfast
Evening Happy Hour with self service
premium full bar, snacks, beer wine
and soft drinks.
Gazebo, heated swimming pool, free
high speed wireless Internet access,
bicycle rentals on property.

1888 Bahamian Conch mansion. Private, tropical. Large rooms with A/C, cable TV, phone, free wireless Internet access, refrigerator and ceiling fans. Walk to all historic sites, museums, Historic Seaport, shopping, restaurants and nightlife.

 CypressKW@aol.com ○ www.CypressHouseKW.com

——

Heron House
512 Simonton St 33040
800-294-1644 305-294-9227
Jeffrey Brannin

169-399 $US BB
23 rooms, 23 pb
Most CC, Cash,
Rated, •
S-ltd/P-no/H-ltd

Continental plus breakfast
Breakfast bar; weekend wine & cheese
hour
Orchid gardens, sun deck, pool, bath
robes, concierge, phones, cable TV,
in-room safes

Located in the heart of the historic district, offering all the intimacy and hospitality of a small southern guesthouse. From the moment guests step on the grounds they are surrounded by colorful orchids and lush, tropical plants. AAA 4 Diamond.

 heronkyw@aol.com ○ www.heronhouse.com/home.htm

——

Island City House Hotel
411 William St 33040
800-634-8230 305-294-5702
Tasha & Gaines Dupree

150-420 $US BB
24 rooms, 24 pb
Most CC, Cash,
Rated, •
C-yes/S-no/P-no/H-ltd

Continental plus breakfast
Widows Walk sun deck with view;
bikes, swimming pool, garden

Choose from three unique houses: the Arch House, the Island City House, and the Cigar House, all of which share lush, tropical gardens with winding, brick pathways throughout. The Island City House Hotel is the oldest operating guesthouse on Key West.

 info@islandcityhouse.com ○ www.islandcityhouse.com

——

Key Lime Inn
725 Truman Avenue 33040
800-549-4430 305-294-5229
Julie Fondriest

119-259 $US BB
37 rooms, 37 pb
Most CC, *Rated*
S-ltd/P-no/H-yes

Continental breakfast
Heated pool, free parking, wireless
Internet, cable TV, room safes, bath
amenities, non-smoking

Key Lime Inn is a 37-room historic hotel in the center of Key West's Old Town area just two blocks from famous Duval Street. You can walk or bicycle to restaurants and nightlife and enjoy the quaint houses in Key West's historic neighborhoods.

 keylime@historickeywestinns.com ○ www.historickeywestinns.com/properties/keyl

——

Knowles House B&B
1004 Eaton St 33040
800-352-4414 305-296-8132
Les Vollmert & Paul Masse

129-279 $US BB
8 rooms, 8 pb
Visa, MC, Disc,
Rated, •
C-ltd/S-ltd/P-no/H-no

Continental plus breakfast
Complimentary wine
Jacuzzis, swimming pool, cable TV,
garden, soothing fountain, shaded
porch, rooftop sun deck

The Knowles House B&B is a charming, restored, and elegantly furnished, mid-1800s conch house centrally located in a handsome residential district of Key West.

 knowleshse@aol.com ○ www.knowleshouse.com

KEY WEST————————————————————————————————

La Mer Hotel & Dewey House
504 & 506 South St 33040
800-354-4455 305-296-6577
Carrie & Matthew Babich

169-465 $US BB
19 rooms, 19 pb
Most CC, *Rated*, •
S-no/P-no/H-yes
French, Spanish

Continental plus breakfast
Afternoon tea, cakes & fruit
Library, dipping pool, access to 3
pools, Jacuzzi, beach

Key West's only luxury oceanfront bed and breakfast emanates island elegance against the backdrop of a white sand beach and lush, tropical flora and fauna.

✉ info@southernmostresorts.com 🌐 www.southernmostresorts.com/la_mer.html

———

La Pensione Inn
809 Truman Ave 33040
800-893-1193 305-292-9923
Freda Erwiin

118-328 $US BB
9 rooms, 9 pb
Most CC, Cash, *Rated*
S-no/P-no/H-yes
Spanish

Continental plus breakfast
Swimming pool, A/C, off-street parking,
bike rentals, non-smoking rooms
available

La Pensione, a grand Classic Revival mansion, dates from Key West's Victorian Age. Sun lovers enjoy the peaceful seclusion of the inn's sparkling pool and lounge deck. Key West's legendary Duval Street is just steps away.

✉ lapensione@aol.com 🌐 www.lapensione.com

———

Lighthouse Court
902 Whitehead St 33040
877 294-9588 305-294-9588
Julie Fondreist

109-349 $US BB
40 rooms, 40 pb
Most CC
C-ltd/S-no/P-no/H-no

Continental breakfast
Large heated pool and pool bar,
wireless Internet, cable TV, room
safes, all rooms non-smoking

Lighthouse Court is a historic hotel with gardens in the center of Key West's Old Town area just two blocks from famous Duval Street. You can walk or bicycle to restaurants and nightlife and enjoy the quaint houses in Key West's historic neighborhoods.

✉ lighthouse@historickeywestinns.com 🌐 www.historickeywestinns.com/properties/ligh

———

Merlin Guesthouse
811 Simonton St 33040
800-642-4753 305-296-3336
Julie Fondriest

109-329 $US BB
20 rooms, 20 pb
Most CC, *Rated*
C-yes/S-no/P-no/H-ltd

Continental breakfast
Private courtyard features cocktail
pool with built-in seating, wireless
Internet access poolside

Merlin is a classic Key West guesthouse providing casual lodging at an ideal location. Just one block from Duval Street, you will be steps away from Key West's best restaurants, nightlife, shopping, and attractions.

✉ merlin@historickeywestinns.com 🌐 www.historickeywestinns.com/properties/merl

———

Ocean Breeze Inn
625 South St 33040
877-879-2362 305-296-2829
Heather Whitehead & Linda Liebig

109 $US BB
15 rooms, 15 pb
Most CC, Cash, Checks
C-ltd/S-ltd/P-no/H-ltd
Czech

Continental breakfast
WiFi, free parking, heated pool, rooms
with kitchen, cable TV, housekeeping,
A/C, courtyard

Ocean Breeze Inn provides an excellent location for your accommodations in Old Town Key West, with Duval Street and tropical South Beach just steps away. Our affordable accommodations and unique charm bring guests back again and again.

✉ info@oceanbreezeinn.com 🌐 www.oceanbreezeinn.com

———

Pilot House Guesthouse
414 Simonton St 33040
800-648-3780 305-294-8719
Scott Ferdinand

115-300 $US EP
14 rooms, 14 pb
Most CC, Cash,
Checks, •
S-ltd/P-no/H-ltd
Spanish, Italian
December 20 – April 30

Fully equipped kitchens &
kitchenettes in rooms
Pool, spa, marble baths, verandas,
gardens, bicycles, TV, A/C, wireless
Internet.

Guest House located in the heart of historic Old Town Key West. A grand two-story mansion and poolside Cabana units beautifully restored with all the comforts and conveniences. Handicap accessible room. Restricted clothing optional pool and spa only!

✉ pilotkw@aol.com 🌐 www.pilothousekeywest.com

KEY WEST――――――――――――――――――――――――――――――――

Simonton Court Inn	150-520 $US BB	Continental plus breakfast
320 Simonton St 33040	30 rooms, 30 pb	Pool, Jacuzzis, patios, air conditioning,
800-944-2687 305-294-6386	Most CC	color cable TV/VCR
Terry Sullivan	C-ltd/S-no/P-no/H-ltd	

Enter the serene setting of Simonton Court Historic Inn & Cottages, and be greeted by fragrant tropical flowers blooming beneath gently swaying palms. One of the most beautiful properties in Key West.

✉ simontoncourt@aol.com ❂ www.simontoncourt.com

The Grand Guest House	98-268 $US BB	Continental plus breakfast
1116 Grinnell St 33040	10 rooms, 10 pb	Concierge, A/C, cable TV, phone,
888-947-2630 305-294-0590	Visa, MC, Disc, *Rated*	refrigerators, iPod player/alarm clock,
Jeffrey Daubman , Jim	C-ltd/S-ltd/P-no/H-no	ceiling fans, free WiFi
Brown & Derek Karevicius	December – May	

Located in the heart of Old Town in a quiet residential neighborhood just 5 blocks from Duval Street and Atlantic beaches. A Frommer's "Find," Superior Small Lodgings "White Glove" winner, Florida Green Lodge, and featured in Nat'l. Geographic Traveler.

✉ info3@grandkeywest.com ❂ www.GrandKeyWest.com

The Key West Bed &	79-265 $US BB	Continental plus breakfast
Breakfast	10 rooms, 6 pb	Sitting room, spa, library, bicycles.
415 William St 33040	Visa, MC, AmEx,	Within walking distance to Duval and
800-438-6155 305-296-7274	*Rated*, •	the docks.
Jody Carlson	S-ltd/P-ltd/H-no	

This lovely 3-story Victorian is located on a quiet, tree-shaded street in the heart of Key West's "Old Town." Walk to the water and the sites and sounds that have made Key West infamous.

✉ relax@keywestbandb.com ❂ www.keywestbandb.com

The Mermaid & The	148-318 $US BB	Full breakfast
Alligator	9 rooms, 9 pb	Complimentary wine served each
729 Truman Ave 33040	Visa, MC, AmEx, •	evening, afternoon lemonade,
800-773-1894 305-294-1894	C-ltd/S-ltd/P-no/H-no	complimentary bottled water & sodas
Dean Carlson & Paul Hayes		Off-street parking, swimming pool,
		tropical gardens, free concierge
		services, beach supplies

An elegant circa 1904 Queen Anne house located in the center of Key West's Old Town, offering the warm hospitality of a traditional bed & breakfast.

✉ kwmermaid@aol.com ❂ www.kwmermaid.com

The Wicker Guesthouse	119-399 $US BB	Continental breakfast
913 Duval St 33040	21 rooms, 24 pb	Kitchen, lounge, heated pool, parking,
800-880-4275 305-296-4275	Most CC, Cash, Checks,	irons, hairdryers, concierge, fridge
Heather Whitehead, Mirka	*Rated*, •	
Miskovska	C-yes/S-ltd/P-no/H-yes	

Our peaceful hideaway lets you enjoy the tranquil island setting, and just outside our front door is Key West's main street. If it's browsing art galleries, shopping, playing water sports, or enjoying the nightlife, it is all within walking distance.

✉ info@wickerguesthouse.com ❂ www.wickerhousekw.com

Tropical Inn	158-414 $US BB	Deluxe expanded continental
812 Duval St 33040	11 rooms, 11 pb	Private, quiet, and lush tropical palm
888-611-6510 305-294-9977	Most CC, •	garden oasis with waterfall pool and
Brandi Gabay	S-ltd/P-no/H-no	hot tub

The Tropical Inn artfully blends the casual warmth of an historic Key West bed & breakfast with the quality appointments, hushed intimacy, and elegantly understated ambience of a romantic small hotel in the European tradition. Lush palm garden, pools.

✉ info@tropicalinn.com ❂ www.tropicalinn.com

The Mermaid & The Alligator, Key West, FL

LAKE WALES

Chalet Suzanne Inn
3800 Chalet Suzanne
Dr 33859
800-433-6011 863-676-6011
Hinshaw Family

129-189 $US BB
26 rooms, 26 pb
Most CC, Cash, Checks,
Rated, •
C-yes/S-no/P-no/H-ltd

Full Country Breakfast Tues-Sun
Lunch 11–2:30, Tues-Fri, 11–3 Sat-Sun;
Dinner 5–8, Fri-Sat, private dining
available on other night
Complimentary sherry in room, fresh
fruit & flowers, pool, airstrip, spa
services available

On National Register of Historic Places, a 26-room oasis for celebrants, travelers and discriminating diners. Each delightfully different guestroom only steps from our sparkling pool, museum, ceramic salon, airstrip, soup cannery and restaurant.

✉ info@chaletsuzanne.com 🌐 www.chaletsuzanne.com

LAKE WORTH

Sabal Palm House
109 N Golfview Rd 33460
888-722-2572 561-582-1090
Colleen & John Rinaldi

99-249 $US BB
7 rooms, 7 pb
Visa, MC, *Rated*
C-ltd/S-no/P-yes/H-no

Full breakfast
Tea & homemade sweets at 3:00 p.m.
Luxury linens, elegant toiletries, spa
robes, nightly turn-down service

The Sabal Palm House Bed and Breakfast in Palm Beach County is honored to be recognized by AAA for our commitment to provide you with the highest hospitality and service. Accommodations include complimentary: gourmet breakfast, afternoon tea and homemade

✉ sabalpalmhouse@aol.com 🌐 www.sabalpalmhouse.com

The Mango Inn
128 N Lakeside Dr 33460
888-626-4619 561-533-6900
Bill, Debbie Null, Judi Flyn

120-275 $US BB
10 rooms, 10 pb
Most CC, *Rated*, •
C-ltd/S-ltd/P-no/H-no

Continental/Full breakfast
Complimentary beverages & sweets
Heated swimming pool, fireplace,
cable TV, VCR, phone with data port,
hairdryer, iron, robes

Located in a quiet & secluded setting surrounded by lush tropical gardens. A heated pool provides an area for quiet relaxation and refreshment. Our charming coastal hamlet is a stone's throw from golfing, scuba diving, snorkeling, fishing, and much more.

✉ info@mangoinn.com 🌐 www.mangoinn.com

LONGBOAT KEY

The Sandpiper Inn
5451 Gulf of Mexico
Dr 34228
941-383-2552
Mary Lou & Richard

99-189 $US EP
11 rooms, 11 pb
Most CC, Cash
C-yes/S-no/P-ltd/H-ltd

Optional breakfast plan available for
Blue Dolphin Cafe across the street
Cable TV, DVD, full bath, private patio,
BBQ, private beach, small heated
pool, beach chairs

One of the most secluded tropical beach settings on Longboat Key. Our spacious studios, one and two bedroom accommodations, come fully equipped with everything to make your stay on Longboat Key exactly what you are looking for in a vacation.

✉ innkeeper@sandpiperinn.com 🌐 www.sandpiperinn.com/FL

LOXAHATCHEE

Southern Palm B&B
15130 Southern Palm
Way 33470
561-790-1413
Cheri Reed

169-259 $US BB
9 rooms, 9 pb
Visa, MC, AmEx,
Rated, •
C-ltd/S-no/P-no/H-yes

Continental plus breakfast
Library, basketball court, unique
collection of animals, wireless
Internet.

Tropical paradise with wildlife nestled on 20 acre wooded estate. Close to Palm Beach Polo Equestrian Club, the equestrian showgrounds, Amphitheater, golf and Lion Country Safari.

✉ creed8559@aol.com 🌐 www.southernpalmbandb.com

MADEIRA BEACH

Snug Harbor Inn
Waterfront B&B
13655 Gulf Blvd 33708
866-395-9256 727-395-9256
T.J. & Susan Gill

80-140 $US BB
8 rooms, 8 pb
Most CC, Cash,
Rated, •
C-yes/S-no/P-yes/H-ltd

Continental plus breakfast
Heated pool, boat docks, WiFi, tiki
hut, full kitchen, cable TV/DVD, pets,
trolley stop, laundry, newspaper.

Snug Harbor Inn is a small, intimate, relaxed waterfront inn located in Madeira Beach, Florida. Sunrise over the bay, Sunset over the Gulf, Snug Harbor Inn is a place to enjoy what you've dreamed your Florida vacation would be. ✉ sharbor@tampabay.rr.com 🌐 snugharborflorida.com

MELBOURNE

Crane Creek Inn
Waterfront B&B
907 E Melbourne Ave 32901
321-768-6416
Andy & Bambi Durik

129-199 $US BB
4 rooms, 4 pb
Most CC, Cash, *Rated*
S-ltd/P-yes/H-no

Full, cooked to order breakfast
Complimentary coffee, teas, soft
drinks, beer, wine, snacks, and water
are also available 24 hours.
Jacuzzi, Htd Pool, Suite, LCD TV,
Hammock, Hot Tub, Hair Dryers, free
WiFi , Iron Boards, Parking

Enjoy our tropical paradise directly on the water. Built in 1925 with hardwood floors and true Florida architecture. Walk to downtown and fabulous restaurants and shops. Fish from our dock, relax in our heated pool or hot tub. WiFi included. ✉ info@cranecreekinn.com 🌐 www.cranecreekinn.com

The Old Pineapple Inn
1736 Pineapple Ave 32935
888-776-9864 321-254-1347
Robert & Celeste Henry

125-175 $US BB
4 rooms, 4 pb
Most CC
C-ltd/S-no/P-no/H-ltd

Full breakfast
Beverage fridge, snacks
Porch, parlor, fireplace, antiques,
wireless Internet, television

Nestled under live oak trees dripping with Spanish moss, The Old Pineapple Inn B&B is housed in the William H. Gleason House, listed on the National Register of Historic Places. Charm, comfort and companion-ability await you . . .

✉ innkeepers@oldpineappleinn.com 🌐 www.oldpineappleinn.com

MELBOURNE BEACH

Port d'Hiver
201 Ocean Ave 32951
866-621-7678 321-722-2727
Linda & Mike Rydson

200-525 $US BB
11 rooms, 11 pb
Most CC, *Rated*
C-ltd/S-no/P-no/H-yes

Full breakfast
At 5:00 complimentary wine and light
hors d'oeuvres are served in the main
house
Complimentary room service,
concierge, flat screen TV, DVD, WiFi,
spa pool, spa tubs, laptop, bikes

Welcome to Port d'Hiver (say port-DEE-vair), a luxury seaside B & B, located 200 feet from the Atlantic Ocean in Melbourne Beach, Florida. Our historic inn consists of 4 Key West-style buildings, connected by winding brick paths. ✉ info@portdhiver.com 🌐 portdhiver.com

MIAMI ——————————————————————————————————

Miami River Inn
118 SW South River Dr 33130
800-HOTEL89 305-325-0045
Jane Caporelli

79-299 $US BB
38 rooms, 38 pb
Visa, AmEx, Disc,
Rated, •
C-yes/S-ltd/P-ltd/H-no

Continental breakfast
Complimentary wine in the evenings
Cable TV, central air/heat, ceiling
fan, private bath, lush gardens, pool,
friendly service

Fresh squeezed paradise! Looking for something completely different? You'll find it at this restored turn-of-the-century hotel on the Miami River. About a 10 minute drive to the Art Deco District.

✉ info@miamiriverinn.com ✪ www.miamiriverinn.com

MOUNT DORA ————————————————————————————

Magnolia Inn
347 E Third Ave 32757
800-776-2112 352-735-3800
Connie & Lori

159-260 $US BB
5 rooms, 5 pb
Visa, MC, *Rated*, •
S-ltd/P-no/H-ltd
Jan – Dec

Full breakfast
spring water, afternoon snacks and
some homemade sweets.
Gazebo with games, TV, stereo, patio,
hammock, swing, WiFi

A circa 1926 Mediterranean Estate. Six comfortable rooms with king/queen beds, TV/CD, private baths, central A/C, full gourmet breakfast. Park and walk to town, enjoy peace and tranquility at the Magnolia Inn and its one acre of tropical gardens. ✉ info@magnoliainn.net ✪ www.Magnoliainn.net

NEW SMYRNA BEACH ————————————————————————

**Night Swan Intracoastal
B&B**
512 S Riverside Dr 32168
800-465-4261 386-423-4940
Chuck & Martha
Nighswonger

110-200 $US BB
15 rooms, 15 pb
Most CC, Cash, Checks,
Rated, •
C-yes/S-no/P-yes/H-yes

Full breakfast
Complimentary Frozen Yogurt and Ice
Cream Espresso & Desserts for Sale
Sitting Room, 4 suites, playground
nearby, 160 foot, 2-story dock on the
Intracoastal Waterway

Free Night w/Certificate: Valid Sunday through Thursday. Room Upgrade.

Located in the Historic District on the Intracoastal Waterway, between Daytona Beach and Kennedy Space Center; just one mile from the beach. Spacious 3-story home; full breakfast.
✉ info@NightSwan.com ✪ www.NightSwan.com

OCALA —————————————————————————————————

Heritage Country Inn
14343 W Hwy 40 34481
888-240-2233 352-489-0023
Christa & Gerhard Gross

69-199 $US BB
7 rooms, 7 pb
Most CC, Cash,
Rated, •
C-yes/S-ltd/P-no/H-yes
German

Full breakfast
Candle light Steak Dinner cooked on a
Stone, Classic or Shrimp Fondue
Dining room, courtyard, gazebo, gas
grill, sitting area, Jacuzzi tubs, satellite
TV, fireplaces, DVD

Located in Ocala, the heart of central Florida's horse country, this delightful B&B is your own private hideaway. Relax in the comfort and charm of one of our seven casually elegant rooms, and enjoy the warmth and convenience of the Heritage Country Inn.
✉ info@heritagecountryinn.com ✪ www.heritagecountryinn.com

ORANGE PARK ————————————————————————————

Club Continental Suites
2143 Astor St 32073
800-877-6070 904-264-6070
Karrie Massee

95-200 $US BB
22 rooms, 22 pb
Most CC, *Rated*, •
C-yes/S-no/P-ltd/H-yes

Continental plus breakfast
Lunch & dinner (Tues – Fri)
Sunday Brunch, bar, restaurant, 7
tennis courts, 3 pools

This romantic, intimate resort nestled on the banks of St Johns River features a Mediterranean style mansion surrounded by Live Oaks draped in Spanish moss, manicured gardens and gurgling fountains. Old World Florida still exists at the Club Continental.
✉ ccsinfo@att.net ✪ www.clubcontinental.com

ORLANDO ————————————————————————————————

The Eō Inn
227 N Eola Dr 32801
888-481-8485 407-481-8485
Rebekah Gimenez & Lesley
Morrison

99-179 $US EP
17 rooms, 17 pb
Most CC, Cash
S-no/P-no/H-ltd

Anyone who enjoys privacy in a relaxed chic atmosphere will appreciate this inn. The Eō Inn & Spa gives every guest a sense of exclusivity and uniqueness that can only be found in a smaller privately owned establishment. ✉ info@eoinn.com ✪ www.eoinn.com

PENSACOLA

Springhill Guesthouse
903 N Spring St 32501
800-475-1956 850-438-6887
Tara Smith

115 $US BB
3 rooms, 3 pb
Visa, MC, Disc,
Rated, •
C-yes/S-no/P-no/H-no

Continental breakfast
Internet connection in each suite,
cable TV/VCR, laundry facilities,
books, games & videos

Free Night w/Certificate: Anytime.

Charming and comfortable, this Queen Anne style home in Historic North Hill is the place to come home to. Conveniently located near downtown Pensacola and 10 minutes to the beaches.

✉ springhillguest@att.net 🌐 www.springhillguesthouse.com

SARASOTA

The Cypress – A B&B Inn
621 Gulfstream Ave. S 34236
941-955-4683
Vicki, Nina, & Robert

150-289 $US BB
5 rooms, 5 pb
Most CC
S-no/P-no/H-no

Full breakfast
Evening hors d'oeuvres & inspired
refreshments served at sunset on
Sarasota Bay
Wireless Internet connection,
concierge services, walking distance
to downtown & marina

Situated on historic grounds overlooking Sarasota Bay, The Cypress offers a unique lodging experience. This tropical oasis reflects the tone and demeanor of a bygone era, attracting the distant traveler, as well as those seeking a romantic getaway.

✉ thecypress@comcast.net 🌐 www.cypressbb.com

SIESTA KEY

Turtle Beach Resort
9049 Midnight Pass Rd 34242
941-349-4554
Gail & David Rubinfeld

175-430 $US EP
20 rooms, 20 pb
Most CC, Cash
C-yes/S-no/P-yes/H-ltd

Discounted package at Ophelia's
Restaurant
Hot tubs in each room, kayaks, bikes,
boats, fishing poles, etc., high speed
wireless Internet

In 1991, we found a bay front property with cottages dating from the 1940s and transformed it into an island paradise. With our private cottages, private hot tubs, and gourmet waterfront dining next door, you'll have a vacation to remember forever!

✉ info@turtlebeachresort.com 🌐 www.turtlebeachresort.com

ST. AUGUSTINE

63 Orange St B&B
63 Orange St 32084
800-605-2063 904-824-6621
Jackie Kent

130-230 $US BB
5 rooms, 5 pb
Visa, MC, AmEx
C-yes/S-no/P-no/H-no

Full breakfast
Afternoon refreshments on weekends,
The Cookie Jar is always full
We are always happy to assist guests
with information about St. Augustine

Set among grand trees, in a quiet residential neighborhood, this grand 1884 home invites you to enjoy a comfortable combination of charming, elegant Victorian antiques & 21st century amenities.

✉ jackie@63orangestreet.com 🌐 www.63orangestreet.com

Alexander Homestead B&B
14 Sevilla St 32084
888-292-4147 904-826-4147
Bonnie Alexander

169-239 $US BB
6 rooms, 6 pb
Most CC, *Rated*, •
C-ltd/S-ltd/P-no/H-no

Full breakfast
After dinner cordials and
complimentary sodas, beer & wine
available
Sitting room, Jacuzzis, fireplaces, cable
TV, luxury linens, bath amenities, etc.

1888 Victorian home restored to exquisite perfection. Five oversized Victorian bedchambers recreate the era when the passionate and the proper, the sensual and the sentimental, the secret and the sensational, combined beautifully in everyday living.

✉ bonnie@alexanderhomestead.com 🌐 www.alexanderhomestead.com

ST. AUGUSTINE

At Journey's End
89 Cedar St 32084
888-806-2351 904-829-0076
Tim Millbern & John
Gallagher

129-229 $US BB
5 rooms, 5 pb
Most CC, •
C-yes/S-ltd/P-ltd/H-ltd

Full breakfast
Complimentary afternoon snacks and
beverages 24/7 including beer, wine
and soda.
Paddle fans, wireless Internet,
porches, side garden, common area,
dining room, many extras offered.

*Not your typical Victorian themed B&B. Journey to exotic destinations in rooms called Safari, Egypt,
China, Key West . . . Built in 1890, the Inn was "reincarnated" in 1996, but still has its original bones:
hardwood floors, porches and more.* ✉ contact@atjourneysend.com ♦ www.atjourneysend.com

---

Bayfront Westcott House
146 Avenida
Menendez 32084
800-513-9814 904-825-4602
Joy & Andrew Warren

119-299 $US BB
15 rooms, 15 pb
Visa, MC, Disc,
Rated, •
C-ltd/S-ltd/P-ltd/H-yes
French

Full breakfast
Complimentary beer & wine happy
hour and evening dessert
Sitting room, games, library, bicycles
available from nearby rental shop

*Bayfront Westcott House is an elegant, romantic, historic district inn w/in walking distance of at-
tractions. Relax on porch w/ views of sailboats, dolphins, & lighthouse. Weddings, reunions, girls
getaways, business retreat. Voted #1 B&B in St. Augustine.*
✉ OnTheBay@WestcottHouse.com ♦ www.westcotthouse.com

Beachfront B&B
One F St 32080
800-370-6036 904-461-8727
Lauren & Rich O'Brien

129-289 $US BB
8 rooms, 8 pb
Most CC, *Rated*, •
S-no/P-no/H-no

Full breakfast
Cookies, coffee & teas
Heated pool, outdoor Jacuzzi in
gazebo, bicycles, robes, beach towels,
beach furniture

*Oceanfront on beautiful St. Augustine Beach and a convenient 10 minutes to the Historic area. En-
joy spectacular sunrises and stunning ocean views. Our guestrooms and suites, each unique, feature
ocean views, dune views or garden views.*
✉ info@beachfrontbandb.com ♦ www.beachfrontbandb.com

Casablanca Inn on the Bay
24 Avenida Menendez 32084
800-826-2626 904-829-0928
Nancy Cloud

89-349 $US BB
30 rooms, 30 pb
Most CC, Cash, Checks
C-ltd/S-ltd/P-ltd/H-ltd

Full Two-Course Breakfast
A complimentary glass of house wine
or beer at our Tini Martini Bar
Antiques, TV/DVD, Jacuzzi tubs,
wireless Internet access, private sitting
areas, sleep number beds

*Thirty luxury suites and rooms in a bayfront location in historic St. Augustine, panoramic Matanzas
Bay views, whirlpools, private porches and sundecks, antique furnishings, decorative fireplaces, private entries, and peaceful luxury.*
✉ innkeeper@casablancainn.com ♦ www.casablancainn.com

Castle Garden
15 Shenandoah St 32084
904-829-3839
Bruce & Brian Kloeckner

89-229 $US BB
7 rooms, 7 pb
Most CC, Cash,
Rated, •
C-ltd/S-no/P-ltd/H-no

Full breakfast
Complimentary bottle of wine or
champagne, whirlpool rooms, picnic
lunches
Bicycles, fresh flowers, 3 bridal rooms
with whirlpools

*St. Augustine's only Moorish Revival dwelling. Former Castle Warden Carriage House built in the
1800's. Restored gardens.* ✉ info@castlegarden.com ♦ www.castlegarden.com

---

Centennial House
26 Cordova St 32084
800-611-2880 904-810-2218
Lou & Beverlee Stines

137-247 $US BB
8 rooms, 8 pb
Visa, MC, *Rated*, •
C-ltd/S-ltd/P-no/H-yes
Summer and Winter

Full Elegant Breakfast
Early morning coffee/tea.
Over-sized whirlpools, fireplaces in
larger rooms, luxury baths.

*Luxury in the Historic District. Featuring private, spacious baths, over-sized whirlpools, gas fireplaces,
cable TV/VCR, sound insulation, and individual room climate control. On the horse-drawn carriage
route.*
✉ innkeeper@centennialhouse.com ♦ www.centennialhouse.com

ST. AUGUSTINE

House of Sea and Sun B&B
2 B St 32080
904-461-1716
Patty Steder

169-229 $US BB
6 rooms, 6 pb
Visa, MC, Disc, *Rated*
C-yes/S-ltd/P-yes/H-ltd

Full breakfast
Social Hour
Beach equipment, private porches,
patios, works of art, beautiful decor,
wedding services, romance

Our goal at the House of Sea and Sun Oceanfront Bed and Breakfast on St. Augustine Beach is to make your stay as wonderful as possible. You may arrive as a stranger, but you'll leave as a friend.

 info@houseofseaandsun.com   🌐 www.houseofseaandsun.com

---

Our House of St. Augustine
7 Cincinnati Ave 32084
904-347-6260
Dave Brezing

159-220 $US BB
5 rooms, 5 pb
Most CC, Cash
C-ltd/S-no/P-no/H-ltd
Some French
Oct. 1 to May 31

Full breakfast
Complimentary bottled spring water is
always available
Free on-site parking and wireless
Internet access, private baths &
verandas, courtyard, kitchenettes

Make Our House your house for a weekend getaway, romantic retreat or cozy stay in the nation's oldest city. Three guestrooms have private baths, verandas and full breakfast in the dining room. Two Studios include in-room full breakfast & kitchenettes.

 ourhouse@ourhouseofstaugustine.com   🌐 www.ourhouseofstaugustine.com

---

Southern Wind Inn
18 Cordova St 32084
800-781-3338 904-825-3623
Scott & Donna Forbes

99-239 $US BB
10 rooms, 10 pb
Most CC, *Rated*, •
C-ltd/S-no/P-no/H-no

Full breakfast
Afternoon dessert, complimentary
wine, iced tea
Spacious verandas, large parlor,
wraparound porch, cable TV, WiFi,
A/C, rooms w/ whirlpool, bicycles

On the Carriage Trail through the historic district of St. Augustine, the Southern Wind Inn is an elegantly-columned 1916 masonry home offering exceptional B&B hospitality and a full breakfast each morning.    innkeeper@southernwindinn.com   🌐 www.southernwindinn.com

---

St. Francis Inn
279 St George St 32084
800-824-6062 904-824-6068
Joe & Margaret Finnegan

129-349 $US BB
17 rooms, 17 pb
Most CC, Cash, Checks,
Rated, •
C-ltd/S-ltd/P-ltd/H-no
American Sign
Language

Full Southern Breakfast
Iced tea, homemade cookies, coffee,
social hour with complimentary wine
& beer, evening desserts
Free on-site parking, swimming pool,
bicycles, WiFi, DVD library, beach
parking and amenities

Antique filled rooms & suites, balconies, fireplaces, kitchenettes, whirlpool tubs, swimming pool, walk to everything, private courtyard & parking. Built in 1791 and located in the Historic District, the inn is rich in old world charm and modern comforts.

 innkeeper@stfrancisinn.com   🌐 www.stfrancisinn.com

---

The Kenwood Inn
38 Marine St 32084
800-824-8151 904-824-2116
Pat & Ted Dobosz

139-259 $US BB
13 rooms, 13 pb
Visa, MC, Disc, *Rated*
C-ltd/S-no/P-no/H-no

Full breakfast
Daily wine hour from 5pm-7pm,
complimentary coffee, tea, lemonade,
iced tea and cookies all day
Several sitting rooms, swimming pool,
walled-in courtyard, bicycles, wireless
Internet, free parking

The Kenwood Inn is a traditional, old fashioned bed and breakfast inn located in the heart of the historic district near the waterfront. Many amenities including a swimming pool and secluded courtyard. Daily wine hour. Beverages and cookies.

 contactus@thekenwoodinn.com   🌐 www.thekenwoodinn.com

---

Victorian House B&B
11 Cadiz St 32084
877-703-0432 904-824-5214
Marc & Jackie Rude

99-199 $US BB
10 rooms, 10 pb
Most CC, Cash,
Rated, •
C-ltd/S-no/P-no/H-no

Full breakfast
Wine, cordials, complimentary soda,
tea, cookies & candies
WiFi, Jacuzzi tubs, suites, cable TV,
hairdryers, ceiling fans, sitting room

Originally built in 1895 and meticulously restored in 1983, Victorian House warmly welcomes guests with its charming stencil decor and tasteful antiques. There are 10 guestrooms in all each lovingly trimmed with unique touches and comforting heirlooms.

 victorianhouse@bellsouth.net   🌐 www.victorianhousebnb.com

ST. PETE BEACH

Inn on the Beach
1401 Gulf Way 33706
727-360-8844
Sheila McChesney

105-395 $US BB
17 rooms, 17 pb
Most CC, Cash
C-ltd/S-ltd/P-no/H-ltd

Continental, weekends only
Coffee service daily
Full climate control, fully equipped
kitchens, expanded cable TV, WiFi,
free parking on site

You'll be right at home in our small, casually elegant Inn with twelve select rooms and 5 cottages designed for your comfort and enjoyment. Feel your cares slipping away with the simple pleasures our beachfront location offers.

info@innonbeach.com www.innonbeach.com

ST. PETERSBURG

Beach Drive Inn B&B
532 Beach Dr NE 33701
727-822-2244
Roland Martino

149-275 $US BB
6 rooms, 6 pb
Most CC, Cash, •
C-ltd/S-ltd/P-ltd/H-no
Hebrew

Full breakfast
Wine & cheese welcome nights, guest
pantry and vending area
Mini-fridges, robes, rooftop sun deck
& garden, guest terrace, free WiFi, and
bicycles

Free Night w/Certificate: Valid June-September 2011. Room Upgrade.

The "stay dreams are made of." Elegant B&B close to everything in downtown St. Petersburg. Our beautifully appointed rooms will take you away to a time when life seemed so much easier and most definitely more comfortable.

info@beachdriveinn.com www.beachdriveinn.com

Inn at the Bay B&B
126 4th Ave NE 33701
888-873-2122 727-822-1700
Dennis & Jewly Youschak

155-290 $US BB
11 rooms, 11 pb
Most CC, Cash,
Rated, •
C-ltd/S-no/P-no/H-yes

Full breakfast
Featherbeds, double whirlpool tubs,
phones & high speed Internet in
rooms

B&B restored in 2001, king and queen allergy-free featherbeds, private baths, double whirlpool tubs, in-room phones and high speed Internet, robes, hot full breakfast, romance, vacation and business.

info@innatthebay.com www.innatthebay.com

Larelle House B&B
237 6th Ave NE 33701
888-439-8387 727-490-3575
Larry & Ellen Nist

129-199 $US BB
4 rooms, 4 pb
Visa, MC, Disc
C-ltd/S-ltd/P-ltd/H-no

Full breakfast
Evening wine & cheese in the
parlor, complimentary soft drinks &
homemade goodies available 24/7.
Wireless Internet, nightly turndown,
garden spa, complimentary bikes,
business services, free parking

The oldest Queen Anne Victorian home on Florida's west coast. A perfect location – nestled in the serenity of the historic Old Northeast residential district – yet less than two blocks away from the always happening St. Petersburg waterfront and downtown.

info@larellehouse.com www.larellehouse.com

Mansion House B&B and Spa
105 & 115 Fifth Ave NE 33701
800-274-7520 727-821-9391
Kathy & Peter Plautz

139-250 $US BB
12 rooms, 12 pb
Visa, MC, *Rated*, •
C-ltd/S-ltd/P-no/H-ltd
Oct-May; June-Sept

Full American Breakfast
Complimentary soda, wine, or water,
cookies, muffins or seasonal treats
Pool, Jacuzzi, WiFi, libraries, gardens,
massage, robes, parking, common
rooms, weddings, meetings

12 luxury rooms with private baths and on-site spa services. Minutes from sunny beaches and the marina, top shopping and dining. Mansion House B&B is a highly rated inn for business and leisure guests. Weddings, reunions and corporate retreats.

 info@mansionhousebb.com www.mansionbandb.com

STARKE

Hampton Lake B&B
Hwy 301, 7 mi south of
Starke 32091
800-480-4522 352-468-2703
Freeman & Paula Register

99-159 $US BB
7 rooms, 7 pb
Most CC, Cash, Checks,
Rated, •
C-ltd/S-ltd/P-no/H-ltd

Full breakfast
Snacks, complimentary drinks
Sitting room, bicycles, lake, fishing,
boating, porch, fireplace

Contemporary lakefront home on a cypress lake. Fish, swim, take a leisurely stroll through the open fields or enjoy a bike ride down country lanes. Relax and watch the sun set across the lake from the back porch.

 HamptonLBB@aol.com ❸ www.hamptonlakebb.com

STUART

Inn Shepard's Park
601 SW Ocean Blvd 34994
772-781-4244
Marilyn Miller

95-200 $US BB
4 rooms, 4 pb
Most CC, Cash, Checks
C-ltd/S-ltd/P-ltd/H-no

Continental plus breakfast
Complimentary bottled waters, sodas,
& snacks
Beach gear, bicycles, kayak for
complimentary use, AC, cable TV,
concierge services available

Key West-style B&B in the heart of historic downtown Stuart. Come discover the hidden jewel of the Treasure Coast . . . Inn Shepard's Park Bed and Breakfast – where your wish is our command!

 marilyn@innshepard.com ❸ www.innshepard.com

Manatee Pocket Inn
4931 SE Anchor Ave. 34997
772-286-6060
Greg & Candy Grudovich

80-110 $US BB
5 rooms, 5 pb
Most CC
C-ltd/S-ltd/P-no/H-yes

Full breakfast
Complimentary beverages available
all day
Sun deck, patio, private bath, TV, WiFi,
refrigerator, microwave

The Manatee Pocket Inn is located in the historic fishing village of Port Salerno, Martin County, Florida. The inn offers 5 guestrooms, each uniquely decorated, and all with private baths.

 manateepocketinn@comcast.net ❸ www.manateepocketinn.com

VENICE

Banyan House B&B
519 S Harbor Dr 34285
941-484-1385
Chuck & Susan McCormick

139-179 $US BB
10 rooms, 10 pb
Visa, MC, *Rated*
C-ltd/S-no/P-no/H-no
Closed in December

Full breakfast
Sitting room, Jacuzzi, bikes, heated
pool, exercise room, pool table,
wireless Internet, gas grill

Historic Mediterranean-style home. Enormous Banyan tree shades courtyard, pool and spa. Sandy beaches nearby for sunning, swimming, fishing and shelling (prehistoric shark's teeth abound).

 relax@banyanhouse.com ❸ www.banyanhouse.com

Horse & Chaise Inn
317 Ponce de Leon 34285
877-803-3515 941-488-2702
Lois Steketee

115-169 $US BB
9 rooms, 9 pb
Visa, MC, *Rated*
C-yes/S-no/P-ltd/H-yes
Oct 1 – July 4

Full breakfast
24 hour cookies & beverages
Bicycles, beach chairs, beach towels,
fireplace, WiFi

Come feel welcome in our 1926 home, an elegant depiction of historic Venice. Enjoy your stay in the Venice of yester-year.

 innkeeper@horseandchaiseinn.com ❸ www.horseandchaiseinn.com

WEIRSDALE

Shamrock Thistle & Crown
12971 SE County Rd 42 32195
800-425-2763 352-821-1887
Brantley & Anne Overcash

95-220 $US BB
7 rooms, 7 pb
Most CC, Cash, Checks,
Rated, •
C-yes/S-ltd/P-no/H-ltd

Full breakfast
Complimentary Klondike Bars,
cookies, sodas, juice, coffee, tea, hot
chocolate, apple cider
Whirlpool spas, fireplaces, heated
pool, porches, cable TV, wireless
Internet, coffee makers

Where romance comes alive. Located in the rolling countryside 20 miles south of Ocala, the original structure, dating to 1887, is a historic landmark. Relax on one of the covered porches or enjoy a spectacular view from this hilltop setting.

 shamrockbb@comcast.net ❸ www.shamrockbb.com

WEST PALM BEACH

Casa Grandview Luxury Inn, Cottages & Suites 1410 George Ave 33401 877-435-2786 561-655-8932 Cheryl Grantham	150-400 $US BB 17 rooms, 17 pb Most CC, • C-yes/S-no/P-ltd/H-no Spanish	Continental breakfast Coffee/Tea Service 6am-6pm; Snacks; full listing of nearby restaurants on website 2 custom pools, Jacuzzi, complimentary daily bicycles, DVD movies, WiFi , LCD HDTV, satellite

Free Night w/Certificate: Room Upgrade.

1925 Mediterranean Revival Casa Grandview Historic Bed & Breakfast Inn, Private Luxury Vacation Resort Cottages, & 1948 Art Deco Cabana Suites offering the Urban Boutique Collection located in Grandview Heights Historic District.

✉ inquiries@casagrandview.com   ◐ www.casagrandview.com

Grandview Gardens B&B 1608 Lake Ave 33401 561-833-9023 Peter Emmerich & Rick Rose	119-199 $US BB 5 rooms, 5 pb Most CC, Cash, Checks, • C-yes/S-ltd/P-ltd/H-yes German, Spanish and French Winter/Spring	European Continental Buffet Innkeepers reception, small snacks and drinks Heated pool, sunbathing terrace, tropical garden, multi-lingual library, bicycles

Luxury B&B located in the historic neighborhood of downtown West Palm Beach, walking distance to City Place, the Palm Beach County Convention Center and the Kravis Performing Arts Center.

✉ grandviewinfo@grandview-gardens.com   ◐ www.grandview-gardens.com

Palm Beach Hibiscus 213 S Rosemary Ave 33401 866-833-8171 561-833-8171 Randy Wills	140-280 $US BB 8 rooms, 8 pb Most CC, Cash C-yes/S-no/P-yes/H-yes	Full breakfast Walking distance to restaurants & night life TV/VCR, phone, high-speed Internet access, porch

Palm Beach Hibiscus is located in the very heart of downtown West Palm beach just 1 block from City Place and its fabulous shops, restaurants & plazas. Our bed & breakfast guestrooms are individually furnished to provide an intimate, relaxed setting.

✉ info@palmbeachhibiscus.com   ◐ www.hibiscushousedowntown.com

Georgia

AMERICUS

Americus Garden Inn	99-129 $US BB	Full 3-course breakfast
504 Rees Pk 31709	8 rooms, 8 pb	Fruit, sodas, tea, coffee, bottled water,
888-758-4749 229-931-0122	Most CC	snacks
Mr. & Mrs. Kim & Susan	C-ltd/S-ltd/P-no/H-yes	Large common areas, 1.3 acre grounds
Egelseer		with gazebo, personal & attentive
		service, wireless Internet

Americus Garden Inn Bed and Breakfast is a romantic, historic pre Civil War 1847 mansion with 8 spacious guestrooms each with king or queen beds, private in-room baths and full hot breakfast near Andersonville and Jimmy Carter National Historic Sites.

✉ info@americusgardeninn.com ◐ www.americusgardeninn.com

ATLANTA

1890 King-Keith House	105-275 $US BB	Full breakfast
B&B	6 rooms, 5 pb	Snacks & beverages including
889 Edgewood Ave NE 30307	C-ltd/S-no/P-no/H-no	wine in mini-kitchen (microwave &
800-728-3879 404-688-7330		refrigerator) for all guests
Windell & Jan Keith		Four porches (one screened), 2 public
		parlors, WiFi & guest computer,
		Jacuzzi in Suite & Cottage

Free Night w/Certificate: Valid Sunday-Thursday only.

Whether your visit to Atlanta is for a Braves game, an evening at the symphony or a convention, your stay will be enriched by Atlanta's 1890 King-Keith House Bed and Breakfast where Southern Hospitality is alive and well. ✉ info@kingkeith.com ◐ www.kingkeith.com

Inman Park-Woodruff	120-150 $US BB	Customized Breakfast
Cottage B&B	3 rooms, 3 pb	Snacks, organic foods, coffee maker,
100 Waverly Way NE 30307	Visa, MC, AmEx,	breakfast features Irish Soda Bread
404-688-9498	*Rated*, •	Exercise equipment or complimentary
Eleanor Matthews	C-ltd/S-no/P-no/H-no	pass to local athletic club, free
		Internet, A/C, cable TV

The Woodruff House has 12-foot ceilings, heart-of-pine floors, 18th and 19th century antiques, a private garden and safe parking. Deluxe, well-appointed rooms and private bathrooms. Stay includes Continental breakfast (customizable for special diets).

✉ info@inmanparkbandb.com ◐ www.inmanparkbandb.com

Laurel Hill B&B	89-150 $US BB	Full breakfast
1992 McLendon Ave 30307	3 rooms, 3 pb	High speed wireless Internet,
404-377-3217	Most CC, Cash, Checks,	terrycloth robes, hairdryers, bath
Dave Hinman	*Rated*, •	products, irons & ironing boards
	C-ltd/S-ltd/P-no/H-no	
	Weekends	

Enjoy 1920's flavor – Two Tudor style homes close to Agnes Scott College, Emory University, City of Decatur, Downtown Atlanta, Georgia State University, Little 5 Points, & Virginia Highlands.

✉ laurel-hill@comcast.net ◐ www.LaurelHill.US

Stonehurst Place	159-399 $US BB	Gourmet Breakfast
923 Piedmont Ave NE 30309	5 rooms, 5 pb	Homemade and gourmet refreshments
877-285-BBINN(2246) 404-	Visa, MC, AmEx,	served around the clock from our
881-0722	*Rated*, •	drinks cabinet in the Music Room.
Barb Shadomy & Caroline	S-ltd/P-ltd/H-no	Spa tubs, Fireplaces, WiFi, iPod
Holder		docking station, flat screen TVs, eco-
		friendly amenities, parking

Atlanta's most award-winning B&B! Best Business Hotel, Best Luxury Hotel, Best Romantic Hotel, Best Amenities, Best Linens Comforters & Pillows, Most Green Conscious. Stonehurst Place features luxurious rooms, five-star service and gourmet breakfasts.

✉ info@StonehurstPlace.com ◐ www.StonehurstPlace.com

ATLANTA

Sugar Magnolia B&B
804 Edgewood Ave,
NE 30307
404-222-0226
Debi Starnes & Jim Emshoff

120-175 $US BB
4 rooms, 4 pb
Visa, MC, *Rated*, •
C-ltd/S-no/P-no/H-no

Full breakfast
Coffee, tea, soft drinks & beer
available any time
Free WiFi, sitting/meeting room,
business center, roof-top deck with
waterfall garden, Jacuzzis

Sugar Magnolia is situated in the heart of the city of Atlanta, a B&B where excellence and comfort are mingled with the Southern charm of yesteryear and the exciting beat of the South's Olympic city.

✉ sugmagbb@aol.com   🌐 www.sugarmagnoliabb.com

BRUNSWICK

Brunswick Manor
825 Egmont St 31520
912-265-6889
Stacy Bass

100-150 $US BB
4 rooms, 4 pb
Visa, MC, *Rated*, •
C-yes/S-ltd/P-yes/H-ltd

Full gourmet breakfast
afternoon refreshments, wine, fruits,
cheese and sherry in rooms, early
coffee
Sitting room, library, veranda with
antique wicker swing, terry cloth
robes, extensive local info

Brunswick Manor B&B is located in the heart of Brunswick's historic Old Town facing one of the original town squares. Elegantly appointed with all the comforts & luxuries of a premier B&B. Enjoy the wrap-around veranda, wrap-around patio & hot tub.

✉ info@brunswickmanor.com   🌐 www.brunswickmanor.com

CLARKESVILLE

Glen-Ella Springs Inn
1789 Bear Gap Rd 30523
877-456-7527 706-754-7295
Ed & Luci Kivett

150-275 $US BB
16 rooms, 16 pb
Most CC, Cash, *Rated*
C-yes/S-ltd/P-no/H-yes
Portuguese

Full country breakfast
Dinner served each evening, by
reservation, wine sold by the glass or
bottle in dining room
Weddings & receptions, meetings,
conference room, pool, gardens,
mountain creek, hiking, WiFi

Secluded and peaceful, Glen-Ella Springs B&B Inn is nestled on 17 acres at the edge of the Blue Ridge Mountains, featuring perennial gardens and distinctive lodging. Enjoy fine dining in our award winning restaurant, open nightly – reservations required.

✉ info@glenella.com   🌐 www.glenella.com

CLAYTON

Beechwood Inn
220 Beechwood Dr 30525
706-782-5485
David & Gayle Darugh

159-219 $US BB
8 rooms, 8 pb
Visa, MC, *Rated*, •
C-ltd/S-no/P-no/H-ltd

Full breakfast
Gourmet dinners & wine tastings by
reservation
Luxury linens, fireplaces, antiques,
private patios & balconies, CD players,
afternoon wine

Georgia's Premier Wine Country Inn. This romantic Inn offers the finest in historic accommodations for those visiting the Georgia Mountains. Selected as the "No. 1 Inn in North America for a Weekend Escape" by Inn Traveler Magazine.

✉ DDarugh@windstream.net   🌐 www.beechwoodinn.ws

CUMBERLAND ISLAND

Greyfield Inn
888-357-7617 904-261-6408
The Ferguson Family

395-595 $US BB
11 rooms, 10 pb
Visa, MC, Disc
C-ltd/S-no/P-no/H-ltd

Full southern-style breakfast
Cocktail Hour hors d'oeuvres, all non-
alcoholic beverages during your stay
Ferry Boat transportation, kayaks
bikes, naturalist-led excursions, fishing
& beach equipment

Turn-of-the-century mansion on pristine, tranquil Cumberland Island. Incredible beaches, marshes, wild horses and many species of birds. Victorian antiques, Tiffany lamps and Chippendale furniture. Large verandah with porch swings and rockers.

✉ seashore@greyfieldinn.com   🌐 www.greyfieldinn.com

Beechwood Inn, Clayton, GA

DAHLONEGA

Dahlonega Spa Resort
400 Blueberry Hill 30533
866-345-4900 706-865-7678
Margaret Nemec

130-175 $US EP
23 rooms, 23 pb
Visa, MC, •
C-yes/S-no/P-ltd/H-yes

Small refrigerator & coffee maker,
breakfast & dinner on request, wine &
beer also available
Spa treatments, Jacuzzi, nature trails

Dahlonega Spa Resort is a B&B and Wellness Retreat Center located on 72 acres near the historic gold-rush town of Dahlonega, in the foothills of the Blue Ridge Mountains, just over an hour north of Atlanta.

✉ guestrelations@puravidausa.com 🌐 www.dahlonegasparesort.com

---

Lily Creek Lodge
2608 Auraria Rd 30533
888-844-2694 706-864-6848
Don & Sharon Bacek

109-199 $US BB
13 rooms, 13 pb
Visa, MC, AmEx,
Rated, •
C-yes/S-ltd/P-no/H-no
Some Spanish & French

Full breakfast
Homemade cookies, wine, hot
chocolate, hot cider
2 hot tubs, pool, fireplace, kitchen,
TV/VCR/DVD, games, gazebo, library,
bocce, hammock, deck, WiFi

Romantic mountain getaway in North Georgia wine country. A fun and relaxing rustic Alpine retreat on nine acres of woods with secluded swimming pool & hot tub. Spa, winery & romance packages. Conference and meeting space for small groups. Wifi, TV, & TLC

✉ lilycreeklodge@windstream.net 🌐 www.lilycreeklodge.com

Long Mountain Lodge
144 Bull Creek Rd 30533
706-864-2337
Dianne Quigley

119-179 $US BB
6 rooms, 6 pb
Most CC, Cash, Checks
C-ltd/S-ltd/P-no/H-yes

Full breakfast
Afternoon snacks
Satellite TV, fireplaces, wireless
Internet access, bathrobes, whirlpool
tubs, writing desks

Luxury guestrooms and suites on Long Mountain. Each room with breathtaking mountain views, beautiful rustic decor and gracious hospitality. Relax in the library with a good book and enjoy gourmet breakfasts by chef and owner, Dianne Quigley.

✉ dquigley@windstream.net 🌐 www.longmountainlodge.com

Lilly Creek Lodge, Dahlonega, GA

DAHLONEGA

**Mountain Laurel Creek Inn
& Spa**
202 Talmer Grizzle Rd 30533
706-867-8134
Dennis Hoover

154-195 $US BB
6 rooms, 6 pb
Most CC, Cash, Checks
S-no/P-no/H-no

Full breakfast
Local wines & beer offered in our pub,
the Copper Penny Pub
Sitting rooms, private balcony,
spa tubs, gas fireplaces, day spa,
massages, facials, pub, WiFi

Featured in Dec. 08 issue of Southern Living Magazine as the place to stay in Dahlonega. Each room is a luxury treat, uniquely decorated with original artwork, fine linens, whirlpool tubs, fireplaces – your place for romance or a quiet mountain getaway

✉ info@mountainlaurelcreek.com 🌐 www.mountainlaurelcreek.com

DARIEN

Darien Waterfront Inn
201 Broad st 31305
912-437-1215
JoAnn Viera

95-139 $US BB
7 rooms, 7 pb
Most CC, Cash
C-ltd/S-ltd/P-ltd/H-no

Continental breakfast
Fresh local seafood. Southern iced
tea. A variety of fine wines and local
brews.
We offer seven rooms that open onto
our spacious porch with gorgeous
river views. Private baths.

We are not your ordinary inn. Sitting at the end of historic Broad Street, we are situated in a 75-year-old warehouse that boast a riverfront porch spanning our establishment from end-to-end.

✉ darienwaterfrontinn@darientel.net 🌐 darienwaterfrontinn.com

The Blue Heron Inn
1346 Blue Heron Ln SE 31305
912-437-4304
Bill & Jan Chamberlain

95-140 $US BB
4 rooms, 4 pb
Most CC, Cash, Checks
C-ltd/S-no/P-ltd/H-ltd

Full breakfast
Home baked goods are provided as
afternoon and evening snacks. Wine
and cheese served each evening.
decks, porches, Jacuzzi tubs,
kitchenette, wireless Internet access,
fireplaces, meeting areas

Located on the edge of a large marsh and tidal creek, ideal for bird watchers and nature lovers. The Blue Heron Inn is perfect for those who want to experience the full beauty and activities of this tidewater community.

✉ blueheroninn@darientel.net 🌐 www.blueheroninngacoast.com

Tell your hosts Pamela Lanier sent you.

ELLIJAY

Hearthstone Lodge
2755 Hwy 282 30705
706-695-0920
Pat & Phil Cunniffe

159-199 $US BB
3 rooms, 3 pb
Most CC, Cash
S-no/P-no/H-no

Full 3 course breakfast
Refreshments each afternoon and a
light desert after dinner
Game room with pool table, spa with
massages, steam room, 1000+ volume
library

Experience gracious hospitality while enjoying privacy, seclusion and romance. Hearthstone offers three unique and distinctively different guest suites, each with a queen bed and private bath. On-site spa services.

✉ hearthstonelodge@windstream.net 🌐 www.thehearthstonelodge.com

HAPEVILLE

Maison LaVigne
3532 South Fulton
Avenue 30354
866-634-1686 404-766-5561
Eileen Randman

120-145 $US BB
5 rooms, 5 pb
Visa, MC, AmEx
C-yes/S-no/P-yes/H-yes

Full breakfast
Demi Pension available – lunch and/
or dinner with overnight stays upon
request
Culinary lessons, WiFi, turn down
service, hot tub & dry sauna,
conference facilities, exercise room

Maison LaVigne is located in the historic neighborhood of Hapeville on a quiet one-way street. Our century-old home offers 3 deluxe accommodations and fine linens from Portugal, France & Belgium. Breakfast is prepared by a Paris-trained chef!

✉ atableoffriends@aol.com 🌐 www.maisonlavigne.com

HELEN

Alpine Hilltop Haus B&B
362 Chattahoochee
Strasse 30545
706-878-2388
Frankie Allen & Barbara
McNary

115-225 $US BB
5 rooms, 5 pb
Visa, MC, *Rated*
S-no/P-no/H-no

Full breakfast
Upon arrival, home-made desserts,
coffee, and tea are often available.
Rooms w/ wood burning fireplaces.
Romantic setting perfect for birthdays,
anniversaries, honeymoons.

Tree-covered, secluded, hilltop location. Short walk to Alpine Village center. Deck overlooking Chattahoochee River. Celebrate special occasions, i.e. anniversaries, birthdays and honeymoons.

✉ hilltop@hemc.net 🌐 www.alpinehilltop.com

**Black Forest B&B and
Cabins**
8902 N Main St 30545
706-878-3995
Art & Lou Ann Connor

135-275 $US BB
12 rooms, 12 pb
Most CC, Cash
S-no/P-no/H-ltd

Full breakfast
Gourmet coffee, homemade desserts
Waterfall weddings, gazebo, deck w/
view, patio with 20' waterfall, koi pond,
concierge services

Black Forest B&B is located on Main Street in the Bavarian village of Alpine Helen, at the foot of the Blue Ridge Mountains in North Georgia. Convenient to restaurants, shopping and activities! Luxurious, intimate accommodations for your romantic getaway!

✉ blackforestbb@aol.com 🌐 www.blackforest-bb.com

LOOKOUT MOUNTAIN

**Chanticleer Inn Bed &
Breakfast**
1300 Mockingbird Ln 30750
866-424-2684 706-820-2002
Rob & Audrey Hart

135-245 $US BB
17 rooms, 17 pb
Most CC, Cash, Checks,
Rated, •
C-ltd/S-no/P-no/H-ltd

Home-made breakfast daily
Afternoon cookies, desserts, coffee,
tea & hot chocolate, soda, bottled
water, boxed Picnic Lunches
Large common Living Room, in
ground pool, antiques, fireplaces,
whirlpool tubs, high speed Internet

10 minutes from downtown Chattanooga and a mountain top away. This Inn offers, luxurious rooms decorated in French Country. Rock City is directly across the street, Ruby Falls and the Incline Railway are within 5 minutes. Special packages and much more . . .

✉ info@stayatchanticleer.com 🌐 www.stayatchanticleer.com

LOOKOUT MOUNTAIN

Garden Walk B&B Inn	90-195 $US BB	Full breakfast
1206 Lula Lake Rd 30750	17 rooms, 17 pb	snacks, coffee, tea
800-617-0502 706-820-4127	Most CC, Cash, Checks	In-room refrigerator, coffee maker,
Erma & Ed Caballero	C-yes/S-ltd/P-yes/H-yes	air conditioning, cable TV, fireplaces,
		Jacuzzi suites

The Garden Walk Bed and Breakfast Inn is Lookout Mountain's newest and finest vacation getaway. Cottage style Bed & Breakfast; plenty of privacy and very unique. Come join us at this beautiful mountain escape.

✉ gardenwalk@gardenwalkinn.com 🌐 www.gardenwalkinn.com

MACON

1842 Inn	149-255 $US BB	Full breakfast
353 College St 31201	19 rooms, 19 pb	Hors d'oeuvres
800-336-1842 478-741-1842	Visa, MC, AmEx,	Nightly turndowns
Ed Olson	*Rated*	
	C-yes/S-no/P-ltd/H-yes	

The Inn boasts 19 luxurious rooms & public areas tastefully designed with fine English antiques, tapestries & paintings. A quaint garden courtyard greets guests for cocktails or breakfast. Nightly turndown, fresh flowers & many other amenities.

✉ management@1842inn.com 🌐 www.1842inn.com

MADISON

Brady Inn B&B	125-175 $US BB	Full breakfast
250 N 2nd St. 30650	7 rooms, 7 pb	Homemade goodies & beverages,
866-770-0773 706-342-4400	Most CC, Cash	complimentary glass of wine in the
Karen & Peter Wibell	C-ltd/S-no/P-no/H-no	evening
		Antiques, WiFi, other business
		services, Georgia Sleep Shop custom-made mattresses

The 1885 Brady Inn Victorian Bed and Breakfast on the Antebellum Trail in the historic district of Madison, Georgia, offers old-fashioned charm, modern amenities, and true Southern hospitality. Seven beautiful guestrooms, each with private bath.

✉ host@bradyinn.com 🌐 www.bradyinn.com/index.php

MARIETTA

Stanley House	90-160 $US BB	Full breakfast
236 Church St NE 30060	5 rooms, 5 pb	We host special events for up to 150,
770-426-1881	Most CC, Cash,	specializing in complete packages at
Lloyd & Cathy Kilday	Checks, •	reasonable prices
	C-ltd/S-no/P-ltd/H-no	

The Stanley House Mansion is a picture of Southern elegance, grace and grandeur of the Victorian era. Constructed in 1895 by the President Woodrow Wilson family, we are also known for our wedding and other special events.

✉ info@thestanleyhouse.com 🌐 www.thestanleyhouse.com

SAUTEE

Lucille's Mountain Top Inn	130-230 $US BB	Gourmet
964 Rabun Rd 30571	10 rooms, 10 pb	Free beverages, snacks & evening
866-245-4777 706-878-5055	Most CC, •	desserts; lunches, dinners or specialty
Lucille & George Hlavenka	C-ltd/S-no/P-no/H-yes	items with advance notice
		360 degree view of mountains &
		valleys, spa, meeting room, retreats, weddings, special events

Free Night w/Certificate: Anytime except Oktoberfest Weekends.

Lucille's Mountain Top Inn is located on a mountain top with over 5 private acres and a 360-degree view of the mountains. We are a new luxury B&B, perfect for romantic getaways and business retreats. On-site spa services available at the Mandala Spa.

✉ stay@lucillesmountaintopinn.com 🌐 www.lucillesmountaintopinn.com

SAUTEE————————————————————————————

Sylvan Valley Lodge	125-175 $US BB	Mon-Sat: Continental, Sun: Brunch
747 Duncan Bridge Rd 30571	10 rooms, 10 pb	On site restaurant
706-865-7371	Most CC, Cash	Rooms and cottages available, Water
John Boyes	C-ltd/S-ltd/P-ltd/H-no	Garden, micro vineyard, private bath

Sylvan Valley Lodge captures the romantic spirit of the Alps. From its alpine architecture to the authentic European cuisine of The Vines restaurant, the Edelweiss is reminiscent of Inns found throughout the mountainous wine regions of Europe.

✉ info@sylvanvalleylodge.com 🌐 www.sylvanvalleylodge.com

The Stovall House Country	98-113 $US BB	Continental plus breakfast
Inn and Restaurant	5 rooms, 5 pb	Restaurant available for groups of 10
1526 Hwy 255 N 30571	Visa, MC, AmEx,	or more.
706-878-3355	*Rated*	Sitting room with books, WiFi, central
Hamilton Schwartz	C-yes/S-ltd/P-no/H-ltd	heating/AC, wraparound porch with
		valley & mountain views

Free Night w/Certificate: Anytime.

Award-winning restoration of 1837 country farmhouse, on 28 serene acres with beautiful mountain views. One of the top 50 restaurants in Georgia. ✉ stovallhouse@hemc.net 🌐 www.stovallhouse.com

SAVANNAH————————————————————————————

118 West	115-200 $US BB	Continental breakfast
118 W Gaston St 31401	1 rooms, 1 pb	Fully equipped kitchen
912-234-8557	*Rated*	Fireplace, satellite TV with premium
Andrea D. Walker	C-ltd/S-no/P-ltd/H-yes	movie channels, private phone line,
		WiFi

One bedroom garden apartment with living room, fully equipped kitchen and a full size bath, located in an 1850 townhouse in Savannah's historic district.

✉ adwalker1@aol.com 🌐 www.118west.com

Amethyst Inn At Sarah's	155-255 $US BB	Full breakfast
Garden	8 rooms, 8 pb	Afternoon social hour with wine and
402 E Gaston St 31401	Visa, MC, *Rated*, •	lemonade & appetizers
912-604-0716 912-234-7716	C-yes/S-no/P-ltd/H-no	Sitting room, swimming pool, suites,
Jane & Rocky Reed		fireplace, cable TV

Beautiful 1888 Victorian home, recently restored to perfection. We are in the Historic District with 4 beautiful suites and 4 luxurious bedrooms with private baths. Beautifully decorated with all the modern conveniences.

✉ sarahsgarden900@bellsouth.net 🌐 www.amethystinnsavannah.com

Azalea Inn and Gardens	159-329 $US BB	Full Southern Gourmet Breakfast
217 E Huntingdon St 31401	11 rooms, 10 pb	Wine and appetizers nightly (except
800-582-3823 912-236-6080	Most CC, Cash, •	Sunday), and every night delight
Teresa & Mike Jacobson	C-ltd/P-ltd/H-no	home-baked dessert
		Complimentary off-street parking,
		swimming pool, WiFi, comfy robes,
		cable TV/DVD, hair dryer, iron

Lighthearted, laid-back southern leisure prevails at Azalea Inn and Gardens' mansion (ca 1889) near Forsyth Park. Off-street parking, WiFi, southern gourmet breakfast, wine & hors d'oeuvres, heritage gardens, balconies & pool. Tips to intimate Savannah.

✉ Azalea.Inn@comcast.net 🌐 www.azaleainn.com

Ballastone Inn	179-335 $US BB	Full Southern Breakfast
14 E Oglethorpe Ave 31401	16 rooms, 16 pb	Afternoon High Tea with scones,
800-822-4553 912-236-1484	Most CC, Cash,	sandwiches, cake & cookies, hot &
Jennifer Salandi	*Rated*, •	cold hors d'ouevres in the evening
	C-ltd/S-ltd/P-no/H-ltd	Gilchrist and Soames toiletries,
		elevator, video library, antique bar

The Ballastone Inn, a four-story Italianate Antebellum mansion built in 1838, combines old-fashioned elegance & charm. The only Inn in Savannah with formal high tea daily, and beer and wine service bar. ✉ inn@ballastone.com 🌐 www.ballastone.com

SAVANNAH

Catherine Ward House Inn
118 E Waldburg St 31401
800-327-4270 912-234-8564
Leslie Larson

139-249 $US BB
9 rooms, 9 pb
Most CC, Cash,
Rated, •
S-no/P-ltd/H-no

Full breakfast
Guests may bring their alcoholic
beverage of choice, we happily supply
glasses & endless ice
Free faxes, WiFi, massages, common
areas, private courtyard, balconies,
Jacuzzi tub, fireplaces, TV

The Catherine Ward House is located on a quiet street in the Victorian District of Savannah, Georgia. This wonderful 19th century inn has had its rooms, its amenities, its policies, and its personality updated.

✉ contact@catherinewardhouseinn.com 🌐 www.catherinewardhouseinn.com

---

Foley House Inn
14 W Hull St 31401
800-647-3708 912-232-6622
Allisen & Grant Rogers

199-349 $US BB
19 rooms, 19 pb
Most CC, Cash, *Rated*
C-ltd/S-ltd/P-yes/H-no

Full breakfast
Complimentary afternoon
refreshments, evening hors d'oeuvre
& wine, bedtime port or sherry
Newspaper, fireplaces, concierge
services, personal itineraries, comp
bottled water, free WiFi

Restored Antebellum mansion furnished with antiques & reproductions. Most rooms have original working fireplaces. Jacuzzis and private balconies in some rooms. Two lush and beautiful courtyards. Walking distance to all major attractions & restaurants.

✉ info@foleyinn.com 🌐 www.foleyinn.com

Green Palm Inn
548 E President St 31401
888-606-9510 912-447-8901
Diane McCray

149-229 $US BB
4 rooms, 4 pb
Most CC, Cash
C-ltd/S-no/P-no/H-no

Full gourmet breakfast
Afternoon dessert bar, plus and
wine and light hors d'oeuvres in the
afternoon
Referrals for the inn's guests to
Savannah's best places, along with
places to enjoy Savannah deals.

Green Palm Inn, a family-owned 4-bedroom B&B in Savannah's historic district, exudes a calm, homey yet smart atmosphere. Guest loyalty attest to the well-traveled innkeepers' devotion to relaxing pleasures. Recommended by Fodor's and American Airlines.

✉ greenpalminn@aol.com 🌐 www.greenpalminn.com

Hamilton-Turner Inn
330 Abercorn St 31401
888-448-8849 912-233-1833
Jim & Gay Dunlop

159-369 $US BB
17 rooms, 17 pb
Most CC, Cash, Checks,
Rated
C-ltd/S-no/P-ltd/H-yes
French

Full Gourmet Southern Breakfast
Afternoon tea & sweets, evening wine
& appetizers, after dinner port
Wireless Internet, turndown, whirlpool
suites, sitting room, fireplace, cable
TV, wheelchair lift

Combining Southern charm and luxurious accommodations with an array of amenities and a knowledgeable staff. Nestled on Lafayette Square, this stately mansion is ideally located for site-seeing, dining and shopping in the Historic District.

✉ innkeeper@hamilton-turnerinn.com 🌐 www.hamilton-turnerinn.com

---

Joan's on Jones B&B
17 W Jones St 31401
888-989-9806 912-234-3863
Joan & Gary Levy

160-185 $US BB
2 rooms, 2 pb
Rated
C-yes/S-no/P-ltd/H-ltd
French

Continental breakfast
Complimentary wine
Heavenly firm mattress bed, goose
down pillows, high count sheets, fresh
flowers

An exquisite "jewel" in the restored 1883 Victorian townhouse that has graced Jones Street, in the heart of Savannah's National Historic Landmark District, for generations.

 joansonjones@comcast.net 🌐 www.joansonjones.com

SAVANNAH

McMillan Inn
304 E Huntingdon St 31401
912-201-2128
Joe & Cindy Celento

190-250 $US BB
5 rooms, 5 pb
Visa, MC, AmEx, •
S-ltd/P-no/H-no

Full Hot Gourmet Breakfast
Home baked goodies &
complimentary snacks in parlor,
bottled water, sodas
Working gas fireplaces, TV/DVD,
phone, CD players, mini fridges

Located in the heart of the Historic District in Savannah, Georgia, the McMillan Inn is a truly wonderful place to either explore . . . or simply hide away.

✉ reservations@mcmillaninn.com   🌐 www.mcmillaninn.com

The Presidents' Quarters Inn
255 E President St 31412
800-233-1776 912-233-1600
Jane Sales, Executive Innkeeper

189-325 $US BB
16 rooms, 16 pb
Most CC, *Rated*
C-yes/S-no/P-yes/H-yes

Continental plus or full breakfast
Hot & cold beverages, evening wine &
hors d'oeuvres, southern pralines or
fresh sweet & cordials
Elevator, WiFi , hair dryer, cable TV,
wet bars, elevator, private balcony,
courtyard, and parking

Named one of the Best B&Bs & Inns in Savannah, "Luxury with a Legacy" prevails on preeminent Oglethorpe Square. The downtown historic Savannah inn features a panoramic courtyard garden, overly-spacious rooms, elevator, generous amenities and free parking

✉ info@presidentsquarters.com   🌐 www.presidentsquarters.com

The Zeigler House
121 W Jones St 31401
866-233-5307 912-233-5307
Jackie Heinz

189-249 $US BB
7 rooms, 7 pb
Most CC, Cash, Checks
C-ltd/S-no/P-no/H-ltd

Continental plus breakfast
Kitchenettes & full kitchens available
WiFi, private baths, hair dryer, cable
TV, CD & DVD player, whirlpools, iron
and ironing board

Mingle with Savannah's gentlefolk from our magnificently situated inn, near historical landmarks and on 'the most beautiful street in America'.

✉ innkeeper@zeiglerhouseinn.com   🌐 www.zeiglerhouseinn.com

SENOIA

The Veranda Historic B&B Inn
252 Seavy St 30276
866-596-3905 770-599-3905
Rick & Laura Reynolds

125-155 $US BB
9 rooms, 9 pb
Most CC, Cash, Checks
C-ltd/S-no/P-no/H-yes

Full breakfast
Tea, snacks, soft drinks; food for
special events
wedding facilities, receptions,
rehearsal dinners, TV room, library,
art gallery, gifts

Listed on the National Register for Historic Places, this historic Greek revival mansion inn was built in 1906 as the Holberg Hotel. Relax & enjoy the wraparound veranda porch with rocking chairs & porch swings or take a stroll through the grounds.

✉ reynolds2803@bellsouth.net   🌐 www.verandabandbinn.com

ST. MARYS

Emma's B&B
300 W Conyers St 31558
877-749-5974 912-882-4199
Angie & Jimmy Mock

119-189 $US BB
9 rooms, 9 pb
Most CC, •
C-ltd/S-no/P-ltd/H-no

Full breakfast
Sack lunches can be made for your
trip to Cumberland Island
Sitting room, formal living & dining
room and porches, wireless Internet,
luxury linens & towels

Emma's Bed and Breakfast, the hidden jewel of St. Marys, is a beautiful escape to tranquility and relaxation. Offering the finest in lodging, hospitality and service, it is your Cumberland Island connection.

 reservations@emmasbedandbreakfast.com   🌐 www.emmasbedandbreakfast.com

ST. MARYS

Goodbread House
209 Osborne St 31558
877-205-1453 912-882-7490
Mardja Gray

89-139 $US BB
6 rooms, 6 pb
Visa, MC, AmEx,
Rated
C-yes/S-no/P-yes/H-no

Full breakfast
Social hour with wine, sodas, coffee or
tea and homemade dessert, afternoon
tea & luncheons
Spa treatments, healing, retreats, golf,
kayaking, fishing, Ferry to the beach,
bikes

Victorian hideaway in quaint historic fishing village off I-95. Ferry to Cumberland Island National Seashore. Golf Cart Community. Healing and Spa Treatments. Personality Consultations.
info@goodbreadhouse.com www.goodbreadhouse.com

Spencer House Inn
200 Osborne St 31558
877-820-1872 912-882-1872
Mary & Mike Neff

125-235 $US BB
14 rooms, 14 pb
Most CC, Cash,
Rated, •
C-yes/S-no/P-no/H-ltd

Full Breakfast with hot entreé
Afternoon tea, sweets & baked goods;
picnic lunches for Cumberland Island.
Elevator, free WiFi, flat screen HDTV
w/DVD, business travel, concierge
assistance, library.

Gateway to Cumberland Island National Seashore. Verandahs with rockers, sunny common areas. Elevator. Quiet, coastal historic village. Walk to restaurants, shops, museums and ferry. Inspected & approved by Select Registry & other national associations.
info@spencerhouseinn.com www.spencerhouseinn.com

ST. SIMONS ISLAND

Beach B&B
907 Beachview Dr 31522
877-634-2800 912-634-2800
Joe McDonough / Melanie
Gerbel

220-350 $US BB
3 rooms, 3 pb
Most CC, Cash, Checks
C-ltd/S-no/P-no/H-no
German, Spanish

made to order
In room complimentary beverages as
well as sweet and salty snacks
porches, balconies, fireplace, wet bar,
Jacuzzi, Endless Pool , beach towels
and chairs, beach bikes

Beach B&B is a beautiful oceanfront Spanish-Mediterranean villa. Suites are furnished with exquisite decor and detail. Guests can take advantage of our endless pool and home theater, and it is within walking distance of the best restaurants.
reserve@beachbedandbreakfast.com www.beachbedandbreakfast.com

Village Inn & Pub
500 Mallory St 31522
888-635-6111 912-634-6056
Kristy Murphy

99-210 $US BB
34 rooms, 34 pb
Most CC, *Rated*, •
C-yes/S-ltd/P-ltd/H-yes

Deluxe Continental breakfast
Intimate pub
Courtyard pool, meeting space,
private balconies, iron/ironing boards,
hairdryers, weddings

Nestled under the ancient live oak trees and between the parks and the historic oceanfront Village and Lighthouse, you will find our unique Inn.
kristy@villageinnandpub.com www.villageinnandpub.com

STONE MOUNTAIN

Village Inn B&B
992 Ridge Ave 30083
800-214-8385 770-469-3459
Ashley Anderson

139-179 $US EP
6 rooms, 6 pb
Most CC, *Rated*, •
C-yes/S-ltd/P-no/H-ltd

Complimentarily soft drinks, water,
snacks and fresh baked cookies
Private bathrooms, whirlpool tubs,
coffee pot, TV w/ VCR, off street
parking, snacks

The Village Inn Bed & Breakfast is one of the oldest surviving houses in Stone Mountain Village. Furnished in 1995 with modern comforts and conveniences, we guarantee that your stay will be as relaxing and comfortable as staying at Grandma's house.
villageb@villageinnbb.com www.villageinnbb.com

THOMASVILLE

1884 Paxton House Inn
445 Remington Ave 31792
229-226-5197
Susie Sherrod

175-375 $US BB
9 rooms, 9 pb
Visa, MC, AmEx,
Rated
C-ltd/S-no/P-no/H-no

Full gourmet
Afternoon and evening refreshments
Phone/data ports, cable TV, robes,
hairdryer, iron, DVD, indoor pool,
computer center

AAA Four Diamond Award Inn with 20 years of service in beautiful historic Thomasville, Georgia. Designed for adults, visited by royalty, perfect for leisure, romance or corporate guests. 30 minutes from Tallahassee.   1884@rose.net www.1884paxtonhouseinn.com

TYBEE ISLAND

DeSoto Beach Bed and Breakfast
210 Butler Avenue 31328
877-786-4542 912-786-4542
Diane Eakins

100-360 $US BB
4 rooms, 4 pb
Most CC, Cash
C-ltd/S-no/P-no/H-no

Full breakfast
Wine & cheese daily
Ocean front pool and sun deck, recreation room, bike-beach chairs-umbrella rentals

This newly renovated Bed & Breakfast on Tybee Island is the closest to the beach! It is adjacent to The World Famous DeSoto Beach Hotel and only steps from Tybee Island's beautiful shores.
✉ diane@desotobeachhotel.com 🌐 desotobeachbandb.com

Savannah Beach Inn
21 Officers Row 31328
800-844-1398 800-844-1398
Christie Register

99-299 $US BB
6 rooms, 6 pb
Most CC, Cash
C-ltd/S-ltd/P-no/H-no

Full breakfast
Wine and cheese reception, milk and cookies in the evening.
Close to the beach, and cozy wrap-around porch

Close to Savannah within two minutes walk of the beach and the Tybee Island Lighthouse, circa 1898. Savannah Beach Inn is 50 ft to the ocean and has six luxurious king and queen rooms with private baths, wireless Internet, cable TV and DVD.
✉ innkeeper@savannahbeachinn.com 🌐 www.savannahbeachinn.com

Tybee Island Inn
24 Van Horn 31328
866-892-4667 912-786-9255
Cathy & Lloyd Kilday

129-269 $US BB
7 rooms, 7 pb
Most CC, •
C-ltd/S-no/P-no/H-no

Full breakfast
Guest refrigerator, snacks or sweets served in the afternoon
TV, king beds, large contemporary tubs/showers for 2, private porch or deck, wedding accommodations

Sleep in king and queen guestrooms inspired by peaceful dreams of the sea. Private baths with tubs for two, private decks or porch, A/C, cable TV. Tybee's number one bed and breakfast.
✉ info@tybeeislandinn.com 🌐 www.tybeeislandinn.com

WASHINGTON

Holly Court Inn
301 S Alexander Ave 30673
866-465-5928 706-678-3982
Philip & Margaret Rothman

120-185 $US BB
4 rooms, 4 pb
Most CC
C-yes/S-ltd/P-no/H-no

Full breakfast
24-hour complementary bar with soft drinks & snacks, catering, candle lit dinner, boxed lunches
Fireplaces, parlor, dining room, veranda, patio, garden, library, weddings & events

The Holly Court Inn has been decorated with period antiques, all the better to immerse yourself in the flavor of the times. All of the rooms have modern amenities and guests are treated every morning to a delicious full breakfast. ✉ info@hollycourtinn.com 🌐 www.hollycourtinn.com

---

Southern Elegance B&B
115 W Robert Toombs
Ave 30673
877-678-4775 706-678-4775
Jeanne Davis Blair

115-225 $US BB
5 rooms, 5 pb
Most CC
C-yes/S-ltd/H-yes

Country Breakfast
Complimentary champagne (Honeymoon Suite), fruit baskets, gourmet dinners (weekends only)
Private garden, cable TV, CD players, robes, fresh flowers

Experience the charm and romance of a bygone era in a beautifully restored Victorian Bed & Break-fast Inn located in historic Washington-Wilkes, Georgia.
✉ info@southernelegancebandb.com 🌐 www.southernelegancebandb.com

---

Washington Plantation
15 Lexington Ave 30673
877-405-9956 706-678-2006
Tom & Barbara Chase

150-220 $US BB
5 rooms, 5 pb
Visa, MC
C-ltd/S-ltd/P-no/H-ltd

Full breakfast
Wine & cheese in the afternoon, goodies outside your door by 7:00 am. Other meals on request.
Fireplaces, telephones, WiFi Internet, cable, robes & slippers, coffeemakers, much more

Free Night w/Certificate: Valid June 2-Sept. 1. Sunday-Thursday. Room Upgrade.

This fine old B&B inn began life in 1828 & grew into its present superb example of Greek Revival architecture. The 7 acres of grounds, planted with magnolias, oaks, dogwood, pecan, hickory, elm and crape myrtle, have served as a backdrop for history.
✉ hoperd@nu-z.net 🌐 www.washingtonplantation.com

Hawaii

BIG ISLAND, CAPTAIN COOK ─────────────────────────────

Hale Ho 'ola B&B	110-150 $US BB	Full breakfast
85-4577 Mamalahoa	3 rooms, 3 pb	Vegetarian, & special requests, light
Hwy 96704	Visa, MC, AmEx,	snacks, coffee & teas are always
877-628-9117 808-328-9117	*Rated*, •	available
Bob & Mary Dahlager	C-yes/S-no/P-no/H-ltd	Sitting room, private lanai, ocean
		views, beach towels, mats, boogie
		boards, some snorkel gear

Hale Ho Ola is located on the Big Island of Hawaii, the unspoiled tropical countryside of Old Hawaii. A two-story, plantation-style home nestled on a ½ acre of tropical gardens with panoramic ocean views. All guests suites are on the ground level.

✉ tlc@hale-hoola.com 🌐 www.hale-hoola.com

Ka 'awa Loa Plantation	125-225 $US BB	Continental plus breakfast
82-5990 Napoo poo 96704	5 rooms, 4 pb	Outdoor hot tub, outdoor lava rock
808-323-2686	Visa, MC, Disc	showers, 1,500 square-foot wrap-
Gregory Nunn & Michael	C-ltd/S-no/P-no/H-ltd	around lanai, spectacular grounds
Martinage		

A Guesthouse and start-up coffee farm in the heart of the Kona Coffee Belt. Nestled in tropical surroundings 1,200 feet directly above Kealakekua Bay, our venue offers a wonderful spot to base your Big Island adventures.

✉ info@kaawaloaplantation.com 🌐 www.kaawaloaplantation.com

Luana Inn	155-195 $US BB	Homemade high quality breakfast
82-5856 Napoopoo	5 rooms, 5 pb	Pool, hot tub, ample parking, wireless
Road 96704	Visa, MC, AmEx, •	access, workstation, common room,
877-841-8120 808-328-2612	C-ltd/S-no/P-no/H-ltd	BBQ & laundry facilities
Ken Okagi & Erin Rene		

Luana Inn offers total comfort in a gorgeous, secluded location within walking distance of Kealakekua Bay in beautiful South Kona on the Big Island of Hawaii. Join us for some of the most expansive, unobstructed ocean views anywhere on the Island.

✉ info@luanainn.com 🌐 www.luanainn.com

Rainbow Plantation B&B	89-109 $US BB	Continental plus breakfast
81-6327 B Mamalahoa	5 rooms, 5 pb	Coffee & tea available any time in
Hwy 96704	Visa, MC, •	our Jungle Kitchen. Pick your own
808-323-2393	C-yes/S-ltd/P-no/H-ltd	Macadamia nuts, all you can ea
Marianna Rainbow & Reiner	German, French	Jungle Kitchen (open Gazebo). High
Schrepfer		speed Internet and wireless access
		with your own laptop.

This private, natural, tropical island retreat is also a wildlife sanctuary for nature lovers on a coffee & macadamia nut farm above Kealakekua Bay. Private accommodations, open gazebo kitchen, BBQ, ocean views, great breakfasts. Wir sprechen Deutsch.

✉ reservations@rainbowplantation.com 🌐 www.rainbowplantation.com

BIG ISLAND, HILO ─────────────────────────────

A Hawaiian Victorian	100-125 $US BB	Full breakfast
Island Princess B&B	4 rooms, 3 pb	A convenient nook for self-serve coffee
160 Kaiwiki Rd 96720	Visa, MC, Disc	or tea at anytime of day or night
866-935-8493 808-935-8493	C-ltd/S-no/P-ltd/H-ltd	Knowledgeable staff, TV/DVD, library,
Dianne Maritt		guest computer, lovely, themed rooms

In the Aloha Spirit, Dianne Maritt welcomes you to VIP B&B and to her acre and a half of Hawaiian heaven. You will enjoy exploring all of what's wonderful on the Big Island and the area surrounding Hilo.

 a.hawaiian.vip.bnb@gmail.com 🌐 www.a-hawaiian-vip-bnb.com

BIG ISLAND, HILO

At the Beach with Friends	150-190 $US BB	Continental plus breakfast
369 Nene St 96720	3 rooms, 3 pb	Complimentary self service tea &
808-934-8040	Visa, MC, AmEx, •	coffee, snacks in the common room
Claudia Rohr & Scott	C-ltd/S-no/P-no/H-no	Beach, gardens, fish, sitting room, CD
Andrews		players, computer kiosk, WiFi, beach
		gear, maps, guide books

Big Island Bed and Breakfast in Hilo. Ocean view rooms. Beach access, swimming, snorkeling. Near to Hilo Airport, restaurants, shopping, farmer's market, waterfalls & historic Downtown Hilo. Close to Hawaii Volcano National Park, Akaka Falls, Mauna Kea

✉ beach@hilo.net 🌐 www.bed-and-breakfast-hilo-hawaii.com

Shipman House B&B	219-249 $US BB	Continental plus breakfast
131 Kaiulani St 96720	5 rooms, 5 pb	Snacks, tropical juices
808-934-8002 808-934-8002	Visa, MC, AmEx,	Historic house tour, library, grand
Barbara & Gary Andersen	*Rated*, •	piano, porch rocking chairs, free
	C-ltd/S-no/P-no/H-ltd	Internet wireless, hula lesson
	Jan. 3 – Dec. 20	

Near Volcanoes, restaurants, gardens, snorkeling. Restored Victorian mansion on Reed's Island in Historic Hilo. Hawaiian koa wood antiques. Exotic flowers and estate-grown tropical fruits. Best breakfast around. Hula classes Thurs. National Reg.   ✉ innkeeper@hilo-hawaii.com 🌐 www.hilo-hawaii.com

The Inn at Kulaniapia Falls	119 $US BB	Full breakfast
#1 Kulaniapia Dr 96721	5 rooms, 5 pb	Sitting room, fireplaces, cable TV,
866-935-6789 808-935-6789	Visa, MC, *Rated*, •	accommodate business travelers,
Len & Jane Sutton	C-yes/S-no/P-no/H-no	pond

Built specifically as a B&B with spacious and comfortable accommodations. Featuring our 120' waterfall, botanical garden area with 3 additional waterfalls, and two miles of walking trails. New Pagoda Guest House.   ✉ waterfall@hilo.net 🌐 www.waterfall.net

BIG ISLAND, HOLUALOA

Holualoa Inn	260-375 $US BB	Full breakfast
76-5932 Mamalahoa	6 rooms, 6 pb	In the afternoon, ice tea, hot tea, and
Hwy 96725	Most CC, *Rated*, •	homemade cookies, guest kitchenette
800-392-1812 808-324-1121	C-ltd/S-no/P-no/H-no	OV Pool, lanai, wireless, labyrinth,
Cassandra Hazen		gazebos, kitchenette, laundry, 30 acres
		of tropical gardens

Stunning Pacific Ocean Views, 30 lush acres of well-tended tropical fruit and flower gardens, 4,300 Kona Coffee trees, custom-tiled mosaic pool, exquisite guestrooms, exceptional service, rooftop, pool and garden gazebos and an abundance of Aloha Spirit.

✉ marketing@holualoainn.com 🌐 www.holualoainn.com

BIG ISLAND, HONAUNAU

Aaahhh … Paradise B&B	95-210 $US BB	Continental breakfast
83-5662 Old Government	3 rooms, 3 pb	Coffee maker with organic 100% Kona
Rd 96725	Visa, MC	coffee in each room
866-567-4375 808-938-3743	C-yes/S-ltd/P-no/H-no	High-speed wireless Internet, local
Miles H. Mulcahy		calls, snorkel equipment/boogie
		boards, bbq for guest use

Located on the Kona Coast of Hawaii's Big Island overlooking Honaunau and Kealakekua Bay. Just minutes away from beaches, restaurants and shopping areas.

✉ miles@aloha.net 🌐 www.ahparadise.com

Dragonfly Ranch: Healing	100-300 $US BB	Healthy alternatives
Arts Center	5 rooms, 5 pb	Organic Kona coffee, teas, high protein
84-5146 Keala O Keawe 96726	Visa, MC, AmEx, •	grains, organic fruit/nuts/seeds,
808-328-2159 808-328-9570	C-yes/S-ltd/P-yes/H-no	sprouted breads
Barbara Moore		Infrared sauna, labyrinth, soft laser,
		lomilomi massage, guided ocean tours
		(friendly wild dolphins)

Kona, Hawaii eco-tourism. Upscale tree house spa hosts romantic honeymoons, B&B families, workshops. Dolphins, snorkeling/diving, labyrinth, birding, yoga studio, lomilomi massage. New 2 bedroom private mini-spa with wheelchair access. Pets. Children.

✉ info@dragonflyranch.com 🌐 www.dragonflyranch.com

BIG ISLAND, HONOKAA ──────────────────────────────────

Waianuhea B&B
45-3503 Kahana Dr 96727
888-775-2577 808-775-1118
Carol Salisbury & Randy
Goff

210-400 $US BB
5 rooms, 5 pb
Most CC, *Rated*, •
C-yes/S-ltd/P-no/H-yes

Full gourmet breakfast
Evening wine hour and appetizers.
Three and Four Course Menu Options
Available for Dinner Service.
Daily maid service, nightly turndowns,
Island Herbal bath products, massage
services, LCD TVs

Getaway to The Big Island of Hawaii, the isle of adventure! Enjoy a peaceful retreat in the tropical paradise that is Waianuhea Bed & Breakfast, located on the lush Hamakua Coast.

✉ info@waianuhea.com 🌏 www.waianuhea.com

BIG ISLAND, KAILUA KONA ──────────────────────────────

Hale Maluhia Country Inn
76-770 Hualalai Rd 96740
800-559-6627 808-329-1123
Ken & Sue Smith cell: 896-
8937

80-120 $US BB
7 rooms, 7 pb
Visa, MC, *Rated*, •
C-yes/S-ltd/P-no/H-yes
Summer

Breakfast W/ Omelet bar & bird watc
Island fresh fruits, fresh bread, omelet
Bar, pastries, cereals, juice, teas &
100% Kona coffee
Japanese spa w/massage jets, tropical
gardens, BBQ area, beach accessories,
library, swimfins, masks

A touch of aloha from old Hawai'i in this secluded, up-country, tropical Eden in the world's best climate. Featuring 2 cottages and 5 bedrooms including private baths, spa with massage jets, Koi ponds, stream, waterfalls, video library.

✉ aloha@hawaii-inns.com 🌏 www.hawaii-bnb.com

Honu Kai B&B
74-1529 Hao Kuni St. 96740
808-329-8676
Wendi & David Wasson

150-195 $US BB
4 rooms, 4 pb
Visa, MC, •
C-ltd/S-no/P-no/H-ltd

Continental plus breakfast
cater to dietary needs and
preferences.
Jacuzzi tub, concierge services,
prearrange tours, massage at the
house.

E komo mai! Welcome! Hawaiian plantation style home with a Zen feel and luxurious amenities. Serene, peaceful, on 1.4 acres of tropical and old growth greenery. Perfect for small conferences, weddings or weekend getaways. Specializing in the Aloha spirit!

✉ wendi@honukaibnb.com 🌏 www.honukaibnb.com

BIG ISLAND, KAMUELA ──────────────────────────────────

Waimea Gardens
808-885-8550
Barbara & Charlie

150-180 $US BB
3 rooms, 3 pb
C-yes/S-no/P-no/H-ltd

Self-serve continental breakfast
Stocked kitchen/kitchenette
Stocked kitchen/kitchenette,
housekeeping, bath essentials,
hardwood floors, private garden

Discover the favored destination of a growing number of savvy travelers – the Big Island of Hawaii and the beautiful upcountry town of Waimea, nestled in the foothills of the Kohala mountains.

✉ contact@waimeagardens.com 🌏 www.waimeagardens.com

BIG ISLAND, KAPOHO ───────────────────────────────────

**Hale O Naia (House of the
Dolphin)**
14-5137 Alapai Point
Rd 96778
808-965-5340
Sally Whitney

90-175 $US BB
3 rooms, 1 pb
Visa, MC
C-ltd/S-ltd/P-no/H-no

Continental breakfast
Jacuzzi hot tub, seclusion, beauty,
sauna, sitting area, large Lanai,
Kapoho Cove, swimming, TV

Lots of room to relax, read a book, write letters or just meditate on the sound of the soothing surf as it laps the back shore from Kapoho Cove. The house decor is tasteful and unique. The guestrooms and Master Suite, are all lavish and luxurious.

✉ dolphinwahine@yahoo.com 🌏 www.hale-o-naia.com

BIG ISLAND, KEAAU

Art and Orchids
16-1504 39th Ave 96749
877-393-1894 808-982-8197
Jerry Gardner & Marklyn
Wilson

95-125 $US BB
3 rooms, 3 pb
Visa, MC, *Rated*, •
C-yes/S-no/P-no/H-ltd
German, Spanish

Continental plus breakfast
Coffee, tea, hot chocolate
Pool & waterfall, hot tub, beach
supplies, satellite TV/DVD, library,
kitchenette, washer/dryer, WiFi

Wake to the sound of rain forest birds in our spacious home on the Big Island of Hawaii. Get away from it all in a quiet, relaxed setting. Enjoy walking through our grounds which include palm, bamboo, fruit, and native Ohia trees with hundreds of flowers.

✉ info@artandorchids.com 🌐 www.artandorchids.com

BIG ISLAND, NAALEHU

Macadamia Meadows Farm B&B
94-6263 Kamaoa Rd 96772
888-929-8118 808-929-8097
Charlene & Cortney Cowan

119-149 $US BB
5 rooms, 5 pb
Visa, MC, Disc,
Rated, •
C-yes/S-ltd/P-no/H-no

Sumptuous tropical breakfast
Snacks, in-room bistro table & chairs,
fridge & microwave
Tropical atmosphere, beaches nearby,
Macadamia nut orchard, tennis courts,
canopy beds, privacy

For those seeking the "real," non-commercialized Hawaii. Located on an 8-acre working macadamia nut farm estate, in the historic Kau area. Complimentary educational orchard tours and sumptuous tropical breakfasts are offered daily.

✉ innkeeper@macadamiameadows.com 🌐 www.macadamiameadows.com

BIG ISLAND, SOUTH KOHALA

Puako B&B
25 Puako Beach Dr 96743
800-910-1331 808-882-1331
Paul Andrade

100-175 $US BB
4 rooms, 4 pb
Visa, MC, AmEx
C-ltd/S-no/P-no/H-ltd

Full Hawaiian breakfast
Fresh Island grown fruits, local baked
goods, island juices and most popular,
100% Kona coffee
King futon, queen bed, private baths
and entrances, A/C, color TV, private
Jacuzzi, maid service

Aloha and welcome to the Puako B&B on the Kohala Coast! Located on Puako Beach on the Island of Hawai'i, complete with luxury accommodations and an aloha with authenticity and style! Come visit us and see!

✉ puakobb@hawaii.rr.com 🌐 www.bigisland-bedbreakfast.com

BIG ISLAND, VOLCANO

A'alani Volcano Heart Hawaii
470 Ulaino Rd 96713
808-248-7725
JoLoyce Kaia

100-125 $US BB
3 rooms, 3 pb
Rated, •
C-ltd/S-no/P-no/H-no

Continental breakfast
Coffee, tea & small treats available
Kitchenette, sitting room with gas
fireplace, honor fee laundry facilities

Free Night w/Certificate: Anytime. Valid only 30 days before intended use.

Your Big Island of Hawaii home away from home. You can rent by the bedroom with sitting area, kitchenette and honor fee laundry facilities.

✉ joloyce@aol.com 🌐 ecoclub.com/hanamaui/volcano.html

Aloha Junction B&B Inn
19-4037 'Olapalapa Rd 96785
888-967-7286 808-967-7289
Robert & Susan Hughes

100-119 $US BB
4 rooms, 4 pb
Visa, MC, AmEx, •
C-yes/S-no/P-yes/H-no

Tropical breakfast
Vegetarian
Free Sauna, wireless Internet &
computer for all guests

Situated just outside Hawaii Volcanoes National Park in Volcano Village, on the Big Island of Hawaii . . . sits the Aloha Junction B&B. Spacious, affordable, with gracious hosts available on site. Delicious, fresh breakfasts and four clean, comfortable rooms.

✉ alohajunction@hotmail.com 🌐 www.bnbvolcano.com

Tell your hosts Pamela Lanier sent you.

BIG ISLAND, VOLCANO

Chalet Kilauea Collection
19-4178 Wright RD, BX
998 96785
800-937-7786 808-967-7786
David Warganich

61-239 $US EP
18 rooms, 12 pb
Visa, MC, Disc,
Rated, •
C-yes/S-ltd/P-no/H-no

$6 Sumptuous Candle-lit Continental
Free Afternoon Tea by fireside from
3–5pm
Living room with fireplace, hot tubs,
Free WiFi, cable TV, free afternoon tea

The collection offers a selection of fine accommodations set immediately outside Hawaii's Volcanoes National Park. The collection is composed of 8 properties situated within Volcano Village and the Olaa rain forest reserve . . . peace and convenience!

✉ d.warganich@volcano-hawaii.com 🌐 www.volcano-hawaii.com

Kilauea Lodge
19-3948 Old Volcano
Rd 96785
808-967-7366
Lorna & Albert Jeyte

170-300 $US BB
14 rooms, 14 pb
Visa, MC, AmEx,
Rated
C-yes/S-ltd/P-no/H-yes
German, Spanish

Full breakfast
Restaurant, bar, dinner 5 – 9pm,
Breakfast 7:30 – 10am, Lunch 10am –
2pm, Sunday Brunch 10am – 2pm
Sitting room, hot tub, garden gazebo,
hot towel racks, robes

Popular mountain lodge with full service restaurant. Nine rooms with fireplaces. Hot tub, gazebos and gardens. One mile from spectacular Volcanoes National Park.

✉ stay@kilauealodge.com 🌐 www.kilauealodge.com

My Island B&B
19-3896 Volcano Rd 96785
808-967-7216 808-967-7110
Gordon & Joann Morse & Kii
Morse

90-175 $US BB
6 rooms, 4 pb
Visa, MC, Disc, •
C-yes/S-no/P-no/H-no

Continental plus breakfast
Inform host of special diets, enjoy
a huge selection of tea & other hot
drinks
Ponds, botanical garden, fireplace,
telephone, wireless Internet, games &
books for children

My Island B&B is a collection of historic bed and breakfast rooms, garden units, cottages and houses. Most are nestled in floral gardens, others in Volcano Village on the edge of Volcanoes National Park on the Big Island of Hawaii.

✉ myislandinn@hawaiiantel.net 🌐 www.myislandinnhawaii.com

Volcano Country Cottages
19-3990 Old Volcano
Rd 96785
808-967-7960
Sandy & Garret Gooding

105-132 $US BB
4 rooms, 4 pb
Most CC, Cash, Checks,
Rated, •
C-yes/S-no/P-no/H-no

Continental breakfast
Kitchen available
Hot tub, larger houses have living
and dining room, art supplies, books,
games

Come share our little piece of paradise. Enjoy the privacy of your own cottage and the friendly advice of your hosts. We have several cottages, surely one will meet your needs.

✉ aloha@volcanocottages.com 🌐 www.volcanocottages.com

Volcano Inn
19-3820 Old Volcano
Road 96785
800-628-3876 808-967-7773
Ron Ober

59-129 $US EP
16 rooms, 15 pb
C-yes/S-no/P-no/H-no

We have rooms with kitchenettes. All
rooms have free coffee and tea. Six
restaurants are nearby.
Hot tub, free wireless, free computer
Internet in lobby, free parking, free
coffee and tea, cable TV

The best value in Volcano. Beautiful rooms at reasonable rates located next to Hawaii Volcanoes National Park. A central location to explore all of East Hawaii. Relax in a hot-tub and enjoy the native forest surroundings. Rooms have private full baths.

✉ info@volcanoinnhawaii.com 🌐 www.volcanoinnhawaii.com

Volcano Rainforest Retreat
11-3832 Twelfth St 96785
800-550-8696 808-985-8696
Kathleen & Peter Golden

140-260 $US BB
4 rooms, 4 pb
Visa, MC, AmEx
C-ltd/S-no/P-no/H-no

Continental plus breakfast
Retreat available for small groups,
gathering place, bodywork,
counseling, cottage, kitchenette

Wander the magical paths of this serene retreat, secluded in a lush native rain forest on the Big Island of Hawaii. Adjacent to Hawaii Volcanoes National Park.

✉ volrain@volcanoretreat.com 🌐 www.volcanoretreat.com

BIG ISLAND, VOLCANO

Volcano Teapot Cottage
19-4041 Kilauea Rd 96785
808-937-4976 808-967-7112
Bill & Antoinette Bullough

195 $US BB
2 rooms, 1 pb
Visa, MC, AmEx
S-no/P-no/H-no

Continental breakfast

Fall under the spell of an enchanting turn-of-the century cottage in the heart of Volcano Village, Hawaii. Nestled on 3 acres of rainforest and surrounded by beautifully landscaped grounds, we invite you to experience the Hawaii of a bygone era.

✉ cottage@volcanoteapot.com ◐ www.volcanoteapot.com

Volcano Village Lodge
19-4183 Road E 96785
808-985-9500
Kay Lee

195-275 $US BB
5 rooms, 5 pb
Most CC, Cash,
Rated, •
C-yes/S-ltd/P-no/H-no
Korean, German

Full Tropical Breakfast
Afternoon Tea, picnic lunch & intimate
dinner in-room by arrangement
Kitchenette, LCD TV/DVD, CD Player,
Free Internet, Phone/fax, luxury
linens, fireplace & hot tub

With flowers, ferns, and trees everywhere, it is hard to imagine a more picturesque village in all of America. We created the lodges for people who want more out of life than a whirlwind tour of the island. ✉ relax@volcanovillagelodge.com ◐ www.volcanovillagelodge.com

KAUAI, HANALEI

Bed Breakfast & Beach in Hanalei
808-826-6111

120-170 $US BB
3 rooms, 3 pb
Rated, •
C-ltd/S-no/P-no/H-no

Continental plus breakfast
Restaurants nearby, supermarket &
health food market nearby
Sitting room, library, TV, coolers,
beach mats/towels, snorkel equipment
available

Elegance, peace & tranquility surrounded by lush mountains, tropical jungles, cascading waterfalls & most beautiful bay in the Hawaiian Island chain. 1 minute walk to Hanalei Bay. Walk to quaint little surfing town, very rural, country like.

✉ hanaleibay@aol.com ◐ www.bestvacationinparadise.com/bandb.htm

---

River Estate
5-6691 Kuhio Hwy 96714
800 390-8444 808-826-5118
Mark Barbanell

275-350 $US EP
5 rooms, 4 pb
Most CC, Cash, Checks,
Rated, •
C-ltd/S-no/P-no/H-no

Gourmet Kitchen
Full gourmet kitchen
Travel agency, activity bookings, area
guide, local concierge who has lived
on Kauai for 40 years.

River Estate is a secluded, romantic, riverfront Kauai estate with two deluxe homes just 2 blocks from the beach on Kauai's north shore. There is nothing like it in the whole area and it has been rated 1 of the 10 most romantic properties in Hawaii.

✉ info@riverestate.com ◐ www.riverestate.com

KAUAI, KAPAA

Hale Lani B&B
283 Aina Lani Pl 96746
877-423-6434 808-823-6434
Ruth Johnson

125-185 $US BB
4 rooms, 4 pb
Most CC, Cash, •
C-yes/S-no/P-no/H-no

Island breakfast delivered daily
Gift basket upon arrival filled with
Kauai treats
Private hot tubs, beach & hiking
equipment, on-site massage, stereo,
TV, DVD, wireless Internet

One of Hawaii's 50 Best" by Frommers, "Best B & B to Recommend to Others" 2006 by Arringtons, featured in Inn Traveler Magazine and Taste of Home 2010, luxury accommodations in Kauai, each with a private hot tub. Famous for their breakfasts!

✉ innkeeper@halelani.com ◐ www.halelani.com

KAUAI, LAWAI

Hale Kua Guests on Kauai
4896 E Kua Rd 96765
800-440-4353 808-332-8570
Bill & Cathy Cowern

110-175 $US EP
5 rooms, 5 pb
•
C-yes/S-ltd/P-no/H-no

Fruit & nut trees available for the
picking!
Kitchens, full baths, washer/dryer, TV,
VCR, DVD, phone, queen bed

Aloha and welcome to the Hale Kua Guest Bed and Breakfast! Our secluded hillside retreat, located on Kauai's sunny south side, offers peace and serenity in one of our five choice accommodations. Looking for the perfect honeymoon spot? You've found it!

✉ treefarm@halekua.com ◐ www.halekua.com

KAUAI, LAWAI

Marjorie's Kauai Inn
3307-D Hailima Rd. 96765
800-717-8838 808-332-8838
Alexis Boilini

130-175 $US BB
3 rooms, 3 pb
Most CC, Cash, *Rated*
C-yes/S-no/P-no/H-no

Continental plus breakfast
High speed wireless Internet, DVD
player and small library of films, coffee
maker and microwave.

Marjorie's is perched above Kauai's Lawai Valley. Although the ambience is rural, you are five minutes from Old Koloa Town for shopping and ten minutes from world-famous Poipu Beach. "Do more than one fun thing in a day!"

✉ alexis@marjorieskauaiinn.com 🌐 www.marjorieskauaiinn.com

KAUAI, POIPU BEACH

Poipu Plantation Resort
1792 Pe'e Rd 96756
800-634-0263 808-742-6757
Chris Moore

120-270 $US BB
13 rooms, 13 pb
Visa, MC, *Rated*, •
C-ltd/S-ltd/P-no/H-ltd

Full breakfast
Full breakfast included for Bed &
Breakfast Suites, not for Vacation
Rental Suites with kitchen
Concierge services, activity & car
discounts, guides to hikes, road trips,
hidden beaches

Poipu Beach Kauai from $125: four B&B Suites or nine Vacation Rental Suites with full kitchen. A/C with many features. Great for couples, honeymoons, families, commitment/wedding groups, reunions and just a great place to stay! Lots of Aloha shared here.

✉ plantation@poipubeach.com 🌐 www.poipubeach.com

MAUI, HAIKU

Maui Dream Cottage
265 W Kuiaha Rd 96708
808-575-9079
Gregg Blue

110 $US EP
2 rooms
Visa, MC, *Rated*, •
C-yes/S-ltd/P-no/H-no
French, Spanish

Full kitchen, washer-dryer, phone, TV/
VCR, cable and high speed wireless
Internet

Two acres of tropical fruits & flowers with ocean & mountain views. Full kitchens, washer/dryer & very private. Haiku itself is the old pineapple center of Maui. There are shops and an excellent restaurant within a minute from the house.

✉ gblue@aloha.net 🌐 www.mauidreamcottage.com

MAUI, HANA

**Hana Maui Botanical
Gardens B&B Vacation
Rental**
470 Ulaino Road 96713
808-248-7725
JoLoyce Kaia

100-125 $US BB
2 rooms, 2 pb
Visa, MC, *Rated*, •
C-ltd/S-no/P-no/H-no

Continental breakfast
Coffee, tea, box juice, Costco muffins
Private kitchens, private baths,
botanical gardens, fruit picking in
season, queen-size bed

Free Night w/Certificate: Anytime. Valid only 30 days before intended use.

Located in a public tropical botanical garden—find the real Hawaii that few visitors see—there are two private studios available with kitchens, private baths and carports the beautiful Hana on the Island of Maui.

✉ joloyce@aol.com 🌐 www.ecoclub.com/hanamaui/hana.html

MAUI, KIHEI

Hale Huanani B&B
808 Kupulau Drive 96753
877-423-MAUI (6284)
Susan

80-90 $US BB
2 rooms, 2 pb
Most CC, Checks
C-yes/S-no/P-no/H-no

Continental breakfast
Coffee, juice, fruit and muffins or
bread
Private bath w/ large shower, HD TV,
DVD player, stocked kitchenette, grill,
WiFi, beach supplies.

Enjoy your own private studio at the Hale Huanani B&B, location in a very quiet and safe, residential neighborhood in south Maui.

✉ susan@halehuananibandb.com 🌐 www.halehuananibandb.com

MAUI, KIHEI

What a Wonderful World B&B
2828 Umalu Place 96753
800-943-5804 808-879-9103
Eva & Jim

99-150 $US BB
4 rooms, 4 pb
Visa, MC
C-yes/S-no/P-yes/H-no

Full breakfast
Free wireless Internet access, use of washer & dryer, use of beach chairs, towels & equipment

Walking distance from one of the most beautiful beaches in the world. The perfect place to rest and enjoy the wonders of the land. We offer lodging and accommodations perfect for a relaxing getaway or a romantic adventure.

athome@amauibedandbreakfast.com   www.amauibedandbreakfast.com

MAUI, LAHAINA

The Plantation Inn
174 Lahainaluna Rd 96761
800-433-6815 808-667-9225
Herb Coyle

169-300 $US BB
19 rooms, 19 pb
Most CC, *Rated*, •
C-ltd/S-ltd/P-no/H-ltd

Continental breakfast
On property is Forbes 4 star award-winning Gerard's Restaurant
Daily maid service, pool, whirlpool spa, comp. video library, comp. self-parking, in-room safe

The Plantation Inn is Maui's premier bed & breakfast. Turn-of-the-century architecture combined with modern amenities offer guests a tranquil oasis in the heart of Maui's historic Lahaina Town. Just two blocks from the beautiful Pacific Ocean.

info@theplantationinn.com   www.theplantationinn.com

MAUI, MAKAWAO

Banyan B&B
3265 Baldwin Ave 96768
808-572-9021
Marty Herling

145-190 $US BB
7 rooms, 7 pb
Most CC, Cash, Checks
C-yes/S-ltd/P-no/H-yes

Continental breakfast
Coffee, tea, herbal tea, hot cocoa, bananas, avocados, other fruit from the property when in season
Wireless Internet, washer/dryer, pool, Jacuzzi, swings & hammocks, handicap accessible room, pool

Cottages and suites in a centrally located shady, quiet retreat. Close, yet wonderfully removed from Maui's resort beachfront crowds. The Banyan B&B simply overflows with peace and Hawaii-ana including a swimming pool, Jacuzzi, yoga studio and gardens.

info@bed-breakfast-maui.com   www.bed-breakfast-maui.com

OAHU, HONOLULU

Aloha Bed and Breakfast
808-395-6694
Phyllis & Donald Young

80-100 $US BB
3 rooms
C-yes/S-no/P-no/H-no

Full breakfast
Willing to accommodate special dietary needs or preferences
Wireless access, swimming pool with natural salt-to-chlorine, cable TV, large deck with patio sets

Perched on Mariners Ridge in Hawaii Kai with wonderful views of the water and mountains. Minutes to famed snorkeling beach, Hanauma Bay. Healthy breakfasts. Salt-filtered pool. Wireless access for laptop computers.

alohaphyllis@hawaii.rr.com   home.roadrunner.com/~alohaphyllis

OAHU, KAILUA

Beach Lane B&B
808-262-8286
Tonic Bille

115-350 $US EP
3 rooms, 3 pb
Visa, MC, *Rated*, •
S-no/P-no/H-no
Danish, Swedish, German

Large sitting and dining room, full kitchen. Families welcome. 3rd day towel change, Beach gear.

Wonderful accommodations on Kailua beach – 60 feet from the water. Experience the romance and solitude at this private getaway.

info@beachlane.com   www.beachlane.com

OAHU, KAILUA ───────────────────────────────────────

Hawaii's Hidden Hideaway B&B	145-195 $US BB	Continental plus breakfast

Hawaii's Hidden Hideaway B&B
1369 Mokolea Dr 96734
877-443-3299 808-262-6560
Janice

145-195 $US BB
3 rooms, 3 pb
•
C-yes/S-no/P-no/H-no

Continental plus breakfast
Each unit is stocked with fruit basket, pastries, yogurt, cereals, juices, coffee, teas & more!
Jacuzzi, cable TV/DVD, WiFi, beach chairs/towels/mats, hairdryers, irons, laundry, telephone, parking

Award Winning, "Most Romantic Hideaway" on Oahu, the fabulous landscaping and gardens make you feel that you are in another world. Ideal for honeymoons, special occasions, family vacations or business. Member: Better Business Bureau & Chamber of Commerce.

✉ hhhideaway@yahoo.com ◐ www.ahawaiibnb.com

Kailua Hawaii Sheffield House
131 Kuulei Rd 96734
808-262-0721
Paul & Rachel Sheffield

115-280 $US BB
2 rooms, 2 pb
Visa, MC, •
C-yes/S-no/P-ltd/H-yes

Continental breakfast
Complementary breakfast is pastry, fruit, juice, coffee & tea
Both rooms have WiFi, microwave, coffee maker, toaster & refrigerator, free parking

Looking for a tropical paradise, a vacation near sandy Kailua Beach? Spend the week in Kailua near Honolulu and Waikiki. Think Sheffield House B&B for your accommodations. A great place for kite surfing, snorkeling, body surfing tours, or hiking.

✉ rachel@hawaiisheffieldhouse.com ◐ www.hawaiisheffieldhouse.com

---

Papaya Paradise B&B
395 Auwinala Rd 96734
808-261-0316
Bob & Jeanette Martz

100-115 $US BB
2 rooms, 2 pb
Rated, •
C-ltd/S-no/P-no/H-no

Self-catered
Hosts provide fresh brewed coffee & tea, cereals, milk, bagels, bread, for guests' breakfast
TV, DVD & movie library, A/C, phone, WiFi, pool, free parking, beach accessories, reading library

Home in residential beach community. Private entry & bath units, 20 miles from the airport & Waikiki. ½ mile to Kailua Beach, 1 mile to Lanakai Beach. Rooms are furnished in rattan and wicker & open to the pool & garden. Easy access to all attractions.

✉ rentme@hawaii.rr.com ◐ kailuaoahuhawaii.com

OAHU, KANEOHE ───────────────────────────────────────

Ali'i Bluffs Windward B&B
46-251 Ikiiki St 96744
800-235-1151 808-235-1124
Donald Munro & L De Chambs

70-85 $US BB
2 rooms, 2 pb
Visa, MC
C-ltd/S-no/P-no/H-ltd

Continental plus breakfast
Tea is served in the late afternoon and ice and glasses are provided in the library in the evenings.
Two double bedrooms, spectacular views and locations, swimming pool, and delicious breakfasts.

Ali'i Bluffs Windward Bed and Breakfast is a luxuriously furnished private home situated on Oahu's beautiful Windward shore, overlooking majestic Kaneohe Bay. At our doorstep is all the beauty of the meandering Windward coast with it's beaches and coves

✉ donm@lava.net ◐ www.hawaiiscene.com/aliibluffs

Idaho

COEUR D'ALENE

The Roosevelt Inn and Spa	89-319 $US BB	Gourmet, full-service breakfast
105 E Wallace Ave 83816	15 rooms, 15 pb	Baked snacks, coffee, teas & hot
800-290-3358 208-765-5200	Most CC, Cash,	chocolate, Murder Mysteries, High
John & Tina Hough	*Rated*, •	Teas & parties
	C-yes/S-no/P-ltd/H-yes	Sitting room, library, fitness center, hot tub, sauna, suites, TV, business travel, meeting rooms, Day Spa.

Free Night w/Certificate: Valid Jan.-May. Room Upgrade.

Historic red brick school house with bell tower, built in 1905. Completely remodeled and furnished in antiques. Meeting facilities for up to 100 people. Beautiful grounds surround the building, bordered by huge Norwegian Maples and giant Ponderosa Pines.

info@therooseveltinn.com 🌐 www.therooseveltinn.com

KAMIAH

Hearthstone Elegant Lodge	125-235 $US BB	Full breakfast
by the River	5 rooms, 5 pb	Afternoon tea, lunch & dinner
3250 Hwy 12 Mile Post	Visa, MC, *Rated*, •	available
64 83536	C-ltd/S-no/P-no/H-no	Spacious suites, guest library, meeting
877-LODGE-4U 208-935-1492	German	space, quality amenities, Internet
Harty & Marjorie Schmaehl		access

An elegant river lodge with fireplaces, Jacuzzis and river view balconies on the historic Lewis and Clark Trail. A 60 acre pine forest setting. Extraordinary hideaway retreat.

visit@hearthstonelodge.com 🌐 www.hearthstonelodge.com

NORTH FORK

100 Acre Wood B&B-Resort	70-130 $US BB	Full breakfast
2356 Highway 93	7 rooms, 5 pb	Dinner close by
North 83466	Visa, MC, *Rated*	WiFi, TV/DVD/VCR, air conditioning,
208-865-2165	C-yes/S-no/P-ltd/H-yes	hot tubs, fishing in our private lake,
Jon & Nancy Cummings		skiing

With 5 suites and two small elegant, unique, and exquisitely decorated rooms our resort in north central Idaho is definitely the place to come to enjoy the beautiful scenery, wonderful fishing and adventurous tours.

acrewood@centurytel.net 🌐 www.100acrewoodresort.com

RIGBY

Blue Heron Inn	109-199 $US BB	Full breakfast
706 N. Yellowstone	7 rooms, 7 pb	Lunch bags available, complimentary
Hwy 83442	Most CC, Cash, Checks,	soft drinks, wine & beer
866-745-9922 208-745-9922	*Rated*, •	Conference Room, library, suites,
Claudia & Dave Klingler	C-yes/S-no/P-ltd/H-yes	fireplaces, hot tub

Relax and unwind at the Blue Heron Inn on the banks of the South Fork of the Snake River. Unmatched hospitality, beautiful views and delicious breakfasts will make your stay memorable.

innkeeper@idahoblueheron.com 🌐 www.idahoblueheron.com

SALMON

Greyhouse Inn	65-124 $US BB	Full gourmet breakfast
1115 Hwy 93 S 83467	10 rooms, 6 pb	Lunch, dinner, afternoon tea upon
800-348-8097 208-756-3968	Most CC, •	request
Sharon & David Osgood	C-ltd/S-no/P-yes/H-no	Snacks, library, bikes, cable, hot tub, tours of Lewis & Clark

Victorian inn with guestrooms, also offers Lewis & Clark log cabins with log beds, private baths, large porch for viewing the beautiful mountains. Lemhi Shoshone and Trapper cabins: kitchenettes, queen beds and lofts with 2 twin beds, and great views.

osgoodd@centurylink.net 🌐 www.greyhouseinn.com

Illinois

ALTON———————————————————————————————————

| **Beall Mansion-An Elegant Bed and Breakfast Inn**
407 E 12th St 62002
866-843-2325 618-474-9100
Jim & Sandy Belote | 119-358 $US BB
5 rooms, 5 pb
Most CC, Cash, •
C-ltd/S-no/P-no/H-no | Gourmet or Self Serve Continental
Delectable catering for weddings &
receptions, meetings and corporate
retreats
Whirlpools for 2, fireplaces, gourmet
chocolates, digital cable TV, DVD,
WiFi, in room massage |

Free Night w/Certificate: Valid Sunday-Thursday; not valid holiday weekends or blackout dates or with any other special, discount, coupon, or credit.

Voted "Best Illinois Bed and Breakfast" -Illinois Magazine Readers Poll. Only 25 minutes from the St. Louis Gateway Arch in historic Alton, Illinois. Whirlpools for two. Fireplaces. 24 Hour "All You Can Eat" Chocolate Buffet. Need we say more?

✉ bepampered@beallmansion.com   🌐 www.beallmansion.com

| **Jackson House**
1821 Seminary St 62002
800-462-1426 618-462-1426
Hope Apple | 120-165 $US BB
4 rooms, 4 pb
Visa, MC, *Rated*
C-ltd/S-no/P-ltd/H-ltd | Full breakfast
Complimentary wine
Sitting room, library, Jacuzzis,
cottages, fireplaces, cable TV |

In town, but with a relaxing and secluded atmosphere. Choose an elegant guestroom or one of our cozy guesthouses, either The Barn or The Cave.

🌐 www.jacksonbb.com

BLOOMINGTON———————————————————————————————

| **The Burr House**
210 E Chestnut 61701
800-449-4182 309-828-7686
Jeff & Mary Ann Brady-Rhodes | 60-105 $US BB
6 rooms, 4 pb
Most CC, Cash, Checks
C-yes/S-ltd/P-no/H-no | Full Breakfast
Evening snack and drink, fruit and
cheese platters for special occasions;
special diets accommodated
Weddings, dinner parties, showers,
business meetings, wireless Internet |

A Civil War-era brick home constructed in 1864, situated near downtown Bloomington. Learn more about the Burr family connection to Abe Lincoln. Great dining, beautiful gardens, perfect for weddings and showers!

✉ burrhouse@hotmail.com   🌐 www.burrhouse.com

CHAMPAIGN———————————————————————————————————

| **The Gold's B&B**
2065 County Rd 525 E 61822
217-586-4345
Rita Gold | 60 $US BB
3 rooms, 1 pb
C-yes/S-no/P-no/H-no | Continental plus breakfast
Cable TV, DVD |

The Golds Bed & Breakfast is located west of Champaign just off Interstate 74. Country charm & hospitality in an 1874 farmhouse. Handy to interstate & university attractions. Furnished with antiques.

✉ ritagold59@gmail.com

CHICAGO————————————————————————————————————

| **China Doll Guest House**
738 W Schubert Ave 60614
866-361-1819 773-525-4967
Jim & Yanan Haring | 245-415 $US EP
3 rooms, 3 pb
Visa, MC, Disc,
Rated, •
C-yes/S-ltd/P-yes/H-no | Guest Prepared Bkfst
Complete private apartment, Jacuzzi,
Steam room, fireplace, cable TV, office
amenities, washer/dryer |

Three private apartments in the Lincoln Park neighborhood with superb personal comfort features including Jacuzzis, steam rooms, fireplaces, and high-end kitchens. Also especially designed for the business traveler including complete in-unit offices.

✉ ChinaDollChicago@Yahoo.com   🌐 chinadollguesthouse.com

CHICAGO

City Scene B&B	150-200 $US BB	Self-serve continental breakfast
2101 N Clifton Ave 60614	2 rooms, 1 pb	Full kitchen allows guest to prepare
800-549-1743 773-549-1743	Visa, MC, Disc	breakfast at leisure
Mary Newman	C-ltd/S-no/P-no/H-no	Sitting room with fireplace, bathroom
		with steam shower, TV/DVD/VCR, free
		high speed Internet access

Comfortable, private suite with one or two bedrooms, sitting room, kitchen and bath on a residential street, in the Sheffield Historic District. Close to dining, shopping, museums, parks, theatres and transportation.

✉ host@cityscenebb.com   🌐 www.cityscenebb.com

Gold Coast Guest House B&B	129-199 $US BB	Continental plus breakfast
	4 rooms, 4 pb	Refreshments Available. Organic
113 West Elm St 60601	Most CC, *Rated*, •	foods and Soy milk, Stevia and herbal/
312-337-0361	C-ltd/S-no/P-no/H-no	regular teas.
Sally Baker		Nearby Health Club $15.00 daily fee,
		garage use available $25/night. Wi-fi
		available throughout!

Guests call our 1873 Victorian row house an "Urban Oasis." in the heart of the city. Featuring A 20 foot high window-wall framing a lush 2 level garden letting the outdoors in.

✉ sally@bbchicago.com   🌐 www.bbchicago.com

The House of Two Urns	109-189 $US BB	Full breakfast
1239 N Greenview Ave 60642	9 rooms, 7 pb	Complimentary coffee & tea service,
877-Two-Urns 773-235-1408	Visa, MC, Disc, *Rated*	all guests have kitchen access for
Kapra Fleming & Miguel	C-ltd/S-no/P-no/H-no	other meals
Lopez Lemus	German, Spanish,	Free WiFi, DISH TV, DVD movie
	French	library, free local phone calls, free
		parking

Filled with antiques & original art, this urban inn is very convenient to shopping, sightseeing, superb restaurants & more. Offers 6 guestrooms, 2 suites in Chicago's vibrant Wicker Park, very close to public transit and the expressway.

✉ info@twourns.com   🌐 www.twourns.com

ELIZABETHTOWN

The Historic Rose Hotel B&B	95-115 $US BB	Full Gourmet Country Breakfast
	5 rooms, 5 pb	Room Service Available (fee);
92 Main St 62931	Most CC, Cash, Checks	Refrigerators & Coffee Maker (with
618-287-2872	C-yes/S-yes/P-no/H-yes	Tea, Coffee provided)
Sandy Vinyard		Flat screen TV/DVD/VCR, fireplaces,
		A/C control, private entrances,
		business accom., video library

Step Back in Time . . . Built in 1812. This 2 story brick building with a veranda upstairs gives you a panoramic view of the Ohio River. The Summerhouse gazebo built in 1882 is waiting for you to sit with a glass of wine and watch river traffic.

✉ therose1@shawneelink.net   🌐 www.rosehotelbb.com

EVANSTON

Margarita European Inn	79-179 $US BB	Homemade baked goods.
1566 Oak Ave 60201	42 rooms, 22 pb	Award-winning Italian restaurant,
847-869-2273	Most CC, Cash,	Pensiero Ristorante, serving dinner.
Michael Pure	*Rated*, •	www.pensieroristorante.com
	C-yes/S-no/P-no/H-ltd	Evening room service, high speed
	Spanish	wireless Internet, English library,
		grand parlor, conference room

The Margarita European Inn offers 42 rooms, each individually appointed & furnished with antiques, providing a unique & memorable atmosphere. Experience the elegance & service of an era you thought only existed in memory. Easy access to Chicago.

✉ info@margaritainn.com   🌐 www.margaritainn.com

Belle Aire Mansion Guest House, Galena, IL

GALENA

Annie Wiggins Guest House 1004 Park Ave 61036 815-777-0336 Wendy & Bill Heiken	95-235 $US BB 7 rooms, 7 pb Most CC, Cash C-ltd/S-no/P-no/H-no	Full breakfast Complimentary lemonade and brandy Sitting room, library, suites, fireplace, porches, refrigerator, wireless Internet

Romantic, historic mansion welcomes you to its whispers of the past. Shhh! Annie still thinks it's 1860. Seven guestrooms with queen size pillow top beds and private baths. Some with romantic soaking tubs for two or fireplaces.

 annie@anniewiggins.com   www.anniewiggins.com

Belle Aire Mansion Guest House 11410 Rt 20 W 61036 815-777-0893 Jan & Lorraine Svec	90-185 $US BB 5 rooms, 5 pb Visa, MC, Disc, • C-yes/S-ltd/P-no/H-no Closed Christmas Day/ Eve	Full breakfast Snacks, chocolate chip cookies in guestrooms, early morning coffee buffet Sitting room, Jacuzzis, suites, fireplaces, Serenity Room with in house massages available

A warm home with the friendliest Innkeepers you'll ever find. Located just minutes from Historic Galena on 11 beautiful acres. Innkeepers have been welcoming guests into their home for 23 years. Be prepared to be pampered!

belleair@galenalink.com   www.belleairemansion.com

Bernadine's Stillman Inn & Wedding Chapel 513 Bouthillier St 61036 866-777-0557 815-777-0557 Dave & Bernadine Anderson	120-280 $US BB 7 rooms, 7 pb Visa, MC, *Rated*, • C-ltd/S-ltd/P-no/H-no	Full breakfast Chocolate chip cookies, ice cream bars, fruit & popcorn Parlor with piano, Wedding Chapel, garden courtyards, close to nature trail & Main St.

Romantic 1858 Victorian Mansion awarded "Best Innkeeper" and "Best Breakfast in the Midwest.) Close to town and located in a residential neighborhood with ample parking. Garden filled courtyards. Seven guestrooms with private baths.

stillman@stillmaninn.com   www.stillmaninn.com

GALENA ————————————————————————————————

Captain Harris Guest House	99-209 $US BB	Full gourmet breakfast
713 S Bench St 61036	5 rooms, 5 pb	Sitting room, library, Jacuzzis, suites,
800-996-4799 815-777-4713	Visa, MC, Disc	fireplaces, cable TV, DVD, WiFi & data
Frank & Anne McCaw	S-no/P-no/H-ltd	ports

Historic home (c.1836) in the heart of Galena. Walk to all restaurants & attractions. Honeymoon cottage with whirlpool for that very special occasion.

✉ captainharris@mchsi.com 🌐 www.captainharris.com

——

Cloran Mansion	99-225 $US BB	Full breakfast
1237 Franklin St 61036	7 rooms, 7 pb	Mini fridge with complementary
866-234-0583 815-777-0583	Most CC, *Rated*, •	soda & water in each room, cookies,
Carmine & Cheryl Farruggia	C-ltd/S-ltd/P-ltd/H-yes	popcorn, candy, tea, coffee
		Bicycles, screened gazebo, video
		library, DVDs, wireless Internet access,
		garaged motorcycle parking

Romantic getaway in an 1880 Victorian Mansion. Relax by the warmth of the fireplace or in one of the whirlpools built for two. A full country style breakfast awaits you in the morning! Simply the best!

✉ innkeeper@cloranmansion.com 🌐 www.cloranmansion.com

——

Farmers' Guest House	119-250 $US BB	Full, hot breakfast
334 Spring St 61036	9 rooms, 9 pb	Snacks, beverages, wine & cheese
888-459-1847 815-777-3456	Most CC, •	served at 6:00 pm
Jess & Kathie Farlow	C-ltd/S-no/P-no/H-ltd	Sitting room, large common areas,
		hot tub, Gift Shop in B&B, massages,
		weddings, retreats

Farmers' Guest House welcomes you with the delight and charm of a by-gone era plus the conveniences of today. We attend to the little things . . . so you can enjoy your stay and make our house your home. ✉ stay@galenabedandbreakfast.com 🌐 www.farmersguesthouse.com

——

Galena Log Cabin	189-249 $US EP	Gas log fireplace, satellite tv,
9401 W. Hart John Rd. 61036	11 rooms, 11 pb	refrigerator, microwave, hike, bike,
815-777-4200	Most CC, Cash, Checks,	canoe/kayak, ski, alpaca farm
Frank & Ruth Netzel	*Rated*	
	C-yes/S-ltd/P-yes/H-yes	

Stay in your very own authentic, hand-made log cabin and begin to cherish the golden sounds of nature. Experience the 45 lovely acres of Galena Log Cabin Getaway and the Adventure Creek Alpaca Farm, owned and operated by Ruth and Frank Netzel.

✉ info@galenalogcabins.com 🌐 www.galenalogcabins.com

——

Goldmoor Inn & Aaron's Cottages and Cabins	155-335 $US BB	Full breakfast
9001 Sand Hill Rd 61036	17 rooms, 17 pb	Complimentary in-room soft drinks,
800-255-3925 815-777-3925	Most CC, Cash, Checks,	juice, tea, coffee & popcorn
Tom & Patricia Smith	*Rated*, •	Massage services, wireless Internet,
	C-ltd/S-no/P-ltd/H-yes	weddings and receptions

Galena, Illinois' most elegant inn. Luxury log cabins, cottages and suites with whirlpools, fireplaces and full breakfast included. Romantic river view. Excellent wedding and reception location. Top rated since 1993. Great hospitality.

✉ goldmoor@galenalink.com 🌐 www.goldmoor.com

——

Park Avenue Guest House	95-145 $US BB	Full breakfast
208 Park Ave 61036	4 rooms, 4 pb	Early morning coffee, afternoon tea,
800-359-0743 815-777-1075	Visa, MC, Disc, *Rated*	snacks
Sharon Fallbacher	C-ltd/S-no/P-no/H-no	Sitting room with TV, 2 parlors,
		gazebo, A/C, fireplaces in rooms

Free Night w/Certificate: Valid Jan. 2-April 1.

Elegant yet comfortable, in quiet residential area. Short walk to beautiful Grant Park, Galena River and Main Street restaurants & shopping.

 parkave@galenalink.com 🌐 www.galenaparkavenue.com

GALENA ─────────────────────────────────

Queen Anne Guest House
200 Park Ave 61036
815-777-3849
Mike & Anita Reese

90-165 $US BB
4 rooms, 4 pb
Most CC, Cash
C-yes/S-no/P-no/H-no

Award winning breakfast
Parlor party with refreshments and
appetizers at 5 pm, a great way to
know other guests
2 parlors & porches, library of books,
games, CDs & movies, garden & fish
pond, wireless Internet

*Located in a quiet neighborhood close to Main Street, Galena River Trail & Grant's Park and Home.
Our B&B has won numerous awards, including best breakfast in the Midwest. Wireless. Come visit us
in our historic, Victorian home and leave as a new friend.*
✉ info@queenanneguesthouse.com   🌐 www.queenanneguesthouse.com

**Ryan Mansion Bed &
Breakfast**
11373 West US Hwy 20 61036
815-777-0336

75-250 $US BB
6 rooms, 6 pb
Most CC, Cash
S-no/P-no/H-no

Full breakfast
Tea & snacks
Wireless Internet access, air
conditioning, private bathrooms,
queen size beds, a full breakfast

Enjoy a romantic bed and breakfast getaway at Galena's finest and largest historic mansion.
✉ annie@anniewiggins.com   🌐 www.ryanmansiongalena.com

The Steamboat House B&B
605 S Prospect St 61036
800-717-2317 815-777-2317
Charlene & Glen Carlson

105-160 $US BB
5 rooms, 5 pb
Visa, MC, Disc
S-no/P-no/H-no

Full breakfast
Evening wine & cheese
Walk to town location, private off-street
parking, billiard room, "wine time"
parlors, WI FI, Gazebo

*Grand Galena Il bed and breakfast mansion offering luxurious Illinois getaways, located only a block
and a half from downtown Galena. Heirloom antiques & historic photographs fill the parlors & five
guestrooms of this premier Galena inn. Special packages*
✉ glenchar@thesteamboathouse.com   🌐 www.thesteamboathouse.com

GRAFTON ─────────────────────────────────

Tara Point Inn & Cottages
1 Tara Point Ln 62037
618-786-3555
Alison Rohan & Sara Meyers

168-216 $US BB
11 rooms, 11 pb
•
C-ltd/S-no/P-no/H-yes

Continental breakfast
Complimentary snacks & beverages
Fireplaces, TV/VCR, whirlpool tubs

*Enjoy the spectacular view of the Mississippi & Illinois Rivers. Watch wintering Bald Eagles. Cottages
with fireplaces. Bike & antique along National Scenic Byway. Visit Lewis & Clark Interpretive Center.*
✉ info@tarapoint.com   🌐 www.tarapoint.com

HENRY ─────────────────────────────────

Mission Oak Inn
1108 County Rd 930E 61537
309-370-4083 309-370-4083
Denny & Jan Reed

155-165 $US BB
2 rooms, 2 pb
Visa, MC, Disc, •
C-ltd/S-no/P-no/H-no

Deluxe full breakfast
Dinners by reservation for our guests.
Complimentary homemade dessert,
one per person.
Private in room bath, private entrance,
private lake, whirlpool, DISH TV/DVD/
CD, fireplace, WiFi

Free Night w/Certificate: Mon-Thurs, excludes Sept and October.

*Mission Oak Inn is an award winning B&B offering a quiet, comfortable getaway from the stress of life.
The inn is located on 120 acres, nestled next to the private 7-acre lake with abundant wildlife. This is
a perfect romantic getaway.*   ✉ innkeepers@missionoakinn.com   🌐 www.missionoakinn.com

JACKSONVILLE ─────────────────────────────────

Blessings On State
1109 W State St 62650
888- 952-9262 217-245-1013
Gwenn Eyer

109-179 $US BB
2 rooms, 2 pb
Most CC, Cash
C-yes/S-no/P-no/H-no

Full breakfast

Free Night w/Certificate: Anytime.

*Blessings on State Bed & Breakfast is located in the prestigious Duncan Park/West State Street historic
district in Jacksonville, Illinois.* ✉ innkeeper@blessingsonstate.com   🌐 www.blessingsonstate.com

KEWANEE

Aunt Daisy's B&B
223 W Central Blvd 61443
888-422-4148 309-853-3300
Glen & Michele Schwarm

99 $US BB
4 rooms, 4 pb
Most CC, Cash,
Rated, •
C-ltd/S-no/P-no/H-no

Full breakfast
Snacks, complimentary dessert in
evenings
Library, suites

Elegant Victorian 1890 home. The many stained glass windows await the opportunity to charm you. Music parlor with a 1929 Aeolian player piano. All beds are king size. Full hot breakfast. Enjoyable surroundings. Great food!

✉ auntdaisybb@verizon.net 🌐 www.auntdaisy.net

MAEYSTOWN

Corner George Inn
1101 Main St 62256
618-458-6660
David & Marcia Braswell

89-169 $US BB
6 rooms, 6 pb
Most CC, Cash
C-ltd/S-no/P-no/H-ltd

Full breakfast
Wine cellar
Air conditioning, ballroom, sitting
rooms, antiques, carriage rides

Located just 35 miles south of St. Louis, Corner George Inn was originally built as a hotel and saloon in 1884 by George Jacob and Sibilla Hoffmann. There are a total of 6 guestrooms, each with a private bath.

✉ cornrgeo@htc.net 🌐 www.cornergeorgeinn.com

METROPOLIS

**Summers Riverview
Mansion B&B**
205 Metropolis 62960
618-524-5328
Colleen and Henk Ahrens

75-185 $US BB
5 rooms, 5 pb
Most CC, Cash
S-no/P-no/H-no
Dutch, German, some
French

Continental plus breakfast
Coffee, tea, juices, bottled water and
snacks
Plenty of parking, Fireplaces, Air
conditioning, TV with cable, All
Service Bar, Bicycles on site

1889 Victorian Mansion features fireplaces, private baths, and two person whirlpool tubs. King and Queen canopy beds. Furnished with period antiques. Golfing, fishing, carriage rides, bicycling along the Ohio River, Casino specials! Home of Superman!!

✉ john@summersbedandbreakfast.com 🌐 www.summersbedandbreakfast.com

MT. VERNON

Sidwell Friends B&B
1812 Richview Rd 62864
618-691-8742
Larry Sidwell

120-160 $US BB
3 rooms, 2 pb
Visa, MC
S-no/P-no/H-no

Full breakfast
Turndown service, WiFi, HDTV, deck,
sunroom, library with fireplace,
heated tile baths, Jacuzzi tub

Sidwell Friends B&B is an historic inn offering luxury amenities . . . heated tile floors & towel racks, Jacuzzi & WiFi. Perfect for a romantic getaway, a fun weekend with friends, an upscale stay for the refined traveler or a relaxing retreat for anyone.

✉ sidwell13@yahoo.com 🌐 www.sidwellfriendsbandb.com

NEBO

Harpole's Heartland Lodge
Rt 1 Box 8A 62355
800-717-4868 217-734-2526
Gary Harpole

178-259 $US MAP
20 rooms, 20 pb
Most CC, Cash, Checks,
Rated, •
C-ltd/S-ltd/P-ltd/H-yes
January – September

Full breakfast
Lunch, snacks, smores, banquet
facilities
Horseback riding, ATVs, fishing,
hayrides, bonfire, conference room,
weddings, game room, clays

An incredible sense of well-being invades your soul as you feel the stress drain out of your body & reality sink in – you'll be enveloped in luxury, with all of nature's beauty just outside the door.

✉ info@heartlandlodge.com 🌐 www.heartlandlodge.com

OAK PARK

Harvey House B&B
107 S Scoville Ave 60302
888-848-6810 708-848-6810
Beth Harvey

175-275 $US BB
5 rooms, 5 pb
Most CC, Cash,
Rated, •
C-ltd/S-no/P-no/H-no

Full Breakfast
Deluxe robes, WiFi Internet access,
color printer, fax/copier, TV/VCR,
licensed massage therapist

Oak Park is 8 miles from the heart of Downtown Chicago. The Inn is just 2 blocks from the train which leaves every 8 minutes to get there! Perfect location for enjoying one of the most beautiful neighborhoods in the country.

✉ harveyhousebb@gmail.com 🌐 www.harveyhousebb.com

The Irish Inn, Ozark, IL

OGLESBY

Brightwood Inn
2407 N State Rt. 178 61354
888-667-0600 815-667-4600
John & Jo Ryan

115-255 $US BB
8 rooms, 8 pb
Most CC, *Rated*, •
C-ltd/S-no/P-ltd/H-ltd

Full breakfast
Complimentary beverages & snacks
Jacuzzi, fireplace, balconies, library,
herb garden, veranda, gathering room
w/bar, TV, DVD, WiFi

Constructed in 1996 in Oglesby, Illinois and nestled on 14 acres within the confines of Mattiessen State Park, the inn was built to resemble a vintage farmhouse complete with verandah. The Inn may be reserved for banquets, small weddings and reunions.

✉ brtwood@starved-rock-inn.com ◑ www.starved-rock-inn.com

OZARK

The Irish Inn
600 Soloman Lane 62972
618-695-5683 618-695-3355
Brian & Lynn McCreery

119-169 $US BB
3 rooms, 2 pb
Most CC, Cash, Checks,
Rated, •
C-yes/S-ltd/P-yes/H-ltd
French, Spanish, Italian,
read/write all European
languages

Full Irish Breakfast
Irish tea is always available, and
gourmet dinners can be arranged at
time of reservation.
King beds / fireplaces in all rooms,
European gourmet dining, fiber optic
WiFi, fun special holiday

Free Night w/Certificate: Mon-Wed; all year; excluding Oct and holidays.

The Irish Inn is a stone and log chalet, built with native rock and full Carolina pines. The Irish Inn sits atop a Frank Lloyd Wright wood foundation, and is accented by pine and bamboo floors, fireplaces, and mementos from lives spent on six continents.

✉ dalianmoore@yahoo.com ◑ irishinn.tripod.com

ROCKFORD

River House B&B Getaway Retreat
11052 Ventura Blvd 61115
815-636-1884
Patty Michalsen

109-229 $US BB
8 rooms, 8 pb
Most CC, Cash, Checks,
Rated
C-yes/S-ltd/P-no/H-ltd

Full breakfast Getaway Lodge only
Getaway Lodge only: Full gourmet
breakfast & complimentary snacks,
coffee, soft beverages included
Jacuzzi, fireplace, satellite TV, private
porch & entrance, group retreats,
weddings, scrapbooking

Two riverfront B&B homes offer both romantic Jacuzzi and fireplace suites for couples or family friendly lodging for vacation travel. Romance extras, weddings, scrapbooking retreats, reunions or rent the entire lodge. ✉ innkeeper@riverhouse.ws ◑ www.riverhouse.ws

ROCKTON

Copperstone Inn	135-455 $US BB	Full breakfast
6702 Yale Bridge Rd 61072	6 rooms, 6 pb	Sitting room, spa, walking paths,
815-629-9999	Most CC, Cash	130 acres, bird & butterfly garden, 2
Saundra Spanton	S-no/P-no/H-yes	stocked ponds, outdoor grill

Copperstone Inn is one of the most luxurious bed and breakfasts you will ever visit. The original limestone home was built in 1858 in traditional Greek revival style. This majestic home exudes an ambience of total elegance and comfort.

✉ admin@copperstoneinn.com 🌐 www.copperstoneinn.com/index.html

ROSELLE

Lynfred Winery B&B	350-400 $US BB	Full breakfast
15 S Roselle Rd 60172	4 rooms, 4 pb	Fresh fruit & cheese tray, a premium
888-298-WINE 630-529-WINE	Most CC, *Rated*	wine tasting, a private tour, fresh
Lisa Klus	S-no/P-no/H-yes	flowers & gourmet breakfast
	Spanish	Fireplaces, winery, gift shop,
		balconies, heated floors, whirlpool
		bath, heated towel racks.

At Lynfred Winery Bed & Breakfast, our friendly, professional team takes great pride in creating the ultimate escape: a historic hideaway where you can forget the pressures of everyday life. Immerse yourself in the beauty of nature and renew your spirits.

✉ wineinfo@lynfredwinery.com 🌐 www.lynfredwinery.com

SHEFFIELD

Chestnut Street Inn	109-179 $US BB	Full breakfast
301 E Chestnut St 61361	4 rooms, 4 pb	Snacks, baked goods; full gourmet
800-537-1304 815-454-2419	Visa, MC, Disc, *Rated*	4-course dinner available upon
Monika & Jeff Sudakov	C-ltd/S-no/P-no/H-no	request
	French, Hungarian	Morning wake up tray, laundry
		available, wireless Internet

Free Night w/Certificate: Anytime.

Award winning B&B featuring gourmet Mediterranean Cuisine using locally grown foods. 4 elegantly appointed guest suites with private bathrooms.

✉ monikaandjeff@chestnut-inn.com 🌐 www.chestnut-inn.com

SULLIVAN

Okaw Valley Orchard Inn	99-125 $US BB	Full breakfast
716 CR 1750N 61951	3 rooms, 3 pb	Complimentary beverages, snacks,
217-728-4093	Visa, MC, Disc	store (store is open mid July – mid
Mike & Jennifer Mitchell	C-ltd/S-no/P-no/H-no	Nov.)
		Wood stove or fireplace, decks
		overlooking orchard, sitting room, TV/
		DVD, DVD library, hot tub, Internet

A simple and relaxing country atmosphere abounds at this barn style B&B, situated on a family run orchard. 3 large rooms decorated in country style with private baths and all of the comforts of home.

✉ jennifer@okawvalleyorchard.com 🌐 www.okawvalleyorchardinn.com

Indiana

ANGOLA

Angola's Tulip Tree Inn B&B
411 N Wayne St 46703
260-668-7000
Katy & Mac Friedlander

85-135 $US BB
4 rooms, 2 pb
Most CC, Cash, •
C-ltd/S-no/P-no/H-no

Full Deluxe Breakfast
High tea available
Free wireless Internet access &
business services, front porch, sun
deck, satellite TV

Return to the peaceful 1890s at the beautiful Tulip Tree Inn Bed & Breakfast, a regal Queen Anne Victorian Mansion, recently renovated, but retaining its original craftsmanship.

✉ tuliptree@tuliptree.com 🌐 www.tuliptree.com

AUBURN

Inn at Windmere
2077 Country Road 40 46706
260-925-3303
Paul & Susie Rexroth

100-140 $US BB
6 rooms, 6 pb
Visa, MC, Disc,
Rated, •
C-yes/S-no/P-no/H-ltd

Full hot breakfast
Home made snacks & beverages
Exercise equip., wireless Internet
access, spa services (extra charge),
fireplaces, bonfires, gazebo

Peaceful, beautifully renovated farmhouse on 40 acres. Great for a romantic getaway, scrapbooking or quilting retreat, church meeting, business travel. Lots of places to relax indoors, 3 rooms with fireplaces, and outdoors a wrap-around porch and gazebo.

✉ inn@innatwindmere.com 🌐 www.innatwindmere.com

BATESVILLE

Stonebridge Inn & Spa
509 N Walnut St 47006
800-966-5914 812-933-1000
Kathy Schuerman

180-240 $US BB
5 rooms, 5 pb
Most CC, Cash,
Checks, •
C-ltd/S-no/P-no/H-no

Full breakfast
Complimentary Snacks & Beverages,
Complimentary Appetizers Friday &
Saturday, Catered Lunch/Dinner
Day Spa, Outdoor Jacuzzi & Pool,
Sauna, Steam Shower, Golf, Meeting
Facility, WiFi, TV/DVD, Bikes

Escape to quiet elegance located less than an hour from Cincinnati, OH and Indianapolis, IN. The 1910 historic estate is located on 3.5 acres of landscaped gardens with a full service spa and five luxury suites featuring private baths and fireplaces.

✉ info@stonebridgeinnandspa.com 🌐 www.stonebridgeinnandspa.com

BLOOMINGTON

Grant Street Inn
310 N Grant St 47408
800-328-4350 812-334-2353
Paul Wagoner

169-329 $US BB
24 rooms, 24 pb
Most CC, Cash, Checks
C-ltd/S-no/P-no/H-ltd

Full breakfast buffet
Snacks, tea, coffee, soda, bottled water
Gathering parlor, books and
periodicals, party room available, high
speed Internet access

Welcome to Grant Street Inn, a 24-room bed and breakfast inn located in the heart of charming Bloomington, Indiana. Just two blocks from Indiana University and four blocks from the courthouse square.

✉ gsi@grantstinn.com 🌐 www.grantstinn.com

Showers Inn
430 N Washington Ave 47408
877-334-9009 812-334-9000
Michael Fierst

159-299 $US BB
12 rooms, 12 pb
Visa, MC, AmEx
C-ltd/S-ltd/P-no/H-ltd

Invigorating continental breakfast
Tea served buffet style afternoons in
the dining room & include a variety of
fresh baked goods
Egyptian cotton sheets, upscale
bathroom amenities, wired/wireless
Internet access, flat screen TVs

We are pleased to announce the opening of the Showers Inn of Bloomington, Indiana. Two historic early 20th century homes have undergone a comprehensive million dollar make-over in order to provide guests with unforgettable service and luxury.

✉ mike@showersinn.com 🌐 www.showersinn.com

BRAZIL

McKinley House B&B
3273 E US Hwy 40 47834
866-442-5308 812-442-5308
Tom & Julie Kinley

90-90 $US BB
3 rooms, 3 pb
C-ltd/S-ltd/P-ltd/H-no

Full breakfast
Snacks are included, picnic lunch &
dinners available for additional fee
Accommodate business travelers,
gatherings, murder mysteries, covered
bridge & other festivals

On the National Road. In 1872 George Green McKinley, one of the contractors of the famed National Road, built a 14 room Italianate style house for his family. The house is built of red brick made on site from clay dug at nearby Croy Creek.

✉ mckinleybandb@gmail.com

BROWNBURG

The Old MG B&B
7579 N State Rd 267 46112
317-852-5923
Pete & Wendy Hylton

95-130 $US BB
3 rooms, 3 pb
Most CC, Cash
C-ltd/S-no/P-no/H-ltd

Continental plus breakfast
Locally roasted coffee including decaf,
and a variety of teas and afternoon
cookies.
Ample parking, WiFi throughout, TV,
DVD player in common room, easy
interstate access, non-smoking,

The historic Old MG B&B was built in the early 1860's and is one of Hendricks County's historic buildings. Today, it houses a small collection of lovingly restored vintage MG sports cars and memorabilia from the golden age of sports car racing.

✉ innkeeper@theoldmg.com 🌐 www.theoldmg.com/index.html

CHESTERTON

At Home in the Woods B&B
898 N 350 E 46304
219-728-1325
Scott & Victoria Phillips

119-149 $US BB
3 rooms, 3 pb
Visa, MC
C-ltd/S-ltd/P-no/H-no

Full 4-course gourmet breakfast
Evening dessert and 24 hour beverage
station included. Dinners are available
upon request.
In-room massage, sitting rooms, Big
screen, outdoor hot tub, pool, hiking
trails, wildlife & WiFi.

Come join us at our Bed and Breakfast in Northwest Indiana and stay the weekend in one of our three national park rooms, all with private baths, an extra large whirlpool or shower, fireplace, and king/ queen beds draped in luxurious linens.

✉ info@athomeinthewoodsbb.com 🌐 www.athomeinthewoodsbb.com

Gray Goose Inn
350 Indian Boundary
Rd 46304
800-521-5127 219-926-5781
Tim Wilk

110-195 $US BB
8 rooms, 8 pb
Most CC, Cash, •
C-yes/S-no/P-yes/H-no

Full gourmet breakfast
Complimentary beverages, tea, coffee,
hot chocolate, snacks, microwave
popcorn, cookies, pastries
Sitting & meeting rooms, telephones
in rooms, free WiFi Internet, business
services

Free Night w/Certificate: Valid Jan.-April.

Located in Indiana Dunes Country. An English country house on 100 acres with a private lake. Charming guestrooms, private baths, fireplaces, Jacuzzis, solarium, gourmet breakfast. Plenty of jogging & hiking trails.

✉ graygoose@verizon.net 🌐 www.graygooseinn.com

COLFAX

Cabins & Candlelight, LLC
7295 N 1100 E 46035
800-864-6717 765-436-2133
Chuck & Rhonda Smith

179-219 $US BB
2 rooms, 2 pb
Visa, MC, AmEx
S-ltd/P-no/H-no

Continental plus breakfast
The kitchen is stocked with breakfast
food, dinnerware & cookware.
Stone gas-burning fireplace, whirlpool
tub, entertainment center, kitchen,
covered porch, grill

Cabins & Candlelight is a romantic getaway for couples featuring luxury log cabins located 45 minutes northwest of Indianapolis. Each cabin features a 15-foot stone fireplace with gas logs, oversize whirlpool tub, screened back porch and kitchen.

 ✉ info@cabinsandcandlelight.com 🌐 www.cabinsandcandlelight.com

EVANSVILLE

Cool Breeze B&B
1240 SE Second St 47713
812-422-9635
Katelin & David Hills

119 $US BB
3 rooms, 3 pb
Most CC, Cash, Checks,
Rated, •
C-ltd/S-ltd/P-no/H-no

Full breakfast
Sitting room, library, off-street parking,
WiFi

Historic 1906 home. American Eclectic style. A quiet, peaceful retreat ideal for a memorable romantic interlude & personal renewal. All rooms have queen beds, private baths, phones & cable TV. Wireless Internet access.

✉ coolbreeze27@juno.com 🌐 www.coolbreezebb.net

FISHERS

The Frederick-Talbott Inn
13805 Allisonville Rd 46038
866-680-6466 317-578-3600
Ed & Nancy

93-167 $US BB
10 rooms, 10 pb
Most CC, Cash, Checks
C-yes/S-no/P-no/H-yes

Cont. on Weekday, Full on Weekend
catering for meetings available
Jacuzzis, fireplaces, cable TV,
conference center, WiFi

Visit a Country Bed & Breakfast complete with spacious rooms, private baths, and beautiful gardens. Over the past 14 years, The Frederick-Talbott Inn has offered quality service, exceptional food, and convenience for those who travel in Indiana.

✉ Innkeeper@fredericktalbottinn.com 🌐 www.fredericktalbottinn.com

INDIANAPOLIS

Nestle Inn
637 N East St 46202
877-339-5200 317-610-5200
Steve & Barb Tegarden

105-140 $US BB
5 rooms, 5 pb
Visa, MC, AmEx
C-yes/S-no/P-no/H-no

Full breakfast
Snack bar
Parlor, library, TV, DVD player
available, microwave, fridge, WiFi

A three story 1896 Victorian home turned into a five room inn (four bedrooms and one suite). Located in the theatre and arts district in downtown Indianapolis. Minutes away from restaurants, shops and sport and entertainment venues.

✉ nestleindy@sbcglobal.net 🌐 www.nestleindy.com

Old Northside Inn
1340 N Alabama St 46202
800-635-9127 317-635-9123
Gary & JoAnne

135-215 $US BB
7 rooms, 7 pb
Most CC
C-yes/S-no/P-ltd/H-ltd

Complete breakfast
A full snack bar including bottled
water, soda, tea, coffee and more
available 24 hours a day
Wireless Internet, computer access,
faxes, music room with piano, parlor,
mini kitchen area for use

The mansion has been renovated in an elegant European turn-of-the-century motif to retain its warm ambience, with the original maple slat flooring and incomparable hand-carved cherry and mahogany woodwork.

✉ Garyh@Hofmeister.com 🌐 www.oldnorthsideinn.com

JEFFERSONVILLE

Market Street Inn
330 W Market Street 47130
888-284-1877 812-285-1877
Carol & Steve Stenbro

109-209 $US BB
7 rooms, 7 pb
Most CC, Cash,
Checks, •
C-ltd/S-no/P-no/H-yes

Full gourmet breakfast
Lunch, dinner, tea by reservation.
Remote control fireplaces, high speed
Internet, in room phones, Cable,
Jacuzzi tubs, fax and copier

A Second Empire 3-story mansion in the city within walking distance of most attractions, offering well appointed rooms with luxurious upscale private baths. Completely restored with every modern amenity in October 2005.

✉ house1877@peoplepc.com 🌐 www.innonmarket.com

Old Bridge Inn
131 W Chestnut St 47130
866-284-3580 812-284-3580
Linda Williams

75-150 $US BB
5 rooms, 5 pb
Most CC, Cash, Checks,
Rated
C-yes/S-no/P-ltd/H-no

Full breakfast
Afternoon tea with 24-hour notice,
snacks
Sitting rooms, Jacuzzis, fireplaces,
accommodates business travelers

This historic home is located in Jeffersonville's historic district, within seconds of I-65 & Louisville, KY. Walk to shops, restaurants, & the Ohio River. Intimate weddings. Corporate rates available.

✉ innbridge@aol.com 🌐 www.oldbridgeinn.com

Arbor Hill Inn & Guest House, La Porte, IN

LAPORTE

Arbor Hill Inn & Guest House 263 W Johnson Rd 46350 219-362-9200 L. Kobat, K. Demoret	79-259 $US BB 12 rooms, 12 pb Most CC, Cash, *Rated* C-yes/S-ltd/P-no/H-yes	Full hot breakfast Lunch & dinner are served with selections made 48 hours in advance, menus available on our website Jacuzzi tubs, suites, fireplaces, cable TV, VCR/DVD, hi-speed Internet, coffee, irons, movies/games

Free Night w/Certificate: Sun-Thurs; excluding holidays; based on availability.

The ultimate in affordable luxury! Historic 1910 Greek Revival Inn. A haven for business & leisure travelers. Nine luxury suites, executive amenities and great packages. Choose from the elegant Main Inn or themed Guesthouse. ✉ info@arborhillinn.com ◔ www.arborhillinn.com

MARION

Burke Place B&B 722 W Fourth St 46952 866-728-7228 765-664-7228 LeRoy Imler & John Lightle	75-95 $US BB 4 rooms, 4 pb Visa, MC, Disc C-ltd/S-no/P-no/H-no	Full breakfast Soft drinks, coffee/decaf, tea, fresh baked cookies & snacks, other meals by special arrangements Cable TV w/remote, telephones, WiFi, fax, copier, lighted off-street parking, whirlpool tubs

Free Night w/Certificate: Anytime.

Burke Place is an urban B&B with a homelike warmth & charm, friendly & relaxed atmosphere, where we cater to your personal needs. Join us for a special get-away time, family visit, to relax after a busy work week, or just a pleasurable experience. ✉ limler@burkeplace.com ◔ www.burkeplace.com

MICHIGAN CITY

Creekwood Inn Route 20-35 At I-94 46360 800-400-1981 219-872-8357 Peggie Wall & Pam Pawloski	105-175 $US BB 13 rooms, 13 pb Visa, MC, AmEx, *Rated*, • C-yes/S-no/P-no/H-yes	Continental plus breakfast Dinner served Wed. – Sat., business meetings & groups by request 33 wooded acres, walking trails, gardens, pond; two-story conservatory

Voted Best B&B in NW Indiana for 10 years running. Secluded 1930 English country manor with 13 rooms on 33 acres of woods & creeks. Fine dining in our historic parlor and a unique meeting site. We have high-speed Internet access. ✉ creekwoodinn@csinet.net ◔ www.creekwoodinn.com

MICHIGAN CITY

The Hutchinson Mansion Inn
220 W 10th St 46360
219-879-1700
Mary DuVal

100-175 $US BB
10 rooms, 10 pb
Visa, MC, *Rated*, •
C-ltd/S-ltd/P-no/H-ltd

Full breakfast
Snacks
Sitting room, piano, whirlpools, fax,
tennis & golf nearby

Elegant Victorian mansion distinguished by outstanding stained glass windows, notable architectural details and magnificent antiques.

🌐 www.hutchinsonmansioninn.com

MITCHELL

Spring Mill Inn
3333 State Road 60
East 47446
877-977-7464 812-849-4081
Brian J. Ferguson

62-114 $US EP
74 rooms, 74 pb
Most CC, •
C-yes/S-no/P-no/H-yes

Bountiful country buffets available.
Full service restaurant, 3 meals daily
& buffets.
Spacious lobbies, indoor/outdoor
pool, fireplaces, game room

Snuggled into a backdrop of stately oaks & scenic hills in Southern Indiana. Built in 1939 of hand-quarried Indiana limestone, the Inn offers 74 cozy country guestrooms. Modern amenities include flat screen TV's and Free WiFi.

✉ springmillinn@dnr.in.gov 🌐 www.in.gov/dnr/parklake/inns/springmill

ROCKPORT

Friendly Farms B&B
2354 S 200 W 47635
270-570-3054
Joan Ramey

75-85 $US BB
5 rooms, 2 pb
C-yes/S-no/P-yes/H-yes

Full or Cont. breakfast
Welcome drink of choice
Porch, horseback riding & stables,
indoor tennis club, pond, canoe, kid
friendly, A/C, antiques

Friendly Farms B&B is located adjacent to the fields of Ramey Riding Stables on Hwy 45. Choose from either the lodge or condo cottage; each adjacent to the fields of Ramey Riding Stables.

✉ jramey66@yahoo.com 🌐 www.rameycamps.com/Site/Bed&Breakfast.htm

VALPARAISO

Inn at Aberdeen, Ltd.
3158 South State Rd 2 46385
866-761-3753 219-465-3753
Bill, Val, Chris, Audrey &
Mandy

106-201 $US BB
11 rooms, 11 pb
Most CC, *Rated*
C-yes/S-no/P-ltd/H-yes

Full gourmet breakfast
Evening dessert, snacks & beverages
Jacuzzi for 2, fireplace, balcony, cable
TV/VCR, lazy ceiling fan, free wireless
Internet

Travel back to the 1800s while enjoying your own Jacuzzi, balcony, cozy fire & truly regal service/ amenities. 18-hole championship golf course.

✉ inn@innataberdeen.com 🌐 www.innataberdeen.com

VEVAY

Schenck Mansion B&B
206 W Turnpike St 47043
877-594-2876 812-427-2787
Jerry & Lisa Fisher

90-200 $US BB
6 rooms, 5 pb
Most CC
C-ltd/S-no/P-no/H-ltd

Full breakfast
TV, private baths, air conditioning,
snack table

A unique, beautifully restored mansion of the 'second empire' located in southeastern Indiana`s Switzerland County. Six, spacious & inviting rooms are complimented by a 4-story tower, copper-lined bath tubs, seven balconies & magnificent details.

✉ jlefisher@hotmail.com 🌐 www.schenckmansion.com

WATERLOO

Maple Leaf Inn	80-90 $US BB	Full breakfast
425 W Maple St 46793	4 rooms, 2 pb	Complimentary soft drinks, bottled
877-402-5393 260-837-5323	Visa, MC	water, juices and homemade goodies,
Ken & Candi Surber	C-ltd/S-no/P-no/H-ltd	Victorian Tea Room
		Hot tub, nightly turn-down service,
		satellite TV, videos, CD player in each
		guestroom with CD's

Escape your hectic world; surround yourself with elegance and peace at the Maple Leaf Inn. This grand home, constructed in 1918, offers many places to relax and be refreshed. Each distinctly decorated room has its own personality.

  mapleleaf425@yahoo.com   🌐 www.visitmapleleafinn.com

WINCHESTER

Winchester Guest House	99-159 $US BB	Full breakfast
Inn	8 rooms, 8 pb	Coffee, wide assortment of teas,
1529 S Old Hwy 27 47394	Most CC, Cash,	evening snacks
765-584-3015	*Rated*, •	Indoor pool, hot tub, theater,
Ted & Debra Davenport	C-yes/S-no/P-no/H-ltd	conferences, golf, free DVD movies,
		massages, flowers, candies

Award winning B&B Resort & Conference Center. Indoor pool, spa, conference room, theater, billiards, table tennis, darts, golf, outdoor games, in-room free DVD movies, massage, fireplace rooms, all private baths. Your private country retreat.

  info@winchester-inn.com   🌐 www.winchester-inn.com

Iowa

BELLEVUE

Mont Rest
300 Spring St 52031
877-872-4220 563-872-4220
Christine & Naomi

125-249 $US BB
12 rooms, 12 pb
Most CC, *Rated*, •
C-ltd/S-no/P-no/H-ltd

Full breakfast
A gourmet dessert is included with
your stay
Murder Mystery, River Cruise, Winery
Tour & Dinner, Golf, Ski, All Grown Up
PJ Party, Massage

*Overlooking the majestic Mississippi River in Bellevue, Iowa, this historic inn is one of the most luxuri-
ous inns in the Midwest. The 12 guestrooms feature queen/king beds, beautiful views, fireplaces, and
2 person whirlpool tubs.*

✉ innkeeper@montrest.com 🌐 www.montrest.com

CEDAR RAPIDS

Belmont Hill Victorian
1525 Cherokee Dr NW 52405
319-366-1343
Ken & Shelley Sullens

95-145 $US BB
5 rooms, 3 pb
Visa, MC, AmEx
C-ltd/S-no/P-ltd/H-ltd

Full breakfast
Afternoon tea by request
Suites, fireplace, accommodate
business travelers, small events,
wooded grounds, gardens

*Experience a unique level of pampering and privacy in a restored 1882 National Register home and
carriage house. Immaculate accommodations and private baths. Lovely secluded grounds, terrace
and gardens.*

✉ shelley@belmonthill.com 🌐 www.belmonthill.com

DUBUQUE

The Hancock House
1105 Grove Ter 52001
563-557-8989
Susan & Chuck Huntley

80-175 $US BB
9 rooms, 9 pb
Most CC, Cash, Checks,
Rated
C-ltd/S-no/P-no/H-no

Full breakfast
Snacks, complimentary – beverage
center
Sitting rooms, Jacuzzis, suites,
fireplaces, cable, wireless Internet, gift
certificates avail.

*Situated on the bluffs overlooking the city of Dubuque to the Mississippi River Valley. Furnished in
Victorian period antiques offering a full breakfast and beverage center.*

✉ chuckdbq@mchsi.com 🌐 www.thehancockhouse.com

The Mandolin Inn
199 Loras Blvd 52001
800-524-7996 563-556-0069
Amy Boynton

85-150 $US BB
8 rooms, 6 pb
Most CC, Cash, Checks,
Rated
C-yes/S-no/P-no/H-yes
Some Spanish & French

Gourmet breakfast
Welcome drink
Cable TV, wireless Internet access,
2 sweet cats, veranda, central air,
fireplace, parlor/music room

Free Night w/Certificate: Valid Sunday-Thursday, except holidays.

*Beautifully restored 1908 Edwardian mansion dedicated to sharing elegance & comfort. Perfect for
kindling romance or unwinding after business, as well as exploring the upper Mississippi River. Handicapped accessible. Wireless Internet access.*

✉ innkeeper@mandolininn.com 🌐 www.mandolininn.com

The Redstone Inn & Suites
504 Bluff St 52001
563-582-1894
Jerry & Kelly Lazore

75-195 $US BB
15 rooms, 15 pb
Most CC, Checks, •
C-yes/S-no/P-yes/H-no

Deluxe Full Breakfast
Afternoon tea, coffee & snacks
available in the parlor
Cable TV, free wireless Internet,
whirlpool suites, laundry services,
business accommodations, fax

*An elegant, intimate boutique hotel, a Queen Ann Victorian in the heart of Cable Car Square. A his-
toric lodging experience with the Mississippi River nearby. Wireless high speed Internet, whirlpool
suites, and private baths. Complimentary breakfast.*

✉ info@theredstoneinn.com 🌐 www.theredstoneinn.com

The Hancock House, Dubuque, IA

DUBUQUE

The Richards House
1492 Locust St 52001
888-557-1492 563-557-1492
Michelle Stuart

40-120 $US BB
6 rooms, 4 pb
Most CC, Cash, Checks,
Rated, •
C-yes/S-ltd/P-ltd/H-no

Full breakfast
Snacks & beverages
Sitting room, antiques, concealed TVs,
phones, fireplaces

An 1883 stick-style Victorian mansion with over 80 stained-glass windows. Seven varieties of wood-work and period furnishings. Working fireplaces in guestrooms.

✉ innkeeper@therichardshouse.com 🌐 www.therichardshouse.com

DURANGO

Quiet Walker Lodge B&B
Inn
18132 Paradise Valley
Trl 52001
800-388-0942 563-552-1034
Mike & Carol Chalberg

99-199 $US BB
7 rooms, 7 pb
Most CC, Cash, Checks,
Rated
S-no/P-no/H-ltd

Full breakfast
After a restful sleep enjoy a hearty
breakfast with fresh brewed coffee,
specialty tea & juice
Whirlpool/bubble tubs (some rooms),
kitchenette, A/C, TVs/VCRs, sound
spas, wireless Internet

Quiet Walker Lodge is nestled in the woods of the Mississippi River Valley a short 8 miles from the city of Dubuque, Iowa, where the peacefulness of the countryside will relax and unwind you.

✉ innkeeper@quietwalkerlodge.com 🌐 www.quietwalkerlodge.com

GRINNELL

Carriage House B&B
1133 Broad St 50112
641-236-7520
Ray & Dorothy Spriggs

65-85 $US BB
6 rooms, 6 pb
Most CC, Cash, Checks,
Rated, •
C-ltd/S-no/P-no/H-no

Full breakfast
Afternoon tea by reservation and
payment, non-alcoholic beverages
Sitting room, library, Jacuzzis,
fireplaces, free wireless Internet
available

Victorian home restored with your comfort in mind; gourmet breakfast; afternoon tea available by reservation. Enjoy the wicker on the porch or read by the fire.

✉ irishbnb@iowatelecom.net 🌐 www.ia-bednbreakfast-inns.com/carriagehouse

IOWA CITY

A B&B Golden Haug
517 E. Washington 52240
319-354-4284
Nila Haug

105-225 $US BB
10 rooms, 10 pb
Most CC, Cash,
Checks, •
C-ltd/S-ltd/P-no/H-ltd

Hearty gourmet breakfast
Bedside chocolates, in-room
refreshment basket
Free WiFi, off-street parking, cable
TV, fridge, microwave in each suite,&
whirlpools, fireplaces in some

Located downtown, this is an ideal place for leisure or business travelers. Ten guestrooms with private baths, free off-street parking and wireless Internet. Convenient breakfast times for our guests. Extended stay rates available.

✉ imahaug@goldenhaug.com 🌐 www.goldenhaug.com

KEOKUK

The Grand Anne B&B
816 Grand Ave 52632
319-795-6990 319-524-6310
Cretia & Rick Hesse

119-159 $US BB
5 rooms, 5 pb
Most CC, Cash, Checks
C-ltd/S-no/P-no/H-ltd

Full Gourmet Breakfast
Parlors, ballroom, billiards, gardens,
private bath, TV/VCR, telephones,
refrigerators, WiFi

Perched on a bluff overlooking the Mississippi River, the Grand Anne B&B redefines "affordable luxury." Designed by George F. Barber, the 22-room 1897 mansion is an elaborate example of Queen Anne style domestic architecture.

✉ grandannekeokuk@yahoo.com 🌐 www.bbonline.com/ia/grandanne

The River's Edge B&B Inn
611 Grand Ave 52632
319-524-1700
Bob & Afton Westwwod

99-139 $US BB
4 rooms, 4 pb
Most CC, Cash,
Checks, •
C-yes/S-no/P-no/H-no

Full breakfast
Snacks
Sitting room, library, suites, cable TV,
accom. bus. travelers

Majestic inn located high above the Mississippi river. Enjoy relaxing in our guestrooms or suites. Breathtaking river view is never out of season.

✉ rooms@riversedgeiowa.com 🌐 www.riversedgeiowa.com

MAQUOKETA

Squiers Manor
418 W Pleasant St 52060
563-652-6961
Virl & Kathy Banowetz

80-195 $US BB
8 rooms, 8 pb
Visa, MC, Disc,
Rated, •
C-yes/S-ltd/P-no/H-no

Full country gourmet breakfast
Complimentary beverages plus a
special candlelight dessert is served
each evening.
Sitting room, library, 3 suites available,
fireplaces, whirlpools, TV's, central air.
in-room coffee

Antique decor, crackling fireplaces and Victorian ambience provide for quiet times and intimate moments at Squiers Manor B&B. Enjoy evening dessert & in-room coffee. All of this & superior service, described recently by a guest as "definitive hospitality."

✉ innkeeper@squiersmanor.com 🌐 www.squiersmanor.com

ST. ANSGAR

Blue Belle Inn
513 West 4th St 50472
877-713-3113 641-713-3113
Sherrie Hansen

70-375 $US BB
10 rooms, 8 pb
Most CC, *Rated*
C-yes/S-no/P-no/H-yes
German (a little)

Full breakfast
Lunch, dinner, a wonderful fondue
feast, popcorn, hot chocolate, coffee,
soda
TV/VCR/DVD, movies, wireless
Internet, kitchenette, library, piano,
conference rooms, spa nearby

Romantic Victorian with gourmet dining, teahouse, fondue, stained glass, maple woodwork, tin ceilings, queen/king beds, A/C, fireplaces, private Jacuzzis. Murder mysteries, weddings, cooking classes, wireless Internet, quaint shops. Handicap accessible.

✉ bluebelle@omnitelcom.com 🌐 www.BlueBelleInn.com

The Castle Inn Riverside, Wichita, KS

Kansas

MANHATTAN

Scenic Valley Inn
610 S Scenic Dr 66503
785-776-6831
Paul & Diana Nickel

125-150 $US BB
3 rooms, 3 pb
Most CC, Cash, *Rated*
C-yes/S-no/P-no/H-ltd
All Year Closed
Holidays

Full 3- course breakfast
Coffee, hot chocolate, cold drinks, &
popcorn in the walk-through pantry,
breakfast served in room
Basketball goal in Barn, church
service every Sunday in Barn, dinner
reservations made for you

Scenic Valley Inn is described within it's name, the scenery & ambience are breathtaking. A charming, private Inn set in a heavily-wooded, romantic and comfortable environment. Located near must see tourist spots and convenient for business travelers.
✉ info@scenicvalleyinn.com ◐ www.scenicvalleyinn.com

WICHITA

**Serenity Bed and
Breakfast Inn**
1018 N Market St 67214
888-788-0884 316-266-4666
Kim Moore

89-149 $US BB
3 rooms, 3 pb
Visa, MC, *Rated*
C-yes/S-ltd/P-ltd/H-ltd
French

Large, full gourmet breakfast
Dinners, desserts, appetizers,
beverage assortments, dessert platters,
caviar platters, champagne . . .
king-size beds, free WiFi, color flat
screen TVs, microwaves, Jacuzzis,
private baths in all rooms.

Free Night w/Certificate: Not valid on major holidays. Room Upgrade.

Serenity Bed and Breakfast Inn is a romantic and historic getaway close to downtown Wichita Kansas, but tucked away on a quiet residential street. King-size beds, Jacuzzis, private baths, free full breakfast, 5-star award winning services, dinners & MORE.
✉ serenitybedandbreakfastinn@yahoo.com ◐ www.serenitybedandbreakfastinn.com

The Castle Inn Riverside
1155 N River Blvd 67203
800-580-1131 316-263-9300
Paula & Terry Lowry

125-275 $US BB
14 rooms, 14 pb
Most CC, Cash, Checks,
Rated, •
C-ltd/S-no/P-no/H-yes

Full breakfast
Light hors d'oeuvres, wine,
homemade desserts on Fri-Sat and
holidays
Parlor, Billiards Room, Library, Jacuzzi
tubs, fireplaces, phones, TV/VCR,
dataport

An architectural masterpiece, this luxurious home has 14 guestrooms, each individually appointed. Guests enjoy a selection of wine, cheese, gourmet coffees, teas, liqueurs, homemade desserts & full breakfast. ✉ *info@castleinnriverside.com* ◐ *www.castleinnriverside.com*

Kentucky

BELLEVUE

Christopher's B&B	125-189 $US BB	Continental plus during week
604 Poplar St 41073	3 rooms, 3 pb	Snacks and water cooler
888-585-7085 859-491-9354	Most CC, Cash, Checks,	WiFi, Suites, cable TV, VCR/DVD
Brenda Guidugli	*Rated*, •	player/movies, Jacuzzi tubs, iron,
	C-ltd/S-ltd/P-no/H-ltd	ironing board, hairdryer

Free Night w/Certificate: Sun-Thurs; based on Jr. Jacuzzi room availability; excludes tax.

Award-winning Christopher's B&B is named after the late 1800's Christian Church & the Patron Saint of Traveler's. Located near the Newport Aquarium and downtown Cincinnati and is easily accessible from many interstates.

✉ christophers@insightbb.com   🌐 www.christophersbb.com

BEREA

Pinnacle View Inn B&B	109-229 $US BB	Full Southern breakfast
491 Log Cabin Road 40403	4 rooms, 4 pb	Homemade delights, bottled water,
859-986-0044	Visa, MC, Disc	soft drinks, premium organic coffee or
Ira J. Bates	C-ltd/S-no/P-no/H-yes	tea are always available
		Fresh flowers, quality linens, Gilchrist
		& Soames amenities, WiFi, comfy
		chairs & beds

Experience a romantic bed and breakfast with spectacular views, offering the finest accommodation in Berea/Richmond, Ky. We are small enough to provide the personal attention you seek, and offer exceptional hospitality and a commitment to service.

✉ PVI@windstream.net   🌐 www.pinnacleviewinn.com

BROWNSVILLE

Serenity Hill B&B	90-130 $US BB	Full breakfast
3600 Mammoth Cave	3 rooms, 3 pb	Homemade cookies in your room.
Rd 42210	Visa, MC	Living room, Satellite TV, WiFi, rooms
270-597-9647	C-ltd/S-no/P-no/H-no	have central heat/air, alarm clocks
James & Debra Lawler		

A modern house decorated with beautiful antiques and family art. They blend together nicely with the casual furnishing to make Serenity Hill a great place to sit back, relax and enjoy the views after a day caving, or visiting the many area attractions.

✉ serenityhill@windstream.net   🌐 www.serenityhillbedandbreakfast.com

GEORGETOWN

Jordan Farm B&B	100-125 $US BB	Continental Plus breakfast
4091 Newtown Pike 40324	4 rooms, 4 pb	Afternoon tea, snacks
859 321-5707	Visa, MC, *Rated*	Eight miles from KY Horse Park, Near
Harold & Rebecca Jordan	C-ltd/S-no/P-no/H-yes	shops, restaurants, Jacuzzis, fridges
		in Suites

Jordan Farm offers a unique opportunity to stay on a beautiful 20-acre working Bluegrass thoroughbred farm. Perfect place for horse enthusiasts to stay and be up close and personal with horses. Charming walks, pond with gazebo for quiet time.

✉ becky@beckyjordan.net   🌐 www.jordanfarmbandb.com

Magnolia Inn	99-159 $US BB	Continental plus breakfast
320 E Main St 40324	3 rooms, 3 pb	TV, WiFi
502-542-0685	Most CC, Cash	
Colleen London	C-yes/S-ltd/P-ltd/H-ltd	

Free Night w/Certificate: Anytime.

Charming 1700's home located in downtown Georgetown. Near shops and restaurants, close to Kentucky Horse park, Georgetown College and I-75. We are cozy yet perfect for individual or group stays. Consider us your home away from home!

✉ info@magnoliainnky.com   🌐 www.magnoliainnky.com

GEORGETOWN

Pineapple Inn
645 S Broadway 40324
502-868-5453
Muriel & Les

80-110 $US BB
4 rooms, 4 pb
Visa, MC, *Rated*, •
C-yes/S-ltd/P-no/H-no

Full breakfast
Snacks, complimentary wine
Sitting room, bar service, Heart of
Bluegrass horse country, spa available

Built in 1876 – on the historical register – gourmet breakfast in country French dining room. Four large private rooms with baths, one with spa, each uniquely decorated with antiques.

⬤ www.pineappleinnbedandbreakfast.com

GHENT

The Poet's House B&B
501 Main St 41045
502-525-3567
David Hendren

95-125 $US BB
4 rooms, 4 pb
Visa, MC, AmEx,
Rated
C-yes/S-no/P-no/H-yes

Full gourmet breakfast
catering by reservation
hot tub, Jacuzzi bath, lovely courtyard,
deck overlooking river

1863 Federal style brick home of Poet and Adjutant General of Kentucky, James Tandy Ellis. Overlooks the beautiful Ohio River. Highway 42 now named Butler-Ellis Highway in honor of James Tandy Ellis. ✉ henghent@gmail.com

HARRODSBURG

Aspen Hall Manor
558 Aspen Hall Dr 40330
888-485-8871 859-734-5050
Jill & Andrew Romero

105-155 $US BB
4 rooms, 4 pb
Most CC, Cash, Checks
C-yes/S-no/P-no/H-no

Full breakfast
Complimentary beverages &
appetizers, lunch & dinner available
Tea room, derby room, porch, private
parties, weddings

Experience the southern elegance of an 1840 Greek Revival Manor House nestled in the quiet hills of Kentucky, in the historic town of Harrodsburg. Just thirty minutes from Lexington, less than one hour from Louisville. ✉ jill@aspenhallmanor.com ⬤ www.aspenhallmanor.com

IRVINE

Snug Hollow Farm
790 McSwain Branch 40336
606-723-4786
Barbara Napier

100-195 $US BB
3 rooms, 3 pb
Visa, MC
C-yes/S-ltd/P-no/H-ltd

Full breakfast
Goodies included; lunch & dinner
available upon request
Massage, fishing, hiking, sitting room,
library, fireplace, sunroom, porches,
forest

"50 Best Girlfriends Getaways of North America" National Geographic. Appalachia at its best! Unique & secluded on 300 acres, restored cozy cabin & farmhouse, porches, peaceful surroundings & gardens. 30 minutes to Berea, 1 hour to Lexington.

✉ info@snughollow.com ⬤ www.snughollow.com

LAGRANGE

Bluegrass Country Estate
1226 Bluegrass
Parkway 40031
877-229-2009 502-222-2902
Cheryl Sabin

160-200 $US BB
5 rooms, 3 pb
Visa, MC, AmEx,
Rated
C-ltd/S-no/P-no/H-no

Full breakfast
Swimming pool, hot tub, patio,
workout room, theater room, game
room, horse barn

Bluegrass Country Estate is a unique Bed and Breakfast in L'Esprit, home of many horse farms. The Estate is on 10 acres with 5 uniquely decorated guestrooms, swimming pool, hot tub, full room theatre, 2 game rooms and gym. Equine lodging available.

✉ relax@bluegrasscountryestate.com ⬤ www.bluegrasscountryestate.com

LOUISVILLE

1853 Inn at Woodhaven
401 S Hubbards Ln 40207
888-895-1011 502-895-1011
Marsha Burton

95-225 $US BB
8 rooms, 8 pb
Most CC, Cash, Checks,
Rated, •
C-ltd/S-no/P-ltd/H-ltd

Full breakfast
Coffee, tea and snacks in each room,
cookies and soft drinks in common
area
Sitting room, library, whirlpool tubs,
steam showers, suites, fireplaces,
cable TV, WiFi

An elegant and comfortable Inn furnished with antiques. Located in a beautiful suburb 8 minutes from downtown Louisville, and close to all attractions including fine dining and shopping. Features include gourmet breakfast, fine linens, beautiful gardens

 woodhavenb@aol.com ⬤ www.innatwoodhaven.com

LOUISVILLE

Austin's Inn Place
915 South 1st St 40203
502-585-8855
Mary & Tom Austin

120-155 $US BB
8 rooms, 8 pb
Most CC, Cash
C-ltd/S-ltd/P-no/H-no

Full breakfast
Meeting rooms, two-person hot tubs,
game room, library, parlor, wireless
Internet and gift shop.

Beyond B&B, Austin's Inn Place is a guest and gathering place in Old Louisville, Kentucky. Featuring eight guestrooms, three dining rooms, parlor, game room, party room and bar all just blocks from the center of downtown.

✉ austinsinnplace@bellsouth.net   🌐 www.austinsinnplace.com

Central Park
1353 S 4th St 40208
877-922-1505 502-638-1505
Robert & Eva Wessels

125-225 $US BB
7 rooms, 7 pb
Most CC, Cash,
Rated, •
C-yes/S-ltd/P-no/H-no

Full breakfast
Complimentary afternoon & evening
beverages, snacks & desserts
Formal parlor, porch & garden,
Jacuzzi, suites, fireplaces, in-room
phones, high speed Internet

Located in the heart of the Old Louisville Historic District, we offer four elegant queen & king guestrooms, one 2 bedroom suite and the Carriage House with kitchenette. All rooms have private baths. Gourmet breakfast every morning.

✉ centralpar@win.net   🌐 www.centralparkbandb.com

Columbine Bed & Breakfast
1707 S Third St 40208
800-635-5010 502-635-5000
Rich May & Bob Goldstein

119-165 $US BB
6 rooms, 6 pb
Visa, MC, *Rated*, •
C-ltd/S-ltd/P-no/H-ltd
Italian

Gourmet breakfast
Snacks, bottled water, juices & soft
drinks
Marble fireplaces, movie library, TV/
VCR/DVD, free WiFi, telephones,
garden, screened porch

Magnificent historic mansion just minutes from Churchill Downs (Kentucky Derby), Louisville International Airport, University of Louisville, and most major attractions.

✉ info@thecolumbine.com   🌐 www.thecolumbine.com

Pinecrest Cottage & Gardens
2806 Newburg Rd 40205
502-454-3800
Nancy Morris

110-165 $US BB
1 rooms, 1 pb
Visa, MC, AmEx
C-yes/S-ltd/P-ltd/H-ltd

Breakfast foods of choice provided
Snacks
Fireplace, free Internet, tennis court,
cable TV, swimming pool

Traditionally decorated, well-appointed guesthouse affording complete privacy. Free Wireless Internet.

✉ pinecrest@insightbb.com   🌐 www.pinecrestcottageandgardens.com

Samuel Culbertson Mansion B&B
1432 S 3rd St 40208
866-522-5078 502-634-3100
Rudy Van Meter

109-179 $US BB
5 rooms, 5 pb
Most CC, Cash,
Checks, •
C-ltd/S-ltd/P-ltd/H-no
German

Full breakfast
Complimentary snacks, lunch/dinner
can be arranged
Cable TV, sitting room, can
accommodate business travel

Louisville's most historic B&B, opulently furnished, southern gourmet breakfasts, close to downtown and Churchill Downs.

✉ rudy@culbertsonmansion.us   🌐 www.culbertsonmansion.com

The Roost Inn (Formerly Inn Off the Alley)
1325 Bardstown Rd 40204
502-451-0121
Annette Saco

105-145 $US BB
3 rooms, 3 pb
Visa, MC
C-yes/S-no/P-ltd/H-no

Continental Breakfast & Snacks
Italian Bistro
Cable TV, wireless Internet, full
kitchen, separate sitting area, desk

Located on the famous Bardstown Rd. in the heart of the historic and eclectic Highlands Neighborhood, where there are hundreds of locally owned shops, restaurants and galleries. The Inn also houses Le Gallo Rosso Italian Bistro, Louisville's hidden gem.

✉ info@theroostinn.com

PARIS

Country Charm Historic Farmhouse
505 Hutchison Road 40361
859-988-1006
David & LaVonna Snell

85-135 $US BB
5 rooms, 4 pb
Visa, MC, Disc
C-yes/S-no/P-no/H-no

Full breakfast
2 acre yard, basketball court, hot tub

Located on seventy acres in the heart of Kentucky Bluegrass country just off US 27/68 between Paris and Lexington. Shady Brook Golf Course is across the road.

✉ dlsnell@dishmail.net 🌐 www.countrycharm.net

PRINCETON

Cadiz Street B&B
209 Cadiz Street 42445
270-625-1314
Charles& Helen Pratt

85 $US BB
2 rooms, 2 pb
Visa, MC
C-ltd/S-no/P-ltd/H-no

Full breakfast

Our completely restored 1895 Victorian home is a charming place to stay for just one night or for a much longer period. Conveniently located just a short walking distance from the beautifully restored downtown area of historic Princeton.

✉ inquiries@cadizstreetbedandbreakfast.com 🌐 www.cadizstreetbedandbreakfast.com

SPRINGFIELD

1851 Historic Maple Hill Manor B&B
2941 Perryville Rd/US 40069
800-886-7546 859-336-3075
Todd Allen & Tyler Horton

119-189 $US BB
7 rooms, 7 pb
Most CC, Cash, Checks,
Rated, •
C-yes/S-ltd/P-ltd/H-ltd

Full Country "Gourmet" Breakfast
Homemade Desserts & Coffee/Tea
Social each evening, 24-hour beverage service, and variety of snacks
Antiques, luxury linens, Jacuzzi for 2, fireplaces, satellite TV/VCR/DVD/CD w/movies, magazines, etc

Free Night w/Certificate: Anytime. Valid Nov-April, Sunday-Thursday.

Historic, award-winning B&B accommodations at a working Alpaca & Llama Farm. Voted #1 in U.S. as the B&B with the Most Historical Charm, Kentucky's Best B&B, Best Breakfast in the Southeast, Best B&B in the South, and Top 10 Best Innkeepers in the U.S.

✉ maplehillmanorbb@aol.com 🌐 www.maplehillmanor.com

VERSAILLES

1823 Historic Rose Hill Inn
233 Rose Hill Ave 40383
800-307-0460 859-873-5957
Alder & Gillian Blackburn

139-184 $US BB
7 rooms, 7 pb
Most CC, *Rated*, •
C-yes/S-no/P-ltd/H-ltd

Full breakfast
Snacks, sodas, after dinner aperitifs, picnic baskets (lunch/dinner) available
Sitting room, library, suites, fireplaces, cookies in room at check-in

Built in 1823, the historic home has been wonderfully renovated, but features of the original mansion are preserved and enhanced. The parlor, library, front porch, and 3 acres of grounds are all for your enjoyment.

✉ Innkeepers@rosehillinn.com 🌐 www.rosehillinn.com

Storybook Inn
277 Rose Hill Ave 40383
877-279-2563 859-879-9993
C Elise Buckley

219-289 $US BB
5 rooms, 5 pb
Most CC, *Rated*
C-yes/S-no/P-yes/H-yes
February thru December

Fresh, gourmet
Daily homemade goodies; bottled water, soft drinks, fruit, tea, coffee, complimentary glass of wine
Hi-Speed Internet, book/movie library, satellite TV, DVD, massage, arrange private horse farm tour

"A delight to the senses! Elegant! Amazing! A real treasure!" are all descriptions used by guests to describe A Storybook Inn. Upscale. Thick ultra comfortable mattresses and bedding. Luscious breakfasts. Private, gorgeous surroundings near Lexington, KY.

✉ stay@storybook-inn.com 🌐 www.storybook-inn.com

Louisiana

BREAUX BRIDGE

Isabelle Inn Bed &	165 $US BB	Full gourmet breakfast
Extraordinary Breakfast	5 rooms, 5 pb	Snacks & refreshments on arrival
1130 Berard St 70517	Most CC	pool, spa, free WiFi, off street parking
337-412-0455	C-yes/S-no/P-no/H-no	
Susan Sabatier		

Family home with 5 luxurious guestrooms and an extraordinary breakfast. Our mission is to provide all the comforts of home along with all the extras of a fine resort. Our little town is big on friendliness; you will feel like family everywhere you go.

✉ karen@isabelleinn.com 🌐 www.isabelleinn.com

Maison Des Amis	100-125 $US BB	Full Cajun breakfast
111 Washington St 70517	4 rooms, 4 pb	Complimentary beverages, muffins,
888-570-3043 337-507-3399	Most CC, Cash, Checks,	candy, granola/oatmeal bars
Ellen Wicker	*Rated*	Laundry, tour information, dinner and
	C-ltd/S-ltd/P-no/H-ltd	swamp tour reservations, cable TV,
	French	wireless Internet,

Historic Creole/Caribbean residence, overlooks legendary Bayou Teche. Lush gardens, gazebo, glassed-in sun porch, private baths, antiques, original artwork. Full Cajun/Creole breakfast. Complimentary beverages, daily maid service, general tour information

✉ seeyou@maisondesamis.com 🌐 www.maisondesamis.com

HAMMOND

Michabelle Inn &	75-125 $US BB	Full breakfast
Restaurant	7 rooms, 7 pb	Full service bar & restaurant, dinner
1106 S Holly St 70403	Most CC, *Rated*	package available
985-419-0550	C-ltd/S-ltd/P-ltd/H-ltd	Library, reception hall, grounds, spa
Chef Michel & Isabel Marcais	French, Portuguese	& fitness center w/ pool, wireless
		Internet

Louisiana's Number 1 Rated Country Inn by AAA, Michabelle is a Greek Revival Estate decorated in authentic French antiques, located in serene surroundings.

✉ michabelle@i-55.com 🌐 www.michabelle.com

HOUMA

A La Maison Crochet Bed	65-85 $US BB	Full breakfast
& Breakfast	2 rooms, 2 pb	wireless Internet, television, laundry
301 Midland Dr 70360	Most CC	facilities, telephone, fax, computer,
888-483-3033 985-879-3033	C-yes/S-ltd/P-yes/H-no	swimming pool, Jacuzzi
Leland & Sally Crochet	Cajun French	

Located in Terrebonne (Good Earth) Parish less than 60 miles from New Orleans, Crochet House is the perfect place to experience the Cajun experience; the people, the culture and their roots.

✉ leesalco@comcast.net 🌐 www.crochethouse.com

LAKE CHARLES

C.A.'s House	165-285 $US BB	Full breakfast
618 Ford St 70601	6 rooms, 5 pb	Snacks, coffee, refreshments
866-439-6672 337-439-6672	Visa, MC, AmEx,	Bikes, hot tub, kayaks, heated
Tanis Robinson	*Rated*	swimming pool
	C-ltd/S-ltd/P-ltd/H-ltd	
	Romanian	

C.A.'s House offers superb luxury accommodations. There are a range of rooms, from single rooms to luxury suites. Located in the heart of Lake Charles' Charpentier Historic District.

✉ waltersatt@aol.com 🌐 cas-house.com

NAPOLEONVILLE

Madewood Plantation House	209-325 $US MAP	Full plantation breakfast
4250 Hwy 308 70390	8 rooms, 8 pb	Wine/cheese reception, candlelight
985-369-7151	Most CC, Cash,	dinner. Vegetarian/dietary needs OK.
Keith & Millie Marshall	*Rated*, •	Lunch by reservation.
	C-ltd/S-ltd/P-ltd/H-ltd	Candlelit dinners included with most
		packages. Canopy beds, private baths,
		parlor, library, porches.

A Greek Revival mansion turned country inn featuring wine & cheese, candlelit dinners with a house party atmosphere. Or choose a more romantic, private dinner, full breakfast, & antique canopied beds. Rated in top 54 inns by National Geographic Traveler.

✉ madewoodpl@aol.com   🌐 www.madewood.com

NATCHITOCHES

Levy-East House	125-200 $US BB	Full gourmet breakfast
358 Jefferson St 71457	4 rooms, 4 pb	Champagne, cream sherry, coffee &
800-840-0662 318-352-0662	Visa, MC, AmEx,	tea, chocolates
Judy & Avery East	*Rated*, •	Sitting rooms, off-street parking, front
	S-no/P-no/H-no	& back galleries, ceiling fans

Enjoy luxurious leisure and elegant accommodations in this grand Antebellum home in the Historic District. Fine antiques, queen size beds with private Jacuzzi baths and gourmet breakfasts.

✉ innkeeper@levyeasthouse.com   🌐 www.levyeasthouse.com

Samuel Guy House	105-135 $US BB	Full breakfast
309 Pine St 71457	5 rooms, 5 pb	Cable TV, phones, coffee makers,
800-984-1080 318-354-1080	Most CC	Jacuzzis, bath & beauty supplies
Keri Fidelak	C-yes/S-no/P-no/H-no	

Witness a piece of Louisiana history being brought back to life at the Samuel Guy House. Rooms are handsomely decorated with antique and reproduction period furniture, comfortable sitting areas, ceiling fans, spacious baths with Jacuzzi tub.

✉ willwill@cp-tel.net   🌐 www.samuelguyhouse.com

The Rusca House	95-135 $US BB	Full breakfast
124 Poete St 71457	4 rooms, 4 pb	Wine, refreshments, snacks
866-531-0898	Most CC	Private entrance, wireless Internet,
Bridget Williams	S-no/P-no	Jacuzzi tubs

Tasteful elegance and charm await you as you step back in time into a lovingly restored 1920's bungalow. From the porch swing to the lovely formal gardens, relaxation and Southern hospitality will grace your visit.

✉ bridget@ruscahouse.com   🌐 ruscahouse.com

NEW ORLEANS

1870 Banana Courtyard	79-165 $US BB	Continental breakfast B&B only
1422 N Rampart St 70116	10 rooms, 10 pb	Main B&B has free soft drinks, bottled
800-842-4748 504-947-4475	Most CC, *Rated*	water, a wine or beer when we're
Mary Ramsey (aka the	C-ltd/S-ltd/P-no/H-ltd	around.
banana lady)	Y'at	Phone, TV, indv. heat &A/C,
		hammock, porch swing, courtyard,
		rooms w/view, balcony, WiFi, biz
		center

Free Night w/Certificate: Rack rate; valid occasion Pirates Attic or Carriage/Quill Room; 6/15-8/15 week nights, excluding holidays, special events, major conventions.

Ooh la la! In 1800s, house was bordello catering to societies elite. B&B in great location, French Quarter 30 yards, Bourbon St. 3 mins. Walk to ALL major attractions. Rooms with view, vacation rental accommodations in New Orleans.

✉ bananacour@aol.com   🌐 www.bananacourtyard.com

NEW ORLEANS

| **A Crescent City Guest House**
612 Marigny St 70117
877-281-2680 504-944-8722
Matthew Harring | 79-179 $US BB
4 rooms, 4 pb
Most CC
C-ltd/S-ltd/P-yes/H-no
September – May | Continental plus breakfast
Extended continental breakfast available 24 hours
Free off-street parking, wireless Internet, movies, patio & hot tub, maid service, tax included |

Enjoy all of the excitement and charm that New Orleans has to offer. We are in the historic Faubourg Marigny, just three blocks from the French Quarter and the Riverfront Street Car Lines. Four guestrooms. Pets welcome, free off-street parking.

✉ matlynccgh@msn.com 🌐 www.crescentcitygh.com

| **Aaron Ingram Haus**
1012 Elysian Fields 70117
504-949-3110
Scott Graves | 119-189 $US EP
4 rooms, 4 pb
Most CC, Cash, •
C-ltd/S-ltd/P-no/H-no | Self catered breakfast
Self-catered kitchen with stove, fridge, coffee maker, microwave & toaster
A/C, free WiFi for your lap top, hairdryers, color cable TV, radio/alarm clocks, laundry facility |

Located only six blocks from world-famous Bourbon Street, within walking distance to most New Orleans attractions. The Frenchmen Street mecca of nightclubs, bars and a number of good and reasonably priced restaurants are within a few blocks of our door.

✉ ingramhaus@yahoo.com 🌐 www.ingramhaus.com

| **Avenue Inn B&B**
4125 St Charles Ave 70115
800-490-8542 504-269-2640
Joe & Bebe Rabhan | 99-399 $US BB
17 rooms, 17 pb
Most CC, Cash,
Rated, •
C-ltd/S-no/P-no/H-yes
Spanish | Continental plus breakfast
Afternoon tea, fruit & cheese upon request, low carb & special diet items available
Grand parlor & master dining room, hardwood floors, Creole porch, private baths, voice mail, WiFi |

1891 Grand Mansion on famed St. Charles Avenue streetcar line, minutes to the French Quarter. Enjoy the "Avenue" in a rocker on our veranda, rest in our restored guestrooms and drift back to the splendor of the past. Don't just visit New Orleans, live it!

✉ stay@avenueinnbb.com 🌐 www.avenueinnbb.com

| **Columns Hotel**
3811 St. Charles Ave 70115
800-445-9308 504-899-9308
Claire & Jacques Creppel | 120-230 $US BB
20 rooms, 20 pb
Most CC, Cash
C-yes/S-no/P-yes/H-no | Full breakfast
Restaurant and lounge on premises
Complimentary daily newspaper, 24 hour front desk staff, Garden District location, in-room service |

If you've ever yearned for grander, more romantic times . . . come to The Columns Hotel in the Garden District of New Orleans. The Columns Hotel, New Orleans' favorite historic hotel, welcomes you to experience a timeless and memorable stay in the South.

✉ columnshtl@aol.com 🌐 thecolumns.com

| **Elysian Fields Inn**
930 Elysian Fields Ave 70117
866-948-9420 504-948-9420
Leigh & Jim Crawford | 109-269 $US BB
9 rooms, 9 pb
Most CC, Cash, Checks,
Rated
C-yes/S-ltd/P-ltd/H-yes | Full breakfast
Coffee & tea bar available all day; bottled water
Flat screen TV, VCR/DVD players, WiFi, daily housekeeping, private Italian marble bathrooms |

Welcome to Elysian Fields Inn, a AAA rated New Orleans B&B . . . a testament to our dedication to our guests. Historic 1850's Urban Inn. 9 tastefully decorated guestrooms each with flat-screen TV, DVD/ VCR player and luxurious private baths.

✉ innkeeper@elysianfieldsinn.com 🌐 www.elysianfieldsinn.com

NEW ORLEANS

Fairchild House B&B
1518 Prytania St 70130
800-256-8096 504-524-0154
Beatriz Aprigliano-Ziegler

75-145 $US BB
9 rooms, 9 pb
Visa, MC, AmEx,
Rated, •
C-yes/S-no/P-no/H-no
Spanish, Portuguese

Continental plus breakfast
Sitting room, suites, cable TV, off-street
parking, courtyard & garden

Classic, comfortable B&B located in the Lower Garden District, one block from streetcar line, 15 blocks to French Quarter.

 info@fairchildhouse.com 🌐 www.fairchildhouse.com

Garden District B&B
2418 Magazine St 70130
504-895-4302
Raynell Dunham

80-225 $US BB
4 rooms, 4 pb
Most CC
C-yes/S-ltd/P-no/H-ltd
Spanish

Continental breakfast
Balconies, courtyard, screened-in
porch, kitchenettes, cable TV, Internet
access

Stay in an 1870 historic home with a great location. Shop, eat, drink & relax on Magazine St or take a quick streetcar ride to the French Quarter. All rooms feature original southern pine floors and 12 foot ceilings.

 info@gardendistrictbedandbreakfast.com 🌐 www.gardendistrictbedandbreakfast.com

---

Gentry House B&B
1031 St Ann St 70116
888-525-2227 504-525-4433
Brian & Charlotte Furness

100-175 $US BB
5 rooms, 5 pb
Visa, MC
C-yes/S-no/P-no/H-ltd

Continental breakfast
Kitchenettes stocked with fruit, cereal
& other snacks
Family friendly, pet visitations in the
courtyard, kitchenettes, romance,
group accommodations

Enjoy New Orleans like a native. Start your days with sinfully flaky fresh croissants delivered to your door daily to enjoy en-suite or in the fountain-splashed courtyard. Stroll out to enjoy beautiful Jackson Square and enjoy the Mighty Mississippi!

 gentryhse@aol.com 🌐 www.gentryhouse.com

La Dauphine
2316 Dauphine St 70117
504-948-2217
Ray Ruiz & Kim Pedersen

85-160 $US BB
3 rooms, 3 pb
Most CC, Cash, *Rated*
S-no/P-no/H-no
French, German and
Danish

SelfServe Toast/Fruit/Yogurt/Cereal
Sitting room, robes, hairdryers, free
WiFi, iMac, free U.S. long distance,
taxes incl, fridge, patio

Stay with a native French heritage New Orleanian. Located in the Faubourg Marigny district, a quieter version of the adjacent French Quarter. We love to host nice, relaxed people- who seek out new surroundings and experiences—who can "go with the flow."

 ladauphine@aol.com 🌐 www.ladauphine.com

Lions Inn
2517 Chartres St 70117
800-485-6846 504-945-2339
Floyd

89-175 $US BB
9 rooms, 6 pb
Most CC
C-yes/S-no/P-no/H-no
French, Italian

Extended Continental Breakfast
Complimentary Wine Hour, 6–7 p.m.
Garden, swimming pool, Jacuzzi,
fireplace, A/C, Internet

Welcome to the Lions' Inn, a romantic bed & breakfast located minutes from the French Quarter. Enjoy the celebrated nightclubs, restaurants & entertainment unique to New Orleans.

 info@lionsinn.com 🌐 www.lionsinn.com

Rose Manor Inn
7214 Pontchartrain
Blvd 70124
504-282-8200
Peter & Ruby Verhoeven

85-195 $US BB
9 rooms, 9 pb
Most CC, Cash, •
C-ltd/S-no/P-no/H-ltd
Chinese, German

Continental plus breakfast
Tea, coffee, soft drinks & snacks, bar
Cable TV, refrigerator, concierge
services, WiFi, meeting/banquet space

All the elegance and decor of an English country house, situated only 10 minutes from the French Quarter, area attractions and convention center. Extremely comfortable, friendly atmosphere.

 info@rosemanor.com 🌐 www.rosemanor.com

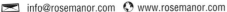

NEW ORLEANS ───

St. Charles Guest House	40-100 $US BB	Continental breakfast
1748 Prytania St 70130	22 rooms, 22 pb	Bakery
504-523-6556	*Rated*	Swimming pool, library, ample reading
	C-ltd/S-ltd/P-no/H-ltd	material (books/magazines)
	Spanish	

Welcome to our lovely guesthouse. We offer comfortable accommodations at a reasonable price and are located near the French quarter in the historic Garden District.

✉ dhilton111@aol.com 🌐 www.stcharlesguesthouse.com

───

Sully Mansion B&B	90-250 $US BB	Continental plus breakfast
2631 Prytania St 70130	8 rooms, 8 pb	Full breakfast on weekends,
800-364-2414 504-891-0457	Most CC, *Rated*, •	complimentary home baked goods,
Nancy & Guy Fournier	C-ltd/S-ltd/P-no/H-no	honor bar
		Concierge services for restaurants,
		tours, outings, voice mail, WiFi, free
		parking, guest baskets

Built as a private home in 1890 the Sully Mansion is an elegant, licensed bed and breakfast in the Garden District. Sully Mansion offers a unique combination of Southern hospitality, gracious accommodations and modern day conveniences. Come be our guest.

✉ sullym@bellsouth.net 🌐 www.sullymansion.com

───

Terrell House B&B	150-200 $US BB	Full breakfast
1441 Magazine St 70130	12 rooms, 10 pb	Coffee makers, bottled water & soft
866-261-9687 504-247-0560	Most CC, Cash	drinks
Linda O'Brien	C-ltd/S-ltd/P-ltd/H-ltd	Cable TV, wireless Internet, robes,
		weddings

At the Terrell House in New Orleans, we invite you to be our guest and experience gracious Southern hospitality and immerse yourself in all New Orleans has to offer.

✉ lobrien@terrellhouse.com 🌐 www.terrellhouse.com

───

The Soniat House	195-650 $US EP	Breakfast Available $12.50 pp
1133 Chartres St 70116	30 rooms, 30 pb	complimentary WiFi, cable TV, daily
800-544-8808 504-522-0570	Most CC, Cash, Checks,	newspapers, wake-up service, self
Rodney & Frances Smith	*Rated*, •	service bar, secure parking
	C-ltd/S-no/P-no/H-yes	
	Spanish, French	

Antiques filled in the quiet residential section of the French Quarter, the Soniat House offers an authentic New Orleans experience. A luxurious boutique hotel, originally three 1830 townhouses, with balconies and lush tropical courtyards.

✉ stay@soniathouse.com 🌐 www.soniathouse.com

OPELOUSAS ───

Country Ridge B&B	85-165 $US BB	Continental plus breakfast
169 Country Ridge Rd 70570	4 rooms, 4 pb	Quiet peaceful setting, pool, patio,
337-948-1678	Most CC, Cash	gardens, yard chess, southern
Sonny & Sheila Ray	S-no/P-ltd/H-no	hospitality.

Free Night w/Certificate: Not valid on Valentines day or the month of Sept. and Oct. Room Upgrade.

Innkeepers Sonny and Sheila Ray invite you to Country Ridge Bed & Breakfast as "your home away from home." Your stay here will be a uniquely southern experience. Pool, comfortable and well appointed rooms, and lovely gardens await at Country Ridge B&B.

✉ countryridge@juno.com 🌐 www.cajunbnb.com

RAYNE

Maison D'Memoire B&B
Cottages
8450 Roberts Cove Rd 70578
866-580-2477 337-334-2477
Lyn & Ken Guidry

109-199 $US BB
4 rooms, 4 pb
Most CC
C-yes/S-no/P-no/H-ltd

Full breakfast
Some suites come with a chilled bottle
of wine
Porch, Jacuzzi, private lake, full
kitchen, TV/VCR, coffeemaker

Recapture the precious memories of the past in our private, authentic Cajun cottages. Each guesthouse has its own pleasing personality. All cottages are at least 100 years old and are restored with love to their former glory.

✉ info@maisonmemoire.com 🌐 www.maisondmemoire.com

SCOTT

The Savoy the Bed and
Breakfast
533 Rue Bon Secours 70583
337-277-8782 337-237-0835
Rodney & Darlene Savoy

70-100 $US BB
2 rooms, 2 pb
C-ltd/S-no/P-no/H-no
French

Full breakfast
Spacious, fully-equipped kitchen,
queen-sized bed, billiard room, private
patio with Jacuzzi

The Savoy is located in a quiet, country atmosphere away from city noises. There is a private patio for guests to enjoy and a full breakfast is served on the patio or in the kitchen each morning, nestled in quiet, cozy neighborhood, off I-10 in Scott, LA.

✉ thesavoybandb@yahoo.com 🌐 www.savoybedandbreakfast.com/local.html

SHREVEPORT

2439 Fairfield B&B
2439 Fairfield Ave 71104
877-251-2439 318-424-2424
Jimmy Harris

145-295 $US BB
4 rooms, 4 pb
Most CC, *Rated*, •
C-yes/S-no/P-yes/H-no

Full breakfast
Whirlpools, private garden, gazebo,
sitting room, library

1905 Victorian with balconies overlook English gardens featuring gazebo, fountain, Victorian swing.

✉ 2439fair@bellsouth.net 🌐 www.shreveportbedandbreakfast.com

Fairfield Place
2221 Fairfield Ave 71104
866-432-2632 318-222-0048
Pat & Mark Faser

109-199 $US BB
8 rooms, 8 pb
Most CC, Cash, Checks,
Rated, •
C-yes/S-ltd/P-yes/H-ltd

Full gourmet breakfast
Bridal Luncheons, Tea Parties, Special
Event Catering, Homemade Goodies
Sitting room, whirlpools, suites, one
acre of gardens & grounds, weddings,
phone, Internet, fax

Casually elegant inn in two lovely, adjoining homes built circa 1870. European and American antiques, gourmet breakfast, exquisite Victorian gardens. Large spacious rooms, king or queen beds and private baths. Ideal for business travelers and tourists.

✉ fairfieldplace@bellsouth.net 🌐 www.fairfieldplace.com

ST. FRANCISVILLE

Butler Greenwood
Plantation
8345 US Hwy 61 70775
225-635-6312
Anne Butler

135-235 $US BB
8 rooms, 8 pb
Visa, MC, AmEx,
Rated, •
C-yes/S-ltd/P-ltd/H-no
Some French

Continental breakfast
Swimming pool, pond, extensive
grounds and gardens, in-room double
Jacuzzis, some fireplaces

8 private cottages with plenty of historic charm, scattered across peaceful, landscaped plantation grounds. All cottages have full kitchens, Jacuzzis, and a porch or a deck. On the National Register of Historic Places.

✉ butlergree@aol.com 🌐 www.butlergreenwood.com

THIBODAUX

Naquin's B&B
1146 W Camellia Dr 70301
985-446-6977
Frank & Joyce Naquin

65-75 $US BB
4 rooms, 4 pb
•
C-yes/S-no/P-ltd/H-ltd
French

Full breakfast
Afternoon tea, snacks
Sitting room, cable TV, accommodate
business travelers

Magic on the Bayou. Enjoy Cajun hospitality with a family of Acadian descent. Four bedrooms with private baths, 50 miles southwest of New Orleans.

✉ naquinsbb@hotmail.com 🌐 www.naquinsbb.com

Maine

ACADIA SCHOODIC

Acadia's Oceanside Meadows Inn
Prospect Harbor,
Rt 195 04669
207-963-5557
Sonja Sundaram, Ben Walter

118-209 $US BB
15 rooms, 15 pb
Most CC, Cash, Checks
C-yes/S-no/P-yes/H-yes

Full gourmet breakfast
Afternoon tea
Sitting room, library, fireplace, lawn games, flowers, private beach

Historic sea captain's home with magnificent oceanviews. 200+ acres with private sand beach, Acadia National Park is 5 minutes away, great hiking, biking, swimming, sea kayaking and canoeing.

✉ oceaninn@oceaninn.com 🌐 www.oceaninn.com

BAILEY ISLAND

Log Cabin, An Island Inn
5 Log Cabin Ln 04003
207-833-5546
Matt & Aimee York

139-329 $US BB
9 rooms, 9 pb
Most CC, *Rated*
C-ltd/S-no/P-no/H-yes
April-October

Full breakfast
A delightful dinner menu as well as a full bar for inn guests only
WiFi, computer for guest to use, beautiful gardens, a heated pool

Nine luxurious rooms, all with private baths & private decks. All have spectacular oceanviews. Some with Jacuzzi tubs, some gas fireplace, some with kitchens. 2 with hot tub, heated pool open late spring to early fall.

✉ info@logcabin-maine.com 🌐 www.logcabin-maine.com

BAR HARBOR

Acadia Hotel
20 Mt Desert St 04609
888-876-2463 207-288-5721
Chris Coston

89-169 $US EP
11 rooms, 11 pb
Most CC, Cash,
Checks, •
C-ltd/S-no/P-no/H-no
Inquire

Cafe Bakery next door
Whirlpool tubs, cable TV, porch & balcony, A/C, private baths

Located on the Historic Corridor in the heart of picturesque Bar Harbor village. Newly and tastefully restored and renovated combining the elegance of a Victorian home with all the comforts appreciated by today's traveler.

✉ acadiahotel@gmail.com 🌐 www.acadiahotel.com

Anne's White Columns Inn
57 Mt Desert St 04609
800-321-6379 207-288-5357
Anne & Robert Bahr

85-165 $US BB
10 rooms, 10 pb
Most CC, Cash, Checks,
Rated
C-yes/S-no/P-no/H-no
May-November

Full breakfast
Late afternoon wine, cheese and crackers
Sitting room, cable TV, private baths, queen beds, covered porch, gardens

Anne's White Columns Inn, an impressive Georgian structure is located in the Historical Corridor in downtown Bar Harbor.

✉ info@anneswhitecolumns.com 🌐 www.anneswhitecolumns.com

Aysgarth Station
20 Roberts Ave 04609
207-288-9655
Jane Holland & Steve
Cornell

70-155 $US BB
6 rooms, 6 pb
Visa, MC, Disc, *Rated*
C-ltd/S-no/P-no/H-no
French

Full breakfast
Afternoon tea & snacks, picnic lunches
Living room, dining room, porch, 3rd floor sun deck

Aysgarth Station offers year round accommodations & extends New England hospitality & quiet comfort in a uniquely casual atmosphere, right in downtown Bar Harbor. Six guestrooms, only a short stroll to the waterfront harbor.

✉ innkeeper@aysgarth.com 🌐 www.aysgarth.com

BAR HARBOR

Bar Harbor Castlemaine Inn B&B
39 Holland Ave 04609
800-338-4563 207-288-4563
Daniel & Diana Daigle

89-289 $US BB
17 rooms, 17 pb
Most CC, Cash, Checks,
Rated
C-ltd/S-no/P-no/H-no
May thru October

Continental plus breakfast
Scones, muffins, breads & coffee
cake, bagels, fresh fruit & a variety of
beverages
A/C, fridge, CATV/DVD/VCR, WiFi,
fax, fireplace, decks. Main St 3 blocks,
ocean 2 blocks, whirlpool

The Inn is nestled on a quiet side street in Bar Harbor Village, surrounded by the magnificent Acadia National Park. AAA 3-Diamond and Mobil 3-Star rating. Well-appointed rooms, some with whirlpool and fireplace. ✉ info@castlemaineinn.com 🌐 www.castlemaineinn.com

Bass Cottage Inn
14 The Field 04609
866-782-9224 207-288-1234
Jeff & Teri Anderholm

200-370 $US BB
10 rooms, 10 pb
Visa, MC, AmEx
C-ltd/S-no/P-no/H-yes
Some Spanish & Italian
Mid May – end of
October

Full gourmet breakfast
Evening wine & hors d'oeuvres during
high season, guest pantry is always
filled with tasty snacks
Free wireless Internet, early coffee
service, piano, library, sun porch,
activity planning

Nowhere in Bar Harbor will you find an inn that blends romantic elegance, comfort and hospitality. The Bass Cottage Inn is a stylish 10-room inn with tasteful decor where guests are treated to a rare blend of luxury and ease. Yankee Mag Editors' Choice.
✉ innkeeper@basscottage.com 🌐 www.basscottage.com

Black Friar Inn & Pub
10 Summer St 04609
207-288-5091
Tom Hulbert

75-175 $US BB
6 rooms, 6 pb
Visa, MC, *Rated*
C-ltd/S-ltd/P-no/H-no
May 1 – Oct 31

Full gourmet breakfast
The Friars Pub with nightly pub fare
& spirits
WiFi, full restaurant & pub

Gothic, mysterious, and down right cool. The rooms are gracious and comfortable all with in-suite baths. The Friar's Pub serves nightly light fare and spirits in the finely crafted Tavern and Grotto. A true gentleman's retreat. ✉ stay@blackfriarinn.com 🌐 www.blackfriarinn.com

Cleftstone Manor
92 Eden St 04609
888-288-4951 207-288-8086
Robert & Anne Bahr

85-195 $US BB
17 rooms, 17 pb
Most CC, Cash, Checks
C-yes/S-no/P-no/H-no
Late April through Oct.

Full breakfast
Afternoon tea & fresh baked cookies
Sitting rooms, library with Internet
access, cable TV, phone, fireplaces

You are invited to stay with us at Cleftstone Manor on your next stay in Bar Harbor, Maine. Where better to experience the splendor of Eden than a stay at a mansion built in 1881. Cleftstone is the only mansion on the west side of Eden Street to survive.
✉ innkeeper@cleftstone.com 🌐 www.cleftstone.com

Coach Stop Inn
715 State Hwy 3 04609
800-927-3097 207-288-9886
Deborah Stahlman

100-165 $US BB
5 rooms, 5 pb
Visa, MC, Disc, *Rated*
C-ltd/S-no/P-no/H-ltd

Full gourmet breakfast
Snacks, complimentary beverages,
afternoon refreshments
Suites, fireplaces, cable TV in common
room

Built in 1804 the Coach Stop is Bar Harbor's oldest inn, dating back to the presidency of Thomas Jefferson. Come see why "Down East" says Coach Stop Inn is "Where to Stay in Bar Harbor." Chef owned and operated.
✉ info@coachstopinn.com 🌐 www.coachstopinn.com

Graycote Inn
40 Holland Ave 04609
207-288-3044
Pat & Roger Samuel

98-185 $US BB
12 rooms, 12 pb
Most CC, Cash, Checks,
Rated, •
C-ltd/S-no/P-no/H-no

Hot Gourmet Breakfast
Early morning coffee tray near room,
afternoon refreshments
Fireplaces, sitting rooms, balconies,
free WiFi, garden, walk to restaurants
& shops

A Retreat from the Everyday. Open year-round. Green certified. Victorian with large rooms, some with fireplaces, sunrooms, or balconies. Large landscaped yard on quiet village street. Full hot breakfast. Walk to shops, galleries, restaurants. Free WiFi.
 innkeepers@graycoteinn.com  www.graycoteinn.com

BAR HARBOR——————————————————————————————————————

Hearthside B&B	85-175 $US BB	Full breakfast
7 High St 04609	9 rooms, 9 pb	Afternoon tea & cookies
207-288-4533	Visa, MC, Disc, *Rated*	All rooms have A/C, 3 rooms with
Susan & Barry Schwartz	C-ltd/S-no/P-no/H-no	fireplaces, 3 baths with whirlpool jets,
	May 1st to October 25th	computer with free WiFi

Small, gracious hostelry in quiet downtown location, elegant and comfortable, blend of antiques and traditional furniture. Rooms with private baths, some with fireplace, whirlpool tub or porch.

✉ bears@hearthsideinn.com 🌐 www.hearthsideinn.com

Holbrook House	89-209 $US BB	Full breakfast
74 Mt Desert St 04609	13 rooms, 13 pb	Afternoon refreshments
800-860-7430 207-288-4970	Visa, MC, AmEx,	Sitting room, library, enclosed bike
Michelle & Eric Allvin	*Rated*	storage, ample parking, A/C, WiFi
	C-ltd/S-no/P-no/H-no	
	May – October	

Relax amid the charm & ambience of Bar Harbor's Golden Years. Holbrook House is a lovely 1876 Victorian showplace on the historic corridor of Bar Harbor. A short walk to downtown and a few miles to Acadia National Park.

✉ info@holbrookhouse.com 🌐 www.holbrookhouse.com

Holland Inn	75-175 $US BB	Full gourmet breakfast
35 Holland Ave 04609	9 rooms, 9 pb	All private baths, A/C, cable TV, sitting
207-288-4804	Visa, MC, *Rated*	rooms, suites, balcony and patios
Evin & Tom Hulbert	C-ltd/S-ltd/P-no/H-ltd	
	May 1-Oct 31	

A delightfully informal, non-Victorian bed and breakfast located within the historic village of Bar Harbor, Maine. Minutes from Acadia National Park and ferry to Nova Scotia.

✉ info@hollandinn.com 🌐 www.hollandinn.com

Ivy Manor Inn & Michelle's	95-275 $US BB	Full off-menu offered
Fine Dining	8 rooms, 8 pb	AAA Four Diamond French Restaurant
194 Main St 04609	Visa, MC, Disc,	open to the public for breakfast, lunch
888-670-1997 207-288-2138	*Rated*, •	& dinner by reservation
Judi & Bob Stanley	C-yes/S-no/P-no/H-yes	Private baths, balconies, fireplaces,
	May through October	cable color TV, outside dining, fax,
		WiFi, private parking

Romance, elegance, antiques & the "finest dining on the island" depicts the Ivy Manor Inn & Michelle's Fine Dining. Fireplaces, balconies, luxurious suites and just one block from the ocean.

✉ info@ivymanor.com 🌐 www.ivymanor.com

Manor House Inn	85-250 $US BB	Full Buffet Breakfast
106 West St 04609	18 rooms, 18 pb	Afternoon tea & freshly baked sweets
800-437-0088 207-288-3759	Most CC, *Rated*	Sitting room, fireplaces, gardens,
Stacey & Ken Smith	C-ltd/S-no/P-no/H-no	whirlpool tubs, gazebo
	Mid April thru late Oct.	

Welcome to Manor House Inn, Bar Harbor's Historic Victorian Inn. Conveniently located within 2 blocks, which is easy walking distance of village shops, restaurants and ocean activities. One mile from Acadia National Park.

✉ manor@me.acadia.net 🌐 www.barharbormanorhouse.com

Mira Monte Inn	99-259 $US BB	Full Breakfast Buffet
69 Mt Desert St 04609	17 rooms, 17 pb	Complimentary late afternoon
800-553-5109 207-288-4263	Most CC, Cash,	innkeeper's social
Marian Burns	Checks, •	Piano, sitting and meeting rooms,
	C-yes/S-no/P-no/H-yes	fireplaces, balcony, private phones,
	Mid-May. through Oct.	A/C, televisions. WiFi

Built in 1864 and named Mira Monte, "Behold the Mountains," for the beautiful surrounding peaks of Acadia National Park. Victorian estate complete with period furnishings and fireplaces. In-town location; within walking distance to the waterfront.

✉ mburns@miramonte.com 🌐 www.miramonte.com

Moseley Cottage Inn, Bar Harbor, ME

BAR HARBOR

Moseley Cottage Inn
12 Atlantic Ave 04609
800-458-8644 207-288-5548
Pam & Scott Allen

68-250 $US BB
18 rooms, 18 pb
Visa, MC, Disc, *Rated*
C-yes/S-no/P-no/H-ltd
April-November

Full breakfast
On-premises parking, parlor with
piano, front porch, courtesy phone,
computer, WiFi

*Beautiful 1894 Victorian Inn in a quiet location just a minute's walk to downtown Bar Harbor. Offer-
ing graciously decorated rooms, period furniture, working fireplaces & private porches. Enjoy your
creative, homemade breakfast on our spacious grounds.*

✉ pamskidog2@aol.com 🌐 www.moseleycottage.net

**Primrose Inn-Historic Bar
Harbor B&B**
73 Mount Desert St 04609
877-TIME-4-BH 207-288-4031
Catherine & Jeff Shaw

99-249 $US BB
15 rooms, 15 pb
Most CC, Cash,
Rated, •
C-ltd/S-no/P-no/H-ltd
May to October

Hearty full breakfast
Afternoon Tea featuring freshly baked
treats from the Primrose kitchen
Wireless Internet access, daily
newspapers delivered to each room,
reserved parking space, spa tubs

*This romantic Bar Harbor Bed and Breakfast is perfectly located just a short stroll from all of the
wonderful restaurants, shops, galleries, and museums that make Bar Harbor a world-class destination
and just a mile from magnificent Acadia National Park.*

✉ relax@primroseinn.com 🌐 www.primroseinn.com

**Saltair Inn Waterfront
B&B**
121 West St 04609
207-288-2882
Matt & Kristi Losquadro

125-355 $US BB
8 rooms, 6 pb
Visa, MC, AmEx
C-ltd/S-no/P-no/H-ltd

Full breakfast
Afternoon refreshments;
complimentary coffee, tea, sodas and
water available 24 hours a day
Water views, fireplaces, Jacuzzi,
balcony, wireless Internet access, TVs,
CD players, dining room

*Open all winter. Come experience the magic of Bar Harbor and Acadia at an elegant, waterfront B&B.
All rooms have elegant private baths en suite. Amenities include luxury linens, gas fireplaces, cable
TV, CD players, and wireless Internet.*

✉ relax@saltairinn.com 🌐 www.saltairinn.com

The Inn at Bay Ledge
150 Sand Point Rd 04609
207-288-4204
Jack & Jeani Ochtera

125-475 $US BB
12 rooms, 12 pb
Visa, MC, *Rated*, •
C-ltd/S-no/P-no/H-ltd
May-Oct/June 15-Oct. 1

Full breakfast
Afternoon tea & treats
Heated pool, fireplaces, sauna, steam
rooms, Jacuzzis, meeting room, garden

*Atop an 80-foot cliff, towering pines and overlooking Frenchman Bay, sits the Inn at Bay Ledge. Liter-
ally clinging to the cliffs of Mount Desert Island with private Maine stone beach is one of the most
breathtaking views that you could ever imagine.*

✉ info@innatbayledge.com 🌐 www.innatbayledge.com

BAR HARBOR

The Willows at Atlantic Oaks 119 Eden St 04609 800-33-MAINE 207-288-5801 David Witham	99-295 $US BB 11 rooms, 11 pb Most CC, Cash, *Rated*, • C-ltd/S-no/P-no/H-ltd May to mid-October	Continental plus breakfast Sitting room, tennis court, indoor swimming pool, suites, cable TV

Restored Bar Harbor summer "cottage" built on the ocean in 1913. Gardens and stone walls recall Bar Harbor's "Cottage Era." 1 mile to downtown Bar Harbor. Pebbled beach, dock, fishing, and ocean views.

✉ reservations@barharbormainehotel.com 🌐 www.barharbormainehotel.com/html/the-willow

BASS HARBOR

Ann's Point Inn Waterfront B&B 79 Ann's Point Rd 04653 207-244-9595 Jeannette & Alan Feuer	235-345 $US BB 4 rooms, 4 pb Visa, MC, AmEx, *Rated* C-ltd/S-no/P-no/H-ltd May – November	Three course gourmet breakfast Afternoon cheese & refreshments, evening fresh baked cookies, 24-hour coffee, tea & snacks Heated indoor pool, hot tub, Finnish sauna, in-room TV/DVD player, WiFi, fireplaces, robes, slippers

This lovely waterfront B&B inn, surrounded by the scenic waters of Bass Harbor, Maine, is a secluded paradise, yet close to all Acadia National Park and Mount Desert Island offer. Four luxurious guestrooms with water views; pool, sauna, hot tub & WiFi.

✉ info@annspoint.com 🌐 www.annspoint.com

BATH

Benjamin F. Packard House 45 Pearl St 04530 866-361-6004 207-443-6004 Amy & Mark Hranicky	90-170 $US BB 4 rooms, 4 pb Most CC, Cash, Checks, *Rated* C-ltd/S-ltd/P-no/H-no	Full breakfast Afternoon tea WiFi, fireplace, private patio library, bicycles, videos, TV, A/C, library, music, hairdryers, etc.

Free Night w/Certificate: Anytime.

Our beautiful 18th century shipbuilder's home is ideally located in the heart of Bath's historic district with easy access to downtown shopping and restaurants. Make the Packard House your premier port for gracious hospitality and unsurpassed service.

✉ benjaminfpackardhouse@yahoo.com 🌐 www.benjaminfpackardhouse.com

Galen C. Moses House 1009 Washington St 04530 888-442-8771 207-442-8771 Jim Haught & Larry Kieft	119-259 $US BB 5 rooms, 5 pb Most CC, Cash, Checks, *Rated*, • C-ltd/S-no/P-yes/H-no	Full breakfast Afternoon tea, wine Turn down service, A/C, wireless Internet

Free Night w/Certificate: Valid midweek Jan. April; excludes holidays and special events.

Built in 1874, the Galen C. Moses House is reminiscent of the 19th century grand Victorian style. Located in Bath, Maine it was selected for the National Register of Historic Homes. This Inn offers all your lodging and accommodation needs.

✉ stay@galenmoses.com 🌐 www.galenmoses.com

Inn at Bath 969 Washington St 04530 800-423-0964 207-443-4294 Elizabeth Knowlton	150-200 $US BB 8 rooms, 8 pb Most CC, Cash, Checks C-ltd/S-no/P-ltd/H-yes Some Spanish	Full breakfast Complimentary tea, coffee Lovely living rooms, terrace & porch; some rooms with fireplaces and/or Jacuzzi

The Inn at Bath is a comfortably elegant B&B, full of color and light, situated in the midcoast region of Maine. Lovingly restored mid 1800's Greek Revival home surrounded by lovely gardens. Located in Bath's Historic District, walking distance to town.

✉ innkeeper@innatbath.com 🌐 www.innatbath.com

BELFAST

Belfast Bay Inn
72 Main St 04915
207-338-5600
Ed & Judy Hemmingsen

198-350 $US BB
8 rooms, 8 pb
Visa, MC, *Rated*
C-yes/S-no/P-no/H-no

Full breakfast
Coffee & tea
Phone, elevator, free parking, gift shop,
WiFi, computer, voicemail, robes,
umbrellas, in-suite spa

You are invited to Belfast, Maine's first and only AAA-Four Diamond Award Winning and Select Registry Boutique Hotel where you will experience the intimacy of a Bed and Breakfast with the services and amenities of a Luxury Hotel.

✉ info@belfastbayinn.com 🌐 www.belfastbayinn.com

Jeweled Turret Inn
40 Pearl St 04915
800-696-2304 207-338-2304
Carl & Cathy Heffentrager

125-165 $US BB
7 rooms, 7 pb
Visa, MC, *Rated*, •
C-ltd/S-ltd/P-no/H-no

Full gourmet breakfast
Afternoon tea & lemonade; evening
Social Hour (5:30–6:30pm) crackers,
cheese & sherry
Sitting rooms, parlors, two verandas
with wicker furniture, antiques, ocean
beach, parks, tennis

Luxurious and historic Belfast B&B. Indulge in romantic guestrooms with poster & brass beds, turrets, whirlpool tub, fireplaces and verandas. Fabulous breakfasts! Midcoast Maine's perfect vacation getaway for honeymoons and windjammer sails.

✉ info@jeweledturret.com 🌐 www.jeweledturret.com

BELGRADE LAKES

Wings Hill Inn &
Restaurant
9 Dry Point Dr 04918
866-495-2400 207-495-2400
Chris & Tracey Anderson

115-195 $US BB
6 rooms, 6 pb
Most CC, Cash, •
C-ltd/S-no/P-no/H-ltd
Some French & Spanish

Full breakfast
Complimentary afternoon tea daily,
award-winning dinner menu available
Thursday through Sunday
Great Room with fieldstone fireplace,
lending library & game collection;
screened lakeview porch

A lakeview inn, with unexpected touches and superb food. Featured in Down East Magazine in 2004, and named to Yankee Magazine's Editors' Choice list in 2005. Hiking, boating & renowned golf in the village; outlets & coastal points within an hour.

✉ wingshillinn@earthlink.net 🌐 www.wingshillinn.com

BETHEL

The Chapman Inn
2 Church St 04217
877-359-1498 207-824-2657
Fred Nolte & Sandra Frye

69-129 $US BB
10 rooms, 8 pb
Most CC, Cash, Checks,
Rated, •
C-yes/S-no/P-yes/H-no

Full breakfast
Wide Screen TV'S, fitness room,
bicycles, billiards, ping pong, darts,
fireplace, sauna, WiFi

The Chapman Inn is a delightfully quaint and charming inn located in the heart of Bethel's historic district, overlooking the town common. We include our world famous full gourmet breakfast, as well as warm, genuine hospitality with every stay.

✉ chapmaninn@roadrunner.com 🌐 www.chapmaninn.com

BOOTHBAY

Hodgdon Island Inn
374 Barters Island
Road 04537
800-314-5160 207-633-7474
Pamela & Richard Riley

119-215 $US BB
9 rooms, 9 pb
Visa, MC, AmEx, •
C-ltd/S-no/P-no/H-no
Some German

Full gourmet breakfast
Enjoy dessert & conversation each
evening, complimentary hot beverages
& bottled water available
Free WiFi, fridge in room, heated
in-ground pool, secret garden, front
porch, water views

Hodgdon Island Inn's spectacular Boothbay location provides the picture perfect Maine getaway with water frontage and picturesque views, a quaint general store with lobster shack and front row seats for beautiful pink sunsets.

✉ stay@boothbaybb.com 🌐 www.boothbaybb.com

BOOTHBAY HARBOR

Atlantic Ark Inn
62 Atlantic Ave 04538
800-579-0112 207-633-5690
Donna

115-215 $US BB
6 rooms, 6 pb
Visa, MC, AmEx,
Rated
C-ltd/S-no/P-no/H-no
May-Oct.

Full Breakfast
Complimentary afternoon beverages,
cheese buffet, snacks & treats
Sitting room, wraparound porch,
terraces, pillow top mattresses, Jacuzzi
WiFi, A/C

*Quaint and intimate, this six guestroom inn offers lovely harbor views, balconies, Oriental rugs, ma-
hogany furnishings, private baths, Jacuzzi, flowers, full breakfast and a short walk to town. Cable TV
available upon request.*

✉ donna@atlanticarkinn.com 🌐 www.atlanticarkinn.com

Blue Heron Seaside Inn
65 Townsend Ave 04538
866-216-2300 207-633-7020
Laura & Phil Chapman

195-265 $US BB
6 rooms, 6 pb
Visa, MC, *Rated*
C-ltd/S-no/P-no/H-ltd
May-December

Full breakfast
Complimentary tea & coffee in rooms,
welcome beverage on arrival
Free use of kayaks from private
dock, free wireless Internet, private
waterfront decks off rooms

*Fully restored 19th c. waterfront B&B. Luxury size A/C rooms, all with water views, furnished with
antiques, all modern amenities and LCD HDTV. Panoramic two-bedroom suite available. Private boat
dock with free boat use. Located in town with parking.*

✉ info@blueheronseasideinn.com 🌐 www.blueheronseasideinn.com

Harbor House Inn
80 McKown St 04538
800-856-1164 207-633-2941
Tom & Monica Churchill

120-175 $US BB
6 rooms, 6 pb
Visa, MC
C-yes/S-no/P-ltd/H-ltd
May – October

Full breakfast
Snacks
Sitting Room, Jacuzzi tubs, Harbor
views, quiet relaxed setting, WiFi, TV/
VCR

*Experience Boothbay Harbor "the way Maine should be," relaxed, quiet & a great value. Each guest-
room is spacious, uniquely designed & furnished with a Queen or King bed. The veranda provides the
perfect place to view the harbor and enjoy breakfast.*

✉ harborhse@ime.net 🌐 www.harborhouse-me.com

**Harbour Towne Inn on the
Waterfront**
71 Townsend Ave 04538
800-722-4240 207-633-4300
Stefanie McElman & Patricia
Richardson

99-299 $US BB
9 rooms, 9 pb
Visa, MC, Disc, *Rated*
C-ltd/S-no/P-no/H-ltd
Please call

Full Breakfast Buffet
We offer homemade treats served with
tea and coffee in the afternoon.
AC, mini-fridge and microwave, free
WiFi, phone, TV

*The Harbour Town Inn is a beautifully refurbished harborfront Inn, with scenic decks and a water-
front dock and float, beautiful flower displays. Come stay with us, read a book on our decks, relax and
see why guests love our location and our delightful Inn*

✉ info@harbourtowneinn.com 🌐 www.harbourtowneinn.com

The Greenleaf Inn
65 Commercial St 04538
888-950-7724 207-633-3100
Jeff Teel

155-265 $US BB
7 rooms, 7 pb
Most CC, Cash, Checks
C-ltd/S-no/P-no/H-yes

Full breakfast
Coffee, tea, juices, soft drinks anytime
Living room, porch, book/video
library, games, hot tub, fitness room,
Internet access, Wi-FI.

*A spacious, restored New England cape style B&B nestled on a knoll overlooking scenic Boothbay
Harbor, the Greenleaf Inn is your ultimate coastal lodging destination for vacations, honeymoons,
anniversary gifts, and romantic getaways.*

✉ inns@greenleaflane.com 🌐 www.greenleaflane.com

The Harborage Inn
75 Townsend Ave 04538
800-565-3742 207-633-4640
Troy & Emery Chapman

155-255 $US BB
11 rooms, 11 pb
Visa, MC, Disc, *Rated*
C-ltd/S-no/P-no/H-no
April-late November

Gourmet Full breakfast
Waterfront lawn with seating,
wraparound porches, Laura Ashley
rooms & suites

*All the modern amenities of a boutique hotel, the Harborage Inn is nestled on the Maine coast with
the charm and attention to detail of a Bed and Breakfast.*

✉ info@harborageinn.com 🌐 www.harborageinn.com

BOOTHBAY HARBOR

Topside Inn
60 McKown St 04538
888-633-5404 207-633-5404
Brian Lamb & Ed McDermott

125-225 $US BB
21 rooms, 21 pb
Most CC, Cash, Checks
C-ltd/S-no/P-no/H-ltd
early May – late
October

Full breakfast
Snacks
Private bath, sitting room, library,
cable TV, hairdryers, irons and ironing
boards

Prime hilltop location with panoramic views of the harbor, islands, lighthouses and ocean. Convenient walk to waterfront village restaurants and area attractions.

info@topsideinn.com   www.topsideinn.com

Welch House Inn
56 McKown St 04538
800-279-7313 207-633-3431
Susan Hodder, Michael
Feldmann

95-220 $US BB
14 rooms, 14 pb
Visa, MC, AmEx,
Rated, •
C-yes/S-no/P-ltd/H-no
German, Spanish

Full breakfast
Beverages always available
Gas fireplaces, whirlpool tub, A/C,
cable TV & VCRs, books & videos,
wireless Internet

Panoramic harbor views, large decks, king beds, private baths, in-room A/C, fireplaces, cable TV and VCRs, library with fireplace, gourmet breakfasts, park and walk to everything, open year round.

info@welchhouseinn.com   www.welchhouseinn.com

BRIDGTON

Noble House Inn
81 Highland Rd 04009
888-237-4880 207-647-3733
Rick & Julie Whelchel

129-259 $US BB
9 rooms, 9 pb
Visa, MC, *Rated*, •
C-yes/S-no/P-no/H-ltd

Wicked-Good Gourmet Breakfast
Famous Bottomless Cookie jar,
gourmet teas, coffee, cocoa, & soda.
Wine list.
Lake, park & beach, fireplaces,
porches, grand piano, games, canoe &
snowshoe, free WiFi, Ski & Stay

Casual luxury in the heart of Maine's Lakes & Mountains region. Offering luxurious guestrooms, dreamy beds, gourmet breakfasts, Bottomless Cookie Jar & exceptional hospitality, we earned Yankee Magazine's "2008 Editors' Choice" award. Refresh your senses.

innkeepers@noblehousebb.com   www.noblehousebb.com

CAMDEN

Blue Harbor House
67 Elm St 04843
800-248-3196 207-236-3196
Annette & Terry Hazzard

99-189 $US BB
11 rooms, 11 pb
Most CC, Cash, Checks,
Rated, •
S-no/P-no/H-no
Basic French

Full breakfast
Cocktail Hour! Enjoy a glass of wine
from our wine list and choice of h'ors
d'oeuvres
Off street parking, daily newspapers,
Spa robes, A/C, Gilchrist & Soames
toiletries, WiFi

Come to the Blue Harbor House whenever you need a place to relax and renew. The Inn is genuinely hospitable and refreshingly casual while Camden, Maine is an irresistible coastal village. Walk to the harbor and restaurants. Sumptuous breakfast. WiFi.

info@blueharborhouse.com   www.blueharborhouse.com

Camden Harbour Inn
83 Bayview St 04843
800-236-4266 207-236-4200
Oscar Verest, Raymond
Brunyanszki

175-700 $US BB
18 rooms, 18 pb
Visa, MC, AmEx
C-ltd/S-no/P-no/H-ltd
Dutch, French, German,
some Indonesian

Full breakfast
Complimentary coffee, tea, and snacks
all day, and room service is available.
Hairdryer, Flat-screen cable TV/
DVD, CD-player, Clock radio, stocked
minibar, coffeemaker, wireless.

Live a dream, indulge your sensibilities, let your imagination soar at the Camden Harbour Inn. An intimate boutique lifestyle hotel, the inn is a sought-out oasis for those who wish to savor the finer aspects of travel, relaxation, discovery, and renewal.

 info@camdenharbourinn.com  www.camdenharbourinn.com

CAMDEN

Camden Hartstone Inn
41 Elm St 04843
800-788-4823 207-236-4259
Mary Jo & Michael Salmon

105-280 $US BB
21 rooms, 21 pb
Visa, MC, *Rated*, •
C-ltd/S-no/P-ltd/H-no

Memorable full breakfast
Internationally recognized cuisine
makes dinner truly memorable,
afternoon tea and cookies
WiFi, guest computer, spa, gameroom,
movie collection, martini mixology
classes

An enchanting hideaway in the heart of Camden village that Fodor's considers "An elegant and so-phisticated retreat and culinary destination", this Mansard style Victorian built in 1835 offers a unique experience in pampered luxury. ✉ info@hartstoneinn.com ◐ www.hartstoneinn.com

Camden Maine Stay Inn
22 High St 04843
207-236-9636
Roberta & Claudio Latanza

115-270 $US BB
8 rooms, 8 pb
Most CC, Cash, Checks,
Rated, •
C-ltd/S-no/P-no/H-no
Italian, Spanish,
German

Full breakfast
Afternoon tea, coffee & cookies
Warm spacious common areas, open
kitchen, exquisite one acre garden

Built in 1802, this historic inn is located in one of America's most beautiful seaside villages. A short walk down tree-lined streets brings one to the harbor & village center.
✉ innkeeper@camdenmainestay.com ◐ www.camdenmainestay.com

Camden Windward House
Bed and Breakfast
6 High St 04843
877-492-9656 207-236-9656
Kristen & Jesse Bifulco

99-265 $US BB
8 rooms, 8 pb
Most CC, Cash,
Rated, •
C-yes/S-no/P-no/H-ltd

Order from menu
Afternoon tea, bar service, bar menu
Sitting room, library, Jacuzzi suites,
fireplaces, cable, WiFi accommodate
business travelers, deck

Camden Windward House, listed on the National Registry of Historic Places, 1 block from Camden Village and Penobscot Bay Harbor. Warm hospitality and bountiful breakfasts await at this 1854 Greek revival. Walking distance to activities, shops and dining.
✉ bnb@windwardhouse.com ◐ www.windwardhouse.com

Captain Swift Inn
72 Elm St 04843
800-251-0865 207-236-8113
Norm & Linda Henthorn

119-245 $US BB
8 rooms, 8 pb
Visa, MC, *Rated*
C-yes/S-no/P-no/H-yes

Full breakfast
Gas logs in some rooms, wireless
Internet available, all ensuite baths,
suites with whirlpool tubs

If you enjoy the warm atmosphere of yesteryear, or are a history or architecture buff, you'll appreci-ate the authenticity of the fully restored Federal period Captain Swift Inn. A short walk to downtown Camden & the harbor. Many outdoor activities nearby.
✉ innkeeper@swiftinn.com ◐ www.swiftinn.com

Inns At Blackberry
Common
82 Elms St 04843
800-388-6000 207-236-6060
Jim & Cyndi Ostrowski

109-289 $US BB
18 rooms, 18 pb
Visa, MC, Disc,
Rated, •
C-ltd/S-no/P-ltd/H-no

Full breakfast
Complimentary seasonal afternoon
refreshments; fine dining for inn
guests; special events.
Three spacious parlors, perennial
gardens, fireplaces, whirlpools, A/C,
cable TV, free wireless.

Our Inns are an oasis set side by side amid splendid perennial gardens in the picture book village of Camden. Blackberry Inn is a gracious 1849 "painted lady" Victorian Inn. The Elms B&B is a stately 1806 Federal Colonial. ✉ innkeepers@blackberryinn.com ◐ www.innsatblackberrycommon.com

Lord Camden Inn
24 Main St 04843
800-336-4325 207-236-4325
Erick Anderson

99-299 $US BB
36 rooms, 36 pb
Visa, MC, AmEx,
Rated, •
C-yes/S-no/P-yes/H-yes

Full breakfast
Hot coffee & freshly baked cookies
available upon your arrival
Large private balconies in most
rooms, fitness room, WiFi, in-room spa
services, free parking

Luxury, historic Inn, fully restored & recently remodeled, 36 individually appointed guestrooms and suites, ocean views, large balconies, gas fireplaces, full breakfast, unsurpassed comfort, elegance & service. A stay worth remembering.
✉ info@lordcamdeninn.com ◐ www.lordcamdeninn.com

CAMDEN

Swan House
49 Mountain St (Rt 52) 04843
800-207-8275 207-236-8275
Lyn & Ken Kohl

95-185 $US BB
6 rooms, 6 pb
Visa, MC, Disc, *Rated*
C-ltd/S-no/P-no/H-no

Full country breakfast
Sitting rooms, gazebo, enclosed
sunporch, mountain hiking trail

Located in a quiet neighborhood, away from busy Route 1. Mountain hiking trail directly behind the inn. Short walk to Camden's – harbor, shops, & restaurants. Swan House is a traditional Bed & Breakfast that is family operated & owner occupied since 1993.

hikeinn@swanhouse.com   www.swanhouse.com

Timbercliffe Cottage B&B Inn
64 High St 04843
866-396-4753 207-236-4753
Karen & Dave Kallstrand

130-255 $US BB
6 rooms, 6 pb
Visa, MC, AmEx
C-ltd/S-no/P-no/H-no

Full breakfast
Cold beverages, coffee & tea available
24 hours
Fireplaces, guest pantry, garden, patio,
parlor, library, wireless Internet &
parking

A warm welcome awaits you at Timbercliffe Cottage B&B Inn. Nestled on a hillside in the shadow of Mt. Battie with a view of Penobscot Bay, this historic home wraps its arms around you and invites you to sit back and relax.

innkeepers@timbercliffecottage.com   www.timbercliffecottage.com

Whitehall Inn
52 High Street 04843
800-789-6565 207-236-3391
Greg & Sue Marquise

99-199 $US BB
45 rooms, 43 pb
Most CC, *Rated*, •
C-yes/S-no/P-no/H-yes
mid-May to late October

Full breakfast
Fine-dining restaurant & pub fare
Restaurant, pub, Internet access,
WiFi, phones, private baths, gardens,
historic neighborhood, gifts

The Whitehall Inn has been the first choice for discerning visitors coming to Camden, Maine since 1901. The historic 45-room full service inn offers a romantic getaway on the side of Mt. Battie, a short walk to Camden Harbor.

reservations@whitehall-inn.com   www.whitehall-Inn.com

CASTINE

The Pentagoet Inn
26 Main St 04421
800-845-1701 207-326-8616
Jack Burke

95-265 $US BB
16 rooms, 16 pb
Most CC, Cash
C-ltd/S-no/P-no/H-no
May – October

Full breakfast

The Pentagoet Inn, a midcoast Maine Bed & Breakfast is a charming Queen Anne Victorian, nestled on a seaside bluff, graced with majestic elms. It overlooks the village and harbor of Castine, Maine.

stay@pentagoet.com   www.pentagoet.com

COREA

Black Duck Inn on Corea Harbor
36 Crowley Island Rd 04624
207-963-2689
Barry Canner & Bob Travers

140-200 $US BB
5 rooms, 5 pb
Visa, MC, Disc, •
C-ltd/S-no/P-ltd/H-no
Danish, some French
late May- mid Oct

Hearty, healthy, gourmet
Special diets catered to with advance
notice
Sitting rooms, library, bicycles, hiking
trails, kayaking services nearby

Romantic settings, casual elegance, antiques and art. Overlooking working lobster harbor. Village charm with rural atmosphere. Near national park and bird sanctuary.

info@blackduck.com   www.blackduck.com

DAMARISCOTTA

Oak Gables B&B & More
36 Pleasant St 04543
800-335-7748 207-563-1476
Martha Scudder

120-300 $US BB
5 rooms, 1 pb
Visa, MC, Disc
C-yes/S-ltd/P-no/H-no

Full breakfast
Afternoon tea
Sitting room, swimming pool, cable
TV, rooms have A/C, WiFi, winterized
cottage & more

A beautiful inn, pristine setting with river frontage and views, hospitality and peaceful surroundings. A secluded 11 acre estate by the Damariscotta River. Charming rooms and guest cottage. Lovely studio apartment and river view apartment. A heated pool.

 martha@oakgablesbb.com   www.oakgablesbb.com

DEER ISLE

Pilgrim's Inn
20 Main St 04627
888-778-7505 207-348-6615
Tina Oddleifson & Tony
Lawless

99-249 $US BB
15 rooms, 15 pb
Visa, MC, Disc, •
C-ltd/S-no/P-ltd/H-no
Mid May-Mid Oct

Full breakfast
On-site restaurant with Tavern menu,
homemade cookies and beverages
throughout the day
3 acres of land, 500-foot waterfront,
library, TV in common room, WiFi,
Adirondack chairs near water

For a respite from the cares and pace of your busy world, come to Pilgrim's Inn on Deer Isle. Listed on the National Register of Historic Places and a member of the prestigious Select Registry, Pilgrim's Inn is sure to please.

✉ innkeeper@pilgrimsinn.com 🌐 www.pilgrimsinn.com

DEXTER

The Brewster Inn
37 Zion's Hill Rd. 04930
207-924-3130
Mark & Judith Stephens

69-139 $US BB
9 rooms, 9 pb
Visa, MC, Disc
C-yes/S-no/P-ltd/H-yes

Full breakfast
Catering for brunch, lunch or dinner
during your stay with a minimum 48
hours notice
Cable TV, AC, fireplaces, whirlpools,
DVD, sitting room, screen porch, WiFi,
bathrobes

Free Night w/Certificate: Anytime. Only valid for rooms valued at more than $100 per night.

The Brewster Inn located in Dexter is less than an hour's drive to Bangor and beautiful Moosehead Lake and the Mt. Katahdin region of Maine. Perfect for romantic getaways, relaxation, weddings, all kinds of outdoor activities and retreats.

✉ innkeeper@brewsterinn.com 🌐 www.brewsterinn.com

DURHAM

The Royalsborough Inn at the Bagley House
1290 Royalsborough
Rd 04222
800-765-1772 207-353-6372
Marianne & Jim Roberts

135-175 $US BB
7 rooms, 7 pb
Visa, MC, Disc,
Rated, •
C-yes/S-no/P-no/H-yes

Full breakfast
Complimentary beverages, cookies,
special event meals may be arranged
Living room w/fireplace, library,
Alpaca Farm & Farm Store on
property, therapeutic massage, WiFi

A country inn, six miles from L.L. Bean & other Freeport shopping. Convenient to major highways, Bates & Bowdoin colleges. The Inn offers a relaxing environment & sumptuous breakfast & has hosted many historical "firsts" in the town.

✉ info@royalsboroughinn.com 🌐 www.royalsboroughinn.com

EAST BOOTHBAY

Five Gables Inn
107 Murray Hill Rd 04544
800-451-5048 207-633-4551
Mike & De Kennedy

140-235 $US BB
16 rooms, 16 pb
Visa, MC, *Rated*, •
C-ltd/S-no/P-no/H-no
Mid-May to End of Oct.

Full breakfast
Tea and lemonade, along with
homemade pastries and cookies,
compliments of your hosts.
Fireplaces, games, wraparound
veranda, pool & boating nearby.

The Five Gables Inn is a beautifully restored bed and breakfast inn in Maine, and the last of the turn-of-the-century summer hotels in the Boothbays. Perched on a garden-framed hillside Five Gables Inn overlooks picturesque Linekin Bay.

✉ info@fivegablesinn.com 🌐 www.fivegablesinn.com

EASTPORT

The Milliken House
29 Washington St 04631
888-507-9370 207-853-2955
Bill & Mary Williams

75-85 $US BB
6 rooms, 6 pb
Visa, MC
C-ltd/S-no/P-ltd/H-no

Full gourmet breakfast
Complimentary wine, snacks, bed-side
chocolates
Sitting room, library, cable TV

Elegant accommodations in a large, gracious 1846 home furnished with ornately carved Victorian marble-topped furniture. Two blocks from the historic waterfront district.

✉ millikenhouse@eastport-inn.com 🌐 www.eastport-inn.com

EASTPORT————————————————————————————————————

Todd House	65-100 $US BB	Full breakfast
1 Capen Ave 04631	6 rooms, 5 pb	BBQ deck with a view
207-853-2328	C-yes/S-ltd/P-yes/H-yes	Library, fireplace, yard with barbecue,
Ruth McInnis		picnic facilities

Step into the past in our Revolutionary War era Cape Cod style home with a wide panorama of Passamaquoddy Bay, listed on the National Register of Historic Places. Children and pets welcome!

🌐 www.virtualcities.com/ons/me/e/mee7501.htm

ELIOT——

Farmstead B&B	70-90 $US BB	Full breakfast
999 Goodwin Rd 03903	6 rooms, 6 pb	All of our rooms are equipped with
207-748-3145 207-748-3145	Visa, MC	private baths air-conditioning, a mini-
John Lippincott	C-yes/S-no/P-yes/H-ltd	fridge and a microwave

Free Night w/Certificate: Valid Sept.-May, and Sunday-Thursday.

'The best kept secret on the seacoast.' Charming Victorian on 2½ acres of lawn and trees. Swing under the pear tree, enjoy the picnic area with gas grill, relax in the hammock or enjoy early morning coffee on the glider after a restful night.

✉ farmsteadb@aol.com 🌐 www.farmstead.qpg.com

FREEPORT————————————————————————————————————

Brewster House B&B	149-199 $US BB	Full, hot, gourmet breakfast
180 Main St 04032	7 rooms, 7 pb	Afternoon snacks & beverages
800-865-0822 207-865-4121	Most CC, *Rated*, •	WiFi Internet access, parlor with
Scott & Ruth Thomas	C-ltd/S-no/P-no/H-ltd	satellite TV, guest computer, suites,
		fireplaces, itinerary plans

Beautifully renovated 1888 historic home. Family suites, large private bathrooms in all rooms, delicious full breakfast with fresh fruit and baked goods. Tastefully decorated with antiques. Fireplaces in three rooms.

✉ info@brewsterhouse.com 🌐 www.brewsterhouse.com/?tracker=lanierbb&utm

Captain Briggs House B&B	100-230 $US BB	Full breakfast
8 Maple Ave 04032	7 rooms, 7 pb	Early breakfast upon request; special
888-217-2477 207-865-1868	Visa, MC, Disc, *Rated*	dietary needs with advance notice
Charles & Beverly Tefer	C-yes/S-no/P-yes/H-no	Common room with cable TV, small
		refrigerator, VCR, and free wireless
		Internet

Historic 1853 Federal home with five beautiful guestrooms & a two-room suite. Located within easy walking distance to many fine shops & restaurants & situated on a large lot off a quiet, dead-end street. Hospitality, convenience & seclusion.

✉ info@captainbriggs.com 🌐 www.captainbriggs.com

Kendall Tavern B&B	140-185 $US BB	Full breakfast
213 Main St 04032	7 rooms, 7 pb	Sweets in the evening
800-341-9572 207-865-1338	Most CC, Cash, Checks,	Fireplaces in library, parlor, free
Tim & Loree Rudolph	*Rated*, •	wireless Internet access, private baths
	C-ltd/S-no/P-no/H-no	

Kendall Tavern Inn is located at the north end of Freeport Village, just a short stroll from shops & restaurants & a perfect location from which to explore the coast of Maine. Great spot for a small wedding or company retreat.

✉ info@kendalltavern.com 🌐 www.kendalltavern.com

Nicholson Inn	90-145 $US BB	Full breakfast
25 Main Street 04032	3 rooms, 3 pb	Central Air Conditioning, Individual
800-344-6404 207-865-6404	C-ltd/S-no/P-no/H-no	Heat Control, Hi-Speed Internet WiFi ,
Jane & Alden		Ample On-site Parking

Nicholson Inn, conveniently located in the heart of Freeport, Maine offers all the amenities a traveler could desire.

 janeandalden@nicholsoninn.com  www.nicholsoninn.com

Peace With-Inn, Fryeburg, ME

FRYEBURG

Admiral Peary House	139-199 $US BB	Full gourmet breakfast
27 Elm St 04037	7 rooms, 7 pb	Complimentary beverages & snacks
877-4ADMPRY 207-935-3365	Most CC, *Rated*, •	24 hours, afternoon tea by prior
Hilary Jones & Derrek	C-ltd/S-no/P-no/H-no	arrangement
Schlottmann	French, German,	Fireplaces, library, pool table, A/C,
	Spanish	free high-speed Internet, WiFi in most
		guestrooms

Quiet historic Inn 15 minutes from all North Conway activities, restaurants & shopping. Offers fireplaces, Jacuzzis, specials and packages, excellent breakfasts & more.

✉ innkeeper@admiralpearyhouse.com 🌐 www.admiralpearyhouse.com

Peace With-Inn	115-185 $US BB	Full Gourmet New England-style
254 W Fryeburg Rd Rte 113	8 rooms, 8 pb	Complimentary refreshments daily
N 04037	Most CC, •	Fine toiletries, fine linens, massage
877-935-7322 207-935-7363	C-ltd/S-no/P-no/H-no	therapy available
The Link Family		

Circa 1750 New England farmhouse. Six guestrooms feature fine linens, fresh flowers, and antiques. Rates include afternoon refreshments and a full New England-style breakfast.

✉ info@peacewithinn.com 🌐 www.peacewithinn.com

The Oxford House Inn	119-189 $US BB	Full breakfast
Rt 302 04037	4 rooms, 4 pb	Excellent restaurant on premise
800-261-7206 207-935-3442	Most CC	featuring local ingredients, full bar and
Jonathan & Natalie Spak	C-yes/S-no/P-no/H-ltd	wine list.
		Restaurant, bar, TV, wireless Internet,
		A/C, game area, back lawn panoramic
		views, grand front porch

Maine B&B and country inn with restaurant located in western Maine Lakes and Mountains Region and the Mount Washington Valley. Mountain views, lodging with superb breakfasts, gourmet dining in a small hotel near the White Mountains.

✉ innkeeper@oxfordhouseinn.com 🌐 www.oxfordhouseinn.com

GEORGETOWN

Coveside B&B
6 Gotts Cove Ln 04548
800-232-5490 207-371-2807
Carolyn & Tom Church

140-205 $US BB
7 rooms, 7 pb
Most CC, *Rated*, •
C-ltd/S-no/P-no/H-ltd
French (limited)
May-Oct.

Full gourmet breakfast
Complimentary beer & soft drinks,
snacks
Screened porch, terrace, rec
room with television and exercise
equipment, canoe, bicycles

Stylish retreat on 5 waterfront acres, reminiscent of turn-of-the-century coastal cottages. All rooms overlook rocky Gotts Cove and Sheepscot Bay; several have fireplaces, private balconies, and spa tub.

✉ innkeeper@covesidebandb.com 🌐 www.CovesideBandB.com

The Mooring B&B
132 Seguinland Rd 04548
866-828-7343 207-371-2790
Penny & Paul Barabe

140-200 $US BB
5 rooms, 5 pb
Visa, MC, AmEx,
Rated
C-ltd/S-no/P-no/H-ltd
May through October

Full breakfast
Cold drinks and snacks homemade
cookies. .Wine and cheese every
afternoon
Sitting room, library, bicycles,
fireplace, cable TV, daily maid service,
business travelers welcome

A quiet, elegant setting on the coast of Maine. Five unique rooms, all with private baths, air conditioning and great ocean views. A wonderful location for that special family reunion, party or wonderful wedding.

✉ mooringbb@midmaine.com 🌐 www.themooringb-b.com

GORHAM

PineCrest B&B Inn
91 South St 04038
877-474-6322 207-839-5843
Matt & Amy Mattingly

99-179 $US BB
7 rooms, 7 pb
Most CC, Cash, Checks,
Rated, •
C-yes/S-no/P-no/H-ltd

Full breakfast
Fine dining with Chef Mo every Friday
from June to November, wine bar and
tastings every Friday
Luxury toiletries, fireplace, wireless
access, living rooms, screened porch,
patio garden

A charming Victorian inn just minutes from Old Port, Portland, coastal beaches, the University of Southern Maine, Freeport Shops, family entertainment and more.

✉ Matt@pinecrestmaine.com 🌐 www.pinecrestmaine.com

GREENVILLE

Blair Hill Inn at
Moosehead Lake
351 Lily Bay Rd 04441
207-695-0224
Dan & Ruth McLaughlin

350-495 $US BB
8 rooms, 8 pb
Visa, MC, AmEx,
Rated, •
C-ltd/S-no/P-no/H-no
May through October

Full Gourmet Breakfast
One of Maine's top 10 restaurants
on premise. Open Thurs, Fri & Sat
evenings from mid-June – mid-Oct
Summer evening concerts, beautiful
gardens, cocktail lounge, concierge
service

A Select Registry, AAA four diamond bed and breakfast inn overlooking Moosehead Lake, Greenville, Maine. The area's finest offers one of Maine's top 10 restaurants, exquisite lodging, renowned views. Stay with us once . . . and we'll stay with you forever.

✉ info@blairhill.com 🌐 www.blairhill.com

Greenville Inn
40 Norris St 04441
888-695-6000 207-695-2206
Jeff & Terry Johannemann

110-450 $US BB
14 rooms, 14 pb
Visa, MC, *Rated*, •
C-yes/S-no/P-no/H-ltd

Full Breakfast
Dinner, extensive wine cellar, full bar,
in-room cheese baskets, tea for two &
so much more
Sitting rooms, fireplaces, lakeviews,
porches, gardens, lounge, concierge,
wireless Internet access

Moosehead Lake's most historic & finest inn, this 1885 restored lumber baron's mansion offers exceptionally appointed guestrooms, suites & cottages featuring fireplaces, upscale amenities, gourmet fine dining, with spectacular lake & mountain views.

✉ innkeeper@greenvilleinn.com 🌐 www.greenvilleinn.com

GREENVILLE

Lodge at Moosehead Lake	195-680 $US BB	Full Gourmet Breakfast
368 Lily Bay Rd 04441	9 rooms, 9 pb	Up North Cuisine dinner; snacks;
800-825-6977 207-695-4400	Most CC, Cash,	cookies, full service pub; wine list; tea;
Dennis & Linda Bortis	*Rated*, •	coffee; bottled water
	C-ltd/S-no/P-ltd/H-ltd	All rooms – a fireplace, Jacuzzi-style
	All year but April	tub, AC, coffee maker, robes, CD
		player, WiFi and TV/VCR/DVD.

Long standing AAA 4 Diamond and Select Registry distinguished inn. Enjoy breathtaking views of Moosehead Lake and the adjacent mountains from our masterfully decorated rooms that reflect the unspoiled natural beauty of the North woods.

✉ innkeeper@lodgeatmooseheadlake.com 🌐 www.lodgeatmooseheadlake.com

GUILFORD

The Trebor Mansion Inn	40-200 $US EP	NE Diner in front yard open 5:30AM;
11 A Golda Ct 04443	5 rooms, 3 pb	Tea & Coffee bar
888-280-7575 207-876-4070	Visa, MC, Disc, •	Sitting room, library, fireplace, 3
The Shaffer Family	C-yes/S-ltd/P-ltd/H-no	acre lawn, 125 ft wrap around porch,
	German, Spanish	balconies every room, WiFi

Private unpretentious luxury with inexpensive rates. Unique and mysterious hilltop mansion on three acres of gardens with mature oaks and maples. near Moosehead & Sebec Lakes. WiFi, balconies on every room. On the National Register of Historic Places.

✉ info@trebormansioninn.com 🌐 www.trebormansioninn.com

HALLOWELL

Maple Hill Farm B&B Inn	90-205 $US BB	Full Country Menu Breakfast
11 Inn Rd 04347	8 rooms, 8 pb	Anytime tea & coffee, homemade
800-622-2708 207-622-2708	Most CC, Cash, Checks,	baked goods; custom catering
Scott Cowger	*Rated*, •	provided for prearranged groups &
	C-ltd/S-no/P-no/H-yes	events
	A little French	Full bar, A/C, sitting room, art gallery,
		trails, whirlpools, farm animals,
		wireless Internet, cable

Maple Hill Farm B&B Inn & Conference Center near Augusta in Hallowell, Maine provides 'green' lodging with the peace & quiet of a country farm that is convenient to Maine's capital with all the services that today's travelers expect. ✉ info@MapleBB.com 🌐 www.MapleBB.com

HARPSWELL

Captains Watch B&B and Sail	155-185 $US BB	Full breakfast
926 Cundys Harbor	4 rooms, 4 pb	Self-serve tea & coffee anytime,
Rd 04079	C-ltd/S-no/P-no/H-ltd	refrigerator to chill beverages, we
207-725-0979		accommodate any special diets
Donna Dillman		Broad Bay views, quiet, 2 rms. access
		cupola, suite w/ fireplace, harbor side
		deck, sailing charter

With expansive water views over authentic lobstering Cundy's Harbor and beyond, our historic B&B offers gracious hospitality to those wishing a true Coastal Maine experience. A scenic 15 minutes from Bath or Brunswick, less from US1, is an unspoiled gem!

✉ cwatch@gwi.net 🌐 home.gwi.net/~cwatch

KENNEBUNK

Waldo Emerson Inn	95-165 $US BB	3-course breakfast
108 Summer St 04043	4 rooms, 4 pb	Complimentary coffee, tea, soft drinks,
877-521-8776 207-985-4250	Most CC, Cash, Checks,	snacks, Poland Springs bottled water,
John & Kathy Daamen	*Rated*, •	Dutch breakfasts
	C-ltd/S-no/P-no/H-ltd	Quilt retreat, antiques, private baths,
	Dutch	fireplaces, complimentary beach
		parking passes, bikes

Free Night w/Certificate: Room Upgrade.

Waldo Emerson Inn is a Colonial style inn listed on the National Register of Historic Places. Antiques, romantic rooms with fireplaces, handmade quilts, bountiful breakfasts. Quilt shop for browsing with 10% guest discount.

✉ innkeeper@waldoemersoninn.com 🌐 www.waldoemersoninn.com

KENNEBUNKPORT————————————————————————————

1802 House Inn	167-369 $US BB	Three-course gourmet breakfast
15 Locke St 04046	6 rooms, 6 pb	Inn-baked cookies, coffee, tea,
800-932-5632 207-967-5632	Visa, MC, AmEx,	lemonade, seasonal refreshments,
Linda Van Goor & Jay	*Rated*, •	Comfort Food Cook-Off weekends
Durepo	C-ltd/S-no/P-no/H-ltd	Concierge, wedding & event planning,
		spa & tee times, dining reservations &
		recommendations

Glorious golf, romantic, peaceful setting. Beautifully restored 1802 Colonial. Luxury rooms, period furnishings, whirlpool tubs, fireplaces, WiFi , cable TV. Gardens. Gourmet three-course breakfast daily. Weddings & honeymoons. Play & Stay golf packages.

✉ info@1802inn.com 🌐 www.1802inn.com

Bufflehead Cove	135-375 $US BB	Full breakfast
Bufflehead Cove Ln 04046	6 rooms, 6 pb	Herbal & regular teas, hot chocolate,
207-967-3879	Visa, MC, Disc, *Rated*	afternoon wine & cheese
Harriet, Jim & Erin Gott	C-ltd/S-no/P-ltd/H-no	Whirlpool tubs, fireplaces, turndowns,
	A little Spanish	concierge service, sitting room, dock,
	May through November	boat access, area maps

Hidden away in the woods, on a bank of the Kennebunkport tidal river, Bufflehead Cove offers peace, privacy and pampering in a beautiful setting. Perfect service with all the amenities: turn downs, wine & cheese hour, delicious breakfasts and soft music.

✉ info@buffleheadcove.com 🌐 www.buffleheadcove.com

Captain Fairfield Inn	146-381 $US BB	Full creative gourmet breakfast
8 Pleasant St 04046	9 rooms, 9 pb	Afternoon chocolate chip cookies,
800-322-1928 207-967-4454	Most CC, Cash,	organic teas & sparkling beverages,
Loryn Kipp & Finn	*Rated*, •	wine list & small plates menu.
MacDonald	C-ltd/S-no/P-no/H-no	WiFi, DVD library, beach towels and
		passes, and much more. Let us take
		care of all the details . . .

A boutique bed and breakfast experience. Featuring a blend of historic and soft modern styling, luxurious amenities, creatively prepared breakfasts and professional, personalized hospitality. Walk to the beach, restaurants, and Kennebunkport's center.

✉ info@captainfairfield.com 🌐 www.captainfairfield.com

Captain Jefferds Inn	149-379 $US BB	3 Course gourmet breakfast
5 Pearl St 04046	15 rooms, 15 pb	Afternoon tea with inn-baked goods,
800-839-6844 207-967-2311	Most CC, Cash, Checks,	cheese & crackers, lemonade or hot
Sarah & Erik Lindblom	*Rated*, •	cider
	C-ltd/S-no/P-ltd/H-no	Queen and king beds, feather beds,
		duvets, fine linens, WiFi, fireplaces,
		gardens, turn-down

Romantic, beautiful, peaceful, "your very special place". Historic residential district. Exceptional luxury amenities, fine linens, fireplaces, whirlpool spas, candlelight gourmet breakfast, afternoon tea.

✉ captjeff@captainjefferdsinn.com 🌐 www.captainjefferdsinn.com

Captain Lord Mansion	179-499 $US BB	Full 3-course breakfast
6 Pleasant St 04046	16 rooms, 16 pb	Afternoon seasonal beverages &
800-522-3141 207-967-3141	Most CC, Cash,	refreshments such as sweets, cheese,
Bev Davis & Rick Litchfield	*Rated*, •	crackers & fresh fruit
	C-ltd/S-no/P-no/H-no	On-prem. spa, htd marble bath floors,
		dbl. Jacuzzi tubs, K/Q 4 poster beds,
		gas F/P, A/C, TVs

An unforgettable romantic experience is your reward when you reserve one of the 16 large, beautifully appointed guestrooms at the Captain Lord Mansion.

✉ innkeeper@captainlord.com 🌐 www.captainlord.com

KENNEBUNKPORT

English Meadows Inn
141 Port Rd 04043
800-272-0698 207-967-5766
Bruce & Valerie Jackson

126-386 $US BB
10 rooms, 10 pb
Visa, MC, *Rated*, •
C-ltd/S-no/P-ltd/H-no

Full gourmet breakfast
Afternoon English Tea served on
Thursday, Friday & Saturday by
reservation only
Library, garden with patio, beach
parking pass, concierge, free wireless
Internet, cottage available

The English Meadows Inn, a Bed & Breakfast Inn in the coastal village of Kennebunkport, Maine offers a unique English "Country House" experience offering different delights regardless of the season.
✉ innkeeper@englishmeadowsinn.com 🌐 www.englishmeadowsinn.com

Kennebunkport Inn
One Dock Square 04046
800-248-2621 207-967-2621
Debra Lennon & Tom Nill

99-439 $US BB
49 rooms, 49 pb
Visa, MC, AmEx,
Rated
C-yes/S-no/P-no/H-yes
French

Complimentary Continental
Pool, spa service, restaurant, flat
screen TVs, fireplace, wireless
Internet, Kuerig coffee makers

The Kennebunkport Inn – Kennebunkport, Maine's quintessential classic New England inn -Old world charm and elegance at the Kennebunkport Inn is a natural blend with the full array of guest services that we provide. ✉ kellykport@roadrunner.com 🌐 www.kennebunkportinn.com

**Shorelands Guest Resort
and Condominiums**
247 Western Ave 04043
800-99-BEACH 207-985-4460
Sonja Haag Ducharme &
Family

59-255 $US BB
25 rooms, 25 pb
Most CC, Cash, •
C-yes/S-no/P-yes/H-no
French, German
April-October

Continental breakfast
Guest Cafe with coffee, tea and muffins
all day
Sitting room, library, bikes, Jacuzzis,
pool, suites, cable TV, gas grills, WiFi,
maid service

A typical Maine country cottage resort, far from noise and congestion. Lawn and garden areas for relaxing, a short walk to a secluded, sandy beach. ✉ info@shorelands.com 🌐 www.shorelands.com

The Maine Stay Inn
34 Maine St 04046
800-950-2117 207-967-2117
Judi & Walter Hauer

129-319 $US BB
17 rooms, 17 pb
Most CC, *Rated*, •
C-ltd/S-no/P-no/H-no
German

Full gourmet breakfast
Afternoon tea, refreshments &
desserts
Fireplace in sitting room, charming
wraparound porch, spacious grounds,
Adirondack chairs, hammock

Distinguished Bed & Breakfast Inn located in Kennebunkport's Historic District. Choose the Victorian romance of a 19th century Inn room or the privacy of a romantic fireplace cottage suite. Walk to shops, restaurants and galleries. Beaches & harbor nearby.
✉ innkeeper@mainestayinn.com 🌐 www.mainestayinn.com

**The Old Fort Inn and
Resort**
8 Old Fort Ave 04046
800-828-3678 207-967-5353

199-495 $US BB
16 rooms, 16 pb
Most CC, Cash, Checks,
Rated
S-no/P-no/H-no
April-December

Continental plus breakfast
A stunning turn of the century bar, the
Club House is the perfect spot to enjoy
a chilled martini
Cable TV, phone in room, WiFi, tennis,
pool, Jacuzzis, A/C, some fireplaces,
spa

A 16 room resort nestled privately amongst turn of the century summer homes. With décor that is stylish yet reminiscent of the estates of yesteryear.Plush bedding, comfortable seating areas and all of the hi tech and high touch amenities necessary.
✉ info@oldfortinn.com 🌐 www.oldfortinn.com

KITTERY

Enchanted Nights B&B
Scenic Coastal Rte 103 03904
207-439-1489
Peter Lamardia & Nancy
Bogenberger

60-350 $US BB
8 rooms, 7 pb
Most CC, *Rated*, •
C-yes/S-ltd/P-yes/H-yes

Full or continental breakfast
Sitting room, family friendly facility,
bikes, tennis, sauna, WiFi, whirlpool
tub

A B&B in Kittery, Maine – one mile to Historic Portsmouth, New Hampshire. French Victorian & Country French ambience. Whimsical, colorful & fanciful, yet elegant.
✉ ceo@enchantednights.org 🌐 www.enchantednights.org

KITTERY

Portsmouth Harbor Inn & Spa
6 Water St 03904
207-439-4040
Lynn Spann Bowditch

160-210 $US BB
5 rooms, 5 pb
Visa, MC, *Rated*
C-ltd/S-no/P-no/H-ltd
Some French

Full gourmet breakfast
Homebaked cookies, afternoon tea, port & sherry
Full day spa, massage, hot tub, sitting room, games, porch, patio, gardens, free WiFi, free parking

Comfortable brick Victorian with beautifully appointed rooms, water and city views, and luxurious day spa, featuring shopping and spa packages. Stroll to historic Portsmouth or Kittery and shop, catch a live performance, and dine. Recommended by NY Times.

info@innatportsmouth.com   www.innatportsmouth.com

LEWISTON

Ware Street Inn
52 Ware St 04240
877-783-8171 207-783-8171
Jan & Mike Barrett

115-210 $US BB
5 rooms, 5 pb
Most CC, Cash, Checks
C-ltd/S-no/P-no/H-no
French

Continental plus breakfast
Bedtime snacks, afternoon tea, etc., pre-arranged gatherings
Turndown service, hairdryer, cable TV/VCR, WiFi, terrace, common living room, den with computer

Refreshing oasis in the heart of the city. Comfort and gracious personal service abound in an inviting, unpretentious atmosphere, creating a feeling of warmth and welcome.

info@warestreetinn.com   www.warestreetinn.com

LINCOLNVILLE

Inn at Sunrise Point
55 Sunrise Point Rd 04843
207-236-7716
Daina Hill

300-595 $US BB
10 rooms, 10 pb
Most CC, Cash, Checks,
Rated, •
C-ltd/S-no/P-no/H-ltd
April through
November

Full gourmet breakfast
Afternoon refreshments & beverages
Library with books, CDs, DVDs, fireplaces, private decks, beach access, massage therapy, free WiFi

The Inn at Sunrise Point, a AAA rated 4 Diamond, Select Registry, award-winning inn invites you to discover a pampered haven for discriminating travelers. Luxury rooms & cottages with ocean views and access, private decks, fireplaces, Jacuzzis and more.

info@sunrisepoint.com   www.sunrisepoint.com

Youngtown Inn & Restaurant
581 Youngtown Rd 04849
800-291-8438 207-763-4290
Manuel & MaryAnn Mercier

140-250 $US BB
6 rooms, 6 pb
Visa, MC, AmEx
C-yes/S-no/P-no

Full breakfast
Beverage station & homemade cookies. Restaurant wine/beer bar on site.
Wireless Internet, Library, fine toiletries, private parking

A classic 1810 farmhouse built proudly upon two centuries of New England heritage. The tastefully decorated guestrooms, sunny verandas, broad pumpkin pine floors, and brick fireplaces capture the warm feel of beautiful rural Maine.

info@youngtowninn.com   www.youngtowninn.com

MONHEGAN ISLAND

The Island Inn
1 Ocean Ave 04852
207-596-0371
Krista Lisajus

130-395 $US BB
32 rooms, 24 pb
Visa, MC
C-yes/S-no/P-no/H-no
French, Russian, Polish
Memorial Day-
ColumbusDay

Full breakfast
Coffeehouse open daily – pastries & light lunches, lunch & dinner available for a fee
Sitting room, library, property overlooking harbor & ocean, suites, family friendly, non-smoking

A turn-of-the-century summer hotel overlooking Monhegan Harbor, the ocean, and the setting sun. Relax in porch chairs or on the lawn overlooking the harbor. Cozy library and fireplaced sitting room. Your hostess, Krista, will be delighted to meet you!

islandin@midcoast.com   www.islandinnmonhegan.com

NAPLES————————————————————————————————————

Augustus Bove House	99-250 $US BB	Full breakfast
Corner of Rts 302 &	7 rooms, 7 pb	Honeymoon/anniversary tray,
114 04055	Visa, MC, Disc,	complimentary coffee & tea
888-806-6249 207-693-6365	*Rated*, •	Sitting room, veranda, lawn, guest
Arlene & David Stetson	C-yes/S-ltd/P-yes/H-ltd	computer & printer available

Recently restored, offers authentic Colonial accommodations in a relaxing atmosphere. Between 2 lakes, 20 minutes from mountain skiing. Let our staff pamper you, with impeccable service, at our beautiful mountainside Country inn!

✉ augbovehouse@roadrunner.com ◐ www.NaplesMaine.com

Inn at Long Lake	120-200 $US BB	Chef-prepared full breakfast
15 Lake House Rd 04055	16 rooms, 16 pb	Complimentary coffee, tea, cocoa &
800-437-0328 207-693-6226	Visa, MC, *Rated*	fresh baked breads & cookies every
Keith A. Neubert	C-ltd/S-ltd/P-no/H-no	afternoon
		Sitting room, library, Great Room with
		fieldstone fireplace, complimentary
		wireless Internet

A unique New England inn celebrating America's grand 1920's & 1930's! Fourteen guestrooms and two suites inspired by and named after luminaries of Classic Hollywood and the American Music scene of the day. "By scratch" home cooking, fresh bread daily.

✉ info@innatlonglake.com ◐ www.innatlonglake.com

Lamb's Mill Inn	110-180 $US BB	Full breakfast
131 Lamb's Mill Road 04055	6 rooms, 6 pb	Afternoon cookies & complimentary
207-693-6253	Visa, MC	beverages
Laurel Tinkham, Sandy Long	C-ltd/S-no/P-no/H-ltd	WiFi, bath amenities, two dining
		rooms, off-street parking, gardens,
		common area, refrigerators,

Lamb's Mill Inn is an inn for all seasons located on a country road in Naples, ME, a small picturesque village situated between Long Lake and Sebago Lake in the foothills of Maine's Western mountains. "Eew hike, ewe bike, ewe ski, ewe zzzzz"!

✉ lambsmil@fairpoint.net ◐ www.lambsmillinn.com

NEW HARBOR————————————————————————————————

Gosnold Arms	115-315 $US BB	Full breakfast
146 State Route 32 04554	26 rooms, 26 pb	Sitting room, wharf, cable TV available
207-677-3727	Visa, MC, *Rated*	in some rooms & cottages
The Phinney Family	C-yes/S-no/P-no/H-ltd	
	May through October	

Charming country inn & cottages, most with harbor or ocean views. Located on the Pemaquid Peninsula of Maine, it is a true working harbor. The wharf is an ideal spot to view the activities of the harbor.

✉ info@gosnold.com ◐ www.gosnold.com

NOBLEBORO————————————————————————————————————

Mill Pond Inn	140 $US BB	Full breakfast
50 Main St 04555	6 rooms, 6 pb	Afternoon gatherings most afternoons
207-563-8014	C-ltd/S-no/P-no/H-ltd	with drinks & "nibbles" shared
Bobby & Sherry Whear		Dock with swim pier, hammocks,
		complimentary canoes & bikes, tie-up
		arrangements for small boats

Relax lakeside in the antique village of Damariscotta Mills. On several occasions the Mill Pond Inn has been referred to as a "magical, mystical place." Six guestrooms with private baths and amazing views invite you to enjoy it's natural surroundings.

✉ millpond@tidewater.net ◐ www.millpondinn.com

NORTH BERWICK

Angel of the Berwicks
2 Elm St 03906
207-676-2133
Sally & Ben Gumm

99-209 $US BB
5 rooms, 5 pb
Most CC, Cash
C-ltd/S-no/P-no/H-ltd

Full breakfast
Late afternoon refreshments offered,
enjoy your own favorite drinks (BYOB)
Baby grand piano in Music Room,
stained glass windows in Library,
fireplaces, private bathrooms

Enter a world of genteel elegance, Victorian romance and gracious hospitality. Experience the grandeur of this 20-room mansion while you enjoy all the Southern Maine Seacoast Region has to offer!

✉ info@angeloftheberwicks.com   🌐 www.angeloftheberwicks.com

NORTH HAVEN ISLAND

Our Place Inn & Cottages
19 Crabtree Pt. Rd. 04853
207-867-4998
Marnelle Bubar

90-275 $US EP
5 rooms, 3 pb
Most CC, Cash, Checks
C-yes/S-ltd/P-ltd/H-ltd

Main house sitting room with
fireplace; cottages have own kitchen,
bedroom

Our Place Inn is a renovated 19th century farmhouse with 4 self-contained cottages. A lighthouse cottage is completed. We offer comfortable accommodations in an informal and relaxed setting.

✉ ourplaceinn@aol.com   🌐 www.ourplaceinn.com

OCEAN PARK

Nautilus By The Sea
Guesthouse
2 Colby Ave 04063
800-981-7018 207-934-2021
Dick & Patte Kessler

70-175 $US BB
12 rooms, 10 pb
Visa, MC, Disc
C-yes/S-no/P-no/H-no
May 20 to October 11

Continental breakfast
Guest living room with cable TV/
VCR and library, enclosed and open
dunefront porch. WiFi.

The Nautilus By The Sea directly on the ocean in historic Ocean Park has 12 rooms, suites, or apartments, with our continental breakfast served on the dunefront enclosed porch. We're 20 minutes from Portland's Jetport, 6 minutes from ME TPK.

✉ info@nautilusbythesea.com   🌐 nautilusbythesea.com

OGUNQUIT

Admiral's Inn
87-95 Main St 03907
888-263-6318 207-646-7093
Ken Holmes

69-299 $US BB
45 rooms, 43 pb
Most CC, *Rated*, •
C-yes/S-ltd/P-no/H-yes
French

Continental breakfast
Lounge
Two heated swimming pools, hot
tubs, gym, sauna, day spa, restaurant/
lounge, and firepit. Location!

Come experience Ogunquit with us! The Admiral's Inn is a resort located on spacious grounds in the center of the village. Stroll to the beach, the Marginal Way, Perkins Cove, The Ogunquit Playhouse and all of the village pleasures. Gym, sauna, restaurant

✉ admirals@gwi.net   🌐 www.theadmiralsinn.com

Beauport Inn on Clay Hill
399 Clay Hill 03907
800-646-8681 207-251-2941
George & Cathy Wilson

130-250 $US AP
5 rooms, 5 pb
Visa, MC
C-ltd/S-no/P-no/H-ltd

Full breakfast
All guestrooms have gas stove, tiled
bath, cable TV, VCR, refrigerators, high
speed Internet

A spectacular newly-constructed stone English manor located on an 11-acre country setting, the Inn is nestled in between the Josiah River, Ogunquit's tennis courts, and rolling, forested hills. Ask about our apartment rental.

✉ gwilson6@maine.rr.com   🌐 www.beauportinn.com

Distant Sands B&B
632 Main St 03907
207-646-8686
Robert Rush

95-175 $US BB
5 rooms, 4 pb
Visa, MC, AmEx,
Rated
C-ltd/S-no/P-no/H-no
Closed Jan 15 to Apr 1.

Full breakfast
Wine & cheese, bottled water for
guests
Patio/deck ocean view, gardens, cable
TV, A/C, robes in room, beach towels
available

Distant Sands Bed & Breakfast offers five beautifully appointed bedrooms in a restored 18th century farmhouse. The house abuts twenty-two acres of conservation land overlooking the Ogunquit River and the ocean in the distance.

✉ innkeeper@distantsands.com   🌐 www.distantsands.com

OGUNQUIT

Leisure Inn
73 School Street 03907
207-646-2737
Pam Batten

129-279 $US BB
6 rooms, 6 pb
Visa, MC
C-ltd/S-no/P-no/H-no
Mem'l - Columbus Day

Expanded Continental Breakfast
Wrap around sun porch, fireplace, free
WiFi, cable TV, A/C, living room and
patio

The Leisure Inn is a two minute walk to Ogunquit's finest restaurants, shops, bars, night clubs and galleries. Clean and comfortable rooms with the finest amenities.

✉ Theleisureinn@aol.com 🌐 theleisureinn.com

Puffin Inn
433 Main St 03907
207-646-5496

85-250 $US BB
10 rooms, 10 pb
Visa, MC, *Rated*
C-ltd/S-no/P-no/H-ltd
April through October

Full breakfast
Afternoon refreshments, wine and
cheese hour available in-season.
Coffee & tea available all day.
All rooms have a private bathroom,
flat screen TV/DVD, A/C, sitting area,
fridge, wireless access.

A charming historic Inn with spacious and comfortable rooms each with a sitting area and private bathroom. Complimentary full breakfast each morning. Located on Main Street a ½ mile from the town center. Walk to the beach, shopping, restaurants.

✉ innkeeper@puffininn.com 🌐 www.puffininn.com

Rockmere Lodge
150 Stearns Rd 03907
888-646-2985 207-646-2985
Andy Antoniuk, Bob Brown
& Doug Flint

125-235 $US BB
8 rooms, 8 pb
Visa, MC, Disc, *Rated*
C-ltd/S-no/P-no/H-no

Full breakfast
Beach towels, chairs & umbrellas,
CD/clock radio, cable TV, VCR/DVD,
movie library, hairdryer, iron

Ogunquit's only ocean-side B&B. Maine shingle-style cottage sitting on a knoll with a commanding view of the Atlantic. Midpoint on the Marginal Way between the town, main beach and Perkins Cove. Decorated with Victorian era antiques. Walk to everything.

✉ info@rockmere.com 🌐 www.rockmere.com

The Terrace by the Sea
23 Wharf Ln 03907
207-646-3232
Sergio Becerra

49-242 $US BB
37 rooms, 37 pb
Visa, MC, *Rated*
C-ltd/S-ltd/P-no/H-yes
Spanish
Mar 23 – Dec 12

Expanded continental breakfast
Pool, tennis nearby, balconies, views,
kitchenette, WiFi, weddings, hair
dryer, ironing board & iron

The Terrace by the Sea combines deluxe motel and suite accommodations along with the elegance of a Colonial inn. Spectacular ocean views in a peaceful, secluded setting at the end of Wharf Lane across from the beach.   ✉ tbts@gwi.net 🌐 www.terracebythesea.com

---

The Trellis House
10 Beachmere Place 03907
800-681-7909 207-646-7909
Pat & Jerry Houlihan

95-225 $US BB
8 rooms, 8 pb
Visa, MC
C-ltd/S-no/P-no/H-no

Full breakfast
Afternoon beverages
Sitting room, porches, ocean views,
trolley stop, A/C, wireless Internet

A year-round inn close to all that is special to Ogunquit. Furnished with an eclectic blend of antiques, coupled with some ocean views and quiet surroundings.

✉ info@trellishouse.com 🌐 www.trellishouse.com

Yardarm Village Inn
406 Shore Rd 03907
888-927-3276 207-646-7006
Scott & Beverlee Drury

95-155 $US BB
10 rooms, 10 pb
Visa, MC, Disc
C-yes/S-ltd/P-no/H-ltd
May – mid October

Continental breakfast
Beer, wine, cheese & cracker shop
Hand-painted Maine blueberry
dinnerware, sailboat charter, Internet,
gift shop, waterfall & gardens

Free Night w/Certificate: Valid Sunday-Thursday; May, June, September, and October; except holiday weekends.

Charming New England Inn adjacent to Perkins Cove. Relax and enjoy ocean breezes from our veranda or find a spot near our bubbling waterfall. Sailing charters, beer, wine, cheese, hand-painted Maine dinnerware and gift shop on premises.

✉ yardarm@maine.rr.com 🌐 www.yardarmvillageinn.com

OLD ORCHARD BEACH

Atlantic Birches Inn	101-192 $US BB	Continental plus breakfast
20 Portland Ave 04064	10 rooms, 10 pb	Teas, coffee, cider, hot chocolate,
888-934-5295 207-934-5295	Most CC, *Rated*, •	juices, water, herbal teas
Ray & Heidi DeLeo	C-yes/S-no/P-no/H-ltd	Sitting rooms, heated pool/beach pool towels, TV/DVD A/C, wraparound porch, picnic table, gazebo

Free Night w/Certificate: Valid November 1st-May 23rd.

The Atlantic Birches Inn B&B located in Old Orchard Beach, Maine is an elegant, romantic, Victorian yet casual Inn. We are a 2 minute walk to, shops, restaurants, fine dining, amusements, arcades, the Pier and 7 miles of flat white sand beach.

✉ Info@atlanticbirches.com 🌐 www.atlanticbirches.com

ORLAND

Orland House B&B	95-143 $US BB	Full breakfast
10 Narramissic River	6 rooms, 6 pb	Complimentary afternoon tea, snacks
Dr 04472	Visa, MC, AmEx,	& wine
207-469-1144	*Rated*, •	Sitting room, library, cable TV,
Cynthia & Alvion Kimball	C-ltd/S-no/P-no/H-no Spanish and some French	business travel accommodations, Internet, fax, private porch

1820s Greek Revival B&B with 20th century amenities. Located on the Narramissic River at the head of Penobscot Bay, 30 minutes from Bangor, 50 minutes to Acadia National Park.

✉ innkeeper@orlandhousebb.com 🌐 www.orlandhousebb.com

POLAND

Wolf Cove Inn	75-250 $US BB	Full breakfast
5 Jordan Shore Dr 04274	10 rooms, 8 pb	Catered meals for group gatherings
207-998-4976	Most CC, Cash,	Sitting room, Jacuzzi, fireplaces, cable
Marie & Steven Struble	Checks, •	TV, WiFi, kayaks, accommodations for
	C-ltd/S-no/P-yes/H-no	business travelers

Wolf Cove Inn is a romantic, elegant country inn with a spectacular lake view and a beautiful, natural setting. The outside deck and terrace are the perfect setting for birdwatching, sunsets and quiet conversations.

✉ info@wolfcoveinn.com 🌐 www.wolfcoveinn.com

PORTLAND

Celtic Cottage	100-120 $US BB	Hearty traditional breakfast
1433 Westbrook Street 04102	3 rooms, 2 pb	Complimentary passes to Total Fitness
207-329-7859 207-773-6072	Visa, MC	Gym, down comforter, free parking,
Mary Kuebler	C-ltd/S-no/P-no/H-no	wireless Internet

Explore the traditional ways of Celtic hospitality. Walk down the road to the Tate House Museum built in 1755 by Captain Tate, mast agent to King George III. Take in a Sea Dogs baseball game at Hadlock Field just 7 minutes from Celtic Cottage.

✉ info@celticcottagemaine.com 🌐 www.celticcottagemaine.com

Inn at St. John	49-215 $US BB	Continental breakfast
939 Congress St 04102	39 rooms, 20 pb	Tea, lemonade & cookies (seasonal)
800-636-9127 207-773-6481	Most CC, *Rated*, •	Family friendly, cable TV, Internet
Paul Hood	C-yes/S-no/P-yes/H-no	connections, bike storage, free parking, A/C

Conveniently located off the West End of Downtown, Portland, ME, the Inn At St. John has been providing travelers with exemplary service for over 100 years, an enjoyable change from the ordinary hotel accommodation. Children and pets are welcome!

✉ theinn@maine.rr.com 🌐 www.innatstjohn.com

Tell your hosts Pamela Lanier sent you.

PORTLAND

Morrill Mansion B&B
249 Vaughan St 04102
888-5morrill 207-774-6900
David Parker

89-239 $US BB
7 rooms, 7 pb
Visa, MC, Disc
C-ltd/S-no/P-no/H-no

Breakfast Buffet
Fresh fruit is available all day, fresh
baked treats can be found in the guest
gathering room
Private baths, TV with DVD players,
AC, CD players, mini-fridges, off-street
parking

*Architectural details that make the Morrill Mansion B&B unique have been restored and modern ame-
nities have been added to make your stay in Portland comfortable. Free off-street parking and Internet
connection are included! We look forward to your visit.*

✉ innkeeper@morrillmansion.com 🌐 www.morrillmansion.com

Percy Inn
15 Pine St 04102
888-41-PERCY 207-871-POET
Dale Northrup, CTC

79-209 $US BB
10 rooms, 10 pb
Visa, MC, •
C-ltd/S-no/P-no/H-no

Continental buffet breakfast
24 hour butler pantry with snacks &
drinks
Parlor with 400 movies & CDs, pantry,
bricked garden courtyard, sun deck

*A stylish and intimate urban inn, situated in the heart of Portland's West End Historic District at Long-
fellow Square. Every room in this 1830 brick rowhouse has its own personality and sense of history,
coupled with the comforts of today.*

✉ innkeeper@percyinn.com 🌐 www.percyinn.com

The Chadwick
140 Chadwick St 04102
800-774-2137 207-774-5141
Buddy Marcum

99-185 $US BB
4 rooms, 4 pb
Visa, MC, Disc, *Rated*
S-no/P-no/H-no

Full breakfast
Fresh baked cookies in the afternoon
upon arrival
Sitting room, library, fireplace, cable
TV, wireless Internet connection

Free Night w/Certificate: Valid January-April.

*"Simple elegance" describes this Queen-Anne located in historic West End. Gourmet breakfasts. Guest-
rooms tastefully decorated. All rooms offer Flat Screen DVD TV's . Only a short walk to the Portland
Harbor and Old Port Shops, art district & Fine Dining.*

✉ info@thechadwick.com 🌐 thechadwick.com

West End Inn
146 Pine St 04102
800-338-1377 207-772-1377
Sara Stempien, Beth Oliver

95-225 $US BB
6 rooms, 6 pb
Most CC, Cash
C-ltd/S-no/P-no/H-no

Full breakfast
Transition from day to night with light
refreshments during Intermezzo from
4:00–6:00 PM.
Wireless, high-speed Internet access;
cable TV, AM/FM clocks w/ipod
docks, free off-street parking.

*A sophisticated, 1871 Georgian-style townhouse B&B nestled within Portland's Western Promenade
neighborhood. Contemporary works by Maine artists adorn colorful walls to provide a delightful oasis
for a romantic interlude or a comfortable business stay.*

✉ innkeeper@westendbb.com 🌐 www.Westendbb.com

Wild Iris Inn
273 State St 04101
800-600-1557 207-775-0224
Diane Edwards

79-159 $US BB
7 rooms, 5 pb
Most CC
C-ltd/S-no/P-no/H-no

Continental plus breakfast
Afternoon snacks & tea at anytime
Sitting room with fireplace, cable,
garden area, business office with high
speed Internet, WiFi

*A cozy seven room bed and breakfast conveniently located within walking distance of downtown
Portland, and a short drive from area beaches and attractions. We are Portland's first certified green
inn.*

✉ diane@wildirisinn.com 🌐 www.wildirisinn.com

Tell your hosts Pamela Lanier sent you.

ROCKLAND

Berry Manor Inn 81 Talbot Ave 04841 800-774-5692 207-596-7696 Cheryl Michaelsen & Michael LaPosta	115-360 $US BB 12 rooms, 12 pb Visa, MC, AmEx, *Rated*, • C-ltd/S-no/P-no/H-ltd	Full breakfast 24-hr guest pantry with homemade pies made by the Berry Manor Inn Pie Moms as seen on Food Network Many common areas for guests' use. Concierge services for boats, golf, restaurants and other needs

Rockland's premier bed and breakfast inn and the only AAA 4-Diamond rated historic inn in mid-coast Maine. Historic Victorian mansion with 12 luxury guestrooms with fireplaces, private baths (many with whirlpool tubs). Green Certified.

info@berrymanorinn.com www.berrymanorinn.com

Captain Lindsey House Inn 5 Lindsey St 04841 800-523-2145 207-596-7950 Capts. Ellen & Ken Barnes	141-215 $US BB 9 rooms, 9 pb Most CC, *Rated*, • C-yes/S-no/P-no/H-ltd French	Full breakfast Afternoon refreshments in our private courtyard or in front of the fire in the winter Deck, private garden, library, wireless Internet

Nestled amongst the historic seaport buildings of downtown Rockland, the 9 room Captain Lindsey House Inn, built in 1837 and one of Rockland's first Inns, offers a quiet, elegant but comfortable & cozy retreat. One block from the harbor and ferry terminal

lindsey@midcoast.com www.lindseyhouse.com

Lime Rock Inn 96 Limerock St 04841 800-546-3762 207-594-2257 P.J. Walter & Frank Isganitis	159-239 $US BB 8 rooms, 8 pb Most CC, • C-ltd/S-no/P-no/H-ltd	Full breakfast Seasonal fruit, homemade breads, regional fruit jams & plenty of freshly brewed coffee Wrap-around porch, gazebo, two parlors, guest pantry, a/c, some rooms with fireplaces, free WiFi

All of the rooms at the Lime Rock Inn are decorated with care to create a home with elegance and luxury, yet have charm and character to ensure comfort and hospitality.

info@limerockinn.com www.limerockinn.com

Old Granite Inn 546 Main St 04841 800-386-9036 207-594-9036 Edwin & Joan Hantz	95-210 $US BB 8 rooms, 8 pb Most CC, • C-yes/S-no/P-yes/H-no	Full breakfast Sitting room, common areas, garden, sunrise deck, guest pantry, in-room TV option, piano, book swap

Comfortable historic inn overlooking a busy harbor filled with boats. We offer eight distinctive rooms, seven with private bath, each furnished with luxurious linens, antiques and contemporary accents. Greet each day with a full gourmet breakfast.   ogi@midcoast.com www.oldgraniteinn.com

ROCKPORT

Island View Inn 908 Commercial Street 04856 866-711-8439 207-596-0040 Dana Burton	79-229 $US EP 15 rooms, 15 pb Visa, MC, AmEx, *Rated* C-yes/S-no/P-no/H-yes May- November	Coffee and tea in the morning Heated pool, large lobby with fireplaces, air conditioned, cozy seating area with cable TV

The only three diamond AAA approved oceanfront property in the Rockland/Camden area offers oversize rooms and large decks. All rooms individually decorated with a coastal theme and views of the beautiful landscape throughout our inn.

info@islandviewinnmaine.com www.islandviewinnmaine.com

Strawberry Hill Seaside Inn 866 Commercial Street 04856 800-589-4009 207-594-5462 Dana Burton	79-199 $US EP 21 rooms, 21 pb Visa, MC, AmEx C-yes/S-no/P-no/H-yes	Coffee & tea in the morning Heated outdoor pool with deck, cable TV, large lobby with fireplaces and cozy seating area, WiFi

Ocean front setting, beautiful landscaping and all rooms have a beautiful ocean view. We offer rooms with one king, one queen, or two full size beds. All rooms are individually decorated with a coastal theme.   info@strawberryhillinn.com www.strawberryhillseasideinn.com

SEARSPORT

Carriage House Inn	110-135 $US BB	Full breakfast
120 E Main St 04974	4 rooms, 4 pb	Coffee & tea in the afternoon
207-548-2167	Visa, MC, Disc	Historic, library, sitting areas, common
Marcia Markwardt	C-ltd/S-no/P-no/H-no	rooms, gardens, antiques, parlor, den, formal dining room

Come stay in one of Maine's most photographed homes! Listed on the National Register of Historic places and Haunted Inns of Maine this 1874 Victorian sea captain's manse was home to Impressionist painter and close friend of Ernest Hemingway, Waldo Pierce.

✉ info@carriagehouseinmaine.com   🌐 www.carriagehouseinmaine.com

SEBASCO ESTATES

Rock Gardens Inn	120-200 $US MAP	Full breakfast
Rt 217 04565	28 rooms, 25 pb	Rates include breakfast & dinner,
207-389-1339	Visa, MC	weekly lobster cookout, picnic
Ona Barnet	C-yes/S-no/P-ltd/H-ltd	lunches available
	June-Sept	Heated pool, kayaks, golf, tennis & boating nearby, ten minutes from sandy beach, art workshops

Enjoy a relaxing vacation in classic Maine-style cottages on a private peninsula facing Casco Bay. Ocean front views, flower gardens, breakfast & dinner daily, lobster cookouts weekly. Art workshops are offered in June, early July, and September.

✉ ona@rockgardensinn.com   🌐 www.rockgardensinn.com

SOUTHWEST HARBOR

Penury Hall	95-130 $US BB	Full breakfast
374 Main St 04679	3 rooms, 3 pb	Complimentary wine, coffee, tea
207-244-7102	Visa, MC	Sitting room, sauna, library, music,
Gretchen Strong	C-yes/S-no/P-no/H-no	fine art, laundry, fridge, porch, garden terrace

Penury Hall is a comfortable, rambling Maine B&B on Mt. Desert Island. The decor reflects your hosts' interests in art, antiques, books, gardening, sailing. Shops and restaurants are within walking distance and Acadia Nat'l Park is only a mile away.

✉ tstrong@penuryhall.com   🌐 www.penuryhall.com

The Birches B&B	135-190 $US BB	Full breakfast
46 Fernald Point Rd 04679	3 rooms, 3 pb	Dining room, living room, croquet
207-244-5182	Visa, MC	court, garden, ocean views
Richard Homer	C-yes/S-no/P-yes/H-no	

Three large airy rooms, private baths, ocean views, gardens, and a croquet court. We have 5 acres of grounds, no traffic noise, just 350 yards to the first tee at the golf course. Separate Old House available for rental. 2 new self contained cottages.

✉ dick@thebirchesbnb.com   🌐 www.thebirchesbnb.com

The Claremont Hotel	152-308 $US BB	Buffet Breakfast
22 Claremont Rd 04679	45 rooms, 44 pb	Dinner & full bar available daily
800-244-5036 207-244-5036	Visa, MC	Cottages, tennis court, croquet courts,
John W. Madiera	C-yes/S-no/P-no/H-ltd	dock, moorings, bicycles, rowboats
	May 24th – October 19th	

Classic Maine shorefront hotel providing summer refuge to visitors of Mt. Desert Island since 1884. Located on Somes Sound, America's east coast fjord, and listed on the National Register.

✉ clmhotel@roadrunner.com   🌐 www.theclaremonthotel.com

The Inn at Southwest	110-190 $US BB	Full breakfast
371 Main St 04679	7 rooms, 7 pb	Afternoon coffee, tea & cookies
207-244-3835	Visa, MC, *Rated*	Down-filled duvets, ceiling fans, fine
Sandy Johnson	C-ltd/S-no/P-no/H-no	linens & towels, gas log stoves, high
	May – November	speed Internet access

Overlooking the serene waters of Southwest Harbor, the Inn at Southwest combines Victorian charm & gracious hospitality. The inn is within walking distance of restaurants, shopping and the marina.

✉ reservations@innatsouthwest.com   🌐 www.innatsouthwest.com

SOUTHWEST HARBOR

The Kingsleigh Inn
373 Main St 04679
207-244-5302
Pamela & Bryan

130-305 $US BB
8 rooms, 8 pb
Most CC, Cash, Checks,
Rated
C-ltd/S-no/P-no/H-ltd
May-October

4 course gourmet breakfast
Afternoon baked goods, in-room
chocolate truffles & Port wine, wine
and hors d'oeurves hour
Living Room & Lounge w/fireplaces,
wraparound porch w/harbor view,
library, robes, slippers, flowers

Overlooking picturesque Southwest Harbor, 4 course gourmet breakfast, some rooms have harbor views & private decks, all have private baths, secluded 3-room turret suite w/fireplace. Enjoy soft robes, slippers, homemade chocolates, wine and hors d'oeurves

✉ relax@kingsleighinn.com 🌐 www.kingsleighinn.com

SPRUCE HEAD

Craignair Inn
5 Third St 04859
800-320-9997 207-594-7644
Michael & Joanne

80-176 $US BB
20 rooms, 14 pb
Most CC, Cash, Checks,
Rated
C-yes/S-no/P-yes/H-no

Full or continental plus breakfast
Restaurant, coffee, tea & full liquor
license, kitchen in Apartment
Library with piano, gardens, coastal
activities, walking, hiking, ocean
swimming, WiFi

In Mid-coast of Maine, overlooking the Atlantic Ocean. Central to Portland – Bangor. Restaurant on premises, outstanding dinners, delicious breakfasts. Out of the way, but not too much! Spectacular views. Pet-Friendly. Fodor's Choice 2008, 2009 and 2010.

✉ innkeeper@craignair.com 🌐 www.craignair.com

TENANTS HARBOR

East Wind Inn
21 Mechanic St 04860
800-241-VIEW 207-372-6366
Tim Watts & Joy Taylor

99-226 $US BB
22 rooms, 16 pb
Visa, MC, AmEx,
Rated, •
C-ltd/S-no/P-ltd/H-ltd
May-November

Full breakfast
Memorable dining with water views,
cocktails, beer & wine, open 7 days a
week, May to November
Water & harbor views from every
antique-filled room in historic Inn and
Meeting House

Our historic seaside inn is in a tiny, tranquil village on a rural peninsula – a peaceful base from which to enjoy Maine's scenic coast and the culturally rich Rockland area.

✉ info@eastwindinn.com 🌐 www.eastwindinn.com

TOPSHAM

Black Lantern B&B
57 Elm St 04086
888-306-4165 207-725-4165
Tom & Judy Connelie

95-110 $US BB
3 rooms, 3 pb
Most CC, Cash, Checks
C-ltd/S-no/P-no/H-no

Full breakfast
Water views, dock, private baths,
antique country furniture &
homemade quilts

Relax in the cozy and comfortable atmosphere of this mid-19th century home on the banks of the Androscoggin River. The Black Lantern Inn is in the historic village of Topsham, ME just 30 minutes north of Portland. ✉ blacklantern@suscom-maine.net 🌐 www.blacklanternbandb.com

WALDOBORO

Blue Skye Farm
1708 Friendship Rd 04572
207-832-0300
Jan Davidson

105-145 $US BB
5 rooms, 4 pb
Visa, MC, •
C-ltd/S-no/P-no/H-ltd

Full breakfast
Lobster dinners by prior arrangement
Picnic tables, hiking trails, outdoor
grills, free wireless Internet

A restored 1770s house with extensive grounds and hundreds of acres of hiking trails, Blue Skye stylishly blends New England simplicity with old world grace. The privacy offered to its discerning guests makes it a favorite with artists & romantics alike.

✉ jan@blueskyefarm.com 🌐 www.blueskyefarm.com

WALPOLE

Brannon Bunker Inn
349 State Route 129 04573
800-563-9225 207-563-5941
Jeanne & Joe Hovance

90-100 $US BB
8 rooms, 6 pb
Most CC, *Rated*, •
C-yes/S-ltd/P-no/H-ltd

Continental plus breakfast
Kitchen facilities available.
Sitting room, porch, antique shop, 3
room suite for family

The Brannon-Bunker Inn offers a welcoming spirit that calls to travelers and families to stay and experience the area's lilac-scented springs, maple-shaded summers, brilliantly colored autumns, or crisp white winters. ✉ brbnkinn@lincoln.midcoast.com 🌐 www.brannonbunkerinn.com

WISCASSET

Snow Squall B&B
5 Bradford Rd 04578
207-882-6892
Paul & Melanie Harris

100-220 $US BB
7 rooms, 7 pb
Visa, MC, *Rated*
C-yes/S-no/P-no/H-ltd
Spanish, Portuguese,
French

Full breakfast
Paul is a professional chef. Full
Breakfast includes fresh fruits, fresh
baked goods and hot entree.
2 sitting rooms, porch with rocking
chairs off breakfast area, private
entrances to carriage suites.

*Voted "Highly Recommended" by Fodors Maine Coast, Snow Squall offers a relaxing and elegant B&B
conveniently located on Route 1 in Wiscasset. All rooms have king or queen beds, A/C, private baths
and a full breakfast is included.Massage and Yoga available*

✉ info@snowsquallinn.com   ◐ www.snowsquallinn.com

YORK

Dockside Guest Quarters
22 Harris Island Rd 03909
800-270-1977 207-363-2868
Eric & Carol Lusty

117-312 $US BB
25 rooms, 25 pb
Visa, MC, Disc,
Rated, •
C-yes/S-no/P-no/H-yes
April- November

Full breakfast buffet
Lunch, dinner & cocktails in adjacent
restaurant, afternoon tea and treats
daily in Maine House
Restaurant, lawn games, boat rentals,
bikes, beach chairs, phones, A/C,
cable TV, wireless Internet

*The essence of Maine is captured at the Dockside overlooking York Harbor. Distinctive accommoda-
tions are offered in a classic New England inn and multi-unit buildings at the waters edge. Dining at
the Dockside is popular with visitors and locals alike.*

✉ eric@docksidegq.com   ◐ www.docksidegq.com

YORK BEACH

The Candleshop Inn
44 Freeman St 03910
888-363-4087 207-363-4087
Barbara Sheff

100-185 $US BB
10 rooms, 3 pb
Most CC, Cash, Checks
C-yes/S-no/P-no/H-ltd
A little French
May 1 to November 1

Full breakfast
Full vegetarian breakfast: vegan/
lactose/gluten free available. Snacks
-fruit, coffee, tea, water
Deck, front porch, ocean views,
meditation garden, massage therapy,
Reiki, Aromatherapy

*With its serene atmosphere and beautiful ocean views, our 10 bedroom home is the perfect setting for
replenishing body, mind and spirit. Wake up to the smells of home cooking, walk the beach at sunrise,
or relax in the meditation garden. Children welcome*

✉ stay@candleshopinn.com   ◐ www.candleshopinn.com

YORK HARBOR

Inn at Tanglewood Hall
611 York St 03911
207-351-1075
Su & Andy Wetzel

115-235 $US BB
6 rooms, 6 pb
Visa, MC, AmEx
C-ltd/S-no/P-no/H-ltd

Full Gourmet Breakfast
Premium Tanglewood brew, select
gourmet teas, hot chocolate & special
treats available all day
Widescreen LCD cable TV & DVD
players, gas fireplaces, updated private
baths, A/C, luxurious linens

*Inn at Tanglewood Hall is a romantic York Harbor Maine B&B along seacoast Route 1A, amidst wood-
land gardens, just beyond the York Beach Lobster Cove bend. Enjoy our casually elegant hospitality,
nearby beaches, Ogunquit, Kennebunkport and Kittery.*

✉ tanglewood@maine.rr.com   ◐ www.tanglewoodhall.com

Maryland

ANNAPOLIS

Annapolis Inn
144 Prince George St 21401
410-295-5200
Joseph Lespier

259-479 $US BB
3 rooms, 3 pb
Visa, MC, *Rated*
C-ltd/S-no/P-no/H-no
Spanish, Italian

Very elegant three-course breakfast
Afternoon tea, chocolates in rooms,
soft drinks
A/C, heated Jacuzzi, towel warmers,
heated marble floors, wireless Internet

The perfect Inn for the perfect getaway. Let us help create the ideal visit to fit your needs. Business, pleasure or vacation, our service is incomparable and our suites are spacious, elegant and luxurious. Pamper or surprise that special someone.

✉ info@annapolisinn.com 🌐 www.annapolisinn.com

Annapolitan B&B
1313 West St 21401
866-990-2330 410-990-1234
John & Joetta Holt

75-260 $US BB
7 rooms, 7 pb
Most CC, Cash
C-yes/S-no/P-ltd/H-yes

Full breakfast
Gourmet meals and private chef
available upon request.
TV Lounge, fax, computer, plus
wireless Internet, laundry facilities

Free Night w/Certificate: Valid Mon.-Thurs. not valid during powerboat show, US sailboat show, navy graduation week, or navy parents weekend. Room Upgrade.

Quaint Colonial architecture, unsurpassed hospitality and unforgettable experiences await at the Annapolitan Bed & Breakfast. Our luxuriously appointed rooms, modern amenities and food offerings exceed the most discerning leisure and business travelers.

✉ annapolitanbandb@yahoo.com 🌐 www.theannapolitan.com

Chez Amis B&B
85 East St 21401
888-224-6455 410-263-6631
Don & Mickie Deline

165-215 $US BB
4 rooms, 4 pb
Visa, MC, AmEx, •
C-ltd/S-no/P-no/H-no

Full breakfast
Soft drinks, beer, wine, peanuts,
M&Ms, cookies, champagne or
chocolate cake for special occasions
Sitting room, European/country
decor, themed rooms, robes, TV, A/C,
antiques, over 200 DVDs & tapes

Former grocery store circa 1900, transformed into a B&B in 1989. Perfect location for enjoying historic area, harbor & Academy. Antiques and quilts decorate this charming, cozy, comfortable and quaint inn. Full breakfast and private baths.

✉ stayatchezamis@verizon.net 🌐 www.chezamis.com

Flag House Inn
24-26 Randall St 21404
800-437-4825 410-280-2721
Charlotte & Bill Schmickle

180-350 $US BB
5 rooms, 5 pb
Visa, MC
C-ltd/S-no/P-no/H-no
Mid-February through
Dec

Continental breakfast
Off street parking on site. Swing on
front porch. Fireplace in guest sitting
room.

1870 Victorian offering free off-street parking, king or twin beds in 4 guestrooms & a 2 room suite, each with private full bath and cable TV. Full hot breakfast in guest dining room. Half-block to Waterfront's City Dock & USNA Visitor's Gate 1.

✉ info@flaghouseinn.com 🌐 www.flaghouseinn.com

Gibson's Lodgings
110 Prince George St 21401
877-330-0057 410-268-5555
Beverly Snyder

129-259 $US BB
21 rooms, 17 pb
Most CC, Cash,
Checks, •
C-ltd/S-ltd/P-ltd/H-yes

Continental plus breakfast
Free Parking in our courtyard,
Free Wireless, Air Conditioning
throughout,All Smoke-Free Rooms.

The location says it all . . . In the heart of the Annapolis Historic District,1 block from the City Dock and Naval Academy, is Gibson's Lodgings Historic Inn and Conference Center. Free Parking, Free Wireless & a Continental Plus Breakfast are Included.

✉ gibsonslodgings@starpower.net 🌐 www.gibsonslodgings.com

ANNAPOLIS

Scotlaur Inn
165 Main St 21401
410-268-5665
Ted & Beth Levitt

85-175 $US BB
10 rooms, 10 pb
Visa, MC, Disc,
Rated, •
C-yes/S-no/P-ltd/H-no
Spanish

Full breakfast
Snacks, lunch and dinner available in
the restaurant
Accommodations for business
travelers, TV, telephones, wireless
Internet access & air conditioning

The Scotlaur Inn offers ten beautifully decorated, old-fashioned guestrooms in the heart of Annapolis. The Scotlaur Inn and Chick & Ruth's Delly (where breakfast is served) have been a family owned business for 3 generations in the historic district. ✉ Info@ScotlaurInn.com ◐ www.scotlaurinn.com

The Tree House
51 Bay Drive 21401
410-260-2801
Patsy Oertli

250-300 $US EP
1 rooms, 1 pb
Visa, MC
C-yes/S-no/P-no/H-no

Terrific views, private beach, fully-
equipped kitchen, sitting rooms,
convenient location, parking

Beautiful bay front "Tree House" apartment with two full baths, kitchen and delightfully designed sitting room with sweeping bay views. Just a few steps away from your very own private pier and sandy beach. ✉ Patsy.oertli@longandfoster.com

BALTIMORE

1840s Carrollton Inn
50 Albemarle St 21202
410-385-1840
Timothy Kline

175-375 $US BB
13 rooms, 13 pb
Most CC, Cash,
Rated, •
C-yes/S-no/P-no/H-yes
Spanish

Full breakfast
Complimentary coffee & tea service
available
WiFi high-speed Internet,flat
screen cable TV,whirlpool
bath,fireplace,refrigerator, microwave
oven.

The Jewel of Jonestown! A block from Little Italy, 4 blocks from the Inner Harbor, boasting luxury rooms and suites with whirlpool tubs, fireplaces & decorator furnishings. Linger over coffee in a tranquil garden courtyard then explore Baltimore's sights.
✉ info@1840scarrolltoninn.com ◐ www.1840scarrolltoninn.com

Blue Door on Baltimore
2023 E Baltimore St 21231
410-732-0191
Roger & Cecelia

149-170 $US BB
3 rooms, 3 pb
Most CC, Cash
C-yes/S-no/P-no/H-no

3 Course Grand Breakfast
Continental breakfast menu on
weekdays, evening turn-down snack,
soda, bottled water & tea service
In-room satellite TV & music, relaxing
common areas, free Internet access
(wireless and cable)

Located in the historic area of Butcher's Hill, and steps away from Patterson Park, you are minutes away from all of Baltimore's business and entertainment venues.
✉ bluedoorbaltimore@verizon.net ◐ bluedoorbaltimore.com

Celie's Waterfront Inn
1714 Thames St 21231
800-432-0184 410-522-2323
Willy Dely

149-349 $US BB
9 rooms, 9 pb
Most CC, Cash
C-ltd/S-no/P-ltd/H-no
French

Continental plus breakfast
Tea, Coffee, Juices, Water
Free wireless Internet, common area
phone with LD, satellite TV, A/C,
whirlpool tubs, fireplaces

The charm of Fells Point, the convenience to Baltimore and the romance of the area's most renowned, historic B&B hotels make Celie's a local favorite. Couples, vacationers and business travelers consider Celie's one of the Baltimore area's hidden gems.
✉ innkeeper@celieswaterfront.com ◐ www.celiesinn.com

Gramercy Mansion
1400 Greenspring Valley
Rd 21153
410-486-2405
Anne Pomykala & Cristin
Kline

150-375 $US BB
11 rooms, 11 pb
Most CC, Cash, •
C-yes/S-no/P-no/H-yes
Spanish

Full breakfast
In-room coffee, tea, soda, bottled
water. Snacks available in lobby.
Gardens, trails, tennis, jacuzzis,
outdoor pool, suites, fireplaces,
meeting rooms, cable, WiFi

A historic Tudor Mansion crowns 45 acres of gardens and woodland trails. Secluded in scenic Greenspring Valley yet just 10 miles from Baltimore, guestrooms and suites offer elegant decor and amenities including whirlpool tubs and fireplaces.
✉ info@gramercymansion.com ◐ www.gramercymansion.com

Mill Street Inn, Cambridge, MD

BALTIMORE

Inn at 2920
2920 Elliott St 21224
877-774-2920 410-342-4450
David Rohrbaugh & Warren
Munroe

175-240 $US BB
5 rooms, 5 pb
Most CC, Cash, •
C-ltd/S-no/P-no/H-no

Full Gourmet Breakfast
Jacuzzi tubs, Satellite TV/VCR, Internet
access

Inn at 2920 is an upscale, contemporary bed and breakfast located in one of downtown Baltimore's most desirable waterfront neighborhoods.

✉ reservations@theinnat2920.com 🌐 www.theinnat2920.com

CAMBRIDGE

Mill Street Inn
114 Mill St 21613
410-901-9144
Skip & Jennie Rideout

125-225 $US BB
3 rooms, 3 pb
Visa, MC, Disc
S-no/P-no/H-no

Full breakfast
Afternoon tea
Cable TV, DVD, WiFi, A/C, water
views, air jet tub

Great getaways begin here, where the pineapple truly signifies welcome, and where visitors will experience Eastern Shore hospitality at its finest.

✉ jennie@millstinn.com 🌐 www.millstinn.com

CHESAPEAKE CITY

Blue Max Inn
300 Bohemia Ave 21915
877-725-8362 410-885-2781
Christine Mullen

100-250 $US BB
10 rooms, 10 pb
Most CC, Cash, Checks,
Rated, •
C-ltd/S-ltd/P-no/H-yes

Full gourmet breakfast
Complimentary teas, coffee and
snacks, chocolates on your pillow
Sitting room, library, Jacuzzi,
fireplace, cable TV/VCR, VHS library,
conference, A/C, WiFi, parking

This elegant bed & breakfast is located in historic Chesapeake City, Maryland, along the shores of the famous Chesapeake and DE Canal. Built in 1854, The Blue Max Inn is a charming and romantic inn located in the heart of this historic town.

✉ innkeeper@bluemaxinn.com 🌐 www.bluemaxinn.com

CHESAPEAKE CITY

Ship Watch Inn
401 First St 21915
877-335-5300 410-885-5300
Gilda Martuscelli

99-245 $US BB
10 rooms, 10 pb
Visa, MC, AmEx
C-yes/S-ltd/P-no/H-yes

Full gourmet breakfast
Complimentary bottled water, juice
& soda, fresh baked goods daily in
addition to snacks & fruit
Foyer lounge, outdoor deck, hot tub,
picnic essentials, restaurant delivery,
weddings, catering

A stunning waterfront view can be enjoyed from all 10 guestrooms which are beautifully appointed in simple, elegant decor. A private bath accompanies each room and 6 feature whirlpool tubs with shower.

 innkeeper@shipwatchinn.com 🌐 www.shipwatchinn.com

CHESTERTOWN

Brampton B&B Inn
25227 Chestertown Rd 21620
866-305-1860 410-778-1860
Danielle Hanscom

169-399 $US BB
12 rooms, 12 pb
Visa, MC, *Rated*
C-ltd/S-no/P-ltd/H-ltd
French, German

Full breakfast
Complimentary refreshments &
cookies and afternoon tea
Majestic front porch with comfortable
seating, sitting room, library, most
rooms with fireplaces

The award-winning Brampton B&B Inn is a quiet oasis just one mile outside the historic town of Chestertown. The inn brilliantly blends the grand elegance of the 19th century country plantation with the comfort and modern amenities you deserve.

 innkeeper@bramptoninn.com 🌐 www.bramptoninn.com

Great Oak Manor
10568 Cliff Rd 21620
800-504-3098 410-778-5943
Cassandra Fedas

169-315 $US BB
12 rooms, 12 pb
Most CC, Cash, Checks,
Rated
C-ltd/S-no/P-ltd/H-yes
Russian

Breakfast includes a hot entree
Afternoon snack, evening port &
sherry, fresh fruit & beverages all
complimentary
Waterfront setting, conference rooms,
massage, golf, bicycles, private beach,
sunset cruises

Come for a romantic getaway to Great Oak Manor where the only honking comes from the geese, where the closest highway is the duck flyway, and where the only traffic you see from your room are the boaters sailing the water of the Chesapeake Bay Waterfront.

 innkeeper@greatoak.com 🌐 www.greatoak.com

DEALE

Creekside B&B
6036 Parkers Creek Dr 20751
410 867-7267
Betty-Carol Sellen & Marti
Burt

100-125 $US BB
3 rooms, 1 pb
Most CC, Cash, Checks
C-ltd/S-no/P-no/H-no
Spanish

Continental plus breakfast
Use of living room, library, canoes,
decks, garden, pool, hot tub

Creekside B&B is located in a small community on the western shore of Chesapeake Bay, 20 miles south of Annapolis. It is tastefully furnished in a blend of old oak & contemporary furniture.

 bcsellen@juno.com

DEEP CREEK LAKE

Carmel Cove Inn
Glendale Rd 21550
301-387-0067
Mary Bender

175-195 $US BB
10 rooms, 10 pb
Visa, MC, Disc, •
C-ltd/S-ltd/P-no/H-yes
Some French & German

Full breakfast
Snacks, complimentary guest beverage
bar with wine, beer, soda & water
Huge English great room with
billiards, bikes, tennis, hot tubs, skiing,
fireplaces, dock, canoe

"Simply the best accommodations and location on the lake." A former Monastery is Deep Creek Lake's premier country inn. Set back in the tranquil woods. Canoes, fishing & swimming and breakfast room service.

 innkeeper@carmelcoveinn.com 🌐 www.carmelcoveinn.com

EASTON

Bishop's House B&B
214 Goldsborough St 21601
800-223-7290 410-820-7290
Diane Laird-Ippolito & John
Ippolito

185-195 $US BB
5 rooms, 5 pb
Most CC, Cash, Checks,
Rated, •
C-ltd/S-no/P-no/H-no
Feb – Dec

Full sumptuous breakfast
Complimentary coffee, selection of
teas, hot chocolate, sodas and snacks
Sitting rooms, bicycles, fireplaces,
whirlpools, wrap around porch &
courtyard with fish pond

Enjoy a memorable visit to MD's Eastern Shore. Romantically furnished, in-town, centrally located for visiting all points of interest. Victorian ambience with 21st century comfort featuring working fireplaces, whirlpool tubs, WiFi & sumptuous breakfasts!

✉ bishopshouse@bishopshouse.com 🌐 www.bishopshouse.com

John S. McDaniel House
14 N Aurora St 21601
877-822-5702 410-822-3704
Mary Lou & Fran Karwacki

149-189 $US BB
5 rooms, 5 pb
Visa, MC, AmEx, •
C-yes/S-no/P-no/H-no

Full Gourmet Breakfast
Please inform us of any food allergies
or preferences, full Snack Center in
Main Dining Room
Central A/C, TV/VCR, cable, ceiling
fans, down comforters & pillows,
library, sitting room, porch

Come experience the tranquil charm of this historic Easton home offering the best of the old and new. We are within walking distance of most of Easton's historical sites.

✉ jsmcdanielhouse@netscape.net 🌐 www.bnblist.com/md/mcdaniel/

ELKTON

Elk Forge B&B
807 Elk Mills Rd 21921
877-ELK-FORGE 410-392-9007
Harry & LeAnn Lendeman

89-269 $US BB
12 rooms, 12 pb
Most CC, Cash, Checks,
Rated, •
C-yes/S-ltd/P-yes/H-yes

Full breakfast
Beer, wine, champagne & various
beverages for sale
Chipping & putting green, reading &
movie library, conference & game
room, outdoor hot tub

Nestled on five acres of beautiful woods and gardens along the Big Elk Creek. The area is rich in history and natural beauty and is just 3 miles from I-95, and minutes from Newark and Wilmington, Delaware. Philadelphia and Baltimore are only an hour away.

✉ reservations@elkforge.com 🌐 www.elkforge.com

GRANTSVILLE

The Stonebow Inn
146 Casselman Rd 21536
800-272-4090 301-895-4250
Julyen Norman & Cathy
Paine

170-210 $US BB
9 rooms, 9 pb
Most CC, Cash,
Rated, •
C-ltd/S-no/P-ltd/H-ltd

Full gourmet breakfast
Complimentary coffee, tea, bottled
water
Steam/dry sauna, porches, rocking
chairs, gas fireplace

Nestled on the banks of the Casselman River in the mountains of western Maryland. Hiking, biking, fishing, skiing, scenic railway, Fallingwater, Deep Creek Lake, all in easy reach.

✉ info@stonebowinn.com 🌐 www.stonebowinn.com

HAVRE DE GRACE

Spencer Silver Mansion
200 S Union Ave 21078
800-780-1485 410-939-1485
Carol Nemeth

85-160 $US BB
5 rooms, 3 pb
Most CC, Cash, Checks,
Rated, •
C-yes/S-no/P-yes/H-yes

Full breakfast
Fresh fruit & candy daily in room,
coffee & tea service with freshly
baked goods
Fireplace, Jacuzzi, massage therapy,
WiFi, parlors

Built in 1896, the Spencer-Silver Mansion offers the perfect lodging while visiting historic Havre de Grace and the upper Chesapeake Bay region.

✉ spencersilver@erols.com 🌐 www.spencersilvermansion.com

MCHENRY

Lake Pointe Inn
174 Lake Pointe Dr 21541
800-523-5253 301-387-0111
Caroline McNiece

232-292 $US BB
10 rooms, 10 pb
Visa, MC, Disc, •
C-ltd/S-no/P-no/H-no

Full breakfast
Evening hors d'oeuvres & wine,
beverage bar, cookies, fresh fruit,
popcorn available all day.
Bicycles, kayaks, canoes, community
tennis court, fire pit, massage room,
steam shower

*The Lake Pointe Inn, the oldest house on Deep Creek Lake in Western Maryland, is perched just 13'
from water's edge & is located across from the Wisp Ski & Golf Resort.*

✉ relax@deepcreekinns.com 🌐 www.deepcreekinns.com

OCEAN CITY

Inn on the Ocean
Boardwalk and 10th
Street 21842
888-226-6223 410-289-8894
The Barretts (Charles)

135-395 $US BB
6 rooms, 6 pb
Most CC, *Rated*
C-ltd/S-no/P-no/H-no

Seated gourmet breakfast
Afternoon refreshments
Salon with fireplace, veranda,
bicycles, Jacuzzis, children over 16,
beach chairs & towels included

*A deluxe, romantic, magnificently restored oceanfront B&B/Inn. Oceanfront wraparound verandah.
Fireplace in winter. Jacuzzis. Romantic getaways, weddings, special occasions, corporate meetings.*

✉ innonoc@aol.com 🌐 www.innontheocean.com

OXFORD

**Sandaway – Waterfront
Lodging**
103 West Strand Rd 21654
888-726-3292 888-SANDAWAY
Ben Gibson

169-299 $US BB
18 rooms, 18 pb
Visa, MC, AmEx,
Rated, •
C-ltd/S-no/P-no/H-ltd

Lite Fare Breakfast
24 hour coffee, tea, hot chocolate, and
snacks located in the Sandaway Sitting
Room
Non-smoking inn, private beach,
waterfront lawn, massage, kayak
rentals

*Chesapeake Bay Romantic B&B featuring waterfront rooms with porches, million dollar views, a
private beach, and great sunsets. Just 7 miles to St. Michaels when you take the car ferry!*

✉ info@sandaway.com 🌐 www.sandaway.com

POCOMOKE CITY

**Friendship Farm Bed &
Breakfast**
32739 Peach Orchard
Rd 21851
800-996-3134 410-957-1094
Russ & Denise Shaner

135-180 $US BB
4 rooms, 4 pb
Visa, MC, Disc
C-yes/S-ltd/P-no/H-no

Full breakfast
24 hr. complementary beverages,
snack basket in each room, dinner
upon arrangement, picnic lunches
Jacuzzi tub, satellite TV, WiFi, patio
with grill, picnic area, water dock

Free Night w/Certificate: Not valid holiday weekends.

*Welcome to Friendship Farm Bed and Breakfast. The inn sits on twelve acres on the banks of the
beautiful Pocomoke River in Somerset County – "nature's masterpiece".*

✉ Info@FriendshipFarmBnB.com 🌐 www.friendshipfarmbnb.com

PRINCESS ANNE

Somerset House B&B
30556 Washington St 21853
410-651-4451
Deborah & Jay Parker

160 $US BB
6 rooms, 6 pb
Most CC, Cash, •
C-yes/S-ltd/P-ltd/H-no

Full breakfast
Afternoon refreshments & gourmet
dinner packages available
Bocce or croquet on the bowling lawn,
gardens, fireplaces, period antiques,
brilliant chandeliers

*Located in the Princess Anne Historic District on the Eastern Shore of Maryland. You will enjoy the
elegant and historic home, the extensive gardens, and the luxury of your own large well-appointed
room, with private bath.*

✉ info@somersethousemd.com 🌐 www.somersethousemd.com

ROCK HALL

Inn at Huntingfield Creek
4928 Eastern Neck Rd 21661
410-639-7779
Joanne Rich

159-279 $US BB
8 rooms, 8 pb
Most CC, Cash
C-yes/S-ltd/P-ltd/H-ltd

Full breakfast
Tea table, cookies and soda available at all times, complimentary wine and beer.
Swimming pool, waterfront dock, conference room, library, great room, WiFi, gardens, event barn.

Elegant & historic 70 acre farm-estate. Beautiful telescoping farmhouse architecture. Ideal for country weddings or retreats. Well-appointed, comfortable rooms with fine linens and excellent beds designed to pamper. 1100' waterfront & dock. ✉ huntingfieldcreek@verizon.net ❍ www.huntingfield.com

Old Gratitude House B&B
5944 Lawton Ave 21661
866-846-0724 410-639-7448
Sandy & Hank Mayer

159-239 $US BB
5 rooms, 5 pb
Most CC
C-ltd/S-no/P-no/H-no

Three-course gourmet breakfast
Beverages & snacks
Private decks, kayaks, bikes, A/C, WiFi, Adirondack chairs

A relaxing, comfortable and elegant B&B that takes full advantage of the soothing water's edge, while also offering access to a variety of activities that will keep you pleasantly busy. Escape to the casual elegance of the Old Gratitude House.
✉ oldgratitudehouse@verizon.net ❍ www.oldgratitudehouse.com

The Inn at Osprey Point
20786 Rock Hall Ave 21661
410-639-2194
Terry Nelson

80-280 $US BB
15 rooms, 13 pb
Most CC, Cash, Checks
C-yes/S-no/P-no/H-no
Spanish, Portuguese

Full breakfast
Romantic fine dining Restaurant open Wed.- Sun. starting at 5 p.m.
Water views, weddings & events, marina, pool, kayaks, gourmet restaurant, bar, volleyball, bicycles

Free Night w/Certificate: Valid Nov-March 31. Cannot be combined with other offers. Room Upgrade.

A luxurious northern Chesapeake Bay adventure destination located on 30 lush acres of waterfront solitude in the village of Rock Hall. On water's edge & delightfully secluded, we offer a wonderful full service destination. ✉ innkeeper@ospreypoint.com ❍ www.ospreypoint.com

SHARPSBURG

Antietam Overlook Farm
800-878-4241 301-432-4200
Mark Svrcek & Philip Graham-Bell

175-240 $US BB
5 rooms, 5 pb
Most CC, Cash,
Rated, •
S-no/P-no/H-ltd

Full breakfast
Complimentary wine, sodas, coffee, tea & snacks
After dinner drinks, sitting room, library, large front porch

Award-winning & extraordinary. Secluded 95-acre mountain top 19th century Country Manor Inn with a four state view at Antietam National Battlefield. Located near Harpers Ferry & Shepardstown.
✉ Reservations@antietamoverlook.com ❍ www.antietamoverlook.com

The Inn at Antietam
220 E Main St 21782
877-835-6011 301-432-6601
Charles Van Metre & Robert LeBlanc

120-185 $US BB
5 rooms, 5 pb
Visa, MC, AmEx,
Rated, •
C-ltd/S-ltd/P-no/H-no
Closed January

Full Breakfast
Sitting room, piano, bicycles, library.

Lovely 1908 Victorian, fully restored and furnished in antiques, on Antietam Battlefield in Civil War historic area. Featuring five suites.
✉ innatantietam@juno.com ❍ www.innatantietam.com

SNOW HILL

River House Inn
201 E Market St 21863
410-632-2722
Larry & Susanne Knudsen

190-250 $US BB
6 rooms, 6 pb
Most CC, *Rated*, •
C-yes/S-no/P-ltd/H-yes

Full breakfast
Lunch & dinner available, complimentary snacks, wine, tea
Porches, A/C, fishing, boating, country club golf, bikes

Come relax at our elegant 1860s riverfront country home in historic Snow Hill. Canoe or bike inn-to-inn. Enjoy Maryland's eastern shore, beaches, bayou, AARP. 6 rooms and suites.
✉ innkeeper@riverhouseinn.com ❍ www.riverhouseinn.com

SOLOMONS

Solomons Victorian Inn
125 Charles St 20688
410-326-4811
Helen & Richard Bauer

110-240 $US BB
7 rooms, 7 pb
Most CC, Cash, Checks,
Rated
C-ltd/S-no/P-no/H-ltd

Full breakfast
Hot & cold drinks, homemade cookies
3 rooms with whirlpool tubs, spa
services, library

Let the Chesapeake romance you at this charming Queen Anne Victorian. Convenient to Washington, Baltimore and Richmond. The Inn has eight queen and king sized rooms, most with views, all with private bath. Larger rooms have whirlpool tubs and fireplaces.

✉ info@solomonsvictorianinn.com ◐ www.solomonsvictorianinn.com

ST. MICHAELS

Aida's Victoriana Inn
205 Cherry St 21663
443-783-2597 410-745-3368
Aida Khalil

99-339 $US BB
7 rooms, 7 pb
Visa, MC, •
C-ltd/S-ltd/P-yes/H-no
Arabic, Spanish,
German

Full breakfast
Friday welcome hour with drinks &
hors d'oeuvres, complimentary non-
alcoholic beverages & snacks
Garden, views, fireplaces, Direct TV &
DVD in sun room and in most of the
bedrooms

Aida's Victoriana Inn is located on the historic St. Michaels harbor. Situated next to the Chesapeake Bay Maritime Museum, we are in walking distance to all attractions. The inn is just 2 blocks from the main street, yet removed from the bustle of town.

✉ info@victorianainn.net ◐ www.victorianainn.net

Five Gables Inn & Spa
209 N Talbot St 21663
877-466-0100 410-745-0100
Heather Sally, Manager

150-425 $US BB
20 rooms, 20 pb
Visa, MC, AmEx
S-no/P-yes/H-ltd

Continental plus breakfast
Afternoon refreshments
Whirlpools, fireplaces, heated indoor
pool, steam room/sauna, Aveda
amenities, Meeting Center, bikes

Rooms feature gas fireplaces, porches & whirlpools with bathrobes & Aveda amenities. Enjoy the heated indoor pool, steam room & sauna Massage, facials and body treatments in the spa by appointment.

✉ info@fivegables.com ◐ www.fivegables.com

George Brooks House B&B
24500 Rolles Range Rd 21663
410-745-8381
Will Workman & Julia
Kuklova

120-240 $US BB
6 rooms, 6 pb
Visa, MC, Disc,
Rated, •
C-ltd/S-no/P-ltd/H-no
Russian

Full breakfast
Guest refrigerator stocked with sodas
& bottled water
Massage by appointment, outdoor hot
tub, 7-speed bikes, swimming pool,
DVD movie library

Restored Gothic Revival Victorian home built in 1908 was designated an Historic Site by Talbot County in 2001. This important county landmark was among two homes selected in 2003 by the State of Maryland for its prestigious "Preservation Award".

✉ georgebrookshouse@atlanticbb.net ◐ www.georgebrookshouse.com

---

Harris Cove Cottages
8080 Bozman Neavitt
Rd 21663
410-745-9701
Alex & Jaimie Locke

145-210 $US EP
8 rooms, 8 pb
Rated
C-yes/S-no/P-no/H-ltd
some American Sign
Language

Catch your own crabs, and we have
steam stations. Have your own full
kitchen
Waterfront cottages, views, A/C, rental
boats, cable, WiFi, kayak, gazebos,
family friendly, bbq

Harris Cove Cottages has eight cottages. Six cottages are individual and form an echelon of sailors saluting our picturesque private driveway. The other two sit majestically as a centerpiece on two acres of bulkheaded waterfront property. ✉ bednboatgetaway@aol.com ◐ www.bednboat.com/index.php

---

Parsonage Inn
210 N Talbot (Rt 33) 21663
410-745-8383
Will Workman

110-215 $US BB
8 rooms, 8 pb
Visa, MC, Disc,
Rated, •
C-ltd/S-no/P-ltd/H-yes

Full gourmet breakfast
Afternoon tea at 4 pm
Parlor with books & menus, special
order wine & cheese or flower
arrangements

Welcome to the Parsonage Inn Bed and Breakfast, a unique brick Victorian in this National Historic District. Within walking distance of the maritime museum, shops and restaurants. Top rated and recommended.

✉ parsinn@atlanticbb.net ◐ www.parsonage-inn.com

ST. MICHAELS

Wades Point Inn on the Bay
10090 Wades Point Rd 21663
888-923-3466 410-745-2500
The Feiler Family

157-269 $US BB
26 rooms, 26 pb
Visa, MC, Disc, *Rated*
C-yes/S-no/P-no/H-yes
March 15-Dec 15

Full breakfast
Water side balconies, air conditioning, some kitchenettes, weddings, meetings

Grand Georgian style home on edge of Chesapeake Bay. Two thousand feet of gently curving shoreline wrap the Inn's private grounds, giving spectacular views to its rooms. Perfect location for weddings and special events.

✉ wadesinn@wadespoint.com 🌐 www.wadespoint.com

SYKESVILLE

Inn at Norwood
7514 Norwood Ave 21784
410-549-7868
Kelly Crum

135-225 $US BB
6 rooms, 6 pb
Visa, MC, AmEx,
Rated
C-ltd/S-no/P-ltd/H-no

Full breakfast
Tea, coffee, homemade cookies, snacks, soft drinks, water
Sitting room, game room, library, movies, Jacuzzi tubs, fireplaces

The Inn at Norwood is a romantic bed & breakfast. We have six spectacular guestrooms, all newly renovated and decorated to reflect Maryland's colorful seasons. It is the perfect escape.

✉ innatnorwood@comcast.net 🌐 www.innatnorwood.com

TANEYTOWN

Antrim 1844 Inc
30 Trevanion Rd 21787
800-678-8946 410-756-6812
Dorothy & Richard Mollett

160-400 $US BB
40 rooms, 40 pb
Most CC, *Rated*
C-ltd/S-ltd/P-no/H-yes

Full breakfast
Afternoon tea, six course dinner, full service bar
Tennis, pool, fireplaces, cable TV, croquet, wireless Internet, bar, gardens

Antrim 1844's luxurious rooms & suites, nationally acclaimed fine dining restaurant & award-winning wine list have earned the Inn a place in connoisseurs' hearts.

✉ info@antrim1844.com 🌐 www.antrim1844.com

TILGHMAN ISLAND

Black Walnut Point Inn
4417 Black Walnut Point Rd 21671
410-886-2452
Bob & Tracy

120-250 $US BB
7 rooms, 7 pb
Visa, MC, Disc, *Rated*
C-ltd/S-ltd/P-no/H-yes

Full breakfast
Tea, snacks, birthday & anniversary cakes, crackers & cheese, grill items, prepared meals.
Bird sanctuary, pool, hot tub, fishing dock, bikes, kayaks, weddings, seminars, retreats.

Free Night w/Certificate: Valid Sept.-May, and Sunday-Thursday. Room Upgrade.

Located at the tip of Tilghman Island on 58 gated acres of a bird sanctuary, Black Walnut Point Inn is a six-acre island of gardens and lawn in the middle of the Chesapeake Bay.

✉ stay@blackwalnutpointinn.com 🌐 www.blackwalnutpointinn.com

Chesapeake Wood Duck Inn
21490 Dogwood Harbor Rd. 21671
800-956-2070 410-886-2070
Kimberly & Jeffrey Bushey

139-249 $US BB
7 rooms, 7 pb
Visa, MC, AmEx,
Rated, •
C-ltd/S-no/P-no/H-no

Full, 3 course, gourmet breakfast
Four-course, prix fix dinner Saturday evenings
Sitting rooms, fireplace, sunroom, 3 porches, kayaking, restaurants & wireless high speed Internet

Enjoy Chesapeake Bay lodging on Tilghman Island. This romantic B&B getaway brims with historic charm and gracious hospitality. The Inn offers a pristine waterfront setting, gourmet cuisine, and a choice of six guestrooms and one cottage suite.

✉ inn@woodduckinn.com 🌐 www.woodduckinn.com

WHITEHAVEN ─────────────────────────────

Whitehaven Hotel	110-250 $US BB	Full breakfast
2685 Whitehaven Rd 21856	7 rooms, 7 pb	2 rooms with fireplaces, kayaks, gift
877-809-8296 410-873-2000	Visa, MC	shop, porches, piano room
Cindy Curran	C-yes/S-no/P-ltd/H-yes	

The Whitehaven Hotel is nestled on the shore of the Wicomico River, about 25 minutes outside Salis-bury. One of the last of its kind, saved from the wrecking ball through cooperative efforts in 1995. Screened porch, working fireplaces.

✉ dotinwhitehaven@aol.com 🌐 www.whitehavenhotel.com

Massachusetts

AMHERST

Allen House Victorian Inn
599 Main St 01002
413-253-5000
Alan Zieminski & Ann King

75-175 $US BB
7 rooms, 7 pb
Visa, MC, *Rated*
C-ltd/S-ltd/P-no/H-no

Full breakfast
Afternoon tea, evening refreshments, specialty seasonal drinks, artisan gourmet chocolates
Sitting room, library, veranda, gardens, A/C, WiFi, concierge service, luxury towels & linens

Authentic 1886 stick-style Victorian on 3 acres opposite the Emily Dickinson Homestead. 7 spacious rooms, private baths, in room computer & writing desks, ceiling fans and central air conditioning. AAA 3-Diamonds rating. Free WiFi and long distance calling

 allenhouse@webtv.net   www.allenhouse.com/gallery/gallery1.html

BARNSTABLE

Ashley Manor
3660 Main St 02630
888-535-2246 508-362-8044
Vince Toreno & Patricia Martin

145-245 $US BB
6 rooms, 6 pb
Most CC, Cash, *Rated*
C-ltd/S-no/P-no/H-no

Full gourmet breakfast
Complimentary brandy, port and hazelnut sherry
Sitting room, A/C, tennis, garden, imported bedside chocolates, whirlpool tubs, gazebo

1699 mansion in the historic district. 6 guestrooms & suites with fireplaces, full in room baths and 2-person Jacuzzis tubs. Walking distance to beach, village & harbor.

stay@ashleymanor.net www.ashleymanor.net

Beechwood Inn
2839 Main St (Rt 6A) 02630
800-609-6618 508-362-6618
Ken & Debbie Traugot

135-209 $US BB
6 rooms, 6 pb
Most CC, Cash,
Rated, •
C-ltd/S-no/P-no/H-no

Full gourmet breakfast
Afternoon snacks & beverages
Parlor, veranda, garden, all rooms have A/C, WiFi, TV/VCR

Award winning romantic Victorian Inn along the historic "Old King's Highway." Six spacious guestrooms furnished with elegant antiques, some with fireplaces or views of Cape Cod Bay. Top rated by AAA and Mobil travel guides.

info@beechwoodinn.com www.beechwoodinn.com

Lamb and Lion Inn
2504 Main St (Route 6A) 02630
800-909-6923 508-362-6823
Alice Pitcher & Tom Dott

165-325 $US BB
11 rooms, 11 pb
Most CC, Cash, Checks,
Rated, •
C-ltd/S-ltd/P-yes/H-no

Continental Breakfast
Enjoy a long, 2,000 calorie breakfast? We are not for you! Ours is quick, easy & gets you moving!
Pool, outdoor hot tub, 12 fireplaces, WiFi, free driving tours, suites with kitchens, total privacy

Located on 4 acres in the historic district. 10 suites, 12 fireplaces, full-sized pool and year-round hot tub spa. Guest privacy is paramount! "Best Mid-Cape B&B/Inn" Cape Cod Life Magazine, 2007–2008. "Best Cape Cod B&B" A-List, 2009.   info@lambandlion.com www.lambandlion.com

BOSTON

Abigayle's Bed and Breakfast
Bay State Rd at Deerfield 02457
888-486-6018 781-449-5302
Marie Kemmler

90-150 $US BB
5 rooms, 5 pb
Visa, MC, Disc, •
C-yes/S-no/P-no/H-no
Chinese

Continental plus breakfast
Direct TV, private phones, WiFi, desks, A/C

Elegant 1896 Victorian Brownstone set on a quiet, tree-lined street in Boston. Near public transportation, Boston University, Fenway Park, restaurants and shops. Modern amenities combined with old world charm.

bnb@bnbboston.com www.bnbboston.com/locations/boston/kenmore-

BOSTON

Adams B&B
14 Edgerly Rd 02115
800-230-0105 617-536-4181
Joe Haley

79-169 $US BB
14 rooms, 10 pb
Visa, MC, AmEx
C-yes/S-no/P-no/H-no

Continental breakfast
TV, living room, deck, fireplace, free
high-speed WiFi Internet, parking
available

Like many of the finer hotels in Boston, we are centrally located in the Back Bay. We are an easy five minute walk to the Prudential/Hynes Convention Centers and the Back Bay/Fenway areas – yet unlike the finer Boston hotels, our rates are greatly less.

info@adamsboston.com   www.adamsboston.com

Aisling B & B
21 E Concord St 02118
617-206-8049
Dympna Moore

175-200 $US BB
3 rooms, 3 pb
Visa, MC
C-yes/S-no/P-no/H-no

Full breakfast

A 19th century Victorian row-house with its original marble fittings, fireplaces and moldings. Located in the South End, each room has its own private bathroom and TV as well as wireless Internet access.

aislingbostonbb@yahoo.com   www.aisling-bostonbb.com

Beacon Hill B&B
27 Brimmer St 02108
617-523-7376
Susan Butterworth

200-250 $US BB
2 rooms, 2 pb
Rated, •
C-yes/S-no/P-no/H-no
French

Home-Cooked
Vegetarian breakfast. Restaurants and
convenience stores one block away
Garage nearby, elevator for luggage,
A/C, flexible arrival time but must be
confirmed. Leave luggage

Superb location in most exclusive, historically preserved downtown neighborhood. Private home in elegant 1869 Victorian townhouse overlooking river. Spacious rooms, private baths, homecooked breakfast. Price varies seasonally. Nearby garage. 3 DAY MIN.

bhillbb@gmail.com   www.beaconhillbandb.com

Beacon Hill Hotel & Bistro
25 Charles St 02114
617-723-7575
Peter Rait

199-405 $US BB
13 rooms, 13 pb
Most CC
C-ltd/S-no/P-no/H-yes

Full breakfast
Breakfast included, lunch & dinner all
available in the Bistro
Plantation shutters, pedestal sinks,
TFT DirecTV (movie channels), WiFi

The privileged location of The Beacon Hill Hotel makes it the perfect choice for travelers, either business or leisure, who would like to make the gas-lit streets and brick sidewalks of Beacon Hill their own, without giving up the comforts they expect.

stay@beaconhillhotel.com   www.beaconhillhotel.com

Clarendon Square Bed & Breakfast
198 W Brookline St 02118
617-536-2229
Stephen Gross

135-455 $US BB
3 rooms, 3 pb
Most CC, Cash, Checks,
Rated
C-ltd/S-no/P-no/H-no
French

Expanded Continental Breakfast
Roof deck hot tub/Jacuzzi, grand
piano, parlor, library, fireplaces, DVD,
WiFi, business services

Clarendon Square is a Boston bed and breakfast with the amenities of a Boston boutique hotel. The Clarendon Square bed and breakfast offers modern furnishings focused on style and sophistication and personalized customer service.

stay@clarendonsquare.com   www.clarendonsquare.com

East Boston B&B
14 Crestway Rd. 02128
617-818-2800
Don Mills

129-450 $US BB
2 rooms, 2 pb
Visa, MC, AmEx
C-yes/S-no/P-yes/H-ltd
French, German, Italian

Old Fashion Breakfast
Dinner made to order, fruit & veggies,
Mills coffee & tea's.
Pick Up/Drop Off to & from Logan
Airport upon request, laundry service,
Justice of Peace on call.

Quiet area for a good night's old fashion sleep and home cooked breakfast made to order, 5 minutes from beach, downtown Boston. One minute from Logan Airport we provide pick up to and from Logan Airport as an extra feature for our guests.

eastbostonbandb@aol.com

BOSTON

La Cappella Suites
290 North St 02113
888-523-9020 617-523-9020
Tricia Muse

95-215 $US BB
3 rooms, 3 pb
Visa, MC, AmEx
C-yes/S-no/P-no/H-no

Continental breakfast
Room rates include a modest,
complimentary, self-serve Continental
breakfast in suite
Cable TV & VCR, complimentary
local phone service, wireless Internet
access, balcony, comp. cribs

Our Inn is located in historic Little Italy, steps from downtown shopping and historic sites, Quincy Market, TD Banknorth Garden, the Aquarium and restaurants. We offer value and convenience in an elegant setting. Great for tourists and business travelers

✉ TriciaMuse@aol.com ○ www.LaCappellaSuites.com

Oasis Guest House
22 Edgerly Rd 02115
800-230-0105 617-267-2262
Joe Haley

99-169 $US BB
30 rooms, 20 pb
Visa, MC, AmEx,
Rated, •
C-ltd/S-ltd/P-no/H-no

Continental breakfast
Complimentary coffee, juice, fruit, and
pastries available every morning
Concierge, sitting room, fax
capabilities, hairdryers, iron/board,
TV, free Internet, maid service

Two townhouses on a quiet residential street in the heart of Boston. Includes amenities such as; telephone, TV, central air, outdoor decks, parking and free wireless Internet.

✉ info@oasisgh.com ○ www.oasisgh.com

Taylor House
50 Burroughs St 02130
888-228-2956 617-983-9334
Dave Elliott & Daryl Bichel

139-349 $US BB
3 rooms, 3 pb
Visa, MC, Disc, *Rated*
C-ltd/S-no/P-ltd/H-no

Continental plus breakfast
Snacks, sodas, coffee station
TV/VCR/DVD in room, movie library,
common room, wireless Internet,
phones

Italianate Victorian home with spacious rooms, high ceilings, private baths, near public transportation, restaurants & shopping. We also offer function space for weddings, receptions and business retreats. ✉ Dave@taylorhouse.com ○ www.taylorhouse.com

---

The Charles Street Inn
94 Charles St 02114
877-772-8900 617-314-8900
Sally Deane & Louise
Venden

250-550 $US BB
9 rooms, 9 pb
Most CC, Cash,
Rated, •
C-yes/S-no/P-yes/H-yes
German; Japanese

Full breakfast
Crackers, juice, bottled water, Roche
chocolates, fresh fruit, nut/fruit and
oatmeal health bars
CD/DVD/VCR library, in-room
whirlpool tub, fireplace, fridge, cable
TV, DSL & wireless Internet

Awards galore, loyal repeat guests, friendly personal attention. Unique amenities like marble fireplaces, antique furniture, private baths with Whirlpool tubs, and breakfast in bed. Watch our video and do 360 degree tour of all nine rooms on our web site.

✉ info@charlesstreetinn.com ○ www.CharlesStreetInn.com

The College Club
44 Commonwealth
Ave 02116
617-536-9510
Edith Toth, Gen. Mgr.

99-279 $US BB
11 rooms, 6 pb
Visa, MC, *Rated*
C-yes/S-no/P-no/H-ltd
Hungarian, Spanish,
French

Continental breakfast
Coffee & tea available 24 hours,
afternoon cookies available
Accommodations for business and
leisure travelers, two adjoining rooms
for meetings & events

Our Victorian townhouse offers old-world charm & modern convenience. Recently renovated, and listed on the National Register of Historic Places. The ideal launching point for your adventures in Boston!

✉ office@thecollegeclubofboston.com ○ www.thecollegeclubofboston.com

---

The Gryphon House
9 Bay State RD 02215
877-375-9003 617-375-9003
Theresa

129-275 $US BB
8 rooms, 8 pb
Most CC, Cash
C-ltd/S-no/P-no/H-no

Continental breakfast
Queen-size beds, gas log fireplaces,
A/C, 27" Sony TV, VCR/DVD, CD/tape
player, a wet bar, free WiFi

The Gryphon House is adjacent to Boston University, between Back Bay and Kenmore Square, near two major art museums, and home of the Red Sox! Enjoy luxury accommodations while exploring the rich history and culture of the Boston area.

✉ innkeeper@gryphonhouseboston.com ○ www.innboston.com

BOSTON

The Victorian House
707 Bennington St 02128
617-818-2800
Don & Joyce Mills

99-225 $US BB
8 rooms, 4 pb
Visa, MC, AmEx
C-yes/S-no/P-yes/H-ltd
French, German

Old Fashion Home Made Meals
Murder Mystery Guest weekends
include Murder Mystery and Dinner
Pick up to and from Logan Airport
upon request, laundry service, Justice
Of The Peace available

The Victorian House is located just minutes away from everything in Boston while providing a haven of peace away from the bustle. Our pampering is sure to make you feel like family. We always go the extra mile to make your stay simply perfect.

✉ eastbostonbandb@aol.com

BREWSTER

Bramble Inn & Restaurant
2019 Main St 02631
508-896-7644
Ruth & Cliff Manchester

158-178 $US BB
5 rooms, 5 pb
Most CC, *Rated*, •
C-ltd/S-no/P-no/H-no
May to December

Full breakfast
Snacks in room, cranberry juice &
granola bars
Air conditioning, outside garden
seating, cable TV, iron, makeup
mirrors, beach towels, hairdryers

The Romantic Bramble Inn is nestled in the heart of Historic Brewster village, just a short stroll to Cape Cod Bay and many attractions. Private courtyard garden, gallery and gourmet dining are part of its charm.

✉ brambleinn@comcast.net 🌐 www.brambleinn.com

Candleberry Inn
1882 Main St 02631
800-573-4769 508-896-3300
Stuart & Charlotte Fyfe

130-200 $US BB
7 rooms, 7 pb
Visa, MC, Disc, *Rated*
C-ltd/S-no/P-no/H-no

Full breakfast
Afternoon tea & refreshments with
homebaked delicacies
Antique furnishings, four poster beds,
fireplaces, suite, patio, gardens

Lovely 200 year-old inn located in the heart of historic Brewster. Antiques, four poster beds, fireplaces, warmth & charm, with all modern amenities. Walk to beach or enjoy almost 2 acres of gardens.

✉ info@candleberryinn.com 🌐 www.candleberryinn.com

Isaiah Clark House
1187 Main St 02631
800-822-4001 508-896-2223
Philomena & Steve

179-229 $US BB
7 rooms, 7 pb
Visa, MC, AmEx,
Rated
C-ltd/S-no/P-no/H-no
April to November

Full breakfast
Special diets, food allergies
Central Air Conditioning, 3 rooms with
fireplaces, cable TV, high speed WiFi.
Queen and King beds.

Experience the history and romance of old Cape Cod in Brewster, MA. A marvelous example of Colonial architecture circa 1785, the Isaiah Clark House is centrally located for easy access to area attractions. One of the few Historic Inns with Central A/C!

✉ stay@isaiahclark.com 🌐 www.isaiahclark.com

Michael's Cottages and B&B
618 Main St 02631
800-399-2967 508-896-4025
Michael Divito

125-250 $US BB
8 rooms, 8 pb
Most CC
C-yes/S-ltd/P-no/H-no

Continental breakfast in B&B rooms
Kitchens, picnic tables, grills, cable
TV, phones, linen service, fireplaces,
sitting room

One house, four cottages, and two B&B rooms located midway on Cape Cod in West Brewster. A quiet, private atmosphere among the pines. Experience the look and charm of old Cape Cod with today's amenities.

✉ info@michaelsinbrewster.com 🌐 www.michaelsinbrewster.com

Old Manse Inn
1861 Main St 02631
866-896-3149 508-896-3149
Karen & Richard Keevers

140-275 $US BB
12 rooms, 12 pb
Visa, MC, AmEx,
Rated
C-ltd/S-no/P-no/H-ltd

Full breakfast
Cookies with afternoon tea /coffee
Bicycles with rail trail just 1 mile.
Beach chairs & umbrellas provide as
Cape Cod Bay only ½ mile

Built in 1801, The Old Manse Inn has been home to generations of legendary seafarers. We offer twelve deluxe luxury rooms, individually decorated and preserved rooms each with private bath.

✉ innkeeper@oldmanseinn.com 🌐 www.oldmanseinn.com

Anthony's Town House, Brookline, MA

BROOKLINE—

Old Sea Pines Inn
2553 Main St 02631
866-444-4552 508-896-6114
Stephen & Michele Rowan

85-185 $US BB
24 rooms, 19 pb
Most CC, *Rated*, •
C-yes/S-no/P-no/H-yes
Italian, German
April-Dec. 22

Full breakfast
Complimentary beverage on arrival, restaurant
Parlor with fireplace, deck, Sunday dinner theatre (summers only)

Early 1900s restored boarding school for young ladies located on Brewer Estate. One of the finest Inns on the New England seacoast, it comes complete with a spacious living room, completely restored formal dining room, and outdoor dining deck.

 info@oldseapinesinn.com ◐ www.oldseapinesinn.com

BROOKLINE—

Anthony's Town House
1085 Beacon St 02446
617-566-3972
Barbara & Viola Anthony

75-118 $US EP
14 rooms
Visa, MC, *Rated*, •
C-yes/S-no/P-no/H-no

Restaurant, stores nearby
Near major league sports, historical sites, sitting room, cable TV, A/C, WiFi

Turn-of-the-century restored Brownstone townhouse with spacious rooms in a Victorian atmosphere; family-operated for over 60 years. Subway at our doorstep, 10 minutes to downtown Boston. Listed on the National Register of Historic Places.

 info@anthonystownhouse.com ◐ www.anthonystownhouse.com

Beacon Inn
1087 & 1750 Beacon St 02446
888-575-0088 617-566-0088

79-149 $US BB
25 rooms, 25 pb
Most CC, Cash, *Rated*
C-yes/S-no/P-no/H-no

Continental breakfast
All rooms include Internet, A/C, telephone, cable TV

The Beacon Inn is two restored 19th century brownstones, offering pleasant accommodations at affordable rates. A convenient location and a high level of service. The T (Boston's subway system) runs right outside our front door!

 info@beaconinn.com ◐ www.beaconinn.com

BROOKLINE

Coolidge Corner Guest House
17 Littell Rd 02146
617-734-4041
Shawn & Jessica LaCount

79-189 $US BB
9 rooms, 4 pb
Most CC, Cash, Checks
C-yes/S-ltd/P-no/H-no

Continental breakfast
Tea, coffee, and snacks are available throughout the day.
Cable TV, WiFi Internet, laundry, on-site parking, gardens, private bath, central A/C

Welcome to the Coolidge Corner Guest House: Bed and Bagel! Our beautiful Victorian home, located just 10 minutes from downtown Boston, is a fresh and affordable alternative to typical inns, hotels and budget motels.

bedandbagel@gmail.com   www.bedandbagel.com

The Beech Tree Inn
83 Longwood Ave 02446
800-544-9660 617-277-1620

119-179 $US BB
10 rooms, 8 pb
Visa, MC, AmEx
C-yes/S-no/P-yes/H-no
Japanese

Continental plus breakfast
Coffee, hot chocolate, tea & home baked cookies in the afternoon
TV/VCR, A/C, hairdryers, video library, dial-up & wireless Internet

The Beech Tree Inn B&B, of Brookline, MA, once a Victorian-style private home, offers warmth and gracious hospitality at affordable prices. Its charming and casual bed and breakfast setting invites the busiest city slicker to come in and relax.

info@thebeechtreeinn.com   www.thebeechtreeinn.com

The Bertram Inn
92 Sewall Ave 02446
800-295-3822 617-566-2234
Kevin & Stephen

99-329 $US BB
14 rooms, 14 pb
Most CC, *Rated*
C-ltd/S-no/P-yes/H-no
Spanish, Italian

Full breakfast
Complimentary, cakes, cookies, cheese and crackers, snacks, coffee & teas offered 24/7
Iron & board, WiFi Internet, fax, TV with digital cable, hairdryers in all rooms, A/C, fireplaces

The Bertram Inn boasts classic Tudor detailing in the historic setting of Brookline, MA, within walking distance of shops, museums, restaurants, colleges, hospitals and public recreation. Enjoy all Boston has to offer, just minutes away.

innkeeper@bertraminn.com   www.bertraminn.com

The Samuel Sewall Inn
143 St Paul St 02446
888-713-2566 617-713-0123
Astrid, Kristen, Stephen

99-349 $US BB
14 rooms, 14 pb
Most CC, *Rated*, •
C-yes/S-no/P-no/H-yes
French, Spanish, Italian, Portuguese

Full Breakfast Buffet
Complimentary cakes, cookies, cheese & crackers, snacks, coffee & tea offered 24/7
Living room, patio, porch, fax available, wireless Internet, turndown service, concierge, cable TV

Built in 1886 as a private residence, The Samuel Sewall Inn boasts beautiful Victorian accommodations in a restored Queen-Anne home, with luxurious amenities, friendly service, and modern conveniences. Just one block away from public transportation.

innkeeper@samuelsewallinn.com   www.samuelsewallinn.com

CAMBRIDGE

A B&B in Cambridge
1657 Cambridge St 02138
800-795-7122 617-868-7082
Doane Perry

95-200 $US BB
3 rooms
Visa, MC, AmEx,
Rated, •
C-ltd/S-no/P-no/H-no
French, German, Greek, Swahili

Crepes, waffles or pancakes, fruit
Afternoon tea & snacks
Small library with antique rocker, nearby pool, cable TV, Wifi, concierge, voicemail

An 1897 Colonial Revival home close to Harvard Square. Affordable elegance with fresh flowers and antiques near museums, theaters and restaurants. Crepes, homemade bread and jam and afternoon tea. WiFi, voicemail, cable TV and concierge services.

DoanePerry@yahoo.com   www.cambridgebnb.com

CAMBRIDGE

A Room at the Top	85-130 $US BB	Continental breakfast
51 Avon Hill St 02140	1 rooms	Milk, juice, coffee, tea, stocked fridge
617-547-6136	C-ltd/S-no/P-no/H-no	in room
Joan Friebely	French	WiFi, flat screen TV, small fridge, microwave, coffee pot, we accept Pay Pal

The beauty of outdoors meets the comfort of the indoors in this 16'x 25' space with windows all across the front, large skylights, cathedral ceiling, and French doors to a private balcony in the trees. Separate entrance from the main house.

 jfriebely@rics.bwh.harvard.edu

Harding House	105-375 $US BB	Hearty continental breakfast
288 Harvard St 02139	14 rooms, 12 pb	Coffee, tea, cookies, goodies, on
877-489-2888 617-876-2888	Most CC, *Rated*	Thursdays enjoy wine & cheese
Briana Pearson	C-yes/S-no/P-no/H-yes	Free DSL access, free parking, TV,
	Portuguese, Korean,	phone, hairdryer, fax, museum passes
	Creole	

We are a beautiful restored and decorated Victorian house, decorated with curious artifacts and original art. We are located in a safe residential neighborhood.

 reserve@harding-house.com 🌐 www.harding-house.com

Irving House at Harvard	65-395 $US BB	Continental plus breakfast
24 Irving St 02138	44 rooms, 29 pb	Afternoon tea with fruit, cookies,
877-547-4600 617-547-4600	Most CC, Cash, •	savory treats
Rachael Solem	C-yes/S-no/P-ltd/H-yes	Sitting room, library, cribs, central
	French, Spanish,	A/C, fax, laundry, conference room
	Russian, Bulgarian	

Since 1945 Irving House has had affordable rates and the best proximity to Harvard Square. It's a large guesthouse that feels like home. Our staff is always ready to help you find your way around town, recommend a restaurant or call a taxi.

 reserve@irvinghouse.com 🌐 www.irvinghouse.com

Parkside on Ellery	135-230 $US BB	Continental breakfast
74 Elllery St 02138	3 rooms, 3 pb	Internet access, cable TV, clock radio,
617-492-5025	Most CC	A/C, telephone with voicemail, hair
David	C-ltd/S-no/P-no/H-no	dryer, iron

Excellent accommodations for the seasoned or casual traveler offer cleanliness, convenience and comfort. Steps from Harvard Square, minutes from Boston. Private entrances, baths, views, with arranged parking and all the requisite amenities.

 info@parksidebb.com 🌐 www.parksidebb.com

Prospect Place B&B	105-200 $US BB	Full breakfast
112 Prospect St 02139	4 rooms, 2 pb	Afternoon tea
800-769-5303 617-864-7500	Visa, MC	Sitting room, business traveler
Eric Huenneke	C-ltd/S-no/P-no/H-no	accommodations, wireless Internet access

Nineteenth century charm at its best, with terrific & discreet modern updates. Gourmet quality full breakfast served on fine china & linens.

 info@prospectpl.com 🌐 www.prospectpl.com

CHATHAM

Captain's House Inn	185-480 $US BB	Full gourmet breakfast
369 Old Harbor Rd 02633	16 rooms, 16 pb	Complimentary afternoon cream tea,
800-315-0728 508-945-0127	Most CC, Cash, Checks,	evening cookies, morning coffee/tea
Jill & James Meyer	*Rated*, •	service
	C-ltd/S-no/P-no/H-no	Lawn croquet, fitness room, outdoor heated pool (seasonal), concierge, laundry, selection of DVD's.

A most distinctive Cape Cod bed and breakfast, the Captain's House Inn is regarded by many respected lodging reviewers as perhaps "The Cape's" finest small inn.

 info@captainshouseinn.com 🌐 www.captainshouseinn.com

CHATHAM

Old Harbor Inn
22 Old Harbor Rd 02633
800-942-4434 508-945-4434
Judy & Ray Braz

129-339 $US BB
11 rooms, 11 pb
Visa, MC, Disc,
Rated, •
C-ltd/S-no/P-no/H-no

Full breakfast
Restaurants nearby, complimentary
coffee & tea service, soft drinks &
water also complimentary
Sitting room with fireplace, sun room,
deck, A/C, Jacuzzi, wireless Internet
access, fitness room

English country decor. King or queen beds. Full breakfast. Walk to seaside village attractions. The Old Harbor Inn is a Select Registry, Distinguished Inns of North America property. A highly-rated, award-winning Inn.

✉ info@chathamoldharborinn.com   🌐 www.chathamoldharborinn.com

---

The Cranberry Inn of Chatham
359 Main St 02633
800-332-4667 508-945-9232
Kay & Bill DeFord

120-395 $US BB
18 rooms, 18 pb
Visa, MC, AmEx,
Rated
C-ltd/S-no/P-no/H-no

Full country breakfast
Afternoon tea with fresh baked treats,
lemonade & iced tea in the summer
Hair dryers, telephone, cable TV, air
conditioning, WiFi, fireplaces, wet
bars, mini-fridges

On the quiet outskirts of Chatham Village, The Cranberry Inn offers a memorable getaway in every season. Its stately presence on Main Street compliments neighboring cottages and shore homes. Lush gardens and a wide veranda make it all the more inviting.

✉ info@cranberryinn.com   🌐 www.cranberryinn.com

CHESTERFIELD

1886 House
202 East St 01012
800-893-2425+44 413-296-0223
Joe & Carol Lingg

95-130 $US BB
3 rooms, 2 pb
Visa, MC, Disc, •
C-yes/S-no/P-ltd/H-no
Spanish, Italian

Full breakfast
Complimentary tea & coffee,
restaurants nearby
Sitting room, library, robes, fireplaces,
cable TV, central air conditioning ,
enclosed porch, WiFi

Free Night w/Certificate: Excluding May and Oct. Room Upgrade.

An authentic New England country farmhouse on 5 acres, in historic Chesterfield just off scenic routes 9 & 143. Cozy, intimate B&B. Beautiful fall colors; many outdoor activities to enjoy. Just 12 miles from Northampton & 8 miles from Look Park.

✉ innkeepers@1886house.com   🌐 www.1886house.com

CONCORD

Colonel Roger Brown House
1694 Main Street 01742
800-292-1369 978-369-9119
Mrs. Lauri Berlied

110-220 $US BB
5 rooms, 5 pb
Visa, MC, AmEx, •
C-ltd/S-no/P-ltd/H-no

Continental plus breakfast
Snacks & beverages
Desks with DSL Internet, voice mail,
individual climate control, kitchenettes

Built in 1775, the house retains the architectural charm of hand-hewn beams and wainscot paneling with modern features such as high-speed DSL & cable TV. All of the suites are newly decorated with a mix of period, reproduction & contemporary furnishings.

✉ InnkeeperCRBH@aol.com   🌐 www.colrogerbrown.com

Hawthorne Inn
462 Lexington Rd 01742
978-369-5610
Marilyn Mudry & Gregory
Burch

129-329 $US BB
8 rooms, 8 pb
Most CC, Cash, Checks,
Rated, •
C-yes/S-ltd/P-ltd/H-no

Multi-course with Inn specialties
Afternoon treats may include: Homemade "Chinese Chews" Brownies,
Cookies with hot or cold beverages.
WiFi, DVD, telephone, bathrobes, hair
dryer, iron, clock-radio, abundant
toiletries, Check-in Welcome Tray.

An intimate New England B&B, where history, literature & nature intertwine, 19 miles from Boston. A favorite for business travelers, families and romantics, the Inn is close to village shops, homes of Hawthorne, Alcott, Emerson, Walden Pond & battle sites.

✉ Inn@ConcordMass.com   🌐 www.ConcordMass.com

CONCORD

North Bridge Inn
21 Monument St 01742
888-530-0007 978-371-0014
Heidi Senkler Godbout

165-275 $US BB
6 rooms, 6 pb
Visa, MC, AmEx
C-yes/S-no/P-ltd/H-no

Full breakfast
Suites with kitchens available
Suites, cable TV, WiFi, business
accommodations, family friendly

European-style B&B located in the heart of historic Concord, MA. Each of the Inn's 6 suites is newly renovated and redecorated in its own distinct style.

✉ info@northbridgeinn.com   🌐 www.northbridgeinn.com

CUMMAQUID

Acworth Inn
4352 Old King's Hwy 02637
800-362-6363 508-362-3330
Lisa Callahan

99-229 $US BB
5 rooms, 5 pb
Visa, MC, AmEx,
Rated, •
C-ltd/S-no/P-no/H-no
German

Full breakfast
Tea & coffee all day, specialty
chocolates, most rooms have
refrigerators
Wireless Internet, robes, concierge
services, beach towels/chairs, books/
games, on site Spa services

Cape Cod 19th century charm in the center of the historic district; especially noted for the hand paint-ed furnishings; easy access to islands. Listed on the National Historic Register. Five romantic rooms, each with private bath and queen size beds. ✉ acworthinn@acworthinn.com 🌐 www.acworthinn.com

DEERFIELD

Deerfield Inn
81 Main Street 01342
800-926-3865 413-774-5587
Karl Sabo & Jane Howard

155-240 $US BB
24 rooms, 24 pb
Visa, MC, AmEx,
Rated
C-yes/S-no/P-no/H-yes
Closed Christmas

Full breakfast
Afternoon tea & cookies for our house
guests, tavern lunch and dinner every
day. Market-driven menus
Free WiFi, local calls, DVD library,
guest PC, museum passes, 1 room hc
accessible, carriage rides

An original 1884 country inn in a National Historic Landmark village, the Deerfield Inn has 24 guest-rooms in two buildings, a fine restaurant and tavern with market-driven menus and a full service bar. A cozy & historic tradition. ✉ frontdesk@deerfieldinn.com 🌐 www.deerfieldinn.com

DENNIS

Isaiah Hall
152 Whig St 02638
800-736-0160 508-385-9928
Jerry & Judy Neal

100-210 $US BB
12 rooms, 11 pb
Most CC, *Rated*, •
C-ltd/S-no/P-no/H-ltd

Continental plus breakfast
Complimentary tea, coffee, chocolate
chip cookies
A/C, TV/VCR, phones, hairdryers,
irons & boards, robes, Wireless
Internet access

This lovely AAA 3 Diamond rated Inn is located in the middle of Cape Cod, an ideal home base for exploring. Walk to beach & village with its restaurants, shops, Cape Playhouse and Cape Museum of Fine Arts. ✉ info@isaiahhallinn.com 🌐 www.isaiahhallinn.com

DENNISPORT

**'By The Sea' Guests Bed &
Breakfast and Suites**
57 Chase Avenue & Inman
Road Extension 02639
800-447-9202 508-398-8685
Helen Kossifos

120-460 $US BB
17 rooms, 17 pb
Most CC, *Rated*, •
C-yes/S-no/P-no/H-yes
Greek, German,
Portuguese, French
May 1- December 30

Full breakfast
Coffee, tea, homemade treats, fresh
fruit, Poland Springs Water
HBO/cable TV, free high speed
Internet connection, private beach,
fully air conditioned

Oceanfront B&B, AAA 3 Diamond property. Breakfast served overlooking private beach. Quaint vil-lages, lighthouses, antique shops, museums, bicycle paths & golf courses all nearby.

✉ info@bytheseaguests.com   🌐 www.bytheseaguests.com

DUXBURY

Winsor House Inn
390 Washington St 02332
800-934-0993 781-934-0991
David & Patricia O'Connell

140-210 $US BB
4 rooms, 4 pb
Most CC, *Rated*
C-yes/S-no/P-no/H-no

Full breakfast
Dinner daily at 4:30 pm (fee)
Fresh flowers, comforters, reading
materials

Charming 19th Century sea captain's home located in the quaint seaside village of Duxbury, 35 miles south of Boston, 10 miles from Plymouth.

 info@winsorhouseinn.com   🌐 www.winsorhouseinn.com

EAST ORLEANS─────────────────────────

Nauset House Inn	80-185 $US BB	Full breakfast with choices
143 Beach Rd 02643	14 rooms, 8 pb	Wine & hors d'oeuvres in the late
800-771-5508 508-255-2195	Visa, MC, Disc, *Rated*	afternoon in our commons room, a
Cindy & John Vessella &	C-ltd/S-no/P-no/H-no	great gathering place
Diane Johnson	April-October	Commons room, conservatory, dining room

Free Night w/Certificate: Valid Sunday-Thursday; excludes July.

Nauset House Inn located on Cape Cod is an intimate 1810 farm house with a unique turn-of-the-century conservatory, just a short walk to Nauset beach. This inn is the answer to those who want a home-away-from-home ambience with a hint of fantasy.

✉ info@nausethouseinn.com ◐ www.nausethouseinn.com

Ship's Knees Inn	90-325 $US BB	Continental plus breakfast
186 Beach Rd 02643	18 rooms, 16 pb	Outdoor pool, courtyard garden patio
888-744-7756 508-255-1312	Visa, MC, Disc,	with gas fire pit, WiFi both indoor &
Peter & Denise Butcher	*Rated*, •	outdoor
	C-ltd/S-no/P-no/H-no	

The Ship's Knees Inn, is a 190-year-old restored sea captain's home, only a five minute walk to beautiful Nauset Beach with rolling sand dunes. Outdoor Pool on the premises.

✉ info@shipskneesinn.com ◐ www.shipskneesinn.com

EASTHAM─────────────────────────

Inn at the Oaks	120-290 $US BB	Full breakfast
3085 County Rd, Rte 6 02642	10 rooms, 10 pb	Dinner occasionally, afternoon tea &
877-255-1886 508-255-1886	Most CC, Cash,	dessert
Pam & Don Andersen	*Rated*, •	Parlor & dining room with fireplaces,
	C-yes/S-no/P-ltd/H-ltd	billiard room, play area, yard games, family suites

The perfect spot for your Cape Cod family vacation. Welcoming families of all ages, we offer suites & amenities for children and adults, including a play area and spa services.

✉ stay@innattheoaks.com ◐ www.innattheoaks.com

EDGARTOWN─────────────────────────

Charlotte Inn	295-1,000 $US EP	Full or continental breakfast available
27 Summer St 02539	25 rooms, 25 pb	for extra fee
508-627-4751	Visa, MC, AmEx	
Gerret & Paula Conover	C-ltd/S-no/P-no/H-no	

In stately Edgartown, on the island of Martha's Vineyard, stands the Charlotte Inn. Within this venerable establishment's walls the proprietors have created a spirited revival of Edwardian era elegance.

◐ www.charlotteinn.net

FALMOUTH─────────────────────────

Captain Tom Lawrence	105-230 $US BB	Full gourmet breakfast
House Inn	7 rooms, 7 pb	Complimentary, afternoon, home-
75 Locust St 02540	Visa, MC, AmEx,	baked snacks
800-266-8139 508-540-1445	*Rated*	Sitting room, free WiFi, A/C, porch,
Anne & Jim Cotter	C-yes/S-no/P-no/H-no	cable TV & refrigerator in each room

Elegant, historic Cape Cod whaling captain's home. Close to sea beaches, numerous golf courses, restaurants, ferries to Martha's Vineyard & Nantucket. Private, fully furnished apartment available.

✉ CaptTomHouse@aol.com ◐ www.CaptainTomLawrence.com

The Palmer House Inn	109-295 $US BB	Full Gourmet Breakfast
81 Palmer Ave 02540	17 rooms, 17 pb	Afternoon & evening refreshments
800-472-2632 508-548-1230	Most CC, Checks,	Sitting rooms, porches, beautiful
Bill & Pat O'Connell	*Rated*, •	grounds, bicycles, turn-down service,
	C-ltd/S-no/P-no/H-yes	WiFi, fireplaces, massages

Quiet elegance surrounds you in this romantic Victorian Inn, located in the Historic District. Beaches, shops, ferry shuttles and restaurants are only a short stroll away. Smoke free premises.

✉ innkeepers@palmerhouseinn.com ◐ www.palmerhouseinn.com

FALMOUTH

Woods Hole Passage
186 Woods Hole Rd 02540
800-790-8976 508-548-9575
Martha Bridgers & Julie
Brienza

139-199 $US BB
5 rooms, 5 pb
Visa, MC, AmEx,
Rated
C-ltd/S-no/P-ltd/H-no

Full breakfast
Tea & sweets in the afternoon
Bicycles, library, spacious grounds &
gardens, outdoor shower, WiFi, child,
dog and Gay Friendly,

Graceful 100 year-old carriage house and renovated barn providing a magical retreat year round. Walk to ocean, bay beaches, Spohr Gardens and Quisset Harbor. Swimming, boating, golf, tennis, shopping, museums and dining all minutes from the Inn.

✉ inn@woodsholepassage.com ☯ www.woodsholepassage.com

FLORENCE

The Knoll B&B
230 N Main St 01062
413-584-8164
Lee & Ed Lesko

-90 $US BB
4 rooms
Rated
C-ltd/S-no/P-no/H-no

Full breakfast
Living room with fireplace and cable
TV, library, WiFi

Large 1910 Tudor house in quiet rural setting, on 16 acres. Near 5 colleges: Smith, Amherst, Mt. Holyoke, University of Massachusetts and Hampshire.

✉ theknoll2@comcast.net ☯ www.theknollbedandbreakfast.com

GLOUCESTER

Inn Magnolia
18 Norman Avenue 01930
978-525-3642
Amanda Nash

89-145 $US BB
18 rooms, 12 pb
Visa, MC
C-yes/S-no/P-ltd/H-no

Continental plus breakfast
Beach passes to a nearby private
beach, discount coupons, decks, A/C,
weddings, private parties

A charming inn offering both old world and modern accommodations at old world prices! Two blocks to beautiful Magnolia Harbor Beach and walking distance to breathtaking conservation land. Available for wedding parties and other elegant events.

✉ innmagnolia@gmail.com ☯ www.innmagnolia.com

Lanes Cove House
6 Andrews St 01930
978-282-4647
Anna Andella

120-130 $US BB
3 rooms, 3 pb
Most CC, Cash, •
C-ltd/S-no/P-no/H-no
mid-April to mid-Nov.

Continental plus breakfast
Afternoon tea & coffee are always
available!
high speed WiFi, Ocean Views,
library, toll-free phone line, and
complimentary computer and printer.

A lovely 1800s Victorian dollhouse on the ocean, quaint, cozy & comfortable, with stunning views of a fishing cove & sunsets. Peacefully located between downtown Gloucester & Rockport, close to Salem & Boston. Modestly priced. Two night minimum, please.

✉ lanescove@comcast.net ☯ www.lanescovehouse.com

GREAT BARRINGTON

Baldwin Hill Farm B&B
121 Baldwin Hill Rd 01230
413-528-4092
Richard & Priscilla Burdsall

118-175 $US BB
4 rooms, 2 pb
Most CC, Cash, Checks
C-ltd/S-no/P-no

Full Country Breakfast
Heated pool, TV, VCR/DVD, piano,
broadband Internet access, gardens

Victorian farm home on a Berkshire hilltop. Convenient access to all Berkshire attractions. Ideal for all types of vacationers! The perfect country setting.

✉ rpburds@aol.com ☯ baldwinhillfarmbandb.com/index.html

Thornewood Inn
453 Stockbridge Rd 01230
800-854-1008 413-528-3828
Terry & David Thorne

99-295 $US BB
13 rooms, 13 pb
Visa, MC, AmEx,
Rated, •
C-yes/S-no/P-ltd/H-no

Full breakfast
Restaurant on site can cater private
functions, reunions etc., full bar.
In-house massage, Jacuzzis, pool,
suites, fireplaces, hot tub, TV, WiFi,
conference facilities, weddings

Exceptional turn of the century Dutch Colonial Inn set in the heart of the Berkshire Hills. Beautiful antique-appointed rooms, views, Jacuzzis, fireplaces, outdoor pool and in-house massage. Specializing in weddings. Near all attractions.

✉ info@thornewoodinn.com ☯ www.thornewood.com

GREENFIELD

Brandt House Inn	95-249 $US BB	Cont. plus weekdays, full weekends
29 Highland Ave 01301	9 rooms, 7 pb	Afternoon tea, complimentary wine,
800-235-3329 413-774-3329	Most CC, *Rated*, •	full breakfast on weekends, snacks
John & Steve	C-ltd/S-ltd/P-ltd/H-no	Sitting room, library, tennis, Jacuzzis,
		cable, fireplaces, fax, phones

An elegant turn-of-the-century Colonial Revival mansion. Beautiful original woodwork and personally selected furnishings and decor. Nine guest suites, seven with private baths. The Brant House Inn is an oasis for tourists and business travelers alike.

✉ info@brandthouse.com 🌐 www.brandthouse.com

HADLEY

Ivory Creek B&B Inn	159-199 $US BB	Gourmet full breakfast
31 Chmura Rd 01035	6 rooms, 6 pb	Guest kitchen available 24/7: coffee,
866-331-3115 413-587-3115	Visa, MC, AmEx,	tea, soda, juice; Hors d'oeuvres 5PM
Tod & Judy Loebel	*Rated*, •	and fresh cookies 8PM
	C-yes/S-no/P-ltd/H-yes	Multiple large comfortable common
		rooms, 11 fireplaces, free wireless
		Internet, spa, soft robes

Elegant but secluded, on 24 wooded acres with beautiful flower gardens & pond with waterfall. Hiking trails throughout the property. Within 5 miles of 5 colleges. Six spacious accommodations each with private bath & fireplace, luxurious beds & linens.

✉ pachaderm@aol.com 🌐 www.ivorycreek.com

HARWICH

Cape Cod Wishing Well	70-250 $US BB	Continental breakfast
212 Route 28 02671	20 rooms, 20 pb	Picnic area for guests to enjoy, award
888-996-9530 508-432-2150	Most CC, •	winning Cape Cod restaurants nearby
Wally Cunningham	C-yes/S-no/P-no/H-no	Renovated guestrooms, picnic area
		with grills, outdoor pool, spectacular
		views, walk to the beach

The Wishing Well caters to families and couples. It is a short walk to the sandy beaches on Nantucket Sound. Located in the middle of The Cape, we are convenient to both Sandwich and Provincetown. Wishing Well guests keep returning year after year.

✉ info@capecodwishingwell.com 🌐 capecodwishingwell.com

HYANNIS

Cape Cod Harbor House Inn	119-520 $US BB	Deluxe continental breakfast
	19 rooms, 19 pb	Fully-equipped kitchens
119 Ocean St 02601	Most CC, Cash, *Rated*	Ocean views, Internet access, DVD
800-211-5551 508-771-1880	C-yes/S-no/P-yes/H-no	player with free movies, online
Ken Komenda	Mid April thru October	concierge, beach shuttle van

Eighteen mini-suites and the Harbor Suite, a honeymoon haven on scenic Hyannis Harbor. All have separate kitchens. Free WiFi. DVD players in rooms with free movies. Free breakfast. Walk to Kennedy Museum and Memorial. Free beach shuttle.

✉ stay@harborhouseinn.net 🌐 www.harborhouseinn.net

Simmons Homestead Inn	110-250 $US BB	Full breakfast
288 Scudder Ave 02601	14 rooms, 14 pb	Complimentary evening wine
800-637-1649 508-778-4999	Most CC, Cash, Checks,	WiFi, sitting rooms, porches, bikes,
Bill Putman	*Rated*, •	billiard room, sports car museum
	C-yes/S-no/P-yes/H-no	

Beautifully restored 1800 sea captain's home. Lovely grounds. Nothing fancy, everything dedicated to just relaxing & fun. Full breakfast, evening wine hour and Toad Hall, a Collection of 50 red classic sports cars is reason enough to visit this unique inn

✉ SimmonsHomestead@aol.com 🌐 www.SimmonsHomesteadinn.com

HYANNIS PORT

Marston Family B&B	390 $US BB	Full Custom Breakfast
70 Marston Ave 02601	3 rooms, 1 pb	Breakfast requests before you arrive,
508-775-3334	C-yes/S-ltd/P-yes/H-ltd	otherwise it's cooks choice
Marcus & Lynette Sherman	June 26 – Oct. 11	Free sailboat rides, sole use of
		bathroom & living room, wireless
		Internet, TV, porch, crib, cot

Full 3 bedroom family suite for six people, 6/24 to 10/11, $390/Day or $2,625/wk. Oldest home in historic Hyannis Port, c.1786. Free WiFi. We host only one party at a time.

✉ marcus334@hotmail.com 🌐 www.catboat.com/b&b

IPSWICH

Ipswich B&B	115-150 $US BB	Full breakfast
2 East St 01938	7 rooms, 6 pb	Vegetarian & special diets on request.
866-IPSWICH 978-356-2431	Visa, MC, AmEx	We feature terrific pancakes & our
Margaret & Ray Morley	C-ltd/S-no/P-ltd/H-no	"special" French toast.
		A/C, private baths, TV, wireless DSL,
		free long distance in USA & Canada, 40
		seat restaurant

The Ipswich Bed and Breakfast is in the heart of Ipswich's historic district. We are within walking distance to town. The house, built by Robert Jordan in 1863, is a wonderful example of a Victorian home, with fine Italianate detail.

✉ ipswichinn@verizon.net 🌐 www.ipswichbedbreakfast.com

Rogers and Brown House	139-195 $US BB	Chef's Choice Entree
B&B	3 rooms, 3 pb	Coffee, tea, gourmet chocolates.
83 County Rd 01938	Visa, MC, •	New mattresses, AC, wireless Internet,
800-585-0096 978-356-9600	C-ltd/S-no/P-no/H-no	TVs, gardens, shop, 2 new bikes &
Frank Wiedenmann &		helmets, painting classes.
Johanne Cassia		

A warm welcome awaits you at historic Rogers and Brown House B&B. A short walk from train & downtown. Close to Crane's Beach & Castle Hill. Enjoy swimming, canoeing/kayaking, biking, bird watching, cross country skiing, fine dining, shopping & folk art.

✉ fjwiedenmann@comcast.net 🌐 www.rogersandbrownhouse.com

The Inn at Castle Hill	115-385 $US BB	Continental plus breakfast
280 Argilla Rd 01938	10 rooms, 10 pb	Afternoon tea with a selection of the
978-412-2555	Most CC	finest quality of loose leaf blended teas
Diana Lannon	C-ltd/S-no/P-no	Plush terry robes, telephone, hair
		dryer, central A/C & heat, bicycles
		available on request

Step into a timeless place of understated elegance and serenity. The Inn at Castle Hill, centrally located on the spectacular 2,100-acre National Historic Landmark Crane Estate, welcomes you to experience its unique and elegant seaside charm.

✉ theinn@ttor.org 🌐 innatcastlehill.thetrustees.org

LEE

Applegate Inn	150-385 $US BB	Full breakfast
279 W Park St 01238	11 rooms, 11 pb	A variety of wine & cheeses are
800-691-9012 413-243-4451	Visa, MC, AmEx,	served nightly; complimentary fine
Gloria & Len Friedman	*Rated*	candies, fruits & nuts
	C-ltd/S-no/P-no/H-yes	Sitting room, library, bicycles,
		Jacuzzis, swimming pool, suites,
		fireplace, sun parlor

Applegate Inn, a true Bed and Breakfast, was built in the grand era of the 1920's. Privacy is all yours with our six acres of groomed trails and yard.

✉ info@applegateinn.com 🌐 www.applegateinn.com

LEE

Chambery Inn
199 Main St 01238
800-537-4321 413-243-2221
Robert & Olga Healey

89-289 $US BB
9 rooms, 9 pb
Most CC, Cash, *Rated*
C-ltd/S-no/P-no/H-yes

Deluxe Continental Breakfast
Adjacent restaurant
Adjacent bar, TV, spa, fireplace,
refrigerator, Jacuzzi for two, wireless
Internet access

Chambery Inn has French-inspired design and nine exceptional rooms. This nineteenth-century parochial school turned country inn possesses a unique character, a truly distinctive landmark in the beautiful Berkshire Hills. ✉ chamberyinn@toole.tc ◑ www.chamberyinn.com

**Devonfield Country Inn
B&B**
85 Stockbridge Rd 01238
800-664-0880 413-243-3298
Bruce & Ronnie Singer

160-375 $US BB
10 rooms, 10 pb
Most CC, *Rated*, •
C-ltd/S-no/P-ltd/H-ltd
Spanish

Full buffet and a hot entree
Brandy, chocolates, bottled water in
rooms; guest pantry with homemade
cookies, tea, coffee
Heated pool, tennis, bicycles, lawn
sports, archery range, exercise room,
library, golf & ski area

A gracious English-style country house in the heart of the Berkshires sits on 32 acres only 2 miles from Main Street, Stockbridge, home of the Norman Rockwell Museum. Ideally situated for exploring the rolling tapestry of the Berkshire Hills. ✉ innkeeper@devonfield.com ◑ www.devonfield.com

**Jonathan Foote 1778
House**
One East St 01238
888-947-4001 413-243-4545
JoAnn Zarnoch

150-225 $US BB
5 rooms, 5 pb
Visa, MC
C-ltd/S-no/P-no/H-ltd

Full homemade breakfast
Homemade coffee cakes at breakfast,
homemade cookies in the afternoon,
Lindt chocolates
Fireplaces, dinner reservations,
help with directions to events and
attractions

Romantic 1778 farmhouse, full of history and charm, provides a country setting that is central to all Berkshire attractions. Fireplaces, antiques, and comfort abound.
✉ innkeeper@1778house.com ◑ www.1778house.com

LENOX

**1897 Hampton Terrace
B&B**
91 Walker St 01240
800-203-0656 413-637-1773
Stan & Susan Rosen

175-345 $US BB
14 rooms, 14 pb
Most CC, Cash, •
C-ltd/S-ltd/P-no/H-yes

Full, hot, candlelit breakfast
Full BYOB bar set-up, in-room Jacuzzis
& fireplaces, cable TV/VCR, WiFi,
concierge

1897 in-town Lenox Gilded Age landmark home. An inn since 1937. After staying here, Traditional Home Magazine declared "enjoy Gilded Age glamour and relaxed elegance at one of the East Coast's premier getaway destinations" and "absolutely perfect."
✉ stan@hamptonterrace.com ◑ www.hamptonterrace.com

Apple Tree Inn
10 Richmond Mt Rd 01240
413-637-1477
Sharon Walker

60-400 $US BB
34 rooms, 34 pb
Most CC, •
C-yes/S-ltd/P-no/H-no
Spanish

Continental breakfast
Hot Breakfast ala carte on weekends,
Dinner served Thurs. – Sat. & Brunch
on Sun., July – August
22 acres, heated outdoor pool, clay
tennis court, paths for short hikes,
weddings/events, tavern

The Apple Tree Inn sits on a twenty-two acre landscaped hilltop estate in the Berkshire Hills of western Massachusetts. It is across the road from Tanglewood, the summer home of the Boston Symphony.
✉ appletreeinn@roadrunner.com ◑ www.appletree-inn.com

Birchwood Inn
7 Hubbard St 01240
800-524-1646 413-637-2600
Ellen G. Chenaux

175-340 $US BB
11 rooms, 11 pb
Visa, MC, AmEx,
Rated
C-ltd/S-ltd/P-yes/H-ltd
French, Spanish

Full award-winning breakfast
Afternoon tea, midnight snack, guest
pantry
Library, den, fireplaces, cable TV,
videos, wireless Internet access,
porch, gardens, hammock

Birchwood Inn Bed and Breakfast, of Lenox, MA, has been welcoming friends, old and new, with warmth and congenial hospitality since 1767. The Inn is renowned for its romantic and comfortable country elegance and memorably decadent breakfasts.
✉ innkeeper@birchwood-inn.com ◑ www.birchwood-inn.com

LENOX

Brook Farm Inn
15 Hawthorne St 01240
800-285-7638 413-637-3013
Linda & Phil Halpern

149-425 $US BB
15 rooms, 15 pb
Most CC, Cash, Checks
C-ltd/S-no/P-no/H-yes
Spanish, Hebrew

Full breakfast
Tea & homemade scones are served
Friday, Saturday and Sunday at 4:00,
guest pantry is open 24 hours
Fireplaces, library, heated pool,
gardens, guest pantry, whirlpools, TV,
wireless Internet

Brook Farm Inn is a graceful Victorian, close to Lenox Center and Tanglewood, in the heart of the
Berkshires of Western Massachusetts. Nestled in a glen surrounded by trees and gardens with heated
outdoor pool, the inn is a 4-season destination.

✉ innkeeper@brookfarm.com 🌐 www.brookfarm.com

Cliffwood Inn
25 Cliffwood St 01240
800-789-3331 413-637-3330
Scottie & Joy Farrely

118-262 $US EP
5 rooms, 5 pb
C-ltd/S-no/P-no/H-no

Fireplace, whirlpool bath & shower,
TV/VCR, outdoor pool, gazebo & deck,
veranda

At Cliffwood Inn, you will find that same spirit of welcome and hospitality in the early 1890s mansion
of belle epoque beauty. Built in the Stanford White style, the B&B features polished, inlaid hardwood
floors, high ceilings and spacious rooms

✉ joy@cliffwood.com 🌐 www.cliffwood.com

Garden Gables Inn
135 Main St 01240
888-243-0193 413-637-0193
Peggy & John Roethel

146-528 $US BB
17 rooms, 17 pb
Most CC, Cash, *Rated*
C-ltd/S-no/P-no/H-ltd

Cooked to order full breakfast
Complimentary sherry, beverages &
freshly baked cookies & biscotti, wine
tasting from owner's winery
Fireplaces, whirlpools, porches,
outdoor pool, spa treatments, yoga
classes, wireless Internet

All the romantic charm of a Berkshire B&B but with four-star amenities! Guests of this historic Inn
near Lenox Village & Tanglewood love the private baths/spa robes, spa room, pool, organic & locally
sourced food and personal service. Green, eco-friendly.

✉ innkeeper@gardengablesinn.com 🌐 www.gardengablesinn.com

Gateways Inn & La
Terrazza Restaurant
51 Walker St 01240
888-492-9466 413-637-2532
Fabrizio/Rosemary
Chiariello

100-380 $US BB
12 rooms, 12 pb
Most CC, Cash, *Rated*
C-ltd/S-no/P-no/H-no
Italian, Spanish

Full breakfast
Restaurant, bar, dinner available
Sitting room with TV, free WiFi,
telephones in room, A/C, fireplaces,
onsite restaurant

Let the Gateways Inn take you to another time and place. The incomparable elegance of the Procter
mansion, infused with the European charm and hospitality of Innkeepers Fabrizio and Rosemary
Chiariello will surely enchant you.

✉ innkeeper@gatewaysinn.com 🌐 www.gatewaysinn.com

Rookwood Inn
11 Old Stockbridge Rd 01240
800-223-9750 413-637-9750
Amy Lindner-Lesser

175-400 $US BB
19 rooms, 19 pb
Most CC, Cash, *Rated*
C-yes/S-no/P-ltd/H-ltd
Spanish

Buffet style with one hot entree
We are happy to meet special dietary
restrictions with advance notice,
afternoon refreshments
Sitting room, fireplaces, TV, phones,
clock radios, robes, hairdryers,
packages, free WiFi

Fairytale Queen Anne Victorian B&B . . . Perfect for your dream getaway. Antique-filled guestrooms
with modern amenities, private baths; comfortable & elegant decor; delicious, heart healthy break-
fasts. An ideal setting for intimate weddings.

✉ stay@rookwoodinn.com 🌐 www.rookwoodinn.com

LENOX ───

Stonover Farm B&B	325-575 $US BB	Full breakfast
169 Under Mountain	5 rooms, 5 pb	Afternoon wine and cheese, we try to
Rd 01240	Most CC, Cash, Checks,	accommodate any dietary preferences
413-637-9100	*Rated*, •	Greenhouse, library, patio, courtyard,
Tom & Suky Werman	C-ltd/S-no/P-ltd/H-yes	pond, private phones w/voicemail,
	French	TV/DVD, CD players, AC, WiFi

Stonover Farm is a 110-year-old Berkshire "cottage" which served as farmhouse to the Stonover Estate, and which has been renovated extensively. Luxury accommodations include 3 suites & 2 self-contained cottages.

✉ stonoverfarm@aol.com 🌐 www.stonoverfarm.com

Summer White House	160-225 $US BB	Continental plus breakfast
17 Main St 01240	6 rooms, 6 pb	Sitting room, library, tennis court,
800-382-9401 413-637-4489	Visa, MC	swimming pool, fireplaces, cable TV,
Mary & Frank Newton	C-ltd/S-no/P-no/H-no	A/C
	Spanish	
	May 20 – October 30	

The Summer White House is just a mile from Tanglewood, in the very heart of historic Lenox. Outstanding recreation of an era (1885) in a house built by John Schermerhorn.

✉ gable@berkshire.net 🌐 www.thesummerwhitehouse.com

The Cornell In Lenox	150-400 $US BB	Full breakfast
203 Main St 01240	28 rooms, 28 pb	Full service pub on premises
413-637-4800	Most CC, Cash, *Rated*	Koi pond, waterfall, expansive decks,
Judith Roszyk	C-ltd/S-ltd/P-no/H-yes	beautiful gardens, wireless Internet,
		Sat TV in all rooms

Free Night w/Certificate: Valid Jan. 3-May 20th; except Feb. 11-14. Room Upgrade.

Our three, uniquely-styled guesthouses feature furnishings in Victorian, country and Colonial decor. Choose a cozy bedroom, a fully equipped suite with fireplace and kitchen or a room featuring a four-poster bed with fireplace and Jacuzzi.

✉ innkeeper@cornellbb.com 🌐 cornellbb.com

Walker House	100-230 $US BB	Continental plus breakfast
64 Walker St 01240	8 rooms, 8 pb	Complimentary wine, afternoon tea
800-235-3098 413-637-1271	*Rated*	Sitting room, piano, computer w/ WiFi,
Peggy & Richard Houdek	C-ltd/S-no/P-yes/H-no	library video theatre, opera & film
	Spanish, French	weekends, verandahs

Peggy & Richard Houdek invite you to share Walker House, their historic Berkshire residence. A landmark in classic American Federal architecture, now in its 3rd decade of welcoming guests.

✉ walkerhouse.inn@verizon.net 🌐 walkerhouse.com

MARBLEHEAD ──────────────────────────────────

A Lady Winette Cottage	125-150 $US BB	Nice Continental Breakfast
B&B	2 rooms	A/C, children over 5 welcome,
3 Corinthian Ln 01945	C-ltd/S-no/P-no/H-no	computer, conference rooms, laundry
781-631-8579		
Susan M. Davies		

A charming Victorian cottage nestled amongst gardens facing Marblehead Harbor. French doors open to your private deck overlooking the harbor. Enjoy breakfast on a large porch furnished with Cape Cod wicker overlooking the sailboats.

✉ Suziwinette@aol.com 🌐 www.aladywinettecottage.com

Brimblecomb Hill	95-125 $US BB	Continental breakfast
33 Mechanic St 01945	3 rooms, 1 pb	Sitting room, fireplace, garden, private
781-631-3172	Visa, MC	entrances
Gene Arnould	C-ltd/S-no/P-no/H-ltd	

Enjoy the charm of this lovingly restored antique home which was featured in both "Better Homes and Gardens" and "Colonial Homes." Three clean, comfortable first floor guestrooms with private or shared baths, two with private entrances.

✉ genearnould@verizon.net 🌐 www.brimblecomb.com/home.html

MARBLEHEAD

Fox Pond B&B
31 Arthur Ave 01945
781-631-1630
Ted Baker

90-250 $US BB
3 rooms, 3 pb
Visa, MC, *Rated*
C-ltd/S-no/P-no/H-ltd

Continental plus breakfast
Breakfast is served from 8:30–9:30am
but coffee is available before breakfast
for early risers
AC, WiFi, washers/dryers, off-street
parking, patios, gardens, HD flat
screen TVs, Jacuzzi for 2

Understated elegance and luxurious details are found throughout this meticulously renovated and expanded cape. Located in an exclusive neighborhood and adjacent to woodlands, Fox Pond provides direct access to meandering trails leading to ocean views.

 foxpond@comcast.net www.foxpondbnb.com

Harbor Light Inn
58 Washington St 01945
781-631-2186
Peter C. Conway

155-365 $US BB
20 rooms, 20 pb
Visa, MC, AmEx,
Rated, •
C-ltd/S-no/P-no/H-no

Continental plus breakfast
Afternoon refreshments, bar & tavern
for lunch & dinner
Sitting room, conference room, double
Jacuzzis, courtyard, heated swimming
pool, free WiFi, Tavern

In the heart of Old Town Marblehead, the Inn offers quick access to the harbor, shops & galleries, historic homes & a variety of restaurants. We look forward to making your stay in Marblehead memorable. Visit our new Tavern with an extensive wine list.

 info@harborlightinn.com www.harborlightinn.com

Harborside House
23 Gregory St 01945
781-631-1032
Susan Livingston

90-120 $US BB
2 rooms
Rated, •
C-ltd/S-no/P-no/H-no
Un petit peu de
Francais

Continental plus breakfast
Harbor Sweets candy, homebaked
cookies, afternoon tea on request
Living room with fireplace, deck,
bicycles, cable TV/VCR, WiFi, off-street
parking

This handsome 1850 home in the historic district overlooks picturesque Marblehead Harbor. Guests enjoy water views from its wood-paneled parlor, period dining room and summer breakfast porch. Two well-appointed guestrooms feature antique furnishings.

 stay@harborsidehouse.com www.harborsidehouse.com

**Notorious Annie's
Waterfront Inn**
115 Front St 01945
781-631-0558
Janet Sheehan

195-295 $US BB
2 rooms, 2 pb
Most CC
C-yes/S-no/P-no/H-no

Continental breakfast
Complimentary coffee & a selection of
teas are always available
Private decks, gardens, private beach,
kayaks, beach towels, hot tub, mini
fridge, wireless Internet

A private cove with the calming sound of waves upon a pebbled shore . . . ocean views, private decks and tubs to soak the cares of the world away while taking in the sea breeze.

 info@notoriousannies.com www.notoriousannies.com

MASHPEE

**Alexander Hamilton
House**
9 Horseshoe Bend
Way 02649
508-419-1584
Barbara Notarius

125-300 $US BB
2 rooms, 2 pb
C-yes/S-no/P-yes/H-no

Continental breakfast
By arrangement: fruit & cheese plate,
chocolate covered strawberries
Waterfront access, King or Queen size
bed, cable TV w/ DVD player, fridge,
coffee maker, microwave

Our Mashpee bed and breakfast offers three guestrooms on Cape Cod. All are spacious, romantic, and private. This B&B is the perfect location to ask the big question, spend your honeymoon, anniversary or birthday.

 ahhcapecod@gmail.com www.alexanderhamiltonhousecapecod.com

MIDDLEBORO

Rock Village B&B	70-130 $US BB	Continental plus breakfast
109 Miller St 02346	6 rooms, 4 pb	Snacks, water and other meals upon
508-947-3413	Visa, MC, Disc	request
Doreen Sullivan	C-ltd/S-ltd/P-no/H-no	Wireless Internet, Toshiba laptop, A/C,
		refrigerators, seasonal pool, library,
		ping pong, pool table

Rock Village B&B is noted for its historical significance to Rock Village. The Rock Mill employed over 90 people from village. The Atwoods legacy left behind the unique architecture, antique tiles, stained glassed windows and wrap around porch.

✉ rockvillagebb@comcast.net 🌐 www.rockvillagebb.com

NANTUCKET

Brass Lantern Inn	125-395 $US BB	Continental plus breakfast
11 N Water St 02554	16 rooms, 16 pb	A wide selection of loose teas & fresh-
800-377-6609 508-228-4064	Most CC, *Rated*, •	baked cookies each afternoon, bottled
Michelle Langlois	C-yes/S-no/P-yes/H-ltd	water in guestrooms
	French	Telephones, TVs, A/C, phones, robes,
		hairdryers, irons, wireless Internet
		access, concierge services

Welcome to Nantucket Island! Enjoy cobblestone streets, rose-covered cottages and miles of sandy beaches. The casually elegant Brass Lantern Inn is perfectly located in the Old Historic District, a 'walk to everything' location. Pet & family friendly.

✉ info@brasslanternnantucket.com 🌐 www.brasslanternnantucket.com

Carriage House	100-200 $US BB	Continental Plus breakfast
5 Rays Ct 02554	7 rooms, 7 pb	Guest refrigerator
508-228-0326	*Rated*, •	Parlor, guest library of local nature
Haziel Jackson & Tomomi	C-yes/S-no/P-no/H-ltd	and history, patio, beach towels,
Sato, Mom Jeanne	French, German,	concierge service
	Spanish, Japanese	

"Adorable and affordable" 1865 B&B on the prettiest, quietest, scallop-shelled country lane; "beautifully quiet, yet right in town." Personal attention for 2 generations. Private baths, parlor, flowered patio, healthy breakfast. Families welcome!

🌐 www.carriagehousenantucket.com

Cliff Lodge B&B	145-475 $US BB	Buffet Breakfast
9 Cliff Rd 02554	12 rooms, 12 pb	Afternoon snacks, tea, wine & cheese
508-228-9480	Visa, MC, AmEx	Fireplaces, art, dining room, garden
Sally Beck	C-ltd/S-no/P-no/H-ltd	patio, A/C, views, open year-round

Built in 1771 as a whaling master's home and situated on a gentle hill only a short walk from the ferry and the town, Cliff Lodge welcomes you to discover with heartwarming comfort, the unforgettable beauty and enchantment of this faraway island.

✉ info@clifflodgenantucket.com 🌐 www.clifflodgenantucket.com

Cliffside Beach Club	295-730 $US BB	Continental breakfast
46 Jefferson Ave 02554	27 rooms, 27 pb	Private bar & cafe
800-932-9645 508-228-0618	AmEx	Private beach, pool, sauna, Internet,
Robert Currie	C-yes/S-no/P-no/H-ltd	daily maid service, massage room,
	French	exercise facility
	May 21 to October 12	

With its breathtaking views of Nantucket Sound and the continued addition of amenities and services, Cliffside offers an intimate resort experience unparalleled by any other.

✉ ackbeach@aol.com 🌐 www.cliffsidebeach.com

House of the Seven Gables	100-250 $US BB	Continental breakfast
32 Cliff Rd 02554	10 rooms, 8 pb	Coffee or tea, juice, fresh baked coffee
508-228-4706	Visa, MC, AmEx	cakes, muffins, or Portuguese rolls
Sue Walton	C-ltd/S-no/P-no/H-no	Sitting room, patio and large back yard
	April-December	

A quiet Victorian in the Old Historic District. Walk to Main Street, beaches, museums and restaurants. A continental breakfast is served to your room or on the patio each morning.

✉ info@houseofthesevengables.com 🌐 www.houseofthesevengables.com

NANTUCKET

Jared Coffin House	125-410 $US BB	Continental Breakfast
29 Broad St 02554	52 rooms, 52 pb	Seasonal restaurant and lounge for
800-248-2405 508-228-2400	Most CC, Cash, •	dinner & take-out
Jim Storey	C-yes/S-no/P-no/H-yes	Business center, telephones, TVs

Three historic buildings in center of Nantucket Town, beautiful patio and garden. Guestrooms with private baths, phone, TV, and some have air conditioning. Seasonal, on-site restaurant and lounge. Downtown location. Walk from the Ferry.
✉ christina@adbmarketing.net 🌐 www.jaredcoffinhouse.com

Martin House B&B	155-405 $US BB	Continental plus breakfast
61 Centre St 02554	13 rooms, 10 pb	Complimentary sherry, afternoon
508-228-0678	Visa, MC, AmEx,	snacks, tea, wine & cheese
Lee Sylva	*Rated*	Sitting room, fireplace, veranda, beach
	C-ltd/S-no/P-no/H-no	towels

Stately 1803 Mariner's home in Nantucket's historic district. Four poster canopy beds, 13 airy rooms. Our spacious accommodations blend the convenience and comforts of today with the romance and nostalgia of the past. ✉ info@martinhouseinn.net 🌐 www.martinhouseinn.net

The Carlisle House Inn	85-395 $US BB	Expanded breakfast buffet
26 N. Water Street 02554	13 rooms, 10 pb	Complimentary weekend wine and
508-228-0720	Most CC, Cash, Checks	cheese parties in summer & special
Heather Sheldon	C-ltd/S-no/P-no/H-no	weekends; guest refrigerator
	some French, Spanish	Free Wifi/Internet, guest computer,
	& Italian	working fireplaces, hair dryers, some
		HDTVs, A/C in all rooms

The island's premier guesthouse located only a short walk from beaches, restaurants and the town center. Fine rooms, canopied beds, fireplaces, a breakfast buffet and an award-winning garden combine to assure the best in New England hospitality.
✉ info@carlislehouse.com 🌐 www.carlislehouse.com

The Veranda House	149-599 $US BB	Continental plus breakfast
3 Step Lane 02554	18 rooms, 18 pb	European style breakfast with gourmet
877-228-0695 508-228-0695	Most CC, Cash, Checks,	bread basket, yogurt, granola, fresh
Scott Allan	*Rated*	fruit, afternoon cookies
	C-ltd/S-no/P-no/H-yes	Harbor views, high-speed Internet,
	Mid- May through	massage therapy on site, flat screen
	October	TV/DVD, turndown service

A retro-chic hotel with sweeping harbor views. Our Nantucket hotel is conveniently located in the heart of Old Nantucket Town. Walk out and explore the Island on foot or by bicycle. Allow our Concierge to arrange your activities and dining reservations.
✉ sherinn@comcast.net 🌐 www.theverandahouse.com

The Wauwinet Inn	380-1,450 $US BB	Full breakfast
120 Wauwinet Rd 02584	33 rooms, 33 pb	Award-winning TOPPER'S Restaurant
800-426-8718 508-228-0145	Most CC, Cash	serving breakfast, lunch, dinner, bar
Eric Landt	C-ltd/S-no/P-no/H-no	menu & Sunday brunch
	May thru October	2 private beaches, private Spa on
		premises, complimentary jitney to
		Nantucket Town, free Internet

Experience The Wauwinet, Nantucket's premier waterfront resort. An idyllic blend of extraordinary service, superior food, gracious comfort and delightful surroundings has earned The Wauwinet critical acclaim.
✉ wauwinet@niresorts.com 🌐 www.wauwinet.com

The White House	150-305 $US BB	Voucher at local restaurant
48 Centre St 02554	4 rooms, 4 pb	Suite has a full kitchen, no breakfast
508-228-9491	Most CC, Cash	voucher given
Sally Beck	C-yes/S-no/P-no/H-no	

Ideally located in the core district of Nantucket town just minutes from Main Street, Steamboat Wharf, shops, restaurants, galleries. Nicely appointed and meticulously clean.
✉ sb@clifflodgenantucket.com 🌐 www.nantucketwhitehouse.com/main.html

NANTUCKET

Union Street Inn
7 Union Street 02554
800-225-5116 508-228-9222
Deborah & Ken Withrow

159-579 $US BB
12 rooms, 12 pb
Visa, MC, AmEx
C-ltd/S-no/P-no/H-no

Full breakfast
Free Wifi, laptop/printer in foyer,
coffee & tea, beach towels, fax,
copying, postage, garden patio

Union Street Inn, a Nantucket hotel, is a classic and striking example of "typical Nantucket" architecture circa 1770. Ideally located in the heart of the historic village just off Main Street's cobblestones and near the harbor. ✉ info@unioninn.com ◐ www.unioninn.com

NEW ASHFORD

Berkshires Shirakaba
20 Mallery Rd 01237
413-458-1800
Louise & Sadao

275-350 $US BB
2 rooms, 2 pb
Most CC, Cash,
Checks, •
C-yes/S-no/P-ltd/H-ltd
Japanese

MTO western or Japanese bkfst.
6 course Japanese dinner in
Traditional tatami mat room or
western table. We cater to special diets
Private Indoor Pool & spa, Wii games,
gazebo, WiFi, sushi lessons, free
nationwide calls

Come away to the ancient hills and cool forests we call the Berkshires. Breathe our clean air, drink our clear water, toss your head back and see stars as if you'd never seen them before.
✉ berkshires.shirakaba@gmail.com ◐ www.berkshires-shirakaba.com

NEW BEDFORD

The Orchard Street Manor
139 Orchard St 02740
508-984-3475
Al & Suzanne Saulniers

125-165 $US BB
3 rooms, 3 pb
Visa, MC, AmEx
C-ltd/S-no/P-no/H-no
French, Spanish

Continental breakfast
Formal parlor, chess & billiard room,
library, gathering room, fine dining
room, deck, guest fridge

Enjoy the luxury of New Bedford's whaling & textile past in a 1845 whaling captain's home, that was renovated in 1903 by a cotton baron to its current, graceful Georgian-Revival style. Eat lunch or dinner at nearby seafood or Portuguese eateries.
✉ theorchardstreetmanor@hotmail.com ◐ www.the-orchard-street-manor.com

NEW MARLBOROUGH

The Old Inn on the Green
134 Hartsville New
Marlborough Rd 01230
413-229-7924
Peter Platt

198-410 $US MAP
11 rooms, 11 pb
Visa, MC, AmEx,
Rated
C-yes/S-no/P-ltd/H-no

Continental breakfast
Restaurant, tap room Dinner is
included with Wednesday, Thursday
and Sunday night din/lodg specials
Antiques, porch, fireplace, Jacuzzi,
sitting rooms, A/C, pool, library, robes,
TV/DVD, WiFi

The Old Inn, once a stagecoach relay, offers authentically restored guestrooms, fine dining in intimate candlelit dining rooms and seasonal al fresco dining on the canopied garden terrace off the taproom. We offer $30 prix fixe menus on Wed, Thurs, Sun. ✉ pplatt@oldinn.com ◐ www.oldinn.com

NEWBURYPORT

Clark Currier Inn
45 Green St 01950
978-465-8363
Bob Nolan

105-195 $US BB
9 rooms, 10 pb
Most CC, Cash, Checks,
Rated
C-ltd/S-no/P-no/H-no

Continental plus breakfast
Afternoon tea
Parlor, fireplace, garden, library, off
street parking, conference room,
wireless Internet

Newburyport is famous for the number of buildings built in the Federal style, and the Clark Currier Inn is one of the city's finer examples. The building is actually two homes in one.
✉ info@clarkcurrierinn.com ◐ www.clarkcurrierinn.com

OAK BLUFFS

Dockside Inn
9 Circuit Ave
Extension 02557
800-245-5979 508-693-2966
Mark & Betsy Luce

150-450 $US BB
22 rooms, 22 pb
Most CC, Cash,
Rated, •
C-yes/S-ltd/P-yes/H-yes
Early Apr through Oct

Continental plus breakfast
Coffee and tea all day
Bicycles, A/C, sitting room, TV, kitchen
suites, garden area, hot tub, beach
accessories, Free WiFi.

The Dockside Inn is located on the enchanted island of Martha's Vineyard, in the seaside village of Oak Bluffs. Overlooking Oak Bluffs Harbor, the Inn is within walking distance to all attractions.
✉ Inns@vineyard.net ◐ www.vineyardinns.com

OAK BLUFFS

Tivoli Inn, On Martha's Vineyard 125 Circuit Ave 02557 508-693-7928 Lisa & Lori Katsounakis	85-265 $US BB 6 rooms, 3 pb Visa, MC, Disc, • C-yes/S-ltd/P-ltd/H-no	in season Assorted teas & spring water available at all times Wireless Internet, porch, TV, guest refrigerator & guest phone, lovely outdoor shower

Located in Oak Bluffs, Martha's Vineyard. The Tivoli Inn is a Victorian gingerbread house with lots of charm & a clean & friendly atmosphere. Walking distance to fine shops & restaurants, beach, nightlife, ferry terminals & much more.

 tivoli@capecod.net   www.tivoliinn.com

ORLEANS

Orleans Inn 3 Old Country Rd 02653 800-863-3039 508-255-2222 Ed & Laurie Maas	250-450 $US BB 11 rooms, 11 pb Most CC, *Rated*, • C-yes/S-no/P-yes/H-ltd	Continental plus breakfast Lunch & dinner available, afternoon tea, snacks, bar service Restaurant, sitting room, bikes, library, suites, fireplaces, cable TV, weddings, packages

Enjoy a special retreat away from the hectic hustle and bustle of everyday life. Create fun-filled memories that will last a lifetime. Escape to this 1875 Sea Captain's Mansion to indulge in quiet comfort and gracious service.

 info@orleansinn.com   www.orleansinn.com

PEABODY

Joan's B&B RR 210 Lynn St 01960 978-532-0191 Joan Hetherington	75-95 $US BB 3 rooms, 1 pb C-ltd/S-no/P-no/H-no All year excluding March	Full breakfast Afternoon tea, snacks Sitting room, patio, laundry, use of whole house, e-mail available

Located 10 minutes from historic Salem, 25 minutes from Boston, and 25 minutes from picturesque Gloucester and Rockport. All bedrooms have A/C, guests have access to wireless Internet, and are served a full breakfast.

 joansbandb@rcn.com

PETERSHAM

Winterwood at Petersham 19 N Main St 01366 978-724-8885 Jean & Robert Day	149-199 $US BB 6 rooms, 6 pb Visa, MC, AmEx, • C-yes/S-no/P-no/H-no	Breakfast with a hot entree Sip a cooling cocktail on one of our screened porches or enjoy tea by the fire in the library Winterwood is available for intimate weddings, birthday & anniversary parties, full liquor license

Winterwood is an elegant 1842 Greek Revival Mansion with 6 beautifully appointed guestrooms, most with fireplaces, all with private baths, A/C, and breakfast. Winterwood is available for intimate weddings, cocktail receptions and rehearsal dinners.

 winterwoodatpetersham@verizon.net   www.winterwoodinn.net

PLYMOUTH

A White Swan B&B 146 Manomet Point Rd 02360 508-224-3759 Christine Cox	99-175 $US BB 4 rooms, 4 pb Visa, MC, Disc C-ltd/S-no/P-ltd/H-no	Full breakfast Special blended coffee, hot tea & snacks Private bathrooms, WiFi, cable TV, off street parking, in room VCR & videos, in room refrigerator

New England historic Farmhouse offering meticulous maintenance and modern amenities. Enjoy walking our beach before breakfast or unwind your day watching the sunset over the ocean. Close to Boston, Cape Cod, Plymouth Rock and Plimoth Plantation.

 relax@whiteswan.com   www.whiteswan.com

PROVINCETOWN ——

Aerie House & Beach Club
184 Bradford St 02657
800-487-1197 508-487-1197
Steve Tait & Dave Cook

45-330 $US BB
11 rooms, 7 pb
Most CC, Cash
C-yes/S-no/P-yes/H-ltd

Continental plus breakfast
All rooms are equipped with a coffee
maker and a supply of coffee and tea.
TV/VCR/DVD/CD players, DVD library,
iPod docks, fireplace, hot tub, WiFi,
laundry, parking, sun deck

Offering a complete range of accommodations including rooms, suites, and efficiencies at either our Guesthouse perched atop Miller Hill, or our bayfront Beach Club, both located in Provincetown's charming East End gallery district.

✉ info@aeriehouse.com   🌐 www.aeriehouse.com

——

Benchmark Inn
6 Dyer St 02657
888-487-7440 508-487-7440
Park Davis

149-395 $US BB
7 rooms, 7 pb
Visa, MC, AmEx,
Rated, •
C-ltd/S-ltd/P-ltd/H-no

Continental Plus breakfast
Complimentary freshly ground/
brewed coffee, tea, spring water, fresh
fruit, yoghurt & snacks daily.
Superb rms: queen/king, fireplace,
dual entrance w/ private space, wet
bar, more. Four w/ Jacuzzi!

Provincetown Cape Cod style and romance, 1850 meets classic contemporary. Features private-use outdoor balconies with water and town views, fireplaces, Jacuzzis, wet bars and attention to detail. Providing superb comfort in America's oldest art colony.

✉ benchmarkinn@aol.com   🌐 www.benchmarkinn.com

——

**Carpe Diem Guesthouse
& Spa**
12 Johnson St 02657
800-487-0132 508-487-4242
Rainer Horn, Jurgen Herzog,
Hans van Costenoble

135-450 $US BB
19 rooms, 19 pb
Most CC, *Rated*, •
S-ltd/P-no/H-no
German, French

Full German Style Breakfast
Wine & cheese hour from 5–6 pm,
pastries, fruit, water, coffee, tea, sherry
& port available all day
Guest office, WiFi, common rooms/
patios, parking, spa, steam room,
sauna, massage, hot tub

Seize the day in our elegant Guesthouse & Spa Resort. Quiet location in center of town. Highest quality amenities, some rooms with fireplaces, whirlpool tubs, private patios. Famous homemade breakfast. On-site massage services, sauna and steam room.

✉ info@carpediemguesthouse.com   🌐 www.carpediemguesthouse.com

——

Christopher's by the Bay
8 Johnson St 02657
877-487-9263 508-487-9263
Dave Rizzo & Jim McGlothlin

70-285 $US BB
10 rooms, 5 pb
Most CC, Cash
C-ltd/S-no/P-ltd/H-no

Continental plus breakfast
Telephones with voicemail and
Dataport, cable TV/VCR, wireless
Internet, fridge & air conditioning

A nineteenth century, Victorian bed & breakfast, located in historic Provincetown, Christopher's by the Bay is a quiet escape to the romance of the past.

✉ info@christophersbythebay.com   🌐 www.christophersbythebay.com

——

**Crowne Pointe Historic
Inn & Spa**
82 Bradford Street 02657
877-276-9631 508-487-6767
David Sanford & Tom Walter

99-627 $US BB
40 rooms, 40 pb
Visa, MC, Disc,
Rated, •
S-ltd/P-no/H-ltd

Full breakfast
Afternoon tea, cookies & wine, on site
restaurant
Library, bikes, Jacuzzis, pool,
fireplaces, cable TV, spa, concierge
services, free wireless

Restored 1800's sea captain's mansion overlooking the harbor in the center of Provincetown. Unsurpassed hot buffet breakfast, spas, romantic in-room fireplaces & whirlpools.

✉ welcome@crownepointe.com   🌐 www.crownepointe.com

——

Fairbanks Inn
90 Bradford St 02657
800-324-7265 508-487-0386
Alicia Mickenberg &
Kathleen Fitzgerald

109-275 $US BB
14 rooms, 12 pb
Visa, MC, AmEx,
Rated
S-no/P-no/H-no

Expanded Continental
Afternoon snacks, guest refrigerator
DVD library, TV, microwave, sun deck,
parking, bike rack, guest computer &
WiFi

Highly recommended by guests and travel writers alike, The Fairbanks Inn is renowned for its unique blend of historic charm, guest amenities, and high standard of hospitality.

✉ info@fairbanksinn.com   🌐 www.fairbanksinn.com

PROVINCETOWN

Gabriel's at the Ashbrooke Inn	120-380 $US BB	Full breakfast
102 Bradford St 02657	17 rooms, 17 pb	Continental breakfast in winter.
508-487-3232	Visa, MC, Disc,	Snacks, cookies, coffee and tea
Elizabeth and Elizabeth	*Rated*, •	available all day.
Brooke	C-yes/S-no/P-yes/H-ltd	Jacuzzi tubs, fireplaces, wet bars, WiFi, free movies, Great Room, Keurig coffeemakers

Centrally located, pet and children friendly, Gabriel's has gorgeously renovated suites and well appointed rooms that offer both comfort and romance. Breakfast in the Great Room is not to be missed.
✉ innkeeper@gabriels.com 🌐 www.gabriels.com

Inn at the Moors	109-239 $US BB	Continental breakfast
59 Provincelands Rd 02657	30 rooms, 30 pb	Near to restaurants & stores, beverage
800-842-6379 508-487-1342	Visa, MC, Disc, •	& snack vending machines
Loretta O'Connor	C-ltd/S-ltd/P-no/H-no	Phone, cable TV, WiFi, refrigerator,
	Mid-May through	ceiling fans, heated pool, BBQ, views,
	October	A/C

All rooms face full view of the moor, a 180 degree view of the expansive salt marsh with sand dunes and Cape Cod on the horizon. This is one of the most captivating views in Provincetown and all of the Cape. ✉ info@innatthemoors.com 🌐 www.innatthemoors.com

Revere Guest House	65-375 $US BB	Continental plus breakfast
14 Court Street 02657	8 rooms, 7 pb	Select coffee & tea, home baked
800-487-2292 508-487-2292	Visa, MC, *Rated*	goodies, fresh jam, fresh fruit
Gary Palochko	C-ltd/S-no/P-no/H-no	Johnathan Williams Salon & Spa, private gardens, outdoor spa, deck with bay views, fireplace

The Revere House is a beautifully restored Colonial house located in the heart of Provincetown. The charm and ambience of the 19th century is seen throughout this historic home. While modern amenities provide the comforts of true luxury accommodations.
✉ info@reverehouse.com 🌐 www.reverehouse.com

Snug Cottage	99-279 $US BB	Sumptuous breakfast buffet
178 Bradford St 02657	8 rooms, 8 pb	Afternoon wine, lemonade/tea/cider
800-432-2334 401-487-1616	Most CC, *Rated*, •	& snacks
Bill and Brian Wilkins	C-ltd/S-no/P-no/H-no	high-speed Internet & Aveda luxury toiletries

Authentic Cape Cod Inn built in 1825 that surrounds you with history. We've preserved the best of the 19th century and added all the comfort and luxury you expect in a first class, modern Inn.
✉ info@snugcottage.com 🌐 www.snugcottage.com

The Brass Key Guesthouse	120-659 $US BB	Continental plus breakfast
67 Bradford St 02657	43 rooms, 43 pb	Poolside lemonade & iced tea, cheese
800-842-9858 508-487-9005	Visa, MC, Disc, •	& cruditas trays, fine wines & beers
Tom, David & Ken	S-ltd/P-no/H-yes	each afternoon
		Courtyard, heated pool, in ground spa, fireplaced guestrooms & common rooms, whirlpool tubs, decks

Provincetown's most unique guesthouse a half-block off Commercial Street, the Brass Key is a cozy retreat in the center of the action. Forty-two guestrooms in six 18th & 19th century houses and three cottages surrounding courtyard pool and in-ground spa. ✉ ken@brasskey.com 🌐 www.brasskey.com

Tucker Inn	135-245 $US BB	Full breakfast
12 Center St 02657	9 rooms, 7 pb	Freshly baked treats served every
800-477-1867 508-487-0381	Most CC, Cash	afternoon; Saturday cocktail party, full
Howard & Thomas	C-yes/S-no/P-yes/H-ltd	bar & great food
	Mid-May—Halloween	Queen bed, AC, fridge, flat panel TV, DVD player, hair dryer, robes, coffeemaker, high speed Internet

The Tucker Inn is one of a handful of stately 2nd Empire Victorian Cottages found in Provincetown. We are a true bed and breakfast inn and our breakfasts go far beyond the ordinary: we offer what may be the best breakfast in Provincetown. ✉ innkeeper@thetuckerinn.com 🌐 www.thetuckerinn.com

PROVINCETOWN──

White Porch Inn
7 Johnston St 02657
508-487-0592
Thomas Shirk

95-365 $US BB
9 rooms, 9 pb
Visa, MC, Disc
C-ltd/S-no/P-no/H-ltd
German
January – December

Continental plus breakfast
Gas fireplaces in most rooms,
luxurious toiletries, A/C, flat screen
TV, DVD + CD/radio, spa tubs.

Provincetown's newest and award winning boutique guesthouse with a contemporary beach atmosphere on the Cape. Conveniently located just steps away from restaurants, shops, galleries, beach, and more. Relax on the porch at this unique Provincetown Inn.
✉ info@whiteporchinn.com 🌐 www.whiteporchinn.com

REHOBOTH──

Gilbert's B&B
30 Spring St 02769
508-252-6416
Jeanne D. Gilbert

69-99 $US BB
5 rooms, 2 pb
Most CC, Cash, Checks,
Rated, •
C-yes/S-no/P-no/H-no

Full breakfast
Afternoon tea, an all organic menu is
available upon request
Sitting room, fireplaces, WiFi,
accommodate business travel

New England farmhouse built in 1830s. Features original floors, windows and hardware. Two guestrooms have private baths and fireplaces. 17 acre tree farm with hiking trails. Gilbert's B&B is designed with comfort in mind.   ✉ JG@gilbertsbb.com 🌐 www.gilbertsbb.com

ROCKPORT──

Emerson Inn by the Sea
1 Cathedral Ave 01966
800-964-5550 978-546-6321
Bruce & Michele Coates

99-379 $US BB
36 rooms, 36 pb
Most CC, *Rated*, •
C-yes/S-no/P-no/H-ltd

Full or continental plus breakfast
Casual & fine dining, Wine Spectator
Award of Excellence, hours & days of
service varies by season
Oceanview accommodations, some
with spa tubs, heated swimming pool,
2 guest cottages, lawn & gardens

Free Night w/Certificate: Valid November-April. subject to availability. Room Upgrade.

The Emerson Inn By the Sea is a newly renovated, handsome white clapboard inn, which once welcomed Ralph Waldo Emerson into its peace and comfort. Also available are two seaside cottages.
✉ info@EmersonInnByTheSea.com 🌐 www.EmersonInnByTheSea.com

Linden Tree Inn
26 King St 01966
800-865-2122 978-546-2494
Tobey & John Shepherd

125-185 $US BB
17 rooms, 17 pb
Most CC, *Rated*, •
C-yes/S-no/P-no/H-no

Full buffet breakfast
Assorted hot beverages available
throughout day and evening,
lemonade in season, cookies
Sun room & living room for guest use,
living room has large TV with DVD/
VCR, parking

Comfortable, romantic Inn with easy access to or from Boston by train. Short stroll to beaches, shops, galleries and restaurants. Lovely view of ocean and mill pond from cupola at top of house.
✉ lindentreeinn@gmail.com 🌐 www.lindentreeinn.com

Seven South Street Inn
7 South St 01966
978-546-6708
Debbie & Nick Benn

89-189 $US BB
9 rooms, 9 pb
Visa, MC, AmEx, •
C-ltd/S-no/P-no/H-no

4-course gourmet breakfast
Afternoon tea, snacks
Sitting room, library, bicycles, pool,
cable TV, business travel, private
baths, wireless Internet

Of all the inn's delights, our elegant four course breakfast is what guests talk about and remember most. Built in 1766, the Inn is ideally located to Rockport's enchanting village. An hour drive from Boston, Portsmouth, Lexington and Concord. ✉ theinn@sevensouth.net 🌐 www.sevensouthstreetinn.com

**The Quarterdeck Inn By
the Sea**
123 Granite St. 01966
877-546-0070 978-546-0050
Randy Marks

124-299 $US BB
8 rooms, 8 pb
Most CC, Cash, Checks
C-yes/S-no/P-no/H-ltd

Full breakfast
Spacious grounds & gardens, gorgeous
Atlantic Ocean views, beach access,
minutes to shops and dining

Whether you want to get away, go on vacation or hold a small business retreat, the Quarterdeck Inn By The Sea is the perfect site.
 info@thequarterdeckinnbythesea.com 🌐 www.thequarterdeckinnbythesea.com

ROCKPORT

The Tuck Inn B&B	89-179 $US BB	Continental plus breakfast
17 High St 01966	11 rooms, 11 pb	Snacks
800-789-7260 978-546-7260	Visa, MC, *Rated*	Sitting room, A/C, swimming pool,
Liz & Scott Wood	C-yes/S-no/P-no/H-no	bicycles, scenic walks, beach, multiple
		flower gardens

Cozy 1790 Colonial home in the quiet seaside village of Rockport. Hospitable & comfortable year' *round lodging. Renowned home-baked breakfast. Antiques, quilts, gardens, pool, non-smoking. 2002* *Editor's Pick Award – Yankee Magazine. AAA rated: 3 DIAMONDS!*

✉ info@tuckinn.com 🌐 www.tuckinn.com

SALEM

The Salem Inn	119-350 $US BB	Hearty continental breakfast
7 Summer St 01970	41 rooms, 41 pb	Complimentary sherry
800-446-2995 978-741-0680	Most CC, Cash,	Private garden, sitting room, A/C,
Richard & Diane Pabich	*Rated*, •	canopy beds, fireplaces, Jacuzzi baths,
	C-yes/S-no/P-ltd/H-ltd	kitchenettes, WiFi

Spacious, luxuriously appointed rooms in three elegantly restored historic homes. Located within easy *walk of city's restaurants, attractions, museums and the waterfront.*

✉ reservations@saleminnma.com 🌐 www.saleminnma.com

SANDWICH

1750 Inn at Sandwich	139-189 $US BB	Full breakfast
Center	5 rooms, 5 pb	Snacks
118 Tupper Rd 02563	Visa, MC, AmEx, •	Central air, gazebo with Jacuzzi,
800-249-6949 508-888-6958	C-ltd/S-no/P-no/H-ltd	fireplaces, robes, 600 TC sheets,
Jan & Charlie Preus		concierge, evening cordials

New England charm with a touch of southern hospitality, in the heart of Cape Cod's oldest seaside *village. This inn, circa 1750, offers charming accommodations, beautiful public rooms, and spacious* *grounds.*   ✉ cpreus@comcast.net 🌐 www.innatsandwich.com

1830 Quince Tree House	125-275 $US BB	Full breakfast
164 Main Street 02563	3 rooms, 3 pb	Bottled water & sodas, wine, sun tea,
866-933-8496 508-833-8496	Visa, MC, AmEx	coffee, tea, hot chocolate & cookies,
Richard & Cecily	C-ltd/S-no/P-no/H-no	after dinner drinks
		Queen bed, fireplace, air conditioning,
		robes, wireless Internet, iron,
		hairdryer, TV/DVD player,

Welcome to the 1830 Quince Tree House, a Georgian Colonial Bed and Breakfast in the historic vil- *lage of Sandwich, Massachusetts on beautiful Cape Cod.*

✉ stay@quincetreehouse.com 🌐 www.quincetreehouse.com

Aaron Burbank's Windfall	85-145 $US BB	Full menu breakfast
House	6 rooms, 4 pb	Afternoon tea
108 Old Main St 02563	Most CC, •	Sitting room, library, suites, fireplaces,
877-594-6325 508-888-3650	C-yes/S-ltd/P-no/H-ltd	cable TV, accommodations for
Ted Diggle		business travelers

A charming 1818 Colonial set in historic Sandwich Village. This gracious antique has retained many *original features, such as wide-board floors and 3 fireplaces, one with a beehive oven.*

✉ windfallhs@aol.com 🌐 www.windfallhouse.com

Belfry Inne & Bistro	145-295 $US BB	Full breakfast
8 Jarves St 02563	15 rooms, 15 pb	Dinner (fee), afternoon tea
800-844-4542 508-888-8550	Visa, MC, AmEx,	Restaurants, bar service, Jacuzzi tubs,
Christopher Wilson	*Rated*, •	fireplaces, conference facilities
	C-yes/S-no/P-ltd/H-no	

In a timeless Cape Cod setting, three architectural masterpieces comprise The Belfry Inn & Bistro, *each from a different time and gracing Jarves Street. twenty suites, some featuring whirlpools, fire-* *place, A/C, TV and balconies.*

✉ info@belfryinn.com 🌐 www.belfryinn.com

SANDWICH

Isaiah Jones Homestead
165 Main St 02563
800-526-1625 508-888-9115
Don & Katherine Sanderson

165-300 $US BB
7 rooms, 7 pb
Most CC, Cash, Checks,
Rated, •
C-ltd/S-no/P-no/H-no

Full gourmet breakfast
Soft drinks, self serve coffee & tea
always available, sherry or port
available in the evening
3 rooms with fireplace, 4 rooms with
glass front stove, 4 with whirlpool tub,
cable TV/DVD

An elegant Victorian B&B in historic Sandwich Village. The inn is furnished almost entirely with antiques. The curved staircase, beautiful woodwork, soft colors tell you you've found "the special place you've been looking for on Cape Cod."

✉ info@isaiahjones.com 🌐 www.isaiahjones.com

SEEKONK

Jacob Hill Inn
120 Jacob Street 02771
888-336-9165 508-336-9165
Bill & Eleonora Rezek

179-459 $US BB
12 rooms, 12 pb
Most CC, *Rated*
S-no/P-no/H-ltd
Polish

Full gourmet breakfast
Cheese plate w/complimentary wine,
24 hour self serve hot/cold beverages
available, cookies & fruit
Billiard room w/plasma home theater,
pool, tennis, fireplaces, large Jacuzzi
tubs, spa, meeting room

Located on a peaceful country estate, a 10 minute drive from downtown, the Convention Center, Rhode Island School of Design & Brown University. Recipient of many prestigious awards.

✉ jacobhillinn@msn.com 🌐 www.Inn-Providence-RI.com

SHEFFIELD

B&B at Howden Farm
303 Rannapo Rd 01257
413-229-8481
Bruce Howden & David
Prouty

119-179 $US BB
3 rooms, 3 pb
Visa, MC
C-ltd/S-no/P-no/H-no

Full breakfast
A/C, WiFi, Cable TV, views of
mountains & meadows

Located three miles below the village of Sheffield Massachusetts, Howden Farm is convenient to the many enriching outdoor and cultural activities that the Berkshires are famous for.

✉ BnB@HowdenFarm.com 🌐 www.howdenfarm.com

SHELBURNE FALLS

Kenburn Orchards B&B
1394 Mohawk Trail 01370
877-536-2876 413-625-6116
Susan and Larry

139-249 $US BB
3 rooms, 3 pb
Visa, MC, *Rated*
C-ltd/S-ltd/P-no/H-ltd

Full breakfast
Candlelight and crystal all home-made
breakfast with fresh local ingredients
from the farm.
Spacious guestrooms, private
bathrooms, parlor, fireplace, porch
rockers, TV/DVD player, 160 acres

Kenburn Orchards is located on a 165 acre farm with Christmas trees and berries. A classic 1877 New England farmhouse with privacy and views. Furnished with beautiful antiques, this slice of history is perfect for a relaxing retreat from modern life.

✉ info@kenburnorchards.com 🌐 www.kenburnorchards.com

SIASCONSET

The Summer House Inns & Cottages
17 Ocean Ave 02564
508-257-4577
Susan Manolis, General
Manager

275-2,000 $US BB
34 rooms, 34 pb
Visa, MC, AmEx, •
C-yes/S-no/P-no/H-no
April-Dec.

Continental plus breakfast
Restaurant, lunch, dinner, bar room
service
Sitting room, swimming pool, suites,
fireplaces, cable TV, accommodations
for business travelers

Romantic cottages on a bluff overlooking the Atlantic, with Jacuzzis and two beautiful inns in Nantucket Town. Two award winning restaurants on site, offering al fresco dining facing the ocean.

✉ reservations@thesummerhouse.com 🌐 www.thesummerhouse.com/summerhouse/index.ht

SOUTH LEE

Federal House Inn
1560 Pleasant St,
Route102 01260
800-243-1824 413-243-1824
Kolleen & Brian Weinrich

150-275 $US BB
9 rooms, 9 pb
Visa, MC, AmEx, •
C-ltd/S-no/P-no/H-ltd

Three Course Candlelight Breakfast
Complimentary wine and hors
d'oeuvres, late evening fresh-baked
cookies
Antiques, A/C, fireplaces, flat screen
TVs, wireless Internet access, stunning
views

Federal House Inn is an historic 1824 Federal Style home with gracious common areas and sunny guestrooms all with private baths and fireplaces. A mile from Stockbridge, minutes to Tanglewood, this elegant B&B is known for its warm hospitality.

info@federalhouseinn.com www.federalhouseinn.com

Historic Merrell Inn
1565 Pleasant St 01260
800-243-1794 413-243-1794
George Crockett

110-295 $US BB
10 rooms, 10 pb
Most CC, Cash,
Rated, •
C-ltd/S-no/P-no/H-no

Full breakfast
Afternoon refreshments
Fireplace rooms, antiques, telephones,
A/C, secure wireless Internet access,
weddings/events

One of New England's most historic stage coach Inns, a few miles from Norman Rockwell Museum and Stockbridge. The only Inn included in the Historic American Buildings Survey.

info@merrell-inn.com www.merrell-inn.com

SOUTH ORLEANS

A Little Inn on Pleasant Bay
654 S Orleans Rd 02662
888-332-3351 508-255-0780
Sandra, Pamela & Bernd

230-315 $US BB
9 rooms, 9 pb
Visa, MC, AmEx, •
C-ltd/S-no/P-no/H-no
German, French
May to September

European Breakfast Buffet
5:00pm Sherry Hour included
Two lounges, patios, bathrooms and
A/C in all rooms

Main house dates back to 1798 and may have been part of the Underground Railroad. Overlooking Pleasant Bay. Chatham and Orleans are minutes away.

welcome@alittleinnonpleasantbay.com www.alittleinnonpleasantbay.com

SOUTH YARMOUTH

Belvedere Inn
167 Old Main St 02664
508-398-1950
Robert and Sue Alexander

125-180 $US BB
3 rooms, 3 pb
Visa, MC, •
C-ltd/S-no/P-ltd/H-no

Full breakfast
Tea, coffee, soft drinks fresh baked
cookies every afternoon
Sitting room, library, screened sun
porch, sundeck, free wireless Internet

Relaxing old Sea Captain's home on the National Register of Historic Homes. Near beaches and all activities, but on quiet street. innkeeper@belvederebb.com www.belvederebb.com

Captain Farris House
308 Old Main St 02664
800-350-9477 508-760-2818
Nancy & Michael

150-250 $US BB
8 rooms, 8 pb
Most CC, Cash, •
S-no/P-no/H-no

Full breakfast
Freshly baked goods, sherry and port
in the parlor, popcorn & soft drinks
Jacuzzi tubs, video library, robes,
fresh flowers, fireplaces, on-site
massage

Tucked away on two acres in the historic Bass River Village of South Yarmouth. This architecturally significant Greek Revival style home has been restored to its former glory. World class antiques and exquisite window treatments adorn all the rooms.

thecaptain@captainfarris.com www.captainfarris.com

STOCKBRIDGE

Conroy's B&B
11 East Street, Rte 7 01262
888-298-4990 413-298-4990
Joanne & James B. Conroy

125-325 $US BB
9 rooms, 6 pb
Visa, MC, •
C-yes/S-no/P-no/H-ltd
A little Spanish
summer, fall

Full breakfast
Gardens, fireplaces, decks, pool, hot
tub

Conroy's B&B, an 1828 farmhouse in the Federal style, sits on three beautiful acres protected by a gi-ant pine hedge. The wide lawn with mature maple trees, wonderful stone walls, old farm foundations and perennial gardens provide four season beauty.

info@conroysinn.com www.conroysinn.com

STOCKBRIDGE

Stockbridge Country Inn	149-499 $US BB	Country Breakfast Made to Order
Rte 183 01262	8 rooms, 8 pb	Afternoon Tea, Complimentary Wine
413-298-4015	Visa, MC, AmEx,	& Assorted Breads & Cheeses, Hand-
Vernon & Diane Reuss	*Rated*, •	dipped Chocolate Strawberries
	C-ltd/S-no/P-no/H-no	WiFi, Bose Radio, Swimming Pool,
		Library, Fireplaces, Bike Storage,
		Studio Gallery, Parlour

Closest Inn to Norman Rockwell Museum, Chesterwood, and Berkshire Botanical Gardens. Federal-style house with up-country furnishings and Audubon's. Poster beds, private baths, full breakfast. Minutes to Tanglewood and skiing. Four acres and a pool.

✉ innkeeper@stockbridgecountryinn.com   ◉ www.stockbridgecountryinn.com

The Inn at Stockbridge	160-385 $US BB	Full candlelight breakfast
30 E St, Rt 7 N 01262	16 rooms, 16 pb	Complimentary wine & cheese,
888-466-7865 413-298-3337	Most CC, Cash, Checks,	butlers pantry, tea, coffee, snacks
Alice & Len Schiller	*Rated*, •	Sitting room, library, antiques, phones,
	C-ltd/S-no/P-no/H-ltd	A/C, pool, fireplace, fitness room,
		massage room, DVD's

Experience peaceful charm and elegance in a 1906 Georgian style mansion secluded on 12 acres. Sixteen well appointed guestrooms, many with a fireplace, double whirlpool and wonderful amenities. Let the cares of the world drift away.

✉ innkeeper@stockbridgeinn.com   ◉ www.stockbridgeinn.com

STURBRIDGE

Sturbridge Country Inn	89-259 $US BB	Continental or Breakfast Basket
530 Main St 01566	15 rooms, 15 pb	Discounted Dinner package available
508-347-5503	Most CC, *Rated*, •	with a local restaurant!
Pat Affenito	C-yes/S-no/P-no/H-no	Whirlpool tubs, fireplaces, pool, free
	Spanish	WiFi, coffee makers, hair dryers,
		CCTV, refrigerators, suites

Historic grand Greek Revival boutique hotel. Each room has a fireplace and a private bath with luxury whirlpool. There's also a studio with full kitchen. Seasonal heated pool. Walk to Old Sturbridge Village, antique shops, cafes. Many specials and pkgs.

✉ info@sturbridgecountryinn.com   ◉ www.sturbridgecountryinn.com

VINEYARD HAVEN

The Doctor's House	150-350 $US BB	Exceptional full country breakfast
60 Mt Aldworth Rd 02568	7 rooms, 7 pb	Iced tea, snacks, afternoon tea, bottled
866-507-6670 508-696-0859	Most CC, *Rated*, •	water, additional meals upon request
Ms. Jilana Abrams	C-yes/S-no/P-ltd/H-no	Cable TV, sauna, bicycles, phone,
	French	fax, wireless Internet, assistance with
		island reservations

A warm, feel at home atmosphere tucked away on two quiet acres, amidst large colorful gardens. Short stroll to village and beach. All rooms with private baths and A/C. A full country breakfast is included too!

✉ info@doctorshouse.com   ◉ www.doctorshouse.com

Thorncroft Inn	195-495 $US BB	Full breakfast
460 Main St 02568	14 rooms, 14 pb	Substantial continental breakfast
800-332-1236 508-693-3333	Most CC, Cash,	delivered to room as alternative to
Karl & Lynn Buder	*Rated*, •	breakfast in the dining room
	S-no/P-no/H-yes	Renowned concierge service, phone,
	Portuguese	TV, air conditioning, Internet access,
	Memorial Day – Labor	parking
	Day	

Romantic country inn. AAA Four Diamond Award every year since 1990. Mobil 3 stars. Fireplaces, central air conditioning, luxury suites with Jacuzzi or private hot tub.

✉ innkeeper@thorncroft.com   ◉ www.thorncroft.com

WAREHAM

Mulberry B&B
257 High St 02571
866-295-0684 508-295-0684
Frances A. Murphy

60-100 $US BB
3 rooms
Most CC, Cash, Checks,
Rated, •
C-yes/S-no/P-no/H-ltd

Full hearty New England breakfast
Afternoon tea, snacks
Sitting room, library, bicycle routes
with maps, restaurant discounts, hot
tub

*Charming 1840s Cape Cod style home originally built by a blacksmith and once a general store oper-
ated by the B&B owner's grandfather. Close to Boston, historic Plymouth, cranberry harvesting and
seaside activities.*

 mulberry257@comcast.net

WELLFLEET

Inn at Duck Creeke
70 Main St 02667
508-349-9333
Bob Morrill & Judith Pihl

95-140 $US BB
27 rooms, 19 pb
Most CC, Cash
C-yes/S-no/P-no/H-ltd
May-October

Continental plus breakfast
Much-reviewed Duck Creeke Tavern
with hip and homey food, lobster,
charm, hospitality and some Jazz
Hospitality, antique charm, family
friendly. Near town galleries &
beaches, restaurant on property

*Enjoy Cape Cod charm. Step a bit back in time. The Inn sits on a knoll overlooking a creek and pond,
near village, bay and beaches. Perfect place to relax and explore the seafaring and artist town. Savor
sweet lobster and more at the town's oldest tavern*

 info@innatduckcreeke.com   www.innatduckcreeke.com

Stone Lion Inn
130 Commercial St 02667
508-349-9565
Janet Loewenstein

195-220 $US BB
5 rooms, 5 pb
Visa, MC, AmEx
S-no/P-ltd/H-no

Full breakfast
WiFi, luxurious bath amenities,
convenient location, pet-friendly
except during summertime

*The Stone Lion Inn Bed and Breakfast is a beautifully restored 19th century former sea captain's home
located in the heart of Wellfleet, Massachusetts on Cape Cod. Come stroll miles of pristine beaches
and swim in the crystal clear ponds.*

 info@stonelioncapecod.com   www.stonelioncapecod.com

WEST BARNSTABLE

High Pointe Inn
70 High St 02668
888-362-4441 508-362-4441
Debbie & Rich Howard

150-295 $US BB
3 rooms, 3 pb
Most CC, Cash,
Checks, •
C-ltd/S-no/P-no/H-no

Full breakfast menu
Afternoon coffee, tea & treats,
complimentary evening cordials
Beach chairs, towels & totes, cable
TV/DVD, WiFi, robes; mini refrigerator,
in-room spa services

*Spacious ocean-view guestrooms feature breathtaking views of the dunes of Sandy Neck Beach with
Cape Cod Bay in the distance. Located just off scenic Route 6A in historic West Barnstable and an easy
one-hour drive from Boston or Providence.*

 info@thehighpointeinn.com   www.thehighpointeinn.com

WEST BOYLSTON

The Rose Cottage
Rts 12 & 140 01583
508-835-4034
Michael & Loretta Kittredge

120-130 $US BB
5 rooms, 5 pb
Rated
C-yes/S-no/P-no/H-ltd
Basic Italian

Full breakfast
Welcoming beverage (when
appropriate)
Sitting room, suites, fireplaces, cable
TV, accommodate business travelers,
WiFi available

*Gracious 1850 Gothic Revival cottage situated on 4 acres of lawn, overlooking Wachusett Reservoir.
Only 45 minutes to Boston and Logan Airport. Just 10 minutes to downtown Worcester.*

 rosecottagebandb@aol.com

WEST FALMOUTH

Chapoquoit Inn
495 Rt 28A 02574
800-842-8994 508-540-7232
Kim & Tim McIntyre

150-275 $US BB
7 rooms, 7 pb
Visa, MC, *Rated*
C-ltd/S-no/P-no/H-ltd
Conversational
Japanese & Spanish

Full breakfast
Tea, coffee & fresh fruit
Bicycles, beach towels, beach chairs &
tennis racquets

Make our home your home at Chapoquoit Inn, an elegant and romantic B&B located on over 3 acres in the heart of Historic West Falmouth Village. Experience the best of old Cape Cod at your doorstep! Enjoy the beautiful Shining Sea Bikeway, only steps away.

✉ info@chapoquoit.com   🌐 www.chapoquoit.com

WEST HARWICH

Cape Cod Fiddlers Green Inn
79 W. Main St. Route
28 02671
508-432-9628
Eileen & Jack

150 $US BB
3 rooms, 3 pb
Most CC, •
S-no/P-ltd/H-no

Full Irish breakfast
We provide in-room refrigerators for
guest convenience
Central climate control, private baths,
garden tubs, cable televisions, A/C, in-
ground pool & deck

Fiddler's Green Inn is set on an acre, away from the hustle and bustle for the romantic. Four poster mahogany queen beds and central climate control, just beautiful! Private baths, color cable TV and A/C all make your stay comfortable.

✉ capecodfiddlersgreen@msn.com   🌐 www.capecodfiddlersgreeninn.com

Tern Inn and Cottages
91 Chase St 02671
800-432-3718 508-432-3714
David & Joan Bruce

99-189 $US BB
8 rooms, 8 pb
Visa, MC
C-yes/S-no/P-no/H-no

Continental plus breakfast
Snacks
Dining & function room, pool, cable
TV, welcome business travelers, house
phone, Internet access

Cape Cod as it should be! Guest rooms offer comfort at a very reasonable price. A unique property offering weekly family cottages or rooms at the Inn for a shorter visit. Queen beds, AC, color TV, private bath, and breakfast in our lovely dining room.

✉ stay@theterninn.com   🌐 www.theterninn.com

WEST STOCKBRIDGE

Shaker Mill Inn
2 Oak St 01266
877-385-2484 413-232-4600
Bob and Mary Thibeault

109-259 $US BB
9 rooms, 9 pb
Visa, MC, AmEx, •
C-yes/S-no/P-yes/H-no

Continental plus breakfast
Complimentary wine, suites w/ full
kitchen
Cable TV, WiFi, fax, in-suite Jacuzzi
tub, rooms w/ fireplace, refrigerators,
patios, balcony

Free Night w/Certificate: Valid Sunday-Thursday. November-June. Room Upgrade.

Welcome to our cozy bed and breakfast inn, a Stockbridge and Lenox Massachusetts area lodging nestled in the beautiful Berkshires. The Shaker Mill Inn offers spacious efficiency suite lodging – with private baths and kitchenettes – at affordable prices.

✉ info@shakermillinn.com   🌐 www.shakermillinn.com

WEST YARMOUTH

The Inn at Lewis Bay
57 Maine Ave 02673
800-962-6679 508-771-3433
Bob & Tanya Liberman

79-169 $US BB
6 rooms, 6 pb
Most CC, Cash, Checks,
Rated, •
C-ltd/S-no/P-no/H-no
Russian

Full breakfast
Afternoon refreshments and snacks
at 4:00 (Wine and crackers, popcorn,
banana nut bread, popcorn, etc)
Wireless Internet, free parking, HD TV
in common rm, water views, beach
chairs & towels, guest computer

Our lovely B&B is just 220 steps from the beach in a quiet seaside neighborhood. Enjoy full breakfast, afternoon refreshments and snacks, and use of our beach chairs and towels. All rooms have private bath, a/c, tv, electric fireplaces, and ocean breezes!

✉ stay@innatlewisbay.com   🌐 www.innatlewisbay.com

WESTFORD

Pine Needles B&B
148 Depot St 01886
978-399-0199
Dave & Claire Davis

100-100 $US BB
3 rooms, 3 pb
Visa, MC, •
C-yes/S-no/P-no/H-no

Full Gourmet Breakfast
BBQ Picnic Basket filled with all the
essentials – small service fee applies
Gas fireplace, A/C, cable TV, sitting
room, game room, fax & copy
machines, access to the Internet

In the heart of historic Massachusetts, close to Boston, Concord & Lowell. A simple country inn providing all the comforts of home and gracious, New England hospitality.

 info@pineneedlesbb.com    www.pineneedlesbb.com

WILLIAMSTOWN

**1896 House Inn & Country
Lodgings**
910 Cold Spring Rd 01267
888-999-1896 413-458-1896
Denise Richer & Suzanne
Morelle

59-289 $US BB
36 rooms, 36 pb
Most CC, Cash,
Rated, •
C-yes/S-no/P-no/H-yes
Summer, Fall, Winter

Full breakfast
Popular and exciting upscale pub, new
menu concept without pricey entrees,
French Restaurant too
Heated outdoor pool, shuffleboard,
gathering room with games, WiFi,
business center, 2 restaurants

Historic 1896 landmark Inn in Williamstown, MA in the Berkshires, with six Barnside luxury bed & breakfast Suites, a great pub, and 2 charming motels. Our romantic inn features Jacuzzis for 2, fireplaces, king beds, WiFi, DVDs, and full breakfasts.

celebrate@1896house.com   www.1896house.com

House On Main Street
1120 Main St 01267
888-750-6849 413-458-3031
Timothy & Donna

79-150 $US BB
6 rooms, 2 pb
Most CC, Cash,
Checks, •
C-yes/S-no/P-ltd/H-ltd

Full, complimentary breakfast
Dietary restrictions easily
accommodated
Sitting room, fireplace in living room,
cable TV, high speed Internet access

The charm of the Victorian era with the luxury of the 21st century. Nestled in a tree-lined setting, with the convenience of walking to the Clark Art Museum, Williams College, Williamstown Theatre Festival, shopping and dining.

Relax@HouseOnMainStreet.com   www.HouseOnMainStreet.com

WILLIAMSTOWN

**The Birches at Steep Acres
Farm**
522 White Oaks Rd 01267
413-458-8134
Daniel Gangemi

100-175 $US BB
3 rooms, 1 pb
Rated
C-ltd/S-no/P-no/H-no

Full gourmet breakfast
Sitting room, swimming, 1½ acre pond,
fishing, hiking trails, boating

This charming B&B is situated on a high knoll, on 50 acres of woods and rolling hills. Relaxing ambience with breathtaking views of the Berkshire Hills and Vermont's Green Mountains. Located 2 miles from Williams College and the center of Williamstown.

thebirchesbb@gmail.com   www.birchesbb.com

YARMOUTH PORT

**Colonial House Inn &
Restaurant**
277 Main St, Rt 6A 02675
800-999-3416 508-362-4348
Malcolm J. Perna

115-160 $US MAP
21 rooms, 21 pb
Most CC, Cash, Checks,
Rated, •
C-yes/S-ltd/P-yes/H-yes
Russian, German,
French, Spanish,
Lithuanian

Continental plus breakfast
Full restaurant and bar available for
Dinner (Dinner included full menu in
room rate)
Bar, indoor pool and Jacuzzi, TV/VCR,
free wireless/DSL, deck, garden,24hr
Free Computer Center

On a street lined, with stately trees, stands the Colonial House Inn. Here the charm of old Cape Cod has been carefully preserved & the tradition of gracious dining & hospitality carried forward.

info@colonialhousecapecod.com   www.colonialhousecapecod.com

The Birches at Steep Acres Farm, Williamstown, MA

YARMOUTH PORT

Olde Captain's Inn
101 Main St, Rt 6A 02675
888-407-7161 508-362-4496
Sven Tilly & Betsy O'Connor

75-120 $US BB
5 rooms, 3 pb
C-ltd/S-no/P-no/H-no

Continental breakfast
Kitchen is fully equipped with
refrigerator, stove, china, kitchen
utensils & condiments.
Maid, concierge service, cable TV,
antiques, honeymooner and intimate
rooms

Olde Captain's Inn is a charming 1812 sea captain's house located in the historic district of the village of Yarmouthport on Cape Cod. Within walking distance of many restaurants, craft and antique shops, and Cape Cod Bay. Modest prices.

 general@oldecaptainsinn.com 🌐 www.oldecaptainsinn.com

The Inn at Cape Cod
4 Summer Street 02675
800-850-7301 508-375-0590
Michael & Helen Cassels

180-365 $US BB
9 rooms, 9 pb
Most CC, *Rated*, •
C-ltd/S-no/P-no/H-no
French

Gourmet breakfast
Afternoon tea with home-baked cakes
& cookies, chocolates in rooms,
refreshments always available
Drawing room & library w/fireplaces,
secure wireless Internet access, cable
& DVD, concierge service

The Inn at Cape Cod is an award winning B&B located on historic route 6A in Yarmouthport, MA. This elegant 1820 mansion is perfectly located in the Mid-Cape and is close to beaches and ferries. Gourmet breakfasts and tempting afternoon treats!

 stay@innatcapecod.com 🌐 www.innatcapecod.com

Michigan

ALLEGAN

Castle in the Country
340 M-40 So. 49010
888-673-8054 269-673-8054
Herb & Ruth Boven

85-269 $US BB
10 rooms, 10 pb
Visa, MC
C-yes/S-no/P-no/H-no

Delightfully presented breakfasts
Complimentary cocoa at bedtime,
gourmet dinners available
Whirlpools, fireplaces; Romance,
Murder Mystery & spa packages;
weddings & receptions; cooking class

Nicknamed "the castle" for its three-story turret and wide wrap-around porch. Guests find it's a place "where enchantment, adventure and romance meet, and memories are made to last forever."

 info@castleinthecountry.com   www.castleinthecountry.com

ALMA

Saravilla B&B
633 N State St 48801
989-463-4078
Linda & Jon Darrow

99-169 $US BB
7 rooms, 7 pb
Most CC, Cash,
Checks, •
C-yes/S-ltd/P-no/H-no

Full breakfast
Snacks & beverages
Fireplaces, pool & ping pong table,
hot tub, piano, A/C, whirlpool tubs,
ballroom, library

Saravilla is an 11,000 sq ft three story Dutch Colonial home built in 1894, and was originally a "summer cottage." Saravilla offers a delightful taste of the Bed and Breakfast experience for everyone.

 Ljdarrow@saravilla.com   www.saravilla.com

ANN ARBOR

First Street Garden Inn
549 S First St 48103
734-741-9786
Kathy Clark & Mike Anglin

140-200 $US BB
2 rooms, 2 pb
Visa, MC
S-no/P-no/H-no

Full breakfast
Gourmet coffee & tea
Free WiFi, piano, afternoon tea

The First Street Garden Inn is an elegant Inn built at the turn of the 20th Century. Nestled on a quiet, tree-lined street, the First Street Garden Inn is convenient to nearby popular attractions, the University of Michigan and downtown Ann Arbor.

 FirstStreetGardenInn@Comcast.net   www.firststreetgardeninn.com

AUBURN HILLS

Cobblestone Manor
3151 University Dr 48326
248-370-8000
Heather & Paul Crandall

179-349 $US BB
9 rooms, 9 pb
Most CC, Cash, •
C-ltd/S-no/P-no/H-yes

Full breakfast
Soft drinks, popcorn, fresh cookies &
mints always available
Whirlpool tubs, fireplaces, high speed
WiFi, indoor chapel, cable TV with
DVD

Voted "Best in Michigan" and "One of the Most Romantic Getaways in the Nation." Built in 1840, recently renovated with the modern amenities required by professional travelers. Offers ten beautifully appointed guestrooms, onsite wedding chapel and gardens.

 stay@cobblestonemanor.com   www.cobblestonemanor.com

AUTRAIN

Pinewood Lodge
906-892-8300
Jerry & Jenny Krieg

130-155 $US BB
5 rooms, 5 pb
Visa, MC, Disc,
Rated, •
C-ltd/S-no/P-no/H-ltd

Full breakfast
Library, sitting room, sauna, beach on
Lake Superior, gazebo, gardens, best
rooms have fireplaces

An exquisite north woods log home surrounded by tall, Norway Pines. A few steps away from the grandeur of the world's largest fresh water lake. Breakfast overlooking the beach, Lake Superior & AuTrain Island.

 pinewood@tds.net   www.pinewoodlodgebnb.com

BIG BAY

Big Bay Lighthouse
3 Lighthouse Rd 49808
906-345-9957
Jeff & Linda Gamble

125-190 $US BB
7 rooms, 7 pb
Rated, •
C-ltd/S-no/P-no/H-no

Full breakfast
Coffee, tea, hot chocolate all day,
evening snack of cookies
Sitting room, library, Jacuzzi,
fireplaces, sauna, WiFi, spa services

Escape the ordinary. High on a cliff overlooking Lake Superior, the Lighthouse beckons you to experience a secluded retreat from modern life, with quiet nights and northern lights.

✉ keepers@BigBayLighthouse.com 🌐 www.bigbaylighthouse.com

BROOKLYN

Dewey Lake Manor B&B
11811 Laird Rd 49230
800-815-5253 517-467-7122
Joe & Barb Phillips

89-139 $US BB
5 rooms, 5 pb
Visa, MC, Disc,
Rated, •
C-ltd/S-ltd/P-ltd/H-no

Full breakfast
Picnic lunch (with prior notice),
snacks, tea, coffee, (lemonade, cider in
season) always cookies
Sitting room, parlor with piano,
fireplace, bonfires, paddle boats,
canoe, grills, massage available

Free Night w/Certificate: Valid November-April.

Century-old historic home on Dewey Lake, a Southern Michigan getaway in the Irish Hills. Discover sparkling lakes, hiking trails, gardens, country air & bird watching. This home furnished with antiques, fireplaces & featherbeds offers a country retreat.

✉ deweylk@frontiernet.net 🌐 www.deweylakemanor.com

CHELSEA

Chelsea House Victorian Inn
118 E Middle St 48118
877-618-4935 734-475-2244
Jim & Kim Myles

115-225 $US BB
5 rooms, 5 pb
Visa, MC
C-yes/S-no/P-no/H-ltd

Full breakfast
Porch, Jacuzzi, fireplace, weddings,
business retreats, private parties, baby
showers

This 1880's Queen Ann Victorian Inn is a full-service Bed and Breakfast with period decorated rooms, an intimate Carriage House suite, a large gathering space, and the finest hospitality imaginable.

✉ innkeeper@chelseahouseinn.com 🌐 www.chelseahouseinn.com

EATON RAPIDS

**The English Inn,
Restaurant and Pub**
677 South Michigan
Road 48827
800-858-0598 517-663-2500
Gary Nelson

104-185 $US BB
10 rooms, 10 pb
Most CC, Cash, Checks
C-ltd/S-no/P-no/H-ltd

Continental plus breakfast
Full service, award-winning restaurant
& pub
Wedding receptions, retreats,
reunions, conferences, pub, wine
cellar, gardens

An historic home built in 1927, this Tudor mansion sits on 15-acres of gardens and woodlands includes two cottages, an award-winning restaurant & Medovue Hall; a 200+ seat banquet hall for banquets, conferences and weddings.

✉ englishinn@comcast.net 🌐 www.englishinn.com

FENNVILLE

Heritage Manor Inn
2253 Blue Star Hwy 49408
888-543-4384 269-543-4384
Ross & Diane Hunter

90-180 $US BB
12 rooms, 12 pb
Most CC, Cash
C-yes/S-no/P-no/H-no

Full Buffet Breakfast
Stocked guest kitchen and homemade
cookies
Heated indoor pool, Jacuzzi,
fireplaces, garden, volleyball court,
playset, wireless Internet

Heritage Manor Inn offers a peaceful country setting for romantic getaways & family gatherings. We welcome guests to enjoy our large backyard volleyball court, basketball hoops, picnic & indoor pool facilities.

✉ rdhunter@heritagemanorinn.com 🌐 www.heritagemanorinn.com

FENNVILLE

J. Paules' Fenn Inn
2254 S 58th St 49408
877-561-2836   269-561-2836
Paulette Clouse

110-165 $US BB
5 rooms, 5 pb
Visa, MC, Disc
C-ltd/S-no/P-yes/H-ltd

Every Morning from 8–10am
Wine & dessert in the evenings.
Coffee, tea & hot chocolate and
cookies all day
Flower gardens, decks, fire pit, picnic
tables all on 2 acres, lots of outdoor
places to lounge

Our Guests say we are the best kept secret in Southwest Michigan. You have 5 rooms to chose from, all with private baths, 4 with fireplaces, 3 with Jacuzzi tubs, full breakfast. Stay three days & get a free bottle of Fenn Valley wine. Non-smoking.

✉ jpaules@accn.org   🌐 www.jpaulesfenninn.com

Kingsley House B&B Inn
626 W Main St 49408
866-561-6425   269-561-6425
David Drees

69-249 $US BB
8 rooms, 8 pb
Most CC, *Rated*, •
C-ltd/S-no/P-no/H-ltd

Full gourmet breakfast
Seasonal snacks & beverages in the
afternoon, bottomless cookie jar, 24-
hour hot and cold beverage
Wrap around porch, bicycles, porch
swing, hammock, wireless Internet
throughout, video library

Free Night w/Certificate: Valid Nov-April, Sunday-Thursday, excluding holidays.

Voted as a Top 12 Inn Worldwide, 2008–2009, just minutes from Saugatuck, Holland & South Haven. Offering romantic lodging with luxury Jacuzzis, fireplaces & gracious hospitality. The peaceful setting & friendly atmosphere make it an ideal getaway.

✉ romanticgetaways@kingsleyhouse.com   🌐 www.kingsleyhouse.com

FLINT

Avon House B&B
518 Avon St 48503
888-832-0627   810-232-6861
Arletta E. Minore

65-65 $US BB
3 rooms
Most CC, Cash, Checks
C-yes/S-no/P-no/H-no

Full breakfast
Breakfast includes beverages, fruit,
baked goods, and a main dish
Sitting room, A/C, play yard, extended
stay rates, small meetings, garden,
wrap-around porch

Enchanting Victorian home close to college and cultural center with art and entertainment. Driving distance to Birch Run Outlets and Frankenmuth. University of Michigan-Flint, Mott and Baker Colleges and Kettering University near by.

✉ avonhsebed@aol.com   🌐 www.avonhousebandb.com

FRANKENMUTH

Bender Haus
337 Trinklein St 48734
989-652-8897
Bev & Elden Bender

95-125 $US BB
4 rooms, 2 pb
Rated, •
C-ltd/S-no/P-no/H-no
German
April-November

Full breakfast
Sitting room, bicycles, cable TV,
central air conditioning and tours
available with advance notice.

Our traditional home is in the center of #1 tourist town. Our home is quiet and peaceful. Two blocks west of Main Street in the beautiful German town of Frankenmuth.

✉ benderjb@juno.com

GRANDVILLE

Prairieside Suites Luxury B&B
3180 Washington Ave
SW 49418
616-538-9442
Cheri & Paul Antozak

179-259 $US BB
5 rooms, 5 pb
Visa, MC, Disc, •
C-ltd/S-no/P-ltd/H-ltd

Full or deluxe continental
An endless supply of cookies & baked
goods, coffee, tea, homemade hot
cocoa & microwave popcorn
Luxury Jacuzzi, Fireplace Suites, King
beds, In-House Massage, Romantic
Packages & Room Services

Voted "3rd Best B&B in North America", "Best in the Midwest" & "Best of the Great Lakes" and "Most Romantic!" Spa Rooms include whirlpool tub, fireplace, King bed, private bath, fridge & microwave, TV/VCR/cable and A/C. Massage services & special packages.

✉ cheri@prairieside.com   🌐 www.prairieside.com

HOLLAND

The Inn at Old Orchard Road 1422 South Shore Dr 49423 616-335-2525 Elizabeth DeWaard	115-125 $US BB 3 rooms, 3 pb Visa, MC, Disc, *Rated* C-ltd/S-no/P-no/H-ltd	Full breakfast Snacks, early morning coffee & tea Cable TV, porch, patio, gazebo, WiFi

Enjoy quiet solitude on a quaint front porch, a spacious patio, or a rustic gazebo at this 1906 Dutch farmhouse. Cozy guestrooms offer queen sized beds, private baths & "wake-up" coffee or tea.

✉ orchardroad@chartermi.net 🌏 www.theinnatoldorchardroad.com

KALAMAZOO

Hall House B&B 106 Thompson Street 49006 888-761-2525 269-343-2500 David & Cathy Griffith	105-180 $US BB 5 rooms, 5 pb Most CC, Cash, *Rated* C-yes/S-no/P-no/H-no	Full breakfast on weekends Deluxe continental breakfast on weekdays, complimentary beverages always available High speed wireless access, DIRECTV, VCRs in rooms, phones, air conditioning (during summer)

Stately 1920s Georgian Colonial home minutes from downtown, Western Michigan University, and on the edge of the Kalamazoo College campus.   ✉ innkeepers@hallhouse.com 🌏 www.hallhouse.com

Kalamazoo House B&B 447 W South St 49007 866-310-0880 269-382-0880 Laurel & Terry Parrott	109-189 $US BB 9 rooms, 9 pb Most CC, Cash, *Rated* C-ltd/S-no/P-no/H-no	Full breakfast Evening refreshments, 24-hour beverage station, bedtime cookies & milk, special diets accommodated WiFi, whirlpool tubs, fireplaces, cable HDTV with DVD & music channels, relaxing parlor and porches.

Victorian elegance and modern convenience in downtown Kalamazoo, just steps from museums, theatres, fine dining and nightlife. Whirlpools and fireplaces provide romantic touches in this highly rated inn, and gracious hospitality brings guests back.

✉ thekalamazoohouse@msn.com 🌏 www.thekalamazoohouse.com

LELAND

Whaleback Inn 1757 N Manitou Trail 49654 800-942-5322 231-256-9090 Scott & Tammie Koehler	109-259 $US BB 19 rooms, 19 pb Visa, MC, *Rated* C-yes/S-ltd/P-no/H-yes	Continental breakfast 24 hour snacks & beverages, breakfast available Memorial through Labor Day Sitting room, hot tubs, sauna, hiking, playground, lake, swimming, basketball, WiFi in all rooms

Relaxing getaway. Beautiful scenic area on Lake Leelanau. All 14 rooms, cottage and 4 cottage suite accommodations are new or recently remodeled, with private baths, WiFi, and ground floor entry.

✉ info@whalebackinn.com 🌏 www.whalebackinn.com

LUDINGTON

The Lamplighter B&B 602 E Ludington Ave 49431 800-301-9792 231-843-9792 Bill & Jane Carpenter	125-170 $US BB 5 rooms, 5 pb Most CC, Cash, *Rated* C-ltd/S-ltd/P-no/H-ltd	Full Gourmet Breakfast Enjoy your morning coffee or tea & breakfast in the dining room or the patio Fireplaces, living room, parlor, antiques, chandeliers, cable TV, Internet, Jacuzzi tubs

The only 3 Diamond AAA rated B&B in the Ludington area. Located minutes from white, sandy beaches and Michigan's most beautiful State Park, The Lamplighter is the B&B of choice for travelers who want to step back in time without losing touch with today.

✉ lamplighter@ludington-michigan.com 🌏 www.ludington-michigan.com

OMER

Rifle River B&B 500 Center Ave 48749 989-653-2543 Gerald & Judie Oboyle	65-75 $US BB 4 rooms C-yes/S-no/P-ltd/H-no	Continental breakfast

For your travels in Omer, Michigan, Rifle River B&B offers great rates, comfortable and clean accom-modations, great views, and friendly service.   ✉ Judiea@Centurytel.net

Bay View Terrace Inn and Restaurant, Petoskey, MI

PENTWATER

Hexagon House
760 6th St 49449
231-869-4102
Tom & Amy Hamel

100-225 $US BB
5 rooms, 5 pb
Visa, MC, *Rated*
C-ltd/S-ltd/P-no/H-no

Full breakfast
Coffee, tea, lemonade, cookies,
brownies, nuts & candies
TV/DVD players, CD/radio, central air
& heat, porches, Jacuzzi tub, electric
fireplaces, massage

The Hexagon House B&B is the perfect romantic destination. Whether enjoying a quiet moment by the fireplace in our Victorian parlor or sharing wine under the stars on our spacious porches, hospitality and ambience will compliment your plans for romance.

✉ innkeepers@HexagonHouse.com 🌐 www.hexagonhouse.com

PETOSKEY

Bay View Terrace Inn and Restaurant
1549 Glendale 49770
800-530-9898 231-347-2410
Mo Rave & Patty Rasmussen

69-169 $US BB
37 rooms, 37 pb
Disc, *Rated*, •
C-ltd/S-no/P-no/H-no
some spanish
June through
September

Expanded continental buffet
Packages for Tea, brunch, picnics and
other specially arranged meals
Massages, manicures, pedicures, can
purchase wine and dinner add-ons,
packages and gifts.

The Bay View Terrace Inn is located in Northwest Michigan in Petoskey, a charming Lake Michigan resort area and inside Victorian BayView, a Chautaugua Association with summer concert series. Rooms are unique and include breakfast and WiFi.

✉ info@theterraceinn.com 🌐 www.theterraceinn.com

SAUGATUCK

Bayside Inn
618 Water St 49453
269-857-4321
Kathy & Frank Wilson

85-240 $US BB
10 rooms, 10 pb
Most CC, Cash, Checks
C-yes/S-no/P-no/H-ltd

Full breakfast
Snacks like popcorn & cookies
available in the afternoon, outdoor
grill
Converted boathouse, private bath
& deck, cable TV, phones, WiFi,
waterfront jetted-spa, A/C

Bayside is a former boathouse, converted to a B&B, on the water near downtown Saugatuck. In-ground outdoor hot tub situated 4 feet from the water's edge. Six rooms and four suites with private baths.

✉ info@baysideinn.net 🌐 www.baysideinn.net

SAUGATUCK

Beachway Resort
106 Perryman St 49453
269-857-3331
Frank & Kathy Wilson

55-320 $US BB
36 rooms, 36 pb
Most CC, *Rated*
C-yes/S-no/P-no/H-yes
May-end of Oct.

Coffee, fruit and doughnuts
Snacks
Swimming pool, cable TV, VCR, video
library, games, sundeck

Overlooking the banks of the Kalamazoo River, the Beachway Resort is the closest hotel to Lake Michigan's award-winning Oval Beach. Enjoy our large heated swimming pool and other fantastic features. The perfect spot for your family's summer get-away!

✉ info@beachwayresort.com 🌐 www.beachwayresort.com

Beechwood Manor Inn & Cottage
736 Pleasant St 49453
877-857-1587 269-857-1587
Gregg Smith & Sal Sapienza

165-195 $US BB
3 rooms, 3 pb
Most CC, Cash
C-ltd/S-no/P-ltd/H-ltd

Full breakfast
Coffeemaker, coffees, teas, hot
chocolate, refrigerator.
Antiques, fireplaces, veranda, A/C,
wireless Internet access, parlor, digital
cable

With our ideal location, gracious hospitality and Innkeepers who have perfected the exact balance between being helpful and present and being discretely in the background, we invite you to come experience Beechwood Manor Inn and Cottage.

✉ beechwoodmanor@comcast.net 🌐 www.beechwoodmanorinn.com

Hidden Garden Cottages & Suites
247 Butler St 49453
888-857-8109 269-857-8109
Daniel Indurante & Gary Kott

135-225 $US BB
4 rooms, 4 pb
Visa, MC, •
S-no/P-no/H-ltd

Continental plus breakfast
Assorted snacks, teas, popcorn
Fireplaces, whirlpool tubs for two, TVs
with DVD/VCR, movies, mini-kitchens,
WiFi, private porches

Luxurious hideaways for two, perfect for guests seeking a more private bed & breakfast. Elegantly furnished, just steps away from shopping, dining and attractions. Perfect for honeymoons or romantic getaways. ✉ indakott@aol.com 🌐 www.hiddengardencottages.com

---

Park House Inn
888 Holland Street 49453
866-321-4535 269-857-4535
Melisa Raywood & Toni Trudell

159-235 $US BB
9 rooms, 9 pb
Most CC, Cash
C-ltd/S-ltd/P-yes/H-yes

Full breakfast
Coffee, tea, soft drinks, bottled
water, snacks & homemade cookies
provided for guests.
WiFi, Jacuzzi, hot tub, fireplace suites,
breakfast inside or outside (weather
permitting).

Stay with us and relive a bit of Saugatuck history. Built in 1857 by H. D. Moore, The Park House is one of Saugatuck's oldest residences. Special packages include romance getaways, spa weekends and much more!

✉ info@parkhouseinn.com 🌐 www.parkhouseinn.com

Sherwood Forest
938 Center St 49453
800-838-1246 269-857-1246
Susan & Keith Charak

110-205 $US BB
5 rooms, 5 pb
Visa, MC, Disc,
Rated, •
C-ltd/S-no/P-no/H-no
Atlantian

Full breakfast
Afternoon tea, snacks
Sitting room, bicycles, heated pool,
skiing, Jacuzzi, cottage

Surrounded by woods, this beautiful Victorian-style home offers fireplace and Jacuzzi suites, heated pool, bicycles, wraparound porch. Half a block to Lake Michigan and spectacular sunsets.
✉ sf@sherwoodforestbandb.com 🌐 www.sherwoodforestbandb.com

The Kirby House
294 W Center St 49453
800-521-6473 269-857-2904
Jim Gowran

110-210 $US BB
8 rooms, 6 pb
Most CC, Cash, Checks,
Rated
C-ltd/S-no/P-no/H-no

Full breakfast
Porch, gardens, fireplaces, heated
in-ground pool, Jacuzzi, parlor, foyer,
butler pantry

The home is graced with quarter-sawn oak woodwork and panels, prismed windows, tall ceilings with gently curved moldings, a six sided tower, wrap-around front porch and beautiful gardens.

✉ jim@kirbyhouse.com 🌐 www.kirbyhouse.com

SAUGATUCK

Twin Gables Inn
900 Lake St 49453
800-231-2185 269-857-4346
Mike & Margaret Hull

100-250 $US BB
15 rooms, 15 pb
Most CC, •
C-ltd/S-no/P-ltd/H-yes

3 course gourmet breakfast
coffee, tea, popcorn, hot cocoa, Chai
Latte, hot cider, chocolates, trail mix,
cocktail crackers
Hot tub, seasonal pool, A/C, bikes,
beach chairs, umbrellas, library, large
common room, pond, gardens

Slip into our charming and romantic Inn on the art Coast of Michigan. Choose one of our 15 beautiful rooms and enjoy a sumptuous breakfast overlooking the harbor. Beautiful ceremony & reception site for weddings & large events. 3 hrs. Chicago/Detroit.

 relaxing@twingablesinn.com  www.twingablesinn.com

SOUTH HAVEN

A Country Place B&B
79 N Shore Dr N 49090
877-866-7801 269-637-5523
John & Cindy Malmstrom

98-155 $US BB
5 rooms, 5 pb
Visa, MC, Disc
C-ltd/S-no/P-no/H-yes
Feb – Nov

Full breakfast
Complimentary refreshments all
day, freshly baked goodies for late
afternoon or evening snack
Fireplace, sitting room, screened
gazebo

Our 140 year old Greek Revival home is situated on 2 acres of woodland with Lake Michigan sandy beach access ½ block away. The focal point of the back lawn is a large screened gazebo where nature can be appreciated to the fullest.

acountryplace@cybersol.com www.acountryplace.net

Carriage House at Harbor
118 Woodman St 49090
269-639-2161
Suzanne & David

125-270 $US BB
12 rooms, 12 pb
Most CC, Cash, Checks,
Rated
S-no/P-no/H-yes

Lavish gourmet breakfast
Afternoon popcorn & homemade
cookies
Massage, concierge services, movie
& reading library, harbor views, living
room, sitting room

Harbor side B&B, open year round, featuring gourmet food, superior service, designer rooms with cozy fireplaces & private baths. Our dining room, screened porch & decks overlook the harbor. Walk to town or across the street to the beach & amazing sunsets.

suzanne@carriagehouseharbor.com www.carriagehouseharbor.com

Inn at the Park B&B
233 Dyckman Ave 49090
877-739-1776 269-639-1776
Carol Ann & Jerry Hall

125-275 $US BB
9 rooms, 9 pb
Visa, MC, Disc, *Rated*
S-no/P-no/H-yes

Full breakfast
Evening hors d'oeuvres & wine in the
pub, freshly baked cookies, coffee, tea,
bottled water, sodas
Parlor, day room and pub with
fireplaces, daily newspapers &
magazines, books, videos

South Haven's Inn at the Park Bed & Breakfast has elegantly appointed guestrooms with cozy fireplaces and whirlpool tubs. Steps from downtown South Haven and Lake Michigan, the ideal place for South Haven getaways.

info@innpark.com www.innpark.com

Martha's Vineyard B&B
473 Blue Star Hwy 49090
269-637-9373
Lou & Ginger Adamson

99-205 $US BB
11 rooms, 11 pb
Most CC, *Rated*
C-ltd/S-no/P-no/H-ltd

Full four-course breakfast
Afternoon refreshments daily, (Lunch
baskets, hors d'oeuvre tray, dinner on
verandah by request)
Parlor, covered veranda, DVD library,
private pond, garden & vineyard,
onsite spa services

We invite you to come & experience our private oasis. Martha's Vineyard offers luxurious accommodations of unparalleled comfort, heartfelt hospitality, service that anticipates and pampers, and soul-inspiring surroundings.

adamson@marthasvy.com www.marthasvy.com

SOUTH HAVEN

Sand Castle Inn
203 Dyckman Ave 49090
269-639-1110
Charles Kindred

125-275 $US BB
10 rooms, 10 pb
Most CC, Cash, Checks,
Rated
C-ltd/S-no/P-no/H-yes

Full buffet style gourmet breakfast
Light evening appetizers, home
baked goods, fresh fruit, hot and cold
beverages always available
Living room, white wicker front porch,
fireplaces, private balconies, pool,
private baths, WiFi

Beautiful, restored, historic Lake Michigan Resort Hotel. 1 block to beach, 3 to downtown, shops, restaurants. Designer decorated. Fireplaces, private decks or balconies. Seasonal heated pool. Full gourmet buffet breakfast, light evening appetizers. WiFi.

✉ innkeeper@thesandcastleinn.com 🌐 www.thesandcastleinn.com

Seymour House
1248 Blue Star Hwy 49090
269-227-3918
Mike & Patty Kirsch

110-205 $US BB
6 rooms, 6 pb
Visa, MC, *Rated*
C-ltd/S-no/P-no/H-no

Full Gourmet Breakfast
Afternoon tea, snacks
Jacuzzis, sitting room, 1-acre pond to
swim in, fireplaces, library with books
and movies

Historic 1862 mansion in picturesque wooded setting, near Lake Michigan's sandy beaches. The Seymour House has been voted one of the Top 15 B&B's with "Best Getaway Packages" by inn-goers in Arrington's Bed & Breakfast Journal's Book of Lists!

✉ info@seymourhouse.com 🌐 www.seymourhouse.com

Victoria Resort B&B
241 Oak St 49090
800-473-7376 269-637-6414
Jan

95-215 $US BB
9 rooms, 9 pb
Visa, MC, Disc, *Rated*
S-no/P-no/H-no

Full breakfast
Bicycles, tennis, basketball, outdoor
fireplace, outdoor pool.

Historic South Haven Michigan bed & breakfast located a block from Lake Michigan and a short walk to downtown South Haven. Guest rooms with fireplaces and whirlpool tubs, full homemade breakfast. Outdoor pool, tennis, bikes, and several cottages as well.

✉ info@victoriaresort.com 🌐 www.victoriaresort.com

Yelton Manor B&B & The
Manor Guest House
140 North Shore Dr 49090
269-637-5220
Elaine & Robert

135-305 $US BB
17 rooms, 17 pb
Visa, MC, AmEx
S-no/P-no/H-no
April through October

Full breakfast
Sweet treats always available, evening
hors d'oeuvres
Porches, parlors, books, Jacuzzis,
fireplaces, WiFi, private baths, TV/
DVDs, lake views, gardens

A fabulous lakeside Victorian mansion, fashioned to be the most lavish and comfortable celebration destination possible. No other South Haven bed and breakfast offers Yelton Manor's unique blend of luxury, location, service, food and affordability.

✉ elaine@yeltonmanor.com 🌐 www.yeltonmanor.com

ST. JOSEPH

The Chestnut House
1911 Lakeshore Dr 49085
269-983-7413
Bob & Lori Stanwood

125-245 $US BB
4 rooms, 4 pb
Most CC, Cash, Checks
C-ltd/S-no/P-no/H-no

Full breakfast
Pool, garden, flat screen TV, wireless
Internet, beach chairs/towels
available, fax/copy, fireplaces

You'll relax and feel pampered in this newly renovated 1920's Arts and Crafts home, our new suites are luxury at its finest. You'll love the sumptuous breakfasts served on the enclosed porch featuring stunning Lake Michigan views.

✉ chestnuthousebandb@comcast.net 🌐 www.chestnuthousebandb.com

SUTTONS BAY

Korner Kottage
503 N. St. Josephs Ave 49682
888-552-2632 231-271-2711
Linda & Jim Munro

106-229 $US BB
4 rooms, 4 pb
C-ltd/S-no/P-no/H-ltd

Full breakfast
24 hour coffee & tea service, snacks &
homemade cookies
Cable TV, refrigerator, ceiling fan,
wireless Internet, guest phone & fax

At the Korner Kottage B&B, living the sweet life is not only possible, it's the rule. Come stay awhile. Feed your soul, inspire your heart. Rest your body. Revel in the romance for which this home was built, and steal away with your true love.

✉ info@kornerkottage.com 🌐 www.kornerkottage.com

THREE RIVERS

Voyager's Inn B&B
210 East St 49093
269-279-9260
Caryn Wilson

85-95 $US BB
3 rooms, 3 pb
Visa, MC, Disc
C-yes/S-no/P-no/H-no

Full breakfast
We use local, farm-fresh eggs, fruits
and vegetables whenever possible
Library, WiFi

Voyager's Inn is a beautiful Queen Anne Victorian home, built c. 1898. We feature touchable elegance and gracious hospitality. Our breakfast includes local fruits, vegetables, eggs and cheese. Savory afternoon snacks, treats and WiFi are complimentary.

✉ reservations@voyagers-inn.com 🌐 www.voyagers-inn.com

UNION PIER

Sandpiper Inn
16136 Lakeview Ave 49129
800-351-2080 269-469-1146
Veronica Lynch & Jim Reilly

120-295 $US BB
9 rooms, 9 pb
Most CC, *Rated*
S-no/P-no/H-no

Full breakfast
Snacks Sunday – Thursday, wine &
hors d'oeuvres Friday & Saturday
Library, bicycles, Jacuzzis, fireplaces,
private beach, 15-person conference &
retreat facilities

Elegant new home 20 feet from terraced stairs to private beach. Luxurious accommodations including screened verandahs, fireplaces, private baths, Jacuzzi tubs, queen size beds & spectacular views.

✉ info@sandpiperinn.net 🌐 www.sandpiperinn.net

WHITEHALL

White Swan Inn
303 S Mears Ave 49461
888-948-7926 231-894-5169
Cathy & Ron Russell

119-179 $US BB
4 rooms, 4 pb
Most CC, Cash,
Checks, •
C-ltd/S-no/P-ltd/H-no

Full breakfast
Coffee area, beverages & homemade
treats
Whirlpool suite, wraparound screened
porch, formal dining room, off-street
parking

Award-winning B&B. Circa 1884, gracious hospitality is the hallmark of White Swan Inn. Located just a few minutes drive to the sugar-sand beaches of Lake Michigan, in a charming resort area, walk to shops. Halfway between Chicago & Mackinac Island

✉ info@whiteswaninn.com 🌐 www.whiteswaninn.com

WILLIAMSTON

Topliff's Tara
251 Noble Rd 48895
517-655-8860
Sheryl & Don Topliff

75-140 $US BB
5 rooms, 3 pb
Visa, MC, Disc, *Rated*
C-ltd/S-no/P-no/H-no

Full breakfast
Snacks, fruit & non-alcoholic
beverages
Hiking, cross country ski trails, hot
tub, llamas

Topliff's Tara is located in a 1905 farmhouse on this 50-acre Grand Country estate. Guests may stroll through the many gardens, or visit the curious llamas at the fences.

✉ info@topliffstara.com 🌐 www.topliffstara.com

Minnesota

AFTON ———————————————————————————————————————

Afton House Inn	79-285 $US BB	Continental plus breakfast
3291 S St Croix Trl 55001	25 rooms, 25 pb	Lunch & dinn 11:30am-10pm, fine
651-436-8883	Most CC, Cash,	dining at the Inn's Wheel Room or
Gordy & Kathy Jarvis	*Rated*, •	Pennington. Swirl Wine Bar & Tapas
	C-yes/S-no/P-no/H-yes	Bar service, Jacuzzis, fireplaces, cable
		TV, antique store, coffee & ice cream
		shop; business travel

Historic country inn overlooking the marina & the scenic St. Croix River. Furnished with antique decor, private baths. Most rooms have gas fireplace & Jacuzzi for two. Views overlook Marina & St. Croix River. Fine dining & casual dining. Romantic getaway!

✉ kathy@aftonhouseinn.com 🌐 www.aftonhouseinn.com

ALEXANDRIA ———————————————————————————————————

Cedar Rose Inn	100-155 $US BB	Full breakfast
422 7th Ave W 56308	4 rooms, 4 pb	Snacks, complimentary wine
888-203-5333 320-762-8430	Visa, MC, *Rated*, •	Sitting room, library, bicycles, hot
Aggie & Florian Ledermann	C-ltd/S-no/P-no/H-no	tubs, swimming, fishing

Cozy 1903 Tudor-Revival style home, walking distance to downtown, many beautiful roses, located in the heart of Minnesota's lake country.

✉ florian@cedarroseinn.com 🌐 www.cedarroseinn.com

ANNANDALE ————————————————————————————————————

Thayer's Historic B&B	185-245 $US BB	Full white linen breakfast
60 W Elm St – Hwy 55 55302	11 rooms, 11 pb	Happy to do vegan, vegetarian, gluten
800-944-6595 320-274-8222	Most CC, Cash, Checks,	& dairy free, plus other special diets
Sharon Gammell	*Rated*	with advance notice
	C-ltd/S-ltd/P-ltd/H-no	Psychic readings, ghost hunting,
		classes in paranormal studies, 2
		friendly cats, wedding officiate

This 1895 award winning Old West Victorian B&B is home to chef & psychic Sharon Gammell & her 2 Maine Coon Cats. Psychic Readings, Ghost Hunting Classes, Murder Mystery Dinners, High Teas, Authentic Antiques & Ghosts, make a Thayer's stay spectacular!

✉ slg@thayers.net 🌐 www.thayers.net

CANNON FALLS ————————————————————————————————

Quill and Quilt B&B	89-209 $US BB	Full breakfast
615 Hoffman Street	5 rooms, 5 pb	Self-serve gourmet hot tea & cocoa
West 55009	Most CC, Cash, Checks	Private baths, fireplaces, A/C and TV/
507-721-1622	C-ltd/S-no/P-no/H-no	DVD combos, spa/massage provided
Polly, Callie, Matt, Jill, JoDell		in separate room

Historic elegance, with modern amenities in charming 1897 home. All 5 beautiful guestrooms have private attached bathrooms, double whirlpools, fireplaces, A/C, TV/DVD, and plenty of character. Spa services available in a private suite on site.

✉ innkeepers@quillandquilt.com 🌐 www.quillandquilt.com

DULUTH ———————————————————————————————————————

A.G. Thomson House	169-299 $US BB	Multi course homemade breakfast
2617 E Third St 55812	7 rooms, 7 pb	Complimentary evening wine
877-807-8077 218-724-3464	Most CC, *Rated*	Whirlpool & fireplace suites, Lake
Tim & Angie Allen	S-no/P-no/H-yes	Superior views, garden walking trail,
		A/C, TV, free wireless

Casual comfort and elegance abounds on two acres of private grounds at A.G. Thompson House in Duluth and Minnesota. The bed and breakfast features spacious whirlpool and fireplace suites with private baths, Lake Superior views and sumptuous breakfasts.

✉ info@thomsonhouse.biz 🌐 www.thomsonhouse.biz

DULUTH

The Olcott House Bed & Breakfast Inn
2316 E 1st St 55812
800-715-1339 218-728-1339
David

135-250 $US BB
6 rooms, 6 pb
Visa, MC, Disc, *Rated*
S-no/P-no/H-ltd

Full breakfast
Afternoon tea, snacks, complimentary wine
Sitting room, library, suites, fireplaces, TV/DVD, AC, CD player, wireless, business travelers

Luxury, elegance, unsurpassed refinement and hospitality await you in this grand 1904 Georgian Colonial Revival mansion. One of Minnesota's architectural gems! 6 lavishly decorated, very private suites w/fireplaces, TV & DVD library. Candlelit breakfasts!

✉ info@olcotthouse.com   🌐 www.olcotthouse.com

ELY

Blue Heron B&B
827 Kawishiwi Trail 55731
218-365-4720
Jo Kovach

120-175 $US BB
5 rooms, 5 pb
Visa, MC, *Rated*
C-yes/S-no/P-yes/H-yes
Japanese

Full breakfast
snacks, tea/coffee/cocoa, lunch, dinner
snowshoes, canoes, sauna, cozy restaurant, 2 sitting rooms, lake views

Blue Heron is located on a pristine lake right on the edge of the million acre Boundary Waters Wilderness. All the comfort of a fine hotel with all the wilderness of a camping trip. Five course dinners optional. Hiking, biking, canoeing and skiing.

✉ info@blueheronbnb.com   🌐 www.blueheronbnb.com

GRAND MARAIS

Poplar Creek Guesthouse B&B
11 Poplar Creek Drive 55604
800-322-8327 218-388-4487
Ted and Barbara Young

95-152 $US BB
3 rooms, 3 pb
Most CC, Cash
C-ltd/S-no/P-no/H-no

Full breakfast
Delicious breakfast, dessert, coffee, tea, hot chocolate
Cabin, vacation rental and yurts, daytrips, packages, wilderness

A short thirty-mile drive up the Gunflint Trail from Grand Marais, you find this exciting new lodging experience. Perched on a glacial esker, the Guesthouse offers a dramatic view of Little Ollie Lake and Poplar Creek below.

✉ bct@boundarycountry.com   🌐 www.littleollielodging.com

LANESBORO

Hillcrest Hide-Away B&B
404 Hillcrest St E 55949
800-697-9902 507-467-3079
Marvin & Carol Eggert

105-139 $US BB
4 rooms, 4 pb
Most CC, Cash, Checks
C-ltd/S-no/P-no/H-ltd

Full breakfast
Awaken to the aroma of just-baked bread outside your door, bottomless cookie jar
WiFi, full A/C, concierge, off-street parking, TV

Immerse yourself in a tranquil setting within 3 blocks of downtown Lanesboro. Just-baked home made bread delivered to your room daily. Our spacious rooms offer a great place for your own personal retreat. Find our mid-week special on our web site.

✉ hillcresthideaway@yahoo.com   🌐 www.hillcresthideaway.com

Mrs. B's Historic Inn
101 Parkway Ave N 55949
507-467-2154
Terry & Meredith Neumann

129-174 $US BB
9 rooms, 9 pb
Visa, MC, Disc
C-ltd/S-no/P-no/H-ltd
April thru October

Gourmet full breakfast
Homemade cookies, or chef's choice, cheese, fresh fruit & assorted crackers on some Fridays
Lobby, guest bar for refreshments, bike storage, garden, patio seating on the Root River, Zen Garden

Mrs B's Historic Lanesboro Inn in Minnesota's Bluff Country offers 9 unique rooms with private baths in its 1872 limestone structure. A/C, WiFi, fireplaces, a sumptuous breakfast prepared by the Inn's personal chef. In town, on the Root River Trail.

✉ mrsbsinn@earthlink.net   🌐 www.mrsbsinn.com

LANESBORO————————————————————————

Stone Mill Hotel & Suites
100 Beacon St E 55949
866-897-8663 507-467-8663
Colleen Lamon

100-180 $US BB
9 rooms, 9 pb
Visa, MC, Disc
C-yes/S-no/P-no/H-yes

Continental plus breakfast
Themed suites, iron-claw fireplaces,
cable, mini micro-fridges, double
whirlpools, 1 block to trail

Free Night w/Certificate: Sun-Thurs.

A Historic Inn at the Lanesboro Feed Mill. Unique lodging experience in 1885 limestone building. 9 suites with themes that depict the history of the building and Lanesboro's irresistible charm. Double whirlpool baths, lofts, and iron-claw fireplaces.

✉ stonemillsuites@hotmail.com 🌐 www.stonemillsuites.com

The Inn at Sacred Clay Farm
23234 Grosbeak Road 55949
866-326-8618 507-467-9600
Sandy & Fred

140-235 $US BB
5 rooms, 5 pb
Most CC, Cash, Checks
C-ltd/S-no/P-no/H-yes

Full breakfast
Freshly brewed coffee & tea
Reading/game room, meditation room,
fireplace, porch, massage tubs, locally
grown foods, piano

The Inn at Sacred Clay Farm is a graceful four-story post-and-beam structure in a stunning, yet peaceful, country setting just two and a half miles from charming, historic Lanesboro.

✉ sacredclayfarm@acegroup.cc 🌐 www.sacredclayfarmbandb.com

MENTOR————————————————————————

Inn at Maple Crossing
14709 Maple Inn Rd SE 56736
218-637-6600
Nancy & James Thomasson

79-125 $US BB
16 rooms, 16 pb
Visa, MC, AmEx
C-yes/S-no/P-no/H-yes

Full breakfast
Scrumptious meals, freshly prepared
daily, and artistically presented in the
dining room.
Library, quiet, country setting, nightly
games, and lakeside porches.

For a romantic get-away, enjoy the quaint, quiet ambience of our lovely country inn, featuring 16 uniquely styled and furnished guestrooms and guest library, conference room, cozy sitting rooms, spacious lakeside porches, fine dining, renowned gift shop.

✉ maplexing@gvtel.com 🌐 www.innatmaplecrossing.com

MINNEAPOLIS————————————————————

Evelo's B&B
2301 Bryant Ave S 55405
612-374-9656
David & Sheryl Evelo

75-95 $US BB
3 rooms
Most CC, *Rated*
C-ltd/S-no/P-no/H-no

Continental plus breakfast
Fresh fruit, assorted fresh breads &
muffins, jam, juice, yogurt, coffee & tea
at breakfast
Free WiFi, TV, refrigerator,
coffeemaker, air conditioning, phone,
maps, newspapers

1897 Victorian with period furnishings. Located on the bus line, walk to Walker Art Center, Minneapolis Art Institute, Children's Theater and downtown. Featured on WCCO TV newscast," Finding Minnesota", Chosen by City Pages as Best in the Twin Cities.

✉ evelosbandb@comcast.net

NEW ULM————————————————————————

The Bohemian
304 S German St 56073
866-499-6870 507-354-2268
Bobbi McCrea

89-199 $US BB
7 rooms, 7 pb
Most CC, Cash
C-yes/S-no/P-no/H-yes

Full breakfast – German specialty
Regional fare with German bacon,
sausages, introductions to local beers,
wine paired with dessert
Parlor, whirlpool, library, carriage
rides, massage, special gift packages,
exceptional hospitality

Featured on HGTV for its Bohemian chic. Weary traveler looking for a romantic inn, getaway or vacation? The Bohemian welcomes guests with comfort and style, offering rest, wine and Old World hospitality.

✉ info@the-bohemian.com 🌐 www.the-bohemian.com

NORTHFIELD

Archer House
212 Division St 55057
800-247-2235 507-645-5661
Todd

79-189 $US EP
36 rooms, 36 pb
Visa, MC, AmEx,
Rated, •
C-yes/S-yes/P-no/H-yes

Full service restaurant
Sitting room, near golf, ski, bike, hike
trails &, whirlpool suites

The Archer House River Inn opened in 1877. The Inn is a grand 4-story red brick building featuring French Second Empire architecture and is situated on the banks of the Cannon River at the center of historic downtown Northfield. ✉ guestservices@archerhouse.com ◐ www.archerhouse.com

PLAINVIEW

Tefft House Bed and Breakfast
20 W Broadway 55964
507-534-3001
Stephen and Marsha
O'Connor

70-140 $US BB
3 rooms, 3 pb
Visa, MC
C-ltd/S-no/P-no/H-no

Full breakfast
Whirlpool tubs, antiques, wireless
Internet, gas fireplaces, A/C, iPod
docking stations

The Tefft House B&B provides luxury accommodations with modern amenities. Every room has just what you need to relax and reconnect with that special someone.
✉ info@teffthouse.com ◐ www.teffthouse.com

RED WING

Moondance Inn
1105 W 4th St 55066
866-388-8145 651-388-8145
Chris Brown Mahoney &
Mike Waulk

125-219 $US BB
5 rooms, 5 pb
Most CC
C-ltd/S-ltd/P-no/H-no

Full breakfast
Complimentary wine & appetizers
on weekends, a tea & sweets service
weekdays
Wireless access, travel information,
golf discounts, seasonal specials,
wedding/event hosting

The Red Wing, MN. Moondance Inn is an architectural gem. Original woodwork, Tiffany and Steuben chandeliers, and a gilded ceiling are on display. All rooms feature private baths with whirlpools and fireplaces. Delicious full breakfasts are served daily.
✉ info@moondanceinn.com ◐ www.moondanceinn.com

Round Barn Farm B&B
28650 Wildwood Ln 55066
866-763-2276 651-385-9250
Robin & Elaine Kleffman

159-249 $US BB
5 rooms, 5 pb
Most CC
C-ltd/S-no/P-no/H-ltd

Full breakfast
Complimentary drinks & ice
Jacuzzis, fireplace, patio, lounge

Come to the country! Come to where old fashioned American and European ambience meet in a 3-story, bracketed country manor farm home.
✉ info@roundbarnfarm.com ◐ www.roundbarnfarm.com

STILLWATER

Ann Bean Mansion
319 West Pine St 55082
877-837-4400 651-430-0355
Jeremy & Erin Drews

139-239 $US BB
5 rooms, 5 pb
Visa, MC, Disc
C-ltd/S-no/P-no/H-ltd

Multi-course gourmet breakfast
Special diets accommodated with
prior notice
Wine or beverage offered on arrival,
fireplaces, private whirlpool baths,
parlor, WiFi, iPod dock

Grand historic Victorian mansion, noted for exceptionally large rooms, gourmet breakfasts (in bed if you wish) and outstanding hospitality! Celebrate an occasion, find retreat, enjoy a get-away . . .
✉ info@annbeanmansion.com ◐ www.annbeanmansion.com

Aurora Staples Inn
303 N 4th St 55082
800-580-3092 651-351-1187
Cathy & Jerry Helmberger

129-249 $US BB
5 rooms, 5 pb
Most CC, Cash, Checks,
Rated
C-ltd/S-no/P-no/H-yes

Full 3 Course Breakfast
Wine & hors d'oeuvres during check-
in time; tray with coffee & tea at 8 am,
full breakfast at 9
In-room massage, library with
fireplace, small weddings & receptions

Queen Anne Victorian close to downtown shopping and restaurants. Wraparound front porch for relaxing, formal English Gardens with a fountain and a view of the river. The Aurora Staples Inn is located in historic Stillwater, Minnesota on the beautiful St Croix river.
✉ info@aurorastaplesinn.com ◐ www.aurorastaplesinn.com

STILLWATER————————————————————————————————————

James Mulvey Inn	99-229 $US BB	Full breakfast
622 W Churchill St 55082	7 rooms, 7 pb	Welcome refreshments & tea on
800-820-8008 651-430-8008	*Rated*	weekends
Terry O'Hara	C-ltd/S-no/P-no/H-ltd	Parlor, balconies, bicycles, Jacuzzis, conference room, fireplaces, wireless Internet, picnic basket

This is an enchanting place. Built by a lumberman, James Mulvey in 1878, this Italianate residence graces the most visited historic river town in the upper Midwest.

✉ info@jamesmulveyinn.com 🌐 www.jamesmulveyinn.com

Lady Goodwood	109-189 $US BB	Delicious four-course breakfast
704 S 1st St 55082	3 rooms, 3 pb	Business services, whirlpool tubs, in-room CD players, fireplace
866-688-LADY(5239) 651-439-3771	Visa, MC	
	C-ltd/S-no/P-no/H-no	
Ron & Cynthia Hannig		

Treat yourself to a restful, romantic stay at Lady Goodwood Bed and Breakfast, located just three blocks from beautiful and historic, downtown Stillwater, Minnesota.

✉ info@ladygoodwood.com 🌐 www.ladygoodwood.com

The Rivertown Inn	175-350 $US BB	Full breakfast
306 W Olive St 55082	9 rooms, 9 pb	Complimentary wine & hors
651-430-2955	Most CC, Cash, Checks,	d'oeuvres served during our nightly
Mary Dieter	*Rated*	social hour from 5:00–6:00pm
	C-ltd/S-no/P-no/H-no	Fireplace, whirlpool baths, Bose Wave Radio/CD, Molton Brown products, robes, beautiful gardens

Built in 1882, this lovingly restored lumber baron mansion features guest quarters that include a private bath with a double whirlpool tub, gas fireplace, and sumptuous decor that pays homage to a great poet or literary figure of the 19th century.

✉ rivertown@rivertowninn.com 🌐 www.rivertowninn.com

Water Street Inn	129-249 $US BB	Full breakfast
101 S Water St 55082	41 rooms, 41 pb	Lavish Sunday Brunch
651-439-6000	Most CC, Cash	Whirlpools, gas fireplaces, balconies
Chuck Doughery	C-yes/S-ltd/P-no/H-yes	

Intimate Victorian charm with historic elegance overlooking the scenic St. Croix River in beautiful downtown Stillwater. Suites, whirlpool baths, balconies and river views. Fine dining and banquets.

✉ info@waterstreetinn.us 🌐 www.waterstreetinn.us

WINONA——

Windom Park	120-195 $US BB	Full breakfast
369 W Broadway 55987	6 rooms, 6 pb	Evening wine & cheese
866-737-1719 507-457-9515	Visa, MC, *Rated*	Fireplaces, Jacuzzis, suites, cable
Craig & Karen Groth	C-ltd/S-ltd/P-no/H-no	TV, business facilities, free wireless
	Polish	Internet

Enjoy the quiet charm of our 1900 Colonial Revival home with classic details, warm woods, and large fireplaces. Come share our home and our dream and get away from today's hectic pace and experience a bit of yesterday's calm and take home a memory.

✉ ckgroth@hbci.com 🌐 www.windompark.com

Mississippi

EUPORA

Dogwood Cottage B&B 35 N Gold St 39744 662-744-0098 (cell) 662-258-4810 Carol Freels	99-149 $US BB 4 rooms, 4 pb Visa, MC, Disc C-yes/S-ltd/P-ltd/H-no	Full breakfast Weddings and special events welcome, bathrobes, hair dryer, iron and board, and toiletries.

A beautiful and charming inn, Dogwood Cottage and Innkeeper Carol are waiting to offer the comfort of home, right down the road from MSU and the historic Natchez Trace Parkway. Come and relax at the Dogwood Cottages, your home away from home.

✉ carol@dogwoodcottagebb.com 🌐 www.dogwoodcottagebb.com

JACKSON

Fairview Inn 734 Fairview St 39202 888-948-1908 601-948-3429 Peter & Tamar Sharp	139-314 $US BB 18 rooms, 18 pb Most CC, Cash, Checks, *Rated*, • C-yes/S-no/P-no/H-ltd Spanish	Full Southern Breakfast 24 hr guest kitchen stocked w/ beverages and snacks, personal fridge, French Country restaurant WiFi, spa, weddings, class/seminars, sitting room, library, meeting facilities, cab & room service

The Fairview Inn & Sophia's Restaurant welcomes you to enjoy its stately elegance. A unique Bed & Breakfast experience awaits you in our 1908 Colonial Revival mansion, one of the few architecturally designed homes of that period remaining.

✉ fairview@fairviewinn.com 🌐 www.fairviewinn.com

NATCHEZ

Bisland House Bed and Breakfast 404 S. Commerce St. 39120 504-913-7498 601-304-5806 Byron & Christine Tims	99-150 $US BB 3 rooms, 3 pb Most CC, Cash C-yes/S-ltd/P-no/H-no	Full breakfast Direct TV, private bath, wireless Internet access, blow dryer, iron and board, refreshments available

This Natchez Bed and Breakfast is a Circa 1904 Colonial Revival Historic home located in the Natchez Historic District. The inn is within walking distance to Main St. shopping, antique stores, restaurants, carriage rides, and Mississippi River Bluffs.

✉ bislandhouse@yahoo.com 🌐 www.bislandhouse.com

Choctaw of Natchez 310 North Wall Street 39120 601-446-7905 Michele Cardneaux	150-300 $US BB 6 rooms, 5 pb Most CC, Cash C-ltd/S-ltd/P-no/H-ltd	Full Southern breakfast Complementary glass of wine Full Southern breakfast, free pickup shuttle for Isle of Capri casino boat, in- room iron and spa robe

Built in 1836 for a planter/philanthropist, as a guest of Choctaw you will enjoy peace, quiet and complimentary southern wine just as a nineteenth century Natchez multimillionaire would have!

✉ mcardneaux2000@yahoo.com 🌐 choctawnatchez.com

Devereux Shields House 709 N Union St 39120 888-304-5378 601-304-5378 Ron & Eleanor Fry	129-179 $US BB 6 rooms, 6 pb Most CC, Cash, *Rated*, • C-ltd/S-no/P-yes/H-ltd	Southern Plantation Breakfast Assorted hot & cold refreshments, special diets happily accommodated TV, central heat & A/C, private baths, WiFi, pool

Escape to quiet times, comfort and history at The Devereaux Shields House c1893, a Queen Ann Victorian located in the beautiful Natchez historic district and just a few blocks from town center or stunning views of the Mississippi River.

 comfort@dshieldsusa.com  www.dshieldsusa.com

Bisland House Bed & Breakfast, Natchez, MS

NATCHEZ

Glenfield Plantation	125-175 $US BB	Full Southern Breakfast
6 Glenfield Lane 39120	4 rooms, 3 pb	Complimentary wine
601-442-1002	Visa, MC, •	Sitting room, banquet facilities, secure
Marjorie & Lester Meng	C-yes/S-ltd/P-ltd/H-ltd	parking, wireless DSL Internet, 180
		channel satellite TV

Family owned for 5 generations, circa 1778 Spanish & 1840 English Gothic architecture. On the National Register of Historic Places. Antiques throughout. Located one and a half miles from downtown Natchez.

✉ glenfieldbb@yahoo.com   🌐 www.glenfieldplantation.com

POPLARVILLE

Jerine's Guest Cottage	85-100 $US BB	Continental breakfast
107 Dauphine St 39470	3 rooms, 1 pb	Flat screen TV, WiFi Internet access,
601-795-4927 601-463-2435	Visa, MC, AmEx, •	living room, dining room, full kitchen
Robert & Bettye Applewhite	C-yes/S-ltd/P-no/H-ltd	

A special cottage with 3 bedrooms, large living room, kitchen & spacious yard. Located in a small town, nice shopping & near major malls on the Mississippi Gulf Coast.

✉ apple_ltd@yahoo.com

Missouri

BLUE EYE————————————————————————————————

White River Lodge	159-209 $US BB	Full breakfast
738 Ozark Hollow Rd 65611	5 rooms, 5 pb	During the afternoon there are a
800-544-0257 417-779-1556	Visa, MC	variety of drinks & snacks available
Becky & Bill Babler	C-ltd/S-no/P-no	Great room with fireplace, sun-room,
		patio, theater room, fitness/game
		room, WiFi, sauna, spa

This spacious log B&B near Branson has a spectacular Table Rock Lake view, luxurious amenities, attention to details and hospitality that will delight even the most discriminating guests.

✉ whiteriverlodge@platwls.com 🌐 www.whiteriverlodgebb.com

BRANSON————————————————————————————————

Red Bud Cove B&B Suites	99-154 $US BB	Full breakfast
162 Lakewood Dr 65672	8 rooms, 8 pb	Reunions, sitting rooms, wireless
800-677-5525 417-334-7144	Visa, MC, Disc,	Internet, hot tub, boat dock, picnic
Carol & Rick Carpenter	*Rated*, •	area
	C-ltd/S-no/P-no/H-yes	

Free Night w/Certificate: Valid Sept-May; Sun-Thurs; holidays excluded.

On beautiful Table Rock Lake only 15 minutes from downtown Branson. Spacious lakefront suites, some with spa and fireplace.

✉ stay@redbudcove.com 🌐 www.redbudcove.com

EXCELSIOR SPRINGS————————————————————————

Inn on Crescent Lake	120-250 $US BB	Full breakfast
1261 St. Louis Ave 64024	10 rooms, 10 pb	Bar service available
866-630-5253 816-630-6745	Most CC, Cash, *Rated*	Swimming pool, paddle boats, hot
Beverly Delugeau	S-no/P-no/H-ltd	tub, ponds, fishing, walking path, spa
	French	services, free WiFi

The Inn on Crescent Lake is a 1915 mansion on 22 acres surrounded by two ponds. There are boats, a swimming pool and a walking path. Enjoy a relaxing and romantic getaway in a luxury suite or room.

✉ info@crescentlake.com 🌐 www.crescentlake.com

FULTON————————————————————————————————

Loganberry Inn	129-199 $US BB	Full gourmet breakfast
310 W 7th St 65251	6 rooms, 6 pb	Fireplace baskets, teas, fireside
888-866-6661 573-642-9229	Visa, MC, Disc,	dinners
Carl & Cathy McGeorge	*Rated*, •	Sitting room, library, fireplace, cable
	C-ltd/S-no/P-ltd/H-no	TV/VCR/DVD, Starlit Spa, wedding
		gazebo

A "nationally recognized award-winning Inn," Loganberry Inn (c. 1899) is strolling distance to downtown Fulton & the historic district, featuring brick streets, unique antiques, art & specialty shops, an old-fashioned soda fountain & live jazz clubs.

✉ info@loganberryinn.com 🌐 www.loganberryinn.com

Romancing the Past B&B	109-169 $US BB	Full breakfast
830 Court St 65251	3 rooms, 3 pb	Tea, coffee, soda, brandy and cookies,
573-592-1996	Most CC, Cash, *Rated*	dinner available or a 'High Tea' social
Cate Richard Dodson	C-ltd/S-ltd/P-no/H-ltd	Sitting room, outdoor hot tub, garden,
		suites, fireplaces, cable TV, DVDs,
		WiFi, fax/copier, parking

Welcome to the historic Jameson home, now on the National Historic Register. Our beautiful B&B, a Missouri Top 10 Inn, offers quaint Victorian enchantments, while only being 3 blocks from the charming brick lined streets of our historic downtown district.

 romancingthepast@sbcglobal.net 🌐 www.romancingthepast.com

HANNIBAL

Dubach Inn
221 North Fifth St 63401
573-355-1167
Kristine and Steve Russell

89-149 $US BB
3 rooms, 3 pb
Most CC, Cash, Checks
C-yes/S-no/P-no/H-yes

Full breakfast
Homemade pastries, fruit dishes, juice,
special dietary needs are honored
with advanced notice

This beautiful Victorian Italianate Villa, built in 1871 has been recently renovated with comfort in mind. The eclectic furnishings will make you feel right at home. With our flexibility you are assured to have one of your most memorable B&B stays.

✉ innkeeper@dubachinn.com 🌐 www.dubachinn.com

Garth Woodside Mansion
11069 New London Rd 63401
888-427-8409 573-221-2789
Col (Ret) John & Julie
Rolsen

175-395 $US BB
11 rooms, 11 pb
Visa, MC, *Rated*, •
C-ltd/S-no/P-ltd/H-yes

Full three course breakfast
Cookies, cider, teas, coffee, cocoa, full
bar in the restaurant
600+ movies, tour planning, restaurant,
WiFi, fireplaces, whirlpool tubs,
gardens, meetings, cottage

Garth Mansion = ideal Hannibal, Missouri bed and breakfast that delights itself on matchless comfort and first-class service. Sitting on almost 40 acres and just 1½ hours from St. Louis in Twain country, Garth is for guests who need a cherished getaway

✉ julier@garthmansion.com 🌐 www.garthmansion.com

HERMANN

Captain Wohlt Inn
123 E 3rd St 65041
573-486-3357
Kent Wilkins

75-185 $US BB
12 rooms, 12 pb
Most CC, Cash, *Rated*
C-ltd/S-ltd/P-no/H-ltd

Full breakfast
Everyone loves Kent's welcome
cookies – they're to die for!
Dining room, living room, patio, deck,
garden, whirlpool tubs

The Captain Wohlt Inn, Hermann's premier historic inn, is located in the heart of Hermann's beautiful Historic National Register District, offering old fashioned charm and comfort, as well as modern conveniences.

✉ captainwohltinn@gmail.com 🌐 www.captainwohltbandb.com

**Hermann Hill Vineyard
& Inn**
711 Wein Street 65041
573-486-4455
Peggy & Terry Hammer

198-444 $US BB
20 rooms, 20 pb
Visa, MC, Disc, *Rated*
C-ltd/S-no/P-ltd/H-yes

Full breakfast
Choice of four unique breakfast
entrees served in your room or the
kitchen, dining room, or deck
Movie library, cable, Jacuzzis,
fireplaces, WiFi, towel warmers, DVD,
VCR, CD players, some hot tubs

Sited on a bluff overlooking the town, vineyard and river; upscale decor enhanced with antiques; lavishly appointed guestrooms; private and quiet. Riverbluff cottages with upscale amenities including hot tubs, 6' Jacuzzis, steam showers and gas grills.

✉ info@hermannhill.com 🌐 www.hermannhill.com

Nestle Inn
215 W 2nd St 65041
573-486-1111
Donna Nestle

135-188 $US BB
3 rooms, 3 pb
Visa, MC, AmEx,
Rated, •
C-yes/S-no/P-no/H-no

Full breakfast
Snacks
River view, sitting room, kings,
Jacuzzis, suites, fireplaces, cable TV,
accommodate business travel

Nestled cozily atop a bluff overlooking the scenic Missouri River, the Nestle Inn is the perfect getaway for romance and relaxation.

✉ harborhaus@yahoo.com 🌐 www.nestleinn.com

Stone Haus B&B
107 Bayer Rd 65041
573-486-9169
Linda & Larry Miskel

110-140 $US BB
4 rooms, 4 pb
Most CC, Cash, Checks
C-ltd/S-ltd/P-no/H-no

Full breakfast
Evening snacks, complimentary soft
drinks
Sitting rooms, fireplace, cable TV, pick-
up from train station

Located in historic Hermann & nestled in the rolling hills of Missouri wine country, the Stone Haus Bed & Breakfast was once a winery built in 1862. You will appreciate our home cooking, welcoming hospitality and beautiful surroundings.

✉ linar@ktis.net 🌐 stonehausbandb.com

HERMANN

Wine Valley Inn
403 Market St 65041
573-486-0706
Sonya Birk & Jeanie Schultz

107-235 $US BB
14 rooms, 14 pb
Most CC, Cash, Checks,
Rated
C-yes/S-no/P-no/H-no

Full breakfast
Conference Room, Wine & Gift
Shop located on site, Jacuzzis, WiFi,
kitchenette, conference room

At the very center of historic Hermann Missouri, Wine Valley Inn, in the historic Begemann & Kimmel Buildings, offers beautifully appointed two-and-three room suites. Guests enjoy all the charm of yesteryear with all the comfort and convenience of today.

✉ winevalleyinn@centurytel.net 🌐 www.wine-valley-inn.com

INDEPENDENCE

Serendipity B&B
116 S Pleasant St 64050
800-203-4299 816-833-4719
Susan Walter

95 $US BB
5 rooms, 5 pb
Most CC
C-yes/S-no/P-yes/H-no

Full breakfast
Cereal, sweet roll, juice, coffee or tea
is available
Library, suites, Beautiful gardens, TV

Step back in time and enjoy the true romance of the Victorian era in our 1887 house, with total Victorian decor. Couples, families, children and pets welcome.

🌐 www.serendipitybedandbreakfast.com

JACKSON

TLC Wellness B&B
203 Bellevue St 63755
573-243-7427
Gus & Trisha Wischmann

55-95 $US BB
4 rooms, 4 pb
Visa, MC, Disc
C-ltd/S-ltd/P-no/H-ltd

Full breakfast
Tea room
Gift shop, parlor, sitting room, TV,
telephones, corporate rates, bay
windows, family heirlooms

Experience our type of hospitality – warm, relaxed and at home. Even though our 1905 Victorian house features turn-of-the-century quality, we think you will find our modern amenities comfortable.

✉ trybnb@yahoo.com 🌐 www.tlcbnb.com

KANSAS CITY

**Southmoreland on the
Plaza**
116 E 46th St 64112
816-531-7979
Mark Reichle & Nancy Miller
Reichle

109-250 $US BB
13 rooms, 13 pb
Visa, MC, AmEx, •
C-ltd/S-no/P-no/H-ltd
Closed December 24-25

Full breakfast
Complimentary wine & hors
d'oeuvres from 4:30 to 6:00
Living room, solarium, fireplaces,
decks, Jacuzzi, gardens, pond, meeting
facilities

This urban inn sets a new standard for hospitality, comfort and convenience. Twelve guestrooms in the main Inn and a luxury suite in the Carriage House offer private baths some with Jacuzzi tubs, telephones and off street parking.

✉ innkeeper@Southmoreland.com 🌐 www.southmoreland.com

LAKE OZARK

Bass and Baskets
1117 Dogwood Rd 65049
573-964-5028
Ed & Debbie Franko

139-159 $US BB
4 rooms, 4 pb
Visa, MC
S-no/P-no/H-no

Full breakfast
Freshly baked cookies, popcorn, soft
drinks and other snacks are always
available.
All rooms have private baths with
whirlpool tubs, fireplaces, WiFi, decks
overlooking the lake

Come away to "Your Home at the Lake" at Bass and Baskets, where the decor will satisfy the inner fisherman in anyone! At this cozy lakeside B&B you can sit quietly by the water, on the deck reading a book, or try a variety of water sports.

✉ stay@bassandbaskets.com 🌐 www.bassandbaskets.com

The Inn at Harbour Ridge, Osage Beach, MO

LIBERTY

The Stone-Yancey House
421 N. Lightburne 64068
816-415-0066
Carolyn & Steve Hatcher

99-149 $US BB
3 rooms, 3 pb
Visa, MC, Disc
C-ltd/S-no/P-no/H-no

Three-course breakfast
Cookies/sweets, iced tea, lemonade,
fridge with sodas and bottled water,
early morning coffee
Wireless Internet, in-room TVs, DVD
players – DVD library, guest parlor,
small event hosting

Enjoy your stay in one of our 3 lovely rooms, each with private baths, queen or king beds, a sitting area, a work area with high speed wireless Internet, TV's with DVD players, and more!

 stay@stoneyanceyhouse.com 🌐 www.stoneyanceyhouse.com

OSAGE BEACH

The Inn at Harbour Ridge
6334 Red Barn Rd 65065
877-744-6020 573-302-0411
Sue & Ron Westenhaver

119-199 $US BB
5 rooms, 5 pb
Visa, MC, *Rated*
C-ltd/S-ltd/P-ltd/H-no

Sinfully delicious breakfast feast
Snacks & soda. 24/7 Flavia coffee/tea
service. Early morning coffee trays
delivered to your door.
Private hot tubs, fireplaces,
paddleboat & swim dock on quiet
Lake cove.

Escape from the hustle and bustle of your hectic life to our award winning bed and breakfast! Located at the Lake of the Ozarks, we want to treat you to a very special B & B experience!

 info@harbourridgeinn.com 🌐 www.harbourridgeinn.com

ROCHEPORT

Yates House
305 Second St 65279
573-698-2129
Conrad & Dixie Yates

179-299 $US BB
6 rooms, 6 pb
Visa, MC, Disc
C-ltd/S-no/P-no/H-no

Full Gourmet Breakfast
Dinner by reservation, fresh cookies
made daily, coffee & tea available 24
hours, catering services
Gardens, locked bicycle parking,
gazebo, sun room, jetted tubs, cooking
classes, wireless Internet

Yates House Bed and Breakfast offers luxurious lodging in Rocheport. Known for fine food, service, and lodging. One block from the Katy Trail along the Missouri River. Excellent local restaurants and shops. One of America's Top Ten coolest small towns.

 yateshouse@socket.net 🌐 www.yateshouse.com

SPRINGFIELD

Virginia Rose	75-125 $US BB	Full breakfast
317 E Glenwood St 65807	4 rooms, 4 pb	In-room breakfast available
800-345-1412 417-883-0693	Visa, MC, Disc,	Sitting room, business traveler
Jackie & Virginia Buck	*Rated*, •	accommodations, large parking area,
	C-ltd/S-no/P-no/H-ltd	airport pick-up service

Lovely country-Victorian hideaway, on tree-covered acre right in town. Private yet close to walking trail, antique and mall shopping and restaurants.

ST. CHARLES

Boone's Lick Trail Inn	115-305 $US BB	Full breakfast
1000 S Main St 63301	7 rooms, 7 pb	In-room beverage service
888-940-0002 636-947-7000	Most CC, *Rated*, •	Hiking, biking, sitting room,
Venetia McEntire	C-yes/S-no/P-yes/H-ltd	conference, folk art, fragrant flower
		gardens, brick patio & porch

Relive the pioneer spirit, enjoy fine lodging along the Lewis and Clark Trail. Experience a feel of Colonial life in Saint Charles, learn about our early pioneers Daniel Boone and Lewis & Clark. Relax amidst flower gardens just steps away from history . . .

 innkeeper@booneslick.com 🌐 www.booneslick.com

Raines Victorian Inn	120-150 $US BB	Full gourmet breakfast
1717 Elm St 63301	3 rooms, 3 pb	A small refrigerator with
636-947-4843	Most CC, Cash	complimentary beverages in your
Ruth Raines Williams	C-ltd/S-no/P-no/H-ltd	room along with snacks.
		Library, perennial gardens & gazebo,
		parlor, period furnishings, whirlpool
		tubs, WiFi access

This elegant Victorian, Queen Anne style, bed and breakfast inn, built in 1904, is the perfect location for an extra special stay. Located just minutes from historic Main Street, shopping, the riverboat casino, and the Katy Trail. ✉ rainesvictorianinn@charter.net 🌐 rainesvictorianinn.com

ST. LOUIS

Fleur-de-Lys Mansion –	150-295 $US BB	Full gourmet breakfast
Luxury Inn at the Park	4 rooms, 4 pb	Coffee, tea, soft drinks, bottled water,
3500 Russell Blvd 63104	Most CC, Cash, Checks,	snacks, complimentary liqueurs,
888-693-3500 314-773-3500	*Rated*	chocolates, cookies
Jan & David Seifert	S-no/P-no/H-no	Jacuzzis, hot tub, fireplaces, meeting
		room, spa services, romantic dinners,
		carriage rides

Honored by TripAdvisor as the #7 Best B&B in the World for 2010, recognized for intimate warmth, luxury and exceptional hospitality; business-friendly. Conveniently located in Historic Compton Hts, 5 minutes from downtown St. Louis;15 minutes from Clayton

 seifert@thefleurdelys.com 🌐 www.thefleurdelys.com

Lehmann House B&B	100-125 $US BB	Full breakfast
#10 Benton Place 63104	5 rooms, 5 pb	Available for weddings, reunions &
314-422-1483	Visa, MC, AmEx	events
Marie Davies	C-yes/S-no/P-no/H-no	

Exquisite historic B&B furnished with antiques located near fine restaurants, museums and more. Formal dining room serving guests a hearty breakfast every morning.

 marie@lehmannhouse.com 🌐 www.lehmannhouse.com

Lodge at Grant's Trail by	90-259 $US BB	Full breakfast weekends
Orlando	9 rooms, 9 pb	Full breakfast on weekends, wine &
4398 Hoffmeister 63125	Visa, MC, Disc, •	cheese at check-in. Chocolate Chip
866-314-STAY 314-638-3340	C-yes/S-no/P-no/H-yes	cookies for bedtime.
Sam & Jan Orlando		Sitting room, suites, fireplaces, satellite
		TV, accommodate business travelers.
		Wireless Internet.

Ten year-old rustic log cabin with 6 uniquely decorated rooms and 2 suites with tubs for two. Suites and some rooms have walk-out balconies. All bedrooms & common areas have fireplaces. Nature trail and interstate accessibility.

 info@lodgeatgrantstrail.com 🌐 www.lodgeatgrantstrail.com

ST. LOUIS

Napoleon's Retreat B&B
1815 Lafayette Ave 63104
314-772-6979
J. Archuleta & M. Lance

105-175 $US BB
5 rooms, 5 pb
Most CC, Cash, Checks,
Rated
C-ltd/S-no/P-no/H-no

Full breakfast
Homemade cookies, tea, soft drinks
Sitting room, courtyard, Jacuzzis,
cable TV, free WiFi, in-room
refrigerators, phones

"One of the ten best urban inns in the nation!" USA Today. In historic Lafayette Square, one mile from downtown. Walk to nine award winning restaurants for dinner, including Bailey's Chocolate Bar. Full Breakfast. Free wireless. ✉ napoleonsretreat@aol.com 🌐 www.napoleonsretreat.com

Park Avenue Mansion
2007 Park Ave 63104
314-588-9004 314-588-9004
Kathy Marks-Petetit & Mike
Petetit

105-285 $US BB
5 rooms, 5 pb
Most CC, Cash, *Rated*
C-ltd/S-no/P-no/H-no

Full gourmet breakfast
Coffee, tea, hot chocolate, soft
drinks, refrigerated water, snacks,
complimentary cognac & brandy
Free WiFi, Jacuzzis, fireplaces, sitting/
meeting room, spa services, romantic
dinners, carriage ride

Award Winning. Luxurious. Comfortable. Historic. Walk into another century filled with elegance, charm & old world graciousness. Our trademark is excellence & superb service. Whether a business or leisure traveler, you won't want to leave us.
✉ info@parkavenuemansion.com 🌐 www.parkavenuemansion.com

STE. GENEVIEVE

**The Inn St. Gemme
Beauvais**
78 N Main St 63670
800-818-5744 573-883-5744
Janet Joggerst

99-189 $US BB
9 rooms, 9 pb
Most CC, Cash, Checks,
Rated
C-yes/S-no/P-no/H-ltd

Full four course breakfast
Tea with dessert, hors d'oeuvres with
wine
Special packages available, whirlpool
tubs, fireplaces, gardens, TV/DVD,
WiFi

Non-intrusive hospitality. All suites with private baths. Individual breakfast tables, waitress service, 8 entree choices! Janet Joggerst, the innkeeper at The Inn St. Gemme Beauvais, serves up a delicious and extremely satisfying breakfast. ✉ innstgemme@sbcglobal.net 🌐 www.stgem.com

TRENTON

Hyde Mansion B&B
418 E 7th St 64683
660-359-1800 (Cell) 660-359-
3300
Caroline

55-98 $US BB
6 rooms, 6 pb
Visa, MC, *Rated*
C-ltd/S-ltd/P-no/H-no

Continental breakfast
Complimentary beverages & snacks
Sitting room, library, baby grand
piano, patio, screened porch, close to
Amish community

Inviting hideaway in rural America, 1949 mansion refurbished for your convenience. Popular with visiting executives, known for its unique rooms and friendly atmosphere.
✉ hydemansion@cebridge.net 🌐 www.virtualcities.com/ons/mo/t/motb501.htm

WARRENSBURG

Cedarcroft Farm & Cottage
431 SE County Rd Y 64093
888-655-9830 660-747-5728
Sandra & Bill Wayne

199-249 $US BB
1 rooms, 1 pb
Visa, MC, Disc, *Rated*
S-ltd/P-no/H-no

Full breakfast
Complimentary evening snack, with
cookies, chocolates, soft drinks, fruit,
more
Cottage, jetted tub, fireplace, dual-
nozzle shower, dish LCD TV, DVD,
WiFi, porch, meadow & trails.

The Cottage on the Knoll at Cedarcroft Farm has all romantic amenities in a secluded meadow. Thermal jetted tub, fireplace, king bed, wireless Internet, breakfast delivered to your door, complete privacy on 80-acre farm! ✉ romance@cedarcroft.com 🌐 www.cedarcroft.com

Gelbach Manor
300 S Holden St 64093
660-747-5085
Douglas & Rhonda Gelbach

90-160 $US BB
4 rooms, 1 pb
Most CC, Checks
C-ltd/P-no

Full breakfast
Pool-side full breakfast when weather
permits.
Marble jetted hot tub, swimming pool,
pergola, patio

Welcome to Warrensburg's newest Bed and Breakfast Inn, Gelbach Manor. Here, you are in easy walking distance from University of Central Missouri, historic downtown Warrensburg, the AMTRAK depot and the Old Drum statue.
✉ rgelbach@embarqmail.com 🌐 www.gelbachmanor.com

Montana

ANACONDA

Hickory House Inn
218 E Park 59711
866-563-5481 406-563-5481
MaryJane Rayfield

80-130 $US BB
5 rooms, 5 pb
Visa, MC, Disc
C-yes/S-ltd/P-ltd/H-yes

Full breakfast
We can accommodate dietary
restrictions, evening tea available
Use of living room, reading area,
sunny porches, spa, gardens

Hickory House Inn prides itself on making sure our guests are comfortable and relaxed. Our rooms are quiet, well appointed and clean. MaryJane's breakfasts are "legend." Two bedroom suite's for families.

✉ hickoryhouseinn@msn.com   🌐 hickoryhouseinn.com

BOZEMAN

Gallatin River Lodge
9105 Thorpe Rd 59718
888-387-0148 406-388-0148
Steve Gamble

150-400 $US BB
6 rooms, 6 pb
Visa, MC, AmEx,
Rated, •
C-yes/S-ltd/P-yes/H-yes

Full Breakfast
Fine dining restaurant for lunch or
dinner, full bar, Wine Spectator Award
wine list
Fly fishing guide service, massage,
conference and wedding services, spa
nearby, library, trout pond

A fine country inn near Bozeman, MT, offering Jacuzzi suites, fine dining and fly fishing guide services, on a secluded ranch near the Gallatin River. Near Yellowstone National Park and Grand Teton Park, close to Big Sky Resort. Select Registry member.

✉ info@grlodge.com   🌐 www.grlodge.com

**Howlers Inn & Wolf
Sanctuary**
3185 Jackson Creek Rd 59715
888-HOWLERS 406-587-5229
Mary-Martha & Chris Bahn

105-195 $US BB
4 rooms, 4 pb
Visa, MC, AmEx,
Rated
C-yes/S-no/P-no/H-no

Full breakfast
Sitting room, Jacuzzi, fireplace, sauna,
game room, exercise facilities, home
theater, pool table

North America's only B&B and wolf sanctuary set on 42 acres in a beautiful alpine canyon. Dramatic log and stone home – each bedroom with full private bath and sweeping mountain views.

✉ howlersinn@Earthlink.net   🌐 www.howlersinn.com

Lehrkind Mansion
719 N Wallace Ave 59715
800-992-6932 406-585-6932
Christopher Nixon, Jon
Gerster

109-229 $US BB
8 rooms, 8 pb
Most CC, Cash, Checks,
Rated, •
C-ltd/S-no/P-ltd/H-no
German

Full breakfast
Tea served whenever you wish
Sitting room, library, large yard,
mountain views, fax, piano, hot tub

An elegant, Queen Anne Victorian mansion furnished in 1890s antiques. Tea served in our music parlor accompanied by the 7 foot tall 1897 Regina music box!

✉ contact@bozemanbedandbreakfast.com   🌐 www.bozemanbedandbreakfast.com

BUTTE

Toad Hall Manor B&B
1 Green Ln 59701
866-443-TOAD 406-494-2625
Jane and Glenn Johnson

115-175 $US BB
4 rooms, 4 pb
Most CC, •
C-ltd/S-ltd/P-no/H-yes
Japanese; a little of
several languages

Full gourmet breakfast
A tray with scones & beverage of
choice delivered to room prior to
breakfast
Wireless Internet, complimentary off-
site gym facility, massage, concierge

An elegant European-style B&B, which takes its name from the children's classic, The Wind In The Willows. All four rooms share views of the Rocky Mountains, the 16th fairway of the Country Club or a private courtyard. We are Montana's premier B&B!

✉ info@toadhallmanor.com   🌐 www.toadhallmanor.com

COLUMBIA FALLS

Bad Rock B&B
480 Bad Rock Dr 59912
888-892-2829 406-892-2829
Serena & Mark Jackson

125-225 $US BB
8 rooms, 8 pb
Most CC, Cash, Checks,
Rated, •
C-yes/S-no/P-no/H-yes

Full breakfast
Complimentary wine & snacks
Exercise room, Internet, small groups,
game room, laundry facilities, gas grill,
ski equipment

Nestled among towering pines, Bad Rock, a Montana Bed and Breakfast Inn, embraces ten private acres of rolling fields and evergreen groves twenty minutes from Glacier National Park, one of Mother Nature's great extravaganzas.

✉ stay@badrock.com ❸ www.badrock.com

EMIGRANT

Paradise Gateway B&B
Guest Log Cabins
2644 Hwy 89 S 59027
800-541-4113 406-333-4063
Pete & Carol Reed

85-350 $US BB
10 rooms, 10 pb
Visa, MC, •
C-ltd/S-ltd/P-ltd/H-ltd
Norwegian

Full breakfast
Afternoon tea & snacks
Sitting room, library, cable TV,
accommodations for business
travelers

Nestled in Paradise Valley, next to the North entrance to Yellowstone Park. Rimmed by majestic mountains, and the Yellowstone River is your front yard.

✉ paradisebandb@wispwest.net ❸ paradisegateway.com

HAMILTON

Deer Crossing B&B
396 Hayes Creek Rd 59840
800-763-2232 406-363-2232
Linda & Stu Dobbins

100-149 $US BB
6 rooms, 6 pb
Visa, MC, AmEx,
Rated, •
C-yes/S-no/P-yes/H-no

Full country breakfast
Fishing guide, shuttle, horseback
riding, two creekside cabins, Dish TV,
WiFi

Experience Old West charm and hospitality. 25 acres of tall pines and lush pastures. Incredible views. Hearty ranch breakfast served in our sunroom.

✉ info@deercrossingmontana.com ❸ www.deercrossingmontana.com

HELENA

The Sanders – Helena's
B&B
328 N. Ewing 59601
406-442-3309
Bobbi Uecker & Rock
Ringling

125-150 $US BB
7 rooms, 7 pb
Most CC, Cash, Checks,
Rated
C-yes/S-no/P-no/H-ltd

Full breakfast
Afternoon cookies, tea, coffee, ice tea,
lemonade, dry sherry
concierge services, wireless Internet,
tv, public radio, piano, library, great
views and MT hospitality

The Sanders offers elegant accommodations in a mansion that dates back to 1875 and is located in the heart of historic Helena.

✉ thefolks@sandersbb.com ❸ www.sandersbb.com

The Sleepy Senator
403 N Hoback St 59601
406-442-2046
Robert N. Clarkson

135-250 $US EP
2 rooms, 1 pb
Most CC, Cash
C-yes/S-no/P-ltd/H-no
Some Spanish

Breakfast, lunch, dinner, available.
Snacks
Entertainment center, computer with
Internet, DVD/VHS, local information,
sauna

Guests are saying: "Excellent!" "Comfortable digs!" "Love the sauna!" The Sleepy Senator Tourist House, just 3 blocks from the State Capitol, is a fully furnished 2 bedroom/3 bed, private townhouse with 'free' hot breakfast, snacks, & off-street parking.

✉ sleepysenator@mt.net ❸ www.clarksonstudio.com/sleepy/index.htm

Walker Creek Retreat
7871 Clausen Road 59601
406-449-2552
Darlene Kechely

115-260 $US BB
5 rooms, 6 pb
Visa, MC
C-ltd/S-no/P-no/H-no

Full breakfast
Freshly brewing coffee & smells of
gourmet cuisine as we prepare a
satisfying breakfast
Rec Room with a pool table, workout
equipment & theatre seating to enjoy
our big screen TV

Whether you are a corporation seeking a majestic meeting place, a family needing to get away from it all, a couple who desires an intimate wedding venue of unspeakable beauty, or any other reason to seek out awestruck wonder, you have found perfection.

✉ info@wcrmt.com ❸ wcrmt.com/index.php

KALISPELL

| **Lonesome Dove Guest Ranch**
1805 Haywire Gulch 59904
800-949-4169 406-756-3056
Sharron Butler | 65-125 $US BB
2 rooms
Most CC, Cash, Checks
C-ltd/S-ltd/P-ltd/H-ltd | Full breakfast
Dinner & entertainment most nights, as well as Sunday Brunch |

Have you ever experienced riding through the abundant wildlife of the Wild Horse Mountains, awakened to the aroma of bacon sizzling over a campfire, heard cowboy poetry under the stars? Lonesome Dove Ranch offers all of these adventures, and more!

✉ sharron@centurytel.net 🌐 www.lonesomedoveguestranch.com

| **The Master Suite**
354 Browns Rd 59901
406-752-8512
Donna McKiernan | 155-235 $US BB
1 rooms, 1 pb
Visa, MC, •
C-ltd/S-ltd/P-yes/H-ltd | Full breakfast
Complimentary afternoon cocktails, hors d'oeuvres upon check in
Special events up to 50, concierge, bicycles, pets allowed in luxury kennel, wireless Internet |

The Master Suite is a private luxury accommodation for two, with million dollar views. Located on 15 acres in the gentle rolling hills overlooking the Flathead Valley in Kalispell, Montana.

✉ donnamck@usamontana.com 🌐 www.mastersuitebedandbreakfast.com

MISSOULA

| **Blue Mountain B&B**
6980 Deadman Gulch Rd 59804
877-251-4457 406-251-4457
Brady Anderson-Wood | 105-155 $US BB
5 rooms, 5 pb
Visa, MC, AmEx, •
C-yes/S-ltd/P-ltd/H-no | Full breakfast
Complimentary beverages & snacks, group dinners, picnic to go, murder mystery dinners
Garden, jetted tubs, views, wildlife, patio, piano, library, koi pond, WiFi, event facilities |

Blue Mountain B&B is nestled on the mountainside among majestic Ponderosa Pines and meditative water gardens, creating a uniquely tranquil experience just minutes away from Missoula's business, sporting and cultural centers.

✉ stay@bluemountainbb.com 🌐 www.missoula-bed-breakfast.com

| **Gibson Mansion**
823 39th Street 59803
866-251-1345 406-251-1345
Tom & Nancy Malikie | 120-155 $US BB
4 rooms, 4 pb
Visa, MC, AmEx
C-yes/S-ltd/P-ltd/H-ltd | Full Gourmet Breakfast
Afternoon snacks, coffee & tea tray with fresh baked scones brought right to your room
Parlor, library, porch, hammock, flower gardens & grounds |

Historic Mansion fully restored with stained glass and hardwood floors. Iron beds with down comforters. Beautiful grounds with flower gardens, an ideal location for weddings and receptions.

✉ info@gibsonmansion.com 🌐 www.gibsonmansion.com

RED LODGE

| **Inn on the Beartooth**
6648 Hwy 212 S 59068
888-222-7686 406-446-1768
Debbie & Ron Van Horn | 100-190 $US BB
6 rooms, 6 pb
Visa, MC
C-yes/S-no/P-no/H-no | Full Country Style Breakfast
Hot tubs, private deck, great room, wood-burning stone fireplace |

Your Ideal Mountain Getaway, the Inn On The Beartooth is a newly built log lodge located at the base of the Beartooth Mountains. Rustic charm with all the modern conveniences.

✉ dnsenterprizes@yahoo.com 🌐 www.bbgetaways.com/innonthebeartooth

STEVENSVILLE

| **Bitterroot River B&B**
501 South Ave 59870
406-777-5205
Tim & Shelley Hunter | 99-129 $US BB
4 rooms, 4 pb
Most CC, Cash
C-ltd/S-yes/P-no/H-ltd | Full breakfast
Fresh fruit, delicious egg casseroles, French toast made with banana bread, fresh coffee & teas
A/C, Internet, Jacuzzi, massage therapy, fireplace, satellite TV, CD player & CD's |

We offer a tranquil country-style setting on river front property, combined with the convenience of being located in a small town. ✉ timothymhunter@msn.com 🌐 www.bitterrootriverbb.com

SUPERIOR————————————————————————————————

Forest Grove Lodge
1107 Mullan Rd E 59872
406-822-6637
Wil & Kelly Mitchell

110-155 $US BB
5 rooms, 5 pb
Visa, MC
C-ltd/S-ltd/P-no/H-no

Full breakfast
Dinner available ($30 per person, with
advanced notice), snacks
Great room, wet bar, covered deck

Nestled near the river in the Lolo National Forest, Forest Grove Lodge is surrounded by peaceful serenity. The Lodge offers five spacious bedrooms with private baths. Come, relax and enjoy a true Montana experience.

info@forestgrovelodge.com   www.forestgrovelodge.com

WHITEFISH————————————————————————————————

Good Medicine Lodge
537 Wisconsin Ave 59937
800-860-5488 406-862-5488
Betsy & Woody Cox

99-250 $US BB
9 rooms, 9 pb
Most CC, Cash, Checks,
Rated
C-yes/S-no/P-no/H-yes
French

Gourmet full breakfast
Homemade, Montana-size cookies
are served with tea, coffee & hot
chocolate on our guest bar
Hot tub, guest laundry, library, TV,
DVD & VHS, common areas, wireless
Internet, ski boot dryer

A classic Montana bed and breakfast with 3 suites and 6 guestrooms. Built of solid cedar, there are balconies with stunning views, crackling fireplaces, an outdoor spa, full breakfasts, a guest laundry and loads of western hospitality.

info@goodmedicinelodge.com   www.goodmedicinelodge.com

Nebraska

The Gandy House   60 $US BB   Continental breakfast
715 5th St 68376   3 rooms
402-862-3278   Visa, MC, Disc
Duaine & Sandy Stalder   C-yes/S-no

Located one block north of Humboldt's Historic City Square. You can relax in the large sun room, on the front porch, by the stone fireplace in the living room, or read a book in the parlor.

 gandyhouse@neb.rr.com   www.gandyhouse.com

Atwood House B&B   85-199 $US BB   Full breakfast
740 S 17th St 68508   4 rooms, 4 pb   Snacks, complimentary soft drinks
800-884-6554 402-438-4567 Most CC, Cash, Checks, Sitting room, library, Jacuzzis, suites,
Ruth & Larry Stoll   *Rated*   fireplace, cable TV
                            C-ltd/S-no/P-no/H-no

Experience the elegance of this 7,500+ sq ft 1894 Neoclassical Georgian Revival mansion. Three suites with 2-person whirlpool (2 with fireplaces), flowers, Victorian furnishings & gourmet breakfasts. Ideal for romantic getaways or business travelers.

 Larry@atwoodhouse.com   www.atwoodhouse.com

Whispering Pines B&B   110-124 $US BB   Full breakfast
2018 6th Ave 68410   5 rooms, 5 pb   All meals are accompanied by
402-873-5850   Most CC, Cash, Checks   seasonal fresh fruit, homemade
Jeanna Stavas   C-ltd/P-ltd   pastries, fruit juices and coffee
                                                    Verandah, porch swing, guest den,
                                                    parlor, outdoor hot tub, garden, cable
                                                    TV, DVD library

The 130 year old home offers modern comforts amongst its many antiques and old Victorian atmosphere. It sits on six and a half acres, is surrounded by 100 year old pine trees, lovely flower gardens, and a water garden with fountains.

jeanna@bbwhisperingpines.com   www.bbwhisperingpines.com

Nevada

CARSON CITY

Bliss Bungalow
408 West Robinson
Street 89703
775-883-6129
Joyce Harrington & Ron
Smith

89-145 $US BB
5 rooms, 5 pb
Most CC, Cash,
Checks, •
C-yes/S-no/P-ltd/H-yes

Self Serve Breakfast Items any hour
WiFi

The Bungalow is Carson City's alternative to casinos and franchise motels the Bungalow is cozy, charming and perfect for the discerning traveler and business person.

✉ innkeeper@blissbungalow.com 🌐 www.blissbungalow.com

Deer Run Ranch B&B
5440 Eastlake Blvd 89704
800-378-5440 775-882-3643
David & Muffy Vhay

99-149 $US BB
2 rooms, 2 pb
Most CC, *Rated*
C-yes/S-no/P-no/H-ltd

Full breakfast
Welcome basket of fruit, wine and
snacks
Snacks, refrigerator, sitting room,
library, TV, VCR, private entry,
wireless broadband, pool.

Western ambience in a unique architect-designed & built ranch house between Reno & Carson City overlooking Washoe Lake.

GENOA

The White House
2274 Genoa Lane 89411
775-783-7208
Phil Stoll

175-225 $US BB
2 rooms, 2 pb
Visa, MC
S-no/P-ltd/H-no

Full breakfast
AC in rooms, fireplace, Internet, TV/
Cable, bike friendly, breakfast, small
pets for just $100 more.

The White House Bed and Breakfast can be found on the eastern side of the Sierra Nevada and nestled in the small town of Genoa. This bed and breakfast is filled with historical charm and located only 20 minutes from Lake Tahoe's world-class skiing.

✉ thewhitehousebandb@yahoo.com 🌐 www.whitehousebandb.net

RENO

Wildflower Village
4275 – 4395 W 4th St 89523
775-747-8848
Pat Campbell

100-125 $US BB
10 rooms, 10 pb
Visa, MC
C-ltd/S-yes/P-no/H-no

Gourmet Champagne Breakfast
Coffee shop for free wireless,
computer/printer, espressos, latte's
teas, bagels muffins and treats.
Ensuite rooms with cooking facilities,
gardens, porches, fireplaces, park at
your room, meetings

Truly a unique village, w/ B&B, plus Artist Studios, Hostels, Apts, Wedding Chapel, Art Galleries, Art Classes & Retreats, Coffee Shop w/Computer, wireless,, printer, & Peets Coffee located on 6+ acres in a country setting . . . just 2 miles from downtown Reno.

✉ patcampbellassoc@sbcglobal.net 🌐 www.wildflowervillage.com

UNIONVILLE

Old Pioneer Garden
2805 Unionville Rd 89418
775-538-7585
David & "Mitzi" Jones

85-95 $US BB
11 rooms, 9 pb
Rated, •
C-yes/S-no/P-yes/H-yes

Full breakfast
Dinner is available for $9.50
Available for wedding or conference,
pool table, gazebo, fireplaces

The Old Pioneer Garden Country Inn is an oasis of Northern Nevada's high desert, dating back to 1861. The inn was built the same year that silver prospectors toured the area & established Unionville. AAA-rated.

✉ oldpioneergarden@att.net

VIRGINIA CITY

B Street House Bed and Breakfast
58 N. B St 89440
775-847-7231
Chris & Carolyn Eichin

99-139 $US BB
3 rooms, 3 pb
Visa, MC
C-ltd/S-no/P-no/H-no
Swiss German, German
Closed winter; call us

Full gourmet breakfast
Afternoon tea with cookies, chocolates, snacks, coffee, tea & cocoa in the parlor.
Deluxe rooms with tub/shower, TV/DVD, free WiFi; mini-fridge, library, gardens, parlor, parking

The B Street House B&B, Virginia City, offers the Elegance of the Old West. Three upstairs guestrooms, full gourmet breakfast, library, gardens, off-street parking, free WiFi , luxury amenities, teatime, & fresh flowers. Near Reno, Carson City, Lake Tahoe

✉ innkeepers@BStreetHouse.com 🌐 www.BStreetHouse.com

New Hampshire

ALBANY

The Darby Field Inn
185 Chase Hill Rd 03818
800-426-4147 603-447-2181
Marc & Maria Donaldson

140-290 $US BB
13 rooms, 13 pb
Visa, MC, AmEx,
Rated, •
C-ltd/S-no/P-no/H-no
Spanish

Full country breakfast
Classic menu and wine list, available
in our mountain view dining room or
in our cozy tavern.
on site-massage, seasonal swimming
pool, hiking, flower gardens,
snowshoeing, sleigh rides, and more

Just 6 miles from North Conway, nestled in the White Mountains. Amenities: spa services, sleigh/carriage rides, award winning gardens, delicious food & friendly people. Local attractions include tax free shopping, Mt. Washington, Kancamaugus Highway.

✉ marc@darbyfield.com 🌐 www.darbyfield.com

ASHLAND

Glynn House Inn
59 Highland St 03217
866-686-4362 603-968-3775
Pamela, Ingrid & Glenn
Heidenreich

149-299 $US BB
13 rooms, 13 pb
Visa, MC, *Rated*, •
C-yes/S-no/P-yes/H-no
German

Full gourmet breakfast
afternoon refreshments, wine & hors
d'oeuvres
4 pet friendly rooms, A/C,
personalized concierge services, WiFi,
fireplaces, dbl. whirlpool baths

"NH's Finest Small Inn" – situated in the heart of the Lakes & Mountains – provides the perfect setting for relaxation, romance & recreation. Guests enjoy scrumptious food and uncompromising service. 4 pet friendly rooms.

✉ innkeeper@glynnhouse.com 🌐 www.glynnhouse.com

BARTLETT

Bartlett Inn
1477 US Rte 302 03812
800-292-2353 603 374 2353
Miriam & Nick Jaques

89-279 $US BB
16 rooms, 16 pb
Most CC, Cash,
Rated, •
C-yes/S-no/P-ltd/H-no
Some Spanish and
French

Full breakfast
Kitchenettes
Kitchenettes, fireplaces, spa tubs,
cottages, family & pet friendly, heated
pool, outdoor hot tub

Discover a Bed & Breakfast & Cottages where hikers, skiers, snowmobilers, families and friends feel welcome. Relax by the fireside, take a hot tub or roast marshmallows under the stars, cross country ski, snowshoe, hike or bike out the back door. ✉ stay@bartlettinn.com 🌐 www.bartlettinn.com

BETHLEHEM

**Adair Country Inn &
Restaurant**
80 Guider Ln 03574
888-444-2600 603-444-2600
Brad & Ilja Chapman

195-375 $US BB
9 rooms, 9 pb
Most CC, *Rated*, •
C-ltd/S-no/P-no/H-no
German, Spanish, Dutch

Gourmet breakfast
Fine New England Style Cuisine,
Afternoon tea with homemade
goodies, complimentary soft drinks
In-room massage, activity rm w/ pool
table, large screen TV, video library,
snowshoes & many trails

Casually elegant country home in a breathtaking setting, with views of the White Mountains. Romantic retreat on 200 acres surrounded by sweeping lawns, gardens, stone walls, woods and wildlife.

✉ innkeeper@adairinn.com 🌐 www.adairinn.com

The Wayside Inn
3738 Main St, Rt 302 03574
800-448-9557 603-869-3364
Victor & Kathe Hofmann

98-128 $US BB
26 rooms, 26 pb
Visa, MC, AmEx,
Rated
C-yes/S-ltd/P-ltd/H-yes
French, German
May-Oct. & Dec.-March

Full breakfast
Dinner available; most popular items
are Veal Zurich, Wiener Schnitzel,
Crab Cakes, Rack of Lamb
Restaurant, common room with
fireplace, cable TV, free wireless
Internet, golf packages

The historic Wayside Inn is a favorite for family vacations, romantic getaways and group gatherings any time of the year. Enjoy golf, hiking, skiing or sightseeing in the White Mountains.

✉ info@thewaysideinn.com 🌐 www.thewaysideinn.com

Glynn House Inn, Ashland, NH

BRIDGEWATER

The Inn on Newfound Lake
1030 Mayhew Tpke, Rt
3A 03222
800-745-7990 603-744-9111
Larry Delangis & Phelps
Boyce

105-355 $US BB
28 rooms, 24 pb
Most CC, •
C-ltd/S-no/P-no/H-no

Continental breakfast
Snacks, restaurant, bar service
Fishing in lake, sitting room, library,
private beach, dock

The Inn has been refurbished and we invite guests to return to the times of relaxation and enjoyment. One of the few remaining true country inns. We have a 240-ft. private beach, private dock & boat moorings on one of the cleanest lakes in the country.

✉ innonlake@metrocast.net 🌐 www.newfoundlake.com

BRISTOL

Pleasant View B&B
22 Hemp Hill Road 03222
888-909-2700 603-744-5547
Heidi Milbrand

110-150 $US BB
7 rooms, 7 pb
Most CC, Cash, Checks,
Rated
S-no/P-no/H-no

Full Country-Style Breakfast
The Inn is also available to rent (up to
30 people) for rehearsal dinners, baby
or bridal showers.

Nestled on a state designated scenic road in New Hampshire's lakes region, Pleasant View Bed and Breakfast, a country Inn, provides a comfortable, cozy atmosphere for guests looking for a touch of home with spectacular mountain views.

✉ theinnwench@metrocast.net 🌐 www.pleasantviewbandb.net

CAMPTON

Colonel Spencer Inn
3 Colonel Spencer Rd 03223
603-536-1755
Mary Jo & Scott Stephens

110-125 $US BB
6 rooms, 6 pb
Visa, MC
C-yes/S-no/P-ltd/H-no

Full homemade country breakfast
Complimentary refreshments &
snacks
Sitting room, cable TV, DVD, VCR,
library, wireless Internet

Experience the charm of a cozy pre-Revolutionary home, now a bed and breakfast steeped rich in America's history. We are perfectly located between Plymouth and Campton in the surrounds of New Hampshire's spectacular White Mountains & Lakes Regions.

✉ innkeeper@colonelspencerbb.com 🌐 www.colonelspencerbb.com

CAMPTON

Mountain Fare Inn
Mad River Rd 03223
603-726-4283
Susan & Nick Preston

105-155 $US BB
10 rooms, 10 pb
Visa, MC, Disc, *Rated*
C-yes/S-no/P-ltd/H-ltd
A little French

Full breakfast
Afternoon tea & snacks
Sitting room, suites, fireplace, cable
TV, conference, sauna, soccer field,
family reunions

Lovely 1830's village farmhouse features the antiques, fabrics and feel of country cottage living. Picturesque gardens in the summer, foliage in the fall, and a true skier's lodge in the winter.

✉ info@mountainfareinn.com   🌐 www.mountainfareinn.com

The Sunny Grange
1354 Rt 175 03223
877-726-5553 603-726-5555
Tami Anderson

119-165 $US BB
5 rooms, 5 pb
Most CC, Cash
C-ltd/S-no/P-no/H-no

Full breakfast
Beverages, snacks, wine, evening treat
Hot tub, wireless Internet, cable TV/
VCR, fireplaces, Jacuzzi tubs, garden,
hammock, A/C, bathrobes

At the Sunny Grange B&B, our guests are our top priority. We're happy to provide those extra touches to make your stay a special one. ✉ reservations@sunnygrange.com 🌐 www.sunnygrange.com

CHOCORUA

Riverbend Inn B&B
273 Chocora Mt.
Highway 03817
800-628-6944 603-323-7440
Craig Cox & Jerry Weiss

100-250 $US BB
10 rooms, 6 pb
Most CC, Cash
C-ltd/S-ltd/P-no/H-no

Full breakfast
Beverages
Guest lounge area, library, fireplace,
decks overlooking river, massage,
yoga, wireless Internet

Chosen "Best Romantic B&B" voted "Best Interior Design and Decor" and "Best Breakfast in New England" by three different magazines. Ten luxurious guestrooms on 15 wooded acres along the Chocorua River. Enjoy breakfast on the deck overlooking the river.

✉ info@riverbendinn.com 🌐 www.riverbendinn.com

The Brass Heart Inn
88 Philbrick Neighborhood
Rd 03817
800-833-9509 603-323-7766
Don & Joanna Harte

80-260 $US BB
16 rooms, 10 pb
Most CC, Cash, Checks
C-yes/S-no/P-no/H-yes

Full breakfast
Fine dining in our restaurant by
reservation; summer/fall dining in the
pub (no reservation needed)
Cottages have microwave oven,
coffeemaker, fridge

We invite you to enjoy the peace and tranquility of our retreat that has delighted guests for over 100 years. Tucked away, yet close to all the Mt. Washington Valley has to offer!

✉ info@thebrassheartinn.com 🌐 www.thebrassheartinn.com

DANBURY

Inn at Danbury
67 NH Route 104 03230
866-326-2879 603-768-3318
Robert & Alexandra Graf

99-160 $US BB
14 rooms, 14 pb
Visa, MC, Disc,
Rated, •
C-ltd/S-no/P-no/H-ltd
Dutch, German and
French

Full breakfast
Award winning German Restaurant
serving Old World and New England
comfort food in a cozy Bistro
WiFi, personal trip planning, massage,
private parties, Ski & Stay, indoor
pool, library, TV

Come visit the Inn at Danbury and experience a New Hampshire Country Inn with amazing down home charm, as well as personalized service and attention to details!

✉ info@innatdanbury.com 🌐 www.innatdanbury.com

DOVER

Silver Fountain
103 Silver St 03820
888-548-6888 603-750-4200
B. Susan Chang

89-149 $US BB
9 rooms, 9 pb
Most CC
C-yes/S-no/P-no/H-yes
Mandarin Chinese

Full breakfast
We will accommodate dietary
restrictions upon request
TV, DVD, robes, alarm clock w/CD,
private bathroom, hairdryer, baby
grand piano, wireless Internet

The Silver Fountain Inn is an elegant early 1870s Victorian that has maintained its original beauty and charm. Rooms range from $89-$149 and include private bath. The large sitting room has a baby grand piano and is ideal for intimate gatherings. ✉ info@silverfountain.com 🌐 www.silverfountain.com

Three Chimneys Inn, Durham, NH

DURHAM

Three Chimneys Inn
17 Newmarket Rd 03824
888-399-9777 603-868-7800
Karen Meyer

129-209 $US BB
23 rooms, 23 pb
Most CC, Cash,
Rated, •
C-yes/S-no/P-no/H-yes

Full breakfast
Snacks, afternoon social hour, lunch
and dinner available in the restaurant,
bar service
Sitting room, library, cable, Jacuzzis,
fireplaces, high-speed Internet

Discover a world of casual elegance at Three Chimneys Inn. This beautifully restored 1649 mansion and carriage house is situated on Valentine Hill overlooking her formal gardens, the Oyster River, and the Old Mill Falls.

✉ info@threechimneysinn.com 🌐 www.threechimneysinn.com

EAST MADISON

Purity Spring Resort
1251 Eaton Rd, Route
153 03849
800-373-3754 603-367-8896

78-230 $US EP
79 rooms, 79 pb
Most CC, Cash
C-yes/S-no/P-no/H-ltd

Meal plans are offered at Purity
Spring's Traditions Restaurant. B&B,
MAP and AP dining available.
Pool & fitness center, porches,
gardens, lake, canoes, sitting rooms,
fireplaces, groups & weddings

Choose from lodge rooms, private lakeside cottages or condominiums, the options will satisfy everyone. With a pristine private lake, family-friendly dining & stunning natural surroundings, Purity Spring Resort is the ideal, four-season destination.

✉ info@purityspring.com 🌐 www.purityspring.com

EATON

Inn at Crystal Lake & Pub
2356 Eaton Rd 03832
800-343-7336 603-447-2120
Bobby & Tim

79-239 $US BB
11 rooms, 11 pb
Most CC, *Rated*
C-ltd/S-no/P-ltd/H-ltd

Full breakfast
Full service dining and full liquor
service; Dining Room and Pub,
cookies
Cable TV/VCRs, CD/radios,
telephones, A/C

Comfortable guestrooms, luxury pampering, hearty breakfasts, central location, irresistible specials and award-winning packages. Now offering dinner and pub menus. Recommended by The Boston Globe and Ski Magazine.

✉ stay@innatcrystallake.com 🌐 www.innatcrystallake.com

ENFIELD

1793 Shaker Hill B&B
259 Shaker Hill Rd 03748
877-516-1370 603-632-4519
Nancy & Allen Smith

90-115 $US BB
4 rooms, 4 pb
Visa, MC
C-ltd/S-no/P-no/H-no

Full breakfast
Afternoon tea, snacks
Sitting room, business travel
accommodations, secure storage for
your bike, weddings

Newly renovated 1790s Colonial farmhouse. Gardens and wraparound porch, newly decorated rooms with down comforters and pillows. All private baths.

✉ shakerhill@earthlink.net 🌐 www.shakerhill.com

Shaker Farm B&B
597 NH Rt 4A 03748
800-613-7664 603-632-7664
Joe & Cathy Gasparik

135 $US BB
6 rooms, 6 pb
Most CC, Cash, Checks
C-ltd/S-no/P-no/H-ltd

Hearty country breakfast
Period furniture, cable TV, A/C,
private baths, deck, wireless Internet

You'll be delighted with the warmth and charm of the lovely rooms in the historic South Family Shaker Farm House. Genuine antique flavor and a warm and friendly atmosphere. A fireplace in the living room, and a deck and screened in area for relaxing.

✉ jgasparik@aol.com 🌐 www.shakerfarm.com

FRANCONIA

Franconia Inn
1300 Easton Rd 03580
800-473-5299 603-823-5542
Richard (Alec) Morris

131-314 $US BB
35 rooms, 34 pb
Visa, MC, AmEx,
Rated, •
C-yes/S-yes/P-no/H-no
Mem. Day—April 1st

Full breakfast
Restaurant, full bar
Lounge with movies, library, bicycles,
heated pool, 4 clay tennis courts,
horse back riding, soaring

Since 1863, The Franconia Inn has welcomed guests with the tranquil appeal of country life, in an elegant setting that is both unpretentious and inviting.

✉ info@franconiainn.com 🌐 www.franconiainn.com

Historic Lovetts Inn
Rt 18 03580
800-356-3802 603-823-7761
Janet & Jim Freitas

135-245 $US BB
18 rooms, 18 pb
Visa, MC, Disc
C-yes/S-no/P-yes/H-ltd

Full country breakfast
Afternoon tea each day at 3:00 pm,
dinner available. Casual and fine
dining
Sitting rooms, outdoor pool, walking/
biking/cross country ski trails, alpine
skiing, pet friendly

Built in 1784 and listed on the National Register of Historic Places. "Where the Art of Fine Dining Remains a Cherished Tradition," Lovetts Inn offers a variety of accommodations in either the historic inn or intimate cottages, most with fireplaces.

✉ innkeepers@lovettsinn.com 🌐 www.lovettsinn.com

FRANKLIN

The Maria Atwood Inn
71 Hill Rd, Rt#3A 03235
603-934-3666
Sandi & Fred Hoffmeister

-127 $US BB
7 rooms, 7 pb
Most CC, Cash, Checks,
Rated, •
C-yes/S-no/P-no/H-no

Full breakfast
Complimentary snacks, beverages,
fruit & cookies
Library, garden, free wireless Internet
access, free long distance phone calls
anywhere in US & CAN

Surrounded by lush green trees and shrubbery lies the Maria Atwood Inn. The allure and mystique of this large Colonial home takes you back into a different time. A relaxed, friendly atmosphere refreshes traveler's physical & mental being as well.

✉ info@atwoodinn.com 🌐 www.atwoodinn.com

GREENFIELD

Greenfield Inn
749 Forest Rd 03047
800-678-4144 603-547-6327
Vic & Barbara

59-159 $US BB
9 rooms, 7 pb
Visa, MC, Disc,
Rated, •
C-yes/S-no/P-no/H-no

Full breakfast
Jacuzzis, Hayloft Suite, Hot Tub,
Hideaway Suite, Free Wireless Internet

Welcome to a four season, southern New Hampshire, Mountain Country mansion. Sleep in Victorian splendor. Breakfast is a party with crystal, china and Mozart. 90 minutes from Boston.

✉ innkeeper@greenfieldinn.com 🌐 www.greenfieldinn.com

HAMPSTEAD

Stillmeadow at Hampstead
545 Main St 03841
603-329-8381
Margaret & Willie Mitchell

135-165 $US BB
3 rooms, 3 pb
C-ltd/S-no/P-no/H-no
Scottish!

Full breakfast, local produce
Fantastic breakfasts using local farm
produce, baked treats
Guests Victorian parlor with
woodstove, patio, individual parking
spaces, flat screen TVs, fridge

Under new ownership. Southern New Hampshire's premier B&B. Beautiful historic 1850 Colonial "Italianate" Style house set on two acres of gardens with many original features combined with the highest levels of modern comfort and amenities.

✉ margaret.mitchell@still-meadow.com 🌐 www.still-meadow.com

HAMPTON

Lamie's Inn & Tavern
490 Lafayette Rd 03842
800-805-5050 603-926-0330
Maureen Mazurkiewicz

99-155 $US BB
32 rooms, 32 pb
Most CC, Checks
C-yes/S-ltd/P-yes/H-yes

Continental breakfast
Tavern and Restaurant on premises
Digital cable television with HBO,
room service, 24-hour fitness club
privileges, newspaper, WiFi

Built in 1740, this family-owned and operated New England Inn continues to deliver quality service to guests from around the world. Whether you are traveling for business or pleasure, it is our goal to make you feel at home!

✉ Maureen@oldsaltnh.com 🌐 lamiesinn.com

HAMPTON BEACH

D.W.'s Oceanside Inn
365 Ocean Blvd 03842
866-OCEANSI 623-2674 603-926-3542
Duane (Skip) & Deb
Windemiller

175-275 $US BB
9 rooms, 9 pb
Most CC, *Rated*, •
S-no/P-no/H-no
Late May to Columbus
Day

Choice of breakfast items off menu
Self-service bar on back deck, sitting
room, library, beach chairs & towels,
WiFi available

D.W.'s Oceanside Inn is a small elegant lodging overlooking the Atlantic Ocean and the beautiful sandy beaches along New Hampshire's 18 mile coastline. The Inn is a quiet respite located at the edge of the busy summer tourist area of Hampton Beach.

✉ info@oceansideinn.com 🌐 www.oceansideinn.com

HANCOCK

Hancock Inn
33 Main St 03449
800-525-1789 603-525-3318
Robert Short

105-260 $US BB
14 rooms, 14 pb
Most CC, *Rated*, •
C-yes/S-no/P-ltd/H-yes

Delicious full breakfast
Restaurant, dinner available
Sitting room, library, Jacuzzis, suites,
fireplace, cable TV, bar

Since 1789, the 1st year of Washington's Presidency, the Hancock Inn has been in continuous operation, hosting thousands of visitors, from cattle drovers & rum runners, aristocracy & a U.S. President. Listed on the National Register of Historic Places.

✉ innkeeper@hancockinn.com 🌐 www.hancockinn.com

HANOVER

The Trumbull House
40 Etna Rd 03755
800-651-5141 603-643-2370
Hilary Pridgen

139-319 $US BB
6 rooms, 6 pb
Most CC, Cash,
Checks, •
C-ltd/S-no/P-ltd/H-no

Sumptuous Breakfast
Swimming pond, meadows, sugar
maple grove, basketball half-court,
trails, Internet access, TV/VCR

Hanover's first and finest Bed & Breakfast offers luxury country lodgings just four miles east of Dartmouth College & three miles from the Dartmouth-Hitchcock Medical Center.

✉ trumbullhouse@gmail.com 🌐 www.trumbullhouse.com

HART'S LOCATION

The Notchland Inn
2 Morey Road 03812
800-866-6131 603-374-6131
Ed Butler & Les Schoof

199-380 $US BB
15 rooms, 15 pb
Visa, MC, Disc,
Rated, •
C-ltd/S-no/P-ltd/H-ltd

Full country breakfast with choices
5-course dinner with choices at each
course, one seating @7PM Wed-Sun;
bar beverages, wines & beer
Comfortable public rooms, library,
piano, wood-burning fireplaces, pet
friendly cottages, Jacuzzis

*Comfortably elegant 1860s granite mansion on 100 forested acres in the middle of the national forest.
8 spacious rooms, 5 suites, & 2 cottages, all with wood burning fireplaces. Wonderful restaurant, 7PM
seating, Wed-Sun. Cottages are pet-friendly!*

 EdoftheNotch@aol.com 🌐 www.notchland.com

HENNIKER

Colby Hill Inn
33 The Oaks 03242
800-531-0330 603-428-3281
Cynthia & Mason Cobb

140-279 $US BB
14 rooms, 14 pb
Most CC, Cash,
Rated, •
C-ltd/S-no/P-no/H-ltd

Full breakfast
Dinner, complimentary beverages, full
bar
Fresh baked cookies, fireplace in
parlor, A/C, croquet, badminton, pool

*A romantic New England country inn. 14 guestrooms, private baths, fireplaces, antiques and two per-
son whirlpool tubs. Candlelit fine dining overlooking perennial gardens and antique barns.*

 innkeeper@colbyhillinn.com 🌐 www.colbyhillinn.com

HOLDERNESS

Squam Lake Inn
28 Shepard Hill Rd 03245
800-839-6205 603-968-4417
Rae Andrews & Cindy Foster

160-185 $US BB
8 rooms, 8 pb
Visa, MC, Disc
C-ltd/S-no/P-no/H-ltd
May 1st to November 15

Full breakfast
Squam Lake Inn Cafe is open for lunch
and dinner, please inquire for hours of
operation
Wine Bar, library w/guest laptop, cozy
lobby w/fireplace, covered porch and
outdoor decks, shopping

*Squam Lake Inn is a charming century old farmhouse located in the quaint village of Holderness, NH.
Relax and enjoy the beautiful surroundings of the Lakes and White Mountain regions while staying
with us! Breakfast included and not easily forgotten!*

 stay@squamlakeinn.com 🌐 www.squamlakeinn.com

INTERVALE

The Old Field House
Rt. 16A 03845
800-444-9245 603-356-5478
Rod & Linea Hopwood

95-195 $US BB
20 rooms, 20 pb
Most CC, Cash
C-yes/S-no/P-no/H-no

Breakfast Buffet
Coffee, tea, hot chocolate, etc.
available 24 hours
Pool, hot tub, sitting areas, game room,
fireplaces, laundry, TV, DVD, solarium

*The Old Field House is a quiet country lodge with the personalized atmosphere of a small inn, but
the amenities of a larger New Hampshire hotel. Both families and couples will appreciate our wide
variety of lodging options.*

 frontdesk@oldfieldhouse.com 🌐 www.oldfieldhouse.com

JACKSON

Carter Notch Inn
163 Carter Notch Rd. 03846
800-794-9434 603-383-9630
Sally Carter & Dick Green

99-250 $US BB
8 rooms, 8 pb
Visa, MC, Disc,
Rated, •
C-ltd/S-no/P-no/H-no

Full breakfast
Afternoon tea & cookies,
complimentary wine & beer
Sitting room with log fire, outdoor hot
tub, WiFi, guest Internet, Jacuzzis,
swimming pool, cable TV

*Beautifully located on a quiet country road overlooking the Wildcat River & golf course, with pan-
oramic mountain views. Wraparound front porch, impeccably clean rooms. Honeymoon suites with
Jacuzzis & balconies, a lounge with fireplace & great breakfasts!*

 info@carternotchinn.com 🌐 www.carternotchinn.com

JACKSON

Inn at Ellis River
17 Harriman Rd 03846
800-233-8309 603-383-9339
Lyn Norris-Baker & Frank
Baker

119-299 $US BB
21 rooms, 21 pb
Most CC, *Rated*, •
C-ltd/S-no/P-no/H-ltd

Full gourmet country breakfast
Afternoon refreshments, packed
lunches, dinner by two day advance
reservation
Atrium with hot tub, sauna, heated
pool, pub, cable TV, gameroom

Nestled by a stream in Jackson village, the inn is a perfect choice for romance and relaxation in the White Mountains. Most rooms have fireplaces, many have Jacuzzi tubs, balconies. Enjoy a gameroom/pub, atrium-enclosed hot tub, gazebo, and outdoor pool.
   ✉ stay@innatellisriver.com 🌐 www.innatellisriver.com

Inn at Jackson
12 Thorn Hill Rd 03846
800-289-8600 603-383-4321
Don & Joyce Bilger

119-259 $US BB
14 rooms, 14 pb
Visa, MC, AmEx,
Rated, •
C-ltd/S-no/P-no/H-ltd

Full 3-course country breakfast
Afternoon snacks & refreshments,
arrival refreshments available by
request
Wireless Internet, fireplaces, A/C, TV,
DVD, hot tub, massage available

The inn maintains 14 spacious guestrooms, many with fireplaces and cozy seating areas. The inn's recently redesigned common rooms provide a romantic setting for our delicious breakfasts and afternoon refreshments. Enjoy mountain views from our hot tub.
   ✉ info@innatjackson.com 🌐 www.innatjackson.com

Inn at Thorn Hill
40 Thorn Hill Rd 03846
800-289-8990 603-383-4242
Jim & Ibby Cooper

169-440 $US BB
25 rooms, 25 pb
Most CC, Cash, Checks
C-ltd/S-no/P-no/H-yes

Full breakfast
3 dining rooms, 3,000 bottle wine list,
lounge featuring New England cuisine,
Afternoon Tea
Fireplaces, Jacuzzis, spa services,
gardens, views, antiques, weddings,
Wine Dinners

The Inn at Thorn Hill & Spa is one of the most outstanding and most romantic inns in the Eastern United States. Located in the classic New England village of Jackson in the heart of New Hampshire's White Mountains.   ✉ stay@innatthornhill.com 🌐 www.innatthornhill.com

Jackson-

The Christmas Farm Inn & Spa
3 Blitzen Way, Route
16B 03846
800-443-5837 603-383-4313
Gary Plourde

179-579 $US BB
41 rooms, 41 pb
Visa, MC, AmEx,
Rated, •
C-yes/S-no/P-ltd/H-ltd

Full breakfast
Snacks, restaurant, dinner, bar
Sitting room, library, Jacuzzis, pool,
suites

Christmas Farm Inn and Spa is a historic country Inn with a rich heritage on a beautiful 15 acre campus in the quaint little town of Jackson, New Hampshire.
   ✉ info@christmasfarminn.com 🌐 www.christmasfarminn.com

Whitney's Inn
357 Black Mountain
Road 03846
800-677-5737 603-383-8916
Don Bilger

109-289 $US BB
27 rooms, 27 pb
Visa, MC, AmEx,
Rated
C-yes/S-no/P-yes/H-ltd

Full breakfast
Whitney's provides two onsite dining
options, the Birches Restaurant & the
Shovel Handle Pub
Cable HD TV, DVD players, CD players,
pool, fireplaces & wireless Internet

Whitney's Inn has been welcoming families and couples since the 1840s. Its charming guestrooms, excellent dining, two pubs and proximity to the Black Mountain ski resort make Whitney's Inn the perfect place for a getaway.
   ✉ info@whitneysinn.com 🌐 www.whitneysinn.com

JACKSON VILLAGE

Wildcat Inn & Tavern
Main St 03846
800-228-4245 603-383-4245
Stewart Dunlop

59-259 $US EP
11 rooms, 11 pb
Visa, MC, AmEx
C-yes/S-no/P-ltd/H-no

Restaurant & tavern on site serving
country dinners, complimentary
coffee, tea & juice
Sitting areas, special events, weddings,
garden, cable TV, A/C

Nestled in the heart of Jackson Village the Wildcat Inn & Tavern has welcomed guests to dine by candlelight, relax by a crackling fire, dance in our tavern and snuggle in our cozy beds for almost 100 years.   ✉ sleep@wildcattavern.com 🌐 www.wildcattavern.com

LINCOLN

The Red Sleigh Inn B&B
191 Pollard Rd 03251
603-745-8517
Bill & Loretta Deppe

75-195 $US BB
6 rooms, 4 pb
Visa, MC, *Rated*
C-ltd/S-no/P-no/H-no

Full Country Breakfast
Complimentary tea & coffee served
Television in the sitting room, library,
summer gardens, activity planning,
sun porch with views

Enjoy the warm relaxed atmosphere of this family-run B&B close to town in the heart of the beautiful White Mountains. Six guestrooms decorated with antiques afford panoramic views of the surrounding mountains. Hearty full country breakfast included.
✉ redsleigh@roadrunner.com 🌐 www.redsleighinn.com

MANCHESTER

Ash Street Inn
118 Ash St 03104
603-668-9908
Darlene & Eric Johnston

139-219 $US BB
5 rooms, 5 pb
Most CC, Cash
C-ltd/S-no/P-no/H-no

Full breakfast
Afternoon tea available (reservations
required)
Complimentary wireless access, cable
TV, phone, off street parking, comp.
airport pickup/drop off

The perfect alternative to Manchester NH hotels. Try the Ash Street Inn on your next trip and see for yourself the difference between Bed and Breakfast Inns and hotels.
✉ innkeeper@ashstreetinn.com 🌐 www.ashstreetinn.com

MEREDITH

Meredith Inn B&B
2 Waukewan St 03253
603-279-0000
Janet Carpenter

114-209 $US BB
8 rooms, 8 pb
Visa, MC, Disc,
Rated, •
C-ltd/S-no/P-no/H-ltd

Full breakfast
Living room with fireplace, books,
games, in-room whirlpool tubs &
fireplace

The Meredith Inn is an 8 room Victorian bed & breakfast with private baths, cable TV, A/C, phones, whirlpool tubs & fireplaces. Full country breakfast. Smoke-free property.
✉ inn1897@metrocast.net 🌐 www.meredithinn.com

NEW LONDON

Inn at Pleasant Lake
853 Pleasant St 03257
800-626-4907 603-526-6271
Linda & Brian MacKenzie

165-225 $US BB
10 rooms, 10 pb
Visa, MC, Disc,
Rated, •
C-yes/S-no/P-no/H-ltd

Full breakfast
Afternoon tea, bar service, restaurant
Sitting room, lake, a wonderful
environment for business retreats &
weddings

Ten well-appointed guestrooms. Full breakfast and afternoon tea included. Panoramic views of Mt. Kearsarge and Pleasant Lake. Reservations required for five course, pre-fixe dinner – available Wednesday to Sunday. ✉ iplreservations@tds.net 🌐 www.innatpleasantlake.com

NORTH CONWAY

1785 Inn & Restaurant
3582 White Mountain
Hwy 03860
800-421-1785 603-356-9025
Becky & Charlie Mallar

69-169 $US BB
17 rooms, 12 pb
Most CC, Cash, Checks,
Rated, •
C-yes/S-ltd/P-no/H-ltd
French

Full country breakfast
Full-service restaurant, lounge/pub,
room service
2 sitting rooms, A/C, swimming pool,
skiing, honeymoon/romance pkgs

Free Night w/Certificate: Valid November-June. Room Upgrade.

Historic inn overlooking famous view of the White Mountains with award-winning restaurant. Fine dining, friendly service, fabulous views, outstanding wine list in a romantic Colonial atmosphere.
✉ the1785inn@aol.com 🌐 www.the1785inn.com

Brookhill B&B
26 Balcony Seat View 03860
888-356-3061 603-356-3061
Susan & Rod Forsman

219-409 $US BB
2 rooms, 1 pb
Visa, MC
C-ltd/S-no/P-no/H-no
Spanish

Full breakfast
Homemade cookies, snacks, juices,
coffee, tea, and sodas available in the
suite's kitchen
Wood fireplace, multi-room suite,
private entrance, views, soaking tub,
WiFi, ski trails, concierge

Brookhill B&B is one of North Conway and Jackson NH's most unique and luxurious lodgings with a private-entrance one or two bedroom suite, a magnificent view of Mt. Washington, and a long list of luxury, upscale amenities. ✉ brookhillbb@roadrunner.com 🌐 www.brookhillbb.com

NORTH CONWAY

Cabernet Inn
3552 White Mountain
Hwy 03860
800-866-4704 603-356-4704
Jessica & Bruce Zarenko

99-239 $US BB
11 rooms, 11 pb
Most CC, *Rated*, •
C-ltd/S-no/P-no/H-yes

Full Country Breakfast
Afternoon refreshments, we try to
accommodate dietary restrictions with
advance notice
Two common living rooms with
woodburning fireplaces, outside deck
& patio, Jacuzzi for two

Enjoy the warmth and elegance of this romantic 1842 country inn set among towering pines, just a stroll away from breathtaking views of Mt. Washington. Unforgettably romantic and exquisitely maintained. Simply . . . elegant! info@cabernetinn.com Ⓦ www.cabernetinn.com

---

Cranmore Inn
80 Kearsarge 03860
800-526-5502 603-356-5502
Bob Prendergast

79-265 $US BB
18 rooms, 18 pb
Visa, MC, *Rated*, •
C-yes/S-ltd/P-ltd/H-no

Full breakfast
Afternoon tea & homemade cookies
Sitting room, library, swimming pool,
exterior hot tub, suites with fireplace,
Jacuzzi & cable TV

The Cranmore Inn is an authentic country inn, continuously operated since 1863. Antique furnishings and country prints lend charm to comfortably modern queen beds and facilities.
 info@cranmoreinn.com Ⓦ www.cranmoreinn.com

Eastman Inn
2331 White Mountain
Hwy 03860
800-626-5855 603-356-6707
Arthur De La Torre

90-220 $US BB
14 rooms, 14 pb
Visa, MC
C-ltd/S-no/P-no/H-no

Full breakfast
Complimentary home baked goodies
daily
Award winning gardens, whirlpool
tubs, private balconies, gas-insert
fireplaces, antiques

Beautiful 14 room inn, situated in the heart of the White Mountains of New Hampshire. Enjoy a full gourmet breakfast, afternoon treats, and warm beverages each evening. Each room is tastefully decorated. Come for the views and enjoy the hospitality.
 BePampered@eastmaninn.com Ⓦ www.eastmaninn.com

Farm By the River B&B
with Stables
2555 West Side Rd 03860
888-414-8353 603-356-2694
Charlene & Rick Davis

95-199 $US BB
9 rooms, 9 pb
Visa, MC, Disc, *Rated*
C-yes/S-no/P-ltd/H-no

Full breakfast
Afternoon baked goodies and
refreshments.
Jac.&/or frplc rms, 2-rm family suites,
yr. rnd horseback/carriage rides,
weddings: 2–80, river: swim/fish

This historic country inn with yr- round horseback riding and sleigh rides has nine rooms some with Jacuzzis &/or fireplaces — family suites also. Two miles from North Conway in the White Mountains of NH. Ski, hike, canoe, Storyland, Conway Railroad.
 info@farmbytheriver.com Ⓦ www.farmbytheriver.com

Kearsarge Inn
42 Seavey St 03860
800-637-0087 603-356-8700
Stewart M. Dunlop

69-349 $US BB
15 rooms, 15 pb
Visa, MC, AmEx,
Rated, •
C-yes/S-no/P-yes/H-ltd

Continental breakfast
Our restaurant, Decades Steakhouse
& Martini Bar is open year round for
dinner
Common sitting area, gas fireplaces,
A/C, Jacuzzi tubs, luxury
accommodations, great farmers porch

Nestled in the heart of North Conway village, the Kearsarge Inn is a romantic B&B within walking distance of sightseeing, shopping, fine dining, and a variety of outdoor activities.
 innkeeper@kearsargeinn.com Ⓦ www.kearsargeinn.com

Old Red Inn & Cottages
2406 White Mountain
Hwy 03860
800-338-1356 603-356-2642
Richard & Susan Lefave

101-204 $US BB
17 rooms, 15 pb
Visa, MC, Disc,
Rated, •
C-yes/S-ltd/P-ltd/H-no
French

Full breakfast
Afternoon Tea and Cookies
gas log fireplaces, coffee makers,
micro-waves WiFi, seasonal pool.
Some cottages have kitchenettes

A romantic get-a-way, or a family trip, North Conway's Old Red Inn & Cottages puts you in the middle of the Mount Washington Valley. You can walk to town for dining, a train ride, outlet-shopping or just plain relaxing. We offer inn rooms or cottages.
 OldRedInn@RoadRunner.com Ⓦ www.oldredinn.com

NORTH CONWAY ───────────────────────────

Red Elephant Inn B&B 28 Locust Ln 03860 800-642-0749 603-356-3548 Rob	110-225 $US BB 8 rooms, 8 pb Most CC, *Rated* C-ltd/S-no/P-no/H-no French	Full breakfast Coffee, tea, fruit, cookies, chocolates, special diet needs accommodated with notice Den w/ LCD TV, library, outdoor pool, fireplaces/stoves, cable TV/DVD/VCR, Jacuzzi tubs, WiFi

A four-season historic bed and breakfast inn tucked away on a quiet wooded lane just off the main route through the Village of North Conway, nestled in the Mount Washington Valley in the heart of the White Mountains of New Hampshire. Private baths and A/C.

✉ info@redelephantinn.com 🌐 www.redelephantinn.com

Riverside Inn B&B 372 Route 16A 03860 866-949-0044 603-356-0044 Kenneth & Chris Lydecker	109-189 $US BB 7 rooms, 6 pb Most CC, Cash, Checks C-ltd/S-ltd/P-no/H-ltd	Full Country breakfast Afternoon tea with home-baked cookies Gas fireplaces, spa tubs, library, four seasons of activity and entertainment.

Newly renovated rooms & suites, romantic fireplaces, spa tubs, private baths, directly on the beautiful East Branch Saco River, central location, near everything, quiet-off the beaten path, small inn with attentive personal service, full country breakfast

✉ riversideinn.nh@gmail.com 🌐 www.riverside-inn-bed-breakfast.com

Spruce Moose Lodge & **Cottages** 207 Seavey St 03860 800-600-6239 603-356-6239 Nellie & Leon Filip	89-299 $US BB 11 rooms, 11 pb Visa, MC C-ltd/S-no/P-ltd/H-no	Full country breakfast Breakfast not included for cottages Groups, cottages, Great Room, private baths, complimentary toiletries, dog friendly

A four-seasons haven for White Mountains travelers almost since its granite foundation was laid more than 150 years ago. Lodge rooms, bungalows, cottages, and Victorian house lodgings available. Dog friendly! ✉ mainmoose@sprucemooselodge.com 🌐 www.sprucemooselodge.com

The Buttonwood Inn 64 Mount Surprise Rd 03860 800-258-2625 603-356-2625 Bill & Paula Petrone	99-299 $US BB 10 rooms, 10 pb Visa, MC, *Rated*, • C-yes/S-no/P-no/H-ltd French, German, Italian	Full breakfast Afternoon tea baked treats, lunch & dinner can be arranged 2 large common rooms with fireplaces, pool, hot tub, TV, DVD's, WiFi, fridge, computer, meetings

Awarded "The Most Perfect Stay" by Arrington's Inn Traveler and an America's Favorite Inns Award winner, this 10-room, 1820's Inn is nestled on six secluded acres on Mount Surprise. Buttonwood Inn is located minutes from North Conway Village.

✉ innkeeper@buttonwoodinn.com 🌐 www.buttonwoodinn.com

Wildflowers Inn 3486 White Mountain Hwy 03860 866-945-3357 603-356-7567 Bob & Emily Koch	90-275 $US BB 9 rooms, 9 pb Most CC, Cash C-yes/S-ltd/P-no/H-yes Chinese & Taiwanese	Full breakfast cooked to order Homemade cookies, brownies, pastries Fireplaces, HDTV in common area, Jacuzzi suites, hot tub, spectacular views of Mt Washington

Wildflowers Inn Bed & Breakfast commands the finest views of Mt Washington. We offer a warm & comfortable home for you to relax and enjoy. A four season Inn that is earning a reputation for fine hospitality and service. ✉ info@wildflowersinn.com 🌐 www.wildflowersinn.com

NORTH WOODSTOCK ───────────────────────────

Wilderness Inn Bed and **Breakfast** 57 S Main St 03262 888-777-7813 603-745-3890 Michael & Rosanna Yarnell	70-180 $US BB 8 rooms, 8 pb Visa, MC, Disc, *Rated*, • C-yes/S-no/P-no/H-no French & Italian	Full gourmet breakfast Afternoon tea, hot cider, cocoa, lemonade Sunporch, central AC, fireplace in living room, fireplace & Jacuzzis in some rooms, cable TV, WiFi

"The quintessential country inn" circa 1912, located in a quaint New England town. The inn has seven family suites and a "honeymoon" cottage. All private baths. Gourmet breakfast.

✉ info@thewildernessinn.com 🌐 www.thewildernessinn.com

The Buttonwood Inn, North Conway, NH

NORTH WOODSTOCK

Woodstock Inn Station & Brewery 135 Main St 03262 800-321-3985 603-745-3951 Scott & Peggy Rice	63-199 $US BB 33 rooms, 31 pb Most CC, *Rated* C-yes/S-yes/P-no/H-ltd	Full breakfast Fine Dining & Family Restaurant on premises Fireplaces, Jacuzzi, cable TV, A/C, in-room phone, indoor pool & exercise room available

One of the most visited country inns in the White Mountains. 33 rooms with cable TV, A/C, and in-room phone; some with Jacuzzis and gas fireplaces. Two restaurants, entertainment and brew pub on premises.

 relax@woodstockinnnh.com 🌐 www.woodstockinnnh.com

PLAINFIELD

Home Hill Country Inn River Rd. 03781 603-675-6165 Paula Snow	80-250 $US BB 11 rooms, 11 pb Most CC, Cash, Checks, *Rated*, • C-ltd/S-no/P-no/H-ltd	Continental plus breakfast We have a renowned farm to table restaurant and a relaxed pub. Sunday Brunch and dinners. Sitting room, bikes, red clay tennis court, heated outdoor pool, WiFi

Welcome to Home Hill Inn a romantic, tranquil retreat set on 25 secluded acres in Plainfield, New Hampshire. Experience the luxury of our beautifully appointed rooms, inventive cuisine, pampering body massage treatments, and a boutique of local wares

✉ homehillinn@gmail.com 🌐 www.homehillinn.com

PORTSMOUTH

Inn at Strawbery Banke 314 Court St 03801 800-428-3933 603-436-7242 Sarah Glover O'Donnell	115-170 $US BB 7 rooms, 7 pb Most CC, Cash, Checks, *Rated* C-ltd/S-no/P-no/H-ltd	Full breakfast Sitting rooms, outdoor garden, all guestrooms have A/C, parking

This historic, Colonial inn charms travelers with its beautiful rooms and outdoor garden. Located in the heart of old Portsmouth.

✉ innatstrawberrybanke@gmail.com 🌐 innatstrawberybanke.com

PORTSMOUTH

Martin Hill Inn
404 Islington St 03801
603-436-2287
Margot Doering

105-210 $US BB
7 rooms, 7 pb
Visa, MC
C-ltd/S-no/P-no/H-no
Spanish

Full breakfast
Dietary needs & preferences are
happily accommodated, including
vegan & gluten free selections
Restaurant reservations, spa
appointments, gift baskets & flowers
arranged on request

*Providing a special retreat to the seacoast of NH for over 30 years, the Inn features 7 unique rooms
with private baths. Walk 10 minutes to downtown Portsmouth's restaurants, boutiques & waterfront.
A full gourmet breakfast & lovely gardens await you.*

✉ reservations@martinhillinn.com 🌐 www.martinhillinn.com

Sise Inn
40 Court St 03801
877-747-3466 603-433-1200
Diane Hodun

119-279 $US BB
34 rooms, 34 pb
Most CC, *Rated*, •
C-yes/S-no/P-no/H-yes

Expanded continental breakfast
All day coffee, tea and spring water,
plus fresh baked cookies every
afternoon
Round-the-clock staffing, oak-paneled
elevator, free parking, new WiFi, TV/
DVD/VCR

*Much larger and more accommodating than a typical Portsmouth Bed and Breakfast, each of the Sise
Inn's 34 guestrooms and suites is uniquely decorated with period furnishings and reproductions. Each
room and suite includes a private bath and amenities.*

✉ info@siseinn.com 🌐 www.siseinn.com

Wren's Nest Village Inn
3548 Lafayette Rd 03801
888-755-9013 603-436-2481
Pamela VanGeystelen

90-275 $US EP
32 rooms, 32 pb
Most CC, Cash
C-yes/S-ltd/P-ltd/H-no

On site restaurant. Breakfast or dinner
pkgs can be added to stay. Romance
pkgs & spa pkgs offered.
Heated pool, hot tub, on-site
restaurant, grills/picnic areas on 4.5
acres

*Located in the heart of the NH seacoast region. You'll find that not only The Wren's Nest, but the entire
area has something to offer every member of the family. O'Reilly, our soft-coated wheaton, greets all
with enthusiasm and charm!*

✉ wrens.nest@comcast.net 🌐 www.wrensnestinn.com

SANBORNTON

**Ferry Point House on Lake
Winnisquam**
100 Lower Bay Rd 03269
603-524-0087
Eric & Andrea Damato

145-260 $US BB
9 rooms, 9 pb
Visa, MC, Disc, *Rated*
C-ltd/S-no/P-no/H-no
Jan 1-Dec 31

Country gourmet
Beverage and snack at check-in
Jacuzzi, gazebo, porch, fireplace,
dining room

*Gracious country Victorian situated on picturesque Lake Winnisquam. Built in 1800's, offers country
gourmet breakfasts.*

✉ info@ferrypointhouse.com 🌐 www.new-hampshire-inn.com

SUGAR HILL

Sugar Hill Inn
116 Route 117 03586
800-548-4748 603-823-5621
Steven Allen

150-410 $US BB
14 rooms, 14 pb
Most CC, Cash,
Rated, •
C-ltd/S-no/P-no/H-no

Full Country breakfast
Dining Thursday – Sunday, Pub,
afternoon tea & crackers/cookies
Swimming pool, spa, gardens, tavern,
restaurant

*Nestled in New Hampshire's White Mountains, Sugar Hill Inn is a romantic getaway known for culi-
nary adventure and warm, inviting guestrooms and Cottages. Yankee Magazine Editor' Choice; DiRo-
NA's Achievement of Distinction in Dining award for 2009–2010.*

✉ info@SugarHillInn.com 🌐 www.sugarhillinn.com

SUGAR HILL

Sunset Hill House	100-499 $US BB	Full breakfast
231 Sunset Hill Rd 03586	30 rooms, 30 pb	Tea, coffee all day, afternoon home
800-786-4455 603-823-5522	Most CC, *Rated*, •	baked cookies or other snacks
Lon & Nancy Henderson	C-yes/S-no/P-ltd/H-yes	On-site heated pool, golf, Nordic ski,
	German, French	snowshoe, fireplaced parlors, fine
		dining, private deck

Free Night w/Certificate: Valid Oct.20-Sept. 20.. Room Upgrade.

For views, food, & ambience, guests & press agree that Sunset Hill House has "New England's most spectacular mountain views," (Yankee Magazine) & "NH's most spectacular Meal," (NH Magazine). Award winning full service inn in the heart of the Mountains.

✉ innkeeper@sunsethillhouse.com   ◯ www.sunsethillhouse.com

SUNAPEE

Dexter's Inn	110-185 $US BB	Full breakfast
258 Stagecoach Rd 03782	19 rooms, 19 pb	On-site restaurant open to both inn
800-232-5571 603-763-5571	Most CC, Cash, Checks,	guests and the general public
John Augustine	*Rated*, •	Commercial xc ski & snowshoe
	C-yes/S-no/P-ltd/H-ltd	center, tennis, swimming, volleyball,
		basketball, game room, lawn games

A family-friendly country resort-inn near Lake Sunapee and Mount Sunapee with an amazing view and idyllic grounds that combines the charm & hospitality of a bed & breakfast with the on-site activities & services of a small resort.

✉ dexters@tds.net   ◯ www.dextersnh.com

SWANZEY

Inn of the Tartan Fox	90-150 $US BB	Four Course Gourmet Breakfast
350 Old Homestead	4 rooms, 4 pb	Picnic lunches on request, gluten free
Hwy 03446	Visa, MC, AmEx	& vegetarian meals with prior notice
877-836-4319 603-357-9308	C-ltd/S-no/P-no/H-yes	Library, gardens, A/C, fireplaces,
Wayne & Meg		gift shop, wireless Internet, student
		discounts, corporate rates

1832 Manor house with Celtic styled rooms. Antiques, private baths, heated marble floors, fireplaces, gift shop. One fully accessible room. Scrumptious gourmet breakfast. Three miles to Main St., Keene.

✉ info@tartanfox.com   ◯ www.tartanfox.com

WALPOLE

Inn at Valley Farms B&B &	175-299 $US BB	Decadent three course breakfast
Cottages	6 rooms, 6 pb	Homemade cookies, coffee, selection
633 Wentworth Rd 03608	Visa, MC	of tea & soft drinks always available
877-327-2855 603-756-2855	C-yes/S-no/P-no/H-ltd	Working organic farm, renown
Jacqueline Caserta		chocolate, beautiful sun room, game
		room, full library, walking trails

Gracious 1774 Colonial home on tranquil 105-acre organic farm. Elegant rooms with three-course gourmet breakfast, 3-bedroom self-sufficient cottages or farmhouse perfect for families. Beautiful grounds with extensive gardens, fine dining and more nearby.

✉ info@innatvalleyfarms.com   ◯ www.innatvalleyfarms.com

WEST CHESTERFIELD

Chesterfield Inn	149-320 $US BB	Full breakfast
20 Cross Road 03446	15 rooms, 15 pb	Full country breakfast is included,
800-365-5515 603-256-3211	Most CC, Cash, Checks,	dinner is served nightly in our
Phil & Judy Hueber	*Rated*, •	candlelit dining room
	C-yes/S-no/P-yes/H-no	TV, phones, fax, wireless Internet,
		mini fridge in room, air conditioning,
		breakfast in bed

Come and relax awhile at this elegant yet comfortable renovated New Hampshire Farmhouse with its cathedral ceilings and rambling views of the Connecticut River Valley. Privacy, and delicious cuisine are yours at one of the best Inns in New England!

✉ chstinn@sover.net   ◯ www.chesterfieldinn.com

New Jersey

ASBURY

Berry Preserve B&B
215 Turkey Hill Rd 08802
610-704-0780
Diann & Steve Berry

90-135 $US BB
3 rooms, 2 pb
Visa, MC
C-ltd/S-no/P-no/H-no
April – December

Full breakfast
Afternoon refreshments.
A/C, cable TV, reading chairs & lights,
vintage films & VCR, hairdryers,
wireless Internet access.

Unwind at the Berry Preserve B&B, a tranquil ten-acre woodland retreat, with genial hosts Steve and Diann Berry. Experience a world of arts and crafts in this unique contemporary lodging with all the comforts of home and easy access to major highways.

✉ berrypreserve@comcast.net   🌐 www.berrypreserve.com

ATLANTIC HIGHLANDS

Blue Bay Inn
51 First Ave 007716
732-708-9600

139-399 $US EP
27 rooms, 27 pb
Visa, MC, AmEx
C-yes/S-no/P-no/H-yes

5 Star restaurant on site

The Blue Bay Inn is the only boutique hotel on the Jersey shore. Its oversized luxurious rooms, deluxe suites and extended stay fully furnished apartments are havens of enlightened comfort.

✉ info@bluebayinn.com   🌐 www.bluebayinn.com

AVON BY THE SEA

Atlantic View Inn
20 Woodland Ave 07717
877-367-6522 732-774-8505
Debbie & Chris Solomita

120-310 $US BB
12 rooms, 12 pb
Visa, MC, Disc, *Rated*
C-ltd/S-no/P-no/H-no

Continental plus breakfast
Early continental, afternoon
refreshments, cookies, bottled water,
snacks, juices, fresh fruit
fireplaces, TV, beach badges, chairs,
towels, umbrellas, bicycles, dinner
reservations . . .

This warm and comfortable B&B was built over a century ago as a grand summer cottage overlooking the ocean. The charm of an English seashore home is captured in furnishings of mahogany, antiques, traditional wicker and hand-painted pieces.

✉ avibb@optonline.net   🌐 www.atlanticviewinn.com

Cashelmara Inn
22 Lakeside Ave 07717
800-821-2976 732-776-8727
Mary Wiernasz, Martin
Mulligan

100-375 $US BB
15 rooms, 15 pb
Visa, MC, Disc, *Rated*
C-ltd/S-no/P-no/H-no
Spanish in am

Full country breakfast to order
Tea & goodie table, ice machine, soda/
bottled water on the honor system
Beach chairs, badges and towels, maid
service, wireless Internet

Our grand staircase, museum quality antiques & golden retriever warmly welcome you. Water views, many from bed, are complimented by designer fabrics & fireplaces. Full country breakfast served daily. In-season free beach badges, towels and chairs.

✉ cashelmara5@aol.com   🌐 www.cashelmara.com

BARNEGAT LIGHT

**Minerva's Beds Breakfasts
and Books by the Sea**
13 W 7th St 08006
609-494-1000
Emma Lapsansky

74-259 $US BB
5 rooms, 5 pb
Most CC, Cash, Checks
C-yes/S-no/P-no/H-yes

Full breakfast
Library, quiet wing, free WiFi, garden,
complimentary bike use, indoor
meeting room, family-friendly

Free Night w/Certificate: Valid Spring and Fall. Room Upgrade.

Only two blocks from beautiful Barnegat Light beaches, and located in a quiet residential neighborhood. Bring the family and enjoy a stroll on the Shore, bike down the beaches, or relax in the comfort of your room. Sun, sea and shore await you!

✉ MinervasBandB@gmail.com   🌐 www.MinervasBandB.com

BEACH HAVEN

Island Guest House B&B Inn
207 3rd St 08008
877-LBI-STAY 609-709-5791
Joanne & Mark Spulock

125-399 $US BB
15 rooms, 12 pb
Visa, MC, *Rated*
C-yes/S-no/P-ltd/H-no

Full breakfast
Afternoon tea time and specialty treats from the kitchen
Outdoor garden, bicycle for two, WiFi, beach chairs/badges, cafe kitchen, A/C, balconies, Jacuzzis

The Island Guest House has been Voted the Best Bed & Breakfast on Long Beach Island. It is a turn-of-the-century historic inn, located oceanside in the heart of Beach Haven, New Jersey. Come and experience the restfulness of a European style guesthouse.

✉ islandguesthouse@comcast.net   🌐 www.theislandguesthouse.com

---

Magnolia House
215 Centre Street 08008
609-492-2226
Cheryl & Tony Curinga

150-300 $US BB
12 rooms, 12 pb
Visa, MC
C-ltd/S-no/P-no/H-no
Italian

Full Served Breakfast
Afternoon Tea, Fresh Iced Tea, Lemonade, Cookies, Crisps, Breads, ect. . 24 Hr Hot Beverages & Fruit.
AC, Beach Badges, Chairs, Towels, Umbrellas, Coolers, Drinks & Snacks, Bikes for guests to borrow.

1867 Romantic Victorian Inn, All Modern Amenities. Located in the Heart of Beach Haven. A short walk to Beach, Theater, Restaurants, Amusement Park & Bay. Beautiful Victorian Garden, Gazebo, Wrap around Porch & Porch Swing. Outdoor Shower & Pool Table.

✉ magnoliahouselbi@comcast.net   🌐 magnoliahouselbi.com

Victoria Guest House
126 Amber St 08008
609-492-4154
Marilyn, Leonard, John & Judy Miller

165-295 $US BB
15 rooms, 15 pb
Visa, MC, Disc
C-ltd/S-ltd/P-no/H-ltd
May thru September

Buffet breakfast
If you have a dietary restriction, let us know, coffee & tea all day, lemonade & iced tea afternoons
Bikes, beach chairs & towels, pool, bottled water, beach badges, wireless Internet, A/C, TV with DVD

Situated four houses from the ocean. We offer spacious guestrooms and a new suite, attractively decorated with cheerful exposure. Linger on our wraparound porches or take a cooling dip in our heated pool.

✉ victoria_guest_house@msn.com   🌐 www.lbivictoria.com

Williams Cottage Inn
506 South Atlantic Ave 08008
609-492-7272
Bette & Merle Vanliere

195-425 $US BB
8 rooms, 8 pb
Most CC, Cash
C-ltd/S-no/P-no/H-yes
Norwegian

Full breakfast
Gourmet coffee & tea, afternoon refreshments
TV, DVD player, WiFi, individual climate control, complimentary use of bicycles & tennis rackets

This 120 year old beach front Victorian mansion has been lovingly restored, lavishly decorated and richly appointed with the finest designer amenities to make it the most luxurious B&B Inn ever to grace the Jersey Shore.

✉ innkeeper@williamscottageinn.com   🌐 www.williamscottageinn.com

BELMAR

A Dream by the Sea
609 9th Ave 07719
732-280-1990
Michelle Sicilio & Carmela Lisi

135-240 $US BB
4 rooms, 4 pb
S-no/P-no/H-no

Full Organic Breakfast
Daily maid service, hypoallergenic beds, hairdryer, robes, wireless, central air & heat, clock radio

Please come and join us for a day or two or maybe a week or few. Experience a most pleasant and relaxing getaway at A Dream by the Sea bed and breakfast in Belmar!

 info@adreambythesea.com   🌐 www.adreambythesea.com

CAPE MAY

Angel of the Sea
5 Trenton Ave 08204
800-848-3369 609-884-3369
Lorie Whissell

95-315 $US BB
27 rooms, 27 pb
Most CC, Cash,
Rated, •
C-ltd/S-no/P-no/H-no

Full breakfast
Early morning coffee service,
afternoon tea & sweets, evening wine
& cheese
Off-street parking, beach chairs,
towels/umbrellas, complimentary
bikes, concierge, cable TV, WiFi

Cape May's most luxurious B&B Victorian mansion. Fabulous oceanviews, ½ block from the beach. Rooms have private baths, ceiling fans, clawfoot tubs, cable TV and WiFi.
✉ info@angelofthesea.com ◐ www.angelofthesea.com

Bayberry Inn
223 Perry St 08204
877-923-9232 609-884-9232
Andy & Toby Fontaine

120-295 $US BB
5 rooms, 5 pb
Most CC, Cash
C-ltd/S-no/P-no/H-ltd

Full, 3 Course Breakfast
Specialties include gourmet delights;
afternoon tea complete with
homemade treats
Guest refrigerator, fireplaces, beach
chairs & towels, on site parking,
dinner reservations, WiFi

Enjoy Cape May's ambience and the serenity of a by-gone era in the historic district. Unwind at our relaxing, romantic seaside B&B inn. Hospitality, Victorian charm and only two blocks from the beach, one block from shopping, dining and theater.
✉ bayberryinnkeeper@comast.net ◐ www.bayberryinncapemay.com

Beauclaire's B&B
23 Ocean St 07675
609-898-1222
Sandy Finnegan

95-255 $US BB
6 rooms, 6 pb
Most CC, Cash, Checks,
Rated
C-ltd/S-no/P-no/H-no

Full gourmet breakfast
Afternoon refreshments & snacks
½ block to beach, off-street parking,
beach chairs, Internet access

Beauclaire's is a renowned Victorian style Bed & Breakfast open all year & located in the historic district in Cape May. Just a half block from the beach & two blocks from the center of town.
✉ innkeeper@beauclaires.com ◐ www.beauclaires.com

Bedford Inn
805 Stockton Ave 08204
866-215-9507 609-884-4158
Archie & Stephanie Kirk

120-255 $US BB
11 rooms, 11 pb
Visa, MC, Disc,
Rated, •
S-no/P-no/H-ltd

Full buffet breakfast
Afternoon refreshments, hot beverage
service 24 hours
Dining room, parlor, 3 porches, limited
on-site parking, private baths, A/C,
TV/DVD, hairdryer

Bedford Inn is an elegant 1883 Italianate seaside inn that has an unusual double staircase, and lovely antique-filled rooms and suites. A full, memorable, breakfast and afternoon refreshments are served daily. ✉ info@bedfordinn.com ◐ www.bedfordinn.com

Carroll Villa Hotel
19 Jackson St 08204
877-275-8452 609-884-9619
Mark Kulkowitz & Pam
Huber

110-299 $US BB
21 rooms, 21 pb
Most CC, Cash, Checks,
Rated, •
C-yes/S-no/P-no/H-no

Full breakfast
Great lunch & dinner served on our
quaint front porch, skylit dining room
or garden terrace
Wireless Internet, happy hour daily,
weddings, corporate retreats, baby
sitting services with notice

Free Night w/Certificate: Valid Oct. 11, 2011-May 24th, 2012. Room Upgrade.

National landmark hotel with critically acclaimed restaurant, located in historic Cape May. We are a small family run business with 21 rooms, all with private bath or shower.
✉ manager@carrollvilla.com ◐ www.carrollvilla.com

Fairthorne B&B
111-115 Ocean St 08204
800-438-8742 609-884-8791
Ed & Diane Hutchinson

230-280 $US BB
10 rooms, 10 pb
Most CC, Cash, Checks,
Rated, •
C-ltd/S-no/P-no/H-no

Full breakfast
Afternoon tea and guest area with
soda, water, ice, coffee & tea
Public library across street, bicycles,
sitting room, near ocean

Voted "Best in the East" B&B by Inn goers. "The Discerning Traveler" chose us as one of the East's most delightful and delicious destinations – Romantic Hideaways 2002.
✉ fairthornebnb@aol.com ◐ www.fairthorne.com

CAPE MAY——————

Gingerbread House	110-335 $US BB	Full breakfast
28 Gurney St 08204	6 rooms, 3 pb	Hot coffee, tea & snacks available
609-884-0211	Visa, MC, *Rated*	throughout the day
Fred & Joan Echevarria	C-ltd/S-ltd/P-no/H-no	Wicker-filled porch, parlor with
	April – December	fireplace, Victorian antiques, A/C, LCD
		flat panel TVs, WiFi

Free Night w/Certificate: Valid October 1-May 26 and Monday-Thursday.

The Gingerbread House is a meticulous and comfortable 1869 inn. It is a woodworkers masterpiece using the innkeepers woodworking talents. It is conveniently located ½ block from the beach, in the heart of Cape May's historic district. ✉ info@gingerbreadinn.com ◑ www.gingerbreadinn.com

John F. Craig House	145-265 $US BB	Full breakfast
609 Columbia Ave 08204	8 rooms, 8 pb	Afternoon tea, snacks & cookies
877-544-0314 609-884-0100	Most CC, Cash, Checks	All rooms have A/C, some fireplaces,
Chip & Barbara Masemore	C-ltd/S-ltd/P-no/H-no	flat screen TV w/dvd, WiFi,
		refrigerators

Welcome to our whimsical yet romantic Bed and Breakfast, an Inn located in the center of Historic Cape May, New Jersey . . . designed for your comfort and our informality. Our inn is rated #8 on Travel Channel's list of Best Beach Communities. ✉ chipbarbara@comcast.net ◑ www.johnfcraig.com

John Wesley Inn &	150-345 $US BB	Full gourmet breakfast
Carriage House	8 rooms, 8 pb	Each afternoon a variety of seasonal
30 Gurney St 08204	Most CC, *Rated*, •	(hot or cold) refreshments are served
800-616-5122 609-884-1012	C-ltd/S-ltd/P-no/H-no	½ block to beach, 2 blocks to mall,
Bonnie & Lance Pontin		parking, Internet, TV, iPod, safes, A/C,
		sunroom/wet bar

"Where Antiques and Amenities Harmonize!" Completely renovated. Centrally located in the Cape May Historic District of Stockton Row, ½ block from beach and 2 blocks from the walking mall. Park your car on-site and forget about it. Walk to fine dining.
✉ info@johnwesleyinn.com ◑ www.johnwesleyinn.com

Leith Hall Historic	105-330 $US BB	Full breakfast
Seashore Inn	8 rooms, 8 pb	Afternoon English tea with cakes &
22 Ocean St 08204	Visa, MC, Disc, *Rated*	cookies. Iced tea and lemonade with
877-884-1400 609-884-1934	C-ltd/S-no/P-no/H-no	cakes & cookies in summer.
Susan & Elan Zingman-Leith	French, Yiddish	Ocean views, whirlpools, fireplaces,
		cable TV/VCRs/DVDs, A/C, large
		porch, wireless Internet, library

Elegantly restored 1880s bed and breakfast in the heart of the Victorian district. Only half block from the beach, with ocean views and a large wraparound porch with rocking chairs.
✉ stay@leithhall.com ◑ www.leithhall.com

Poor Richard's Inn of Cape	110-185 $US BB	Continental plus breakfast
May	8 rooms, 8 pb	Hot water available for tea most of the
17 Jackson St 08204	Most CC, Cash, Checks,	day
609-884-3536	*Rated*	Sitting room, porches, near beach
Harriett Sosson	C-ltd/S-no/P-no/H-no	
	Valentines-New Year's	

Classic gingerbread guesthouse offers accommodations with eclectic Victorian and country decor. A wonderful eight-room Victorian on gorgeous Jackson Street, less than a minute's walk to Cape May's main beach. ✉ harriettsosson@comcast.net ◑ www.poorrichardsinn.com

Rhythm of the Sea	215-395 $US BB	Full breakfast
1123 Beach Ave 08204	9 rooms, 9 pb	Beverage service daily, dinner by
800-498-6888 609-884-7788	Most CC, *Rated*	prior arrangement
Robyn & Wolfgang Wendt	C-ltd/S-no/P-no/H-no	Gathering rooms, parking, bikes,
	German	beach towels, beach chairs, concierge

With the ocean as the front yard, fragrant breezes and a wealth of seaside activities, Rhythm of the Sea is an ideal location for a Cape May getaway. Savor sumptuous meals, relaxed and peaceful privacy and 'gemuetlichkeit.'
✉ stay@rhythmofthesea.com ◑ www.rhythmofthesea.com

CAPE MAY

The Abbey B&B Inn
34 Gurney St @ Colombia
Ave 08204
866-884-8800   609-884-4506
Jay Schatz

95-200 $US BB
7 rooms, 7 pb
Visa, MC, Disc, *Rated*
C-ltd/S-ltd/P-no/H-no
Easter-Dec.

Full buffet breakfast dining room
Afternoon tea, wine & baked goods
offered in dining room each day
Daily housekeeping, wireless Internet,
onsite parking, beach tags & chairs,
flat screen TV in parlor

Free Night w/Certificate: Buy one night and get one included; valid Sunday or Monday thru Thursday; April, May, June, or October.

Elegantly restored Gothic Revival villa. Period antiques. Genuine merriment in a warm unobtrusive atmosphere. Rooms with A/C in season. Flat screen TV in parlor. One block from the Atlantic Ocean in the heart of the historic district. On site parking.

✉ theabbey1@verizon.net   🌐 www.abbeybedandbreakfast.com

The Dormer House
800 Columbia Ave 08204
800-884-5052   609-884-7446
Lucille & Dennis Doherty

99-250 $US BB
14 rooms, 14 pb
Most CC, Cash, Checks,
Rated
C-ltd/S-no/P-no/H-ltd

Full breakfast
Afternoon Tea & Treats
Sitting room, glass enclosed breakfast
porch, bikes, Jacuzzi room, comp.
beach chairs/towels, WiFi

One of the great summer houses of the 1890s. Enjoy your full breakfast and tea all year long on our sun porch. An inn for all seasons. "Come for the tea, stay for the night."

✉ dormerhouse@gmail.com   🌐 www.dormerhouse.com

The Mainstay Inn
635 Columbia Ave 08204
609-884-8690
Diane Clark

175-360 $US BB
13 rooms, 13 pb
Visa, MC, *Rated*
C-ltd/S-no/P-no/H-yes
April-Janurary 1st

Full breakfast (Sept-June)
4–5 p.m. daily: hot/iced tea, home
made sweets, fresh fruit & tea
sandwiches or cheese spreads.
12 A/C rooms, piano, 3 sitting rooms

An elegant Victorian Inn within a lovely garden setting. The Inn and adjacent Cottage feature wide rocker-lined verandas and large rooms, which are lavishly and comfortably furnished.

✉ mainstayinn@comcast.net   🌐 www.mainstayinn.com

The Mooring B&B
801 Stockton Ave 08204
609-884-5425
Leslie Valenza & Vince
Casale

150-275 $US BB
11 rooms, 11 pb
Visa, MC, •
C-ltd/S-no/P-no/H-no
French
Mid-April to October

Full & Continental breakfast avail
Afternoon tea
On-site parking, guest kitchen, WiFi
access, outside showers, beach towels

Victorian mansard structure furnished in original period antiques with contemporary upgrades. One block to ocean and easy walking distance to fine restaurants and shopping.

✉ leslie@themooring.com   🌐 www.themooring.com

The Queen Victoria B&B
102 Ocean Street 08204
609-884-8702
Anna Marie & Doug McMain

115-595 $US BB
34 rooms, 34 pb
Visa, MC, Disc, *Rated*
C-ltd/S-no/P-no/H-ltd

Full buffet breakfast
Afternoon tea with sweets & savory,
in the English fashion, 24 hr. pantry,
complimentary beverages
Bicycles, beach chairs, evening
turndown, wireless Internet, TV/DVD
& refrigerator in all rooms

Renowned historic Cape May B&B open all year with thirty-two antique-filled rooms & luxury suites, all with private bath, many with a whirlpool tub and/or fireplace.

✉ stay@queenvictoria.com   🌐 www.queenvictoria.com

The Queen Victoria B&B, Cape May, NJ

CAPE MAY

Victorian Lace Inn	125-350 $US BB	Full breakfast
901 Stockton Ave 08204	8 rooms, 8 pb	Freshly baked afternoon treats &
609-884-1772	Visa, MC, Disc, *Rated*	refreshments, kitchenettes in each
Carrie & Andy O'Sullivan	C-yes/S-no/P-no/H-no	suite
		Spa, Jacuzzis, library, wireless
		Internet, fax service, beach towels &
		chairs, fireplaces

Beautiful all-suite Colonial Revival inn, with oceanviews and fireplaces. The Cottage has a fireplace and Jacuzzi. The Victorian Lace Inn is a classic, cedar-sided B&B by the sea. Open year around and family friendly. ✉ innkeeper@VictorianLaceInn.com 🌐 www.victorianlaceinn.com

Wilbraham Mansion	120-365 $US BB	Full breakfast
133 Myrtle Ave 08204	22 rooms, 22 pb	Afternoon tea
609-884-2046	Visa, MC	Indoor heated pool (20 X 40), 3 dining
Doug Carnes	C-ltd/S-no/P-no/H-yes	rooms, 1 parlor, 2 porches, Jacuzzi
		tubs, fireplaces, TVs

Experience today's comforts & yesterday's Victorian elegance in one of Cape May's oldest & finest homes overlooking Wilbraham Park. Stay in one of the historic Mansion's ten rooms, or stay in one of twelve new Suites with Jacuzzi tubs and fireplaces.
✉ wilbrahammansion@verizon.net 🌐 www.wilbrahammansion.com

CLINTON

Riverside Victorian	95-130 $US BB	Full breakfast
66 Leigh St 08809	6 rooms, 4 pb	Afternoon refreshments
908-238-0400	Most CC, Cash	TV/VCR, A/C, telephone & in-room
Monita & Owen McElroy	C-ltd/S-no/P-no/H-no	high-speed Internet service, fireplace,
		fridge, fax machine

Step back in time and enjoy Victorian splendor in an inviting, friendly atmosphere. Whether your stay is business related or simply to get away for awhile, you will find a warm welcome waiting for you here!
✉ mail@riversidevictorian.com 🌐 www.riversidevictorian.com

FLEMINGTON

Main Street Manor Bed & Breakfast Inn
194 Main St 08822
908-782-4928
Donna & Ken Arold

130-215 $US BB
5 rooms, 5 pb
Most CC, *Rated*
C-ltd/S-no/P-no/H-no

Fresh, Full Country Breakfast
Afternoon tea, 24 hour coffee & tea,
baked goodies & seasonal fruits,
complimentary wine & cordials
Personal service, many books, board
games, cards, DVD library

Relax and feel at home in this magical Victorian Manor House, nestled in the heart of Flemington's residential historic district. Fireplaces, featherbeds and an elegant candlelight breakfast are a few of the indulgences awaiting your arrival.

✉ innkeeper@mainstreetmanor.com 🌐 www.mainstreetmanor.com

Silver Maple Organic Farm B&B
483 Sergeantsville Rd 08822
908-237-2192
Steven Noll

75-175 $US BB
5 rooms, 5 pb
Most CC, Cash,
Rated, •
C-yes/S-no/P-yes/H-ltd

Full homemade country breakfast
Complimentary soft drinks, coffee, tea,
waters, fruits & snacks 24/7
Robes, A/C, down comforters, rec
room, living room, fireplace, gardens,
pool, deck, hot tub, tennis

Historic Country Farmhouse minutes to New Hope, Lambertville, Frenchtown, Doylestown & Flemington. We embrace diversity & we are kid & pet friendly. Pool, hot tub, tennis & a full breakfast in a rural country setting. Extra comfortable rooms and rates.

✉ silvermaplebandb@gmail.com 🌐 www.silvermaplebandb.com

FRENCHTOWN

Widow McCrea House
53 Kingwood Ave 08825
908-996-4999
Burt Patalano, Lynn Marad

110-320 $US BB
6 rooms, 6 pb
Visa, MC, *Rated*
C-ltd/S-no/P-ltd/H-yes

Gourmet Candlelit 3 Course
Complimentary bottle of wine en suite
upon arrival, evening cordials.
Private cottage with garden &
fountains, parlor, fireplaces, Jacuzzis,
cable TV/DVD/CD, free WiFi

Charming 1878 Victorian Inn features spacious suites with fireplaces/Jacuzzis. English cottage with private garden, statuary & fountains. Six elegant guestrooms. Fine antiques, queen size featherbeds, private baths, candlelight breakfast. Private dining.

✉ widowmccrea@sprintmail.com 🌐 www.widowmccrea.com

HADDONFIELD

Haddonfield Inn
44 West End Ave 08033
800-269-0014 856-428-2195
Nancy & Fred Chorpita

159-339 $US BB
9 rooms, 9 pb
Most CC, Cash, •
C-ltd/S-no/P-yes/H-yes

Full gourmet breakfast
Snacks, cookies, tea, coffee, wine,
soda
Fireplaces, elevator, free calls,
concierge service, parking, cable,
WiFi, whirlpool baths

Elegant hotel for business or pleasure in an historic village near Philadelphia. Comforts include fireplaces, luxury linens & robes, WiFi, cable, private baths, whirlpools, concierge, elevator and a full breakfast served on individual tables. ✉ Innkeeper@haddonfieldinn.com 🌐 www.haddonfieldinn.com

HIGHLANDS

SeaScape Manor
3 Grand Tour 07732
732-291-8467
Sherry Ruby, Gloria Miller,
Robert Adamec

145-245 $US BB
4 rooms, 4 pb
Visa, MC, AmEx,
Rated
C-ltd/S-no/P-yes/H-ltd

Full breakfast
Complimentary wine
Panoramic ocean views, sitting room,
library, bikes, ocean swimming,
fireplaces, beach passes

Secluded manor nestled in the tree covered hills, overlooking the blue Atlantic and Sandy Hook National Recreation area. Once a private nineteenth century home, it still retains all its original charm. Escape to elegance. 45 minutes from NYC.

✉ seascape25@comcast.net 🌐 www.seascapemanorbb.com

LAMBERTVILLE

BridgeStreet House
75 Bridge St 08530
800-897-2503 609-397-2503
Dolores Holmes

100-185 $US BB
5 rooms, 5 pb
Visa, MC, AmEx
C-ltd/S-ltd/P-no/H-no

Continental plus breakfast
Snacks, beverages,
Cable color TV, A/C, bathrobes, fine
English soaps, free WiFi

Our beautiful bed & breakfast is a pre-Victorian Federal style row home situated in the heart of historic Lambertville, NJ. ✉ bridgestinn@comcast.net 🌐 www.bridgestreethouse.com

LAMBERTVILLE

York Street House
42 York St 08530
888-398-3199 609-397-3007
Laurie & Mark Weinstein

125-275 $US BB
6 rooms, 6 pb
Most CC, Cash,
Checks, •
C-ltd/S-no/P-no/H-no

Full breakfast
Complimentary hot and cold
beverages, homemade cookies
Common rooms, fireplaces, gardens,
cable TV, Jacuzzi tubs, free high speed
Internet access

Quiet, elegant Georgian Colonial Revival Inn. Fireplaces, canopies, Jacuzzi tubs, Waterford chandelier, and complimentary beverages. Full gourmet breakfast every morning.

 innkeeper@yorkstreethouse.com 🌐 www.yorkstreethouse.com

LONG VALLEY

Neighbour House B&B
143 W Mill Rd 07853
908-876-3519
Rafi & Iris Kadosh

85-145 $US BB
4 rooms, 2 pb
Visa, MC, AmEx, •
C-ltd/S-no/P-no/H-no
Hebrew

Full breakfast
Afternoon tea
Sitting room, bicycles, fireplaces, cable
TV, hiking, antique shops, fishing

Our guests enjoy elegantly furnished rooms in an enchanting, pastoral setting (we're surrounded by 800 beautiful green acres).

 neighbourhouse@comcast.net 🌐 www.neighbourhouse.com

NEW EGYPT

Inn at Laurita Winery
19 Archertown Rd 08533
609-752-0303
Diana Lee Black

135-310 $US BB
10 rooms, 10 pb
Most CC, *Rated*
C-yes/S-no/P-no/H-ltd

Full breakfast
Afternoon coffee, tea & snack
Sitting room, library, bicycles, suites,
fireplaces, cable TV, accommodations
for business travelers

Warmth and comfort, with that "welcome home" attitude, envelopes you as you are shown to your guestroom or suite. Leave any thought of schedule behind as your agenda now includes only "rest and relaxation!"   innkeeper@lauritawinery.com 🌐 www.innatlauritawinery.com

NEWTON

The Wooden Duck B&B
140 Goodale Rd 07860
973-300-0395
Beth & Karl Krummel

139-299 $US BB
10 rooms, 10 pb
Most CC, *Rated*, •
C-ltd/S-no/P-no/H-yes

Full breakfast
Snacks & beverages available 24/7
Game room, living room, swimming
pool, hiking, fireplaces, satellite TV,
free wireless Internet

Country estate on 10 wooded acres adjacent to a beautiful State Park. Outdoor activities year-round. Full country breakfast served in dining room. Perfect romantic getaway, yet all amenities required by business travelers including wireless Internet.

 woodenduckinn@aol.com 🌐 www.woodenduckinn.com

NORTH WILDWOOD

Candlelight Inn
2310 Central Ave 08260
800-992-2632 609-522-6200
Bill & Nancy Moncrief

110-265 $US BB
10 rooms, 10 pb
Visa, MC, AmEx, •
C-ltd/S-no/P-no/H-no

Full breakfast
Afternoon refreshments including
wine; soft drinks and bottled water,
Murder Mystery dinners
WiFi, hot tub, TV/DVD (DVDs free),
CD player & fireplaces in all rooms, 3
suites, whirlpool tubs

Seashore Queen Anne Victorian B&B with genuine antiques, fireplaces, wide veranda. Getaway specials & murder mystery parties available. Close to the beach & boardwalk.

 info@candlelight-inn.com 🌐 www.candlelight-inn.com

**Summer Nites 50's Theme
B&B**
2110 Atlantic Ave 08260
866-ROC-1950 609-846-1955
Sheila & Rick Brown

115-280 $US BB
8 rooms, 8 pb
Most CC, *Rated*, •
S-ltd/P-no/H-yes

Full breakfast
Afternoon refreshments of root beer
floats, milkshakes & soft pretzels
Wrap-around porch, game room,
Jacuzzi, Internet access, pool table,
bicycles, beach towels

Summer Nites, located in beautiful North Wildwood, NJ has all of the modern amenities, while retaining and capturing the excitement and uniqueness of the early days of Rock-and-Roll. Choose from the Elvis Suite, Marilyn Room, 60's Suite and 5 more rooms.

 info@summernites.com 🌐 www.summernites.com

OCEAN CITY

Brown's Nostalgia B&B
1001 Wesley Ave 08226
866-223-0400 609-398-6364
Harmon & Marjorie Brown

113-180 $US BB
8 rooms, 8 pb
C-ltd/S-no/P-no/H-ltd

Full breakfast
Afternoon snacks & drinks
Fireplaces, Jacuzzis, decks, porch,
powder room, parking, exercise room,
hot tub, bikes, beach tags

A circa 1900 inn providing accommodations in the center of Ocean City, New Jersey. Just walking distance from the beach and boardwalk. Newly renovated and offering a nostalgic atmosphere combined with modern conveniences.

brownsnj@comcast.net www.brownsnostalgia.com

Inn the Gardens B&B
48 Wesley Rd 08226
609-399-0800
Jennifer Torres

99-189 $US BB
7 rooms, 7 pb
Visa, MC
C-yes/S-no/P-no/H-ltd
Spanish

Continental plus breakfast
Afternoon beverages
Porches, balconies, outdoor enclosed
shower, garden patio, beach tags, free
WiFi access,

Beautiful balconies to enjoy the ocean breezes. Located in the quiet, north end of the island. Spacious side yard & backyard with a beautiful patio & gardens. Old fashion charm and modern conveniences make you feel right at home.

innthegardens@aol.com www.innthegardens.com

Northwood Inn
401 Wesley Ave 08226
609-399-6071
Marj & John Loeper

130-315 $US BB
7 rooms, 7 pb
Visa, MC, *Rated*
C-ltd/S-no/P-no/H-no

Full breakfast
Afternoon cookies and iced tea.
Roof-top deck with year round
whirlpool, bikes, game room, pool
table, fireplace, Free WiFi, DVD's

Award winning 1894 Victorian with 21st century comforts including Jacuzzis, central air, wireless Internet. Located between Atlantic City & Cape May. Enjoy our romantic rooftop whirlpool spa with magnificent sunsets in all seasons.

info@northwoodinn.com www.northwoodinn.com

Scarborough Inn
720 Ocean Ave 08226
800-258-1558 609-399-1558
Gus & Carol Bruno

110-255 $US BB
24 rooms, 24 pb
Visa, MC, Disc,
Rated, •
C-ltd/S-ltd/P-no/H-no
Italian
May to October

Continental plus wkdays/Full wkends
Afternoon refreshments
Free wireless Internet, concierge, high-
speed computer & beach tags, parking
on premises

Experience the true luxury of our Ocean City, NJ, Bed & Breakfast that artfully combines vintage charm with modern amenities. Stroll to beach, boardwalk, shopping, and dining from our centrally located Historic District neighborhood.

scarboroughinn@comcast.net www.scarboroughinn.com

**Serendipity Bed &
Breakfast**
712 Ninth St 08226
800-842-8544 609-399-1554
Karen Morella

105-215 $US BB
5 rooms, 5 pb
Most CC, Cash, Checks,
Rated, •
C-ltd/S-ltd/P-no/H-no

Full breakfast
Snacks, beverages all day
Free parking, electric fireplace in most
rooms, video library, beach passes &
chairs

Welcome all year round to our light and airy oasis by the sea, where you can stroll to the beach and Ocean City Boardwalk, just a half block away!

info@serendipitynj.com www.serendipitynj.com

The Inn at Laurel Bay
400 Atlantic Ave 08226
609-814-1886
Sharon & John Szabo

100-200 $US BB
6 rooms, 4 pb
C-yes/S-ltd/P-no/H-ltd

Continental breakfast
Afternoon fresh brewed herbal iced
teas & savory snacks, full service cafe
downstairs
A/C, newspaper, grand porch, beach
tags & chairs, sports equipment

Your comfort is our commitment at The Inn at Laurel Bay. Every detail, from the morning paper to the grand porch, is chosen to enhance your experience.

laurelbay400@aol.com web.mac.com/laurelbay400

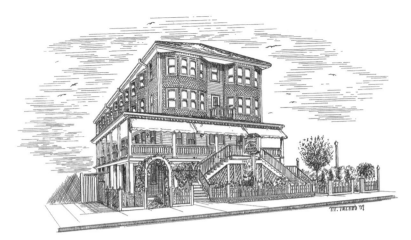

Scarborough Inn, Ocean City, NJ

OCEAN GROVE

Carriage House B&B
18 Heck Ave 07756
732-988-3232
Kathi & Phil Franco

125-190 $US BB
8 rooms, 8 pb
Most CC, Cash, Checks
C-ltd/S-no/P-no/H-no

Full breakfast
Cold drinks, snacks
Disc't beach badges, beach chairs/
towels, library/sitting room, cable TV/
VCR/DVD, wireless Internet,

Intimate eight-room B&B overlooking the Atlantic Ocean & one block from the center of town. Winner of The Historical Society Restoration Award.

✉ carriagehouseog@aol.com 🌐 www.carriagehousenj.com

House by the Sea
14 Ocean Ave 07756
732-774-4771
Sally & Alyn Heim

90-135 $US BB
18 rooms, 10 pb
Visa, MC
C-ltd/S-no/P-no/H-no
Memorial Day – Labor
Day

Continental breakfast
Guest may keep their food in
refrigerators to share in our lower
lounge. Afternoon high tea.
2 sitting rooms, 3 porches, 2 color TVs

At House by the Sea, you can realize your fantasy of oceanfront living. Walk to restaurants, shops & the Great Auditorium. Close to Jersey shore events & New York City attractions.

✉ housebysea@monmouth.com 🌐 www.travelguides.com/home/house_by_the_sea

---

Ocean Plaza
18 Ocean Pathway 07756
732-774-6552
Bob Valente

90-425 $US BB
19 rooms, 19 pb
Most CC, Cash
C-yes/S-no/P-no/H-yes

Continental breakfast
Coffee, Tea, Snack Bar
Air Conditioning, Cable TV, WiFi,
Guest Computer

This grand century old Victorian Bed & Breakfast located just one block from the beach provides the perfect setting for family vacations, relaxing getaways, corporate travel, family or group get togethers and weddings. 1½ hrs. from NYC and Philadelphia

✉ info@TheInnsofOceanGrove.com 🌐 www.TheInnsofOceanGrove.com

The Lillagaard Inn
5 Abbott Ave 07756
732-988-1216
Dick & Jane Wehr

120-175 $US BB
22 rooms, 19 pb
Most CC, Cash, Checks
C-ltd/S-no/P-no/H-no

Full breakfast
Our Victorian Tea Room serves
afternoon tea with delicious scones &
lunch
Library, game room, front porch,
formal dining room, wireless Internet,
romance, conference

This historic inn features 22 enchanting guestrooms, each named for its unique theme. Imagine yourself surrounded by the tranquility of an earlier time, soothed by the soft murmur of the ocean . . . .

✉ lillagaard@aol.com 🌐 www.lillagaard.com

PLAINFIELD

The Pillars of Plainfield B&B Inn 922 Central Ave 07060 908-753-0922 Lamont Blowe & Nancy Fiske	125-190 $US BB 7 rooms, 7 pb Most CC, Cash, *Rated*, • C-yes/S-no/P-yes/H-no	Full breakfast Complimentary cordials, home baked cookies, soda Living room, library, fireplaces, free Internet access

Close to NYC and Newark Liberty International Airport. An 1870 Victorian mansion in the Van Wyck Brooks Historic District, where homes on acre lots offer "sylvan seclusion with urban access."

✉ info@pillars2.com ◯ www.pillars2.com

POINT PLEASANT BEACH

Tower Cottage 203 Forman Ave 08742 877-766-2693 732-892-2070 Tony & Maureen Haddad	275-425 $US BB 5 rooms, 5 pb Most CC, Cash, Checks S-no/P-no/H-no	Full gourmet breakfast Early morning cup of coffee, afternoon freshly baked treats, and evening glass of wine. fireplace, luxurious MicroFiber Robes, HD flat screen TVs, iPod docking station, luxury toiletries

The Tower Cottage is a meticulously restored Queen Anne Victorian inn. It is ideally located for guests traveling for pleasure or business to Point Pleasant Beach at the Jersey Shore or surrounding communities of Bay Head, Spring Leak, or Manasquan.

✉ Stay@TheTowerCottage.com ◯ www.thetowercottage.com

SPRING LAKE

Chateau Inn & Suites 500 Warren Ave 07762 877-974-5253 732-974-2000 Scott Smith	89-359 $US BB 37 rooms, 37 pb Most CC, *Rated*, • C-yes/S-no/P-no/H-ltd	Gourmet Continental Breakfast Gourmet coffee bar with herbal teas and flavored syrups, afternoon cookies, ice tea & lemonade Spa & Fitness Center Passes, WiFi Internet, bicycles, DVD movie rentals, beach & tennis passes

The historic Chateau Inn and Suites offers elegance and romance unmatched at the Jersey Shore. Enhancements include Fireplaces, Jacuzzis, balconies overlooking "The Lake" and just a short walk to Spring Lake's prestigious beaches, shopping and boardwalk.

✉ info@chateauinn.com ◯ www.chateauinn.com

Spring Lake Inn 104 Salem Ave 07762 732-449-2010 Barbara & Andy Seaman	99-599 $US BB 16 rooms, 16 pb Most CC, Cash, *Rated*, • C-yes/S-no/P-no/H-ltd Spanish	Great breakfast Jersey fresh fruit, candy, smoked salmon, bagels Wireless Internet, cable TV, beach badges, fireplaces, ocean views

Circa 1888 Victorian with 80-foot porch, fireplaces, parlor, ocean views, digital cable, the heart of an intimate hotel and the soul of a B&B. One short block to the ocean & boardwalk. Quiet. Great breakfast! ✉ springlakeinn@aol.com ◯ www.springlakeinn.com

The Ocean House 102 Sussex Ave. 07762 888-449-9094 732-449-9090 Nancy & Dennis Kaloostian	125-295 $US BB 20 rooms, 20 pb Visa, MC C-ltd/S-no/P-no/H-ltd	Gourmet candlelight breakfast Cooking Class Weekends Wrap-around porch, bicycles, beach chairs & umbrellas, ice & soda machine, cable TV, WiFi

The tradition began over 100 years ago and since that time, the Ocean House has brought to each season the promise of elegant surroundings, peaceful days, and lasting friendships.

✉ oceanhouse0762@aol.com ◯ www.theoceanhouse.net

SPRING LAKE ───────────────────

The Sandpiper Inn	109-259 $US BB	Full breakfast
7 Atlantic Ave 07762	15 rooms, 15 pb	Afternoon snacks
732-449-6060	Most CC, Cash	A/C, TV with DVD, Jacuzzis, bikes,
Harold & Chris Cullison	C-ltd/S-no/P-no/H-no	beach passes, beach towels & chairs,
	Summer	veranda, heated indoor pool.

Whether it be romance, recreation or relaxation; a getaway weekend, extended vacation or corporate meeting, The Sandpiper Inn provides the commitment to excellence you deserve. Grand and spacious, comfortable and welcoming, the Sandpiper Inn awaits you . . .

✉ ubhappy@sandpiperinn.com 🌐 www.sandpiperinn.com

Villa Park House	100-375 $US BB	Full breakfast
417 Ocean Rd 07762	11 rooms, 7 pb	Parlor, porch, weddings, WiFi, A/C,
732-449-3642	Visa, MC, AmEx,	refrigerator, bikes, beach badges,
Matthew & Dara Schmid	*Rated*	chairs, towels & umbrellas
	C-yes/S-no/P-no/H-no	

A grand Victorian era home that has been a welcome retreat for visitors since 1886. We have been the choice for many wanting to relax & rejuvenate near the Atlantic Ocean.

✉ info@villaparkhouse.com 🌐 www.villaparkhouse.com

White Lilac Inn	139-359 $US BB	Full breakfast
414 Central Ave 07762	9 rooms, 9 pb	Afternoon refreshments, early bird
732-449-0211 732-974-0568	Most CC, Cash, •	coffee
Mari Kennelly	C-ltd/S-no/P-no/H-no	Beach badges, bicycles, parking, A/C,
		cable TV/VCR, fireplaces, whirlpool

A Romantic, Victorian Inn with southern charm and triple-tiered porches awaits your arrival. Enjoy the warm hospitality, relax by the fireplace, start your day with our delicious breakfasts.

✉ Mari@whitelilac.com 🌐 www.whitelilac.com

STOCKTON ───────────────────

Woolverton Inn	145-435 $US BB	Full country breakfast
6 Woolverton Rd 08559	13 rooms, 13 pb	Snacks, catering, complimentary soft
888-264-6648 609-397-0802	Visa, MC, AmEx,	drinks and bottled water
C. McGavin, M. Lovette, M.	*Rated*, •	Sitting room, suites, fireplaces,
Smith	C-ltd/S-no/P-no/H-ltd	Jacuzzis, gardens, meeting facilities,
	Some Spanish and	weddings
	German	

A 1792 stone manor house on 10 acres of lawns and gardens, surrounded by 400 acres of rolling farmland. So close to everything, but a world away. Elegant hearty breakfasts.

✉ sheep@woolvertoninn.com 🌐 www.woolvertoninn.com

WILDWOOD ───────────────────

The Sea Gypsy B&B	110-185 $US BB	Full breakfast
209 E Magnolia Ave 08260	10 rooms, 10 pb	Old fashioned candy cupboard with
609-522-0690	Most CC	candy, cookies, popcorn & goodies,
Todd & Natalie Kieninger,	C-yes/S-no/P-no/H-no	wine & other drinks
Anna Grimm		Sitting room, bicycle, Jacuzzi, suites,
		TV/DVD/VCR, VHS/DVD library, maid
		service, verandah, shuttle

The Sea Gypsy B&B is a quiet B&B get-away in the heart of Wildwood on the Jersey seaside. A charmingly restored 1903 Victorian with a turret, sun deck, wide porches and a hot tub. Bring the entire family for seaside fun, adventure and comfort.

✉ info@theseagypsy.com 🌐 www.theseagypsy.com

New Mexico

ALBUQUERQUE

Adobe Garden at Los Ranchos B&B
641 Chavez NW 87107
505-345-1954
Lee & Tricia Smith

115-135 $US BB
6 rooms, 6 pb
Visa, MC
C-yes/S-no/P-no/H-no

Full breakfast
Afternoon tea
Grand old cottonwoods, adobe-walled
courtyard, swimming pool, fireplace

At Adobe Garden you are steeped in the richness of Colonial Spanish architecture and the private, semi-rural village of Los Ranchos de Albuquerque. Wake up to the warmth of New Mexico sunshine and a sumptuous breakfast prepared to perfection.

✉ adobegarden@spinn.net 🌐 www.adobegarden.com

Casita Chamisa B&B
850 Chamisal Rd NW 87107
505-897-4644
Arnold Sargeant

105-125 $US BB
3 rooms, 2 pb
Visa, MC, AmEx
C-yes/S-no/P-yes/H-no

Continental plus breakfast
Sitting room, patio, decks, indoor pool,
hot tub

Albuquerque's first B&B. Two bedroom country guesthouse and 19th century adobe house with two large bedrooms each with a fireplace and private bath. Archaeological site, indoor heated swimming pool, TV's and high speed Internet.   ✉ chamisainn@aol.com 🌐 www.casitachamisa.com

---

Downtown Historic B&B of Albuquerque
207 & 209 High St. NE 87102
888-342-0223 505-842-0223
Steve & Kara Grant

89-209 $US BB
9 rooms, 7 pb
Most CC, Cash, Checks
C-ltd/S-no/P-no/H-ltd

Full Gourmet Breakfast
Afternoon tea, homemade snacks &
fresh fruit provided
Cable TV, telephones, central heat/air,
free wireless Internet

Historic Dutch Colonial/Bungalow style homes offering beautifully decorated rooms and gourmet breakfast, in Albuquerque's Historic Huning Highland neighborhood, near downtown restaurants and other attractions. Weddings and special events welcome as well.

✉ info@albuquerquebedandbreakfasts.com 🌐 www.albuquerquebedandbreakfasts.com

---

Los Poblanos Inn
4803 Rio Grande Blvd
NW 87107
866-344-9297 505-344-9297
Armin & Penny Rembe

155-300 $US BB
20 rooms, 19 pb
Most CC, Cash,
Checks, •
C-yes/S-ltd/P-no/H-ltd
Spanish, French, Italian

Gourmet full organic breakfast
Private dining options available upon
prior arrangement. Cooking classes,
picnic lunches an option
in-room phones, organic farm, bikes,
cable TV, wireless Internet & daily
delivery of New York Times

Listed in both the National & NM Register of Historic Places, Los Poblanos is set amidst 25 lush acres. Exquisitely decorated rooms, gourmet organic breakfasts.

✉ info@lospoblanos.com 🌐 www.lospoblanos.com

Old Town B&B
707 17th St NW 87104
888-900-9144 505-764-9144
Nancy Hoffman

85-120 $US BB
2 rooms, 2 pb
Rated, •
C-yes/S-no/P-no/H-no

Full breakfast
Refreshment in room
Garden patio, kiva fireplace, private
baths

Old Town B&B provides the comforts of home in a quiet, secluded garden setting with a wealth of interesting activities just minutes away from its doorstep.

✉ nvrhoffman@gmail.com 🌐 www.inn-new-mexico.com

Sarabande B&B
5637 Rio Grande NW 87107
888-506-4923 505-345-4923
Janie Egers

99-159 $US BB
6 rooms, 6 pb
Most CC, Cash, Checks
C-ltd/S-ltd/P-yes/H-no

Full breakfast

Sarabande Bed and Breakfast's enchanting casa features sculptured adobe walls, ceilings crafted from hand hewn vigas and slender latillas, one-of-a-kind antique stained glass windows and uniquely charming guestrooms more peaceful than a Spanish lullaby.

✉ janie@sarabandebnb.com 🌐 www.sarabandebnb.com

Downtown Historic B&B, Albuquerque, NM

ALBUQUERQUE

The Mauger Estate B&B	89-209 $US BB	Full breakfast
701 Roma Ave NW 87102	8 rooms, 8 pb	Snacks, complimentary wine, sweets
800-719-9189 505-242-8755	Most CC, Cash,	Sitting room, family friendly facility,
Tammy Walden	*Rated*, •	satellite TV, free hi-speed wireless
	C-yes/S-no/P-ltd/H-no	Internet, free parking

The Mauger Estate B&B (pronounced Major) is a wonderfully intimate, restored Queen Anne residence, where high ceilings and rich woodwork offer an old-fashioned and rewarding experience. It is Albuquerque's most centrally located bed and breakfast.

 maugerbb@aol.com 🌐 www.maugerbb.com

ALGODONES

Hacienda Vargas B&B Inn	89-189 $US BB	Full country breakfast
1431 Hwy 313 El Camino	7 rooms, 7 pb	Evening snacks, hot tea dinner by
Real 87001	Visa, MC, AmEx,	reservation
800-261-0006 505-867-9115	*Rated*, •	Sitting room, library, fireplaces golf
Cynthia & Richard Spence	C-ltd/S-ltd/P-ltd/H-ltd	course nearby, private Jacuzzi tubs,
	some Spanish	gardens (hairdryer, iron

Conveniently located between Albuquerque and Santa Fe, NM. Southwest Hacienda in a historic 17th c. setting. All 7 rooms and suites have private baths, private entrances, most with fireplaces and some with Jacuzzis. On-site wedding chapel.

 stay@haciendavargas.com 🌐 www.haciendavargas.com

ARTESIA

Heritage Inn B&B	88-104 $US BB	Continental breakfast
209 W Main 88210	11 rooms, 11 pb	Business traveler accommodations,
866-207-0222 575-748-2552	Most CC, *Rated*	use of health club, wireless Internet,
Sue Kehoe	C-yes/S-no/P-ltd/H-yes	cable TV, deck with grill
	Spanish	

In SE New Mexico, crossroads to adventure, located downtown, convenient to shops and restaurants. 2nd story property, quiet, very clean and comfortable. Preferred by business and leisure travelers, "a gem in the desert."

 innkeeper@artesiaheritageinn.com 🌐 www.artesiaheritageinn.com

CEDAR CREST ───────────────────────────────

Elaine's, A B&B
72 Snowline Rd-SL
Estates 87008
800-821-3092 505-281-2467
Elaine O'Neil

99-149 $US BB
5 rooms, 5 pb
Most CC
C-ltd/S-no/P-no/H-no

Full breakfast
Tea, coffee, hot chocolate, drinks
Fireplace, European antiques, Jacuzzi
tubs in some rooms and outside,
wireless Internet

Charm, elegance, and gracious hospitality in a beautiful three-story log home, nestled in the evergreen forests. Breathtaking alpine views make this a perfect location for a romantic rendezvous. High speed Internet keeps the business traveler connected. ✉ elaine@elainesbnb.com 🌐 www.elainesbnb.com

CHAMA ───────────────────────────────

The Parlor Car B&B
311 Terrace Ave 87520
888-849-7800 575-756-1946
Wendy & Bonsall Johnson

79-159 $US BB
3 rooms, 3 pb
Most CC, *Rated*, •
C-yes/S-no/P-no/H-no

Full breakfast
Box lunches on request, snacks,
welcome basket
Sitting room, library, Jacuzzi in 1 room,
cable TV, gardens

Luxuriate in cool, clean mountain air in an historic Victorian banker's home. Guests are treated to the luxury enjoyed by the socially elite of the early 20th century at economy pricing.
🌐 www.parlorcar.com

CHIMAYO ───────────────────────────────

Casa Escondida Bed & Breakfast
64 County Rd 0100 87522
800-643-7201 505-351-4805
Belinda Bowling

105-165 $US BB
8 rooms, 8 pb
Visa, MC, •
C-yes/S-no/P-yes/H-ltd

Full, hot, sit-down breakfast
Snacks, teas, coffees, lemonade
Outdoor hot tub, fireplaces, private
decks & patios, woodburning stove

Free Night w/Certificate: Valid Sunday-Thursday nights: May-October; Valid any night: November-April; Holiday periods & special events exculded all year.

Secluded mountain B&B on 6 acres, in the historic village of Chimayo, just 35 minutes north of Santa Fe. Ideal central location for splendid day trips & ski outings throughout northern NM. Four of 8 rooms are pet-friendly. ✉ info@casaescondida.com 🌐 www.casaescondida.com

CIMARRON ───────────────────────────────

Casa del Gavilan
Hwy 21 South 87714
800-GAVILAN 575-376-2246
Robyn Parris

94-154 $US BB
6 rooms, 4 pb
Visa, MC, Disc, *Rated*
C-yes/S-ltd/P-no/H-ltd

Full breakfast
Dinners available with reservation &
additional charge

Casa del Gavilan (also known as the Nairn Place) offers exceptional views of the Sangre de Cristo mountains, hiking trails, and the peace and tranquility so rare these days. The guestrooms all have private baths and a full breakfast is served daily.
✉ robyn@casadelgavilan.com 🌐 www.casadelgavilan.com

CORRALES ───────────────────────────────

Chocolate Turtle B&B
1098 W. Meadowlark
Ln. 87048
877-298-1800 505-898-1800
Dallas & Nancy Renner

119-149 $US BB
4 rooms, 4 pb
Most CC, Cash, Checks,
Rated
C-ltd/S-no/P-no/H-ltd

Full breakfast
Chocolate turtles in each room,
complimentary snacks & cookies
available
Great Room, Portal & Patio, TV in Great
Room, WiFi, CD players in guestrooms

Classic adobe style home with 4 colorful guestrooms in picturesque Corrales, a historic farming community in the Rio Grande river valley of New Mexico. Country-like setting, incredible mountain views, horses, and golf. Weddings, meetings. AAA 3 Diamonds.
✉ Innkeeper@chocolateturtlebb.com 🌐 www.chocolateturtlebb.com

Nora Dixon Place B&B
312 Dixon Rd 87048
888-667-2349 505-898-3662
Norris & Cynthia C. Tidwell

104-170 $US BB
3 rooms, 3 pb
Visa, MC, AmEx,
Rated, •
C-yes/S-no/P-ltd/H-ltd

Full breakfast
Fresh ground coffee, brewed teas &
milk
Sitting room, suites, fireplaces,
conference facilities, TV, phones

Quiet New Mexico Territorial Style B&B, facing Sandia Mountain in Corrales. Located on the north-side of Albuquerque where historic sites are easily visited on day excursions. Rural peacefulness just 35 minutes from the Albuquerque airport.)✉ noradixon@comcast.net 🌐 www.noradixon.com

Casa del Gavilan, Cimarron, NM

EDGEWOOD

Lazy K Ranch Bed & Breakfast
27 Autumnwood Ct 87015
877-281-2072 505-281-2072
Lisa & Andrew Kwas

99-250 $US BB
4 rooms, 4 pb
Rated
C-ltd/S-no/P-yes/H-no

Full breakfast
Wine or tea with refreshments, snacks are always available
Game room, pool table, parlor, fireplace, Jacuzzi, garden, deck, patio, private log cabin

Come and enjoy the peaceful hospitality of mountain living. Just minutes from Albuquerque and Santa Fe along the historic Turquoise Trail. Four bedrooms all with private bathrooms, some with Jacuzzi tubs. Romantic getaway with gorgeous views.

✉ lisa@lazykranchbb.com 🌐 www.lazykranchbb.com

EL PRADO

Dobson House
575-776-5738
Joan and John Dobson

118-140 $US BB
2 rooms, 2 pb
C-ltd/S-no/P-no/H-no

Full breakfast
Afternoon refreshments of local goat cheeses, focaccia, fresh fruit & assorted beverages.
Extensive library, superb food, private bathrooms w/ shower, self-contained stoves, down comforters

Dobson House sits at 7,000 feet on a 100 foot hill in a rift valley overlooking the Rio Grande Gorge, near natural hot springs. Enjoy luxurious accommodations in this beautiful adobe structure, surrounded only by mountains, desert and sky.

✉ dobhouse@newmex.com 🌐 www.new-mexico-bed-and-breakfast.com

ESPANOLA

Inn at the Delta
243 N Paseo De Onate 87532
800-995-8599 505-753-9466
Emery & Dolores Maez

110-165 $US BB
10 rooms, 10 pb
Most CC, Cash, *Rated*
C-yes/S-no/P-ltd/H-ltd
Spanish

Continental plus breakfast
Wireless Internet, in-room massage therapy, whirlpools tubs, kiva fireplaces

Featuring hand made Mexican tile floors, the authentic Adobe structure is considered to be one of the most beautiful structures in Northern New Mexico. The Inn is centrally located between eight northern New Mexico Pueblos. ✉ emery.maez@gmail.com 🌐 www.innatthedelta.biz

FARMINGTON

Casa Blanca B&B Inn
505 E La Plata St 87401
800-550-6503 505-327-6503
David and Shirley Alford

125-175 $US BB
8 rooms, 8 pb
Most CC, Cash, Checks, *Rated*, •
C-yes/S-no/P-no/H-yes
Spanish

Full gourmet breakfast
fresh fruit, cookies, coffee, snacks
library, afternoon snacks, Jacuzzi tubs, fireplaces, cable TV, WiFi, business travelers welcome

Beautiful Mediterranean-style home built and handcrafted by the original owner's father in the 1950s; has made a perfect transition to a bed & breakfast inn. AAA three diamond rating.
✉ info@casablancanm.com 🌐 www.casablancanm.com

GILA

Casitas de Gila Guesthouses
50 Casita Flats Rd 88038
877-923-4827 575-535-4455
Becky & Michael O'Connor

140-225 $US BB
5 rooms, 5 pb
Most CC
C-ltd/S-ltd/P-no/H-yes

Continental plus breakfast
Stocked kitchen
Hot tub, art gallery, fireplaces, free
WiFi, full kitchens, spotting scope,
library of books

Southwestern guesthouses & art gallery on 260 acres overlooking Bear Creek and the Gila Wilderness, near Silver City, New Mexico. Our Stress-Free Zone was selected by Sunset Magazine as a "Top 10 Hidden Getaway." Explore by day, relax at night!

✉ info@casitasdegila.com 🌐 www.casitasdegila.com

JEMEZ SPRINGS

Desert Willow
15975 Hwy 4 87025
575-829-3410
Leone Wilson

149-169 $US BB
1 rooms, 1 pb
Most CC, *Rated*, •
C-yes/S-no/P-yes/H-ltd

Full breakfast
Deck overlooking river, fully equipped
kitchen, 2 bedroom cottage with
fireplace

Tucked into a quiet, mountain canyon with sheer cliffs rising from the river along New Mexico's Jemez Mountain Trail, the Dragonfly Cottage at the Desert Willow B&B in Jemez Springs, New Mexico is a nature-lovers' delight!

✉ wilsons@desertwillowbandb.com 🌐 www.desertwillowbandb.com

LAS CRUCES

DreamCatcher Inn B&B de Las Cruces
10201 Starfly Rd 88011
866-298-1935 575-522-3035
Ken & Anita McLeod

115-145 $US BB
4 rooms, 4 pb
Most CC, Cash, *Rated*
C-ltd/S-no/P-ltd/H-yes

Full breakfast
Coffee & tea are provided for all to
enjoy, popcorn, guest kitchen
TV, DVD/VCR, small sound system,
phone, high-speed Internet connection
in each room

Minutes from the lights, hustle, and bustle of Las Cruces, NM. Close to fine dining, shopping, NM State University, NASA. Three guestrooms, on 10 acres, for those who love to hike and enjoy the peace and tranquility of the beautiful High Desert.

✉ dreamcatcherinn@yahoo.com 🌐 www.dreamcatcherinn.com

Hilltop Hacienda B&B
2600 Westmoreland
Ave 88012
877-829-7142 575-382-3556
Bob and Teddi Peters

115-145 $US BB
3 rooms, 3 pb
Most CC, *Rated*, •
C-ltd/S-ltd/P-ltd/H-yes
Spanish, Portuguese
minimal

Full breakfast
Special diet needs will be
accommodated as best we can
Sitting room, library, fireplace, cable
TV, 20 acres of peace & quiet

Lodging in Las Cruces includes a secluded, romantic B&B with breathtaking sunrises and sunsets, atop 20 beautiful acres with 360 degree views of mountains, Las Cruces, and Mesilla Valley.

✉ thehilltophacienda@yahoo.com 🌐 www.zianet.com/hilltop

MESILLA

Casa de Rosie B&B
2140 Calle del Norte 88046
888-361-3699 575-523-0821
Rosie Martinez

99-125 $US BB
3 rooms, 3 pb
Visa, MC, AmEx
C-ltd/S-ltd/P-yes/H-ltd

Full breakfast

A beautiful bed and breakfast in Old Mesilla, it is located about 100 steps from the Plaza and the Basilica of San Albino. Casa de Rosie is in walking distance to all the shops and restaurants but still secluded and quiet.

✉ rosie@casaderosie.com 🌐 www.casaderosie.com

PLACITAS

Blue Horse B&B
300 Camino de las
Huertas 87043
877-258-4677 505-771-9055
Tom & Cathy Hansen

99-135 $US BB
3 rooms, 3 pb
Visa, MC, Disc
C-ltd/S-no/P-ltd/H-no

Full breakfast
Complimentary beverages & snacks
Fireplaces, inviting courtyard,
whirlpool jetted tub, surrounded by
mountains, unique furnishings

Nestled in the beautiful high desert foothills of Albuquerque's Sandia Mountain. Relax in comfortable Southwestern rooms amidst glorious mountains, mesas, sunsets and stars.

✉ info@bluehorsebandb.com 🌐 www.bluehorsebandb.com

SANTA FE

Bobcat Inn
442 Old Las Vegas
Hwy 87505
505-988-9239
Amy & John Bobrick

99-139 $US BB
7 rooms, 7 pb
Visa, MC, Disc, *Rated*
C-yes/S-no/P-no/H-yes

Full breakfast
High tea available (summer),
homemade cookies & hot chocolate
(winter)
Fireplace, great room, gardens,
complimentary wireless Internet
access

Nature lovers dream with old world ambience. Located in the foothills of Santa Fe. Beautiful gardens, stunning views of the mesa, gourmet breakfast.Authentic Southwestern style.

✉ res@nm-inn.com 🌐 www.nm-inn.com

Don Gaspar Inn
623 Don Gaspar Ave 87505
888-986-8664 505-986-8664
Shirley Isgar

165-385 $US BB
10 rooms, 10 pb
Visa, MC, Disc, *Rated*
C-yes/S-no/P-no/H-yes

Gourmet Southwestern Buffet
Homemade granola and fresh fruit in
the breakfast room daily. afternoon
treats, tea, coffee.
Private gardens and courtyards; DVD
library, local activities & information.

Three historic homes in the heart of Santa Fe, just a short walk to the Plaza. Selected as a "Top 10 Romantic Inns for 2003" and Travel & Leisure's "Top Lodging Secret in Santa Fe." This charming Inn offers large suites, private patios and hospitality.

✉ info@dongaspar.com 🌐 www.dongaspar.com

Dunshee's B&B and Casita
986 Acequia Madre 87505
505-982-0988
Susan Dunshee

112-162 $US BB
2 rooms, 2 pb
Visa, MC, *Rated*
C-yes/S-no/P-no/H-no

Continental plus breakfast
Continental plus in casita, full
breakfast in suite, homemade cookies
Sitting room, refrigerator, TV, private
patio & gardens

Romantic hideaway in adobe compound in historic zone. Choice of 2-room suite or 2-bedroom guest-house furnished with antiques.

✉ sdunshee@aol.com 🌐 www.dunshees.com

El Farolito
514 Galisteo St 87501
888-634-8782 505-988-1631
Walt Wyss & Wayne Mainus

150-275 $US BB
8 rooms, 8 pb
Most CC, Cash, Checks,
Rated, •
C-yes/S-ltd/P-no/H-no

Full breakfast
Light afternoon refreshments, Dietary
restrictions honored with notice
Lounge, A/C, family friendly, private
entrances, fireplaces, garden patios,
onsite parking, wireless

In the city's historic district, just a short walk to the Plaza, numerous restaurants and museums, El Farolito offers 8 romantic casitas. All accommodations feature patios, fireplaces, private entrances, AC, authentic Southwestern decor & art. ✉ innkeeper@farolito.com 🌐 www.farolito.com

---

El Paradero B&B
220 W Manhattan Ave 87501
866-558-0918 505-988-1177
Sue Jett & Paul Elliott

110-200 $US BB
15 rooms, 15 pb
Visa, MC, AmEx,
Rated
C-ltd/S-no/P-ltd/H-ltd

Full Gourmet Breakfast
Afternoon tea time with homemade
cookies, fresh-baked pastries, and
other savories
Open courtyard w/garden, common
rooms, central cooling in rooms, guest
computer with Internet access

Experience old Santa Fe charm in this 200 year-old adobe farmhouse bed & breakfast. Located in the historic downtown district just a few minutes walk from the Plaza, museums, shops & restaurants.

✉ info@elparadero.com 🌐 www.elparadero.com

Four Kachinas Inn
512 Webber St 87501
800-397-2564 505-982-2550
Wayne Mainus & Walt Wyss

130-240 $US BB
6 rooms, 6 pb
Most CC, Cash, Checks,
Rated, •
C-yes/S-ltd/P-no/H-ltd
Spanish (limited)

Full breakfast
Complimentary afternoon baked
goods, soft drinks, water, tea & coffee
Sitting room, garden courtyard,
concierge services

Only 4 blocks from the historic Plaza. Furnished with handcrafted furniture and regional art. Serving a full breakfast. Enjoy our peaceful garden areas. The inn is within a short walk to numerous restaurants, art galleries, museums, and historic sites.

✉ info@fourkachinas.com 🌐 www.fourkachinas.com/home.htm

SANTA FE——

Guadalupe Inn
604 Agua Fria St. 87501
505-989-7422
Dolores Myers & Henrietta
Quintana

145-195 $US BB
12 rooms, 12 pb
Most CC, Cash, Checks,
Rated, •
C-yes/S-no/P-no/H-yes
Spanish and ASL

Full breakfast
Breakfast burritos, huevos rancheros,
eggs (almost any style), pancakes or
French toast
A/C, satellite TV, telephone, some
whirlpool baths, DSL/wireless

Located in the oldest district of Santa Fe, referred to as the historic Guadalupe District. Come visit our historic downtown plaza . . . a nice six-block stroll from our B&B.

✉ office@guadalupeinn.com   🌐 www.guadalupeinn.com

Hacienda Nicholas B&B
320 E Marcy St 87501
888-284-3170 505-992-0888
Carolyn Lee

125-240 $US BB
7 rooms, 7 pb
Visa, MC, *Rated*, •
C-yes/S-no/P-yes/H-yes
French

Full breakfast with local cuisine
Wine and appetizers are served each
evening; afternoon cookies and teas.
Award-winning spa, garden, outdoor
kiva fireplace, wireless Internet, cable
TV, A/C

Unwind in the peace and tranquility afforded by extra thick adobe walls and the heavenly scent of a luscious rose garden. We are now operating as a "Green Inn" and find new ways every day to operate in a more eco-friendly fashion.

✉ info@haciendanicholas.com   🌐 www.haciendanicholas.com

Inn of the Turquoise Bear
342 E Buena Vista St 87505
800-396-4104 505-983-0798
Ralph Bolton & Robert Frost

130-365 $US BB
10 rooms, 8 pb
Most CC, Cash, Checks,
Rated, •
C-ltd/S-ltd/P-ltd/H-ltd
Spanish, French,
German, Norwegian,
American Sign
Language

Full Breakfast to order
Complimentary afternoon
refreshments
Sitting room, library, cable TV/VCRs,
book & film library, concierge services

Six blocks to the Plaza. An acre of terraced gardens. Eleven guestrooms/suites with southwest style. Private entrances & romantic courtyards. Kiva fireplaces & Viga ceilings. Many more amenities.

✉ bluebear@newmexico.com   🌐 www.turquoisebear.com

Inn On the Paseo
630 Paseo De Peralta 87501
800-457-9045 505-984-8200

89-239 $US BB
18 rooms, 18 pb
Most CC, *Rated*, •
C-yes/S-no/P-no/H-ltd

Continental breakfast
Private entrances, antiques, large
accommodations, Jacuzzi tub,
fireplace, A/C, wireless Internet

Inn on the Paseo, discover our Southwestern charm and hospitality conveniently located in the Historic District of Santa Fe, you will find yourself within walking distance to the Plaza, Canyon Road, shops, galleries and gourmet restaurants.

✉ stay@innonthepaseo.com   🌐 www.innonthepaseo.com

Las Palomas B&B
460 W San Francisco
St 87501
877-982-5560 505-982-5560

99-498 $US BB
63 rooms, 63 pb
Most CC, *Rated*, •
C-yes/S-no/P-yes/H-yes

Deluxe Continental Breakfast
Breakfast & coffee bar
Wireless Internet access, hot tub &
sauna, fitness center, kids play area

Nestled amongst a secluded tree covered compound just 3 short blocks from Santa Fe's Historic Plaza. The historic casitas of Las Palomas built of traditional adobe bricks have been maintained to preserve the authentic feel of Santa Fe.   ✉ stay@laspalomas.com   🌐 www.laspalomas.com

Madeleine B&B Inn
106 Faithway St 87501
888-877-7622 505-982-3465
Carolyn Lee

120-250 $US BB
7 rooms, 7 pb
Visa, MC, Disc,
Rated, •
C-ltd/S-ltd/P-no/H-no
French

Full breakfast
Afternoon tea & cookies, nightly wine
& appetizer hour
Award-winning on-site spa, luxuriously
soft robes, privileges at El Gancho
Health & Tennis Club

This elegant 1886 Victorian, set in a secluded garden near the Plaza & Convention Center offers full breakfasts & an evening wine & appetizer hour. Our Balinese-inspired spa, staffed with master-level therapists offers the ultimate in spa treatments.

✉ info@madeleineinn.com   🌐 www.madeleineinn.com

SANTA FE

Pueblo Bonito B&B Inn
138 W Manhattan Ave 87501
800-461-4599 505-984-8001
Herb & Amy Behm

70-185 $US BB
18 rooms, 18 pb
Most CC, Cash, Checks,
Rated, •
C-yes/S-no/P-no/H-ltd

Breakfast Buffet
Happy Hour- "Pueblo Margaritas,"
wine, lemonade, tea, salsa & chips
served 4:00–6:00 pm daily.
On-site parking, in-room DSL, kiva
wood burning fireplace, coffee set ups,
laundry, downtown locale.

"Our favorite B&B in Santa Fe for the past 15 yrs. We love this little inn, from its massive adobe structure to the red brick paths, secluded grounds, huge adobe wall, southwest style rooms, morning breakfasts and afternoon margaritas!" B. Mulnich.

pueblo@pueblobonitoinn.com   www.pueblobonitoinn.com

Water Street Inn
427 W Water St 87501
800-646-6752 505-984-1193
Dee Ann Skidmore

190-275 $US BB
11 rooms, 11 pb
Most CC, Cash, Checks,
Rated
C-yes/S-no/P-yes/H-ltd
Spanish

Full breakfast
Evening appetizers with
complimentary wine at Vanessie, our
restaurant right next door
Sitting room, hot tub, suites, fireplaces,
flat screen cable TV DVD/VCR,
wireless, room service

Water Street Inn is three blocks from the Plaza; providing guests with superior accommodations and amenities, convenience and a fun, relaxed atmosphere.

info@waterstreetinn.com   www.waterstreetinn.com

SILVER CITY

The Inn on Broadway
411 W Broadway 88061
866-207-7075 575-388-5485
Sandra Hicks

115-160 $US BB
4 rooms, 4 pb
Most CC
C-ltd/S-ltd/P-no/H-ltd

Full breakfast
Sodas, snacks, guest refrigerator
Library, shady veranda, walk to
restaurants

The Inn on Broadway is located in Silver City's Historic District. Walk to restaurants, art galleries and shops. Relax on our shady veranda overlooking the garden or in our cozy library. Enjoy a delicious, homemade breakfast after a restful night's sleep.

info@innonbroadwayweb.com   www.innonbroadwayweb.com

TAOS

Adobe & Pines Inn
4107 Road 68 87557
800-723-8267 505-751-0947
Katherine & Louis Costabel

98-225 $US BB
8 rooms, 8 pb
Visa, MC, •
C-yes/S-ltd/P-yes/H-no

Full gourmet breakfast
Private entrance/baths, fireplaces,
whirlpools, TV/VCR/DVD/CD players,
video/CD library, spa service

Historic adobe hacienda transformed into one of the most charming/luxurious hideaways in the Southwest, says Frommers, Fodors, HGTV, and many more. Private entrances/baths, fireplaces, whirlpools, gardens, full breakfasts, Cable TV/VCR/DVD, video/CD library.

mail@adobepines.com   www.adobepines.com

Adobe and Stars
584 State Hwy 150 87571
800-211-7076 575-776-2776
Judy Salathiel

95-180 $US BB
8 rooms, 8 pb
Most CC, Cash,
Rated, •
C-yes/S-no/P-yes/H-yes
Spanish

Full breakfast
Coffee, tea & soda
Beautiful common area, hot tub under
the stars, Jacuzzi, robes, hairdryers,
fireplaces, WiFi

Southwestern pueblo, adobe style Inn with kiva fireplaces, beamed ceilings, hot tub under the stars and Jacuzzi tubs. 360 degree mountain views, full breakfasts, skiing, mountain biking and hiking access.   jsalathiel@yahoo.com   www.TaosAdobe.com

Country Inn of Taos
720 Karavas Rd & Upper
Ranchitos Rd 87571
800-866-6548 575-758-4900
Yolanda Deveaux & Judd
Platt

145-175 $US BB
8 rooms, 8 pb
Visa, MC
C-ltd/S-no/P-no/H-no

Full breakfast
Hand-carved furniture, kiva fireplaces,
private baths, TVs, down comforters,
leather sofas

Enjoy an extraordinary vacation at our historic Taos bed and breakfast hacienda, nestled among beautiful gardens and towering trees on 22 acres in Taos, New Mexico.

info@taos-countryinn.com   www.taos-countryinn.com

TAOS

Dreamcatcher B&B
416 La Lomita Rd 87571
888-758-0613 575-758-0613
John & Prudence Abeln

115-175 $US BB
7 rooms, 7 pb
Visa, MC, AmEx,
Rated
C-ltd/S-no/P-no/H-yes
Some Spanish

Full breakfast
Tea & snacks available 24 hours a day
Sitting room, fireplaces, hammocks,
150 channel satellite TV

Dreamcatcher B&B is the perfect Taos B&B to designate as your starting point to all of what Taos and northern NM have to offer. Our adobe home sits nestled in a serene, wooded area just a short walk from Historic Taos Plaza.

✉ dream@taosnm.com 🌐 www.dreambb.com

Hacienda Del Sol
109 Mabel Dodge Ln 87571
866-333-4459 575-758-0287
Gerd & Luellen Hertel

145-325 $US BB
11 rooms, 11 pb
Most CC, Cash,
Rated, •
C-yes/S-no/P-ltd/H-ltd
German, French

Afternoon sweets
Complimentary snacks
Library, fireplaces, gallery, outdoor
hot tub, robes, gardens, health club
access, computer & WiFi

200-yr-old adobe hideaway purchased by Taos' legendary art patroness Mabel Dodge for her Indian husband, Tony. Adjoins vast Indian lands, close to Taos Plaza. Tranquility, mountain views. "One of the US's top 10 romantic inns," USA Today.

✉ sunhouse@newmex.com 🌐 www.taoshaciendadelsol.com

Inn on La Loma Plaza
315 Ranchitos Rd 87571
800-530-3040 575-751-0178
Jerry & Peggy Davis

165-450 $US BB
10 rooms, 10 pb
Most CC, Checks,
Rated
C-yes/S-no/P-yes/H-ltd

Full breakfast
Private entrances, baths, sitting areas,
fireplaces, patios, phones, cable TV,
CD, radio, kitchenettes

A historic Taos landmark, an intimate and luxurious setting 2 blocks from downtown Taos. Each room has its own distinctive ambience created by a combination of handcrafted furniture, antiques and southwestern fabrics.

✉ laloma@vacationtaos.com 🌐 www.taos-bed-breakfast.com

La Dona Luz Inn
206 Des Georges Lane 87571
575-758-9000
Paul "Paco" Castillo

59-229 $US BB
9 rooms, 9 pb
Visa, MC, Disc
C-yes/S-ltd/P-yes/H-ltd

Deluxe continental breakfast
Rooftop private hot tub, wood burning
adobe fireplaces, Jacuzzi baths, patios

"The Essence of Old Taos." Delight in the ambience of this quaint & colorful adobe inn with rooms richly decorated in the Taos tradition. Fine art work & Indian & Spanish antiques are displayed throughout the house. The closest B&B to the old plaza.

✉ info@stayintaos.com 🌐 www.stayintaos.com

La Posada de Taos
309 Juanita Ln 87571
800-645-4803 575-758-8164
Brad Malone

124-219 $US BB
6 rooms, 6 pb
Most CC, Cash,
Rated, •
C-ltd/S-ltd/P-yes/H-yes

Full Gourmet Breakfast
Afternoon Tea, beverages, snack
service
Sitting room, patios, sun room, portals,
fireplaces, courtyards, WiFi, Jacuzzi
baths, outdoor views

La Posada de Taos is a historic adobe inn just two blocks west of 400-year old Taos Plaza. You'll enjoy nothing less than excellence each morning when breakfast is served. Our focus is your comfort, so come and join us any time of year.

✉ contact@laposadadetaos.com 🌐 www.laposadadetaos.com

Mabel Dodge Luhan House
240 Morada Ln 87571
800-846-2235 575-751-9686
Maria Fortin

98-245 $US BB
19 rooms, 19 pb
Visa, MC, AmEx
C-ltd/S-no/P-no/H-ltd

Full gourmet breakfast
Private baths, fireplaces, kitchen
facilities, cottages, views, patios,
classes & workshops

Charming, elegant, historic 1920s adobe inn and conference center, once the home of a wealthy patron of the arts and creative sanctuary for many artists. Panoramic view. Quiet patios and a tree-lined acequia. Many art and creativity workshops offered.

✉ mabel@mabeldodgeluhan.com 🌐 www.mabeldodgeluhan.com

TAOS

Orinda B&B	104-289 $US BB	Full breakfast
461 Valverde 87571	5 rooms, 5 pb	Afternoon tea & snacks
800-847-1837 505-758-8581	Visa, MC, AmEx,	Sitting room, library, spa services,
John & Cathryn Ellsworth	*Rated*	some rooms feature kiva fireplace &
	C-ltd/S-no/P-ltd/H-no	Mexican tiled private bath

Orinda B&B is a 70+ year old adobe hacienda combining unequaled mountain views in a country setting. We're a short 10-minute walk to center of town with its famed plaza, excellent restaurants, galleries and museums.

✉ orinda@newmex.com   🌐 www.orindabb.com

The Historic Taos Inn	75-275 $US EP	Award-winning Doc Martins
125 Paseo del Pueblo	44 rooms, 44 pb	Restaurant, Adobe Bar features
Norte 87571	Most CC, Cash,	Margaritas & a New Mex bistro menu
800-TAOS-INN 575-758-2233	*Rated*, •	Fine Dining, Live Music, Kiva
Carolyn Haddock	C-yes/S-ltd/P-no/H-ltd	Fireplaces, Internet, comp. passes to
		fitness center, packages

Free Night w/Certificate: Anytime. Room Upgrade.

Founded on a rich legacy of excellence. Our guests are eager to sample the atmosphere of old Taos yet expect modern amenities. The Historic Taos Inn has everything a visitor to Taos wants under one roof. Southwestern rooms, bar and fine dining.

✉ marketing@taosinn.com   🌐 www.taosinn.com

TAOS SKI VALLEY

Columbine Inn &	69-189 $US BB	Continental plus breakfast
Conference Center	20 rooms, 20 pb	Sitting room, hot tub, board games,
1288 Hwy 150 87525	Most CC, •	frequent stay program, free ski shuttle,
888-884-5723 575-776-5723	C-yes/S-no/P-ltd/H-no	free WiFi
Susie & Paul Geilenfeldt	May-Oct, Nov-April	

Beautiful timber-frame lodge nestled in the Taos Mountains. Enjoy hiking, biking, riding the chair lift, horseback riding, visiting museums, and shopping. Stay in the mountains with cool weather and a relaxing atmosphere. Friendly, Fun, & Convenient.

✉ psgeilen@taosnet.com   🌐 www.columbineinntaos.com

New York

ADAMS BASIN ─────────────────────────────

Adams Basin Inn	115-145 $US BB	Gourmet and freshly baked pastries
425 Washington St 14410	4 rooms, 4 pb	Tea or coffee served upon arrival;
888-352-3999 585-352-3999	Visa, MC, *Rated*	bottled water, sodas available in guest
Pat & Dave Haines	C-ltd/S-no/P-no/H-no	refrigerator
		Common area of parlor, tavern and
		porch are open to guests; available for
		weddings & showers

Nestled next to the historic towpath of the Erie Canal, Adams Basin Inn is a delight to lovers of antiques, exceptional food and relaxation.

✉ hainespat@gmail.com   🌐 www.adamsbasininn.com

ALFRED STATION ─────────────────────────────

Country Cabin Manor B&B	94-149 $US BB	Full breakfast
1289 SR 244 14803	4 rooms, 4 pb	Tea, soft drinks, bottled water, hot
607-587-8504	Visa, MC, Disc	chocolate
Judy Burdick	C-ltd/S-no/P-no/H-ltd	Deck, pond, fishing, whirlpool tub,
		dining room, fireplace, sitting room,
		high speed Internet, fax

Located ¾ mile from Alfred, NY, in the scenic foothills of the Allegheny Mountains. Quiet, romantic getaway, year round vacation spot, many recreational activities in the area.

✉ jaburdalburd@juno.com   🌐 www.countrycabinmanor.com

AMENIA ─────────────────────────────

Hilltop House B&B	175-240 $US BB	Full breakfast
Depot Hill Rd 12501	5 rooms, 3 pb	Tea and hot chocolate available
845-789-1354	Most CC, Cash, Checks	WiFi
Sandra Johnson	C-ltd/S-ltd/P-no/H-no	

The inn has five delightful guestrooms quaintly furnished with antiques & quilts, each offering their own distinctive charm. Common areas at the Inn are wonderful places to relax and visit with fellow guests.   ✉ info@hilltophousebb.com   🌐 www.hilltophousebb.com

AUBURN ─────────────────────────────

10 Fitch	200-325 $US BB	Full breakfast
10 Fitch Ave. 13021	3 rooms, 3 pb	Complimentary snacks, beverages,
315-255-0934	Most CC, Cash	bottled water, Sally's homemade choc
Cheryl Barber	C-ltd/S-ltd/P-no/H-ltd	chip cookies
		Fireplaces, library, sun room, garden,
		A/C, antiques, Jacuzzi hot tub,
		balcony, breakfast in suite,

Free Night w/Certificate: Valid Nov.-May; Except holiday weekends; not valid with any other discount or offer; subject to availability.

A luxurious romantic inn conveniently located between the wineries and Skaneateles, NY. Professionally decorated and adorned with Mac-Kenzie Childs home furnishings, antiques, original artwork, designer fabrics and decadent silk draperies.

✉ innkeeper@10fitch.com   🌐 www.10fitch.com

AVON ─────────────────────────────

White Oak B&B	105-125 $US BB	Full breakfast
277 Genesee St 14414	3 rooms, 3 pb	On request: vegetarian, non-dairy, low
585-226-6735	Visa, MC	cholesterol, or low carb
Barbara B. Herman	C-ltd/S-no/P-no/H-no	Cable TV/DVD, sitting room, library,
		business travelers, wireless Internet,
		all rooms with A/C

The White Oak is a splendid example of Second Empire Victorian architecture: a peaceful retreat located in Avon, NY. Avon is situated on the eastern bank of the Genesee River, near New York's Finger Lakes, Rochester, Letchworth State Park.

✉ avon-bnb@frontiernet.net   🌐 www.whiteoakbandb.com

BAINBRIDGE

Berry Hill Gardens
242 Ward-Loomis Rd 13733
800-497-8745 607-967-8745
Jean Fowler

125-185 $US BB
8 rooms, 8 pb
Most CC, Cash, Checks
C-yes/S-ltd/P-no/H-no
Spanish, German,
Italian, French

A full, healthy-living breakfast
Coffee, tea; guest convenience kitchen
Ceiling fans, bathrobes, eco-friendly,
library, WiFi

A country B&B situated high on a hilltop overlooking miles of rural beauty in Central New York. Museums, golf, fishing, hunting, artisans & fascinating history. Five comfortable guestrooms in the Inn and three rooms in our lodge with over 300 acres to roam.

✉ info@berryhillgardens.com 🌐 www.berryhillgardens.com

BALLSTON SPA

Lewis House
38 E High St 12020
518-884-9857
Preston Lewis

100-250 $US BB
4 rooms, 4 pb
Visa, MC, AmEx
C-yes/S-no/P-no/H-no

Full breakfast
Homemade treats, refreshments
Fireplace, living room, dining
room, games, books, videos, HDTV,
telephone, WiFi

Romantic 1871 Victorian landscaped with perennials can be found in the historic Saratoga district. Enjoy comfortable accommodations in one of the three guestrooms or the Garden Suite. Sleep in tranquility while enjoying Saratoga Springs and our area.

✉ info@lewishouse.com 🌐 www.lewishouse.com

BARRYVILLE

ECCE Bed & Breakfast
19 Silverfish Road 12719
888-557-8562 845-557-8562
Alan Rosenblatt

150-285 $US BB
5 rooms, 5 pb
Visa, MC, Disc
C-ltd/S-ltd/P-no/H-no

Full breakfast
Complimentary in room snacks and
beverages. Afternoon Tea
Large outdoor decks, views, wildlife,
60 acres, fireplace, sunroom,
weddings, events, hiking trails.

An award winning mountain house perched on a bluff 300 feet above the Upper Delaware River. Located on 60 acres w/ hiking trails, ECCE offers panoramic views of both the NY and PA mountain ranges. The five elegantly appointed rooms all have private baths.

✉ eccebandb@frontiernet.net 🌐 www.eccebedandbreakfast.com

BLOOMING GROVE

Dominion House
50 Old Dominion 10914
845-496-1826
Joe & Kathy Spear

125-199 $US BB
4 rooms, 2 pb
Most CC
C-yes/S-no/P-no/H-ltd

Full breakfast
Specialties of the house are caramel
sticky buns, peach French toast and
scones, snacks 24 hours
Large parlor, slate top pool table, hot
tub, swimming pool, library, business
accommodations

"A Taste of Elegant Country Living!" Built in 1880 by Benjamin H. Strong, a local farmer whose family settled in Orange County in the seventeen hundreds. Situated on 4.5 acres, at the end of a country lane in central Orange County.

✉ kathy@thedominionhouse.com 🌐 www.thedominionhouse.com

BLUE MOUNTAIN LAKE

The Hedges
Hedges Rd 12812
518-352-7325
Patricia Benton

205-320 $US MAP
31 rooms, 31 pb
Rated
C-ltd/S-no/P-no/H-yes
May through October

"Made to order" breakfast
Iced tea, lemonade, coffee during day.
Evening snack. Full bar service at
dinner.
Canoes, kayaks, beach, tennis
court, library, game/common room,
housekeeping service, WiFi

On the shores of Blue Mountain Lake, in the heart of America's largest State Park, The Hedges offers the relaxation & recreation of an historic Adirondack Great Camp.

✉ thehedges@frontiernet.net 🌐 www.thehedges.com

BOLTON LANDING

Boathouse Bed & Breakfast
44 Sagamore Rd 12814
518-644-2554
Joe & Patti Silipigno

150-395 $US BB
7 rooms, 7 pb
Visa, MC, AmEx,
Rated
C-ltd/S-no/P-no/H-no

Full breakfast
Some rooms have whirlpools,
fireplaces & microwaves, all Lakeview
Rooms have balconies

Historic B&B located directly on Lake George and open year round. This famous and unique B&B has been featured in publications like Motor Boat and Sailing, The Great and the Gracious, and Unique Homes. Also featured on the PBS special Rustic Living.

✉ Stay@boathousebb.com ◐ www.boathousebb.com

BOUCKVILLE

Ye Olde Landmark Tavern
6722 State Route 20 13310
315-893-1810
Stephen Hengst

90-140 $US BB
5 rooms, 5 pb
Most CC, Cash
C-yes/S-no/P-no/H-no
April-December

Continental breakfast
Dinner, restaurant, bar service
Suites, cable TV, private baths,
traditional early America decor,
canopy bed, wireless Internet

Historic cobblestone building on National Register of Historic Places, in antique center of New York State. Near Colgate University and Hamilton College. Ye Olde Landmark Tavern serving the needs of both area residents and travelers for over 150 years.

✉ yeoldelandmark@yahoo.com ◐ www.yeoldelandmark.com

BRANCHPORT

Gone With the Wind on Keuka Lake
14905 West Lake Rd 14418
607-868-4603
Linda Lewis

109-169 $US BB
8 rooms, 8 pb
C-ltd/S-no/P-no/H-ltd

Full breakfast
Fruit, home-baked Rhett's Rhubarb
coffee cake, one of Aunt Pitti Pat's
many flavors of pancakes
Private cove, gazebo, canopy of trees,
Log Lodge, retreats, reunions

A stately stone mansion set above Keuka Lake, serving guests since 1989. Designed around the epic story, "Gone with the Wind" it is a luxurious getaway for the weary traveler and B&B adventurer alike! The Stone Mansion and "The Sequel" await!

✉ gwwkeukalake@hotmail.com ◐ www.gonewiththewindonkeukalake.com

BROCKPORT

The Victorian
320 Main St 14420
585-637-7519
Sharon M. Kehoe

80-150 $US BB
5 rooms, 5 pb
•
C-yes/S-no/P-no/H-ltd
Spanish

Full breakfast
Afternoon tea
Sitting room, library, fireplace, fax,
cable TV, wireless Internet access, in-
room phone, phone card

Late 19th-century Queen Anne home, with pleasing blend of antiques & modern furnishings. Short walk from historic Erie Canal. ✉ sk320@aol.com ◐ www.victorianbandb.com

BRONX

The Bronx Guesthouse
East 233 St 10466
718-881-7022
Chef Denisey

75-160 $US BB
4 rooms
Most CC, •
C-ltd/S-no/P-yes

Self-serve Continental
Satellite TV, board games, fax machine,
Internet

The Guest House offers an eclectic and peaceful retreat. Built at the turn of the century, the house retains much of the old world flavor. Explore the proximity of local attractions.

✉ reservations@bronxguesthouse.com ◐ www.bronxguesthouse.com

BUFFALO

Beau Fleuve B&B Inn
242 Linwood Ave 14209
800-278-0245 716-882-6116
Ramona & Rik Whitaker

155-175 $US BB
4 rooms, 4 pb
Most CC, Cash,
Rated, •
C-ltd/S-no/P-ltd/H-no
Some Spanish
Closed January

Full breakfast
Complimentary snacks, cookies,
soft drinks, juices, coffee, tea, hot
chocolate & cider
In-room TV/DVD, fireplace, robes,
WiFi, guest parlor, central A/C, fridge/
microwave/toaster

Forget hotels! Enjoy the serene and comfortable elegance of Buffalo's finest B&B, where your hosts have provided gracious hospitality, delectable candlelight breakfasts, and complimentary concierge services for 20 years in this beautiful 1882 property.

✉ beaufleuve@verizon.net ◐ www.beaufleuve.com

CANANDAIGUA

1795 Acorn Inn	160-275 $US BB	Full gourmet breakfast
4508 Rt 64 S 14424	5 rooms, 5 pb	Complimentary hot & cold beverages
866-665-3747 585-229-2834	Most CC, *Rated*	& snacks
Sheryl Mordini	C-ltd/S-no/P-no/H-no	Common room w/large fireplace,
	German	library, outdoor hot tub, small
		weddings/reunions, family gatherings

Thoroughly renovated & beautifully appointed with fine furnishings & antiques, the 1795 Acorn Inn offers the simple elegance of the past seamlessly integrated with modern comfort & luxury. AAA Four Diamond rated for fourteen consecutive years.

✉ info@acorninnbb.com 🌐 www.acorninnbb.com

1840 Inn on the Main	145-210 $US BB	Full Gourmet breakfast
176 N Main St 14424	5 rooms, 5 pb	Beverages available all day, and
877-659-1643 585-394-0139	Most CC, Cash,	freshly baked treats available in the
Jaynee & Guy Straw	*Rated*, •	afternoon.
	C-ltd/S-ltd/P-no/H-no	Wireless, Jacuzzi tubs, fireplaces, A/C,
		TV/DVD, porch, suite for families.

Elegant 1840's Second Empire Victorian tastefully decorated in period furnishings & offers discriminating travelers the elegance of days gone by with the conveniences of today. 4 beautifully appointed guestrooms (en suite baths) & independent family suite

✉ questions@innonthemain.com 🌐 www.innonthemain.com

Chambery Cottage B&B	129-179 $US BB	Full breakfast
6104 Monks Rd 14424	4 rooms, 4 pb	Tea, coffee, cookies, snacks
585-393-1405	Visa, MC, *Rated*	Green & organic, sitting room, library,
Zora & Terry Molkenthin	C-ltd/S-no/P-no/H-no	video/DVD, CD, garden seating areas,
	Czech	central air-conditioning

Chambery Cottage is a fully renovated, 100 year-old farmhouse. The decor is Old World or French country. All four guestrooms feature private bath, TV/VCRs, DVD, CD players, alarm clocks, some fireplaces, Jacuzzi. Central air, green, organic & all natural.

✉ euroctge@frontiernet.net 🌐 www.chamberycottage.com

CANDOR

The Edge of Thyme, A B&B	90-145 $US BB	Full breakfast
Inn	5 rooms, 3 pb	High tea by appointment
6 Main St 13743	Most CC, Cash, Checks,	Sitting rooms w/fireplaces, AC, piano,
800-722-7365 607-659-5155	*Rated*, •	indoor games, lawn games, gift shop,
Frank & Eva Mae Musgrave	C-yes/S-no/P-no/H-no	wireless Internet

Free Night w/Certificate: Not Valid in month of May or Family weekends at Colleges. Room Upgrade.

Featured in Historic Inns of the Northeast. Visit a turn-of-the-century Georgian home. Enjoy a leaded-glass windowed porch, marble fireplaces, period sitting rooms, gardens, pergola and the gracious atmosphere.

✉ innthyme@twcny.rr.com 🌐 www.edgeofthyme.com

CANTON

Ostrander's B&B	75-90 $US BB	Full breakfast
1675 State Hwy 68 13617	4 rooms, 4 pb	Evening dessert, beverages, in-room
315-386-2126	Visa, MC, AmEx,	fridge
Al & Rita Ostrander	*Rated*, •	Sitting room, free wireless Internet,
	C-ltd/S-no/P-no/H-no	cable TV, VCR, DVD, phones, A/C,
		cottages with full kitchen

Whether you arrive for business or for pleasure, we offer the perfect combination of convenience & quiet comfort. Visit the sheep barn, play with border collie dogs or shop in our gift shop.

✉ info@ostranders.com 🌐 www.ostranders.com

Tell your hosts Pamela Lanier sent you.

CAZENOVIA

Brae Loch Inn
5 Albany St 13035
315-655-3431
James & Valerie Barr

95-170 $US BB
12 rooms, 12 pb
Most CC, Cash,
Rated, •
C-yes/S-no/P-ltd/H-no
Spanish

Continental breakfast
Dinner available seven nights a week,
fine dining or casual pub menu
Brunch on Sunday
Fireplaces, gift shop, lounge with pool
table, full bar, dinners nightly

Family owned & operated since 1946. As close to a Scottish Inn as you will find this far west of Edinburgh! Serving exquisite fine dining and casual pub menu nightly. Specializing in warm, comfortable accommodations.

✉ braeloch1@aol.com 🌐 www.braelochinn.com

Brewster Inn
6 Ledyard Ave 13035
315-655-9232
Richard Hubbard

80-235 $US BB
17 rooms, 17 pb
Most CC, Cash, *Rated*
C-yes/S-no/P-no/H-yes

Continental breakfast
Dinner 7 nights a week 5–9 p.m. and
Brunch on Sundays 10:30–1:30 p.m.
Jacuzzis, fireplaces, TV, air
conditioning

The Brewster Inn is a truly beautiful country inn catering to discerning diners and travelers. Offering fine dining and lodging on the south shore of Cazenovia Lake.

✉ thebrewsterinn@aol.com 🌐 www.thebrewsterinn.com

CHAUTAUQUA

Spencer Hotel
25 Palestine Ave 14722
800-398-1306 716-357-3785
Helen Edgington

175-250 $US BB
24 rooms, 24 pb
Visa, MC, *Rated*, •
C-yes/S-no/P-no/H-yes

Full breakfast
Tea, gourmet breakfast included with
stay, catered dinner buffets
Spa services, enrichment workshops,
special events

A literary-themed, four-season boutique resort in the heart of the historic Chautauqua Institution begins its second century by offering refreshed spa services and enrichment workshops, and adding more modern amenities in this historic venue.

✉ marketing@thespencer.com 🌐 www.thespencer.com

CHERRY CREEK

Cherry Creek Inn B&B
1022 West Rd 14723
716-296-5105
Sharon Howe Sweeting

85-150 $US BB
4 rooms, 4 pb
Visa, MC, Disc
C-yes/S-no/P-no/H-no

Full breakfast
refrigerator (avail. 24/7) w/ drinks,
catering for conf., afternoon tea, Amish
luncheons
WiFi, hot tub, gardens, lawn games,
pub room, events facility, Victorian
library

Luxurious accommodations on 31 acres in Amish country. Experience Chautauqua County through literary pursuits, indoor & outdoor games, antiquing, birding, hiking and snow sports. Library, hot tub and WiFi.

✉ innkeeper@cherrycreekinn.net 🌐 www.cherrycreekinn.net

CHESTERTOWN

Friends Lake Inn
963 Friends Lake Rd 12817
518-494-4751
John & Trudy Phillips

299-499 $US MAP
17 rooms, 17 pb
Most CC, *Rated*, •
C-ltd/S-no/P-no/H-yes

Full country breakfast
Full dinner service available, full wine
bar
Library, swimming, Adirondack suites
with view, outdoor sauna, massages,
hiking, snowshoeing

Fully restored 19th century Inn with lakeviews and 4 rooms with working fireplaces. Award-winning restaurant & wine list, on premise hiking and x-country skiing, snowshoeing, private beach canoes & kayaks on Friends Lake.

✉ trudy@friendslake.com 🌐 www.friendslake.com

CHESTERTOWN

The Fern Lodge
46 Fiddlehead Bay
Road 12817
518-494-7238
Sharon Taylor

275-525 $US BB
5 rooms, 5 pb
Visa, MC, AmEx,
Rated, •
S-no/P-no/H-no

Full multi-course breakfast
A small menu of in-room options
available
Pool table, wine cellar, game table,
nine-person theatre, sauna, exercise
equipment, honor bar, WiFi.

Free Night w/Certificate: Valid midweek non-holiday only Sun.-Thurs.. Jan.-June. October
20-Dec.20. Room Upgrade.

In the midst of the Adirondack Mountains, overlooking Friends Lake, there stands a wondrous guest-house where luxurious lodging, indulgent baths and unforgettable breakfasts join in an atmosphere of rustic elegance and lakeside living.

 sharon@thefernlodge.com    www.thefernlodge.com

CLARENCE

Asa Ransom House
10529 Main St, Rt 5 14031
800-841-2340 716-759-2315
Robert & Abigail Lenz

125-330 $US BB
10 rooms, 10 pb
Visa, MC, Disc,
Rated, •
C-yes/S-no/P-ltd/H-yes

Full Breakfast
Bar, Snacks, Dinner (except Mondays),
Lunch on Wednesday, High Tea on
Tuesday, Thursday, Saturday.
Fireplaces, cable TV, free WiFi ,
refrigerators, porches, balconies,
whirlpool tub, pets limited

Free Night w/Certificate: Room Upgrade..

Awarded #1 B&B in Buffalo News. Top three in food, service, hospitality, and historic charm in Bee Readers Survey. Historic Village Inn with herb garden, regional dishes & wine, homemade breads & desserts, and gift shop.

innfo@asaransom.com   www.asaransom.com

CLAVERACK

1805 House
775 Snydertown Rd 12513
518-929-5923
Tom & Maria Elena Benton

135 $US BB
3 rooms, 3 pb
Most CC, Cash, •
C-yes/S-no/P-yes/H-ltd
Spanish

Full breakfast
Pond, dining room

Set on over 100 acres of natural beauty, our historic eyebrow Colonial home offers a quiet, pastoral getaway conveniently situated between the Berkshire and Catskill Mountains.

1805house@gmail.com   www.1805house.com

COLD SPRING

The Pig Hill Inn
73 Main St 10516
845-265-9247
David Vitanza

150-250 $US BB
9 rooms, 9 pb
Most CC, Cash
C-ltd/S-no/P-no/H-yes
Czech, Slovak, Russian

Full breakfast
Tea & pastries, wine & beer cash bar
Conservatory, terraced garden,
luxurious four-poster beds, privacy,
romance, trolley services nearby

At The Pig Hill Inn, we have raised self-indulgence to a fine art. Experience our warm hospitality and relax from the pressures of your everyday routine. Enjoy privacy and romance for a weekend escape or stay for a whole week.

pighillinn@aol.com   www.pighillinn.com

COLD SPRING HARBOR

Swan View Manor
45 Harbor Road 11724
631-367-2070
Lisa & Geraldine

132-225 $US BB
18 rooms, 18 pb
Most CC, Cash
C-ltd/S-no/P-no/H-no

Continental breakfast
Complimentary coffee, soft drinks,
fruit & snacks, formal afternoon tea
available upon request
Sitting room with fireplace, A/C,
cable TV, phone, wireless Internet,
refreshments

At the Swan View, the comfort & enjoyment of your stay is of the utmost importance to us. This bed & breakfast, nestled on the North Shore of Long Island in Cold Spring Harbor, a town that is truly enchanting.

info@swanview.com   www.swanview.com

COOPERSTOWN

Diastole B&B
276 Van Yahres Rd 13326
607-547-2665
Brigitte Priem

159-239 $US BB
4 rooms, 4 pb
Visa, MC, Disc,
Rated, •
C-ltd/S-no/P-no/H-no
February 5-October 31

Cooked to order breakfast
Sitting room with fireplace, hot tub,
WiFi, refrigerator, microwave, hiking
trails

Enjoy Luxurious accommodations at this mountain top B&B. All rooms have a spectacular view of the lake. Fireplace in most rooms. Jacuzzi suites available. Outdoor hot tub. New addition has log cabin furnishings that are exquisite.

✉ diastole@hughes.net   🌐 www.diastolebb.com

Main Street B&B
202 Main St 13326
800-867-9755 607-547-9755
Ron & Susan Streek

109-169 $US BB
3 rooms, 3 pb
C-yes/S-ltd/P-no/H-no

Full breakfast
Family friendly facility, sitting room,
TV, A/C, WiFi

A Victorian B&B within walking distance to Baseball Hall of Fame and the highlights of Cooperstown. Lovely front porch for relaxation.   ✉ rms202@stny.rr.com   🌐 www.mainstreetbandb.info

---

Overlook B&B
8 Pine Blvd 13326
607-547-2019
Jack & Gayle Smith

139-174 $US BB
3 rooms, 3 pb
C-yes/S-no/P-no/H-no

Continental plus breakfast
Breakfast: coffee, juices, fresh fruits,
cereals, yogurt, hard boiled eggs,
homemade baked goods
Warm hospitality, TV/VCR in common
area, fireplace in living room, parking,
families welcome, WiFi

Overlook B&B rises in Victorian splendor on stately Pine Boulevard. Accommodations are offered in light and spacious rooms, all with private baths. A short stroll from the Baseball Hall of Fame, The Farmers' Museum, Fenimore House and Main Street.

✉ information@OverlookBB.com   🌐 www.overlookbb.com

Rose & Thistle B&B
132 Chestnut St 13326
607-547-5345
Patti D'Esposito

125-200 $US BB
4 rooms, 4 pb
Most CC, Cash, Checks
S-ltd/P-no/H-no

Full breakfast
Snacks, cookies, cakes, chips, pretzels,
coffee & tea are available
Parlor, porch, Internet access, A/C, TV

An enchanting experience awaits at this turn-of-the-century Victorian B&B. Old world charm & new world luxury combines to let you experience "Bed & Breakfast in an elegant tradition."

✉ stay@rosenthistle.com   🌐 www.rosenthistle.com

The Cooper Inn
15 Chestnut St 13326
800-348-6222 x2 607-547-2567
John D. Irvin

115-260 $US BB
15 rooms, 15 pb
Visa, MC, AmEx, •
C-yes/S-no/P-no/H-no

Continental breakfast
Special breakfast price &
complimentary bottle of wine with
dinner at nearby Otesaga Resort
Free WiFi, cable TV, heat, A/C, pool
& fitness ctr at nearby Otesaga Hotel,
reduced golf green fee

The Cooper Inn has 15 rooms, each with modern amenities including phone, free wireless Internet access, cable TV, central heat, air conditioning, and private baths. Use of the facilities at Otesaga Hotel in season.

✉ Reservation1@Otesaga.com   🌐 www.CooperInn.com

The Inn at Cooperstown
16 Chestnut St 13326
607-547-5756
Marc & Sherrie Kingsley

105-525 $US BB
18 rooms, 18 pb
Visa, MC, AmEx, •
C-yes/S-no/P-no/H-ltd

Continental plus breakfast
Coffee, tea, and other hot drinks
available; iced tea & lemonade served
on the porch in the summer
Guestrooms have A/C, CD/clock radio,
hairdryer, iron/ironing board, wireless
Internet access

Beautifully restored Victorian inn providing genuine hospitality and spotless, comfortable guestrooms. The only Select Registry property in Cooperstown, the inn is just a short walk from the National Baseball Hall of Fame, shopping and fine dining.

✉ info@innatcooperstown.com   🌐 www.innatcooperstown.com
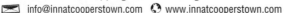

COOPERSTOWN

The White House Inn	95-215 $US BB	Full gourmet breakfast
46 Chestnut St 13326	6 rooms, 6 pb	All guestrooms have cable TV,
866-547-1980 607-547-5054	Visa, MC, AmEx,	telephone, Internet access and private
Marjorie & Ed Landers	*Rated*, •	baths, in-ground pool
	C-yes/S-no/P-no/H-yes	

The White House Inn provides the comforts of home, the elegance of fine lodgings, gracious hospitality, and the convenience of parking on-site and walking to local attractions. Enjoy the seclusion of our private garden with a swimming pool.

✉ reserve@thewhitehouseinn.com   📞 www.thewhitehouseinn.com

Tunnicliff Inn	55-360 $US BB	Hot buffet breakfast
34-36 Pioneer St 13326	17 rooms, 17 pb	"The Pit" restaurant on premises
607-547-9611	Visa, MC, Disc	A/C, cable TV, DVD player with movie
Tom	C-yes/S-no/P-no/H-no	library, wireless Internet, mini-fridge,
		coffee makers

Historic 17 room Inn built in 1802 located in the center of Downtown Cooperstown. Restaurant & Tavern known as the "Pit" on the premises. We have banquet facilities for rehearsal dinners, birthdays and anniversaries.

✉ TUNNICLIFFINN@Verizon.net

CORINTH

Agape Farm LLC	135-170 $US BB	Full breakfast
4839 Rt 9 N 12822	3 rooms, 3 pb	Snacks
518-654-7777	Visa, MC, Disc, *Rated*	Gardens, trout stream, farm animals,
Fred & Sigrid Koch	C-yes/S-no/P-no/H-ltd	dogs, cats, family friendly facility

Nestled in the Adirondacks, Agape Farm is a country farmhouse on 33 scenic acres. Enjoy true country hospitality, relax on the charming wraparound porch, enjoy fellowship in the inviting living room, or sing around the piano. Children welcome.

✉ agapefarmbnb@roadrunner.com   📞 www.agape-farm.com/index.html

CORNWALL

Cromwell Manor Inn	165-380 $US BB	Full breakfast
174 Angola Rd 12518	12 rooms, 12 pb	Chocolate chip cookies, continental
845-534-7136	Visa, MC, AmEx,	breakfast available, picnic baskets
Jack Trowell & Cynthia	*Rated*, •	Fireplaces, in-room massage, spa
Krom	C-ltd/S-no/P-no/H-yes	options, patio/fountain, wireless
		Internet, computers

Free Night w/Certificate: Valid Sunday-Thursday; Holidays excluded.

Top 10 Inn of NY, "Highly recommended"…USA Today. "A fantastic B&B!"… CBS Early Show. This stunning 1820 Greek Revival Mansion is set on 7 lush acres with scenic Hudson Valley views.

✉ cmi@hvc.rr.com   📞 www.cromwellmanor.com

CROTON-ON-HUDSON

The Alexander Hamilton	120-299 $US BB	Full gourmet breakfast
House	8 rooms, 8 pb	Wonderful homemade cookies.
49 Van Wyck St 10520	Most CC, Cash, Checks,	Optional candlelight dinner.
914-271-6737	*Rated*, •	Big whirlpool tubs, swimming pool,
Barbara Notarius & Tom	C-yes/S-no/P-yes/H-no	suites, fireplaces, TV, Free Wifi, iPod
Morrissey	French	Docking Stations with CD.

We are a romantic Victorian Inn close to all the attractions of the lower Hudson Valley, 48 minutes from the heart of NYC. River view, village setting, with pool.

✉ alexanderhamiltonhouse@gmail.com   📞 www.alexanderhamiltonhouse.com

DRYDEN

Candlelight Inn	95-165 $US BB	Full breakfast
49 W Main St 13053	5 rooms, 5 pb	Air conditioning, fireplace, in-ground
800-579-4629 607-844-4321	Visa, MC	heated pool, in-room TVs, Jacuzzi
Doris Nitsios	C-yes/S-no/P-ltd/H-no	suite

Relax in antique filled and cozy rooms in our circa 1828 Federal home. Surround yourself in style and comfort. Five charming rooms with private baths, TVs, and air conditioning.

✉ Innkeeper@CandlelightInnNY.com   📞 www.candlelightinnny.com

Mill House Inn, East Hampton, NY

DUNDEE

1819 Red Brick Inn	105-139 $US BB	Full breakfast
2081 Rt 230 14837	5 rooms, 5 pb	Complimentary beverages, snack
607-243-8844	Visa, MC, Disc	served in evening.
Wendy & Robert Greenslade	C-ltd/S-no/P-no/H-ltd	Parlour with Satellite TV and DVD player, Hammock under our majestic pines for relaxing, Pond

We invite you to spend a relaxing interlude in our charming 1819 Federal style home, located in a tranquil country setting in the heart of the Finger Lakes.

✉ redbrickinn@frontiernet.net   🌐 www.1819inn.com

Sunrise Landing B&B	150-215 $US BB	Full breakfast
4986 Apple Rd Ext 14837	3 rooms, 3 pb	Refrigerator with complimentary
866-670-5253 607-243-7548	Most CC, Cash,	non-alcoholic beverages, along with
Robert & Barbara Schiesser	Checks, •	bagged snacks, in your room.
	C-ltd/S-no/P-no/H-ltd	Large dock & waterfront, paddle boat, row boat, and canoe, piano, A/C, wood burning fireplace, WiFi

Enjoy the peaceful seclusion of Sunrise Landing on Seneca Lake, offering pristine accommodations, luxurious amenities, warm hospitality right on the lake. Enjoy being located on the Wine Trail and close to many area attractions; near Watkins Glen.

✉ relax@sunriselandingbb.com   🌐 www.sunriselandingbb.com

EAST HAMPTON

Getaway House	100-425 $US BB	Continental breakfast
4 Neighborhood House	4 rooms, 2 pb	Large pool, central air conditioning,
Dr 11937	Visa, MC, AmEx, •	bicycles, beach passes, fireplace
631-324-4622	C-ltd/S-no/P-no/H-ltd	
Johnny Kelman		

A charming bed and breakfast nestled in a wooded setting, yet close to the village and ocean beaches. Central air conditioning and 20 x 40' swimming pool. Continental breakfast served on the patio.

✉ windsigh@earthlink.net   🌐 www.getawayhouse.com

Mill House Inn	275-1,275 $US BB	Best Breakfast in the Hamptons!
31 N Main St 11937	10 rooms, 10 pb	Homemade cookies around the clock,
631-324-9766	Most CC, *Rated*, •	hot & cold beverages all day. Room
Sylvia & Gary Muller, Lee	C-yes/S-no/P-yes/H-ltd	service available in suites.
Ellis	Spanish	Full Concierge Services, A/C, gas fireplaces, whirlpool baths, high speed wireless Internet

A luxurious Bed & Breakfast Inn in the heart of historic East Hampton Village. Beautifully appointed rooms & spectacular dog-friendly suites. Walk to superb beaches restaurants antiques galleries theaters & shops. Enjoy the best breakfast in the Hamptons!

✉ innkeeper@millhouseinn.com   🌐 www.millhouseinn.com

EAST HAMPTON

The 1770 House	209-1,495 $US BB	Full & Continental
143 Main St 11937	7 rooms, 7 pb	Restaurant, Tavern & seasonal garden
631-324-1770	Visa, MC, AmEx	dining
Demi Reichart	C-ltd/S-no/P-no/H-ltd	Hand pressed Frette linens, plasma
		TVs, gas fireplaces, parlor & garden

Historic Colonial inn offers seven guestrooms with private baths, antiques and modern indulgences, and separate 2 bedroom Carriage House with loft. On site restaurant with downstairs tavern. Wine Spectator Award of Excellence, 2009.   ✉ innkeeper@1770house.com 🌐 www.1770house.com

The Baker House	275-950 $US BB	Full breakfast
181 Main Street 11937	5 rooms, 5 pb	Local organic produce & farm
631-324-4081	Most CC, Cash, Checks	products, well-stocked bar, continental
Antonella & Bob Rosen	S-yes/P-no/H-ltd	breakfast option
		Pool, facilities for weddings, library
		with books, magazines and DVDs,
		private helicopter service

The Baker House 1650 is recognized as one of the finest luxury inns in the United States. Featuring elegant rooms, sumptuous breakfasts, a lovely pool, garden area and spa facilities, guests are sure to enjoy their stay at The Baker House.   ✉ info@bakerhouse1650.com 🌐 www.bakerhouse1650.com

EAST MARION

Coffey House Bed &	225-375 $US BB	3 Course, Gourmet Breakfast
Breakfast	4 rooms, 4 pb	Afternoon tea, soft drinks, and a light
5705 Main Rd 11939	Most CC, Cash, *Rated*	snack to enjoy on our deck or front
631-477-2107	C-ltd/S-no/P-no/H-ltd	porch.
Ellie & Rick Coffey	German	Full private bath w/ tub, vanity &
		shower, AC, cable TV/DVD, hair dryer,
		alarm clock, fireplace

The Coffey House Bed and Breakfast is a romantic and restful retreat located on the beautiful North Fork of Long Island in East Marion, New York.
✉ info@thecoffeyhouse.com 🌐 www.thecoffeyhouse.com

Quintessentials B&B &	265-310 $US BB	Full breakfast
Spa	5 rooms, 5 pb	Seasonal goodies including afternoon
8985 Main Rd 11939	Most CC, *Rated*	refreshments, snacks & fruit basket
800-444-9112 631-477-9400	C-ltd/S-no/P-no/H-no	Full-service Spa on site, steam room,
Sylvia Daley	German, Portuguese,	internet, garden, gazebo, whirlpool,
	Spanish	fireplaces, DVDs, books

Quintessentials B&B and Spa is a romantic inn on the North Fork in Long Island Wine Country. Features a full-service Spa, elegant rooms with fireplaces, private sundecks, whirlpool baths, near fine beaches & 33 wineries & just 90 miles from New York City
✉ innkeeper@quintessentialsinc.com 🌐 www.QuintessentialsInc.com

EASTPORT

Seatuck Cove House	100-475 $US BB	Full breakfast
Waterfront Inn	5 rooms, 5 pb	Full amenities, clock radio, TV,
61 South Bay Ave. 11941	Most CC, Cash	wireless Internet access, balcony,
631-325-3300	S-no/P-no/H-no	fireplace
Colleen McGrath		

Seatuck Cove House is Long Island's most romantic, elegant bed and breakfast. This spacious waterfront inn offers breathtaking panoramic water views, overlooking Moriches Bay and Seatuck Cove.
✉ info@seatuckcovehouse.com 🌐 www.seatuckcovehouse.com

ELLICOTTVILLE

Jefferson Inn of	89-229 $US BB	Full breakfast
Ellicottville	7 rooms, 7 pb	Sitting room, parlor, suites, fireplace,
3 Jefferson St 14731	Most CC, Cash, Checks,	cable TV, wireless Internet, afternoon
800-577-8451 716-699-5869	*Rated*, •	sweets, hot tub
Jean Kirsch	C-ltd/S-ltd/P-ltd/H-yes	

Charming 1800's Victorian Inn located in the center of Ellicottville just steps from shops, spas and restaurants. Rock in a chair on the wrap around porch or soak in the outdoor hot tub. Enjoy local golf, antiquing, hiking, skiing, and Amish country.
✉ info@thejeffersoninn.com 🌐 www.thejeffersoninn.com

FAIRPORT

Clematis Inn
2513 Penfield Rd 14450
585-388-9442
Theda Ann Burnham

135-145 $US BB
3 rooms, 2 pb
C-yes/S-no/P-yes/H-no

Vegetarian fare, no refined sugar
Attention given to special diets,
afternoon tea
Sitting room, library, sunroom, terry
cloth robes, hairdryers

A 1900 Historic National Folk House is the perfect lodging for your comfort, when you visit Upstate New York. The warm hospitality of The Clematis Inn will make your stay most Inn-joyable.

✉ clematis@rochester.rr.com   🌐 www.clematisinn.com

FLEISCHMANNS

Breezy Hill Inn
835 Breezy Hill Rd 12430
845 254-5615
Michelle & Alan Sidrane

125-280 $US BB
6 rooms, 4 pb
Visa, MC
C-ltd/S-no/P-no/H-yes
French, Portuguese,

Full breakfast
We accommodate food allergies
and offer a gluten free breakfast, if
requested
recreation room w/pool table, byob
bar, exercise and steam rooms, porch,
den, internet, Flatscreen DirecTV

Located 2 hours from NYC in the heart of the Catskills, minutes from skiing, hiking, antiquing and swimming, Breezy Hill Inn, a newly restored Victorian Catskills bed and breakfast provides restful getaways, gourmet breakfasts and luxury in the country.

✉ info@breezyhillinn.com   🌐 www.breezyhillinn.com

FORESTBURGH

Inn at Lake Joseph
162 St Joseph Rd 12777
845-791-9506
Ivan & Ru Weinger

145-405 $US BB
17 rooms, 17 pb
Most CC, Cash, Checks,
Rated, •
C-ltd/S-ltd/P-yes/H-yes
Spanish and Portuguese

Full breakfast
All day help yourself lunch and snack
bar.
Private lake

High in the Catskill Mountains, just two hours from New York City, exists a romantic, 140-year-old country estate on a 250 acre private lake, within thousands of acres of forest and wildlife preserve.

✉ ivan@lakejoseph.com   🌐 www.lakejoseph.com

GALWAY

Wyndbourne B&B
1631 Hermance Rd. 12074
518-882-1790
Nancy & Ralph Caparulo

95-150 $US BB
3 rooms, 1 pb
C-ltd/S-no/P-no/H-no

Full breakfast
Local focus in season. Tea in
afternoon. Aperitif selection.
Double fireplace, apple orchard, no-
tech atmosphere, antiques, warmth,
history, art, and character.

Sitting high on a hill at the edge of the Adirondack foothills, at Wyndbourne Bed & Breakfast we offer travelers a convenient and lovely location for enjoying the natural beauty and cultural opportunities of upstate New York.

✉ innkeeper@wyndbourne.com   🌐 www.wyndbourne.com

GREENPORT

Stirling House
104 Bay Avenue 11944
800-551-0654 631-477-0654
Clayton Sauer

175-295 $US BB
3 rooms, 3 pb
Most CC, *Rated*, •
C-ltd/S-ltd/P-no/H-ltd
French

Full breakfast
Afternoon tea, gourmet snacks,
lemonade, assorted beverages, guest
fridge.
Wraparound porch, expansive
waterviews, breakfast/sitting room,
WiFi ,i-pod docking station

Free Night w/Certificate: Valid January 1-March 31; Monday-Thursday; special offers cannot combine with any other special offers.

Your 1880's-era Victorian "home-away-from-home." Relax & enjoy Greenport & our beautiful environs with our unobstructed water views from our front porch and rooms. The highest concentration of lighthouses in the US. Beach passes available. Immaculate.

✉ info@stirlinghousebandb.com   🌐 www.thestirlinghouse.com

GREENPORT

The Bartlett House Inn
503 Front St 11944
631-477-0371
Jack & Diane Gilmore

159-299 $US BB
10 rooms, 10 pb
Visa, MC, Disc, *Rated*
C-ltd/S-ltd/P-no/H-no

European Breakfast
snacks and bottled water always
available
Fireplace, conferences, wireless
Internet, porch, gardens

Stately Classic Revival home featuring 10 guestrooms, all with private bath & furnished with one of a kind pieces. Located near North Fork wineries, beaches, Greenport Village & Shelter Island. A special place to get away from it all and feel pampered.

✉ info@bartletthouseinn.com   ◐ www.bartletthouseinn.com

GREENVILLE

Greenville Arms 1889 Inn
Rt 32 South St 12083
888-665-0044 518-966-5219
Kim & Mark LaPolla

115-235 $US BB
16 rooms, 15 pb
Visa, MC, Disc,
Rated, •
C-ltd/S-no/P-ltd/H-ltd
Spanish

Full breakfast from menu
Gourmet chocolate shop on site,
Afternoon Tea, dinner by reservation
on most nights
Wireless Internet access, art
workshops, quilt workshops, secluded
50' pool, sitting room

Historic 1889 Victorian Inn welcoming guests for 50 years. Gardens, outdoor pool, chocolate shop and an atmosphere of warmth and charm invite guests to relax. A delicious breakfast completes a memorable stay.   ✉ stay@greenvillearms.com   ◐ www.greenvillearms.com

GREENWICH

Country Life B&B
67 Tabor Rd 12834
518-692-7203
Richard & Wendy Duvall

95-180 $US BB
4 rooms, 4 pb
Rated, •
C-yes/S-no/P-no/H-ltd
Spanish, German,
French

Full breakfast
Candy dish & sherry in room, coffee &
tea maker in parlor
Patio, library, swimming hole, sunsets,
sitting room, hammock, porch swing,
picnic table, birding,

Free Night w/Certificate: Valid Nov. -June; Sundays-Thurs; not valid holidays, special events, and weekends.

A unique experience awaits you around Saratoga Springs. Our 1829 farmhouse B&B is situated in Washington County within the towns and villages of the Battenkill Valley on 118 acres of woodlands, meadows, waterfalls and a swimming hole   ✉ stay@countrylifebb.com   ◐ www.countrylifebb.com

HAGUE

Ruah B&B
9221 Lake Shore Dr 12836
800-224-7549 518-543-8816
Judy & Peter Foster

120-225 $US BB
4 rooms, 4 pb
Most CC, Cash, Checks
C-ltd/S-no/P-no/H-no

Full breakfast
Sitting rooms, mountain views,
fireplace, balcony, lounge, WiFi in all
rooms

Ruah B&B has large, bright common rooms with massive windows that bring "The Queen of the Lakes" and the surrounding Adirondack Mountains into every room.

✉ ruahbb@aol.com   ◐ www.ruahbb.com

The Locust Inn
Rts. 8 & 9N 12836
888-593-7712 518-543-6934
Carolyn & David Dunn

89-185 $US BB
5 rooms, 5 pb
Visa, MC, AmEx
S-no/P-no/H-no

Full breakfast
Sitting room, WiFi, TV/VCR, near
public beach; shops & restaurants,
swimming, boating, fishing

The Inn is nestled on the shores of crystal clear Northern Lake George where you can enjoy a nature-oriented hideaway in the Adirondack Mountains.

✉ relax@locustinn.com   ◐ www.locustinn.com

HAMLIN

The Country Corner
317 Redman Rd 14464
585-964-9935
Linda DeRue

100 $US BB
3 rooms, 1 pb
C-ltd/S-no/P-no/H-no

Continental breakfast
Complimentary beverages & snacks
Wrap-around porch, sun room, sitting
room, air conditioning

If you love the country and history and are looking for a relaxing getaway, this is the place for you. Country Corner in Hamlin, NY is close to the Rochester area, near Brockport; very close to Hamlin Beach State Park and a short drive to Niagara Falls.

✉ jderue1@rochester.rr.com   ◐ thecountrycorner.com

HAMMONDSPORT

Park Inn Hotel
37-39 Sheather St 14840
607-569-9387
John Jensen

99-109 $US BB
5 rooms, 5 pb
Visa, MC, Disc
C-ltd

Full breakfast
Restaurant & tavern
Private dining/conference room, A/C,
sitting room, phone, TV

The Park Inn is an authentic village inn, situated on Hamondsport's charming Village Square, that has been providing food, drink & lodging to travelers for more than a century.

🌐 www.parkinnhotel.biz

HERKIMER

Bellinger Rose B&B
611 W German St 13350
866-867-2197 315-867-2197
Chris & Leon Frost

129-169 $US BB
4 rooms, 4 pb
Most CC, •
C-yes/S-ltd/P-no/H-no

Breakfast Menu
Tea, coffee, soft drinks, snacks
Hot tub, on-site massage therapy, heat/
AC control, TV/DVD, robes and bath
amenities, Jacuzzi tubs

Our quiet, romantic surroundings afford a Victorian experience unlike all others, complete with on-site massage services. Escape from the hectic world of the city. Relax by the fire, or enjoy our stone patio complete with fountains, waterfalls & pond.

✉ bellingerrose@hotmail.com 🌐 www.bellingerrose.com

Portobello Inn
5989 State Route 5 13350
315-823-8612
Roland S. Randall

110-150 $US BB
5 rooms, 5 pb
Most CC, Cash, Checks
C-ltd/S-no/P-no/H-no

Full breakfast
Coffee, tea, juices, soft drinks,
homebaked cookies, desserts &
snacks
Fireplaces, wireless Internet, fax,
antique shop, library, country club
use – golf, tennis & pool

Enjoy a gracious B&B experience! Classic Italianate inn overlooking the Mohawk River Valley & the Erie Canal since the 1840s. From our wraparound porch & Victorian veranda, enjoy views reminiscent of the Tuscan hills of Italy. ✉ stay@portobelloinn.com 🌐 www.portobelloinn.com

HIGH FALLS

Captain Schoonmaker's B&B
913 State Rte 213 12440
845-687-7946
Judy & Bill Klock

140-195 $US BB
5 rooms, 5 pb
Most CC, Cash, Checks,
Rated, •
C-ltd/S-no/P-no/H-no

Fireside Gourmet Breakfast
Coffee, tea & yummy homemade
cookies always available!
3 common rooms with fireplaces, trout
stream, waterfalls, gardens, fireside
dining, wireless Internet

Fall asleep to the sound of the stream and waterfall. Hear the rooster softly crowing while you snuggle under your down comforter. The scent of wood burning fireplaces, luscious breakfasts, and country air will keep you returning to this country B&B!

✉ schoonmkr1@aol.com 🌐 www.captainschoonmakers.com

Whispering Pines B&B
60 Cedar Hill Rd 12440
845-687-2419
Celia & HD Seupel

119-169 $US BB
5 rooms, 5 pb
Visa, MC, Disc, *Rated*
C-ltd/S-no/P-no/H-no
German, French

Weekend Full, Weekday Continental
Afternoon tea
Sitting room, library, VCR/DVD, 2
rooms with Jacuzzis, outdoor Jacuzzi
spa, deck

Light-filled B&B on 50 acres of woods. Historic sightseeing, crafts, woodland-walking, fine dining, antiquing, biking; enjoy the quiet.

✉ whisperingpinesbb@gmail.com 🌐 www.whisperingpinesbb.com

HILLSDALE

Swiss Hutte Country Inn & Restaurant
Rte 23 12529
518-325-3333
Gert & Cindy Alper

100-210 $US BB
14 rooms, 14 pb
Visa, MC, *Rated*
C-yes/S-no/P-yes/H-yes
German

Full breakfast
Award winning restaurant, bar service,
patio dining, fridge
Views, rooms with porch or balcony,
TV, phones, parlor, tennis, swimming
pool, catering, weddings

Swiss Hutte is just what you would expect from a country inn with a Swiss Innkeeper. It's clean, charming, friendly, comfortable and it features an outstanding kitchen. Nestled in a hidden, wooded valley in the Berkshires.

✉ 8057@msn.com 🌐 www.swisshutte.com

HONEOYE

Greenwoods B&B Inn
8136 Quayle Rd 14471
800-914-3559 585-229-2111
Lisa & Mike Ligon

119-169 $US BB
5 rooms, 5 pb
Most CC, *Rated*, •
C-ltd/S-no/P-no/H-ltd
May thru October

Full gourmet breakfast
Sitting room, library, Jacuzzis, suites,
fireplaces, cable TV, WiFi, Robes &
slippers, irons

Greenwoods is a country inn displaying influences from the "Great Camps" of yesterday. A hilltop setting provides panoramic lake and valley views from a rustic log home. Experience a peaceful retreat, the best of yesterday the tasteful comforts of today!

✉ innkeeper@greenwoodsinn.com 🌐 www.greenwoodsinn.com

HOPEWELL JUNCTION

Bykenhulle House
21 Bykenhulle Rd 12533
845-242-3260
Bill & Florence M. Beausoleil

185-215 $US BB
5 rooms, 5 pb
Most CC, Cash,
Checks, •
C-ltd/S-no/P-no/H-ltd

Full breakfast
tea, coffee, hot chocolate
Wireless Internet access in common
area and in 2nd floor rooms,
reservations, books, magazines, etc.

Hudson Valley's historic Bykenhulle House B&B is Dutchess County's most romantic Bed & Breakfast in upstate New York. Our location is perfect if you want to go to Millbrook, Hyde Park, Rhinebeck, or even Kent, CT. A perfect distance for a day trip to NYC.

✉ stay@bykenhullehouse.com 🌐 www.bykenhullehouse.com

HUNTER

The Fairlawn Inn
7872 Main St 12442
518-263-5025
Chuck Tomajko

129-249 $US BB
9 rooms, 9 pb
Most CC, Cash, •
C-ltd/S-no/P-ltd/H-ltd

Full breakfast
Snack basket, cookie jar,
complimentary soft drinks
Flat Screen TV with cable & DVD in all
rooms, A/C, four common area rooms,
pool table & fireplace

Beautifully restored country home in the Catskills. In the shadow of Hunter Mountain, a four season resort area. Three story corner turret, wraparound porches, sumptuous breakfast. Concierge services – many things to do within walking distance.

✉ finn1@hvc.rr.com 🌐 www.fairlawninn.com

Washington Irving Inn
6629 Rt 23A 12442
518-589-5560
The Jozic Family

140-190 $US BB
15 rooms, 15 pb
Visa, MC, AmEx,
Rated, •
C-yes/S-no/P-no/H-no

Full breakfast
Victorian tea on Saturday & Sunday,
restaurant on premises, cocktail
lounge
Outdoor pool, TV/VCR, whirlpool
baths, garden, wrap-around porch,
mountain views

The inn's distinctive architectural charm and informal atmosphere make everyone feel welcome. Suitable for romantic getaways, family outings or reunions, weddings, group and corporate retreats.

✉ washingtonirvinginn@verizon.net 🌐 www.washingtonirving.com

HYDE PARK

Costello's Guest House
21 Main St 12538
845-229-2559
Patsy Newman Costello

65-85 $US EP
2 rooms
Rated
C-ltd/S-no/P-no/H-no

No breakfast is served, however, there
are several restaurants nearby
Near Roosevelt Home & Library, CIA,
Vanderbilt's, Vassar, Marist & Bard
colleges, wireless Internet

Federal style home built in the 1850's. Located in the Historic District of the Village of Hyde Park. Comfortable and convenient with air-conditioning in guestrooms. Surrounded by historic sites and elegant estates, close to restaurants and shopping.   ✉ Patsyc97@AOL.com

Le Petit Chateau Inn
39 W Dorsey Lane 12538
845-437-4688
Valerie Hail

165-250 $US BB
4 rooms, 4 pb
Visa, MC, AmEx
C-yes/S-no/P-ltd/H-no
French

Full breakfast
A welcome gift of refreshments and
cheese from France
Fireplaces, Cooking Classes, Robes,
Internet access, Walkway Across the
Hudson, Private Chef Events,

Small European style inn located ½ mile from the renowned Culinary Institute of America. Every room is named after a French wine region. Full gourmet breakfast prepared by CIA graduate chefs.

✉ info@lepetitchateauinn.com 🌐 www.lepetitchateauinn.com

ITHACA───

Log Country Inn	70-275 $US BB	Full breakfast
800-274-4771 607-589-4771	13 rooms, 9 pb	Afternoon tea in winter, vegetarian
Wanda Grunberg	Visa, MC, *Rated*, •	and vegan breakfast available on
	C-yes/S-no/P-ltd/H-ltd	request
	Polish, Russian	Sitting room, library, sauna, fireplace,
		Jacuzzi, computer, Internet access in
		some rooms

Enjoy Wanda's blintzes and Russian pancakes. Rest in cozy rooms furnished with custom made furniture. Family friendly and pets are welcome too. Historic, sulfur spring water, walking trails on the property as well as ponds and 100 acres of woods.

✉ wanda@logtv.com 🌐 www.logtv.com/inn

───

The Hound & Hare	110-250 $US BB	Full gourmet breakfast
1031 Hanshaw Rd 14850	4 rooms, 4 pb	Afternoon tea, snacks
800-652-2821 607-257-2821	Most CC, *Rated*	Sitting room, library, bicycles, Jacuzzi,
Zetta Sprole	C-yes/S-no/P-no/H-no	cable, suites, fireplaces, whirlpool
		tubs, WiFi

White brick Colonial built on land given to my forebears by General George Washington for service in Revolutionary War. Four tastefully decorated guestrooms with heirlooms and antiques, with fresh flowers for your pleasure.

✉ info@houndandhare.com 🌐 www.houndandhare.com

JAY───

Book & Blanket B&B	80-99 $US BB	Full breakfast
12914 State Route 9N 12941	3 rooms, 1 pb	Afternoon tea on request
518-946-8323	AmEx	Wireless Internet, sitting room, library,
Kathy, Fred, Sam & Zoe the	C-yes/S-no/P-no/H-no	fireplace, porch swing, piano
Basset Hound		

Free Night w/Certificate: Valid January 10 to May 15; Not valid President's Weekend.

1850s Greek Revival near Lake Placid. Picturesque Adirondack hamlet with village green, covered bridge and swimming hole. Bedrooms honor famous authors.

✉ bookinnjay@aol.com 🌐 www.bookandblanket.com

KEENE VALLEY───

Trail's End Inn	100-230 $US BB	Full breakfast
62 Trail's End Way 12943	12 rooms, 8 pb	Snacks, lunch
800-281-9860 518-576-9860	Most CC, •	Sitting room, library, Jacuzzis, suites,
David Griffiths & Susan	C-ltd/S-no/P-ltd/H-no	fireplaces, cable TV, WiFi, Internet
Lindtelgen		

Secluded 1902 lodge & cottages in the Adirondack mountains; clawfoot tubs, patchwork quilts, wood floors, fireplaces. Hike, bike, ski, visit Lake Placid Olympic sites. Weddings and groups hosted.

✉ innkeeper@trailsendinn.com 🌐 www.trailsendinn.com

LAKE LUZERNE───

Lamplight Inn B&B	135-249 $US BB	Full breakfast menu
231 Lake Ave 12846	15 rooms, 15 pb	Complimentary tea & coffee available
800-262-4668 518-696-5294	Visa, MC, AmEx,	any time, cookies at check in time,
Gene & Linda Merlino	*Rated*, •	wine & beer licensed
	C-ltd/S-no/P-no/H-yes	Guest sitting room with games, coffee
		& tea, service bar for wine, special
		romance packages

Laniers' 1992 "Inn of the Year" is still going strong. Between Lake George & Saratoga Springs. Romantic 1890 Victorian & Carriage House, fireplace bedrooms. Suites with Jacuzzi & fireplace. TVs, phones. Full breakfast menu. Romance packages. Free WiFi.

✉ stay@lamplightinn.com 🌐 www.lamplightinn.com

LAKE PLACID

Brooks' Sunshine Cottage B&B
15 Maple St 12946
518-523-3661
Bernadine & Joe Brooks

85-130 $US BB
5 rooms, 5 pb
Visa, MC
C-yes/S-no/P-no/H-ltd

Buffet
2 Living rooms w/fireplaces, gas grills, lounge chairs, off-street parking, kitchens in all suites

Charming European Style Bed & Breakfast, located on quiet Maple Street, bordering Hillcrest Avenue Park. Entire, century old, traditional house with spacious areas for relaxation, reading, or game playing is available for groups.

✉ brooks@brookssunshine.com ◐ www.brookssunshine.com

Paradox Lodge
2169 Saranac Ave 12946
877-743-9078 518-523-9078
Chef Moses & Nan
LaFountaine

135-245 $US BB
8 rooms, 8 pb
Visa, MC
C-ltd/S-no/P-no/H-no

Full breakfast
Restaurant & full bar
WiFi, A/C, fireplace, Jacuzzi, kayaks, canoe, restaurant

Paradox Lodge was built in 1890 on Paradox Bay in Lake Placid, NY. Paradox Lodge provides a quiet and comfortable atmosphere for guests. Featured in Rachel Ray's Tasty Travels on the Food Network; if that doesn't say good food, we don't know what does!

✉ paradoxlodge@roadrunner.com ◐ www.paradoxlodge.com

South Meadow Farm Lodge
Rt 73 (Cascade Rd) 12946
800-523-9369 518-523-9369
Tony & Nancy Corwin

115-170 $US BB
7 rooms, 6 pb
Most CC, Cash,
Checks, •
C-yes/S-no/P-no/H-ltd

Full breakfast
Family style dinner for parties of 6 adults or more and trail lunch are optional
Free x-country skiing and mountain biking; beautiful, peaceful views; wood-fired suana

Come hike, bike or cross country ski out our back door. Your stay includes a full breakfast served family style. Our 7 room lodge sits down in a meadow with fantastic mountain views. Smoke free. Be sure to visit our maple sugar house.

✉ ncorwin@southmeadow.com ◐ www.southmeadow.com

LEW BEACH

Beaverkill Valley Inn
7 Barnhart Rd 12758
845-439-4844
Chris Jurgens

105-340 $US BB
20 rooms, 20 pb
Most CC
C-yes/S-ltd/P-no/H-yes

Full breakfast
Afternoon Tea, lunch & dinner available
Game room, lounge & bar, sundeck, tennis courts, casting pond, ice skating, skiing, hiking, fishing

What do people enjoy here? It's the year-round access to outdoor activities & a chance to relax & reconnect with nature, take a break from the city or to enjoy a romantic getaway.

✉ innkeeper@beaverkillvalleyinn.com ◐ www.beaverkillvalleyinn.com

LEWISTON

Sunny's Roost B&B
421 Plain St 14092
716-754-1161
Sunny Matthews

100-100 $US BB
4 rooms, 3 pb
Most CC, Cash, Checks
C-yes/S-no/P-yes/H-ltd

Full breakfast
Pet Friendly, walk to River, many historical sights near by, delicious home cooking by Sunny

Free Night w/Certificate: Not available July and August.

This building was a convent in it's previous incarnation. We have turned it into what some of us call "Grandma's House" – comfortable while still being right in the middle of all the action. Communal dining table, queen beds, and wide front porch.

✉ sunny@sunnysroost.com ◐ www.sunnysroost.com

LISBON

North Fork B&B
219 Baker Rd 13658
315-528-0175
Lisa B. Gardner

80-85 $US BB
2 rooms, 2 pb
Most CC, Cash
C-yes/S-ltd/P-yes/H-no

Full breakfast
In-room coffee, homemade sour dough
bread, freshly roasted coffee
Ceiling fan, cable/satellite TV, VCR,
DVD, fridge, clock radio, ironing board
& iron, hair dryer, A/C

Relaxing getaway situated on 46 acres in the heart of Amish country. Children are always welcome. Close to several area universities. Pet friendly. Close to Canadian border and the St. Lawrence River. Come to "the place where everyone feels at home."

✉ northforkbandb@hughes.net 🌐 www.northforkbandb.net

LITTLE FALLS

Gansevoort House Inn
42 W Gansevoort St 13365
315-823-3969
Linda Stivala

115-200 $US BB
3 rooms, 3 pb
Most CC
C-yes/S-no/P-no/H-ltd
Fluent in Spanish,
Familiar with Italian,
German and French
May-October

Full breakfast
Afternoon Tea, snacks.
TV in sitting & reading room

The Gansevoort House Inn in the foothills of the Adirondack Park, between Albany & Syracuse on I-90, offers three guestrooms, 2 with private baths, and a separate guest suite in the carriage house.

✉ info@gansevoorthouse.com 🌐 www.gansevoorthouse.com

LIVINGSTON MANOR

The Guest House
408 Debruce Rd 12758
845-439-4000
Shaun & Andrea Plunket

150-245 $US BB
6 rooms, 6 pb
Most CC, Cash,
Rated, •
C-yes/S-ltd/P-yes/H-no
French, German,
Portuguese, Spanish,
Italian, Hungarian

All essentials provided in cottage
Tea, coffee & fruit, evening drinks
offered in hosts house, cooking facility
Jacuzzis, Massages, BBQ, fly fishing,
hiking, heated pool in summer,
practice tennis court, cable Tv

Rustic luxury on this 40-acre Catskill estate. All rooms with private bath or Jacuzzi. Full breakfast, hiking and fly fishing on the property. Six cottages available. First class dining and antique stores are just minutes away.

✉ andrea@theguesthouse.com 🌐 www.theguesthouse.com

LOCKPORT

Maplehurst B&B
4427 Ridge Rd 14094
716-434-3502
Mark & Peggy Herbst

65-85 $US BB
4 rooms, 3 pb
Most CC, *Rated*, •
C-ltd/S-ltd/P-no/H-no
Some German

Full breakfast
Afternoon tea, snacks
Sitting room, cable TV, accommodate
business travelers

Historic, spacious, antique-filled country bed & breakfast located minutes from world famous scenic and historic sites. Large, comfortable guestrooms tastefully decorated.

✉ maplehurstmkh@earthlink.net 🌐 www.maplehurst.us/index.html

MARIAVILLE

Mariaville Lake B&B
176 Batter St 12137
518-864-5252
Rick & Lorrie Runnels

125-195 $US BB
5 rooms, 5 pb
Visa, MC, Disc
C-yes/S-no/P-no/H-no

Full breakfast
We welcome vegetarians, local and
organic fare whenever possible
Hiking nearby, dock, canoe, kayaks,
swimming, antiques, deli within
walking distance

Welcome to Mariaville Lake Bed & Breakfast, a 5 room Upstate New York Inn with a great vibe. Just minutes from I-88 and I-90 and near Schenectady, Albany and Saratoga. Mariaville Lake B & B is lakeside lodging at its best.

✉ innkeeper@mariavillelakebb.com 🌐 www.mariavillelakebb.com

MILLERTON

Simmons' Way Village Inn
53 Main St 12546
518-789-6235
Jay & Martha Reynolds

199-240 $US BB
9 rooms, 9 pb
Most CC, Cash, Checks
C-yes/S-no/P-no/H-no

Full breakfast
Number 9 Restaurant
Porches, fireplaces, draped canopy
beds, sitting areas

Located in the center of the quaint country village of Millerton, NY, listed by Frommer's as one of the "Top 10" villages in America. Close to all Berkshire and Hudson Valley destinations. Shop, dine, play and relax.

✉ info@simmonsway.com 🌐 www.simmonsway.com

MUMFORD

Genesee Country Inn B&B
948 George St 14511
800-697-8297 585-538-2500
Deborah & Richard
Stankevich

120-200 $US BB
10 rooms, 10 pb
Visa, MC, Disc,
Rated, •
C-ltd/S-no/P-no/H-ltd

Full country breakfast
Coffee, tea, snacks, and cookies; guest
pantry
A/C, phones, fax, wireless Internet,
TV/DVD, library, deck by pond,
gazebo, sun room, meeting room

The Genesee Country Inn was built in 1833. This historic stone mill inn has 10 guestrooms with private baths located on Spring Creek. Ponds, waterfall, patio decks and gazebo are situated on 8 acres. We are located at the beginning of the Finger Lakes.

✉ stay@geneseecountryinn.com 🌐 www.geneseecountryinn.com

NEW PALTZ

Mountain Meadows B&B
542 Albany Post Rd 12561
845-255-6144
Corinne D'Andrea & Art
Rifenbary

145-155 $US BB
4 rooms, 4 pb
Most CC, Cash, Checks
C-yes/S-no/P-ltd/H-ltd

Full breakfast
Afternoon refreshments, delicious
home-baked goods daily
Recreation room with pool table, guest
kitchen, large in-ground pool, hot tub,
lawn games, A/C

Beautiful grounds and panoramic views of the Shawangunk Mountains provide the backdrop for our contemporary B&B. An ideal place for nature lovers who enjoy casual and comfortable living.

✉ mtnmead542@aol.com 🌐 www.mountainmeadowsbnb.com

NEW YORK CITY

1291 Bed & Breakfast
337 W 55th St 10019
212-397-9686
Roland Solenthaler

38-280 $US BB
31 rooms, 9 pb
Visa, MC
C-ltd/S-no/P-yes/H-no
German, French, Italian,
Spanish, Swiss German

24 hour self service
Coffee, tea, milk, toast, peanut butter,
jelly
Lounge with big screen TV, Internet
access, bike/scooter rentals, phone
with free local calls

A young, highly professional and motivated team greets you at 1291 Bed & Breakfast. We are located on 55th Street between 8th and 9th Avenues, right in the heart of Manhattan. Times Square and Central Park are within walking distance. ✉ 1291@1291.com 🌐 www.1291.com

36 Riverside Wyman House
36 Riverside Dr 10023
212-799-8281
Pamela & Ron Wyman

199-349 $US BB
6 rooms, 6 pb
Rated, •
C-ltd/S-no/P-no/H-no

Breakfast Basket
Complimentary "get started" breakfast
basket for first morning only.
Luxury, outstanding attention to detail,
sleep sofas, kitchenette, Cable TV,
WiFi, maid service

Located on sunny Riverside Park, Wyman House has been lauded by hundreds of happy travelers for its gracious hospitality. You'll find the finest accommodations with the utmost attention to detail.

✉ pam@wymanhouse.com 🌐 www.wymanhouse.com

Chelsea Inn
46 W 17th St 10011
800-640-6469 212-645-8989
Harry Chernoff

89-279 $US BB
33 rooms, 5 pb
Most CC, Cash, •
C-yes/S-no/P-no/H-no
Spanish, Polish, Italian

Continental breakfast
Voucher for breakfast at Nana's Treats,
the charming coffee shop downstairs
Refrigerator, coffeemaker, safe, alarm
clock, hair dryer, WiFi-free in each
room

Chelsea Inn is a four story walk-up NYC Hotel which offers a choice of suites or single rooms, private or shared baths – all with refrigerator, coffee maker and sink. The rooms are generously large and suites are huge. ✉ reservations@chelseainn.com 🌐 www.chelseainn.com

NEW YORK CITY

Chelsea Pines Inn
317 W 14th St 10014
888-546-2700 212-929-1023
Jay Lesiger, Tom Klebba, Al
Ridolfo

169-329 $US BB
23 rooms, 23 pb
Most CC, Cash, •
C-ltd/S-no/P-no/H-ltd

Continental plus breakfast
Complimentary concierge service
Outdoor patio, greenhouse, A/C, color
TV with HBO, phone, fridge, WiFi,
business center

Chelsea Pines is charmingly decorated with original vintage film posters from the Golden Age of Hollywood. 1 bedroom suites are available.

✉ mail@chelseapinesinn.com 🌐 www.chelseapinesinn.com

East Village B&B
244 E 7th St, Apt. #5-6 10009
212-260-1865
Betty-Carol Sellen

135-175 $US BB
2 rooms
Visa, MC, AmEx
C-ltd/S-no/P-no/H-no

Self-serve continental breakfast
Coffee, tea available anytime
Hairdryers, alarm clocks, New York
guidebooks, TV, video player & stereo

Newly renovated apartment in a period building. Contemporary furniture & art. Two bedrooms are suitable for one to two guests per room. Living room & dining area available to guests. There are two shared bathrooms.

✉ evbandb@juno.com

Mount Morris House
12 Mount Morris Park
West 10027
917-478-6214
Vasili

150-295 $US BB
5 rooms, 5 pb
Visa, MC, AmEx
C-ltd/S-no/P-no/H-no

Continental plus breakfast
Fireplaces, cable TV, DVD players,
WiFi, radio, alarm clock, in-house
laundry service, maid service

Historic 1888 Victorian NYC Mansion restored with every amenity. We invite you to stay in one of our spacious bedroom suites and make yourself at home in this historic New York residence with grand reception rooms and a private garden.

✉ vasilias007@yahoo.com 🌐 www.mountmorrishouse.com

Rooms to Let
83 Horatio St 10014
212-675-5481
Marjorie Colt

170-230 $US BB
4 rooms, 1 pb
C-ltd/S-no/P-no/H-no
Portuguese, Spanish,
Italian

Vouchers to a local restaurant
Continental breakfast offered with
vouchers to a local restaurant, pantry
with fridge, tea & coffee
Parlor with cable TV available to all
guests, lovely garden

Greek Revival residence, c.1840, retains much of its original feeling. In historic Greenwich Village, moments away from the trendy Meatpacking District with designer shops and fashionable clubs. A calm, quiet retreat from the action found all around.

✉ margecolt@aol.com 🌐 www.roomstolet.net

Stay the Night
18 E 93rd St 10128
212-722-8300
Nick Hankin

75-245 $US EP
7 rooms, 5 pb
Visa, MC
C-yes/S-no/P-no

Jacuzzis, fireplace, beautifully
maintained garden, walking distance
to many major attractions

Fully renovated and very secure, on a tree-lined block between 5th and Madison Avenues two minutes from Central Park. Four suites with ensuite baths, two guestrooms, and a 1 bedroom apartment with full kitchen and bath with Jacuzzi.

✉ nick@staythenight.com 🌐 www.staythenight.com

The Inn on 23rd
131 W 23rd St 10011
877-387-2323 212-463-0330
Annette Fisherman

250-399 $US BB
14 rooms, 14 pb
Most CC, Cash, Checks,
Rated
C-yes/S-no/P-no/H-yes
Spanish, German

Continental plus breakfast
Complimentary wine & cheese in the
afternoon
Sitting room, library, cable, suites,
fax, copier, hairdryers, iron, A/C,
newspapers, Internet

A sumptuous B&B in the heart of New York City. Enjoy the conveniences of a first class Manhattan hotel, in a setting one might expect in Martha's Vineyard or Vermont.

✉ reservations@innon23rd.com 🌐 www.innon23rd.com

NEWBURGH

Goldsmith Denniston B&B
227 Montgomery
Street 12550
845-562-8076
Nancy Billman

165 $US BB
4 rooms, 4 pb
Most CC
C-ltd/S-no

Full breakfast
Private baths, air conditioning, patio,
lawn for badminton or croquet, library

Denniston House is an elegant bed and breakfast in the heart of the historic district of Newburgh, New York the gateway to the Hudson Valley. Denniston House offers comfort, elegance and good food in a setting convenient to the many area attractions.

✉ dennistonbb227@aol.com 🌐 www.dennistonbb.com

NIAGARA FALLS

Butler House B&B
751 Park Pl 14301
866-706-8199 716-284-9846
Mike & Marcia Yoder

99-139 $US BB
4 rooms, 4 pb
Visa, MC, Disc,
Rated, •
C-ltd/S-no/P-no/H-no

Homemade Breakfasts
A/C, cable TV, clock radio, hairdryers
and ironing boards, wireless Internet

Snuggled amongst the beautiful trees and homes, on a quiet two way street in the heart of Niagara Falls. Within walking distance to the Majestic Niagara Falls, Seneca Niagara Casino and Canada.

✉ butlerhousebb@yahoo.com 🌐 www.butlerhousebb.com

Hanover House B&B
610 Buffalo Ave 14303
800-381-6496 716-278-1170
Barbara & Richard

80-145 $US BB
5 rooms, 4 pb
Visa, MC, Disc
C-ltd/S-no/P-ltd/H-no

Full breakfast
Bottle water, Tea & cookies always
available to guests
Wi-Fi, Internet access, private off-street
parking, TV, refrig, microwave, sitting
room, porch

A ten minute walk to the Falls, Maid-of-the-Mist, Cave-of-the-Winds, Aquarium, Seneca Niagara Casino, and many of the natural scenic parks of the area. Large rooms, Queen size beds, private baths, private parking, cable TV, bottled wtr, refrig & microwave.

✉ barbara@hanoverhousebb.com 🌐 www.hanoverhousebb.com

The Red Coach Inn
2 Buffalo Ave 14303
866-719-2070 716-282-1459
Tom Reese

99-419 $US BB
32 rooms, 32 pb
Most CC, Cash, Checks,
Rated, •
C-ltd/S-no/P-no/H-ltd

Full breakfast
Restaurant for breakfast, lunch, dinner
or snacks
Restaurant, bar service, sitting room,
library, Jacuzzis, suites, kitchenettes

Affordable luxury! Modeled after the Old Bell Inn, in Finedon, England, The Red Coach Inn has been welcoming guests to Niagara Falls since 1923.

✉ innkeeper@redcoach.com 🌐 www.redcoach.com

OLIVEREA

Slide Mt. Forest House
805 Oliverea Rd 12410
845-254-4269 845-254-5365
Ralph Combe, Jr.

85-225 $US BB
19 rooms, 15 pb
Rated
C-yes/S-no/P-no/H-no
German

Full breakfast
Lunch & dinner available (fee)
Restaurant, bar, pool, sitting room,
hiking, tennis courts, fishing, wireless
Internet, game room

Free Night w/Certificate: Anytime. Not valid Memorial Day, July 4th, Labor Day or Columbus Day Weekends.

Fresh air, nature and a touch of Old World charm await you at Slide Mt. Forest House, a German American, Catskill Mountains Inn. We offer the activities of a large resort with the congenial atmosphere of a small inn. ✉ slide_mtn@yahoo.com 🌐 www.slidemountain-inn.com

PALENVILLE

The Clark House
3292 Rt 23A 12463
518-678-5649
Michael & Christine Clark

105-225 $US BB
5 rooms, 5 pb
Visa, MC, AmEx
C-ltd/S-no/P-no/H-no

Full breakfast
10 person hot tub, sitting room,
fireplace, conference, on-site caterer,
weddings, Jacuzzis, WiFi

Magnificent Victorian guesthouse located in the heart of the Catskill Mountains – only 2 hours north of NYC. Easily accessible by bus. Hiking trails and skiing are minutes away. Two deluxe suites with fireplace and whirlpool available.

 theclarkhousebb@yahoo.com 🌐 www.catskillsbb.com

PECONIC

Home Port
2500 Peconic Ln 11958
631-765-1435
Peter and Cheryl Castiglione

150-250 $US BB
4 rooms, 4 pb
Visa, MC, AmEx
C-yes/S-no/P-no/H-no

Full Gourmet Breakfast
Coffee and teas
Free WiFi, formal candlelit dining
room, wrap around porch

Come relax with us!! Home Port is surrounded by 13 acres of park property, offering a walking or running track that takes you by wine vineyards, and 6 tennis courts that are yours to use day or evening!

 info@homeportbandb.com ⊕ www.homeportbandb.com

PENN YAN

Finton's Landing On Keuka Lake
661 E Lake Rd 14527
315-536-3146
Doug & Arianne Tepper

179 $US BB
4 rooms, 4 pb
Visa, MC, Disc, *Rated*
C-ltd/S-no/P-no/H-no
Dutch
Weekends, June-
Harvest

Full breakfast
Wrap-around porch, 165' beach, two-
person hammock, gazebo, canoe,
paddleboat, swim, WiFi

A waterfront Victorian with private baths & A/C, by a secluded beach on Keuka Lake. Romantic porch, gazebo, fireplace, canoe and paddleboat. Garage space for your bicycles! Bring your kayak! Gardens and wireless access.

 tepperd@eznet.net ⊕ home.eznet.net/~tepperd

Fox Inn
158 Main St 14527
800-901-7997 315-536-3101
Cliff & Michele Orr

109-214 $US BB
6 rooms, 6 pb
Visa, MC, AmEx,
Rated, •
C-yes/S-ltd/P-no/H-no

Full breakfast
Bar service, catering available
Sitting room, library, Jacuzzis for
two, fireplaces, cable TV/VCR, Suite
available, A/C, business

1820 Greek Revival Inn furnished with Empire furnishings, marble fireplaces, sun porch, parlor with billiards table and formal rose gardens.

 info@foxinnbandb.com ⊕ www.foxinnbandb.com

Trimmer House B&B
145 E Main St 14527
800-968-8735 315-536-0522
Gary Smith

99-349 $US BB
7 rooms, 7 pb
Visa, MC, AmEx,
Rated
C-ltd/S-ltd/P-no/H-ltd
Chinese

Full breakfast
Snacks
Sitting room, library, Jacuzzis, suites,
fireplaces, cable TV, wireless Internet

1891 Queen Anne Victorian. Romantic atmosphere in the heart of New York wine country. Let us pamper you in our luxurious surroundings. Close to wineries, shops and restaurants. Adjacent Guesthouse.

 innkeeper@trimmerhouse.com ⊕ www.trimmerhouse.com

Tudor Hall B&B on Keuka Lake
7603 E Bluff Dr 14527
315-536-9962
Priscilla & Don Erickson

175-215 $US BB
3 rooms, 3 pb
Visa, MC, AmEx
C-ltd/S-no/P-no/H-no
spring, summer and fall

Full candle lit breakfast
Complimentary sherry and chocolates
private beach, air conditioned suites
w/private baths, boats, bikes, spa,
TVs, wireless network

Elegant English Tudor home with terraced gardens & private beach on Keuka Lake, in the heart of NY State's Finger Lakes wine region. Fall asleep to the soothing sound of the lake lapping outside your window.   tudorhall@hotmail.com ⊕ www.p-port.com/tudorhallbb

PENNELLVILLE

River Edge Mansion
One County Route 10 13132
315-695-3021
Anne & Steve Hutchins

139-179 $US BB
3 rooms, 3 pb
Visa, MC, Disc
C-yes/S-no/P-ltd/H-no

Full breakfast
Beverage, cheese and crackers
provided in the evenings on arrival,
lunch & dinner upon request
Featuring whirlpool suites, fireplaces,
air conditioning and private docking
on the Oneida River.

Come experience this romantic 1818 Greek revival mansion. Featuring whirlpool suites, fireplaces, and private docking on the Oneida River. Inn is located on the scenic Erie Canal near Oneida Lake and is listed in the National Register of Historic Places.

 innkeeper@riveredgemansion.com ⊕ www.riveredgemansion.com

PINE BUSH

Pine Bush House Bed and Breakfast
215 Maple Ave 12566
845-744-3641
Mark & Barbara Grey

135-250 $US BB
5 rooms, 5 pb
Visa, MC, *Rated*
C-ltd/S-no/P-no/H-no

Full breakfast
Coffee & tea station, lemonade or iced tea, homemade cookies 4:00pm – 6:00pm
Steam showers, Jacuzzi, bidet, wireless Internet, flat screens with movies, A/C, fireplaces, piano

Welcome to Pine Bush House B&B, a charming and romantic Victorian home built in 1904. The Inn's quiet elegance has long made it a favorite for honeymoons, anniversaries, and other special getaways. Visit us and enjoy our white glove treatment!

✉ Barbara@PineBushHouse.com 🌐 www.pinebushhouse.com

PINE ISLAND

Cider Mill Inn B&B
207 Glenwood Rd 10969
845-258-3044
Robert and Clara Lipinsky

120-250 $US BB
3 rooms, 3 pb
Most CC, Cash
C-ltd/S-no/P-no/H-no

Full breakfast
All rooms with private bath, outdoor hot tub available all year, pool during summer months

The Cider Mill Inn is a country retreat in the heart of the Hudson Valley. A beautifully restored 1865 Victorian farmhouse offering a tranquil setting for a special getaway.

✉ info@cidermillinn.com 🌐 www.cidermillinn.com

Glenwood House B&B
49 Glenwood Rd 10969
845-258-5066
Andrea & Kevin Colman

150-295 $US BB
5 rooms, 5 pb
Visa, MC, Disc, *Rated*
C-yes/S-ltd/P-ltd/H-ltd
Italian, German

Many Options!
Jacuzzi tubs, fireplaces, candles, outdoor hot tub, sauna, pool, massage services, library

Beautifully restored Victorian farmhouse. Cottage rooms and suites with Jacuzzi tubs, fireplaces, antiques, canopy beds, candles and candlelit full breakfasts. Weddings hosted. Minutes from historic Warwick and Mountain Creek Ski and Water Resort.

✉ info@glenwoodhouse.com 🌐 www.glenwoodhouse.com

PITTSFIELD

Sunrise Farm B&B
331 County Hwy 17 13411
607-847-9380
Janet Schmelzer

80-100 $US BB
2 rooms, 1 pb
C-yes/S-no/P-ltd/H-no

Full breakfast
Complimentary wine
Well-behaved dogs accepted, A/C, WiFi

Quiet farm on a hill with lovely views of the rural community in Pittsfield. Swimming/hiking at nearby State Parks. Short drive to Cooperstown. Dog-friendly with dog-sitting available. Fields and woods for walking. Small enough for hosts to be flexible.   ✉ jluddite@frontiernet.net

PURLING

The Bavarian Manor Country Inn & Restaurant
866 Mountain Ave 12470
518-622-3261
Suzanne & Stanley Oldakowski

109-199 $US BB
18 rooms, 18 pb
Visa, MC, Disc
C-yes/S-no/P-yes/H-no
German, Polish

Full breakfast
Restaurant, dinner available, bar service
Jacuzzis, fireplaces, cable TV, massage sessions, WiFi Internet

Nestled on 100 acres in the Catskill Mountains, this 4-story Victorian Inn overlooking a private lake has been welcoming guests since 1865 with its friendly, relaxed, casual atmosphere. Eighteen guestrooms with private baths.

✉ innkeeper@bavarianmanor.com 🌐 www.bavarianmanor.com

RED HOOK

The Grand Dutchess
7571 Old Post Rd 12571
845-758-5818
Elizabeth Pagano & Harold Gruber

150-195 $US BB
5 rooms, 5 pb
Visa, MC, AmEx
C-ltd/S-no/P-no/H-no

Full breakfast
Hot & cold drinks always available
Parlors, porches, great room, dining room, living room, private baths

The Grand Dutchess boasts the perfect setting for your leisurely or romantic getaway, meetings, corporate retreats & other gatherings. A breathtaking backdrop of the magnificent Hudson River Valley, relaxing atmosphere & attention to detail.

✉ dutchessinnkeeper@earthlink.net 🌐 www.granddutchess.com

RHINEBECK

Olde Rhinebeck Inn c.1745	195-295 $US BB	Full gourmet country breakfast
340 Wurtemburg Rd 12572	4 rooms, 4 pb	Coffee station, guest fridge stocked
845-871-1745	Visa, MC	with complimentary beverages
Jonna Paolella	C-ltd/S-no/P-no/H-no	Sitting room, Jacuzzi, suites, satellite TV, country atmosphere, unique antiques, private entrances

Chosen as one of the top 10 inns in North America by Forbes.com, Olde Rhinebeck Inn is ideally located to enjoy the highlights of the Hudson River Valley. Authentic, elegant, rustic and intimate this lovely little inn is a genuine find, see for yourself!
✉ innkeeper@rhinebeckinn.com ◐ www.rhinebeckinn.com

Primrose Hill B&B	150-175 $US BB	Full breakfast
567 Ackert Hook Rd 12572	2 rooms, 2 pb	Cable TV, CD/DVD players, large
845-698-0370	Most CC	selection of movies, wireless Internet
Dave & Karen O'Riley	C-ltd/S-ltd/P-no/H-no	service

Primrose Hill B&B is located on a private 3 acre setting in the scenic Primrose Hill area of Rhinebeck. Picture yourself spending a leisurely getaway in one of two beautifully appointed guestrooms. Wake up pampered to a hearty country breakfast.
✉ doriley@hvc.rr.com ◐ www.primrosehillbb.com

Stone Church Road B&B	95-125 $US BB	Full breakfast
339 Stone Church Rd 12572	4 rooms, 2 pb	Fresh fruit, soft drinks, bottled water,
845-758-2427	Most CC	candy, homemade cookies
Richard and Marsha DeBlasi	C-yes/S-ltd/P-no/H-no	Sitting room, library, satellite TV, nature trail, outdoor games, patios, board games, private entrance

Lovely country setting 10 minutes north of the center of Rhinebeck; convenient to area attractions. Four comfortable rooms with scenic views. A common room with a variety of games and satellite TV. Private guest entrances. Flexible breakfast time.
✉ stay@stonechurchroadbedandbreakfast.com ◐ www.stonechurchroadbedandbreakfast.com

Veranda House	150-215 $US BB	Full gourmet breakfast
6487 Montgomery St 12572	5 rooms, 5 pb	Breakfast on terrace
877-985-6800 845-876-4133	Visa, MC, AmEx	Sitting room, library, central A/C,
Yvonne Sarn	C-ltd/S-no/P-no/H-no	concierge service, veranda with wicker, in room phones

Charming 1842 Federal house located in the scenic town of Rhinebeck, NY, in the heart of the Hudson Valley. Restaurants, fairs, antiques. Gourmet breakfasts. ◐ www.verandahouse.com

ROCHESTER

A B&B at Dartmouth House	149-199 $US BB	Full breakfasts by candlelight
215 Dartmouth St 14607	5 rooms, 5 pb	Bottomless cookie jar filled with
800-724-6298 585-271-7872	Most CC, Cash, Checks,	home-baked cookies, complimentary
Ellie & Bill Klein	*Rated*	beverages available at all times
	C-ltd/S-no/P-no/H-no	High speed wireless Internet, grand piano, AC, movies, guest computer, TV/VCRs, parking, porches

Welcome to A B&B at Dartmouth House-a quiet, spacious Tudor in Rochester's cultural Park-East Ave. district. Hosts are well-traveled and love people. Located in an architecturally fabulous residential neighborhood, just a short walk to downtown.
✉ stay@dartmouthhouse.com ◐ www.dartmouthhouse.com

ROCK CITY FALLS

The Mansion of Saratoga	125-295 $US BB	Served every morning from 8:30–10am
801 Rte 29 12863	9 rooms, 9 pb	Innkeepers reception every evening
888-996-9977 518-885-1607	Most CC, Cash, •	from 5–7pm, coffee, tea, water & fruit
Lori Wodicka	C-ltd/S-no/P-no/H-ltd	available 24/7
	Closed in January only.	Public phone in hallway, cable TV, free wireless Internet, 4-acres w/pond, ducks, waterfalls, fountain

Step back in time & experience the romance of the 19th Century. Built in 1866, the historic Mansion is a luxurious villa located 7mi from the action of Saratoga Springs & 25 minutes from spectacular Lake George. ✉ infodesk@themansionsaratoga.com ◐ themansionsaratoga.com

SALISBURY MILLS

Caldwell House B&B
25 Orrs Mills Rd 12577
800-210-5565 845-496-2954
Gene Sheridan

160-260 $US BB
5 rooms, 5 pb
Visa, MC, AmEx,
Rated, •
C-ltd/S-ltd/P-no/H-no
Spanish, Italian

Full 3 course breakfast
Free sodas, homemade baked goods,
coffee, tea, chai latte, cafe mocha hot
chocolate-24 hours
Front porch, sitting room, 2 fireplaces,
TV/VCR, room phones, Jacuzzi, air
conditioning, gift shop

Winner of the 2010 Best Bed & Breakfast in Hudson Valley, this elegant & romantic 1803 Colonial on 3 landscaped acres furnished w/antiques, fine linens and fresh flowers. Located near West Point, Storm King Art Center, wineries, hiking & designer outlets.

info@caldwellhouse.com   www.caldwellhouse.com

SARANAC LAKE

Sunday Pond B&B
5544 State Rte 30 12983
518-891-1531
Lesley & Dick Lyon

89 $US BB
4 rooms, 4 pb
Most CC
C-yes/S-no/P-no/H-no

Hearty Adirondack Breakfast
Trail lunches and complete dinner
menus are available for guests,
catering
Great room w/fireplace, stereo/ DVD;
laundry services, activity planning,
picnic area w/gas grill

Adirondack style lodging in a peaceful forest setting. Enjoy Summer, Winter, Spring and Fall with us in the heart of the Northern Adirondacks. Experience the scent of balsam, the haunting cry of the loon and the tranquility of nature in comfort.   info@sundaypond.com   www.sundaypond.com

SARATOGA SPRINGS

Batcheller Mansion Inn
20 Circular St 12866
800-616-7012 518-584-7012
Daniel Del Gaudio

165-475 $US BB
9 rooms, 9 pb
Most CC, Cash
C-ltd/S-no/P-no/H-no

Full breakfast
WiFi, TV, phone, refrigerator, robes,
irons/boards, concierge services,
conference facilities

A Saratoga Springs New York Bed and Breakfast Inn, The Batcheller Mansion Inn has a notable history. Built in 1873 by George Sherman Batcheller, it sits majestically on the corner of Circular Street and Whitney Place.

mail@batchellermansioninn.com   www.batchellermansioninn.com

Fox 'n' Hound B&B
142 Lake Ave 12866
866-369-1913 518-584-5959
Marlena Sacca

169-375 $US BB
5 rooms, 5 pb
Visa, MC, *Rated*
C-ltd/S-ltd/P-no/H-no

Gourmet Breakfast
Beverages & snacks in the afternoon,
24 hour tea and chocolates
Sitting room with fireplace, music
room with piano and games, WiFi

Off Season rates start November 1st plus AAA/AARP members receive a 10% discount. Visit our Packages and Specials page for your special getaway.

innkeeper@foxnhoundbandb.com   www.foxnhoundbandb.com

Geyser Lodge
182 Ballston Ave 12866
518-584-0389
Sandra Macica & Norman
Bovee

109-249 $US BB
5 rooms, 5 pb
Visa, MC
C-ltd/S-no/P-no/H-ltd

Full Weekends, Continental Weekdays
Homemade pastries, muffins, scones
or breads, fresh fruit, juice, coffee/tea,
yogurt and cereals
Free WiFi, bottled water and snacks,
fireplace, AC, in-ground swimming
pool, bicycles for guest use

The backyard in-ground pool, spacious sitting porch, water gardens, and gazebo welcome you on a warm summer day. In the winter enjoy a warm drink and a good book as you relax by the warmth of one of our fireplaces.

mail@geyserlodge.com   www.geyserlodge.com

Union Gables B&B
55 Union Ave 12866
800-398-1558 518-584-1558
Tom

150-400 $US BB
13 rooms, 13 pb
Visa, MC, AmEx
C-yes/S-no/P-yes/H-no

Continental breakfast
Sitting room, porch, weddings

A century-old residence just strolling distance from dining and browsing in an eclectic downtown. Experience the sparkling natural springs, exuberant Congress Park and the exhilarating thoroughbred racetrack, all nearby. Pet friendly!   stay@uniongables.com   www.uniongables.com

SARATOGA SPRINGS

Westchester House B&B
102 Lincoln Ave 12866
888-302-1717 518-587-7613
Bob & Stephanie Melvin

140-495 $US BB
7 rooms, 7 pb
Most CC, *Rated*, •
C-ltd/S-ltd/P-no/H-no
French, German
April thru November

Continental Plus breakfast
Complimentary beverages, snacks
Fireplace, guest fridge, in-room phones
w/voice mail, data ports, WiFi

Gracious, Queen Anne Victorian Inn surrounded by old fashioned gardens. Elegant bedrooms combine old world ambience with modern comforts. Walk to all Saratoga Springs' attractions. Wireless Internet available.

✉ innkeeper@westchesterhousebandb.com 🌎 www.westchesterhousebandb.com

SCHROON LAKE

**Schroon Lake Bed &
Breakfast**
1525 US Rte 9 12870
518-532-7042
Mark & Sharon Piper

125-155 $US BB
5 rooms, 5 pb
Visa, MC, AmEx,
Rated
C-ltd/S-no/P-no/H-ltd

Full Country Breakfast
4 p.m. afternoon refreshments
Private sitting rooms, cable TV, DVD,
refrigerator, microwave, hair dryer,
iron in all rooms, WiFi

Modern amenities meet antique charm at this romantic inn located in the Adirondack Park in Upstate NY. Open year round for all your Adirondack adventures. Relax on the grand front porch and enjoy a scrumptious, full breakfast each morning. Just Be Away!

✉ info@schroonbb.com 🌎 www.schroonbb.com

Silver Spruce Inn
2005 Rt 9 12870
518-532-7031
Phyliss Rogers

100-150 $US BB
8 rooms, 8 pb
Visa, MC
C-ltd/S-no/P-no/H-ltd

Full breakfast
Porch, dining room, parlor, perennial
gardens, gazebo

The Silver Spruce Inn is a spacious Adirondack country home, rich in local history with large, very nicely appointed and tastefully decorated guestrooms.

✉ info@silverspruce.com 🌎 www.silverspruce.com

SHARON SPRINGS

Edgefield B&B
153 Washington St 13459
518-284-3339
Daniel M. Wood

135-235 $US BB
5 rooms, 5 pb
•
C-yes/S-no/P-ltd/H-no
May – November

Full breakfast
Afternoon tea, complimentary evening
refreshments
Living room, veranda, library,
fireplace, friendly host & cat

A well-appointed Edwardian home in an historic village near Cooperstown & Glimmerglass Opera. Comfortable, elegant English country-house decor and antiques. Five guestrooms (queen or twin) with private baths.

✉ info@edgefieldbb.com 🌎 www.edgefieldbb.com

SHELTER ISLAND HEIGHTS

Olde Country Inn
11 Stearns Point Rd 11965
631-749-1633
Jeanne & Franz Fenkl

135-325 $US BB
12 rooms, 12 pb
Most CC, Cash
C-ltd/S-no/P-no/H-ltd

Full breakfast
Pub serving dinner & wine
Garden pavilion, A/C, ceiling fan,
smoke-free

This charming Victorian inn, originally built circa 1886, is located on beautiful Shelter Island nestled between the North and South Forks of Long Island, New York.

✉ info@oldecountryinn.com 🌎 www.oldecountryinn.com

SKANEATELES

1899 Lady of the Lake
2 W Lake St 13152
888-685-7997 315-685-7997
Sandra Rademacher

132-175 $US BB
3 rooms, 3 pb
Most CC, Cash, Checks
C-ltd/S-no/P-yes/H-no

Gourmet breakfast
Complimentary bottled water, soda &
beer
Sitting room, porch, library, cable TV
& DVD in guestrooms, complimentary
Internet access

An elegant 19th century Queen Anne Victorian located in the heart of this historic village, on the shore of Skaneateles Lake.

✉ sandra@ladyofthelake.net 🌎 www.ladyofthelake.net

SKANEATELES

Hobbit Hollow Farm
3061 W Lake Rd 13152
315-685-2791
Richard Flynn

120-295 $US BB
5 rooms, 4 pb
Visa, MC, AmEx,
Rated
C-ltd/S-no/P-no/H-no

Full breakfast
Afternoon tea, snacks, wine, cheese,
coffee
Sitting room, library, Jacuzzis,
fireplace, cable TV

Restored turn-of-the-century home. Elegantly refurbished in a quiet country setting on 320 acres. Equestrian stables nearby. Elegant dining within 2 miles.

✉ innkeeper@hobbithollow.com 🌐 www.hobbithollow.com

SOUTH WORCESTER

Charlotte Valley Historic Inn
Charlotte Valley Rd 12197
607-397-8164
Lawrence & Joanne
Kosciusko

125-200 $US BB
5 rooms, 3 pb
Rated
C-yes/S-no/P-no/H-ltd

Full breakfast
Afternoon tea, snacks, other
refreshments, complementary wine
Sun room, tennis court, outdoor
seating, fireplace, satellite TV, DVDs,
videos, quilts, books

The Inn is nearly 200 years old, and an important example of Greek Revival Architecture as a Stage-coach Stop built in 1832. Fine period antiques. Songbird mornings and brilliant sunsets. Good food. "The best of both worlds" in a private country setting.

✉ charlottevalley@yahoo.com 🌐 www.cooperstownchamber.org/CVINN

SOUTHAMPTON

1708 House
126 Main Street 11968
631-287-1708
Skip & Lorraine Ralph

195-675 $US BB
15 rooms, 15 pb
Visa, MC, AmEx
C-ltd/S-no/P-no/H-ltd

Continental breakfast
Beach passes, access to tennis courts,
info on golf, wineries, shopping, events
and horseback riding

This cozy Colonial home actually dates from 1708 and you can stay in the original 18th-century rooms. The inn has beautiful rooms; great for any guests.

✉ 1708house@hamptons.com 🌐 www.1708house.com

Mainstay B&B
579 Hill St 11968
631-283-4375
Elizabeth Main

150-625 $US BB
6 rooms, 5 pb
Most CC, *Rated*, •
C-ltd/S-no/P-no/H-no

Continental breakfast
Restaurant nearby; waffles
Sitting room, tennis courts in area,
water sports, swimming pool on
premises, all rooms have A/C

A Hampton B&B extraordinaire on Hill Street in Southampton. Charming, cozy, friendly & warm. Gardens, pool, A/C, continental breakfast included. Featuring a 2 bedroom suite, and a king master suite with fireplace.

✉ elizabeth@themainstay.com 🌐 www.TheMainstay.com

Village Latch Inn
101 Hill St 11968
800-545-2824 631-283-2160
Lois Dale

195-650 $US BB
35 rooms, 35 pb
Most CC, Cash
C-yes/S-no/P-ltd/H-ltd
May through October

Continental breakfast
Fireplaces, decks, private balconies,
heated swimming pool, tennis court &
private baths

Situated on the Village's Tony Hill Street is the famed celebrity hideaway, The Village Latch & Villas. The home away from home for countless of the rich and famous seeking the ultimate in country chic and privacy.

✉ mail@villagelatch.com 🌐 www.villagelatch.com

SPENCER

A Slice of Home B&B
178 N. Main Street 14883
607-589-6073
Beatrice Fulmer

80-200 $US BB
5 rooms, 5 pb
Visa, MC, *Rated*
C-ltd/S-ltd/P-ltd/H-no
Some German
Closed Dec 27-May 1

Full breakfast
Drinks, snacks available
Sitting room, hot tubs, suites, cable TV,
wireless Internet, accommodations for
business travel

We are located in the Finger Lakes Winery District, and specialize in self-tour planning, hiking, winery tours, and huge, delicious breakfasts. All rooms have private baths, A/C, TV, use of hot tub. An 18 hole golf course is within walking distance!

✉ info@sliceofhome.com 🌐 www.sliceofhome.com

ST. JOHNSVILLE

Inn by the Mill	150-375 $US BB	Deluxe Continental Breakfast
1679 Mill Rd 13452	5 rooms, 5 pb	Unlimited 24/7 complimentary ice
866-568-2388 518-568-2388	Visa, MC, AmEx,	cream, gourmet desserts
Ron & Judith Hezel	*Rated*	Sitting room, library, fireplaces,
	C-ltd/S-no/P-no/H-ltd	bicycles, waterfall, gardens, hot tub,
	5/1-11/1; winter breaks	smoke-free, WiFi, AC

*Welcome to Inn by the Mill, a romantic upscale B&B, located in upstate-central New York! An histori-
cal 1835 stone grist mill, miller's home, flower and water gardens, elegant rooms and private baths.
Complimentary ice cream and desserts 24/7.* ✉ stay@innbythemill.com ◐ www.innbythemill.com

STONE RIDGE

Victorian Knoll B&B	135-175 $US BB	Full breakfast
30 Peak Farm Rd 12484	3 rooms, 3 pb	Afternoon tea
866-262-0100 845-687-9639	Visa, MC	Verandah, pond, gazebo, gardens,
Patti & Tom Habersaat	C-ltd/S-no/P-no/H-no	Jacuzzi, parlor, dining area

*Victorian Knoll offers you access to a vast array of excellent dining, historical, cultural & natural
entertainment adventures. Let the charm of a bygone era embrace you today & throughout the year.*
✉ info@victorianknoll.com ◐ www.victorianknoll.com

TRUMANSBURG

Halsey House B&B	199-289 $US BB	Full breakfast
2057 Trumansburg Rd 14886	5 rooms, 5 pb	Game room, library, TV/DVD/VCR,
800-387-5590 607-387-5428	Visa, MC, Disc	A/C, wireless Internet access, plush
KC Christopher & Mitch	C-ltd/S-ltd/P-no/H-ltd	bathrobes
Clarke		

*A Federal style historic mansion located in the Finger Lakes region of New York. Stunning scenery,
expansive lakes, gorges, waterfalls and scenic wine trails surround us. A perfect romantic, restful
getaway featuring luxury and comfort.*
✉ kc@halseyhouse.com ◐ www.halseyhouse.com

Taughannock Farms Inn	105-250 $US BB	Continental breakfast
2030 Gorge Rd 14886	22 rooms, 22 pb	A 145 seat fine dining restaurant
888-387-7711 607-387-7711	Most CC, Cash, Checks	featuring American cuisine
Tom & Susan	C-yes/S-no/P-no/H-yes	Many of our rooms have Internet
	April 1st- December 31st	access and several have Jacuzzis

*Since 1873, only three families have owned Taughannock Farms. We think that's one of the reasons
history and tradition have remained so strong here. Our guests arrive eagerly and leave reluctantly,
savoring an experience few other inns can offer.*
◐ www.t-farms.com

UNADILLA

Westwood Guest Cottage	165-185 $US EP	Full kitchen & outside gas BBQ grill
286 Fred Braun Rd 13849	1 rooms, 1 pb	Living room, VCR with tapes, linens,
212-579-9685	Visa, MC, AmEx,	picnic area, 20'x 40' pool, canoe
Lisa Moskowitz & Doren	*Rated*, •	
Slade	C-yes/S-ltd/P-yes/H-no	
	Spanish	
	May – November	

*Private 2-bedroom hideaway with fully equipped kitchen, nestled on 11 acres of woods. Near Oneonta
& Cooperstown. Charming antiques, patio, grill, pool and phone. Relax and explore. $25 pet fee for
entire stay.*
✉ westwoodguestcottage@nyc.rr.com ◐ www.westwoodguestcottage.com

UTICA

The Pratt Smith House	75 $US BB	Full breakfast
10497 Cosby Manor	2 rooms, 2 pb	Cable TV, sitting room, high-speed
Rd 13502	*Rated*	wireless Internet
315-732-8483	C-yes/S-no/P-no/H-no	
Anne & Alan Frederick		

*1815 brick Colonial, wide plank floors, antiques; set on 22 acres in a woodsy residential area conve-
nient to city, area attractions, NY's thruway.*
✉ alannem@roadrunner.com

WARRENSBURG

Cornerstone Victorian B&B	99-194 $US BB	Five-Course Gourmet Breakfast
3921 Main St. 12885	5 rooms, 5 pb	Homemade Dessert daily and
518-623-3308	Most CC, Cash, •	Complimentary 24-Hour Beverage
Doug & Louise Goettsche	C-ltd/S-no/P-no/H-no	Pantry
	German	Concierge, Victorian Lobby with
		Fireplace, WiFi, Cable TV, Wraparound
		Porch, Perennial Gardens

Awarded Lanier's "Inn of the Year-2004" and Voted #1 "B&B with Best Breakfast" Grand Victorian with gleaming woodwork & perennial gardens. Delightful rooms with Two-Person Whirlpool/Fireplace. Near Lake George, Saratoga Springs & Gore Mountain Ski Area

✉ stay@cornerstonevictorian.com ❂ www.cornerstonevictorian.com

Country Road Lodge Bed & Breakfast	105-115 $US BB	Full breakfast
115 Hickory Hill Rd 12885	4 rooms, 4 pb	Lemonade, iced or hot teas & coffee
518-623-2207	•	available at all times, fresh muffins
Steve & Sandi Parisi	C-ltd/S-no/P-no/H-no	(chef's choice) at 7 AM.
		Scenic sitting room with Franklin
		stove, books, screened gazebo,
		perennial garden paths, free WiFi.

A cottage on 40 acres at the end of a short country road. Idyllic setting on Hudson River in Adirondack Mountains, near Lake George. Sociable hosts. No traffic. Common room with comfortable seating, Franklin stove. Perennial gardens, birds, hiking trails.

✉ mail@countryroadlodge.com ❂ www.countryroadlodge.com

Seasons B&B	120-205 $US BB	Full breakfast
3822 Main St 12885	5 rooms, 3 pb	Afternoon tea/coffee with sweets,
518-623-3832	Visa, MC, AmEx,	evening beverages available
Eileen M. Frasier	*Rated*, •	Personal robes, hairdryers, cable TV,
	C-ltd/S-no/P-no/H-no	A/C and Wireless Internet. massage
		therapist available

Italian-villa style residence, c.1830, with comfortable, unique accommodations. The house is situated at the top of a small hill & mostly surrounded by a dense landscape of trees & evergreens. Minutes from Lake George, Saratoga and Gore Mountain Ski area.

✉ eileen@seasons-bandb.com ❂ www.seasons-bandb.com

The Glen Lodge B&B	124-149 $US BB	Full breakfast
1123 Route 28 12885	8 rooms, 8 pb	Sauna, large porches, quiet
800-867-2335 518-494-4984	Visa, MC	sitting room, stone fireplace & air
Aimee & Douglas Azaert	C-yes/S-no/P-no/H-yes	conditioning

Take in the beauty and nature of the Adirondack Mountains of Upstate New York, at The Glen Lodge & Market. From the beautiful stone fireplace to the Adirondack styled cedar wood furniture, we invite you to indulge yourself in total relaxation and comfort.

✉ info@TheGlenLodge.com ❂ www.theglenlodge.com

WARWICK

Peach Grove Inn	140-225 $US BB	Full breakfast
205 Route 17A 10990	6 rooms, 6 pb	Afternoon tea
845-986-7411	Most CC, Cash, Checks	Fireplaces, whirlpool tubs, central AC,
John Mastropierro	C-ltd/S-no/P-no/H-ltd	some rooms with TV/VCR/DVD

The Peach Grove Inn is one of the most majestic lodgings in the lower Hudson Valley. The Peach Grove Inn offers richly appointed antiques, spacious private rooms and baths, Jacuzzis and more.

✉ peachgrv@warwick.net ❂ www.peachgroveinn.net

Warwick Valley Bed & Breakfast, Warwick, NY

WARWICK

Warwick Valley Bed & **Breakfast** 24 Maple Ave 10990 888-280-1671 845-987-7255 Loretta Breedveld	120-185 $US BB 6 rooms, 6 pb Most CC, Cash, Checks, • C-yes/S-ltd/P-no/H-no	Full breakfast Sitting room w fireplace, kitchen use, bicycles, covered porch, WiFi, DVD, video & book library, spa

Free Night w/Certificate: Anytime.

Begin discovering the Hudson Valley along the historic tree-lined district of Warwick in upstate New York. The Warwick Valley B&B provides guests with the comfort and warmth of an elegant home setting with hospitality at its finest! ✉ loretta@warwick.net ◐ www.wvbedandbreakfast.com

WATER MILL

Box Farm 78 W. Mecox Rd 11976 508-479-6364 Sean Farrell	250-650 $US BB 5 rooms, 5 pb Visa, MC, *Rated*, • C-yes/S-ltd/P-yes/H-ltd French and German	Full breakfast Cocktails & cheese in the evening Living room, deck, lawn, swimming pool, beach passes, parking permits

The Inn at Box Farm is located in the center of the Hamptons on Long Island, New York. A 300 year-old home provides six beautiful guestrooms a short distance from the beach.

✉ inn@boxfarm.com ◐ www.boxfarm.com

WATERLOO

Through the Grapevine **B&B** 108 Virginia St 13165 866-272-1270 315-539-8620 Michael & Joan Smith	110-120 $US BB 2 rooms, 2 pb Most CC, Cash, Checks C-yes/S-ltd/P-no/H-no	Full breakfast Sitting room, spas, fireplaces

Our charming 1870 Italianate is your own private retreat, offering a gourmet breakfast and fresh home-roasted and ground coffee. We are convenient to Finger Lakes, wineries and fine restaurants.

✉ info@throughthegrapevinebnb.com ◐ www.throughthegrapevinebnb.com

WESTHAMPTON BEACH

1880 Seafield House B&B
2 Seafield Ln 11978
800-346-3290 631-288-1559
Elsie Collins

150-250 $US BB
3 rooms, 3 pb
Visa, MC, *Rated*, •
C-yes/S-no/P-no/H-no

Continental Plus
Complimentary sherry, muffins, fresh
baked goodies, and sweets, wine for
special occasions
Sitting room, piano, tennis court,
library, swimming pool, fireplace

*Built back in 1880, this Victorian home is conveniently located in the village of Westhampton Beach,
on Long Island, near some of the finest shops and restaurants. This exquisite bed and breakfast features two guest suites complete with private baths.*

✉ elsie.collins@verizon.net 🌐 www.1880seafieldhouse.com

South Winds B&B
91 Potunk Ln 11978
866-332-3344 631-288-5505
Rosemary & Randy Dean

180-325 $US BB
3 rooms, 3 pb
Visa, MC, *Rated*
C-ltd/S-no/P-no/H-no

Continental plus breakfast
Afternoon beverage, cookies, fruit
Pool, parlor, porch, refrigerators, cable
TV

*The former estate of New York Governor A. Smith. Newly renovated and featuring up-to-date amenities and plenty of space. Relax in our spacious rooms, country parlor, or on the large front porch, with
the ocean a brisk walk away. Pool on the property.*

✉ info@southwindsbnb.com 🌐 www.southwindsbnb.com

WESTPORT

**The Inn on the Library
Lawn**
1234 Stevenson Rd 12993
888-577-7748 518-962-8666
Anthony & Alexandra
Wheeler

80-210 $US EP
11 rooms, 11 pb
Most CC, Cash, Checks,
Rated
C-yes/S-no/P-no/H-no

Restaurant on-site
TV/VCR in room, free wireless
high speed Internet access, Cafe &
Bookstore

*Elegant Victorian inn with period decor & furnishings. Lake Champlain views. Walk to restaurants,
marina, beach, golf, theater & shopping.* ✉ innmail@hotmail.com 🌐 www.theinnonthelibrarylawn.com

WILLSBORO

Champlain Vistas
3295 Essex Rd. 12996
518-963-8029
Barbara & Bob Hatch

75-140 $US BB
5 rooms, 3 pb
Visa, MC
C-ltd/S-no/P-no/H-yes

Full breakfast
Snacks, afternoon tea
Sitting room, trails for hiking & biking
nearby, near golf, swimming

*Lake and mountain views with antiques throughout; wraparound porch and stone fireplace. Special
wedding site; artists' paradise.*

✉ rdehatch@aol.com 🌐 www.virtualcities.com/ny/champlainvistas.ht

WOODSTOCK

**Enchanted Manor of
Woodstock**
23 Rowe Rd 12401
845-679-9012
Claudia & Rolan

170-335 $US BB
4 rooms, 4 pb
Visa, MC, Disc, •
C-ltd/S-no/P-ltd/H-no

Full healthy breakfast
Tea, wine, fruit, vegan and vegetarian
available
Heated salt water pool, outdoor hot
tub, massage therapy, gym, steam
room, Jacuzzi tubs, wireless

Free Night w/Certificate: Valid November-April and weekdays only from May-October.
Room Upgrade.

*Elegant yet comfortable home with beautiful furnishings, on eight storybook acres. Extraordinary
6-level deck overlooking pond with cascading waterfall, heated salt water pool and outdoor hot tub.*

✉ enchantedmanor@gmail.com 🌐 www.enchantedmanorinn.com

**The Woodstock Inn on the
Millstream**
48 Tannery Brook Rd 12498
800-420-4707 845-679-8211
Karen Pignataro

129-245 $US BB
18 rooms, 18 pb
Visa, MC, AmEx,
Rated
C-yes/S-no/P-no/H-ltd
Italian, French

Bountiful Continental Breakfast
HBO, A/C, stream, private pond for
recreational use, continental breakfast,
free WiFi

*Your retreat in the heart of Woodstock. Relax by the stream or amidst our exquisite gardens, sunny
lawns and towering pines, then stroll into the lively village of Woodstock for shopping, dining, and
galleries.* ✉ info@woodstock-inn-ny.com 🌐 www.woodstock-inn-ny.com

North Carolina

APEX

B&B Country Garden Inn
1041 Kelly Rd 27523
800-251-3171 919-363-0888
Bud & Beth McKinney

100-150 $US BB
3 rooms, 3 pb
Most CC
C-yes/S-no/P-no/H-no

Full breakfast
Afternoon tea, snacks
Sitting room, suites, cable, Internet,
gazebo, fishing

Our secluded, cozy inn is perfect for a romantic weekend getaway, on eight plus acres of ponds and gardens in the North Carolina countryside. Convenient to Research Triangle Park and the Triangle area. Wine tastings, weddings, retreats and events hosted.

✉ inn@budnbeth.com 🌐 www.bnbcountrygardeninn.com

ASHEVILLE

1889 WhiteGate Inn & Cottage
173 E Chestnut St 28801
800-485-3045 828-253-2553
Ralph Coffey & Frank Salvo

169-379 $US BB
11 rooms, 11 pb
Visa, MC, AmEx,
Rated
C-ltd/S-ltd/P-ltd/H-yes

Full 3-course gourmet breakfast
Evening refreshments
Award-winning gardens, parlor,
fireplaces, games, koi pond, solarium,
family & dog friendly

Circa 1889 shingle-style house, surrounded by beautifully landscaped grounds with a greenhouse conservatory filled with orchids and tropical plants. ✉ innkeeper@whitegate.net 🌐 www.whitegate.net

A Hill House B&B Inn
120 Hillside St 28801
800-379-0002 828-232-0345
Bill & Terry Erickson

155-230 $US BB
9 rooms, 9 pb
Visa, MC, Disc, *Rated*
C-ltd/S-no/P-no/H-no

Full breakfast
Afternoon wine, tea, home-baked
treats & cookies
Sitting room, wrap-around porch,
Jacuzzi, suites, fireplace, cable TV,
DVD players, WiFi

Hill House Bed and Breakfast in Asheville is renowned for its comfortable and casual feel. We enjoy taking care of our guests and strive to provide those special touches from exceptionally restful beds to delightful breakfasts. ✉ info@hillhousebb.com 🌐 www.hillhousebb.com

Abbington Green B&B
46 Cumberland Circle 28801
800-251-2454 828-251-2454
Valerie Larrea

165-425 $US BB
8 rooms, 8 pb
Visa, MC, AmEx,
Rated, •
C-ltd/S-no/P-ltd/H-ltd

Full breakfast
Beverages available 24/7
All king beds, whirlpools, fireplaces,
HDTVs, a/c, WiFi access, English
gardens, library, piano

Elegant, award-winning, historic home and carriage house—English theme throughout with prize-winning English gardens. Rooms and suites with king bed, whirlpool& shower, fireplace, HDTV, WiFi. Sumptuous candlelit breakfast served on crystal and china.

✉ info@abbingtongreen.com 🌐 www.abbingtongreen.com

Albermarle Inn
86 Edgemont Road 28801
800-621-7435 828-255-0027
Cathy and Larry Sklar

145-370 $US BB
11 rooms, 11 pb
Visa, MC, AmEx,
Rated, •
C-ltd/S-no/P-no/H-no

Full gourmet breakfast
Afternoon refreshments
Concierge, wireless Internet, in-room
massages, sitting room, sun porch,
veranda, English garden

AAA four-diamond rated. Elegant 1907 Greek Revival mansion on landscaped grounds in the residential Grove Park section of Asheville. Features exquisite carved oak staircase and spacious guestrooms with luxurious linens, robes and amenities.

✉ info@albemarleinn.com 🌐 www.albemarleinn.com

Applewood Manor Inn B&B
62 Cumberland Circle 28801
800-442-2197 828-254-2244
Nancy & Larry Merrill

150-225 $US BB
6 rooms, 6 pb
Most CC, Cash, Checks,
Rated
C-ltd/S-ltd/P-ltd/H-no
Spanish

Full breakfast
Afternoon complimentary
refreshments from 5–6 pm
Sitting room, suites, fireplaces, TVs/
DVDs, fresh flowers, chocolates,
balconies, arbor with swing

Welcome to Applewood Manor Inn B&B! Your new hosts Larry and Nancy Merrill will make your trip to Asheville, cozy and comfortable. Their beautiful Inn will bring you the comforts of home and hospitality fit for royalty! ✉ innkeeper@applewoodmanor.com 🌐 www.applewoodmanor.com

ASHEVILLE

At Cumberland Falls Bed and Breakfast Inn
254 Cumberland Avenue 28801
888-743-2557 828-253-4085
Patti & Gary Wiles

145-260 $US BB
6 rooms, 6 pb
Visa, MC, Disc,
Rated, •
C-ltd/S-no/P-no/H-no
Spanish

Three course candlelit gourmet
Afternoon tea, baked goods,
complimentary wine & cheese on
Saturday by request.
Jacuzzis, fireplaces, king beds, lux.
linen, cable, business travelers,
concierge services, WiFi

We are a turn-of-the-century home located in Historic Asheville. Our home features waterfalls and magnificent gardens, Jacuzzis and fireplaces. Totally renovated property insures your comfort. Concierge services complete with printed directions.   ✉ fallsinn@aol.com ✺ www.cumberlandfalls.com

Beaufort House Inn
61 N Liberty St 28801
800-261-2221 828-254-8334
Christina and Jim Muth

199-289 $US BB
11 rooms, 11 pb
Visa, MC, AmEx,
Rated, •
C-ltd/S-no/P-no/H-ltd

Full breakfast
Weekend Afternoon tea with abundant
desserts
Jacuzzi tubs, fireplaces, tea gardens,
balconies, decks, private entrances

National Historic property. Lovely tea garden & manicured lawns. All homemade baked goods.
✉ innkeeper@beauforthouse.com ✺ www.beauforthouse.com

Bent Creek Lodge
10 Parkway Crescent 28704
877-231-6574 828-654-9040
Doug & Jodee Sellers

135-185 $US BB
10 rooms, 10 pb
Visa, MC, Disc, •
C-ltd/S-no/P-no/H-yes

Full breakfast
Afternoon snacks, dinner by
reservation for groups of 6 or more
Walking trails, pool table, gardens,
concierge service, two sitting rooms
with satellite TV, lodge

Stay in the heart of the mountains you came to see in this elegantly, rustic lodge, only yards from the Blue Ridge Parkway and 10 miles from downtown Asheville. Enjoy the mountain views, the fireplace, the scrumptious breakfast & hiking trails on site.
✉ bentcreek@ioa.com ✺ www.bentcreeknc.com

Biltmore Village Inn
119 Dodge St 28803
866-274-8779 828-274-8707
Aaron Hazelton

199-335 $US BB
7 rooms, 7 pb
Most CC, Cash,
Rated, •
C-ltd/S-no/P-ltd/H-ltd
Spanish

Gourmet 3-Course Breakfast
Soft drinks, water, ice, coffeemaker,
glassware, champagne buckets,
complimentary wine & cheese
Wireless Internet, concierge service,
whirlpool tubs, fireplaces, pet-friendly
cottage

Built by Vanderbilt's lawyer, this Victorian mansion is a landmark on the National Register. It is the closest B&B to the Biltmore Estate. Guests enjoy mountain views, spacious rooms, private baths, Jacuzzi tubs and fireplaces.   ✉ info@biltmorevillageinn.com ✺ www.biltmorevillageinn.com

Black Walnut B&B
288 Montford Ave 28801
800-381-3878 828-254-3878
Peter & Lori White

150-320 $US BB
8 rooms, 8 pb
Visa, MC, AmEx,
Rated
C-ltd/S-no/P-ltd/H-yes

Full gourmet breakfast
Afternoon tea at 5, wine, cheese, hors
d'oeuvres, pastries, complimentary
guest beverages
Living room, koi pond, terrace &
porch, movie library, VCR en-suite,
cable TV, WiFi, pet friendly

Historic property, beautifully restored. Featured in "1000 Places to See Before You Die." Interiors are luxurious, with 8 guestrooms with king or queen beds, fireplaces, private baths en suite, and a newly renovated carriage house.   ✉ info@blackwalnut.com ✺ www.blackwalnut.com

Bridle Path Inn
30 Lookout Rd. 28804
828-252-0035
Carol & Fred Halton

98-150 $US BB
8 rooms, 8 pb
Visa, MC, AmEx
C-yes/S-ltd/P-no/H-yes

Full breakfast
Dinner by great cooks, picnic baskets,
gourmet Wisconsin cheeses and soft
drinks
Sitting room, verandah, hiking trails,
small refrigerators, private bathrooms

The Inn is comfortable, quaint & secluded on a hill overlooking downtown Asheville. Enjoy an elegant, full breakfast in front of the fireplace in winter or in summer on the wide verandah . . . savoring the moment . . . while viewing the surrounding mountains.
✉ Innkeeper@BridlePathInn.com ✺ www.BridlePathInn.com

ASHEVILLE ───

Carolina B&B
177 Cumberland Ave 28801
888-254-3608 828-254-3608
James & Susan Murray

135-225 $US BB
7 rooms, 7 pb
Most CC, Cash, *Rated*
C-ltd/S-no/P-no/H-no

Full breakfast
Air conditioning, gardens, fireplaces,
pet friendly rooms, Jacuzzis

Designed in 1900 by Richard Sharp Smith, its pebbledash finish, unique rooflines and abundant porches blend art and nature in the true Arts and Crafts tradition. Situated on a gently rolling one-acre lot within walking distance of downtown Asheville.

✉ info@carolinabb.com 🌐 www.carolinabb.com

North Lodge on Oakland
84 Oakland Rd 28801
800-282-3602 828-252-6433
Greg Adkins & Gregg Guertin

105-190 $US BB
6 rooms, 6 pb
Visa, MC, Disc, *Rated*
C-ltd/S-no/P-no/H-no

Gourmet three-course breakfast
Guest refrigerator with complimentary
water and sodas, snack pantry &
freshly baked cookies
Gardens with lighted gazebo &
fountain, in-room massages available,
concierge assistance

Visiting Asheville? Looking for relaxation and convenience? Come to North Lodge and enjoy the peace and serenity of this 1904 house, nestled on an acre of gardens and featuring six tastefully appointed guestrooms, two with gas fireplaces.

✉ stay@northlodge.com 🌐 www.northlodge.com

Oakland Cottage B&B
74 Oakland Rd 28801
866-858-0863 828-994-2627
Mary & Byron Bridges, Jim
Reid

80-150 $US BB
5 rooms, 5 pb
Most CC, Cash, Checks
C-yes/S-no/P-ltd/H-no

Full breakfast
Coffee & teas available all day
WiFi, guest laundry, DVD library,
books & games, crib & high chair
available

Oakland Cottage is an Arts & Crafts style historic home, circa 1910, with 5 Guest Rooms and Suites all with private baths and many in-room amenities, including Cable TV & Wireless Internet Access. Convenient in-town location.

✉ info@VacationInAsheville.com 🌐 www.oaklandcottage.com

Pinecrest B&B
249 Cumberland Ave 28801
888-811-3053 828-281-4275
Janna & James Martin &
Stacy Shelley

130-210 $US BB
5 rooms, 5 pb
Visa, MC, Disc,
Rated, •
C-ltd/S-no/P-no/H-no

Full gourmet breakfast
Afternoon tea, snacks, complimentary
wine
Sitting room, library, fireplaces, TV,
sunroom, fine linens, lush robes,
welcome business travelers

Turn-of-the-century residence with European elegance. A parlor with fireplace, sunroom, and five beautifully appointed guestrooms. Stone patio and landscaped gardens for outdoor enjoyment and relaxation.

✉ innkeeper@pinecrestbb.com 🌐 www.pinecrestbb.com

Princess Anne Hotel
301 E Chestnut St 28801
866-552-0986 828-258-0986
Howard Stafford

129-289 $US BB
16 rooms, 16 pb
Most CC, Cash, *Rated*
C-ltd/S-no/P-no/H-ltd

Full breakfast
Complimentary coffee, tea, biscotti
& truffles in room, sodas & ice,
afternoon wine & hors d'oeuvres
Wireless Internet, computer station,
access to Grove Park Inn Sports
complex, library, veranda

Asheville's Historic Treasure Circa 1924. Friendly, relaxed, and refined the Princess Anne Hotel offers a comforting blend of luxury and intimacy, where contemporary sophistication is touched with old-world charm. Uniquely Asheville. ✉ info@princessannehotel.com 🌐 www.princessannehotel.com

---

The Lion and The Rose
276 Montford Ave 28801
800-546-6988 828-255-7673
Jim & Linda Palmer

135-225 $US BB
5 rooms, 5 pb
Visa, MC, AmEx,
Rated
C-ltd/S-no/P-no/H-no

Full breakfast
Hot & cold drinks and snacks
available 24 hours a day
Antiques, park like garden, fireplaces,
Jacuzzi, cable TV, CD/DVD player,
Wifi, luxury soaps & linens

Beautiful Queen Anne Mansion, leaded/stained glass & antiques throughout. Sumptuous gourmet breakfast, morning coffee/tea delivered to your door. In Montford Historic District. Walking distance to downtown Asheville. ✉ info@lion-rose.com 🌐 www.lion-rose.com

ASHEVILLE

Wright Inn & Carriage House
235 Pearson Dr 28801
800-552-5724 828-251-0789
Barbara & Bob Gilmore

125-280 $US BB
11 rooms, 11 pb
Most CC, *Rated*, •
C-ltd/S-no/P-no/H-no

Full breakfast
Snacks, complimentary beverages
around the clock, Friday & Saturday
afternoon social hour
Sitting room, 3 Zone central A/C,
whirlpools, fireplaces, TVs, wireless
Internet, phones

The Wright Inn & Carriage House represents one of the finest examples of Queen Anne architecture found in the Historic Montford District. The Wright Inn offers some of the finest lodging in Asheville, NC.

 info@wrightinn.com  www.wrightinn.com

BANNER ELK

Blueberry Villa and Banner Elk Winery
60 Deer Run Ln 28604
828-898-9099 828-260-1790
Dede Walton & Dick Wolfe

175-289 $US BB
8 rooms, 8 pb
Most CC, Cash, Checks
C-ltd/S-ltd/P-no/H-yes

Full breakfast
Complimentary wine tasting at our
own Banner Elk Winery
Daily Maid Service, Jacuzzi bathtubs,
TV, terrace, private trout pond, front
porch with a view

Inn, vineyard & winery on 7 acres in the heart of Carolina High Country. Eight distinctive bedrooms with private baths & Jacuzzis. Terrace overlooks private trout pond. Intimate weddings, family retreats, corporate gatherings hosted. On-site catering.

info@blueberryvilla.com www.blueberryvilla.com

Perry House B&B
153 Klonteska Dr 28604
877-806-4280 828-898-3535
Robin & Mike Dunn

59-129 $US BB
5 rooms, 5 pb
Most CC, *Rated*
C-ltd/S-no/P-ltd/H-ltd

Full breakfast
Snacks, soda, bottled water, tea, wine.
Wireless Internet access, Deli,
views, cable TVs, VCRs, individually
controlled heat & A/C

The Perry House was built in 1903 and recently restored into a beautiful country inn complete with custom designed furnishings by master craftsmen, Carl and Jim Stanton of Linville, North Carolina.

perryhouse@skybest.com www.perryhouse.com

The Banner Elk Inn B&B
407 Main Street East 28604
888-487-8263 704-898-6223
Beverly Lait

110-250 $US BB
10 rooms, 10 pb
Visa, MC
C-ltd/S-ltd/P-ltd/H-yes

Full breakfast
The cozy Coffee & Tea, self-service
room is always open for guests 24
hours a day
Wireless, TV/DVD, down comforters,
A/C, whirlpools, fireplaces, porches

High in the Blue Ridge Mountains, within the village of Banner Elk, behind a white picket fence, a park-like setting and views to pastoral mountain meadows, lies the beautiful, charming, historic The Banner Elk Inn.

bannerelkinn@skybest.com www.bannerelkinn.com

BEAUFORT

Captains' Quarters Bed & Biscuit
315 Ann St 28516
800-659-7111 252-728-7711
Ms. Ruby & Captain Dick Collins

85-135 $US BB
3 rooms, 3 pb
Rated
C-ltd/S-ltd/P-no/H-ltd

Full English Style Breakfast
"Toast the Sunset" complimentary
beverages, Ms. Ruby's famous "Riz"
biscuits with breakfast
Parlor & formal dining room,
fireplaces, ceiling fans, WiFi & fax,
courtesy airport shuttle

Our Historic Victorian "Home of Hospitality with Quiet Elegance" located in the heart of the historic district is furnished with family heirlooms & antiques. The wrap-around front Veranda faces South West into the prevailing summer breeze.

captqtrs@coastalnet.com www.captainsquarters.us

BEAUFORT

Langdon House B&B
135 Craven St 28516
252-728-5499
Lizzet Prest

137-220 $US BB
4 rooms, 4 pb
Most CC, *Rated*
C-ltd/S-ltd/P-ltd/H-no
Spanish

Two course gourmet breakfast
Gourmet Breakfast incl. vegetarian
Mexican breakfast, Mexican brunch on
request, coffee, tea, snack
Refreshments, sitting room, bicycles,
fishing and beach supplies, whirlpool
tub with massaging jets

Guests at the Langdon House come first. We want you to enjoy your visit and leave contented, feeling that you made the best of your time in Beaufort – be it fine dining, fishing, sailing, exploring or simply relaxing with a good book. ✉ innkeeper@coastalnet.com 🌐 www.langdonhouse.com

---

Pecan Tree Inn
116 Queen St 28516
800-728-7871 252-728-6733
David & Allison DuBuisson

100-180 $US BB
7 rooms, 7 pb
Most CC, Cash, Checks,
Rated, •
C-ltd/S-no/P-no/H-ltd

Continental plus breakfast
Cold drinks
Jacuzzis, bikes, beach equipment,
patio seating, large garden, wireless
Internet

Romantic, antique-filled 1866 Victorian home in the heart of Beaufort's Historic District. A warm & comfortable lodging from which to discover Beaufort, the gem of the southern Outer Banks. The Inn provides a restful oasis for guests. ✉ innkeeper@pecantree.com 🌐 www.pecantree.com

BELHAVEN

Belhaven Water Street B&B
567 E Water St 27810
866-338-2825 252-943-2825
Karen & Andrew Fisher

85-115 $US BB
3 rooms, 3 pb
Visa, MC, *Rated*
C-ltd/S-no/P-no/H-yes

Full breakfast
Complimentary soft drinks & bottled
water are available at anytime in the
butler's pantry, BYOB
Front porch with harbor view,
fireplaces, Jacuzzi, wireless Internet,
Marina Pick Possible!

100-year-old home offers three guestrooms, all with private baths, view of harbor, & working fireplaces. The Belhaven Room features a Jacuzzi. The spacious living room has a cozy fireplace, piano, books, games, and a TV. Butler's Pantry with drinks.
✉ ahfisher@embarqmail.com 🌐 www.belhavenwaterstreetbandb.com

BLACK MOUNTAIN

Black Mountain Inn
1186 Old US Hwy 70 W 28711
828-669-6528
June Bergeron

128-169 $US BB
7 rooms, 7 pb
Visa, MC, •
C-yes/S-ltd/P-yes/H-no

Breakfast buffet
Gardens, pet friendly, family
accommodations, on-site spa services,
gardens

Discover a peaceful retreat steeped in the spirit of the North Carolina Mountains. More than 5,000 square feet of interior space and 3 landscaped and wooded acres offer our guests room to discover the antiquity and feeling of the Blue Ridge Mountains.
✉ jbergeron@mindspring.com 🌐 blackmountaininn.com

Red Rocker Inn
136 N Dougherty St 28711
888-669-5991 828-669-5991
Doug & Jenny Bowman

105-210 $US BB
17 rooms, 17 pb
Visa, MC, Disc
C-ltd/S-no/P-no/H-no
Closed January
weekdays

Full breakfast buffet
Casual Fine Southern dining nightly
except Sunday, homemade cookies,
strawberries & champagne
Sitting room, gardens, large porch,
suites, fireplaces, antiques, elegant
accommodations, A/C, safes

Named the Best B&B in Asheville and all of Western North Carolina 6 years in a row. Voted by the readers of Southern Living Magazine as one of the top three inns in the South. Recommended by The New York Times. Exceptional lodging and Southern dining!
✉ info@redrockerinn.com 🌐 www.redrockerinn.com

BLOWING ROCK

Crippen's Country Inn
239 Sunset Dr 28605
877-295-3487 828-295-3487
Carolyn & Jimmy Crippen

99-159 $US BB
9 rooms, 9 pb
Visa, MC, Disc
C-ltd/S-ltd/P-no/H-no

Full breakfast
Complimentary Beverage Station
serving water, soda, coffee and hot tea.

Your gourmet getaway in the NC mountains. At Crippen's it's all about the food! Located in Historic Downtown Blowing Rock, walking distance to Main Street's shops, galleries, bars and restaurants.
✉ jimmycrippen@crippens.com 🌐 www.crippens.com

Crippen's Country Inn, Blowing Rock, NC

BOONE

Lovill House Inn B&B
404 Old Bristol Rd 28607
800-849-9466 828-264-4204
Anne & Scott Peecook

139-219 $US BB
6 rooms, 6 pb
Visa, MC, *Rated*, •
C-ltd/S-no/P-no/H-no
Spanish

Full hot breakfast with choices
Hors d'oeuvres at social hour, and
beverages anytime, early coffee and
tea service each morning
Evening turndown, evening social
hour, beer, wine, soda and lemonade
available 24 hours

Historic AAA Four Diamond Inn conveniently located on eleven wooded acres, less than one mile from Old Town Boone NC and Appalachian State University, just off the Blue Ridge Parkway. Where old world charm combines with today's modern amenities.

 innkeeper@lovillhouseinn.com 🌐 www.lovillhouseinn.com

BREVARD

The Inn at Brevard
315 E Main St 28712
828-884-2105
Faye & Howard Yager

99-260 $US BB
15 rooms, 15 pb
Visa, MC, *Rated*
C-yes/S-ltd/P-yes/H-ltd
French

Full breakfast
Dinner on Thursday, Friday, Saturday,
& Sunday by reservation, fine wines,
full bar
Sitting rooms, access to private
camping, hiking, fishing, waterfalls

The Inn at Brevard, beautifully located in the heart of Brevard, North Carolina. Antiques, shopping, dining, & more are just minutes away. Come join us & experience the magic of the mountains!

 brevard@theinnatbrevard.com 🌐 www.theinnatbrevard.com

BRYSON CITY

Folkestone Inn
101 Folkestone Rd 28713
888-812-3385 828-488-2730
Steve & Eva Clayton

99-163 $US BB
10 rooms, 10 pb
Most CC, Cash, *Rated*
S-no/P-no/H-no
Spanish

Full Bountiful Breakfast
Complimentary snacks, soft drinks,
cookies, water
Guest computer, library, game room,
porch, rocking chairs, balconies,
beautiful grounds, A/C, WiFi,

An old-fashioned bed & breakfast at the Deep Creek entrance to the Great Smoky Mountains National Park just two miles north of Bryson City, a sleepy mountain town.

 innkeeper@folkestone.com 🌐 www.folkestone.com

BRYSON CITY

Fryemont Inn
245 Fryemont St 28713
800-845-4879 828-488-2159
Monica & George Brown

125-270 $US MAP
46 rooms, 46 pb
Visa, MC, Disc, *Rated*
C-yes/S-no/P-ltd/H-no
Suites open all year

Full breakfast and dinner menu.
Bar Menu offered in Fireside Bar, rates
include breakfast & dinner
Full service fireside bar, billiards,
fireplaces, rocking chair porch,
swimming pool, patio

A mountain tradition in lodging and fine dining since 1923. Serving a full country breakfast and excellent four course dinner. Casual elegance and rustic beauty, overlooking the Great Smoky Mountains National Park. ✉ fryemont@dnet.net ☏ www.fryemontinn.com

BURNSVILLE

Terrell House B&B
109 Robertson St. 28714
888-682-4505 828-682-4505
Mike & Laura Hoskins

90-100 $US BB
6 rooms, 6 pb
Most CC, Cash, Checks
C-ltd/S-no/P-no/H-no
French

Full breakfast
Parlor, formal dining room, large
back porch, gazebo, gardens, nearby
attractions

The Terrell House is a restored, early 1900's Colonial, built as a girl's dormitory for the Stanley McCormick School. The bed and breakfast inn has six lovely guestrooms, each with private bath, sitting area, and queen or twin beds. ✉ terrellhouse@hotmail.com ☏ www.terrellhousebandb.com

CAPE CARTERET

Harborlight Guest House
332 Live Oak Dr 28584
800-624-VIEW 252-393-6868
Bob Pickens & Debbie
Mugno

165-315 $US BB
6 rooms, 6 pb
Visa, MC, *Rated*, •
C-ltd/S-no/P-no/H-yes
German

Full breakfast
Snacks, coffee & tea all day, in-suite
breakfast
Fireplaces, Jacuzzis, TV/VCR,
refrigerator, WiFi, in-suite massages,
cable TV, kayaks avail.

Romantic coastal inn located on the central NC coast. Luxury suites feature two-person whirlpools, fireplaces, waterviews, & in-suite breakfast. Recently named a top undiscovered inn in America!
✉ info@harborlightnc.com ☏ www.harborlightnc.com

CAROLINA BEACH

The Beacon House
715 Carolina Beach Ave
N 28428
877-BEACON6 910-458-6244
David & Tammy Doriot

79-300 $US BB
7 rooms, 7 pb
Visa, MC, Disc,
Rated, •
C-ltd/S-no/P-ltd/H-no

Full Southern Breakfast
Private catering for large groups can
be arranged with our local caterers.

Enjoy the relaxing charm of an original 1950's Boarding House just steps from the beach! Relax on one of our verandas or head out for a day at the beach; there are plenty of activities to keep you busy. Cottages for families with kids and pets.
✉ innkeeper@beaconhouseinnb-b.com ☏ www.beaconhouseinnb-b.com

CHAPEL HILL

Inn at Bingham
Mebane Oaks Rd 27514
800-566-5583 919-563-5583
Francois & Christina

150-195 $US BB
4 rooms, 4 pb
Most CC, Checks,
Rated, •
C-yes/S-ltd/P-no/H-no
French, Spanish

Full breakfast
Snacks, complimentary wine & cheese
Sitting room, library, small meetings,
wedding facilities

This 208-year-old B&B inn is tucked away on 10 acres under large pecan trees. Just west of Chapel Hill and the University of North Carolina. Once was the homestead for the headmaster of the Bingham School. ✉ fdeprez@mebtel.net ☏ www.chapel-hill-inn.com

CHARLOTTE

The Duke Mansion
400 Hermitage Rd 28207
888-202-1009 704-714-4400
Becky Farris

99-219 $US BB
20 rooms, 20 pb
Visa, MC, *Rated*
C-yes/S-no/P-no/H-yes

Gourmet, made-to-order breakfast
Dinner, beverages, snacks
Sitting room, library, cable TV/VCR,
voice mail, wireless Internet, meetings,
groups

Dedicated to offering fine cuisine, beautiful amenities, relaxing atmosphere and remarkable service. With an emphasis on Southern charm, our historic home is a welcome alternative to large, impersonal corporate campuses or hotels.
✉ frontdesk@dukemansion.org ☏ www.dukemansion.com

Inn at Bingham, Chapel Hill, NC

CHARLOTTE

The Vanlandingham Estate
2010 The Plaza 28205
888-524-2020 704-334-8909
Billy Maddalon

149-249 $US BB
9 rooms, 9 pb
Most CC, Cash, Checks,
Rated, •
C-yes/S-no/P-no/H-no

Full breakfast
Catering for events, complimentary
water, coffee, tea & soft drinks
Meeting Rooms available for seminars,
weddings & luncheons

The VanLandingham Estate Inn & Conference Center is a beautiful place to rest your soul, host spectacular events or gather for productive meetings. The Estate welcomes guests with its unique combination of warm hospitality, grace and Southern elegance.

✉ reservations@vanlandinghamestate.com 🌐 www.vanlandinghamestate.com

CULLOWHEE

The River Lodge B&B
619 Roy Tritt Rd 28723
877-384-4400 828-293-5431
Cathy Sgambato

135-240 $US BB
6 rooms, 6 pb
Visa, MC, *Rated*
C-ltd/S-no/P-no/H-no

Full breakfast
Afternoon tea, snacks &
complimentary wines
Greatroom, 1923 antique Brunswick
Billiard table, giant fireplace, games,
gardens and acreage, cozy

On a bend in the Tuckasegee River sits this elegant Smoky Mountain lodge built with 100 year old hand-hewn logs taken from old barns and cabins in the Smoky Mountains region. A comfy bed and a mouth-watering breakfast make for a memorable escape.

✉ cathy@riverlodge-bb.com 🌐 www.riverlodge-bb.com

DAVIDSON

Davidson Village Inn
117 Depot St 28036
800-892-0796 704-892-8044
Gordon & Rebecca Clark

125-175 $US BB
18 rooms, 18 pb
Most CC, Cash,
Rated, •
C-yes/S-no/P-no/H-yes

Continental plus breakfast
Afternoon tea & fresh baked goodies;
our kitchen is stocked with a wide
variety of drinks & snacks
Conference/banquet room, library,
sitting room, concierge services

"Where Old World Charm Meets New World Comforts!" Amidst the gently rolling hills of the Carolina Piedmont lies the village of Davidson. Remember a time when small towns offered a slower pace and a friendly welcome to all visitors? Davidson still does.

✉ reservations@davidsoninn.com 🌐 www.davidsoninn.com

Tell your hosts Pamela Lanier sent you.

DILLSBORO

The Chalet Inn	96-200 $US BB	Full breakfast
285 Lone Oak Dr 28789	11 rooms, 11 pb	Snacks, complimentary imported beer
800-789-8024 828-586-0251	Most CC, Cash, Checks,	or wine
George & Hanneke Ware	*Rated*, •	Fireplaces, Jacuzzis for 2, private
	C-ltd/S-no/P-no/H-yes	balconies, A/C, WiFi, pool & sauna/
	German, Dutch, French	tennis privileges, some TVs

Closest B&B and Boutique Hotel to Great Smoky Mountains National Park. Jacuzzi & fireplace suites, large or economy rooms, all with private baths, A/C, free WiFi. Mountain views, private flower-be-decked balconies, babbling brook beckon you to this AAA Inn.

✉ paradisefound@chaletinn.com 🌐 www.chaletinn.com

The Dillsboro Inn	125-275 $US BB	Continental breakfast
146 N River Rd 28725	7 rooms, 7 pb	Suites, waterfall, campfire, fireplaces,
866-586-3898 828-586-3898	Visa, MC, •	river views, trout fishing
T. J. Walker	C-ltd/S-ltd/P-ltd/H-ltd	

On white water river next to waterfall and riverfront park, within walking distance of Dillsboro's craft shops, restaurants, and the Great Smokey Mountain Railroad. Seven riverfront suites with porches overlooking the waterfront. Nightly campfires.   ✉ info@dillsboroinn.com 🌐 www.dillsboroinn.com

DURHAM

Arrowhead Inn	135-325 $US BB	Full breakfast
106 Mason Rd 27712	9 rooms, 9 pb	Dinner will be served (extra), wine,
800-528-2207 919-477-8430	Most CC, Cash, Checks	beer available.
Philip & Gloria	C-yes/S-no/P-no/H-ltd	Six wedding arches, weddings/reunion
		packages, whirlpools, experience in
		hospitality for 25 years.

Relax in the grace and allure of a historic plantation estate at the Arrowhead Inn, a Durham bed and breakfast. Resting on six acres of gardens and lawns, this North Carolina bed & breakfast has been renovated to provide the best comfort and amenities.

✉ info@arrowheadinn.com 🌐 www.arrowheadinn.com

The Blooming Garden Inn	110-225 $US BB	Full gourmet breakfast
513 Holloway St 27701	5 rooms, 5 pb	Complimentary wine, tea & snacks
888-687-0801 919-687-0801	Most CC, Cash, Checks,	Library, antiques, 2-person Jacuzzi
Frank & Dolly Pokrass	*Rated*, •	suites, smoke-free, Internet
	C-yes/S-no/P-no/H-no	connections, free WiFi, cable TV

Vibrant colors and floral gardens transform this restored, gated Victorian inn into a cozy, memorable retreat, in downtown historic Durham. Smoke-free. Smaller events arranged. Very personable hosts. Close to the new Durham Performing Arts Center.

✉ bloominggardeninn@msn.com 🌐 www.bloominggardeninn.com

EDENTON

Captain's Quarters Inn	99-135 $US BB	Full breakfast
202 W Queen St 27932	8 rooms, 8 pb	Welcome refreshments, afternoon
800-482-8945 252-482-8945	Visa, MC, *Rated*	beverages & snacks, gourmet dinners
Don & Diane Pariseau	C-ltd/S-no/P-no/H-yes	offered with or without wine
		Jacuzzi, parlor, dining room, porch,
		living room, wine list, wireless Internet

Our inn is located in the historic district of "The South's prettiest town," Edenton, North Carolina. We offer Wine & Dine and Sailing Packages. Coming soon – Captain Cook Package, which includes a cooking demonstration with chef Diane.

✉ wq.202@hotmail.com 🌐 www.captainsquartersinn.com

Granville Queen Inn	95-135 $US BB	Varied breakfast choices
108 S Granville St 27932	7 rooms, 7 pb	Coffee, tea, and hot chocolate always
252-482-5296	Most CC	available
David & Dora	C-ltd/S-no/P-no/H-yes	Fireplaces, private balconies, cable
		TV, VCRs, and telephones

From the moment you step in the door at the Granville Queen Inn, it will be our pleasure to see that your visit is a memorable escape from the daily routine. 1907 neoclassical manor offering 7 guest-rooms with private bath and deluxe sit-down breakfast.

✉ stay@granvillequeen.com 🌐 www.granvillequeen.com

EDENTON

The Pack House Inn
103 East Albemarle
Street 27932
252-482-3641
Giuliano Giannone &
Michael Scalpi

89-135 $US BB
9 rooms, 9 pb
Most CC, Cash, •
C-yes/S-ltd/P-yes/H-yes

Full breakfast
Complimentary wine & cheese, 24
hour guest kitchen, four-course dinner
by reservation
Complimentary refreshments, 3
parlors with fireplaces, library,
porches

Edenton's oldest and most elegant inn offering the finest dining in eastern North Carolina. Enjoy our luxurious guestrooms with fireplaces and whirlpool tubs, located in Edenton's historic district.

✉ info@thepackhouse.com 🌐 www.thepackhouse.com

FLETCHER

Chateau On The Mountain
22 Vineyard Hill Dr. 28732
888-591-6281 828-651-9810
Lee & Jeanne Yudin

185-350 $US BB
6 rooms, 6 pb
Most CC, Cash, Checks
C-ltd/S-no/P-yes/H-ltd

Full breakfast
Complimentary beverages Picnic
Lunches with advance notice Candlelight dinner with notice
Balcony, spa tubs, private hot tub,
wireless DSL, outdoor view, concierge,
weddings, in room massage

Looking for an Asheville Bed and Breakfast? Then review our elegant mountain retreat. Considered one of Asheville's and Hendersonville's most romantic Bed and Breakfast our goal is to make it your favorite home away from home.

✉ innkeepers@chateauonthemountain.com 🌐 www.chateauonthemountain.com

FRANKLIN

Buttonwood Inn
50 Admiral Dr 28734
828-369-8985
Liz Oehser

99-119 $US BB
3 rooms, 3 pb
Visa, MC, Disc, *Rated*
C-yes/S-no/P-no/H-ltd

Full breakfast
Sitting room, king bed, loveseat,
decorative fireplace, and private
bathroom, Amish decor

Completely surrounded by tall pines, small and cozy Buttonwood will appeal to the person who prefers simplicity and natural rustic beauty.

✉ lizp1939@frontier.com 🌐 www.buttonwoodbb.com

FUQUAY VARINA

Fuquay Mineral Spring Inn
333 S Main St 27526
866-552-3782 919-552-3782
John & Patty Byrne

139-225 $US BB
5 rooms, 5 pb
Visa, MC, *Rated*
C-ltd/S-ltd/P-no/H-ltd
Some Spanish and
French

Full breakfast
Tea, wine, beer, coffee, soda, espresso
& juice
Sitting room, library, garden; cable
TV, wireless Internet & Bose radios,
weddings & special events

The Fuquay Mineral Spring Inn and Garden is an Historic Landmark Inn and Garden located in the heart of the Fuquay Springs Historic District across from the Fuquay Mineral Spring Park. Chefs offer cooking classes on most Wednesday evenings at the Inn.

✉ jbyrne@fuquayinn.com 🌐 www.fuquayinn.com

GRANITE FALLS

Thistle House B&B
25 Hillside Ave 28630
888 256 0745 828-313-3989
Phyllis Esler

85-125 $US BB
4 rooms, 4 pb
Most CC, Cash
C-ltd/S-no/P-ltd/H-no

Full breakfast
Hot Chocolate or gourmet tea for two
in room upon request, scones, pastries
& snacks
Gift shop, books for sale, crafts, games,
puzzles, TV DVD VHS in common
room, WiFi

Free Night w/Certificate: Any time except July 8-11, 2011 and July 24-August 9, 2011.
Room Upgrade.

A peaceful place of beauty and relaxation nestled in the quaint and quiet little town of Granite Falls. A place to stay for a night, a weekend or a week.

 manager@thistlehousebb.com 🌐 www.thistlehousebb.com

HENDERSON

Lamplight Inn	90-120 $US BB	Full breakfast
1680 Flemingtown Rd 27536	4 rooms, 4 pb	Parlor, TV lounge, wraparound porch,
877-222-0100 252-438-6311	Visa, MC	fireplace, fine collection of old books
Shirley Payne	C-yes/S-no/P-ltd/H-yes	& tobacco memorabilia.

Free Night w/Certificate: Valid March-September.

Step back from the fast pace of today, and join us by the fire in the Parlor. Located 45 minutes from the Raleigh-Durham airport and less than 2 miles from interstate 85, The Lamplight Inn resides on a 150 year old, 5 acre tobacco farm.    inn@lamplightbnb.net   🌎 www.lamplightBnB.net

HENDERSONVILLE

Claddagh Inn	95-175 $US BB	Full breakfast
755 N Main St 28792	16 rooms, 16 pb	Afternoon wine & light refreshments
866-770-2999 828-693-6737	Most CC, Cash, *Rated*	Private bath, air conditioning, cable
Sinikka Bell	C-yes/S-no/P-no/H-ltd	TV, telephone, wireless Internet, in-room fireplaces

The Claddagh Inn is an excellent launching point for short drives to witness the breathtaking beauty of the Great Smoky Mountains National Park, Pisgah National Forest, Dupont State Forest, Blue Ridge Parkway and Chimney Rock Park.   ✉ innkeepers@claddaghinn.com   🌎 www.claddaghinn.com

HIGHLANDS

4-1/2 Street Inn	125-170 $US BB	Gourmet breakfasts
55 4-½ St 28741	10 rooms, 10 pb	Homemade cookies, wine, appetizers,
888-799-4464 828-526-4464	Visa, MC	juice, fruit, hot tea, hot chocolate,
Helene & Rick Siegel	C-ltd/S-no/P-no/H-yes	surprise treats
	March – December	Hot tub, bicycles, parlor with books, music, games, birdwatching, gardens, concierge, morning paper

A perfect combination of romantic country charm and understated elegance, the 4½ Street Inn offers a secluded sanctuary within walking distance to town.
✉ relax@4andahalfstinn.com   🌎 www.4andahalfstinn.com

Colonial Pines Inn B&B	75-160 $US BB	Full breakfast
541 Hickory St 28741	7 rooms, 7 pb	Cider, hot chocolate, tea, sherry,
866-526-2060 828-526-2060	Visa, MC, AmEx	cookies, snacks
Chris & Donna Alley	C-ltd/S-no/P-no/H-no	Free wireless Internet, suites, kitchens, fireplaces, grand piano, cable TV, videos, library.

Perched on a 2-acre hillside in-town with a soothing mountain view from a breezy wrap-around veranda. Moderately priced rooms, spacious suites, private cottages. Sumptuous breakfasts, afternoon refreshments and berry gardens.   ✉ sleeptight@colonialpinesinn.com   🌎 www.colonialpinesinn.com

Fire Mountain Inn	205-385 $US BB	Full country breakfast
800-775-4446 828-526-4446	15 rooms, 15 pb	Breakfast not included in rates for
Hiram Wilkinson & Mathew	Visa, MC, AmEx, •	cabins, lunch & dinner available by
Gillen	C-yes/S-no/P-yes/H-ltd	advance order
		Guests receive a guide to dining & all activities in the area

One of the most unique & spectacular mountaintop hideaways in America. On hundreds of acres with long range mountain views, just outside the upscale mountain village of Highlands, NC.
✉ reservations@firemt.com   🌎 www.firemt.com

Main Street Inn	135-245 $US BB	Full breakfast
270 Main St 28741	20 rooms, 20 pb	Afternoon tea, on-site full service
800-213-9142 828-526-2590	Most CC, Cash, *Rated*	restaurant & bar
Gary Garner	C-ltd/S-no/P-yes/H-no	Piano, tapas bar, fireplaces, cable TV, A/C in rooms, wireless Internet, off street parking

Rated #2 top inn in the US, The Main Street Inn has been welcoming guests for over 135 years. An 1881 Federal Farmhouse renovated in 1998, the inn offers 20 charming, cozy rooms with private baths, piano, bar with appetizers, private off street parking.
✉ info@mainstreet-inn.com   🌎 www.mainstreet-inn.com

KILL DEVIL HILLS──────────────────────────────

Colington Creek Inn
1293 Colington Rd 27948
252-449-4124
Bob & Mae Lunden

168-198 $US BB
4 rooms, 4 pb
Visa, MC, Disc
S-no/P-no/H-yes
Closed – Jan, Feb. &
Mar

Full breakfast
Evening hors d'oeuvres and snacks
at night
The Atlantic Ocean, great dining,
shopping, airport & the Wright
Brothers Memorial within 1 mile

*Pamper yourself with a luxury bed and breakfast experience. Panoramic views from every room!
Located in the heart of Kill Devil Hills just 1 mile from the public beach access and shopping.*
✉ info@colingtoncreekinn.com 🌐 www.colingtoncreekinn.com

KITTY HAWK──────────────────────────────

Cypress Moon Inn
1206 Harbor Ct 27949
877-905-5060 252-202-2731
Greg and Linda Hamby

135-210 $US BB
3 rooms, 3 pb
Visa, MC
C-ltd/S-no/P-no/H-no

Full breakfast
Vegetarian dishes are available upon
request.
Sitting room, porches, kayaks,
windsurfing, sailing & surfing lessons,
satellite TV, room fridges.

*The Cypress Moon Inn rests on the shore of The Albemarle Sound, in the village of Kitty Hawk, NC.
There are three guestrooms all with a spectacular view over the Sound. The beach is just one mile
away.* ✉ info@cypressmooninn.com 🌐 www.cypressmooninn.com

KURE BEACH──────────────────────────────

Darlings by the Sea
329 Atlantic Ave 28449
800-383-8111 910-458-1429
Jim and Dee Gabriel

149-269 $US BB
5 rooms, 5 pb
Most CC, Cash
S-ltd/P-no/H-no

Continental breakfast basket
Bikes, Beach Chairs, Beach Towels,
Whirlpool, Cable TV, WiFi, Fitness
center, Ocean Front Balcony

*Fabulously appointed, Oceanfront, Whirlpool suites. King beds, King Pillows Down and Acrylic, Terry
Robes, Down comforters, Plush towels. Cable TV, VCR, DVD Player, Romantic, Mirrored whirlpool
and shower for two. Oceanfront fitness center.*
✉ reservations@darlingsbythesea.com 🌐 www.darlingsbythesea.com

LEICESTER──────────────────────────────

Wildberry Lodge B&B
135 Potato Branch Rd 28748
866-863-2525 828-683-2525
Ken & Glenda Cahill

149-399 $US BB
6 rooms, 6 pb
Most CC
C-ltd/S-no/P-no/H-ltd

3 course gourmet breakfast
Afternoon tea, fruit, non-alcoholic
beverages, snacks, dinner with
reservation by your Personal Chef
Library, satellite TV DVD/VCR, pool
table, decks, dry heat sauna

*Experience the casual sophistication of Wildberry Lodge. Constructed of handcrafted red pine logs,
nestled in the Newfound Mountains, 15 miles from Asheville, NC.*
✉ innkeepers@wildberrylodge.com 🌐 www.wildberrylodge.com?ref=lanierbb.com

MAGGIE VALLEY──────────────────────────────

Brooksong B&B
252 Living Waters Ln 28751
866-926-5409 828-926-5409
Betty & Cletis Wagahoff

135-160 $US BB
5 rooms, 5 pb
Visa, MC, Disc
C-ltd/S-no/P-no/H-no

Full breakfast
WiFi, fireplaces, refrigerators, jetted
tubs, separate showers & cable TV

*Nestled in the heart of the Great Smoky Mountains on the banks of Jonathan Creek in the scenic little
town of Maggie Valley, North Carolina is Brooksong, a Victorian bed and breakfast.*
✉ info@brooksong.com 🌐 www.brooksong.com

MANTEO──────────────────────────────

The White Doe Inn B&B
319 Sir Walter Raleigh
St 27954
800-473-6091 252-473-9851
Bebe & Bob Woody

199-335 $US BB
8 rooms, 8 pb
Visa, MC, *Rated*
C-ltd/S-no/P-no/H-ltd

Full Four-Course Served Breakfast
Gourmet teas, coffee, cappuccino,
espresso, desserts & sherry available
afternoons & evenings
Whirlpools, gas fireplaces, balconies,
wireless access, spa services,
weddings, bicycles & more

*Enjoy island life in this beautiful Victorian Inn that provides spacious and comfortable surroundings.
Amenities include fireplaces, private baths, 2-person whirlpools, four-course breakfast, spa services,
balconies, gardens and concierge service.*
✉ whitedoe@whitedoeinn.com 🌐 www.whitedoeinn.com

MATTHEWS

803 Elizabeth B&B
803 Elizabeth Ln 28105
704-841-8900
Martha & Will Krauss

80-100 $US BB
3 rooms, 2 pb
Visa, MC, AmEx, •
C-ltd/S-no/P-no/H-no
conversational German

Full breakfast
At no extra charge, upon request we
will provide a vegetarian or other
special diet
antiques, gardens, free wireless
Internet, fax, flatscreen TV, sun room

803 Elizabeth is a small B&B tucked among many trees and gardens on five acres. Many family antiques furnish the B&B in a very comfortable and homelike atmosphere. The yard features seasonal gardens of roses, flowers, herbs, vegetables and fruits.

✉ martha@803elizabeth.com 🌐 www.803elizabeth.com

MOUNT AIRY

Sobotta Manor B&B
347 W Pine St 27030
336-786-2777
Thurman & Robin Hester

139-159 $US BB
4 rooms, 4 pb
Most CC, Cash, •
C-ltd/S-no/P-ltd/H-ltd

Full breakfast
Coffee, soda & snacks, evening social
Porch, parlor, garden, business center,
wireless Internet, library, games, cable
TV, concierge asst.

North Carolina welcomes you to visit and fall in love with Mount Airy or Mayberry, as it is known to many, with grace and hospitality we are located in the heart of Yadkin Valley wine country and just 15 miles from the Blue Ridge Parkway.

✉ sobottamanor@aol.com 🌐 www.sobottamanor.com

The Thompson House
702 E.Pine St. 27030
336-719-0711
Mark Smith

80-140 $US BB
3 rooms, 3 pb
Visa, MC, *Rated*
C-ltd/S-ltd/P-ltd/H-no

Full breakfast
Complimentary soft drinks and snacks
are available. Special breakfast upon
request: green eggs & ham
Cable TV, Internet, board games,
books, badminton, volleyball, croquet,
horse shoes

The Thompson House B&B is a two-story Victorian located in the Flat Rock area of Mt. Airy. Outside the house, the wraparound porch has plenty of rocking chairs. There is also a small outdoor balcony upstairs.

✉ markcsmith666@roadrunner.com

MOUNT HOLLY

Robin's Nest B&B
156 N Main St 28120
888-711-NEST 704-827-2420
Robin & Jerry Williams

80-105 $US BB
4 rooms, 4 pb
Most CC, Cash
C-ltd/S-no/P-no/H-no

Full breakfast
Beverages and homemade treats
available.
Wireless Internet Available

The Robin's Nest Bed and Breakfast is a 1914 Classical Revival home located on 1.5 acres atop a hill in the Heart of Mt. Holly.

✉ robinsbb@bellsouth.net 🌐 www.robinsnestbb.com

NAGS HEAD

Nags Head Beach Inn
303 East Admiral St 27959
800-421-8466 252-441-8466
Ken & Lisa Muglia

75-200 $US BB
8 rooms, 8 pb
Most CC
S-no/P-no/H-no
Spring, Summer, Fall

Continental plus breakfast
Great restaurants nearby
Lobby, Jacuzzi tub, pool, individual
temp control, TV, 125 yds to beach,
bikes, beach chairs

Welcome to Nags Head Beach Inn, located in the heart of Nags Head, North Carolina, just 125 yards from the beach! Walk to restaurants and shopping, take a ride on the bike path, or just grab a chair and umbrella and relax. Great Shingle Style Inn.

 nagsheadbeachinn@aol.com 🌐 www.nagsheadbeachinn.com

NAGS HEAD

The First Colony Inn
6720 South Virginia Dare
Trail 27959
800-368-9390 252-441-2343
Sarah Close

109-329 $US BB
26 rooms, 26 pb
Visa, MC, *Rated*
C-yes/S-no/P-no/H-yes

Continental breakfast
Breakfast served with at least one hot
item, Manager's Social each afternoon
Library, verandas, pool, croquet,
ocean, fishing, weddings, beach,
computer, Internet, weddings

Elegant 26-room inn with Southern hospitality, verandahs along all 4 sides; English antiques, wonderful big beds. Walkway to our private gazebo on the dune; ocean view & sound views on third floor.

 innkeeper@firstcolonyinn.com 🌐 www.firstcolonyinn.com

NEW BERN

Hanna House B&B
218 Pollock St 28560
866-830-4371 252-635-3209
Joe & Camille Klotz

89-150 $US BB
5 rooms, 5 pb
Most CC, Cash, Checks
C-ltd/S-no/P-no/H-no

Full breakfast
An extensive gourmet breakfast
menu, afternoon snacks & beverages,
evening aperitif & biscotti
High speed Internet connection, full
gourmet breakfast, complimentary
bath amenities

Welcome to the Hanna House Bed and Breakfast. Recently renovated and furnished in the finest antiques and oriental carpets. Located in New Bern's register of historic places and designated an historic home, we are steps away from all major attractions.

 hannahouse@suddenlinkmail.com 🌐 www.hannahousenc.net

Harmony House Inn
215 Pollock St 28560
800-636-3113 252-636-3810
Ed & Sooki Kirkpatrick

119-185 $US BB
10 rooms, 10 pb
Visa, MC, Disc,
Rated, •
C-yes/S-no/P-no/H-ltd
Korean

Full homemade breakfast
Wine & cheese hour from 6PM to 7PM,
sodas available throughout guests'
stay
Two-person Jacuzzis in some suites,
parlor, games, porch with swings &
rocking chairs

Comfortable yet elegant. Unusually spacious c.1850 home. Rockers/swings on porch. In historic district near Tryon Palace, Fireman's Museum, Historic Trolley Tour, antique shops, and restaurants. Most of our guests park and walk throughout their stay.

 harmony@cconnect.net 🌐 www.harmonyhouseinn.com

Meadows Inn B&B
212 Pollock St 28560
877-551-1776 252-634-1776
John & Betty Foy

99-169 $US BB
8 rooms, 7 pb
Visa, MC, AmEx,
Rated
C-yes/S-no/P-no/H-no

Full breakfast
Hot and cold beverages, homemade
cookies, snacks
Spacious gathering room with a large
screen TV, TV/VCRs in all rooms, free
WiFi, spa services

Nestled peacefully in the heart of the downtown historic district, this c 1847 Antebellum inn has been welcoming guests since 1980. Accommodations to suit the business or family traveler. Perfect for that romantic getaway you have been planning.

 meadowsinnbnb@earthlink.net 🌐 www.meadowsinn-nc.com

Sail Inn
714 Pollock St 28562
866-731-6036 252-259-8507
Michael McMillan & Karen
Snyder

85-125 $US BB
3 rooms, 2 pb
Most CC, Cash
C-ltd/S-ltd/P-no/H-no

Continental Plus breakfast
24/7: Complementary hot coffee, or
tea, chilled sodas or water, fresh fruit
too.
Cable TV, DVDs, free WiFi, iPod
station, iron w/ironing board,
hairdryer, coffee maker, games, books

"A Simple Inn Reflecting A Quieter Time." We strive to provide a quaint, quiet, intimate setting for our overnight guests in a lovely, historic home. Come on in to the Sail Inn.

 sailinn@yahoo.com 🌐 www.sailinn.biz

NEW BERN

The Aerie B&B
509 Pollock St 28562
800-849-5553 252-636-5553
Michael & Marty Gunhus

129-199 $US BB
7 rooms, 7 pb
Most CC, *Rated*, •
C-ltd/S-no/P-no/H-no

Full gourmet breakfast
Early-evening wine and hors
d'oeuvres, coffee, tea, hot cocoa, water
& sodas available 24 hours
Wireless High-Speed Internet
throughout, massage by appointment,
cable TV/VCR/DVD, feather beds

Relax and share the warmth and charm of this turn-of-the-century Victorian home, one block from the Tyron Palace in the heart of the historic district.

✉ info@aeriebedandbreakfast.com 🌐 www.aeriebedandbreakfast.com

OCRACOKE

The Castle on Silver Lake
Silver Lake Rd 27960
800-471-8848 252-928-3505
Castle Innkeeper

159-279 $US BB
11 rooms, 11 pb
Visa, MC
C-ltd/S-no/P-no/H-no
Closed January

Full breakfast
A/C, cable TV/VCR/CD, whirlpool
tubs, private entrances, library,
fireplaces, business accommodation

Relax in the comfortable rooms of this three-story inn. The rooms are tastefully decorated with antiques and each has its own private bath. The Castle, located on Ocracoke Island, North Carolina offers elegant amenities and so much more!

✉ innkeeper@thecastlebb.com 🌐 www.thecastlebb.com

Thurston House Inn
685 Irvin Garrish Hwy 27960
252-928-6037
Donna Boor

95-155 $US BB
10 rooms, 10 pb
Visa, MC, Disc, •
C-ltd/S-no/P-no/H-ltd

Full breakfast
Wireless Internet, hot tub, ice
machine, TV, phone, massages on site,
outside shower

Covered porches with swing and rockers, private grounds with lush native plants and graying cedar shake buildings set the scene for a perfect island retreat.

✉ stay@thurstonhouseinn.com 🌐 www.thurstonhouseinn.com

PILOT MOUNTAIN

Pilot Knob Inn
361 New Pilot Knob Ln 27041
336-325-2502
Will & Jennifer Allen

129-249 $US BB
12 rooms, 12 pb
Visa, MC, AmEx,
Rated, •
S-no/P-ltd/H-yes

Full breakfast
6 acre lake-fishing, boating, hiking &
biking on site, sauna, whirlpools for
two, hot tub, fireplace

Cabins with whirlpool tubs for two, a lake with boats and fishing, honeymoon suites, hiking, mountain areas, local wineries and full breakfast located near the Yadkin Valley Wine Trail and Blue Ridge Parkway.

✉ pilotknobinn@surry.net 🌐 www.pilotknobinn.com

PISGAH FOREST

Key Falls Inn
151 Everett Rd 28768
828-884-7559
C & P Grosvenor & J
Fogleman & B Grosvenor

96-232 $US BB
5 rooms, 5 pb
Visa, MC, Disc
C-ltd/S-no/P-no/H-yes
Spanish

Full breakfast
Afternoon tea & cookies. Lunches,
dinners, pizza available with advance
notice. Catering and events
Sitting room, cable TV, VCR, DVD, trail
to waterfall, tennis ct., fishing pond

Charming, restored Victorian farmhouse furnished with antiques on 26 acres near Brevard. Porches, mountain view, waterfall, wooded setting & sumptuous breakfasts.Luxury cabin, event services and catering available.

✉ keyfallsinn@citcom.net 🌐 www.keyfallsinn.com

PITTSBORO

Rosemary House B&B
76 West St 27312
888-643-2017 919-542-5515
Karen Pullen

100-175 $US BB
5 rooms, 5 pb
Visa, MC, Disc
C-yes/S-no/P-no/H-no

Vegetarian
Cookie jar, complimentary drinks, hot
chocolate & tea
Wireless high-speed Internet, cable TV,
rocking chairs on huge porch

Welcome to our gracious 1912 Colonial Revival Bed & Breakfast, listed on the National Register of Historic Places. Comfortable accommodations, personal service, delicious breakfasts.

✉ karen@rosemary-bb.com 🌐 www.rosemary-bb.com

RALEIGH

Cameron Park Inn B&B	139-199 $US BB	Full breakfast
211 Groveland Ave 27605	5 rooms, 5 pb	Complimentary soft drinks and snacks
888-257-2171 919-835-2171	Most CC, *Rated*	Sitting room and guest lounge,
Nikki D'Ambrose	C-ltd/S-no/P-no/H-ltd	wireless Internet, copy & fax available,
		bicycles

Nestled along a quiet tree-lined street in the secluded elegance of the historic Cameron Park, there's the most delightful place to stop and spend the night, take a mid-week break or settle in for a weekend's relaxation. ✉ innkeeper@cameronparkinn.com ◐ www.cameronparkinn.com

The Oakwood Inn B&B	119-209 $US BB	Full breakfast
411 N Bloodworth St 27604	6 rooms, 6 pb	Complimentary snacks, soda,
800-267-9712 919-832-9712	Most CC, Cash,	homemade cookies
Doris & Gary Jurkiewicz	*Rated*, •	Sitting room, piano, parlor, porch,
	C-ltd/S-no/P-no/H-no	massage therapist, date night
		packages, dinner/theatre packages

Victorian retreat nestled in the heart of Raleigh's Historic Oakwood District. Six guestrooms, each with private bath, remote control fireplaces, cable TV w/DVD, free WiFi.
✉ innkeepers@oakwoodinnbb.com ◐ www.oakwoodinnbb.com

RIDGECREST

Inn On Mill Creek	149-199 $US BB	Full breakfast
3895 Mill Creek Rd 28770	7 rooms, 7 pb	Baked goods, fresh fruit & juice from
877.735.2964 828.668.1115	Visa, MC, Disc, *Rated*	our orchards
Dave & Brigette Walters	C-yes/S-no/P-yes/H-ltd	In-room massages, paddle boats for
		the lake, organic fruit orchard, Jacuzzi
		tubs, fireplaces

This Asheville, Black Mountain area B&B and orchard on 7 acres is literally surrounded by North Carolina's Pisgah National Forest. It is centrally located between the Biltmore Estate in Asheville, Mount Mitchell, Chimney Rock and Lake Lure. ✉ info@innonmillcreek.com ◐ www.innonmillcreek.com

ROBBINSVILLE

Blue Waters Mountain	155-185 $US BB	Full breakfast
Lodge	9 rooms, 9 pb	All rooms include King or Queen beds,
292 Pine Ridge Rd 28771	Most CC, Cash,	private bath, satellite TV and wireless
888-828-3978 828-479-8888	Checks, •	high speed Internet
Mike & Maury Stewart	C-yes/S-no/P-no/H-yes	

Relaxing escape in the heart of the Blue Ridge Mountains of NC. Known for its natural splendor, outdoor lifestyle and deep serenity, this majestic setting offers a wealth of activities or the perfect backdrop to do nothing at all.
✉ bluewaters@webworkz.com ◐ www.bluewatersmtnl.com

Snowbird Mountain Lodge	205-365 $US AP	Full breakfast
275 Santeetlah Rd 28771	25 rooms, 25 pb	Lunch & dinner included
800-941-9290 828-479-3433	Most CC, *Rated*	Sitting room, piano, vegetarian meals,
Robert Rankin	C-ltd/S-ltd/P-no/H-ltd	wildflower hikes
	April 15-Nov. 6	

An unspoiled, hidden vacation oasis tucked away in the Appalachian Mountains of western North Carolina. Explore the National Forest by foot, bike, horseback or car, go fishing, hiking, rafting or birdwatching. Maybe just relax at the lodge with a massage?
✉ innkeeper@snowbirdlodge.com ◐ www.snowbirdlodge.com

SEAGROVE

The Duck Smith House	135-135 $US BB	We serve a complete breakfast
465 North Broad	4 rooms, 4 pb	Beverage with cheese tray served to
Street 27341	Most CC, *Rated*	you on a silver tray. All very special
888-869-9018 336-873-7099	C-yes/S-no/P-yes/H-ltd	just for you.
Sisters Barbara & Suzanne		Small in-room TV, large common room
Murphy & Daisy Mae		TV, natural scenery, wrap around
		porch with wicker furniture

Escape, relax and recharge with the Duck Smith House Bed & Breakfast. Nothing but the best while you are our guests! We serve a complete breakfast which may include Stuffed French Toast, which is Barbara's signature dish, or another breakfast favorite!
 suzanne@ducksmithhouse.com ◐ www.ducksmithhouse.com

SUNSET BEACH

Sunset Inn
9 North Shore Dr 28468
888-575-1001 910-575-1000
Andrea Price

99-199 $US BB
14 rooms, 14 pb
Visa, MC
C-ltd/S-no/P-no/H-yes

Hot Buffet
Fresh brewed coffee and hot tea, an
endless supply of popcorn
Beach chairs, umbrellas, bikes, and
small coolers available to rent, WiFi,
book and video library

Sunset Beach offers one of the widest beaches on the east coast with white fine grained sand that soothes your senses. Perfectly located, Sunset Beach, NC is convenient and yet provides a feeling of "escape from it all."

✉ info@thesunsetinn.net 🌐 www.thesunsetinn.net

TRYON

**1906 Pine Crest Inn &
Restaurant**
85 Pine Crest Ln 28782
800-633-3001 828-859-9135
Carl Caudle (Owner/GM)

89-599 $US BB
35 rooms, 35 pb
Most CC, Cash, Checks,
Rated, •
C-yes/S-ltd/P-ltd/H-ltd

Full 3-course hot breakfast
Afternoon refreshments & early
evening port & sherry, 4-Diamond
restaurant & bar
Library, fireplaces, gazebo, golf,
spa services, weddings/receptions,
corporate retreats & meetings

Elegant mountain inn with views of the Blue Ridge Mountains. Near the Blue Ridge Parkway and Biltmore House. Gourmet restaurant, library, bar and wide verandas add to the casual elegance.

✉ lanierbb@pinecrestinn.com 🌐 www.pinecrestinn.com

VALLE CRUCIS

Lazy Bear Lodge
315 Lazy Bear Tr 28692
828-963-9201
Anne Winkelman

145-160 $US BB
5 rooms, 5 pb
Visa, MC
C-ltd/S-no/P-no/H-yes

Full breakfast
Restaurant opens for Saturday night
dining for overnight guests sometimes
Gas fireplaces, sitting areas, porches,
TV, CD/radio, fans, jetted/claw footed
tub & spa room

Overlooking historic Valle Crucis in the North Carolina High Country, minutes from the Blue Ridge Parkway, Boone and Blowing Rock, Lazy Bear Lodge is a mountain retreat built from the ground up and beautifully furnished with guest's comfort in mind.

✉ mawinkelman@skybest.com 🌐 www.lazy-bear-lodge.com

The Mast Farm Inn
2543 Broadstone Rd 28691
888-963-5857 828-963-5857
Sandra Deschamps Siano &
Danielle Deschamps

99-459 $US BB
14 rooms, 14 pb
Most CC, Cash, •
C-yes/S-no/P-no/H-yes
French & Spanish

Full gourmet breakfast
Restaurant featuring fresh, organic
regional cuisine; espresso & wine bar
in the inn
A large wraparound porch, spacious
grounds, organic gardens, pond and
creek

The Mast Farm Inn has been welcoming guests since the 1800s; while we have added modern amenities, the hospitality remains the same: attentive and sincere. Eight spacious guestrooms and six romantic getaway cottages offered. Come make yourself at home.

✉ henri-deschamps@mastfarminn.com 🌐 www.mastfarminn.com

WARRENTON

Ivy Bed and Breakfast
331 N Main St 27589
800-919-9886 252-257-9300
Jerry & Ellen Roth

70-120 $US BB
4 rooms, 3 pb
Most CC, *Rated*, •
C-yes/S-ltd/P-no/H-no

3-course, candlelit breakfast
A guest refrigerator with bottled water
provided, coffee and tea available 24
hours
Sitting room, working fireplaces in
dining room & parlor, wireless high
speed Internet access

Free Night w/Certificate: Anytime. Room Upgrade.

An elegant 1903 Victorian home furnished with beautiful antiques, in historic Warrenton, North Carolina, a short drive from Raleigh, NC & Richmond, VA. Relax by the fireplace on those cool mornings or rock on the wraparound front porch.

✉ info@ivybedandbreakfast.com 🌐 www.ivybedandbreakfast.com

WARRENTON

Magnolia Manor Plantation B&B
128 Pet Burwell Rd 27589
252-257-6055
Larry & Sheila Carver

150-250 $US BB
6 rooms, 6 pb
Most CC, Cash
C-yes/S-ltd/P-no/H-no

Full breakfast
Evening dessert or appetizers
Satellite TV, cozy sitting areas and two
telephone lines in all suites

Magnolia Manor Plantation Bed & Breakfast is a newly refurbished plantation manor house south of historic Warrenton, North Carolina, on thirteen secluded acres. Antebellum treasure.

✉ innkeepers@magnoliamanorbnb.com   🌐 www.magnoliamanorbnb.com

WASHINGTON

Moss House
129 Van Norden St 27889
252-975-3967
Rebecca & Scott Sipprell

90-135 $US BB
4 rooms, 4 pb
Visa, MC, AmEx,
Rated, •
C-ltd/S-ltd/P-no/H-no
January 1-Dec. 31

Full breakfast with elegance
Our guest refrigerator is stocked with
bottled water and sodas free to our
guests. Ice buckets.
Living room, sitting area, in room
cable TV's ,Wifi, private baths, central
A/C, extra pillows, garden

Washington NC's Premier Bed and Breakfast, located in the historic district, one block from the Pamlico River. Walking distance to local restaurants and shops. Original artwork and antiques in a comfortable and relaxing, coastal style with fine details.

✉ info@themosshouse.com   🌐 www.themosshouse.com

Pamlico House
400 East Main Street 27889
252-946-5001
Virginia Finnerty

135-147 $US BB
5 rooms, 5 pb
Most CC, Cash, •
C-ltd/S-ltd/P-ltd/H-ltd

Full breakfast
Complimentary coffee/tea & soft
drinks.
Refrigerator, large screen cable TV
in family room, free local calls, spa
services, bikes, grounds

Quintessential bed and breakfast, The Pamlico House offers a choice of five luxury rooms with private baths, and all the amenities that our guests associate with the world's finest boutique hotels.

✉ info@PamlicoHouseBB.com   🌐 www.PamlicoHouseBB.com

WAYNESVILLE

Andon-Reid Inn Bed and Breakfast
92 Daisy Ave 28786
800-293-6190 828-452-3089
Ron & Rachel Reid

119-199 $US BB
5 rooms, 5 pb
Visa, MC, Disc, *Rated*
C-ltd/S-ltd/P-no/H-no

Our special fully served breakfast
Complimentary sodas, water, coffee
& snacks all day & evening, freshly
baked goods offered daily.
Wine Menu, TV/DVD, Wireless
Internet, Recreation Room, Darts, Wii
Sports, Fitness Studio, Sauna, Billiard

The beauty of the mountains, the quaint town of Waynesville, the comfort & relaxation of the romantic, historical Andon-Reid Inn is yours, and just a phone call away. Unwind and relax. Plan your special event with us and let us pamper you.   ✉ info@andonreidinn.com   🌐 www.andonreidinn.com

Brookside Mountain Mist Inn
142 Country Club Dr 28786
877-452-6880 828-452-6880
Carolyn Gendreau & Dina Giunta

129-169 $US BB
5 rooms, 5 pb
Most CC, Cash,
Checks, •
C-ltd/S-ltd/P-no/H-no

Full breakfast
Evening socials on Fridays 5–6PM
with wine & hors d'oeuvres; afternoon
drinks, snacks & baked goods
In-room massages, video library,
fireplace, Jacuzzi, cable w/26" LCD
TV's, WiFi, turndown service

Overlooking the Great Balsam Mountains, this one-story luxury inn provides the peacefulness and elegance you deserve. Enjoy the quaint town of Waynesville with its assortment of shoppes, cafes and restaurants along with golf right across the street.

✉ info@brooksidemountainmistbb.com   🌐 www.brooksidemountainmistbb.com

Can't Find It Inn
879 Mountain Side Dr 28786
828-734-1088 828-452-4186
Pat Puckett

150-150 $US BB
2 rooms, 2 pb
Visa, MC
S-ltd/P-no/H-no

Full breakfast
Snacks & soft drinks
Satellite TV, DVD, CD players, coffee
makers & fridge, luxurious bath robes,
wireless Internet

A secluded 2-suite B&B specializing in romance & privacy. No crowds, no community meals, no children. Enjoy life the way it was meant to be.   ✉ cantfinditinn@hotmail.com   🌐 www.cantfinditinn.com

WAYNESVILLE—————————————————————————————

Herren House B&B
94 East St 28796
800-284-1932 828-452-7837
Gerry Shields & Roland
Labadan

110-170 $US BB
6 rooms, 6 pb
Most CC, Cash, Checks,
Rated, •
C-ltd/S-no/P-no/H-yes
French, German,
Turkish

Full gourmet breakfast
A/C, cable TV, WiFi, private
bathrooms, rocking chair wraparound
porch, courtyard & garden gazebo

Unique 19th century boarding house, completely & exquisitely restored with full modern amenities. A special place filled with Victorian charm & casual elegance. Delicious breakfasts, afternoon refreshments. Closest B&B to downtown.

BedandBreakfast@HerrenHouse.com   www.herrenhouse.com

—————————————————————————————————————

Inn at Iris Meadows
304 Love Lane 28786
888-466-4747 828-456-3877
Becky & George Fain

225-300 $US BB
7 rooms, 7 pb
Most CC, *Rated*, •
C-ltd/S-no/P-ltd/H-no

Full breakfast
Mid-afternoon refreshments with
coffee or tea.
Fluffy robes, hairdryers, irons and
ironing boards, TV/VCR's, phone, and
clock radios, WiFi.

Located in the heart of the Great Smoky Mountains, the inn is nestled amidst five rolling acres overlooking the picturesque town of Waynesville. Perfect location for romantic getaways, anniversaries, birthdays, celebrations!

irismeadows@aol.com   www.irismeadows.com

—————————————————————————————————————

Oak Hill on Love Lane
224 Love Ln 28786
888-608-7037 828-456-7037
Deb & Shell Isenberg

150-235 $US BB
5 rooms, 5 pb
Visa, MC, AmEx
C-ltd/S-no/P-no/H-no

Full breakfast
Butler pantry, afternoon treats
nightly turndown,

The best of Western NC. 3,600 feet above sea level in The Great Smoky Mountains, we're just minutes from Asheville, The Biltmore Estate and The Blue Ridge Parkway. Experience "All the service and amenities of a fine hotel in the quiet comfort of a B&B."

oakhillonloveln@bellsouth.net   www.oakhillonlovelane.com

—————————————————————————————————————

**Old Stone Inn Mountain
Lodge & Restaurant**
109 Dolan Rd 28786
800-432-8499 828-456-3333
David Gardner

99-175 $US BB
18 rooms, 18 pb
Most CC, Cash,
Checks, •
C-ltd/S-ltd/P-yes/H-no

Full, hot breakfast included
Award-winning, fine dining restaurant
with full-service bar open six nights a
week
Guest sitting room with fireplace &
full-service bar, wireless Internet

Tucked away on 6½ wooded acres yet within walking distance of downtown Waynesville, this rustic mountain lodge offers 18 comfortable guestrooms and unsurpassed dining. Tranquil and secluded yet close to everything!

reservations@oldstoneinn.com   www.oldstoneinn.com

—————————————————————————————————————

**The Windover Inn Bed and
Breakfast**
117 Old Hickory St 28786
866-452-4411 828-452-4411
Glenn & Jennifer Duerr

110-180 $US BB
8 rooms, 8 pb
Most CC, Cash, Checks
C-ltd/S-ltd/P-no/H-no

Full breakfast
Freshly baked cookies, Fri. and Sat.
PM munchy food, complimentary
bottled water, organic coffees
Refrig. every flr, AM coffee on every
flr, teas, hot choc., in suite brkfst, TV/
DVD player, firepit

Rejuvenate your spirit in our North Carolina luxury accommodations. Nestled in the quaint historic town of Waynesville, between the Blue Ridge Mountains of western North Carolina and the Smoky Mountains, we're just 30 minutes from Asheville!

 relax@windoverinn.com    www.windoverinn.com

WAYNESVILLE

The Yellow House
89 Oakview Dr 28786
800-563-1236 828-452-0991
Shawn Bresnahan

165-265 $US BB
10 rooms, 10 pb
C-ltd/S-no/P-ltd/H-yes

Full breakfast
Coffee, tea, soft drinks & snacks,
appetizers each evening. Picnics and
special occasion desserts.
Sitting room, library, Jacuzzi s, 5 acres
of gardens and grounds. Hammocks,
rocking chairs, WiFi .

Located in the Blue Ridge and Great Smoky Mountains. You will enjoy the restful, relaxing and roman-
tic mood of The Yellow House B&B as well as the mountain atmosphere. The stars shine brighter on
our guests at 3,000 ft elevation and five minutes outside.

info@theyellowhouse.com   www.theyellowhouse.com

WEAVERVILLE

Inn on Main Street
88 S Main St 28787
877-873-6074 828-645-4935
Dan & Nancy Ward

125-165 $US BB
7 rooms, 7 pb
Most CC, Cash,
Rated, •
S-no/P-no/H-no
Spanish, some German
& French

Full breakfast
Complimentary evening refreshments,
plus snacks, soft drinks always; picnic
lunches sold
Mountain views, WiFi, fireplaces,
whirlpool tubs, Biltmore tickets,
rafting, twin & king beds

A romantic eco-friendly getaway near Asheville and the Biltmore Estate in quiet, artsy Weaverville.
Enjoy incredible mountain views from the back porch during breakfast and afternoon beverages.
Walk to cafes, live music, galleries and a mountain lake.

relax@innonmain.com   www.innonmain.com

WEST JEFFERSON

Buffalo Tavern
958 W Buffalo Rd 28694
877-615-9678 336-877-9080
Brian "Doc" Adams

89-159 $US BB
4 rooms, 4 pb
Visa, MC
C-ltd/S-ltd/P-no/H-no

Full breakfast
Complimentary wine
Warmth and friendly hospitality,
fireplaces, Turkish bathrobes, private
baths, satellite available

Elegant Southern Colonial circa 1872. A popular tavern during prohibition with patrons such as for-
mer NC Governors. All rooms have A/C. 1 suite available.

buffalotravernbnb@aol.com   www.buffalotavern.com

WILLIAMSTON

Big Mill B&B
1607 Big Mill Rd 27892
252-792-8787
Chloe G. Tuttle

75-135 $US BB
4 rooms, 4 pb
Most CC, Cash
C-ltd/S-ltd/P-no/H-ltd
Some Spanish
May 1-October 15

Continental plus breakfast
Breakfast served in-room, catered
candlelight gourmet dinners & picnic
lunches available
Bicycles, fireplace, cable TV in rooms,
DVD, wireless Internet, coin laundry,
phone every room, iron

Featured in Our State magazine, this coastal Carolina countryside B&B is a favorite of romantics and
those who seek privacy. Just minutes from major highways, it is the perfect stopover to the Outer
Banks.

info@bigmill.com   www.bigmill.com

WILMINGTON

C.W. Worth House B&B
412 S 3rd St 28401
800-340-8559 910-762-8562
Margi & Doug Erickson

144-184 $US BB
7 rooms, 7 pb
Visa, MC, *Rated*, •
C-ltd/S-no/P-no/H-no

Full breakfast
Complimentary beverages & snacks
2 sitting rooms with TV/DVD, free WiFi
Internet, porches, gardens, 1 room
with whirlpool

The C. W. Worth House Victorian Bed & Breakfast, located in the Historic District, is known for its
striking Queen Anne architecture, romantic atmosphere and gardens. Your hosts greet you warmly
and make you feel at home.

 relax@worthhouse.com   www.worthhouse.com

WILMINGTON

Front Street Inn
215 S Front St 28401
800-336-8184 910-762-6442
Richard & Polly Salinetti

139-239 $US BB
12 rooms, 12 pb
Most CC, *Rated*
C-ltd/S-ltd/P-ltd/H-ltd

Continental plus breakfast
Complimentary cookies & seasonal
snacks, Sol y Sombra honor bar, room
service, wet bars
Robes, phones, TVs, DVD players,
wireless, massages, game room,
parking, balconies, fresh flowers

*One of Our State magazine's 21 perfect places to stay in NC & Encore magazine's best bed & breakfast
in Wilmington (2006 & 2007). Intimate European style inn with privacy and charm. One block from
river in historic downtown. Abundant, healthful breakfast.*

✉ richard@frontstreetinn.com 🌐 www.frontstreetinn.com

Graystone Inn
100 S Third St 28401
888-763-4773 910-763-2000
Rich & Marcia Moore

169-379 $US BB
9 rooms, 9 pb
Most CC, Cash,
Rated, •
C-ltd/S-no/P-no/H-no
German, Italian

Full & continental plus breakfast
Complimentary wine & snacks
WiFi, sitting room, piano, robes,
library, fitness center, phones with
voice mail

*Recently named "One of America's Top 10 Most Romantic Inns" by American Historic Inns. The Gray-
stone Inn is an AAA 4 Diamond property and member of Select Registry.*

✉ contactus@graystoneinn.com 🌐 www.graystoneinn.com

Rosehill Inn B&B
114 S Third St 28401
800-815-0250 910-815-0250
Tricia & Bob Milton

139-199 $US BB
6 rooms, 6 pb
Most CC, *Rated*, •
C-ltd/S-no/P-no/H-no

Full breakfast
Sitting room, library, premium cable
TV in rooms, some VCRs, luxurious
bathrobes, wireless Internet

*Romantic lodging at its best! Beautifully restored 1848 Victorian Neo-classical home, six guestrooms
with period antiques & private baths. In the heart of Wilmington's historic district, near Cape Fear
River, beaches, shopping, dining and entertainment.*

✉ rosehill@rosehill.com 🌐 www.rosehill.com

The Verandas
202 Nun St 28401
910-251-2212
Dennis Madsen, Charles
Pennington

169-269 $US BB
8 rooms, 8 pb
Visa, MC, AmEx,
Rated, •
C-ltd/S-no/P-no/H-no
American Sign
Language

Full breakfast
Complimentary wine, beer, sherry,
sodas, snacks, homemade cookies
Sitting room, cable TV, piano, wireless
Internet, verandas, gardens

*Grand, affordable luxury on a quiet street two blocks from riverwalk, restaurants and shopping. Large
corner rooms with private baths, phone, TV & wireless Internet. The Verandas is for traveling executives as well as a comfortable weekend retreat.*

✉ verandas4@aol.com 🌐 www.verandas.com

Ohio

ALEXANDRIA

Willow Brooke Bed 'n Breakfast
4459 Morse Rd 43001
800-772-6372 740-924-6161
Sandra Gilson

115-270 $US BB
5 rooms, 5 pb
Visa, MC, Disc
C-ltd/S-no/P-no/H-ltd

Full breakfast
Balconies, fireplaces, outdoor hot tub, wireless Internet, sauna, satellite TV, Jacuzzi suites

Secluded, elegant English Tudor Manor House with separate Guest House in 34 acres of woods. Large luxurious suites with candlelight, fireplaces, feather beds & Jacuzzi tubs add to the romantic atmosphere.

innkeeper@willowbrooke.net   www.willowbrooke.com

AVON LAKE

Sunset Shores B&B
32708 Lake Rd 44012
440-933-6393
Denny & Bobbie Potonic

98-160 $US BB
4 rooms, 4 pb
Most CC, Cash, Checks, •
C-ltd/S-ltd/P-no/H-no

Extended Continental breakfast breakfast, snacks, soft drinks and a shared refrigerator on our delightful porch.
cable TV, AC, music room, scenic patio and lakefront deck

Drive down a tree lined lane to Sunset Shores Bed and Breakfast, a century old house on the shores of Lake Erie. Beautiful and relaxing describe the surroundings of Sunset Shores with the coziness of a private home and a residential neighborhood.

sunsetshores@oh.rr.com   www.sunsetshoresbb.com

BELLEVUE

The Victorian Tudor Inn
408 W Main St 44811
419-483-1949
Richard E. Stegman, Jr.

99-120 $US BB
4 rooms, 4 pb
Visa, MC, AmEx
C-yes/S-ltd/P-ltd/H-ltd

Full breakfast
Coffee, teas, sodas, bottled water and "munchies" always available
Business services, hot tub room, robe & slippers, iPod docks, wireless Internet, down comforters

Majestic 7,000 sq. ft. Tudor style B&B in the vacationland of North Central Ohio minutes from Lake Erie. A truly unique experience offering the elegance of yesterday & the comforts & amenities of today. Most rooms are spacious suites with large bathrooms.

richard@victoriantudor.com   www.victoriantudor.com

BERLIN

Coblentz Country Cabin
5130 TR 359 44610
877-99-SLEEP 330-893-1300
Elvin Coblentz

65-249 $US EP
7 rooms, 7 pb
Visa, MC, Disc
C-yes/S-no/P-no/H-no

Kitchenette
Fireplace, Jacuzzi, A/C, heat, cable TV/VCR, Internet, great rooms, billiards, hot tub

Welcome to Coblentz Country Cabins, beautiful country lodging nestled on a wooded hillside in the heart of Ohio's Amish Country, the largest Amish settlement in the world.

amishcountrylodging@verizon.net   www.amishcountrylodging.com

Donna's Premier Lodging
5523 East St 44610
800-320-3338 330-893-3068
Johannes & Donna Marie Schlabach

99-369 $US BB
17 rooms, 17 pb
Visa, MC, Disc, *Rated*
C-ltd/S-ltd/P-no/H-ltd

Please inquire about breakfast
Fresh fruit & pastry platter along with sparkling apple cider
Pamper your sweetie with a relaxing in room massage, ask about our other sweetheart packages

Welcome to Donna's Premier Lodging located in Berlin, Ohio! Experience a romantic, luxurious stay in one of our beautifully appointed honeymoon and anniversary cottages, cedar log cabins, chalets, bridal suites or villas, and enjoy all of our amenities.

 info@donnasb-b.com    www.donnasofberlin.com

Willow Brooke Bed n' Breakfast, Alexandria, OH

BERLIN

Graystone Cottages
5572 N Market St 44610
877-231-2912 330-231-4495
Mark & Dorothy Yoder

89-179 $US BB
4 rooms, 4 pb
Visa, MC
C-yes/S-no/P-no/H-yes

Pasties, fresh fruit, juice, coffee
½ block from all the best Amish
Country shopping, Jacuzzis,
kitchenettes, fireplaces

Graystone Cottages is located in Berlin, the heart of Holmes County Ohio. In the midst of horse-drawn Amish buggies and local gift shops, the private cottages offer a quiet and warm environment.

 dorothy@graystone-cottages.com 🌐 www.graystone-cottages.com

---

The Lamplight Inn B&B
5676 TR 362 44610
866-500-1122 330-893-1122
Larry & Helen Wilgus

103-179 $US BB
7 rooms, 7 pb
Most CC, Cash, Checks,
Rated
C-ltd/S-no/P-no/H-no

Full breakfast
Singing Innkeeper, spacious dining
room, gazebo, wrap around porch,
gardens, 10,000 tulips, 160-DVD'

"BEST B&B NE Ohio" and Home of the "Singing Innkeeper" in Berlin Ohio's Amish Country offers country luxury at it's best! King & queen beds, fireplaces, Jacuzzi tubs, A/C, private entrances, seasonal gardens, gazebo, spectacular views! Walk to shops.

info@thelamplightinn.com 🌐 www.thelamplightinn.com

BUCYRUS

HideAway Country Inn
1601 State Rt 4 44820
800-570-8233 419-562-3013
Debbie A. Miller

169-299 $US BB
11 rooms, 11 pb
Visa, MC, Disc,
Rated, •
C-yes/S-ltd/P-ltd/H-yes
Spanish

Breakfast by Chef to 12 Presidents
Private Candlelight Dinner, Chef's
Table Chef to Dr Oz. & 12 Presidents,
wine cellar, cocktails
Fireplace, Jacuzzi for 2, spa, birding,
wedding site/group activities

Central Ohio's premiere location for all your get-away needs. Weddings, elopements, spa & massage services, girlfriend get-aways, corporate retreats, wine cellar, full bar and culinary classes. Featured in New York Times and Travel & Leisure magazine.

innkeeper@hideawayinn.com 🌐 www.HideAwayInn.com

BURTON

Red Maple Inn
14707 S Cheshire St 44021
888-646-2753 440-834-8334
Gina N. Holk

119-200 $US BB
18 rooms, 18 pb
Most CC, *Rated*, •
C-yes/S-yes/P-no/H-yes

Deluxe Continental Breakfast
Wine & cheese, light appetizers, in-
room chocolates, Friday night Amish
style family dinners
Meeting room, fitness room, Amish
furniture, library, Jacuzzis, bikes,
balconies, suite with kitchen

Overlooking peaceful Amish country. Relax, refresh, & recharge in our 17 rooms and 1 suite with Jacuzzis, balconies, fireplaces, library, all with great staff. Fitness center and conference room. Near antique & Amish craft shops, 7 golf courses, and more.

✉ info@redmapleinn.com ◐ www.redmapleinn.com

CLEVELAND

Brownstone Inn Downtown
3649 Prospect Ave 44115
216-426-1753
Mr. Robin Yates

75-95 $US BB
4 rooms, 4 pb
Most CC, Cash,
Rated, •
C-ltd/S-no/P-ltd/H-no

Full breakfast
Snacks, kitchenette for guests to use
Sitting room, fireplaces, cable TV,
business services, high speed WiFi,
central A/C, laundry service

Brownstone Inn Downtown staff is here to provide unique adventures for any occasion (almost). Beautiful townhouse located minutes from all cultural, educational and musical activities.

✉ ryates1@mindspring.com ◐ www.brownstoneinndowntown.com

Emerald Necklace Inn
18840 Lorain Rd 44126
440-333-9100
Gloria Kemer

99-149 $US BB
3 rooms, 3 pb
Visa, MC, Disc
C-yes/S-ltd/P-yes/H-no

Tea Room setting
View our Tea Tasting Menu. We
specialize in Bridal Showers,
Rehearsal dinners, & small Weddings.
Salon & Spa, Tea Room lunch,
adjacent to Cleveland Metro Parks,
Golf, cycling. Gift Shop. Small Pets

The Emerald Necklace is one of Cleveland's historic treasures. The restored building and gardens that surround the Inn reflect the talent of the innkeeper.

✉ stay@emeraldnecklaceinn.com ◐ www.emeraldnecklaceinn.com

Stone Gables B&B
3806 Franklin Blvd 44113
877-215-4326 216-961-4654
Richard Turnbull & James
Hauer

110-190 $US BB
5 rooms, 5 pb
Most CC, Cash, Checks
C-yes/S-no/P-ltd/H-no
Spanish

Elegant gourmet full breakfast
Vegetarian meals on request, tea,
coffee, snacks always available.
Deck, gardens, library, sitting room,
parlor, piano, high speed Internet,
WiFi, massage schedulable.

Stone Gables Bed & Breakfast is in Ohio City, a historic neighborhood near the west side of Cleveland, only 1 mile to downtown. Our 5 elegant rooms are designed with your comfort in mind. Romantic whirlpool tub rooms, cozy suites all with private baths.

✉ stonegablesbnb@yahoo.com ◐ www.stonegables.net

CLEVELAND HEIGHTS

Crest B&B
1489 Crest Rd 44121
216-382-5801
Clark & Phyllis Gerber

75-85 $US BB
2 rooms, 1 pb
Visa, MC, •
C-yes/S-ltd/P-no/H-no
Some German

Continental plus breakfast
Afternoon tea, complimentary wine
Sitting room, accommodations for
business travelers, tennis nearby

Affordable housing near cultural activities and excellent restaurants. Continental plus breakfast served in dining room. ✉ crest1489@yahoo.com

COLUMBUS

50 Lincoln-Short North B&B
50 E. Lincoln St 43215
800-516-9664 614-299-5050
Sandy Davis

129-149 $US BB
7 rooms, 7 pb
Most CC
C-ltd/S-no/P-no/H-no

Full breakfast
Cable TV, wireless Internet, private
parking, small business retreats

Urban delight in the Short North Arts District. Minutes from Downtown Columbus, Ohio State University and the Columbus Convention Center. We're just steps away from the best galleries, restaurants, specialty shops, clubs and pubs that the city offers.

✉ shortnorthbb@gmail.com ◐ www.columbus-bed-breakfast.com

COLUMBUS

Harrison House
313 W 5th Ave 43201
800-827-4203 614-421-2202
Lynn Varney

129-169 $US BB
4 rooms, 4 pb
Most CC, Cash, *Rated*
C-yes/S-ltd/P-yes/H-no

Full breakfast
Vegetarian and special diets meal
planning. Please advise in advance.
Guest parlor, free parking, cable TV,
free WiFi

Welcome to Harrison House Bed & Breakfast, a historic inn located near central Columbus, OH, where you will experience a unique ambience for rest and relaxation. Take a step back in time, relax & enjoy. ✉ harrisonhousecolumbus@gmail.com ○ www.harrisonhouse-columbus.com

House of the Seven Goebels
4975 Hayden Run Rd 43221
614-761-9595
Pat & Frank Goebel

125 $US BB
2 rooms, 2 pb
Visa, MC, AmEx
C-ltd/S-no/P-no/H-no

Full & Continental Breakfast
Music room, parlor, woodburning
fireplace, Oriental rugs

From the pineapple hospitality sign above the front walk, to the warmth of the music room and parlor, The House of the Seven Goebels beckons to those that enjoy and appreciate the past.
✉ fgoebel@columbus.rr.com

DANVILLE

Red Fox Country Inn
26367 Danville Amity
Rd 43014
877-600-7310 740-599-7369
Denny Simpkins

85-115 $US BB
6 rooms, 6 pb
Most CC, *Rated*, •
C-yes/S-no/P-ltd/H-ltd

Full breakfast
Coffee, tea or soft drinks and home
made cookies and treats are available
Sitting room, library, cable TV,
accommodates business travelers

Experience this lovely 1830s Inn located in the scenic Ohio countryside. Less than 30 minutes from Amish country or Mohican County, it's sure to offer a unique and relaxing vacation.
✉ sudsimp@aol.com ○ www.redfoxcountryinn.com

The White Oak Inn
29683 Walhonding Rd 43014
877-908-5923 740-599-6107
Ian & Yvonne Martin

135-220 $US BB
12 rooms, 12 pb
Most CC, Cash,
Rated, •
S-no/P-yes/H-yes
Some French

Full breakfast
Dinner with notice, fruit &
cheese platters, chocolate dipped
strawberries, cookies, soft drinks
Common room with books,
boardgames and fireplace, porch with
swings, screen house, gazebo

Central Ohio Bed and breakfast inn in Ohio's Amish area offering romantic getaways, murder mysteries, fine dining, elopement and other wedding packages. Two luxury log cabin cottages have whirlpool tubs and fireplaces. Pet friendly. ✉ info@whiteoakinn.com ○ www.whiteoakinn.com

DAYTON

Inn Port Bed & Breakfast and Suites
22, 137-139 Brown St 45402
937-224-7678
Leslie & Jeff Gonya

79-149 $US BB
6 rooms, 4 pb
Most CC, •
C-ltd/S-no/P-ltd/H-no

Continental breakfast
Complimentary soda & water
High speed Internet, satellite/cable TV,
CD player in each guestroom, guest
kitchen

Free Night w/Certificate: Available anytime expect special event weekends.

Within walking distance of many of the tastes, sights and sounds of downtown Dayton, Inn Port is your lodging oasis in the heart of the historic Oregon District. Ideal for a romantic getaway, girls' night out or a visit to the University of Dayton.
✉ innport@sbcglobal.net ○ www.innport.com

DELAWARE

Welcome Home Inn
6640 Home Rd 43015
800-381-0364 740-881-6588
Forrest & Brenda Williams

95-160 $US BB
5 rooms, 5 pb
Most CC, Cash, Checks
C-yes/S-no/P-no/H-ltd

Full Breakfast
Snacks in rooms & Inn Home Bakery
goods to order
Sitting room, porch, accommodate
business travelers, antiques, grand
piano, walking trail thru woods

A Southern farmhouse style home located on six wooded acres. Wraparound wicker filled porch. Oak antiques. Grand piano in large dining room.
 info@welcomehomeinn.com ○ www.welcomehomeinn.com

DELLROY

Whispering Pines Bed & Breakfast
1268 Magnolia Rd SW 44620
866-452-5388 330-735-2824
Bill & Linda Horn

179-245 $US BB
9 rooms, 9 pb
Most CC, Cash, Checks,
Rated, •
C-ltd/S-no/P-no/H-yes

Full breakfast
Afternoon home-made chocolate chip
cookies, tea & coffee
2-person whirlpool tubs, fireplace,
balcony, lakeviews, great food,
romance, in-room massage

Your dream place on the lake, nestled on 7 rolling acres with a perfect view of beautiful Atwood Lake. Relax in a 2-person whirlpool-tub, sip wine on your balcony and wake up to a delicious breakfast.

✉ whisperingpines@atwoodlake.com 🌐 www.atwoodlake.com

FRANKLIN FURNACE

RiverView Inn B&B
91 Riverview Dr 45629
888-388-8439 740-355-4004
George & Bobbie Sich

99-129 $US BB
4 rooms, 4 pb
Most CC, Cash, Checks,
Rated
C-yes/S-no/P-no/H-ltd

Full breakfast
Packaged snacks, soft drinks, iced
teas, bottled water
Exercise room, outdoor hot tub,
whirlpool tub, satellite TVs, wireless
Internet, business center.

The Riverview Bed & Breakfast Inn is a modern, spacious California-style home with a large elevated wraparound deck, outdoor hot tub, and upstairs balcony. All rooms have wall-to-wall carpeting, satellite TV, and private baths.

✉ riverviewbb@roadrunner.com 🌐 www.riverhost.com

FREDERICKTOWN

Heartland Country Resort
3020 Township Rd. 190 43019
800-230-7030 419-768-9300
Dorene Henschen

90-240 $US BB
4 rooms, 4 pb
Most CC, Cash, Checks,
Rated, •
C-yes/S-ltd/P-yes/H-ltd

Full breakfast
Afternoon tea, snacks, lunch and
dinner available
Sitting room, screened porch, Jacuzzis,
fireplaces, luxury suites, wooded trails
& stalls for horses

Hospitality, adventure, and romance await you at this luxury horse ranch northeast of Columbus, Ohio. Scenic woods, hills, pastures, and recreation or relaxation on over 70 acres. Family and pet friendly. Groups are welcome. Reservations are required.

✉ heartbb@bright.net 🌐 www.heartlandcountryresort.com

GLENMONT

Annie's Place at Nature's Retreat
12061 TR 252 44628
330-231-0108 330-377-4783
Bob & Karen Hunter

150-175 $US BB
3 rooms, 2 pb
Visa, MC
C-yes/S-ltd/P-ltd/H-no

Continental plus breakfast
Enjoy fresh Amish baked pie and a
loaf of bread from our local Amish
Bakery in addition to breakfast
Hot tub, satellite dish, fireplace, trails,
hay rides, horse rental available, catch
& release pond.

This Civil War era farmhouse has 3 bedrooms and 2 baths and can sleep up to 6 people. Kitchen, reading room, fireplace, gazebo with hot-tub. Reservations are for the whole house, not individual rooms. Special arrangements possible for more than 6 persons.

✉ info@naturesretreat.net 🌐 www.naturesretreat.net

KELLEYS ISLAND

A Water's Edge Retreat, Luxury Bed & Breakfast
827 E Lakeshore Dr 43438
800-884-5143 419-746-2333
Tim & Beth

179-350 $US BB
6 rooms, 6 pb
Visa, MC, *Rated*, •
C-ltd/S-no/P-ltd/H-ltd
Some French, ASL
April through October

Gourmet Breakfast Buffet
Our Packages include hors d'ouvres &
wine each evening
Weddings & Minister, Parlor w library,
firepl, Jacuzz's, Beach decks, bikes,
veranda, Garden Spa.Golf Carts

Waterfront, elegant Queen Anne Victorian style. Travel & Leisure rated "...best of the Great Lakes." Only AAA 3-diamond inn in the area. Prices listed above are nightly. Package getaways include Cruising, bikes, massage and more. Call or email for detail.

✉ awatersedgebnb@aol.com 🌐 WatersEdgeRetreat.com

LEBANON

Hardy's Bed and Breakfast Suites
212 Wright Ave 45036
877-932-3266 513-932-3266
Phyllis & Al Hardy

155-185 $US BB
10 rooms, 9 pb
Visa, MC
C-ltd/S-ltd/P-no/H-ltd

Full breakfast
Fresh baked desserts in your room on arrival, tea & coffee in room, group luncheons
Suites, massage therapy, parlor with fireplace, flower gardens & porches, murder mysteries

Enjoy our four beautifully furnished Victorian homes and gardens, all at one location in the Floraville District of historic Lebanon, OH. Experience one of eight private suites for your romantic special occasion or relaxing getaway.

✉ hardys@go-concepts.com ○ www.hardysproperties.com/hardy's_haven.html

LOGAN

A Georgian Manner Bed & Breakfast
29055 Evans Rd 43138
800-606-1840 740-380-9567
B.J. King

105-219 $US BB
5 rooms, 3 pb
Visa, MC, *Rated*, •
S-ltd/P-no/H-yes

Full breakfast
Coffee, tea, fruit, snacks, sodas
Jacuzzi Suites, fireplace, canoeing, trails, kitchen, Wedding Pavilion, library, sitting room, BBQ

A Georgian Manner B&B is premier lodging in the Hocking Hills on Lake Logan. Outdoor weddings are our specialty and the Ohio Honeymoon Suite/Jacuzzi is perfect for honeymoons, romantic getaways, elopements, proposals or a special anniversary.

✉ ageorgianmanner@hocking.net ○ www.georgianmanner.com

Inn & Spa at Cedar Falls
21190 State Rt 374 43138
800-653-2557 740-385-7489
Ellen Grinsfelder & Terry Lingo

125-414 $US BB
26 rooms, 26 pb
Visa, MC, AmEx, •
C-ltd/S-no/P-yes/H-yes
Rooms closed on X-mas

Full breakfast
Lunch & dinner at restaurant on premises
Spa, gift shop, bar service, sitting room, WiFi, business retreats welcome

Log cabins, secluded cottages and antique furnished rooms. Three cabins with whirlpool tubs; 12 cottages with whirlpool tubs. Gourmet meals prepared from the inn's organic garden. Gift shop, spa, meeting room & restaurant. ✉ info@innatcedarfalls.com ○ innatcedarfalls.com

LONDON

Alexandra's B&B
117 N Main St 43140
740-852-5993
Ron & Susan Brown

85-179 $US BB
8 rooms, 7 pb
Visa, MC, AmEx,
Rated, •
C-ltd/S-no/P-no/H-ltd

Full breakfast
Porches, Jacuzzi, wedding accommodations, company retreats, family reunions

Walking into Alexandra's B&B may give the feeling of stepping back in time, but among the beautiful antiques you will find all the necessities of modern life including wireless Internet, cable TV and Jacuzzi tubs. We serve a full breakfast. ✉ info@alexandrasbb.com ○ www.alexandrasbb.com

MIAMISBURG

English Manor
505 E Linden Ave 45342
937-866-2288
Julie & Larry Chmiel

99-125 $US BB
5 rooms, 3 pb
Most CC, Cash, Checks,
Rated
C-ltd/S-no/P-ltd/H-no

Full breakfast
Teas, luncheons & dinners for groups with advance reservations
Wireless available throughout the property

A Tudor style mansion. Tranquility in a setting of elegance, hand-rubbed wood, leaded glass windows and antique furnishings. Step back in time.

✉ englishmanorohio@yahoo.com ○ www.englishmanorohio.com

MILLERSBURG

Fields of Home Guest House
7278 CR 201 44654
330-674-7152
Mervin & Ruth Yoder

65-145 $US BB
7 rooms, 7 pb
Visa, MC, Disc, *Rated*
C-yes/S-ltd/P-ltd/H-ltd
Limited German

Continental plus breakfast
Snacks, complimentary sodas
Suites, fireplaces, hot tubs, whirlpool baths, kitchenettes, wireless Internet

Our log cabin B&B invites you to relax and enjoy the peace and quiet of rural Amish Country. Enjoy perennial gardens, fish pond and paddle boat. We offer such amenities as fireplaces, kitchenettes, whirlpool bathtubs, and two-person hot tubs.

○ www.fieldsofhome.com

MILLERSBURG

Garden Gate Get-a-Way B&B	105-185 $US BB	Homemade Breakfast Buffet
6041 Township Rd 310 44654	5 rooms, 5 pb	Homemade evening snack, coffee,
330-674-7608	Visa, MC, Disc, *Rated*	tea, hot chocolate, popcorn, in-room
Carol Steffey	C-ltd/S-no/P-no/H-ltd	bottled water.
	All year; Closed Sunday	Common room with refrigerator, microwave, video library, books & magazines; Games & Cards

Amish Country Ohio bed and breakfast, Named One of the Top 10 Bed and Breakfasts in the United States. Wine tasting weekends, murder mystery weekends, Amish Country Tours & more. Best noted for perennial gardens & evening campfire.   ✉ info@garden-gate.com ◐ www.garden-gate.com

Guggisberg Swiss Inn/ Amish Country Riding Stables	89-220 $US BB	Continental breakfast
	24 rooms, 24 pb	Complimentary wiener roast/country
5025 State Rt #557 44654	Visa, MC, Disc, *Rated*	picnic Sunday evenings weather
877-467-9477 330-893-3600	C-ltd/S-no/P-no/H-yes	permitting (June – August)
Eric & Julia Guggisberg		Horseback riding stable on premises, horse-drawn sleigh rides in winter, wireless Internet

The Guggisberg Swiss Inn is family owned and operated. We invite you to join us at this unique lodging facility, in one of the largest and friendliest Amish communities in the world. Live entertainment most weekends April through October. Packages.
✉ innkeeper@guggisbergswissinn.com ◐ www.guggisbergswissinn.com

Holmes With A View	118-245 $US BB	Continental breakfast
3672 TR 154 44654	6 rooms, 6 pb	Whirlpool tub, gas fireplace, kitchen,
877-831-2736 330-893-2390	Most CC, Cash	wireless Internet, 1 outdoor hot tub, 2
Paul & Miriam Grossi	C-ltd/S-no/P-no/H-yes	king-sized beds

Our exquisite hillside Inn offers views of the amazing Amish farmland of Holmes County, Ohio. You are secluded above Berlin and Millersburg, yet close enough to enjoy day trips and adventures in neighboring cities.   ✉ pagrossi@juno.com ◐ www.holmeswithaview.com

The Barn Inn	99-219 $US BB	Full Country Breakfast
6838 CR 203 44654	11 rooms, 11 pb	Coffees, tea, baked items, popcorn
877-674-7600 330-674-7600	Most CC, Cash, •	Fireplaces, satellite TV, double size
Paul & Loretta Coblentz	C-ltd/S-ltd/P-no/H-yes	Jacuzzis, suites, recliners, DVD/VCR, WiFi

Awarded top 10 B&B in the nation and top 12 worldwide. Generous hospitality, country breakfasts served daily, fine accommodations with private entrances in a beautifully restored barn. Travel tips and cultural stories are shared daily after breakfast.
✉ reservations@thebarninn.com ◐ www.thebarninn.com

The Inn at Honey Run	99-349 $US BB	Continental plus breakfast
6920 Country Rd #203 44654	38 rooms, 38 pb	Casual fine dining for lunch & dinner
800-708-9394 330-674-0011	Most CC	Game & reading room, fireplaces,
Jason Nies	C-ltd/S-no/P-no/H-yes	deck gardens, spa treatments, bird watching, fine dining, concierge

Nestled in the heart of the Ohio Amish Country, The Inn at Honey Run is a serene oasis of nature and wildlife, comfort and privacy, fine dining and warm hospitality.
✉ info@innathoneyrun.com ◐ www.innathoneyrun.com

MOUNT VERNON

The Chaney Manor B&B Inn	125-150 $US BB	Full breakfast OR discount without
	3 rooms, 3 pb	Dinners with advance reservations,
7864 Newark Rd 43050	Visa, MC, Disc, •	snacks, romantic stays with heart
740-392-2304	C-ltd/S-no/P-ltd/H-ltd	cakes, candies!
Freda & Norman Chaney	French and German (limited)	Deep seated 2 person Jacuzzi, therapeutic massage, warm stones for self-therapy

Winner of 3 awards for North America!! One of the most unusual, romantic, historic Inns in Ohio. Huge suites, gourmet meals, Roman Jacuzzi room, massage. Six acres with gardens, pond, covered dock and bridge. Honeymoons, reunions, meetings, etc.
✉ chaney@ecr.net ◐ sites.google.com/site/thechaneymanorbandbco

NAPOLEON

The Augusta Rose B&B
345 W Main St 43545
877-590-1960 419-592-5852
Ed & Mary Hoeffel

85-96 $US BB
4 rooms, 4 pb
Most CC, Cash, Checks,
Rated, •
C-yes/S-no/P-no/H-no

Full breakfast
Snacks, soda and ice water are
available in the sitting room
2 sitting rooms – one with TV,
recreational assistance, wireless
Internet access, central AC

Stately Victorian with wraparound porch, located one block from scenic Maumee River. Tranquil small town.

✉ innkeepers@augustarose.com   🌐 www.augustarose.com

NORWALK

Georgian Manor Inn
123 W Main St 44857
800-668-1644 419-663-8132
Judy & Gene Denney

125-200 $US BB
4 rooms, 4 pb
Visa, MC, AmEx,
Rated, •
C-ltd/S-no/P-no/H-no
Closed Christmas

Full breakfast
Soft drinks, snacks, 5 minutes from
great casual, family-owned restaurant
Large library, sun porch, fireplace,
gardens, 2 patios, near day spa,
wireless Internet

AAA 4 Diamond rated, stately mansion on historic West Main St., 1.3 acres with gardens, near Lake Erie and Sandusky vacation hot spots. Plush surroundings & elegant accommodations with 4 guest-rooms & 5 public rooms. Spa, dining, shopping & golf nearby.

✉ GeorgianManor@neo.rr.com   🌐 www.georgianmanorinn.com

OBERLIN

1830 Hallauer House B&B
14945 Hallauer Rd 44074
877-774-3406 440-774-3400
Joe & Sue Woodward

125-185 $US BB
3 rooms, 3 pb
Visa, MC, Disc
S-no/P-no/H-no

Full breakfast
Mini-fridge stocked with
complimentary snacks & beverages
Music room, in-room fridge, free WiFi,
pool, gardens, sauna, whirlpool, TV,
exercise room, A/C

An award winning Ohio B & B on 2 acres offering 3 bedrooms, 1 of which is a suite that will sleep 7, each with private bath, satellite TV, A/C, and mini frig. Secluded, pool, gardens, music room, exercise room, full breakfast. Near Oberlin College.

✉ hallauerhouse@gmail.com   🌐 www.hallauerhousebnb.com

Ivy Tree Inn & Garden
Oberlin
195 S Professor St 44074
440-774-4510
Ron Kelly & Steve Coughlin

84-135 $US BB
4 rooms, 4 pb
Visa, MC, •
C-yes/S-no/P-no/H-no

Full breakfast
Afternoon tea, catered small meetings
& events
Sitting room, cable TV, garden tours,
small meetings

Oberlins's First B&B, established 16 years ago. 1850's historic home, award winning inn and garden with designer guestrooms, private baths and gorgeous gardens. 2 blocks to Oberlin College. "Best Scenic View in Oberlin."

✉ conorr12@yahoo.com

PAINESVILLE

Fitzgerald's Irish B&B
47 Mentor Ave 44077
440-639-0845
Debra & Tom Fitzgerald

105-150 $US BB
4 rooms, 4 pb
Visa, MC, Disc, *Rated*
C-ltd/S-no/P-no/H-no

Full breakfast on weekends
Beverages and continental breakfast
on weekdays
Sitting room, cable TV room, fireplace,
games available

Free Night w/Certificate: Monday-Thurs; Nov 1-April 29; excluding holidays; Mayo & Dublin room only.

Irish hospitality awaits you in our 16-room French Tudor home, charming you with its unique castle-like architecture. Just 3 miles from Lake Erie beaches, 15 mins from 25+ wineries and 30 minutes from Cleveland.

✉ fitzbb@gmail.com   🌐 www.fitzgeraldsbnb.com

POMEROY

Carpenter Inn & Conference Center
39655 Carpernter Dyesville Rd 45769
800-644-2422 740-698-2450
Pnina Sabel

95-200 $US BB
14 rooms
Visa, MC
C-ltd/S-no/P-no/H-ltd

Continental breakfast
We offer a full-body, hour-long massage for $65 by advance reservation only. Non-Smoking

Accommodations are available to suit every preference. We have worked to ensure that visits at the Carpenter Inn are tranquil and re-energizing. Therefore our rooms are free of television and telephones, though we do provide clock radios.

✉ info@carpenter-inn.com 🌐 www.carpenterinn.com

ROCKBRIDGE

Glenlaurel Inn
14940 Mount Olive Rd 43149
800-809-REST (7378) 740-385-4070
Greg & Kelley Leonard

149-339 $US BB
19 rooms, 19 pb
Most CC, Cash,
Rated, •
S-no/P-no/H-yes

Gourmet breakfast
We offer a dining experience like no other . . . we serve fine cuisine with a Scottish flair
Hot tubs, secret gardens, fireplaces, conference facility, weddings, walking trails, gift shop & spa

Welcome to the Glenlaurel Inn, a Scottish Country Inn with wooded cottages and crofts, labeled the "premier romantic getaway in the Midwest" and conveniently located just one hour southeast of Columbus, Ohio in the Hocking Hills.

✉ michael@glenlaurel.com 🌐 www.glenlaurel.com

SAGAMORE HILLS

Inn at Brandywine Falls
8230 Brandywine Rd 44067
888-306-3381 330-467-1812
George & Katie Hoy

139-325 $US BB
6 rooms, 6 pb
Most CC, *Rated*, •
C-ltd/S-ltd/P-ltd/H-yes

Full Candlelight Breakfast
Wine or Juice on arrival. Fruit, cookies, coffee and tea after dinner
Library, sitting room, fireplaces, Jacuzzi

Built in 1848, the Inn at Brandywine Falls is an impeccable country place, part of the tapestry of 33,000 acres of parkland and Cuyahoga Valley National Park, adjacent to the Brandywine waterfall. Six rooms, all with well-appointed private baths.

✉ brandywinefallsinn@windstream.net 🌐 www.innatbrandywinefalls.com

SALESVILLE

Pine Lakes Lodge B&B
61680 Buskirk Ln 43778
740-679-3617
Dionne Bell

99-250 $US BB
5 rooms, 5 pb
Most CC
C-ltd/S-ltd/P-ltd/H-no

Country Style breakfast
Complimentary snacks & drinks, picnic lunch or dinner for additional charge
2 person Jacuzzi in each room, sauna, hot tub, massage therapist, flat screens & DVD player

Enjoy our beautiful Hilltop Lodge with a panoramic view from which you can see for miles. Elegant suites, weddings, conferences. Sparkling ponds & meadows, working cattle ranch.

✉ peacefulretreat@pinelakeslodge.com 🌐 www.pinelakeslodge.com

SANDUSKY

Wagner's 1844 Inn
230 E Washington St 44870
419-626-1726
Barbara Wagner

70-125 $US BB
3 rooms, 3 pb
Visa, MC
C-ltd/S-no/P-yes/H-ltd

Continental plus breakfast
Complimentary chocolates
Billiard room with TV, air conditioning, screened in porch, patio, fireplaces, WiFi

Step back into history with a quiet retreat from the hustle and bustle of today's world at Wagner's 1844 Inn in Sandusky, Ohio. Elegantly restored Victorian home. Listed on National Register of Historic Places. Near Lake Erie attractions.

✉ wagnersinn@sanduskyohio.com 🌐 www.lrbcg.com/wagnersinn

TOLEDO ————————————————————————————————————

Mansion View Inn B&B	129-149 $US BB	Full gourmet breakfast
2035 Collingwood Ave 43620	4 rooms, 4 pb	Historic mansion & neighborhood,
419-244-5676	Visa, MC	walking tours, gourmet breakfast, art,
Don & Brenda Spurlin	S-no/P-no/H-no	antique shopping, WiFi, TV

Enjoy splendor in a historic 1887 eighteen room Victorian Mansion with four beautiful bed & breakfast rooms. Mansion View can also host special events. It is situated near the Toledo Museum of Art, the Convention Center, dining and shopping.

✉ innkeeper@mansionviewtoledo.com 🌐 www.mansionviewtoledo.com

Oklahoma

ARDMORE

Shiloh Morning Inn
2179 Ponderosa Rd 73401
888-554-7674 580-223-9500
David & Jessica Pfau

159-299 $US BB
9 rooms, 9 pb
Most CC, Cash, Checks,
Rated, •
S-no/P-no/H-yes

Three Course Breakfast
Private Dinner for Two in your Suite or
Cottage, available by reservation most
evenings
Walking trails throughout property,
TV/DVD (with over 200 movies), mini-
fridge, whirlpool tubs

An oasis to leave cares behind as you enjoy the rural Oklahoma countryside. Romantic, secluded get-away; soak in a private hot tub, stroll on 73 acres of gated privacy, & enjoy life as it was meant to be.

✉ innkeepers@ShilohMorning.com 🌍 www.ShilohMorning.com

BROKEN BOW

Lago Vista B&B
Hwy 259A 74728
580-494-7378
Chandra Rickey

200-250 $US BB
4 rooms, 4 pb
Most CC, Cash, Checks
S-ltd/P-yes/H-no

Full breakfast
Girls Gone Wine and Beer served each
evening. Snacks and non alcoholic
beverages during entire stay.
Jacuzzi tub, bath amenities, fireplace,
WiFi, hot tub, balconies, Satellite TV,
game room, conf.room

A Tuscan style house where all 4 guestrooms have balconies with views of Broken Bow Lake. Each room has a fireplace, Jacuzzi tub, walk-in shower and luxury bed linens. While visiting Lago Vista enjoy Beavers Bend State Park and Broken Bow Lake.

✉ lagovistabedandbreakfast@yahoo.com 🌍 www.lagovistabedandbreakfast.com

COOKSON

Terrapin Peak B&B
20965 W 921 Rd 74427
918-457-4906
Genny Maiden

139-169 $US BB
6 rooms, 6 pb
Visa, MC, Disc
C-ltd/S-ltd/P-no/H-ltd

Continental breakfast
Hot Breakfast available Dinner
available 2 weeks notice requested
Menus posted on website
Theater Room w/1000+ movies Pool
table Dining Area

Terrapin Peak Bed, Breakfast and Beyond was designed to deliver a contemporary, rustic, secluded, charming experience in manicured woods with a clean environment in every room. Located 2 miles from Lake Tenkiller.

✉ info@terrapinpeakbbb.com 🌍 www.terrapinpeakbbb.com

EDMOND

**Aaron's Gate Country
Getaway**
877-540-1300 405-282-0613
Gary & Martha Hall

270-330 $US BB
3 rooms, 3 pb
Visa, MC, AmEx
S-no/P-no/H-no

Self-cooked breakfast
Drinks, popcorn, famous Maple
Walnut Cookies
Full kitchens, grill, fireplaces, Jacuzzis,
hot tubs

Private honeymoon cottages for two. Exclusive retreat for magical romance. Jacuzzis for two, fire-places, full entertainment centers, European spa showers, and screened porches with hot tubs for two.

✉ innkeeper@arcadianinn.com 🌍 www.aaronsgate.com/aarons-gate-about

Arcadian Inn B&B
328 E First 73034
800-299-6347 405-348-6347
Martha & Gary Hall

170-260 $US BB
8 rooms, 8 pb
Most CC, *Rated*, •
S-no/P-no/H-no

Full breakfast
Dinner by reservation, complimentary
sodas, water & snacks
Sitting room, hot tubs, Fireplace,
wireless Internet

Luxurious, romantic setting, sumptuous homemade breakfast. Intimate getaway for couples, perfect for the business traveler. Specializing in preferential treatment.

✉ innkeeper@arcadianinn.com 🌍 www.arcadianinn.com

GUTHRIE

Stone Lion Inn	66-147 $US BB	Full breakfast
1016 W Warner 73044	16 rooms, 16 pb	Snacks, lunch & dinner available
405-282-0012	Visa, MC, *Rated*, •	Sitting room, library, fireplaces, cable
Rebecca Luker & Grant	C-ltd/S-no/P-no/H-ltd	TV
Aguirre		

Historic Guthrie is centrally located near 8 universities. Four 18-hole golf courses only 10 minutes away. Inn is famous for murder mystery weekends!

✉ stonelioninn@aol.com   🌐 www.stonelioninn.com

NORMAN

Montford Inn	104-239 $US BB	Full breakfast
322 W Tonhawa 73069	16 rooms, 16 pb	Early evening wine, soft drinks,
800-321-8969 405-321-2200	Most CC, Cash, Checks,	homemade cookies, lemonade &
William & Ginger Murray,	*Rated*, •	snacks
Phyllis & Ron Murray	C-yes/S-no/P-no/H-yes	Fireplaces, 2 outdoor private hot tubs,
		six cottages with 2-person whirlpools

Nestled in the heart of Norman, OK, the Montford Inn B&B invites you to experience the comfort of being at home, yet be a part of something special. Urban 16-room inn with 6 cottage suites. Restaurants, shops, parks, University of Oklahoma nearby.

✉ innkeeper@montfordinn.com   🌐 www.montfordinn.com

Whispering Pines Inn and	125-195 $US BB	Full breakfast
Restaurant	7 rooms, 7 pb	Restaurant with full service bar
7820 E Hwy 9 73026	Visa, MC, AmEx	Weddings, gazebo, wrap-around
405-447-0202	C-ltd/S-ltd/P-no/H-ltd	porch, kitchenettes, jet tubs, fireplaces
Kchao Family		

Built in 1994, this bed and breakfast has the look and feel of a 1900's mansion, accompanied by a wrap-around porch, gazebo, and grand staircase. Baskets of goodies are found in every room, from the elegant house suites to the rustic Pine Cone Cottage.

✉ whisperingpinesbb@sbcglobal.net   🌐 www.thewhisperingpinesinn.com

OKLAHOMA CITY

Grandison Inn at Maney	109-199 $US BB	Full Breakfast on weekends
Park	8 rooms, 8 pb	In-room dinners, picnic baskets,
1200 N Shartel Ave 73103	Most CC, Cash, Checks	snacks & stocked refrigerator
888-799-4667 405-232-8778	C-ltd/S-no/P-ltd/H-ltd	Airport pickup, romantic amenities &
Claudia & Bob Wright		packages available

Free Night w/Certificate: Valid Sunday-Thursday. except for holidays. Room Upgrade.

Each bedroom has its own personality & story, decorated with handsome antiques. Rooms are complete with private bath including luxurious Jacuzzi tubs & an abundance of romantic amenities!

✉ grandison@coxinet.net   🌐 www.grandisoninn.com

STUART

Wakefield Country Inn &	160-350 $US MAP	Full breakfast
Winery	3 rooms	Fresh homemade cookies upon
8297 Diagonal 1500 Rd 74570	Visa, MC, Disc	arrival. Lunch included in 2-day
580-513-0707 580-513-0707	S-ltd/P-no/H-no	packages
Steve & Pam Wakefield		Winery/Wine tasting, Hydrotherapy
		spa, in-ground swimming pool,
		wireless Internet, 5-course dinner

Our Mission Statement: From the moment you arrive, our goal is to make you feel at home in comfortable surroundings where you can relax, rejuvenate, and renew your spirit.

✉ info@wakefieldcountryinn.com   🌐 www.wakefieldcountryinn.com

SULPHUR ———————————————————————————————————————

Echo Canyon Resort
549 Lawton Ave 73086
580-421-5076
Carol Ann & Joe Van Horn

129-249 $US MAP
13 rooms, 13 pb
Most CC
C-ltd/S-ltd/P-no/H-ltd

3 course gourmet breakfast
Renown triple entre, four-course
dinner, extra charge! Find out more
about our gourmet meals.
Spa, massages, Jacuzzis, sitting rooms,
private balconies, corporate retreats &
family reunions

*A unique spa resort on twenty-seven private gated acres, with five star dining. An ideal romantic,
luxury destination for relaxation and rejuvenation. An excellent location for corporate retreats and
family reunions.*

✉ ecmanor@brightok.net 🌐 www.echocanyonresort.com

Oregon

ALBANY

Edelweiss Manor
1708 Springhill Dr. 97321
800-531-4306 541-928-0747
Linda & Larry

150-250 $US BB
1 rooms, 1 pb
Visa, MC
S-no/P-no/H-ltd
Spanish

Full breakfast
Guest room offers a mini fridge with assorted beverages
Queen size bed, closet, and a private bath with shower, sink, and dressing area. Access to sauna.

Edelweiss Manor is an historic landmark located on several acres of landscaped gardens, lawns, water features and gazebos. Separate buildings house a day spa and gift boutique featuring local artisans work, studio and art class room, near Country Club.

✉ info@edelweissmanor.com 🌐 www.edelweissmanor.com

ARCH CAPE

Arch Cape Inn
31970 E Ocean Lane 97102
800-436-2848 503-436-2800
Cynthia & Stephen
Malkowski

149-399 $US BB
10 rooms, 10 pb
Most CC, Cash,
Checks, •
C-ltd/S-no/P-ltd/H-yes

Gourmet Breakfast
Gardens, Jacuzzi, oceanview deck, WiFi, 2 min walk to beach, spa/sauna room, fine dining

The setting of Arch Cape is between a forest and the sea, creating a feeling of tranquility and peacefulness. The beach is a 2 minute walk from the inn, and six of the rooms have an ocean view.

✉ innkeeper@archcapeinn.com 🌐 www.archcapeinn.com

At Ocean's Edge B & B
80199 Pacific Rd. 97102
503-791-2499
Lucy and Daryl Eigen

145-365 $US BB
3 rooms, 3 pb
Visa, MC

Full organic breakfast
Private bath, IPod docking station, complimentary WiFi, TV/DVD/cable, and iron and ironing boards.

At Ocean's Edge is a new luxury boutique bed and breakfast located in the Cannon Beach area. Enjoy the calm and serenity this well-appointed B&B offers you: excellence in accommodations, epicurean delights, and expansive ocean vistas.

✉ eigencst@gmail.com 🌐 atoceansedge.com

ASHLAND

A Midsummer's Dream
496 Beach St 97520
877-376-8800 541-552-0605
Lisa Beach

150-230 $US BB
5 rooms, 5 pb
Most CC, Cash, Checks
C-ltd/S-no/P-no/H-yes
February – October

Full breakfast
All suites have fireplaces & spa tubs; finest linens, towels & robes, gardens

Housed in a completely restored 1901 Victorian, all five rooms boast a king-size bed, fireplace, and a large private bathroom with a two person jetted tub and glass block shower. Within walking distance of town and the university in a quiet neighborhood.

✉ info@amidsummer.com 🌐 www.amidsummer.com

Albion Inn
34 Union St 97520
888-246-8310 541-488-3905
Cyd and Gary Ropp

124-164 $US BB
5 rooms, 5 pb
Visa, MC, Disc,
Rated, •
C-ltd/S-ltd/P-yes/H-yes
All year; OSF season

Full breakfast
Coffee is available at 7 AM; tea anytime. Afternoon cookies. Most of our food is fresh and organic.
Spacious, comfortable rooms, inviting common areas filled with fine art, privacy of our gardens.

Free Night w/Certificate: Anytime. Room Upgrade.

Historic 1905 farmhouse offers peaceful serenity in quiet residential neighborhood only one block from Ashland's restaurants, galleries, and shops. Guests enjoy delicious, organic breakfasts out on the patio or indoors overlooking the rose garden.

 info@albion-inn.com 🌐 www.albion-inn.com

ASHLAND——————————————————————————————

Arden Forest Inn 261 W Hersey St 97520 800-460-3912 541-488-1496 William Faiia	149-245 $US BB 5 rooms, 5 pb Visa, MC S-no	2 course family-style breakfast Complimentary coffee, tea, iced refreshments Library, art, guest kitchen, high-speed Internet, garden, fountains, gazebo, heated pool, sundeck

Providing a sanctuary for theatre lovers, our unique Ashland bed & breakfast is situated on an acre of lush, park-like gardens & offers over 20 years of hospitality excellence. Breathtaking grounds offer a casual and relaxed atmosphere unlike any other. ✉ info@afinn.com ◐ www.afinn.com

Chanticleer Inn 120 Gresham St 97520 800-898-1950 541-482-1919 Ellen Campbell	169-199 $US BB 6 rooms, 6 pb *Rated* C-ltd/S-no/P-ltd/H-ltd Spanish, French and Japanese	Full breakfast Cookies, sherry and port Living room with fire place, NY Times, A/C & TV-DVD in each room, WiFi, gardens, koi pond & hammock

Elegant 1920 Craftsman in Ashland's historic neighborhood a short stroll to the Oregon Shakespeare Festival, restaurants, galleries, and Lithia Park. The Chanticleer offers mountain views, comfortable quiet rooms, full gourmet breakfasts, A/C & more
✉ comfy@ashlandbnb.com ◐ www.ashland-bed-breakfast.com

Country Willows B&B Inn 1313 Clay St 97520 800-945-5697 541-488-1590 Kara & Dan Burian	120-275 $US BB 9 rooms, 9 pb Most CC, Cash, *Rated* C-ltd/S-no/P-no/H-yes	Full breakfast Complimentary cookies, quick breads and scones; selection of local whole- leaf organic teas. Porches, heated pool, Jacuzzi, wireless, lawns & gardens, barn-style suites, fireplaces, hiking

The ultimate resort-style Oregon B&B inn, snuggled against a rolling hillside on a lush 5 acres of farmland. Surrounded by magnificent southern Oregon Siskiyou and Cascade Mountain ranges. Nine unique rooms and suites furnished with antiques. Pool & spa.
✉ innkeeper@countrywillowsinn.com ◐ www.countrywillowsinn.com

Hersey House & Bungalow 451 N Main St 97520 888-343-7739 541-482-4563 Lorraine Peterson	99-275 $US BB 6 rooms, 6 pb Visa, MC, Disc, • C-ltd/S-no/P-ltd/H-no	Full Gourmet Breakfast Cookies, afternoon beverage & truffles each evening WiFi, deck, gardens

A beautifully preserved Craftsman home surrounded by lush gardens within walking distance of downtown theaters. Five guestrooms with king/queen beds & private baths or a fully equipped cottage. A delightful gourmet breakfast is served each morning.
✉ innkeeper@herseyhouse.com ◐ www.herseyhouse.com

McCall House 153 Oak St 97520 800-808-9749 541-482-9296 Nola O'Hara	105-250 $US BB 10 rooms, 10 pb Most CC, Cash, *Rated*, • C-ltd/S-no/P-no/H-ltd	Full sumptuous breakfast Afternoon treats High-speed Internet access, guest phones, off-street parking, fireplaces

Just one block from the acclaimed Oregon Shakespeare Festival, our lovingly restored Italianate mansion offers luxurious accommodations in Victorian-inspired suites and guestrooms.
✉ mccall@mccallhouse.com ◐ www.mccallhouse.com

Oak Street Cottages 171 Oak St 97520 541-488-3778 Constance Dean	184-295 $US BB 4 rooms, 4 pb Visa, MC, AmEx, • C-yes/S-no/P-yes/H-yes Nov – March off-season	Full breakfast Each cottage has a full-sized and fully equipped kitchen, dining room and living room. All cottages have HVC and A/C, fireplace, free wireless, phones, TV, DVD, patio, BBQ, private parking

Gather your family and friends for your very own "Ashland Experience.) Our four cottages sleep 6, 8 or 11, and children are welcome. Let Oak Street Cottages be your family's "home away from home." Stay 6 nights, 7th night is free! We specialize in groups.
✉ osc@mind.net ◐ www.oakstreetcottages.com

ASHLAND

Pelton House B&B
228 B Street 97520
866-488-7003 541-488-7003

95-185 $US BB
5 rooms, 5 pb
Visa, MC, *Rated*
C-ltd/S-no/P-no

Full breakfast
Afternoon tea, dessert, non-alcoholic
beverages included; optional lunch
and dinner available

In Ashland's Railroad District near the Shakespeare theater, the historic Pelton House Bed & Breakfast has all the amenities. AAA rated, wireless Internet, a scrumptious breakfast, exquisite bathrooms, turn-down service and wonderful hospitality.

✉ info@peltonhouse.com 🌐 www.peltonhouse.com

The Iris Inn
59 Manzanita St 97520
800-460-7650 541-488-2286
Vicki & Greg Capp

95-180 $US BB
5 rooms, 5 pb
Visa, MC, *Rated*, •
C-ltd/S-no/P-no/H-ltd
Spanish, Italian, French

Elegant full breakfasts
Lemonade & sun tea for hot summer
days, wine at 5 p.m.; sherry, port &
chocolates after theater
Mountain views, cottage garden, WiFi,
custom amenities, robes, nightly
turndown, great reading light

Our tradition of 28 years of excellence continues! On a quiet street near theaters & town, relax in the garden or enjoy a winter escape. View rooms & delectable breakfasts! AAA 3 diamond inn. WiFi.

✉ innkeeper@irisinnbb.com 🌐 www.irisinnbb.com

The Winchester Inn,
Restaurant & Wine Bar
35 South Second St 97520
800-972-4991 541-488-1113
Michael & Laurie Gibbs

140-299 $US BB
19 rooms, 19 pb
Most CC, Cash, Checks,
Rated, •
C-yes/S-no/P-no/H-ltd
German, some Spanish

Two course gourmet breakfast
Full service restaurant & wine bar
Garden, gazebo, jetted tubs, fireplaces,
balcony, antiques, afternoon treats
delivered to room

Victorian hideaway complete with lush gardens & fine dining. This enchanting Inn is within walking distance of the Oregon Shakespeare Festival, Lithia Park, restaurants & shopping.

✉ innkeeper@thewinchesterinn.com 🌐 www.winchesterinn.com

ASTORIA

Astoria Inn
3391 Irving Ave 97103
800-718-8153 503-325-8153
Mickey Cox

85-100 $US BB
4 rooms, 4 pb
Visa, MC, •
S-ltd/P-no/H-no

Hearty breakfasts
Fresh baked cookies
Veranda overlooks the Columbia
River, sitting room, cable TV

Often mentioned as the best location in Astoria, the inn's new make-you-smile colors on the outside make you feel welcome and relaxed inside. A happy place with good food for happy times.

🌐 www.astoriainnbb.com

Grandview B&B
1574 Grand Ave 97103
800-488-3250 503-325-5555
Charleen Maxwell

66-188 $US BB
9 rooms, 7 pb
Most CC, *Rated*, •
C-ltd/P-no

Full breakfast
Snacks
Sitting room, canopy beds, books,
games, binoculars, liquor not
permitted

Light, airy, cheerful Victorian close to superb Maritime Museum, Lightship, churches, golf, clam-digging, fishing, beaches and rivers.

✉ grandviewbedandbreakfast@usa.net 🌐 www.pacifier.com/~grndview

---

Rose River Inn B&B
1510 Franklin Ave 97103
888-876-0028 503-325-7175
David & Pam Armstrong

85-150 $US BB
5 rooms, 5 pb
Visa, MC
C-ltd/S-no/P-no/H-no

Full breakfast
Breakfast is served at 8:30 a.m.
Sitting room, suites, fireplaces, cable
TV, DVD, wireless Internet, bicycle
storage

Historic bed and breakfast in Astoria, Oregon on the Columbia River. The Rose River Inn is a beautiful 1912 Craftsman style home in a National Historic district of Astoria, Oregon, the oldest American city west of the Rockies.

✉ roseriverinn@charter.net 🌐 www.roseriverinn.com

AURORA

Anna Becke House B&B
14892 Bobs Ave 97002
866-383-2662 503-678-6979
Terri Roberts

130-130 $US BB
2 rooms, 2 pb
Visa, MC, Disc
C-ltd/S-ltd/P-no/H-no

Full gourmet breakfast
"Serve yourself" afternoon & evening
refreshment guest lounge
Cable TV, DVDs, wireless Internet &
guest robes

Spend a night in a classic craftsman bungalow that could be right out of the pages of your favorite decorating magazine! And just a short stroll from its quiet historic neighborhood to the heart of Oregon's Antiques Capital.

info@annabeckehouse.com www.annabeckehouse.com

BEAVERTON

Cornerstone B & B
17290 SW Alvord Ln. 97007
503-747-2345
Harold & Margaret Meyering

95 $US BB
3 rooms, 3 pb
Most CC, Cash, Checks
C-ltd/S-no/P-no/H-yes

Buffet Breakfast
Buffet offers main entree and other,
refrigerator available on request for
guest use.
Flat Panel Televisions, Private Baths,
Private Entrances, Queen beds or
twins, heat and A/C

Cornerstone Bed and Breakfast welcomes you to the fresh and relaxing atmosphere at the base of Cooper Mountain in Washington County, Oregon. The Cornerstone B&B is a warm and friendly place with the happiness and comfort of guests in mind.

info@cornerstonebedandbreakfast.com www.cornerstonebedandbreakfast.com/index.htm

BEND

Cabin Creek B&B
22035 Hwy 20 East 97701
888-572-5856 541-318-4798
Dave & Melody Spicer

99-165 $US BB
3 rooms, 3 pb
Most CC, Cash
C-ltd/S-no/P-no/H-no

Full breakfast
Fresh baked cookies at 8:30 p.m.
Beverages and snacks available 24/7
The 14 acres offers plenty of room to
park boats, snowmobiles, and safe out
of the weather storage.

This custom log home B&B was built in 2007 and is surrounded by more than 13 acres of woods and pasture land. It was designed with your comfort and privacy in mind. The moment you step into the grand entrance of this log home, you will not want to leave.

innkeeper@cabincreekbandb.com cabincreekbedandbreakfast.com

Lara House Lodge B&B
640 NW Congress St 97701
800-766-4064 541-388-4064
Lynda Clark

149-329 $US BB
6 rooms, 6 pb
Most CC, Cash, Checks,
Rated
S-no/P-no/H-no

Multi-course gourmet breakfast
Pacific Northwest wines and hors
d' ouevres are served daily from
4:30–5:30
Sun room, fireplace, outdoor sunny
deck and shady front porch, historic
neighborhood near park

Lara House Lodge is a magnificent 1910 Craftsman Style Historic Home conveniently located in downtown Bend's historic district, across the street from beautiful Mirror Pond & Park. Enjoy our luxurious furnishings, exquisite bedding, and gourmet breakfast

info@larahouse.com www.larahouse.com

BORING

Fagan's Haven B & B
503-658-2010
Jane McClain

65-85 $US BB
3 rooms, 1 pb
C-ltd/S-no/P-ltd/H-ltd

Full breakfast
TV/VCR, extensive library of craft
and quilt books, craft room, skylights,
microwave, and fridge.

Fagan's Haven has been described at the best kept B&B secret in Oregon. A wonderful place to indulge your creative passion, spend time with friends, work on that secret Christmas present, or find a temporary respite.

 info@FagansHavenBnb.com faganshavenbnb.com

BRIGHTWOOD

Brightwood Guesthouse
64725 E Barlow Trail
Rd 97011
503-622-5783
Bonnie Rames

145-175 $US BB
1 rooms, 1 pb
Rated, •
C-ltd/S-ltd/P-no/H-ltd

Full 5-course breakfast
Snacks, beverages; complimentary
wine or bubbly when notified of
special occasion
Living room, library, washer & dryer,
TV/VCR, games, flowers, art supplies

Peaceful, private, romantic cabin of your own in the river valley forest of Mt Hood. Huge hot soaking tubs outdoors; pretty territorial views from each window, fantastic breakfasts. Everything provided for your comfort and convenience.

✉ brightwoodbnb@hotmail.com   🌐 www.Mounthoodbnb.com

BROOKINGS

A Beachfront B&B by Lowden's
14626 Wollam Rd 97415
800-453-4768 541-469-7045
Gary & Barbara Lowden

109-139 $US BB
2 rooms, 2 pb
Visa, MC
C-yes/S-no/P-no/H-no

Continental breakfast
Coffee, tea, popcorn, milk, hot
chocolate, orange juice, water, jams &
peanut butter
Ambiance fireplace with remote
control, free WiFi, 2 night & 5 night
discounts

Ocean and river frontage with easy beach access. Near a redwood forest. Lovely ocean front suites with fireplace, private entry and private bath. Located where the Winchuck River meets the Pacific Ocean.

✉ glowden@charter.net   🌐 www.beachfrontbb.com

A Country Retreat B&B
16980 Coho Dr 97415
800-856-8604 541-661-3773
Bill & Evelyn

100-147 $US BB
2 rooms, 2 pb
Visa, MC, •
C-ltd/S-no/P-no/H-ltd

Full Country Breakfast
Afternoon Tea, coffee & cookies
Cable TV/DVD/VCR, free wireless
Internet, Billiard Room, Grand Piano,
Fireplace

Two private, large luxury guestrooms with high window views, private baths and entrances, robes Jacuzzi, wireless Internet, a Billiard Room, grand piano and fireplaces. Private park for reunions and weddings, lots of amenities and close to the beach.

✉ info@countryretreatbnb.com   🌐 www.countryretreatbnb.com

Holmes Sea Cove B&B
17350 Holmes Dr 97415
888-290-0312 541-469-3025
Lorene Holmes

150 $US BB
2 rooms, 2 pb
Visa, MC
C-yes/S-no/P-no/H-ltd

Continental plus breakfast
Hot tub/spa with ocean view, gazebo,
scenic trail, semi-private beach

Overlooking the beautiful Oregon coast with a scenic trail to a semi-private beach. Holmes Sea Cove B&B is a place of peace and privacy. Cottage and 2 room suite available. 3 night minimum stay on the Pacific Suite.

🌐 personal.kitusa.com/holmes

CARLTON

Lobenhaus B&B and Vineyard
6975 NE Abbey Rd 97111
503-864-9173
Joe & Shari Lobenstein

160-190 $US BB
6 rooms, 6 pb
Visa, MC, Disc
C-ltd/S-no/P-no/H-ltd

Full Oregon Bounty Breakfast
Refreshments & snacks provided at
check-in, wine for purchase, guest
refrigerator in dining area
Wireless Internet, fireplace, satellite
big screen HD TV DVD, large common
areas, grounds, vineyard

Nestled in a peaceful wooded setting on 27 acres, our unique tri-level lodge has 6 beautifully appointed guestrooms, each with a private bathroom. View the woods and spring fed creek from your window or open your door to step onto the expansive deck.

✉ innkeeper@lobenhaus.com   🌐 www.lobenhaus.com

Lobenhaus B&B and Vineyard, Carlton, OR

CARLTON

R.R. Thompson House
517 N. Kutch St. 97111
503-852-6236
Roselyn and Mike

150-245 $US BB
5 rooms, 5 pb
Most CC, Cash
C-ltd/S-no/P-no/H-no

Full breakfast
The guest refrigerator holds a
selection of sodas and water for your
enjoyment anytime.
Wireless Internet, HDTV, AC,
Whirlpool Tubs, Parking, Gardens,
Living Room and Board Games

Stroll from the Thompson House to any of Carlton's two dozen tasting rooms, offering the finest Oregon wines. Return to the warmth of an historic inn with modern amenities, private baths and whirlpool tubs. Wake up to a hearty gourmet breakfast.

 innkeeper@rrthompsonhouse.com  www.rrthompsonhouse.com/index.htm

CAVE JUNCTION

Vertical Horizons
Treehouse Paradise
3305 Dick George Rd. 97523
541-592-4751
Phillip & Jodie Moskios

200-225 $US BB
3 rooms, 1 pb
Most CC, Cash, Checks
C-yes/S-ltd/P-no/H-ltd

Continental plus breakfast
BBQ/gas grill, disk golf course,
volleyball, horse shoes, fishing, rafting,
technical tree climbing+

Sleep in state of the art luxury tree houses! Each unique in design. Disc golf, fishing, technical tree climbing and more on site. Serving local organic whenever possible.

verticalhorizons@frontiernet.net treehouseparadise.com

CENTRAL POINT

The Willows
3347 Old Stage Rd 97502
866-664-1425 541-665-3020
Joe & Sandra Dowling

150-225 $US BB
5 rooms, 5 pb
Visa, MC, AmEx,
Rated, •
C-ltd/S-no/P-ltd/H-no

Full breakfast
Afternoon tea/snacks during summer
season
In-room TV and DVD/VCR, telephone/
data port, WiFi, A/C, in-ground pool,
tennis, croquet, classes

Experience the modern yet historic accommodations at this authentic Rogue Valley Orchard Mansion. The upscale bed and breakfast resort is listed in the National Register and has a wonderful history. Each room is appointed with elegant furnishings and art.

scu73@aol.com thewillowsbedandbreakfast.com

COOS BAY

Old Tower House B&B	75-165 $US BB	Continental & Gourmet
476 Newmark Ave 97420	4 rooms, 4 pb	Tea & coffee available upon request
541-888-6058	Visa, MC, •	TV/DVD, video library, antiques, sun
Thomas & Stephanie Kramer	C-ltd/S-no/P-no/H-no	porch

Historic home in Coos Bay filled with history, antiques, and ambience. Gourmet breakfasts served in the main house. The Old Tower House is listed on the National Register of Historic Places, and is set a few yards from the Bay.

✉ oldtowerhouse@yahoo.com 🌐 www.oldtowerhouse.com

CORVALLIS

Harrison House	129-149 $US BB	Full breakfast
2310 NW Harrison	5 rooms, 5 pb	Willamette Valley wines, afternoon tea,
Blvd 97330	Most CC, Cash, Checks,	cold sodas, spring water & snacks
800-233-6248 541-752-6248	*Rated*, •	Sunroom/library, in-room WiFi,
Hilarie Phelps & Allen	C-yes/S-no/P-no/H-no	phones, TV with DVD, local truffles,
Goodman		hazelnuts & spring water

Gracious hospitality & comfort in a beautifully furnished, historic Dutch Colonial home. 4 rooms with private baths & a lovely detached Cottage Suite. Walk to OSU, restaurants, and shopping. Seasonal breakfasts, local wines, & all business amenities.

✉ stay@corvallis-lodging.com 🌐 www.corvallis-lodging.com

The Hanson Country Inn	125-175 $US BB	Full breakfast
795 SW Hanson St 97333	4 rooms, 4 pb	Sitting rooms, private decks, garden
541-752-2919	Most CC	area, library, Internet access
Patricia Covey	C-ltd/S-no/P-ltd/H-ltd	

Charming country home with splendid architectural details. Brimming with cozy warmth, unique charm and elegant ambience. A truly wonderful experience that you will want to enjoy again and again!

✉ hcibb@aol.com 🌐 www.hcinn.com

DAYTON

Wine Country Farm	150-225 $US BB	Full country breakfast
6855 Breyman Orchards	12 rooms, 12 pb	Home baked cookies, complimentary
Rd 97114	Visa, MC, Disc,	tasting wine.
800-261-3446 503-864-3446	*Rated*, •	Indoor & outdoor sitting areas,
Joan Davenport	C-ltd/S-no/P-no/H-yes	Jacuzzi, sauna, fireplaces, massage
	Spanish	services, horseback riding, wine.

Surrounded by vineyards and magnificent views, we provide warm gracias hospitality and comfortable accommodations in the heart of Oregon's famous Dundee Hills wine country. You can find us in "1000 Places To See Before You Die" by Patricia Schultz.

✉ jld@winecountryfarm.com 🌐 www.winecountryfarm.com

DEPOE BAY

An Ocean Paradise Whales	295-385 $US BB	Full breakfast
Rendezvous B&B	2 rooms, 2 pb	We provide coffee, tea, hot chocolate,
147 NW Hwy 101 97341	Most CC, Cash	water, soda, popcorn, and other treats,
541-765-3455	S-no/P-no/H-no	all complimentary.
Joe and Dian Forbis		Each suite has a PRIVATE large
		outdoor area with a fire pit to enjoy
		while watching the ocean waves.

A unique, one of a kind find right on the ocean with nothing to block your amazing view. Two elegant suites each with private entrances, and private outdoor areas with firepits. Each has an elegant private bathroom.

✉ info@WhalesRendezvous.com 🌐 www.whalesrendezvous.com

Wine Country Farm, Dayton, OR

EUGENE

C'est La Vie Inn
1006 Taylor St 97402
866-302-3014 541-302-3014
Anne-Marie Lizet

125-250 $US BB
4 rooms, 4 pb
Visa, MC, AmEx,
Rated
C-ltd/S-ltd/P-ltd/H-no
French

Full breakfast
Coffee, tea, cold beverages & beer,
cookies in the butler's pantry, wine
available to purchase
Flat screen TV with CD player & DVD,
free WiFi, computer, library, fireplaces,
robes, hair-dryers

All of the guest offerings, from the cozy Gauguin room to the opulent Casablanca, are uniquely deco-
rated, and all have private en-suite baths and fireplaces. Elegant features include individual cooling/
heating controls, robes, cable TV/DVD, and free WiFi.

✉ contact@cestlavieinn.com 🌐 www.cestlavieinn.com

Lorane Valley B&B
86621 Lorane Hwy 97405
541-686-0241
Esther & George Ralph

125-145 $US BB
1 rooms, 1 pb
Visa, MC, AmEx
C-yes/S-ltd/P-no

Full breakfast
Fresh cut flowers, book loans, PBS
documentaries, Jacuzzis

Three and a half miles from the hustle and bustle of Eugene is a haven of tranquility. Our corner of the
world is a beautiful, two level cedar home set on 15 acres overlooking the Lorane Valley.

✉ LoraneValleyBandB@att.net 🌐 www.loranevalleyBandB.com

River Walk Inn
250 N Adams St 97402
800-621-2904 541-344-6506
Richard & Donna Cribbs

100-120 $US BB
3 rooms, 3 pb
Visa, MC
C-ltd/S-no/P-no/H-no

Full breakfast
Tea & snacks are available in the
dining room at all times, evening port
in the library
Wireless Internet with a laptop
available for guest use, bicycles

River Walk Inn Bed and Breakfast is located in a quiet residential neighborhood on the edge of down-
town Eugene. We consider it the perfect location for out-of-town guests.

✉ innkeeper@ariverwalkinn.com 🌐 www.ariverwalkinn.com

Tell your hosts Pamela Lanier sent you.

FLORA

North End Crossing Barn and Bed
80903 College Lane 97828
888-897-8020 541-828-7010
Dan & Vanessa

85-85 $US BB
2 rooms
C-yes/S-ltd/P-yes/H-ltd
Memorial wknd – New
Yrs

Full country breakfast
Refreshments offered throughout the
day, coffee, tea, hot chocolate, scones,
fruit & more
Learn the old ways and pioneer skills,
sitting room, library, antiques, hiking
& walking . . . more

*Early risers may help milk the cows or gather eggs, slop the hogs and feed the drafts. Or sleep in
covered with old time quilts. But be sure to wake in time for a hearty country breakfast cooked on a
wood cookstove.*

✉ northendcrossing@tds.net 🌐 www.northendcrossing.com

FOSSIL

Wilson Ranches Retreat B&B
16555 Butte Creek Rd 97830
866-763-2227 541-763-2227
Phil & Nancy Wilson

79-109 $US BB
6 rooms, 2 pb
Visa, MC, AmEx
C-yes/S-ltd/P-no/H-ltd

Full 'cowboy' breakfast
Fully equipped kitchen
Satellite television, business traveler
accommodations

*Welcome to the Wilson Ranches Retreat Bed and Breakfast in North Central Oregon. A 9,000 acre
working cattle ranch takes you off the beaten track to our rustic hideout.*

✉ info@wilsonranchesretreat.com 🌐 www.wilsonranchesretreat.com

GOLD BEACH

Endicott Gardens
95768 Jerry's Flat Rd 97444
866-212-1220 541-247-6513
Patrick & Beverly Endicott

80-210 $US BB
4 rooms, 4 pb
Most CC, Cash
C-ltd/S-ltd/P-no/H-ltd

Full or Continental plus breakfast
Seasonal fruit, coffee & tea
Fireplace, gardens, pond, decks
overlooking the gardens

*Spectacular grounds with several fruit trees, flowers, shrubs and exotic plants. The home features four
guestrooms in a separate wing, each with private bath.*

✉ kittyscott@comcast.net 🌐 www.endicottgardens.com

Tu Tu' Tun Lodge
96550 N Bank Rogue 97444
800-864-6357 541-247-6664
Kyle Ringer

125-595 $US EP
20 rooms, 20 pb
Visa, MC, *Rated*, •
C-ltd/S-ltd/P-no/H-ltd
May—October

Meal plans: breakfast only, $18, b'fast
& dinner, $57.50, lunch $15, outside
guests by reservation
Library, sitting room, swimming pool,
games, 2 outdoor hot tubs

*Secluded lodge nestled on banks of the Rogue River, with country inn hospitality, gourmet meals,
white water excursions and guided fishing. Two houses, two suites, and sixteen rooms available.*

✉ tututunlodge@charter.net 🌐 www.tututun.com

GOLD HILL

Rogue River Guest House
41 Rogue River Hwy 97525
877-764-8322 541-855-4485
Joan Ogilvie & Doug Rowley

65-170 $US BB
2 rooms, 2 pb
•
C-yes/S-no/P-ltd/H-no

Full breakfast
Lunch & dinner by request;
complimentary wine
Jacuzzi suite with oceanview,
business services, family friendly, kids
welcome, pet friendly

*A completely refurbished 1890's farmhouse along the Rogue River in Southern Oregon, halfway be-
tween Medford and Grants Pass. Comfortable surroundings with all the amenities.*

🌐 www.rogueriverguesthouse.com

GRANTS PASS

Flery Manor B&B
2000 Jumpoff Joe Creek
Rd 97526
541-476-3591
Marla & John Vidrinskas

120-220 $US BB
5 rooms, 4 pb
Visa, MC, *Rated*, •
C-ltd/S-no/P-no/H-no
Lithuanian, Russian

Full 3 course gourmet breakfast
Afternoon tea, coffee, snacks, wine
Library, Suties/fireplace, Jacuzzi,
robes, fresh flower, piano, gazebo,
waterfalls, pond, trails, rafting

*"Get away from the hurried world..." Elegant, Romantic, Secluded." 7 mountain view acres near the
famous Rogue River. Suites, king bed, fireplace, Jacuzzi, private balcony. Library, parlor w/piano,
huge balcony/extraordinary view.* ✉ flery@flerymanor.com 🌐 www.flerymanor.com

Flery Manor B&B, Grants Pass, OR

GRANTS PASS

The Lodge at Riverside	125-325 $US BB	Continental breakfast
955 S.E. 7th St 97526	32 rooms, 32 pb	Evening wine & cheese reception,
877-955-0600 541-955-0600	Most CC, *Rated*, •	bedtime milk & cookies
Tamara Bushnell	C-yes/S-no/P-no/H-yes	Outdoor pool & spa, fireplaces,
		Jacuzzis, meeting rooms, restaurant,
		catering & special events

Let the scenic Rogue River become your backyard as you catch your breath in richly decorated, over-sized rooms. Experience the best of Grants Pass, Oregon for quiet pleasures, whirlwind vacations or corporate meetings.

 tamara@thelodgeatriverside.com   🌐 www.thelodgeatriverside.com

Weasku Inn	199-329 $US BB	Continental plus breakfast
5560 Rogue River Hwy 97527	17 rooms, 17 pb	Wine & cheese reception each
800-4-WEASKU 541-471-8000	Most CC, Cash,	afternoon, fresh baked cookies each
Kirt Davis	*Rated*, •	night
	C-yes/S-ltd/P-no/H-yes	Sitting room, fireplaces, cable TV,
		wireless Internet, conference facility &
		outdoor deck

Free Night w/Certificate: Excluding weekends and holidays May 15-Sept 15. Room Upgrade.

A cozy riverfront inn built around a colorful, historic fishing lodge. Decorated with locally hand-crafted furniture, one of a kind lamps, pillow top beds with feather duvets, chairs & fishing memorabilia.

 kirt@countryhouseinns.com   🌐 www.weasku.com

HOOD RIVER

Hood River BnB	85-135 $US BB	Full breakfast
918 Oak St 97031	4 rooms, 2 pb	Tea, snacks & cookies, all in a great
541-387-2997	Visa, MC, Disc	home
Jane & Jim Nichols	C-ltd/S-no/P-ltd/H-yes	Sitting rooms, guest-use computer
	French	with Internet access, library, deck,
		hammock, grill, picnic table

Just 3 blocks from downtown Hood River, OR, our B&B is ideal for those who want a comfortable place to relax & call home during your stay in the Gorge or at Mount Hood. Large, comfortable rooms with local fruit and good breakfasts.

 jane@hoodriverbnb.com   🌐 www.hoodriverbnb.com

HOOD RIVER

Inn At The Gorge	119-159 $US BB	Full breakfast
1113 Eugene St. 97031	5 rooms, 5 pb	Wraparound porch, backyard terrace,
877-852-2385 541-386-4429	Visa, MC	free wireless Internet service, DVDs,
Frank & Michele Bouche	C-ltd/S-no/P-no/H-ltd	off-street parking

Free Night w/Certificate: Valid November–April; except Holidays and Spring Break.

Built in 1908, this Queen Anne style home has operated as a Bed and Breakfast since 1987. We are located within walking distance to downtown shops and restaurants.

✉ stay@innatthegorge.com 🌐 www.innatthegorge.com

IDEYLD PARK

Steamboat Inn	170-300 $US EP	Evening dinner available, aperitif and
42705 N Umpqua Hwy 97447	19 rooms, 19 pb	hors d'oeuvres
800-840-8825 541-498-2230	Visa, MC, *Rated*, •	Library, fireplaces, decks, A/C, fly-
Sharon & Jim Van Loan	C-yes/S-no/P-ltd/H-yes	fishing guides,
	March through	
	December	

Commanding a breathtaking view of the North Umpqua River, the Steamboat Inn is nestled among the towering firs of the Umpqua National Forest. We are about two hours by car from airports at Eugene and Medford.

✉ patricialee@hughes.net 🌐 www.thesteamboatinn.com

JACKSONVILLE

Country House Inns	99-295 $US BB	Danish/Juice or Other as Below
Jacksonville	40 rooms, 40 pb	Stage Lodge guests receive a danish &
240 E California St 97530	Most CC, *Rated*, •	juice breakfast. Others receive a cert
800-367-1942 541-899-2050	C-yes/S-no/P-yes/H-yes	to a local restaurant.
Lydia Gibson		Fax, copy, Premium bath products,
		coffee makers, microwaves, mini-
		fridges

Combining five unique properties, Country House Inns Jacksonville has an accommodation for every taste or budget. Stay at the historic McCully House, the budget friendly Stage Lodge, the one of a kind Wine or Pine Cottages or the B&B-style Reames House.

✉ innkeeper@countryhouseinnsjacksonville.com 🌐 countryhouseinnsjacksonville.com

Elan Guest Suites &	160-250 $US BB	Gift card to local coffee shop
Gallery	3 rooms, 3 pb	Coffee, teas, chocolate and bottled
245 West Main St. 97530	Most CC, Cash, *Rated*	water are complimentary. Local wines
877-789-1952 541-899-8000	C-ltd/S-ltd/P-no/H-no	offered for sale in rooms.
Duane Sturm and Cherie		
Reneau		

Elan's executive lodging is a jewel box of comfort, technology and pure panache. In the Wild West backdrop of historic Jacksonville, Elan exceeds the expectations of our most distinguished guests. Luxurious suites, complimentary WiFi and private garage.

✉ contact@elanguestsuites.com 🌐 www.elanguestsuites.com

Jacksonville Inn	159-465 $US BB	Full breakfast
175 E California St 97530	12 rooms, 12 pb	Restaurant, lounge, wine tasting, lunch
800-321-9344 541-899-1900	Most CC, Cash,	& dinner additional, gourmet catering
Jerry & Linda Evans	*Rated*, •	on and off premises
	C-yes/S-no/P-ltd/H-yes	Luxurious cottages with many
	Greek, Danish, Italian,	amenities available; a connoisseur's
	Spanish	wine shop with over 2,000 wines

The Inn offers its guests elegance in a historic setting, with gourmet dining, a connoisseur's wine cellar, luxurious hotel accommodations, and 4 honeymoon cottages that are "suites extraordinaire."

✉ jvinn@mind.net 🌐 www.jacksonvilleinn.com

Tell your hosts Pamela Lanier sent you.

JACKSONVILLE

Jacksonville's Magnolia Inn
245 N 5th St 97530
866-899-0255 541-899-0255
Robert & Susan Roos

99-169 $US BB
9 rooms, 9 pb
Most CC, *Rated*
C-ltd/S-no/P-yes/H-yes

Continental breakfast from bakeries
Gourmet coffees, teas, European
pastries, homemade baked goods,
yogurt, waffles, oatmeal, fruit
TV/VCR/extended cable, high-speed
wireless Internet, guest kitchen,
outdoor veranda

Featured in Sunset Magazine and AAA's Via magazine. Located across from the museum, just two short blocks to town. Park your car and walk to award winning restaurants. Comfortable elegance in the heart of Jacksonville, voted 1 of 10 coolest US small towns

✉ maginn@charter.net 🌐 www.magnolia-inn.com

TouVelle House B&B
455 N Oregon St 97530
800-846-8422 541-899-8938
Gary Renninger Balfour

139-189 $US BB
6 rooms, 6 pb
Visa, MC, Disc,
Rated, •
C-ltd/S-no/P-no/H-no
German

Full breakfast/continental
Tea & hot beverages
Beautiful gardens, swimming pool,
sauna, spacious verandas, high speed
wireless Internet, fridge, AC

TouVelle House Bed & Breakfast is ready to welcome you with a gentle, serene environment where you can relax knowing that all of your needs have already been anticipated.

✉ info@touvellehouse.com 🌐 www.touvellehouse.com

LAFAYETTE

Kelty Estate B&B
675 3rd St 97127
800-867-3740 503-560-1512
Nicci Stokes

129-179 $US BB
5 rooms, 5 pb
Most CC, Cash, Checks
C-ltd/S-ltd/P-ltd/H-ltd

3-Course Gourmet Breakfast
Complimentary wine & cheese
Concierge services, corporate retreats,
weddings, wireless Internet

The Kelty Estate is a historic B&B in the heart of Oregon's wine country, one hour from Portland and the coast. As a guest of the Kelty, you are welcome to book our limousine to chauffeur you around the lush landscape or your own private wine tour. ✉ info@keltyestate.com 🌐 www.keltyestatebb.com

LINCOLN CITY

Coast Inn B&B
4507 SW Coast Ave 97367
888-994-7932 541-994-7932
Rosie Huntemann

109-198 $US BB
4 rooms, 4 pb
Visa, MC, AmEx
C-ltd/S-ltd/P-ltd/H-no

Full breakfast
Smoked salmon, wine & cheese,
lemonade & Fresh Lemon English
Shortbread
Library, WiFi

Welcome to Coast Inn Bed & Breakfast! We're only 2–2½ hours from Portland International Airport. Located in the historic Taft Heights district of Lincoln City. A short walk from Siletz Bay and beach access. Our pristine, level beach beckons you.

✉ coastinn@oregoncoastinn.com 🌐 www.oregoncoastinn.com

MCMINNVILLE

A'Tuscan Estate
809 NE Evans 97128
800-441-2214 503-434-9016
Jacques & Liz Rolland

140-250 $US BB
5 rooms, 5 pb
Most CC, Cash, Checks
C-ltd/S-no/P-no/H-no
French, Spanish

Full breakfast
Afternoon coffee, tea & fresh baked
cookies, private dinners
Sitting parlor, morning coffee room,
fireplace

1928 historic estate, 5 blocks from historic downtown. Close to Linfield College, Delphian School, antique shopping & wineries. 45 minutes to coast, 50 minutes to Mt. Hood ski resorts.

✉ innkeeper@a-tuscanestate.com 🌐 www.a-tuscanestate.com

Baker Street B&B Inn
129 SE Baker St 97128
800-870-5575 503-472-5575
Cheryl Hockaday

99-159 $US BB
5 rooms, 5 pb
Most CC, *Rated*
C-ltd/S-ltd/P-ltd/H-no

Light healthy breakfast
Restaurants nearby
One block from city park, jetted tub,
clawfoot tubs with showers, cottages

In the heart of Wine Country, Baker Street Inn is a downtown B&B with 3 guestrooms and 2 private cottages, near Linfield College and historic downtown. Three breakfast options. Midway between the Coast and Portland. Ask about La Nouveau Chateau!

✉ cheryl@bakerstreetinn.com 🌐 www.bakerstreetinn.com

MCMINNVILLE

Joseph Mattey House	150-225 $US BB	Full breakfast
10221 NE Mattey Ln 97128	4 rooms, 4 pb	Refreshments & cookies in the
877-434-5058 503-434-5058	Visa, MC, AmEx	afternoon, local wines available by the
Jack & Denise Seed	C-ltd/S-no/P-no/H-no	glass
	German, French, some	Sitting rm, parlor, porch swing, vine-
	Italian	yard, orchard, indoor & outdoor games

An 1892 Queen Anne Victorian surrounded by stately cedars and overlooking the vineyard, the Joseph Mattey House offers a secluded setting in the heart of the Oregon wine country. Centrally located for all wineries, restaurants and local attractions.

✉ mattey@matteyhouse.com 🌐 www.josephmatteyhouse.com

Steiger Haus	95-150 $US BB	Full seasonal breakfast
360 SE Wilson St 97128	5 rooms, 5 pb	Early continental breakfast baskets,
503-472-0821	Visa, MC, Disc, *Rated*	cheese & fruit plates, seasonal picnics,
Dale & Susan DuRette	C-ltd/S-no/P-no/H-ltd	honor bar
		Sitting room, movies & games, English
		garden, WiFi, honor bar, regional wine
		list, wine tours

In the heart of Oregon Wine Country. Unique architecture in a park-like town setting. Walking distance to gourmet restaurants. Charm and hospitality plus!

✉ reservations@steigerhaus.com 🌐 www.steigerhaus.com

Youngberg Hill Vineyards & Inn	200-350 $US BB	Full breakfast
10660 SW Youngberg Hill	8 rooms, 8 pb	Full Wine Tasting included with each
Rd 97128	Visa, MC, *Rated*, •	stay.
888-657-8668 503-472-2727	C-ltd/S-no/P-no/H-ltd	Library, lounging salon, dining rooms,
Nicolette Bailey		& wine tastings.

Oregon's premier wine country inn and one of Wine Spectator's favorite locations; set on a 50 acre hilltop surrounded by organic vineyards. We will take your breath away with the most beautiful views, warm luxurious Inn, and exceptional estate wines.

✉ info@youngberghill.com 🌐 www.youngberghill.com

MEDFORD

Under the Greenwood Tree	120 $US BB	Full breakfast
3045 Bellinger Ln 97501	4 rooms, 4 pb	Complimentary tea & treats
541-776-0000	Most CC	Pond, gazebo, garden, llamas,
Joseph & Barbara Lilley	C-ltd/S-no/P-yes/H-no	weddings, hammocks, massage
		services

This Country B&B Inn is set on 10 quiet and peaceful acres of idyllic grounds. It is surrounded by gracious Oregon gardens and interesting antique farm buildings dating to the Civil War Era.

✉ utgtree@qwest.net 🌐 www.greenwoodtree.com

MT. HOOD

Mt. Hood Hamlet B&B	145-165 $US BB	Full breakfast
6741 Hwy 35 97041	4 rooms, 4 pb	Complimentary juice, soft drinks,
800-407-0570 541-352-3574	Visa, MC, Disc, •	coffee & tea. House red or white wine
Paul & Diane Romans	C-ltd/S-no/P-ltd/H-ltd	may be purchased
		Private baths, 4 rms with fireplaces,
		2 with Jacuzzis, outdoor spa, library,
		WiFi, guest computer

Reach out & touch Mt. Hood from our 18th century New England Colonial style home with modern conveniences & amenities. 13 miles mountain top to rooftop, and a world apart from your daily cares. WiFi hotspot & DSL for those who must!

✉ info@mthoodhamlet.com 🌐 www.mthoodhamlet.com

NEWBERG

University House of Newberg B&B
401 N. Meridian St 97132
866-538-8438 503-538-8438
Leigh Wellikoff

175-275 $US BB
3 rooms, 2 pb
Visa, MC
C-ltd/S-no/P-no/H-no

Continental breakfast
Tea, popcorn, chocolate, crackers, juice, other snacks.
Hot tub, massage therapy available, full business center with WiFi, concierge service, etc.

University House provides the quintessential Oregon wine country experience. We offer the intimate charm of a beautifully restored 1906 home furnished with the warmth of stunning family antiques. There are no other guests in the house during your stay.

✉ hostess@universityhousenewberg.com 🌐 www.universityhousenewberg.com

NEWPORT

Ocean House, An Oceanfront Inn
4920 NW Woody Way 97365
866-495-3888 541-265-3888
Charmaine & Lex

135-250 $US BB
8 rooms, 8 pb
Most CC, Cash, Checks,
Rated, •
C-ltd/S-no/P-no/H-yes

Full breakfast
Complimentary beverages including wine, sodas, teas, bottled water, popcorn & homemade cookies too
All rooms with ocean views & fireplaces, 4 rooms with whirlpool, oceanfront gardens, WiFi

Unforgettable in any season, Ocean House offers gracious lodging for adult travelers. Spectacular views of the ocean and the incomparable Oregon coastline can be seen from every room as well as the Great Room, dining area and the spacious decks.

✉ oceanhouse@gmail.com 🌐 www.oceanhouse.com

The Lightkeeper's Inn B&B
811 SW 12th St. 97365
541-265-5642
Cheryl Lalack

195-248 $US BB
2 rooms, 2 pb
Visa, MC, AmEx
C-ltd/S-no/P-ltd/H-no

Full breakfast
Hor d'ovres and wine in your suite
Laundry room, soda, bottled water, microwaveable popcorn, hot tea, and coffee

Spectacular bay views from all rooms in the house. Close to attractions, events, shopping, beach, and more. Enjoy one of innkeeper Cheryl's fantastic breakfasts in our dining room, or enjoy a quiet breakfast in your private suite.

✉ innkeeper@thelightkeepersinnbb.com 🌐 www.thelightkeepersinnbb.com

Tyee Lodge Oceanfront B&B
4925 NW Woody Way 97365
888-553-8933 541-265-8953
Charmaine & Lex

99-210 $US BB
6 rooms, 6 pb
Most CC, *Rated*, •
C-ltd/S-no/P-no/H-ltd

Full Course Breakfast
Complimentary hot & cold beverages, wines, fresh baked cookies, popcorn; special diets accommodated
Private trail to beach, outdoor fire pit, sitting room, WiFi, TV on request

Come and enjoy our natural setting along the bluffs of peaceful Agate Beach in Newport. Our park-like setting is unequaled on the Oregon Coast. Sit by your window or by the fire and watch the waves. All 6 rooms have gas fireplaces.

✉ reservations@tyeelodge.com 🌐 www.tyeelodge.com

OTIS

Lake House B&B
2165 NE East Devils Lake Rd 97368
888-996-8938 541-996-8938
Mary Sell

95-220 $US BB
3 rooms, 3 pb
Visa, MC, Disc
C-yes/S-ltd/P-no/H-no

Full breakfast
Fireplace, sitting room, private hot tub, rowboat or canoe, dock, fishing

Cedar home and guest cabin located on a 680-acre freshwater lake, only two miles from the Pacific coastline & downtown Lincoln City. Very quiet area, large rooms, private entrance.

✉ lakehousebnb@charter.net 🌐 www.lakehousebb.com

PACIFIC CITY

The Craftsman Bed & Breakfast
35255 4th St 97135
503-965-4574
Michael Rech

110-170 $US BB
4 rooms, 4 pb
Most CC, Cash
C-ltd/S-ltd/P-no/H-no

Full breakfast
Baked goodies upon arrival and throughout the day. Miele Nespresso coffee machine. Wine list.
Game table, hot tub, sun deck, DVD library, fireplace, reading inglenook, WiFi, fisherman's sink

The Craftsman B&B welcomes you to experience the beautiful Oregon Coast in style, grace and comfort. Everything in town is within walking distance. Park your car, relax and unplug. No lace, no doilies!

✉ innkeeper@craftsmanbb.com 🌐 www.craftsmanbb.com

PORT ORFORD

WildSpring Guest Habitat
92978 Cemetery Loop 97465
866-333-9453 541-332-0977
Michelle & Dean Duarte

198-306 $US BB
5 rooms, 5 pb
Most CC, Cash, *Rated*
C-ltd/S-no/P-no/H-yes

Healthy Buffet
Coffee, teas, hot chocolate, juices, fruit, popcorn, chocolates
LCD TV/DVD, CD/iPod stereo, refrig, 500 DVDs, massage table, wine glasses, candles, spa robes

WildSpring Guest Habitat is a small, ecofriendly resort in Port Orford overlooking the spectacular south Oregon coast. On 5 secluded acres, it offers luxury accommodations in a peaceful, naturally beautiful environment. ✉ info@wildspring.com 🌐 www.wildspring.com

PORTLAND

A Painted Lady Inn
1927 N.E. 16th Ave. 97212
503-335-0070
Jody Runge

109-179 $US BB
5 rooms, 3 pb
Visa, MC, Disc
C-yes/S-no/P-no/H-ltd

Full breakfast
Delightful garden patio & covered front porch with swing, Central City Location!

Located in vibrant, hip Northeast Portland, A Painted Lady Bed and Breakfast Inn offers a calm oasis in the heart of the city. Just steps from wonderful shops and fine restaurants, A Painted Lady will be your Portland home-away-from-home.

✉ jrunge15@comcast.net 🌐 www.apaintedladyinn.com

Bellaterra B&B
3935 SW Corbett Avenue 97239
503-332-8125
Ellen

95-150 $US BB
5 rooms, 5 pb
Most CC, Cash
C-ltd/S-no/P-ltd/H-no
Some Spanish

Full breakfast

Newly-remodeled Victorian with ample common spaces, reading nook, traditional moldings and custom carvings, and five nature- and culture-themed guestrooms, each furnished with antiques and having its own glass or stone-tiled bathroom. ✉ bellaterrainfo@gmail.com 🌐 bellaterrabnb.com

Bluebird Guesthouse
3517 SE Division St 97202
866-717-4333 503-238-4333

60-105 $US BB
7 rooms, 2 pb
Visa, MC
C-ltd/S-no/P-no/H-no

Simple Continental Breakfast
A full kitchen guests can use to prepare meals
In-room A/C & heat controls.
Complementary: WiFi, Internet computer, local phone, maps.

Charming, friendly & reasonably priced, the Bluebird Guesthouse is located in the heart of Southeast Portland. Visit our website to see an availability calendar and to make reservations.

✉ info@bluebirdguesthouse.com 🌐 www.bluebirdguesthouse.com

PORTLAND

Britannia at Terwilliger Vista	110-200 $US BB	Full breakfast
515 SW Westwood Dr 97201	5 rooms, 5 pb	Complimentary sodas & water
888-244-0602 503-244-0602	Visa, MC, *Rated*, •	Sitting room, library, suites, fireplaces,
Carl & Irene	C-ltd/S-no/P-no/H-ltd	cable TV, wireless Internet

An elegant Georgian Colonial located in the West Hills of Portland. Situated on over a ½ acre of gardens, manicured lawns, and mature trees. This inn features blonde Honduran mahogany woodwork and Waterford crystal chandeliers throughout.

✉ terwilligervista@gmail.com 🌐 www.terwilligervista.com

Clinton Street Guesthouse	70-115 $US BB	Continental plus breakfast
4220 SE Clinton Street 97206	4 rooms, 2 pb	Coffee & tea, special diets and early
503-234-8752	Most CC, Cash, Checks	risers accommodated with prior
Ann Skvarek & Jason Fayen	C-yes/S-ltd/P-no/H-ltd	notice
		Front porch, living room, dining room,
		WiFi, books & DVDs, luxury linens, 20
		minutes from airport

A lovely 1913 craftsman style B&B that offers authentic residential ambience in a casual setting. Located in southeast Portland.

✉ everettandclintonstreet@gmail.com 🌐 www.clintonstreetguesthouse.com

Evermore Guesthouse	90-150 $US BB	Continental Breakfast
3860 SE Clinton St 97022	5 rooms, 5 pb	Included: off-street parking, fast
503-206-6509	C-ltd/S-no/P-no/H-no	Internet computer/ WiFi, area maps,
Chris & Cecily		local & long distance calls

Charming and relaxed accommodations in the heart of Southeast Portland. Furnished comfortably and simply – just enough of what you'd like without the clutter. Minutes to city attractions and a short walk to some of the best restaurants, cafes & shops

✉ info@evermoreguesthouse.com 🌐 www.evermoreguesthouse.com

Hostess House	75-85 $US BB	Full gourmet breakfast
5758 NE Emerson St 97218	2 rooms	Afternoon tea
877-760-7799 503-282-7892	Most CC, *Rated*	Outstanding hospitality since 1988,
Milli Laughlin	C-yes/S-ltd/P-no/H-ltd	sitting rm, fireplace, park like backyard

An affordable tranquil getaway (since 1988). Gourmet breakfasts. Our inn is not for the conspicuous consumer but for the lower-maintenance person who is looking for quality accommodations with a smile. You'll not be disappointed.

✉ hostess@hostesshouse.com 🌐 www.hostesshouse.com

Lion & the Rose Victorian B&B	99-224 $US BB	Full breakfast
1810 NE 15th Ave 97212	7 rooms, 7 pb	Complimentary beverages, light
800-955-1647 503-287-9245	Most CC, *Rated*	refreshments
Steven Unger	C-ltd/S-no/P-no/H-no	Telephones, free local & long distance,
		cable TV, data ports, high-speed
		wireless Internet access

Exceptional B&B on the National Register of Historic Places, this majestic 1906 Queen Anne Victorian mansion takes you to another time. Seven unique guestrooms, with private baths, emanate Victorian charm.

✉ innkeeper@lionrose.com 🌐 www.lionrose.com

Mt. Scott Manor	90-150 $US BB	Family style
12570 SE Callahan Rd 97086	4 rooms, 4 pb	Minutes from surrounding attractions,
503-477-4949	Visa, MC	but located in a peaceful setting of
Virgil and Della	C-yes/S-no/P-ltd/H-no	nature and serenity

Mt. Scott Manor is a three-story, modern home with 6,000 sq. ft. guest area. Inspired by the grand old Tudor manor houses of England, you would think you were there. Placed between a breathtaking mountain view and a private forest complete with resident deer.

 mt.scottmanorbandb@comcast.net   mtscottmanor.com

PROSPECT

Prospect Historic Hotel –
Motel and Dinner House
391 Mill Creek Drive 97536
800-944-6490 541-560-3664
Fred & Karen

70-150 $US BB
24 rooms, 24 pb
Visa, MC, Disc,
Rated, •
C-yes/S-no/P-yes/H-yes

Hearty breakfast
Dinner House offers superb American
Cuisine from May through October.
Prime Rib, Salmon, Shrimp, etc
Closest Historic Hotel B&B to Crater
Lake. Modern Motel & Restaurant

This spectacular Crater Lake lodging is located just 28 miles from Crater Lake National Park and ¼ mile from the Rogue River, offering warm and inviting accommodations in the natural beauty of Oregon.

info@prospecthotel.com www.prospecthotel.com

SAINT PAUL

Inn at Champoeg
8899 Champoeg Rd NE 97137
503-678-6088
Paterese & West Livaudais

149-169 $US BB
2 rooms, 2 pb
Visa, MC, AmEx
C-ltd/S-no/P-no/H-no

Full breakfast

Free Night w/Certificate: Anytime.

Located among the rolling hills and fields of the north Willamette Valley, The Inn at Champoeg is uniquely suited as a destination of quiet repose. The spacious elegance of the Inn welcomes each visitor with open arms.

info@innatchampoeg.com www.innatchampoeg.com

SEAL ROCK

Caledonia House B&B
6575 NW Pacific Coast
Hwy 97376
541-563-7337
Dee Brodie & Belinda Goody

119-169 $US BB
5 rooms, 5 pb
Visa, MC
C-ltd/S-no/P-no/H-no

Full breakfast
In room coffee or tea and "Welcome" treats.
luxurious linens, flat screen TVs, in room temp. control, WiFi or PC, guest kitchen, Tub for Two . . .

Our Scotland-inspired B&B is perfectly located between the Pacific Ocean and the temperate coastal rain forests that encompass over 2 acres of our certified wildlife habitat and nature trails. We are also centrally located on the scenic Oregon coast.

caledoniabnb@peak.org caledoniabb.com

SEASIDE

Gilbert Inn
341 Beach Drive 97138
800-410-9770 503-738-9770
Gilbert Inn LLC

69-229 $US EP
6 rooms, 6 pb
Most CC, Cash, *Rated*
S-no/P-no/H-no

In-room coffee. Many restaurants within 5 minute walk from the Inn
Sitting room, games, books

Enjoy a unique opportunity to stay in the Historic Home of Alexandre Gilbert. This Queen Anne Victorian is located in Seaside, Oregon. One block from the beach and downtown, this Seaside oasis is quiet and relaxed, offering guests a home away from home.

gilbertinn@seasurf.net www.gilbertinn.com

SOUTH BEACH

Stone Crest Cellar Bed &
Breakfast
9556 South Coast
Hwy. 97366
541-867-6621
Judy & Craig Joubert

145-195 $US BB
2 rooms, 2 pb
Most CC, Cash, Checks
C-ltd/S-ltd/P-no/H-ltd

Full breakfast
Evening wine & appetizers
Ocean views, private baths, sitting room, deck

A spectacular ocean front Inn & venue for relaxing get-aways, weddings, elopements & receptions. Full service wedding packages for al budgets. Voted 2010 Bride's Choice Award Wedding Wire.

jjoubert@charter.net www.stonecrestbb.com

ST. HELENS

Nob Hill Riverview B&B
285 S 2nd St 97051
503-396-5555
Matthew & Tana Phemester

110-210 $US BB
3 rooms, 3 pb
Most CC, Cash, Checks,
Rated, •
C-ltd/S-no/P-no/H-ltd
Some Spanish

Full Hot Organic Gourmet Breakfast
In the late afternoon guests can enjoy
a complimentary Afternoon Tea and
appetizers upon request
Gathering rooms, wood-burning
fireplace, sunroom filled with flowers,
TV, business accommodations

Nob Hill Riverview Bed and Breakfast loves to pamper our guests! The home is newly restored, fresh and beautiful. Listed on historical places. A true 1900 Arts and Craft home. Beautiful views of the river from most rooms. Upscale and luxury.

 stay@nobhillbb.com 🌐 www.nobhillbb.com

SUN RIVER

DiamondStone Guest Lodges
541-536-6263
Doug & Gloria Watt

99-139 $US BB
10 rooms, 10 pb
Most CC, Cash, Checks,
Rated, •
C-yes/S-ltd/P-yes/H-no

Full breakfast
Coffee, tea, complimentary beverages
– beer, wine, juices.
Western art, hot tub, outdoor BBQ,
free movie library.

DiamondStone manages several luxurious, comfy, rural Vacation Rentals. DS B&B offers private baths, TV/DVD/VCRs/phones, outdoor spa. Featured in "Northwest Best Places" it is at the heart of the recreational mecca that is Central Oregon – golf, fish, ski!

 diamond@diamondstone.com 🌐 www.diamondstone.com

WALDPORT

Cliff House B&B
1450 SW Adahi Rd 97394
541-563-2506
Sharon Robinson

125-225 $US BB
4 rooms, 4 pb
Visa, MC, *Rated*
C-ltd/S-no/P-no/H-no
Dutch

Full breakfast
Afternoon tea, coffee, fresh lemonade,
cookies
Sitting room, hot tubs, decks, ocean
gazing, wireless Internet, massage
services, outdoor weddings

Cliff House Bed and Breakfast, a luxuriously restored historic home, overlooks the Pacific Ocean and Alsea Bay on the Central Oregon Coast. Experience a renaissance of elegance and old world charm transposed into the 21st century.

 innkeeper@cliffhouseoregon.com 🌐 www.cliffhouseoregon.com

WHEELER

Wheeler On The Bay Lodge
580 Marine Dr 97147
800-469-3204 503-368-5858
Pat Scribner

85-225 $US BB
11 rooms, 11 pb
Visa, MC, Disc, *Rated*
C-yes/S-ltd/P-no/H-yes

Limited breakfast
Complimentary teas, coffee, spiced
cider, cocoa
Spa, fireplace, TV, DVD/VHS movies,
massage, fridge, micro, coffee maker,
telephones, kayaks, WiFi

Two hours west of Portland is a rare find on the Oregon Coast. Wheeler on the Bay Lodge on Nehalem Bay Estuary has water & mountain views. Services include free WiFi, spas, massages, movies, kayaks and a private boat dock. Charter boat, fishing or crabbing

 WheelerLodge@nehalemtel.net 🌐 www.wheeleronthebay.com

YACHATS

SeaQuest Inn
95354 Highway 101 97498
800-341-4878 541-547-3782
Kelley Essoe & Nerina Perez

150-275 $US BB
7 rooms, 7 pb
Most CC, Cash, *Rated*
C-ltd/S-no/P-no/H-ltd
Prime and Winter

Full Gourmet Breakfast
All day home-baked goodies, coffee,
tea, hot cocoa & cider, fresh fruit,
cheese & crackers
Jacuzzi tubs, private decks, ocean
views, great room, sitting room, 2
ponds, sandy beach, vast lawn

As our most welcomed guest—indulgent comfort, ocean views, the crashing surf, and your own warm, inviting Jacuzzi tub await your arrival at the oceanfront SeaQuest Inn Bed and Breakfast in Yachats, Oregon.

 info@seaquestinn.com 🌐 www.seaquestinn.com

Pennsylvania

BARTO

Landhaven B&B
1194 Huffs Church Rd 19504
610-845-3257
Ed & Donna Land

95-150 $US BB
5 rooms, 5 pb
C-ltd/S-no/P-no/H-yes

Full Country Breakfast
TV, fax & telephones available in the
common seating area; library

Converted 1871 General Store offering quaint comfortable rooms with specialty baths and showers for each room. Homemade country-style breakfasts. Calming country views. On-site concerts, antique shop. Many packages available, or create your own!

✉ info@landhavenbandb.com 🌐 www.landhavenbandb.com

BEDFORD

Golden Eagle Inn
131 East Pitt St 15522
814-624-0800
Oralee Kieffer

150-185 $US BB
12 rooms, 12 pb
Visa, MC
C-yes/S-no/P-no/H-no

Full breakfast
Elegant guestrooms & suites furnished
with antiques, WiFi available in most
rooms

An historic Colonial tavern in beautiful downtown Bedford, Pennsylvania, famous for heritage and hospitality. Extensively renovated to preserve the original beauty and warmth.

✉ oralee@bedford.net 🌐 www.bedfordgoldeneagle.com

The Chancellor's House B&B
341 South Juliana
Street 15522
866-535-8414 814-624-0374
Lynn and Steve George

125-150 $US BB
3 rooms, 3 pb

Full breakfast
Coffee and juice are accompanied by
fresh fruit, fresh scones.
New private baths, state-of-the-art
kitchen, ceiling fans, cable TV and
high speed wireless Internet

We have lovingly restored this grand old house into a Bed and Breakfast, saving the traditional architectural features and adding all new modern conveniences.

✉ reservations@thechancellorshouse.com 🌐 www.thechancellorshouse.com

BELLEFONTE

Our Fair Lady
313 E Linn St 16823
814-355-1117
Robert and Tami Schuster

120-150 $US BB
5 rooms, 3 pb
C-ltd/S-no/P-no/H-no

special dietary needs accommodated
Afternoon wine and cheese,
Historic home w/5 guestrooms, queen
size feather beds, full breakfast, high
speed WiFi, event venue

Start your morning rocking on one of our historic porches, or in the gazebo with a cup of freshly ground coffee and a good book. You may even find yourself returning in the late afternoon or evening relaxing with a glass of wine.

✉ ofl.schuster@gmail.com 🌐 www.ourfairladybnb.com

The Queen
176 E Linn St 16823
888-355-7999 814-355-7946
Nancy Noll & Curtis Miller

95-245 $US BB
5 rooms, 5 pb
Visa, MC, AmEx,
Rated, •
C-yes/S-no/P-yes/H-no

Full breakfast
champagne bucket & glasses, flowers
& candy are available
Sitting room, suites, fireplaces, cable
TV, business travelers, shower w/
massage jets, WiFi

The Queen is a Queen Anne-style Victorian home ornately decorated with the many collectibles of its owners. Collections include Santas, Victorian memorabilia and hunting and fishing items.

✉ thequeenbnb@psualum.com 🌐 www.thequeenbnb.com

BETHLEHEM

The Sayre Mansion
250 Wyandotte St. 18015
877-345-9019 610-882-2100
Carrie Ohlandt

150-325 $US BB
18 rooms, 18 pb
Most CC
C-yes/S-no/P-ltd/H-yes

Full breakfast
Refrigerators & coffee makers in
Carriage House
Parlors, fireplace, air conditioning,
private baths, telephones, wireless
Internet access, cable TV

Meticulously restored, this bed and breakfast Inn offers luxury and comfort in 18 guestrooms each preserving the architectural details of the mansion.

 innkeeper@sayremansion.com   ◐ www.sayremansion.com

BIRD IN HAND

**Bird-in-Hand Village Inn &
Suites**
2695 Old Philadelphia
Pike 17505
800-914-2473
Jim & John Smucker

89-229 $US BB
24 rooms, 24 pb
Most CC, *Rated*
S-no/P-no/H-ltd
February-December

Continental plus breakfast
Evening snacks
Sitting room, 2-hour Dutch Country
bus tour, suites w/hot tub, fireplace,
refrigerator, meeting room

Beautifully restored historic inn located in Pennsylvania Dutch Country. Victorian-style architecture and furnishings in a rural setting. Complimentary tour of PA Dutch country.

 sscharmer@bird-in-hand.com   ◐ www.bird-in-hand.com/index.php/places_to_st

**Greystone Manor Victorian
Inn**
2658 Old Philadelphia
Pike 17505
717-393-4233
Angela Skiadas

79-189 $US BB
10 rooms, 10 pb
Most CC, Cash, Checks,
Rated, •
C-yes/S-no/P-yes/H-yes

Full breakfast
Snacks & beverages, pool side menu,
catering menu, family reunion &
special dinners available
Pool & hot tub, sitting rooms, pantry,
numerous patios & balconies, picnic
area, dining room

Free Night w/Certificate: Valid January-April 1st for standard room and November–December weekdays.

1883 Victorian Mansion in the heart of Amish country. Only a stones throw away to all of the shopping, food, and entertainment. Perched atop a hill on 2 beautiful acres this inn has award winning gardens, a pool, Jacuzzi, & is surrounded by 3 Amish farms.

 angela@greystonemanor.com   ◐ www.greystonemanor.com

BLOOMSBURG

The Inn at Turkey Hill
991 Central Rd 17815
570-387-1500
Andrew Pruden

109-225 $US BB
23 rooms, 23 pb
Most CC
C-yes/S-ltd/P-yes/H-ltd

Continental breakfast
Dinner every evening, catering
available
Cozy tavern, whirlpools & fireplaces,
duck pond & gazebo, meeting facility

The Inn at Turkey Hill is a moment's drive from Interstate 80 in Bloomsburg, an oasis along the highway, a world of peaceful strolls by the pond, personal wake-up calls, gourmet cuisine and beautifully appointed guestrooms.

 andrew@innatturkeyhill.com   ◐ www.innatturkeyhill.com

BOALSBURG

B&B at The Rock Garden
176 Brush Valley Rd 16827
888-620-7625 814-466-6100
Joe Thomas & Laura
Stephenson

110-225 $US BB
5 rooms, 5 pb
Visa, MC
C-ltd/S-no/P-no/H-yes

Full Breakfast
Tea & coffee available through the day
Internet, fax, gardens, available for
meetings & celebrations, events

Welcome to The Rock Garden, a State College Bed & Breakfast located at the base of Mt. Nittany just minutes from the Penn State campus. Situated between the village of Lemont and Historic Boalsburg, we offer relaxation in a beautiful country setting.

 info@therockgardenbandb.com   ◐ www.therockgardenbandb.com

BOALSBURG

Earlystown Manor
2024 Earlystown Rd. 16827
877-466-6481 814-466-6491
Anne & Zane Smilowitz

125-495 $US BB
8 rooms, 8 pb
Visa, MC, Disc
C-ltd/S-no/P-no/H-no

Full breakfast
Coffee, tea, soft drinks & snacks are
always available for our guests
Guests & friends are welcome to use
our indoor and outdoor facilities

Located in Central Pennsylvania, the Earlystown Manor Bed & Breakfast offers modern day conveniences in a relaxing and traditional setting. The facilities are air conditioned with private baths. Each room offers a splendid view of the countryside & WiFi.

✉ zxs@psu.edu 🌐 www.earlystownmanor.com

BOILING SPRINGS

Gelinas Manor Victorian B&B
219 Front St 17007
866-297-2588 717-258-6584
Lee & Kity Gelinas

79-139 $US BB
4 rooms, 3 pb
Most CC, Cash,
Checks, •
C-yes/S-no/P-no/H-no

Full breakfast
Coffee, cocoa, tea 24/7
Sitting room, library, suites, A/C, email
& fax services

Guests will find the highest levels of service, comfort, ambience, and elegance in this circa 1870 home in an historic village. Fly fishing, car shows, Appalachian trail, are all nearby. Midway between Hershey & Gettysburg.

✉ Lee@gelinasManor.com 🌐 www.GelinasManor.com

BUTLER

Locust Brook Lodge B&B
179 Eagle Mill Rd 16001
724-283-8453
Carol Pawlowicz & Ed
Pawlowicz

80-150 $US BB
7 rooms, 7 pb
Most CC, Cash, Checks
C-yes/S-ltd/P-ltd/H-ltd

Full Breakfast
Afternoon tea, milk and cookies
Wifi Internet, in-room telephones,
horse trails and stabling area,
recreation room with pool table

Come spend a night or a week in this tranquil lodge, located in the heart of a 100 acre farm, but just minutes from major highways. Enjoy our desks, rustic living room and a welcoming outdoor area with hiking trails.

✉ locustbrooklodge@earthlink.net 🌐 home.earthlink.net/~locustbrooklodge

CANADENSIS

Brookview Manor
4534 RR 447 18325
800-585-7974 570-595-2451
Gaile & Marty Horowitz

130-225 $US BB
10 rooms, 10 pb
Most CC, Cash, *Rated*
C-ltd/S-no/P-no/H-no

Full gourmet breakfast
Casual to gourmet dinner by award
winning chef, reservations required in
our restaurant
Bar, sitting room, TV/DVD, lawn
games, hiking, Jacuzzi, fireplaces,
enclosed wrap-around porch

Recapture the art of relaxation in an enchanting country Inn. The Brookview Manor is nestled in the heart of the Poconos across from Brodhead Creek. Romantic accommodations with Jacuzzis and fireplaces. Intimate lounge and Gourmet Restaurant on premise.

✉ innkeepers@TheBrookviewManor.com 🌐 www.thebrookviewmanor.com

CARLISLE

Carlisle House B&B
148 S Hanover St 17013
717-249-0350
Mary & Alan Duxbury

119-219 $US BB
10 rooms, 10 pb
Most CC, Cash, *Rated*
C-ltd/S-no/P-no/H-no

Full breakfast
Teas and Coffee, Fruit
Free wireless Internet, fax, voicemail
in each room, in room TV and DVD
players, off-street parking.

A unique Bed and Breakfast experience in a historic 1826 Carlisle home. Voted "Best of Carlisle" 2004 through 2010, located in the Downtown Carlisle Historic District, walk to great restaurants, antiques, and Dickinson College!

✉ stay@thecarlislehouse.com 🌐 www.thecarlislehouse.com

CARLISLE

Pheasant Field
150 Hickorytown Rd 17015
877-258-0717 717-258-0717
Dee Fegan & Chuck
DeMarco

129-219 $US BB
8 rooms, 8 pb
Most CC, Cash, Checks,
Rated, •
C-ltd/S-no/P-ltd/H-yes

Full breakfast
Snacks, soft drinks available anytime
Sitting room, tennis court, pet friendly,
horse boarding available, labyrinth on-
site, VCR/DVD movie

Lovely 200 year-old brick farmhouse in a country setting. History, antiques, fly fishing, car shows. Appalachian trail nearby. Labyrinth on-site for quiet meditation. Extended-stay apartment available.

✉ stay@pheasantfield.com 🌐 www.pheasantfield.com

CHADDS FORD

Fairville Inn
506 Kennett Pike, Rt 52 19317
877-285-7772 610-388-5900
Rick & Laura Carro

170-295 $US BB
15 rooms, 15 pb
Most CC, Cash, Checks,
Rated
C-ltd/S-ltd/P-no/H-yes

Full and Continental Breakfasts
Afternoon tea with a selection of
cheeses, fruit & inn-baked goods
Satellite TV, telephone, and wireless
Internet in each room. Most rooms
have a fireplace and deck.

Elegant accommodations in the heart of Brandywine Valley. Just minutes from world-famous Longwood Gardens, the Winterthur Estate and Gardens, the Nemours Estate, the Brandywine River ("Wyeth") Museum, wonderful local wineries and more. Enjoy the elegance!

✉ info@fairvilleinn.com 🌐 www.fairvilleinn.com

CHURCHTOWN

Inn at Twin Linden
2092 Main St 17555
866-445-7614 717-445-7619
Sue & Norm Kuestner

130-275 $US BB
8 rooms, 8 pb
Most CC, Cash, Checks,
Rated, •
C-ltd/S-no/P-no/H-no

Full breakfast
Complimentary snacks, soft drinks,
coffee & tea available 24/7. Fine
dinning on Saturday evenings.
Jacuzzi tubs, fireplaces, cable, VHS/
DVD, free WiFi, private dining tables,
business meeting space

Elegant accommodations in an historic estate for discriminating inn-goers. Private baths and dining tables, Jacuzzis, fireplaces, and renowned gourmet cuisine.

✉ innattwinlinden@comcast.net 🌐 www.innattwinlinden.com

CLARK

Tara—A Country Inn
2844 Lake Rd 16113
800-782-2803 724-962-3535
Laura Ackley

200-425 $US BB
27 rooms, 27 pb
Most CC, Cash
C-ltd/S-no/P-no/H-ltd

Full breakfast
Ashley's Gourmet Dining Room,
Stonewall's Tavern, Atlanta Lounge,
Sunday Brunch & Breakfast
All rooms have a gas fireplace,
T.V., and D.V.D. player. Weddings,
banquets, and corporate events.

Tara is the ultimate in World Class Country Inns, devoted to guests who expect the exceptional and appreciate the best. Inspired by the movie Gone With the Wind, Tara offers you Southern Hospitality and a chance to enjoy the luxuries of days gone by.

✉ info@tara-inn.com 🌐 www.tara-inn.com

CLEARFIELD

Christopher Kratzer House
101 East Cherry St 16830
888-252-2632 814-765-5024
Bruce & Ginny Baggett

65-90 $US BB
3 rooms, 2 pb
Most CC, Checks,
Rated, •
C-yes/S-ltd/P-yes/H-no

Full breakfast
Fine dining restaurants just around the
corner
Snacks, sitting room, library, attic flea
market for browsing, A/C

As the oldest home in Clearfield, The Christopher Kratzer Bed and Breakfast is a Classic Revival house in the Old Town Historic District. ✉ bbaggett@pennswoods.net

CRESSON

The Station Inn
827 Front Street 16630
800-555-4757 814-886-4757
Tom Davis

80-180 $US BB
7 rooms, 7 pb
C-ltd/S-no/P-no/H-no

Continental plus breakfast
Restaurant, bar service, sitting room,
library

Lodging in a classic mountain resort hotel providing comfortable lodging, good company, and hearty breakfasts for rail enthusiasts since 1993. A historic 1865 hotel.

🌐 www.stationinnpa.com

DENVER

Farm Folk Bed and Breakfast
2184 West Route 897 17517
717-629-0300
Matt & Heather Martin

69-149 $US BB
2 rooms, 2 pb
Visa, MC, Disc
C-yes/S-ltd/P-ltd/H-yes

Full breakfast
Breakfast brought to your door
Seclusion & relaxation in a rural
location, private entrances & private
baths

Hospitality is our tradition and we stand by every word of it. Service with a smile and amenities that make you smile. This is why people keep coming year after year. Privacy, luxury, and a new perspective on life is what guests find at Farm Folk.

heather@thefarmfolk.com   www.thefarmfolk.com

EAGLES MERE

Crestmont Inn
180 Crestmont Dr 17731
800-522-8767 570-525-3519
Fred & Elna Mulford

110-220 $US BB
15 rooms, 15 pb
Visa, MC, *Rated*, •
C-yes/S-no/P-no/H-no

Full country breakfast
Dinner, restaurant, bar service
Commons room, bicycles, tennis
court, private whirlpool, lake access,
cable TV

Free Night w/Certificate: Valid November, December, January, February, March, and April.

A hidden treasure nestled in the Endless Mountains in "the town that time forgot, Eagles Mere, Pennsylvania."

crestmnt@epix.net   www.crestmont-inn.com

Eagles Mere Inn
Corner of Mary & Sullivan
Ave 17731
800-426-3273 570-525-3273
Toby Diltz

179-259 $US MAP
19 rooms, 19 pb
Visa, MC, Disc,
Rated, •
C-yes/S-no/P-no/H-yes

Full Country breakfast
5 course dinner included, excellent
wine list
Pub, warm hospitality, gourmet
meals, outstanding wines & peaceful
relaxation

Ultimate stress relief! Eagles Mere is the "last unspoiled resort", featuring boating, hiking, horseback riding, and much more. Guests enjoy warm hospitality, gourmet meals included in rates, outstanding wines and peaceful relaxation.

relax@eaglesmereinn.com   www.eaglesmereinn.com

EAST BERLIN

Bechtel Victorian Mansion
400 West King St 17316
800-331-1108 717-259-7760
Carol & Richard Carlson

115-175 $US BB
6 rooms, 6 pb
Visa, MC, AmEx,
Rated, •
C-yes/S-ltd/P-no/H-no

Full breakfast
Complimentary tea
Sitting room, TV with VCR and DVD,
movies, A/C, meeting room, garden

Free Night w/Certificate: Valid Sunday-Thursday.

1897 Victorian mansion with 6 guestrooms. All rooms have private bath & A/C. Beautifully decorated in country Victorian style, furnished with period antiques, accented with porcelain dolls, teddy bears & toys.

bechtelvictbb@aol.com   www.bechtelvictorianmansion.com

EAST EARL

A Suite Escape
417 Fairview Street 17519
877-273-7227 717-445-5649
Joanne Martin

139-169 $US BB
2 rooms, 2 pb
Most CC, Cash
C-yes/S-no/P-no/H-ltd

Full breakfast
Breakfast is in your room or on your
patio
Hot tub, flat screen TV's, fireplaces

Come and escape the hustle and bustle of everyday life and enjoy the heart of PA Dutch Country. Enjoy our beautiful view and private suites, creating the perfect getaway for the romantic or family vacation. Soak in our hot tub under the stars.

 sjmartin@dejazzd.com   www.asuiteescape.com/index.htm

EASTON

The Lafayette Inn
525 W Monroe St 18042
800-509-6990 610-253-4500
Paul & Laura Di Liello

125-225 $US BB
18 rooms, 18 pb
Most CC, *Rated*
C-yes/S-no/P-ltd/H-yes
Italian

Full breakfast
Complimentary snacks, sodas, coffee,
teas, fresh fruit.
Sitting room, whirlpools, suites,
fireplaces, cable TV, DVDs, fax, free
WiFi access

Our 18 antique filled rooms and landscaped grounds offer distinctive accommodations in Pennsylvania's historic Lehigh Valley. Romantic suite getaways; family-friendly guestrooms.

✉ info@lafayetteinn.com 🌐 www.lafayetteinn.com

EPHRATA

Kimmell House B&B
851 S State St 17522
800-861-3385 717-738-3555
Dave & Bonnie Harvey

95-135 $US BB
4 rooms, 4 pb
Visa, MC, Disc
C-ltd/S-no/P-no/H-no

Full breakfast
Early coffee & afternoon tea available
Fireplace, patio and garden, private
baths, free wireless Internet, AC, open
hearth fireplace

Kimmell House B&B is a charming Georgian sandstone built in 1795 located in Ephrata, PA. The B&B offers four rooms and is conveniently located within minutes of historic areas, antique markets, shopping outlets, fine restaurants and wineries.

✉ info@kimmellhouse.com 🌐 www.kimmellhouse.com

The Hurst House
154 East Farmersville
Road 17522
800-603-9227 717-355-5151
Rich & Bert Hurst

130-180 $US BB
5 rooms, 5 pb
Visa, MC
C-ltd/S-ltd/P-no/H-yes
Pennsylvania Dutch

Full breakfast
Coffee, tea, hot chocolate and cookies
waiting for you in the Gathering Room
WiFi, fireplaces, A/C, exercise room,
accommodating business meetings &
parties, private balconies

We invite you to The Hurst House B&B, in Ephrata, Lancaster County, PA. An elegant Victorian Mansion located on top of the Katza Buckle overlooking hundreds of beautiful Amish & Old Order Mennonite farms in the heart of the Pennsylvania Dutch Country.

✉ TheHurstHouse@gmail.com 🌐 www.hursthousebedandbreakfast.com

Twin Pine Manor B&B
1934 W Main St 17522
888-266-0099 717-733-8400
Norm Kurtz

119-225 $US BB
8 rooms, 8 pb
Most CC, Cash
C-ltd/S-ltd/P-no/H-ltd
April to Mid-December

Full breakfast
Exercise room/sauna, Cable TV/DVD
players, Jacuzzis, Great room/piano,
Rec room/pool table, Internet

Twin Pine Manor is a spacious 15 room mansion with 8 guestrooms with private baths. Six rooms have Jacuzzis (for 2) and fireplaces. Located in the heart of Pennsylvania Dutch Country, we offer a countryside retreat setting for bed & breakfast guests.

✉ twinpinemanor@hotmail.com 🌐 www.twinpinemanor.com

ERIE

The Boothby Inn LLC
311 West 6th Street 16507
866-BOOTHBY 814-456-1888
Wally & Gloria Knox

130-170 $US BB
4 rooms, 4 pb
Most CC, *Rated*
S-no/P-no/H-no

Full breakfast
Ice machine, microwave, refrigerator
stocked with refreshments & snacks
and a coffee machine
Phone, wireless Internet, cable TV
w/ VCR, desk, CD player and new
exercise facility a walk away!

Experience the finest accommodations downtown Erie has to offer. Catering to the business traveler and vacationer, the Inn boasts warm and sophisticated hospitality.

✉ info@theboothbyinn.com 🌐 www.theboothbyinn.com

ERWINNA

Golden Pheasant Inn
763 River Rd 18920
800-830-4474 610-294-9595
Barbara & Michael Faure

95-225 $US BB
8 rooms, 8 pb
Visa, MC, *Rated*, •
C-ltd/S-ltd/P-ltd/H-ltd
French, Spanish, Italian

Continental plus breakfast
Dinner (Tuesday-Sunday), wine in
room
Restaurant, bar, canoes, Delaware
Canal & River, hiking/biking

1857 magical country bed and breakfast inn & restaurant situated between river and canal. The rooms are furnished with incredible blend of antiques. "A bite of France in Bucks County."

 barbara@goldenpheasant.com 🌐 www.goldenpheasant.com

The Boothby Inn LLC, Erie, PA

FAIRFIELD

The Historic Fairfield Inn	130-225 $US BB	Continental plus breakfast
15 W Main St 17320	6 rooms, 6 pb	Fine dining restaurant & casual tavern
717-642-5410	Most CC, Cash,	both serving lunch, brunch & dinner
Joan & Sal Chandon	*Rated*, •	in a historic stone inn
	C-yes/S-no/P-no/H-no	Civil War dinner theatre, banquets,
		conferences, history & underground
		RR tour, WiFi, whirlpools

A tradition of exceptional service, fine cuisine & luxury accommodations since the 1700's. Guestrooms & suites with private baths, A/C, TV, wireless Internet. On-site tavern & restaurant. 8 fireplaces during the winter and outdoor dining in summer.

 innkeeper@thefairfieldinn.com   🌐 www.thefairfieldinn.com

FRANKLIN

The Lamberton House	70-130 $US BB	Full breakfast
1331 Otter St 16323	5 rooms, 5 pb	Evening dinners are available at
866-632-7908 814-432-7908	Visa, MC, AmEx	an additional charge- advance
Mary & Jim Nicklin	C-yes/S-no/P-no/H-no	reservations required.
		Library, drawing room, wireless
		Internet

Restored 1874 Queen Anne Victorian mansion, a delightful refuge from the stress of modern life. Five gracious guest bedrooms with a full breakfast provided each morning. Located mid-way between Pittsburgh and Erie, PA. Event facilities for up to 40.

 info@lambertonhouse.com   🌐 lambertonhouse.com

GETTYSBURG

A Sentimental Journey B&B	85-99 $US BB	24 hour Continental breakfast
	6 rooms, 5 pb	Plus snacks on your schedule
431 Baltimore St 17325	Visa, MC, Disc	Cable TV, AC, queen beds, porch,
888-337-0779 717-420-0058	C-ltd/S-no/P-no/H-ltd	living room, free parking, 24 hr
Barbara & Steve Shultz		breakfast room, walk to everything

Nostalgic guestrooms in Gettysburg's historic district. Low rates plus discounts for weeknights, multiple nights or off-season. All rooms are unique and you are within walking distance to everything

 aceshigh@embarqmail.com   🌐 www.asentimentaljourneybb.com

GETTYSBURG

Baladerry Inn at Gettysburg	155-260 $US BB	Full country breakfast
40 Hospital Rd 17325	10 rooms, 10 pb	Baked Goods, Coffee and Tea
717-337-1342	Visa, MC, Disc,	Sitting room, library, fireplace,
Judy & Kenny Caudill	*Rated*, •	conferences, private bathrooms with
	C-ltd/S-ltd/P-no/H-no	showers, hiking and biking

Private, quiet, historic and spacious country location at the edge of the Gettysburg National Historic Park. Three miles from the center of town and ½ mile from the Visitor Center off of RT 97 look for Granite Schl House Road.

✉ innkeeper@baladerryinn.com   🌐 www.baladerryinn.com

Battlefield Bed & Breakfast	125-299 $US BB	Delicious full hot breakfast
2264 Emmitsburg Rd 17325	8 rooms, 8 pb	Afternoon cookies, lemonade, coffee,
888-766-3897 717-334-8804	Most CC, Cash, Checks,	and tea
Florence Tarbox	*Rated*, •	Daily Civil War history programs, WiFi,
	C-yes/S-no/P-yes/H-yes	TV, fireplaces, romance packages, row boat, petting zoo

Our Civil War home and private 30 acre location makes us especially suitable for history travelers, families with children, and travelers with pets. We host weddings, receptions, and commitments in our historic barn and gardens. We are the friendly inn!

✉ battlefieldbnb@gmail.com   🌐 www.gettysburgbattlefield.com

Brickhouse Inn	115-184 $US BB	Full breakfast
452 Baltimore St 17325	14 rooms, 14 pb	Lemonade, mulled cider, homemade
800-864-3464 717-338-9337	Visa, MC, Disc,	sweets, cookies
Tessa Bardo & Brian Duncan	*Rated*, •	Sitting rooms, beautiful garden, easy
	C-ltd/S-ltd/P-no/H-ltd	walk to restaurants, museums, shops and battlefield

1898 brick Victorian & adjacent c.1830 bullet-scarred historic Welty House, nestled in the historic district. Walk to battlefields, great restaurants, antique and gift shops.

✉ stay@brickhouseinn.com   🌐 www.brickhouseinn.com

Inn at Herr Ridge	169-259 $US BB	Full breakfast
900 Chambersburg Rd 17325	16 rooms, 16 pb	Gourmet Fine Dining & Casual Upscale
800-362-9849 717-334-4332	Most CC, Cash,	Spa services: massages, manicures &
Steven Wolf	*Rated*, •	pedicures
	C-ltd/S-no/P-no/H-ltd	

The enchanting atmosphere of the Inn at Herr Ridge is unforgettable. The inn offers a rare experience to every guest who crosses the threshold, and it is only minutes from town. If you are searching for a relaxing and romantic getaway, search no further!

✉ info@herrtavern.com   🌐 www.herrtavern.com

James Gettys Hotel	140-250 $US BB	Continental breakfast
27 Chambersburg St 17325	12 rooms, 12 pb	Fresh ground coffee & imported
888-900-5275 717-337-1334	Most CC, Cash, Checks,	British teas, homemade cookies and
Stephanie Stephan	*Rated*	fresh chocolates with turndown
	C-yes/S-no/P-no/H-yes	Suites, wireless Internet service, cable
	French	TV, telephones, kitchenettes, and all conveniences of home

This fully renovated circa 1804 historic hotel in downtown Gettysburg offers twelve tastefully appointed suites with living rooms, kitchenettes, bedroom and private bath. Gracious amenities, warm hospitality and exceptional service.

✉ info@jamesgettyshotel.com   🌐 www.jamesgettyshotel.com

Keystone Inn	99-169 $US BB	Full breakfast
231 Hanover St 17325	7 rooms, 7 pb	Coffee, tea, afternoon snacks
717-337-3888	Most CC, Cash, Checks,	Parlor, extensive library
Michael & Marjorie Day	*Rated*	
	C-yes/S-no/P-no/H-ltd	

A wonderful late Victorian. Great house near the historic battlefields. Lovely flower gardens. Comfort is our priority. Country breakfasts.

✉ keystoneinn@comcast.net   🌐 www.keystoneinnbb.com

GETTYSBURG ──────────────────────────────

| **The Gaslight Inn**
33 East Middle Street 17325
800-914-5698 717-337-9100
Mike & Becky Hansen | 115-170 $US BB
9 rooms, 9 pb
Most CC, Cash, Checks,
Rated, •
C-ltd/S-ltd/P-no/H-yes | Full breakfast
Snackbar stocked with soda, hot water
for tea, coffee & hot choc., spring
water & beer, and sweets.
Sitting room, library, Jacuzzis,
fireplaces, cable, conference room,
WiFi, handicap accessible room. |

Luxurious touches, wonderful outdoor living spaces & gardens, & the best food in town are compli-
mented by hosts' who are anxious to help you make your visit to Gettysburg memorable.

✉ info@thegaslightinn.com   🌐 www.thegaslightinn.com

| **The Inn at White Oak**
1 White Oak Trail 17325
866-500-7072 717-334-8448 | 175-249 $US BB
5 rooms, 5 pb
Most CC, Cash, Checks
C-ltd/S-ltd/P-no/H-ltd | Delicious, Full breakfast
Afternoon treats with hot and cold
beverages and snacks 24 hrs. in our
Guest Kitchen.
Full Spa, WiFi ,Cable TVs, Luxury
linens, Jacuzzi's, Fireplaces, Packages,
12 Common Rooms, 30 Acres |

A grand Gettysburg Estate and Spa with gracious accommodations surrounded by luxury, romance,
tranquility and Gettysburg's history on 30 private acres of gardens, ponds, pasture, woodlands and
waterfalls. Just minutes from all of the historic attractions!

✉ info@innatwhiteoak.com   🌐 www.InnatWhiteOak.com

GLEN MILLS ──────────────────────────────

| **Sweetwater Farm**
50 Sweetwater Rd 19342
800-793-3892 610-459-4711
Sean & Farrell Kramer | 150-370 $US BB
14 rooms, 14 pb
Visa, MC
C-ltd/S-no/P-ltd/H-no | Full breakfast
Billiard room, library, swimming pool,
fitness center, massage |

1734 stone mansion on 50 manicured acres. Seven elegantly decorated rooms in the main house with
fireplaces & canopied beds. There are 7 cottages – 5 of which are child and pet friendly.

✉ info@sweetwaterfarmbb.com   🌐 www.sweetwaterfarmbb.com

GORDONVILLE ──────────────────────────────

| **After Eight B&B**
2942 Lincoln Hwy E 17529
888-314-3664 717-687-3664
Robert Hall | 109-200 $US BB
10 rooms, 10 pb
Most CC, Cash, *Rated*
C-ltd/S-ltd/P-no/H-ltd | Full breakfast
Coffee, tea, fruit, fruit drinks, sodas,
water and snacks throughout the day
Sitting room, antique decor, game
table, guest Internet, WiFi, gardens,
fountains, gazebo |

Renovated Colonial brick home from 1809, in the center of the Pennsylvania Dutch, Amish heartland.
Elegantly decorated and antique filled guestrooms with modern amenities and private baths.

✉ info@aftereightbnb.com   🌐 www.aftereightbnb.com

HANOVER ──────────────────────────────

| **Beechmont Inn**
315 Broadway 17331
800-553-7009 717-632-3013
Kathryn & Thomas White | 119-174 $US BB
7 rooms, 7 pb
Most CC, Cash, Checks,
Rated, •
C-ltd/S-no/P-no/H-yes | Full breakfast
Help yourself cookie jar with
homemade cookies, soft drinks,
bottled water
Wireless Internet, guest computer
station, library, in-room telephones,
fax, copier, guest fridge |

Selected as Pennsylvania's Innkeeper of the Year 2009, the Whites extend excellent hospitality to each
guest. Whether on vacation, a wedding, or business, enjoy comfortable rooms and hearty breakfasts
designed to create treasured memories of your stay.

✉ innkeeper@thebeechmont.com   🌐 www.thebeechmont.com

HANOVER

Sheppard Mansion
117 Frederick St 17331
877-762-6746 717-633-8075
Timothy Bobb, GM

140-250 $US BB
5 rooms, 5 pb
Most CC, *Rated*
C-ltd/S-no/P-no/H-no

Full breakfast
Fine Dining in our Restaurant, Weds
thru Saturday nights
Cable TV, WiFi, Express Check-In/Out,
Event & Meeting Space

Restored to its original elegance and splendor, our 1913 neo-classical mansion located in the historic district is perfect for a romantic getaway or the weary business traveler. Delectable menu, full bar and wine list, and excellent service await you.
✉ kathryn@sheppardmansion.com ◐ www.sheppardmansion.com

HERSHEY

1825 Inn Bed & Breakfast
409 S Lingle Ave 17078
877-738-8282 717-838-8282
Will McQueen

114-239 $US BB
8 rooms, 8 pb
Most CC, Cash, •
C-ltd/S-no/P-no/H-no

Full breakfast
Evening homemade treat with snacks,
hot cocoa, tea's & hot cider
Gardens, enclosed Breakfast Porch,
parlor, gazebo

Our historical Inn offers you the tranquility and comfort of the country along with lovely gardens and inviting surroundings. The Cottages are perfect for a honeymoon getaway. We are also near to all the Hershey city conveniences.   ✉ info@1825inn.com ◐ www.1825inn.com

Berry Patch
115 Moore Rd 17046
888-246-8826 717-865-7219
Bunny Yinger

129-229 $US BB
7 rooms, 7 pb
Most CC, Cash
S-ltd/P-ltd/H-ltd

Full breakfast
Snacks – cookies, crackers, popcorn,
etc.
Weddings, parties, Jacuzzi, fireplaces,
patio, cable TV, VCR, gourmet gifts,
wireless Internet

The Berry Patch Bed and Breakfast is pleased to offer a variety of Lebanon, PA accommodations. We invite our guests to choose one of the beautifully decorated guestrooms from our Pennsylvania Dutch Country Inn. ✉ bunny@berrypatchbnb.com ◐ www.berrypatchbnb.com

HUMMELSTOWN

The Inn at Westwynd Farm
1620 Sand Beach Rd 17036
877-937-8996 717-533-6764
Carolyn Troxell

109-189 $US BB
10 rooms, 10 pb
Most CC, Cash, •
C-ltd/S-no/P-no/H-yes

Full breakfast
Afternoon refreshments, snacks,
complimentary bottled water, sodas,
wine & beer
Sitting rooms, library, Jacuzzis,
fireplaces, cable TV, WiFi, guest
computer, horse farm

An unforgettable bed and breakfast experience amidst rolling hills, horses and pastures. Enjoy lovely country views, gourmet breakfasts and comforting amenities accented by antiques, fireplaces and luxurious linens. ✉ innkeeper@westwyndfarminn.com ◐ www.westwyndfarminn.com

HUNTINGDON

The Inn at Solvang
301A Stonecreek Rd (Rte
26) 16652
888-814-3035 814-643-3035
Stephanie Lane

100-135 $US BB
5 rooms, 5 pb
Visa, MC, AmEx,
Rated
C-ltd/S-no/P-no/H-yes

Full 3-course breakfast
Sitting room, library, deck, cable
TV, music room, 3rd floor terrace,
conference facilities

The Inn at Solvang is a gracious, secluded, southern Colonial style house noted for exceptional gourmet breakfasts. Unwind, enjoy a stroll through our woods, fish our private trout stream at Stone Creek, or play 18 holes at Standing Stone Golf Course.
✉ innkeeper@solvang.com ◐ www.solvang.com

INTERCOURSE

Carriage Corner
3705 E Newport Rd 17534
800-209-3059 717-768-3059
Gordon & Gwen Schuit

68-99 $US BB
5 rooms, 5 pb
Visa, MC, *Rated*, •
C-ltd/S-no/P-no/H-no

Full breakfast
Afternoon tea available, use of guest
refrigerator
Common room, central A/C, library,
cable TV, gazebo, outdoor deck,
bathrobes, wireless Internet

Located in the hub of the Amish farmland and tourist area in a relaxing country atmosphere. Dinner with an Amish family can be arranged. The B&B is a unique blend of hospitality, laughter and kindness. ✉ gschuit@comcast.net ◐ www.carriagecornerbandb.com

INTERCOURSE

The Inn & Spa at Intercourse Village
3542 Old Philadelphia Pike 17534
800-664-0949 717-768-2626
Ruthann Thomas

159-399 $US BB
9 rooms, 9 pb
Most CC, Cash, *Rated*
S-no/P-no/H-no

5 Course Candlelit Breakfast
Fruit, pretzels, sodas, coffee & tea
Grand Suites w/Jacuzzi for Two,
Separate sitting Room, Gas burning
fireplaces, cable TV, WiFi

Winner of the "Top Ten Romantic Inns" Award. A Romantic Inn & Spa for Couples in the Historic Village of Intercourse. K/Q beds, private in-suite baths, gas burning fireplaces, Grand Honeymoon suites with Jacuzzi for two. ✉ innkeeper@inn-spa.com ○ www.inn-spa.com

JIM THORPE

The Inn at Jim Thorpe
24 Broadway 18229
800-329-2599 570-325-2599
David Drury

103-259 $US BB
49 rooms, 49 pb
Most CC, *Rated*, •
C-yes/S-no/P-no/H-yes

Continental plus breakfast
Full hot breakfast buffet on the
weekend. New Broadway Grille & Pub!
Spa services, whirlpools, fireplaces,
balcony, game room, bike storage.

Nestled in the folds of several dramatic mountains, Jim Thorpe is one of the country's most scenic and historic towns. Our historic hotel is one of our town's landmark treasures.

✉ reservations@innjt.com ○ www.innjt.com

LAHASKA

Golden Plough Inn of Peddler's Village
Route 202 & Street Rd 18931
215-794-4004
Matthew Knol

165-470 $US BB
71 rooms, 71 pb
Most CC, Cash, Checks,
Rated, •
C-yes/S-ltd/P-no/H-ltd

Continental breakfast
Restaurant for lunch, dinner, bar
service, snacks
Library, fireplaces, cable TV, Day spa,
accommodates motor coach travelers,
shopping

Free Night w/Certificate: January-April 2012; Sunday-Friday.

Beautifully appointed rooms throughout charming, landscaped shopping village. Pampering amenities & warm, genuine service. Coffee, tea, bottled water & refrigerators in all rooms.
✉ lodging@peddlersvillage.com ○ www.goldenploughinn.com

LANCASTER

Apple Bin Inn
2835 Willow Street
Pike 17584
800-338-4296 717-464-5881
Steve & Jamie Shane

99-199 $US BB
5 rooms, 5 pb
Most CC, Cash
C-yes/S-no/P-no

Full country breakfast
Complimentary soft drinks & snacks
Library, cable TV with DVD, wireless
Internet access, free parking, private
cottage with fireplace

In the heart of Lancaster County & PA Dutch Country, our inn features 5 delightful guestrooms and scrumptious breakfasts! Just minutes from "Sight & Sound" Theatre, Strasburg Railroad, outlet malls, quilt & antique shopping, and all Amish attractions!
✉ stay@AppleBinInn.com ○ www.AppleBinInn.com

Australian Walkabout Inn
837 Village Rd 17602
888-WALKABT 717-464-0707
Lynne & Bob Griffin

109-269 $US BB
5 rooms, 5 pb
Visa, MC, *Rated*
C-ltd/S-no/P-no/H-no

Full breakfast
Complimentary beverages
In-room whirlpools/hot tub, fireplaces,
TV/DVD, mini fridge, bathrobes

Built in 1925 by a famous local master cabinet maker, featuring superior construction methods such as native chestnut pocket doors and inlaid flooring. Large front porch with inviting swing. Luxury suites, cozy rooms, cottages, all with private baths.
✉ stay@walkaboutinn.com ○ www.walkaboutinn.com

King's Cottage B&B
1049 E King St 17602
800-747-8717 717-397-1017
Janis Kutterer, Ann Willets

160-295 $US BB
8 rooms, 8 pb
Visa, MC, AmEx, •
C-ltd/S-no/P-no/H-ltd

Full Gourmet Breakfast
Afternoon refreshments
Massage room, 47 jet therapeutic
Spa/Hot Tub, sunroom, piano, guest
kitchen, water garden, patio,

A Top 10 Most Romantic Inn, in the heart of PA Dutch Country. An elegant B&B with whirlpools, fireplaces and gourmet breakfasts. Resident Massage therapist available to guests. Near Amish farms, antique & quilt shops, outlets & Sight & Sound Theater.
✉ info@kingscottagebb.com ○ www.kingscottagebb.com

LANCASTER

Pheasant Run Farm B&B	125-175 $US BB	Full breakfast
200 Marticville Rd 17603	4 rooms, 4 pb	Coffee & tea
717-872-0991	Visa, MC, AmEx	Reception room, rose gardens, porch
Bob & Vivian Abel	C-ltd/S-no/P-no/H-ltd	

Pheasant Run Farm is a beautifully converted barn B&B in picturesque Lancaster County. The bed and breakfast features four rooms with private baths and combines today's modern luxuries with the barn's original architectural features.

✉ vivianbob@earthlink.net   🌐 www.pheasantrunfarmbb.com

Silverstone Inn & Suites	149-289 $US BB	Homemade Fresh 2 course breakfast
62 Bowman Rd 17602	8 rooms, 8 pb	Bar snacks & complimentary drinks
877-290-6987 717-290-6987	Most CC, Cash,	Events, marble bathrooms, flat-screen
Toni & Lorin Wortel	*Rated*, •	TV/DVD, free WiFi, individual heat/
	C-ltd/S-ltd/P-no/H-ltd	AC, unique decor, gardens
	Dutch	

Welcome to Silverstone Inn and Suites B&B! A romantic and award-winning historic limestone house c. 1750, nestled quietly in the heart of the Amish area of Lancaster County, PA, on its own 15 acre maple syrup and sheep farm. Eight rooms and suites.

✉ toni@theplacetostay.com   🌐 www.silverstoneinn.com

LEWISBURG

Pineapple Inn	145-185 $US BB	Full country breakfast
439 Market St 17837	5 rooms, 5 pb	Complimentary tea, snacks
570-524-6200	Most CC, Cash, Checks,	A/C, pool nearby, piano, tea room,
Charles & Deborah North	*Rated*	sitting room, tennis, wonderful
	C-yes/S-no/P-no/H-no	restaurants, wireless Internet
	German	

The beautifully restored 1857 Federal Victorian home rests in the Historic District. Just blocks from Bucknell University. Susquehanna University and Penn State University are a short but scenic drive form the inn. Beautiful architecture, great antiquing.

✉ pineappleinn@dejazzd.com   🌐 www.pineappleinnbnb.com

LIGONIER

Campbell House B&B	90-165 $US BB	Full breakfast
305 E Main St 15658	6 rooms, 6 pb	Complimentary snacks & beverages
888-238-9812 724-238-9812	Most CC, *Rated*, •	House phone, fax, High speed wireless
Patti Campbell	S-no/P-no/H-no	Internet

Charming accommodations, with a Victorian & eclectic flavor, await those who long for a smoke-free, peaceful retreat, a romantic interlude, or are visiting the Laurel Highlands.

✉ innkeeper@campbellhousebnb.com   🌐 www.campbellhousebnb.com

LINFIELD

Shearer Elegance B&B	109-165 $US BB	Full breakfast
1154 Main St 19468	7 rooms, 7 pb	private baths, Jacuzzi tubs, WiFi, TV,
800-861-0308 610-495-7429	Most CC, Cash, Checks,	massage therapy, venue for weddings,
Sue Tator	*Rated*, •	parties, showers
	C-ltd/S-no/P-no/H-ltd	

10,000 sq. ft. Victorian with 3 acres of gardens in summer, and 35 decorated Christmas trees in winter. After more than 10 years serving travelers and vacationers in the suburban Philadelphia area, Shearer Elegance Bed & Breakfast is bigger and better than ever.

✉ contact@shearerelegance.com   🌐 www.shearerelegance.com

LITITZ

Speedwell Forge B&B	125-250 $US BB	Full breakfast
465 Speedwell Forge	5 rooms, 5 pb	Whirlpool tubs, fireplaces, private
Road 17543	Most CC, Cash,	bath, antique furnishings, sitting areas
877-378-1760 717-626-1760	Checks, •	and more.
Dawn Darlington	C-ltd/S-no/P-no/H-no	

Built in 1760 on 120 acres, and listed on the National Register of Historic Places. We offer 3 elegant guestrooms and 2 cottages, all with private baths, central air, and wireless Internet. Many rooms include a fireplace, whirlpool tub, and kitchenette.

✉ stay@speedwellforge.com   🌐 www.speedwellforge.com

LOCK HAVEN

Aurora Leigh Bed and Breakfast 302 W Church St 17745 570-748-6530 Tracy & Peter	95-155 $US BB 4 rooms, 4 pb Most CC, Cash C-yes/S-no/P-no/H-no	Full Three Course Breakfast High Tea every afternoon includes sandwiches, sweets, teas and other drinks. Wireless Internet, housekeeping with green program, concierge service, off street parking, high tea.

Welcome to the Aurora Leigh Bed & Breakfast, a 27-room Queen Anne Victorian mansion in historic Lock Haven, gateway to the Pennsylvania Wilds. We are 3½ hours away from Pittsburgh, Philadelphia, and New York City and only minutes from the scenic beauty.

✉ owners@auroraleighbandb.com 🌐 www.auroraleighbandb.com

LORETTO

Spring Hill Bed and Breakfast 246 Spring Hill Lane 15940 814-886-2020 Kathy & Larry Hoover	105-125 $US BB 3 rooms, 3 pb Visa, MC, Disc C-ltd/S-no/P-no/H-no April 1st – December 1st	Gourmet Breakfast Complimentary refreshment upon arrival, coffee, tea, soft drinks and homemade dessert. Wifi throughout property, private bath, wonderfully appointed rooms, Carriage House.

Welcome! Spring Hill B&B is located in Loretto, Pennsylvania, overlooking the neighboring ridges, and minutes away from St. Francis University and Mount Aloysius College. Come and enjoy the relaxing atmosphere and pleasant getaway of Spring Hill B&B.

✉ info@springhillBB.com 🌐 www.springhillbb.com

MANHEIM

Rose Manor 124 S Linden St 17545 800-666-4932 717-664-4932 Susan	99-140 $US BB 5 rooms, 4 pb Visa, MC, *Rated*, • C-ltd/S-no/P-no/H-no	Full breakfast Complimentary sherry Picnic baskets, sitting room, gardens, gift shop

Lancaster County 1905 manor house. Comfortable, elegant English manor house decor & cooking reflect herbal theme. Surrounded by rose & herb gardens. Full breakfast included.

✉ rosemanor@paonline.com 🌐 www.rosemanor.net

MARIETTA

B.F. Hiestand House B&B 722 E Market St 17547 877-560-8415 717-426-8415 Pam & Dallas Fritz	110-250 $US BB 6 rooms, 6 pb Most CC, Cash, Checks C-ltd/S-no/P-ltd/H-ltd	Full breakfast Complementary after work beverage and munchies Cable TV w/DVD, private baths w/ whirlpool tubs steam showers video library, veranda, fireplaces, A/C

An historic 1887 High Queen Anne Victorian. Experience the elegance of a bygone era. Enjoy breakfast in our charming dining room. Exquisite parlors with 12-foot ceilings, pocket doors and fireplaces.

✉ info@bfhiestandhouse.com 🌐 www.bfhiestandhouse.com

Lavender Patch 190 Longenecker Ave 17547 717-426-4533 Marian & Chet Miller	115-125 $US BB 3 rooms, 3 pb Visa, MC C-yes/S-no/P-no/H-ltd	Full breakfast Afternoon tea WiFi, pool, gazebo & gardens, cable TV & VCR

Welcome to the charming Lavender Patch Bed and Breakfast in Marietta, Lancaster County, Pennsylvania. With an eye for detail, this lovely home features 3 rooms, delicious breakfast, afternoon tea, pool, hand painted decorative walls and gardens.

✉ lavpatch@desupernet.net 🌐 www.lavenderpatch.com

MCCLURE

Mountain Dale Farm 330 Hassinger Way 17841 570-658-3536 Ken & Sally Hassinger	50-90 $US EP 12 rooms, 10 pb Visa, MC C-yes/S-ltd/P-no/H-no	Meals may be provided if schedule permits, but only with prior arrangements, extra charge for meals Kitchen available for guest use, individual cabins offer privacy

If you're looking for a wholesome, family-oriented environment for overnight lodging, an extended vacation, family reunion or other special event then you've come to the right place. Scenic rolling country, animals, fishing, hiking. ✉ mountaindale@mountaindale.net 🌐 www.mountaindale.net

MCCONNELLSBURG

Crampton Manor B&B
270 Country Lane 17233
717-491-2813
Linda & Michael Crampton

75-135 $US BB
5 rooms, 4 pb
C-ltd/S-no/P-no/H-no

Full breakfast
Please advise us in advance of any
dietary restrictions
Wireless high speed Internet, porch,
private entrance, cathedral ceiling, TV,
kitchen, fireplace

Crampton Manor B&B is a private, mountain retreat located on 100 breathtaking acres. Comprised of The Main House, The Hayloft and The Carriage House. All of our accommodations offer heat and A/C with ceiling fans and free wireless Internet.

✉ cramptonmanor@embarqmail.com   ◐ www.cramptonmanor.com

MERCERSBURG

The Mercersburg Inn
405 S Main St 17236
866-628-7401 717-328-5231
Lisa & Jim McCoy

140-395 $US BB
17 rooms, 17 pb
Visa, MC, Disc,
Rated, •
C-ltd/S-no/P-no/H-no
Russian

Full breakfast – 3 course gourmet
Byron's Dining Room on premise; fine
dining Thurs-Sun, full bar, fireplaces

A stately, 20,000 sq ft Georgian mansion on 5 acres of terraced lawns. Once the private residence of Ione & Harry Byron, the home is now a 17 guestroom country inn.

✉ lisa@mercersburginn.com   ◐ www.mercersburginn.com

MOUNT JOY

Hillside Farm
607 Eby Chiques Rd 17552
888-249-3406 717-653-6697
Gary Lintner

90-250 $US BB
5 rooms, 5 pb
Most CC, *Rated*, •
C-ltd/S-no/P-no/H-no

Full breakfast
Afternoon & evening snacks
Sitting room, book library, baby grand
piano, A/C, 6-person spa, balcony

A quiet, secluded, bed & breakfast, farm stay located in the heart of Lancaster, Pennsylvania Amish Country. Overlooks Chickies Creek with dam and waterfall and entirely surrounded by working farms.

✉ innkeeper@hillsidefarmbandb.com   ◐ www.hillsidefarmbandb.com

NAZARETH

**Classic Victorian Estate
Inn**
35 N New St 18064
610-759-8276
Irene & Danny Sokolowski

105-240 $US BB
4 rooms, 4 pb
Visa, MC, AmEx,
Rated
C-yes/S-no/P-no/H-ltd

Full breakfast
Low fat-special diet
Historic District, private baths,
corporate rates, feather duvets,
fireplace

You need a place to stay that is relaxing and private. Bring yourself to a well deserved renewal. Come and be pampered with a gourmet breakfast and turn-of-the-century ambience.

✉ clasicvictorianbnb@msn.com   ◐ www.classicvictorianbnb.com

NEW HOPE

1790 Pineapple Hill Inn
1324 River Rd 18938
888-866-8404 215-862-1790
Kathryn & Charles "Cookie"
Triolo

94-249 $US BB
9 rooms, 9 pb
Most CC, *Rated*, •
C-ltd/S-no/P-no/H-no

Full breakfast
Afternoon tea, snacks, evening sherry
Sitting room, library, pool, cable
TV, fireplaces, telephones, wireless
Internet

Enjoy the charm of a beautifully restored, Colonial manor house built in 1790. Set on almost 6 acres, this Bucks County B&B rests between New Hope's center and Washington Crossing Park.

✉ innkeeper@pineapplehill.com   ◐ www.pineapplehill.com

**1870 Wedgwood Bed &
Breakfast Inn of New
Hope, PA**
111 W Bridge St 18938
215-862-2570
Carl & Nadine Glassman

95-325 $US BB
10 rooms, 10 pb
Visa, MC, AmEx,
Rated, •
C-yes/S-ltd/P-yes/H-yes
French, Hebrew, Dutch,
Italian

Continental plus breakfast in bed
Guest Pantry available 24/7, Hot/
cold drinks, just-baked cookies, hard
candies & fruit, Saturday Tea
Victorian gazebo, double Jacuzzis,
inroom massage, fireplaces, Snack
baskets, WiFi, breakfast in bed

Bucks County New Hope, Pa Victorian bed and breakfast inn. 1989 "Inn Of The Year!" On 2 private, park-like acres in New Hope. Open year round. Walk to vibrant village center just steps away from Inn. Gracious accommodations with all modern amenities: WiFi

 stay@WedgwoodInn.com   ◐ www.WedgwoodInn.com

Fox and Hound B&B, New Hope, PA

NEW HOPE

Fox and Hound B&B of New Hope
246 W Bridge St 18938
215-862-5082
Lisa Menz

95-195 $US BB
8 rooms, 8 pb
Visa, MC, Disc, *Rated*
C-ltd/S-no/P-no/H-no
French, Spanish, German

Full hot gourmet breakfast
Afternoon refreshments
A/C, cable TV, some w/ fireplace, private patio, balcony/sundeck, WiFi, parking, conference room

Elegant 1840 stone farmhouse. Short walk to New Hope & Lambertville, near all Bucks County attractions. All rooms with private bath, A/C, some with fireplace, patio, balcony or sundeck. Reduced midweek rates. Wireless Internet.

✉ innkeeper@foxhoundinn.com 🌐 foxhoundinn.com

Wishing Well Guest House
144 Old York Rd 18938
215-862-8819
Dan Brooks

99-150 $US BB
6 rooms, 6 pb
Visa, MC
C-yes/S-ltd/P-ltd/H-yes

Full on Wkends, Continental M-F
Afternoon brings lemonade or tea, and later a late night snack.
Roof deck, garden, patio, fireplaces, dining area, living room

The property originally functioned as a farm and owned all of the surrounding land to the south. In contrast to city life, you'll find that our "home sweet home," is a beacon of tranquility.

✉ wishingwell8819@comcast.net 🌐 www.wishingwellguesthouse.com

NEW OXFORD

Chestnut Hall B&B
104 Lincoln Way West 17350
888-886-5660 717-624-8988
Tina & Steve McNaughton

115-160 $US BB
4 rooms, 4 pb
Visa, MC, *Rated*
C-ltd/S-no/P-no/H-no

Full breakfast
Snacks & beverages, daily afternoon baked snack
Private bath, plush robes, cable TV, A/C, electric controlled fireplace, gardens, wireless Internet

Chestnut Hall is embodied in Victorian style at its finest. Our Mission is to offer you the opportunity and setting to be transported back in time to relive the mood and elegance of the late 19th century with all the comforts and amenities of today.

✉ chestnuthallbb@yahoo.com 🌐 www.chestnuthallbb.com

NEW TRIPOLI

Dockside B&B
6089 Herring Ct 18066
610-698-2448
Robert & Donna Herring

120-195 $US BB
4 rooms, 4 pb
Visa, MC
C-ltd/S-no/P-no/H-ltd

Full breakfast
Snacks, fruit, soda, bottled water
Deck, waterfront, Jacuzzis, compact refrigerators, Internet access, A/C, fresh flowers

Every effort has been made for our guests to enjoy a quiet, comfortable, and memorable stay. Take a stroll around our 6 acre waterfront property, or just rest in the gentle breeze and enjoy the view from our three level deck

✉ herringr@ptd.net 🌐 www.docksidebed.com

NORTH EAST

Grape Arbor B&B
51 E Main St 16428
866-725-0048 814-725-0048
Dave & Peggy Hauser

95-175 $US BB
8 rooms, 8 pb
Visa, MC, Disc
C-ltd/S-ltd/P-no/H-ltd

Full breakfast
Free beverages & treats
Library with games, videos, outside
patio & porch, free wireless, Jacuzzi
tubs, kitchen facilities

Two neighboring historic 1830s brick mansions. Elegant rooms and suites with private baths, antiques, some with Jacuzzi or private entrance. Four-course breakfast and many special touches.

✉ grapearborbandb@aol.com 🌐 www.grapearborbandb.com

ORRTANNA

Hickory Bridge Farm
96 Hickory Bridge Rd 17353
717-642-5261
Robert & Mary Lynn Martin

115-165 $US BB
9 rooms, 8 pb
Visa, MC, Disc, *Rated*
C-ltd/S-no/P-no/H-ltd

Full breakfast
Dinner available Fri.& Sat. evenings,
Sunday's midday. Banquets,
Rehearsals, Weddings & Elopements.
Whirlpools, wood burning fireplaces,
fishing, country store, farm museum,8
miles west of Gettysburg

Relax in the country by enjoying a cozy cottage by the stream, a hearty breakfast at the farmhouse, and dining in restored PA barn on weekends. Historic and romantic setting.

✉ info@hickorybridgefarm.com 🌐 www.hickorybridgefarm.com

PHILADELPHIA

Morris House Hotel
225 S 8th St 19106
215-922-2446
Gabriela Buresova

179-389 $US BB
15 rooms, 15 pb
Most CC
C-yes/S-no/P-no/H-no

Continental breakfast
An Afternoon Tea
A/C, CD, clock radio, TV/DVD,
wireless Internet, garden, sitting room,
library, suites, antiques

This registered national historic landmark has been renovated into a luxury boutique hotel which offers the coziness of a bed and breakfast, in an 18th century setting, combined with the luxuries of today.

✉ info@morrishousehotel.com 🌐 www.morrishousehotel.com

Silverstone B&B
8840 Stenton Ave 19118
800-347-6858 215-242-3333
Yolanta Roman

115-155 $US BB
3 rooms, 3 pb
Visa, MC, *Rated*
C-yes/S-no/P-no/H-ltd
Polish, French

Full breakfast
Cable TV, VCR in rooms, wireless
Internet, swimming pool, fitness
center, Tempur-Pedic mattresses

This stunning Victorian Gothic B&B is located in historic Chestnut Hill and features spacious bedrooms with private baths, a kitchen and a laundry room for guests, and an elevator. We are in walking distance to shops, restaurants and the train.

✉ yolanta@silverstonestay.com 🌐 www.silverstonestay.com

The Gables B&B
4520 Chester Ave 19143
215-662-1918
Warren Cederholm & Don
Caskey

125-225 $US BB
10 rooms, 8 pb
Most CC, •
C-ltd/S-no/P-no/H-no

Full breakfast
Snacks
Sitting room, fireplaces, cable TV,
business travelers, private phones,
WiFi, computer station, iron

One of Pennsylvania's finest, restored Victorian mansions. Winner of the Historic Preservation Award. Near University of PA, Drexel University, hospitals and museums, 12 minutes to center city Philadelphia by easy public transportation. Free Parking.

✉ gables@gablesbb.com 🌐 www.gablesbb.com

The Thomas Bond House B&B
129 South 2nd St 19106
800-845-2663 215-923-8523
Dan Weese

115-190 $US BB
12 rooms, 12 pb
Most CC, Cash, Checks,
Rated, •
C-ltd/S-no/P-no/H-no

Full breakfast
Full breakfast weekends, continental
plus weekdays, evening wine &
cheese, fresh baked cookies
Hairdryer, TV, phone, fireplace,
whirlpool, local calls, free WiFi

Circa 1769, listed in National Register. Individually decorated rooms. Only lodging in Independence National Historical Park. One of top 25 historic inns, AAA & Mobile rated.

 info@thomasbondhousebandb.com 🌐 www.thomasbondhousebandb.com

PITTSBURGH

Morning Glory Inn	155-450 $US BB	Full breakfast
2119 Sarah St 15203	6 rooms, 6 pb	Wine
412-431-1707	Most CC, Cash, •	Sitting room, library, bicycles, suites,
Nancy Eshelman	C-yes/S-ltd/P-ltd/H-yes	fireplaces, conferences, cable TV,
		WiFi, fax/copy machine

Tucked away in the city's South Side, Pittsburg, PA's most eclectic, diverse and dynamic neighborhood, is a delightful discovery: an 1862 Italianate style Victorian brick townhouse since 1996 a downtown Pittsburgh B&B, the Morning Glory Inn.

✉ nancy@gloryinn.com 🌐 www.gloryinn.com

The Priory Hotel	140-240 $US BB	Continental plus breakfast
614 Pressley St 15212	42 rooms, 42 pb	Complimentary wine & snacks
866-377-4679 412-231-3338	Most CC, *Rated*, •	Honor bar, cable TV, accommodations
John Graf	C-yes/S-no/P-no/H-ltd	for business travelers, WiFi

A European style hotel in Pittsburgh with 42 guestrooms, carefully restored to Victorian elegance. Offers the modern amenities of a larger facility and the charm and personal service that only a small boutique hotel can offer.

✉ info@thepriory.com 🌐 www.thepriory.com

POINT PLEASANT

Tattersall Inn	130-215 $US BB	Full breakfast by fireplace/patio
37 River Rd, Rt 32 18950	6 rooms, 6 pb	On weekends, afternoon tea & light
800-297-4988 215-297-8233	Visa, MC, *Rated*	snack, complimentary glass of wine
John & Lori Gleason	C-ltd/S-no/P-no/H-no	1750s Common Room, walk-in
		fireplace, multiple porches, gardens,
		A/C, TV, wireless Internet

Beautiful, historic c. 1753 manor home. Porches, fireplaces, antiques, breakfast, tea, private baths. Centrally located in Bucks County by the Delaware River, within 7–8 miles to New Hope, Lambertville, Frenchtown, Peddler's Village and Doylestown.

✉ info@tattersallinn.com 🌐 www.tattersallinn.com

READING

B&B on the Park	129-249 $US BB	Continental plus breakfast
1246 Hill Rd 19602	5 rooms, 4 pb	Antiques, parlor, chandeliers, porch,
610-374-4440	Most CC	cable TV, A/C, & WiFi
George & Cindy Heminitz	C-ltd/S-no/P-no/H-ltd	

We would like to invite you to come to Reading, PA, to relax in our gracious hospitality with Victorian style at Bed & Breakfast on the Park. ✉ parkbandb@comcast.net 🌐 www.parkbandb.com

ROCKWOOD

The Gingerbread House	80-95 $US BB	Full breakfast
B&B	5 rooms, 2 pb	Snacks and drinks always available
156 Rockdale Rd 15557	C-ltd/S-no/P-no/H-no	High speed Internet, comfortable
814-926-2542		rooms, private baths available
Marianne Shurtz		

A lovely 1903 Victorian Home with wrap around porch. near the Allegheny Passage Trailhead, just a short drive from Seven Springs and Hidden Valley Mountain Resorts. Also near Frank Lloyd Wright's Falling Water and Kentucky Knob.

✉ mshurtz@shol.com 🌐 thegingerbreadhousebandb.com/contact.html

Trenthouse Inn	87-169 $US BB	Candlelight Breakfast
2008 Cooper Kettle	5 rooms, 4 pb	Night time treats, coffee and tea,
Hwy 15557	Most CC, Cash, Checks	delicatessen available to purchase
888-352-8221 814-352-8222	C-yes/S-ltd/P-no/H-ltd	other items
Juliann & Maryann		Sitting room, outdoor patio and firepit,
		deli, wireless Internet, Direct TV

Trenthouse is a historic Inn with an exciting story to tell. The Inn includes a marketplace and delicatessen that was built in 1884. The Trenthouse is on the grounds of the old village of Trent. The Trenthouse Inn is a comfortable, beautiful destination.

✉ browns@trenthouseinn.com 🌐 www.trenthouseinn.net

RONKS

Candlelight Inn B&B
2574 Lincoln Hwy E 17572
800-77-CANDL 717-299-6005
Tim & Heidi Soberick

89-179 $US BB
7 rooms, 7 pb
Visa, MC, Disc,
Rated, •
C-ltd/S-no/P-no/H-no
French, Italian

Full breakfast
Afternoon tea & snacks
Sitting room, antiques, oriental rugs,
Victorian style, Jacuzzi, fireplaces,
A/C, suites, romantic

Free Night w/Certificate: Valid December-May and Sunday-Thurs.

The Candlelight Inn Bed & Breakfast, an Amish Country B&B, is centrally located in Lancaster County, PA making it the perfect destination. This large Georgian B&B is enclosed by farmland & offers a gracious, romantic & relaxing retreat.

✉ candleinn@aol.com 🌐 www.candleinn.com

Olde Homestead Suites
3515 B West Newport
Rd 17572
717-768-3300
Merlin & Mary Lou Yutzy

99-169 $US BB
9 rooms, 9 pb
Visa, MC, Disc
C-yes/S-no/P-no/H-ltd

Full breakfast
Sunday-Continental breakfast
Patio, common room, DVD/VHS
players, Jacuzzi tubs, massage therapy

Olde Homestead Suites features 8 suites and one private cottage with private baths, some with king beds, Jacuzzi, waterfall shower/tubs and fireplaces in the heart of Dutch Country Pennsylvania.

✉ innkeeper@oldehomesteadsuites.com 🌐 www.oldehomesteadsuites.com

SELINSGROVE

Selinsgrove Inn
214 N Market St 17870
866-375-1700 570-374-4100
Scott

139-179 $US BB
24 rooms, 24 pb
Most CC, Cash
C-ltd/S-no/P-no/H-yes

Full breakfast
kitchenette, Jacuzzis, Internet

A stay at the Selinsgrove Inn allows guests to enjoy downtown Selinsgrove and all of its surroundings restaurants, shops, and attractions while indulging in the finest accommodations of the area.

✉ scott@selinsgroveinn.com 🌐 www.selinsgroveinn.com

SHARON

**Buhl Mansion Guesthouse
& Spa at Tara**
422 E State St 16146
866-345-2845 724-346-3046
Donna Winner

300-450 $US BB
10 rooms, 10 pb
Most CC, Cash
S-no/P-no/H-no

Full breakfast
Heating/cooling, gas fireplace, TV,
VCR, DVD & CD player, telephone &
Internet access

The Buhl Mansion is one of America's most romantic inns, perfect for romantic getaways, indulgent spa escapes, exclusive executive retreats and castle weddings. Steeped in history, built & maintained on love, promising grand memories of a lifetime.

✉ info@buhlmansion.com 🌐 www.buhlmansion.com/index.htm

SHAWNEE ON DELAWARE

Santosha on the Ridge
Mosier's Knob Road 18356
570-476-0203
Leslie Underhill

145-200 $US BB
4 rooms, 4 pb
Visa, MC, AmEx
C-ltd/S-no/P-no/H-no

Organic
Afternoon cookies or pastries with hot
tea, coffee or juice
All rooms have A/C, TV/DVD player,
robes. Yoga and massage available by
appointment

Located 72 miles west of Manhattan, perched on the edge of the Delaware Water Gap Recreation Area, Santosha on the Ridge is a secluded B&B where you can explore the Pocono Mountains. Enjoy skiing, golf, hiking, theatre, shopping, canoeing, or just relax.

✉ info@santoshaontheridge.com 🌐 www.santoshaontheridge.com

Tell your hosts Pamela Lanier sent you.

SHAWNEE ON DELAWARE

Stony Brook Inn
5 River Rd 18356
888-424-5240 570-424-1100
Rose Ann Whitesell & Pete
Ferguson

100-160 $US BB
4 rooms, 4 pb
Visa, MC, Disc
S-no/P-no/H-no

Full country breakfast
Afternoon tea, snacks, complimentary
beverages
WiFi, cable TV, large living room with
stone fireplace, large screened in
porch, swimming pool

*Built in 1853, we offer 4 rooms highlighted with antiques. All rooms are A/C and have private baths.
A full country breakfast is served in our cheery dining room or screened-in porch. Stony Brook Inn is
a gracious, comfortable inn with modern amenities.*

✉ sbinn@ptd.net 🌐 www.stonybrookinn.com

SHIPPENSBURG

Dykeman House
6 W Dykeman Rd 17257
717-530-1919 717-530-1919
John & Rachelle Davidson

120-129 $US BB
3 rooms, 3 pb
Visa, MC, *Rated*
C-ltd/S-no/P-no

Full country breakfast
Complimentary beverage, late
afternoon cheese & crackers
Balcony, yards

*The Dykeman House today sits on approximately 4 acres of what once was a 450 acre estate estab-
lished in 1740. The land next to and surrounding the house contains numerous springs, and has been
known as Indian Springs and today as Dykeman Spring.*

✉ innkeeper@dykemanhouse.com 🌐 www.dykemanhouse.com

SMOKETOWN

Homestead Lodging
184 Eastbrook Rd 17576
717-393-6927
Bob & Lori Kepiro

51-82 $US BB
5 rooms, 5 pb
Most CC, Cash,
Checks, •
C-ltd/S-no/P-no/H-no

Continental breakfast
Microwave available & refrigerators in
rooms with "pay as you use" sodas,
water, juices, snacks
Wireless Internet, AC/heat, cable TV,
refrigerator, hair dryers, clock radio,
iron/board available

*Christian family owned B&B where you can rest, relax & recharge. Bob & Lori provide personal atten-
tion, warm hospitality & knowledge of the area. Centrally located in heart of Amish farms & country.*

✉ lkepiro@comcast.net 🌐 www.homesteadlodging.net

SPRING MILLS

Inn on the Sky
538 Brush Mountain
Road 16875
814 422 0386
Jere McCarthy and Paula
Martin

139-399 $US BB
5 rooms, 5 pb
Visa, MC
C-yes/S-ltd/P-ltd/H-no
French

Full breakfast
Indoor & outdoor fireplaces, wrap-
around deck, full breakfast, TV,
Jacuzzi tubs, sitting areas

*Relax and stay a while at the Inn On the Sky, located in Spring Mills, where mountain views, fine
architecture and an easy going atmosphere create the perfect home away from home.*

✉ innkeeper@innonthesky.com 🌐 www.innonthesky.com

STARLIGHT

The Inn at Starlight Lake
289 Starlight Lake
Road 18461
800-248-2519 570-798-2519
Sari & Jimmy Schwartz

100-255 $US BB
21 rooms, 19 pb
Visa, MC, •
C-yes/S-no/P-ltd/H-ltd

Delicious breakfast
Full service restaurant & bar offering
breakfast, lunch, dinner, selection of
wines & cocktails
Lake front, swimming, tennis boating,
bicycles, hiking, fishing, cross country
skiing, snowshoeing

*Surrounded by rolling hills, wood and lakes, the Inn is a perfect country retreat. Enjoy recreation from
swimming to skiing, romantic rooms, excellent food & spirits and congenial atmosphere.*

✉ info@innatstarlightlake.com 🌐 www.innatstarlightlake.com

STATE COLLEGE──────────────────────────────────

Limestone Inn Bed and
Breakfast
490 Meckley Road 16801
888-922-8944 814-234-8944
Karen Patzer

95-185 $US BB
5 rooms, 5 pb
Visa, MC, Disc
C-ltd/S-ltd/P-ltd/H-no

Full breakfast
A full, mouth watering breakfast and
complimentary snacks and beverages
are included.
private baths, sitting area, and central
AC, TV, VCR, small collection of
movies

Come enjoy old-fashioned style with modern comfort in the brick, Federal style farmhouse built in
1800 and renovated in 1992. Our rooms have queen size beds, private baths, sitting area, and central
air conditioning. Wireless Internet is available on site

✉ kpatzer@psualum.com 🌐 www.limestoneinn.com

STRASBURG──────────────────────────────────

The Limestone Inn
33 E Main St 17579
800-278-8392 717-687-8392
Denise & Richard Waller &
daughters

89-129 $US BB
6 rooms, 5 pb
Most CC, Cash, *Rated*
C-ltd/S-no/P-no/H-no

Full gourmet breakfast
Tea, coffee, snacks, cold drinks
Sitting rooms, library, bicycle storage,
patio

The Limestone Inn B&B (circa 1786) is listed in the National Register of Historic Places and is situ-
ated in the heart of Lancaster's Amish country. Enjoy life in the slow lane at one of the most beautiful
homes in Lancaster County.

✉ limestoneinn@yahoo.com 🌐 www.thelimestoneinn.com

TERRE HILL──────────────────────────────────

Artist's Inn & Gallery
117 East Main Street 17581
888-999-4479 717-445-0219
Jan & Bruce Garrabrandt

125-260 $US BB
5 rooms, 5 pb
Most CC, Cash, Checks,
Rated, •
C-ltd/S-ltd/P-no/H-no

Four-course gourmet breakfast
Snacks, cold and hot beverages,
bottomless home-made cookie jar –
available 24/7
Art gallery, sitting room, culinary
tours, tennis, wireless, gardens,
cottage and carriage house

Make your getaway picture perfect – spend the night in an art gallery! Romantic B&B in small town
surrounded by Amish farms. Enjoy passing Amish buggies, Jacuzzi's, fireplaces, candlelight break-
fasts. Three guestrooms, 2 separate private cottages nearby.

✉ relax@artistinn.com 🌐 www.artistinn.com

UNION DALE──────────────────────────────────

Stone Bridge Inn &
Restaurant
306 Sugar Hill Rd. 18470
570-679-9200

90-205 $US BB
13 rooms, 13 pb
Most CC
C-yes/S-no/P-no/H-ltd

Continental breakfast
Casual, fine dining restaurant on
premises, tavern menu also available
with lighter fare
Indoor pool, hot tub, Internet access,
catering, massages & manicures
available with appointment

We will remind you of a quaint, alpine hide-away. Here, vacationing is synonymous with relaxation.
Fine dining and pleasantly inviting accommodations are yours on 200 scenic acres of forests and
pastureland overlooking the rolling mountains.

✉ sbinn@nep.net 🌐 www.stone-bridge-inn.com

UNIONTOWN──────────────────────────────────

Inne at Watson's Choice
234 Balsinger Rd 15401
888-820-5380 724-437-4999
Nancy & Bill Ross

130-225 $US BB
12 rooms, 12 pb
Visa, MC, Disc,
Rated, •
C-ltd/S-no/P-no/H-yes
French

Four course breakfast
Continental breakfast served at 7:00
a.m. for early tours at Frank Lloyd
Wright homes
Sitting room, library, accommodations
for business travelers, WiFi at the
Harvest House

Restored circa 1800 Western Pennsylvania farmhouse offering charm & ambience of yesteryear and
just a short drive to Frank Lloyd Wright's "Fallingwater" and "Kentuck Knob" located in the Laurel
Highlands of southwestern Pennsylvania.

✉ innkeeper@watsonschoice.com 🌐 www.watsonschoice.com

VALLEY FORGE

Great Valley House of Valley Forge
1475 Swedesford Rd 19355
610-644-6759
Pattye Benson

94-129 $US BB
3 rooms, 3 pb
Most CC, Cash, Checks,
Rated
C-yes/S-no/P-ltd/H-no
Limited French

Full Gourmet Breakfast
Swimming pool, free wireless Internet,
cable TV, guest refrigerator &
microwave, sitting room

Built before the Revolutionary War, the 300 year old Great Valley House retains original fireplaces, antiques and random-width wood floors. As you enjoy breakfast, there may be a fire in the old kitchen walk-in fireplace.

✉ stay@greatvalleyhouse.com ◐ www.greatvalleyhouse.com

WARFORDSBURG

Buck Valley Ranch
1344 Negro Mountain
Road 17267
800-294-3759 717-294-3759
Nadine Fox

75-90 $US MAP
4 rooms
AmEx, Disc, •
C-yes/S-ltd/P-no/H-no

Full breakfast
Lunch
horseback riding, outdoor pool, hot
tub, air conditioned

Buck Valley Ranch LLC is a year round resort located in the Appalachian Mountains of south central Pennsylvania and offers trail riding and other outdoor activities in a magnificent secluded setting.

✉ info@buckvalleyranch.com ◐ www.buckvalleyranch.com

WELLSBORO

Kaltenbach's B&B
743 Stonyfork Rd & Kelsey
St 16901
800-722-4954 570-724-4954
Lee Kaltenbach

90-150 $US BB
10 rooms, 10 pb
Visa, MC, *Rated*, •
C-yes/S-no/P-no/H-no
Spanish

Full breakfast
Afternoon tea, snacks, wine
Lunch/dinner by reservation, sitting
room, library, tennis court, Jacuzzis,
free WiFi in all rooms

Featuring antique quilts made by the owner's grandmother 95 years ago. Nearby rails to trails, hiking and biking through the Grand Canyon.

◐ www.kaltenbachsinn.com

Puerto Rico

CEIBA

Ceiba Country Inn
Carr 977 KM 1.2 00735
888-560-2816 787-885-0471
Michael A Marra

85-115 $US BB
9 rooms, 9 pb
Most CC, Cash,
Rated, •
C-yes/S-ltd/P-no/H-yes
Spanish

Continental plus breakfast
Lounge with TV, lending library,
games, microwave, free WiFi. Patio w/
gas grill.Daily maid service.

Pastoral setting with a view of the sea. Centrally located for trips to the rain forest, beaches, outer islands and San Juan.

✉ prinn@juno.com 🌐 www.ceibacountryinn.com

OLD SAN JUAN

The Gallery Inn
204 Norzagaray 00901
866-572-ARTE(2783)
787-722-1808
Manuco Gandia & Jan
D'Esopo

145-410 $US BB
22 rooms, 22 pb
Visa, MC, AmEx, •
C-yes/S-ltd/P-yes/H-no
Spanish

Continental plus breakfast
A full breakfast menu is available for
an additional fee
Sitting room, conference room, music
room, gardens, ocean view decks

The Gallery Inn is a stunning twenty-two room boutique hotel, that sits above the Old City's North Wall, commanding sensuous Atlantic Ocean breezes and gorgeous views over San Juan Bay and the mountainous central regions of Puerto Rico.

✉ hgandia@thegalleryinn.com 🌐 www.thegalleryinn.com

RINCON

Blue Boy Inn
556 Black Eagle Street 00677
787-823-2593
Marc Tremblay

155-190 $US BB
6 rooms, 6 pb
Visa, MC, •
C-ltd/S-ltd/P-ltd/H-yes
French, Spanish

Gourmet Breakfast
High speed Internet & wireless, daily
maid service, 2 BBQ areas, many
outside sitting areas

Welcome to Rincon, a wonderful and relaxed beach town in the west of Puerto Rico called 'la Porta del Sol.' Spectacular sunsets, a variety of outdoor activities, and an ample selection of restaurants will make your stay unforgettable.

✉ info@blueboyinn.com 🌐 www.blueboyinn.com

Tres Sirenas Ocean Front
26 Sea Beach Dr 00677
787-823-0558
Harry & Lisa Rodriguez

170-300 $US BB
4 rooms, 4 pb
Visa, MC
C-yes/S-no/P-ltd/H-no
Spanish

Full gourmet breakfast
Pool, Jacuzzi, cable TV, A/C & fans,
beach towels, lounge chairs, in room
spa services.

Our classic beachfront accommodations offer comfort and elegance in a casual setting. We offer a variety of rooms and apartments. Each unit was designed to provide awesome beach views and intimate settings.

✉ lisamasters@mac.com 🌐 www.tressirenas.com

SAN JUAN

Hosteria Del Mar Beach Inn
Tapia St #1 Ocean Park 00911
877-727-3302 787-727-3302
Loisse

99-239 $US BB
23 rooms, 23 pb
Most CC, Cash,
Rated, •
C-yes/S-ltd/P-yes/H-yes
Spanish

Continental plus breakfast
Uvva offers International & Caribbean
Cuisine, open daily for breakfast,
lunch & dinner -8am to 10pm
Cable TV, A/C, free WiFi in lobby,
beach lounge area, room service, in
house restaurant.

An intimate beachfront boutique hotel with ocean view rooms & private balconies at the shore of Ocean Park, the most beautiful beach in San Juan! A casual & easygoing ambience with a modern twist combining the old with new in a chic Bohemian style.

 hosteriadelmar@hotmail.com 🌐 www.hosteriadelmarpr.com

404   Puerto Rico

SAN JUAN————————————————————————————

Tres Palmas Inn
2212 Park Blvd 00913
888-290-2076 787-727-4617
Manuael Peredo

81-175 $US BB
18 rooms, 18 pb
Visa, MC, AmEx,
Rated, •
C-yes/S-ltd/P-no/H-yes
Spanish

Continental breakfast
Sitting room, Jacuzzis, swimming pool,
suites, cable TV, phone with dataport

This quaint beachfront inn, recently renovated, is a refreshing alternative to traditional high priced and crowded hotels.

✉ info@trespalmasinn.com 🌐 www.trespalmasinn.com

VIEQUES ISLAND————————————————————————

Hacienda Tamarindo
4.5 Km, Rt 996 00765
787-741-0420
Burr & Linda Vail

135-335 $US BB
16 rooms, 16 pb
Most CC, Cash,
Rated, •
C-ltd/S-ltd/P-no/H-yes
Spanish

Full breakfast
Honor bar, picnic lunch packed in
an insulated back pack, coffee & tea
buffet at 6:30 am
Wireless Internet, sitting room, library,
tennis court, swimming pool, exercise
room, Bio-bay Tours

"Extraordinary small hotel . . . the nicest place to stay on Vieques." Spectacular Caribbean views, 16 charming rooms decorated with art, antiques & collectibles. Gorgeous gardenside pool. Breakfast awarded best for all Puerto Rican small hotels.

✉ hactam@aol.com 🌐 www.haciendatamarindo.com

Rhode Island

BLOCK ISLAND──────────────────────────────────

1661 Inn	75-450 $US BB	Champagne Buffet Breakfast
800-626-4773 401-466-2421	9 rooms, 9 pb	
Rita Draper	Visa, MC	
	C-yes/S-no/P-no/H-ltd	
	Spanish	

Taking in the spectacular ocean view of the Atlantic, one can't help but feel that this is what vacation should be. These nine spacious and elegant rooms offer combinations of ocean views, decks, canopy beds, whirlpool tubs, or gas fireplaces.

 office@biresorts.com ✪ www.blockislandresorts.com/guest_rooms/1661

───

The Atlantic Inn	160-435 $US BB	Fresh Cooked Breakfast Buffet
High St 02807	22 rooms, 22 pb	Romantic, Candlelit Dinners in the Inn,
800-224-7422 401-466-5883	Visa, MC, Disc, *Rated*	Tapas, Cocktails and Sunsets on the
Anne & Brad Marthens	C-yes/S-no/P-no/H-ltd	Inn's Veranda and Law
	Limited German,	Tennis, Ocean and beaches, nature
	French, Spanish	walks, antiques, horseback riding,
	Mid Apr. – Oct.	shopping and art galleries

An 1879 Victorian inn set high on a hill overlooking the ocean & harbor. The Atlantic Inn is surrounded by 6 landscaped acres, sloping lawns, numerous gardens & two of six tennis courts on the island.

 AtlanticInn@BIRI.com ✪ www.atlanticinn.com

───

The Rose Farm Inn	159-309 $US BB	Continental plus breakfast
1005 Roslyn Rd 02807	19 rooms, 17 pb	Afternoon tea
401-466-2034	Most CC	Bicycle, beach chair and umbrella
Judith B. Rose	C-ltd/S-no/P-no/H-yes	rental, on-site florist
	April-October	

The Rose Farm Inn is known for its natural setting, romantic rooms and informal hospitality. A working farm until 1963, the twenty acres of farmland are now home to marsh hawks, ring-necked pheasant and white-tailed deer.

 rosefarm@riconnect.com ✪ www.rosefarminn.com

BRISTOL──

Point Pleasant Inn & Resort	375-625 $US BB	Full breakfast
333 Poppasquash Rd 02809	6 rooms, 6 pb	Tea, open bar, snacks, complimentary
800-503-0627 401-253-0627	Visa, MC, *Rated*, •	wine
Trish & Gunter Hafer	C-ltd/S-ltd/P-no/H-ltd	Sitting room, library, bikes, tennis,
	German, Spanish,	Jacuzzis, swimming pool, suites,
	Latvian, Portuguese	fireplaces, landscaped garden
	April-November	

Point Pleasant Inn & Resort is located on Poppasquash Point, a peninsula located in Bristol, Rhode Island. An English country manor house from another era, the Inn offers a rare look at life from the pages of a romance novel.

 trishwwi1@aol.com ✪ www.pointpleasantinn.com

LITTLE COMPTON─────────────────────────────────

The Edith Pearl Bed and Breakfast	175-350 $US BB	Full breakfast
250 West Main Rd 02837	3 rooms, 1 pb	Wireless Internet, Bicycles and
401- 592-0053	C-ltd/S-no/P-yes/H-no	helmets, Beach towels and chairs,
Deborah LeLevier		library, fenced dog yard

Surrounded by 200 acres of preserved and working farmland. The picturesque grounds have ancient, shading maple trees, rolling lawns, perennial gardens, and views of farm, woodland and pond plus peeks of the Sakonnet River.

 stay@edithpearl.com ✪ www.edithpearl.com

NARRAGANSETT

The Richards
144 Gibson Ave 02882
401-789-7746
Steven & Nancy Richards

150-230 $US BB
4 rooms, 4 pb
Rated, •
C-ltd/S-no/P-no/H-ltd

Full gourmet breakfast
Complimentary sherry in room
Library with fireplace, tennis courts
nearby, fireplaces in bedrooms, air
conditioning, WiFi

Gracious accommodations in an English country setting. Awaken to the smell of gourmet coffee and freshly baked goods. Water garden with Koi.

✉ therichards144@hotmail.com 🌐 www.therichardsbnb.com

NEWPORT

1 Murray House B&B
1 Murray Pl 02840
888-848-2048 401-846-3337
Noreen O'Neil

99-255 $US BB
2 rooms, 2 pb
Visa, MC, Disc, *Rated*
C-ltd/S-ltd/P-yes/H-ltd
10 months

Gourmet breakfast
In room tea & coffee
Koi pond, swimming pool, hottub,
flower gardens, TV/VCR, A/C, private
patios, in-room breakfast

Located in the lovely Newport Mansion & Cliff Walk district. 5 minute walk to beach, 4 minutes to downtown Newport. Private baths & patios with room. Swimming pool, hot tub & flower gardens. Gourmet breakfast served to your charming room. Pets welcome.

✉ murrayhousebnb@aol.com 🌐 www.murrayhouse.com

Admiral Fitzroy Inn
398 Thames St 02840
866-848-8780 401-848-8000
Angela Craig

105-325 $US BB
18 rooms, 18 pb
Most CC, Cash
C-yes/S-no/P-no/H-ltd

Continental breakfast
Tea kettle with the fixings, small fridge
Phone, TV, A/C, hair dryer, private full
bath – 2 with whirlpool tub, private
deck with harbor views

Located in Newport, Rhode Island, the Admiral Fitzroy Bed & Breakfast Inn offers rooms decorated and furnished in a distinctive fashion to please the eye and lift the spirits.

✉ info@admiralfitzroy.com 🌐 www.admiralfitzroy.com

Almondy Inn
25 Pelham St 02840
800-478-6155 401-848-7202
Evelyne Valkenberg

155-380 $US BB
5 rooms, 5 pb
Visa, MC, AmEx,
Rated, •
C-ltd/S-no/P-no/H-no
Dutch, Spanish, French,
German

Full Gourmet Breakfast
In-room coffee service; afternoon wine
& cheese
Off-street parking provided, Jacuzzis,
fireplaces, suites, wireless Internet
access, TV, VCR

The Almondy Inn, built in the 1890's is an elegantly restored B&B conveniently located in downtown Newport, RI, just steps from Bannister's Wharf, historic downtown restaurants, shops and galleries and minutes from Newport Beaches and Mansions.

✉ info@almondyinn.com 🌐 www.almondyinn.com

Beech Tree Inn
34 Rhode Island Ave 02840
800-748-6565 401-847-9794
Jim & Cindy Mahood

129-379 $US BB
8 rooms, 8 pb
Most CC, *Rated*, •
C-ltd/S-ltd/P-yes/H-no
Russian
Apr 30 through Nov 14.

Biggest breakfast in town
Snacks, complimentary wine
Sitting room, library, Jacuzzis, suites,
fireplaces, cable TV, soda machine, ice
machine, garden

This charming Victorian home, built in 1887, was lovingly renovated, and offers spacious rooms with private baths, cable TV, air conditioning, lovely gardens and sundecks.

✉ cmquilt13@cox.net 🌐 www.beechtreeinn.com/bt/btindex.html

Belle View Inn
22 Freebody St 02840
800-722-6354 401-849-8211
Lorna & Anthony Zaloumis

89-275 $US BB
2 rooms, 2 pb
Most CC, Cash, Checks
C-ltd/S-ltd/P-no/H-no

Continental breakfast
Afternoon cookies & snacks
Private baths, relaxing garden deck &
porches, free wireless Internet, cable
TV, DVD, free parking.

Located between the spectacular Cliff Walk at Newport Beach and downtown Newport, RI. Built in 1900 and beautifully restored in 2003, our B&B is surrounded by an elegant, wrought-iron fence reminiscent of the opulent Newport mansions.

✉ innkeeper@belleviewinn.com 🌐 www.belleviewinn.com

NEWPORT————————————————————————

Black Duck Inn	99-314 $US BB	Full breakfast
29 Pelham St 02840	8 rooms, 7 pb	Sitting room, cable, Jacuzzis,
800-206-5212 401-841-5548	Most CC, Cash, Checks,	fireplaces, A/C
Lisa & Garry Foisy	*Rated*, •	
	C-ltd/S-no/P-no/H-no	

This large, well-appointed, newly renovated in art deco and traditional design is conveniently located opposite Bowen's Wharf in downtown Newport. Shops, restaurants, historic mansions and sailing are all in walking distance.

✉ innkeeper@newportbedandbreakfast.com 🌏 www.blackduckinn.com

Chestnut Inn	125-175 $US BB	Continental breakfast
99 3rd St 02840	2 rooms	Sitting room, library, tennis, suites,
401-846-0173 401-847-6949	•	cable TV, fishing, swimming
Bill, Eileen & Cheryl Nimmo	C-yes/S-yes/P-yes/H-no	

One block from Narragansett Bay, in Newport's historic "Point" section. A perfect getaway for couples and families. Children and pets are welcome.

✉ chstnut99@aol.com 🌏 www.newportchestnutinn.com

Hydrangea House Inn	295-475 $US BB	Full breakfast buffet
16 Bellevue Ave 02840	10 rooms, 10 pb	afternoon wine & cheese
800-945-4667 401-846-4435	Most CC, Cash, Checks,	Sitting room, parlor w/fireplace, A/C,
Dennis & Grant	*Rated*, •	private parking
	S-no/P-no/H-no	

(Within Newport's "Old Quarter.") A gratifying hot breakfast buffet served in our formal dining room. All Fireplace suites with 2-person whirlpools & queen & king bed.

✉ hydrangeahouseinn@cox.net 🌏 www.hydrangeahouse.com

Ivy Lodge	99-479 $US BB	Full breakfast
12 Clay St 02840	8 rooms, 8 pb	Fresh fruit, bread pudding, baked
800-834-6865 401-849-6865	Most CC, Cash, *Rated*	apples, homemade breads & granola
Daryl & Darlene McKenzie	C-yes/S-ltd/P-no/H-ltd	Cable TV, A/C, CD/radio, direct-dial
		phone with data port, VCR or DVD
		player

Welcome to Ivy Lodge! Located in the heart of Newport's Mansion District, romantic Ivy Lodge provides luxurious family suites with off-street parking and a leisurely breakfast served daily.

✉ innkeepers@ivylodge.com 🌏 www.ivylodge.com

Newport Blues Inn	99-350 $US BB	Full breakfast
96 Pelham St 02840	12 rooms, 12 pb	Coffee and Tea
800-206-5212 401-847-4400	Most CC, Cash, Checks	Large porch, garden patio, parlor, A/C,
Jean Ryan	C-ltd/S-no/P-no/H-no	cable TV, refrig in rooms, wireless,

The Newport Blues Inn, one of Newport's finest Inns, offers our guests an experience of classic Rhode Island charm with a modern day style and appeal. We are only a block away from the action, you can walk to all that Newport offers.

✉ innkeeper@newportbluesinn.com 🌏 www.newportbluesinn.com

Pilgrim House Inn	105-265 $US BB	Continental plus breakfast
123 Spring St 02840	11 rooms, 11 pb	Complimentary sherry, shortbread
800-525-8373 401-846-0040	Most CC, *Rated*, •	Deck with view of harbor, living room
Barry & Debbie Fonseca	C-ltd/S-no/P-no/H-no	with fireplace, cable TV in all rooms,
		free wireless Internet

Elegant Victorian inn two blocks from the harbor in Newport's historic district. Rooftop deck with view of Newport Harbor. Walking distance to shops, dining & sights, Cliff Walk.

✉ Innkeeper@PilgrimHouseInn.com 🌏 www.pilgrimhouseinn.com

NEWPORT

Samuel Durfee House 352 Spring St 02840 877-696-2374 401-847-1652 Heather & Michael de Pinho	110-295 $US BB 5 rooms, 5 pb Visa, MC, • C-ltd/S-no/P-no/H-no	Full breakfast Afternoon refreshments & snacks including coffee, tea, sodas WiFi throughout the inn, TV, phone & refrigerator in guest sitting room, some rooms have TV's

An elegant 1803 Federal period bed and breakfast Inn located downtown, just a block from the harbor and two blocks from Bellevue Avenue. All rooms are spacious and tastefully decorated. Perfect for a romantic getaway.

✉ innkeeper@samueldurfeehouse.com 🌐 www.samueldurfeehouse.com

The Clarkeston 27 Clarke St 02840 800-524-1386 401-848-5300 Rick & Tamara Farrick	109-289 $US BB 9 rooms, 9 pb Visa, MC C-ltd/S-no/P-no/H-no	Full breakfast Air Conditioning, all private baths, romantic fireplaces, luxurious Jacuzzi tubs, off-street parking

Welcome to The Clarkeston, located in scenic Newport Rhode Island. Enjoy the historical 1700's Colonial feel of wide plank floors and period doors while still having all the modern amenities to ensure a relaxing and comfortable stay.

✉ newportinn@aol.com 🌐 www.innsofnewport.com/innclarkeston.html

Victoria Skylar Bed and Breakfast 107 2nd St 02840 866-752-1653 401-855-8701 Ann Coulton	199-259 $US BB 4 rooms, 4 pb Visa, MC, *Rated*, • S-no/P-no/H-no	Full Gourmet Breakfast Godiva chocolates, premium bottled waters, snacks, wine & cheese, sherry & brandy in the eves Rose garden, pillow-top mattresses, luxury linens, Jacuzzi, eco-friendly fireplaces, A/C, toiletries

An elegant, romantic, Victorian bed and breakfast, located in the quiet, historic Point District of Newport, RI. One block from the harbor and a short walk to restaurants, parks, and shopping in Newport's downtown area.

✉ victoriaskylarbb@aol.com 🌐 www.victoriaskylar.com

Weatherly Cottage B&B 30 Weatherly Ave 02840 401-849-8371 Patti Toppa	99-145 $US BB 3 rooms, 3 pb Visa, MC C-ltd/S-no/P-no/H-no	Full breakfast A bottomless cup of coffee Parking, full breakfast, queen, full or twin bed, satellite TV

A lovely, traditional bed and breakfast, located in the quiet residential southern end of Newport, RI. We're just 2 blocks from Salve Regina University and within walking distance to downtown and a majority of attractions.

✉ weatherlycottage@aol.com 🌐 www.weatherlycottage.com

PROVIDENCE

The Old Court B&B 144 Benefit St 02903 401-751-2002 Max Gallagher	145-215 $US BB 10 rooms, 10 pb Most CC, *Rated*, • C-ltd/S-no/P-no/H-no	Full breakfast Complimentary tea, assorted breads Antiques, cable TV in every room, private bath in every room, wet bars in some rooms, free WiFi

The Old Court B&B was built in 1863, Italianate in design and in ornate details; the B&B combines tradition with contemporary standards of luxury. The Old Court is filled with antique furniture and chandeliers.

✉ reserve@oldcourt.com 🌐 www.oldcourt.com

SOUTH KINGSTOWN

Admiral Dewey Inn 668 Matunuck Beach Rd 02879 800-457-2090 401-783-2090 Joan LeBel	110-160 $US BB 10 rooms, 8 pb Visa, MC, *Rated* C-ltd/S-ltd/P-no/H-no Polish	Continental plus breakfast Snacks Sitting room, bicycles, cable TV

The past comes alive in this 1898 Victorian, which has been lovingly restored and furnished with antiques in the Victorian style. Listed on the National Historic Register.

🌐 www.admiraldeweyinn.com

WAKEFIELD ───

Sugar Loaf Hill B&B
607 Main St 02879
401-789-8715
Stephanie & David Osborn

95-159 $US BB
4 rooms, 3 pb
Visa, MC
C-yes/S-no/P-no/H-ltd
Some Greek & Spanish

Full breakfast. Continental avail.
Dining room, living room, parlor, guest
fridge, porch, fireplaces

Sugar Loaf Hill Bed and Breakfast is nestled on 1½ acres in a charming historic area, peacefully surrounded by stone walls, hollies, rhododendrons, and large shade trees. Just 3 miles from University of Rhode Island and close to beaches.

✉ sugarloafhill@verizon.net 🌐 www.sugarloafhillbandb.com

WESTERLY ───

The Villa
190 Shore Rd 02891
800-722-9240 401-596-1054
Michael & Barbara Cardiff

125-320 $US BB
8 rooms, 8 pb
Most CC, Cash, Checks,
Rated
S-no/P-no/H-ltd

Gourmet
Afternoon snacks available during the
on-season
Outdoor hot tub, heated swimming
pool, 4 fireplaces, All Jacuzzi suites,
cable TV & DVDs

Escape to our Mediterranean style villa. We set the stage for your romantic getaway. You'll fall in love and want to return. Outdoor heated pool and hot tub. Adjacent to golf course. Private and romantic. Gourmet breakfast. In-room hot tubs. Fireplaces.

✉ villa@riconnect.com 🌐 www.thevillaatwesterly.com

Woody Hill B&B
149 S Woody Hill Rd 02891
401-322-0452
Ellen L. Madison

125-165 $US BB
3 rooms, 3 pb
Most CC, Cash,
Rated, •
C-yes/S-no/P-no/H-ltd

Continental breakfast
Winter hearth cooking
Porch with swing, pool, wireless
Internet

Relaxed 18th century ambience on 20 country acres, with a 40' in-ground pool and furnished with antiques. Two miles from ocean beaches.

✉ woodyhillbandb@verizon.net 🌐 www.woodyhill.com

WICKFORD ───

Haddie Pierce House
146 Boston Neck Rd 02852
866-4HADDIE 401-294-7674
Darya & John Prassl

140-160 $US BB
5 rooms, 5 pb
Most CC, Cash
C-ltd/S-no/P-no/H-no

Full breakfast
Tea, coffee, soft drinks
Double parlor, front porch & patio,
walk to the beach or village

The Haddie Pierce House is a restored Victorian home in historic Wickford Village. Five rooms with private baths. Antiques and period furnishings provide a casual elegance. Walk to the beach or village shops. Listed on the National Historic Register.

✉ info@HaddiePierce.com 🌐 www.HaddiePierce.com

WOONSOCKET ───

Pillsbury House B&B
341 Prospect St 02895
800-205-4112 401-766-7983
Roger Bouchard

95-135 $US BB
4 rooms, 4 pb
Most CC, Cash, Checks
C-ltd/S-no/P-no/H-no

Full breakfast
Complimentary wine & beverages
Sitting room, suite, fireplace,
accommodate business travelers, high
speed wireless Internet

Built in 1875, The Pillsbury House is tucked away on quiet and historic Prospect Street in Woonsocket's fashionable North End. Close to Boston, Providence and Newport.

✉ rogerwnri@prodigy.net 🌐 www.pillsburyhouse.com

South Carolina

BEAUFORT

Beaulieu House at Cat Island
3 Sheffield Ct 29907
866-814-7833 843-770-0303
Diann Corsaro

125-235 $US BB
5 rooms, 5 pb
Most CC, Cash
C-yes/S-no/P-yes/H-yes

Full breakfast
Refreshments on the veranda
Jacuzzi, verandas, private baths,
ceiling fans, kitchenette

Beaulieu House is the only waterfront B&B in Beaufort. Five minutes from the Historic District and adjacent to the Sanctuary at Cat Island & fine dining at the British Open Pub. Stay at the Beaulieu House where South Carolina meets Paradise.

✉ beaulieubb@aol.com 🌐 www.beaulieuhouse.com

The Old Point Inn
212 New St 29902
843-524-3177
Julie & Paul Michau

125-175 $US BB
5 rooms, 5 pb
Most CC, Cash,
Rated, •
C-ltd/S-ltd/P-no/H-no
French, Afrikaans

Full gourmet breakfast
Complimentary wine & soft drinks
each evening
Access to golf, tennis & beach; boating,
kayaking & bicycling

This late Victorian Queen Anne home built in 1898 as a wedding gift, the Old Point Inn is the only Inn located in the historic Point neighborhood. Away from the noise of downtown, it is a very easy stroll to restaurants, shops and Waterfront Park.

✉ oldpointinn@yahoo.com 🌐 www.oldpointinn.com

BENNETTSVILLE

Breeden Inn, Cottages, & Retreat on Main
404 E Main St 29512
888-335-2996 843-479-3665
Wesley & Bonnie Park

120-180 $US BB
13 rooms, 13 pb
Most CC, Cash, Checks,
Rated, •
C-ltd/S-no/P-no/H-no

Full breakfast
Beverage offered upon arrival.Bed
chocolates.Snack basket & stocked
fridge in each house.
Pool. Whirlpools.Winding garden
walks. WiFi.TV/VCR/DVD/Blu-Ray.
Video library.Bikes.Southern porches

Comfortable, elegant, romantic & historic Inn midway between NY&FL, near the NC/SC beaches. Four 19th-century houses offer thirteen guestrooms, luxurious bedding, whirlpools, kitchens, winding garden walks, a large in-ground pool, wonderful Southern porches & WI-Fi.

✉ info@breedeninn.com 🌐 www.breedeninn.com

CHARLESTON

1807 Phoebe Pember House
26 Society St 29401
843-722-4186
Anne G. Shue

140-250 $US BB
6 rooms, 6 pb
Visa, MC, AmEx
C-ltd/S-no/P-no/H-no

Continental breakfast
Wine reception on Friday
Business traveler accommodations,
concierge, turn-down service, yoga
studio

200 year-old Federal-style Charleston property with carriage and coach houses, with beautiful piazzas overlooking private walled gardens. In the heart of the Historic District with private parking. On-site retreat center and yoga studio.

✉ info@phoebepemberhouse.com 🌐 www.phoebepemberhouse.com

1843 Battery Carriage House Inn
20 S Battery 29401
800-775-5575 843-727-3100
Elizabeth Kilminster

99-299 $US BB
11 rooms, 11 pb
Most CC, *Rated*, •
S-no/P-no/H-no

Continental breakfast
Complimentary wine
Free wireless Internet access available
in some rooms and the lobby

For a truly memorable Charleston experience, stay in the Battery Carriage House Inn, located in the garden of the Stevens-Lathers house, one of the most gracious houses on the city's historic harbor front. Eleven intimate rooms and continental breakfast.

 batterych@bellsouth.net  🌐 www.batterycarriagehouse.com

CHARLESTON ───

36 Meeting Street
36 Meeting St 29401
843-722-1034
Vic & Anne Brandt

125-200 $US BB
3 rooms, 3 pb
Visa, MC, *Rated*
C-ltd/S-ltd/P-no/H-no

Continental breakfast
Sitting room, kitchenettes, TV &
phones in rooms

Experience the intimacy of being a resident in the most exclusive part of Charleston's Historic Residential District. Suites have private entrance, elegant furnishings, four poster mahogany rice beds.

✉ info@36meetingstreet.com 🌐 www.36meetingstreet.com

A B&B at 4 Unity Alley
4 Unity Alley 29401
843-577-6660
Donald Smith

150-300 $US BB
4 rooms, 4 pb
Visa, MC
C-ltd/S-no/P-no/H-no
Spanish

Full breakfast
Small garden, cable TV, telephone, fax
machine, off-street parking, tennis, golf
& swimming nearby

The only B&B located in the heart of Charleston's French Quarter. Large rooms with antiques and a beautiful garden. Breakfast served in our formal dining room. Park in our garage and walk everywhere.

✉ unitybb@aol.com 🌐 www.unitybb.com

Ashley Inn B&B
201 Ashley Ave 29403
800-581-6658 843-723-1848
Barry Carroll

119-249 $US BB
7 rooms, 7 pb
Visa, MC, •
C-ltd/S-ltd/P-no/H-no

Full breakfast
Afternoon tea, sandwiches & cookies,
complimentary sherry
Sitting room, fireplace, complimentary
bikes, free off-street parking

Sleep until the fragrance of southern cooking lures you to the garden for breakfast. Featured in Gail Greco's Nationally Televised "Country Inn Cooking." Charleston's Gourmet Breakfast Place.

✉ reservations@ashleyinnbb.com 🌐 www.charleston-sc-inns.com/ashley

Cannonboro Inn B&B
184 Ashley Ave 29403
800-235-8039 843-723-8572
Diane Mott

99-249 $US BB
8 rooms, 8 pb
Most CC, •
C-ltd/S-no/P-no/H-no

Full breakfast
Afternoon tea, sandwiches, goodies
Sitting room, garden, complimentary
bikes, free off-street parking, WiFi,
cable TV, suite w/ kitchen

Antebellum home c.1850 in Charleston's historic district. Breakfast served on a piazza overlooking a country garden. Fireplaces in rooms. A place to be pampered with very special southern hospitality.

✉ reservations@cannonboroinnbb.com 🌐 www.charleston-sc-inns.com/cannonboro

Governor's House Inn
117 Broad St 29401
800-720-9812 843-720-2070
Mary Kittrell

195-595 $US BB
11 rooms, 11 pb
Most CC, Cash, Checks,
Rated
C-ltd/S-ltd/P-no/H-ltd

Full breakfast
Lowcountry Tea of local recipes Wine
and cheese hour Evening sherry
3 living rooms, whirlpools, wet bars,
concierge, veranda, free parking, free
wireless Internet

The Governor's House Inn is a National Historic Landmark reflecting the Old South's civility and grandeur. Praised by one national publication as "Charleston's most glamorous and sophisticated Inn," the Inn blends historic splendor and romantic elegance.

✉ governorshouse@aol.com 🌐 www.governorshouse.com

King George IV Inn
32 George St 29401
888-723-1667 843-723-9339
Terry & Debra Flowers

89-230 $US BB
10 rooms, 8 pb
Most CC, Cash, Checks,
Rated, •
C-ltd/S-no/P-no/H-ltd

Southern style/stuffed croissants
Refreshments are available all day in
the Breakfast Room
Three levels of porches, off street
parking, cable TV & refrigerators in
every room

A four story Federal style home furnished in antiques, originally the 1790's home of a Charleston journalist & Jeffersonian politician, Peter Freneau. All rooms have decorative fireplaces, hardwood floors, high ceilings with moldings.

 info@kinggeorgeiv.com 🌐 www.kinggeorgeiv.com

CHARLESTON—

Palmer Home B&B
5 E Battery 29401
843-853-1574
Francess Palmer

200-425 $US BB
5 rooms, 5 pb
Visa, MC, *Rated*
C-ltd/S-no/P-ltd/H-no

Full breakfast
Refreshments available during the day.
Afternoon wine & cheese reception
daily.
Sitting room, piazzas, historic district,
pool, parking, wine & cheese

Enjoy a room with a view. One of the fifty famous homes in the city; furnished in period antiques; piazzas overlook harbor & Fort Sumter where the Civil War began.

✉ palmerbnb@aol.com

Palmer's Pinckney Inn
19 Pinckney St 29401
866-722-1733 843-722-1733
Cindy Brunell

150-250 $US BB
5 rooms, 5 pb
Visa, MC
C-ltd/S-ltd/P-yes/H-ltd

Continental breakfast
Homemade cookies & muffins,
lemonade & soft drinks are available
anytime
Free off street parking, gas fireplaces,
Jacuzzi tubs, concierge services

Centrally located in the historic Market area in downtown Charleston, within walking distance to shops and restaurants. Five bedrooms with private baths, two with Jacuzzi tubs, four with fireplaces. Free off street parking!

✉ pinckneyinn@comcast.net 🌐 www.pinckneyinn.com

The Cabell House
8 Church St 29401
843-723-7551
Ms. Randy Cabell

165-275 $US BB
4 rooms, 4 pb
Visa, MC, AmEx, •
C-ltd/S-no/P-ltd/H-no
French

Eggs, bacon, grits, fresh fruit etc
Wine and Iced tea available on
request.
Complimentary parking, WiFi, digital
flat-screen TVs, Keurig coffee makers,
Porch w/rockers, Liv.Rm.

Free Night w/Certificate: Anytime.

The Cabell House puts you in the heart of Charleston, steps away from the High Battery with views of the Harbor and Ft Sumter. We're happy to help you with recommendations & reservations, for restaurants, tours & entertainment. Easy walk to everything!

✉ info@cabellhouse.com 🌐 www.cabellhouse.com

The Indigo Inn
8 Cumberland St. 29401
800-845-7639 843-577-5900
Ignatius Nazareth

139-239 $US BB
40 rooms, 40 pb
Most CC, Cash, Checks
C-yes/S-ltd/P-ltd/H-ltd

Continental plus breakfast
Late afternoon hors d'oeuvres &
beverages
Lobby, sitting areas, courtyard, private
baths

The Charleston Inn of distinction offers superior accommodations and lodging in the heart of the city's historic district featuring 19th century style with 21st century comfort.

✉ info@indigoinn.com 🌐 www.indigoinn.com

The Jasmine House
64 Hasell St. 29401
800-845-7639 843-577-5900
Ignatius Nazareth

149-316 $US BB
11 rooms, 11 pb
Most CC, Cash, Checks
S-no/P-no/H-no

Continental plus breakfast
Courtyard, patio, fireplace, private
bath

The Jasmine House offers luxurious accommodations in a Southern Style. Within walking distance to the bustling City Market and surrounded by Charleston's finest restaurants, specialty shops and historic sights. ✉ info@jasminehouseinn.com 🌐 www.jasminehouseinn.com

---

**The Thomas Lamboll
House B&B**
19 King St 29401
888-874-0793 843-723-3212
Marie & Emerson Read

135-195 $US BB
2 rooms, 2 pb
Visa, MC
C-ltd/S-no/P-no/H-no

Continental plus breakfast
Tennis and golf nearby, off-street
parking

Built in 1735 in the historic district of Charleston. Bedrooms have queen size beds, private baths and French doors leading to the piazza.

✉ lamboll@aol.com 🌐 www.Lambollhouse.com/home.htm

The Moore Farm House B&B, Conway, SC

CHARLESTON

Two Meeting Street Inn B&B
2 Meeting St 29401
888-723-7322 843-723-7322
Pete & Jean Spell, Karen Spell Shaw

225-479 $US BB
9 rooms, 9 pb
Rated
C-ltd/S-no/P-no/H-no
Closed December 24 – 26

Full hot Southern breakfast
Lowcountry afternoon tea featuring recipes from Charleston cookbooks. Evening sherry to end the day. Newspapers, bathrobes, complimentary WiFi, iPod docks, professional concierge services, free parking.

Overlooking Battery park, Charleston's signature Meeting Street inn showcases curved piazzas, Tiffany windows, and its distinctive white turret. Originally a wedding gift, the Inn continues its legacy of luxury accommodations and Southern hospitality.

✉ innkeeper2meetst@bellsouth.net 🌐 www.twomeetingstreet.com

CONWAY

The Cypress Inn
16 Elm St 29526
800-575-5307 843-248-8199
Carol & Hugh Archer, Anne & George Bullock

145-235 $US BB
12 rooms, 12 pb
Most CC, Cash,
Rated, •
C-ltd/S-no/P-no/H-yes

Full breakfast
Snacks, bottled water, soda, iced tea, lemonade, wine & beer
Jacuzzi, heat/air, plush robes, TV/VCR, phones with data ports & voice mail, WiFi

The Cypress Inn is tucked away in the charming town of Conway, SC; just 12 miles from Myrtle Beach. Near golfing, shopping, beaches and great restaurants. Voted the "Most Elegant" on the SC Coast.

✉ info@acypressinn.com 🌐 www.acypressinn.com

The Moore Farm House B&B
3423 Hwy 319 29526
866-MOORE BB 843-365-7479
Harry & Cathy Pinner

109-149 $US BB
4 rooms, 4 pb
Visa, MC
C-ltd/S-no/P-no/H-no

Full breakfast
Welcome drinks & cookies at check-in, guest fridge with free drinks & snacks
WiFi connection, ceiling fans, TV & DVD, plush terrycloth robes, whirlpool tubs, library, pool table

The Moore Farm House B & B continues a long tradition of warm hospitality in a rural setting, minutes from the charming old river town of Conway & 15 miles from Myrtle Beach. Enjoy all Myrtle Beach has to offer and sleep well away from the noise.

✉ info@TheMooreFarmHouse.com 🌐 www.TheMooreFarmHouse.com

Tell your hosts Pamela Lanier sent you.

FOLLY BEACH

Water's Edge Inn
79 W 2nd St 29439
800-738-0884 843-588-9800
Paul Lauer/Dawn Goldman

199-279 $US BB
8 rooms, 8 pb
Visa, MC, AmEx, •
C-ltd/S-ltd/P-no/H-ltd

Continental plus breakfast
Complimentary bottled water & other
beverages, cocktails & light hors
doeuvres
Fireplaces, down comforters, plasma
flat screen TV, iPod ports, wireless
telephone & Internet

Nestled on the scenic marsh and just two short blocks from the pristine beaches of the Atlantic Ocean, Water's Edge offers a truly unique experience like no other in the area. Many extras invite you to relax, unwind and enjoy your surroundings. ✉ info@innatfollybeach.com 🌐 www.innatfollybeach.com

GEORGETOWN

Harbor House B&B
15 Cannon St 29440
843-546-6532
Meg Tarbox

159-199 $US BB
4 rooms, 4 pb
Visa, MC, *Rated*, •
S-ltd/P-no/H-no

Full South Carolina breakfast
Afternoon refreshments of shrimp or
crab dip, complimentary wine, beer,
soft drinks & juices
Bicycles, fireplaces, WiFi & flat screen
TVs, waterfront, newly updated
bedding

Harbor House is the only waterfront bed and breakfast in Georgetown, SC. Enjoy the breezes from the harbor on our porch. Stroll through the historic district and dine on the waterfront.
✉ info@harborhousebb.com 🌐 www.harborhousebb.com

Mansfield Plantation B&B
1776 Mansfield Rd 29440
866-717-1776 843-546-6961
Kathryn Green

150-200 $US BB
9 rooms, 9 pb
Most CC, •
C-yes/S-ltd/P-yes/H-no
German

Full breakfast
Dinner by reservation
Sitting room, library, suites, fireplaces,
boat dock, pets welcome

Historic Antebellum plantation house & guesthouses nestled amid moss-laden oaks, marshes & 900 private acres. Enjoy antique furnishings, paintings, collectibles; hammocks, swings, & bird watching.
✉ mightymansfield@aol.com 🌐 www.mansfieldplantation.com

GREENVILLE

Pettigru Place
302 Pettigru St 29601
877-362-4644 864-242-4529
Lori Donaldson

119-199 $US BB
5 rooms, 5 pb
Most CC, *Rated*, •
C-ltd/S-no/P-no/H-no

Full gourmet breakfast
Snacks, wine & cheese, tea service
Free wireless Internet, suites, fireplace,
cable TV, conferences

Voted Greenville's Favorite B&B and one of the Nation's Top 3 for Business. Set on a peaceful, tree-lined street in the Historic District, an easy stroll to 50 restaurants, theaters and the business district. Free wireless Internet. ✉ info@pettigruplace.com 🌐 www.pettigruplace.com

LANDRUM

The Red Horse Inn
45 Winston Chase
Court 29356
864-895-4968
Mary Wolters

175-320 $US BB
12 rooms, 12 pb
Visa, MC, Disc,
Rated, •
C-ltd/S-ltd/P-ltd/H-ltd

Continental plus breakfast
Each cottage has a kitchen, four-
course meals available upon request,
selection of wines, pizza
Dining area, living room, fireplace,
bedroom, bath, sitting area, TV, A/C,
massage, weddings

Sweeping mountain views, pastoral vistas and endless sky provide the perfect setting for 6 charming cottages. The Main Inn offers 6 luxurious rooms. Whirlpools, outdoor spas, fireplaces and more make The Red Horse Inn the South's most romantic retreat.
✉ theredhorseinn@aol.com 🌐 www.theredhorseinn.com

LATTA

Abingdon Manor Inn & Restaurant
307 Church St 29565
888-752-5090 843-752-5090
Michael & Patty Griffey

180-225 $US BB
7 rooms, 7 pb
Most CC, Cash, Checks,
Rated, •
C-ltd/S-ltd/P-ltd/H-ltd

Full breakfast
Fine dining, full service liquor, beer &
wine, AAA 4 Diamond rating
Sitting rooms, library, gardens
turndown service, cable TV

Experience the grandeur of Abingdon Manor. The only luxury inn (AAA-4 diamond) with such close proximity to I-95 in Georgia or the Carolinas (5 miles east). Historic, elegant, and comfortable.
✉ abingdon@bellsouth.net 🌐 www.abingdonmanor.com

MARION

The Grove
408 Harlee St 29571
843-423-5220
Denley & Ann Caughman

95-190 $US BB
5 rooms, 5 pb
Visa, MC, AmEx,
Rated, •
C-ltd/S-no/P-no/H-no

3 Course Gourmet Breakfast
Afternoon tea, snacks
Lunch, dinner (fee), sitting room,
library, bikes, hot tub

1893 Victorian manor in historic village between I-95 and Myrtle Beach. Dramatic architecture, stunning rooms.

✉ theinnonharlee@bellsouth.net ◎ www.montgomerysgroveinn.com

MYRTLE BEACH

Serendipity Inn
407 N 71st Ave 29572
800-762-3229 843-449-5268
Kay & Phil Mullins

55-149 $US BB
15 rooms, 15 pb
Most CC, Cash, *Rated*
C-yes/S-no/P-no/H-yes

Continental plus breakfast
Pool, hot tub, grill, garden room, living
room, kitchen, Internet access, TV,
DVD, fridge, A/C

Unique and secluded, this Spanish Mission-style inn offers a totally different approach to beach accommodations. A deluxe continental breakfast is served daily in the sunny garden room.

✉ serendipity-inn@att.net ◎ www.serendipityinn.com

SUMMERVILLE

Flowertown B&B
710 S Main St 29483
843-851-1058
Veronique & Gregory Elam

100-145 $US BB
5 rooms, 5 pb
Visa, MC, AmEx
C-ltd/S-no/P-no/H-no
French

Continental breakfast
Complimentary drinks
Sitting room, fireplace, cable TV,
computer, wireless Internet access

Historic Victorian house, c. 1889, with beautiful southern porches, bountiful gardens, a pond and cottage. Across from beautiful Azalea Park in the historic district. Downtown Charleston 20 minutes away. Beaches, lakes, golf and plantations are nearby.

✉ innkeeper@flowertownbandb.com ◎ www.flowertownbandb.com

Price House Cottage B&B
224 Sumter Ave 29483
843-871-1877
Jennifer & David Price

165 $US BB
1 rooms, 1 pb
Visa, MC, AmEx
C-ltd/S-ltd/P-ltd/H-ltd

Full gourmet breakfast on weekends
Kitchen stocked with soft drinks, juice
& teas
Tennis court, Jacuzzi, fireplace,
cable TV, complimentary high speed
Internet access, CD player

Restored 1812 servants' quarters, gourmet continental breakfast in cottage weekdays, full gourmet breakfast by candlelight chandelier in Main House weekends. Luxurious appointments & decor in Summerville's historic district.

✉ phcbb@knology.net ◎ www.pricehousecottage.com

UNION

The Inn at Merridun
100 Merridun Pl 29379
888-892-6020 864-427-7052
Peggy Waller

109-125 $US BB
5 rooms, 5 pb
Most CC, *Rated*, •
C-ltd/S-no/P-no/H-ltd

Full breakfast
Meals by prior arrangement, evening
dessert
Sitting room, library, 1 room with
whirlpool bath

Welcome . . . We invite you to make Merridun your home away from home. Join us in a small Southern college town where you are offered the opportunity to savor life at a more leisurely pace.

✉ info@merridun.com ◎ www.merridun.com

WINNSBORO

Honeysuckle Acres
70 Honeysuckle Ln 29180
800-387-1112 803-635-7583
Harold & Patricia Frish

90-130 $US BB
3 rooms, 2 pb
Visa, MC, *Rated*
C-ltd/S-no/P-no/H-no
Italian, French

Full breakfast
Epicurean picnic baskets available,
complimentary soft drinks, wine
Cable TV/VCR/DVD, in-room CD
player, library, turndown service,
picnic grove with outside fireplace

Honeysuckle Acres is a massive four-column Colonial home built in 1927. The house is reminiscent of an Antebellum mansion. It is set on seven park-like acres and is complete with the original stables and the original carriage stone in front.

✉ honeysuckleacresbb@yahoo.com ◎ clickbrochure.com/honeysuckleacres/brochure

South Dakota

CARPENTER

Possibility Farm
18653 408th Ave 57322
888-759-9615 605-352-6356
Darla & Harold Loewen

85-180 $US BB
2 rooms
C-yes/S-no/P-no/H-no

Full breakfast
Possibility Farm is some distance from
town, noon and evening meals are
served upon request.

*Harold and Darla Loewen welcome you to Possibility Farm. We look forward to having you come visit
and share our life on the farm, where you can relax and enjoy the rural lifestyle, learn about agriculture and farming, and marvel at the buffalo!*

✉ farmadventure@santel.net 🌐 www.possibilityfarm.com

CUSTER

Custer Mansion
35 Centennial Dr 57730
877-519-4948 605-673-3333
Bob & Pat Meakim

80-130 $US BB
5 rooms, 5 pb
Visa, MC, *Rated*, •
C-yes/S-no/P-no/H-no

Full breakfast
Afternoon tea, full cookie jar with
refreshments
Library, bikes, tennis, horseback
riding, golf nearby, year round hot tub,
wireless Internet

*Historic 1891 Victorian on 1 acre in heart of beautiful and scenic Black Hills. The area is famous for
its breath taking monuments, and Custer Mansion is well known for providing Western hospitality,
and delicious, homebaked food.*

✉ cusmanbb@gwtc.net 🌐 www.custermansionbb.com

DEADWOOD

Black Hills Hideaway
11744 Hideaway Rd 57732
605-578-3054
Kathy & Ned Bode

129-199 $US BB
8 rooms, 8 pb
Visa, MC, Disc,
Rated, •
C-ltd/S-ltd/P-no/H-ltd

Full breakfast
Snacks, cookies, Dinner (add fee)
Sitting rooms, bikes, Jacuzzis,
fireplaces, decks, views, hot tubs,
meetings, reunions, honeymoons

*Mountain inn with cathedral ceilings & wood interior, tucked in National Forest. You'll be pampered
on 67 wooded acres with fresh mountain air, the aroma & whispering of pines, peace & solitude.*

✉ hideaway@enetis.net 🌐 www.enetis.net/~hideaway

HILL CITY

Coyote Blues Village B&B
23165 Horsemans Ranch
Rd 57745
888-253-4477 605-574-4477
Christine & Hans-Peter
Streich

65-160 $US BB
10 rooms, 10 pb
Most CC, Cash, Checks,
Rated, •
C-yes/S-ltd/P-ltd/H-ltd
German, French

Swiss no need for lunch Breakfast
Espresso, cappuccino, tea, dinner,
vegetarian dining
Satellite TV, wireless Internet, fridge,
private hot tubs and patios

*European styled bed and breakfast, tucked away on 30 wooded acres north of Hill City. Swiss specialty
breakfast. Patios and hot tubs. Near Mount Rushmore, Crazy Horse, and Custer State Park. Located in
the Black Hills, South Dakota.*

✉ coyotebb@wildblue.net 🌐 www.coyotebluesvillage.com

RAPID CITY

Hisega Lodge
23101 Triangle Trail 57702
605-342-8444
Kenn & Carol Duncan

99-299 $US BB
9 rooms, 9 pb
Most CC, Cash, Checks
C-ltd/S-no/P-no/H-no

Full breakfast
We are happy to accommodate special
diets. Please let us know in advance.
Free WiFi, non-smoking

*If you're looking for a Black Hills bed and breakfast that is rustic, unique and real, book a stay at
Hisega Lodge. This centrally located inn sits next to beautiful Rapid Creek. For simple comfort, delicious food and great atmosphere, visit Hisega*

✉ info@hisegalodge.net 🌐 www.hisegalodge.net

Willow Springs Cabins, Rapid City, SD

RAPID CITY

Peregrine Pointe B&B
23451 Peregrine Pointe
Place 57702
877-388-8378   605-388-8378
Eileen Rossow & Warren
Meyer

140-160 $US BB
5 rooms, 5 pb
Visa, MC
C-ltd/S-ltd/P-no/H-ltd

Full breakfast
Snacks, cookies & nonalcoholic
beverages are provided in the evening.
Lunch & dinner for added cost.
Library, queen beds, private baths,
AC, exit to a deck, double dead-bolt
locks, free WiFi, AAA 3DIA.

Peregrine is a Latin word which means wanderer, nomadic, roving, and tending to travel. Come join us at our contemporary getaway for those looking for simple relaxation, great adventure, and quiet pleasures.

peregrineptbb@msn.com   www.peregrinebb.com

Willow Springs Cabins
11515 Sheridan Lake
Rd 57702
605-342-3665
Joyce & Russell Payton

165-180 $US BB
2 rooms, 2 pb
Rated
S-no/P-no/H-no
April-November

Gourmet Basket Breakfasts
Coffee, tea, hot chocolate, popcorn,
cookies. Outdoor gas grill provided for
your use.
TV/DVD, stereo, fridge, microwave,
outdoor hot tubs, hiking trails,
mountain stream, itinerary plans

Privacy at its best! Secluded, antique filled, log cabins in the beautiful Black Hills National Forest. Great views, gourmet breakfasts in your cabin, private outdoor hot tubs. A relaxing romantic retreat! Willow Springs requires a minimum two night stay.

info@willowspringscabins.com   www.willowspringscabins.com

WEBSTER

Lakeside Farm
13476 437th Ave 57274
605-486-4430
Glenn & Joy Hagen

60 $US BB
3 rooms, 2 pb
Rated
C-yes/S-no/P-no/H-no

Full breakfast
Tea or coffee, cookies, snacks
Sitting room, bicycles, museum,
factory outlet

Sample country life with us, a family-owned farm in the Northeastern South Dakota lakes area. Fresh air, open spaces, fresh milk and homemade cinnamon rolls.

gjhagen@venturecomm.net

Tennessee

ATHENS

Majestic Mansion B&B
202 E Washington Ave 37303
423-746-9041
Elaine Newman

95-135 $US BB
3 rooms, 3 pb
Visa, MC, Disc
C-yes/S-no/P-no/H-no

Full breakfast
Afternoon tea
Spa services, A/C, transportation,
closed in sun-porch, TV-WiFi in all
rooms, dog boarding closeby

This historic downtown Athens landmark was built in 1909 and is located just one block from the McMinn County Courthouse and two blocks from Tennessee Wesleyan College.

✉ info@themansionbnb.com   🌐 www.themansionbnb.com

COSBY

Creekwalk Inn at
Whisperwood Farm
166 Middle Creek Rd 37722
800-962-2246 865-696-2222
Janice & Tifton Haynes

129-259 $US BB
9 rooms, 9 pb
Most CC, *Rated*, •
C-ltd/S-no/P-no/H-ltd

Fresh fruit, local foods, gourmet
Dinner by reservation, picnic lunches
by request (extra fee), welcome
baskets, fruit and desserts
Romantic and casual, romance
packages, massage, nature trails,
elopements, reserve for wedding
venue

The natural charm of a log home on a private estate. Romantic, award-winning B&B in the Smoky Mountains near Gatlinburg. Serving gourmet food and offering romance, honeymoon & elopement specials. Whirlpools, fireplaces, and breakfast arrives at your door.

✉ janice@creekwalkinn.com   🌐 www.whisperwoodretreat.com

CROSSVILLE

Cumberland Mountain
Lodge
1130 Clint Lowe Rd 38572
919-599-5712
John & Susan Looney

175 $US BB
3 rooms, 3 pb
Visa, MC
C-ltd/S-no/P-ltd/H-ltd

Continental breakfast
On-site spa & beauty services by
request. Weddings, Receptions,
Events.

Three bedroom B&B Lodge. All rooms have private baths. Peaceful and quiet getaway with panoramic views of one of Tennessee's most beautiful farms and the surrounding mountains. Packages available.

✉ Info@CumberlandMountainLodge.com   🌐 www.cumberlandmountainlodge.com

DUCKTOWN

The Company House Bed
& Breakfast Inn
125 Main St 37326
800-343-2909 423-496-5634
Margaret Tonkin & Mike
Fabian

79-99 $US BB
7 rooms, 7 pb
Visa, MC, Disc,
Rated, •
C-ltd/S-ltd/P-ltd/H-no

Full breakfast
Soft drinks, tea, coffee & sweets
Deck overlooking water garden,
rocking chair front porch, selection of
books, piano, big screen TV

Circa 1850 inn located in the Copper Basin Area of the Southern Appalachian Mountains near the Ocoee River Olympic Whitewater Center. The breakfasts get rave reviews. Enjoy the big screen TV in the parlor or the rocking chair on the front porch.

✉ companyhouse@etcmail.com   🌐 www.companyhousebandb.com

ERIN

Five Oaks B&B
51 Averitt Dr 37061
931-289-5533
Margaret Mann

75 $US BB
4 rooms
C-ltd/S-ltd/P-no/H-ltd

Full breakfast
Refreshments included
Cable TV, refrigerator, ceiling fan,
clock radio, coffeemaker, turn-down
service, WiFi

Historic lodging, luxurious rooms & a taste of Ireland are all genuinely offered at this 19th-century Victorian home that sits on the hill above the village of Erin.

FRANKLIN

Butterfly Meadows Inn & Farm
6775 Bethesda Arno Road 37179
877-671-4594 615-671-4594
Darlene & Norman Bobo

149-219 $US BB
7 rooms, 7 pb
Visa, MC
C-yes/S-no/P-no/H-yes
Sign Language

Full Gourmet Breakfast
Unlimited coffees, teas & hot chocolates, lunch & dinner available for an extra fee
Fireplaces, Rocking Chair porch, nature walking trails, library, sitting rooms, WiFi, DVDs, Games

A place for you to relax and unwind. Take the time to slow down and catch a breath of fresh country air. Built to replicate the charm and comfort of a 100 year old farmhouse. Feel at home in one of our seven comfortable rooms and suites.

✉ relax@butterflymeadowsinn.com 🌐 butterflymeadowsinn.com

Magnolia House B&B
1317 Columbia Ave 37064
866-794-8178 615-794-8178
Robbie Smithson

130-150 $US BB
4 rooms, 4 pb
Most CC, Cash, Checks
C-ltd/S-no/P-no/H-no

Full breakfast

Craftsman style home built circa 1905, situated on the site of the Battle of Franklin and within walking distance to historic downtown. Furnished with antiques and fine linens.

✉ magnoliabnb@bellsouth.net

GATLINBURG

Berry Springs Lodge
2149 Seaton Springs Rd 37862
888-760-8297 865-908-7935
Patrick & Sue Eisert

149-249 $US BB
11 rooms, 11 pb
Visa, MC, Disc, •
C-ltd/S-no/P-no/H-yes

Bountiful Breakfast Served
24 hour complimentary beverages & snacks, nightly signature desserts
In-room Jacuzzis, turndown service, massage service, balconies, spectacular sunrises and sunsets, TV

Newly built Lodge. Relaxing luxury & first class service. Close to Dollywood; minutes to hiking trails, shopping & horseback riding. Romantic rooms & suites, some with Jacuzzi. Spa services.

✉ stay@berrysprings.com 🌐 www.berrysprings.com

Buckhorn Inn
2140 Tudor Mtn Rd 37738
866-941-0460 865-436-4668
Lee & John Mellor

115-295 $US BB
24 rooms, 24 pb
Most CC, Cash, Checks,
Rated
C-ltd/S-ltd/P-no/H-yes
Spanish, French, Latin

Hearty Breakfast
Romantic Gourmet Dinner, Picnic Lunches, Afternoon Refreshments, Receptions, Private Parties, Fireplaces, Jacuzzis, fitness center, massages, WiFi , TV/DVD, nature trail, bathrobes, coffeemakers

Facing spectacular mountain views, Buckhorn Inn is a private 30-acre tranquil retreat for the discriminating traveler. The area's most historic inn, it offers all modern amenities and is the only inn in the area that serves dinner every evening.

✉ info@buckhorninn.com 🌐 www.buckhorninn.com

Eight Gables Inn
219 N Mountain Trl 37738
800-279-5716 865-430-3344
Lee Bennett

140-270 $US BB
19 rooms, 19 pb
Most CC, Cash,
Rated, •
C-ltd/S-ltd/P-no/H-no

Full breakfast
Evening dessert, complimentary coffee, tea, non-alcoholic beverages & bottled water
All rooms have cable TV, CD & video players, bathrobes, imported soaps, concierge services & WiFi

Minutes from Gatlinburg and Pigeon Forge; our casual elegance will win you over. Our unique charm, warm hospitality and gracious service are the perfect compliment to your stay here in the mountains. 19 luxurious rooms and suites. AAA 4 Diamond Award.

✉ Eightgablesinn@aol.com 🌐 www.eightgables.com

GATLINBURG

Four Sisters Inn
425 Stuart Ln 37738
866-914-3687 865-430-8411
Jackie Price

125-220 $US BB
6 rooms, 6 pb
Most CC, Cash, Checks
C-yes/S-ltd/P-no/H-yes

Continental breakfast on request
Guest room phones, cable TV, HBO,
Internet, WiFi, free parking downtown

Come experience the best small inn in town. The Four Sisters' Inn is a luxuriously appointed six-room inn located at the end of a quiet wooded street. Private, quiet, yet close to everything.

✉ jackie@4sistersinn.com 🌐 www.4sistersinn.com

Laurel Springs Lodge B&B
204 Hill St 37738
888-430-9211 865-430-9211
Karen and Dan Berry

109-159 $US BB
5 rooms, 5 pb
Visa, MC, Disc, *Rated*
C-ltd/S-ltd/P-no/H-no
January to December

Full breakfast
Cookies, snacks, evening desserts
and beverages. Special diets
accommodated with advance notice.
Free WiFi, in room mini-fridge, movie
library, in room elec. fireplaces,
discount attraction tickets

Authentic Historic 1930s Smoky Mountain Lodge. Nestled on a wooded hillside in Gatlinburg, TN, an easy walk to downtown Gatlinburg & 3 miles to the entrance to the Smoky Mountain National Park or Arts & Crafts Community. Overlooks the Little Pigeon River.

✉ relax@laurelspringslodge.com 🌐 www.laurelspringslodge.com

The Foxtrot B&B
1520 Garrett Lane 37738
888-436-3033 865-436-3033
Bob & Shirley Price

165-205 $US BB
4 rooms, 4 pb
Most CC, *Rated*
C-ltd/S-no/P-no/H-ltd
French

3 course gourmet breakfast
Evening desert, 24 hour gourmet
coffee & tea service, soft drinks &
bottled water in the room
Library with fireplace, on-site spa
services, access to pool, tennis courts,
fitness center

Nestled in the trees at the crest of the mountain, the Foxtrot B&B offers 2 suites with fireplaces and balconies, and 2 luxurious, deluxe king rooms with private baths and Jacuzzi tubs. Spectacular views of the Great Smoky Mountains.

✉ information@thefoxtrot.com 🌐 www.thefoxtrot.com

GREENEVILLE

Nolichuckey Bluffs
295 Kinser Park Ln 37743
800-842-4690 423-787-7947
Brooke & Patricia Sadler

95-155 $US BB
8 rooms, 8 pb
Most CC, Cash,
Checks, •
C-yes/S-no/P-ltd/H-no

Full breakfast
Afternoon tea, snacks
Weddings in new wedding chapel
Library, Jacuzzis, fireplaces, disc golf,
reunions, groups

Free Night w/Certificate: Anytime except holidays and special events.

Quiet luxury cabins in a country setting. Fireplaces, full kitchens, trails, English garden and spectacular mountain and river views. Disc golf and grist mill on property.

✉ cabins@usit.net 🌐 www.tennessee-cabins.com

KINGSPORT

**Fox Manor Historic B&B
Inn**
1612 Watauga St 37664
888-200-5879 423-378-3844
Susan & Walter Halliday

110-175 $US BB
6 rooms, 6 pb
Most CC, *Rated*
S-no/P-no/H-no
French

Full breakfast
Bottomless cookie jar, fresh
homemade popcorn
Sitting rooms, English pub bar,
fireplaces, library, veranda, gazebo,
guest computer, Free WiFi

Free Night w/Certificate: Valid anytime except during Nascar Race Weeks and Story Telling Festivals. Room Upgrade.

Upon arrival, you will notice the original carriage steps used by passengers to disembark from their horse-drawn carriages. This is your first clue that you've arrived at a truly unique & historic inn.

✉ shalliday@foxmanor.com 🌐 www.foxmanor.com

Tell your hosts Pamela Lanier sent you.

Fox Manor Historic B&B Inn, Kingsport, TN

KINGSTON

Whitestone Country Inn
1200 Paint Rock Rd 37763
888-247-2464 865-376-0113
Paul and Jean Cowell

165-325 $US BB
22 rooms, 22 pb
Most CC, *Rated*
C-ltd/S-ltd/P-no/H-yes

Full breakfast
Lunch & Dinner (fee), complementary
snacks, event catering
Whirlpool tubs, fireplaces, DVD
Players, conference center, wedding
chapel, spa treatment, marina

Whitestone Country Inn's 360 secluded acres lies on the shores of Watts Bar Lake. Enjoy views of the Smoky Mountains. Experience luxurious lodging, whirlpool tubs, gourmet dining, and take advantage of our weddings and event services.

 info@whitestoneinn.com 🌐 www.whitestoneinn.com

Woodland Cove
144 Helton Vojtkofsky
Lane 37763
877-700-2683 865-717-3719
Bruce & Della Marshall

125-165 $US BB
3 rooms, 3 pb
Visa, MC, Disc
C-yes/S-no/P-no/H-no

Full breakfast
Accommodations include evening
dessert, complimentary beverages
Satellite TV and VCRs, full use of dock,
swimming, canoeing, and paddle
boating, and private baths.

Nestled on the shores of beautiful Watts Bar Lake; come enjoy leisure hours on this peaceful, secluded woodland cove; do some canoeing, paddle boating or just relaxing by the lake. You will be made to feel right at home with us!

 info@woodlandcovebb.com 🌐 www.woodlandcovebb.com

MONTEAGLE

Monteagle Inn
204 W Main St 37356
931-924-3869
Jim Harmon

165-265 $US BB
13 rooms, 13 pb
Visa, MC, Disc,
Rated, •
C-ltd/S-no/P-no/H-yes

Full, hot gourmet breakfast
snacks, cheese & fruit plates for
wine; chocolates with roses in room,
customized dinners & function
The perfect romantic experience
or just a refreshing get-a-way to our
beautiful mountain beauty

Monteagle Inn is a romantic B&B situated atop the beautiful Cumberland Plateau in Monteagle, Tennessee. Beautifully appointed interiors, balconies, patios, courtyards, gardens, and a wonderful front porch create a comfortable European atmosphere.

✉ suites@monteagleinn.com 🌐 www.monteagleinn.com

MOUNTAIN CITY

Prospect Hill B&B Inn	99-245 $US BB	Full breakfast, always fresh fruit
801 W Main St/ Hwy	5 rooms, 5 pb	Snack basket in rooms, chocolates,
67 37683	Most CC, Cash,	coffee/tea 24/7, filtered & bottled
800-339-5084 423-727-0139	*Rated*, •	water, other snacks.
Robert & Judy Hotchkiss	C-ltd/S-ltd/P-ltd/H-ltd	Porch & balcony, fireplaces, A/C,
		whirlpool tubs, cable TV, garden,
		views, fireflies, concierge

Large, comfortable, very private and luxurious rooms. Perfect for a romantic getaway or nature-lover's vacation. Elopements for 2 or weddings for 100. Perfect tranquility, views, whirlpools and fireplaces in this c.1889 mansion. Relax. Reconnect. Romance.

✉ inn@prospect-hill.com ◐ www.prospect-hill.com

MURFREESBORO

Hastings House B&B	112 $US BB	Full breakfast
223 N Academy St 37130	2 rooms, 2 pb	Cable TV and DVD player
615-907-3364	*Rated*	
Jane Blakey	C-ltd/S-ltd/P-ltd/H-ltd	

The Hastings House Bed and Breakfast in Murfreesboro welcomes you to Rutherford County, TN. Enjoy the cats in the house; dogs are welcome in the Big Springs Cabin. Close to downtown. Owner is very connected to the community!

✉ hastingshousetn@bellsouth.net ◐ www.hastingshousebb.com

NASHVILLE

The Big Bungalow B&B	125-185 $US BB	Full Hot Breakfast
618 Fatherland Street 37206	3 rooms, 3 pb	Cable TV, free WiFi, computer,
615-256-8375	Visa, MC, Disc	massage therapist on site, screened-in
Ellen Warshaw	C-ltd/S-ltd/P-no/H-no	porch, monthly house concerts

You are all invited to visit my home. The guestrooms are welcoming and cozy, but so is the dining room and living room. Enjoy the comfort each place in the house has to offer.

✉ stay@thebigbungalow.com ◐ www.thebigbungalow.com

NEWPORT

Christopher Place	165-330 $US BB	Full breakfast
1500 Pinnacles Way 37821	8 rooms, 8 pb	Gourmet 4 course dinner, picnic
800-595-9441 423-623-6555	Most CC, Cash, Checks,	lunches & snacks
Marston Price	*Rated*, •	Swimming, tennis, sauna, exercise
	C-ltd/S-no/P-no/H-ltd	room, videos, library, fireplaces

On 200 acres near Gatlinburg in the Smoky Mountains. Voted best bed and breakfast in the area. Named one of the 10 most romantic in the country. AAA 4 Diamond. Fine dining. Luxury rooms. Personal service.

✉ marston@christopherplace.com ◐ www.christopherplace.com

ONLY

Chestnut Hill Ranch B&B	129-285 $US BB	Full gourmet-country breakfast
3001 Browns Bend Rd 37140	4 rooms, 4 pb	3 course dinners, luncheons, gourmet
931-729-0153	Visa, MC, *Rated*	picnics, specialty desserts, catering for
Cher Boisvert-Tanley &	C-ltd/S-ltd/P-no/H-yes	groups & businesses.
George Tanley	Spanish, French	Jacuzzi in outdoor Gazebo. Private
		baths, Fireplaces, Gift Baskets,
		Romance packages, massage etc

Southern hospitality in a beautiful ranch setting. Romance, comfort, pampering, relaxation, fabulous meals, themed rooms, private baths, sumptuous breakfast, romance packages for celebrations, gazebo with hot tub, fireplaces, amenities sure to please.

✉ chestnuthillranch@earthlink.net ◐ www.chestnuthillranch.com

RED BOILING SPRINGS

| **Armour's Red Boiling Springs Hotel**
321 E Main St 37150
615-699-2180
Dennis & Debra Emery | 49-129 $US BB
14 rooms, 14 pb
Most CC, Cash, Checks
C-yes/S-no/P-no/H-yes | Full Country Breakfast
Dinner available with advance notice;
full country luncheons and dinners
available for groups of 12+
Mineral Baths, Steam Bath, Massage
by CMT (advance notice required),
Suites, large Dining Room (80) |

National Historic Registry 85 year old hotel. 12 rooms & 2 suites, furnished with antiques, private baths. Porches with rockers on 2 levels overlooking Salt Lick Creek, WiFi , Mineral & Steam Baths available, massages available by CMT's by appointment.
✉ armourshotel@yahoo.com 🌐 www.armourshotel.com

ROAN MOUNTAIN

| **Mountain Harbour B&B**
9151 Hwy 19 E 37687
866-772-9494 423-772-9494
Terry & Mary Hill | 80-135 $US BB
3 rooms
Visa, MC
C-yes/S-no/P-yes/H-no | Full breakfast
Pet friendly, peaceful and rural,
bordering Appalachian Trail |

We are a rural B&B and Hostel situated a quarter of a mile from the Appalachian Train. The Roan Mountain is over 6000 feet in elevation and famous for their rhododendron gardens.
✉ welcome@mountainharbour.net 🌐 www.mountainharbour.net

SEVIERVILLE

| **Ancient Oaks B&B**
431 Thomas Loop Rd 37876
888-735-2951
Allen Hood | 125-275 $US EP
5 rooms, 5 pb
Visa, MC, AmEx
S-ltd/P-no/H-yes | Concierge services, over 90 acres,
business center, fitness center, game
room, gardens, theater |

Experience Ancient Oaks Bed & Breakfast in the Smoky Mountains of East Tennessee just minutes from Gatlinburg, Pigeon Forge, and Sevierville. We offer exclusivity, sophistication and personalized service combined with an unrivaled relaxing atmosphere.
✉ info@myrestandrelaxation.com 🌐 www.myrestandrelaxation.com

SMITHVILLE

| **The Inn at Evins Mill**
1535 Evins Mill Rd 37166
800-383-2349 615-269-3740
Tina Clark | 240-300 $US MAP
12 rooms, 12 pb
Most CC, Cash, •
C-ltd/S-ltd/P-no/H-no | Full breakfast
Dinner and Breakfast included. Light
snacks, beer, soft drinks, bottled water.
12 rooms with creek side decks, TVs/
VCRs, CD, coffeemaker, hairdryers,
guest computer with Internet |

Evins Mill rests on a scenic 40-acre property, featuring waterfalls, hiking trails, bluff view rooms with creek side decks, a historic lodge and gristmill, and delicious, Southern gourmet cuisine.
✉ info@evinsmill.com 🌐 www.evinsmill.com

TOWNSEND

| **Gracehill B&B**
1169 Little Round Top Way
37882
866-448-3070 865-448-3070
Kathleen Janke | 250-325 $US BB
4 rooms, 4 pb
Visa, MC, AmEx,
Rated, •
C-ltd/S-no/P-no/H-ltd | 3 Course Full Breakfast
Complimentary snack area, coffee, tea,
soda, fruit drinks & water, chocolates
& crunchy-munchies!
WiFi, guest computer, SAT TV,
VCR/DVD, fitness center, massage,
whirlpool, steam shower, fireplaces |

Award-winning 3 years in a row "Best Scenic View from a B&B in the U.S." – Inn Traveler Magazine. Blount County's Bravo Award for Beautiful Gardens. 360-degree view of the Great Smoky Mountains National Park. Near Gatlinburg, Pigeon Forge and Townsend.
✉ bestview@gracehillbandb.com 🌐 www.gracehillbandb.com

WARTRACE

| **Ledford Mill**
1195 Shippmans Creek
Rd 37183
931-455-2546
John & Mildred Spear | 95-125 $US BB
3 rooms, 3 pb
Visa, MC
C-yes/S-no/P-ltd/H-no
January – December | Full breakfast
Refreshments & snacks available
Waterfalls, garden, sitting area, video
library, antiques |

Relax at historic Ledford Mill at the headwaters of Shipman's Creek, an 1884 gristmill listed on the National Register of Historic Places and the Tennessee Heritage Trail. 3 unique rooms with private baths. Waterfalls, gardens and antique shop. ✉ spears_games@msn.com

Texas

AMARILLO

Adaberry Inn
6818 Plum Creek Dr 79124
806-352-0022

125-195 $US BB
9 rooms, 9 pb
Most CC, Cash, •
C-ltd/S-no/P-no/H-yes

Full breakfast
Complimentary Snacks and Beverages!
Game room with putting greens, darts,
pool table, Movie theatre, Movie
library, & Fitness Room

Adaberry Inn was a modernized constructed boutique bed & breakfast specifically designed to accommodate business travelers as well as vacationers with the comfort and security of a larger-than-life private home and the amenities of a first-class hotel.

✉ adaberryinn@yahoo.com 🌐 www.adaberryinn.com

AUROA

MD Resort B&B
601 Old Base Rd 76078
866-489-5150 817-489-5150
Donna Davis

77-497 $US BB
18 rooms, 14 pb
Visa, MC, AmEx,
Rated, •
C-yes/S-yes/P-ltd/H-yes

Full breakfast
Country picnic baskets for two, or a
romantic dinner for two in suite
Pool, spa, hay rides, game room,
sitting area, outdoor sports, carriage
rides, pecan orchard

A Texas ranch B&B conveniently located in the Dallas/Fort Worth area. MD Resort offers modern conveniences with an Old West atmosphere. Close to the big city, yet quietly secluded from the bustling workday world.

✉ customerservice@mdresort.com 🌐 www.mdresort.com

AUSTIN

Austin Folk House
506 W 22nd St 78705
866-472-6700 512-477-9639
Sylvia Mackey

85-225 $US BB
9 rooms, 9 pb
Most CC
C-ltd/S-ltd/P-no/H-yes
Spanish

Full breakfast
Afternoon sweets and evening wine
Cable TV and VCR, private phone
lines and voice mail, robes, fine
toiletries

Beautifully restored in 2001, this B&B offers historic charm without sacrificing modern comfort and convenience. Decorated with antiques and a large collection of folk art. Centrally located.

✉ sylvia@austinfolkhouse.com 🌐 www.austinfolkhouse.com

Mansion at Judge's Hill
1900 Rio Grande 78705
800-311-1619 512-495-1800
Lisa Wiedemann

129-399 $US EP
48 rooms, 47 pb
Most CC, Cash,
Rated, •
C-yes/S-no/P-yes/H-yes
Spanish

Judges' Hill Restaurant & Bar, private
stocked minibar, free breakfast with
mention of this listing
High speed wireless Internet,
hairdryer, iron & board, CD/DVD,
luxury bathrobes

Mansion at Judges' Hill is a premier 4 star, 48-room boutique hotel & restaurant in Austin, TX. We bestow an exquisite hotel & a luxurious restaurant that is affordable & inviting.

✉ reservations@judgeshill.com 🌐 www.judgeshill.com

Star of Texas Inn
611 W 22nd St 78705
866-472-6700 512-477-9639
Sylvia

95-225 $US BB
10 rooms, 10 pb
Most CC
C-ltd/S-no/P-ltd/H-ltd

Full breakfast
Wraparound porch, balcony, high
speed wireless Internet, parlor

Star of Texas Inn is a Victorian mansion built in 1897. A relaxed and comfortable place to stay in central Austin. Near to downtown and the University of Texas.

✉ sylvia@austinfolkhouse.com 🌐 www.staroftexasinn.com

BOERNE

Paniolo Ranch B&B Spa
1510 FM 473 78006
866-726-4656
Judy Kennell

230-325 $US BB
4 rooms, 4 pb
Visa, MC, AmEx
S-no/P-no/H-ltd

Full breakfast
Dinner is also available
Spa Services, room service, satellite
TV, WiFi, hot tub, lake views, gift shop,
art gallery

The Paniolo Ranch Bed and Breakfast Spa offers a resort retreat overlooking the picturesque Texas Hill Country lake and hills. This B&B Spa offers outstanding recreation and relaxation, whether for a honeymoon, anniversary, or weekend getaway.

 paniolo@panioloranch.com 🌐 www.panioloranch.com

BRENHAM

Far View
1804 S Park St 77833
888-FAR-VIEW 979-836-1672
Steve & Linda

95-205 $US BB
9 rooms, 9 pb
Most CC
C-ltd/S-ltd/P-no/H-yes

Full breakfast
Lighter fare, low fat, low carbohydrate
& vegetarian meals are available upon
request
Air conditioning, swimming
pool, outdoor fireplace, 24 hr
complimentary hot & cold drinks,
WiFi

Warm hospitality awaits in this restored 1925 prairie-style home, a Texas Recorded Historical Landmark on a 2-acre retreat. Far View features elegant rooms, dedicated to your comfort. Near Historic Brenham, TX, 70 miles from Houston, 90 from Austin.

 stay@farviewbedandbreakfast.com 🌐 www.farviewbedandbreakfast.com

Mariposa Ranch B&B
8904 Mariposa Ln 77833
877-647-4774 979-836-4737
Johnna & Charles
Chamberlain

99-239 $US BB
11 rooms, 11 pb
Most CC, Cash, Checks
C-yes/S-ltd/P-no/H-no
Spanish

Full breakfast
Snack baskets, picnic baskets, dinners
available
Weddings, business services, library,
TV/VCR/DVD, video library, Jacuzzi,
swimming pool

Private cabins, cottages and suites including an 1860 Texas Plantation home, and an early Texas antique log cabin. All with private baths, some with Jacuzzis-for-two or antique claw foot tubs. Swimming pool, weddings, special occasions are our specialty.

 info@mariposaranch.com 🌐 www.mariposaranch.com

Murski Homestead B&B
1662 Old Independence
Rd 77833
877-690-0676 979-830-1021
Pamela Murski

115-245 $US BB
3 rooms, 3 pb
Visa, MC, Disc, *Rated*
C-ltd/S-ltd/P-no/H-ltd

Full Self Serve breakfast
Cooking classes, Foodie Events
Elopements, Concierge, satellite TV,
Electric Fireplaces, Private Baths,
IPhone Dock, Ceiling Fans

Intimate Ranch Elopements, Foodie Events, Romantic Getaways! Experience True Texas Hospitality! 1896 ranch homestead, beautiful hills & views, cooking classes, front porch swing & outdoor living areas, wildlife/birding, gardens, history, shopping, theater

 pmurski@sbcglobal.net 🌐 www.murskihomesteadbb.com

CANTON

Redbird Retreat B&B
10025 FM 1255 75103
903-829-9632
Peggy & Jim Cox

95-150 $US BB
5 rooms, 5 pb
S-no/P-no/H-no

Full gourmet or country breakfast
Videos, books. ceiling fans & A/C in
every room; small groups

Redbird Retreat is nestled on seven acres of woods adjoining a private lake. Just 10 minutes from Canton's World Famous Trade Days. A fantastic place to hold business meetings, retreats, or other small groups.

 reservations@redbirdretreat.com 🌐 www.redbirdretreat.com

CAT SPRING

BlissWood Bed & Breakfast
13300 Lehmann Legacy Ln 78933
713-301-3235
Carol L. Davis

179-299 $US BB
21 rooms, 21 pb
Visa, MC, Disc, •
C-yes/S-no/P-ltd/H-ltd
German

Continental breakfast
Restaurant, snacks, complimentary wine
Bicycles, swimming pool, suites, fireplaces, cable TV, accommodate business travel, outdoor sports

Spend a day, a week, or longer at BlissWood B&B, an unbelievable Texas getaway at Lehmann Legacy Ranch, a 650 acre ranch an hour west of Houston. Unwind in a peaceful country setting amidst majestic Live Oaks in your choice of charming guesthouses.
✉ carol@blisswood.net 🌐 www.blisswood.net

CLEBURNE

River Rock B&B Cottages
206 W. Dabney 76033
817-774-6248
Danielle Petty

125-149 $US BB
2 rooms, 2 pb
Most CC, Cash, *Rated*
C-yes/S-no/P-no/H-ltd

Continental breakfast
SOME Food, snacks & beverages provided
Covered Parking * Fully Equipped 2 Bedroom Cottage * Garden Area with Hot Tub * Flat Screen

River Rock Bed & Breakfast Cottage is a place to turn off the stress, relax in our quiet cottage in peace. We are happy to accommodate all schedules.
✉ daniellepetty@riverrockbbcottages.com 🌐 riverrockbbcottages.com/Home.aspx

COMFORT

Idlewilde Lodge B&B
115 Highway 473 78013
830-995-3844
Connie & Hank Engel

87-132 $US BB
2 rooms, 2 pb
Rated
C-yes/S-ltd/P-ltd/H-ltd

Full breakfast
Lunch & dinner available, snacks
Complimentary wine, sitting room, library, tennis court, pool, pavilion

Free Night w/Certificate: Anytime. Room Upgrade.

Customized service is our motto and our specialty is a large, full country breakfast complete with table linens, candlelight, fine china, and classical music.
✉ idlewilde@hctc.net

Meyer B&B on Cypress Creek
845 High St 78013
888-995-6100 830-995-2304
Shane Schleyer

99-210 $US BB
28 rooms, 28 pb
Most CC, Cash, Checks
C-yes/S-no/P-no/H-ltd

Full breakfast
Fresh fruit in season, hot brewed coffee & an assortment of herbal teas
Swimming pool, creek, Jacuzzi, hot tub, dining room, fireplace, WiFi

Meyer Bed & Breakfast offers one of the most scenic, peaceful & romantic getaways in the Texas Hill Country. ✉ info@meyerbedandbreakfast.com 🌐 www.meyerbedandbreakfast.com

DALLAS

Corinthian B&B
4125 Junius St 75246
866-598-9988 214-818-0400
Dan Tucker

129-229 $US BB
5 rooms, 5 pb
Visa, MC, AmEx,
Rated, •
S-no/P-no/H-no

Full plated gourmet breakfast daily
Afternoon snacks, cookies, pastries, soft drinks & bottled water
Bathrobe, quality linen, hairdryer, phone, TV, DVD, VCR, CD, off street parking

The Corinthian B&B is a home near the heart of Dallas, in the Peak-Suburban Historic District near the Swiss Ave. area of famous homes. We are eager to make your stay at The Corinthian memorable, relaxing and fun. ✉ innkeeper@corinthianbandb.com 🌐 www.corinthianbandb.com

Hotel St. Germain
2516 Maple Ave 75201
800-683-2516 214-871-2516
Claire Heymann

290-650 $US BB
7 rooms, 7 pb
Visa, MC, AmEx,
Rated, •
C-ltd
French, Spanish

Continental plus breakfast
Room service, bar service, dinner, snacks, complimentary wine, restaurant
Concierge, butler service, turndown, valet parking, Internet & fax, library, Jacuzzis, fireplaces

Award-winning boutique hotel. A European oasis in the century-old French Hotel Particulie in uptown Dallas. New Orleans gardened courtyard, Old World style, with New World conveniences and luxury.
✉ genmgrstgermain@aol.com 🌐 www.hotelstgermain.com

FORT DAVIS

Old Schoolhouse B&B
401 N Front St 79734
432-426-2050
Carla & Steve Kennedy

93-101 $US BB
3 rooms, 1 pb
Visa, MC, Disc
C-ltd/S-no/P-no/H-no
German

Full breakfast
Free sodas, water, tea, coffee & snacks
Microwave oven, refrigerator,
hairdryers, robes, library

This century old adobe schoolhouse sits in shaded comfort near the Fort Davis National Historic Site. Star gaze at the McDonald Observatory, hike at Davis Mountain State Park, or swim at Balmorhea State Park. We are a gateway to Big Bend National Park.

 kennedys@schoolhousebnb.com ❂ www.schoolhousebnb.com

FORT WORTH

Lockheart Gables
Romantic B&B
5220 Locke Ave 76107
888-224-3278 817-738-5969
David & Marilyn Lewis

189-229 $US BB
6 rooms, 6 pb
Most CC, Cash, Checks
S-ltd/P-no/H-ltd

Full breakfast
Cookies, special drinks,
complimentary picture
Jacuzzi tubs, fireplaces, wedding
accommodations, tea room, parlor,
music room, romance, common area

Lockheart Gables Romantic B&B, located in Fort Worth, Texas, is the choice for couples planning their honeymoon, an anniversary, a birthday or just wanting a private, peaceful romantic getaway.

 david@lockheartgables.com ❂ www.lockheartgables.com

The Texas White House
1417 8th Ave 76104
800-279-6491 817-923-3597
Jamie & Grover McMains

129-249 $US BB
5 rooms, 5 pb
Most CC, Cash, Checks,
Rated, •
C-ltd/S-ltd/P-ltd/H-ltd

Full, gourmet breakfast
Snacks and cold drinks
Sitting room, porches, gazebo, garden,
business accommodations, fireplace,
sauna, whirlpool tub

Historically designated, award winning, country-style home has been restored to its original 1910 grandeur with simple yet elegant decor. Centrally located, within 5 minutes of downtown Fort Worth. Two suites, three rooms.

 txwhitehou@aol.com ❂ www.texaswhitehouse.com

FREDERICKSBURG

115 Austin Place
115 Austin St 78624
888-991-6749 830-997-0443
Ron Maddux

119-169 $US BB
2 rooms, 2 pb
Most CC
S-ltd/P-no/H-ltd

Continental breakfast
Coffee & tea bar
Hot tub, patio, authentic 1930's
furnishings

Austin Place offers a memorable experience, different from the Victorian or Country Style that so typifies most bed & breakfasts today.

 stay@fredericksburg-lodging.com ❂ www.fredericksburg-lodging.com/Austin-place

A Way of the Wolf Country
Inn
458 Wolf Way 78624
888-WAY-WOLF 830-997-0711
Ron & Karen Poidevin

115-145 $US BB
7 rooms, 5 pb
Rated
C-ltd/S-ltd/P-no/H-no

Full breakfast
Coffee, tea, soft drinks
Living room, kitchen, pool, screened
porches, gas grills, prayer center,
conference facility

60 acres in Texas Hill Country. Tastefully furnished with antiques. Ideal for a romantic getaway or retreat. Restored Civil War cabin and restored Amish barn with full baths and mini kitchens.

 waywolf@ctesc.net ❂ www.wayofthewolf.com

A.L. Patton Suites on Main
332 W Main St 78624
888-991-6749 830-997-0443
Ron Maddux

119-179 $US BB
2 rooms, 2 pb
Most CC
S-no/P-no/H-no

Continental breakfast
Complimentary cheese, chocolates &
fresh fruit plate, coffee & tea bar
Fireplace, Jacuzzi, climate controlled
rooms, DVD player, off street parking,
king-size beds

This historic building was built in 1853 & sits on Main Street, only 2 blocks from the Central shopping district. The decorator has captured the essence of nostalgic "Days Gone By" in both of our suites.

 stay@fredericksburg-lodging.com ❂ www.fredericksburg-lodging.com/A-l-patton2

FREDERICKSBURG

Alte Welt Gasthof
142 E Main St 78624
888-991-6749 830-997-0443
Ron & Donna Maddux

150-159 $US BB
2 rooms, 2 pb
Most CC, *Rated*, •
C-ltd/S-no/P-no/H-no
German

Continental breakfast
Afternoon tea, snacks, complimentary wine
Jacuzzis, suites, cable TV, accommodations for business travelers

Beautiful European and antique decor. Vintage fabrics and fine linens enhance the Old World ambience of this historic inn. It's only a block away from Fredericksburg's historic Marktplatz.

 stay@texas-bed-n-breakfast.com **◐** www.texas-bed-n-breakfast.com

Cat's Meow B&B
9848 Hwy 290 West 78624
830-997-0888
Pauline Scott

95-265 $US BB
4 rooms, 4 pb
Visa, MC, Disc, •
S-ltd/P-ltd/H-no

Continental breakfast
On site massages, outdoor gazebo, romantic packages & intimate weddings, whirlpool tubs, fireplaces

Located in the beautiful Hill Country, the Cat's Meow features luxury, secluded cabins with 2 person whirlpool tubs and fireplaces. Romantic packages, on site massages and intimate weddings are our specialty.

 catsmeow@beecreek.net **◐** www.catsmeowbedandbreakfast.com

Corner Cottage B&B
305 S. Orange St 78624
830-990-8265
Marsha Thompson

89-139 $US BB
3 rooms, 3 pb
Visa, MC, Disc
C-ltd/S-ltd/P-no/H-no

Full Gourmet Breakfast
Free romantic picnic basket lunch for two with a three night stay!
Wireless Internet, old-fashion bicycles, hammock, porch swing, ice machine, cable TV, DVD/VCR movies

Full Gourmet Breakfast, Private Entrance, Jacuzzi tub, Wireless Internet, and Gas Fireplace with each suite. No wonder, Corner Cottage was featured in Country Decorating Ideas Magazine twice! Come and visit a time where the clock loses importance.

 rthompson1134@austin.rr.com **◐** www.fredericksburgcornercottage.com

Magnolia House
101 E Hackberry St 78624
800-880-4374 830-997-0306
Claude & Lisa Saunders

110-165 $US BB
5 rooms, 5 pb
Most CC, *Rated*, •
C-ltd/S-ltd/P-no/H-ltd

Two course gourmet breakfast
Fresh baked goodies every afternoon, complimentary wine & soft drinks
Two sitting rooms, patio, waterfall, koi pond, large front porch

A bed & breakfast known for gracious Southern hospitality and their 2 course gourmet breakfasts. This elegant historic home features 5 guestrooms (2 are suites with fireplaces) tastefully decorated and appointed with guests' comfort in mind.

 stay@magnolia-house.com **◐** www.magnolia-house.com

Schandua Suite
205 E Main St 78624
888-990-1415 830-990-1415
Sharla & Jonathan Godfrey

175-300 $US BB
1 rooms, 1 pb
Visa, MC, Disc, *Rated*
S-ltd/P-no/H-no

Continental plus breakfast
Snacks, complimentary hors d'oeuvres on arrival, chocolates
Sitting room, library, suites, cable TV, robes, phone, fine antiques & family heirlooms

Luxury suite located in the heart of the historic district. Pullman kitchen, quaint shops all within walking distance, private balcony overlooking secluded courtyard.

 sharla44@hctc.net **◐** www.schandua.com

GALVESTON

Avenue O B&B
2323 Ave O 77550
866-762-2868 409-762-2868
Connie & Jim Porter

95-159 $US BB
5 rooms, 4 pb
Most CC
C-yes/S-no/P-yes/H-no

Full breakfast
Outdoor grill available, tasty treats delivered to your room daily
Video library, gardens, patio, living room, dining room, Jacuzzi, wireless Internet

Located in the historic Silk Stocking District just blocks from the beach, and minutes from the Strand, this 1923 Mediterranean-style bed and breakfast exhibits a comfortable elegance throughout.

 connie@avenueo.com **◐** www.avenueo.com

GALVESTON

Grace Manor B&B	99-199 $US BB	Full breakfast
1702 Post Office St. 77550	4 rooms, 4 pb	Champagne with Strawberries and
800-810-8590 409-621-1662	Most CC, Cash, *Rated*	Chocolates – $39.95 Wine & Cheese
Barb Gatlin	S-no/P-no/H-no	Basket with Fruit – $39.95
		Breakfast, wireless Internet, private
		Jacuzzi tub in rooms, free parking for
		cruise guests.

"The phrase, "sleeping in a museum," fits Grace Manor, a stately Victorian mansion at 1702 Postoffice Street in Galveston." – Coast Magazine, The Daily News, (Cozy Coastal Comforts) – September 2009

✉ barbgatlin@hotmail.com 🌐 www.gracemanor-galveston.com

Lost Bayou Guesthouse	125-200 $US BB	Continental plus breakfast
1607 Ave. L 77550	5 rooms, 3 pb	Fresh made Croissant w/egg, cheese &
832-613-5884 409-770-0688	Most CC, Cash, Checks	bacon or Kolache, or Breakfast Taco,
Phil DeMarco	C-ltd/S-ltd/P-no/H-no	fresh fruits, cereals
		Each room has own A/C & heater w/
		remote, cold drinks & juice, bottled
		water, ice, wireless

This 1890 Bed and Breakfast is a survivor of the great hurricane of 1900. A historical Victorian home located in the Lost Bayou historic district, in Galveston Texas. With 5 large bedrooms this B&B is centrally located on the East end of Galveston.

✉ sales@lostbayou.com 🌐 www.lostbayou.com

The Mermaid & The	149-279 $US BB	Full breakfast
Dolphin	8 rooms, 8 pb	Tropical Buffet – Saturday & Sunday
1103 33rd St 77550	Most CC, Cash	only.
800-930-1866 409-762-1561	S-no/P-no/H-no	
Jeff		

Water . . . It's the essence of life. So naturally, it's one of the greatest sources of relaxation. Relax your body, rejuvenate your mind and re-discover yourself at Galveston's Tropical Romantic Getaway.

✉ info@mermaidanddolphin.com 🌐 www.mermaidanddolphin.com

The Victorian Inn	125-175 $US BB	Gourmet
511 17th St 77550	6 rooms, 3 pb	Butler Pantry: nuts, fruit, candies,
409-762-3235	Visa, MC, AmEx,	cookies, popcorn, iced tea, and
Marcy Hanson	*Rated*, •	gourmet coffee.
	C-ltd/S-ltd/P-no/H-no	Personal reservations for all events
		and dinning, roses or Champagne,
		carriage rides, or adventures.

Free Night w/Certificate: Valid Oct, 2011-April 2012. Room Upgrade.

Official 2011 Best of Texas Historical B&B! Elegant Victorian Mansion on a private estate. Gardens are an Official Wildlife habitat, butterfly waystation and bunny sanctuary. Period antiques, private balconies, gourmet breakfasts! Enjoy the Peace!

✉ Marcy.Hanson@att.net 🌐 www.vicbb.com

GLEN ROSE

Country Woods Inn	100-250 $US BB	Barn breakfast buffet plus
420 Grand Ave 76043	13 rooms, 13 pb	Kitchens, cookout patios, campfire
888-849-6637 817-279-3002	Visa, MC	circles in every unit
Helen Kerwin	C-yes/S-ltd/P-ltd/H-ltd	Campfire circles, swimming hole,
		petting barnyard, horseshoes,
		porches, fishing, riverwalk downtown

Award-winning, family friendly Inn on the Paluxy River. 40 acres surrounded by nature. 13 cabins, and century-old guesthouses. Walk to Downtown Square. Breakfast in the barn. Enjoy fishing, swimming and the barnyard.

✉ countrywoodsinn@yahoo.com 🌐 www.countrywoodsinn.com

GRANBURY

Inn on Lake Granbury
205 W Doyle St 76048
877-573-0046 817-573-0046
Jim Leitch & Cathy Casey

215-375 $US BB
9 rooms, 9 pb
Most CC, •
C-ltd/S-no/P-no/H-yes

Full breakfast
Appetizers & beverages each
afternoon at 5:30pm
Weddings & events, fireplaces,
porches, balconies, robes, TV,
Internet, fire pits, pool

Featuring almost two acres of landscaped gardens, a flagstone pool, and scenic lakefront views. Imagine a romantic walk down winding pathways to Lake Granbury's water's edge.

✉ info@innonlakegranbury.com   ◐ www.innonlakegranbury.com

GRAPEVINE

Garden Manor B&B Inn
205 E College St 76051
877-424-9177 817-424-9177
Judy & Gunther Dusek

115-195 $US BB
4 rooms, 4 pb
Visa, MC, AmEx
C-ltd/S-no/P-no/H-no

Full breakfast
Bottled water, soft drinks, morning
coffee service,
Wireless cable & Internet connections,
mini-fridge with free soft drinks &
water

Garden Manor B&B Inn is 7 minutes from DFW Int'l Airport and designed for both business and leisure travel. 1 block from Main Street with shops, restaurants, theatre, live music & wine tasting rooms. 3 guestrooms, 1 suite. Weddings and receptions hosted.

✉ info@gardenmanorbandb.com   ◐ www.gardenmanorbandb.com

HILLSBORO

1895 Tarlton House
211 N. Pleasant St 76645
888-808-1895 254-582-3422
Teresa & David Stoops

99-159 $US BB
6 rooms, 6 pb
Most CC, Cash
C-ltd/S-no/P-yes/H-no
Spanish

Full breakfast
4 PM afternoon social hour with
beverages and snacks at your request
7 fireplaces, wrap around porch,
music parlor, wireless Internet, luxury
linens

Looking for an historic getaway in a luxury mansion with an exquisite breakfast? The 1895 Tarlton House is the place for you. Victorian architecture, themed decor, and modern amenities reward you with a pleasurable stay, and refreshment of the soul.

✉ innkeeper@1895tarltonhouse.com   ◐ www.1895tarltonhouse.com

HUNTSVILLE

The Whistler
906 Avenue M 77340
800-404-2834 936-295-2834
Mary Thomason Clegg

155-175 $US BB
4 rooms, 3 pb
Visa, MC, AmEx
C-ltd/S-no/P-no

Full breakfast
Complete gourmet breakfast

An elegant home, built in 1859, fully restored to its Victorian Splendor. Located in historic Huntsville, the Mount Vernon of Texas and home of Texas hero Sam Houston.

✉ mtclegg@sbcglobal.net   ◐ www.thewhistlerbnb.com

IRVING

Jefferson Street B&B Inn
512 S Jefferson St 75060
972-253-2000
Lee Lowrie

99-380 $US EP
10 rooms, 10 pb
Most CC, *Rated*
C-ltd/S-no/P-no/H-yes

Full breakfast
Breakfast is optional, the cost is $7 per
person
Cable TV with 160+ channels, wireless
Internet, free private off-street parking,
conference room

AAA-Approved. Between Dallas & Ft Worth. Charming quiet neighborhood, just 6 miles from DFW and Love Field Airports. Wonderful, clean and fun Texas themed rooms with great Stearns & Foster mattresses, WiFi, cable TV and climate control.

✉ jeffersonstreetbnb@hotmail.com   ◐ www.jeffersonstreetbnb.com

JASPER

Swann Hotel B&B
250 N Main 75951
877-489-9717 409-489-9010
Mary Silmon

119-129 $US BB
8 rooms, 6 pb
Visa, MC
C-ltd/S-ltd/P-ltd/H-yes

Full breakfast
Snacks & soft drinks
Parlour, baby grand piano, balconies,
porches, massage facility nearby,
antiques, wireless Internet

1901 restored Victorian boutique hotel in downtown Jasper. Walk to art galleries, massage therapy, quaint shops, lovely park with a creek and lighted jogging trail. Minutes from Lake Sam Rayburn and Martin Dies Park for golf, bird watching & canoeing.

✉ swannhotel2005@yahoo.com 🌐 www.hotelswann.com

JEFFERSON

Carriage House B&B
401 N. Polk 75657
903-665-9511
Stephanie Lester

89-139 $US BB
7 rooms, 7 pb
Most CC, Cash, Checks
C-ltd/S-ltd/P-yes/H-no

Multi-course gourmet breakfast
Continental breakfast on weekdays,
free water & sodas available,
homemade cookies
Free Wi-FI, home-made cookies in
the room, flat screen TVs with cable,
sodas and waters

The Carriage House is a beautiful historic home only two blocks from all of the shops and restaurants in the Historic Riverfront District.

✉ info@carriagehousejefferson.com 🌐 www.carriagehousejefferson.com

The Hale House Inn B&B
702 S Line St. 75657
903-665-9955
Timm & Karen Jackson

89-149 $US BB
6 rooms, 6 pb
Most CC, Cash, Checks,
Rated, •
C-ltd/S-ltd/P-ltd/H-no

Full breakfast
Sitting rooms, such as Media Room,
Library, Music Room, porches and
gazebo, gardens

The Hale House Inn offers six beautifully appointed guestrooms with private baths, a charming veranda and gazebo where you can choose to have breakfast. This Jefferson Texas bed and breakfast Inn is a delightful setting for an ideal getaway.

✉ mystay@thehalehouseinn.com 🌐 www.thehalehouseinn.com

KEMAH

Clipper House Inn
710 Bradford Ave 77565
866-887-3534 281-334-2517
Barbara & Jerry Hopper

99-259 $US BB
8 rooms, 8 pb
Most CC, Cash
C-yes/S-no/P-no/H-ltd

Continental breakfast
Complimentary spring water, sodas,
and juice, wine & cheese, Breakfast
basket each day
Landscaped gardens, phone, fax,
modem hookup available, wireless
Internet, winery tours, antiques

Free Night w/Certificate: Valid Monday-Wednesday.

Nestled in the heart of Kemah and close to all the Boardwalk attractions lies The Clipper House Inn. Situated on nearly and acre of manicures gardens are seven 1930s cottages filled with antiques and treasures from the owners world travels.

✉ innkeeper@clipperhouseinn.com 🌐 www.clipperhouseinn.com

KYLE

Inn Above Onion Creek
4444 FM 150 W 78640
866-745-1617 512-268-1617
Amy Dolan

199-399 $US MAP
12 rooms, 12 pb
Visa, MC, AmEx
C-ltd/S-ltd/P-no/H-yes

Full breakfast
Endless cookies, hot and cold
beverages; 3 course dinner included,
served at 6pm
Dining room, whirlpool, library, spa
services, hiking and biking trails,
weddings, conferences

We are a 12 room country inn and spa on 100 acres located 25 miles from Austin, in Kyle, Texas. The inn sits on a hill above Onion Creek, offering beautiful views of the Hill Country. 3 course Dinner and breakfast included in rate.

✉ info@innaboveonioncreek.com 🌐 www.innaboveonioncreek.com

MARFA

Arcon Inn B&B
215 N Austin 79843
432-729-4826
Mona & Rodolfo

75-225 $US EP
6 rooms, 2 pb

The Arcon Inn is a turn of the century Victorian adobe full of museum quality antiques and South American Colonial art. The house is warm and comfortable. Guests are treated with all the amenities you would expect in a fine B&B. Breakfast served daily.

✉ arconinn@yahoo.com

MARSHALL

Wisteria Garden
215 E Rusk 75670
903-938-7611
John & Mary Lynn Vassar

75-95 $US BB
4 rooms, 4 pb
Visa, MC, Disc
C-yes/S-no/P-no/H-no

Full breakfast
Cable, WiFi, coffee maker and mini fridge in rooms.

Built in 1884, by a Marshall Merchant, this beautiful Inn sits only two blocks from the historical downtown courthouse and town square.

✉ john@wisteriagarden.com 🌐 wisteriagarden.com

MATADOR

Hotel Matador Bed and Breakfast
1115 Main Street 79244
806-347-2939
Linda Roy

85-125 $US BB
9 rooms, 9 pb
Most CC, Cash, Checks
C-ltd/S-no/P-no/H-no

Full cowboy gourmet breakfast
Afternoon tea, non-alcoholic beverage
Wireless Internet, individual climate control, private baths, cable TV, landscaped courtyard

A historic 1914 hotel recently restored to meet the needs of today's traveler, Hotel Matador B&B provides cable TV, wireless Internet, a beautifully landscaped courtyard, a cowboy gourmet breakfast, and West Texas hospitality in the Caprock foothills.

✉ reflect@hotelmatador.com 🌐 www.hotelmatador.com

MCKINNEY

Dowell House c. 1870 B&B
1104 S Tennessee St 75069
972-562-2456
The Muellers

145 $US BB
2 rooms, 2 pb
Most CC, Cash,
Checks, •
S-no/P-no/H-no

Full breakfast – 9 AM
Snacks, complimentary beverage
Hot tub, whirlpool bath, satellite TV, guest parlor, desks, free wireless Internet, business rate

Romantic and elegant, this historic B&B is near the quaint town square in McKinney, Texas, the perfect place to escape from the city. The house was a filming location for the original "Benji" movie.

✉ lookin4ancestrs@sbcglobal.net 🌐 www.dowellhouse.com

MINEOLA

Munzesheimer Manor
202 N Newsom 75773
888-569-6634 903-569-6634
Bob & Sherry Murray

90-120 $US BB
7 rooms, 7 pb
Most CC, Cash, Checks,
Rated, •
C-ltd/S-ltd/P-no/H-ltd

Full gourmet breakfast
Hot cider, cold lemonade, fresh baked cookies
Two parlors, fireplaces, cable TV, refrigerators, accommodate business travelers, weddings & events

1898 Victorian with wraparound porches. Victorian nightgowns, gourmet breakfasts, and special pampering. Featured in national magazines and named as one of "Best Twelve B&Bs in Texas."

✉ innkeeper@munzesheimer.com 🌐 www.munzesheimer.com

NEW BRAUNFELS

Acorn Hill B&B
250 School House 78132
800-525-4618 830-907-2597
Pam Thomas

145-170 $US BB
6 rooms, 6 pb
Most CC, *Rated*, •
C-yes/S-no/P-ltd/H-no

Full breakfast
Dining room, antiques, organ, porches, pool, hot tub, garden, weddings

Just five minutes from the Guadalupe River and downtown Gruene, and ten minutes from historic New Braunfels, find an old log Schoolhouse, a 1905 Victorian house and three romantic cottages. Enjoy our beautiful pool, hot tub and country setting.

✉ acornhill@acornhillbb.com 🌐 www.acornhillbb.com

NEW BRAUNFELS————————————————————

Gruene Mansion Inn	180-340 $US BB	Breakfast buffet
1275 Gruene Rd 78130	30 rooms, 30 pb	Porch, antiques, clawfoot tubs,
830-629-2641	Visa, MC, AmEx	fireplaces, flat screen TVs
Cecil & Judi Eager	C-yes/S-no/P-no/H-ltd	

Sitting on the banks of the Guadalupe River, & adjacent to Gruene Hall, the Gruene Mansion Inn offers you the opportunity to enjoy lodging in the most unique Texas style.

✉ frontdesk@gruenemansioninn.com 🌐 www.gruenemansioninn.com

Hunter Road Stagecoach Stop	115-200 $US BB	Full gourmet breakfast
	4 rooms, 4 pb	Sitting room, dog trot, porches, TV,
5441 FM 1102 78132	Most CC, *Rated*, •	walking & bike trails
830-620-9453	C-ltd/S-ltd/P-ltd/H-yes	
Bettina		

Texas landmark constructed 150 years ago by Amish settlers. Authentically restored Fachwerk house and log cabin. All are surrounded by gardens of antique roses and herbs.

✉ stagecoach@satx.rr.com 🌐 www.stagecoachbedandbreakfast.com

Kuebler Waldrip Haus B&B	125-300 $US BB	Full candlelight breakfast 9:30am
	11 rooms, 11 pb	Enjoy complimentary homemade
1620 Hueco Springs	Most CC, Cash, Checks,	cookies, snacks, drinks, Blue Bell Ice
Loop 78132	*Rated*, •	Cream. Use BBQ pits or kitchens.
800-299-8372 830-625-8300	C-yes/S-ltd/P-ltd/H-yes	Free copy/fax, WiFi, book & movie
Margaret K. Waldrip & son,	Spanish	library, playground, lounge areas,
Darrell Waldrip		fishing pond & bird watching.

This New Braunfels Texas Bed and Breakfast lodging is on 43 acres just 3–6 min. from Gruene and New Braunfels. Three beautifully restored buildings have 11 rooms that sleep 2 per room or some up to 5. Hot breakfast, bird watch, playground, fishing pond.

✉ kueblerwaldripinfo@att.net 🌐 www.kueblerwaldrip.com

Lamb's Rest Inn	150-225 $US BB	Full breakfast
1385 Edwards Blvd 78132	6 rooms, 6 pb	Breakfast served Sun/Thurs buffet
888-609-3932 830-609-3932	Visa, MC, Disc, •	9–10:30am. Fri/Sat breakfast is served
Judy & George Rothell	C-ltd/S-ltd/P-no/H-no	in dining room at 9am
		Jacuzzi, pool, hot tub, river access,
		quality bathroom products, bathrobes,
		fireplace, luxury linens

Enjoy true Texas hospitality on the Guadalupe River near the historic village of Gruene. A peaceful, romantic atmosphere awaits you in tranquil gardens.

✉ info@lambsrestinn.com 🌐 www.lambsrestinn.com

Prince Solms Inn B&B	125-195 $US BB	Full breakfast
295 E San Antonio St 78130	14 rooms, 14 pb	Snacks and bottled water in room
800-625-9169 830-625-9169	Most CC, Cash	upon arrival.
Al Buttross	C-ltd/S-no/P-no/H-ltd	Romantic, full service bar, parlor,
		phone, cable, and courtyard.

Experience pampered hospitality at Prince Solms Inn, one of Texas' most historic treasures, offering eight guestrooms, four luxurious suites & two cottages, and serving a scrumptious country breakfast every morning. ✉ innbox@princesolmsinn.com 🌐 www.princesolmsinn.com

PITTSBURG————————————————————

Pecan House	89-110 $US BB	Full Gourmet English Breakfast
212 College St 75686	6 rooms, 6 pb	Special English home-cooked lunches
903-856-5504	Most CC, Cash, Checks	and dinners, High Teas, wine available
Peter Jessop	C-ltd/S-ltd/P-ltd/H-yes	at dinner
		Victorian decor, library & sitting
		room, free wireless Internet, cable TV,
		library, decks

Elegant Victorian home, with all the grace of traditional English & European ambience. The English owners provide a wonderful service, you will think you were in Europe! Peace and relaxation is served with English Afternoon Tea! The best B&B in Pittsburg!

✉ support@pecanhousedesign.com 🌐 www.pecanhousebnb.com

SALADO

The Inn at Salado	85-160 $US BB	Full breakfast
7 N Main St 76571	12 rooms, 12 pb	Sitting room, fireplaces, cable TV,
800-724-0027 254-947-0027	Most CC, Cash	conference, weddings & receptions,
Rob & Suzanne Petro	C-ltd/S-no/P-no/H-no	whirlpool tub

The Inn displays both a Texas Historical Marker and a National Register listing. Walking distance to shopping and dining. The Inn is a great place for couples to get away and for business retreats.

✉ rooms@inn-at-salado.com 🌐 www.inn-at-salado.com

SAN ANTONIO

1908 Ayres Inn	99-299 $US BB	Continental Breakfast and Hot Items
124 W. Woodlawn Ave 78212	5 rooms, 5 pb	Baked Fresh Hot Pepper Turkey,
210-736-4232	Most CC, Cash	Feta Cheese and Spinach stuffed
M. Eifler & H. Llanas	C-ltd/S-ltd/P-no/H-no	Croissants. Cinnamon Rolls, Espresso
	Spanish	Gated Parking, WiFi, Fax, Copy
		Machine, & Printer, Books, Magazines,
		Games, Porch, Pond & Garden

San Antonio Bed and Breakfast. Located in the historic neighborhood of Monte Vista, this two-story neoclassic home built in 1908 by the renowned architect Atlee B. Ayres at 124 West Woodlawn is listed in the National Registry of Historic Places.

✉ sa1908ayresinn@msn.com 🌐 www.1908ayresinn.com

A Beckmann Inn &	109-189 $US BB	Gourmet breakfast with dessert
Carriage House	5 rooms, 5 pb	Butter cookies, welcome "tea"
222 E Guenther St 78204	Most CC, Cash, *Rated*	Convenient location, trolley, porches,
800-945-1449 210-229-1449	C-ltd/S-no/P-no/H-no	refrigerators, TVs, phones, hairdryers,
Lisa Cantu		irons

Set in the beautiful King William historic district, A Beckmann Inn & Carriage House is a "hidden treasure," the perfect location for enjoying San Antonio at its very best, whether for business or leisure travel.

✉ stay@beckmanninn.com 🌐 www.beckmanninn.com

Bullis House Inn	69-159 $US BB	Full breakfast
621 Pierce St 78208	5 rooms, 1 pb	Guest kitchen located next to Bullis
877-477-4100 210-223-9426	Visa, MC, *Rated*, •	House Inn.
Steven & Alma Cross	C-yes/S-ltd/P-no/H-no	Information area next door;Free
		WiFi;high speed Internet, free
		parking;pool;BBQ;hair dryers, lockers.

Affordable Elegance in the Classic Southern Style. Located across Fort Sam Houston quadrangle. Easy access from San Antonio Airport and downtown by car. Guest rooms have 14-foot ceilings, chandeliers, cable TV, clock radios, small fridges, fireplaces . . .

✉ APSMCross@aol.com 🌐 www.bullishouseinn.com

Christmas House B&B	85-125 $US BB	Full breakfast
2307 McCullough 78212	4 rooms, 4 pb	Two restaurants within walking
800-268-4187 210-737-2786	Visa, MC, Disc,	distance Tex-Mex & Italian
Penny Estes	*Rated*, •	Sitting room, private/semi private
	C-ltd/S-ltd/P-no/H-ltd	veranda, private bathrooms, TV

Free Night w/Certificate: Valid Sunday-Thursday; Holidays excluded.

Christmas House B&B is near San Antonio's famous Alamo and Riverwalk (1.5 miles) with bus service available close to the door. Built in 1908, it is located in the historic Monte Vista District.

✉ christmashsb@earthlink.net 🌐 www.christmashousebnb.com

SAN ANTONIO

Dr. Yrizarry's B&B	129-159 $US BB	Full breakfast
115 W Ashby Pl 78212	3 rooms, 3 pb	Refrigerator in room with refreshments
210-733-5899	Most CC, Cash, Checks,	and small basket of goodies
Ada C. Yrizarry	*Rated*	Sitting room, steam room, bicycles as
	C-ltd/S-no/P-no/H-no	requested
	Spanish	

This unique San Antonio, TX B&B, you will be captivated by ponds and water fountains, herbs , and the sounds of native and exotic birds, a few blocks from the newly opened Riverwalk Extension, the Pearl Brewery Development, and Museum Reach Urban Segment

✉ yrizarry@swbell.net 🌐 www.historicsanantoniobandb.com

Inn on the Riverwalk	99-299 $US BB	Full breakfast
129 Woodward Pl 78204	13 rooms, 13 pb	Water, fruit juice, teas & coffees,
800-730-0019 210-225-6333	Most CC, *Rated*, •	snacks
Johanna Gardner & Scott	C-yes/S-no/P-yes/H-ltd	River views from porches, free
Kiltoff	Spanish	parking, free WiFi, TV, A/C,
		refrigerators, desks, spa tubs

Located in the heart of downtown San Antonio, we're situated on the famous San Antonio Riverwalk. We'll book your romantic getaway from Champagne and Chocolates on your bed, to reservations for a fabulous dinner on the Riverwalk, and a carriage ride home.

✉ innkeeper@innontheriverwalksa.com 🌐 www.innontheriverwalksa.com

Noble Inns – Oge Inn	169-399 $US BB	Full or Continental
Riverwalk	19 rooms, 19 pb	Afternoon refreshments & cookies,
209 Washington St 78204	Most CC, Cash,	evening port & sherry, appetizers,
800-242-2770 210-224-7300	*Rated*, •	honor bar in lobby
Don & Liesl Noble	C-ltd/S-no/P-no/H-no	Sitting room, library, A/C, cable TV,
		phone, 1½ acres of gardens on the
		Riverwalk downtown, WiFi

Elegant, romantic, Antebellum mansion on 1.5 acres on the Riverwalk in the King William Historic District. European antiques, quiet comfort & luxury. Shopping, dining, Alamo & Convention Center, 2 to 4 blocks. Trolley service to all downtown attractions.

✉ stay@nobleinns.com 🌐 www.nobleinns.com/oge.html

O'Casey's Bed & Breakfast	90-125 $US BB	Full breakfast
225 West Craig Place 78212	7 rooms, 7 pb	Sitting room, cable TV, garden,
800-738-1378 210-738-1378	Most CC, Cash, •	carriage house, Internet access
John & Linda Fay Casey	C-yes/S-no/P-yes/H-no	

Friendly, home-style B&B in a quiet, residential historic district. Five guestrooms and two carriage house apartments with private baths, hearty full breakfast, reasonable rates and families are welcome. ✉ jpcasey@grandecom.net 🌐 www.ocaseybnb.com

The Inn at Craig Place	125-205 $US BB	3 course gourmet breakfast
117 W Craig Pl 78212	5 rooms, 5 pb	Hospitality corner with light snacks,
877-427-2447 210-736-1017	Visa, MC, Disc, *Rated*	coffee, tea & soft drinks along with a
Gregg & Kelly Alba	S-ltd/P-no/H-no	bedtime snack
	French	Evening sweet, romance & celebration
		packages, wireless high speed
		Internet, fireplaces, Jacuzzis

The Inn sets the scene for romance, comfort & indulgence for your special occasion. The Inn provides the peaceful retreat you've earned for recovery and relaxation following a day of meetings.

✉ stay@craigplace.com 🌐 www.craigplace.com

SAN MARCOS

Crystal River Inn	95-175 $US BB	Full breakfast
326 W Hopkins 78666	12 rooms, 12 pb	Complimentary brandy, chocolates
888-396-3739 512-353-3248	Most CC, •	Fireplaces, courtyard, piano, fountain,
Mike, Cathy & Sarah Dillon	C-ltd/S-ltd/P-no/H-yes	bikes, 2-room suites, picnics

A romantic, luxurious Victorian that captures the matchless spirit of Texas Hill Country. Fresh flowers, homemade treats. 4-room garden cottage available with fireplace.

✉ info@crystalriverinn.com 🌐 www.crystalriverinn.com

SEABROOK ────────────────────────────────

Beacon Hill B&B	109-150 $US BB	Hot plated breakfast at the B&B
3701 Nasa Rd One 77586	4 rooms, 4 pb	Refreshments
281-326-7643	Most CC, Cash	WiFi, cable, private fishing pier
Delaina Hanssen	C-ltd/S-no/P-ltd/H-ltd	(lighted 2Q11), in-room coffee/frig,
		books, walk-to restaurants

Free Night w/Certificate: Valid Sun-Thurs. excluding holidays & special events. Room Upgrade.

Celebrate, romance your partner or bring the entire family for a refreshing getaway on the water, let the sea breeze and mild climate soothe your soul. Relax on Clear Lake, fish on our private, lighted pier and walk to local restaurants.

✉ delaina.hanssen@gmail.com ○ www.beaconhillbnb.com

The Old Parsonage Guest	105-185 $US BB	Continental plus breakfast
House	2 rooms, 1 pb	A goodie basket filled with chips,
1113 Hall St 77586	Visa, MC, AmEx	cookies, pretzels, a bottle of wine and
713-206-1105	C-yes/S-no/P-no/H-yes	delicious snacks
Stevie Jones		

This professionally designed guesthouse features a living room, fully equipped kitchen, utility room, two spacious bedrooms with queen size beds and one large bath. A beautifully landscaped backyard is home to squirrels, birds and butterflies.

✉ info@seabrookaccommodation.com ○ www.seabrookaccommodation.com

SMITHVILLE ────────────────────────────────

9E Ranch B&B	85-225 $US BB	Full breakfast basket delivered
2158 Highway 304 78957	4 rooms, 4 pb	Coffee & tea in cabins
512-497-9502	Visa, MC, *Rated*, •	Heat & A/C, woodburning stoves,
Joan Bohls	C-yes/S-no/P-yes/H-no	footed tub, antiques, CD/clock radio,
		private cabins, weddings

Experience the beauty and tranquility of Texas by staying in the Texas Lone Star, Eagles' Nest log cabin, Michelle's Log Cabin or 2 bedroom Daisy Cottage on a hill at the 9E Ranch in Lost Pines, Bastrop. Available for weddings.

✉ joan9e@gmail.com ○ www.9eranch.com

TOLAR ────────────────────────────────

The Windmill Farm B&B	125-150 $US BB	Full breakfast delivered to cabin
6625 Colony Road 76476	3 rooms, 3 pb	
817-279-2217	Visa, MC, Disc	
Cell 254-835-4168	C-yes/S-no/P-yes/H-ltd	
Chuck & Ruby Rickgauer		

Three private cabins on 26 country acres with over 40 windmills. We offer a great view of Texas with beautiful sunsets as the porches face west. The Windmill Farm is located 7 miles from Granbury and 20 miles from Glen Rose.

✉ crickgauer@itexas.net ○ www.thewindmillfarm.com/BedBreakfast.htm

TYLER ────────────────────────────────

Rosevine Inn	120-195 $US BB	Full breakfast
415 S Vine 75702	7 rooms, 7 pb	Snacks & refreshments on arrival,
903-592-2221	Most CC, Cash, Checks,	picnic lunch for fee with notice
Bert & Rebecca Powell	*Rated*, •	Sitting room, library, spa, outdoor hot
	C-ltd/S-no/P-no/H-no	tub, courtyard, game room, free WiFi,
	French, Spanish	TV in all rooms

Return to your carefree days when your biggest worries were when can we go out to play? When do we go to bed? What's for Breakfast? One minute you are relaxing, the next you are playing, then you meet a new friend! Rosevine Inn, the "best" in Tyler!

✉ rosevine@dctexas.net ○ www.rosevine.com

VICTORIA

Friendly Oaks B&B
210 E. Juan Linn St. 77901
361-575-0000
Bill & CeeBee McLeod

65-95 $US BB
4 rooms, 4 pb
Most CC, Cash, *Rated*
C-ltd/S-no/P-no/H-ltd

Full breakfast
Conference room, complimentary
wireless Internet, A/C, cable TV, BBQ
grill,

Friendly Oaks B&B is nestled among several huge live oak trees in a quiet preserved historic area. Close to banks, courts, restaurants, antique shops and the new Performing Arts Center. Scrumptious full breakfasts feature Texas produce.

✉ innkprbill@aol.com 🌐 www.friendlyoaksbandb.com.

WACO

The Livingston at Heritage Square
330 Austin Ave 76701
800-651-1664 254-722-5721
Mary Baskins

169-255 $US EP
6 rooms, 6 pb
Most CC, Cash
C-yes/S-ltd/P-yes/H-ltd

$10 voucher given to guests for the
local coffee shop
High speed Internet, comfortable
rooms with luxury furnishings, king
beds and balconies.

Situated in the heart of Downtown Waco, The Livingston at Heritage Square is a luxury boutique inn offering beautifully appointed one, two, and three bedroom suites.

✉ marybaskin@hotmail.com 🌐 www.the-livingston.com

WIMBERLEY

Blair House Inn
100 Spoke Hill Rd 78676
877-549-5450 512-847-1111
Mike & Vickie Schneider

150-289 $US BB
11 rooms, 11 pb
Most CC, Cash,
Rated, •
C-ltd/S-no/P-no/H-yes

Full 3 course breakfast
Homemade dessert, beverages, 5
Course Dinner offered on Saturdays,
picnic baskets available
Living room, lounge, library, spa
services, sauna, massage, nature trail,
bicycles, cooking school

Rejuvenate your soul & spirit by surrounding yourself with the blissful views of the Texas Hill Country. Named one of the "Top 5 B&B's" by Texas Highways Magazine, the Blair House Inn provides ultimate comfort with attentive service and warm hospitality!

✉ info@blairhouseinn.com 🌐 www.blairhouseinn.com

Creekhaven Inn
400 Mill Race Ln 78676
800-827-1913 512-847-9344
Pat & Bill Appleman

150-275 $US BB
14 rooms, 14 pb
Most CC
S-ltd/P-no/H-yes

Breakfast Buffet
Welcome reception for Friday night
arrivals
Massages available, great room,
library, swimming creek, swing, fire
pits, patios, hot tub

Texas Hill Country elegance is yours at this romantic waterfront haven, lush in its natural setting and gracious hospitality. With 14 rooms, expansive decks, patios and gardens, this is a great place to hold your next reunion, business retreat or wedding.

✉ pat@creekhaveninn.com 🌐 www.creekhaveninn.com

Prow'd House B&B
304 Rocky Springs Rd 78676
866-720-7666 512-847-1900
Donna & Dave Kyte

125-150 $US BB
6 rooms, 6 pb
Visa, MC
C-ltd/S-no/P-no/H-no

Full breakfast
Breakfast is served each morning
in the dining area or on the patio,
weather permitting
Queen bed, private full baths, TV, DVD
player, Internet access, coffee pot,
hairdryer, private patio

A beautiful example of a "Lindal Cedar Home" with a cedar lined towering cathedral ceiling and huge prow windows that open up a panorama of Hill Country views.

✉ prowdhouse@anvilcom.com 🌐 www.prowdhouse.com

Wimberley Inn
200 Ranch Road 3237 78676
877-447-3750 512-847-3750
Denese & Dan Washam

79-199 $US BB
21 rooms, 21 pb
Visa, MC, AmEx
C-ltd/S-no/P-no

Continental breakfast
High-speed Internet available,
individually controlled A/C and
heating, select DVD & CD collection

Wimberley Inn provides a tranquil, intimate and quiet stay, surrounded by live oaks and cedars in the Hill Country. At the same time the Inn is within walking distance to the galleries, gift shops and restaurants of Wimberley Square.

✉ wimberley_inn@yahoo.com 🌐 www.wimberleyinn.com

Utah

CEDAR CITY

1897 Iron Gate Inn B&B
100 N 200 W 84720
800-808-4599 435-867-0603
Susan & CR Wooten

99-159 $US BB
10 rooms, 10 pb
Most CC, Cash, •
C-yes/S-no/P-ltd/H-yes

Full Gourmet Breakfast
Complimentary glass of wine,
lemonade or soft drink each afternoon
in the garden or dining room.
Secluded terrace for outdoor dining
and relaxing, parlor, living room, fine
linens & beds, free WiFi

Not cluttered or too frilly, this casually elegant B&B offers dreamy king & queen bedrooms w/private baths and fabulous breakfasts! Close to Zion Nat'l Park and Bryce Canyon, 2 blocks to the Shakespeare Festival. Free afternoon wine or lemonade; WiFi.

info@theirongateinn.com 🌐 www.TheIronGateInn.com

Amid Summer's Inn B&B
140 South 100 West 84720
888-586-2601 435-586-2600
Charlene & Gary Elsasser

99-179 $US BB
10 rooms, 10 pb
Most CC, Cash,
Rated, •
C-ltd/S-ltd/P-no/H-ltd

Full warm gourmet breakfast
Fruit smoothies, home baked cookies,
chocolates, fresh fruit, assorted
beverages & tea served daily
Nightly turn down service, daily room
service, dinner reservations, massage/
manicure by appointment

Amid Summer's Inn Bed and Breakfast is an award-winning Tudor inn located in historic, downtown Cedar City, Utah. Walk to The Utah Shakespearean Festival. Close to Zion National Park & Bryce Canyon. Specials and romance packages on website.

info@amidsummersinn.com 🌐 www.amidsummersinn.com

Willow Glen Inn
3308 N Bulldog Rd 84721
866-586-3275 435-586-3275
Violet & Phil Carter

79-225 $US BB
8 rooms, 8 pb
Most CC, Cash,
Rated, •
C-yes/S-no/P-no/H-no

Full breakfast
Catered parties for groups of 20 or
more by reservation
Sitting room, suites, fireplace,
conference facilities

Willow Glen has 8 unique rooms on 9 acres of landscaped yards & gardens. The perfect base for trips to 3 national parks, the Utah Shakespearean Festival & winter skiing at Brian Head Resort.

info@willowgleninn.com 🌐 www.willowgleninn.com

GLENDALE

Historic Smith Hotel B&B
295 N Main St 84729
800-528-3558 435-648-2156
Rochelle & Mike

74-94 $US BB
7 rooms, 7 pb
Visa, MC, *Rated*, •
C-yes/S-no/P-ltd/H-ltd

Full breakfast
Sitting room, screened porch, 2 acres
to roam, swing, BBQ & picnic table

Historic 1927 hotel with a lovely view of nearby bluffs from the guest porch. Located in beautiful Long Valley between Zion and Bryce Canyon National Parks. Two acres to roam.

smith_hotel@email.com 🌐 www.historicsmithhotel.com

Windwhisper Cabin B&B
Hwy 89 Mile Marker 92
84729
435-632-8410 435-648-2162
Terry & Audrey Behling

99-139 $US BB
3 rooms, 2 pb
Visa, MC, Disc
C-yes/S-ltd/P-no/H-ltd
Closed winter

Full breakfast
Preserved fruits & jams from our
garden, fresh eggs from Candy, the
sweetest senorita in the valley.
Garden, patio, wildlife, nature, down
comforters, private entrance, beautiful
flagstone patio, cabin

People are attracted to our inn, offering 2 guestrooms and 1 private cabin, because of our location, between Zion National Park and Bryce Canyon, but are pleasantly surprised to find a peaceful home-away-from-home!

windwhisper@color-country.net 🌐 www.windwhisperbb.com

HUNTSVILLE

Jackson Fork Inn, LLC	85-160 $US BB	Continental breakfast
7345 East 900 S 84317	7 rooms, 7 pb	Restaurant on premises
800-255-0672 801-745-0051	Most CC, Cash,	Whirlpool tubs in some rooms,
Vicki Petersen	*Rated*, •	hair dryer, soaps, lotion, shampoo,
	C-yes/S-no/P-yes/H-no	conditioner, DVD

Free Night w/Certificate: Anytime.

Old dairy barn renovated into a restaurant & inn. Quiet getaway without phones. Private whirlpool tubs for that special occasion. Our meals are prepared to order with fresh seasonal ingredients.

✉ info@jacksonforkinn.com 🌐 www.jacksonforkinn.com

KANAB

Purple Sage Inn	125-155 $US BB	Full breakfast
54 S Main St 84741	4 rooms, 4 pb	Porch with rocking chairs, patio,
877-644-5377 435-644-5377	Most CC, Cash	garden, private baths, living room, TV
Kathy Brock	C-ltd/S-no/P-no/H-no	

Purple Sage Inn aka The William Derby Johnson, Jr. House is listed on The National Register of Historic Places and is the winner of the Utah Heritage Foundation's 2002 Heritage Award. The home was also featured in five issues of Victorian Homes magazine.

✉ PurpleSageInn@Kanab.net 🌐 www.purplesageinn.com

MANTI

Yardley Inn & Spa	65-150 $US BB	Full breakfast
190 S 200 West 84642	5 rooms, 5 pb	Spa, library, fireplaces, Jacuzzi
800-593-1312 435-835-1861	Most CC, Cash, Checks	
Gill & Marlene Yardley	C-ltd/S-no/P-ltd/H-yes	

Built before the turn-of-the-century, this Bed and Breakfast has all the warmth and charm of an old English Country Inn, with European-style spa amenities. Elegantly furnished with antiques combine the convenience of today with the ambience of yesteryear.

✉ myinnspa@mail.manti.com 🌐 www.yardleyinnandspa.com

MIDWAY

Johnson Mill B&B	159-220 $US BB	Full breakfast
100 N. Johnson Mill	10 rooms, 10 pb	Tea, evening treats
Rd 84049	Most CC, *Rated*, •	Lake, streams, paths, 25 acres,
888-272-0030 435-654-4466	C-ltd/S-no/P-no/H-no	fireplaces, jetted tubs, waterfalls, TV/
Lani Lively		VCR

Nestled in a pristine high mountain valley surrounded by a crystal blue lake and a meandering river flowing with rainbow trout. Whether staying a week or only a night, Johnson Mill provides an unforgettable experience guaranteed to last a lifetime.

✉ info@johnsonmill.com 🌐 www.johnsonmill.com

MOAB

Cali Cochitta B&B	85-165 $US BB	Full breakfast
110 South 200 E 84532	6 rooms, 6 pb	Custom catered dinner, afternoon tea
888-429-8112 435-259-4961	Visa, MC, Disc,	Sitting room, library, Hot Tub,
David & Kim Boger	*Rated*, •	cable TV, business traveler
	C-yes/S-no/P-no/H-ltd	accommodations, WiFi

Located in the heart of spectacular "Red Rock Country . . . a wonderland of breathtaking panoramas", Cali Cochitta, the "House of Dreams", is secluded yet close to local shops and activities.

✉ info@moabdreaminn.com 🌐 www.moabdreaminn.com

Castle Valley Inn	95-185 $US BB	Full breakfast
424 Amber Lane 84532	8 rooms, 8 pb	Fresh ground coffee, tea and juices, all
888-466-6012 435-259-6012	Most CC, Cash	breakfasts are suitable to vegetarian
Jason & Jeanette Graham	C-yes/S-no/P-no/H-ltd	diets
		Free WiFi, outdoor hot tub, room
		refrigerators & coffee makers, robes,
		TV monitors & free movies

Five acres of carefully tended orchards, lawns, and fields nestled in the heart of the American West. Lodging at Castle Valley Inn is an experience with a touch of a Bed and Breakfast atmosphere and that of a Country Inn.   ✉ info@castlevalleyinn.com 🌐 www.castlevalleyinn.com

MOAB

Sunflower Hill Luxury Inn
185 N 300 E 84532
800-662-2786 435-259-2974
Stucki family

175-245 $US BB
12 rooms, 12 pb
Most CC, Cash, Checks,
Rated, •
C-ltd/S-no/P-no/H-no

Full breakfast
Evening refreshments, 24 hour
beverage service and snacks available.
Outdoor Pool, Hot Tub, A/C, Robes,
spa amenities, CD players, Cable TV/
DVD/VCR, WiFi , BBQ grill.

Inviting country retreat adorned with antiques and a most tasteful decor. Serene setting with lush flower gardens, shade trees and a spectacular outdoor pool. Healthy homemade breakfast. Sunflower Hill is Moab's top rated property (1998 to present – AAA).

✉ innkeeper@sunflowerhill.com 🌐 www.sunflowerhill.com

MT. CARMEL

**Arrowhead Country Inn
and Cabins**
2155 S State St 84755
888-821-1670 435-648-2569
Jane & Jim Jennings

79-269 $US BB
12 rooms, 12 pb
Most CC, Cash, •
C-yes/S-ltd/P-ltd/H-yes
March 1st to January 2

Farm Fresh Breakfast Feast
Restaurants in nearby towns and
parks.
3 Major National Parks nearby, great
views of the White Cliffs, casual
atmosphere & friendly hosts

Arrowhead Country Inn & Cabins is a Bed & Breakfast Inn located centrally between Zion National Park, Bryce Canyon National Park and the pristine Grand Canyon North Rim and across the street from the Historic Maynard Dixon Home and Studio.

✉ duelj1@color-country.net 🌐 www.arrowheadbb.com

PARK CITY

Old Town Guest House
1011 Empire Ave 84060
435-649-2642 435-649-2642
Deb Lovci

99-250 $US BB
4 rooms, 4 pb
Visa, MC, AmEx,
Rated, •
C-ltd/S-no/P-no/H-no

Healthy "Park City" breakfast
Afternoon snacks, tea, and other items
depending on the season
Hot tub, common room, boot dryers,
ski storage, robes, business center,
wireless, eco-friendly Inn

Free Night w/Certificate: Subject to availability, not valid during holidays. Room Upgrade.

Nestled in the heart of Park City, Old Town Guest House is the perfect place for active skiers, hikers & bikers wishing to enjoy the mountains of Utah. We are Park City's best for comfort, convenience & affordability. You won't find a better deal!

✉ Dlovci@cs.com 🌐 www.oldtownguesthouse.com

The Blue Church Lodge
424 Park Ave 84060
800-626-5467 435-649-8009
Louise Wismer

150-550 $US BB
26 rooms, 24 pb
Rated, •
C-yes/S-no/P-no/H-no

Continental breakfast in Winter
Kitchens available for guest use.
Hot tub, gameroom, fireplaces, ski
lockers, sitting room, WiFi, laundry
facility, daily maid service

An eleven suite and townhouse property nestled between the Wasatch Mountains and Park City's Historic Main Street. Just steps away from award-winning restaurants, trendy shops, pubs, live theatre and skiing, there's truly something for everyone.

✉ bcl@qwestoffice.net 🌐 www.thebluechurchlodge.com

Washington School Inn
543 Park Ave 84060
800-824-1672 435-649-3800
Jessica Davis

150-620 $US BB
15 rooms, 15 pb
Visa, MC, AmEx,
Rated, •
C-ltd/S-no/P-no/H-ltd

Full breakfast
Afternoon wine & appetizers
Spa, sauna, ski lockers, mezzanine
area, dining room

In the heart of Park City, Utah, a most elegant, luxurious & full service bed & breakfast style Inn can be found, the Washington School Inn. It's just a block from Town Lift & Main Street.

✉ info@washingtonschoolinn.com 🌐 www.washingtonschoolinn.com

SALT LAKE CITY

Ellerbeck Mansion B&B	119-169 $US BB	Full breakfast
140 N B St 84103	6 rooms, 6 pb	Water, soft drinks, hot chocolate and
800-966-8364 801-355-2500	Most CC, *Rated*, •	snacks available
Debbie	C-ltd/S-no/P-no/H-ltd	Telephone, TV, turndown service,
		sitting room, fireplace, wireless
		Internet, library, ski storage

Short 5 block walk to Temple Square and downtown Salt Lake City. 20 minutes from ski resorts. Historic 1892 mansion built by Thomas Ellerbeck, chief clerk to Brigham Young. Built in historic avenues neighborhood.

✉ ellerbeckmansion@qwestoffice.net 🌐 www.ellerbeckbedandbreakfast.com

Haxton Manor	120-200 $US BB	Continental plus breakfast
943 E South Temple 84102	7 rooms, 7 pb	Tea, candy and fresh baked snacks
877-930-4646 801-363-4646	Visa, MC, AmEx,	Sitting room, library, Jacuzzi tubs,
Buffi & Douglas King	*Rated*, •	fireplaces, cable TV, free wireless
	C-ltd/S-no/P-no/H-yes	Internet
	Spanish	

Tucked neatly within the heart of the Salt Lake Valley, and minutes away from city center and many world famous canyon ski areas, is historic Haxton Manor. English-style, historic country Inn conveniently located within walking distance of the university.

✉ innkeepers@haxtonmanor.com 🌐 www.haxtonmanor.com

Parrish Place B&B	99-139 $US BB	Continental plus breakfast
720 E Ashton Ave 84106	5 rooms, 5 pb	Complimentary beverages
801-832-0970	Most CC, Cash, Checks,	Cable TV/VCR, video library, free
Jeff & Karin Gauvin	*Rated*, •	WiFi, hot tub, robes, guest telephone
	S-ltd/P-no/H-no	
	Swedish	

Come and experience the elegance of a hundred plus years of architectural beauty recaptured at the Parrish Place. Parrish Place is within walking distance to shopping, restaurants, parks, and golfing, and just a short drive to the downtown area (4 miles).

✉ info@parrishplace.com 🌐 www.parrishplace.com

Silver Fork Lodge	90-200 $US BB	Full breakfast
11332 E Big Cottonwood	7 rooms, 7 pb	Restaurant, bar service
Canyon 84121	Most CC	Sitting room, library, sauna, outdoor
888-649-9551 801-533-9977	C-yes/S-no/P-no/H-no	hot tub in winter, cable TV, conference
Dan Knopp & Melissa		room, weddings
Reddell		

Rustic log ski lodge nestled in the Wasatch National Forest. Full service restaurant on premises, outdoor Jacuzzi in winter and indoor sauna. The restaurant was voted "best food with a view."

✉ silverforklodge27@sisna.com 🌐 www.silverforklodge.com

Wildflowers B&B	85-145 $US BB	Full breakfast
936 E 1700 S 84105	5 rooms, 5 pb	Restaurant nearby
800-569-0009 801-466-0600	Most CC, *Rated*, •	Sitting room, library, deck, stained
Cill Sparks & Jeri Parker	C-ltd/S-no/P-no/H-no	glass windows
	French	

National Historic 1891 Victorian offering delights of the past and comforts of the present. Wildflower gardens, close to park, downtown and ski resorts. ✉ lark2spur@aol.com 🌐 www.wildflowersbb.com

SPRINGDALE

Under the Eaves B&B	85-185 $US BB	Complementary at local Oscar's Cafe
980 Zion Park Blvd 84767	6 rooms, 6 pb	Close to Park, shops, restaurants,
866-261-2655 435-772-3457	Most CC, Cash, Checks,	stunning surroundings, gardens,
Joe Pitti & Mark Chambers	*Rated*	common rooms, parking, Free Wi-fi
	C-ltd/S-no/P-no/H-no	

Historic 1931 home in Springdale, Utah surrounded by Zion National Park. Wonderful, warm atmosphere with an eclectic mix of art and antiques. Surrounded by beautiful gardens and lovely shade trees. Close proximity to restaurants, shops, shuttle and Park.

✉ info@undertheeaves.com 🌐 www.undertheeaves.com

Muley Twist Inn, Teasdale, UT

ST. GEORGE

Green Gate Village	99-259 $US BB	Full breakfast
Historic Inn	14 rooms, 14 pb	Lunch of home-made soups,
76 W Tabernacle 84770	Most CC, Cash,	sandwiches & sweat treats available
800-350-6999 435-628-6999	*Rated*, •	Mon-Sat at Judd's General Store
Lin & Ed Sandstrom	C-ltd/S-no/P-no/H-ltd	Pool, business & reception centers,
		meeting rooms, restaurant, snack bar,
		gift shop

Welcome to the Green Gate Village Historic Inn. Behind our green gates you'll discover 14 unique buildings including nine beautifully restored pioneer homes, nestled in a garden-like setting around our "Village Green" and swimming pool.

✉ stay@greengatevillageinn.com   🌐 www.greengatevillageinn.com

TEASDALE

Muley Twist Inn	99-140 $US BB	Full breakfast
249 West 125 St 84773	5 rooms, 5 pb	Afternoon tea, snacks
800-530-1038 435-425-3640	Disc, *Rated*, •	Sitting room, library, accommodations
Eric & Penny Kinsman	C-yes/S-no/P-no/H-yes	for business travelers, wheelchair
	April 1 – Oct 15	accessible, WiFi, A/C

Distinctive lodging at the edge of the world. Newly built, 5-room B&B with private baths, delicious breakfasts, gourmet coffee and magnificent views from large porches. Come and enjoy the quiet!

✉ muley@rof.net   🌐 www.muleytwistinn.com

Vermont

ARLINGTON ───────────────────────────────

Arlington Inn
3904 Historic Rt 7A 05250
800-443-9442 802-375-6532
Eric & Elizabeth Berger

129-319 $US BB
17 rooms, 17 pb
Most CC, Cash,
Rated, •
C-yes/S-no/P-ltd/H-yes

Full breakfast
Afternoon snack & hot mulled cider,
gourmet dining, full service tavern
with wine list
gardens, gazebo, carriage barn,
porches & patios, Jacuzzis, fireplaces,
Internet

Experience elegance and style in this Village Estate decorated with beautiful antiques. 17 luxurious rooms, fireplaces, Jacuzzi's, and full breakfast. Editor's Pick Yankee Travel Guide.

✉ stay@arlingtoninn.com 🌐 www.arlingtoninn.com

Arlington's West Mountain Inn
144 West Mountain Inn Rd 05250
802-375-6516
The Carlson Family

155-340 $US BB
20 rooms, 20 pb
Most CC, Cash, Checks,
Rated, •
C-yes/S-no/P-ltd/H-yes
French

Full breakfast
5-Course dinner served nightly, dining
room for gatherings, catering
150 acres – Hiking, fishing,
snowshoeing. Tavern, game room,
living room, elegant dining, VIEWS.

150-acre hillside estate; hike or snowshoe woodland trails. Fish the Battenkill. Hearthside dining, charming rooms. Relax and enjoy the lawns, gardens and alpacas. 2009 "Fodor's Choice," Yankee Travel Guide "Editor's Pick," Frommers "Highly Recommended"

✉ info@westmountaininn.com 🌐 www.westmountaininn.com

Country Willows c.1850
332 E Arlington Rd 05250
800-796-2585 802-375-0019
Anne & Ron Weber

146-185 $US BB
3 rooms, 3 pb
Visa, MC
C-ltd/S-no/P-no/H-no

Award winning, bountiful breakfasts
Late afternoon light refreshments,
optional
Parlor with fireplace, library. suites,
in-room fireplaces, coffee. Also,2BR
Self-catered Cottage.

Gracious Queen Anne Victorian Inn, c.1850 on the National Register of Historic Places. Intimate, romantic and family-owned! Arlington is a charming and historic village. Ski Bromley or Stratton. Famed BattenKill, "home" river of Orvis headquarters!

✉ cwillows332@comcast.net 🌐 www.countrywillows.com

Hill Farm Inn
458 Hill Farm Rd 05250
800-882-2545 802-375-2269
Lisa & Al Gray

110-250 $US BB
15 rooms, 15 pb
Most CC, Cash,
Rated, •
C-yes/S-ltd/P-no/H-no

Full country breakfast
Afternoon/evening tea
Nature trails along the river, farm
animals, views, fireplaces, A/C, cable
TV, weddings

200 year old dairy farm on 50 acres along the Battenkill River, walking trails, farm animals, spectacular views. Full country breakfast. Suites, cabins, fireplaces, kitchens. Families welcome. Minutes to Manchester, VT. Country weddings.

✉ stay@hillfarminn.com 🌐 www.hillfarminn.com

BARNARD ───────────────────────────────

The Fan House
Rt 12 N 05031
802-234-6704
Sara Widness

160-240 $US BB
3 rooms, 3 pb
Visa, MC, •
C-ltd/S-no/P-ltd/H-no
Italian, some German

Full breakfast
Beverages, cheese & crackers
Sitting room, library, garden, lake
within 3 minute walk, massage service

Free Night w/Certificate: Valid Jan.-June and Nov. 1-Dec. 20th.

Enveloped in understated elegance, sensuous comfort and style, guests visibly relax upon entering the 1840 country kitchen. They're at home and sense they will sleep well at The Fan House.

 swidness@aol.com  🌐 www.thefanhouse.com

Hill Farm Inn, Arlington, VT

BARNARD

The Maple Leaf Inn	140-290 $US BB	Full gourmet breakfast
5890 Vermont Rt 12 05031	7 rooms, 7 pb	Complimentary coffee, tea, sodas,
800-516-2753 802-234-5342	Most CC, Cash, Checks,	snacks, afternoon wine & beer
Nancy & Mike Boyle	*Rated*, •	Sitting room, library, whirlpool tubs,
	C-ltd/S-no/P-no/H-yes	fireplaces, satellite TV, WiFi, computer
		for guest use

A Victorian-style farmhouse nestled snugly within sixteen acres of maple and birch trees is The Maple Leaf Inn. The inn is located in Barnard, VT. A quintessential village with steepled churches, general store, country lanes and back roads.

✉ innkeeper@mapleleafinn.com 🌐 www.mapleleafinn.com

BELLOWS FALLS

Readmore Bed, Breakfast & Books	150-250 $US BB	Full gourmet breakfast
1 Hapgood St 05101	5 rooms, 4 pb	Afternoon tea on request
802-463-9415	Visa, MC	Robes, turn down service, flowers,
Stewart & Dorothy Read	S-no/P-no/H-ltd	chocolate on pillows, fireplaces &
	A little French	Jacuzzi, gift shop, concierge.

Start the day at our "Green Hotel" with a full, gourmet breakfast. Come stroll through our gardens, relax in our gazebo or on the front porch. Sample the tea offerings. On chilly days, cuddle up by the fire with a book or snuggle under a quilt.

✉ read@sover.net 🌐 www.readmoreinn.com

BENNINGTON

Alexandra B&B Inn	125-215 $US BB	Full Gourmet Breakfast
Historic Route 7A 05201	12 rooms, 12 pb	Afternoon tea; full bar & bistro dining
888-207-9386 802-442-5619	Most CC, Cash,	for guests exclusively
Daniel Tarquino & Melissa Martin	*Rated*, •	Cable TV, phones, gas fireplaces, A/C,
	C-ltd/S-no/P-no/H-ltd	whirlpool tubs, WiFi, sitting areas,
	Spanish, Hebrew,	terrace, garden, gazebo
	Arabic	

1859 Vermont Farm House & Barn with splendid views overlooking the Bennington Monument & Green Mountains of Vermont, the Alexandra Inn offers elegant & modern English Country accommodations to all travelers.

✉ alexandr@sover.net 🌐 www.alexandrainn.com

BENNINGTON

Eddington House Inn	99-179 $US BB	Full gourmet breakfast
21 Main St 05257	3 rooms, 3 pb	Afternoon refreshments, endless
800-941-1857 802-442-1511	Most CC, Cash, Checks	desserts, in room chocolate truffles
Patti Eddington	C-ltd/S-no/P-no/H-ltd	Fireplaces, air conditioning, Wifi,
		bicycle storage

Elegantly restored Southern Vermont bed and breakfast nestled in the heart of North Bennington Village. Walk to Bennington College, award winning restaurants and waterfalls. Close to Covered Bridges, Green Mountains & Shopping. Great VT Getaway Packages.
✉ edhousevt@comcast.net 🌐 www.eddingtonhouseinn.com

Four Chimneys Inn &	125-295 $US BB	Full breakfast
Restaurant	11 rooms, 11 pb	Casual fine dining, full wine list and
21 West Rd Rte 9 05201	Most CC, Cash,	cocktails
802-447-3500	*Rated*, •	Dinner & bar, patios, beautiful
Lynn & Pete Green	C-ltd/S-no/P-no/H-yes	grounds, in-room massage, in-room
	Polish	high speed Internet, private baths

One of New England's premier inns located on 11 magnificent acres, in historic Old Bennington, VT. 11 uniquely appointed rooms each with private bath, TV, phone & A/C, Internet. Full breakfast. Casual fine dining with full bar. Warm & friendly atmosphere.
✉ innkeeper@fourchimneys.com 🌐 www.FourChimneys.com

South Shire Inn	125-265 $US BB	Full breakfast
124 Elm St 05201	9 rooms, 9 pb	Afternoon tea & homemade cookies.
888-201-2250 802-447-3839	Visa, MC, *Rated*	A/C, telephone, fireplaces, whirlpool
George & Joyce Goeke	S-no/P-no/H-no	bath, TVs with VCR. Wireless Internet.
		Wake up.

Elegant Victorian Inn offering luxurious accommodations, private baths, A/C and fireplaces. Walk to restaurants, shops and historic sites. Full breakfast served.
✉ relax@southshire.com 🌐 www.southshire.com

BOLTON VALLEY

Black Bear Inn	89-350 $US BB	Full Country Breakfast
4010 Bolton Access Rd 05477	25 rooms, 25 pb	Candlelit dinners, full bar, reasonably
800-395-6335 802-434-2126	Visa, MC, Disc, •	priced wine list granted Wine
Brian & Jill Drinkwater	C-yes/S-no/P-yes/H-ltd	Spectator Award of Excellence
		Free WiFi, parlor, public and private
		hot tubs, outdoor pool, suites,
		fireplaces, cable

Mountaintop country inn, featuring 25 individually decorated rooms and suites. Many have private hot tubs & firestoves. Pet-friendly, family-friendly, the only ski-in/ski-out inn in Vermont! Full Country breakfasts each day and gourmet candlit dinners. ✉ blkbear@wcvt.com 🌐 www.blackbearinn.travel

BONDVILLE

Bromley View Inn	99-300 $US BB	Full breakfast
RR1, Box 161, Route	17 rooms, 17 pb	Lunch & dinner, restaurant, bar
30 05340	Most CC, Cash	service
877-633-0308 802-297-1459	C-yes/S-no/P-yes/H-no	Sitting room, library, pool,
Kami & Kevin Golembeski		suites, fireplaces, business travel
		accommodations

While staying with us, guests will awaken to scenic mountain views with a warm hardy Vermont breakfast including daily specials such as egg scrambles, Stuffed French Toast, homemade baked breads and muffins, as well as cereals, juices, fruit and more.
✉ info@bromleyviewinn.com 🌐 www.bromleyviewinn.com

BRATTLEBORO

1868 Crosby House	150-185 $US BB	Full gourmet breakfast
175 Western Avenue 05301	5 rooms, 5 pb	Early coffee/tea tray brought to your
800-638-5148 802-257-7145	•	room. Snacks & afternoon tea.
Lynn Kuralt	C-ltd/S-no/P-no/H-no	Sitting room, library, whirlpool, suites,
		cable TV, fireplaces, wireless Internet,
		train pickup/drop

Historic home decorated with family heirlooms and collected antiques, luxurious accommodations, elegant gourmet breakfasts. Private baths, fireplaces, whirlpool, wireless Internet, Landscaped gardens, walking trails, close to town shops & restaurants.
✉ lynn@crosbyhouse.com 🌐 www.crosbyhouse.com

BRATTLEBORO

Green River Bridge House
2435 Stage Road 05301
800-528-1868 802- 257-5771
Joan Seymour

175-235 $US BB
3 rooms, 3 pb
Most CC, Cash, Checks
C-ltd/S-ltd/P-no/H-no

Full breakfast
Afternoon tea & snacks
Spa services, Jacuzzi, game room

Built in 1830, this charming B&B once housed the Green River Post Office and is nestled against the meandering river that gave it its name. It is luxurious in comfort and sensuous in visual appeal.

✉ grbh@sover.net ◐ www.greenriverbridgehouse.com

Meadowlark Inn B&B
Orchard St 05303
800-616-6359 802-257-4582
Lucia Osiecki & Deborah
Jones

149-239 $US BB
8 rooms, 8 pb
Visa, MC, AmEx,
Rated
C-yes/S-no/P-ltd/H-ltd
Spanish

Cooked to order
Afternoon tea & snacks, in-room
chocolates
Sitting room, library, fireplaces, cable
TV, free wireless Internet access

Fully restored 1870's Vermont country inn with amenities that will surprise and delight guests! Relaxing & quiet with panoramic views all around. A delicious full breakfast prepared & served by the owners who just happen to be trained chefs.

✉ innkeeper@meadowlarkinnvt.com ◐ www.meadowlarkinnvt.com

BRIDGEWATER CORNERS

October Country Inn
362 Upper Rd 05035
800-648-8421 802-672-3412
Edie & Chuck Janisse

165-195 $US BB
10 rooms, 10 pb
Visa, MC, *Rated*, •
C-yes/S-no/P-no/H-ltd
Spanish

Full country breakfast
Coffee, tea, cookies, beer & wine
licensed; Dinner (when available) is
$30.00 per person.
Pool, gardens, library, games, hiking,
bicycling, skiing, snowboarding

October Country Inn is loved because guests feel like they're at home here. Experience genuine Vermont hospitality—enjoy the relaxed atmosphere and farmhouse charm surrounded by the scenic splendor of the Green Mountains. ✉ innkeeper@octobercountryinn.com ◐ www.vermontinns.net

BURLINGTON

Lang House on Main Street
360 Main St 05401
877-919-9799 802-652-2500
Kim Borsavage

145-245 $US BB
11 rooms, 11 pb
Most CC, Cash
C-yes/S-no/P-no/H-yes

Gourmet breakfasts
Afternoon snack of cookies, coffee, tea
or lemonade. Vermont cheese plates,
beer & wine for sale.
Robes for guest use, in-room AC/
heat control, alarm clocks, off-street
parking, wireless Internet

Beautifully kept period furnishings and antiques. Soaring ceilings, stained glass windows, and stunning woodwork and plaster detailing, with a rosette pattern repeated throughout the house.

✉ innkeeper@langhouse.com ◐ www.langhouse.com

Willard Street Inn
349 South Willard 05401
800-577-8712 802-651-8710
Larry and Katie Davis

140-235 $US BB
14 rooms, 14 pb
Most CC, Cash
C-ltd/S-no/P-no/H-no

Chef-prepared, plated breakfast
Fresh baked chocolate chip cookies
delivered daily to rooms. Tea/coffee
bar available all hours.
Free WiFi , cable TV, 1.5 acres of lawn/
English Gardens, Solarium sitting room

Historic 1881 Victorian mansion, offering 14 rooms with private baths and free WiFi, views of Lake Champlain, Adirondacks & English Gardens. Gourmet breakfasts in our sunny, marble-floored solarium. Service of yesteryear with the amenities of today.

✉ info@willardstreetinn.com ◐ www.willardstreetinn.com

CHESTER

Henry Farm Inn
2206 Green Mountain
Tpke 05143
800-723-8213 802-875-2674
Patricia & Paul Dexter

100-170 $US BB
9 rooms, 9 pb
Most CC, Cash, Checks,
Rated, •
C-yes/S-ltd/P-no/H-ltd

Full breakfast
Fireplace, sitting room, swimming &
skating pond, cross-country ski trail

1700s Colonial in country setting, 1 mile from Chester Village. Fifty-six acres including pond, meadow, woods & river. Nine spacious guestrooms all with private baths. Children very welcome.

✉ info@henryfarminn.com ◐ www.henryfarminn.com

Fox Creek Inn, Chittenden, VT

CHESTER ───────────────────────────────────────

Hugging Bear Inn &	125-150 $US BB	A delicious country breakfast
Shoppe	5 rooms, 5 pb	Afternoon snack of Vermont cheddar
244 Main St 05143	Most CC, Cash, Checks,	cheese, cider, tea and coffee
800-325-0519 802-875-2412	*Rated*	A/C, 2 living rooms, library, computer,
Georgette Thomas	C-yes/S-no/P-no/H-no	wireless Internet, games, toys, gift
		shop, collectibles

Vermont family B&B and teddy bear shop. Elegant Victorian in National Historic District. Largest selection of Steiff, Muffy Vanderbear and Artist bears in New England.

 inn@huggingbear.com 🌐 www.huggingbear.com

───────────────────────────────────────

Inn Victoria	120-295 $US BB	Full gourmet breakfast
321 Main St 05143	8 rooms, 8 pb	Afternoon tea, dinner by prior
802-875-4288	Most CC, Cash, *Rated*	arrangement. High Tea on weekends.
Penny & Dan Cote	C-ltd/S-no/P-no/H-yes	Victorian parlor, cable Flat screen TV',
	French	DVD, Jacuzzi, fireplaces, A/C, WiFi
		Internet, hot tub,

Free Night w/Certificate: Not valid during holidays or fall foliage (Sept. 22-Oct. 22). Room Upgrade.

You've found us!! Rated in the Top Ten Bed and Breakfast Inns in the USA. Rated the top B&B in Vermont 2006 2007. Rated by Yankee Magazine as Best Romantic B&B. Romantic and Luxurious blended with charm and friendly service. The epitome of B&B experience

 innkeeper@innvictoria.com 🌐 www.innvictoria.com

CHITTENDEN ───────────────────────────────────────

Fox Creek Inn	175-325 $US BB	Full breakfast
49 Dam Road 05737	8 rooms, 8 pb	Dinner by reservation, complimentary
800-707-0017 802-483-6213	Visa, MC, AmEx,	soft drinks, tea, coffee, snacks upon
Sandy & Jim Robertson	*Rated*, •	request
	C-ltd/S-no/P-ltd/H-yes	Full bar & wine cellar, sitting room,
		library, dining room

Small sophisticated country inn hidden away in the Green Mountains. Excellent dining, first class wine list and full bar. Wonderfully spacious and comfortable rooms offering peace and quiet.

 innkeeper@foxcreekinn.com 🌐 www.foxcreekinn.com

CHITTENDEN

Mountain Top Inn & Resort	160-575 $US BB	Full breakfast
195 Mountain Top Rd 05737	30 rooms, 30 pb	Lunch, dinner available; morning &
800-445-2100 802-483-2311	Visa, MC, AmEx, •	afternoon snacks
Khele Sparks	C-yes/S-no/P-yes/H-yes	Beach, pontoon boat, kayaks, pool, horseback riding, xc ski & snowshoe, sleigh rides, dog sledding.

Classic mountain resort set on 350 acres with breathtaking lake & mountain views, endless outdoor adventures. Equestrian & Nordic Ski & Snowshoe Center with miles of trails. Casual dining; tastefully decorated rooms. Affordable packages. Pets welcome!

✉ diane@mountaintopinn.com 🌐 www.mountaintopinn.com

DANBY

Silas Griffith Inn	97-299 $US BB	Custom cooked homemade breakfast
178 Main St 05739	10 rooms, 10 pb	Emma's Restaurant, 24 hr advance
888-569-4660 802-293-5567	Most CC, *Rated*, •	reservations required, New England
Catherine & Brian Preble	C-yes/S-no/P-yes/H-yes	home-cooked, fresh and local Seasonal gazebo spa & outdoor pool, library, WiFi & DSL, cable TV, organic gardens, walking paths

Built by VT's 1st millionaire, this romantic 1891 Victorian has 10 antique-filled rooms, comfortable beds, private baths, gas fireplaces in the bedrooms, mt. views, seasonal outdoor gazebo-spa and pool, warm and friendly hosts.

✉ stay@silasgriffith.com 🌐 www.silasgriffith.com

DORSET

Barrows House	125-235 $US BB	Full breakfast
Route 30 05251	28 rooms, 28 pb	Full-service gourmet restaurant and
800-639-1620 802-867-4455	Most CC, Cash	tavern
Jim & Linda McGinnis	C-yes/S-no/P-ltd/H-yes	Weddings, business meetings, fireplace, porch/terrace, bicycles, tennis courts, heated outdoor pool

Barrows House is your Vermont inn for all seasons and for all reasons. Our unique facilities and extensive grounds make us a special place for a family gathering, a wedding, a small business meeting or a spur-of-the-moment vacation.

✉ innkeepers@barrowshouse.com 🌐 www.barrowshouse.com

Inn at West View Farm	135-210 $US BB	Full breakfast
2928 Route 30 05251	9 rooms, 9 pb	Restaurant serving dinner from 6 p.m.,
800-769-4903 802-867-5715	Visa, MC, AmEx	Thurs-Mon, full bar and extensive
Christal Siewertsen	C-ltd/S-no/P-no/H-no	wine list

A traditional inn and restaurant rich in comfort, romance and history. Once a working dairy farm and welcoming guests for nearly a century. The Inn's restored 1870 farmhouse offers the amenities of a full service inn in a beautiful pastoral setting.

✉ stay@westviewfarm.com 🌐 www.innatwestviewfarm.com

The Dorset Inn on the Green	170-475 $US BB	Full breakfast
8 Church St & Rt 30 05251	25 rooms, 25 pb	Luxury linens, flat screen TV, plush
802-867-5500	Most CC, Cash,	bath robes, fireplaces, heated marble
Steve & Lauren Bryant	*Rated*, •	floors, ample storage
	C-ltd/S-no/P-ltd/H-yes	

For more than 200 years, The Dorset Inn has offered traditional New England hospitality. Gracious lodging, gourmet dining, fine wines and great spirits, are all trademarks of Vermont's oldest continually operating inn.

✉ Info@dorsetinn.com 🌐 www.dorsetinn.com

EAST DOVER

Cooper Hill Inn
117 Cooper Hill Rd 05341
800-783-3229 802-348-6333
Charles & Lee Wheeler

120-240 $US BB
10 rooms, 10 pb
Visa, MC, Disc
C-yes/S-no/P-no/H-no
Mandarin, Spanish
Closed April and
Novembe

Full breakfast
We provide all meals for group
reunions & catering for weddings of
up to 200 people
Sitting room, Jacuzzis, fireplaces, game
room, satellite TV, wireless Internet

A hilltop inn with one of the most spectacular views in New England. Watch the Moon rise in the East while watching the Sun set in the West. The perfect place for weddings, retreats, or family reunions.

 coopinn@sover.net 🌐 www.cooperhillinn.com

GAYSVILLE

Cobble House Inn
1 Cobble House Rd 05746
802-234-5458
Tony Caparis

110-160 $US BB
4 rooms, 4 pb
•
C-yes/S-no/P-ltd/H-ltd

Please advise of special needs.
Afternoon snack, tea & coffee.
Lunches and dinners are also
available with advance notice.
Free WiFi, Laundry, TV, Massage,
woodstove, large porch, library,
snowshoes, gold pans available

Cobble House Inn is a grand 1860's late-Victorian mansion, set in a hillside on the White River bank. Enjoy swimming, tubing, kayaking, fishing, snowshoeing, X-country skiing. The only bed and breakfast in the Village of Gaysville and Town of Stockbridge.

 unwind@cobblehouseinn.com 🌐 www.cobblehouseinn.com

HARDWICK

Kimball House
173 Glenside Ave 05843
802-472-6228
Sue Holmes

89-99 $US BB
3 rooms
C-ltd/S-no/P-no/H-ltd

Full breakfast
Light supper available with prior
arrangement
Kitchen, porches, gardens, dining
room

The house has a warm comfortable feeling and is situated on large well-groomed and garden filled grounds. There is a timeless beauty that surrounds the house and grounds that makes leaving difficult.

 holmesue@aol.com 🌐 www.kimballhouse.com

HINESBURG

The Hidden Gardens B&B
693 Lewis Creek Rd 05461
802-482-2118
Marcia C. Pierce

80-145 $US BB
2 rooms
Most CC
C-ltd/S-no/P-no/H-no

Full breakfast
Cookies, shortbread, tea, soda, Garden
Tea parties
Living room & sunroom, pond, DSL
wireless Internet, bicycles, camp,
gardens, private bath option

Contemporary large-timbered post and beam home with vaulted ceilings, surrounded by 26 acres of woods and gardens. Great getaway for adults visiting Vermont's Champlain Valley and Green Mountains.

 info@thehiddengardens.com 🌐 www.thehiddengardens.com

HUNTINGTON

**Sleepy Hollow Inn, Ski &
Bike Center**
1805 Sherman Hollow
Rd 05462
866-254-1524 802-434-2283
Molly Peters

105-155 $US BB
8 rooms, 6 pb
Visa, MC, AmEx
C-yes/S-no/P-no/H-yes

Full breakfast
Swimming pond, wood-fired sauna,
weddings, events, sitting rooms,
fireplaces, trail passes

Welcome to Sleepy Hollow, a Vermont Country Inn featuring acclaimed Nordic skiing and mountain biking, in a beautiful setting. Moose, deer, wild turkey, and other wildlife abound.

 info@skisleepyhollow.com 🌐 www.skisleepyhollow.com

HYDE PARK

Fitch Hill Inn
258 Fitch Hill Rd 05655
800-639-2903 802-888-3834
Julie & John Rohleder

99-189 $US BB
6 rooms, 6 pb
Most CC, Cash, Checks,
Rated, •
C-ltd/S-no/P-no/H-ltd
German

Full breakfast
Tea, cocoa, cider or lemonade, and
cookies in the afternoon
TVs, video & DVD library, board
games, Internet computer, WiFi, CD
players, CD library

Quiet retreat on 3 acres overlooking Green Mountains. Beautifully renovated 200 yr-old house with 4 guestrooms with private baths & 2 one-room suites with fireplaces and whirlpool tubs. Full hot breakfast each morning. TVs, Free WiFi

✉ innkeeper@fitchhillinn.com 🌐 www.fitchhillinn.com

The Governor's House In Hyde Park
100 Main St 05655
866-800-6888 802-888-6888
Suzanne Boden

95-265 $US BB
8 rooms, 6 pb
Most CC, Cash,
Checks, •
C-yes/S-no/P-no/H-yes
French
June- March

Full breakfast
Afternoon tea, snacks, dinner &
picnics by request
In-room fireplaces, WiFi, cable/VCR/
DVD, movie library, bedtime snacks,
Ben & Jerry's ice cream

Centerpiece of quiet Hyde Park village, Governor's House offers modern comfort with the gracious elegance of an earlier time. Bedroom fireplaces. Full afternoon tea. Intimate weddings. Jane Austen weekends. Many specials and the perfect elopement package.

✉ info@OneHundredMain.com 🌐 www.OneHundredMain.com

JAMAICA

Three Mountain Inn
Main St, Rt 30 05343
800-532-9399 802-874-4140
Jennifer & Ed Dorta-Duque

165-370 $US BB
15 rooms, 15 pb
Most CC, *Rated*
C-ltd/S-no/P-ltd/H-ltd
Spanish

Full breakfast
AAA 4-Diamond dining room, fully
stocked bar, award winning wine list
All rooms have A/C and heat,
augmented with gas fireplaces,
wireless Internet

The Three Mountain Inn, located in the unspoiled village of Jamaica, VT, is a perfect choice to spend a few days of rest and relaxation. We invite you to enjoy a warm and comfortable atmosphere, with exceptional food and the finest personal service.

✉ stay@threemtn.com 🌐 www.threemountaininn.com

JEFFERSONVILLE

Smuggler's Notch Inn
55 Church St 05464
866-644-6607 802-644-6607
Patrick & Lisa Martin

89-129 $US BB
11 rooms, 11 pb
Visa, MC, AmEx,
Rated
C-yes/S-no/P-no/H-no

Breakfast is $5 per person
Full breakfast, lunch, pub & dinner
menus
Dining room, tavern, bakery, Jacuzzi
tubs, fireplaces, deck, hot tub, SAT-TV,
discount lift tickets

The Smugglers' Notch Inn is a family-friendly, 11-room Inn complete with a 65-seat dining room, full-service bakery & a 60-seat tavern. Our executive chef, Lorri Dunn, has been featured in Gourmet magazine & our inn has been featured in Yankee Magazine.

✉ info@smuggsinn.com 🌐 www.smuggsinn.com

JERICHO

Homeplace B&B
90 Old Pump Rd, Essex
Jt. 05465
802-899-4694
Mariot Huessy

115-125 $US BB
6 rooms, 4 pb
C-yes/S-no/P-ltd/H-no

Full breakfast
Common room with puzzles, piano

A quiet spot in a hundred acre wood. The large house is filled with European & American antiques. Near Burlington & Mt. Mansfield. There are friendly house & barn animals residing here.

 mariot@homeplacebandb.com 🌐 www.homeplacebandb.com

KILLINGTON

Birch Ridge Inn
37 Butler Rd 05751
800-435-8566 802-422-4293
Bill Vines & Mary Furlong

90-325 $US BB
10 rooms, 10 pb
Most CC, *Rated*, •
C-ltd/S-no/P-no/H-yes

Full breakfast
Dinner plans available
Restaurant, fireplace lounge, many
rooms are air conditioned & have
fireplaces & whirlpool tubs

Experience Vermont in style. 10 rooms surrounded by gardens, nestled in the Green Mountains. Start with a country breakfast, finish with fine dining. Killington Ski and Golf Resort is less than 1 mile away. Handicap accessible.

✉ innkeepers@birchridge.com   🌐 www.birchridge.com

Inn at Long Trail
Rt 4, Sherburne Pass 05751
800-325-2540 802-775-7181
Murray & Patty McGrath

79-300 $US BB
19 rooms, 19 pb
Visa, MC, AmEx,
Rated, •
C-yes/S-no/P-ltd/H-ltd
Summer, fall, winter

Full breakfast
Irish pub (lunch/dinner), or candlelit
dining Fall and Winter in main dining
room
Sitting room, hot tub, weekend Irish
music

A classic Vermont ski lodge/bed & breakfast offering country bedrooms, whirlpool rooms and fireplace suites. Candlelit dining fall and winter. McGrath's Irish Pub serves food daily, with live Irish music weekends.

✉ ilt@innatlongtrail.com   🌐 www.innatlongtrail.com

Snowed Inn
104 Miller Brook Rd 05751
800-311-5406 802-422-3407
Manfred & Jeanne Karlhuber

110-385 $US BB
20 rooms, 20 pb
Most CC, *Rated*, •
C-yes/S-no/P-no/H-ltd
German
6/15-4/15

Continental plus breakfast
Sitting room, Jacuzzis, suites, WiFi
throughout inn, cable TV, fireplaces
outdoor hot tub

Distinctive country rooms and suites complemented by a fieldstone fireplace lounge, greenhouse breakfast room and outdoor hot tub overlooking the wooded brook.

✉ snowedinn@vermontel.net   🌐 www.snowedinn.com

LONDONDERRY

The Frog's Leap Inn
7455 Route 100 05148
877-FROGINN 802-824-3019
Kraig & Dorenna Hart

69-170 $US BB
8 rooms, 8 pb
Visa, MC, AmEx, •
C-yes/S-no/P-yes/H-yes

Full breakfast
bakery using organic products(pre-
order or Internet order only) Dinner
by Advance reservation only
Catering for weddings and special
events, WiFi, pool, guest computer,
fireplace

Historic Inn with a natural, rural setting. Centrally located between Okemo, Stratton, Bromley and Magic Mountain. Comfortable rooms with private baths. Casual setting, quiet retreat that is pet-friendly. Perfect for getaways and special events.

✉ froggemail@gmail.com   🌐 www.frogsleapinn.com

LOWER WATERFORD

Rabbit Hill Inn
Lower Waterford Rd 05848
800-76-BUNNY 802-748-5168
Brian & Leslie Mulcahy

199-399 $US BB
19 rooms, 19 pb
Most CC, Cash, Checks,
Rated, •
S-no/P-ltd/H-yes

Full candlelit breakfast
Afternoon tea & pastries, multi-course
dinner available
Pub & game room, candlelit
turndown service, in-room massage,
personalized concierge, free WiFi

Stylish country inn established in 1795. We invite you to this tranquil place — an oasis of unparalleled comfort, heartfelt hospitality, soul-inspiring surroundings, and service that anticipates and pampers.

✉ info@rabbithillinn.com   🌐 www.rabbithillinn.com

LUDLOW

Andrie Rose Inn	110-330 $US BB	Continental and full breakfast
13 Pleasant St 05149	15 rooms, 15 pb	Dinner Friday and Saturday by
800-223-4846 802-228-4846	Most CC, Cash,	reservation, snacks, beer, fairly priced
Michael & Irene Maston	*Rated*, •	and well-rounded wine list
	C-yes/S-no/P-yes/H-no	Sitting room, library, Jacuzzi, suites,
		fireplace, cable TV VCR/DVD, outdoor
		hot tub, weddings

Beautiful historic property in elegant c.1829 country village, near Okemo Ski Mountain. Offering a choice of romantic whirlpool tub suites and family suites.

 innkeepers@andrieroseinn.com   www.andrieroseinn.com

The Combes Family Inn	86-196 $US BB	Full breakfast
953 E Lake Rd 05149	11 rooms, 11 pb	Coffee, tea, hot chocolate, cold drinks
800-822-8799 802-228-8799	Most CC, Cash,	on request, Ruth's delicious dinners
Ruth & Bill Combes	Checks, •	by reservation, BYOB
	C-yes/S-no/P-ltd/H-no	TV lounge & quiet reading room, fire
	French	places, games, piano, library, videos,
	Closed 4/1-5/1	wireless Internet

Free Night w/Certificate: Not valid Martin Luther King Day, President's weekend, Columbus Day weekend, Christmas week (Dec.26-Jan.1).

The Combes Family Inn is a century-old farmhouse nestled on a quiet country backroad off Vermont's scenic Route 100. 50 acres of woods and meadows for exploring.

 billcfi@tds.net   www.combesfamilyinn.com

The Governor's Inn	169-309 $US BB	Full 3 course breakfast
86 Main St 05149	8 rooms, 8 pb	Afternoon tea, gourmet picnics
800-468-3766 802-228-8830	Most CC, *Rated*, •	Fully air-conditioned, fireplace & cable
Jim & Cathy Kubec	C-ltd/S-no/P-no/H-no	TV in most rooms, luxurious robes,
	French	wireless Internet access

Circa 1890 romantic, 8-room B&B inn in Ludlow, Vermont, on village green. Full breakfast and afternoon tea. Near Okemo skiing. Walk to shops and restaurants. Luxury rooms, fireplaces, antiques, cable TV, whirlpool tubs. Wireless Internet access.

 info@thegovernorsinn.com   www.thegovernorsinn.com

The Okemo Inn	120-230 $US BB	Full breakfast
61 Locust Hill Rd 05149	10 rooms, 10 pb	Complimentary coffee, tea & hot
800-328-8834 802-228-8834	Visa, MC, AmEx	spiced cider each evening
Ron & Toni Parry	C-ltd/S-ltd/P-no/H-no	Pool, public rooms, cable TV, library,
		games & puzzles, fireplace

Nestled on the northern edge of Ludlow, the Okemo Inn features 10 comfy guestrooms, all with private bath and air conditioners. Each guestroom is uniquely furnished and decorated, including either a King Bed, a Queen Bed or 2 Double Beds.

 okemoinn@okemoinn.com   www.okemoinn.com

MANCHESTER

The Inn at Manchester	155-295 $US BB	Full Breakfast
3967 Main St 05254	18 rooms, 18 pb	Fully licensed pub
800-273-1793 802-362-1793	Most CC, Cash, Checks,	Sitting rooms, library, fireplaces, pool,
Frank & Julie Hanes	*Rated*, •	porch, A/C, gardens, free Internet
	C-ltd/S-no/P-no/H-no	access, Flat TV in each

A Gem in the Green Mountains. Casual elegance & warm hospitality. Charming guestrooms, comfortable & inviting common areas. Beautiful grounds, gardens, pool, patio & fully licensed pub.

 innkeepers@innatmanchester.com   www.innatmanchester.com

MANCHESTER CENTER

The Inn at Ormsby Hill
1842 Main St 05255
800-670-2841 802-362-1163
Ted & Chris Sprague

205-535 $US BB
10 rooms, 10 pb
Visa, MC, AmEx,
Rated, •
C-ltd/S-no/P-no/H-yes

Full gourmet breakfast
Afternoon refreshments; welcome
cookies upon arrival in room; wine
and Vermont beers
Sitting room, library, all rooms have a
fireplace & Jacuzzi for two, flat-screen
TV, beer & wine

Romantic and luxurious, this historic Manchester inn offers bed chambers w/canopies, fireplaces, Jacuzzis for two. Spectacular mountain views. "A breakfast that'll knock your socks off" – Yankee Magazine. Only Manchester, Vermont AAA 4 Diamond Inn.

 stay@ormsbyhill.com 🌐 www.ormsbyhill.com

The Manchester View
77 High Meadow Way & Rt
7 05255
800-548-4141 802-362-2739
Pat & Tom Barnett

85-350 $US EP
36 rooms, 36 pb
Most CC, Cash, *Rated*
C-yes/S-no/P-no/H-yes

$3 Continental Breakfast
Wine & cheese baskets by request,
coffee, muffins & juice to order,
Birthday Cake to order
WiFi, phone, fax, spa tubs, outdoor
heated pool, cribs, fireplaces,
breakfast room delivery, Suites

Best AAA accommodations in the Manchester area. This 36 Room & Suite luxurious property offers the best of a classic Vermont Country inn or a small hotel. Know for it many Fireplaces & In Room 1 & 2Person Jacuzzi's it is a Romantic Vermont Destination

 Stay@manchesterview.com 🌐 www.manchesterview.com

MENDON

The Vermont Inn
69 Route 4 05701
800-541-7795 802-775-0708
Mitchell & Jennifer Duffy

100-255 $US BB
16 rooms, 16 pb
Most CC, Cash, Checks,
Rated, •
C-yes/S-no/P-no/H-yes
Memorial Day-April 1

Full country breakfast
Dinner Meal plans avail.: 3 course
is $25 pp, 4 course dinner is $30 pp.
Afternoon cookies & cider.
Fitness room, sauna, hot-tub, suites,
family suites, business services,
outside pool, televisions

Mitchell & Jennifer Duffy are pleased to welcome you to the Vermont Inn. Please join us at our circa 1840 small country inn on five acres in the Green Mountains. We offer the charm of a family run inn with excellent New England and Continental cuisine.

 relax@vermontinn.com 🌐 www.vermontinn.com

MONTGOMERY CENTER

English Rose Inn
195 Vermont Rt 242 05471
888-303-3232 802-326-3232
Gary & Mary Jane Bouchard-
Pike

95-165 $US BB
14 rooms, 14 pb
Visa, MC, Disc
C-yes/S-no/P-ltd/H-ltd

Deluxe Gourmet Breakfast
Fine dining restaurant, award winning
chefs
3 sitting areas w/ wood burning
fireplace, WiFi, cell phone reception,
TV/VCR, movie channels

Nestled within the gorgeous Vermont Green Mountains, our location provides a beautiful backdrop for any special family or business occasion.

 englishroseinn@fairpoint.net 🌐 www.englishroseinnvermont.com

---

Phineas Swann B&B Inn
195 Main St 05471
802-326-4306
John Perkins & Jay Kerch

119-319 $US BB
9 rooms, 9 pb
Most CC, Cash, Checks,
Rated, •
C-ltd/S-no/P-yes/H-ltd
German and French

Full gourmet breakfast
Free soda, icemakers in rooms, free
snacks, fabulous "all day" afternoon
tea, gourmet dinners
Flat screen TVs, private phones,
Internet access + WiFi, baby grand
player piano

AAA 3 Diamond Rated – one of Vermont's most elegant country inns, right in the heart of a charming New England village. We are just 12 miles from the Canadian border, and very popular with skiers and fall foliage visitors. We are also very pet-friendly!

 info@phineasswann.com 🌐 www.phineasswann.com

MONTGOMERY CENTER────────────────────────────────────

The Inn on Trout River	104-184 $US BB	Full breakfast menu
241 Main St 05471	10 rooms, 10 pb	Sitting room, library, bicycles, tennis
800-338-7049 802-326-4391	Most CC, *Rated*, •	court, fireplaces
Lee & Michael Forman	C-yes/S-no/P-no/H-no	

Vermont Historic District, 7 covered bridges, downhill and cross-country skiing, vast snowmobile trails. 10 rooms, private baths, queen beds, down comforters.

✉ info@troutinn.com 🌐 www.troutinn.com

MONTPELIER────────────────────────────────────

Betsy's B&B	85-150 $US BB	Full breakfast
74 E State St 05602	12 rooms, 12 pb	Snacks, fruit
802-229-0466	Most CC, Cash, Checks,	Suites, in-room voice mail & data
Jon & Betsy Anderson	*Rated*, •	ports, wireless Internet access, front
	C-yes/S-no/P-ltd/H-no	porch, terraced gardens
	Some Spanish	

Set in a quiet historic district just two blocks from town, Betsy's is both comfortably homey & romantically Victorian. The beds are so comfortable that breakfast just has to be good.

✉ betsysbnb@comcast.net 🌐 www.BetsysBnB.com

The Inn at Montpelier	145-250 $US BB	Generous continental plus breakfast
147 Main St 05602	19 rooms, 19 pb	Full bar, snacks
802-223-2727	Most CC, *Rated*	Sitting room, fireplaces, cable TV,
John & Karel Underwood	C-ltd/S-no/P-no/H-no	accommodate business travelers, free
		wireless Internet access

An elegant, historic Inn in the capital city. Each room is furnished with unique antiques, art and fine reproductions. Best porch in Vermont.

✉ innatmontpelier@comcast.net 🌐 www.innatmontpelier.com

NEWFANE────────────────────────────────────

Four Columns Inn on the	175-400 $US BB	Full breakfast buffet
Green	15 rooms, 15 pb	Afternoon tea, dinner available,
21 West St 05345	Most CC, Cash,	restaurant
800-787-6633 802-365-7713	*Rated*, •	Bar service, sitting room, Jacuzzis,
Debbie & Bruce Pfander	C-yes/S-no/P-ltd/H-ltd	pool, suites, massage, fireplaces, cable
		TV, DVD library

Innkeepers are friendly and hospitable, making the Inn a happy and comfortable place to be. Recently featured in Country Home Magazine, Travel Holiday and Country Inns Magazine, "...a magical handful of buildings on the Green of a fairytale village."

✉ innkeeper@fourcolumnsinn.com 🌐 www.fourcolumnsinn.com

NORTH HERO ISLAND────────────────────────────────────

Charlie's Northland Lodge	90-115 $US BB	Full breakfast
3829 US Rt 2 05474	4 rooms, 2 pb	Complimentary sherry
802-372-8822	Visa, MC, *Rated*, •	Sitting room, biking, lake, sailing,
Dorice Clark	C-ltd/S-no/P-no/H-no	canoeing, fishing, kayakingon both.
		Direct lake access

A snug B&B in a quiet village setting on Lake Champlain. A place to go to fish, sail, bike or just plain relax. Our cottage sleeps six is at Pelot Bay on North Hero Island.

✉ clark_dorice@yahoo.com 🌐 www.charliesnorthlandlodge.com

NORTHFIELD────────────────────────────────────

Northfield Inn	119-179 $US BB	Full gourmet breakfast
228 Highland Ave 05663	12 rooms, 9 pb	Pastries, fresh fruit, assorted hot &
802-485-8558	Most CC, Cash, Checks,	cold beverages & snacks available all
Aglaia Stalb	*Rated*, •	day, plus evening wine.
	C-ltd/S-no/P-no/H-no	Guest PC, WiFi, TV, videos, DVD/
	Greek	VCR, library, Koi pond, hiking trails,
		bicycles, Pool & River nearby

This turn-of-the-century mansion, once occupied by a Royal Princess, has been restored to its original Victorian elegance, tastefully decorated with period furnishings, beautiful gardens, peaceful koi pond, antique apple orchard & surrounded by woodlands.

✉ thenorthfieldinn@aol.com 🌐 www.TheNorthfieldInn.com

NORWICH

The Norwich Inn
325 Main St. 05055
802-649-1143
Joe and Jill Lavin

139-239 $US EP
38 rooms, 38 pb
Most CC, Cash
C-yes/S-no/P-yes/H-yes

Come join us in the dining room,
brewery, pub, or wine cellar!
cellar, library, terrace, private bath,
TV, wireless Internet, telephone, wine
room, brewery, pub

The Norwich Inn is a historic, full-service Vermont country inn located in Norwich, just across the river from Hanover, New Hampshire.

✉ innkeeper@norwichinn.com 🌐 www.norwichinn.com

PERKINSVILLE

The Inn at Weathersfield
1342 Rt 106 05151
802-263-9217
Dave & Jane Sandelman

140-285 $US BB
12 rooms, 12 pb
Most CC, *Rated*
C-ltd/S-no/P-no/H-ltd

Full breakfast
24 hr coffee, tea & hot chocolate, full
restaurant & bar, catering
21 acres w/ walking trails &
amphitheater, massage services, WiFi,
concierge, weddings, whirlpools

Known for its distinctive style of lodging and dining, it is the perfect choice for a quiet getaway in Southern Vermont. The Inn at Weathersfield is more than a simple B&B, it is more like a small European style or boutique hotel.

✉ stay@weathersfieldinn.com 🌐 www.weathersfieldinn.com

PERU

Johnny Seesaw's
3574 VT Route 11 05152
800-424-CSAW 802-824-5533
Gary Okun

80-240 $US BB
22 rooms, 22 pb
Visa, MC, Disc, *Rated*
C-yes/S-yes/P-yes/H-ltd
French
Closed April—May

Full breakfast
Dinner every night, full bar
Tennis, swimming pool, library, sitting
room, formal dining room, center
fireplace, private cottages

Welcome to Johnny Seesaw's! This unique country lodge features cozy rooms, 3 room suites, and cottages with 2 bedrooms, 2 baths and living room with fireplace; restaurant, wine list, Olympic sized pool, tennis court and welcomes children and pets.

✉ jseesaws@sover.net 🌐 www.jseesaw.com

PITTSFIELD

Casa Bella Inn
3911 Rt 100 North 05762
877-746-8943 802-746-8943
Susan & Franco Cacozza

95-125 $US BB
8 rooms, 8 pb
Visa, MC, AmEx,
Rated
C-ltd/S-no/P-no/H-no
Italian, German, and
Spanish

Full breakfast
Chef owned restaurant/bar service,
afternoon refreshments
Sitting room with potbelly stove, mini
suites, self-guided tours

Travel to our scenic mountain valley location and enjoy one of Vermont's finest full service inns. Looking for lodging near Killington? Give us a call. Considering a hotel or motel? Try our B&B for personal service in the heart the Green Mountains.

✉ info@casabellainn.com 🌐 casabellainn.com

PLAINFIELD

Comstock House B&B
1620 Middle Road 05667
802-272-2693
Warren Hathaway & Ross
Sneyd

115-185 $US BB
4 rooms, 3 pb
Visa, MC
C-ltd/S-no/P-no/H-no

Full breakfast
Panoramic views, wireless Internet,
private baths, home made breakfast,
generous rooms

Beautiful B&B with stunning panoramic views of the Green Mountains from every room. Enjoy large rooms with private baths, farm-fresh breakfasts, WiFi. Conveniently located in central VT, near the state capitol, and many attractions. Informative hosts.

✉ stay@ComstockHouseBB.com 🌐 www.comstockhousebb.com

PLYMOUTH

Hawk Inn & Mountain Resort
Route 100 05056
800-685-4295 802-672-3811
Jessica Alberty

150-600 $US BB
50 rooms, 50 pb
Most CC, *Rated*, •
C-yes/S-no/P-no/H-yes

Full breakfast
The River Tavern Restaurant serving breakfast, lunch and dinner.
Library w/ Fireplace, Spa, Indoor & Outdoor Heated Pools, Hiking, Tennis, Fishing, Bicycles

On 1,200 pristine acres in the heart of Vermont's breathtaking Green Mountains, Hawk has created one of the most peaceful and unspoiled family-friendly resorts in the world. Luxurious villas and a 50-room inn offer an elegant setting for a great getaway.

✉ hawkinn@hawkresort.com 🌐 www.hawkresort.com

PUTNEY

Hickory Ridge House
53 Hickory Ridge Rd S 05346
800-380-9218 802-387-5709
Gillian Pettit

150-235 $US BB
8 rooms, 8 pb
Visa, MC
C-ltd/S-no/P-ltd/H-ltd

Full breakfast
Complimentary tea, coffee, cold soft drinks & snacks
Sitting rooms, fireplaces, cable TV, DVD players, WiFi

Located on a quiet country road in Putney, VT, and listed in the National Register of Historic Places, Hickory Ridge House offers modern convenience in a private, rural setting.

✉ mail@hickoryridgehouse.com 🌐 www.hickoryridgehouse.com

QUECHEE

Inn at Clearwater Pond
984 Quechee-Hartland Road 05059
888-918-4INN (4466) 802-295-0606
Christine DeLuca

175-295 $US BB
5 rooms, 5 pb
•
C-yes/S-ltd/P-yes/H-ltd

Full breakfast
Assorted cookies and sweets, fruits, granola bars, biscotti, tea, coffee
Hot air ballooning, swimming pond, massage therapy, workout room, weddings, outdoor equipment rentals

Romance, beauty & a bit of adventure – you've discovered our hidden gem! Just down the road from Woodstock is our bit of paradise, close to town but nestled in the country. Need to escape from city life? We have exactly what you're looking for.

✉ innatclearwaterpond@gmail.com 🌐 www.innatclearwaterpond.com

READING

Bailey's Mills
1347 Bailey's Mills Rd 05062
800-639-3437 802-484-7809
Barbara Thaeder

120-199 $US BB
3 rooms, 3 pb
•
C-yes/S-no/P-ltd/H-no

Full breakfast with hot entree.
Afternoon tea, refreshments
Sitting room, library, fireplaces, pond, stream, walking paths; 50 acres

History-filled country home overlooking "Spite Cemetery.) Colorful breakfast in Colonial dining room, solarium or on the front porch.

✉ info1@baileysmills.com 🌐 www.baileysmills.com

RICHMOND

The Richmond Victorian Inn
191 E Main St 05477
888-242-3362 802-434-4410
Frank & Joyce Stewart

129-169 $US BB
5 rooms, 5 pb
Visa, MC, Disc, *Rated*
C-ltd/S-no/P-no/H-no
French (limited)

Full gourmet breakfast
British-style afternoon teas served Sundays, Sept-May. Private Dinners-See website for more info!
Free WiFi, books, magazines, TV/VCR, good conversation, dinner reservations, discount ski passes.

Free Night w/Certificate: Valid November-April 30; subject to availability, not valid on holidays.

Lovely, restored 1850s Queen Anne Victorian, 12 miles from Burlington. Private bathrooms, comfortable antique furnishings, full gourmet breakfasts. Historic Round Church, shops, excellent restaurants within walking distance. Convenient to many activities.

✉ innkeeper@richmondvictorianinn.com 🌐 www.richmondvictorianinn.com

ROCHESTER

Liberty Hill Farm
511 Liberty Hill 05767
802-767-3926
Bob & Beth Kennett

90-180 $US MAP
7 rooms
C-yes/S-no/P-no/H-no

Full breakfast & dinner
Full dinner served at 6 pm with farm
fresh local foods, eggs, maple syrup,
cheese, vegetables, fruits
Sitting rooms, library, river tubes,
MT bike trails, cribs and high chairs;
snowshoes, XC ski rental

There is always a warm welcome at Liberty Hill Farm. This working dairy farm, nestled between the White River and the Green Mountains, provides excellent meals and family activities year round.
beth@libertyhillfarm.com www.libertyhillfarm.com

RUTLAND

Harvest Moon
1659 N. Grove St 05701
802 773-0889
Susan Lipkin

105-125 $US BB
2 rooms, 2 pb
C-yes/S-no/P-ltd/H-ltd

local and organic
Hot tea always available. Refrigerator
and micro wave in parlor.
Living room with TV/VCR, parlor with
electric flame stove, antique piano and
antiquarian books

At Harvest Moon Bed & Breakfast you'll enjoy a truly organic getaway. This classic 1835 Vermont farmhouse is furnished throughout with comfortable antique decor and spectacular mountain views. Our intimate setting will make you feel right at home.
relax@harvestmoonvt.com www.harvestmoonvt.com

SAXTONS RIVER

The Saxtons River Inn
27 Main St 05154
802-869-2110
Bob Thomson

99-159 $US BB
16 rooms, 16 pb
Most CC, Cash
C-yes/S-no/P-yes/H-no

Continental breakfast
Pub & restaurant on the premises
Wireless Internet, TV, phone,
housekeeping

Charming, historic 16 room inn with restaurant and pub. Very close to some fantastic ski mountains with prices that can't be beat. We think of the Inn as both a place to relax and as a base for exploring the pleasures of Southern Vermont.   innatsr@vermontel.net www.saxtonsriverinn.com

SHAFTSBURY

Meadowood Farm
557 Bennett Hill Road 05262
800-935-2440
Clifford & Donna Ward

145-190 $US BB
4 rooms, 4 pb
Visa, MC
C-yes/S-no/P-yes/H-ltd
January – October

Full breakfast
Dinner by reservation
TV, private baths, suite with sitting
area & wet bar, panoramic views,
stable, horse & pet friendly

There is a place in southwestern Vermont where back roads lead to lush horse farms, where peace and quiet abound. The air is cool all summer long and vistas stretch for miles. That place is Meadowood Farm, a decidedly unique mountaintop experience.
sonny@meadowoodvt.com www.meadowoodvt.com

SHREWSBURY

Crisanver House
1434 Crown Point Rd 05738
800-492-8089 802-492-3589
Michael & Carol Calotta

155-395 $US BB
9 rooms, 9 pb
Visa, MC, AmEx,
Rated, •
C-ltd/S-no/P-no/H-no
Italian
Closed in April and Nov.

Gourmet country breakfast
Afternoon Tea, Dinner by reservation
Conservatory, Library, Jacuzzi, Heated
Pool, Tennis, Snowshoeing, Wireless
Internet, Skiing, Porch

Escape to a cherished experience with gracious hospitality, marvelous accommodations, great food, wonderful service, magnificent views/surroundings and blissful setting. Be relaxed, revived, refreshed and rekindled in spirit-all as described by our guests
info@crisanver.com www.crisanver.com

Maple Crest Farm
2512 Lincoln Hill Rd 05738
802-492-3367
William & Donna Smith

60-100 $US BB
9 rooms, 2 pb
Most CC, *Rated*
C-ltd/S-no/P-no/H-yes
February-December

Full breakfast
Afternoon tea, snacks
Sitting room, library, suites, fireplaces

1808 Federal style, 27 room home, high in the Green Mountains, lovingly preserved for 7 generations. 320 acres to hike/walk. Furnished with antiques, 10 miles south of Rutland, 12 miles to Ludlow.
maplecrestbnb@gmail.com www.smithmaplecrestfarm.com/Bed_and_Breakfa

STOWE

Auberge de Stowe	79-199 $US BB	Continental plus breakfast
692 Main St 05672	8 rooms, 8 pb	Sitting room, Jacuzzi, swimming pool
800-387-8789 802-253-7787	Visa, MC, AmEx	(seasonal), fireplace, wireless Internet
Chantal & Shawn Kerivan	C-yes/S-no/P-no/H-no	
	French, German	

An 8 room country inn. Relax by the fireplace or hot tub in the winter, cool down in the swimming pool or river in the summer. Enjoy your stay with us here in Stowe, the way life and family vacations were meant to be.

✉ info@aubergedestowe.com 🌐 aubergedestowe.com

Bears Lair Inn	119-199 $US BB	Full breakfast
4583 Mountain Rd 05672	10 rooms, 10 pb	Afternoon tea during regular & high
800-821-7891 802-253-4846	Most CC, Cash,	season
Carolyn & Bill Cook	*Rated*, •	Large living room, satellite TV room,
	C-ltd/S-no/P-no/H-no	heated pool (summer), 2 hot tubs, WiFi

Warm hospitality awaits you in our cozy 3 diamond awarded B&B, nestled at the base of Mount Mansfired the highest mountain in Vermont. Babbling brook, waterfall, wooded walking trail on our 9 beautiful acres. Full breakfast, afternoon tea, free WiFi.

✉ bearslairinn@gmail.com 🌐 www.bearslairinn.com

Brass Lantern Inn	99-225 $US BB	Full country breakfast
717 Maple St 05672	9 rooms, 9 pb	Tea with fresh baked cookies &
800-729-2980 802-253-2229	Visa, MC, AmEx,	pastries are available every afternoon
Mary Anne & George Lewis	*Rated*, •	Fireplaces, whirlpool, patio, wireless
	C-ltd/S-no/P-no/H-no	Internet access, cable TV upon request, individual heat & A/C

An authentic B&B inn in the quaint village of Stowe Vermont. Award winning breakfast. Charming and romantic bed and breakfast with country quilts and antique furniture. Outdoor hot tub, fireplaces and whirlpool tubs and magnificent mountain views.

✉ info@brasslanterninn.com 🌐 www.brasslanterninn.com

The Gables Inn	80-250 $US BB	Full breakfast
1457 Mountain Rd 05672	18 rooms, 18 pb	Complimentary apres ski in winter
800-GABLES-1 802-253-7730	Most CC, Cash,	Sitting room, fireplace, swimming pool
Annette Monachelli & Randy Stern	*Rated*, •	(summer), hot tub, ping pong, A/C
	C-yes/S-no/P-ltd/H-ltd	

Stowe's classic Vermont country inn. Antiques, wood floors, nice views. Rooms range from cozy inn rooms to luxury accommodations with Jacuzzis and fireplaces. Our breakfast is legendary.

✉ info@gablesinn.com 🌐 www.gablesinn.com

Three Bears at the Fountain	115-300 $US BB	Full breakfast
1049 Pucker St. Rte.	6 rooms, 6 pb	Afternoon sweets, tea, coffee, guests
100 05672	Visa, MC, Disc	have access to the one dollar store for
802-253-1882	C-ltd/S-no/P-ltd/H-no	soda, mixers, snacks
Suzanne Vazzano		Plush robes, hot tub, swimming pool, mountain views, WiFi, cable TV, fireplaces, bath amenities

Free Night w/Certificate: Valid Sunday-Thurs., non-holiday (foliage period).

A six-room B&B located 1 mile north of the village of Stowe. Full mountain views. Newly renovated with updated amenities, Queen & King rooms & two suites.

✉ threebears@stowevt.net 🌐 www.threebearsbandb.com

Tell your hosts Pamela Lanier sent you.

STOWE

Timberholm Inn
452 Cottage Club Rd 05672
800-753-7603 802-253-7603
Tom & Susan Barnes

90-225 $US BB
9 rooms, 9 pb
Visa, MC, •
C-ltd/S-no/P-no/H-no

3 course country breakfast
Afternoon treats, locally blended teas
& homemade cookies
Weddings, civil unions, cable TV, small
refrigerator, microwave, hot tub, WiFi,
outside deck, pub

Free Night w/Certificate: Not valid 2/11/11-2/21/10. 9/16/11-10/22/11.. 12/18/11-
1/1/12. 2/10/12-2/20/12. Room Upgrade.

*Tucked into a wooded hillside in Stowe, Vermont, The Timberholm Inn is a country inn with the am-
bience of a bygone era and the warm interior of rich knotty pine. Built in 1949, it remains one of the
most popular year round lodging properties to this day.*

✉ info@timberholm.com 🌐 www.timberholm.com

TAFTSVILLE

Apple Hill Inn
10 Hartwood Way 05073
802-457-9135
Beverlee Cook

135-200 $US BB
3 rooms, 3 pb
Most CC, Cash, Checks
C-yes/S-no/P-yes/H-yes

Hearty, healthy buffet breakfast
Catered afternoon teas, brunches,
receptions, small dinners by
arrangement
Tea Room, solarium, deck, views, free
wireless Internet, facility for weddings,
special events

*Apple Hill Inn offers its guests the ultimate in hospitality. From the time you arrive until the time you
depart your experience is Vermont at its very best. Located high on a hill in the Green Mountains,
overlooking the Ottaquechee River and waterfalls.*

✉ applehill1@aol.com 🌐 www.applehillinn.com

WAITSFIELD

Mad River Inn
243 Tremblay Rd 05673
800-832-8278 802-496-7900
Luc Maranda

115-175 $US BB
9 rooms, 9 pb
Visa, MC, AmEx, •
C-yes/S-no/P-no/H-no
French

Full breakfast
Afternoon tea
Cable TV, business traveler
accommodations, Hot Spring outdoor
hot tub

*From the moment you enter the sunny front room or our Inn, with white wicker furniture and pastel
floral prints, the flower-bedecked back porch overlooking the gazebo, and lush gardens in open fields,
you will know you have arrived in heavenly Vermont.*

✉ madriverinn@madriver.com 🌐 www.madriverinn.com

**Millbrook Inn &
Restaurant**
Route 17 05673
800-477-2809 802-496-2405
Joan & Thom Gorman

110-190 $US BB
7 rooms, 7 pb
Visa, MC, AmEx,
Rated
C-ltd/S-no/P-yes/H-no
Some French
Closed April-May &
Nov.

Full cooked-to-order breakfast
Complimentary refreshments, full
dinner from restaurant
3 sitting rooms, vegetarian dining
menu, high speed wireless Internet,
fireplace

*Charming hand-stenciled guestrooms with handmade quilts, country gourmet dining, vegetarian
choices, in our small candlelit restaurant. Chef-owned and operated since 1979. Large, landscaped
back yard for relaxing.*

✉ gorman@millbrookinn.com 🌐 www.millbrookinn.com

Mountain View Inn
1912 Mill Brook Rd 05673
802-496-2426
Fred & Susan Spencer

100-145 $US BB
7 rooms, 7 pb
Most CC
C-yes/S-no/P-no/H-no

Full breakfast
WiFi, common rooms, private baths,
games, books, fireplace, piano

*An 1826 farmhouse made into a comfortable inn with private baths and family heirlooms. Comfort-
able accommodations in the country just minutes from the quaint shops in Waitsfield or the hiking
trails and ski slopes at Sugarbush and Mad River Glen.*

 info@vtmountainviewinn.com  www.vtmountainviewinn.com

Mountain View Inn, Waitsfield, VT

WAITSFIELD

The Inn at Round Barn Farm	165-315 $US BB	Full breakfast
1661 E Warren Rd 05673	12 rooms, 12 pb	Afternoon cookies & evening hors
802-496-2276	Visa, MC, AmEx,	d'oeuvres, full service catering
Anne Marie DeFreest & Tim Piper	*Rated*, •	company on premise for events
	C-ltd/S-no/P-no/H-ltd	Sitting room, library, Jacuzzis, swimming pool, fireplace, cable TV

Vermont's premiere B&B has been a landmark in the Sugarbush Mad River Valley for over 20 years. A hospitable staff, wonderful food, amazing landscaping, organic gardens, well-decorated guestrooms and a beautiful setting on 245 acres await you.

Info@InnattheRoundBarn.com   www.theroundbarn.com

The Waitsfield Inn	119-179 $US BB	Full breakfast
5267 Main St 05673	12 rooms, 12 pb	Common rooms, games, TV, VCR,
800-758-3801 802-496-3979	Most CC, Cash	fireplaces, free WiFi, walk to shops &
John & Vickie Walluck	C-ltd/S-no/P-no/H-no	restaurants, shuttle to slopes
	French and some German	

The Waitsfield Inn is a historical 1825 Vermont Farmhouse in the center of Waitsfield Village. All our rooms have private baths and most have A/C. This Bed and Breakfast is home to both Sugarbush and Mad River Ski Resorts and many outdoor activities.

lodging@waitsfieldinn.com   www.waitsfieldinn.com

Weathertop Mountain Inn	115-289 $US BB	Full prepared-to-order breakfast
755 Mill Brook Rd, Rt 17 05673	8 rooms, 8 pb	Evening dining, Southeast Asian
800-800-3625 802-496-4909	Most CC, Cash, Checks	specialties, local microbrews, fine
Lisa & Michael Lang	C-ltd/S-no/P-ltd/H-no	wine & quality sake available
	Spanish	Hot tub, sauna, game room with fireplace, great room with fireplace, wireless DSL, evening dining

Not your typical country inn . . . . Asian antiques & art, eclectic evening cuisine & thoughtful amenities to enhance your visit to Vermont's Mad River Valley. Visit us to discover why Weathertop Mountain Inn is not your typical country inn.

stay@weathertopmountaininn.com   www.weathertopmountaininn.com

WAITSFIELD

Wilder Farm Inn	110-145 $US BB	Country Gourmet breakfast
1460 Main St 05673	8 rooms, 8 pb	Fresh baked afternoon snacks, evening
800-496-8878 802-496-9935	Visa, MC, AmEx, •	cordials, fireside s'mores, veg/vegan
Luke & Linda Iannuzzi	C-ltd/S-no/P-no/H-no	breakfast available
		Library, 2 fireplaces, WiFi, cable
		TV, swim hole & Mad Path, lovely
		grounds, on-site pottery studio

Come and relax at the Wilder Farm Inn (c. 1860) with spectacular views no matter what season. Surrounded by the Green Mountains, the Mad River Valley boasts beauty beyond belief, true country living at its best. Come as Guests . . . Leave as Friends

✉ info@wilderfarminn.com 🌐 wilderfarminn.com

Yellow Farmhouse Inn	119-239 $US BB	Full gourmet breakfast
550 Old County Rd 05673	8 rooms, 8 pb	Morning coffee or tea & afternoon
877-257-5767 802-496-4263	Visa, MC	snacks
Mike & Sandra Anastos	C-ltd/S-no/P-no/H-yes	Vermont Castings stoves, Jacuzzis,
		whirlpool tubs, air conditioners, WiFi
		Internet

Romantic and secluded, the Yellow Farmhouse Inn is nestled on 10 acres just minutes from Sugarbush Ski Resort, Mad River Glen Ski Area, restaurants, shopping, nightlife & all the Mad River Valley has to offer.

✉ innkeeper@yellowfarmhouseinn.com 🌐 www.yellowfarmhouseinn.com

WARREN

Beaver Pond Farm Bed &	159-204 $US BB	Full Gourmet Breakfast
Breakfast	4 rooms, 4 pb	Coffee, tea, afternoon treat; wine &
1225 Golf Course Rd 05674	Visa, MC, AmEx, •	beer extra
800-685-8285 802-583-2861	C-ltd/S-no/P-no/H-no	Fireplace, hot tub, wireless Internet,
Kim and Bob Sexton		TV/DVDs, coffee bar, beer & wine bar,
		sleds, snowshoes

Rejuvenate your spirit at our distinctive and intimate Vermont farmhouse. Pamper yourself with gourmet breakfasts and treats, glorious views and a soothing hot tub. Stroll or snowshoe our 5 rolling acres.

✉ innkeeper@beaverpondfarminn.com 🌐 www.beaverpondfarminn.com

Sugar Lodge	79-189 $US BB	Continental breakfast
2197 Sugarbush Access	22 rooms, 22 pb	Homemade cookies, beer & wine bar
Rd 05674	Visa, MC, AmEx	Hot tub, outdoor pool, central A/C,
800-982-3465 802-583-3300	C-yes/S-no/P-no/H-yes	fireplaces, wine & beer bar, laundry
Susan & Robert Cummiskey		facilities, ice machine

A classic mountain lodge next to the Sugarbush Resort. Nestled in the Green Mountains & within an hour of Burlington, Montpelier & all of Vermont's most popular attractions.

✉ mail@sugarlodge.com 🌐 www.sugarlodge.com

West Hill House B&B	140-250 $US BB	Award-winning full breakfast
1496 West Hill Rd 05674	8 rooms, 8 pb	Coffee, tea, snacks, accessible cookie
800-209-1049 802-496-7162	Most CC, *Rated*, •	jar, cash bar, dinner by advance notice
Peter & Susan MacLaren	C-ltd/S-no/P-no/H-ltd	Wine cellar, library, TVs & movies,
		in-room fireplaces, Jacuzzis, phones,
		WiFi, snowshoes & sleds

Free Night w/Certificate: Not valid Sept.16-Oct.15,2011; Dec.23-Jan. 1, 2012; Feb.17-Feb.25, 2012.

Comfortable, well-appointed 1850 home on quiet lane near Sugarbush Resort. Gardens, ponds, gazebo. Near fine restaurants, quaint villages. Guestrooms have fireplaces & whirlpool or steam shower. A lovely spot to relax, romance, refresh.

✉ innkeepers@westhillbb.com 🌐 www.westhillbb.com

Old Stagecoach Inn, Waterbury, VT

WATERBURY

Grunberg Haus B&B Inn & Cabins	90-180 $US BB	Full cooked breakfast
Route 100 S 05676	14 rooms, 8 pb	Refreshments, snacks in self-serve
800-800-7760 802-244-7726	Visa, MC, Disc, •	pub/gameroom
Jeff & Linda Connor	C-yes/S-ltd/P-ltd/H-no	Forest trails, deck, balconies, self-serve pub/gameroom with woodstove, living room fireplace

Austrian chalet offering romantic guestrooms with balconies, antiques, quilts and summer cabins. Rural, casual, quiet . . . Often described by guests as "cozy, relaxing, hospitable." Located on the edge of a large forest but just 5 miles from the highway.

 info@grunberghaus.com 🌐 www.grunberghaus.com

Moose Meadow Lodge	189-229 $US BB	Full breakfast
607 Crossett Hill 05676	4 rooms, 4 pb	Green Mountain coffees, Vermont
802-244-5378	Visa, MC	Liberty teas and herbals
Greg Trulson & Willie Docto	C-yes/S-ltd/P-no/H-ltd Tagalog	Free high-speed Internet (Wi-Fi), Private Baths & Steam rooms, Five-person hot tub, 86 private acres

Nestled in 86 secluded acres in the Green Mountains, the Adirondack style Moose Meadow Lodge in Waterbury, Vermont invites you to enjoy a truly unique experience.

 relax@moosemeadowlodge.com 🌐 www.moosemeadowlodge.com

Old Stagecoach Inn	80-140 $US BB	Full Country Breakfast
18 N Main St 05676	11 rooms, 8 pb	Bar Service
800-262-2206 802-244-5056	Most CC, Cash, *Rated*	Sitting room, library, bar, family/group
John Barwick	C-yes/S-no/P-ltd/H-no German	travel, A/C, parlor, antiques, WiFi, wood burning fireplace

Meticulously restored village Inn on the National Register of Historic Places. Located in Waterbury – the home of Ben & Jerry's, the heart of the Green Mountains on scenic Route 100, right between the resort areas of Stowe, Sugarbush and Mad River Glen.

 lodging@oldstagecoach.com 🌐 www.oldstagecoach.com

WEST DOVER

Red Oak Inn	69-259 $US BB	Full breakfast
45 Route 100 05356	24 rooms, 24 pb	Snack & soda machines available
866-573-3625 802-464-8817	Most CC, *Rated*, •	Outdoor pool, hot tub, suites, 2
Robert & Debra Buehler	C-yes/S-ltd/P-yes/H-ltd	fireplace lounges, cable TV, exercise room, game room, BYOB tavern

Fall in love with our impeccably landscaped, 4 season country inn. You'll enjoy a New England vacation in the picture postcard setting you've always dreamed of at the Red Oak Inn.

 info@redoakinn.com 🌐 www.redoakinn.com

WEST DOVER

The Snow Goose Inn
Rt 100 05356
888-604-7964 802-464-3984
Cyndee & Ron Frere

125-375 $US BB
13 rooms, 13 pb
Most CC, Cash, Checks,
Rated, •
C-yes/S-no/P-yes/H-yes

Full country breakfast
Complimentary wines & snacks in
early evening, catered meals & bar
service available
Fireplaces, gardens, Jacuzzis, WiFi,
meeting space, guest computer, full
housekeeping, fax

Ideal for a romantic getaway from the hassle of city life. Comfort & charm amid 3 wooded acres, pond & natural gardens. Most of our antique filled rooms have wood fireplaces & 2 person Jacuzzis.

✉ stay@snowgooseinn.com   🌐 www.snowgooseinn.com

WEST GLOVER

Rodgers Country Inn
582 Rodgers Rd 05875
800-729-1704 802-525-6677
Nancy Rodgers

50-70 $US BB
5 rooms
Most CC
C-yes/S-no/P-no/H-no

Full breakfast
Dinner is offered for guests
Sitting room, TV/VCR, lake, country
cooking

Peace, quiet and a friendly atmosphere. Located in the Northeast Kingdom of Vermont. Dinner is also offered to our guests. Family operated for over 40 years.

✉ jnrodger@together.net   🌐 www.rodgerscountryinn.com

WEST WARDSBORO

**Edelweiss at Snow
Mountain Farms**
758 Sheldon Hill Road 05360
877-771-0877 802-896-6530
Mary Lyn Bourque

105-225 $US BB
2 rooms, 2 pb
Visa, MC, •
C-ltd/S-no/P-no/H-ltd
late May through mid-
Oct

Vermont Breakfast by Candlelight
Afternoon tea or happy hour
refreshments each day, dinner
available by reservation
Wood fireplace, TV/VCR/DVD, 24-hour
coffee & snacks, concierge, small
business services, WiFi

The Inn is located on one of the most scenic roads in America in southern Vermont. Nearby are many of the top Vermont attractions, including the majestic Green Mountains, many outdoor recreational activities, music, art and unending shopping and antiquing

✉ esmfbnb@verizon.net   🌐 www.edelweissbandb.com

WESTMORE

WilloughVale Inn
793 VT Route 5A
South 05860
800-594-9102 802-525-4123
Roy Clark

105-320 $US BB
18 rooms, 18 pb
Most CC, Cash,
Rated, •
C-yes/S-no/P-yes/H-yes

Continental breakfast
Continental Breakfast for guests only,
restaurant on-site open seasonally
June to mid-October
Bicycles, 1 double kayak, 1 single
kayak, 2 canoes for rent, fireplaces,
Jacuzzis, playground

The perfect getaway in Vermont's Northeast Kingdom with lakeside and lakeview accommodations and stunning mountain views. The Inn offers 10 unique guestrooms, 4 lakefront + 4 lakeview cottages, all fully-equipped on the hill above the Inn.

✉ info@willoughvale.com   🌐 www.willoughvale.com

WESTON

The Inn at Weston
630 Main St. 05161
802-824-6789
Bob & Linda Aldrich

185-325 $US BB
13 rooms, 13 pb
Visa, MC
C-ltd/S-no/P-yes/H-ltd

Full breakfast
Restaurant, fine dining on site,
afternoon refreshments
A/C, TV, CD & VCR players, fireplaces,
orchid greenhouse, whirlpool tubs,
decks, weddings, reunions

An 1848 farmhouse on 7 acres, nestled in a quintessential southern Vermont village offers warm, friendly service. Most of the rooms have Jacuzzi tubs, fireplaces, feather beds & some offer private decks. The dining room serves locally harvested cuisine.

 theinnatweston@comcast.net   🌐 www.innweston.com

WILLISTON

Catamount B&B
592 Governor Chittenden
Rd 05495
888-680-1011 802-878-2180
Jim & Lucy McCullough

85-125 $US BB
3 rooms, 1 pb
Visa, MC, Disc
C-yes/S-no/P-no/H-ltd

Continental plus breakfast
Sitting room, bikes, fireplace, suites,
accommodate business travelers,
WiFi, activity rental

Free Night w/Certificate: Valid November-April. Room Upgrade.

This beautiful 1796 historic home in the country is located just minutes from Lake Champlain, Burlington shops, restaurants and area attractions. Trail side activities include mountain biking, trail running/walking, cross country skiing, and snowshoeing.

✉ bandb@catamountoutdoor.com 🌐 www.bbonline.com/vt/catamount/index.html

WILMINGTON

Shearer Hill Farm B&B
297 Shearer Hill Rd 05363
800-437-3104 802-464-3253
Bill & Patti Pusey

85-115 $US BB
6 rooms, 6 pb
C-yes/S-ltd/P-no/H-yes

Baked Apples with Vermont Syrup
Vermont Breakfast, Coffee
Delicious baked apple breakfast every
morning, warm and cozy rooms,
private baths, ceiling fans

At Shearer Hill Farm B&B, great hospitality is our top priority. Come help farmer Bill gather sap and boil syrup. It's a truly wonderful experience! We're more than simply a Vermont bed and breakfast because there's so much to do right outside our door!

✉ ppusey@shearerhillfarm.com 🌐 www.shearerhillfarm.com

WINDSOR

Juniper Hill Inn
153 Pembroke Rd 05089
800-359-2541 802-674-5273
Ari Nikki & Robert Dean

165-350 $US BB
16 rooms, 16 pb
Most CC, Cash, Checks,
Rated, •
C-ltd/S-no/P-ltd/H-ltd
Finnish

Cooked to order country breakfast
Romantic Dinner by reservation
Thurs-Monday, our famous coffee, tea,
homemade afternoon snack
Restaurant, bar, sitting room, library,
swimming pool, fireplace, walking
nature trails, golf, more

Luxurious and romantic historic Colonial mansion with unsurpassed location featuring richly appointed guestrooms, working fireplaces, four poster beds, canopies & numerous amenities. Woodstock and Dartmouth nearby. Surrounded by nature.

✉ Innkeeper@juniperhillinn.com 🌐 www.juniperhillinn.com

WOODSTOCK

Applebutter Inn
7511 Happy Valley Rd 05091
800-486-1734 802-457-4158
Barbara Barry & Michael
Pacht

100-225 $US BB
6 rooms, 6 pb
Visa, MC, *Rated*, •
C-ltd/S-no/P-no/H-ltd

Full gourmet breakfast
Homemade cookies & complimentary
teas in the afternoon, vegetarian &
vegan meals on request
WiFi throughout, library, cable TV,
fireplace sitting room, Music Room
with grand piano

Fantastic candlelight gourmet breakfast. Beautiful gardens. Historic 1854 country home with six gorgeous air-conditioned guestrooms (4 with fireplaces), centrally located between the villages of Woodstock and Quechee.

✉ aplbtrn@comcast.net 🌐 www.applebutterinn.com

Canterbury House
43 Pleasant St 05091
800-390-3077 802-457-3077
Bob & Sue Frost

135-200 $US BB
7 rooms, 7 pb
Visa, MC, *Rated*
C-ltd/S-no/P-no/H-no

Gourmet full plated breakfast
Sitting room, WiFi, Internet access,
TVs, patio, fishing, golf, skiing, hiking

An 1880 Victorian townhouse restored to offer modern comfort & historic authenticity. All 7 rooms have private baths and summer air conditioning. The house is within walking distance of the Village Green.

✉ lodginginfo@thecanterburyhouse.com 🌐 www.thecanterburyhouse.com

WOODSTOCK

Carriage House of Woodstock	100-195 $US BB	Full breakfast
Route 4 West 05091	9 rooms, 9 pb	Homemade cookies & tea
800-791-8045 802-457-4322	Most CC	Parlor with fireplace, wrap-around
Debbie & Mark Stanglin	C-ltd/S-no/P-no/H-ltd	porch, private parking lot, whirlpool tubs, WiFi

1865 Victorian B&B located just one mile west of the village of Woodstock. Nine uniquely decorated rooms, all with private baths – one with fireplace. Several with TV & whirlpool tub. The Carriage House is on the Vermont Register of Historic Places.

 stanglin@sover.net ○ www.carriagehousewoodstock.com

Deer Brook Inn	120-195 $US BB	Full breakfast
535 Woodstock Rd 05091	5 rooms, 5 pb	Afternoon tea
802-672-3713	Visa, MC, AmEx,	Sitting room, suite, fireplace, A/C,
David Kanal	*Rated*	cable TV, in-room music systems,
	C-ltd/S-no/P-no/H-no	WiFi, porch, lawns & gardens

Indulge yourself in our historic inn set on 5 acres of lawns, gardens, and wooded areas. Spacious, romantic accommodations with private baths, music systems and wireless Internet. Includes a 3 course breakfast in the dining room or on the terrace.

 deerbrook@vermontel.net ○ www.deerbrookinn.com

The Blue Horse Inn	160-350 $US BB	Fresh & Local Ingredients
3 Church St. 05091	10 rooms, 10 pb	Library, Pool, Tennis Court
802-221-4238	Most CC, Cash	
Keri Cole & Anna	S-no/P-yes/H-no	
Kolchinsky	German, French	

The Blue Horse Inn is uniquely situated in Woodstock Village. Our sweeping grounds overlook the Ottauquechee River and Mt. Tom, and guests can enjoy our clay tennis court and heated outdoor pool.

 keri@thebluehorseinn.com ○ www.thebluehorseinn.com

The Charleston House	135-290 $US BB	Full breakfast
21 Pleasant St 05091	9 rooms, 9 pb	A/C in the summer, Jacuzzis,
888-475-3800 802-457-3843	Visa, MC, AmEx	fireplaces
Dieter & Willa Nohl	C-ltd/S-no/P-no/H-ltd	
	French, German,	
	Spanish	

The Charleston House is part of what makes Woodstock special. At The Charleston House, comfort and warm hospitality are yours to enjoy. Visit us for a vacation you will love to remember.

 charlestonhousevermont@comcast.net ○ www.charlestonhouse.com

---

The Jackson House Inn	175-295 $US BB	Full breakfast
114-3 Senior Lane 05091	11 rooms, 11 pb	sitting room, library, WiFi, satellite TV,
800-448-1890 802-457-2065	Most CC, Cash, Checks	suites, massage tubs, gas fireplaces,
Richard and Kathy Terwelp	C-ltd/S-no/P-no/H-yes	pond

Immaculate 1890 Victorian manor just outside charming historic Woodstock. 11 rooms, all with private bath. Suites offer gas fireplaces, some with massage tubs. Gourmet breakfast included. 3 acres with pond and secluded park-like gardens, A/C, WiFi.

 info@jacksonhouse.com ○ www.jacksonhouse.com

The Lincoln Inn at the Covered Bridge	125-175 $US BB	Full breakfast
Rte 4 W 05091	6 rooms, 6 pb	Restaurant, bar service, biking, sitting
802-457-3312	Most CC, Cash	room, library
Amy Martsolf	C-ltd/S-no/P-no/H-no	

The Lincoln Inn in Woodstock is a warm, cozy country inn located 2.5 miles west of the Woodstock Village Green. Far enough from the village of Woodstock to be quiet, yet close enough to go to town in a few short minutes.

 stay@lincolninn.com ○ www.lincolninn.com

WOODSTOCK—————————————————————————————

The Village Inn of Woodstock	150-335 $US BB	Full breakfast
	8 rooms, 8 pb	Champagne by the glass or Mimosas
41 Pleasant St 05091	Visa, MC, *Rated*	to purchase for a special occasion
800-722-4571 802-457-1255	C-ltd/S-no/P-no/H-no	Victorian parlor & tavern, sitting room,
Evelyn & David Brey	German	perennial shaded garden, spa tubs,
		fireplaces, WiFi

Eight elegant, romantic rooms with period antiques, private baths, A/C & cable TV in our restored Victorian gem in the Village. Rates include a 3 course breakfast with pastries made in-house. It's your time away, let us help you make the most of it!

✉ stay@villageinnofwoodstock.com 🌐 www.villageinnofwoodstock.com

The Woodstocker Inn	130-395 $US BB	Hot cooked to order full breakfast
61 River St 05091	9 rooms, 9 pb	European breakfasts British specialties
866-662-1439 802-457-3896	S-no/P-no/H-no	such as boiled eggs soldiers, beans on
Dora Foschi, David Livesley	Italian	toast, smoked salmon
& Daisy Doo the hound!		WiFi, wood stove, car parking, sitting
		room, library, mainly organic supplies,
		recycled paper goods

2010 Lanier INNKEEPERS OF THE YEAR. Multi-award winning eco 1830's village Cape home. Organic food, recycled paper goods, eclectic European boutique style + indulgent bathrooms Accredited Green inn 2009/10 B&B Innkeepers of the Year. 2008/9 World Top 12

✉ innkeeper@woodstockervt.com 🌐 www.woodstockervt.com

Virgin Islands

ST. CROIX, CHRISTIANSTED

Carringtons Inn St. Croix
56 Estate Herman Hill 00820
877-658-0508 340-713-0508
Claudia & Roger Carrington

100-165 $US BB
5 rooms, 5 pb
Visa, MC, AmEx,
Rated, •
S-no/P-no/H-no

Full breakfast
Snacks, Welcome Cocktail
Sitting room, swimming pool, cable TV,
accommodate business travelers

Welcome to Carrington's Inn – your home in the Caribbean. Five spacious and beautifully decorated rooms surround the pool and patio. Personalized service is our trademark.

✉ info@carringtonsinn.com 🌐 www.carringtonsinn.com

Villa Greenleaf
11 Estate Montepellier 00821
888-282-1001 340-719-1958
Jeff Teel

200-300 $US BB
5 rooms, 5 pb
Most CC, Cash, Checks,
Rated, •
C-ltd/S-no/P-no/H-no

Full breakfast
Tropical drinks and hors d'oeuvres at
sunset
Private screened porches, roof decks,
living room, pool, concierge, included
in the nightly rate.

Where the annual temperature is 82 degrees, with cool breezes and breathtaking sunsets, we welcome you to Villa Greenleaf on St. Croix. Come join us in the most relaxed atmosphere that the Caribbean has to offer.

✉ stay@villagreenleaf.com 🌐 www.villagreenleaf.com

ST. JOHN, CRUZ BAY

The Hillcrest Guest House
#157 Enighed 00831
340-998-8388, cell 340-776-
6774
Phyllis Hall

137-245 $US BB
5 rooms, 5 pb
Most CC, Cash, Checks,
Rated, •
C-yes/S-no/P-no/H-no
A little Spanish

Breakfast items are placed in Suite
Bagels, muffins, tea, coffee, bacon,
eggs, juice, snacks, drinks & liquor,
red & white wine
A/C, free WiFi, snorkel, fins, beach
chair, umbrella, kitchenette/kitchen,
near beach

"Perfect place to feel human again." Hillcrest Guest House is one of the oldest and established Bed and Breakfast, vacation rentals on St. John and is located on a hill overlooking Cruz Bay with spectacular, "Million Dollar" romantic views.

✉ hillcrestguesthouse@yahoo.com 🌐 www.HillcrestStJohn.com

ST. THOMAS, CHARLOTTE AMALIE

**At Home In The Tropics
Bed & Breakfast Inn**
1680 (25) Dronningens
Gade 00802
340-777-9857
Pam Eckstein

205-245 $US BB
4 rooms, 4 pb
Visa, MC, AmEx
C-ltd/S-no/P-no/H-no
German
November 1 to August 1

Full breakfast
Honor bar & packaged snacks
Living room, dining room, porch,
library, WiFi, pool-side decks and
picnic facilities, parking, view

Bright and airy restored c 1803 St Thomas courtyard property located on Government House steps on Blackbeard's Hill. Swimming pool and water views from every room and deck. Easy walk down old Danish steps to historic harbor, restaurants, yachts & ferries.

✉ athomeinthetropics@earthlink.net 🌐 www.athomeinthetropics.com

---

Bellavista B&B
2713 Murphy Gade 12-14
00802
888-333-3063 340-714-5706
Wendy Snodgrass

175-265 $US BB
4 rooms, 4 pb
Most CC
C-ltd/S-ltd/P-no/H-no

Full breakfast
Complimentary bottled water, fresh
fruit and granola bars
Concierge, turn down service, flowers
in room, swimming pool, tropical
garden

A delightfully inviting estate overlooking the harbor at Charlotte Amalie. Experience the personalized service and quality amenities of a traditional B&B with distinctive Caribbean style.

 mail@bellavista-bnb.com 🌐 www.bellavista-bnb.com

At Home in the Tropics B&B, Charlotte Amalie, VI

ST. THOMAS, CHARLOTTE AMALIE

Bunker Hill Hotel
2307 Commandant Gade
00802
340-774-8056
Angela Rawlins

79-125 $US BB
15 rooms, 15 pb
Visa, MC, AmEx, •
C-yes/S-ltd/P-no/H-no

Full breakfast
Restaurant, lunch & dinner available
Swimming pool, suites, cable TV,
accommodates business travelers

A small, unique, clean, & comfortable B&B Inn, conveniently located in the historic district area of Charlotte Amalie, just a few minutes walking distance to many points of interest.

✉ info@bunkerhillhotel.com   🌐 www.bunkerhillhotel.com

Galleon House
4 C Commandant Gade 00804
800-524-2052 340-774-6952
Martha & Sandy

75-159 $US BB
12 rooms, 11 pb
Visa, MC, AmEx,
Rated, •
C-yes/S-no/P-ltd/H-no

Full breakfast
A/C, pool, wireless Internet, phone in
room, small pet designated rooms

Located in the Historic District of the Danish King's Quarters on Government Hill. Just steps away from the historic downtown duty free shopping area. Offering island charm in a relaxed and lush, tropical setting. Small pets welcome in certain rooms.

✉ info@galleonhouse.com   🌐 www.galleonhouse.com

**Miller Manor Hotel &
Guesthouse**
2527 Prindcesse Gade 00804
888-229-0762 340-774-1535
Marj & Harry

85-171 $US EP
10 rooms, 9 pb
Most CC, Cash, •
C-yes/S-ltd/P-no/H-no

Enjoy complimentary coffee or
tea from 7:00 – 10:00 a.m, breakfast
available during high season
Satellite TV, microwave, small fridge
A/C, wireless Internet, fax service,
laundry facilities, decks

Charming and historic Danish Manor house built in the 1800's has a wonderful view of St. Thomas harbor. Close to the airport, and within walking distance to shopping and ferries to nearby islands. Amenities include AC, wireless Internet and satellite TV.

✉ info@millermanor.com   🌐 www.millermanor.com

Virginia

ABINGDON

Shepherd's Joy
254 White Mill Road 24210
276-628-3273
Joyce & Jack Ferratt

135-155 $US BB
4 rooms, 4 pb
Visa, MC
C-ltd/S-ltd/P-no

Full breakfast

Situated in the Historic District of Abingdon Virginia, Shepherd's Joy offers an opportunity to experience the rare Victorian charm of an in-town farm. You can escape here to rest, relax and enjoy the pleasures of an unhurried life.

 stay@shepherdsjoy.com   www.shepherdsjoy.com

ALEXANDRIA

The Peake Fairfax House B&B
Cameron St 22314
888-549-3415 703-549-3415
Linda Egerton

120-225 $US BB
2 rooms, 2 pb
Most CC, •
C-ltd/S-no/P-no/H-no

Continental breakfast
Air conditioning, WiFi, fireplace,
library, TV, wedding facilities

A lovely way to experience a little of life in Alexandria as it was in the early Federal Period. This 1816 Old Town Alexandria Townhouse, elegantly furnished with period antiques and modern amenities, is on the Historic Registry.

 bbinfo@aabbn.com

AMHERST

Crump's Mountain Cottage
2150 Indian Creek Rd 24521
866-868-4118 434-277-5563
Carolyn & Curtis Crump

69-130 $US BB
2 rooms, 1 pb
Rated, •
C-yes/S-no/P-yes/H-no

Continental plus breakfast
Tea, coffee and popcorn
Stocked fishing pond, hiking trails,
games, music, movie videos, cards,
puzzles & guided nature tour

Solitary Cottage nestled in Blue Ridge Mountains, on 243 wooded acres, panoramic views from deck. Refresh your spirit with nature's sights & sounds. Enjoy the quiet & solitude. Hike on the property or in nearby G.W. National Forest. Guided tours offered

 crumpmtcottage@pngusa.net   www.crumpmtncottage.com

APPOMATTOX

Spring Grove Farm
3440 Spring Grove Rd 24522
877-409-1865 434-352-7429
Emily & Joe Sayers

125-250 $US BB
12 rooms, 12 pb
Most CC, Cash, Checks
C-yes/S-ltd/P-no/H-yes

Full breakfast
Snacks
Sitting room, library, Jacuzzis, steam
showers, suites, fireplaces, cable TV,
accommodate bus. trvl.

Spring Grove Farm is a restored 1842 plantation on 200 country acres. Eleven rooms & suites plus a cottage, all with private baths, many with whirlpools or steam showers. Perfect for weddings, receptions, retreats, reunions, or conferences.

 springgrovefarm@msn.com   www.springgrovefarm.com

ARRINGTON

Harmony Hill
929 Wilson Hill Rd 22922
434-270-8776
Mark Norris

119-159 $US BB
6 rooms, 6 pb
Most CC, Cash, Checks,
Rated, •
C-yes/S-no/P-yes/H-ltd
Arabic

Full country breakfast
24-hour complimentary sodas, iced
tea, coffee, juice, and freshly baked
goodies
Whirlpool tubs, fireplaces, big screen
HDTV, highspeed wireless Internet,
sun room, rocking chairs

Experience the charm of the Virginia Blue Ridge Mountain Area with a relaxing stay in a cozy log cabin bed & breakfast. Kick back in a comfy setting without pulling the plug on modern living. All rooms include HDTV, and there is an extensive DVD library.

 innkeepers@harmony-hill.com  www.harmony-hill.com

ASHLAND

The Henry Clay Inn
114 N Railroad Ave 23005
804-798-3100
Ann-Carol M. Houston

95-195 $US BB
14 rooms, 14 pb
Most CC, *Rated*
C-yes/S-no/P-ltd/H-yes

Continental buffet breakfast
Parlor, large porches, Jacuzzi in suites,
fireplaces in common areas, small
town pleasures, WiFi

Southern charm with fireplaces, a large front porch with rocking chairs, 14 period furnished rooms, a gallery featuring local artists and a Parlor that opens onto a balcony overlooking the old Ashland train station.

✉ information@henryclayinn.com   🌐 www.henryclayinn.com

BASYE

Sky Chalet Mountain Lodge
259 Sky Chalet Lane, Rt
263 22810
877-867-8439 540-856-2147
Ken & Mona Seay

69-155 $US BB
6 rooms, 6 pb
Visa, MC, Disc, •
C-yes/S-yes/P-yes/H-no

Continental breakfast
Mountain views, stone fireplaces,
kitchens, kitchenettes, decks, sitting
rooms, Jacuzzi for two

Renovated mountaintop Bed and Breakfast Lodge in the Shenandoah Valley with spectacular mountain and valley views. Private baths, private decks, fireplaces, kitchens, kitchenettes, Jacuzzi for two. The Mountain Lovers' paradise in the Shenandoah Valley!

✉ skychalet@skychalet.com   🌐 www.skychalet.com

BEDFORD

Vanquility Acres Inn
105 Angus Terrace 24523
540-587-9113
Ellen V. Everett

95-155 $US BB
4 rooms, 3 pb
C-yes/S-ltd/P-no/H-ltd

Full breakfast
Coffee/tea station, beverage/snack
baskets
Large rooms & suites, private baths,
cable TV, WiFi, VCR/DVD, central air,
refridge, microwave

A country home, nestled on a 10-acre family estate with beautiful views of the Blue Ridge Mountains and Peaks of Otters. Set in tranquil surroundings where you and your loved ones can enjoy a quiet and relaxing stay.

✉ Lodging@vanquilityacresinn.com   🌐 www.vanquilityacresinn.com

BLACKSBURG

Clay Corner Inn
401 Clay Street SW 24060
540-552-4030
Joanne Anderson

119-139 $US BB
8 rooms, 8 pb
Visa, MC, AmEx
C-ltd/S-ltd/P-ltd/H-ltd

Full breakfast
Cookie bar, Fridays, 2–9 p.m.
Homemade cookies any time. Bottled
water, coffee, tea, soda.
WiFi, luxury linens, cable TV, Virginia
wines, dog friendly, cafe style
breakfast 7:30–10 daily.

Embracing sustainable patterns of living and lodging, the inn offers the comforts of home, amenities of a fine hotel and friendly atmosphere of a small inn.

✉ stay@claycorner.com   🌐 claycorner.com

Maison Beliveau
5415 Gallion Ridge Rd 24060
540-961-0505
Joyce Beliveau

225-299 $US BB
5 rooms, 5 pb
Most CC, Cash
C-ltd/S-no/P-no/H-yes
French

Signature Gourmet Breakfast
Nightly wine and cheese hour. Lunch
and dinner with prior notice. 24 hour
snacks & beverages station
Free WiFi, outside deck, jetted tub,
heated bathroom tile floor, fireplace,
bath robes, TV, CD, DVD

Treat yourself to the experience of Maison Beliveau! Situated on 165 acres of rolling land, this unique inn provides incredible views and a calming atmosphere to help you relax and unwind during your stay.

✉ Joyce@maisonbeliveau.com   🌐 www.maisonbeliveau.com

BOSTON

The Inn on Thistle Hill
5541 Sperryville Pike 22713
540-987-9357
Seane Malone

145-195 $US BB
4 rooms, 4 pb
Visa, MC, Disc, •
C-ltd/S-ltd/P-ltd/H-ltd

Delicious cooked-to-order breakfast
Completely candle-lit (about 75
candles!), gourmet 5-course dinner by
advance reservation
Raindrop Aromatherapy Massage,
Aquachi Foot Spa, Consults, Energy
Balancing, Aromatherapy Classes

Thistle Hill sits on ten acres of both wooded & open land in the foothills of the Blue Ridge Mountains. Visit wineries, go antiquing, hike Old Rag Mountain or simply relax in the garden or ramble through our woods. Ask about our special packages.

✉ theinnonthistlehill@earthlink.net 🌐 www.theinnonthistlehill.com

BRIDGEWATER

Bridgewater Inn & Cottage
104 W College St 22812
540-828-4619
Mary Stevens Ayers

105-170 $US BB
3 rooms, 2 pb
Visa, MC, *Rated*
C-yes/S-no/P-yes/H-no

Full breakfast
Snacks, complimentary wine
Library, tennis, pool, fireplace, cable,
business accommodations, hot tub,
sun room on site

Bridgewater Inn and Cottage has two suites that offer ultimate comfort and each detail has been carefully considered for our guests. Romance, elegance, tranquility, and privacy describe the ambience of Bridgewater Inn and Cottage.

✉ bridgewaterinn_cottage@msn.com 🌐 www.bridgewaterinnandcottage.com

CAPE CHARLES

Cape Charles House B&B
645 Tazwell Ave 23310
757-331-4920
Bruce & Carol Evans

140-200 $US BB
5 rooms, 5 pb
Most CC, Cash, Checks,
Rated, •
C-ltd/S-ltd/P-no/H-no

Full gourmet breakfast
Complimentary tea & sweets, wine
and cheese, special dietary needs by
arrangement
Parlors, formal dining room, antiques,
wrap-around porch, wireless Internet,
Jacuzzis, cable TV

Cape Charles House received the Governor's Award for Virginia Hospitality. A comfortably elegant, romantic getaway in 1912 Colonial Revival. Oriental rugs, antiques and collections are incorporated into the beautifully decorated, lovingly restored home.

✉ stay@capecharleshouse.com 🌐 www.capecharleshouse.com

CHARLOTTESVILLE

Dinsmore House Inn
1211 W Main St 22903
877-882-7829 434-974-4663
Ryan & Denise Hubbard

119-279 $US BB
8 rooms, 8 pb
Most CC, Cash, Checks
C-ltd/S-no/P-no/H-ltd

Full breakfast
Complimentary beverages & snacks,
evening social hour w/ wine & cheese,
afternoon tea
Pool, hot tub, fitness center, courtyard,
wrap-around windows, elegant
atmosphere, free Internet

The Dinsmore House Bed & Breakfast combines a perfect location with luxurious comfort, creating a unique Charlottesville experience.

✉ info@dinsmorehouse.com 🌐 www.dinsmorehouse.com

**Prospect Hill Plantation
Inn & Restaurant**
2887 Poindexter Rd 22906
800-277-0844 540-967-0844
The Sheehan Family since
1977

195-395 $US BB
13 rooms, 13 pb
Most CC, Cash, Checks,
Rated, •
C-ltd/S-ltd/P-no/H-ltd

Full brkfast-in-bed or Dining Rm
Elegant dining Sun-Thur 7pm, Fri-Sat
8pm, w/comp. wine reception ½ hr.
prior, snacks in rm on arr.
Jacuzzis in 8 rms, all with fireplaces,
40+ acres of manicured grounds,
bicycles, honeymoon packages

Historic plantation manor on 50 acres with 13 romantic rooms & cottages just 15 mi East of Charlottesville. Working fireplaces in all rooms, 8 w/Jacuzzis. Outdoor pool.

✉ info@prospecthill.com 🌐 www.prospecthill.com

CHINCOTEAGUE

1848 Island Manor House 4160 Main St 23336 800-852-1505 757-336-5436 Sam and lin Mazza	120-215 $US BB 8 rooms, 8 pb Most CC C-ltd/S-ltd/P-no/H-no	Gourmet water & snacks Beach Lunches $9.95 person Afternoon Tea $18.00 @ person dinner@ $35. for 3 courses 3 common rooms, fireplace, brick courtyard with fountain, AC, Wireless Internet

Chincoteague Island's most elegant and gracious Inn providing comfort, hospitality and the best food on the island. 5 minutes from beautiful Assateague National Seashore and Chincoteague Wildlife Refuge.

✉ hosts@islandmanor.com 🌐 www.islandmanor.com

Channel Bass Inn 6228 Church St 23336 800-249-0818 757-336-6148 David & Barbara Wiedenheft	125-225 $US BB 7 rooms, 7 pb Most CC, Cash, Checks, *Rated*, • C-yes/S-no/P-yes/H-ltd French, Dutch, German, Spanish Late March thru November	Full breakfast English afternoon tea at a special rate of $10.00/person for inn guests, complimentary coffee, tea Parlor, piano, library, bikes, beach gear, cooler, TV, Tea Room, English gardens, meals on the porch

A world of peaceful elegance surrounds you when you enter the Channel Bass Inn. Originally built as a private home in 1892, the Inn was converted to a small hotel in the 1920s. Today it offers a wonderful respite to travelers from all over the world.

✉ barbara@channelbassinn.com 🌐 www.channelbassinn.com

Miss Molly's Inn 4141 Main St 23336 800-221-5620 757-336-6686 Sam & Lin Mazza	120-185 $US BB 7 rooms, 5 pb Most CC, Cash, *Rated*, • C-ltd/S-no/P-ltd/H-no	Gourmet breakfast Cool refreshments, tea, cocoa & coffee, snacks, vegetarian breakfast available Sitting room, bicycles, beach items, screened gazebo, library, garden

Miss Molly's Inn sits on the bay and has five wonderful porches with plenty of rocking chairs and a large deck on the second floor that overlooks the bay. We also have a beautiful screened-in gazebo full of flowers. We aim to anticipate your every need.

✉ missmollysinn@verizon.net 🌐 www.missmollysinn.com

CHURCH VIEW

Dragon Run Inn B&B 35 Wares Bridge Rd 23032 804-758-5719 Sue & Ivan Hertzler	100-150 $US BB 4 rooms, 4 pb C-yes/S-ltd/P-ltd/H-no	Country style breakfast Picnic baskets, additional meals (lunch & dinner) available with fee Fresh flowers, Fruit basket, Video library, Library

Country farmhouse built from local cypress in 1913. Themed rooms with private baths including Jacuzzi tubs. We offer yesterday's atmosphere coupled with today's conveniences.

✉ runninn@oasisonline.com 🌐 www.dragonruninn.com

COPPER HILL

Bent Mountain Lodge 9039 Mountain View Dr 24079 540-651-2500 Bonnie & Jesse Lawrence	110-130 $US BB 10 rooms, 10 pb Visa, MC C-yes/S-no/P-yes/H-yes Portuguese	Continental breakfast Tea any time Decks, 5 Jacuzzi tubs, gazebo, wedding facilities, kitchen, fireplaces, new sun rooms, TV, Internet

15000 Sq. Ft. with 10 suites, king or queen with private bath, many with private decks or porches and great views at 3200 Ft. overlooking Blue Ridge Parkway 15 miles south of Roanoke, VA. Excellent location for weddings. Accessible suites and ramps.

✉ mscmom74@swva.net 🌐 www.bentmountainlodgebedandbreakfast.com

CROZET

Montfair Resort Farm
2500 Bezaleel Dr. 22932
434-823-5202
Leoral Vincenti

130-176 $US EP
6 rooms, 6 pb
Visa, MC
C-yes/S-no/P-yes/H-no

Organic coffees & teas
Cottages are fully equipped w/
modern appliances. Gas heaters,
utensils, linens, towels, free WiFi.

Montfair Resort Farm is an eco-friendly vacation retreat with cozy A-frame and cedar timber frame cottages which overlook our tranquil 6 acre lake. Our retreat offers a perfect combination of comfort, simplicity and nature for couples and small families.

✉ montfair@ntelos.net 🌐 www.montfairresortfarm.com

The Inn at Sugar Hollow Farm
6051 Sugar Hollow Rd 22932
866-566-7388 434-823-7086
Dick & Hayden Cabell

170-290 $US BB
9 rooms, 9 pb
Visa, MC, AmEx,
Rated
C-ltd/S-no/P-no/H-no

Full breakfast
Beverages, butlers' pantries, catered
lunches and dinners for meetings &
retreat groups available
Fireplaces, double whirlpool tubs,
several common rooms, 2 terraces,
WiFi, TV Den, gardens, massages

Serene, romantic country retreat, mountain streams near Shenandoah Park, Blue Ridge Mountains and wineries. Fireplaces, double whirlpool tubs, hiking, biking, near Monticello and University of Virginia. ✉ theinn@sugarhollow.com 🌐 www.sugarhollow.com

CULPEPER

Fountain Hall
609 S East St 22701
800-29-VISIT 540-825-8200
Steve & Kathi Walker

125-175 $US BB
6 rooms, 6 pb
Most CC, *Rated*, •
C-yes/S-no/P-no/H-yes

Continental plus breakfast
Complimentary beverages, fresh fruits
Common rooms, books, fireplaces,
movies, porches, golf nearby, hiking,
rooms with whirlpool, WiFi

Gracious accommodations for business & leisure. Centrally located in historic Culpeper, between Washington D.C., Charlottesville & Skyline Drive.

✉ visit@fountainhall.com 🌐 www.fountainhall.com

DUBLIN

Rockwood Manor
5189 Rockwood Rd 24084
540-674-1328
Frank Drummund

120-170 $US BB
8 rooms, 6 pb
Most CC
C-ltd/S-ltd/P-no/H-ltd

Full breakfast
Complimentary drinks & snacks,
evening social with appetizers on the
porch, catering
Historic grand staircase, fireplace,
sitting area, weddings, receptions,
grand patio, bright decor

Welcome to Rockwood Manor in the beautiful New river Valley, Virginia! Experience A Southern Tradition. Romantic elegance and superb tranquility in an incomparable Virginia gem. Located near many attractions, Claytor Lake, New River Trail, VT, RU and Floyd.

✉ info@rockwood-manor.com 🌐 www.rockwood-manor.com

DYKE

Cottages at Chesley Creek Farm
2390 Brokenback Mountain
Rd 22935
866-709-9292 434-985-7129
Chuck Swinney & Stu White

175-200 $US EP
4 rooms, 4 pb
S-no/P-no/H-no

Jacuzzi, fireplace, solitude, fully
equipped kitchen, dishes towels and
linens provided, pool

Four secluded cottages in the Blue Ridge Mountains of VA, completely furnished with exception of food. To ensure your privacy there is no TV or phone. There is a stereo & lots of books, gas fireplace, Jacuzzi & queen bed. Enjoy trails & mountain views.

✉ info@chesleycreekfarm.com 🌐 www.chesleycreekfarm.com

FREDERICKSBURG

Inn At The Olde Silk Mill
1707 Princess Anne St 22401
540-371-5666
Ed or Anna

85-145 $US BB
27 rooms, 27 pb
Most CC, Cash, *Rated*
C-yes/S-no/P-no/H-yes

Continental breakfast
Evening Tea and Cookies in Parlor.
Conference room avail., honeymoon/
anniversary, Victorian Suites

The Inn at the Olde Silk Mill is over 80 years old and reflects a casual elegance enriched with an era gone by. Our 27 room historic Inn is the perfect setting for weddings, events, business retreats and romantic getaways. ✉ innkeeperfci1@aol.com 🌐 www.innattheoldesilkmill.com

FREDERICKSBURG

La Vista Plantation
4420 Guinea Station
Rd 22408
800-529-2823 540-898-8444
Michele & Edward Schiesser

145-165 $US BB
2 rooms, 2 pb
Visa, MC, Disc, •
C-yes/S-no/P-no/H-no

Full breakfast
Complimentary soft drinks, bottled
water, ice, fresh brown eggs from
resident hens
Free WiFi, fridge, library, A/C, TV,
VCR/DVD/CD player, fishing, gardens,
radio, fireplaces, videos

Lovely 1838 National Register Classical Revival bed &breakfast on 10 acres outside historic Fredericksburg, VA.Antiques, fireplaces, gardens & old trees.Stocked pond with dock & row boat.Formal room or 2 bedroom apartment.Fresh brown egg breakfast- our hens.

✉ info@lavistaplantation.com 🌐 www.lavistaplantation.com

GLEN ALLEN

The Virginia Cliffe Inn
2900 Mountain Rd 23060
877-254-3346 804-266-7344
Margaret Clifton

125-150 $US BB
4 rooms, 4 pb
Visa, MC, AmEx
C-yes/S-no/P-no/H-no

Full breakfast
Special requests accepted, food and
catering available
We are a major venue for weddings.
Facilities up to 200 people for wedding
parties.

Styled in the tradition of grand plantation homes of the eighteenth century! The Virginia Cliffe Inn is nestled among the trees in Glen Allen, 12 miles north of Richmond, Virginia.

✉ innkeeper@vacliffeinn.com 🌐 www.vacliffeinn.com

GORDONSVILLE

Wolftrap Farm
17379 Wolftrap Dr 22942
540-832-1803
Keith Cuthrell

110-250 $US BB
5 rooms, 5 pb
Most CC
C-yes/S-no/P-ltd/H-ltd

Full breakfast
Continental breakfast served in the
cottage.
Hot tub, ponds, horse stables, patio,
porch, kitchen, trails

On a 584-acre horse and cattle farm, with mountain views, miles of forest trails, rolling pastures, abundant creeks and brooks, nine ponds, and easy access to all the attractions of Charlottesville and the Central Virginia area.

✉ wolftrapfarm@yahoo.com 🌐 www.thewolftrapfarm.com

GOSHEN

Hummingbird Inn
30 Wood Ln 24439
800-397-3214 540-997-9065
Dan & Patty Harrison

145-175 $US BB
5 rooms, 5 pb
Visa, MC, AmEx, •
C-ltd/S-ltd/P-ltd/H-no

Full breakfast
Beverages & baked goods, dinners
available Friday & Saturday, snack
basket in room
Comfy rooms, whirlpool tubs, Internet
radio, fireplaces, verandas, computer
w/free Internet access

Free Night w/Certificate: Anytime.

Unique Carpenter Gothic house surrounded by an acre of grounds, a deck next to the stream, comfortable furnishings, modern amenities & warm hospitality await you. Want to relax? This is the perfect place.. watch the hundreds of hummingbirds visiting us!

✉ stay@hummingbirdinn.com 🌐 www.hummingbirdinn.com

HARRISONBURG

**Stonewall Jackson Inn
B&B**
547 E Market St 22801
800-445-5330 540-433-8233
Dr. Wayne Engel

89-189 $US BB
10 rooms, 10 pb
Visa, MC, Disc,
Rated, •
C-ltd/S-ltd/P-ltd/H-ltd

Full Gourmet Quality Breakfast
Homemade treats, in-room snacks,
chocolates, etc. We accommodate
vegan and special dietary requests.
Superb Amenities: Off-Street Parking,
FREE WiFi, Luxury Linens, Climate
Control Rooms, Patio Dining

"A Night's Delight & Breakfast to Remember"...is our mission, and succinctly describes the legendary Award Winning "Stonewall Jackson Experience"! We are a Certified Virginia Green, 3-Diamond Inn & Trip Advisor's top rated B&B in the Central Shenandoh.

✉ info@stonewalljacksoninn.com 🌐 www.StonewallJacksonInn.com

HUME

Marriott Ranch
5305 Marriott Ln 20186
877-324-7344 540-364-2627
Kelly Barrett

129-229 $US BB
10 rooms, 9 pb
Visa, MC, AmEx
C-yes/S-no/P-no/H-ltd

3 course breakfast
Guests are welcomed with a
complimentary tray of delicious
cheeses as well as refreshing
beverages
Meetings, retreats, weddings, company
picnics, on-site riding stable with 25
horses & full catering.

The 10 comfortable bedrooms along with afternoon beverage service and three course breakfasts serve to remind guests of the true meaning of hospitality. Perfect for hosting company picnics, executive meetings & retreats, weddings and other social events.

✉ kelly.barrett@marriott.com 🌐 www.marriottranch.com

IRVINGTON

The Hope and Glory Inn
65 Tavern Rd 22480
800-497-8228 804-438-6053
Peggy & Dudley Patteson

175-395 $US BB
35 rooms, 35 pb
Visa, MC, AmEx,
Rated
C-yes/S-no/P-ltd/H-no

Full breakfast
Catered events
Sitting room, massages, bikes, tennis
court, croquet & bocce on premises,
pool

Travel & Leisure ranks us one of this country's Great Inns. Frommer's Travel Guide – three stars – its highest rating! Historic schoolhouse, quaint cottages, lush gardens, waterfront village.

✉ inquiries@hopeandglory.com 🌐 www.hopeandglory.com

KILMARNOCK

Kilmarnock Inn
34 East Church St 22482
804-435-0034
Sandra & Shawn Donahue

150-250 $US BB
16 rooms, 16 pb
Most CC, Cash, Checks
C-yes/S-ltd/P-ltd/H-yes

Full breakfast
Full on-site catering available
Gathering room, onsite massage,
bicycles, full service bar & lounge

Kilmarnock Inn, celebrating our Presidential Heritage with each of our cottages and our main house named for the 8 Virginia Presidents. The Main House was built circa 1884 & the cottages were designed to replicate the facades of the president's homes.

✉ Innkeeper@kilmarnockinn.com 🌐 kilmarnockinn.com

LEXINGTON

1868 Magnolia House Inn
501 S Main St 24450
866.751.8664 540.463.2567
Russ and Mary Stuart
Harlow

139-189 $US BB
5 rooms, 5 pb
Most CC, Cash, Checks,
Rated
C-ltd/S-no/P-no/H-no

Full breakfast
Soft drinks, bottled water, crackers,
homemade cookies
Parlor with library & fireplace,
porches, garden, WiFi

A short walk from downtown restaurants, museums, and boutiques, this 1868 Shenandoah Victorian style Inn, with its high ceilings, tall windows, porches and fireplaces, offers a comfortable mix of antiques, Oriental rugs, and traditional furnishings.

✉ magnolia@rockbridge.net 🌐 www.magnoliahouseinn.com

Applewood Inn & Llama Trekking
Buffalo Bend Rd 24450
800-463-1902 540-463-1962
Chris & Linda Best

140-169 $US BB
3 rooms, 3 pb
Visa, MC
C-ltd/S-no/P-yes/H-ltd
German
April-November

Full breakfast
Hot cider, beverages, fridge, pantry,
snacks; limited dinner availability
(please inquire)
Fireplaces, sitting room, library,
porches, pool, hiking, llama treks
(with optional picnic lunch)

Spectacular passive solar home on 36 acres. Mountain views. Close to historic Lexington and Natural Bridge. Miles of trails for hiking and llama treks. Full in-ground swimming pool. Heart healthy breakfasts. Nature lovers retreat.

✉ inn@applewoodbb.com 🌐 www.applewoodbb.com

Brierly Hill, Lexington, VA

LEXINGTON

Autumn Ridge Cottages
Autumn Ridge Ln 24450
866-900-3387 540-463-3387
Norm & Barbara
Rollenhagen

175-195 $US EP
3 rooms, 3 pb
Visa, MC, Disc, •
C-ltd/S-no/P-no/H-no

A breakfast basket is available for your
first morning for $20.
King beds, oversize double whirlpool
tubs, fully equipped kitchens, satellite
TV, fireplaces.

The Autumn Ridge Cottages are located on a private, secluded 40-acre ridge just outside of Historic Lexington. It's the best of both worlds- easy to town and the privacy of the country! Come stay at Autumn Ridge and renew your hearts and clear your minds.

info@autumnridgecottages.com   www.autumnridgecottages.com/index.html

Brierley Hill
985 Borden Rd 24450
800-422-4925 540-464-8421
Ken & Joyce Hawkins –
Diana Bragg, Asst Innkeeper

139-379 $US BB
6 rooms, 6 pb
Visa, MC, AmEx,
Rated
C-ltd/S-ltd/P-no/H-yes

Full breakfast
Afternoon refreshments
refrigerator, DVD library, central heat
& air, free high-speed Internet

English country house atmosphere. Magnificent views of Blue Ridge Mountains & Shenandoah Valley. Experience this relaxed elegance just five minutes from downtown Lexington.

relax@brierleyhill.com   www.brierleyhill.com

House Mountain Inn
455 Lonesome Dove
Tr 24450
540-464-4004
Jeff & Jamie Irvine

138-365 $US MAP
9 rooms, 9 pb
Visa, MC, AmEx
C-ltd/S-ltd/P-ltd/H-yes

Hearty gourmet breakfast
Wine & cheese reception every
afternoon at 4:00; dinner available for
extra fee
On-site trails, 2 fishing ponds, horse
stalls, pub, massage; cabin also
available; conferences

Secluded on a private mountain near Lexington, Virginia, the House Mountain Inn offers gracious bed and breakfast hospitality and rustic lodging elegance in a breathtakingly beautiful Shenandoah Valley location.   housemtninn@hughes.net   www.housemountaininn.com

Stoneridge B&B
246 Stoneridge Ln 24555
800-491-2930 540-463-4090
Jim, Evelyn, John & Sandy
Stallard

90-150 $US BB
5 rooms, 5 pb
Most CC, Cash, Checks,
Rated
C-yes/S-no/P-ltd/H-no
German, French

Full gourmet breakfast
Afternoon refreshments
Sitting room, library, whirlpools, suite,
fireplaces, Direct TV, catering, free
WiFi, gardens, patio

A touch of elegance in an historic setting. Once the center of a 400 acre Shenandoah Valley farm, Stoneridge offers a glimpse of Antebellum life. The original house was built in 1829 with bricks made on the property.   stoneridge@ntelos.net   www.stoneridge-inn.com

LOCUST DALE

Inn at Meander Plantation
2333 N James Madison
Hwy 22948
800-385-4936 540-672-4912
S. Thomas, S. Blanchard

175-285 $US BB
10 rooms, 10 pb
Most CC, Cash, •
C-ltd/S-no/P-yes/H-no

Full gourmet breakfast
Fine dining restaurant
Fireplaces, sitting rooms, porches,
A/C, river trails, spa services

Escape to The Inn at Meander Plantation bed and breakfast—centrally located an hour from Washington, DC, Fredericksburg VA and Charlottesville, VA. Rest, unwind and enjoy the pleasures of a simpler life in true Virginia country inn style.

✉ inn@meander.net ◐ www.meander.net

LYNCHBURG

Carriage House Inn
404 Cabell St 24504
800-937-3582 434-846-1388
Mike and Kathy

149-249 $US BB
6 rooms, 5 pb
Visa, MC, •
C-ltd/S-no/P-no/H-no

Full breakfast
Welcoming refreshments
Off street parking, airport and train
pick up-drop off service, evening turndown service

Free Night w/Certificate: Valid Jan.-April; June-July, November-December; not valid on holidays or 3-day weekends.

Award winning B&B located within walking distance to historic downtown. A treasure trove, rich with architectural detail including many of the original fireplaces, mantels, light fixtures, moldings, intricately carved woodwork, doors, bath tubs and sinks.

✉ info@TheCarriageHouseInnBandB.com ◐ www.thecarriagehouseinnbandb.com

Federal Crest Inn B&B
1101 Federal St 24504
800-818-6155 434-845-6155
Ann & Phil Ripley

85-235 $US BB
5 rooms, 4 pb
Most CC, *Rated*, •
C-ltd/S-no/P-no/H-no

Full breakfast
Snack basket in every room,
complimentary evening beverages &
cookies
In room fireplaces, TV, private
bathrooms, WiFi, airport
transportation, conference center,
quiet

Free Night w/Certificate: Valid January-April. Room Upgrade.

Romantic and elegant! This unique and spacious 1909 mansion with seven fireplaces and antiques offers charm, comfort and modern conveniences. Theater with 60 inch TV on the 3rd floor. Conference center available.

✉ info@federalcrest.com ◐ www.federalcrest.com

Ivy Creek Farm
2812 Link Rd 24503
800-689-7404 434-384-3802
Marilyn & Lynn Brooks

159-199 $US BB
3 rooms, 3 pb
Visa, MC, AmEx
C-ltd/S-no/P-no/H-ltd

Full gourmet breakfast
Afternoon wine, refreshments &
snacks; evening chocolates; 24 hr
beverages
Turn-down w/ candy, library, laundry,
gym, A/C, flat screen room tv, WiFi,
indoor pool/lap lane, spa

Welcome to Ivy Creek Farm, the quintessential Virginia bed and breakfast with memorable, gourmet breakfasts and luxurious accommodations. Casually elegant three-bedroom B&B, standing on ten private wooded acres in the city of Lynchburg.

✉ info@ivycreekfarm.com ◐ www.ivycreekfarm.com

MANASSAS

Bennett House Bed and Breakfast
9252 Bennett Dr 20110
800-354-7060 703-368-6121
Jean & Curtis Harrover

115-150 $US BB
2 rooms, 2 pb
Most CC, Cash, Checks,
Rated, •
C-ltd/S-no/P-ltd/H-no

Full breakfast
Wine, cheese, cookies and tea are
available at the time of check-In.
Sitting room, library, fireplaces, cable
TV, hot tub, A/C, business services,
free WiFi

Charming Victorian setting characterized by exceptional gourmet breakfasts, tastefully appointed facilities, and attentiveness to guests' needs. A warm welcome awaits you at the Bennett House Bed and Breakfast!

 jharrover@aol.com  ◐ www.virginia-bennetthouse.com

MIDDLEBURG

Briar Patch B&B Inn
23130 Briar Patch Ln 20117
866-327-5911 703-327-5911
Ellen Goldberg & Dan
Haendel

95-270 $US BB
9 rooms, 3 pb
Most CC
C-yes/S-ltd/P-yes/H-ltd

Full weekends, continental weekdays
Continental breakfast on weekdays,
complimentary snacks & drinks
Free high speed wireless Internet,
pool, hot tub, suites, fireplaces,
accommodates business traveler

Free Night w/Certificate: Anytime. Room Upgrade.

Historic farm (c. 1805) on 47 rolling acres in the heart of Virginia horse & wine country. Large pool, hot tub, mountain views, & grazing horses. We host weddings, retreats, business meetings, and other social & business events.

info@BriarPatchBandB.com www.BriarPatchBandB.com

**The Goodstone Inn &
Estate**
36205 Snake Hill Rd 20117
877-219-4663 540-687-4645
Emily

235-610 $US BB
17 rooms, 17 pb
Visa, MC, AmEx, •
C-ltd/S-no/P-no/H-no
Spanish

Deluxe continental & full breakfast
Afternoon Tea daily, 3 course dinner,
5 nights a week at our Hilltoppers
Restaurant, 6–9 pm
Outdoor pool, Jacuzzi, hiking,
mountain bikes, canoeing, golf,
massages, trail riding

Set amidst a 265-acre country estate with the Blue Ridge Mountains in the distance. The natural unspoiled beauty of the estate makes Goodstone an oasis in the country where guests can rest, relax, and rejuvenate.

information@goodstone.com www.goodstone.com

MT. JACKSON

Widow Kip's Country Inn
355 Orchard Dr 22842
800-478-8714 540-477-2400
Betty & Bob Luse

110-135 $US BB
7 rooms, 7 pb
Visa, MC, •
C-yes/S-no/P-yes

Family style breakfast
Courtyard, original fireplaces, pool,
bicycles, WiFi available

Your hosts welcome you to their 1830 restored Victorian homestead. It is nestled on 7 rural acres that offer a birds-eye view of the Shenandoah River – just 50 yards away.

widokips@shentel.net www.widowkips.com

NELLYSFORD

The Mark Addy Inn
56 Rodes Farm Dr 22958
434-361-1101
Leslie & Rafael Tal

99-229 $US BB
10 rooms, 10 pb
Visa, MC, AmEx,
Rated, •
C-yes/S-ltd/P-ltd/H-yes
French, German, Italian,
Hebrew

Full country breakfast
Dinner offered Tues through Sat by
reservation; a stocked, guest kitchen is
also available for use
Sitting room, library, tennis court,
Jacuzzi, pool, suites, cable TV,
lounge. pool table, free WiFi

The Mark Addy B&B Inn is situated in Virginia's magnificent Blue Ridge Mountains, near the Parkway, Skyline Drive, Thomas Jefferson's Monticello and the home of the University of Virginia.

info@mark-addy.com www.mark-addy.com

NEW CHURCH

Garden and Sea Inn
4188 Nelson Road 23415
800-824-0672 757-894-9097
Dorothee & Thomas Renn

110-225 $US BB
9 rooms, 9 pb
Most CC, Cash, Checks,
Rated, •
C-yes/S-ltd/P-yes/H-yes
German, French
January thru November

Full breakfast
Snacks, cookies, soft drinks, sherry or
port, gourmet restaurant
Pool, sitting room, library, Jacuzzis,
suites, fireplaces, TV/DVD,
refrigerators, coffeemakers

Romantic Victorian B&B near Chincoteague and Assateague Islands, yet perfectly located for those visiting the Eastern Shores quaint towns and marinas. Large rooms, heated pool, TV/DVD, A/C, refrigerators, gardens, full gourmet breakfast & pets welcome!

innkeeper@gardenandseainn.com www.gardenandseainn.com

Garden and Sea Inn, New Chuch, VA

NEW MARKET

Apple Blossom Inn
9317 N Congress St 22844
540-740-3747
Betty Karol Wilson

135-185 $US BB
2 rooms, 1 pb
Visa, MC
C-ltd/S-no/P-no/H-no

Full breakfast
Vegetarian & Diabetic menus are
available upon request & any food
allergies will be accommodated
Gourmet meals, award winning
gardens, unmatched privacy &
hospitality

Located in historic New Market, Virginia, in the beautiful Shenendoah Valley, this quaint and charm-
ing 1806 eight-room house is entirely yours. Rent the entire inn for the same price as a single room!

 appleinn@shentel.net   www.appleblossominn.net

NEWPORT NEWS

Boxwood Inn
10 Elmhurst St 23603
757-888-8854
Kathy Hulick

105-145 $US BB
4 rooms, 4 pb
Visa, MC, Disc, *Rated*
C-ltd/S-no/P-no/H-ltd

Full breakfast
Dinner packages available. on-site
catering
Antiques, weddings, catering

We invite you to stay in this gracious & charming circa 1896 Inn featuring 4 antique-filled rooms.
Complimentary breakfast in the "Blue Willow" Tea Room. Enjoy the old world style and ambience.

boxwoodinn@yahoo.com www.Boxwood-Inn.com

NORFOLK

**B&B at Historic Page
House Inn**
323 Fairfax Ave 23507
800-599-7659 757-625-5033
Charles & Debbie

150-230 $US BB
7 rooms, 7 pb
Most CC, Cash,
Rated, •
C-ltd/S-no/P-yes/H-no

Full breakfast
In-room breakfast, afternoon tea,
snacks, fruit, candy, wine & sherry
Cable TV, suites with fridge, wireless
Internet, yard games Southern
hospitality . . . and much more!

Award-winning restoration. Elegantly appointed. "Year's Best Inn Buy," Country Inns Magazine. Many
amenities. Perfect location. AAA 4 Diamond Award.Norfolk's hidden gem. Small, pet friendly; chil-
dren over 8 years of age welcome.

innkeeper@pagehouseinn.com www.pagehouseinn.com

ONANCOCK

Colonial Manor Inn
84 Market St 23417
757-787-3521
Linda Nicola

99-139 $US BB
6 rooms, 6 pb
Visa, MC, Disc, *Rated*
C-yes/S-no/P-yes/H-yes

Full Southern gourmet breakfast
Local, organic and vegetarian food
offered. Assistance with special diets.
Private entrance, gazebo, free Internet
access, private baths, queen beds,
concierge services.

The Colonial Manor Inn offers 4,500 sq ft of guest area, all private baths, unlimited on site parking and manicured grounds spanning 2 acres. Relax & enjoy the newly renovated, enclosed front porch that is furnished to accommodate you year round

✉ Colonial.Manor.Inn@gmail.com ◐ www.colonialmanorinn.com

ORANGE

Chestnut Hill B&B
236 Caroline St 22960
888-315-3511 540-661-0430
Kathleen Ayers

179-295 $US BB
6 rooms, 6 pb
Most CC, Cash, Checks
C-yes/S-ltd/P-yes/H-yes

Full breakfast
Bottled flat or sparkling water, homemade confections, afternoon tea &
wine
Turn-down service, Jacuzzi tub,
pillow-top beds, HDTV, complimentary
WiFi, library & business center

This nearly 150 year-old bed and breakfast is situated in a luxurious setting, with unparalleled customer service always included in your stay. Enjoy our new remodel complete with a Jacuzzi & all the modern amenities that allows any traveler relaxation.

✉ kayers1214@aol.com ◐ www.chestnuthillbnb.com

Greenock House
249 Caroline Street 22960
800-841-1253 540-672-3625
Lill Shearer & Dria Conyers

145-235 $US BB
5 rooms, 5 pb
Most CC, Cash, Checks,
Rated
S-no/P-no/H-ltd

Elegant Gourmet Breakfast
Evening hors d'oeuvres and wine by
request, dinner available
Parlor, library, whirlpool tubs, A/C,
fireplaces, cable TV

Stay in a restful, relaxing setting. Enjoy genteel company and gourmet meals including evening hors doeuvres. In the morning, indulge in a gourmet breakfast before enjoying your day exploring Orange! Convenient to D.C. and Richmond.

✉ reservations@greenockhouse.com ◐ www.greenockhouse.com

Holladay House
155 W Main St 22960
540-672-4893
Sam & Sharon Elswick

111-249 $US BB
6 rooms, 6 pb
Most CC, Cash, Checks
C-yes/S-ltd/P-ltd/H-ltd

Full breakfast
Beverages, homemade cookies &
refreshments
In-room massage, fireplaces,
whirlpools, TV/DVD, alarm clock/CD,
robes, wireless Internet, computer

This Federal style B&B (c. 1830) is located in the heart of Orange, a quintessential historic Virginia town. Enjoy an elegant breakfast, curl up by the nineteenth-century marble fireplace, grab a homemade cookie, or relax in a luxurious whirlpool tub.

✉ innkeeper@holladayhousebandb.com ◐ www.holladayhousebandb.com

Inn on Poplar Hill
278 Caroline St 22960
866-767-5274 540-672-6840
Victoria & Marty Tourville

139-199 $US BB
6 rooms, 6 pb
Visa, MC, •
C-ltd/S-no/P-ltd/H-no

Gourmet country breakfast
Afternoon refreshments, stocked
cookie jar
Garden weddings, murder mystery
dinners, wildflower trails, fishing pond,
antiques, billiards

Free Night w/Certificate: Anytime.

A casually elegant Queen Anne Victorian built in the 1890's by the great granddaughter of Thomas Jefferson. The Inn overlooks the historic town of Orange, VA. Surrounded by 28 acres with an abundance of wildflowers, walking trails and country charm.

 stay@innonpoplarhill.com  www.innonpoplarhill.com

ORANGE

Mayhurst Inn
12460 Mayhurst Ln 22960
888-672-5597 540-672-5597
Jack & Pat North

169-239 $US BB
8 rooms, 8 pb
Most CC, Cash, Checks,
Rated, •
C-yes/S-no/P-yes/H-yes

Full, 3-course breakfast
Evening refreshments, selected fine
Virginia wines, crackers & gourmet
cheeses, cookies & sweets
In-room massages, fireplaces, double
whirlpools tubs, luxury linens,
extensive amenities on 37 acres

Free Night w/Certificate: Valid July 5-August 31, 2011.

*We invite you to experience Luxury, Romance and Civil War History in this marvelously preserved
and restored plantation home. A stay at Mayhurst will transport you far away from today's stresses
and let you experience true Southern Hospitality.*

✉ mayhurstbandb@aol.com 🌐 www.mayhurstinn.com

PEARISBURG

Inn at Riverbend
125 River Ridge Dr 24134
540-921-5211
Janet and Jimm Burton

179-259 $US BB
7 rooms, 7 pb
Most CC, Cash, •
C-ltd/S-ltd/P-no/H-ltd
Some Spanish and
French
Year Round ex Jan 2-9

Full breakfast
Refreshments on arrival,
complimentary guest refrigerator,
coffee, tea
Living room, TV Game Room, Outdoor
decks and terraces, walking areas

*Overlooking the Appalachian Mountains and the New River, this Virginia B&B awaits your arrival!
Seven guestrooms with great views, whirlpool tubs, WiFi, TV's offer a relaxing getaway to Southwest
Virginia. Perfect for elopements and reunions.*

✉ stay@innatriverbend.com 🌐 www.innatriverbend.com

THE PLAINS

Grey Horse Inn
4350 Fauquier Ave 20198
877-253-7020 540-253-7000
John & Ellen Hearty

119-210 $US BB
6 rooms, 6 pb
Most CC, Cash, Checks,
Rated, •
C-yes/S-ltd/P-yes/H-yes
French, Spanish, Arabic

Full breakfast
Hunt country upgrade – wine &
cheese plate
Jacuzzi, private balcony, queen/king
beds, antiques, gardens, TV/video,
A/C

*Grey Horse Inn is in The Plains, VA near Middleburg & Warrenton & close to Washington. Minutes
from the Blue Ridge Mountains, Civil War sites, Great Meadow & wineries. Fine dining is nearby.*

✉ innkeeper@greyhorseinn.com 🌐 www.greyhorseinn.com

PORT HAYWOOD

**Inn at Tabb's Creek
Landing**
Rt 14 23138
804-725-5136
Greg & Lori Dusenberry

99-189 $US BB
6 rooms, 6 pb
Visa, MC, *Rated*, •
C-ltd/S-ltd/P-no/H-ltd

Full breakfast
Saturday afternoon wine & cheese
Relax on our dock, deck or screened-
in porch, swimming pool, lawn games,
canoe, library, board games

*Ancient magnolias taller than main house, screened porches overlooking the water, fragrance drift-
ing from the rose garden all around. Aqua gem beauty of pool and your own cottage enclosed by a
picket fence.*

✉ innattabbscreek@gmail.com 🌐 www.innattabbscreek.com

RICHMOND

Grace Manor Inn
1853 W Grace St 23220
804-353-4334
Dawn & Albert Schick

150-225 $US BB
4 rooms, 4 pb
Most CC
S-ltd/P-no/H-no

Gourmet, 3-Course Breakfast
Complimentary bottle of wine &
cheese plate upon arrival
Concierge, reservations, sight seeing
& dinner recommendations & driving
directions

*"Let us pamper you" is our motto, and Grace Manor Inn will do just that. Step back in time as you
enter this historical mansion decorated in period pieces. Enjoy complimentary wine and cheese in
your suite. Leave feeling relaxed and rejuvenated.*

 innkeeper@thegracemanorinn.com 🌐 www.thegracemanorinn.com

RICHMOND

Maury Place at Monument
3101 West Franklin
Street 23221
804-353-2717
Jeff Wells & Mac Pence

159-289 $US BB
4 rooms, 4 pb
Most CC, Cash, Checks
S-no/P-no/H-no

Full gourmet breakfast
Complimentary beverages & snacks,
tea & coffee
Concierge services, off-street parking,
pool & hot tub, en suite baths, flat
screen TVs, Internet

Relax in the refined elegance of this historically preserved 1916 home. Four, unique guest suites feature modern amenities including private baths and secure wireless Internet. Centrally located to shopping, dining, and local universities.  innkeeper@mauryplace.com ● www.mauryplace.com

ROCHELLE

Ridge View
5407 S Blue Ridge
Tpke 22738
866-852-4261 540-672-7024
Eleanor & Frank Damico

129-149 $US BB
3 rooms, 3 pb
Visa, MC, Disc,
Rated, ●
C-yes/S-no/P-no/H-no

Full breakfast
Lunch, with 48 hours notice
Whirlpool tub, cable TV,
accommodations for business
travelers

Free Night w/Certificate: Valid Jan-April and July-August.

Ridgeview is nestled in Madison County on 17 rolling acres with breath taking views of the Blue Ridge Mountains. Enjoy the relaxing atmosphere and delicious gourmet breakfast. A Perfect Retreat!
edamico@virginia-ridgeview.com ● www.virginia-ridgeview.com

SPERRYVILLE

Hopkins Ordinary
47 Main St 22740
540-987-3383
Sherri Fickel, Kevin Kraditor

129-289 $US BB
6 rooms, 6 pb
Visa, MC
C-ltd/S-no/P-ltd/H-ltd
Spanish

Full breakfast
Beverages are offered in the afternoon,
port, cookies or other sweets in the
evening
Fireplaces, wrap-around porches,
wireless Internet access, private
balconies, gardens, dining room

Hopkins Ordinary is a bed and breakfast inn located in the historic village of Sperryville in the foothills of the Blue Ridge Mountains near Shenandoah National Park. Surrounded by wineries and farms in Rappahannock County, Virginia.
innkeeper@hopkinsordinary.com ● www.hopkinsordinary.com

STANARDSVILLE

The Lafayette Inn
146 E Main St 22973
434-985-6345
Alan & Kaye Pyles

139-199 $US BB
7 rooms, 7 pb
Most CC, Cash, *Rated*
C-yes/S-ltd/P-no/H-yes

Full breakfast
Tavern, dinner available. Private
Chef's tasting for two under
candlelight! Full catering service.
Gas fireplaces, gazebo, cable TV,
wireless Internet. Concierges service-
wine tours, in room massage.

As in the past, The Lafayette offers the best of Virginia; a nineteenth century setting with fine foods, comfort and hospitality. We will have your gas fireplace blazing and lights set romantically.
alan@thelafayette.com ● www.thelafayette.com

STANLEY

Milton House B&B Inn
113 W Main Street 22191
540-778-2495
John Carria

85-215 $US BB
5 rooms, 5 pb
Visa, MC, Disc, *Rated*
S-no/P-no/H-no

Full Breakfast-may be en suite
Afternoon teas, dinners, specialty
trays, raw food, vegan & vegetarian
cuisine upon prior request
Cable TV, DVD/VCR, in-room coffee
& tea, alarm clocks, Jacuzzis, in-room
refrigerators, fireplaces

This unique 1913 historic Southern Colonial home was ordered from the Sears Roebuck catalogue. Located in the bucolic town of Stanley, 7 miles south of Luray in the Shenandoah River Valley near the famous Luray Caverns and Skyline Drive.
miltonhouseinn@yahoo.com ● www.miltonhouseinn.com

STANLEY

White Fence B&B	155-175 $US BB	Full country breakfast
275 Chapel Rd 22851	4 rooms, 4 pb	Snacks, soft drinks, breakfast baskets
540-778-2115	Visa, MC, Disc,	Jacuzzi, fireplace, microwave, cable
Sally and Mike Dixon	*Rated*, •	TV, high speed Internet access, clock/
	C-ltd/S-no/P-ltd/H-no	radio, air conditioning
	French	

Lovely 1845 Victorian on 3 beautiful acres in the Shenandoah Valley near Luray & Shenandoah National Park. Luxury accommodations include cottage, carriage house & suites. We offer a Virginia Elopement Package & other special romantic packages.

✉ sallyandmikedixon@gmail.com 🌐 www.whitefencebb.com

STAUNTON

Frederick House	100-295 $US BB	Full hot homemade breakfast
28 N New St 24401	25 rooms, 25 pb	Outside dining on a terrace or porch,
800-334-5575 540-885-4220	Most CC, *Rated*, •	a party in a private dining room, a
Joe & Evy Harman	C-yes/S-no/P-no/H-no	special cake or meal
		Five historic residences offer sitting
		rooms, library, conference facilities,
		private dining rooms

Frederick House has five restored 19th century residences with 25 rooms and suites in the heart of historic downtown Staunton, a culturally rich district with theatre, dining and shopping. Breakfast is served in Chumleys Tearoom in the reception building.

✉ stay@frederickhouse.com 🌐 www.frederickhouse.com

The Staunton Choral	100-250 $US BB	Multi-course
Gardens B&B	6 rooms, 6 pb	Snacks available all the time, guest
216 W Frederick St 24401	Visa, MC, Disc	microwaves & refrigerators
540-885-6556	C-ltd/S-no/P-yes/H-no	TV lounge, front parlor, fireplace in 3
Carolyn Avalos		rooms, several gardens & courtyard
		with large water garden

Walk to everything from our historic B&B in downtown Staunton. Packages include Shakespeare Theater Special; Wedding/Elopement; Girlfriend Getaways; Christian Retreat and Couples Weekends. Specials available! Pet friendly accommodations also.

✉ reservations@stauntonbedandbreakfast.com 🌐 www.StauntonBedandBreakfast.com

STEELES TAVERN

Sugar Tree Inn	148-248 $US BB	Full breakfast
145 Lodge Trail, Hwy	13 rooms, 13 pb	Three course gourmet dinner by
56 24483	Visa, MC, *Rated*	reservation on weekends, casual fare
800-377-2197 540-377-2197	C-ltd/S-no/P-no/H-ltd	dinner most weekdays
Jeff & Becky Chanter	February – December	Woodburning fireplaces, whirlpool
		tubs, ceiling fans, VCRs/video tapes

Less than a mile from the Blue Ridge Parkway, & located on 28 acres at 2,800 feet, the Inn is a place of rustic elegance, peace & tranquility. All of our rooms feature woodburning fireplaces.

✉ innkeeper@sugartreeinn.com 🌐 www.sugartreeinn.com

URBANNA

Atherston Hall B&B	100-200 $US BB	Full breakfast
250 Prince George St 23175	4 rooms, 4 pb	Dinner by arrangement Sun – Wed in
804-758-2809	Visa, MC, Disc	winter, Afternoon Tea by arrangement
Bill & Judith Dickinson	C-yes/S-no/P-yes/H-ltd	English toiletries, wireless Internet, 2
		sitting rooms, 1 with TV/DVD; small
		dogs OK by arrangement

Nestled one block away from the main street and the harbor, Atherston Hall is just around the corner from all Urbanna has to offer. The elegance of English country living in the heart of historic Urbanna. Wonderfully restored. Great hospitality.

✉ judith@atherstonhall.com 🌐 www.atherstonhall.com

URBANNA

Inn at Urbanna Creek	95-160 $US BB	Full breakfast
210 Watling St 23175	4 rooms, 4 pb	Refreshments, ice beverages,
804-758-4661	C-yes/S-no/P-yes/H-no	High speed Internet, satellite TV,
Suzanne Corwell Chewning		refreshments & ice beverages,
		massage by appointment.

A classic 1870's river town home and cottage located in historic Urbanna Va. This charming getaway exudes warm hospitality and gracious service.

✉ innaturbannacreek@verizon.net 🌐 www.innaturbannacreek.com

VIRGINIA BEACH

Barclay Cottage Bed and	95-225 $US BB	Full multi-course breakfast
Breakfast	5 rooms, 3 pb	Breakfast sunrise picnic by prior
400 16th St 23451	Most CC, Cash,	request, complimentary hot & cold
866-INN-1895 757-422-1956	*Rated*, •	beverages & snacks 24/7
Stephen & Marie-Louise	S-ltd/P-no/H-ltd	Broadband WiFi, extensive library of
LaFond	French	books, DVDs, VHS videos, games, ABC
		license, gift shop

This award-winning historic Inn, only 2 minutes walk to the beach, welcomes you with open arms from the moment you arrive. Antiques, handmade quilts, high-quality bedding, thirsty towels, luxurious robes, & sweet surprises await you in each room.

✉ innkeepers@barclaycottage.com 🌐 www.barclaycottage.com

Beach Spa Bed and	109-249 $US BB	Multi-Course Gourmet Breakfast
Breakfast	8 rooms, 8 pb	Vegan & Vegetarian
2420 Arctic Ave 23451	Most CC, Cash, Checks,	Internet access, WiFi, heated spa
888-422-2630 757-422-2621	*Rated*	pool, weddings, anniversaries, jet tub,
Danny and Debbie Santos	C-yes/S-no/P-no/H-yes	massage shower

Centrally located 2 blocks from the Virginia Beach Resort. Majestic porches, butterfly bushes and a cascading waterfall welcome guests into the enchanting retreat. A great alternative to hotel accommodations and perfect for a romantic getaway.

✉ innkeeper@beachspabednbreakfast.com 🌐 www.beachspabednbreakfast.com

Country Villa B&B Inn and	169-320 $US BB	3 course custom, brkfast w/dessert
Day Spa	2 rooms, 2 pb	Cakes, gourmet baskets, caramel
2252 Indian River Rd 23456	Visa, MC, *Rated*	apples, dipped berries, champagne,
757-721-3844	S-no/P-no/H-no	wine, picnic basket, specialty dessert
Teresa & Phil Bonifant	Some French	Compl. wine, hot cookies, stocked
		fridge, hot tub, pool, beach equip,
		Onsite Spa, balloons, Gift Cert.

Country Villa Inn is Virginia Beach's unique 4 acre lodging choice. A quiet refuge with onsite Spa, custom gourmet breakfast, pool, hot tub and personalized service. Activities, restaurants, shopping only minutes away. Pampering at its best with privacy!

✉ innkeeper@countryvillainn.com 🌐 www.countryvillainn.com

WARM SPRINGS

The Inn at Gristmill	95-160 $US BB	Continental breakfast
Square	17 rooms, 17 pb	Bar, dinner & Sunday brunch at The
124 Old Mill Road 24484	Visa, MC, Disc,	Wheelwater Restaurant
540-839-2231	*Rated*, •	Sauna, swimming pool, tennis courts,
The McWilliams Family	C-yes/S-yes/P-no/H-ltd	spa services, Country Store

Casual country hideaway, historic original mill site dating from 1800's. Each room individually decorated.

✉ grist@tds.net 🌐 www.gristmillsquare.com

Black Horse Inn, Warrenton, VA

WARRENTON

Black Horse Inn
8393 Meetze Rd 20187
540-349-4020
Lynn Pirozzoli

200-375 $US BB
9 rooms, 9 pb
Most CC, *Rated*, •
C-ltd/S-ltd/P-ltd/H-no

Full breakfast
Afternoon Hunt Country tea offers
wine, sherry, port, hors d'oeuvres and
cookies
Complimentary wine, bar service,
sitting room, library, fishing, rooms
with Jacuzzis, horse facility

Historic Southern plantation style mansion with nine guestrooms, in the heart of hunt country. Elegant grand ballroom seats 200 for weddings, and corporate events. Stone fireplaces. Outdoor terraces, pond, bridge, gazebo, manicured gardens, and stables.

✉ relax@blackhorseinn.com   🌐 www.blackhorseinn.com

WASHINGTON

Caledonia Farm – 1812
47 Dearing Rd 22747
800-BNB-1812 540-675-3693
Phil Irwin

140-140 $US BB
2 rooms, 2 pb
Visa, MC, Disc,
Rated, •
C-ltd/S-no/P-no/H-ltd
German, Danish (basic)

Full breakfast from menu
Complimentary beverages and snacks
in suites and upon arrival.
Sitting room, library, bikes, piano,
porch views, lawn games, birding trail,
fishing pond, turndown.

Free Night w/Certificate: Not valid Friday, Saturdays, and holidays.

National Register stone home on a cattle farm adjacent to Shenandoah National Park mountains. Skyline Drive views, history, recreation, hospitality, fireplaces, comfortable furnishings. Acclaimed B & B for 25 of its 200 years . . . quiet, cozy and romantic. .

✉ rphilipirwin@gmail.com   🌐 www.bnb1812.com

Fairlea Farm Bed and Breakfast
636 Mt Salem Ave 22747
866-FAIRLEA 540-675-3679
Susan & Walt Longyear

155-205 $US BB
4 rooms, 4 pb
Rated, •
C-ltd/S-no/P-no/H-no
French

Hearty full country breakfast
Afternoon refreshments, including
tea, fresh local cider or lemonade &
homemade baked goods
Parlor fireplace, views, terrace,
gazebo, gardens, farm, miniature
donkeys, national park

Free Night w/Certificate: Valid Sunday thru Thursday; year round; subject to availability.

Our guests enjoy spectacular Blue Ridge Mountain views, lush pasture land and perennial gardens. A short stroll to the historic village of Little Washington to find wineries, antiques, art galleries and the restaurant, The Inn at Little Washington.   ✉ longyear@shentel.net   🌐 www.fairleafarm.com

WASHINGTON

Foster Harris House
189 Main St 22747
800-874-1036 540-675-3757
Diane & John MacPherson

199-339 $US BB
5 rooms, 5 pb
Visa, MC, AmEx,
Rated
C-ltd/S-no/P-no/H-ltd

4-course lavish breakfast
Evening wine or beer
Luxury linens, spa robes, bicycle
rentals, breathtaking views, 2 blocks to
Inn at Little Washington

Nestled in the foothills of the Blue Ridge Mountains, minutes from Shenandoah National Park & steps from the world-renowned Inn at Little Washington, the Foster Harris House offers comfortable, refined accommodations in an enchanting country setting.

✉ stay@fosterharris.com 🌐 www.fosterharris.com

Middleton Inn
176 Main St 22747
800-816-8157 540-675-2020
Mary Ann Kuhn

275-575 $US BB
7 rooms, 7 pb
Visa, MC, AmEx,
Rated
C-ltd/S-no/P-ltd/H-no

Full breakfast
Afternoon wine & cheese, tea, evening
port
Nightly turndown service, twice daily
maid service, massages, fireplaces,
complimentary newspapers

An historic country estate, Middleton Inn has received the prestigious Four Diamond AAA Award for excellence in accommodations & service in an elegant atmosphere for over 10 years. Nine fireplaces, mountain views, marble baths. Select Registry member.

✉ innkeeper@middletoninn.com 🌐 www.middletoninn.com

WILLIAMSBURG

A Primrose Cottage
16538 Chickahominy Bluff
Rd 23185
800-522-1901 804-829-5441
Inge Curtis

200-300 $US BB
2 rooms, 1 pb
Visa, MC, *Rated*, •
C-ltd/S-no/P-ltd/H-no
German

Self Catered Breakfast
Water access, minutes to boat rental &
launching ramp

A self-catering, private vacation cottage on the Chickahominy River. A peaceful hideaway just 15 short minutes from Williamsburg.

✉ ingecurtis@aol.com 🌐 www.primrose-cottage.com

Bentley Manor Inn
720 College Terrace 23185
877-334-0641 757-253-0202
Fred & Jane Garland

125-185 $US BB
4 rooms, 4 pb
Visa, MC
C-ltd/S-no/P-no/H-no

Full country breakfast
Sitting room, suites, cable TV, free
wireless Internet access, business
traveler accommodations

Charming classic brick Colonial in the heart of historic Williamsburg, VA, adjacent to William and Mary College, a leisurely stroll to Colonial Williamsburg, a short drive to Jamestown and Yorktown . . . Capture the timeless essence of Colonial Williamsburg.

✉ info@bentleymanorinn.com 🌐 www.bentleymanorinn.com

Colonial Gardens B&B
1109 Jamestown Rd 23185
800-886-9715 757-220-8087
Karen & Ron Watkins

155-185 $US BB
4 rooms, 4 pb
Most CC, Cash,
Rated, •
C-ltd/S-ltd/P-no/H-ltd

Full Gourmet Breakfast
Wine & Cheese hour, snacks & drinks
available 24 hours in stocked guest
refrigerator
Concierge service for dining
reservations, golf, fax, copier, pilot-
friendly!

Colonial Gardens is an enchanting escape into old world European romance and elegance. With its silks and satins, fine Italian linens, richly ornate furniture, and the allure of over an acre of gardens.

✉ innkeeper@colonial-gardens.com 🌐 www.colonial-gardens.com

Fife & Drum Inn
441 Prince George St 23185
888-838-1783 757-345-1776
Billy & Sharon Scruggs

165-325 $US BB
9 rooms, 9 pb
Most CC, *Rated*, •
C-ltd/S-no/P-no/H-ltd

Full breakfast
Snacks
Cable TV, VCRs, individual phone
lines, free WiFi, soft bathrobes, many
other amenities

Historic Williamsburg's only downtown lodging. Located adjacent to The College of William & Mary, Merchants Square, and Colonial Williamsburg. For guests seeking their own private address the Drummers Cottage is offered.

✉ bscruggs@FifeAndDrumInn.com 🌐 www.FifeAndDrumInn.com

WILLIAMSBURG

Governor's Trace	150-175 $US BB	Full breakfast
303 Capitol Landing	3 rooms, 3 pb	Antiques, fireplaces, porches, common
Rd 23185	Visa, MC, Disc, •	area, library, free wireless Internet
800-303-7552 757-229-7552	S-no/P-no/H-no	
Richard Lake		

Closest B&B to historic Colonial Williamsburg. "...vies for the most romantic (in Williams-burg)"—Washington Post. Candlelit breakfast served in your room. One room has woodburning fireplace. Two rooms have private screened-in porches.

✉ govtrace@cavtel.net 🌐 www.governorstrace.com

Magnolia Manor Inn	155-215 $US BB	Full breakfast
700 Richmond Rd 23185	4 rooms, 4 pb	Coffee, tea, muffins & cookies
800-462-6667 757-220-9600	Visa, MC, AmEx	Suites, fireplaces, fresh flowers,
Scott & Jennifer Carter	C-ltd/S-no/P-no/H-no	whirlpool tubs, turn-down service,
		living room, WiFi

At Magnolia Manor experience Colonial Williamsburg history and hospitality. Each morning begins with a gourmet breakfast in the lovely dining room by the fireplace. It is the perfect setting for a romantic getaway or a relaxing retreat.

✉ magnoliamanorinn@yahoo.com 🌐 www.magnoliamanorwmbg.com

Williamsburg Sampler B&B Inn	160-215 $US BB	Full breakfast
922 Jamestown Rd 23185	4 rooms, 4 pb	Wet bar & fridge in suites,
800-722-1169 757-253-0398	Visa, MC, *Rated*, •	complimentary sodas
Ike Sisane	C-ltd/S-no/P-no/H-no	18th century carriage house, antiques,
		pewter, samplers, suites, fireplaces

Williamsburg's finest plantation style Colonial home. Richly furnished. Guests have included descendants of John Quincy Adams, Capt. John Smith and Charles Dickens.

✉ info@williamsburgsampler.com 🌐 www.williamsburgsampler.com

WOODSTOCK

Candlewick Inn	130-180 $US BB	Full breakfast
127 N Church St 22664	4 rooms, 4 pb	Five o'clock tea, lemonade or hot
540-459-8008	Visa, MC	cider
Sharon & Dennis Pike	S-no/P-no/H-no	A/C, parlor, player piano, Jacuzzi in
		suite, sitting areas in all rooms

The Candlewick Inn is a beautifully restored pre-Civil War home located in picturesque Shenandoah County, Virginia. The Inn is on the National Historic Registry.

✉ candlewickinnllc@hotmail.com

WOOLWINE

Dutchies View B&B	85-125 $US BB	Full breakfast
10448 Woolwine Hwy 24185	6 rooms, 6 pb	Popcorn & crackers, decadent
276-930-3701	Most CC, Cash, Checks	desserts, juice, soda, coffee & tea
Patrick & Crystal Powell	C-ltd/S-no/P-no/H-ltd	available all day, microwave
		Library, satellite TV,

Dutchies View is located high on a grassy knoll with an unsurpassed panoramic view of the Blue Ridge Mountains in lovely Woolwine, VA. Sunrise and sunset may be enjoyed from the oversized windows in our guestrooms or from the spacious deck outside.

✉ innkeepers@dutchiesview.com 🌐 www.dutchiesview.com

Washington

ABERDEEN

A Harbor View Inn
111 W 11th St 98520
877-533-7996 360-533-7996
Cindy Lonn

119-225 $US BB
5 rooms, 5 pb
Visa, MC, AmEx,
Rated, •
C-ltd/S-no/P-no/H-ltd
Little Spanish &
German

Full Country Breakfast
Huge selection of afternoon tea,
organic snacks & coffee
Sitting room, tennis court, suites,
fireplace, cable TV, accommodates
business travelers

Historic Colonial Revival home, antiques, every room with waterview, located in a historic district, walking homes tour included with your stay and breakfast in the sunroom overlooking the harbor.

✉ info@aharborview.com ◉ www.aharborview.com

ASHFORD

**Alexander's Country Inn,
Restaurant & Day Spa**
37515 State Rd 706 E 98304
800-654-7615 360-569-2300
Bernadette Ronan/Jerry
Harnish

99-175 $US BB
12 rooms, 12 pb
Visa, MC, Disc,
Rated, •
C-yes/S-no/P-no/H-ltd

Full breakfast
Complimentary wine & seasonal fresh
fruits, acclaimed restaurant
Day Spa offering massage. Parlor with
fireplace. Hot tub, Media Room w/big
cable TV. Free WiFi

One mile from Mount Rainier National Park. Retains its historic charm and character while providing modern amenities. Full breakfast, evening wine, media room and hot tub are included in the daily rate. 2 self-catered vacation cabins. Popular Restaurant.

✉ info@alexanderscountryinn.com ◉ www.alexanderscountryinn.com

BAINBRIDGE ISLAND

Holly Lane Gardens
9432 Holly Farm Ln 98110
206-842-8959
Patti Dusbabek

90-135 $US BB
5 rooms, 4 pb
Most CC, Cash, Checks
C-yes/S-ltd/P-ltd/H-ltd

Full breakfast
Beverages, homemade international
desserts, organic eggs/vegetables/
fruit/herbs
Reading, entertainment center,
libraries, hot tub, 8.6 acres, private
cottage, fire pit, gardens

Olympic Mountain views, flowers, woodlands. Cottage and Suite offer bedroom, front room, kitchen and bath. Clerestory Room on the 2nd floor of the house, has a spectacular mountain & garden view as does the 3rd floor bedroom.

✉ patty.dusbabek@comcast.net ◉ www.hollylanegardens.com

BELFAIR

Selah Inn on Hood Canal
130 NE Dulalip
Landing 98528
877-232-7941 360-275-0916
Bonnie & Pat McCullough

95-195 $US BB
4 rooms, 4 pb
Visa, MC, *Rated*, •
C-ltd/S-no/P-no/H-ltd

Full breakfast
Lunch & dinner available, bar service
Conference room, sitting room, library,
Jacuzzi, fireplaces, cable TV, ensuite
massage, deck hot tub

An elegant NW lodge with a majestic view of the Hood Canal. Access to the beach for digging clams; we'll steam them for your first of five courses at dinner. A perfect spot for a destination wedding! Small groups and business travelers are welcome.

✉ innkeeper@selahinn.com ◉ www.selahinn.com

BELLEVUE

A Cascade View
13425 NE 27th St 98005
888-883-7078 425-883-7078
Marianne & Bill Bundren

130-150 $US BB
2 rooms, 2 pb
Visa, MC, AmEx,
Rated
C-yes/S-ltd/P-no/H-no

Full breakfast
Afternoon tea if requested
Sitting room, library, fireplaces, cable
TV, accommodate business travelers,
wireless home

Panoramic views of the Cascade Mountains with extensive colorful and fragrant gardens. 2 beautiful rooms with private baths and extra amenities, fireplace, TV/VCR, sitting room, full breakfasts. The perfect location for the tourist or business traveler

✉ innkeepers@acascadeview.com ◉ www.acascadeview.com

Inn at Barnum Point, Camano Island, WA

BIRCH BAY

Cottages by the Beach
4813 Lora Lane 98230
425-339-8081
Kelvin & Patti Barton

150-285 $US BB
2 rooms, 3 pb
Visa, MC, Disc
C-yes/S-no/P-no/H-no
October – May

Brioche, cinnamon rolls, fruit
Cheese & egg layer casserole baked in
a brioche shell, cinnamon rolls, fruit,
coffee & tea
Firewood & firestarters provided,
custom soaps, dishwasher, full
kitchen, washer/dryer, RV parking

Two fully furnished cottages beautifully decorated with full kitchens in the heart of Birch Bay, a resort area for over 100 years. Romantic lace and French Country adorn the 2 bedroom "Lora's Cottage" while "Seashell Cottage" is great for golfing getaways

✉ info@ilovecottages.com   🌐 www.ilovecottages.com

CAMANO ISLAND

Inn at Barnum Point
464 S Barnum Rd 98282
800-910-2256 360-387-2256
Carolin Barnum

125-225 $US BB
3 rooms, 3 pb
Visa, MC, Disc,
Rated, •
C-yes/S-no/P-no/H-no

Full breakfast brunch
Complimentary beverages
books, VCR tapes, sidewalks,
landscaping, outside lighting,
waterfront views from every window

All rooms have spectacular water and mountain views. Enjoy our spacious 900 sq ft suite. A Cape Cod house on a bluff overlooking Port Susan Bay and the Cascade Mountains. Private bath and fireplaces. A tranquil place to relax, beachcomb, enjoy the birds.

✉ barnumpoint@camano.net   🌐 www.innatbarnumpoint.com

CAMAS

Camas Hotel
405 NE 4th Avenue 98607
360-834-5722
Thomas and Karen Hall

79-130 $US BB
10 rooms, 10 pb
Most CC, Cash, •
C-ltd/S-no/P-ltd/H-no
German, Spanish,
French (limited)

Continental plus breakfast
On site restaurant
Free WiFi, free parking, concierge
service

Situated near Portland & the Columbia River Gorge! 100 year old hotel set amidst historic tree-lined shopping district of Camas. Restored to its original 1911 charm with added comfort of European style hospitality & American warmth.   ✉ reservations@camashotel.com   🌐 www.camashotel.com

COLVILLE

Lazy Bee B&B
3651 Deep Lake Boundary
Rd 99114
509-732-8917
Bud Budinger & Joann
Bender

129 $US BB
2 rooms
Visa, MC
C-ltd/S-ltd/P-ltd/H-ltd

Continental breakfast
Lunch, dinner, afternoon tea, snacks
Library, bicycles, fireplaces,
accommodate business travelers, new
outdoor romantic bedroom

The Lazy Bee is a rustic lodge nestled at the base of Red Mountain with a view of Stone Mountain near the Canadian border. We've deliberately slowed the pace of life in order to give guests less stress and a sense of tranquility.   ✉ budinger.bender@plix.com   🌐 www.travelguides.com/home/Lazy_Bee

COUPEVILLE

Anchorage Inn	89-149 $US BB	Full breakfast
807 N Main St 98239	7 rooms, 7 pb	Cookies, popcorn, coffee, tea, cider,
877-230-1313 360-678-5581	Visa, MC, *Rated*, •	hot chocolate & cold beverages
Dave & Dianne Binder	C-ltd/S-ltd/P-ltd/H-ltd	WiFi, cable TV, VCR, DVD, telephone,
		dinner reservations, porch & patio,
		maps, umbrellas

Awarded the best B&B in the Pacific NW, the Victorian Anchorage Inn B&B is located on beautiful Whidbey Island, in the historic town of Coupeville, Washington. Perfect for privacy, group retreats, weddings, anniversaries and as an escape for lovers.

✉ crowsnest@anchorage-inn.com   🌐 www.anchorage-inn.com

The Blue Goose Inn	119-149 $US BB	Scrumptious full breakfast
702 N Main St 98239	6 rooms, 6 pb	Fresh baked cookies & hot beverages
877-678-4284 360-678-4284	Visa, MC, *Rated*	all day; cheese platters, wine &
Sue & Marty	S-no/P-no/H-ltd	champagne available on request
		Centrally located on Whidbey Island
		just a short walk to Coupeville's
		waterfront shops & restaurants

Free Night w/Certificate: Anytime. Room Upgrade.

Named "Best in the West 2010–2011" — for the second year in a row! The Blue Goose Inn graciously combines history and comfort in neighboring 1880's Victorian homes.

✉ stay@bluegooseinn.com   🌐 www.bluegooseinn.com

DEER HARBOR

The Place at Cayou Cove	125-495 $US BB	Full Breakfast
161 Olympic Lane 98243	3 rooms, 3 pb	Coffee & teas, wine & hors d'oeuvres
888-596-7222 360-376-3199	Visa, MC	are offered each evening during the
Charles & Valerie Binford	C-yes/S-no/P-yes/H-yes	summer season
		Complimentary ferry & airport pickup,
		organic garden, private hot tubs, self-
		service rates available

Nestled on the shore of Deer Harbor between Cayou Valley's two mountain ridges at the southwest tip of Orcas Island, The Place At Cayou Cove takes full advantage of the southerly views across the Harbor to the Olympic Mountains in the distance.

✉ stay@cayoucove.com   🌐 www.cayoucove.com

EASTSOUND

Kangaroo House B&B on	100-195 $US BB	Full delicious 3 course breakfast
Orcas Island	5 rooms, 5 pb	Early risers get breakfast to go if you
1459 North Beach Rd 98245	Most CC, Cash,	can't sit down with us in the morning
888-371-2175 360-376-2175	*Rated*, •	Special diets on request, living room
Charles & Jill	C-ltd/S-no/P-no/H-no	fireplace, sitting room, hot tub in
	Spanish	garden

1907 Craftsman B&B near Eastsound on beautiful Orcas Island in WA state's San Juan Islands. Offering comfortable beds, delicious full breakfasts, and a relaxing atmosphere. This stately Orcas Island landmark has been hosting guests for over 100 years.

✉ innkeeper@KangarooHouse.com   🌐 www.KangarooHouse.com

FORKS

Miller Tree Inn	115-215 $US BB	Full breakfast
654 E Division St 98331	8 rooms, 8 pb	Lemonade, coffee, tea, cocoa and
800-943-6563 360-374-6806	Most CC, Cash, Checks,	cookies, pre-dawn breakfast during
Bill & Susan Brager	*Rated*, •	fishing season available
	C-ltd/S-no/P-ltd/H-ltd	Off-street parking, TV, DVDs, books,
		piano, board games, fireplace, wireless
		net, some jetted tubs

Free Night w/Certificate: Valid Oct 1-May 15.

Come and share our beautiful 1916 farmhouse, located on the edge of town and bordered by trees and pasture lands. We offer a warm welcome, hearty breakfasts, spacious common areas, and quiet, comfortable rooms for a reasonable price.   ✉ millertreeinn@centurytel.net   🌐 www.millertreeinn.com

FRIDAY HARBOR

Bird Rock Hotel
35 First St 98250
800-352-2632 360-378-5848
Laura Saccio

87-345 $US BB
15 rooms, 11 pb
Visa, MC, AmEx,
Rated, •
C-yes/S-no/P-no/H-yes
Spanish, French,
German, Dutch,
Japanese

Gourmet breakfast delivered to you
Afternoon snacks and refreshments
Rooms have ipod-docking radio,
beach cruiser bikes for use, free WiFi,
flat-panel hdtv

An exquisitely crafted, eco-intelligent collection of stylishly modern rooms ranging from simple, European-style sleeping rooms to deluxe, harbor-view suites.

 stay@birdrockhotel.com 🌐 www.birdrockhotel.com

Harrison House Suites B&B
235 C St 98250
800-407-7933 360-378-3587
Anna Maria de Freitas, David Pass, Michael Buckle

99-395 $US BB
5 rooms, 6 pb
Most CC, Cash, Checks,
Rated, •
C-yes/S-ltd/P-yes/H-ltd

Full breakfast
On-site catering & dinner at Coho,
the Inn's restaurant, cookies, cooking
classes & wine dinners
Use of bikes, kayaks, laundry facilities,
off-street parking, reading and movie
library, massages

Free Night w/Certificate: Valid Oct.-May except holidays.

A hillside retreat conveniently located 1½ blocks from the ferry terminal and historic downtown Friday Harbor. Old world charm combined with contemporary conveniences offer one of a kind accommodations in this historic residence.

 innkeeper@harrisonhousesuites.com 🌐 www.harrisonhousesuites.com

GIG HARBOR

Bear's Lair B&B
13706 92nd Ave Ct NW 98329
877-855-9768 253-857-8877
Giulio & Jenny Santori

115-215 $US BB
4 rooms, 4 pb
Visa, MC, *Rated*
C-ltd/S-ltd/P-no/H-yes
Spanish, Italian

Full breakfast
Homemade baked goods throughout
the day, self-service coffee & tea 24 hrs
Upscale accommodations, private
cottage, gardens, suites, fireplaces,
video library

Come enjoy our luxurious five acre country estate-style B&B. Stay at the private carriage house, perfect for romantic getaways or one of the three luxurious rooms in the main house. Breathtaking gardens, island gazebo, duck pond and minutes from downtown.

 bearslairbb@aol.com 🌐 www.bearslairbb.com

Waterfront Inn
9017 N Harborview Dr 98332
253-857-0770
Steve & Janis Denton

140-229 $US BB
7 rooms, 7 pb
Visa, MC
C-ltd/S-no/P-no/H-ltd
Spanish

Continental breakfast
Complimentary tea, hot chocolate &
popcorn to go with free DVDs, catering
available
Huge over-the-water sitting pier,
complimentary kayak use, lovely
garden, Jacuzzi tub, Internet

Located at the head of Gig Harbor Bay, the Waterfront Inn offers private, luxurious rooms in a beautiful historic home. Each room has a private entrance, a large bath with Jacuzzi tub, & many rooms have a fireplace with a sitting area & awesome views.

 info@waterfront-inn.com 🌐 www.waterfront-inn.com

GREENBANK

Guest House Log Cottages
24371 SR 525 98253
800-997-3115 360-678-3115
Peggy Walker

125-350 $US BB
6 rooms, 6 pb
Visa, MC, Disc, *Rated*
C-ltd/S-no/P-no/H-ltd

Generous continental breakfast
TV/DVD/VCR, CD player, exercise
room, pool, spa, retreat & honeymoon
spot, free WiFi, fireplaces

Free Night w/Certificate: Valid Oct. 15, 2011-April 30,2012; Sundays-Thursdays-mid-week winter.

Spark and rekindle your romance at Guest House Log Cottages B&B, a place where your pleasure and comfort are a priority. These beautifully furnished, cozy cottages are scattered on 25 acres of forest on Whidbey Island in Puget Sound.

 stay@guesthouselogcottages.com 🌐 www.guesthouselogcottages.com

ILWACO

China Beach Retreat Inn
222 Robert Gray Dr 98624
800-INN-1896 360-642-5660
David Campiche & Laurie
Anderson

179-299 $US BB
4 rooms, 4 pb
Visa, MC, AmEx,
Rated, •
S-no/P-no/H-ltd
German

Full breakfast
Coffee & tea service available all day.
Freshly baked cookies upon arrival.
Group retreats, weddings, views, spa
tubs. Audubon Cottage is perfect for
honeymoons and anniversary

China Beach Retreat is a nest of delights, where your senses receive all that they can demand of nature. This B&B retreat is elegantly and comfortably furnished in antiques. The decor is an eclectic enhancement of the beautiful views.

✉ innkeeper@chinabeachretreat.com   🌎 www.chinabeachretreat.com

LA CONNER

La Conner Country Inn
107 S. 2nd St. 98257
888-466-4113 360-466-3101
Cindy Nelson

109-189 $US BB
28 rooms, 28 pb
Most CC, Cash,
Rated, •
C-yes/S-no/P-yes/H-yes

Continental plus breakfast
Freshly baked cookies, coffee & tea
served in the library every afternoon
Business Center, Wireless Internet,
meeting facilities

Spacious and cozy guestrooms feature fireplace, wooden accents and charm. Wireless Internet and full service conference facilities available. Expansive breakfast includes fresh fruit, pastries, home made granola, hard boiled eggs and much more.

✉ reservations@laconnerlodging.com   🌎 www.laconnerlodging.com/laconner-country-in

LAKEWOOD

Thornewood Castle Inn
8601 N Thorne Lane
SW 98498
253-584-4393
Deanna Robinson, J B
Douglas

250-550 $US BB
8 rooms, 8 pb
Most CC, Cash,
Checks, •
C-ltd/S-no/P-no/H-ltd

Full breakfast
In room refrigerator & microwave, TV/
VCR, jetted tubs, fireplaces, murder
mystery evenings

Thornewood Castle is World Class, Historic & One of a Kind. Experience another time, another space with an overnight visit to this magnificent estate. Perfect for a honeymoon, romantic evening with someone special, or to treat yourself to rest & renew.

✉ info@thornewoodcastle.com   🌎 www.thornewoodcastle.com

LANGLEY

Country Cottage of Langley
215 6th St 98260
800-713-3860 360-221-8709
Jacki Stewart

139-189 $US BB
5 rooms, 5 pb
Visa, MC, AmEx,
Rated, •
C-yes/S-no/P-ltd/H-ltd

Full gourmet breakfast
A full, hot breakfast served in your
cottage, on the deck, or in our four
seasons dining room
Scenic dining room, WiFi, view, deck,
living room, gardens, gazebo, croquet
& bocce ball

A classic, 1920 farmhouse with 5 romantic & distinctly designed cottages with private decks on 2 acres of beautiful gardens. Amazing view of Puget Sound, 2-person Jacuzzis, fireplaces, gourmet breakfast delivered to cottage, short walk to the village.

✉ stay@acountrycottage.com   🌎 www.acountrycottage.com

Saratoga Inn
201 Cascade Ave 98260
800-698-2910 360-221-5801
Kayce Nakamura

145-325 $US BB
16 rooms, 16 pb
Most CC, Cash,
Rated, •
C-yes/S-no/P-no/H-yes

Full breakfast
Afternoon wine, tea & hors d' oeuvres,
freshly-baked cookies, drinks available
throughout the day
Porch with rocking chairs, bicycles to
borrow, sitting room, conference room

The stunning beauty of Puget Sound and its many islands is the setting for the Saratoga Inn. Your journey begins with a scenic, 20 minute, car-ferry ride from the mainland to Whidbey Island.

✉ info@saratogainnwhidbeyisland.com   🌎 www.saratogainnwhidbeyisland.com

LEAVENWORTH

Abendblume Pension
12570 Ranger Rd 98826
800-669-7634 509-548-4059
Randy & Renee Sexauer

145-269 $US BB
7 rooms, 7 pb
Visa, MC, Disc,
Rated, •
S-no/P-no/H-ltd

Full breakfast
Fireplaces, down comforters,
balconies, whirlpool tubs

Inspired by fine European country inns, Abendblume is one of Leavenworth's finest award-winning bed and breakfasts. "A very private world to escape and rejuvenate."

✉ info@abendblume.com 🌐 www.abendblume.com

All Seasons River Inn
8751 Icicle Rd 98826
800-254-0555 509-548-1425
Susan & Dale Wells

165-230 $US BB
7 rooms, 7 pb
Visa, MC, *Rated*
C-ltd/S-no/P-no/H-yes

Full breakfast
Dessert
Game table area, TV room,
bicycles, Jacuzzis, suites, fireplaces,
refrigerators, wireless Internet

Set on a quiet wooded riverbank, this gracious inn offers spacious riverview suites with jetted tubs, private bath, comfortable riverview seating; decks, and some fireplace. And oh, what a breakfast!

✉ info@allseasonsriverinn.com 🌐 www.allseasonsriverinn.com

Enchanted River Inn
9700 E Leavenworth
Rd 98826
877-548-9797 509-548-9797
Bill & Kathy Lynn

230-250 $US BB
3 rooms, 3 pb
Visa, MC, AmEx
S-no/P-no/H-no

3 course gourmet breakfast
Pillow top king beds, binoculars for
watching the area wild life and river
features, guest robes

Situated on a rapidly flowing river with awesome views of nature encircled by tall mountains yet only a short walk to the Bavarian Village of Leavenworth. Sleep to the peaceful sounds of the river and awaken to the aroma of a gourmet breakfast.

✉ river.inn@verizon.net 🌐 www.enchantedriverinn.com

Haus Rohrbach Pension
12882 Ranger Rd 98826
800-548-4477 509-548-7024
Carol & Mike Wentink

105-200 $US BB
10 rooms, 8 pb
Most CC, Cash, Checks
C-yes/S-no/P-no/H-ltd

Full country breakfast!
Wine dinner series, Theatre dinners
Seasonal pool and year-round spa,
and incredible gardens, scrapbooking
weekends

A European-style Country Inn overlooking the beautiful Leavenworth Valley celebrating 34 years of service in 2008. Where hospitality, recreation and relaxation are a tradition.

✉ info@hausrohrbach.com 🌐 www.hausrohrbach.com

Mountain Home Lodge
8201 Mountain Home
Rd 98826
800-414-2378 509-548-7077
Kathy & Brad Schmidt

130-530 $US BB
12 rooms, 12 pb
Visa, MC, Disc, *Rated*
C-ltd/S-no/P-no/H-ltd
Spanish

Full breakfast
Four course dinner, gourmet breakfast
& lunch included in winter
Fireplace, Jacuzzi, robes, stereo
systems, heated pool, hot tub, tennis
court, weddings, plasma TVs

On a secluded 20 acre meadow overlooking the Cascades, & surrounded by forest, our luxurious 12 guestroom lodge & cabins combine superb cuisine, year-round outdoor activities and total pampered relaxation.

✉ info@mthome.com 🌐 www.mthome.com

River Haus in the Pines
9690 E Leavenworth
Rd 98826
509-548-9690
Mike & Cindy Hendricks

189-225 $US BB
3 rooms, 3 pb
Visa, MC
C-ltd/S-no/P-no/H-ltd

Full breakfast
River & mountain views, fireplace,
private decks, private bathrooms with
soaking tub, TV/DVD/CD

River Haus in the Pines B&B is a craftsman style home beautifully situated on the Wenatchee River with seasonal shoreline access. Ideal setting for both peaceful relaxation and outdoor adventures.

 info@riverhausinthepines.com  🌐 www.riverhausinthepines.com

LEAVENWORTH

Run of the River 9308 E Leavenworth Rd 98826 800-288-6491 509-548-7171 Steve & Jan Bollinger	230-265 $US BB 6 rooms, 6 pb Visa, MC, Disc, *Rated* S-no/P-no/H-yes	Hearty, healthy and fresh! Afternoon tea, treats Complimentary tandem, mountain bikes & snowshoes, expert tips on discovering the magic of the Valley

As Washington's only 4-star inn rated by NW Best Places, Run of the River Inn has earned its distinction for peaceful romance and luxury surroundings. Six suites offer a haven of privacy, with fireplaces, Jacuzzi tubs and decks to view the refuge.

info@runoftheriver.com   www.runoftheriver.com

LONG BEACH

Boreas B&B Inn 607 N Ocean Beach Blvd 98631 888-642-8069 360-642-8069 Susie Goldsmith & Bill Verner	179-199 $US BB 5 rooms, 5 pb Most CC, Cash, Checks, *Rated*, • C-ltd/S-no/P-no/H-no Some Spanish	Full 3 course gourmet breakfast Triple chocolate brownies, organic Boreas coffee, extensive tea selection, pistachios & chocolates! Concierge service, two living rooms with fireplaces, glorious ocean views, hot tub by the sand dunes

If you love three-course gourmet breakfasts created from local delicacies, glorious ocean vistas, beautiful surroundings, and award-winning gracious service, Boreas Inn is your getaway. The ambience at Boreas entices you to never go home again!

info@boreasinn.com   www.boreasinn.com

LOPEZ ISLAND

Edenwild Inn 132 Lopez Rd 98261 800-606-0662 360-468-3238 Kris Weinshilboum	170-195 $US BB 8 rooms, 8 pb Visa, MC, *Rated* C-ltd/S-no/P-no/H-yes	Self serve breakfast Patio, living room, dining room, unique decor, comfortable accommodations, marina views, fireplaces

Experience friendly service and the warm atmosphere of Lopez Island from our premium accommodations, nestled in the heart of Lopez Village.

edenwild@rockisland.com   www.edenwildinn.com

LUMMI ISLAND

Full Bloom Farm 2330 Tuttle Ln 98262 360-758-7173 Elisabeth Marshall	120-150 $US EP 2 rooms, 2 pb C-ltd/S-no/P-ltd/H-yes	Deck, full kitchen, fireplaces, bicycles, award-winning gardens, cottage & apartment rentals

At Full Bloom Farm, enjoy the relaxing ambience of our lovely cottage and apartment in our beautiful, award-winning garden setting. We raise herbaceous and intersectional peonies – in Spring, the fields are a stunning sight in full bloom.

info@fullbloomfarmpeonies.com   www.fullbloomfarmpeonies.com/vacation/index

The Celtic Mariner B&B 1611 Seacrest Dr. 98262 360-758-2270 James & Tammy Strong	100-120 $US BB 1 rooms, 1 pb Visa, MC C-ltd/S-no/P-no/H-no	Full breakfast Private entrance, queen sized bed, leather sofa, kitchenette with mini refrigerator, fireplace

The Celtic Mariner offers you an escape from urban intensity! Our B&B has a picnic and relaxation area on the seacliff with splendid views of Hale Passage, Mt Baker, The Sisters, Portage Island and incredible sunrises.

jmtbstrong@msn.com   www.thecelticmarinerbandb.com

MT. BAKER

Mt. Baker Lodging, Inc. 7463 Mt Baker Hwy 98244 800-709-SNOW (7669) 360- 599-2453 Guest Services	109-509 $US EP 95 rooms, 95 pb Most CC, *Rated*, • C-yes/S-ltd/P-ltd/H-ltd	All properties are self-catered. Fully equipped kitchens with cookware. Catering available upon request! All bed & bath linens provided

A delightful alternative to the traditional Mt. Baker area bed & breakfast or inn, Mt. Baker Lodging proudly offers private, self-catered, fully equipped vacation home rentals, located in Glacier and Maple Falls at the gateway to Mount Baker, Washington.

reservations@mtbakerlodging.com   www.mtbakerlodging.com

MUKILTEO

Hogland House B&B
917 Webster St 98275
888-681-5101 425-742-7639
Kay Scheller

85-125 $US BB
2 rooms, 2 pb
Visa, MC
C-yes/S-ltd/P-yes/H-no

Full breakfast or "On Your Own"
Hot tub, porches, sitting room, TV/
DVD, wireless Internet, in-room coffee

A National Historic Register waterfront home with Old World finishes, overlooking Puget Sound in Old Mukilteo. Includes a hot tub, collectibles, wooded trails on five acres at the end of a quiet road.

 romance@hoglandhouse.com  www.hoglandhouse.com

NORTH BEND

Roaring River B&B
46715 SE 129th St 98045
877-627-4647 425-888-4834
Herschel & Peggy Backues

109-195 $US BB
5 rooms, 5 pb
Most CC, *Rated*, •
C-ltd/S-no/P-no/H-no

Full breakfast
Warm full breakfast baskets delivered
to the door each morning
Jacuzzis, WiFi, fireplaces, cable TV,
business travelers, private entrances,
sitting areas, decks

Choose a hot tub, sauna, or Jacuzzi room. Very romantic, very private, wonderful restaurants and incredible views of mountains, rivers, forests and occasional wildlife.

 roaringriver@comcast.net  www.theroaringriver.com

OCEAN PARK

Charles Nelson Guest House
26205 Sandridge Rd 98640
888-862-9756 360-665-3016
Ginger Bish

160-180 $US BB
3 rooms, 3 pb
Visa, MC, AmEx
C-yes/S-no/P-yes/H-no

Full breakfast
Smoked oyster or salmon with
seasonal fruit, cheese & fruit plate
Sunroom, fireplace, hammocks,
freshly pressed sheets, soft robes &
thirsty towels, wine @ 5:00 pm

Free Night w/Certificate: Valid September-June 30th. Room Upgrade.

On the edge of Ocean Park and just within the boundaries of Nachotta, our inn overlooks Willapa Bay and the Wildlife Refuge of Long Island.

 cnbandb@charlesnelsonbandb.com  www.charlesnelsonbandb.com

George Johnson House B&B
26301 'N' Place 98640
866-665-6993 360-665-6993
Charlotte Killien

125-165 $US BB
3 rooms, 3 pb
Visa, MC
C-ltd/S-no/P-no

Full Country Breakfast
Antique accessories, high-speed
wireless Internet, wraparound porch,
library & perennial gardens

Experience the Peninsula's historic spirit in this beautiful 1913 Craftsman home. Nestled on a quiet street, it's just a short walk to the ocean beach or to nearby attractions. Each of the three guestrooms offer private bathrooms and wireless Internet.

 stay@georgejohnsonhouse.com  www.georgejohnsonhouse.com

PORT ANGELES

Colette's B&B
339 Finn Hall Rd 98362
877-457-9777 360-457-9197
Karen & Richard Fields

195-395 $US BB
5 rooms, 5 pb
Visa, MC, *Rated*
S-no/P-no/H-ltd

Multi-Course Gourmet Breakfast
Afternoon Tea, evening wine & hors
d'oeuvres
Romantic getaway, concierge services,
Jacuzzis, fireplaces, king suites, DVD
library, very private

Breathtaking 10-acre oceanfront estate, nestled between the Olympic Range and the Strait of Juan de Fuca. Luxury oceanfront king suites w/Jacuzzi spas for two and romantic fireplaces. Fodors "Top Choice.) Best Places to Kiss-"Utopian Oceanfront Hideaway".

 colettes@colettes.com  www.colettes.com

Domaine Madeleine
146 Wildflower Ln 98362
888-811-8376 360-457-4174
Jeri Weinhold

150-310 $US BB
5 rooms, 5 pb
Most CC, Cash, Checks,
Rated
C-ltd/S-ltd/P-no/H-no

Full breakfast
24 hour coffee, tea, hot chocolate,
cider, cookies, candy
Sitting room, library, Jacuzzi, games,
fireplaces, cable TV, DVDs, maps,
guidebooks, panoramic views

Serene, romantic, contemporary estate with panoramic mountain and waterviews. Exquisite gardens, Monet garden replica, European/Asian antiques, fireplace, Jacuzzi, private entrance, renowned 5-course breakfast.

 stay@domainemadeleine.com  www.domainemadeleine.com

PORT ANGELES

Eden by the Sea 1027 Finn Hall Rd. 98362 360-452-6021 David & Evelyn Brown	150-185 $US BB 3 rooms, 3 pb Visa, MC C-ltd/S-no/P-no/H-ltd	Multiple course gourmet breakfast Afternoon Tea, lemonade & cookies, fruit, fresh veggies, crackers, chips, nuts Great room & library downstairs, large conversation room with TV upstairs

A unique Eden by the Sea experience awaits you, secluded on the Olympic Peninsula, in the land of the Great Northwest. This waterfront property will provide you with a peaceful rest in rooms with private baths and views of the water and mountains.
✉ info@edenbythesea.net ◐ www.edenbythesea.net/index.html

Inn at Rooster Hill 112 Reservoir Rd 98363 877-221-0837 360-452-4933 Peggy Frehner	119-189 $US BB 7 rooms, 7 pb Visa, MC, Disc, *Rated*, • C-ltd/S-ltd/P-ltd/H-no	Full breakfast Jacuzzi tub, antique beds, luxury bedding, TV, fridge, coffee, wireless

Inn at Rooster Hill is a quiet, French-country bed and breakfast set on a 2½ acre piece of wooded property in Port Angeles, Washington. All of our rooms have great amenities and with all new, high-quality bedding, you are assured of a good night's sleep.
✉ info@innatroosterhill.com ◐ www.innatroosterhill.com

Sea Cliff Gardens Bed & Breakfast 397 Monterra Dr 98362 800-880-1332 360-452-2322 Bonnie & Phillip Kuchler	135-245 $US BB 5 rooms, 5 pb Visa, MC, Disc, *Rated*, • S-no/P-no/H-ltd	Full breakfast Breakfast-to-go is available for early-starters, daily fresh-baked cookies, coffee, teas, hot cocoa Fireplace, two-person Jacuzzi or hot tub, TV, DVD, CD, hi-speed wireless Internet access

Quiet waterfront luxury near Olympic National Park. Roam through two acres brimming with ocean-front flower gardens and towering cedars, then relax on a bench-for-two and watch the sunset over the Salish Sea. Spacious rooms feature spectacular water views.
✉ info@SeaCliffGardens.com ◐ www.seacliffgardens.com

PORT ORCHARD

Reflections – A B&B 3878 Reflection Lane East 98366 360-871-5582 Cathy Hall	65-110 $US BB 4 rooms, 2 pb Visa, MC, *Rated* C-ltd/S-no/P-no/H-no	Full breakfast evening snack, wine or tea on arrival TV/VCR, fireplace, ceiling fans, meeting rooms, washer/dryer, library.

Free Night w/Certificate: Anytime.

Just a short distance from downtown Port Orchard, Reflections Bed & Breakfast Inn is a perfect place for an overnight or weekend stay. ✉ jimreflect@wavecable.com ◐ www.reflectionsbnb.com

PORT TOWNSEND

Commander's Beach House 400 Hudson St 98368 888-385-1778 360-385-1778 Gail Dionne Oldroyd	99-225 $US BB 4 rooms, 3 pb Visa, MC C-ltd/S-no/P-no/H-ltd	Full breakfast Gourmet hot chocolate, teas, coffee, and spiced cider with biscottis for dunking Ocean views, living room, fireplaces, verandah, weddings

This quiet and relaxing Cape Cod style beach house offers the best of both worlds. We are located on the water with miles of beach to explore And.. just three blocks from downtown shops and restaurants. "Come relax and solve nothing."
✉ stay@commandersbeachhouse.com ◐ www.commandersbeachhouse.com

Holly Hill House B&B 611 Polk Street 98368 800-435-1454 360-385-5619 Nina & Greg Dortch	99-178 $US BB 5 rooms, 5 pb Visa, MC, *Rated* C-ltd/S-ltd/P-no/H-no	Full breakfast at 9:00am Tea, cocoa, homemade marshmallows, snacks, wine Parlor with TV, DVD & video, gardens, views, patio, packages

Holly Hill House is an 1872 Victorian B&B in the historic uptown district. Providing comfortable and relaxing accommodations that pamper our guests.
✉ info@hollyhillhouse.com ◐ www.hollyhillhouse.com

PORT TOWNSEND

Quimper Inn
1306 Franklin St 98368
800-557-1060 360-385-1060
Sue & Ron Ramage

98-160 $US BB
4 rooms, 4 pb
Visa, MC
C-ltd/S-no/P-no/H-ltd

Full breakfast
Please inform us if you have special
dietary requirements or restrictions.

Since 1991 our guests have enjoyed staying in our home. Our 4 guestrooms reflect unique, elegant, uncluttered decor, beautiful woodwork, high ceilings and period fixtures.

✉ rooms@quimperinn.com 🌐 www.quimperinn.com

POULSBO

Morgan Hill Retreat
1921 Northeast Sawdust Hill
Rd 98370
800-598-3926 360-598-4930
Marcia Breece

125-175 $US BB
3 rooms, 3 pb
Visa, MC, •
C-ltd/S-no/P-ltd/H-yes

Full breakfast
We'll stock the refrigerator – just let us
know in advance! (however, additional
charges apply)
Labyrinth, trout pond, fly fishing or
lavender cooking lessons, in-room
massage, free WiFi, wildlife

Morgan Hill Retreat features comfortably sophisticated accommodations created to inspire relaxation and renewal. With an emphasis on privacy, this refuge will indulge visitors craving rest, solitude and inspiration.

✉ marcia@morganhillretreat.com 🌐 www.morganhillretreat.com

PUYALLUP

Hedman House
502 9th St SW 98371
866-433-6267 253-848-2248
Neil & Normajean Hedman

105-145 $US BB
2 rooms, 1 pb
Visa, MC, *Rated*
C-ltd/S-no/P-no/H-no

Full breakfast
Covered porch, courtyard, spa tub,
fireplace, wireless Internet, central air

Hedman House, a B&B, located in Puyallup, Washington is a comfortable and romantic lodging alternative to the hotels and motels in Seattle and Tacoma. Perfect for romantic weekend getaways, antiquing, the Fair or business.

✉ hedman-house@msn.com 🌐 www.hedmanhouse.com

REDMOND

A Cottage Creek Inn
12525 Avondale Rd NE 98052
425-881-5606
Steve & Jeanette Wynecoop

110-160 $US BB
5 rooms, 5 pb
Visa, MC, AmEx,
Rated
C-ltd/S-ltd/P-no/H-no
Very little German

Full breakfast
Afternoon tea on request
Sitting room, Jacuzzis, suites, hot tub,
pond, creek, conference facilities,
WiFi, phones, wineries

Romantic English Tudor in beautiful, tranquil garden setting. Five lovely rooms/suites w/ private baths & cable TV. Many fine wineries & restaurants nearby. Phones & high speed WiFi are comp. Private nature trail, Hot Tub, Full Breakfast included.

✉ innkeepers@cottagecreekinn.com 🌐 www.cottagecreekinn.com

SEATTLE

11th Avenue Inn Bed & Breakfast
121 11th Avenue E 98102
800-720-7161 206-720-7161
David Williams

69-169 $US BB
8 rooms, 8 pb
Most CC, *Rated*
C-ltd/S-no/P-no/H-no

Full breakfast
50 restaurants within a 15 minute walk
Free parking, free WiFi & guest
Internet computers & printer, TV/DVD,
living room, den, front porch.

Walk to the Pike Place Market and to the other downtown Seattle attractions from a charming 1906 Seattle bed and breakfast on a tree-lined side street in Seattle's Capitol Hill neighborhood. We're near dozens of restaurants, shops, a popular park, and bus

✉ info@11thavenueinn.com 🌐 www.11thavenueinn.com

B&B on Broadway
722 Broadway Ave E 98102
206-329-8933
Russel Lyons & Don Fabian

145-175 $US BB
4 rooms, 4 pb
Most CC, Cash, Checks
S-no/P-no/H-no

Continental breakfast

First, you notice the finely carved banister and staircase, then the oversize stained glass window over the landing. Facing the stairway, block glass panels frame the doorway in the roomy foyer. Welcome to the B&B on Broadway, your B&B on Capitol Hill.

✉ info@bbonbroadway.com 🌐 www.bbonbroadway.com

SEATTLE ───────────────────────────────────

Bacon Mansion B&B 959 Broadway E 98102 800-240-1864 206-329-1864 Daryl J. King	99-234 $US BB 11 rooms, 9 pb Most CC, Cash, *Rated* C-ltd/S-no/P-ltd/H-ltd	Continental plus breakfast Tea & cookies in the afternoon Sitting room, library, conference room, cable TV, hairdryer, private telephone, bathrobe, free WiFi

Stay in Seattle's leading Bed and Breakfast and enjoy the charm and comfort of yesterday, with all the convenience of today. One of Capitol Hill's gracious mansions c. 1909.

 info@baconmansion.com 🌐 www.baconmansion.com

───────────────────────────────────

Bed & Breakfast Inn Seattle 1808 E Denny Way 98122 206-412-REST 206-412-REST Seleima Silikula, Shannon Seth	85-165 $US BB 14 rooms, 1 pb Visa, MC, Disc C-ltd/S-no/P-ltd/H-ltd	Full Breakfast Access to our gourmet kitchen, wireless, off-street parking, laundry facility and bike rental

An Urban Inn for the savvy traveler. Located just 10 blocks from downtown Seattle. 10 minute bus ride to Space Needle and Waterfront. Your home away from home.

 Stay@BnBInnSeattle.com 🌐 www.SeattleBednBreakfast.com

───────────────────────────────────

Chambered Nautilus Bed and Breakfast Inn 5005 22nd Ave NE 98105 800-545-8459 206-522-2536 Joyce Schulte	104-204 $US BB 10 rooms, 10 pb Visa, MC, AmEx, *Rated* C-ltd/S-no/P-ltd/H-no French	Full 3-course breakfast Tea, coffee, fruit & cookies Fireplaces, porches, A/C, private baths, robes, HDTV, hairdryer, in room WiFi, guest computer

An elegant Inn near the University of Washington campus. Minutes from downtown. Features spacious, quiet and comfortable rooms with amazing breakfasts and homemade cookies! Fireplaces in winter, gardens for spring and summer. WiFi throughout.

 stay@chamberednautilus.com 🌐 www.chamberednautilus.com

───────────────────────────────────

Chelsea Station Inn B&B 4915 Linden Ave N 98103 206-547-6077 Bennett, Lauren, Maureen and Toni	159-275 $US BB 4 rooms, 4 pb Visa, MC C-yes/S-ltd/P-no/H-no	Full breakfast Kitchenette stocked with treats Suites with living room, dining room, kitchenette, powder room & sumptuous master suite

Located just 10 minutes from downtown Seattle and right across the street from the Woodland Park Zoo, Chelsea Station Inn B&B features four luxurious suites, each can accommodate up to four guests!

 info@chelseastationinn.com 🌐 chelseastationinn.com

───────────────────────────────────

Gaslight Inn 1727 15th Ave 98122 206-325-3654 Stephen Bennett	98-168 $US BB 8 rooms, 6 pb Visa, MC, AmEx, *Rated* C-ltd/S-no/P-no/H-ltd	Seasonal Continental Breakfast A wet bar, microwave and under counter refrigerator are the only food storage/preparation facilities Heated pool, sun deck, living room, fireplace, library

In restoring Gaslight Inn, we have brought out this bed and breakfast's original turn-of-the-century ambience and warmth, while keeping in mind the additional conveniences and contemporary style needed by today's travelers.

 innkeepr@gaslight-inn.com 🌐 www.gaslight-inn.com

───────────────────────────────────

Greenlake Guest House 7630 E Green Lake Dr N 98103 866-355-8700 206-729-8700 Blayne & Julie McAferty	134-214 $US BB 4 rooms, 4 pb Visa, MC, Disc, *Rated* C-ltd/S-no/P-no/H-no	Full breakfast Tea, coffee, homemade cookies, guest refrigerator with sodas & bottled water Dining room, fireplace, living room, sunroom, wireless Internet, TV/DVD, large DVD library

1920 Craftsman style B&B, located across the street from Green Lake. All rooms include private bath with Jacuzzi tub/shower & heated tile floors, lake views or gas fireplace, TV/DVD, wireless Internet, full breakfast. 10 minute drive to downtown Seattle.

 stay@greenlakeguesthouse.com 🌐 www.greenlakeguesthouse.com

SEATTLE

Inn at Harbor Steps
1221 First Ave 98101
888-728-8910 206-748-0973
David Huynh

175-250 $US BB
28 rooms, 28 pb
Most CC, Cash, •
C-yes/S-no/P-no/H-yes

Full breakfast
Afternoon wine, tea & hors d' oeuvres,
freshly-baked cookies, drinks available
throughout the day
High speed Internet, fireplaces, jetted
tubs, on-site parking, indoor pool,
basketball court, gym

Nestled in the heart of Seattle's sleek arts and business district and crowned by the glamorous Harbor Steps Park, the Inn at Harbor Steps is perfectly located to the best Seattle has to offer.
 innatharborsteps@foursisters.com 🌐 www.innatharborsteps.com

Inn of Twin Gables
3258 14th Ave W 98119
866-466-3979 206-284-3979
Katie Frame

100-250 $US BB
4 rooms, 4 pb
Visa, MC, AmEx
C-ltd/S-no/P-ltd/H-ltd
Spanish & French

Full gourmet breakfast
We serve a full gourmet breakfast
using herbs from our garden.
Enclosed sun porch, living room,
fireplace, convenient to attractions,
dining, shopping, WiFi

The Inn of Twin Gables offers 3 comfortable guestrooms and a Garden Suite with 2 BRs, bath, full kitchen, private entrance; and a substantial gourmet breakfast. Personal attention and an ambience of welcome and comfort make it your home away from home.
 innkeepers@innoftwingables.com 🌐 www.innoftwingables.com

Mildred's B&B
1202 15th Ave E 98112
800-327-9692 206-325-6072
Melodee Sarver

125-225 $US BB
4 rooms, 4 pb
Visa, MC, AmEx,
Rated
C-yes/S-ltd/P-no/H-no

Full breakfast
Afternoon tea or coffee, homemade
cookies
Sitting room, fireplace, library,
veranda, grand piano, queen beds,
front yard putting green

1890 Victorian. Wraparound veranda, lace curtains, red carpets. City location near bus, electric trolley, park, art museum, flower conservatory. innkeeper@mildredsbnb.com 🌐 www.mildredsbnb.com

---

Olympic View Bed & Breakfast Cottage
2705 SW 164th Pl 98166
206-200-8801
Dave & Eileen Schmidt

165-220 $US BB
1 rooms, 1 pb
Visa, MC, *Rated*
C-ltd/S-ltd/P-no/H-no

Full breakfast
Sodas, snacks, fresh fruit, afternoon
tea, requests are taken for special
meals in the cottage
Private cottage & hot tub, king bed,
free WiFi, laundry facilities, cable TV,
CD/DVD, videos

Awarded "Most Scenic View" & "Best Kept Secret.) Private cottage with hot tub overlooking spectacular water and mountain views. Full kitchen, breakfast, king bed, living area, TV, DVD, stereo, private bath, walk to beach and close to Seattle attractions.
 innkeeper@olympicviewbb.com 🌐 olympicviewbb.com

Shafer Baillie Mansion
907 14th Ave E 98112
800-985-4654 206-322-4654
Mark Mayhle & Ana Lena
Melka

139-219 $US BB
8 rooms, 8 pb
Most CC, Cash, Checks
C-yes/S-no/P-no/H-no

Expanded Continental breakfast
Coffee & tea available all day
Sitting room, fireplaces, weddings
hosted

Magnificent 1914 Tudor Revival 14,000 sq ft mansion on Seattle's original Millionaires' Row. Capitol Hill location, central to all major attractions and amenities: downtown, waterfront, Pike Place Market, Seattle Center, Washington Convention Center. sbmansion@gmail.com 🌐 www.sbmansion.com

---

Sleeping Bulldog B&B
816 19th Ave. South 98144
206-325-0202
Korby Kencayd and Randal
Potter

116-206 $US BB
3 rooms, 3 pb
Most CC, Cash, Checks
C-ltd/S-no/P-no/H-no
some German

Full breakfast
fresh baked cookies, or cupcakes
flat-screen TVs, DVD players, iHome
radios, and Keurig coffee makers.

We are an intimate B&B located in a quiet neighborhood close to Downtown and Seattle's Sports Stadiums. Enjoy the dramatic view of Downtown, Puget Sound, Qwest Field and the Olympic Mountain. A Full Gourmet breakfast awaits you in the morning.
 innkeepers@sleepingbulldog.com 🌐 www.sleepingbulldog.com

Soundview Cottage B&B
17600 Sylvester Rd SW 98166
888-244-5209 206-244-5209
Annie Phillips

190-200 $US BB
1 rooms, 1 pb
Most CC, Cash, Checks,
Rated
C-ltd/S-no/P-no/H-ltd

Self-prepared breakfast
Stereo, DVD, CD player, Cable TV,
hi-speed Internet connection, and an
outdoor deck and hot tub

Soundview Cottage Bed & Breakfast is a self-contained, absolutely private, charming guesthouse. With amazing views of Puget Sound, islands, and mountains from your cozy, intimate hideaway, you will be assured of a memorable visit.   ✉ annie@soundvcottage.com   🌐 www.seattlecottage.net

---

Three Tree Point
17026 33rd Ave SW 98166
888-369-7696 206-669-7646
Penny & Doug Whisler

150-250 $US BB
2 rooms, 2 pb
Visa, MC, AmEx
C-yes/S-ltd/P-yes/H-ltd

Full breakfast
Snacks
A/C, terry robes & slippers, stereo
w/CD player, in-room cable TV/VCR,
morning paper

Escape to one of Seattle's most enjoyable bed and breakfast getaways. Located on a quiet hillside overlooking Puget Sound and Three Tree Point, this is a true Northwest retreat.
✉ whislers@comcast.net   🌐 www.3treepointbnb.com

Villa Heidelberg B&B
4845 45th Ave SW 98116
800-671-2942 206-938-3658
Judy Burbrink

100-250 $US BB
6 rooms, 2 pb
Visa, MC, AmEx,
Rated, •
C-ltd/S-no/P-no/H-no

Full breakfast
Cable TV, WiFi & fax access, each
bathroom has Noevir products, a
hairdryer & bathrobes in each room

1909 Craftsman home, just minutes from the airport & downtown Seattle. Two blocks to shops, bus & a variety of ethnic restaurants. Great view of Puget Sound and Olympic Mountains with marvelous sunsets. Close to Lincoln Park and Alki Beach.   ✉ info@villaheidelberg.com   🌐 www.villaheidelberg.com

Shelburne Inn
4415 Pacific Way 98644
800-INN-1896 360-642-2442
Laurie Anderson & David
Campiche

115-195 $US BB
15 rooms, 15 pb
Visa, MC, AmEx,
Rated, •
C-yes/S-no/P-no/H-ltd
German

Full country breakfast
Freshly baked cookies upon arrival.
Shelburne Restaurant and Pub serve
breakfast, lunch and dinner.
Lobby and main dining room have
fireplaces. Guest computer available in
library. Wireless Internet.

The oldest surviving hotel in Washington state, with the time-honored tradition of superb service, decor and cuisine. Can accommodate small meetings of up to 30. The restaurant serves breakfast, lunch and dinner making creative use of local ingredients.
✉ innkeeper@theshelburneinn.com   🌐 www.theshelburneinn.com

Groveland Cottage B&B
4861 Sequim-Dungeness
Way 98382
800-879-8859 360-683-3565
Simone Nichols

125-155 $US BB
5 rooms, 5 pb
Most CC, Cash, Checks
C-ltd/S-no/P-ltd/H-no

Full breakfast
Snacks in the afternoon. Breakfast to
go if early departure is needed
High speed wireless Internet, Cable TV
and lush gardens

Groveland Cottage is located in the Sequim-Dungeness Valley along the Strait of Juan de Fuca on Washington's beautiful North Olympic Peninsula. Sequim offers convenient access to Olympic National Park, Dungeness Spit National Wildlife Refuge, & the ferry.
✉ simone@olypen.com   🌐 www.grovelandcottage.com

Juan de Fuca Cottages
182 Marine Dr 98382
866-683-4433 360-683-4433
Missy & Tom Rief

99-315 $US EP
14 rooms, 14 pb
Visa, MC, Disc, *Rated*
C-yes/S-no/P-ltd/H-ltd

Self serve- purchase own food
Complimentary coffee & tea
Whirlpool tub, CabTV/VCR/DVD/
CD, robes, slippers, 2 fireplace suites,
kayak rentals, 200 movies free

Free Night w/Certificate: Valid Sept. 15-June 15, Sundays through Thursdays. Not valid with any other specials. Room Upgrade.

Charming, completely equipped cottages and suites perched on a 50-foot bluff overlooking Dungeness Spit. We have our own private beach on Dungeness Bay. Prepare your own breakfast in cozy kitchens.
✉ juandefuca@olypen.com   🌐 www.juandefuca.com

SEQUIM

Lost Mountain Lodge	189-349 $US BB	Farmer's Market Gourmet Breakfast
303 Sunny View Dr 98382	5 rooms, 5 pb	Complimentary lattes & espresso,
888-683-2431 360-683-2431	Visa, MC, AmEx,	welcome tray of wine & hors
Dwight & Lisa Hostvedt	*Rated*, •	d'oeuvres, evening treats, free
	C-ltd/S-no/P-no/H-ltd	popcorn
	French	Free WiFi , spa services, hydrotherapy
		spa, free movies & DVDs, library

Discover why newest Best Places to Kiss gave us their only, highest 4-kisses rating on the Olympic Peninsula. 9+ acres of mountain views & idyllic ponds. Romantic fireplace suites, king beds & superb amenities. Gourmet breakfast, lattes, hydrotherapy spa.

✉ getaway@lostmountainlodge.com 🌐 www.lostmountainlodge.com

Red Caboose Getaway B&B	155-210 $US BB	Full gourmet breakfast
24 Old Coyote Way 98382	6 rooms, 6 pb	Vegan, vegetarian, etc. just let us know
360-683-7350	Most CC	when making reservations
Charlotte & Olaf	S-no/P-no/H-no	Queen featherbed, large whirlpool
	All Year -closed January	tubs, robes, hairdryer, fireplace, mini-fridge, TV/DVD, WiFi

Stay in one of six themed luxury cabooses in the beautiful town of Sequim, in the shadow of the Olympic mountains & minutes away from John Wayne Marina. Our gourmet breakfast are elegantly served in our private 1937 Zephyr dining car, "The Silver Eagle".

✉ info@redcaboosegetaway.com 🌐 www.redcaboosegetaway.com

SNOHOMISH

Countryman B&B	105-135 $US BB	Full or continental breakfast
119 Cedar Ave 98290	3 rooms, 3 pb	Breakfast includes a choice of menu
800-700-9622 360-568-9622	Visa, MC, Disc, •	and time served
Larry & Sandy Countryman	C-yes/S-no/P-yes/H-no	Private baths, balconies, queen twin/king bed, wireless Internet, cable t.v., historic driving tour

1896 Queen Anne Victorian, located in the historic district of Snohomish, antique capital of the Pacific Northwest – private baths, queen, or twin/king beds, choice of breakfast menu and time. See the best of Pacific Northwest without changing rooms!

✉ sandy@countrymanbandb.com 🌐 www.countrymanbandb.com

Pillows & Platters B&B	80-100 $US BB	Full breakfast
502 Avenue C 98290	3 rooms, 1 pb	High speed wireless Internet access,
360-862-8944	Visa, MC	porch swing
Shirley & Dennis Brindle	C-ltd/S-no/P-no/H-ltd	

Welcome to this cheery house, built in 1892 as the original Methodist Parsonage for the city of Snohomish. Three intriguing rooms available, one with private bath, friendly hosts, and a romantic and relaxing atmosphere. Enjoy your trip! ✉ pillowsandplatters@gmail.com 🌐 www.pillowsandplatters.com

SPOKANE

Roberts' Mansion	140-200 $US BB	Full breakfast
1923 W 1st Ave 99201	5 rooms, 5 pb	Wireless Internet service, weddings &
509-456-8839	Visa, MC	events, gardens, parlor, billiard room,
Mary Moltke	C-yes/S-no/P-no/H-no	library, sunroom

Nestled proudly in Spokane's historic Browne's Addition, the meticulously restored Roberts Mansion celebrates its Victorian heritage in grand style. Suited as a Bed & Breakfast and Event facility, consider holding your wedding, or other event with us.

✉ manager@ejrobertsmansion.com 🌐 www.ejrobertsmansion.com

TACOMA

Branch Colonial House	135-209 $US BB	Full or continental breakfast
2420 N 21st St 98406	6 rooms, 6 pb	Sitting room, jetted tubs, fireplace,
877-752-3565 253-752-3565	Visa, MC, AmEx,	cable TV, Bose Wave radio/CD, DVD
Robin Korobkin	*Rated*, •	players, wireless Internet
	C-yes/S-no/P-no/H-no	

Nestled above Tacoma's historical Old Town district and over looking Commencement Bay, the Branch Colonial House offers romantic views, antique furnishings, and easy access to all of Puget Sound area dinning and attractions.

 stay@branchcolonialhouse.com 🌐 www.branchcolonialhouse.com

TACOMA

Plum Duff House
619 North K St 98403
888-627-1920 253-627-6916
Peter & Robin Stevens

90-150 $US BB
4 rooms, 4 pb
Most CC, Cash, *Rated*
C-ltd/S-no/P-ltd/H-no

Full breakfast
Tea, coffee, hot chocolate, cookies, cold drinks, fruit
Gardens, sitting room, sun room, Jacuzzi, fireplaces, WiFi, cable TV/ videos, local phones

Built in 1900 and listed on the Tacoma Historic Register, this unique, charming home has high ceilings, arches, and lovely gardens. We invite you to relax and enjoy genuine hospitality in a casual, leisurely atmosphere.

✉ plumduffhouse@gmail.com 🌐 www.plumduff.com

VASHON ISLAND

Artist's Studio Loft B&B
16529 91st Ave SW 98070
206-463-2583
Jacqueline Clayton

119-215 $US BB
5 rooms, 5 pb
Most CC, Cash, Checks, *Rated*
C-ltd/S-no/P-no/H-no

Full or expanded continental
Bicycles, Jacuzzi, suites, fireplace, conference facilities, kitchenette, hot tub

An enchanting, romantic getaway nestled on five acres with flower gardens & hot tub, on beautiful Vashon Island, minutes from Seattle. Cottages with fireplaces & Jacuzzis. Healing, serene atmosphere, private entrances & baths. Rated 3 diamonds by AAA.

✉ info@vashonbedandbreakfast.com 🌐 www.vashonbedandbreakfast.com

Swallow's Nest Guest Cottages
6030 SW 248th St 98070
800-269-6378 206-463-2646
Bob Keller

105-145 $US EP
7 rooms, 7 pb
Most CC, *Rated*, •
C-yes/S-no/P-ltd/H-ltd

Cottages with kitchens; coffee, tea, cocoa
Some hot tubs, fireplaces, golf, boating nearby

The Swallow's Nest affords travelers the opportunity to sojourn to a private country retreat on Vashon Island. There are 7 charming cottages in 3 separate locations each furnished in a comfortable & warm manner, some with views.

✉ anynest@vashonislandcottages.com 🌐 www.vashonislandcottages.com

WENATCHEE

Apple Country B&B
524 Okanogan Ave 98801
509-664-0400
Angie and David Lawrence

85-120 $US BB
6 rooms, 4 pb
Most CC, Cash, Checks
C-ltd/S-no/P-no/H-no

Full breakfast
Sitting room, Bicycle Storage, Cable TV all rooms, Accommodate Business travelers, Wireless Internet

Charming 1920 Craftsman home. Gourmet breakfast served daily. Close to downtown, Convention Center, riverfront and skiing. 18 miles from Leavenworth, WA. Five guestrooms, separate Carriage House.

✉ innkeepers@applecountryinn.com 🌐 www.applecountryinn.com

YAKIMA

A Touch of Europe
220 N 16th Ave 98902
888-438-7073 509-454-9775
Chef Erika & James A. Cenci

129-137 $US BB
2 rooms, 2 pb
Most CC, *Rated*, •
C-ltd/S-no/P-no/H-no
German

Full breakfast
Afternoon high tea, fine dining onsite with prior arrangement for multi-course luncheons & dinners
Nearby tennis court & pool, library, museums, wineries, farmers market, farms, orchards

Pamper yourself with luxurious surroundings, enjoy a signature, candlelit breakfast included in rates, arrange optional three course candlelit signature dinner prepared fresh by 3-time cookbook author-award winning chef/owner – unforgettable flavors

✉ atoeurope@msn.com 🌐 www.winesnw.com/toucheuropeb&b.htm

West Virginia

BERKELEY SPRINGS

Highlawn Inn
171 Market St 25411
888-290-4163 304-258-5700
Sandra M. Kauffman

98-225 $US BB
12 rooms, 12 pb
Visa, MC
S-ltd/P-no/H-no

Full gourmet breakfast
Delectable snacks & beverages are
always available
Wrap-around veranda, gardens, A/C,
color TV, some whirlpools & fireplace

The flavor of a more gracious time saturates this elaborate Victorian bride's house, with its wrap around veranda overlooking the historic spa town of Berkeley Springs, West Virginia.

✉ info@highlawninn.com 🌐 www.highlawninn.com

CABINS

North Fork Mountain Inn
Smoke Hole Rd 26855
304-257-1108
Ed & Carol Fischer

130-245 $US BB
10 rooms, 10 pb
Visa, MC, *Rated*
C-ltd/S-ltd/P-ltd/H-no

Full breakfast
Dinner available on most evenings for
an additional fee
Sitting room, hot tub, billiards, video
& music library, Jacuzzis, fireplaces,
WiFi, Direct TV

An outpost of luxury in the wilderness. Secluded, non-resort getaway located on the North Fork Mt. within Monongahela National Forest. Wraparound porches, breathtaking views. Hiking and caverns nearby.

✉ nfmi@wildblue.net 🌐 www.northforkmtninn.com

CHARLES TOWN

Hillbrook Inn
4490 Summit Point Rd 25414
800-304-4223 304-725-4223
Carissa & Christopher
Zanella

149-369 $US BB
10 rooms, 10 pb
Visa, MC, AmEx,
Rated
C-yes/S-ltd/P-ltd/H-ltd
Open all year Mon. –
Sun

Two-course Gourmet breakfast
Choice between a sumptuous 5-course
dinner or 3-course dining experience
created by Chef Christine.
Restaurant, sitting room, library,
antiques, art collection, gardens,
weekend weddings, quilting

Elegant B&B accommodations in an award-winning European style inn. Romantic 5-course. Extensive grounds and gardens with a stream, ponds, and a terrace with a fountain. Eclectic art, antiques and books in beautiful, old-world surroundings.

✉ info@hillbrookinn.com 🌐 www.hillbrookinn.com

ELKINS

Tunnel Mountain B&B
Old Rt 33 26241
888-211-9123 304-636-1684
Anne & Paul Beardslee

89-99 $US BB
3 rooms, 3 pb
Most CC, Cash, Checks,
Rated
C-ltd/S-no/P-no/H-no

Full breakfast
Restaurant nearby
Sitting room with fireplace, patio,
wooded paths, A/C, scenic views,
cable TV

Free Night w/Certificate: Valid November-March and Sunday-Thursday.

Romantic country fieldstone B&B nestled in scenic West Virginia Mountains next to National Forest and recreational areas. Also, a vacation cottage available along the river next to national forest. Sleeps up to six people, large deck, private setting.

GLEN DALE

Bonnie Dwaine
505 Wheeling Ave 26038
888-507-4569 304-845-7250
Bonnie & Sidney Grisell

95-135 $US BB
5 rooms, 5 pb
Most CC, Cash, Checks,
Rated, •
C-ltd/S-ltd/P-no/H-no

Full Sat-Sun/Continental Plus M-F
Complimentary snacks, soft drinks, ice
machine
Great room, living room, library,
fireplaces, A/C, spacious, wireless
Internet, whirlpool

Victorian warmth & elegance with the convenience of modern amenities. This beautiful home displays many antiques. Five guestrooms, each with fireplace, private ensuite bath, whirlpool tub & shower and more. Candlelight gourmet breakfast on weekends.

✉ Bonnie@Bonnie-Dwaine.com 🌐 www.Bonnie-Dwaine.com

HARPERS FERRY

Harpers Ferry Guest House	95-125 $US BB	Full breakfast
800 Washington St 25425	3 rooms, 3 pb	Snacks, cold drinks
304-535-2101	Visa, MC, *Rated*	Sitting room, cable TV, mini theater,
Al & Alison Alsdorf	C-ltd/S-no/P-no/H-ltd	free wireless, frame shop, off-street parking

A wonderfully friendly B&B located right in Historic Harpers Ferry, WV. Walk to shops, restaurants, and Harpers Ferry National Park.

✉ hfgh@comcast.net 🌐 www.harpersferryguesthouse.com

The Town's Inn	70-140 $US EP	Fridge & coffee/tea basket or tray in
175 & 179 High St 25425	7 rooms, 3 pb	each room
877-489-2447	Visa, MC	WiFi, in-room microwaves & fridge,
	C-yes/S-no/P-no/H-no	babysitting, laundry & shopping services, shuttle, catering

The Town's Inn consists of two pre-Civil War stone residences, Heritage House and the Mountain House, which are situated in the heart of historic Harper's Ferry and surrounded by the Harper's Ferry National Historic Park.

✉ info@thetownsinn.com 🌐 www.TheTownsInn.com

LEWISBURG

Historic General Lewis Inn	110-155 $US EP	Breakfast, lunch & dinner are not
301 E Washington St 24901	25 rooms, 25 pb	included in the rate but are served in
800-628-4454 304-645-2600	Most CC, Cash, Checks,	our dining room
Jim & Mary Noel Morgan	*Rated*, •	A/C, phones, TV, private baths, garden
	C-yes/S-no/P-no/H-yes	

The General Lewis Inn & Restaurant is a unique blend of the old and new, established and operated by the same family since 1928. The ideal setting for your weekend getaway, adventure on crystal blue water or a trip back in time.

✉ info@generallewisinn.com 🌐 www.generallewisinn.com

MARTINSBURG

Aspen Hall Inn	100-150 $US EP	Microwave & refrigerator available for
405 Boyd Ave 25401	4 rooms, 4 pb	guest use
304-260-1750	C-ltd/S-no/P-no/H-ltd	Breakfast room, cable TV, wireless
Charles Connolly		Internet access, grounds, creek, gazebo, A/C, massage therapy

Hospitality meets history in this magnificent 260-year-old inn. At the gateway to the Shenandoah Valley, 80 mi from Washington, DC. and at the hub of a wide variety of activities and historic sites. Specializing in monthly rentals.

✉ aspenhallinn@wvdsl.net

Wisconsin

ALGOMA

At the Water's Edge B&B
N7136 Hwy 42 54201
920-203-9584
Kari & Dave Anderson

109-159 $US BB
7 rooms, 7 pb
Visa, MC, Disc, *Rated*
S-ltd/P-no/H-ltd
May – November

Full breakfast
Coffee bar featuring tasty syrups and
sugars. Tea is also available.
All rooms have private entrance and
private bath. Enjoy our 1500 sqft deck
overlooking Lake Michigan

*The perfect B&B to enjoy a romantic get-a-away, anniversary or just a break from it all. Located just
south of historic Algoma. Each suite has its own theme. Enjoy the 1500 sqft deck overlooking Lake
Michigan.*

 info@atthewatersedgebnb.com  www.atthewatersedgebnb.com

ASHLAND

**Second Wind Country Inn
B&B**
30475 Carlson Road 54806
715-682-1000
Mark and Kelly Illick

79-159 $US BB
3 rooms, 3 pb
Visa, MC
C-ltd/S-no/P-no/H-yes

Full breakfast
Candlelight dinners for two or a
luncheons or dinner for group. Family
style dinners with our Family
Gathering room w/ board games,
outdoor bonfire, breakfast on the deck
or in your room, library, WiFi

*Second Wind is in a lovely rural setting just minutes from downtown Ashland and Lake Superior's
Chequamegon Bay area. Our name, Second Wind, reflects just what we want for you, our guests, to
experience. Farm animals and wildlife are an everyday sight.*

 catchyourbreath@secondwindcountryinn.com  www.secondwindcountryinn.com

---

The Inn at Timber Cove
1319 Sanborn Ave 54806
715-682-9600
Brian & Tina Miller

75-135 $US BB
5 rooms, 5 pb
Visa, MC
C-ltd/S-no/P-no/H-no
Portuguese

Full breakfast
Evening dessert & tea served in your
cottage or suite
Fireplace room, tea room, porches,
refrigerator, air conditioning, bicycles

*A 20-acre northern Wisconsin estate and a name that conjures up images of peaceful seclusion, of
quiet and cozy reflection. These are the things we desire all our guests to experience.*

 timbercove@mailstation.com  www.innattimbercove.com

BARABOO

Pinehaven B&B
E 13083 Hwy 33 53913
608-356-3489
Lyle & Marge Getschman

99-145 $US BB
5 rooms, 4 pb
Visa, MC, Disc, *Rated*
C-ltd/S-ltd/P-no/H-no

Full breakfast
Fishing, A/C, fridge, gazebo, rowboat,
paddle boat, cottage w/ whirlpool tub
& TV/DVD, Internet

*Beautiful view of the bluffs and a small private lake. Tranquil setting. Take a stroll, fish, admire the
Belgian draft horses. Relax. Acres to roam. Guest cottage available with double whirlpool, TV/DVD/
VCR, kitchen & dining area, fireplace & A/C.*

 www.pinehavenbnb.com

BELLEVILLE

**Cameo Rose Victorian
Country Inn**
1090 Severson Rd 53508
866-424-6340 608-424-6340
Dawn & Gary Bahr

159-249 $US BB
5 rooms, 5 pb
Visa, MC, Disc, *Rated*
C-ltd/S-no/P-no/H-ltd

Full Award Winning Breakfast
Snacks during check-in, 4–6 PM
120 scenic acres, gardens, views,
pond, waterfalls, woodland, trails,
suites, whirlpools, fireplaces

*What a difference a night makes at a genuine Madison, Wisconsin B&B getaway on 120 scenic acres
near vibrant Madison, University of Wisconsin, New Glarus – Little Switzerland and Mount Horeb –
Little Norway. "Best breakfast in Midwest" Award.*

 innkeeper@cameorose.com  www.cameorose.com

CAMP DOUGLAS

Sunnyfield Farm
N6692 Batko Rd 54618
888-839-0232 608-427-3686
John & Susanne Soltvedt

80-120 $US BB
4 rooms, 2 pb
Most CC, Cash, Checks,
Rated
C-yes/S-no/P-yes/H-no

Full breakfast
Tea, coffee, snacks
Sitting room, porch, cat & dog on the
premises

Nature lover's paradise. Choose from three bedrooms on second floor or a third floor studio. Aroma of coffee and fresh baked rolls start the day. There are 160 acres to hike, or settle in for a snooze on the porch.

✉ soltvedt@mwt.net 🌐 www.sunnyfield.net

CEDARBURG

The Washington House Inn
W62 N573 Washington
Ave 53012
888-554-9545 262-375-3550
Wendy Porterfield

100-315 $US BB
34 rooms, 34 pb
Most CC, Cash, Checks,
Rated, •
C-yes/S-no/P-no/H-yes

Continental plus breakfast
Afternoon wine & cheese social hour
Sitting room, fireplaces, whirlpool
baths, steam showers, sauna, wet bars,
wireless Internet

Country Victorian elegance found in the center of the Historical District. Breakfast in our charming gathering room. Shopping, golf, winter sports. Gift certificates and spa packages available.

✉ info@washingtonhouseinn.com 🌐 www.washingtonhouseinn.com

EAU CLAIRE

Otter Creek Inn
2536 Hwy 12 54702
866-832-2945 715-832-2945
Shelley & Randy Hansen

110-210 $US BB
6 rooms, 6 pb
Most CC, Cash, *Rated*
S-no/P-no/H-no

Full breakfast
Beverages during check-in times
Rooms have TVs/VCRs, video library
for your use

Each guestroom has a whirlpool for 2! Many with fireplaces. Choice of breakfast entree, serving time, breakfast in bed. Spacious 3-story English Tudor, antiques, in-ground pool. Many restaurants nearby.

✉ info@ottercreekinn.com 🌐 www.ottercreekinn.com

EPHRAIM

Eagle Harbor Inn
9914 Water St 54211
800-324-5427 920-854-2121
Nedd & Natalie Neddersen

98-269 $US BB
9 rooms, 9 pb
Visa, MC, Disc, *Rated*
C-yes/S-no/P-no/H-yes

Continental Plus Breakfast
Homemade afternoon treats
Indoor pool, sauna, fitness room,
croquet, gardens, playground, grills,
beach, golf nearby, WiFi

A gracious, New England-style inn on Ephraim's main street filled with antiques & warm hospitality, books & a fireplace reading room. An excellent breakfast served garden side in summer! Walk to boating, beach, golf, antiquing, galleries and restaurants.

✉ nedd@eagleharbor.com 🌐 www.EagleHarborInn.com

FISH CREEK

**Thorp House Inn &
Cottages**
4135 Bluff Ln 54212
920-868-2444
Christine & Sverre Falck-
Pedersen

95-235 $US BB
11 rooms, 11 pb
Rated
C-ltd/S-no/P-ltd/H-no
Norwegian

Continental plus breakfast
Restaurants nearby
Sitting room with fireplace, some
guestrooms & cottages with fireplace,
some with whirlpool

Antique-filled, historic Inn backed by wooded bluff, overlooking bay. Listed in the National Register of historic Places. 5 elegant guestrooms, some with fireplace, 3 with whirlpool. Also, 6 private, housekeeping cottages. Walk to beach. Open year-round

✉ innkeeper@thorphouseinn.com 🌐 www.thorphouseinn.com

White Gull Inn
4225 Main St. 54212
888-331-8601 920-868-3517
Andy & Jan Coulson

155-295 $US BB
17 rooms, 17 pb
Most CC, Cash
C-ltd/S-no/P-no/H-ltd

Hearty breakfasts
lunch, candlelight dinner, traditional
Door County fish boils
Inn rooms, suites and cottages.
Antiques, fireplaces and fabulous food.

Established in 1896, the White Gull Inn has provided accommodations with character and unforgettable dining to generations of visitors to the Door Peninsula.

✉ innkeeper@whitegullinn.com 🌐 www.whitegullinn.com

GREEN BAY

The Astor House
637 S Monroe Ave 54301
888-303-6370 920-432-3585
Greg & Barbara Robinson

89-165 $US BB
5 rooms, 5 pb
Most CC, Cash, Checks,
Rated, •
C-ltd/S-no/P-no/H-no

Continental plus breakfast
Complimentary wine
Double whirlpools, gas fireplaces,
phone, TV, stereo, VCR, DVD players,
WiFi Internet

Luxurious and romantic, close to all of Green Bay's major attractions. Our five uniquely styled guest-rooms indulge our guests in comfort with amenities that include; private baths, double whirlpool tubs, fireplaces, TV with VCR and DVD, and WiFi.

✉ astor@execpc.com 🌐 www.astorhouse.com

GREEN LAKE

McConnell Inn
497 S Lawson Dr 54941
888-238-8625 920-924-6430
Mary Jo & Scott Johnson

80-175 $US BB
5 rooms, 5 pb
Visa, MC, Disc
C-ltd/S-no/P-no/H-no

Full breakfast
Afternoon homemade cookies or
sweets

Free Night w/Certificate: Valid November-April only, excluding holidays.

Experience why McConnell Inn has been a Wisconsin favorite for over 25 years, receiving local and state honors and awards. Arrive at the inn and leave your cares and your vehicle at the curb – we are an easy walk to all that Green Lake has to offer.

✉ info@mcconnellinn.com 🌐 www.mcconnellinn.com

HARTFORD

Westphal Mansion Inn B&B
90 S Main St 53027
262-673-7938
Pam & Garret Terpstra

99-229 $US BB
8 rooms, 8 pb
Visa, MC, Disc
C-ltd/S-no/P-no/H-yes

Full breakfast
Wine & tea social hour,
complimentary beverages, homemade
cookies, bedside decadent chocolates
Full concierge service, formal living
and dining rooms, gardens & porches,
game & book library

This historic 1913 English Tudor mansion offers 8 elegant antique appointed suites, each with a private attached bath. The inn is furnished in an old world French Country style. Romantic, luxurious accommodations and amenities create a European ambience.

✉ terpstra7938@sbcglobal.net 🌐 westphalmansioninn.com

HARTLAND

Monches Mill House
W301 N9430 Hwy E 53029
262-966-7546
Elaine Taylor

50-85 $US BB
4 rooms, 2 pb
C-yes/S-no/P-yes/H-yes
French

Continental plus breakfast
Lunch in summer by reservation, fixed
menu with set price
Sitting room, hot tub, bikes, tennis,
canoeing, hiking

House built in 1842, located on the bank of the mill pond. Furnished in antiques, choice of patio, porch or gallery for breakfast enjoyment. Jacuzzi, barn, pond, Oconomowoc River and pond canoeing, tennis court, hiking on Ice Age trail.

HAZEL GREEN

Wisconsin House
2105 E Main St 53811
877-854-2233 608-854-2233
Ken & Pat Disch

85-145 $US BB
8 rooms, 6 pb
Most CC, Cash, Checks,
Rated, •
C-yes/S-no/P-no/H-no

Hearty Full Breakfast
Complimentary soft drinks, beverages
& delicious cookies always available
Library with piano, garden, gazebo,
porches

Free Night w/Certificate: November-August excluding holiday weekends. Type of room depending on availability. Room Upgrade.

An historic, comfortably furnished bed and breakfast, we're located just 10 miles north of Galena, Illinois, 13 miles west of Dubuque, Iowa, and 15 miles south of Platteville, Wisconsin. So close, so different! Stay with us and enjoy each of them.

✉ wishouse@mhtc.net 🌐 www.wisconsinhouse.com

LAKE GENEVA

Eleven Gables Inn on Lake Geneva 493 Wrigley Dr 53147 262-248-8393 Annabelle	119-330 $US BB 8 rooms, 8 pb Most CC, *Rated* C-yes/S-no/P-yes/H-ltd	Continental Plus breakfast Lake Front, Private pier to swim or fish, all rooms private baths.Free WI-Fi. Dog friendly.

Lakeside historic inn. Romantic bedrooms, bridal chamber, and now with country cottage and family coach house. Fireplaces, down quilts, wet bars, TVs, balconies. Live web cam of Lake Geneva.

✉ lakefront@lkgeneva.com   🌐 www.lkgeneva.com

French Country Inn W 4190 West End Rd 53147 262-245-5220 Mary Haggermaker	155-295 $US BB 33 rooms, 33 pb Visa, MC, Disc C-yes/S-ltd/P-no/H-ltd	Full breakfast Award-winning Kirsch's Restaurant is located on the premises, late afternoon tea in the parlour Dining room, parlour, fireplaces, armoires, whirlpools, balconies, pool, gathering room

Our B&B is located in the heart of Wisconsin's famous Geneva Lakes area on the south shore of Lake Como. The Lake Geneva area is both romantic and picturesque with its lazy winding country roads filled with many fine old homes and mansions.

✉ innkeeper@frenchcountryinn.com   🌐 www.frenchcountryinn.com

Lazy Cloud Lodge W4033 State Road 50 53147 262-275-3322 Keith and Carol Tiffany	129-235 $US BB 19 rooms, 19 pb Most CC, Cash, Checks, *Rated* S-no/P-no/H-yes	Continental plus breakfast Picnic basket dinner, complimentary wine & snacks Double whirlpool with view of fireplace, bubble bath, fridge, microwave, private entrance, candles

"Lazy Cloud . . . imagine your perfect romantic getaway in Lake Geneva Wisconsin. Our romantic getaway offers double whirlpools, fireplaces, candles, champagne and chocolate dipped strawberries!"

✉ love@lazycloud.com   🌐 www.lazycloud.com

The Geneva Inn N-2009 S Lake Shore Dr 53147 800-441-5881 262-248-5680 Teresa D'Amato	155-375 $US BB 37 rooms, 37 pb Most CC C-yes/S-no/P-no/H-yes German, French, Spanish	Continental buffet breakfast Lunch, Dinner, Sunday Brunch Free weekday newspaper, exercise facility, wireless Internet, bedtime chocolates, private pier.

Come to The Geneva Inn and discover intimate accommodations and distinctive European charm at a luxurious retreat located directly on the shores of Geneva Lake!

✉ luxury@genevainn.com   🌐 www.genevainn.com

MADISON

Annie's Bed and Breakfast 2117 Sheridan Drive 53704 608-244-2224 Annie & Larry Stuart	179-229 $US BB 1 rooms, 1 pb Most CC, Cash, Checks, *Rated* C-ltd/S-no/P-no/H-no	Full breakfast Snacks available Library, fireplace, dining rm, Jacuzzi rm, & theater, bicycle storage, nearby tennis court & beach

Beautiful garden B&B with views all seasons in a 300 acre park. Walk the lake shore, meadows, or woods. One 2-bedroom suite with private bath. Six minutes to downtown and campus.

✉ innkeeper@anniesinmadison.com   🌐 www.anniesinmadison.com

Arbor House, An Environmental Inn 3402 Monroe St 53711 608-238-2981 John & Cathie Imes	125-230 $US BB 8 rooms, 8 pb Visa, MC, AmEx, *Rated* C-yes/S-no/P-no/H-yes	Full breakfast on weekends Continental breakfast weekdays, drinks & appetizers, evening sweet treat Cable, massage services, fireplaces, sauna & sunroom, meeting space, mountain bikes, computer access

Historic landmark across from UW Arboretum with an environmental emphasis. Minutes from the Capitol & UW campus. Corporate rates.

✉ arborhouse@tds.net   🌐 www.arbor-house.com

OSCEOLA

Pleasant Lake B&B
2238 60th Ave 54020
800-294-2545 715-294-2545
Richard & Charlene Berg

109-159 $US BB
3 rooms, 3 pb
Visa, MC, Disc, *Rated*
C-ltd/S-no/P-no/H-no

Full breakfast
Help yourself to some complimentary
snacks throughout the day
Jacuzzis, fireplaces, complimentary
use of canoe, private bathrooms with
whirlpool tub, lake access

Nestled on 12 wooded acres overlooking quiet, semi-private Pleasant Lake. Three guestrooms offer queen beds, double whirlpool tubs, lake views & crackling campfires with the stars reflecting on the moonlit lake.

✉ plakebb@centurytel.net 🌐 www.pleasantlake.com

St. Croix River Inn
305 River St 54020
800-645-8820 715-294-4248
Ben & Jennifer Bruno,
Cheryl Conarty

135-250 $US BB
7 rooms, 7 pb
Visa, MC
C-ltd/S-no/P-no/H-ltd

Full gourmet breakfast
Comp. coffee, tea, snacks & fresh
baked treats. 5 course dinner avail Fri
and Sat
River views, fitness room, wireless
Internet, central heat/air, movies, CDs,
games, turndown service

Stay in one of our luxurious suites and enjoy breathtaking panoramic river views, turndown service, and a delicious gourmet breakfast served in your room. Experience timeless luxury on the river.

✉ innkeeper@stcroixriverinn.com 🌐 www.stcroixriverinn.com

REEDSBURG

Parkview B&B
211 N Park St 53959
608-524-4333
Tom & Donna Hofmann

85-105 $US BB
4 rooms, 2 pb
Visa, MC, Disc,
Rated, •
C-ltd/S-no/P-no/H-no

Full breakfast
Snacks, wake-up coffee, cheese & wine
on Saturday evenings
Sitting room, bicycle storage,
park across the street, WiFi,
accommodations for special diets

1895 Victorian home with comfortable antiques, across from City Park. Central to Wisconsin Dells, Baraboo, Spring Green, bike trails. Located in the Park Street Historic District, one block from Main Street.

✉ info@parkviewbb.com 🌐 www.parkviewbb.com

**Pine Grove Park B&B
Guest House**
S2720 Hwy V 53959
866-524-0071 608-524-0071
Jean & Kurt Johansen

140-185 $US BB
4 rooms, 4 pb
Most CC
S-no/P-no/H-ltd

Full breakfast
High speed WiFi , walking trails,
snowshoeing, large pond, whirlpool
tubs, fireplace, private.

Enjoy a private romantic getaway in one of our guesthouses with covered porch surrounded by woodlands, wetlands, and native wildflowers, a perfect travel destination for your Wisconsin honeymoon or romantic vacation.

✉ info@pinegroveparkbb.com 🌐 www.pinegroveparkbb.com

STEVENS POINT

Dreams of Yesteryear
1100 Brawley St 54481
715-341-4525
Bonnie & Bill Maher

85-160 $US BB
6 rooms, 4 pb
Most CC, *Rated*
C-ltd/S-ltd/P-no/H-no

Full breakfast
Afternoon tea, snacks
Sitting room, library, tennis court, hot
tub, bike trail map, pool, 2 3-room
suites

Three story antique embellished National Historic Register Victorian Queen Anne. Only B&B within designated Historic Downtown Main Street Business District. Conveniently located, still Dreams is set in a quiet historic neighborhood surrounded by gardens.

✉ bonnie@dreamsofyesteryear.com 🌐 www.dreamsofyesteryear.com

White Lace Inn, Sturgeon Bay, WI

STURGEON BAY

Black Walnut Guest House
454 North 7th Ave 54235
877-255-9568 920-743-8892
Geri Ballard & Mike
Shatusky

99-160 $US BB
4 rooms, 4 pb
Visa, MC, Disc
C-ltd/S-ltd/P-no/H-no

Continental plus breakfast
Fresh home made Cookies always in
the cookie jar. Afternoon cold drinks,
evening tea, hot chocolate
Private bath, Central AC, queen bed,
whirlpool tub, in-room refrigerator,
fireplace, balcony, TV/DVD

*The Black Walnut Guest House features 4 uniquely individual guestrooms, detailed with charm &
romance. Sumptuous surroundings, a whirlpool tub, a fireplace and a delicious breakfast served to
your room each morning set the mood for your romantic getaway.*

 stay@blackwalnut-gh.com 🌐 www.blackwalnut-gh.com

Chanticleer Guest House
4072 Cherry Rd 54235
866-682-0384 920-746-0334
Bryon Groeschl & Darrin
Day

140-400 $US BB
12 rooms, 12 pb
Most CC, Cash, Checks
S-no/P-no/H-yes

Continental plus breakfast
Snacks
Double whirlpools, fireplaces, heated
swimming pool and walking trails on
70 private acres

*Nestled among the orchards of Door County, comfort, relaxation and romance were foremost on the
owners' minds when they created Chanticleer Guest House. Get the best of both worlds-rustic charm
and the pampered feel of a Bed and Breakfast.*

 information@chanticleerguesthouse.com 🌐 www.chanticleerguesthouse.com

---

Inn at Cedar Crossing
336 Louisiana St 54235
920-743-4200
Steve & Kelly Hellmann

75-195 $US BB
9 rooms, 9 pb
Visa, MC, Disc, *Rated*
C-ltd/S-no/P-no/H-no

Full hot breakfast with choices
Complimentary afternoon tea, coffee,
lemonade & fresh baked cookies each
day
Restaurant & pub on site offering
casual & fine dining, as well as happy
hour specials

*Elegant 1884 inn situated in historic district near shops, restaurants, and museums. Nine romantic
rooms feature antique decor, fireplaces, whirlpools, and all the modern amenities. Full hot breakfast
with entree choices and afternoon cookies included.*

innkeeper@innatcedarcrossing.com 🌐 www.innatcedarcrossing.com

STURGEON BAY

White Lace Inn
16 N 5th Ave 54235
877-948-5223 920-743-1105
Dennis Statz, Mary & Marcia

70-235 $US BB
18 rooms, 18 pb
Most CC, Cash, Checks,
Rated
C-ltd/S-ltd/P-no/H-ltd

Full breakfast
Complimentary cookies, beverages
Sitting room, gazebo, gardens,
fireplaces, whirlpools, TV/VCRs, WiFi

The White Lace Inn's four historic homes are nestled in a friendly old neighborhood, bordered by a white picket fence, surrounded by gardens. We have 18 rooms and suites – 15 have fireplaces – 12 have whirlpools – 9 have both a fireplace and whirlpool.

 Romance@WhiteLaceInn.com 🌐 www.whitelaceinn.com

TURTLE LAKE

Canyon Road Inn
575 W Town Line Rd 54889
888-251-5542 715-986-2121
Patti & Turner

140-180 $US BB
6 rooms, 6 pb
Visa, MC, Disc
S-no/P-no/H-yes

Full breakfast
Snack area with full-size fridge &
microwave for guests use
Large deck off the living room on the
lakeside, trails in the woods & by the
lake, watercraft

Enjoy casual elegance in one of our six spacious guest suites. Each feature a comfy king size bed, private bathroom, relaxing double whirlpool tub, a cozy fireplace and private patio or deck overlooking the lake or woods. info@canyonroadinn.com 🌐 www.canyonroadinn.com

VIROQUA

Viroqua Heritage Inn B&B
220 E Jefferson St 54665
888-4-HERINN 608-637-3306
Nancy L. Rhodes

75-135 $US BB
8 rooms, 6 pb
Most CC, Cash
C-yes/S-no/P-no/H-ltd

Full breakfast
Porches, fireplace, woodwork, dining
room, balcony, garden, pond

Located in Wisconsin's Hidden Valley Region, these two elegant Victorian-era B&Bs offer a unique and memorable opportunity to simply relax or enjoy the many activities available around Vernon County.
 rhodsent@mwt.net 🌐 www.herinn.com

WAUSAU

Rosenberry Inn
511 Franklin St 54403
800-336-3799 715-842-5733
Barry & Linda Brehmer

90-150 $US BB
8 rooms, 8 pb
Visa, MC
C-yes/S-no/P-no/H-no

Full breakfast
We can accommodate most special
diets
Antiques, refrigerators, coffee makers,
CD players, free wireless Internet,
fireplaces, TV, library

The historic-home-turned-B&B features beautiful stained-glass windows, wide halls, a carved oak stairway that leads to the second floor, and a sweeping front porch overlooking Franklin Street – making it ideal for lodging accommodations.
 rosenberryinn@charter.net 🌐 www.rosenberryinn.com

WILTON

Amil's Inn B&B
27038 State Highway
131 54670
608-435-6640
David & Anita Reeck

79-119 $US BB
4 rooms, 4 pb
Visa, MC, Disc
C-ltd/S-no/P-no/H-no

Full breakfast
Comp. soda, juice, water, signature
cookies. Afternoon tea and sweets.
high speed wireless Internet, central
A/C, library

An historic home that captures the allure of times gone by with all the comforts of today. Nestled in the heart of the Elroy-Sparta Bike Trail in Wilton Wisconsin.
 stay@amilsinn.com 🌐 www.amilsinn.com

WISCONSIN DELLS

Bowman's Oak Hill B&B
4169 St Hwy 13 North 53965
888-253-5631 608-253-5638
David & Nancy Bowman

95-175 $US BB
5 rooms, 5 pb
Most CC, Cash,
Rated, •
C-ltd/S-no/P-no/H-no
some Spanish

Full breakfast
Afternoon & evening snacks
Robes, spa showers, TV/VCR, video
library, large deck with fire pit, sitting
room & sun porch

Ranked #1 on tripadvisor.com and the proud Grand Prize Winners of the Wisconsin Bed and Breakfast Cook-Off. We are only minutes from all of the Dells area attractions. It is our goal to help you have a fun filled restful vacation or weekend getaway.
 bowmansoakhillbb@aol.com 🌐 www.bowmansoakhillbedandbreakfast.com

Nagle Warren Mansion, Cheyenne, WY

Wyoming

CHEYENNE

Nagle Warren Mansion
222 E 17th St 82001
800-811-2610 307-637-3333
Jim Osterfoss

138-195 $US BB
12 rooms, 12 pb
Most CC, Cash, Checks,
Rated, •
C-yes/S-no/P-ltd/H-yes
Spanish, German

Full breakfast
Afternoon tea; full bar; luncheons,
dinners & reception, Poor Richards &
Capitol Grill for dinners
Hot tub, fireplaces, TV, phone,
wireless, bicycles, parlour, garden,
exercise facility

Ideally situated, the mansion offers all of today's needs in a comfortable & elegant ambience. Let us spoil you while you explore the original West.

✉ jim@nwmbb.com 🌐 www.naglewarrenmansion.com

DEVILS TOWER

Devils Tower Lodge
#34 State Road 110 82714
888-314-5267 307-467-5267
Frank Sanders

125-225 $US BB
4 rooms, 4 pb
Visa, MC, *Rated*
C-yes/S-ltd/P-no/H-ltd

Full breakfast
Dinner served on request for a small
fee.
Outdoor spa, living room, piano,
indoor climbing wall, exercise room

Our unique B&B is nestled on 21 acres of prairie and pine, at the base of Devils Tower. Each room has dramatic vistas of Devils Tower National Monument, queen beds, open-air view decks and private baths. A full country breakfast is served. ✉ frank@devilstowerlodge.com 🌐 www.devilstowerlodge.com

Lytle Creek Inn B&B
289 Lytle Creek Rd 82714
307-467-5599
Dee & Peter Kim Carroll

95-135 $US BB
3 rooms, 3 pb
Visa, MC, AmEx
C-ltd/S-no/P-no/H-ltd

Full breakfast
Fresh baked goods always available,
afternoon refreshments, additional
meals available for fee
Free wireless Internet, over-sized
decks for your viewing and relaxing
pleasure

Lytle Creek Inn B&B is nestled at the edge of the western Black Hills in northeastern Wyoming among the oak and pine that line Lytle Creek. Quiet peaceful rural landscape, comfortable accommodations and star gazing just 4 miles from Devils Tower.

✉ info@lytlecreekinn.com 🌐 www.lytlecreekinn.com

JACKSON

A Teton Tree House
6175 Heck of a Hill Rd 83014
307-733-3233
Denny & Sally Becker

205-285 $US BB
6 rooms, 6 pb
Visa, MC, Disc,
Rated, •
C-ltd/S-no/P-no/H-no
A little Spanish
May through October

"Healthy Heart"—no eggs or meat
Juices, coffee, teas, beer & wine are
available
A Grand Room with games & books
galore

Tucked away, and yet close to two national parks and the town of Jackson, this B&B offers a quiet retreat amidst the trees with unique, comfortable rooms and a warm, friendly atmosphere.

 atetontreehouse@aol.com 🌐 www.atetontreehouse-jacksonhole.com

---

Bentwood Inn B&B
4250 Raven Haven Rd 83001
307-739-1411
Peter & Jennifer Tignor

205-335 $US BB
5 rooms, 5 pb
Most CC, *Rated*
C-yes/S-no/P-no/H-yes

"Hearty & Sumptuous" Full brkfst
Afternoon tea, hors d'oeuvres,
evening wine & cheese, personal chef
prepared meals available
Great Room w/ 3-story river rock
fireplace, library, deep Jacuzzi
bathtubs, private fireplace & deck

Award-winning "architectural marvel" (Frommer's 2003), a 6,000 sq. ft. log inn with five guest suites, constructed using massive 200 year old logs brought in from Yellowstone Nat'l Park after the great fire of 1988, on 3 old growth acres.

 info@bentwoodinn.com 🌐 www.bentwoodinn.com

Teton View B&B
2136 Coyote Loop 83014
307-733-7954
Carol & Franz Kessler

189-325 $US BB
3 rooms, 3 pb
Visa, MC, Disc
C-yes/S-no/P-ltd/H-no
German
Summer and Fall

Guests love our full breakfasts!
Afternoon treats
Outdoor hot tub, indoor Jacuzzi, daily
housekeeping, free WiFi, friendly &
peaceful atmosphere

Experience the grandeur of the Grand Tetons in our family environment, blending Western hospitality with a European flair. A visit to Teton View B&B in Jackson Hole, neighbor to Yellowstone and Grand Teton National Parks, will bring you back!

 info@tetonview.com 🌐 www.TetonView.com

The Wildflower Inn
3725 N Teton Village
Rd 83002
307-733-4710
Ken & Sherrie Jern

280-380 $US BB
5 rooms, 5 pb
Visa, MC, *Rated*, •
C-yes/S-no/P-no/H-no

Fantastic breakfast
A casual afternoon beverage & snack,
homemade lemonade, teas, lovely
wines, fresh cookies
WiFi Internet access, trekking poles,
bikes, day packs, great advice on
things to see & do

Named "Best of the West" by Sunset Magazine and featured in "Cooking with Paula Deen" the Wild-flower Inn is a beautiful log inn on 3 gorgeous acres with mountain views. Famous for fantastic food, luxurious rooms and wonderful attention to detail.

 jhwildflowerinn@cs.com 🌐 www.jacksonholewildflower.com

MOOSE

Lost Creek Ranch
Old Ranch Road 83012
307-733-3435
Anne

$US AP
13 rooms, 13 pb
Visa, MC
C-yes/S-no/P-no/H-yes
May – October

Full breakfast
All meals included. Special requests or
dietary needs can be accommodated
through prior arrangement.
Horses, full spa, skeet, hiking, airport
shuttle, cardio equip, hot tub, pool,
Kid's Club

Privately owned ranch between Grand Teton Nat'l Park and Bridger-Teton Nat'l Forest. All the excitement of a traditional ranch + luxurious comforts of a full-service spa in the region's most spectacular location. Weekly stays only. Inquire about rates.

 ranch@lostcreek.com 🌐 www.lostcreek.com

SARATOGA ───────────────────────────────────

Wolf Hotel
101 E Bridge St 82331
307-326-5525
Doug & Kathleen Campbell

67-110 $US EP
10 rooms, 10 pb
Visa, MC, AmEx
C-yes/S-no/P-no/H-no

Lunch: 11:30–2, Mon-Sat. Dinner: 6–9
(9:30 Summer), Mon-Th, 6–9:30, Fri-Sat
(10 Summer), Sun Closed
Five Suites, semi-private room for
meetings and private parties, porch,
pool table, restaurant, bar

Built in 1893 as a stage coach stop and listed in the National Register, the hotel is noted for its fine food and convivial atmosphere. Wolf Hotel anchors Saratoga, one of America's top ten small towns. No stop lights, but a warm, friendly town.

 kcampbel@union-tel.com   🌐 www.wolfhotel.com

WILSON ───────────────────────────────────

Sassy Moose Inn
3895 W Miles Road 83014
800-356-1277 307-413-2995
Craig Kelley

79-229 $US BB
5 rooms, 5 pb
Most CC, Cash, Checks
C-yes/S-no/P-yes/H-no

Full breakfast
Wireless Internet & cable TV, hot tub,
firepit, daily housekeeping, fireplaces

Each of our five guestrooms has its own charm in our comfortable 4800 square foot western-style log home and petit spa. Perfect for a romantic getaway or the ideal family vacation. You can even Rent-The-Inn for your family reunions, or business retreats.

✉ craigerwy@aol.com   🌐 www.sassymoose.com

Canada

Alberta

BANFF

Rocky Moutain B&B
223 Otter St. T0L 0C0
403-762-4811
Ashley Schneider

70-170 $US BB
10 rooms, 6 pb
Visa, MC
C-yes/S-no/P-no/H-no

Full breakfast

Welcome to the Rocky Mountain B&B in beautiful Banff. We are an intimate, high-country inn situated in a quiet residential neighbourhood. The building dates from 1918 and has 10 guestrooms and a gorgeous main lounge and dining room.

✉ reservations@rockymtnbb.com 🌐 www.rockymtnbb.com

CALGARY

1910 Calgary Historic B & B at Twin Gables
611-25 Ave SW T2S 0L7
866-271-7754 403-271-7754
Henry & Deirdre

89-225 $CAN BB
3 rooms, 3 pb
Visa, MC, AmEx,
Rated, •
C-ltd/S-no/P-no/H-no

Full breakfast
Special diets, stocked fridge,
chocolates, misc snacks in room
Computer, WiFi, Business Center,
telephone, iron, robes, A/C, fans, bath
amenities

Calgary's only Canada Select 5 Star Inn. Private entrance to gracious, tastefully decorated suites. Walk to downtown, Convention Center, Stampede park. 1 block from the Elbow River, restaurants and shopping. Delightful bed and breakfast accommodations.

✉ stay@twingables.ca 🌐 www.twingables.ca

Along River Ridge
1919 52 Street NW T3B 1C3
888-434-9555 403-247-1330
Dianne Haskell

79-149 $CAN BB
3 rooms, 3 pb
Visa, MC, AmEx,
Rated
C-ltd/S-no/P-no/H-ltd

Full breakfast
Afternoon tea, snacks, lunch & dinner
available, beverage station
Solarium, library, Jacuzzis, fireplaces,
Cable TV, VCR, DVD, Large screen TV,
WiFi, Steam shower

Experience 'A Touch of Country in the City', with the Bow River at your doorstep, city center less than 15 minutes away, and the majestic Rocky Mountains less than one hour away. Canada Select 4 star – restful, romantic "all seasons" retreat.

✉ haskell@alongriverridgebb.com 🌐 www.alongriverridgebb.com

Calgary Westways Guesthouse
216 25th Ave SW T2S 0L1
866-846-7038 403-229-1758
Jonathon Lloyd & Graham McKay

79-169 $CAN BB
5 rooms, 5 pb
Visa, MC, AmEx,
Rated, •
C-ltd/S-no/P-yes/H-no
French

Full breakfast
Romantic dinner for two
Sitting room, free WiFi, Jacuzzis,
fireplaces, high definition TV, office
center, bicycles

1912 Arts & Craft style Heritage Home, it is a 20 minute walk to downtown Calgary. All rooms have en suite or private baths and modern amenities. The only 3 Diamond AAA/CAA rated B&B in Calgary. Close to restaurants, pubs & river walks

✉ westways@shaw.ca 🌐 www.westways.ab.ca

Hughes House B&B
315 11th Ave NE T2E 0Z2
403-804-4431
Kelly Smith

65-140 $CAN BB
4 rooms, 3 pb
C-yes/S-no/P-ltd/H-no

Continental breakfast
Beverages & snacks on arrival
guest hospitality room[frig, micro,
laundry ect]free WiFi and long
distance calling, piano, fireplace,

Hughes House is an elegantly renovated 1914 Victorian home. From the moment you enter the foyer you'll feel the difference.For your comfort and safety guestrooms are all located on the 2nd and 3rd floors; above the foot and vehicular traffic.

✉ info@hugheshouse.ca 🌐 www.hugheshouse.ca

COCHRANE

Mountview Cottage
27 Mount View Est T4C 2B2
877-433 8193 403-932-4586
Neil & Marilyn Degraw

95-125 $CAN BB
3 rooms, 2 pb
Visa, MC, *Rated*, •
C-ltd/S-no/P-no/H-ltd
April 01 to December 30

Full breakfast
Evening tea or coffee or hot chocolate
with home-baked pastries
Sitting area w/fireplace, fridge, library,
pool table, garden patio, BBQ, horse
shoes, horse corral

Valley view with Rocky Mountains 180 degrees on the horizon. Beautiful park-like gardens with fish pond & benches to relax on 4 acres in the foot hills. Enjoy a stroll through wild flowers, tumbleweed & prairie wool. Experience a gourmet breakfast.

✉ degraw@nucleus.com 🌐 www.bbcanada.com/3681.html

JASPER

Astoria Hotel
404 Connaught Dr T0E 1E0
800-661-7343 780-852-3351
George Andrew

121-215 $CAN BB
35 rooms, 35 pb
Visa, MC, AmEx,
Rated, •
C-yes/S-no/P-no/H-no
French, German

Full breakfast
Restaurant, lunch, dinner, tea, snacks,
liquor store, pub food, liquor, beer,
wine, gourmet coffee
TV, DVD, mini fridge, coffee & tea,
hairdryer, iron, guest laundry, air
conditioning, free WiFi

The Astoria is a small hotel of character & charm located in the center of the village of Jasper in the largest National Park in the Canadian Rockies. It boasts clean comfortable rooms, an excellent restaurant and a popular pub.

✉ info@astoriahotel.com 🌐 www.astoriahotel.com

JASPER EAST

Overlander Mountain Lodge
Hwy 16 T7V 1X5
877-866-2330 780-866-2330
Garth & Kathy Griffiths

145-475 $CAN BB
27 rooms, 27 pb
Most CC, Cash,
Rated, •
C-yes/S-no/P-no/H-ltd
French, Spanish

Continental breakfast
Breakfast included mid-October to
mid-June. Seasonal lunch menu.
Dinner service starts at 5:30 pm.
Lounge, seasonal patio, library,
fireplaces, conference & wedding
facilities

Beautiful, romantic lodge overlooking Jasper National Park & the Canadian Rockies. Spectacular views & casual fine dining. Weddings, mountain biking/hiking trails, special packages.

✉ overland@telusplanet.net 🌐 www.overlandermountainlodge.com

ROCKY MOUNTAIN HOUSE

The Prairie Creek Inn
Box 22, Site 12, RR 2 T4T
2A2
403-844-2672
Terri & Larry Cameron

150-300 $US BB
10 rooms, 10 pb
Visa, MC, AmEx
C-yes/S-no/P-ltd/H-yes

Full breakfast
Cakes, cheese & crackers, chocolates,
etc. available for additional fee
Fireplace, satellite TV, wireless
Internet, breakfast delivery, weddings,
corporate meetings

In the heart of West Central Alberta near Rocky Mountain House lies a small but very special luxury bed and breakfast country inn called The Prairie Creek Inn. This handsome getaway is open year round and offers Canada Select 4.5 Star accommodations.

✉ theprairiecreekinn@telus.net 🌐 www.theprairiecreekinn.com

British Columbia

ANMORE

The Silver Door
1075 Thomson Rd V3H 4X9
604-949-1322
Reesa Devlin

150-195 $CAN BB
2 rooms, 2 pb
Visa, MC, *Rated*, •
C-ltd/S-no/P-no/H-no

Full breakfast
Snacks, fridge for personal items,
refreshments, bed snacks, fruit basket,
tea, juices coffee
Heated pool, hot tub, steam room,
infra red sauna, exercise room, pool
table, home theater, library

A retreat where the mountains touch the stars, where the deer roam and the black bear comes to call. This is our home. The color silver denotes an air of sophistication and excellence and defines the exemplary service and amenities that you will find.

✉ rdevlin@thesilverdoor.ca 🌐 www.thesilverdoor.ca

BRENTWOOD BAY

Benvenuto B&B
1130 Benvenuto Ave. V8M
1J6
888-544-1088 250-544-1088
Carrie & Clint Coleman

99-175 $CAN BB
3 rooms, 3 pb
Visa, MC, AmEx, •
C-ltd/S-ltd/P-ltd/H-no

Full breakfast
Coffee, variety of teas, hot chocolate,
water, etc.
Private entrances, high quality beds,
cable T.V.,free WiFi, bathrobes, extra
toiletries and much more!

Benvenuto Bed and Breakfast is located "next door to world famous Butchart Gardens." We are a three suite peaceful oasis with nature at your doorstep while being minutes away from downtown Victoria BC and many world class destinations!

✉ reservations@benvenutobandb.com 🌐 www.benvenutobandb.com

CLINTON

Poolside Paradise B&B
405 Spruce Ave V0K 1K0
250-459-7990
Lorne & Luan Bernhardt

80-100 $CAN BB
3 rooms, 3 pb
C-yes/S-ltd/P-no/H-ltd
American Sign
Language, some simple
Spanish

Full Gourmet breakfast
Also available special diet &
vegetarian meals. Beverage bar
(coffee, tea, cocoa) & popcorn
provided
Indoor pool, hot tub, guest den &
dining room, WiFi, in-room VCRs/TVs,
micro & refrig, library, BBQ

Themed bedrooms, queen beds, private baths, indoor pool, hot tub, gardens, solarium, guest dining room, den with movies. Full gourmet breakfast, will accommodate special diet & vegetarians. Romantic, private little paradise in Clinton, British Columbia

✉ poolsideparadisebb@bcwireless.com 🌐 www.poolsideparadisebb.com

COBBLE HILL

Cobble House B&B
3105 Cameron-Taggart
Rd V0R 1L6
866-743-2672 250-743-2672
Ingrid & Simon Vermegen

115-125 $CAN BB
3 rooms, 3 pb
Visa, MC, •
C-yes/S-ltd/P-no/H-ltd
Dutch, German

Full breakfast
Complimentary tea or coffee
Wireless Internet, sitting room,
Jacuzzi, cable TV, bar fridge in each
room, individual heat control

Cobble House is a peaceful haven in the heart of Vancouver Island's growing wine and culinary region in the Cowichan Valley. Centrally located on a forested acreage, we are still only 45 minutes north of Victoria.

✉ cobblehouse@shaw.ca 🌐 www.cobble-house.com

GABRIOLA

Marina's Hideaway
RR1, Site 14, C64 V0R 1X2
888-208-9850 250-247-8854
G. Brunell & R. Hayward

125-165 $US BB
3 rooms, 3 pb
Most CC, Cash, Checks
C-ltd/S-ltd/P-ltd/H-ltd

Full breakfast

We offer all of the amenities of a luxury hotel without the hassles or the pricing! If you are looking for a special treat, whether it's an anniversary, birthday, or just the need to get away, you will love the privacy and luxury of Marina's Hideaway.

✉ Georgene@marinashideaway.com 🌐 www.marinashideaway.com

Cobble House, Cobble Hill, BC

GABRIOLA ISLAND

WurHere B&B
3200 Coast Rd V0R 1X7
250-247-7345
Ken & Merrillee Wur

89-120 $US BB
2 rooms, 2 pb
Visa, MC, *Rated*, •
C-ltd/S-yes/P-no/H-no

Full breakfast
Coffee or tea, juice, breads, bar fridge, microwave
Self-contained rooms, cabins with private entrances, individual en-suites

Share the moments, share the days, share the love! Enjoy a unique bed and breakfast experience on this enchanted acreage. Each cabin is self-contained with a private entrance, kitchen area and an ensuite with heated floors. ✉ wurhere@shaw.ca ◐ www.wurherebandbgabriola.com

HALFMOON BAY

Rockwater Secret Cove Resort
Ole's Cove Rd V0N 1Y0
877-296-4593 604-885-7038
Kevin Toth

119-429 $CAN EP
38 rooms, 38 pb
Most CC, Cash, Checks
C-yes/S-no/P-ltd/H-yes

Cocktail bar, restaurant, catering, Sunday Brunch from 11 am to 1 pm
Patio, games room, outdoor heated pool, massage & spa services

The best kept secret among Sunshine Coast Accommodations is Rockwater Secret Cove Resort. What was once the Lord Jim's Resort Hotel, this magical oasis has been transformed into a private paradise for distinguished guests.

✉ reservations@rockwatersecretcoveresort.com ◐ www.rockwatersecretcoveresort.com

KELOWNA

A Lakeview Heights B&B
3626 Royal Gala Dr V4T 2N9
800-967-1319 250-707-1234
Anne & Mike Murphy

105-155 $CAN BB
3 rooms, 3 pb
Visa, MC, *Rated*
C-ltd/S-no/P-no/H-ltd
French, some German & Italian.

Extensive gourmet breakfast
Vegetarian or special diets by advance request, welcoming beverage on arrival, in-room tea & coffee
Guest living room, view patio with outdoor furniture, local area touring assistance & reservations

Imagine . . . a Canada Select 4-star B&B with spectacular lake, mountain & vineyard views, where you can enjoy luxury accommodations with private bathrooms, warm hospitality and gourmet breakfasts at an affordable price . . . that's A Lakeview Heights B&B.

✉ info@mountainsideaccommodations.com ◐ www.mountainsideaccommodations.com/lakeview

A Touch of English
5 Alameda Ct V1V 1C6
888 338-1054 250 448-6250
Clare & Kelly Sucloy

125-155 $CAN BB
4 rooms, 4 pb
Visa, MC, *Rated*
C-ltd/S-ltd/P-ltd/H-no

4 Course – Gourmet Breakfast
All dietary needs met, gluten free, celiac, vegetarian, afternoon Tea served upon arrival. Enjoy !
Elegant guest living room, patio overlooking swimming pool, English gardens, views of downtown

Welcome to A Touch of English B&B – afternoon tea with home-made scones and fresh fruit, amazing views of the valley & city lights, relax in the large swimming pool, newly renovated rooms with king size beds + self-contained full suite, private entrance.

✉ clare@touchofenglish.com ◐ www.touchofenglish.com

KELOWNA

Aaron's Pool & Spa B&B
2160 Wilkinson St V1Y 3Z8
250-860-6814
Rick & Marie Gruenke

95-150 $CAN BB
2 rooms, 2 pb
Visa, MC, *Rated*
C-yes/S-no/P-no/H-ltd

Continental plus breakfast
In-room coffee & fridge
In-ground swimming pool, spa-suite,
TV/DVD movies & cable Internet in
rooms, pampering inclusions

We are tucked into a nice, quiet residential area, conveniently located close to the lake, shopping and downtown Kelowna. Enjoy breakfast in the privacy of your own suite or when weather permits, on the patio by the pool.   ✉ info@kelownabb.com 🌐 www.kelownabb.com

MALAHAT

Prancing Horse Retreat
573 Ebedora Ln V0R 2L0
877-887-8834 250-743-9378
Elaine & Allan Dillabaugh

99-275 $CAN BB
5 rooms, 5 pb
Visa, MC, *Rated*, •
C-yes/S-no/P-no/H-ltd

Full breakfast
Restaurant
Tennis, Jacuzzis, pool, suites,
fireplace, cable TV, accommodations
for business travelers

Our Victorian Villa is located just 20 minutes north of Victoria, overlooking the ocean and snow-capped Olympic mountain range. Our luxury suites offer double tubs and fireplaces.

✉ stay@prancinghorse.com 🌐 www.prancinghorse.com

NANAIMO

Copper Kettle
465 Stewart Ave V9S 4C7
877-740-3977 250-740-3977
Fiona & Maurice

100-125 $CAN BB
3 rooms, 3 pb
Visa, MC, *Rated*
C-ltd/S-no/P-no/H-no

Full breakfast
Tea and Coffee maker in each Room.
Discuss special diets or allergies if
required.
Clean rooms, ensuite bathrooms/
shower, bathrobes, slippers, radio/
alarm clock, kettle, coffeemaker,

We invite you to come for a comfortable and peaceful stay with us where you can enjoy the natural atmosphere where the city meets the sea shore. 5 min walk to downtown.

✉ info@copperkettlebc.com 🌐 www.copperkettlebc.com

Flying Cloud B&B
581 Cumberland Pl V9T 4S5
888-303-2413 250-758-2083
Vivian & Neil Reinhart

125-175 $CAN BB
3 rooms, 3 pb
Visa, MC
C-ltd/S-ltd/P-no/H-no

Full breakfast
West Coast theme lounge, wine &
cheese reception on deck 4–6pm,
cookies, tea, coffee, popcorn, water
Four fireplaces, billiard room, views of
the bay, three decks, hot tub, infared
sauna, Internet

An amazing Nanaimo location with views on Vancouver Island. Come and experience Vancouver Island hospitality with hosts Neil & Vivian Reinhart in their lofty Flying Cloud Bed & Breakfast.

✉ info@flyingcloudbedandbreakfast.com 🌐 www.flyingcloudbedandbreakfast.com

Hammond Bay Oceanside B&B
3804 Hammond Bay Rd V9T 1G3
250-618-4300 250-751-1409
Karen & Bill Stant

100-125 $US BB
2 rooms, 2 pb
Visa, MC
C-ltd/S-no/P-no/H-no

Full breakfast
Private kitchen facilities, picnic area
available to guests, morning coffee on
our private patio.
Picturesque views of Georgia Strait
and the Coastal Mountains, private
entrances.

Two comfortable oceanside rooms with private entrances, bathrooms and kitchen facilities in Nanaimo. Private beach is at your doorstep. Quiet peaceful retreat on the east coast of Vancouver Island.

✉ hammondbaybb@Shaw.ca 🌐 www.hammondbaybb.com

Long Lake Waterfront B&B
240 Ferntree Place V9T 5M1
877-758-5010 250-758-5010
Gordie & Janice Robinson

100-175 $CAN BB
3 rooms, 3 pb
Visa, MC, *Rated*, •
C-ltd/S-ltd/P-ltd/H-no

Full breakfast
Fresh fruit, yogurt, refreshments and
hot entree varying every day.
Air-conditioning, fridge, ensuite with
shower and/or Jacuzzi, WiFi, canoe,
kayaks and pedal boat

Retreat to an old growth forest in the middle of thriving Nanaimo! Long Lake Waterfront B&B features 3 private luxury suites, and guests rave about our exceptional customer service, privacy, lakeside fun, excellent breakfasts and wonderful conversation!

✉ frontdesk@LodgingNanaimo.com 🌐 www.lodgingnanaimo.com

NORTH SAANICH

The Glenelg B&B
9574 Glenelg Ave V8L 5H2
250-656-3629
Eric & Hayato

110-135 $CAN BB
2 rooms, 2 pb
Visa, MC
C-ltd/S-no/P-no/H-no

Full breakfast
Complimentary coffee or tea in our
Guest Lounge
King or Queen beds, Finnish Sauna
Use, fluffy bathrobes, private patio, in-
house laundry

The Glenelg is a beautiful West Coast, contemporary home with separate area for guests including a beautiful private lounge and patio. Surrounded by nature and enjoying clean air and close proximity to the Butchart Gardens and all other amenities.

✉ akabane@telus.net 🌐 www.theglenelg.com

NORTH VANCOUVER

Crystal's View
420 Tempe Crescent V7N
1E6
604-987-3952
Crystal Davis

135-295 $CAN BB
3 rooms, 3 pb
Visa, MC, *Rated*, •
C-ltd/S-no/P-no/H-no

Full home cooked breakfast
Tea, coffee, cookies, refreshments
Panoramic views, double Jacuzzi,
sundeck, fireplace, plasma TV/DVD

Outstanding panoramic views from every room from this luxurious Bed and Breakfast. Experience modern comforts and fine European hospitality. Centrally located in a quiet neighborhood. Canada Select 4½ Stars!   ✉ Crysview@shaw.ca 🌐 www.bc-bedandbreakfast.com

**Lockhaven Waterfront
B&B**
2136 Lockehaven Rd V7G
1X6
604-928-8225
Denise and Noulan Bowker

165-339 $CAN BB
2 rooms, 2 pb
Visa, MC, AmEx,
Rated, •
S-no/P-no/H-no

Continental Mon-Sat, full Sunday
In-suite kitchenettes
private outdoor Jacuzzi hot tubs,
shared laundry, in-suite computers,
wireless Internet & phones

Right by the ocean with stunning views, Lockehaven offers luxury and privacy with 2 large self-contained suites with exterior hot tubs. Located in idyllic Deep Cove, it is only a 25 minute drive to downtown Vancouver.   ✉ hosts@lockehaven.ca 🌐 www.lockehaven.ca

ThistleDown House
3910 Capilano Rd V7R 4J2
888-633-7173 604-986-7173
Rex Davidson

110-295 $CAN BB
6 rooms, 6 pb
Visa, MC, *Rated*, •
C-ltd/S-no/P-no/H-no
German
February to November

Full Gourmet Breakfast
Afternoon tea of homemade pies,
cakes or pastries served in the lounge
or the garden; sherry & port
Goose down or silk-filled duvets,
antiques, fireplaces, library, gardens,
WiFi, full concierge

Internationally acclaimed, ThistleDown is a 1920 Craftsman-style, heritage-listed home, restored with great care & filled with antiques, handcrafted furnishings & works of art from around the world. Breakfast is deliciously gourmet, service is impeccable.

✉ info@thistle-down.com 🌐 www.thistle-down.com

PEMBERTON

Greenwood Country Inn
1371 Greenwood St V0N 2L0
604-894-5607
Margit de Haan

120-175 $CAN BB
3 rooms, 3 pb
Visa, MC
C-yes/S-no/P-ltd/H-ltd
German

Full breakfast
Home-cooked dinners by request
Kitchenette, small weddings, local art,
decks, fireplace, lounge, Jacuzzi suite,
deck with hot tub

Nestled on a bluff high above the village of Pemberton, British Columbia, offering unparalleled views from every direction. Take your breath away beauty!

✉ reserve@greenwoodcountryinn.com 🌐 www.greenwoodcountryinn.com

PENDER ISLAND

Oceanside Inn
4230 Armadale Rd V0N 2M0
800-601-3284 250-629-6691
Bill & Maggie Rumford

139-239 $CAN BB
3 rooms, 3 pb
Visa, MC
S-no/P-no/H-no
May thru October

Full breakfast
Complimentary beverages in room
Sitting room, library, private hot tubs/
deck, suites, fireplaces, restaurants
nearby

Oceanside is nestled on 3 acres of oceanfront, with beach access where our guests can retreat from the rapid pace of city life. Privacy is characteristic of life at Oceanside. Private outdoor hot tubs for all rooms.

✉ oceanside@penderisland.com 🌐 www.penderisland.com

PRINCE RUPERT

Eagle Bluff Lighthouse B&B
201 Cow Bay Rd V8J 1A2
800-833-1550 250-627-4955
Mary Allen & Bryan Cox

80-125 $CAN BB
7 rooms, 5 pb
Visa, MC, *Rated*
C-yes/S-no/P-no/H-ltd

Full breakfast
Tea, coffee & kitchen facilities, common area
Full decks and sitting room, phone/fax and Internet

Experience Prince Rupert's waterfront. Fully renovated heritage home in historic Cow Bay with comfortable rooms and extraordinary views! ✉ eaglebed@citytel.net ◐ www.citytel.net/eaglebluff

RICHMOND

Doorknocker B&B
13211 Steveston Hwy V6W 1A5
866-877-8714 604-277-8714
Jeanette & Chris

89-139 $CAN BB
3 rooms, 3 pb
Visa, MC, AmEx, •
C-ltd/S-no/P-no/H-no
German

and special diets
Coffee & assorted teas, filtered water, cookies
Free wireless Internet, free onsite parking, gardens, gazebo, heated indoor pool, sauna, art gallery

The Doorknocker B&B is a Tudor-style Mansion on an estate surrounded by gardens and mountain views. Central to everything in Vancouver, a luxurious quiet getaway in the city. Beautiful rooms, fantastic breakfasts, great rates, the best place to stay.
✉ thedoorknocker@shaw.ca ◐ www.thedoorknocker.com

SALT SPRING ISLAND

Sky Valley Inn
421 Sky Valley Rd V8K 2C3
866-537-1028 250-537-9800
Richard Slosky

170-220 $CAN BB
3 rooms, 3 pb
Visa, MC, *Rated*
C-ltd/S-no/P-no/H-ltd

Gourmet breakfast
A complimentary decanter of sipping Sherry
Gardens, pool, fireplace, fresh cut flowers, a complimentary decanter of sipping Sherry, robes

Sky Valley is a Salt Spring Island Bed and Breakfast and the island's only luxury French country retreat, on eleven acres of natural beauty.
✉ info@skyvalleyinn.com ◐ www.skyvalleyinn.com

SIDNEY

Beacon Inn at Sidney
9724 Third St V8L 3A2
877-420-5499 250-655-3288

119-259 $CAN BB
9 rooms, 9 pb
Visa, MC, AmEx,
Rated, •
C-ltd/S-no/P-no/H-no
French

Full gourmet breakfast
Common area guest fridge & coffee/tea station with snacks.
Guest lounge w/fireplace, newspapers, free off-street parking, concierge, afternoon Sherry, WiFi.

The Area's only 5-Star property. Near Victoria, Butchart Gardens, ferries & airport. Luxurious guestrooms with spa-like ensuite bathrooms, soaker or jetted tubs, A/C, F/P's, WiFi , CD player/radios. Stroll to local shops, restaurants & the waterfront.
✉ info@beaconinns.com ◐ www.thebeaconinn.com

SOOKE

Cape Cod B&B
5782 Anderson Cove Rd V0S 1N0
888-814-7773 250-642-3253
Gwendolyn Ginman

130-160 $CAN BB
1 rooms, 1 pb
Visa, MC, AmEx, •
C-yes/S-ltd/P-no/H-ltd
French, German

Full breakfast
Snacks, fresh fruit, complimentary sherry
Sitting room, library, kitchen, BBQ, satellite TV/PPV/VCR/DVD, private patio.

Cape Cod style home nestled in two wooded acres with spectacular ocean and forest views on the south-west coast of Vancouver Island. Self-contained suite is totally private and peaceful. A scenic forty minute drive from Victoria and the Butchart Gardens.
✉ capecodbb@shaw.ca ◐ www.capecodbnb.bc.ca

Sooke Harbour House
RR #4 V9Z 0T4
800-889-9688 250-642-3421
Sinclair & Frederique Philip

259-659 $CAN BB
28 rooms, 28 pb
Visa, MC, *Rated*, •
C-yes/S-no/P-yes/H-yes
French

Full or continental breakfast
Dinner, restaurant
Wet bars ,fireplaces, sitting room, piano, steam showers, Jacuzzi, infared sauna, library, bikes, cooking

Romantic little inn right on the water, located 45 minutes southwest of Victoria on Vancouver Island, BC. Wonderful attention to detail in every area of the inn.
✉ info@sookeharbourhouse.com ◐ www.sookeharbourhouse.com

SPENCES BRIDGE

The Inn at Spences Bridge
3649 Hwy #8 V0K 2LO
877-354-1997 250-458-2311
Ray Nigalis

68-118 $CAN BB
12 rooms, 5 pb
Visa, MC, AmEx,
Rated, •
C-yes/S-ltd/P-ltd/H-yes
Limited French

Continental breakfast
Restaurant open 11am – 9pm, full
menu, vegetarian
Lounge, riverside dining, gift shop,
library, hiking, bicycles

A beautiful country inn and B&B on the scenic Thompson River. Comfortable lodging & fine vegetarian dining in BC's oldest operating hotel, just 3.5 hrs NE of Vancouver through the Fraser Canyon.

✉ theinn@spencesbridge.ca 🌐 www.spencesbridge.ca

SURREY

Apple Creek B&B
14686 32nd Ave V4P 2J2
604-760-7077
Beverley Olafson

100-175 $CAN BB
3 rooms
Visa, MC, •
C-yes/S-no/P-ltd/H-no

hearty, home-cooked breakfast
Tea, coffee, beverages & light evening
snacks, special diet meal preparation
may be arranged
Free wireless Internet, indoor
swimming pool, Jacuzzi, TV/DVD/VCR
entertainment area

Regarded as one of the premier homes in the Vancouver region, on five landscaped acres. Furnished with a world class collection of Canadian antiques, fireplaces, squash court & indoor pool. Beach & golf nearby. A luxury private or corporate retreat stay.

✉ info@applecreekbb.com 🌐 www.applecreekbb.com

B&B on the Ridge
5741 146th St V3S 2Z5
888-697-4111 604-591-6065
Dale & Mary Fennell

80-140 $CAN BB
3 rooms, 3 pb
Rated
C-ltd/S-ltd/P-no/H-no
Hungarian

Full breakfast
Snacks, refreshments upon arrival,
nightly goodies, coffee & tea making
facilities
Cable TV/VCR/DVD, wireless Internet
Access, Tourist Info, Free Local Calls,
Free Parking, Sundeck

Escape from the city to a delightful, tastefully decorated B&B situated on ½ acre, with a quiet country atmosphere. This comfortable escape from the city is conveniently located to everything the Greater Vancouver area has to offer.

✉ stay@bbridgesurrey.com 🌐 www.bbridgesurrey.com

VANCOUVER

A TreeHouse B&B
2490 W 49th Ave V6M 2V3
877-266-2960 604-266-2962
Barb & Bob Selvage

109-199 $CAN BB
4 rooms, 2 pb
Visa, MC, AmEx,
Rated, •
C-ltd/S-ltd/P-no/H-no

Full gourmet breakfast
Courtesy beverage for celebrations,
chocolates on the pillow, in room tea,
coffee, filtered water
Wireless Internet, free calls to
US&Canada, TV/DVDs, Entertainment
Books, parking, concierge service

"Bauhaus Mood, Zen Spirit": modern contemporary home featuring contemporary art, warm hospitality, personalized service, and substantial, gourmet breakfasts. A TreeHouse offers refined simplicity in a beautiful, exclusive neighborhood.

✉ bb@treehousebb.com 🌐 www.treehousebb.com

AAA Catherine's B&B
668 E 29 Ave V5V 2R9
800-463-9933 604-875-8968
Catherine Vong

59-169 $CAN BB
12 rooms, 10 pb
Visa, MC, AmEx, •
C-yes/S-no/P-no/H-no
most Asian languages

Full breakfast
Internet, VCR/cable in guest lounge,
discounted local tour rates and car
rental

We offer year round, affordable bed and breakfast accommodations with spectacular views near all major Vancouver tourist attractions, transportation, parks and recreation. Free computer use and unlimited wireless Internet. Mini gym for your use.

✉ bnbvancouver@gmail.com 🌐 www.aaabedandbreakfast.com

VANCOUVER

Barclay House
1351 Barclay St V6E 1H6
800-971-1351 604-605-1351
Maria Siy

145-275 $CAN BB
6 rooms, 6 pb
Visa, MC, AmEx,
Rated, •
C-ltd/S-no/P-no/H-no

Full 3-course gourmet breakfast
Assorted pastries and fruit
Wifi, cable, DVD, alarm, fridge, coffee/
tea, robes, hairdryers, safes, free
parking & local calls

Downtown! AAA 3 Diamonds!Voted best Vancouver B&B by The Independent! Best Lodging in Vancouver by The Vancouver Sun! Recommended by Los Angeles Times!

✉ info@barclayhouse.com ◐ www.barclayhouse.com

English Bay Inn
1968 Comox St V6G 1R4
866-683-8002 604-683-8002
Boban Vuckovic

149-299 $CAN BB
6 rooms, 6 pb
Most CC, Cash,
Rated, •
C-ltd/S-no/P-no/H-no
Spanish, Greek Korean,
Malay, Serbian, Italian
etc.

Full breakfast
Tea, coffee, port, sherry
Sitting rooms, library, fireplace,
laundry, concierge, restaurant
reservations etc.

Tucked away between high-rise apartments in a quiet corner of Vancouver's Downtown West End offering an unexpected hideaway in the heart of the city. Walk to Stanley Park, English Bay Beach, and downtown.

✉ stay@englishbayinn.com ◐ www.englishbayinn.com

House on Dunbar B & B
3926 20 Ave West V6S 1G4
604-224-6355
Joanne Renwick

110-165 $CAN BB
3 rooms, 3 pb
Visa, MC, AmEx, •
S-no/P-no/H-no

Full or Healthy Heart breakfast
Full kitchen for guest use,
complimentary tea, coffee, soft drinks
and snacks available
Computer with high speed and
wireless Internet, 50' plasma TV, free
laundry, luscious yard

House On Dunbar is a spacious, contemporary and comfortable B&B that offers guests the warmth and comforts of home and provides an ideal home base to explore all Vancouver has to offer. We provide everything you want and more . . . Indulge yourself.

✉ houseondunbarbandb@gmail.com ◐ houseondunbarbandb.com

Kings Corner B&B
4006 Glen Dr V5V 4T3
604-879-7997
Anne & Christopher King

70-150 $CAN BB
2 rooms, 2 pb
C-yes/S-no/P-ltd/H-no

Full breakfast
Wireless Internet, hot tub, kitchenette,
privates entrance

You'll always receive a warm welcome at King's Corner 1912 heritage Vancouver bed and breakfast home. With our central location in a quiet residential neighborhood it is the perfect place to stay!

✉ talkischeap@shaw.ca ◐ www.kingscornerbb.com

Manor Guest House
345 West 13th Ave V5Y 1W2
604-876-8494
Brenda Yablon

95-310 $US BB
26 rooms, 20 pb
Visa, MC, *Rated*
C-ltd/S-no/P-no/H-no
French, German

Full gourmet vegetarian breakfast
Guest kitchen use, dinner by prior
arrangement
Conference facilities for up to 25,
parlor & music room, English garden,
decks, guest lounge

An Edwardian mansion on the southeastern edge of downtown Vancouver, in a safe & elegant neighborhood. Spacious rooms, private baths, free parking. Top-floor suite sleeps six. Close to shopping, restaurants & public transit. ✉ info@manorguesthouse.com ◐ www.manorguesthouse.com

---

Nelson House B&B
977 Broughton St V6G 2A4
866-684-9793 604-684-9793
David Ritchie

88-198 $CAN BB
6 rooms, 4 pb
Visa, MC
C-ltd/S-ltd/P-no/H-no
French
Closed 12/24,25,31 & 1/1

Full Canadian Breakfast
Mini-refrigerators & filtered water
in some rooms, tea & coffee in the
Shangri-La Suite
Off-street parking included, 3 decks,
garden, fireplaces, library, WiFi,
hairdryers, ensuite Jacuzzi

Downtown, where you want to be! West End location only steps to the best of Vancouver, near Stanley Park and Robson Street shopping. Character, comfort, convenience for business and vacation.

✉ info@downtownbedandbreakfast.com ◐ www.downtownbedandbreakfast.com

VANCOUVER

Stanley Park Inn
1030 Chilco St V6G 4R6
604-683-8063
Bob Chapin

250-350 $CAN BB
3 rooms, 3 pb
Visa, MC, AmEx
C-yes/S-no/P-no/H-ltd

Full breakfast
Sherry & port in the afternoon &
evening
Parlour, library, high-speed wireless
Internet

Experience the elegance of bygone eras and Vancouver's natural appeal. Exquisite 18th and 19th century English and French antiques in a restored 1930s Tudor-style home, 1 block from Stanley Park, English Bay.

✉ info@stanleyparkinn.com 🌐 www.stanleyparkinn.com

VERNON

Lakeside Illahee Inn
15010 Tamarack Dr V1B 2E1
888-260-7896 250-260-7896
Peter & Debbie Dooling

114-379 $CAN BB
5 rooms, 5 pb
Visa, MC, *Rated*, •
C-ltd/S-no/P-no/H-ltd
German

Full breakfast
Lakeshore sunset dining by
reservation May to October of each
year. Corporate boardroom services.
Day lounge, outdoor hot-tub,
lakeshore patio, on the water sitting
dock, kayaks, firepit, sand beach WiFi

Free Night w/Certificate: Not valid July-Aug. Room Upgrade.

A superlative Waterfront Boutique Inn on Lake Kalamalka. Awarded the "6th Best on the Waterfront" for B&B/Country Inns throughout North America. Distinguished as "the Jewel of the Okanagan" for fine accommodations, and amenities by North American Inns.

✉ info@illahee.com 🌐 www.illahee.com

VICTORIA

Abbeymoore Manor
1470 Rockland Ave V8S 1W2
888-801-1811 250-370-1470
Anne, Ian & Michelle

139-249 $CAN BB
7 rooms, 7 pb
Visa, MC, *Rated*, •
C-ltd/S-no/P-ltd/H-no

Gourmet Breakfast
Tea & coffee station, guest refrigerator
with complimentary soft drinks, fresh
fruit & snacks
High-speed Internet access, library,
2 daily newspapers, Aveda beauty
products in every room

Choose from 5 gorgeous heritage B&B rooms or for the ultimate in privacy several self-contained suites at ground level. We are a short drive to downtown and a block from Craigdarroch Castle and the 36 acre estate. TripAdvisor's #1 B&B in Victoria since '05

✉ innkeeper@abbeymoore.com 🌐 www.abbeymoore.com

Abigail's Hotel
906 McClure St V8V 3E7
800-561-6565 250-388-5363
Nick Saklas

169-349 $CAN BB
23 rooms, 23 pb
Visa, MC, AmEx,
Rated, •
C-yes/S-no/P-ltd/H-no

Full gourmet breakfast for two
Complimentary light evening hors
d'oeuvres at 5:00 pm, plus coffee and
tea 24 hours a day.
Wine, Beer & Champagne Service; Spa
services, gift shop; 24 hr concierge,
free parking & Internet

Experience the charm of this unique bed & breakfast boutique hotel, just steps from Victoria's famous attractions, museums and parks! Includes a 3-course gourmet breakfast, evening appetizers, local calls, parking & Internet.

✉ innkeeper@abigailshotel.com 🌐 www.abigailshotel.com

Albion Manor Bed & Breakfast
224 Superior St V8V 1T3
877-389-0012 250-389-0012
Don Halton & Fernando
Garcia

99-199 $CAN BB
8 rooms, 8 pb
Visa, MC, *Rated*, •
C-ltd/S-ltd/P-ltd/H-ltd

Full gourmet breakfast
We are happy to provide for your
dietary needs be they vegetarian
gluten free, etc.
Gardens, patios, balconies, fireplaces,
Jacuzzis, special packages & surprises
available

Our gracious 1892 Heritage Home is located on a peaceful oak-tree lined street in the historic James Bay district, a 5 minute walk from the US ferry terminal, the ocean, shopping and Victoria's major venues. The crowning touch to your Victoria visit.

✉ info@albionmanor.com 🌐 www.albionmanor.com

Abigail's Hotel, Victoria, BC

VICTORIA

Ambrosia Historic B&B	135-285 $CAN BB	Full breakfast
522 Quadra St. V8V 3S3	4 rooms, 4 pb	Jetted tubs for two, rain showers,
877-262-7672 250-380-7705	Visa, MC, AmEx,	concierge, Aveda products, Frette
Bob & Dawna Bailey	*Rated*, •	linens, in-room spa services
	S-no/P-no/H-no	

The historic Ambrosia B&B offers the ultimate in luxury, romance and relaxation, in the heart of Victoria's Downtown. Our spacious rooms have private en-suite bathroom, renovated in 2004. Gourmet breakfast, our amenities set the tone for a great time.

✉ stay@ambrosiavictoria.com 🌐 www.ambrosiavictoria.com

Amethyst Inn at Regents Park	149-399 $CAN BB	Full Gourmet Breakfast
1501 Fort St V8S 1Z6	13 rooms, 13 pb	Bottled water & soft drinks, evening
888-265-6499 250-595-2053	Most CC, *Rated*, •	sherry, tea, coffee & cookies in the
Abel	C-ltd/S-no/P-no/H-no	parlour
	Japanese, Mandarin	High speed wireless Internet,
		telephone, cable TV, DVD, CD player
		in all rooms

Built in 1885, Amethyst Inn authentically reflects the Victorian era. Victoria's exceptionally romantic inn, awarded "Best Breakfast in Canada," Inn Traveler, 2005.

✉ innkeeper@amethyst-inn.com 🌐 www.amethyst-inn.com

Ashcroft House B&B	109-199 $CAN BB	Full breakfast
670 Battery St V8V 1E5	5 rooms, 5 pb	Coffee, tea, bottled water, fresh fruit
866-385-4632 250-385-4632	Most CC, Cash, Checks	TV, VCR, electric fireplace, kitchenette,
Paulanne & David	C-ltd/S-ltd/P-no/H-no	WiFi, guest computer, laundry
		facilities, bike storage

The little touches and attention to details at our Victoria bed and breakfast will leave you wishing you had more time here! At Ashcroft House B&B, we know you will enjoy its unmistakable sense of comfort, peace and all those sunny windows!

✉ Paulanne@AshcroftHouseBandB.com 🌐 www.AshcroftHouseBandB.com

---

Tell your hosts Pamela Lanier sent you.

VICTORIA

Binners'...A **Contemporary Oasis** 58 Linden Ave V8V 4C8 888-409-5800 250-383-5442 Binners & Edward Davidson	89-245 $CAN BB 3 rooms, 3 pb Most CC, Cash, *Rated*, • C-ltd/S-ltd/P-no/H-ltd Some French	Gourmet multi-course breakfast In-room microwave, coffeemaker, bar fridge with soft drinks, spring water; in-room coffee & teas WiFi, guest computer, concierge services, in-room phones, in-room spa services, jetted tubs

4.5 star boutique-style B&B with elegant, comfortable suites & rooms. Fireplaces, Jacuzzis, gourmet 3-course breakfast. Just 3 minutes from downtown and ½ block to stunning ocean & mountain views & walkways. Concierge & spa services available.

✉ hosts@binners.com 🌐 www.BinnersVictoria.com

Cycle Inn B&B 3158 Anders Rd V9B 4C4 877-829-2531 250-478-6821 Joanne Cowan	75-125 $CAN BB 3 rooms, 2 pb *Rated* C-yes/S-ltd/P-ltd/H-ltd French, German, Spanish,	Delicious breakfast Drinks on the deck, or English style tea Rec room fridge, sauna, VCR, library, games, bicycle lock up, maps, swings, BBQ, deck, boats, quiet

A lovely waterfront residence located on the famous Galloping Goose Trail. Whether you have come to see your child safely into the new school, you are on a golfing holiday, or in business meetings, by evening this is a must stay! ✉ stay@cycleinn.com 🌐 www.cycleinn.com

Dashwood Manor Seaside **Heritage B&B** 1 Cook St V8V 3W6 800-667-5517 250-385-5517 Dave & Sharon Layzell	109-289 $CAN BB 11 rooms, 11 pb Visa, MC, *Rated*, • C-ltd/S-no/P-no/H-no French	Full gourmet breakfast Knowledgeable and experienced owners offer valuable assistance with trip planning and reservations.

Best ocean views in Victoria! Dashwood Manor is Victoria's only seaside heritage B&B in walking distance to downtown. Breathtaking views of the ocean and snow-capped mountains of Washington's Olympic Peninsula from each guestroom.

✉ info@dashwoodmanor.com 🌐 www.dashwoodmanor.com

Gazebo Bed & Breakfast 5460 Old W Saanich Rd V9E 2A7 877-211-2288 250-727-2420 Linda & Martin Vernon	155-220 $CAN BB 3 rooms, 3 pb Visa, MC, *Rated*, • C-ltd/S-no/P-no/H-ltd	Full breakfast Complimentary beverages Wireless Internet, guest computer & printer, massages, double Jacuzzis, fireplaces, glorious garden

Relax at a Victorian manor house near the Butchart Gardens in a quiet central location. Stay in a secluded cottage or elegant rooms surrounded by lovely gardens. Massages, packages available. WiFi. Canada Select 5 Stars at 4 star prices.

✉ stay@gazebo-victoria.com 🌐 www.gazebo-victoria.com

Humboldt House B&B Inn 867 Humboldt St V8V 2Z6 888-383-0327 250-383-0152 David & Vlasta Booth	129-295 $CAN BB 6 rooms, 6 pb Visa, MC, AmEx, *Rated*, • C-ltd/S-no/P-no/H-no Czech, German, French	Full Gourmet breakfast Afternoon tea, complimentary sparkling wine, truffles Sitting room, library, Jacuzzis, suites, fireplaces, cable TV

Victoria's most romantic and private B&B. Relax by firelight in your Jacuzzi, and feast on a gourmet breakfast in the privacy of your room. Large windows offer a peaceful view of neighbouring St. Ann's Academy and its apple orchard. ✉ rooms@humboldthouse.com 🌐 www.humboldthouse.com

Marketas B&B 239 Superior St V8V 1T4 250-384-9844 Marketa	85-155 $CAN BB 7 rooms, 6 pb Visa, MC, AmEx, *Rated*, • C-yes/S-ltd/P-ltd/H-ltd Czech, French	Full breakfast of choice from menu Home made muffins, tea, coffee during the day, complimentary Port wine Jacuzzis, fireplaces, full gourmet breakfast of your choice from the menu and free parking.

Marketa runs a warm and friendly hostelry accommodation with European flair, close to downtown Victoria. Whether you're visiting Victoria on a family break, romantic getaway, or business, this bed and breakfast's uniquely decorated rooms will enchant you!

✉ info@marketas.com 🌐 www.marketas.com

VICTORIA

**Spinnakers Brewpub &
Guest House**
308 Catherine St V9A 3S8
877-838-2739 250-386-2739
Paul Hadfield

149-279 $CAN BB
10 rooms, 10 pb
Visa, MC, AmEx,
Rated, •
C-ltd/S-no/P-ltd/H-ltd

Gourmet Breakfast Basket
Lunch served from 11am to 4pm,
dinner from 4pm to 10:30pm
Restaurant, Bar, Free Wireless Internet
Access, Free Parking, Water & Truffles
on Arrival

From Canada's oldest brewpub, the guesthouses offer heritage and contemporary accommodations in luxurious rooms with queen beds and deluxe bedding, Jacuzzi tubs, wood or gas fireplaces, original art and breakfast.

✉ fdmanager@spinnakers.com 🌐 www.spinnakers.com

WHISTLER

Cedar Springs B&B Lodge
8106 Camino Drive V0N 1B8
800-727-7547 604-938-8007
Joern & Jackie Rohde

99-279 $CAN BB
8 rooms, 6 pb
Visa, MC, AmEx, •
C-yes/S-no/P-no/H-ltd
German

Full breakfast
Home baked snacks for afternoon tea,
complimentary tea & coffee. Iced tea
in the summer
Guest lounge with TV/DVD/VCR, wet
bar, hot tub, decks, gardens, bike
rentals;shuttle;free wireless

Casual Canadian hospitality and comfort. Sumptuous breakfasts, seasonal afternoon teas and dinners; fireside living and dining room. Comfortable rooms; sauna, hot tub. Canada Select 3 Star Rating.

✉ info@whistlerinns.com 🌐 www.whistlerbb.com

Golden Dreams
6412 Easy St V0N 1B6
800-668-7055 604-932-2667
Ann & Terry Spence

115-175 $CAN BB
3 rooms, 1 pb
Visa, MC, •
C-ltd/S-ltd/P-ltd/H-no
German, French

Homecooked nutritious breakfast
Will cater to vegetarian/special diets,
complimentary snacks for apres ski,
welcome drink in summer
Free wireless Internet. Daily
housekeeping. Eco-friendly B&B,
recycling, composting, chemical-free!

Serving GREAT B&B memories since 1987 with our true west coast hospitality! Be surrounded by mountain beauty, choose one of our unique THEME rooms and awaken to a wholesome breakfast. In hosts words: "Arrive as strangers, leave as friends."

✉ ann@goldendreamswhistler.com 🌐 www.goldendreamswhistler.com

Marshlands Inn, Sackville, NB

New Brunswick

LAKEVILLE

Auberge Wild Rose Inn	99-250 $CAN BB	Full breakfast
17 Baseline Rd E1H 1N5	16 rooms, 16 pb	The inn provides dinner by
888-389-7673 506-383-9751	Visa, MC, AmEx,	reservation only from 5:30 to 8:00 in
dennis wu	*Rated*, •	the evening
	C-ltd/S-no/P-no/H-no	Sitting room, whirlpools, suites,
	French	fireplaces, cable LCD HD TV, business
		travelers, wireless Internet

Cozy, comfortable inn exudes romance from the warm fireplaces to the quaint antiques. This, coupled with a gourmet breakfast makes for a memorable stay. Canada Select 4½ star rating, jet whirlpool, LCD HD TV, free Internet, licensed restaurant, view.

✉ wildroseinn@hotmail.com 🌐 www.wildroseinn.com

SACKVILLE

Marshlands Inn	99-205 $CAN EP	Licensed fine dining
55 Bridge St E4L 3N8	18 rooms, 18 pb	Parlours, fireplaces, gardens,
800-561-1266 506-536-0170	Visa, MC	verandas, antique store
Lucy & Barry Dane	C-yes/S-no/P-ltd/H-ltd	
	Spanish, Italian	

The Marshlands Inn is one of Canada's best known country inns. This pre-Confederation home, operating as an inn for over 60 years, has been the stopping place for many of Canada's notables and visiting celebrities. Even the Queen of England has stayed.

✉ info@marshlands.nb.ca 🌐 www.marshlands.nb.ca

SHEDIAC

Auberge Maison Vienneau	85-109 $CAN BB	Full breakfast
Inn	5 rooms, 5 pb	Antiques, Grand Salon, fireplace,
426 Main St E4P 2G4	Most CC, *Rated*, •	bicycles
866-532-5412 506-532-5412	C-ltd/S-no/P-no/H-no	
Marie & Norbert Vienneau	French	

A charming B&B that will offer you good taste, wholesome maritime hospitality and together with the Shediac region, cultural and sport activities that will fulfill your stay. Ideal as a romantic escape, business trip or family reunion.

✉ info@maisonvienneau.com 🌐 www.maisonvienneau.com

Newfoundland and Labrador

L'ANSE AUX MEADOWS

Viking Village B&B	62-78 $CAN BB	Full hot breakfast
A0K 2X0	5 rooms, 5 pb	Dinner available, complimentary
877-858-2238 709-623-2238	Visa, MC, *Rated*, •	snack
Thelma Hedderson	C-yes/S-no/P-ltd/H-no	Sitting room, cable TV, accommodate
		business travelers, suites

Viking Nest B&B serves a full breakfast every day. Complimentary evening snack also available, and we will recommend our favorite restaurants. Single rates available.

✉ vikingnest@nf.aibn.com 🌐 www.vikingvillage.ca

PORT BLANDFORD

Terra Nova Hospitality	75-138 $CAN BB	Full breakfast
Home & Cottages	21 rooms, 21 pb	Lunch, dinner, afternoon tea, snacks,
A0C 2G0	Visa, MC, AmEx, •	restaurant, bar service
888-267-2373 709-543-2260	C-yes/S-no/P-no/H-yes	Sitting room, library, Jacuzzis,
Rhoda Parsons		suites, fireplaces, cable, sauna, BBQ,
		conference facility

Terra Nova offers a full breakfast with homemade jams and bread. The property overlooks the ocean and is a spacious and luxurious home with cottages offered as well.

✉ terranovahosp@nf.aibn.com 🌐 www.terranova.nfld.net

Nova Scotia

CANNING

The Farmhouse Inn
9757 Main St B0P 1H0
800-928-4346 902-582-7900
Andrea Kelly

90-160 $CAN BB
6 rooms, 6 pb
Visa, MC, AmEx,
Rated, •
C-yes/S-no/P-no/H-ltd

Full breakfast
Afternoon tea
A/C, guest parlor, 2-person whirlpool
tubs, fireplaces, cable TV, VCR

Charming country getaway in a historic village. Cozy renovated 1860 farmhouse close to wineries, hiking & highest tides. Queen, king or 2 twin bedrooms, A/C, wireless Internet, TV/VCR, ensuite washroom. Suites have 2-person Jacuzzi &/or fireplace.

 farmhous@ns.sympatico.ca ◐ www.farmhouseinn.ca

CENTREVILLE

Delft Haus
1942 Hwy 359 B0P 1J0
866-851-4333 902-678-4333
Ray & Debra Ridley

115-145 $CAN BB
4 rooms, 4 pb
Visa, MC, AmEx,
Rated, •
C-yes/S-no/P-no/H-ltd
French and German

Full breakfast
Try our new 'Goodchild's Tea Room'.
High tea in the afternoon is such a
treat!
Aveda Spa services, free vacation
guide online, library, bikes, wireless
Internet

A luxurious classic Victorian B&B and Tea Room now incorporates onsite Aveda Spa services for that special relaxing getaway or romantic vacation. We can help you plan your perfect holiday in Nova Scotia so that you see everything and miss nothing.

 info@delfthaus.com ◐ www.delfthaus.com

GUYSBOROUGH

DesBarres Manor Inn
90 Church Street B0H 1N0
902-533-2099
Victoria

149-259 $CAN BB
10 rooms, 10 pb
Visa, MC, AmEx,
Rated
C-yes/S-no/P-no/H-no

Full breakfast
Chef's complimentary Taste of Nova
Scotia reception, afternoon tea,
gourmet evening dining
WiFi, phone, cable TV, private baths,
hair dryers, robes, Gilchrist & Soames
bath amenities

"The crowning jewel of a fabulous trip to Nova Scotia", DesBarres Manor blends the elegance of the past with modern luxury. Nestled in the charming seaside village of Guysborough, the stately 1837 inn pampers with luxury accommodations and gourmet dining.

 reservations@desbarresmanor.com ◐ www.desbarresmanor.com

HALIFAX

Heritage Hideaway B&B
36 Rutledge St B4A 1W9
877-437-4433 902-835-3605
Diane Gillis

115-139 $CAN BB
2 rooms, 2 pb
Visa, MC
C-yes/S-no/P-no/H-no

Full breakfast
Queen beds, feather pillows, robes/
towels, hair dryer, CBTV, DVD, clock
radio/CD player, stationary

Welcome to Heritage Hideaway, one of Halifax's most romantic B&Bs. Relax and unwind in our circa 1870 Victorian home and experience tranquil ambience and gracious hospitality; making for a memorable Nova Scotia stay.

 info@heritagehideaway.com ◐ www.heritagehideaway.com

The Halliburton
5184 Morris St B3J 1B3
888-512-3344 902-420-0658
Robert Pretty

150-350 $CAN BB
29 rooms, 29 pb
Visa, MC, AmEx,
Rated, •
C-yes/S-no/P-no/H-no

Continental plus breakfast
Dinner nightly, cocktails in library or
courtyard, restaurant, bar
Suites, fireplace, cable, LCD TV,
garden, courtyard, unique decor,
wireless Internet access

Halifax's historic boutique hotel with fine dining and gracious lodging. The Halliburton offers accommodations and Maritime hospitality in a trio of heritage townhouses. 29 guestrooms and suites with private baths.

 information@thehalliburton.com ◐ www.thehalliburton.com

HUBBARDS

Pleasant View B&B
9301 St. Margaret's Bay
Rd B0J 1T0
902-857-1201
Marian & Gene Foster

115-135 $CAN BB
6 rooms, 6 pb
•
C-yes/S-no/P-yes/H-ltd

Full breakfast
Breakfast included in Main House only
Lounge, decks, patio, shared kitchen
in Guest House

Pleasant View Guest House and Bed & Breakfast is centrally located in the heart of Nova Scotia's scenic Lighthouse Route, Hwy. #3, on the South Shore.

✉ thefosters@pleasantviewbandb.com 🌐 www.pleasantviewbandb.com

LUNENBURG

1826 Maplebird House
36 Pelham St B0J 2C0
888-395-3863 902-634-3863
Susie Scott & Barry Chappell

95-125 $CAN BB
4 rooms, 4 pb
Visa, MC, *Rated*
C-ltd/S-no/P-no/H-no

Full breakfast
Pool, Internet, wood burning stove,
TV/DVD/CD, piano, patio, books,
games & family room

A restored heritage home (circa 1826) once used as a dairy farm, this year celebrating its 185th birthday and 19 years as a bed and breakfast. Enjoy a relaxed atmosphere in our home, catching sunrises and sunsets on the verandah. ✉ barry.susie@maplebirdhouse.ca 🌐 www.maplebirdhouse.ca

Atlantic Sojourn
56 Victoria Rd B0J 2C0
800-550-4824 902-634-3151
Sebelle Deese & Susan Budd

100 $CAN BB
4 rooms, 4 pb
Visa, MC
C-yes/S-no/P-no/H-no
May 1 – November 1

Full breakfast
Complimentary coffee, tea & cookies
Living room with cable TV, VCR, DVD,
games, movies, magazines, parlour,
deck, garden with koi pond

Enjoy a stay in one of four rooms with ensuite bath and full breakfast. Let Lunenburg be your hub for day trips along the South Shore, Halifax, Peggy's Cove, Annapolis Royal, or Bay of Fundy. Off street parking, wireless Internet, secure bike storage.
✉ atlanticsojourn@eastlink.ca 🌐 www.atlanticsojourn.com

Boscawen Inn
150 Cumberland St B0J 2C0
800-354-5009 902-634-3325
Johnny & Linda Power

99-255 $CAN BB
20 rooms, 20 pb
Visa, MC, AmEx,
Rated, •
C-yes/S-no/P-ltd/H-ltd
French

Continental breakfast
Catering for events available
Conference facilities, deck with
harbour view, antiques

The Boscawen Inn is Lunenburg's premier facility. Only the Boscawen boasts a genuine and elegant Victorian ambience with licensed parlors, deck, dining room, lounge and bar. It is located in the heart of historic, UNESCO, "Old Town" Lunenburg.
✉ reservations@boscawen.ca 🌐 www.boscawen.ca

PARRSBORO

The Maple Inn
2358 Western Avenue B0M
1S0
877-627-5346 902-254-3735
Ulrike Rockenbauer

90-170 $CAN BB
8 rooms, 8 pb
Visa, MC, AmEx,
Rated, •
C-yes/S-no/P-no/H-no
German
1st May to 31st October

Breakfast Menu Card
Living Room for guests, afternoon
refreshments with cakes or other
sweets

This beautifully restored 1893 Italianate style home is located a few steps from the World's Highest Tides. We offer you the hospitality of a B&B and the privacy of an Inn. Choose one of our 8 rooms (all with antiques) or our 2 bedroom suite! ✉ office@mapleinn.ca 🌐 www.mapleinn.ca

WOLFVILLE

In Wolfville Luxury B&B
56 Main Street B4P 1B7
888-542-0400 902-542-0400
Gordon & Pamela Townsend

99-160 $CAN BB
4 rooms, 4 pb
Visa, MC, *Rated*, •
C-ltd/S-no/P-no/H-no
Ukrainian

Full gourmet breakfast
Guest refrigerator with complimentary
bottled water, coffee makers with
complimentary tea & coffee
Cable TV, DVD & VCRs, Internet, fax
machine available, robes & slippers,
iron & ironing board

People say there is no place like the Annapolis Valley. Lush greenery, vast orchards, pristine vineyards and peaceful ambience are sure to please all who discover it. When you are visiting Wolfville, at the heart of the valley, come and stay in luxury!
✉ inwolfville@ns.sympatico.ca 🌐 www.inwolfville.ns.ca

Ontario

ANCASTER

Tranquility Base
110 Abbey Close L9G 4K7
877-649-9290 905-648-1506
Shirley & Larry Woods

85-95 $CAN BB
3 rooms, 2 pb
Visa, MC, AmEx,
Rated
C-ltd/S-no/P-no/H-no

Full breakfast
Refreshments & dinner on request
Family room, library, robes, slippers,
hair dryer, fridge, coffee maker, water
& juice

Tranquility Base is on a quiet cul-de-sac and is ideal for guests who come to the area for weddings and family visits. It has lovely Victorian dolls, art, and other antiques. Your hosts enjoy history, antiques, traveling and meeting people.

✉ tranquilitybnb@cogeco.ca 🌐 www.tranquilitybase.on.ca

BELWOOD

Riverwood Retreat Centre
& Bed and Breakfast
6885 Fifth Line RR #1 N)
B 1J0
519-843-9982
Bert & Marilyn Peel

85-105 $CAN BB
4 rooms, 4 pb
Visa, MC, *Rated*
S-no/P-no/H-ltd

Full breakfast
Special diets accommodated with
advance notice.
Ensuite baths. Hair drier in room.

A new country home nestled in 12 acres of woods with the Irvine River meandering through the back of the property and surrounded by spruce trees and tall pines. The perennial gardens are spectacular, and have a walking trail to the river.

✉ info@riverwoodretreatbb.com 🌐 www.riverwoodretreatbb.com

CHELTENHAM

The Top of the Hill B&B
14318 Creditview Rd L7C
1N4
905-838-3790
Shelley & Steve Craig

80-105 $CAN BB
2 rooms, 2 pb
Visa, MC
C-yes/S-no/P-no/H-no

Full breakfast
Dinners by special request, vegetarian
meals available
Air conditioning, cable TV, wireless
Internet, hot tub, guest refrigerator

The Top of the Hill is an historic home located on two lush acres of the Niagara Escarpment. It offers all the charm of days gone by and the modern amenities guests would expect today. Voted Best Breakfast in Canada by Arrington's Inn Traveler.

✉ thetopofthehill@rogers.com 🌐 www.thetopofthehillbb.ca

DORSET

The Nordic Inn
1019 Nordic Inn Rd L0R 2C0
705-766-2343
Jane & Andre Tieman

80-125 $CAN EP
12 rooms, 12 pb
Visa, MC, AmEx, •
C-yes/S-no/P-yes/H-ltd
Dutch, French

Lunch available, snacks
Fire pit, playground, llamas, 20 miles
of trails, snowmobiling, canoeing,
hiking, suite w/ whirlpool

Family outdoor adventures in Muskoka – Haliburton – Algonquin – Lake of Bays. Excellent value for modern, clean, cozy accommodations located high on a hill overlooking the quaint hamlet of Dorset.

✉ info@thenordicinn.com 🌐 www.thenordicinn.com

GANANOQUE

Trinity House Inn
90 Stone St S K7G 1Z8
800-265-4871 613-382-8383
J. O'Shea

99-250 $CAN BB
8 rooms, 8 pb
Visa, MC, *Rated*
C-ltd/S-no/P-ltd/H-ltd
Closed mid- Jan.-12 Feb.

Country Buffet
Dinner, restaurant, bar service
Sitting room, suites, cable TV, waterfall
gardens, rocking chair veranda, WiFi,
guest computer

Trinity House Inn is for those who appreciate Old World charm and hospitality, together with genuine beauty and the comfort it brings. Eight guestrooms, award-winning Victorian waterfall gardens, fine dining and a terraced patio.

✉ info@trinityinn.com 🌐 www.trinityinn.com

GUELPH

Walkerbrae House
57 Walkerbrae Trail N1H 6J4
519-240-0308
Mary Hughes

175-225 $CAN BB
1 rooms, 1 pb
Visa, MC, *Rated*, •
C-yes/S-no/P-yes/H-ltd

Full breakfast
Your suite has coffee, tea and hot
chocolate at your fingertips by using
our Keurig beverage maker
kitchenette, 42" flat screen tv, hot tub

Exclusive retreat for two nestled in a one-acre retreat on the edge of Guelph. Luxuriate in the 600 square foot private suite with your own entrance.

✉ stay@walkerbrae.ca 🌐 www.walkerbrae.ca

Willow Manor
408 Willow Rd N1H 6S5
866-763-3574 519-763-3574
Donna Cooper

100-130 $CAN BB
5 rooms, 5 pb
Most CC, Cash, Checks
C-ltd/S-no/P-ltd/H-no

Full breakfast
Specialty diets can be accommodated
by prior arrangement at time of
reservation
Fireplace, antique baby grand piano,
Oriental rugs, gardens, pool & patio

Willow Manor is a premier, award-winning bed & breakfast in Guelph. Proven performance over 16 years and an international reputation for quality. An outdoor swimming pool and landscaped gardens on 2.5 acres. Business and tourist guests welcome!

✉ willowmanor1@on.aibn.com 🌐 www.willowmanorbb.com

HAMILTON

Rutherford House B&B
293 Park St S L8P 3G5
905-525-2422
David & Janis Topp

115-120 $CAN BB
2 rooms, 2 pb
Visa, MC, AmEx,
Rated
C-ltd/S-no/P-no/H-no

Full breakfast
Sitting room, central A/C, parking,
wireless Internet, TV/VCR, fridges,
coffeemakers, secret garden

Late Victorian home, downtown Hamilton Heritage District. B&B luxury and comfort-ensuite baths, down duvets, breakfast to spoil you, dining/sitting room with fireplace. Easy walk to everything downtown offers. 65km drive to Niagara Falls.

✉ david.janis.topp@sympatico.ca 🌐 www.rutherfordbb.com

KINGSTON

Rosemount Inn & Spa
46 Sydenham St K7L 3H1
888-871-8844 613-531-8844
Holly Doughty

169-299 $CAN BB
11 rooms, 11 pb
Visa, MC, •
S-no/P-no/H-no

Gourmet breakfast
Welcoming Afternoon Tea and Freshly
Baked Home Made Cookies and Cake
in the Living Room.
Vinotherapy Spa, phone, voice mail,
high speed Internet, fireplace, A/C,
Meeting room

1850 Tuscan Villa in Kingston. D'Vine Spa at the Rosemount with products of wine and chocolate for your indulgence. The inn is a short walk of 3 blocks from shops, museums, restaurants, theatres, 1000 Islands Cruises and the University.

✉ rosemt@kingston.net 🌐 www.rosemountinn.com

NEW HAMBURG

Waterlot Restaurant & Inn
17 Huron St N N3A IKI
519-662-2020
Leslie Elkeer

100-130 $CAN BB
3 rooms, 1 pb
Visa, MC, AmEx
C-ltd/S-ltd/P-no/H-ltd

Continental breakfast
Lunch & dinner available, bar, fine
dining restaurant, snacks, hors
d'oeuvres, evening wine tasting
Library, TV/VCR, sitting room, large
deck/porch, flower garden, fireplace,
fine antiques

Nestled along a millpond, in the quaint village of New Hamburg, stands the Waterlot Restaurant and Inn. Built as a stately, private residence in 1847, the Waterlot has been a culinary landmark in the region since 1974.

✉ waterlot@waterlot.com 🌐 www.waterlot.com

NIAGARA FALLS

Kilpatrick Manor B&B
4601 Second Ave L2E 4H3
866-976-2667 905-321-8581
Kevin & Nance Kilpatrick

129-199 $CAN BB
4 rooms, 4 pb
Visa, MC, *Rated*, •
S-no/P-no/H-no

Two course Chef prepared breakfast
Decadent nightcaps delivered to your
room with silver tray service
In-room massages, breakfast-in-bed,
decadent nightcaps, excellent custom
packages

Romantic, luxurious & delicious. The Kilpatrick Manor is a beautiful 1891 Victorian home with 4 guestrooms all with ensuite bathrooms, fireplace & seating area, TV & DVD, bathrobe, slippers and fresh flowers. Chef Kevin creates scrumptious breakfasts.

✉ stay@kilpatrickmanor.com ◗ www.kilpatrickmanor.com

NIAGARA ON THE LAKE

6 Oak Haven
6 Oak Dr L0S 1J0
866-818-1195 905-468-7361
Christine Rizzuto

110-150 $CAN BB
3 rooms, 3 pb
Visa, MC, •
C-ltd/S-ltd/P-ltd/H-ltd

Gourmet food
Tea, snacks & coffee
Garden oasis, pond, gazebo, great
room, fridge, spa services, fireplaces,
bikes, wireless Internet

Welcome to 6 Oak Haven, where our motto is "There are no strangers here, only friends we have not yet met!" Located in a quiet area of Niagara on the Lake, 6 Oak Haven is a 5 minute walk to the Lake, amazing sunsets & 15 minute walk to the Old Town.

✉ info@oakhavenbb.com ◗ www.niagaraonthelakeoakhaven.com

Apple Tree Historic B&B
263 Regent St L0S 1J0
866-625-8862 905-468-8687
Gail Wardle

135-185 $CAN BB
3 rooms, 3 pb
Visa, MC
S-no/P-no/H-no

Full breakfast
Soft drinks, bottled water, minibar for
our guests convenience.
Centrally air conditioned, featherbeds
with fabulous linens, private en-suite
bathroom

Excellently located in the center of Niagara-on-the-Lake, this charming home is perfect for your romantic getaways just one block to shopping, restaurants, and theaters. Free parking and wireless Internet for our guests! ✉ relax@appletreebb.ca ◗ www.appletreebb.ca

Brockamour Manor
433 King St. L0S 1J0
905-468-5527
Rick Jorgensen & Colleen
Cone

145-250 $CAN BB
6 rooms, 6 pb
Visa, MC, AmEx
C-ltd/S-ltd/P-no/H-no

Full breakfast
Games room with billiards table &
wood burning fireplace. covered front
porch, complimentary water

Our Niagara on the Lake Bed and Breakfast (circa 1809) is a perfect location for a romantic getaway or to escape the everyday. Enjoy theatre, restaurants, quaint shops and wineries! Or, relax amongst the trees on an acre of designated heritage property. ✉ info@brockamour.com ◗ www.brockamour.com

Downhome B&B
93 William St L0S 1J0
888-223-6433 905-468-3173
James Down

165-195 $CAN BB
3 rooms, 3 pb
Visa, MC, AmEx
S-no/P-no/H-no
Russian, Ukrainian

Full three course gourmet breakfast
Coffee, tea, cookies & sweets available
24/7
Garden sitting areas, mini-fridge in
rooms, Jacuzzi, gas fireplace, lounge
sitting room

Our Georgian home is in the heart of Old Town, only four blocks from boutique shops, theatres, & fine restaurants. All of our bedrooms have 15" pillow top mattress queen beds with sitting area. Wake to the aroma of a freshly prepared gourmet breakfast.

✉ info@downhomeniagara.ca ◗ www.downhomeniagara.ca

Grand Victorian
15618 Niagara Parkway L0S
1J0
905-468-0997
Eva Kessel

170-225 $CAN BB
6 rooms, 6 pb
Visa, MC
C-ltd/S-no/P-no/H-ltd
Polish and German

Brunch style
Start your day with a brunch style
breakfast served in the conservatory
or dining room
Fireplace, verandah, fabulous
antiques, private porch, tennis court,
gardens

Whispers of time gone by. This historic circa 1870s mansion has grandiose interiors with fireplaces, 4 poster beds and antiques. Wrap around verandah. A parkland setting with tennis, surrounded by Reif Estates Vineyards. Across from Niagara River. ✉ Eva@grandvictorian.ca ◗ www.grandvictorian.ca

NIAGARA ON THE LAKE

Historic Inns of Niagara – **Post House** 95 Johnson St L0S 1J0 877-349-POST 905-468-9991 Barbara Ganim	149-379 $CAN BB 11 rooms, 11 pb Visa, MC, AmEx, • C-yes/S-no/P-ltd/H-ltd	Full Epicurean Breakfast Homebaked coffee cakes, muffins with local fresh fruits, early coffee; will assist with diet needs "Amenities of a Five Star Hotel in a bed & breakfast setting"; romantic packages offering privacy

This home is one of a collection of two fine historic homes in the Heritage District, offering a 2 minute stroll to Main Street. Amenities of a Five Star hotel in a bed & breakfast setting. Our homes have been completely restored with in-room baths.

✉ post@posthouseinn.com 🌐 www.historicinnsofniagara.com

John's Gate Gourmet B&B 155 John St W L0S 1J0 866-566-4283 905-468-4882 Meheroo Jamshedji	95-150 $CAN BB 3 rooms, 3 pb Visa, MC, *Rated*, • C-yes/S-no/P-no/H-no Hindi	Full gourmet breakfast Juice, soft drinks, 24-hour tea & coffee station Wireless Internet, fax, computer facilities, will help with other travel & dinner arrangements

Custom-built Pre-Victorian style home with private entrance and living and dining rooms for the comfort of our guests. Located just off the main road into Niagara-on-the-Lake and the Niagara Parkway. We are 1 km from downtown Queen Street.

✉ info@johnsgate.com 🌐 www.johnsgate.com

Schoolmaster's House B&B 307 Mississiaugua St L0S 1J0 866-863-3303 905-468-1299 Jane & Steven Vasil	145-175 $CAN BB 3 rooms, 3 pb Visa, MC, AmEx S-no/P-no/H-yes	Full breakfast 7:30 am coffee & tea service to your door with a copy of the day's newspaper Computer, fax machine, Internet access, library, telephone

Early 19th c. Heritage B&B in the heart of Niagara Wine Country, a short stroll to theatres, shops & fine dining. Enchanting accommodations & sumptuous breakfasts. Wake well-rested & feeling refreshed; walk, hike, bike or drive the scenic lake front.

✉ info@schoolmastershouse.com 🌐 www.schoolmastershouse.com

Simcoe Manor 242 Simcoe St L0S 1J0 866-468-4886 905-468-4886 John Gartner	189-300 $CAN BB 5 rooms, 5 pb Visa, MC C-ltd/S-ltd/P-no/H-ltd	Full gourmet breakfast Complimentary tea, coffee and water on arrival Common room with fireplace, reading materials, heated swimming pool, cable TV, DVD, verandah

Stately "Old Town" home graciously harmonizes tradition, ambience and friendliness with modern comfort. Park setting, steps away from attractions, theatre, dining, shopping and golf. A/C, fireplaces, and porch.

✉ stay@simcoemanor.com 🌐 simcoemanor.com

The Grange at Stag Hollow 50 Firelane 11A RR3 L0S 1J0 905-938-0698 Philip Thornber & Bibi Adams	185-285 $CAN BB 3 rooms, 3 pb Visa, MC, *Rated* S-no/P-no/H-ltd French	Gourmet Breakfast Guests can pre-arrange for wine and cheese trays in their rooms Patios, fireplaces, whirlpool tubs, balconies, TV lounge, fridge, ice maker, free Internet, glasses

A private vintage, 2 acre lakefront estate located amidst the vineyards, restaurants, theaters and sights of Historic Niagara-on-the-Lake, Ontario, Canada: the only B&B on Lake Ontario. Luxury and gourmet breakfasts combine with a cozy lakeside setting.

✉ thegrange@staghollow.ca 🌐 www.staghollow.ca

Simcoe Manor, Niagara-on-the-Lake, ON

NIAGARA ON THE LAKE

Wishing Well Historical Cottage Rental 156 Mary St L0S 1J0 866-226-4730 905-980-0346 Maria Rekrut	150-250 $CAN BB 2 rooms, 2 pb *Rated*, • C-yes/S-no/P-no/H-ltd Italian, Spanish, French	Continental plus breakfast Gourmet coffee & tea, juices, full use of kitchen with ingredients for preparation Spa bath amenities, robes, slippers, fireplaces, wireless Internet, phone & A/C

Niagara on the Lake an historical cottage rental. Great for a family and friends' getaway while visiting Niagara Falls and Niagara on the Lake. A well-known region for wineries and to view Niagara Falls, Ontario. Niagara on the Lake is open year round.

✉ info@celebritybb.com 🌐 www.niagaracottage.com

ORANGEVILLE

McKitrick House Inn & Guest Suites B&B 255 & 257 Broadway L9W 1K6 877-625-4875 519-941-0620 Sheila Kalyn	56-190 $CAN BB 10 rooms, 8 pb Visa, MC, *Rated*, • C-yes/S-no/P-ltd/H-ltd	We offer vegetarian meals, just ask Lunch, dinner, vegetarian & diet restricted meals available, refreshments served upon arrival Our private dining room is available for brunch & dinner parties, showers, meetings & weddings

These two beautiful Victorian homes offer exquisite accommodations to travelers from over 70 countries. The Inn is furnished with fine antiques of the 1870's period and The Guest Suites decor is contemporary sophistication.

✉ info@mckitrickhouseinn.com 🌐 www.mckitrickhouseinn.com

ORONO

Willow Pond Country 7570 Best Rd L0B 1M0 905-442-0992 Lynn & Randy Morrison	99-235 $CAN BB 4 rooms, 3 pb Visa, MC, AmEx, • C-yes/S-ltd/P-ltd/H-ltd Polish, German	Full breakfast Coffee, tea, milk, fresh fruit, dinner available (MAP rates) Hot tub, sauna, spa treatments, private lake & creek, destination Weddings, retreats, honeymoons.

Peace, tranquility & a touch of luxury await you on 40 acres of countryside. Elopement & Wedding packages available. Spot the Great Blue Heron & Canada Geese around our private lake & creek. Relax in your private suite with Jacuzzi, hot tub or sauna

✉ lynn@willowpondbedandbreakfast.ca 🌐 www.willowpondbedandbreakfast.ca

OTTAWA

Albert House Inn
478 Albert St K1R 5B5
800-267-1982 613-236-4479
Cathy & John Delroy

104-180 $CAN BB
17 rooms, 17 pb
Visa, MC, AmEx,
Rated, •
C-ltd/S-no/P-ltd/H-no
Closed for Christmas

Full breakfast cooked to order
Complimentary beverages & room
service menu
Lounge with fireplace, guest computer
desk, wireless Internet, fax/scanner/
copier

Downtown Victorian inn where guests can walk to Parliament, Canadian War Museum, National Archives Library, shopping, dining, entertainment and business meetings. Fabulous breakfasts, free wireless & Internet desk. Parking available. CAA/AAA approved.

✉ contact@albertinn.com ◐ www.albertinn.com

Ambiance B&B
330 Nepean St K1R 5G6
888-366-8772 613-563-0421
Maria Giannakos

99-129 $CAN BB
4 rooms, 2 pb
Visa, MC, AmEx
C-yes/S-no/P-no/H-no
French and Greek

Full Gourmet breakfast
Complimentary coffee, teas, hot cocoa,
soft drinks and snacks
WiFi, Parking, Private lounge, A/C,
iron & board, hairdryers, slippers &
robe, fridge, free calls

Our downtown Victorian B&B (c 1904) is only a ten minute walk to Parliament Hill and less than 5–20 minutes from restaurants, shopping and all other major attractions. Parking, WiFi and a full gourmet breakfast is included in all our affordable rates.

✉ info@ambiencebandb.com ◐ www.ambiencebandb.com

Auberge McGee's Inn
185 Daly Ave K1N 6E8
800-262-4337 613-237-6089
Jason, Judy, Sarah & Ken
Armstrong

108-198 $CAN BB
14 rooms, 14 pb
Visa, MC, •
C-yes/S-no/P-no/H-ltd
French, Spanish

Full breakfast
Free local calls, Jacuzzi tubs, cable TV,
fireplaces, voicemail, wireless Internet,
free parking

Located downtown, this award winning 1886 historic Victorian inn is on the east side of the Rideau Canal in Sandy Hill. Walking distance to Parliament Hill, museums, theatre, bike paths & the ByWard Market. Please join us! You will not be disappointed.

✉ contact@mcgeesinn.com ◐ www.mcgeesinn.com

Shirley Samantha's B&B
28 Carlotta Ave K1L6S6
613-745-2105
Cynthia King and Paul
Zendrowski

85-115 $CAN BB
2 rooms, 2 pb
C-yes/S-no/P-no/H-no
French, Spanish

Full breakfast
Home-made cookies, juice, soft drinks.
Special diets accommodated with
advance notice.
Free WiFi, locked bike/ski storage
avail., use of desk and phone in Study,
books & magazines

The perfect location from which to tour the National Capital. Walk to downtown, close to public transportation, ½ block from Rideau River Walking/bike path.

✉ shirleysamantha@sympatico.ca

Swiss Hotel
89 Daly Ave K1N 6E6
888-663-0000 613-237-0335
Sabina & Josef Sauter

99-258 $CAN BB
22 rooms, 22 pb
Visa, MC, AmEx,
Rated
C-ltd/S-no/P-no/H-no
French, Swiss-German,
German, Spanish

Swiss breakfast buffet (optional)
Breakfast is optional.
Garden patio, A/C, Meeting &
Conference Room, laundry services,
weddings, free WiFi, Internet access

Uniquely designed Swiss Hotel offers simple elegance and tranquility in the heart of Ottawa. This stylish historical inn offers free WiFi, an ideal domicile for vacationers, business travelers and conventioneers. Enjoy typical Swiss charm since 1985.

✉ info@swisshotel.ca ◐ www.swisshotel.ca

STRATFORD

Stewart House Inn
62 John St N N5A 6K7
866-826-7772 519-271-4576
Marc Armstrong

199-379 $CAN BB
6 rooms, 6 pb
Visa, MC, AmEx,
Rated, •
C-ltd/S-no/P-no/H-no

Full gourmet breakfast
In-room early coffee or tea service, 24-
hr complimentary espresso machine,
fresh fruit, cookies
Sitting room, library, salt water pool,
fireplaces, cable TV, wireless Internet,
evening turn-down

This magnificent 1870 Victorian mansion is situated on an acre of beautiful residential woodlands, overlooking the tranquil Avon River parklands, and is a short two-block stroll to the Theatre District and Downtown Stratford. Seasonal saltwater pool.

✉ reservations@stewarthouseinn.com 🌐 www.stewarthouseinn.com

Stone Maiden Inn
123 Church St N5A 2R3
866-612-3385 519-271-7129
Pat & Kim Walsh

99-265 $CAN BB
14 rooms, 14 pb
Visa, MC, AmEx
C-ltd/S-no/P-no/H-ltd

Full plated hot breakfast
Complimentary coffee/tea bar
available to guests 24/7. Lunches
available with advance reservation.
A/C, TV, fireplaces, whirlpool
tubs, phones, mini-bar, WiFi, guest
computer, free parking

Our Heritage Mansion offers quiet Victorian elegance with superior accommodation and the utmost in personal service in a quiet residential area within easy walking distance to all theatres, shopping, restaurants and dining. ✉ reservations@StoneMaidenInn.com 🌐 www.StoneMaidenInn.com

TORONTO

312 Seaton – A Toronto B&B
312 Seaton St M5A 2T7
866-968-0775 416-968-0775
Ted Bates & Nick Franjic

105-210 $CAN BB
5 rooms, 3 pb
Visa, MC, *Rated*
C-ltd/S-no/P-no/H-ltd

Full breakfast
Bottled water, tea, coffee are all
available at all times.
High speed Internet, wireless & hard
wire, computer, A/C, TV, mini-fridge

A detached Victorian home on a quiet tree-lined street, in downtown Toronto's historical "Cabbagetown." Four guestrooms, 2 with private baths, and one fully furnished apartment. Parties and meetings hosted. ✉ info@312seaton.com 🌐 www.312seaton.com

---

Banting House Inn
73 Homewood Ave M4Y 2K1
800-823-8856 416-924-1458
Paul Hyde

89-155 $CAN BB
7 rooms, 1 pb
Visa, MC, *Rated*, •
C-ltd/S-no/P-ltd/H-no
French

Full breakfast
Sitting room, library, suites, fireplace,
cable TV, parking

An elegant Edwardian home offering a peaceful respite to the hustle and bustle of downtown Toronto. Secluded garden, patio, secure on-site parking, cable TV, made to order breakfast.

✉ bantinghs@aol.com 🌐 www.bantinghouse.com

Bonnevue Manor B&B Place
33 Beaty Ave M6K 3B3
416-536-1455
Glenn & Dorothy Dodds

99-119 $CAN BB
4 rooms, 4 pb
Visa, MC, AmEx, •
C-yes/S-no/P-no/H-ltd
French

Full or continental breakfast
Tea & snacks
Sitting room, patio & deck, BBQ

An elegant, eclectic, spacious city mansion in downtown Toronto with a homey ambience, a sumptuous breakfast, comfortable beds, warm and friendly hospitality.

✉ bonne@interlog.com 🌐 www.bonnevuemanor.com

By The Park B&B
92 Indian Grove M6R 2Y4
416-520-6102 416-761-9778
Margo Rygier

95-215 $CAN BB
8 rooms, 8 pb
Visa, MC, AmEx
C-yes/S-no/P-no/H-ltd

Full Vegetarian Breakfast
Private kitchen in one-bedroom suite
or shared kitchenettes with some
suites
Living room, wood-burning fireplace,
cable TV, garden, fountain, porch,
parking, wireless Internet

Selected as top 5% of "The Best Places to Bed and Breakfast in Ontario." We offer traditional B&B serving a full vegetarian/vegan breakfast as well as self-contained one-bedroom suites and bedrooms with ensuite bathrooms and a shared kitchen.

✉ bytheparkbb@rogers.com 🌐 www.bythepark.ca

TORONTO ───

Pimbletts Guest House	65-105 $CAN BB	Full breakfast
B&B	12 rooms, 12 pb	Wireless Internet, parking, telephone,
242 Gerrard St E M5A 2G2	Visa, MC, AmEx,	fax machine, copier, deck
416-921-6898	*Rated*	
Geoffrey Pimblett	C-yes/S-no/P-no/H-no	

Pimblett's B&B – another illustrious house of repute. Charles Dickens and Oscar Wilde would most certainly have stayed here. An Englishman's home in the heart of downtown Toronto. Free parking, close to public transport, private bathrooms.

✉ pimbletts@sympatico.ca 🌐 www.pimblett.ca

───

Victoria's Mansion	99-139 $US EP	Private three or four-piece bathrooms,
68 Gloucester St. M4Y 1L5	22 rooms, 22 pb	air conditioning, fridge, cable TV, free
416-921-4625	Visa, MC	wireless Internet
Kathy	C-yes/S-no/P-no/H-no	

Built in the 1880s, this beautifully-renovated historic mansion is nestled on a quiet, tree-lined street just steps away from the excitement and culture that Toronto has to offer.

✉ info@victoriasmansion.com 🌐 www.victoriasmansion.com

WATERLOO ───

Hillcrest House	125-135 $CAN BB	Full breakfast
73 George St N2J 1K8	3 rooms, 3 pb	Enjoy our specially selected meals
866-624-3534 519-744-3534	Visa, MC	and snacks
Stefan & Wendy	C-ltd/S-no/P-ltd/H-ltd	Concierge service, spa, library, games,
		outdoor areas, weddings, high speed
		Internet, fireplaces

Whether you're here for business or pleasure, we welcome you to rejuvenate your body and soul in our peaceful and charming home. You'll find Hillcrest House in the heart of Uptown Waterloo, just steps from many shops, restaurants and activities.

✉ info@hillcresthouse.ca 🌐 www.hillcresthouse.ca

Prince Edward Island

CHARLOTTETOWN

Colonial Charm Inn B&B	85-175 $CAN BB	Full breakfast
9 Euston St C1A 1V5	7 rooms, 7 pb	Complimentary tea is available
866-892-8934 902-892-8934	Visa, MC, *Rated*, •	anytime for our guests
Gary & Shelley MacDougall	C-yes/S-no/P-no/H-ltd	Sitting room with Internet access,
		laundry service is available for guests

Award-winning 4 star B&B in historic downtown Charlottetown. A 5 minute walk to the centre of our capital city. Walking distance to theatres, waterfront, dining, shopping and all downtown attractions. Suites available with private balconies.

✉ colonialcharminn@eastlink.ca ✪ www.colonialcharminn.com

Elmwood Heritage Inn	99-275 $CAN BB	Full fresh gourmet breakfast
121 North River Rd C1A 3K7	7 rooms, 7 pb	Complimentary coffee, tea service,
877-933-3310 902-368-3310	Most CC, Cash,	pop & juice, bubbly and bedside
Jay & Carol Macdonald	*Rated*, •	chocolates for celebrations
	C-yes/S-no/P-no/H-no	Informed, personalized Concierge
		service, 8 fireplaces, whirlpools, A/C,
		TV/VCR, irons/boards, WiFi

5 Star Elmwood Heritage Inn is on a secluded acre estate in historic Charlottetown PEI. Quiet Victorian elegance, modern amenities(WiFi), gourmet breakfast (veg & celiac available) and friendly informative concierge service for planning daily excursions.

✉ elmwood@pei.sympatico.ca ✪ www.elmwoodinn.pe.ca

Heritage Harbour House	99-219 $CAN BB	Full breakfast with all home baking
Inn	21 rooms, 21 pb	Off-street parking, bike storage,
9 Grafton St C1A 1K3	Visa, MC, AmEx,	laundry facilities, wireless Internet,
800-405-0066 902-892-6633	*Rated*, •	public computer, A/C
Arie & Jinny van der Gaag	C-yes/S-no/P-no/H-yes	
	Spanish, Japanese,	
	French	

The elegance and character of a stately old family dwelling, combined with today's modern amenities. Our inn's twenty one rooms and suites all have different decor and are furnished in a warm, home style atmosphere.

✉ reservations@hhhouse.net ✪ www.hhhouse.net

Quebec

CHATEAU RICHER

Auberge Baker	79-150 $CAN BB	Full breakfast
8790 Royale G0A 1N0	8 rooms, 8 pb	Fine dining restaurant is located on
866-824-4478 418-824-4478	Most CC, *Rated*, •	ground level, MAP also available
Gaston Cloutier	C-yes/S-no/P-no/H-ltd	Sitting room, bar terrace, fine cuisine
	French	dining room, free parking lot, WiFi
		Internet access

In 1935, Alvin A. Baker converted the LeFrancois home, built in 1840, into a country inn. Restored with great attention, each room of the old house has a private bathroom as well as antique furniture.

✉ gcloutier@auberge-baker.qc.ca 🌐 www.auberge-baker.qc.ca/introang.html

LEVIS

Au Gre du Vent B&B	115-145 $CAN BB	Full breakfast
2 rue Fraser G6V 3R5	5 rooms, 5 pb	Breakfast made with natural, organic
866-838-9070 418-838-9020	Visa, MC, AmEx,	products
Michele Fournier & John	*Rated*, •	Central air, sitting room, pool & patio,
L'Heureux	C-yes/S-no/P-ltd/H-no	bicycle storage facilities, free parking
	French	

Highest Quebec Province classification "5 Stars." Only 5 minutes from Hwy 20 and within walking distance to the ferry leading you to the heart of Old Quebec City (crossing time: 10 minutes). An authentic & charming B&B facing Old Quebec City.

✉ augreduvent@msn.com 🌐 www.au-gre-du-vent.com/introang.html

MAGOG

A Tout Venant	70-115 $CAN BB	Gourmet International Breakfast
20 rue Bellevue J1X 3H2	5 rooms, 5 pb	Complimentary tea, coffee & herbal
888-611-5577 819-868-0419	Visa, MC, *Rated*, •	tea.
Sylvie & Robert	C-yes/S-no/P-no/H-no	Kitchen, TV, , stereo and fireplace,
	French	massage therapy onsite, wireless
		Internet

A Tout Venant B&B will fulfill all desires, with 5 rooms with private baths, hearty breakfasts, free WiFi, a massage therapy room with 2 tables, a peaceful garden, getaway packages and great location.

✉ info@atoutvenant.com 🌐 www.atoutvenant.com

La Maison Hatley	85-115 $CAN BB	Full breakfast
48 Hatley St J1X 3G4	4 rooms, 4 pb	Tea or coffee
888-995-6606 819-868-6606	Visa, MC, *Rated*, •	Air conditioning, exterior hot tub open
Christiane & Vincent Arena	C-ltd/S-no/P-no/H-no	year round
	French, Italian	

La Maison Hatley B&B offers comfortable lodging, in a quaint, ancestral home built in 1875. Come and enjoy the outdoor hot tub, open all year around.

✉ info@lamaisonhatley.com 🌐 www.lamaisonhatley.com

MONTREAL

Accueil Chez Francois	120-150 $CAN BB	Hearty breakfast
4031 Papineau H2K 4K2	5 rooms, 3 pb	Coffee, hot chocolate, herbal tea,
514-239-4638	Visa, MC, AmEx,	juices
Francois Baillergeau	*Rated*	Wireless Internet access, A/C,
	C-yes/S-no/P-no/H-no	television, non-allergic quilts,
	French	hairdryer, slippers

In the heart of Montreal, we are located in the Plateau Mont-Royal where restaurants, lively bars, fashion designers & well-known theatres are all waiting for your enjoyment.

✉ info@chezfrancois.ca 🌐 www.chezfrancois.ca

MONTREAL

Armor Manoir Sherbrooke	99-149 $CAN BB	Continental breakfast
157 Sherbrooke E St H2X	22 rooms, 22 pb	Complimentary coffee
1C7	Visa, MC, •	24 hour reception, 3 rooms with
800-203-5485 514 845 0915	C-yes/S-yes/P-no/H-no	whirlpool, TV, iron & hairdryer, lake
Annick Legall	French	swimming, bicycles, concierge

A century-old home transformed into an exquisite and charming hotel, located near Saint-Denis and Saint-Laurent streets, renowned for their fine restaurants, boutiques and bistros. Newly remodeled.

✉ info@armormanoir.com 🌐 www.armormanoir.com

Auberge De La Fontaine	99-368 $CAN BB	Full healthy buffet breakfast
1301 Rachel E St H2J 2K1	21 rooms, 21 pb	Free access to the kitchen for a
800-597-0597 514-597-0166	Visa, MC, AmEx,	snacks, coffee and juice; (bar service
Jean Lamoth	*Rated*, •	$$)
	C-yes/S-ltd/P-no/H-ltd	Terrace, complimentary WiFi, dry-
	French	cleaning service (fee), meeting room,
		guest computer available.

Facing a magnificent park and ideally located in the heart of the Plateau Mont-Royal district. Our delightful, elegant rooms and suites will charm you. The Auberge de La Fontaine is a three star, 3 diamond hotel with over sixteen years of experience.

✉ info@aubergedelafontaine.com 🌐 www.aubergedelafontaine.com/site/montreal-hotel/index.cfm

Le Cartier	60-125 $CAN BB	Continental breakfast
1219 Rue Cartier H2K 4C4	7 rooms, 4 pb	Kitchen facilities (except no cooking),
877-524-0495 514-917-1829	Visa, MC, AmEx,	microwave, refrigerator, etc. are
Richard Lemmetti	*Rated*, •	available
	C-yes/S-no/P-no/H-no	Laundry service (extra cost), A/C,
	French	cable TV, HS wireless Internet, airport
		shuttle at discount

Beautiful Montreal downtown (Village) Bed and Breakfast with private studio-suite style and nice back yard. 1 min from subway. Walking distance to all city attractions.

✉ bb_le_cartier@hotmail.com 🌐 www.bblecartier.com

Manoir Ambrose	75-200 $CAN BB	Continental breakfast
3422 Stanley St H3A 1R8	22 rooms, 20 pb	Complimentary coffee or tea in the
888-688-6922 514-288-6922	Visa, MC, AmEx,	afternoon
Antonietta Carriero	*Rated*, •	Phone, cable TV, sitting room, air
	C-yes/S-no/P-no/H-no	conditioning, wireless Internet access,
	French	laundry

Victorian-style lodge in downtown Montreal on the slope of Mount Royal, close to Peel Metro station, McGill University Museum, restaurants, Montreal underground shopping. Quiet surroundings & friendly atmosphere. Personality, comfort & affordable prices.

✉ info@manoirambrose.com 🌐 www.manoirambrose.com

SUTTON

Le Domaine Tomali-	125-200 $CAN BB	Continental breakfast
Maniatyn	5 rooms, 5 pb	Garden, reading room, conference
377 Chemin Maple J0E 2K0	Visa, MC, *Rated*	room, indoor/outdoor swimming pool,
450-538-6605	C-ltd/S-no/P-no/H-ltd	TV, WiFi, weddings
Alicja Bedkowska	French, Polish	

In Sutton (QC), our B&B is a 5 suns "Certified B&B and Country Inn", Quebec Tourism's highest rating. Amenities include: 5 cozy antique furnished suites with a panoramic view, a tropical indoor swimming pool, on-site access to skiing, biking and hiking.

✉ info@maniatyn.com 🌐 www.maniatyn.com

Saskatchewan

Backroads Bed and Breakfast
Main Street S0K 0G0
306-598-2141
Shirl and Les Kunz

60-200 $CAN BB
5 rooms
MC
C-yes/S-no/P-ltd/H-no

Full breakfast
Deck, movie library

Affordable, comfortable accommodations for the traveler, vacationer or people who want to escape to a place of solitude with good service. We also have a guesthouse with all the amenities of home. Deck and firepit in the backyard.

lskunz@bogend.ca www.backroadsbb.ca

Worldwide

Antigua / Barbuda
ST. JOHN'S

Long Bay Resort Inn	350 – 800 $US BB	Full breakfast
800-291-2005 268-463-2005	25 rooms, 25 pb	Lunch, Dinner, Restaurant, Cocktail
Christian J. Lafaurie	Visa, MC, AmEx,	Bar Service
	Rated, •	Beach resort, water sports, tennis,
	C-yes/S-yes/P-no/H-no	billiards, library, games room,
	English	2 water fronts, 2 restaurants, 2
		cocktail lounges, snorkeling equip,
		windsurfers, ocean kayaks

A Caribbean Beach Resort that is peaceful, friendly and family oriented. Offering tennis, water sports, a library and a games room. Owner operated since 1966, now guided by the 2nd generation.

✉ info@longbayhotel.com 🌐 www.longbayhotel.com

Argentina
BUENOS AIRES

B&B Olleros 3000	62 – 86 $US BB	Continental breakfast
+54-11-4554-7269	2 rooms, 2 pb	Tea, beer, mineral water
Claudine & Juan	*Rated*, •	Sitting room, newspapers, fax,
	C-ltd/S-no/P-no/H-no	computer, WiFi, fridge, hairdryer,
	Spanish, French,	laundry, travel advice & information
	English, Italian	on tours, shows & activities in town

Stylish guesthouse located in a central, quiet neighborhood within walking distance of trendy Palermo in Buenos Aires. Sophisticated & comfortable accommodations hosted by Claudine, a professional in hospitality & Juan, an architect & art historian.

✉ info@claudinehomes.com 🌐 www.claudinehomes.com/olleros/index.php?page=home&locale=en_EN

Australia
SYDNEY

Bet's B&B	140 AUD BB	Self-catered
+61-2-9660-8265	1 rooms, 1 pb	Breakfast ingredients provided in the
Bet Dalton	Visa, MC, *Rated*	kitchenette
	C-no/S-no/P-no/H-no	Queen bed, modern bathroom &
	English, Filipino	laundry, fully-equipped kitchenette,
		dining table, lounge area w/sofa,
		armchairs, coffee table, TV/DVD,
		writing desk, private entrance

Just 2 miles from the heart of Sydney, Bet's B&B is a modern, fully self-contained artist-style studio, beautifully designed and furnished, with a modern kitchen, spotless bathroom and laundry. Secure private entrance. 15 minutes by bus or train to city.

✉ stay@betsbandb.com.au 🌐 www.betsbandb.com.au

Simpsons of Potts Point	235 – 345 AUD BB	Continental breakfast
+61-2-9356-2199	12 rooms, 12 pb	Complimentary port & sherry, in-room
Ree Daly	MostCC, Cash,	tea & coffee
	Rated, •	A/C, ceiling fans, wake-up calls,
	C-ltd/S-no/P-no/H-ltd	hairdryer, iron facilities & laundry
	English	(near by), library, drawing room (w/
		computer), in-room dial-up & WiFi
		throughout, conservatory

"Simpsons of Potts Point" the first choice for boutique hotels in Sydney! This small and exclusive, luxury accommodation secret is waiting to be discovered for your stay in Sydney Australia!

✉ hotel@simpsonshotel.com 🌐 www.simpsonshotel.com

Austria

INNSBRUCK

Hotel Weisses Kreuz	100 – 132 € BB	Breakfast Buffet
+43-5125-94790	40 rooms, 31 pb	A small selection of drinks is available
Dr. Josef Ortner	Visa, MC, AmEx,	Direct dial telephone, radio, cable TV,
	Rated, •	Internet access & WiFi, wonderful
	C-yes/S-ltd/P-yes/H-ltd	views, city centre
	English, French, Italian,	
	German	

A traditional Austrian inn established 1465, situated in Innsbruck's Gothic old town. There is a cozy, familiar atmosphere, wooden ceilings, antique furniture and friendly service. Mozart stayed here in 1769. All major sights within easy walking distance.

✉ hotel@weisseskreuz.at 🌐 weisseskreuz.at/en/index.php

OBERALM BEI HALLEIN

Schloss Haunsperg	140 – 220 € BB	Full breakfast
+43-6245-80662	8 rooms, 8 pb	Snacks, complimentary wine
Family Von Gernerth	Most CC, *Rated*, •	Sitting room, library, bicycles,
	C-yes/S-yes/P-yes/H-no	barbeque, chapel, gardens & private
	English, Italian, German	clay tennis court, golf, horseback
		riding, squash & winter sports all
		close by

Schloss Haunsperg is a 14th century, country manor house offering elegantly appointed rooms and suites with period furniture. Surrounded by secluded gardens with a friendly, family-owned atmosphere, it is just 15 minutes from Salzburg.

✉ info@schlosshaunsperg.com 🌐 www.schlosshaunsperg.com

SALZBURG

Altstadthotel Amadeus	100 – 200 € BB	Large breakfast buffet
+43-6628-71401	26 rooms, 26 pb	Free afternoon coffee & tea
Margo Weindorfer	MostCC, Cash,	Cable TV, safe, telephone
	Rated, •	
	C-yes/S-yes/P-yes/H-ltd	
	German, English,	
	French, Italian	

Free Night w/Certificate: Valid Jan.-April, 2011. except Fridays and Saturdays. Room Upgrade.

Traditional and unique. The Hotel Amadeus is a small, exclusive hotel with charming and fully equipped rooms in the heart of Salzburg. The Amadeus is a family run hotel. A large breakfast buffet is included. It is walking distance to most sights.

✉ salzburg@hotelamadeus.at 🌐 www.hotelamadeus.at

Hotel Walkner	39 – 60 € BB	Full breakfast
+43-6217-5550	22 rooms, 22 pb	Lunch, afternoon tea, complimentary
Hilda Haberl	Visa, MC, AmEx,	wine, snacks
	Rated, •	Restaurant, bar, heated swimming
	C-yes/S-ltd/P-yes/H-no	pool, sauna, game room, bikes, safe
	English, French,	deposit box, chapel/shrine, WiFi/
	German	wireless LAN, child care services,
		laundry

The province of Salzburg is very special with its mountains, hills, meadows, lakes, nature in all forms, and, of course, the cultured, unspoiled Salzburg way of life. Hotel Walkner is situated in the middle of all this perfection – welcome to our hotel!

✉ office@hotel-walkner.at 🌐 www.hotel-walkner.at

VIENNA ─────────────────────────────────────

Apartments Rothensteiner	85 – 225 € BB	Full breakfast
+43-1523-9643	18 rooms, 18 pb	Full-service restaurant on the
Bernd Rothensteiner	MostCC, Cash,	premises
	Rated, •	Completely furnished apartments, TV,
	C-yes/S-yes/P-yes/H-yes	telephone, private baths, free Internet
	English, German, Italian	access, room safes & safe deposit
		boxes, rooftop terrace, parking

Apartments Rothensteiner is a traditional Viennese property meeting the highest standards of excellent accommodation. The studio and family apartments are decorated in beautiful, classic furnishings. It is within walking distance to Vienna's city center.

✉ hotel@rothensteiner.com 🌐 www.rothensteiner.com

Central Apartments &	110 – 130 € EP	Fully equipped modern kitchens,
Vacation Rentals Vienna	2 rooms, 1 pb	cable TV, DVD & CD player, telephone,
+43-6991-1406665	Visa, MC, *Rated*	fax, answering machine, PC with
Mr. Daryoush Voshmgir	C-yes/S-ltd/P-ltd/H-no	Internet access, ironing board, hair
	English, German,	dryer
	Italian, Farsi	

Four-star, self-catering apartments in prime location in the city center in Vienna, Austria: Family friendly, modern and fully furnished business and vacation apartments suitable for short-term or long-term accommodation in the center of Vienna, Austria.

✉ office@central-apartments-vienna.com 🌐 www.central-apartments-vienna.com

Hotel Kugel	65 – 120 € BB	Buffet Breakfast
+43-1523-3355	25 rooms, 25 pb	Beer, wine, soft drinks, tea, coffee,
Johannes Roller	*Rated*, •	champagne
	C-yes/S-ltd/P-no/H-no	Garage, bar service, library, free baby
	German, English,	cot, mini-bar, hairdryer, TV, free LAN-
	Italian, French, Spanish,	access
	Polish	
	March 1st 2011 until 8th	
	of January 2012	

Situated in an historic part of Vienna between St. Stephen's Cathedral and Schönbrunn Palace, Hotel Kugel offers its guests a traditional, relaxed Viennese atmosphere. Romantic canopy bedrooms and budget rooms are moderately priced.   ✉ office@hotelkugel.at 🌐 www.hotelkugel.at

Pension Wild	53 – 97 € BB	Buffet Style Breakfast
+43-1406-5174	26 rooms, 13 pb	Sauna, exercise room gyms, swimming
Peter Wild	Visa, MC	pools, Fitness center 1 minute
	C-yes/S-no/P-yes/H-no	
	German	

The house was built in 1907 and has recently been renovated. My family founded the hotel in 1960 and we've modernized and extended the facilities several times since to offer our guests maximum comfort.   ✉ info@pension-wild.com 🌐 www.pension-wild.com

Bahamas

ANDROS ─────────────────────────────────────

Small Hope Bay Lodge	470 – 520 $US AP	All Inclusive
800-223-6961 242-368-2013	21 rooms, 21 pb	Savory Dinner, all drinks & bar drinks
Jeff Birch	MostCC, Cash,	Ceiling fans, private baths, A/C (in
	Rated, •	all bedrooms), hot tub, scuba &
	C-yes/S-yes/P-yes/H-yes	snorkeling packages, bicycles, kayaks,
	English	windsurf, sailboat, private beach,
	Closed Sept.	solarium, lodge, patio

ALL INCLUSIVE-Small Hope Bay Lodge-scuba diving, snorkeling, fishing, relaxing! 21 beachfront cottages! Couples, singles, families- all are welcome! Unspoiled & virtually undiscovered, Andros Island is the most established dive resort in the Caribbean.

✉ shbinfo@smallhope.com 🌐 www.smallhope.com

NASSAU

Arawak Inn	75 – 125 $US EP	Complimentary tea selection in your
242-322-2638	5 rooms, 5 pb	room
Lloyd & Elizabeth Ann Gay	Visa, MC, *Rated*	Microwave, refrigerator, cable TV, A/C,
	C-ltd/S-no/P-no/H-no	private bathroom, daily maid service,
	English	cabana, gift shop, book exchange

Enjoy a family island experience at our cozy little inn situated within easy reach of downtown Nassau. In a garden with hummingbirds and butterflies, and close to the local zoo, historic sites and the famous Fish Fry.

✉ arawakinn@gmail.com 🌐 www.arawakinnbahamas.com

Orange Hill Inn	110 – 159 $US EP	Meals available in restaurant –
888-399-3698 242-327-7157	32 rooms, 32 pb	breakfast $7-$8
Judy & Brandon Lowe	Visa, MC, *Rated*	Restaurant, beach side relaxation,
	C-yes/S-no/P-no/H-ltd	evening activities, scuba diving, boat
	English	charters, laundry, maid, TV, in-room
		phone, fee based safe use, Internet
		access

Welcome to Orange Hill Beach Inn, your Bahamas hotel destination with the charm of the family islands and all the conveniences of home.

✉ info@orangehill.com 🌐 www.orangehill.com

Barbados

CHRIST CHURCH

Meridian Inn	69 – 99 $US EP	Restaurant nearby, beverages for sale
246-428-4051	16 rooms, 16 pb	A/C, balcony, microwave, TV,
Graham Turner	Visa, MC, *Rated*	kitchenette, daily maid service, ceiling
	C-ltd/S-ltd/P-no/H-no	fans
	English	

This sixteen room apartment hotel is situated at the quiet end of St. Lawrence Gap, on the south coast of the island, close to nightlife, dining, water sports and activities. Just 100 steps along a sandy path to the beach – crystal-clear turquoise water. ✉ meridianinn@sunbeach.net 🌐 meridianinn.com

ST. MICHAEL

Sweetfield Manor Bed and	245 – 495 $US BB	Full multi-course breakfast
Breakfast	7 rooms, 6 pb	Welcome drinks, ice tea & fresh baked
246-825-0050 246-429-8356	MostCC, Cash,	goods!
George & Ann Clarke	*Rated*, •	Swimming pool with waterfall & spa,
	C-ltd/S-ltd/P-no/H-no	full access for guests to all main rooms
	English, German	and decks of Manor like at home,
		minutes to port, beaches, shopping,
		restaurants, and sights

An authentic island Plantation Great House Bed & Breakfast in Barbados. Casual elegance, premium rooms with award winning multi-course, gourmet breakfasts. "Sweetfield Manor is the best kept secret in Barbados!" – Caribbean Travel & Life Magazine

✉ clarke@sweetfieldmanor.com 🌐 www.sweetfieldmanor.com

Belgium

BRUGGE

Alegria B&B
+32-50-330937
Veronique De Muynck

90 – 160 € BB
6 rooms, 6 pb
Visa, MC, *Rated*, •
C-ltd/S-no/P-no/H-no
English , French,
Dutch, small amount of
German & Italian

Continental breakfast
fresh orange juice & fruitsalad,
homemade jams
Garden, private garage, bike storage
9km from sea, 3km from the country ,
free welcome (bruges card) discounts.
Bruges Map & info 3 nights = incl
walking guidebook

Alegria is a stylish renovated Manor House with a beautiful inner garden and coach house. Alegria is just steps away from the historical area and Market Square of Brugge. A small boutique B&B created with flair offering a delicious buffet breakfast.

✉ alegriabb@skynet.be ◉ users.skynet.be/alegriabb

Hotel Heritage Bruges
+32-50-444444
Johan Creytens

167 – 451 € EP
24 rooms, 24 pb
Visa, MC, AmEx,
Rated, •
C-ltd/S-no/P-no/H-no
English, French,
German, Dutch

Room Service, Hot & Cold Buffet
Breakfast 20
Health center, sauna & Turkish steam
bath, sun bed (fee), sun deck, fitness
room with cardio systems, baggage
room, parking, WiFi, babysitting,
stroller, highchair

A 19th century mansion house, recently renovated into a small, luxurious, family run hotel, 20 rooms and 4 suites, with modern facilities and personal service, in the historic city center.

✉ info@hotel-heritage.com ◉ www.hotel-heritage.com

Hotel Prinsenhof
+32-50-342690
Thierry Lemahieu

172 – 359 € EP
19 rooms, 19 pb
Visa, MC, AmEx,
Rated, •
C-yes/S-no/P-yes/H-ltd
Flemish/Dutch, French,
German, English

Full Hot & Cold Buffet Breakfast   19pp
A/C, TV, DVD, CD, mini-bar, trouser
press, safe, bathrobe, hairdryer, WiFi,
reception, cozy lounge, breakfast
room, baggage room, private parking
for fee

A family run hotel with a warm ambience and a feeling that all guests are important. All bedrooms are peaceful and beautifully furnished in a traditional and elegant style.

✉ info@prinsenhof.com ◉ www.prinsenhof.com

WIJNENDALE-TORHOUT

Woodside Bed & Breakfast
+32-50-223777
Luc & Stacey Van de Velde

75 € BB
3 rooms, 3 pb
Rated
C-yes/S-ltd/P-no/H-no
English, French,
German, Dutch

Continental breakfast
Free tea & coffee
Internet, fax, private parking, baby
cot, books & games, outdoor heated
swimming pool

Flemish/English couple offers you a beautiful b&b near Brugges. 3 modern rooms with private bathroom, seating area with free coffee and tea, WiFi, TV-DVD. Free use of private parking and swimming pool. Many possibilities for day trips and activities !

✉ info@woodside.be ◉ www.woodside.be/english.html

Belize

BELIZE CITY ──────────────────────────────

The Great House Inn +501-223-3400 Steve Maestre	100 – 150 $US EP 16 rooms, 16 pb MostCC, Cash, *Rated*, • C-yes/S-no/P-no/H-no English, Spanish	In house Smoky Mermaid Restaurant & Bar, 6am-10pm Free WiFi, air conditioning, private bath, hair dryer, refrigerator, coffee maker, direct dial telephone, cable Tv, alarm clocks, safety deposit box, bottle water, cookie

The look and feel of yesterday with today's modern conveniences make The Great House, Belize's most desirable "outpost" away from home. Meticulously appointed, spacious rooms with all the amenities for your comfort and convenience.

✉ greathouse@btl.net   ◐ www.greathousebelize.com

Villa Boscardi Bed and Breakfast +501-223-1691 Francoise Lays	75 – 89 $US BB 7 rooms, 7 pb MostCC, Cash, *Rated*, • C-yes/S-ltd/P-no/H-ltd English, French, Spanish and Italian.	Full breakfast Eggs, bacon, toast, fruits, coffee and fresh juice Cable TV, A/C, private bathroom, hair dryer, fan, mini refrigerator, telephone, wireless Internet, free breakfast, enclosed parking, laundry services, tours.

Villa Boscardi is a tasteful B&B located in a safe, quiet residential area. We are just a block away from the beautiful Caribbean Sea, with easy access to downtown Belize City, the marinas, and the International Airport. Children under 8 stay for free.

✉ boscardi@btl.net   ◐ www.villaboscardi.com

CAYE CAULKER ──────────────────────────────

Anchorage Resort +501-206-0304 David & Soledad Heredia	75 $US EP 18 rooms, 18 pb MostCC, Cash C-yes/S-no/P-no/H-no English, Spanish	Free WiFi, TV, private balcony. All rooms have AC.

2 private acres of white, sandy beaches where you can relax under the coconut palms. Snorkel or swim off our pier. Children under 10 stay free.

✉ anchorageresort@yahoo.com   ◐ www.anchorageresort.com

Morgan's Inn +501-226-0178 Ellen McRae	25 – 45 $US EP 3 rooms, 3 pb Visa, MC C-yes/S-ltd/P-ltd/H-ltd English, Spanish	No food is offered Stove & refrigerator in all cabins, butane is guest's responsibility, hot water showers in all cabins

Morgan's Inn has 3 Belizean-style cabins available. All cabins are beach-front, with plenty of coconut trees on the land. All have hot/cold showers and large covered porches for relaxing. Marine biologist guide on-site. Lower rates for longer stays.

✉ sbf@btl.net

Tree Tops +501-226-0240 Doris Creasey	50 -100 $US EP 6 rooms, 4 pb Visa, MC C-ltd/S-ltd/P-no/H-no	Coffee, tea High ceilings, large fans, double rooms have cable TV & refrigerators, two rooms with shared baths and four rooms with en suite

Tree Top's Guesthouse can be found on the windward side of picturesque Belize. The six room guesthouse offers luxurious accommodations, featuring a mixture of traditional, Colonial Caribbean style with just a touch of the tropical Mediterranean.

✉ treetopsbelize@hotmail.com   ◐ www.treetopsbelize.com

COROZAL

**Serenity Sands Bed and
Breakfast**
+501-669-2394
Penny & Don Lebrun

80 – 120 $US BB
5 rooms, 5 pb
Visa, MC, *Rated*
C-ltd/S-ltd/P-no/H-no
English

Full breakfast
Alarm clock, BBQ grill, board games,
DVD player, Internet access, library,
satellite/cable TV, telephone, washer/
dryer, A/C, ceiling fans, private
bathroom & entrance

*Serenity Sands Bed and Breakfast is a comfortable, environmentally friendly Bed and Breakfast
where travelers can come for stunning scenery, beautiful sunrises and the peace and tranquility of a
secluded beach.*

✉ info@serenitysands.com   ◔ www.serenitysands.com

SAN IGNACIO

**Mountain Equestrian
Trails**
800-838-3918 +501-669-1124
Marguerite Bevis

65 – 132 $US BB
10 rooms, 10 pb
Visa, MC, AmEx,
Rated, •
C-yes/S-yes/P-ltd/H-ltd
Spanish, English

Full breakfast
Lunch & Dinner
Intimate atmosphere, private thatched-
roof cabanas, intimate kerosene
lighting, Cantina Restaurant, Bar

*Deep in the rain forest setting overlooking a private valley with incredible views of the Maya Moun-
tains in Cayo, at the heart of the Slate Creek Preserve, you'll find an intimate atmosphere, and quali-
fied staff providing outstanding service and more.*

✉ metbelize@pobox.com   ◔ www.metbelize.com

SAN PEDRO TOWN

Mata Rocks Resort
888-628-2757 +501-226-2336
Terry Anderson & Liz
Cechini

110 – 231 $US BB
17 rooms, 17 pb
Visa, MC, AmEx,
Rated, •
C-yes/S-ltd/P-no/H-yes
English/Spanish

Continental Breakfast
Snacks, beachfront bar serves casual
lunches
Free wireless, complimentary bicycles,
free taxi transport, beachfront, pool

*The soft sandy beach just outside your door at Mata Rocks Resort beckons you to enjoy the sparkling
blue Caribbean Sea. Whether you want privacy or access to adventure, our peaceful and serene
beachfront hotel invites you to Ambergris Caye in Belize.*

✉ reservations@matarocks.com   ◔ www.MataRocks.com

Cayman Islands

BODDEN TOWN

The Retreat at Lookout
705-719-9144 705-719-9144
Harvey & Betty Stephenson

99 – 179 $US BB
8 rooms, 8 pb
Visa, MC, Disc, *Rated*
C-ltd/S-no/P-no/H-yes
English

Caribbean Breakfast
Sitting room, pool, kitchen, dining
Room, veranda with rocking chairs,
hot tub, lush landscape, cable TV,
WiFi, A/C, hairdryer, mini-fridge, radio,
iron/board, walking

*Welcome to the Retreat at Lookout, Caymans first Agritourism hotel. A unique guesthouse and an oa-
sis of tranquility within easy reach of the very best of the Cayman Islands. Our charming guestrooms
are nestled on the island within a lush working farm*

✉ reservations@retreatatlookout.com   ◔ www.retreatatlookout.com

SNUG HARBOUR

Annie's Place
345-945-5505
Annie Multon

125 – 140 $US BB
2 rooms, 2 pb
MostCC, Cash, *Rated*
C-yes/S-no/P-no/H-ltd
English

American or English
Ceiling fan, cable TV, refrigerator &
safe, two sitting rooms, library, TV,
VCR, stereo, daily maid service, tennis
& volleyball facilities available

*Annie's Place is a select guesthouse located in the upscale residential area of Snug Harbour, only 3.5
blocks from the famous Seven Mile Beach. The Brittania Golf Club by Jack Nicklaus is within walking
distance.*   ✉ ampm@candw.ky   ◔ www.anniesplace.ky

WEST BAY───────────────────────────

Shangri-La B&B 345-526-1170 Eileen Davidson	119 – 189 $US BB 8 rooms, 8 pb MostCC, Cash, *Rated* C-ltd/S-no/P-no/H-ltd English	Full breakfast Guests may use the kitchen for snacks TV, hairdryers, pool, Jacuzzi, A/C, in–room safes, telephone, iron & laundry services, bicycles, beach chairs & towels

Shangri-La B&B is a tropical lakeside retreat, with six Caribbean style, en suite bedrooms, an exotic pool and Jacuzzi offering dreamy scenery and a lush garden.

✉ info@shangrilabandb.com 🌐 www.shangrilabandb.com

China

BEIJING─────────────────────────────

China Beijing Hutong Courtyard B&B +86-1366-121-9901 Sally Roese	45 – 85 $US BB 4 rooms, 3 pb *Rated* C-yes/S-no/P-no/H-no Chinese, English	Traditional Chinese Breakfast Complimentary tea & coffee, lunch & dinner for fee TV, DVD Player, A/C, heating, safe in each room, guest fridge, microwave, washing machine, common living Room, dining room, free Internet, free local phone calls

A typical Beijing traditional Hutong courtyard house in historic residential area in central Beijing. Traditional carved Chinese furniture in every room. Walking distance to several main tourist attractions. The house and area are full of character.

✉ sally@bb-china.com
🌐 www.bb-china.com/book-online/8-Hutong-Courtyard-Bed-and-Breakfast-Beijing-Shichahai-Nanluoguxiang-Maoer.html

BEIJING - DONGCHENG DISTRICT──────────────────

Red Wall Garden Hotel +86-1051-692-222	120 -250 $US BB 40 rooms, 40 pb Most CC, • C-yes/S-no/P-no/H-yes English, Chinese	Continental plus breakfast On site restaurant, cafe, tea room & winery Trained butler service, cell phone service, airport pick up, babysitting, specialized diet available, shopping & wellness guides, etc.

When you arrive in the most ancient and the most mystical country of ceremonies, the moment you find the one brush of purple red in the bustling metropolis, please hold your footsteps, we welcome you . . .

✉ redwallgardenhotel@gmail.com 🌐 www.redwallgardenhotel.com

Colombia

CARTAGENA───────────────────────────

Hotel Casa La Fe 251-589-6802 Geoff Chew	115 – 200 $US BB 14 rooms, 14 pb Visa, MC, *Rated*, • C-yes/S-ltd/P-no/H-ltd English & Spanish	Full breakfast 24 hr self-service espresso machine rooftop terrace, plunge pool, WiFi, bikes, hotel's own printed maps and guides for restaurants, typical cuisine, light meals and bars.

Beautifully restored elegant hotel located in the historic centre of Cartagena. The hotel has been twice recommended in the Travel Section of the NYT, by the Times of London and was recently categorized as Top Value Hotel in Cartagena by Trip Advisor.

✉ hotelcasalafe@gmail.com 🌐 www.casalafe.com

Costa Rica

ALAJUELA

Orquideas Inn	69 – 160 $US BB	Full breakfast
+506-2433-7128	26 rooms, 26 pb	Lunch & dinner available in the
Liseth Alean	Visa, MC, AmEx,	restaurant
	Rated	Friendly English speaking staff, pool,
	C-yes/S-no/P-ltd/H-ltd	secluded outdoor Jacuzzi, TV, phone,
	Spanish, English	coffee maker, hairdryer, safe, A/C, bar,
		spa, gift shop, laundry service, luggage
		storage

The Inn is nestled on over 10 acres of lush natural tropical gardens teaming with exotic tropical fruits, flowers, birds and butterflies. From the minute you arrive, your cares melt away as you take a dip in the pool or relax in the outdoor Jacuzzi.

✉ info@orquideasinn.com 🌐 www.orquideasinn.com

Pura Vida Retreat and Spa	77 – 1,370 $US AP	Continental breakfast
888-767-7375 770-483-0238	50 rooms, 30 pb	Wholesome, delicious meals included,
Innkeeper	Visa, MC, *Rated*	5 night rate
	C-yes/S-no/P-no/H-no	Pool, Jacuzzi, indoor and outdoor
	English, Spanish	meditation sites, gardens, coffee
		makers

Welcome to Pura Vida Retreat and Spa in Costa Rica. We look forward to being your host at this beautiful resort. Pura Vida Retreat and Spa is considered by some as the Wellness & Yoga destination of choice outside the United States.

✉ reservations@puravidaspa.com 🌐 www.puravidaspa.com

CIUDAD DE CARIARI

The Cariari Bed &	80 – 100 $US BB	Full Breakfast Menu
Breakfast	6 rooms, 5 pb	Fresh fruit always available, beverage
866-224-8339 +506-2239-2585	Visa, MC, *Rated*, •	& bocas
Laurie Blizzard	C-yes/S-ltd/P-yes/H-yes	WiFi, computer, TV, refrigerators,
	Spanish, English, some	ceiling fans, deck for meetings and
	German & French	friends, laundry facilities, Spanish
		classes, tour information, reservations,
		auto rentals, massage

This beautiful Spanish style home in a safe residential area, has a patio and a warm friendly atmosphere. Our huge roof-deck is available for meditation, yoga, massage, bird watching or just relaxing. Access to the Cariari C.C. just 10 min.to SJO airport.

✉ laurie@cariaribb.com 🌐 www.cariaribb.com

ESCAZU

Boutique Hotel Out of	85 – 280 $US BB	Full breakfast
Bounds and Vacation	8 rooms, 8 pb	Fresh fruit drink or coffee
Rental	MostCC, Cash,	A/C, cable TV, fridge, coffeemaker,
+506-2288-6762	*Rated*, •	WiFi, yards, bbq
Meranda Glesby & Matteo	C-yes/S-ltd/P-ltd/H-yes	
Brancacci Soto	English, Spanish, Italian	

Out of Bounds Hotel and Vacation Rental is nestled in the Escazu Mountains on a beautiful property overlooking the Central Valley. With an amazing view of Volcanoes Irazu, Barva and Poas. Enjoy the view from the Terrace or from your rocking chairs.

✉ info@bedandbreakfastcr.com 🌐 www.bedandbreakfastcr.com

Tell your hosts Pamela Lanier sent you.

QUEPOS

La Mansion Inn	125 – 850 $US BB	Full breakfast
800-360-2071 +506-2777-3489	22 rooms, 22 pb	Restaurant and Bar on premises.
Rosalie Maas	Most CC, *Rated*, •	A/C, in-room spa, room service, bar,
	C-ltd/S-no/P-yes/H-no	concierge, daily house keeping, free
	Spanish, English, Dutch	calls to the U.S. and Canada from the
		V.I.P Lounge and reception.

Chosen as a "Best for Romance" and "Best for Luxury" Hotel by TripAdvisor® in its 2009 Travelers' Choice® awards, we provide stunning 360° views of the Pacific Ocean, rainforest and Manuel Antonio National Park.

✉ reservations@lamansioninn.com 🌐 www.lamansioninn.com

SAN JOSE

Adventure Inn Hotel	89 – 109 $US BB	Full breakfast
866-258-4740 +506-2239-2633	34 rooms, 34 pb	Delicious lunches & dinners at
Eric & Mike Robinson	MostCC, Cash,	reasonable rates
	Rated, •	Solar-heated swimming pool, Jacuzzi,
	C-yes/S-no/P-yes/H-yes	WiFi, Internet, guest computers, fully
	Spanish, English	equipped gym, rain forest & volcano
		tours, car and 4WD rentals, A/C, free
		airport transfer

Value-priced smoke-free hotel/B&B between San Jose and airport, huge rooms with A/C, cable, WiFi, full American breakfast, 4 guest computers, sports bar, gym, pool and Jacuzzi, tour rain forests, volcanoes, car rentals, outstanding guest comments.

✉ lanier2@adventure-inn.com 🌐 www.adventure-inn.com/?r=LanierBB

Casa Lima B&B	65 – 75 $US BB	Continental plus breakfast
305-964-6017 786-991-8112	23 rooms, 23 pb	On-site restaurant offers local, Int. &
Nelson Ruiz	Visa, MC, Disc, *Rated*	Cuban food
	C-yes/S-ltd/P-ltd/H-ltd	WiFi Internet access, cable TV, DVD
	English, Spanish	player, comfortable beds, private full
		bathroom with accessories.

"Un pequeño paraiso" is what we often hear from our guests . . . "A small-paradise." Casa Lima is an exclusive bed and breakfast nestled in one of Costa Rica's most unique and privileged neighborhoods, Rohomoser.

✉ info@casalimacr.com 🌐 www.casalimacr.com

SANTA CRUZ

The Painted Pony Guest Ranch	95 – 145 $US BB	Full Ranch breakfast
+506-2653-8041	4 rooms, 3 pb	A variety of meal plans included in
Kay and Esteban	C-yes/S-ltd/P-ltd/H-ltd	packages
	English, Spanish	Splash pool, Hi speed Internet, WiFi,
		Beach and Mountain extensions,
		Horseback riding tours, lessons,
		demonstrations and training. High
		Season Fiestas

The Painted Pony Guest Ranch is a beautiful 50 acre working horse ranch minutes from Costa Rica's most popular Pacific beaches and offers B&B accommodations, riding packages, vacation planning and a variety of riding and other tours.

✉ contact@paintedponyguestranch.com 🌐 www.paintedponyguestranch.com/home

TAMARINDO

Los Altos de Eros	395 – 595 $US BB	Full breakfast
786-866-7039 +506-8850-4222	5 rooms, 5 pb	Gourmet Lunch also included Daily
Calvin & Jacqueline Haskell	MostCC, Cash,	Mountaintop, views of jungle/ocean.
	Rated, •	Pool, library/TV, luxurious tropical
	C-no/S-no/P-no/H-yes	spa

Imagine If You Will- A Luxury Inn & Spa incorporating "world class" features & benefits located in a paradise-like setting in one of the most beautiful of all countries . . . Costa Rica.

✉ info@losaltosdeeros.com 🌐 www.losaltosdeeros.com

TAMARINDO————————————————————————————————

Villa Alegre B&B on the Beach +506-2653-0270 Suzye & Barry Lawson	150 – 230 $US BB 7 rooms, 7 pb Visa, MC, AmEx C-yes/S-ltd/P-no/H-yes English, Spanish	Full breakfast Bocas(appetizers) are often served in the evening Beachfront, pool, library, A/C, shuffleboard, horseshoes, private patios, kitchenettes, wheelchair accessible, phone & fax, secure parking, safe deposit boxes

Villa Alegre B&B offers luxury accommodations in a Spanish style villa on the beach of Playa Langosta in Tamarindo. Vacation and rest in our peaceful tropical garden setting adjacent to natural parkland and just a few steps to the Pacific Ocean.

✉ vialegre@racsa.co.cr ◐ www.villaalegrecostarica.com

Denmark
AEROSKOBING————————————————————————————————

Pension Vestergade +45-625-2229 Susanna Grene	440 DRK BB 6 rooms, 4 pb C-yes/S-no/P-no/H-no English, German, Danish	Full breakfast lunch, dinner (fee) Afternoon tea, complimentary wine, bar service, bicycles, hot tub, sitting room

Extremely beautiful classified house from 1784 in the middle of classified small town, furnished with antiques. Parks and gardens. Scandinavian light, colors and warmth with an English host.

✉ contact@vestergade44.com ◐ www.vestergade44.com/index_uk.html

Dominica
PORTSMOUTH————————————————————————————————

Picard Beach Cottages 767-445-5131 Janice Armour	80 – 220 $US BB 18 rooms, 18 pb Visa, *Rated*, • C-yes/S-no/P-no/H-no English	Continental breakfast Lunch, Dinner, Snacks (fee) Laundromat, childcare, security, tour desk, restaurant, bar, entertainment, afternoon tea, sitting room, pool, fridge, phone, room service, A/C, balcony, wake-up calls

Explore the glorious nature of Dominica staying in luxury and comfort at Picard Beach Cottages. Wooden cottages with traditional Dominican 18th Century architecture and furnishings, cottages are spacious and feature many modern amenities.

✉ picardbeach@cwdom.dm ◐ www.avirtualdominica.com/picard.htm

ROSEAU————————————————————————————————

Anchorage Hotel 767-448-2638 Janice Armour	105 – 160 $US BB 32 rooms, 32 pb Visa, *Rated*, • C-yes/S-no/P-no/H-ltd English	Full American Breakfast Restaurant, lunch, dinner, p.m. tea Sitting Room, bar service, snacks, swimming pool, dive center, TV, A/C, telephone, Internet access

The Anchorage is an informal, elegant hotel. The lounge, pool, terrace and restaurant open out to a wide expanse of the Caribbean Sea and brilliant sunsets.

✉ reservations@anchoragehotel.dm ◐ www.anchoragehotel.dm

Portsmouth Beach Hotel 767-445-5142 Janice Armour	66 – 132 $US BB 80 rooms, 80 pb Visa, *Rated*, • C-yes/S-no/P-no/H-yes English	Continental breakfast Lunch, dinner, afternoon tea, snack available Sitting room, bar service, swimming pool, A/C, cable TV, telephone, wireless Internet, refrigerator access

Portsmouth Beach Hotel is located on a golden sand beach on the northwest coast of Dominica, just half a mile from Portsmouth. Set in a tropical garden, there are eighty rooms, each with a private bathroom and veranda. ✉ pbh@cwdom.dm ◐ www.avirtualdominica.com/pbh.htm

England, U.K.

BATH

Bath Paradise House Hotel	65 – 200 £ BB	Full breakfast
+44-122-531-7723	11 rooms, 11 pb	Complimentary tea, coffee & biscuits
General Manager	Visa, MC, AmEx,	in room
	Rated	Sitting room, walled gardens, TV/DVD,
	C-yes/S-no/P-no/H-ltd	radio, hospitality tray, WiFi, Internet,
	English	Molton Brown products

Behind the classic and dignified exterior, Paradise House conceals more than half an acre of splendid walled gardens. Panoramic views overlook the City of Bath, Royal Crescent and the Abbey below.
✉ info@paradise-house.co.uk 🌐 www.paradise-house.co.uk

Bathwick Gardens	90 – 130 £ BB	Full breakfast
+44-122-546-9435	3 rooms, 3 pb	Bike rentals available.
Julian & Mechthild Self von	C-ltd/S-no/P-no/H-no	
Hippel	English, German	

Welcome to our stunning Regency Bed & Breakfast in the World Heritage City of Bath. Perfectly located for your stay in the Georgian City.
✉ visitus@bathwickgardens.co.uk 🌐 www.bathwickgardens.co.uk

Dorian House	85 – 160 £ BB	Full English & Buffet Breakfast
+44-122-542-6336	12 rooms, 12 pb	Near to Spa, drawing room, garden,
Kathryn Hugh	Most CC, *Rated*, •	small bar, car park, free WiFi
	C-yes/S-no/P-no/H-no	
	English	

Enter an atmosphere of period charm in Dorian House. Panoramic views overlooking Bath. Five diamond rating by AA/RAC/ETC. Licensed. Off-street parking. Ten minute walk to Roman Baths and City Center. ✉ info@dorianhouse.co.uk 🌐 www.dorianhouse.co.uk

Marlborough House	95 – 130 £ BB	Abundant vegetarian breakfast
+44-122-531-8175	6 rooms, 6 pb	Marlborough House specializes in
Peter Moore	Visa, MC, *Rated*, •	organic foods
	C-yes/S-no/P-ltd/H-ltd	Fabulous hosts, antiques, history,
	English	tours, walks, music, theater, advice
	Closed Christmas Eve	
	and Christmas Day	

An enchanting warm and friendly Victorian house close to the Royal Crescent, Assembly Room, Guild Hall, Jane Austen Centre, Roman Baths and Thermal Spas. We are renowned for our relaxed atmosphere, excellent breakfasts and easy conversations.
✉ mars@manque.dircon.co.uk 🌐 www.marlborough-house.net

Oldfields Hotel	49 – 210 £ BB	Full breakfast
+44-122-531-7984	16 rooms, 16 pb	Smoked salmon, English & Vegetarian
General Manager	Visa, MC, AmEx,	breakfast
	Rated	Drawing room, garden, car park,
	C-yes/S-no/P-no/H-no	Jacuzzi tub, TV, DVD, telephones,
	English	wireless Internet, A/C

An elegant & traditional B&B with panoramic views of Bath & only 10 minutes walk to Bath city center. Magnificent drawing room & dining room with spectacular views of Bath.
✉ info@oldfields.co.uk 🌐 www.oldfields.co.uk

LASTINGHAM

Lastingham Grange	125 – 195 £ BB	Full breakfast
+44-175-141-7345	11 rooms, 10 pb	Morning Coffee, Lunch, Afternoon Tea
The Wood Family	Visa, MC, *Rated*, •	& Dinner
	C-yes/S-no/P-yes/H-no	Lounge, terrace, 10 acres of gardens
	English, Spanish, Thai	and fields on the edge of the North
	Open March – end Nov	York Moors

A family run country inn on the edge of the North York Moors National Park located in the historic village of Lastingham, a peaceful backwater in the heart of the National Park. Lastingham is the perfect base for exploring the moors, York and the coast.
✉ Reservations@lastinghamgrange.com 🌐 www.lastinghamgrange.com

LONDON

Barry House
+44-207-723-7340
Bobby Bhasin

80 – 105 £ BB
17 rooms, 15 pb
MostCC, Cash,
Rated, •
C-yes/S-no/P-no/H-no
English

English breakfast
Tea & coffee making facilities en suite
TV, phone, hair dryer, free wireless
Internet access in all rooms

The Barry House offers family friendly accommodations in central London. It is close to Hyde Park, Marble Arch and many of London's famous sights. A recommended hotel with a 3 star guest rating by Visit Britain.   ✉ hotel@barryhouse.co.uk ◐ www.barryhouse.co.uk

---

Europa House Hotel
+44-207-723-7343
Francisca Perez

80 – 88 £ BB
20 rooms, 20 pb
Visa, MC, *Rated*, •
C-yes/S-no/P-no/H-no
English, Spanish

English Breakfast
Tea & coffee making facilities
En suite baths with shower, telephone,
TV, non-smoking rooms available

The Europa House has been a family run bed and breakfast since 1974. We are situated in the heart of London, in the Paddington – Hyde Park area.
✉ europahouse@enterprise.net ◐ www.europahousehotel.com

Lincoln House Hotel
+44-207-486-7630
Joseph Sheriff

89 – 139 £ BB
25 rooms, 23 pb
MostCC, Cash, Checks,
Rated, •
C-yes/S-yes/P-no/H-yes
English, Deutch,
Francois

Full Breakfast
Choice of full, vegetarian, continental
or in-room
Wireless Internet, en-suite bathrooms,
mini fridge, trouser press, unlimited
tea & coffee, satellite TV, telephone,
hair dryer, close to lots of restaurants

A delightfully charming and affordable Georgian B&B hotel, located in the heart of London's West End. Near to all the diverse scenes and activities London has to offer, ideal for shopping, leisure and business trips. Includes a superb English breakfast.
✉ reservations@centrallondonbandb.co.uk ◐ www.centrallondonbandb.co.uk

---

Marble Arch Gloucester
Place Hotel
+44-207-486-6166
Dean Sheriff

99 – 149 £ € BB
19 rooms, 19 pb
MostCC, Cash,
Rated, •
C-yes/S-ltd/P-no/H-no
English

Continental breakfast
Cooked Breakfast and Vegetarian or
Vegan Breakfast
Direct phone, Sat-TV, tea & coffee
stations, mini-fridge, iron/board, WiFi,
hairdryer, safe deposit box upon
request, non-smoking rooms available

Marble Arch Hotel is a comfortable Bed & Breakfast hotel with spacious ensuite bedrooms with free WiFi Internet at fantastic Prices. Located in the heart of Central London next to Oxford Street, next to all major sites and the Airport Bus Stop
✉ reservations@gloucesterplacehotel.com ◐ www.gloucesterplacehotel.com

---

Tudor Court Hotel
+44-207-723-5157
Mr. C. Gupta

99 £ BB
38 rooms, 31 pb
MostCC, Cash, *Rated*
C-yes/S-no/P-no/H-no
English, French,
German, Italian

Full breakfast
Coffee & Tea
LCD TV with 45 channels, safes, WiFi,
24 hour reception, direct dial phones,
hairdryers, irons/adapters, secure
luggage storage

Built originally in the 1850's, this elegant Victorian listed building is ideally situated within minutes from Paddington Station, taking you into the heart of the capital home to the most famous restaurants, theaters, shopping, and historic exhibits.
✉ reservations@tudorcourtpaddington.co.uk ◐ www.tudorcourtpaddington.co.uk

---

The Way to Stay
+44-207-385-4904
Sohel & Anne Armanios

52 £ BB
3 rooms, 1 pb
Rated
C-yes/S-no/P-no/H-no
English

Continental breakfast
Central heating and TV in all rooms

B&B centrally located in London, comfortable family homes, all within short walking distance of the underground station. TV in all rooms, direct transport to all attractions, airports and Euro Star.
◐ www.thewaytostay.co.uk

France

BAYEUX

Clos de Bellefontaine +33-6-8142-2481 +33-6-8142-2481 Carole Mallet	95 – 150 € BB 2 rooms, 2 pb *Rated*, • C-yes/S-no/P-ltd/H-no English, French	Fruits, homemade cakes Sitting room, garden & terrace, gated parking, free computer & WiFi access

Located within the Historic Bayeux, also within walking distance from the Historical Center, near the D.day Beaches, one and a half hour drive from Honfleur or Le Mont-Saint-Michel. In a quiet garden enclosed by walls.

✉ clos.bellefontaine@wanadoo.fr 🌐 clos.bellefontaine.monsite.wanadoo.fr

La Foulerie +33-2-3177-7953 Jean Luc & Irene Tallec	65 € BB 3 rooms, 3 pb Visa, MC, *Rated* C-yes/S-no/P-no/H-yes French, English	Continental breakfast Billiard room, TV/DVD, fireplace, garden

La Foulerie is one of a group of old farmhouses and is over 250 years old. It has been lovingly and artistically restored to maintain its original architecture.

✉ jean.tallec@wanadoo.fr 🌐 www.lafoulerie.net

BIRON

Le Prieure' du Chateau de Biron +33-5-5361-9303 Elisabeth Vedier	120 – 180 € BB 6 rooms, 6 pb Visa, MC, *Rated*, • C-ltd/S-no/P-ltd/H-no French, English, German, some Spanish April thru mid-November	Continental plus breakfast Dinner (on request) with wine Jacuzzi, bathrobes, hairdryers, fine bed linens, fans, tea & coffee facilities, Internet access, sitting room, terrace & stunning views, all beds are twin, Queen or King

A Luxury Bed and Breakfast in Dordogne, Perigord, in village of Biron just below the Château de Biron. Le Prieuré is a large historic building from the early 16th C., offering 6 elegant rooms with en-suite modern bathrooms. Bergerac Airport

✉ leprieurebiron@yahoo.com 🌐 www.leprieurebiron.com

CAUNES-MINERVOIS

L'Ancienne Boulangerie +33-4-6878-0132 Roy Compton & Gareth Armstrong	55 – 85 € BB 6 rooms, 5 pb *Rated* C-yes/S-no/P-yes/H-no English, a little French	Continental breakfast Evening meals provided on request Sitting Room, library, bicycles, terrace

Comfortable, renovated bakery with a pleasant terrace, more than three centuries old in the heart of a medieval village with a 1,200-year-old abbey, surrounded by vineyards and a communal forest.

✉ ancienne.boulangerie@free.fr 🌐 www.ancienneboulangerie.com

EZE

Bastide aux Camelias B&B +33-4-9341-1368 Sylviane Mathieu	110 – 240 € BB 5 rooms, 5 pb C-no/S-ltd/P-no/H-no English, Italian, French	Continental breakfast Outdoor hot tub, sauna, pool, library, lounge

A charming 4★★★★ guesthouse on the French Riviera between Nice and Monaco in the middle of the park Grande Corniche. Located in one of the most beautiful medieval villages of France overlooking the Mediterranean Sea. Special "well-being" package.

✉ sylviane.mathieu@libertysurf.fr 🌐 www.bastideauxcamelias.com

PARIS ───

Hotel Britannique	160 – 221 € EP	Full buffet breakfast available
+33-1-4233-7459	39 rooms, 39 pb	Sound proof rooms, AED
Jean Francis Danjou	Visa, MC, AmEx,	(defibrillator) in the Hotel, bar service,
	Rated, •	sitting Room, A/C, free WiFi, direct dial
	C-yes/S-no/P-no/H-no	phone, safe, flatscreen TV, hairdryer,
	English, Spanish,	cribs . . .
	French	

Completely renovated, the Britannique is an authentic, charming hotel located in the historical center of Paris. Ideal for walking the oldest districts such as the Louvre, les Halles, le Marais, Saint Germain des Pres & the Latin Quarter. ✉ danjou@hotel-britannique.fr ◐ www.hotel-britannique.fr

Le Clos Medicis	150 – 495 € EP	Buffet Breakfast 13 , Afternoon Tea
+33-1-4329-1080	38 rooms, 38 pb	A/C, phone, safe, hairdryer, bar
Olivier Meallet	MostCC, Cash,	service, sitting room, bathrobes,
	Rated, •	fireplace, garden, complimentary WiFi,
	C-yes/S-yes/P-no/H-yes	non-smoking rooms available
	English, Italian, Spanish,	
	French, Portuguese	

Hotel Clos Médicis is a charming, boutique hotel (3 stars) located in Paris on the Left Bank in Saint Germain des Prés. Once a private residence dating back to 1860, it has been tastefully renovated with all the modern comforts and conveniences.
✉ message@hotelclosmedicisparis.com ◐ www.hotelclosmedicisparis.com

ST-SATURNIN-LES-APT ──────────────────────────────

Le Mas Perreal	110 – 130 € BB	Full breakfast
+33-4-9075-4631	5 rooms, 5 pb	Just let us know about special diets
Elizabeth & Kevin Widrow	Visa, MC, *Rated*	Bikes, French lessons, pool, gardens,
	C-yes/S-no/P-no/H-yes	private terraces, en suite bathrooms,
	French, English,	panoramic views
	Spanish, Portuguese,	
	touch of Provencal	

Le Mas Perreal is a luxurious B&B set amidst 17 acres of vineyards and cherry orchards in the Luberon Park, the heart of Provence and offers 5 beautifully decorated rooms, a fantastic breakfast and the perfect base for exploring Provence.
✉ elisabeth-kevin@masperreal.com ◐ www.masperreal.com

French Polynesia

RANGIROA ─────────────────────────────────────

Pension Bounty	126 € BB	Continental plus breakfast
+68-996-0522	4 rooms, 4 pb	Equipped kitchenettes, half board
Alain Ruiz	Visa, MC, AmEx,	possible
	Rated, •	Bathroom with hot water, safe, large
	C-ltd/S-ltd/P-ltd/H-no	deck, ceiling fan, free WiFi, library,
	English, Spanish, Italian	bicycles

Welcome to Pension Bounty in French Polynesia. A private road leads directly from our family lodging to the nearby beach on the beautiful bay of Ohotu. At one end of this beach find taxiboats to ferry guests to the village of Tiputa and other sights.
✉ contact@pension-bounty.com ◐ www.pension-bounty.com

Guatemala
ANTIGUA——

Casa Encantada	54 – 275 $US BB	Full breakfast
866-837-8900 713-344-2344	10 rooms, 10 pb	Wrought iron king & queen poster
Julia Sole	MostCC, Cash,	beds, armoire fridges, safes, TV,
	Rated, •	signature bathrobes, imported
	C-yes/S-no/P-no/H-no	amenities, rooftop terrace, bar, dining,
	Spanish, English,	courtyard, lily pond
	French	

Casa Encantada, a luxurious hotel in the 16th century Spanish Colonial City of Antigua Guatemala, defines elegant, understated hospitality with the utmost in personal service and a staff conversant in Spanish, French and English.

✉ info@casaencantada-antigua.com 🌐 www.casaencantada-antigua.com

Casa Madeleine B&B Spa	105 – 305 $US BB	Guatemalan, Mexican, or American
877-325-9137 +502-7832-9348	6 rooms, 6 pb	Two complementary bottles of water
Perla Reyes	MostCC, Cash, *Rated*	provided daily
	C-yes/S-ltd/P-no/H-ltd	Cable TV, broadband Internet & WiFi,
	Spanish, English	mini-bar, hairdryer, room safe, steam
		room, Jacuzzi, concierge, daily maid
		service, airport shuttle service, special
		tour packages

Casa Madeleine is a distinctive boutique hotel with an exclusive spa offering an intimate experience for guests. Nestled in the historical district of the beautiful Colonial city of La Antigua, Guatemala; Casa Madeleine offers a magical retreat.

✉ frontdesk@casamadeleine.com 🌐 www.casamadeleine.com

Hostal Las Marias	70 – 110 $US BB	Continental plus breakfast
+502-5516-9147	10 rooms, 10 pb	Cable TV, Internet access, shuttle from
Monica Estrada	MostCC, Cash, *Rated*	airport, walk around tours, parking
	C-yes/S-ltd/P-no/H-yes	area, hairdryer (upon request),
	Spanish, English	fireplace

Hostal Las Marias is an Inn with a mixture of styles, the Colonial folklore of Guatemala and today's modern amenities. A home built with personal touches and traditional details with everything you need in place.

✉ reservations@hostallasmarias.com 🌐 www.hostallasmarias.com

Hostal San Nicolas	80 – 110 $US BB	Continental plus breakfast
+502-7832-2915	4 rooms, 4 pb	We offer delicious light sandwiches,
Rossana Pons	Most CC, *Rated*, •	soups
	C-yes/S-ltd/P-no/H-ltd	Hot water, mini-bar, microwave,
	Spanish, English	coffeemaker, cable TV, cozy living
		room with wood-burning fireplace,
		spacious dining room for guests, small
		bar, WiFi

Enjoy Antigua Guatemala's unique atmosphere while staying at Hostal San Nicolas. Its historic and cozy spaces are the ideal haven for the city's visitors. You will find a perfect place to relax in the beautiful garden, corridors or resting areas.

✉ mail@hostalsannicolas.com 🌐 www.hostalsannicolas.com

India
JAIPUR

Umaid Bhawan (A Heritage Home) +91-141-220-1276 Ranvijay	2,400 – 3,500 INR BB 40 rooms, 40 pb Visa, MC, AmEx, *Rated*, • C-yes/S-ltd/P-ltd/H-ltd English, Hindi	Continental breakfast A delectable range of Indian cuisine is offered A/C, TV, alarm clock, hairdryer, wake up service, pool, business center, Internet cafe, laundry service, private balconies, folk dance/puppet show, library, BBQ grill

Built on traditional Rajput style, the balconies are intricately carved, there are many courtyards, terraces, a beautiful garden and the rooms are furnished with antiques. An exotic attraction of traditional Rajasthani ambience and modern luxuries.

✉ info@umaidbhawan.com   🌐 www.umaidbhawan.com

Ireland
CARLOW

Barrowville Town House +353-599-143324 Anna & Dermot Smyth	80 – 120 € BB 7 rooms, 7 pb Visa, MC, AmEx, *Rated*, • C-yes/S-ltd/P-no/H-no English.	Traditional Breakfast Several restaurants are within walking distance Sitting room, car park, gardens, direct dial phone, TV, hairdryer, non-smoking

The Barrowville Town House is a premier quality guesthouse, a three Star Georgian listed property. There are antique furnishings throughout. A traditional Irish breakfast is served in the conservatory overlooking the gardens. ✉ barrowvilletownhouse@eircom.net   🌐 www.barrowville.com

COUNTY GALWAY

Cashel House Hotel +353-953-1001 McEvilly Family	190 – 390 € BB 29 rooms, 29 pb Visa, MC, AmEx, *Rated*, • C-yes/S-ltd/P-ltd/H-ltd English, French, German	Full breakfast Lunch, dinner, afternoon tea, snacks, restaurant Bar service, sitting room, library, bicycles, tennis court, horseback riding, small beach, television, hairdryers

Cashel House Hotel is an elegant country manor set in a beautiful garden by the sea. Connemara pony breeding & horseback riding on site. Near a huge wilderness touring area. There are 19 rooms & 13 suites with a fine dining restaurant on the premises.

✉ res@cashel-house-hotel.com   🌐 www.cashel-house-hotel.com

MOUNTRATH

Roundwood House +353-578-732120 Hannah & Paddy Flynn	120 – 130 € BB 10 rooms, 10 pb Disc, *Rated*, • C-yes/S-ltd/P-ltd/H-no English, Spanish, French Closed 25 December	Full breakfast Dinner available Drawing room, Library of "The History of Civilization" for book lovers, bar service, gardens, acres of park and woodland, Croquet, Boule, Mountain Walks nearby

Beautiful Palladian villa surrounded by woods. A piece of warm and welcoming history. We aim to create a special place where personal attention and service comes naturally and life is taken at a relaxed pace.

✉ info@roundwoodhouse.com   🌐 www.roundwoodhouse.com

Italy

ARZACHENA

B&B Costa Smeralda	70 – 130 € BB	Continental plus breakfast
+39-0789-99811	3 rooms, 3 pb	Mini fridge, external kitchen and BBQ
Luciana Pedrotti	C-yes/S-ltd/P-ltd/H-no	Private bath, A/C, satellite TV, free Internet

In welcoming a new Gallura Bed and Breakfast near Porto Cervo and the wonderful beaches of the Costa Smeralda. Piero & Luciana opened their house to show you this amazing land and its sea, coasts, perfumes and colours! Welcome!

✉ info@bbcostasmeralda.com   🌐 www.bbcostasmeralda.com

ASCIANO

Podere Finerri	100 – 140 € EP	Full Breakfast available for 12 Euros
+39-0577-704475	11 rooms, 9 pb	Linen & towels, daily cleaning,
Daniela Di Cesare &	*Rated*	laundry, child care, dog sitting, private
Malcolm Ayres	C-yes/S-ltd/P-yes/H-ltd	dinners & chef
	Italian, English	

Podere Finerri is a 1700's farmhouse with breathtaking views over the Siena hills, totally surrounded by fields of wheat, vineyards and olive groves. Finerri Olive Grove produces organic olive oil.

✉ info@thelazyolive.com   🌐 www.thelazyolive.com

BUONCONVENTO

Podere Salicotto	140 – 220 € BB	Continental breakfast
+39-0577-809087	7 rooms, 7 pb	In room coffee & tea
Silvia Forni	Visa, MC, *Rated*, •	Plush linens, tea/coffee & tisanes,
	C-ltd/S-no/P-no/H-no	private safe, hairdryer, A/C, Heating,
	Italian, English, German	bathrobes, pool towels, daily cleaning,
		BBQ, salt water pool, bicycles, WiFi

Podere Salicotto features panoramic views of the rolling Tuscan hills, magnificent sunrises and sunsets, intimate ambience and located near Montalcino and Siena. A warm welcome to Podere Salicotto, from Silvia & Paolo, its owners and hosts.

✉ info@poderesalicotto.com   🌐 www.poderesalicotto.com

CASTIGLIONE D'ORCIA

Castello di Ripa d'Orcia	130 – 195 € BB	Continental breakfast
+39-0577-897376	13 rooms, 13 pb	Dinner – by reservation
The Aluffi Rossi Family	Visa, MC, *Rated*, •	Rustic Tuscan furniture, pool, terrace,
	C-ltd/S-ltd/P-no/H-no	restaurant, fireplace, wedding chapel,
	English, French, Italian	meeting room, tasting room – Orcia
		Wines & Extra Virgin Olive Oil, bikes
		on request, phone

The castle of Ripa d'Orcia dates back to and is set in a 12th Century Medieval Hamlet. Restored to a comfortable country residence bed & breakfast which offers hospitality along with the discovery of its fine wines and Extra Virgin Olive Oil production.

✉ info@castelloripadorcia.com   🌐 www.ripadorcia.it

CETONA

La Frateria Di Padre Eligio	240 – 300 € BB	Full breakfast
+39-0578-238261	7 rooms, 7 pb	Lunch and dinner in our elegant
Maria Grazia Daolio	Visa, MC, AmEx,	restaurant
	Rated	Lounge, gardens, woods, restaurant,
	C-yes/S-ltd/P-no/H-no	period antiques, privacy, peaceful,
	Italian, English, French	authentic atmosphere, mystic aura,
		no TV

Padre Eligio's "La Frateria" has been created in one of the most beautiful monuments made by man, the convent of Saint Francis, founded by the Saint in 1212, an example of late middle ages convent life, still intact.

✉ info@lafrateria.it   🌐 www.lafrateria.it

COLLE DI VAL D'ELSA

Le Tre Perle B&B	70 – 110 € BB	Continental breakfast
+39-3478-302033	5 rooms, 5 pb	Home cooked meals are available
+39-0577-921489	MostCC, Cash	upon request
Elisabetta	C-yes/S-no/P-no/H-no	Daily room cleaning, towels & bed
	English & Italian	linens, heating & A/C, TV, hair dryer
		(on request)

Centrally located, Le Tre Perle B&B offers accommodations at affordable prices, combined with a comfortable and relaxing atmosphere. Choose from 5 rooms with a combination of doubles, triples, and quadruples – all with private bathrooms.

✉ elisabetta@letreperle.com 🌐 www.letreperle.com

CORTINA D'AMPEZZO

Hotel Menardi	53 – 140 € BB	Continental plus breakfast
+39-0436-2400	49 rooms, 49 pb	Lunch, Dinner (fee), Afternoon Tea
The Menardi Family	MostCC, Cash,	Wellness Center, sauna, steam bath,
	Rated, •	whirlpool, massage, bar, restaurant,
	C-yes/S-no/P-no/H-yes	complimentary wine, sitting room,
	English, German,	library
	French, Italian	

At the turn of century it was an ancient family house, an inn with a stable and a bar, a post-house on the route connecting the Habsburg Empire to the Kingdom of Italy.

✉ info@hotelmenardi.it 🌐 www.hotelmenardi.it

CORTONA

Casa Bellavista B&B	120 – 140 € BB	Sumptuous Buffet Breakfast
+39-0575-610311	4 rooms, 4 pb	Traditional Tuscan dinners on request
Simonetta Demarchi	Visa, MC, *Rated*, •	Sitting Room offers comfort to enjoy
	C-yes/S-yes/P-ltd/H-no	music, read or plan the next day's
	Italian, English	travels, relax in a hammock or at the
		pool, free Vespa use for guests

Nestled on a hilltop in the Val di Chiana, amid fields of sunflowers, olive groves and vineyards Casa Bellavista is your Tuscan dream. Experience Tuscan country life while you enjoy views of the Abbazia di Farneta, Montepulciano, Lucignano and Cortona.

✉ info@casabellavista.it 🌐 www.casabellavista.it

Le Gelosie Bed & Breakfast	85 – 180 € BB	Full breakfast
info@legelosie.com +39-0575-	7 rooms, 7 pb	
630005	MostCC, Cash	
Andrea Bruni	C-yes/S-no/P-no/H-no	
	English, Italian, German,	
	Spanish, French	

This lovely bed and breakfast is the result of a flight of fancy of its young owner: he wanted to offer a sophisticated alternative for the cosmopolitan tourist.

✉ info@legelosie.com 🌐 www.legelosie.com

FASANO

Masseria Marzalossa	80 – 250 € BB	Continental breakfast
+39-0804-413780	12 rooms, 12 pb	Daily menu prepared by Mistress
Mario & Maria Teresa	Visa, MC	Maria Teresa
Guarini	C-ltd/S-no/P-no/H-no	Cookery course on request, swimming
		pool, lemon grove

The Farm House "Marzalossa" was built in the XVIIth century and is one of the historical homes of Apulia. The Guarini family has owned it for over two centuries and it is directly managed by them.

✉ masseriamarzalossa@marzalossa.it 🌐 www.marzalossa.it

FLORENCE───────────────────────────────────────

B&B Villa La Sosta	79 – 130 € BB	Continental breakfast
+39-3358-349992	5 rooms, 5 pb	We serve healthy breakfasts.
+39-0554-95073	Visa, MC, *Rated*, •	Billiard Room, Panoramic Windowed
Antonio & Giuseppina	C-yes/S-no/P-no/H-ltd	Attic, Private Parking, TV, WiFi ,
Fantoni	Italian, English, Spanish	Internet, Daily Cleaning, Provision of
		Tourist Information

A charming and elegant B&B situated in one of Florence's most exclusive residential areas. Only 10 minutes walking distance from the historic city center.

✉ info@villalasosta.com   🌐 www.villalasosta.com

───────────────────────────────────────

Casa Rovai	70 – 200 € BB	Buffet Breakfast
+39-3474-852643	6 rooms, 6 pb	Mineral water, tea & coffee, healthy
+39-0552-001647	Most CC, *Rated*	food
Anna Maria Meo	C-yes/S-no/P-no/H-ltd	Free Internet corner, private car
	Italian, English, French,	parking, bike rental, dry cleaning/
	German, Spanish,	washing service, wine & food tasting/
	Portuguese	private dinners (min 4 people),
		cooking classes (min 4 people)

Tastefully decorated with original 18th and 20th century furniture and recently renovated, the property has been under this family's ownership since the turn of the 1900's. 6 elegant guestrooms with painted ceilings and walls. Only steps from the Uffizi.

✉ info@casarovai.com   🌐 www.casarovai.it

───────────────────────────────────────

Florence Dream Domus	125 – 165 € BB	Typical Italian breakfast
Bed and Breakfast	6 rooms, 6 pb	Air-conditioned, satellite TV, savory
+39-0552-95346	C-yes/S-no/P-no/H-no	food with express service, tours,
Perla		proximity to Duomo, Internet
		connection, Jacuzzi

An inviting and comfortable house furnished with antiques, Florentine tapestry and refined marble floors. Ready to welcome many friends from all over the world and make sure their stay becomes, as for me, a "Florence Dream".

✉ info@florencedream.it   🌐 www.florencedream.it/inglese/florencedream.htm

───────────────────────────────────────

La Casa Dei Tintori	80 – 150 € BB	Full breakfast
+39-0552-639771	5 rooms, 5 pb	Espresso coffee, yogurt, chocolate, tea,
+39-3287-665169	C-yes/S-no/P-ltd/H-no	juice
Alfredo Ingegno	Italian	Free and fast Internet, tourist info,
		private bathroom, TV, air conditioning,
		hairdryer, safe-deposit box

If you are looking for clean, warm, friendly hospitality and personal service the Casa dei Tintori B&B in Florence, Italy is your answer. With the friendly help of your hosts, Alfredo and Valeria, this B&B can truly be your home away from home.

✉ alfredoingegno@casadeitintori.it   🌐 www.casadeitintori.it/en

───────────────────────────────────────

Hotel Casci	80 – 150 € BB	Buffet style breakfast
+39-0552-11686	24 rooms, 24 pb	Bar/cafe in lobby, breakfast in Fresco
Paolo Lombardi	Visa, MC, AmEx,	Room
	Rated	A/C, fridge, direct phone, TV, DVD,
	C-yes/S-ltd/P-ltd/H-yes	free movies, radio, hairdryer, safe
	English, French,	box, lobby WiFi, tour & car rental
	German, Spanish	desk, concierge reservations, laundry
		service

Situated in a 15th century palace in central Florence, originally the home and property of the infamous composer, G. Rossini, this small, welcoming hotel, run by the Lombardi Family, is perfect for the individual traveler, families and small groups alike.

✉ info@hotelcasci.com   🌐 www.hotelcasci.com

FLORENCE

Hotel Morandi Alla Crocetta
+39-0552-344747
Paolo Antuono

80 – 220 € BB
10 rooms, 10 pb
MostCC, Cash,
Rated, •
C-yes/S-no/P-yes/H-no
English, French, Italian,
German

Continental plus breakfast
Sitting room, library, garage, antiques,
A/C, WiFi & Internet access, SAT-TV,
mini-bar

Following an ancient tradition of hospitality the Morandi Alla Crocetta offers a quiet, comfortable and distinguished atmosphere in the former convent of the Crocetta. It is today a place where one can enjoy a really pleasant and relaxed Florentine stay.

✉ welcome@hotelmorandi.it 🌐 www.hotelmorandi.it

La Paggeria de Villa Mazzini
+39-0554-01362
Paolo Verzelletti

120 – 170 € BB
4 rooms, 5 pb
Visa, MC
C-yes/S-ltd/P-yes/H-no
Italian, English, French

Continental breakfast
Gourmet meals are available also.
Private parking, daily cleaning of
the room. children under 2 free,
heating, A/C, fireplace and satellite TV.
Swimming pool, Jacuzzi.

The Paggeria Bed and Breakfast is a stone villa in the Florence hills that has been popular for centuries with visitors and Florentines alike for its cool temperatures during the summer months, clean air and splendid views over Florence and Fiesole.

✉ info@lapaggeria.com 🌐 www.lapaggeria.com

Villa Antea
+39-0554-84106
Serena Lenzi

80 – 200 € BB
6 rooms, 6 pb
Visa, MC, *Rated*, •
C-yes/S-no/P-yes/H-yes
Italian, English, French

Continental Plus Breakfast
Vegetarian or gluten free meals upon
request
Semi-canopy king bed, rain shower
with body sprays, air conditioning,
free WiFi, satellite TV LCD, minibar,
private safe, blackout curtains, table
& chair

Villa Antea is a charming and romantic small Relais in Florence. The building is beautiful, authentic and individual, a true gem. The rooms are very spacious and elegant, all decorated with original furnishing and modern amenities. The bathrooms are huge!

✉ info@villaantea.com 🌐 www.villaantea.com

Villa Ulivi
+39-0554-00777
Maria Grazia Furnari

60 – 130 € BB
10 rooms, 10 pb
Visa, MC, *Rated*, •
C-yes/S-ltd/P-ltd/H-ltd
Italian, French, Spanish

Buffet Breakfast
Excellent regional wines
Garden, free parking, roof top terrace,
backyard patio, barbecue grill, chapel,
wine cellar and wine tasting

Villa Ulivi is a beautiful Florentine mansion that combines town and countryside as well as ancient and modern facilities. It is located in a prestigious residential area of Florence, very close to the center and to the main monuments and attractions.

✉ info@villaulivi.com 🌐 www.villaulivi.com

GARGAGNAGO

Villa Monteleone
+39-0457-704974
Lucia D. Raimondi

85 – 90 € BB
3 rooms, 3 pb
Visa, MC, *Rated*
C-yes/S-ltd/P-no/H-ltd
Italian, Spanish, English
March to November

Full breakfast
Free tours of the cellar and guided
wine tastings
San Vito Suite has a full bath & sauna,
the Santa Lena Suite has a splendid
terrace & just added the San Paolo
Suite. A/C and small refrigerators in
all rooms

Villa Monteleone is set in a 17th century villa surrounded by vineyards and a beautiful park that has been designated a national monument.

✉ bedandbreakfast@villamonteleone.com 🌐 www.villamonteleone.com

LEVANTO

Hotel Nazionale
+39-0187-808102
Angela Lagomarsino

90 – 138 € BB
38 rooms, 38 pb
MostCC, Cash,
Rated, •
C-yes/S-no/P-yes/H-no
English, German,
French
Open from April
through November

Buffet breakfast
. . . includes local Ligurian Focaccia
Bar service, Garden, panoramic roof
terrace, sitting room, parking, suites,
phone, hairdryer, room safe, TV,
minibar, A/C, WiFi, lift

Friendly, family-run hotel, conveniently situated close to town, the beach, train, boats & "Cinque Terre." The Hotel Nazionale has been a symbol of the resort town of Levanto's hospitality for more than a century. ✉ hotel@nazionale.it ✆ www.nazionale.it

LUCCA

Ai Cipressi
+39-3482-432729
Gabriele

69 – 99 € BB
3 rooms, 3 pb
MostCC, Cash,
Rated, •
C-ltd/S-no/P-no/H-ltd
Italian, English, French,
German

Breakfast Buffet
A/C, hairdryer, Satellite TV, free
private parking, WiFi

Free Night w/Certificate: Valid Nov-April. Room Upgrade.

Whatever takes you to Lucca, there is surely a moment that you'll spend visiting some pretty corner of our precious city. Whatever the reason for your visit, Ai Cipressi is ideally situated right in the heart of it all. ✉ info@aicipressi.it ✆ www.aicipressi.it/default.asp

Albergo San Martino
+39-0583-469181
Mr. Andrea Morotti

90 – 170 € BB
10 rooms, 10 pb
Visa, MC, AmEx,
Rated, •
C-yes/S-no/P-no/H-ltd
Italian, German, French,
English

Buffet breakfast
Snacks, tea, wine, beer, etc . . .
Parking, bike rental, laundry service,
room service, wake-up system,
hairdryer, credit cards/Bancomat, bar,
A/C, outdoor living area, living room,
fax, safe at reception

A small intimate hotel located on a quiet narrow street within the city walls in the heart of Lucca's Historic Center. The interiors of the rooms, lounge and hallways are stylishly decorated in warm, inviting colors, which complement the kind hospitality.
✉ info@albergosanmartino.it ✆ www.albergosanmartino.it

MERANO

Castle Fragsburg Relais & Chateaux
+39-0473-244071
Alexander Ortner

266 – 650 € BB
20 rooms, 20 pb
Visa, MC, AmEx,
Rated, •
C-yes/S-no/P-no/H-yes
Italian, German, French,
English
April – November

Full breakfast buffet
1-Star-Michelin restaurant:á la carte
lunch&dinner
Spa, sauna, heated outdoor pool,
library, smoking lounge, terrace with
panoramic view, W-LAN, private park,
bathrobes, terrycloth slippers

The old hunting lodge Relais & Chateaux Castel Fragsburg is located in a fantastic setting above Merano, surrounded by gorgeous nature and spectacular mountains. Enjoy the cuisine and relaxing Spa of the smallest First-Class-Hotel in the Dolomites.
✉ info@fragsburg.com ✆ www.fragsburg.com

MONTEBELLUNA

Villa Serena
+39-0423-300210
Serena

85 – 110 € BB
22 rooms, 22 pb
Visa, MC, AmEx,
Rated
C-yes/S-no/P-no/H-yes
Italian, English

Buffet Breakfast
A/C, private bathrooms – some w/
Jacuzzi, mini bar, tv, isdn, adsl WiFi,
all rooms are non-smoking, wheelchair
accessible rooms available

The soft profile of the Costa d'Oro hills is the natural back drop of Villa Serena: an elegant country mansion, in eighteenth century style. Surrounded by the green Treviso country, Villa Serena is situated in Montebelluna, a dynamic city. ✉ info@villaserenaonline.com ✆ www.villaserenaonline.com

PALERMO

Casa Giuditta Palermo
+39-3282-250788
Salvatore Gallo

39 – 250 € BB
4 rooms, 4 pb
Visa, MC, AmEx,
Rated, •
C-yes/S-yes/P-yes/H-yes
English, Italian, Russian,
French, German

Italian Breakfast
Coffee & tea maker
A/C, SAT-TV, cradle if required,
personal driver (upon request),
washer/dryer, dishwasher, nearby
restaurants, bar, stores & supermarket

Casa Giuditta offers travelers beautiful 17th century apartments in the center of the town of Palermo. The fully furnished and air-conditioned apartments may be rented by the day or week and can accommodate 1 to 6 people.

✉ casagiuditta@yahoo.com 🌐 www.casagiuditta.com

PERUGIA

San Felicissimo
+39-0756-919400
Alberto Spagnolli

70 – 80 € BB
10 rooms, 10 pb
Visa, MC, *Rated*
C-yes/S-ltd/P-yes/H-ltd
Italian, English, German,
Spanish

Continental plus breakfast
Fridge, mini bar, patio, terrace, pool,
Internet, WiFi, Sat-TV

San Felicissimo, a farm vacation B&B, is an elegantly renovated early 19th century farm house, in the Umbrian countryside. Nestled in the lovely hillside of Poggio Pelliccione, just 4 km from the centre of Perugia.

✉ info@sanfelicissimo.net 🌐 www.sanfelicissimo.net

PIENZA

Fonte Bertusi
+39-0578-748077
Manuela Rosati

100 – 130 € BB
8 rooms, 8 pb
Visa, MC, AmEx
C-yes/S-yes/P-yes/H-ltd
english

Full breakfast
Pool, wine shop, massage available.

The Pisano family has been running the farmhouse since 1991 offering its guests warm hospitality. You will discover a unique place to spend a different holiday, flavouring the pleasure of the many sensations the simple natural things can give you.

✉ info@fontebertusi.it 🌐 www.fontebertusi.it

POLCANTO

Porcigliano B&B
+39-0558-409903
Gabbriella Papini & Family

70 – 80 € BB
3 rooms, 3 pb
Rated, •
C-yes/S-no/P-no/H-no
Italian, English, French
Closed November –
February

Continental plus breakfast
complimentary afternoon coffee/tea,
wine/beverages
Hair dryer, iron/ironing board
available on request at no charge.
Complimentary Internet WiFi, and
car parking. Possibility to use the
breakfast corner for picnic.

A cosy country house just a few kilometers from Florence and the Etruscan town of Fiesole in the beautiful Florence hills. Porcigliano is an excellent base for anyone wishing to visit Florence and the most interesting places of Tuscany.

✉ info@porcigliano.it 🌐 www.porcigliano.it

POSITANO

B&B Villa Mary Positano
+39-0898-75216
Tiziana Mastellone

80 – 180 € BB
3 rooms, 3 pb
Visa, MC, AmEx,
Rated, •
C-yes/S-ltd/P-no/H-no
Italian, English, French

Continental breakfast
TV SAT, air conditioning, safety box,
hair dryer, hydro-massage

Villa Mary Bed & Breakfast is located in Positano, one of the most exclusive gems of the Divine Amalfi coast. Declared by UNESCO a World Heritage Site, with an atmosphere characterized by strong scents, colours, traditions & unique artistic masterpieces.

✉ info@villamary.it 🌐 www.villamary.it

ROME

Casa Franci Bed & Breakfast
+39-3934-191484
Francesca

45 – 120 € BB
3 rooms, 3 pb
Visa, MC, *Rated*, •
C-yes/S-ltd/P-no/H-no
English, Italian, Spanish, French

Continental breakfast
Tea & coffee, cappuccino, espresso, cereals, fruit
TV, DVD, movies, PC for small fee, balcony, wake-up call, non-smoking rooms, cot, coffee maker, mini-bar, central heating, hairdryer

If you are looking for a quiet, centrally-located, yet affordable place in Rome, come and enjoy breakfast with a view of St. Peter's Dome from our cozy bed and breakfast, Casa Franci.

✉ hellotomymail-casafranci@yahoo.com 🌐 www.casafrancibedandbreakfast.com

---

Hotel Modigliani
+39-0642-815226
Marco & Giulia Di Tillo

80 – 280 € BB
24 rooms, 24 pb
Most CC, *Rated*
C-yes/S-no/P-no/H-ltd
English, German, French, Italian, Spanish

Continental plus breakfast
Homecakes, cheese, ham, salami, eggs, cappuccino
Luxury Lounge and Bar, Inner garden, view from top floor suites, sitting room, Wireless area, library, art, copier, fax, mini bar, Sat-TV, safe, A/C, hairdryer

A charming boutique Hotel in the center of Rome, near The Spanish Steps and Via Veneto, with inner garden, luxury salon, dramatic view from superior rooms on the top floor, including independent apartments, and family rooms.

✉ info@hotelmodigliani.com 🌐 www.hotelmodigliani.com

Looking at St. Peter
+39-0335-261571
Roberto Paparelli

70 – 100 € BB
2 rooms
C-yes/S-yes/P-ltd/H-no
english , french and italian

Full breakfast
In the room: a fully stocked minibar, satellite television, computer with Internet, hair dryer, and full breakfast in the morning.

Allow us the pleasure of welcoming you to our home, located virtually two steps from St. Peter's Square. Discover the eternal city in a comfortable and friendly lodging space, adjacent to the whole of Rome.

✉ roberto@lookingatstpeter.com 🌐 www.lookingatstpeter.com

SIENA

Locanda del Loggiato
+39-3354-30427
+39-0577-888925
Sabrina & Barbara Marini

90 -180 € BB
6 rooms, 6 pb
Visa, MC, AmEx
C-yes/S-no/P-yes/H-ltd
Italian, English, French

Traditional Tuscan Breakfast
Sweets, chocolate biscuits, tea, nuts, wine
Sitting room, piano, AC, loft, antiques, private baths

The stone building dates to the 1300s. There are six, romantic, double bedrooms and a large living room with a loft and grand piano. Very cozy and purposely old-fashioned in feeling.

✉ locanda@loggiato.it 🌐 www.loggiato.it

Villa Fiorita
+39-3918-9000
Gabriele Fontani

50 – 130 € BB
10 rooms, 10 pb
C-yes/S-yes/P-no/H-no
Italian

Continental breakfast
On request, breakfast served in room or in garden.
Front desk service from 8am-8pm, guided tours, free street parking, garden area, satellite TV, A/C & Central heating

Villa Fiorita Bed & Breakfast is located in Siena in a liberty-style villa built from 1912 to 1916. Inside the villa it is possible to find the elegance and originality of an ancient residence and the traditional welcoming of Siena.

✉ bebvillafiorita@gmail.com 🌐 www.villafiorita-siena.com

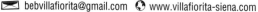

SINALUNGA

Relais La Leopoldina
+39-0577-623447
Angela Meattini

95 – 180 € BB
6 rooms, 6 pb
Visa, MC, AmEx,
Rated, •
C-yes/S-ltd/P-ltd/H-no
Italian, english, french

Continental plus breakfast
Warm croissants homemade cakes jam
cheese salami
Satellite TV, telephone, minibar, safe,
air conditioning, wireless Internet, en-
suite bathroom with Jacuzzi shower,
hairdryer, outdoor swimming pool

A comfortable and elegant B&B in the heart of the Siena countryside, ideally located for daily tours to many close historical towns. The manor house dates back to the 18th century, has 6 nice double rooms, a swimming pool and a very well-known restaurant.

✉ info@relaislaleopoldina.it   🌐 www.relaislaleopoldina.it

SIRACUSA

Giuggiulena Villa
+39-0931-468142
Sabrina Perasole

90 – 110 € BB
6 rooms, 6 pb
MostCC, Cash,
Rated, •
C-yes/S-no/P-ltd/H-yes
Italian, English

Buffet Breakfast
A rich buffet breakfast with local
specialties
Air conditioning, heating, mini-bar,
satellite TV, Sky TV, Internet WiFi,
daily room cleaning, free parking, a
beautiful terrace and access to the sea,
bicycles

The Giuggiulena Hotel, classified as a Bed and Breakfast in the tourist literature, is a shelter carved into a cliff overlooking a bay off the ocean on the east coast of Sicily.

✉ info@giuggiulena.it   🌐 www.giuggiulena.it

Palazzo del Sale
+39-0931-65958
Sabrina Perasole

90 – 120 € BB
7 rooms, 7 pb
MostCC, Cash, *Rated*
C-ltd/S-no/P-no/H-no
Italian, English

Continental breakfast
Satellite TV, A/C-heating, mini bar,
fridges, communal cooking space,
Internet, bicycles, sun terrace

Palazzo del Sale known as the Salt or White Gold building, has high ceilings and walls of stone embedded with details in a unique and pleasant style, gives an authentic feel to the place. All seven rooms furnished with beautiful original appointments.

✉ info@palazzodelsale.com   🌐 www.palazzodelsale.it

TAORMINA

La Pensione Svizzera
+39-9422-3790
Pancrazio Vinciguerra

60 – 150 € BB
22 rooms, 22 pb
Visa, MC, AmEx,
Rated, •
C-yes/S-no/P-yes/H-no
Italian, English, German,
French

Breakfast Buffet
The bar is open from 10.00a.m. until
1.00a.m.
Child care, bar, Free WiFi, hair dryer,
safe, 24hr front desk, attraction &
reservation assistance, SAT-TV-LCD,
A/C, garden, laundry service, ocean/
sea views, parking

A perfect example of a small charming hotel located on the Via Pirandello, one of the most beautiful panoramic roads of Taormina. A short walk to the center (Corso Umberto) as well as to the cable car and the main bus terminal.

✉ info@pensionesvizzera.com   🌐 www.pensionesvizzera.com

VENICE

B&B Sandra
+39-0417-20957
Alessandra Soldi

85 – 130 € BB
2 rooms, 2 pb
Rated
C-yes/S-no/P-no/H-no
English, French, Italian

Buffetl breakfast
Kettle & cups are available in guest-
rooms
Terrace, A/C, very quiet & romantic

B&B Sandra stands along one of the main canals in the Old City Center, close to the most important sites in Venice.

✉ info@bbalessandra.com   🌐 www.bbalessandra.com

VENICE

Ca' Arco Antico
+39-0412-411227
Marco Angelini

80 – 160 € BB
8 rooms, 8 pb
Visa, MC, AmEx,
Rated, •
C-yes/S-no/P-no/H-no
English, Spanish,
French, German

Continental breakfast
Safe deposit box, hairdryer, alarm
WiFi, Internet, TV, A/C, heat

An old arch and a lovely Venitian courtyard shelters the Inn "Ca'Arco Antico", an oasis of peace and tranquility on the main floor of a Venetian house where all the charm and elegance of the yesteryear has been preserved.

✉ info@arcoanticovenice.com ◯ www.arcoanticovenice.com

Casanova ai Tolentini
+39-3498-782995
Alberto & Monica

70 – 400 € BB
19 rooms, 19 pb
Visa, MC, *Rated*
C-yes/S-no/P-yes/H-no
Italian, English, French,
Spanish

Buffet Breakfast
Half board service upon request
A/C, heating, safe, WiFi, Internet,
flat Screen SAT TV, courtesy kit,
hairdryers, luggage storage, private
baths, laundry service on request,
partner restaurant

The Venice of your dreams is welcoming and accessible at the B&B Casanova ai Tolentini, just two minutes from the Piazzale Rome car park, near the direct boat line for San Marco and Rialto.

✉ info@casanovaaitolentini.com ◯ www.casanovaaitolentini.com/en/index.htm

---

Hotel Bernardi Semenzato
+39-0415-227257
Maria Teresa Pepoli

68 – 98 € BB
25 rooms, 18 pb
MostCC, Cash, •
C-yes/S-ltd/P-yes/H-no
Italian, English, French,
German Spanish

Continental breakfast
Snacks
Sitting room, hot tub, terrace on the
roof, exchange, A/C, Sat-TV, in-room
tea & coffee stations, free Internet &
WiFi connection

Welcome to the Hotel Bernardi Semenzato, a delightful hotel, situated in the heart of the old city, in a safe and quiet area, close to all major attractions and shopping sites. Completely renovated rooms, some with views, private baths & antiques. ✉ info@hotelbernardi.com ◯ www.hotelbernardi.com

Jamaica

KINGSTON

Anchorage Jamaica
866-978-6806 876-925-1067
Jennifer Tame

70 – 80 $US BB
8 rooms, 6 pb
Rated
C-no/S-no/P-no/H-no
English

Continental Jamaican Breakfast
Jamaican Breakfast $10 extra for
apartment guests
Fans, A/C, TV, coffee & tea facilities,
WiFi connection available

The Anchorage Bed & Breakfast property is set in the beautiful residential foothills on the outskirts of Kingston, Jamaica's commercial and cultural capital, just ten minutes away from New Kingston.

✉ anchorage@flowja.com ◯ www.anchoragejamaica.com

LITTLE BAY

Coral Cove Resort
876-457-7594 217-649-0619
Steve Zindars

299 – 349 $US AP
15 rooms, 15 pb
Most CC, •
C-yes/S-ltd/P-no/H-ltd
English, Spanish,
French

Full breakfast
All meals and drinks included Fresh
baked deserts
Room service, Internet access,
bicycles, bar/lounge, library,
snorkeling gear & instruction, laundry
service, child care, meeting & banquet
facilities, wedding coordinator

Coral Cove Resort is a place that holds everything that is magical about the island of Jamaica. A secluded, All-Inclusive Beach Resort perfect for weddings and gatherings of family and friends. A little piece of paradise for relaxation, fun and romance.

 cclbayj@yahoo.com ◯  www.coralcovejamaica.com

NEGRIL

White Sands	47 – 540 $US BB	Continental breakfast
876-957-4291	45 rooms, 45 pb	Bar and grill restaurant on site
Mr. Francis Williams	C-yes/S-yes/P-yes/H-yes	Air-conditioning, refrigeration, choose either a balcony or porch

Negril hotels vary greatly with respect to style and price. White Sands Negril is the most unique hotel beach resort in Jamaica, offering true Jamaican charm and ambience. Owned and operated by the same family for 30 years.

✉ whitesands@cwjamaica.com   🌐 www.whitesandsjamaica.com

Xtabi B&B	40 – 250 $US EP	Restaurant serves breakfast, lunch & dinner
876-957-0524 876-957-0121	24 rooms, 24 pb	
David Prebble	Most CC, *Rated*, •	Pool, lagoon, diving packages & tours,
	C-yes/S-yes/P-no/H-no	cable TV, A/C, kitchenettes in some
	English	rooms, all rooms & cottages have private baths with a veranda or deck

Xtabi, meeting place of the gods, the name as exotic as the quaint cottages and octagon shaped bungalows lying across the land and on rocky terraces above a turquoise sea. In Negril tourism is not set apart from Jamaican life because everyone is family.

✉ xtabiresort@cwjamaica.com   🌐 www.xtabi-negril.com

OCHO RIOS

Hibiscus Lodge Hotel	137 – 161 $US BB	Full breakfast
876-974-2676	26 rooms, 26 pb	Restaurant, bar, lunch, dinner
Michelle Doswald	MostCC, Cash,	AC, pool, tennis, hot tub, TV room,
	Rated, •	laundry service, gardens
	C-yes/S-yes/P-no/H-ltd	
	English	

Set amid 3 acres of lush gardens on a cliff overlooking the ocean. Centrally located in the heart of Ocho Rios. Where your vacation can be as relaxing, or active as you want it to be!

✉ mdoswald@cwjamaica.com   🌐 www.hibiscusjamaica.com

PORT ANTONIO

Hotel Mocking Bird Hill	138 – 600 $US EP	Mille Fleurs our on-site restaurant
876-993-7134 876-993-7267	10 rooms, 10 pb	Coffee stations, clock radio, hairdryer,
Barbara Walker, Shireen Aga	Visa, MC, *Rated*, •	vanity mirrors, Suite with WiFi station,
	C-yes/S-no/P-no/H-ltd	DVD-flat screen PC, iPod dock, cozy
	German, English,	reading corner, in-Room safe, pool,
	French	library

Hotel Mocking Bird Hill, Jamaica's award winning environmentally friendly luxury boutique hotel is romantic, peaceful, gracious and comfortable, the perfect Jamaican holiday hideaway nestled in the foothills of the Blue Mountains, minutes from the beach.

✉ info@hotelmockingbirdhill.com   🌐 www.hotelmockingbirdhill.com

ST. ANN'S BAY

High Hope Estate	110 – 185 $US EP	Complimentary afternoon tea, A la
876-972-2277	5 rooms, 5 pb	carte menu.
Ludovica & Dennis	Visa, MC, *Rated*, •	Pool, private beach club, nature trails,
	C-ltd/S-ltd/P-no/H-no	massages, facials, in-room coffee, turn
	English, Italian, and	down service, golf, tennis, sailing and
	some German	diving . . . .all nearby, cooking classes

Five beautifully furnished guestrooms located on 40 acres of botanical gardens. Highly acclaimed restaurant featuring Jamaican and Italian specialty dishes. High Hope offers guests peace, tranquility and natural beauty.

✉ info@highhopeestate.com   🌐 www.highhopeestate.com

Mexico

AJIJIC

Casa Del Sol Bed & Breakfast Inn
866-403-9275 +52-376-766-0050
Cathy Roberts

90 – 150 $US BB
11 rooms, 11 pb
Rated
C-yes/S-ltd/P-no/H-yes
Spanish, English

Full breakfast
Purified water, guest mini kitchen
Fabulous breakfasts, TV/DVD, free
phone & WiFi, ceiling fans, cozy bar,
heated pool, purified-pressurized
water, smoke-free environment, guest
mini kitchen

Welcome to the comfort and hospitality of Casa del Sol, a beautiful small Inn located in the heart of the 16th century village of Ajijic, Mexico.

✉ info@casadelsolinn.com 🌐 www.casadelsolinn.com

Estrellita's Bed & Breakfast
+52-376-766-0917
Lorraine Pasini

55 – 85 $US BB
6 rooms, 6 pb
Rated
C-ltd/S-no/P-yes/H-no
English, Spanish

Continental breakfast
Many excellent restaurants close by
Casitas w/kitchens, private baths,
swimming pool, gardens, fans, cable
TV, sitting areas, roof-top patio,
purified Water, WiFi, free calls to US &
Canada, eclectic art

Located in the heart of the enchanted village of Ajijic, bordered by the Lake Chapala Society, a beautiful estate with lush gardens, views, fine artwork and warm hospitality.

✉ lorrainepasini@yahoo.com 🌐 www.estrellitasinnajijic.com

BUCERIAS

Casa Cielito Lindo
+52-329-298-2440 705-447-1104
Sandi & Brian Barkwell

125 – 225 $US BB
4 rooms, 4 pb
Rated, •
C-ltd/S-ltd/P-no/H-no
English
October – May

Full Hot Breakfast
Lunch & Dinner available on request
Egyptian cotton bedding, private
baths, maid service daily, safes, street
parking, private pool & terraces

Casa Cielito Lindo is situated on the north shore of the Bay of Banderas on the longest, most beautiful stretch of Pacific Coast beach. The hand crafted Cherub fountain inside the yard, the gleaming marble floors, the attention to detail are delightful.

✉ info@waterfrontdreamvacations.com 🌐 www.waterfrontdreamvacations.com

---

Casa Loma Bonita
415-310-5435
David Pantoja

125 – 235 $US BB
4 rooms, 4 pb
Rated
C-yes/S-ltd/P-no/H-no
English, Spanish

Full breakfast
On site restaurant with authentic
Mexican cuisine
Luxurious king size bed, comfortable
sitting area, refreshing swimming
pool, large private bathroom, rich
marble floors, stunning balcony views,
relaxing porch & patios

Casa Loma Bonita is just minutes North of Puerto Vallarta in Bucerias. This is a unique villa property overlooking Bahia de Banderas, close to championship golf courses, white sand beaches, one-of-a-kind shops and a variety of dining experiences.

✉ Noemipantoja@gmail.com 🌐 www.casalomabonita.com

CANCUN

B&B Quinta Bianca
423-373-0740 +52-988-482-096
Bianca Buchel

30 – 60 $US BB
8 rooms, 2 pb
Rated
C-yes/S-ltd/P-no/H-ltd
English, German,
Spanish

Mexican or Fitness Breakfast
Double futon bed, make-up area, A/C,
ceiling fans, nicely decorated rooms,
additional water closet in each house,
daily housekeeping, phone for local
calls

Located in a safe residential area of Cancun, Quinta Bianca offers accommodations split into three houses. Each house has three bedrooms and one of them has a large private bathroom, the other two guestrooms share a big bath.

✉ quintabianca@hotmail.com

CHAPALA

Quinta Quetzalcoatl
+52-376-765-3653
Rob Cracknell

75 – 150 $US BB
9 rooms, 9 pb
Rated
C-no/S-ltd/P-no/H-no
English, Spanish

Full breakfast
Many restaurant selections & shops
near by
Swimming pool & private sunning
areas, BBQ, outside tables & chairs,
parking, private car rental, tours &
chauffeur services, an honor bar, fax,
Internet access

Totally restored & decorated, this villa has become a fine, romantic small Inn featuring 5 Suites and 3 Casitas. Located on the north shore of beautiful Lake Chapala, Mexico, QQ is "the" place to indulge yourself in peace and relaxation.

✉ qqinnchapala@yahoo.com 🌐 www.accommodationslakechapala.com

COZUMEL

Summer Place Inn
+52-987-872-6300
Henny Watts

65 – 95 $US BB
7 rooms, 7 pb
Most CC, *Rated*, •
C-yes/S-ltd/P-no/H-ltd
English, Spanish,
Danish

Self-help 24 hours a day
Full kitchen stocked with breakfast
foods
TV, DVD player, bicycles, full kitchen,
stocked fridge, A/C, laundry, Internet
phone, wireless Internet, wave
boards, library, beach towels, coolers,
International Calls

Conveniently located downtown in Cozumel, the Summer Place Inn offers private units and a charming condo. Competitively priced, the accommodations can be booked nightly, weekly or monthly.

✉ info@summerplaceinn.net 🌐 www.summerplaceinn.net

GUANAJUATO

Casa Estrella de la Valenciana
866-983-8844 +52-473-732-1784
Sharon Schaap Mendez

185 – 235 $US BB
6 rooms, 6 pb
Most CC, *Rated*
C-ltd/S-no/P-ltd/H-ltd
Spanish, English

Full breakfast served from 9 to 10
Other meals available by advance
request
Luxury linens, Sat-TV, DVD/VHS
player, CD/clock radio, hairdryer,
bathrobes, iron/board

Perched on a hillside, with spectacular panoramic city and mountain views, Casa Estrella de la Valenciana welcomes you to experience Colonial Mexico and its treasures.

✉ info@mexicaninns.com 🌐 www.mexicaninns.com

HUATULCO

Agua Azul la Villa B&B
+52-958-581-0265
Richard Gazer

119 – 139 $US BB
6 rooms, 6 pb
Visa, MC, *Rated*
C-no/S-no/P-no/H-no
English, Spanish

Continental plus breakfast
Honor Bar, bottled water
Cascade swimming pool, large
terrazas, library, gardens, private
ocean view terrace, A/C, fans, phone

With stunningly beautiful ocean views & spacious private terraces off of every guestroom, Agua Azul la Villa offers a tranquil vacation destination in a tropical paradise for adults. Your Canadian host will be glad to orient you to the area.

✉ gaurei@hotmail.com 🌐 www.bbaguaazul.com

LA PAZ

El Angel Azul
+52-612-125-5130
Esther Ammann

105 – 195 $US BB
10 rooms, 10 pb
Visa, MC, *Rated*
C-ltd/S-ltd/P-no/H-no
Spanish, English,
German

Full breakfast
Our Bar is open in the afternoon
Bar&Lounge, WiFi, garden, cable
TV for guests in lounge, A/C, tour
planning, afternoon tea & early bird
coffee, English Book Store and Art
Shop

A fascinating place that recaptures the spirit and culture of La Paz. In the heart of the city, the building was formerly the town's courthouse. Completely renovated and redesigned as a B&B inn. A Historic landmark & enviornmentally friendy.

✉ hotel@elangelazul.com 🌐 www.elangelazul.com

MANZANILLO

Pepe's Hideaway
+52-314-333-0616
Pepe Telarana

200 – 250 $US AP
6 rooms, 6 pb
Visa, MC, *Rated*, •
C-no/S-ltd/P-no/H-no
Spanish, English

Full breakfast
An all inclusive gourmet experience!
Swimming pool, Jacuzzi, bar,
restaurant, private baths, ceiling
fans, mini bar, hammock on private
veranda, massage service, Internet &
telephone access

*A private nature reserve in Manzanillo, Mexico. Accommodations in luxury thatched-roof bungalows
with spectacular views and awesome sunsets. Pepe's Hideaway is a handmade paradise.*

✉ pepeshideaway1@mac.com   🌐 www.pepeshideaway.com

MAZATLAN

Captain Moe's B&B
866-252-6364 +52-669-914-3319
Captain Moe & Dorothy

60 -75 $US BB
4 rooms, 4 pb
Most CC, *Rated*, •
C-ltd/S-ltd/P-ltd/H-ltd
English, Spanish

Continental plus breakfast
Guests may use our courtyard kitchen
& gas grill
Private entrance, free calls to USA
Canada & Europe, WiFi, refrigerators,
wonderful sunset, ocean view from
rooftop terrace, courtyard kitchen

*Located in the "Golden Zone" of Mazatlan, walking distance to the best beaches, restaurants, shops
and transportation. This relaxing Bed & Breakfast offers smoke-free rooms and is situated amongst a
tropical courtyard and rooftop terrace.*

✉ moeanddorothy@captmoe.com   🌐 www.captmoe.com

**Casa de Leyendas Bed and
Breakfast**
866-391-2301 602-445-6192
Glenn & Sharon Sorrie

89 – 115 $US BB
6 rooms, 6 pb
Visa, MC, *Rated*, •
C-ltd/S-ltd/P-ltd/H-no
English/Spanish

Full Breakfast
Pool/spa, honor bar, maid/laundry
service, A/C, safes, WiFi, free calls to
U.S./Canada, free concierge, purified
water, bikes, boogie/surf boards, SAT-
TV, DVD, hairdryers

*Located in Centro Historico, the beach on one side and the museum on the other! 4 short blocks to
the plaza Machado where you will find wonderful restaurants and enjoy the flavors of Mexico; just sit
back and relax or set out for a fun filled exciting day*

✉ reservations@casadeleyendas.com   🌐 www.casadeleyendas.com

Meson De Cynthia
+52-669-918-0194 +52-669-136-
0560
Cynthia Romero

70 – 100 $US BB
7 rooms, 7 pb
Visa, MC
C-ltd/S-no/P-no/H-ltd
Spanish, English

Continental breakfast
Mexican snacks and dinners by
arrangement
A/C, microwave, cable TV, coffee
maker, Internet, maid service, laundry
service, special accommodation
requests, patio with view

*Located in the heart of Mazatlan in the Historic District, the recently restored, historic building, the
Meson De Cynthia, is a five room, two suite B&B, embedded amidst continuous cultural and traditional events.*

✉ cynthia@mesondecynthia.com   🌐 www.mesondecynthia.com

Olas Altas Bed & Breakfast
775-293-4446 +52-669-668-
4395
Bill McGrady

105 $US BB
6 rooms, 6 pb
Visa, MC
C-ltd/S-ltd/P-no/H-ltd
Spanish, English

Full breakfast
In room refrigerators filled with
refreshments
Pool, pressurized/purified water
system, sunny/shaded dining and
sitting areas, formal dining for 12, full
service pool bar, international phone,
laundry, A/C, cable TV

*Come and enjoy a very unique and exclusive bed and breakfast featuring all the amenities of a first-
class boutique hotel. Sitting just steps away from the famous Olas Altas (high waves) beach known for
its great surfing, fishing and hospitality.*

✉ reservations@olasaltasmaz.com   🌐 www.olasaltasmaz.com

MERIDA

Casa Ana B&B
+52-999-924-0005
Ana Ilano

40 – 50 $US BB
5 rooms, 5 pb
Rated
C-yes/S-ltd/P-ltd/H-ltd
Spanish, English

Continental breakfast
Home-cooked meals on request
Tropical garden, swimming pool,
palapa, A/C, ceiling fans, hammocks,
daily maid service

Five immaculate spacious rooms, each with a private bath and air conditioning, offering peace and tranquility a heartbeat from the Plaza Principal in El Centro. Casa Ana is in the White City, as Merida is known, centrally located with great rates.

✉ info@casaana.com   🌐 www.casaana.com

Casa Del Balam
+52-999-924-8844
+52- 999-924-2150
Carmen Barbachano &
Gomez Rul

100 – 188 $US BB
51 rooms, 51 pb
Visa, MC, AmEx,
Rated, •
C-yes/S-ltd/P-no/H-ltd
Spanish, English

American breakfast
Las Palomas Bistro & Bar
Pool, elevators, boutique, silver shop,
parking service, safe, access to golf
club, fee services include massages,
babysitter, crib, room service, laundry,
WiFi cards

Hotel Casa del Balam is one of the oldest and most distinguished hotels in Merida on the Yucatan Peninsula. It is one of the few original Mexican Art Deco buildings left in this Colonial City. The hotel is newly renovated with modern conveniences.

✉ hotelbalam@prodigy.net.mx   🌐 www.hotelcasadelbalam.com

Hotel Casa San Angel
+52-999-928-1800
Alberto Banuet

140 – 210 $US BB
15 rooms, 15 pb
Visa, MC, AmEx,
Rated, •
C-no/S-no/P-no/H-ltd
English and Spanish

American Breakfast
Private parking, WiFi, beautiful setting,
A/C, ceiling fans, TV, hammocks, safe
deposit box, two world class boutiques
exclusive to the Yucatan.

Welcome to Hotel Casa San Angel, a family owned boutique hotel in the heart of Merida, Yucatan, Mexico. The historical building has been restored with love and care with beautiful murals in the interior, while still conserving the original architecture.

✉ info@hotelcasasanangel.com   🌐 www.hotelcasasanangel.com

**In Ka'an Bed & Breakfast
& Other Accommodations**
+52-999-943-4156
Bonnie Wrenshall

90 $US BB
3 rooms, 3 pb
Rated
C-yes/S-ltd/P-yes/H-ltd
English

Full breakfast
Lunch served with prior notice
Large pool w/22m lap pool, extensive
library, videos, DVD, SAT-TV, poolside
palapa, Internet access, barbecue,
secure parking

"In Ka'an," is a happy blending of Mexican architecture and ambience with Canadian/American standards of comfort. Enjoy your breakfast on the terrace overlooking the pool. For those who prefer their own space, we also offer fully furnished guesthouses.

✉ bonnie@inkaan.com   🌐 www.inkaan.com

OAXACA

Casa Colonial
800-758-1697   +52-951-516-5280
Jane Robison

40 – 118 $US BB
15 rooms, 12 pb
Visa, MC, *Rated*
C-yes/S-yes/P-yes/H-yes
Spanish, English

Full breakfast
Lunch, Dinner (fee)
Sitting room, library, verandas, tropical
gardens, limited secure parking,
phone, fax, Internet service, including
WiFi

An inn that is run very much as a country manor. The extensive library, friendly Oaxacan staff, lush gardens, personal service, excursion arrangements and superior food have made Casa Colonial a destination in itself for 30 years!

✉ reservations@casa-colonial.com   🌐 www.casa-colonial.com

OAXACA

La Casa de Mis Recuerdos	65 – 120 $US BB	Two course Oaxaquenian breakfast
877-234-4706 +52-951-515-8483	8 rooms, 6 pb	Special dietary meals with advance
William & Nora Gutierrez	Visa, MC, *Rated*, •	notice
	C-no/S-no/P-no/H-no	Cool Refreshments on Arrival, Non-
	Spanish, English	smoking, WiFi, daily housekeeping,
		low-cost LD calls, purified bottled
		water, optional cooking classes,
		private dinner parties

Nestled in the emerald hills of Mexico's state of Oaxaca, lies a romantic gem of a city by the same name. This charming Colonial town is one of Mexico's national treasures, a showcase of the real Mexico, an authentic Mexican experience.

✉ misrecue@hotmail.com ◖ www.misrecuerdos.net

PASO DEL GUAYABO

House of Wind and Water	85 – 120 $US BB	Full breakfast
941-932-8543 +52-322-222-6719	5 rooms, 5 pb	Dinner options for additional cost
Andy Marcus & Kathleen	MostCC, Cash, Checks,	Access to art studio, private gardens,
Carrillo	*Rated*	ponds, DVD library, dipping pool on
	C-ltd/S-no/P-no/H-no	premises, river access downstairs

Join hosts Kathleen Carrillo & Andrew Marcus in their lovely bed and breakfast retreat on the Rio Cuale. They invite you to participate in relaxing outdoor activities and specialized art retreats. You will be delighted with the charm of Puerto Vallarta.

✉ kathleencarrillo80@hotmail.com ◖ www.houseofwindandwater.com

PATZCUARO

La Casa Encantada B&B/	90 – 135 $US BB	Full breakfast
Boutique Hotel	12 rooms, 12 pb	Nearby restaurants serving regional
619-819-8398 +52-434-342-3492	*Rated*, •	style food
Cynthia de la Rosa	C-ltd/S-ltd/P-yes/H-yes	8 am to 4 pm bilingual office staff,
	English & Spanish daily	computer & printer, wireless Internet,
	from 8 am to 4 pm for	free calls to U.S. & Canada and 60
	guests of La Casa	other countries, daily maids, fireplaces
		& heated rooms

La Casa Encantada is an idyllic place to get away from it all. Inside the adobe walls there is an abundance of color in the lush gardens, patios and portals. The setting is tranquil. The house is a masterpiece of Colonial architecture.

✉ cynthia@lacasaencantada.com ◖ www.lacasaencantada.com

PUERTO MORELOS

Rancho Sak Ol Libertad	65 – 145 $US BB	Continental plus breakfast
+52-998-871-0181	14 rooms, 14 pb	Self-serve breakfast buffet
Valente Quintana	Visa, MC, *Rated*, •	Large common room, fans, AC,
	C-ltd/S-yes/P-no/H-ltd	common kitchen, massage, bikes,
	English, Spanish	snorkel equipment, hammocks,
		thatched roofs

A true vacation away from the fast pace. A place to set your own pace, enjoy, play, explore, or just relax in the hammocks. A place to reflect and renew.

✉ reservations@ranchosakol.com ◖ www.ranchosakol.com

PUERTO VALLARTA

Casa Amorita	145 – 175 $US BB	Full breakfast
+52-322-222-4926	5 rooms, 5 pb	Roof Top Terrace, sun decks, balcony,
Rita Love	MostCC, Cash, *Rated*	garden, Pool, WiFi, free calling to
	C-ltd/S-no/P-no/H-no	United States & Canada
	Spanish, English	

Casa Amorita is in the heart of Puerto Vallarta with an incredible view of Banderas Bay, the Cathedral Guadalupe and the Sierra Madre Mountains.

✉ ritalove@hotmail.com ◖ www.casaamorita.com

PUERTO VALLARTA

Casa Corazon 866-648-6893 George T. Tune	58 – 111 $US BB 42 rooms, 42 pb MostCC, Cash, *Rated* C-yes/S-ltd/P-no/H-no Spanish, English	Full breakfast Sliding door with terrace, private entry bath, maid service, some rooms with TV, A/C, mini fridges, 9 person elevator, kitchenettes include table, fridge & stove

Welcome to Casa Corazon Hotel, "House of Hearts,) a quaint B&B that has grown into a small family hotel on the beach in beautiful Puerto Vallarta, Mexico. Casa Corazon Hotel sits on a hillside overlooking beautiful Bandera Bay.

✉ casacorazon1@yahoo.com 🌐 www.casacorazonvallarta.com

Los Cuatro Vientos Hotel +52-322-222-0161 Gloria Whiting	69 – 79 $US BB 15 rooms, 15 pb Visa, MC, *Rated* C-yes/S-yes/P-no/H-no English & Spanish	Buffet breakfast on Garden Patio Meals available at Chez Elena, on-site restaurant Refreshingly cool deep pool, the town's best venue for super sized margaritas, spectacular sunsets, 3 scenic levels with stair access, roof top bar, WiFi

Walk to shops & beaches. A tropical paradise amidst a profusion of flowers. A favorite with guests seeking a traditional Mexican setting. Deep & refreshing pool. Rooftop terrace for sunning by day and Margaritas at sunset. WiFi .

✉ fourwinds@cuatrovientos.com 🌐 www.cuatrovientos.com

Quinta Maria Cortez 888-640-8100 801-263-9500 Margaret Parrish & Jon C. Jones	120 – 260 $US BB 7 rooms, 7 pb Visa, MC, AmEx C-ltd/S-ltd/P-no/H-ltd	Full breakfast ceiling fans, A/C, bathrobes, free wi-Fi, in room safes

Located on a spectacular beach just minutes south of the Puerto Vallarta. A favorite destination for travelers from around the world searching for a relaxing getaway in a unique setting.

✉ info@villasinvallarta.com 🌐 www.quinta-maria.com

SAN FRANCISCO

Casa Obelisco 415-655-1714 +52-311-258-4315 Judi & John Levens, Barbara & Bill Kirkwood	200 $US BB 4 rooms, 4 pb Visa, MC, *Rated* C-no/S-no/P-no/H-no English, Spanish, German	Full breakfast Soft drinks, beer, wine, cocktails, snacks, lunch Pool, pool bar, sun decks, roof top lounge area, beach, horseback riding, snorkeling, hiking, great restaurants close by, romantic beach setting, perfect getaway

The exotic get away you've been dreaming about, an exquisite, two story oceanfront home overlooking a deserted white sand beach. Surrounded by tropical palms in a quaint little village with great restaurants nearby in the new Riviera Nayarit.

✉ reservations@casaobelisco.com 🌐 www.casaobelisco.com

SAN JOSE DEL CABO

Villa del Faro Devora Wise	140 – 425 $US BB 5 rooms, 6 pb Most CC, *Rated* C-yes/S-ltd/P-no/H-ltd Spanish, English, French Open October to August	Full breakfast Full bar and wine list. Gourmet dinner on request. Pool, terrace, fountains, custom rugs, private balcony, Sat-TV, private beach, canopy king bed, kitchen, fireplaces, outdoor shower

Exquisitely off the grid! An Eco-Hotel, Villa del Faro is a unique oasis nestled on a deserted beach. It was created as a labor of love by artisans and architects. One hour north of the Los Cabos Airport, but a world away in seclusion and serenity.

✉ rental@villadelfaro.net 🌐 www.villadelfaro.net

SAN MIGUEL DE ALLENDE

Casa Maria
+52-415-185-8388
Catalina Lopez

120 – 220 $US BB
6 rooms
Visa, MC, AmEx,
Rated
C-ltd/S-ltd/P-no/H-no
Spanish

Mexican Breakfast
Private terrace, garden, Jacuzzi, SAT-TV, computer room with WiFi, in-room massage & yoga, 7/24 front desk

Casa María is the coziest of places in San Miguel de Allende. At Casa María, you will enjoy the old style atmosphere of San Miguel el Grande: its hospitality, the cordiality of its people, and zealous personal attention.

info@casamariabb.com www.casamariabb.com

Hacienda de las Flores
817-717-3534 +52-415-152-1859
A. Franyutti, C. Finkelstein

96 – 200 $US BB
16 rooms, 16 pb
Visa, MC, AmEx,
Rated, •
C-yes/S-no/P-yes/H-ltd
English, Spanish

Full breakfast
Catering on request for weddings, 1–120 people
Bar, garden, pool, 2 conference rooms, executive meetings, accommodations for business travelers, wireless Internet, catering for weddings, parties, out door pool

Hacienda de las Flores is an exclusive, tranquil and casual hotel which is a stimulus to modern life. It has beautiful gardens in the heart of town that are reminders of a serene way of life of yesteryear. New excercise equipment and remodeled rooms.

info@haciendadelasflores.com www.haciendadelasflores.com

Hotel Villa Mirasol
+52-415-152-8057
Amparo Rivas

100 – 150 $US BB
12 rooms, 12 pb
MostCC, Cash, Checks,
Rated
C-ltd/S-no/P-no/H-ltd
English, Spanish

Continental plus breakfast
Tea Time (Merienda), lunch service, wine
Living room, library, access to local country club, free wireless Internet.

Free Night w/Certificate: Anytime. Room Upgrade.

Villa Mirasol is located only five minutes from the "Jardin" our main square and a very short distance to Bellas Artes, The Angela Peralta Theatre and Instituto Allende (Arts School).

amparo@villamirasolhotel.com www.villamirasolhotel.com

Susurros B&B
+52-415-152-1065
Robert Waters

155 – 185 $US BB
4 rooms, 4 pb
MostCC, Cash, Checks,
Rated
C-ltd/S-ltd/P-no/H-no
Spanish, English

Mexican Breakfast
Honor Bar
Lush towels, cotton robes, hairdryer, hot bottled water, shoeshine kit, umbrella, personal safe, laundry srvs, fireplaces, antiques, folk/fine art, purified water, WiFi

Susurro provides the ultimate romantic getaway for those seeking a luxurious escape. Rooms offer elegance with luxury and comfort. Relax by the pool or on your terrace. There is always a space for you to enjoy your privacy or to socialize with our guests.

rwaters@earthlink.net susurro.com.mx

TLAQUEPAQUE

Casa de las Flores
888-582-4896 +52-333-659-3186
Stan Singleton & Jose Gutierrez

95 – 105 $US BB
7 rooms, 7 pb
Visa, MC, *Rated*
C-ltd/S-ltd/P-no/H-ltd
Spanish, English

Continental plus breakfast
Inquire about other meals offered
Shopping or sightseeing trips, translating, available for small events

This B&B is just 15 minutes away from the center of Guadalajara and just three blocks from the famous historic center of Tlaquepaque one of the largest crafts and arts capitals of Mexico.

 info@casadelasflores.com  www.casadelasflores.com

TLAQUEPAQUE

Casa del Retoño B&B
+52-333-635-7636
Eslye Berenice Panduro

850 – 950 MXN BB
9 rooms, 9 pb
Visa, MC, AmEx,
Rated
C-yes/S-no/P-yes/H-no
English, Spanish

Continental breakfast buffet
Terrace with books, garden with lawn,
flowers & fruit trees, Cable/SAT TV,
radio alarm clock, fan, telephone,
fax, computer with DSL Internet, WiFi
Internet & printer

Enjoy the comfort, tranquility & warmth of a Mexican family house, built with typical Mexican materials, which guarantee you an unforgettable stay. Two blocks away from downtown Tlaquepaque.

✉ info@lacasadelretono.com.mx 🌐 www.lacasadelretono.com.mx

Quinta Don Jose Boutique Hotel
866-629-3753 +52-333-635-7522
Arturo & Estela Magana

80 – 155 $US BB
18 rooms, 18 pb
Visa, MC, AmEx,
Rated, •
C-yes/S-ltd/P-ltd/H-ltd
Spanish, French

Continental included/full menu extr
Gourmet restaurant TlaquePasta
5–10pm. Light lunch
Courtesy airport pick-up, fine dining
at our restaurant "TlaquePasta") area
tours, intimate bar, pool, tree shaded
patio, free WiFi, guest computer desk

An oasis in the heart of Tlaquepaque, the decorative arts and crafts capital of Mexico in the greater Guadalajara area. We are a boutique hotel that specializes in personal service to our guests while sharing our local traditions, food, people and Fiesta!

✉ info@quintadonjose.com 🌐 www.quintadonjose.com

TRONCONES

Casa Las Piedras
Effy Weisfield

100 – 285 $US BB
4 rooms, 4 pb
MostCC, Cash, *Rated*
C-yes/S-no/P-ltd/H-no
Spanish, English

Full breakfast
Vaulted ceilings, cooling fans, pool,
garden, beach front, suite with bar and
fridge, entertainment center, open air
shower, outdoor pergola

Casa Las Piedras is a luxuriously appointed bed & breakfast inn and vacation rental house located on the beach in beautiful Playa Troncones, nestled on the Pacific Coast of Mexico near Ixtapa and Zihuatanejo.

✉ casalaspiedras@gmail.com 🌐 www.casalaspiedras.com

Present Moment Retreat
916-580-3418
Tom Morisette

115 $US BB
10 rooms, 10 pb
MostCC, Cash, *Rated*
C-yes/S-no/P-ltd/H-ltd
Spanish, English

Full Gourmet Breakfast
Lunch & Dinner, spa cuisine available
Private decks, meditation gardens,
awe-inspiring views, massage therapy,
spiritual renewal and healing retreat

Located just north of Ixtapa, with the amenities of a 5 Star Hotel and the privacy of a deserted island, Present Moment Retreat uniquely combines the luxuries of a health spa & beach resort with the tranquility of an intimate Spiritual Life & Yoga Center.

✉ reserve@presentmomentretreat.com 🌐 www.presentmomentretreat.com

Morocco

HARHOURA, RABAT

Villa Bourdoud
416-769-8041
Doris & Bouchta El Harchali

50 – 100 CAD BB
5 rooms
C-yes/S-ltd/P-ltd/H-ltd
English, French &
Arabic

Full breakfast
Optional lunches & dinners upon
request
Large salon, rooftop sunroom,
gardens, terrace, gated property,
carport

A Moroccan family bed and breakfast on the Atlantic coast near Rabat – stay with us any time of the year and experience Moroccan hospitality. Enjoy our gardens, terrace, rooftop sunroom and magnificent ocean views.

 athomeinnmorocco@yahoo.ca   www.athomeinnmorocco.com

MARRAKECH───

Riad Azenzer	55 – 65 € BB	Full breakfast
+212-524-386353	5 rooms, 5 pb	Moroccan dinner & lunch available on
Cécile & Said	Visa, MC, •	request
	C-yes/S-no/P-no/H-no	A/C, pool
	French, English, Arabic	

In the authentic heart of old Marrakech enjoy life and relax on the terrace with its wonderful view on the snowy Atlas mountain tops. Be seduced by its simple architecture and the warm atmosphere of Riad Azenzer.

✉ riadazenzer@gmail.com ◍ www.riadazenzer.com

Riad Karmela	80 – 150 € BB	Continental plus breakfast
+212-524-387937	19 rooms, 19 pb	Breakfast, meals, hamam
Joel Castrec	Visa, MC, AmEx	Summer plunge pool, orange trees,
	C-ltd/S-ltd/P-no/H-ltd	shopping, spacious terraces, lounge
		areas, sun beds & Jacuzzi

Charming 19 bedroom riad in the middle of the Marrakech Medina, close to the main square and short walk from the Souks. Beautiful terraces, hammam, spa, massages, a summer plunge pool and a restaurant.

✉ info@riadkarmela.com ◍ www.riadkarmela.com

Riad Le Clos des Arts	90 – 165 € BB	Moroccan breakfast
+212-658-360-475	6 rooms, 6 pb	Mint tea with pastries on arrival, fresh
+212-524-375159	AmEx	fruits
Giorgina & Massimo	C-ltd/S-ltd/P-no/H-ltd	A/C, safe, Internet & WiFi,
Tumiotto	English, French, Italian,	entertainment with live traditional
	German, Spanish,	music, dancing on request, sitting
	Swahili	room, dining room, terrace pool,
		sunbeds

A charming Arab house renovated in pure Moresque style. Be seduced by this fascinating Oriental atmosphere, be tempted by the authenticity of traditional Moroccan flavors, be refreshed by a plunge into the small pool on the terrace.

✉ contact@leclosdesarts.com ◍ www.leclosdesarts.com

Netherlands

AMSTERDAM──

Amsterdam B&B Barangay	68 – 148 € BB	Full breakfast
+31-62-504-5432	2 rooms, 2 pb	Breakfast in bed or in nice breakfast
GD Yosalina-Bouman &	Visa, MC, AmEx,	kitchen
Willem Bouman-Yosalina	*Rated*, •	Fridge, TV, radio-alarm, VHS, DVD, CD,
	C-ltd/S-ltd/P-no/H-no	cell phone on request, private external
	English, Dutch, German,	bathroom for patio rooms and shared
	Filipino, Visayan, Little	bathroom for upper rooms
	Spanish	

An award winning guesthouse. Your very friendly tropical style hide-away in the historic center of Amsterdam. Close to Central Station and all attractions are literally just around the corner. The best location to explore Amsterdam & beyond.

✉ rooms@barangay.nl ◍ www.barangay.nl

B&B Amsterdam	80 – 120 € BB	Cereals & fresh milk
+31-06-376-0967	3 rooms, 2 pb	Coffee & tea facilities
Paul & Karen Galdermans	*Rated*	Canal side location, rates based on
	C-ltd/S-no/P-no/H-no	length of stay
	English, Dutch, German,	
	French, Spanish	

Romantic rooms on a lovely canal opposite the Vondelpark. Convenient location, reasonable prices & recommended by various guide books. Some rooms with private baths. Easy-going hospitality make this a charming place to stay in Amsterdam.

✉ pgaldermans@chello.nl ◍ www.bedandbreakfastamsterdam.net

AMSTERDAM

Logement Hanna Penso
+31-20-626-3163
Beatrijs Stemerding

110 € BB
2 rooms, 2 pb
Visa, MC, *Rated*
C-ltd/S-no/P-no/H-no
English, Dutch, German,
French

Guests may make own breakfast
Ingredients for self serve included in
price
Kitchenette, TV & Internet connection

Hanna Penso is located in an 18th century canal-side property. Two ground-floor rooms, including a romantic garden room. Close to many major tourist attractions. Very attractive and quiet surroundings.

✉ info@hannapenso.nl   🌐 www.hannapenso.nl

Maes B&B
+31-20-427-5165
K. B. Harrison

95 – 195 € BB
4 rooms, 4 pb
Visa, MC, AmEx,
Rated
C-ltd/S-no/P-no/H-no
English, Dutch, Russian,
some French & German

Continental plus breakfast
Tea, coffee, fruit, snacks in guest
kitchen
Private baths. Apartments are also
available.

In the center of Amsterdam, only minutes away from the museums and within walking distance from all major sights and nightlife spots, yet in a quiet residential area.

✉ maesinfo@xs4all.nl   🌐 www.bedandbreakfastamsterdam.com

LEIDEN

Leon & Ingrid B&B
+31-64-378-6005
Leon & Ingrid

75 – 125 € BB
4 rooms, 2 pb
C-yes/S-no/P-no/H-no
English, German,
French, Dutch

Full dutch breakfast
Drinks, wine, beer, snacks. Lunch
package possible
Roof terrace, terrace, mini-bar, Jacuzzi,
city center, historic canal mansion
(1605), fireplace

Beautiful ancient canal mansion built in 1605 and situated in the city center of Leiden. Old features and details are preserved. The house is along the famous canals. Minutes from the restaurants, museums, shops and other historic sites.

✉ info@leon-ingrid.nl   🌐 www.leon-ingrid.nl

New Zealand

AUCKLAND

The Ambers
+64-9-426-0015
Diane & Gerard Zwier

160 – 200 NZD BB
4 rooms, 3 pb
Visa, MC, *Rated*, •
C-ltd/S-no/P-no/H-no
English, Dutch, German,
French

Full breakfast
Complimentary tea, coffee & wine
En-suites, gardens, lounge, formal
dining, breakfast to order, fine linens
& towels, tranquil country setting,
evening drinks

Our B&B is a charming old-style European country house with formal rose gardens, fountains, mature trees and olive grove. There are beautiful beaches, golf courses, and sophisticated cafes and restaurants nearby. All our bedrooms have their own en suite.

✉ gzwier@xtra.co.nz   🌐 www.the-ambers.co.nz

**Ascot Parnell Fine
Accommodation**
+64-9-309-9012
Bart & Therese Blommaert

195 – 365 NZD BB
3 rooms, 3 pb
Visa, MC, *Rated*, •
C-ltd/S-no/P-no/H-ltd
English, French,
German, Dutch

Cooked to order breakfasts
Complimentary refreshments offered
Guest rooms are bright & airy,
tastefully furnished, parking, WiFi
Internet, balconies with views,
tranquility guaranteed, meet & greet
from Airport

Parnell-Village, near downtown Auckland is an elegant, small B&B hotel. Offering luxury accommodations in central Auckland, yet so quiet. Walk to all attractions. Garden surroundings with city and sea views. Living at its best, book well in advance.

✉ info@ascotparnell.com   🌐 www.ascotparnell.com

DUNEDIN

27 Pitt St B&B
+64-3-477-5133
Jan Taylor

130 – 170 $US BB
2 rooms, 2 pb
C-no/S-no/P-ltd/H-no

Continental breakfast

Quiet and private location situated within easy walking distance of downtown Dunedin city and main street with huge selection of shops, including renowned Otago boutique fashion designers.

✉ 27pitt@xtra.co.nz   🌐 www.27pitt.co.nz

Glendinning House
+64-3-477-8262

325 – 400 NZD BB
2 rooms, 2 pb
Visa, MC
C-yes/S-no/P-no/H-no

Gourment Breakfasts
Wines, spirits, fruit, baked goods, teas & coffees
Large luxury suite, dressing room, ensuite bathroom, quality toiletries, bathrobes, slippers, designer linens, tiled fireplaces, central heating, Internet, fax & phone

Glendinning House offers all the atmosphere of the period with the highest levels of luxury and comfort. Business and leisure travelers accustomed to superior standards of service and appointments will enjoy finer comforts as well as the prime location.

✉ info@glendinninghouse.co.nz   🌐 www.glendinninghouse.co.nz

NELSON

Boutique Hotel Warwick House
0800-022233 in NZ
+64-3-548-3164
Nick Ferrier

149 – 395 NZD BB
5 rooms, 5 pb
Visa, MC, *Rated*, •
C-ltd/S-ltd/P-no/H-yes
English, German, Spanish, French

Full gourmet breakfast
Home made foods, dinner for groups may be arranged
Luxury accommodation, en-suite lounges, library, clawfoot baths, Grand Ballroom. Massage and Aroma therapy on site Local info. Free WiFi, secure off street parking

Warwick House offers luxurious, boutique B&B accommodation in Nelson's well-known, turreted castle. 5–10 mins. walk from Nelson Ctr. Intriguing history, impressive architectural features and graceful ambience in one of Nelson's most fascinating buildings.

✉ info@warwickhouse.co.nz   🌐 www.warwickhouse.co.nz

QUEENSTOWN

Pencarrow B&B
+64-3-442-8938
Bill & Kari Moers

595 NZD BB
4 rooms, 4 pb
MostCC, Cash,
Rated, •
C-ltd/S-ltd/P-no/H-ltd
English

Four course breakfast
Complimentary drink, afternoon sweets
Lounge, Bar, Games room, Concierge room, library, tea, coffee, mini bars, sweets, flowers, spa pool, 4 acres of gardens, WiFi & laptops, turn down service with gifts

Pencarrow offers luxury accommodations with magnificent views of Lake Wakatipu and the Remarkables Ranges. Luxury suites with lavish baths. Located on four acres, private, and quiet with Spa.

✉ info@pencarrow.net   🌐 www.pencarrow.net

WANAKA

Riversong B&B
+64-3-443-8567
Ann & Ian Horrax

160 – 180 NZD BB
3 rooms, 2 pb
Visa, MC, *Rated*, •
C-yes/S-no/P-yes/H-no
English

Continental plus cooked breakfast
Evening meal $55.00 per person by arrangement
Tea & coffee facilities, balconies, SKY TV, WiFi, fishing guidance, tourist information, on-site parking, historic riverside setting, library, outstanding views

On the banks of the Clutha River, one of the most historic areas of Central Otago, Riversong offers the ultimate in a relaxed, friendly, satisfying and scenic B&B home stay.

✉ info@riversongwanaka.co.nz   🌐 www.riversongwanaka.co.nz

Panama

BOQUETE

Cabanas B&B Momentum
+507-7204-385
Ken Neal

66 $US EP
2 rooms, 2 pb
MostCC, Cash, Checks
C-yes/S-ltd/P-yes/H-ltd
English, Spanish

Full kitchen, BBQ, kitchen stocked
with all your cooking needs, laundry
on-site, hot water showers, queen-
sleeper sofa

*Comfortable 14'x14' room, features queen size bed with orthopedic mattress. Private in-suite bath-
room with hot water shower. Guests enjoy all facilities including free WiFi, heated pool, gym and trails.*

✉ stay@momentum-panama.com 🌐 www.momentum-panama.com

COSTA DEL ESTE

**Bariloche Panama Via
Argentina Apartments**
+34-695-097-612 +34-695-097-
612
Paul

99 – 165 $US EP
16 rooms, 16 pb
C-yes/S-no/P-no/H-no
Spanish, English

Meals can be prepared at an extra
cost.
Living-room, dining-room, bathroom,
fully equipped kitchen, cable TV,
Internet & WiFi, queen bed, walk-in
closet, air-conditioning, 24h security,
daily cleaning

*Just a walk away from main avenues, the business district, the center, the best clubs in town, and the
best restaurants, Bariloche is located in the heart of dynamic Panama City, Via Argentina.*

✉ paub@barcelona-guide.info 🌐 panama-apartment.com

PANAMA CITY

The Balboa Inn
+507-6618-4414 +507-3141-520
Saskia Swartz & Thorwald
Westmaas

75 – 105 $US BB
9 rooms, 9 pb
Visa, MC, *Rated*, •
C-yes/S-ltd/P-yes/H-no
English, Spanish, Dutch,
German

Full breakfast
Early departure breakfast (5–7 a.m),
vegetarian b.
Private bathrooms, WiFi, satellite TV,
A/C, ceiling fans, big covered terrace,
gardens, airport pickup, taxi service or
a trusted private driver

*The Balboa Inn sits at the foot of Panama's landmark, Ancon Hill & is one of the most frequently rated
B&B's. In a quiet residential & very safe area between downtown, Amador Causeway Casco Viejo &
just minutes from the domestic airport & Panama Canal.*

✉ innkeepers@thebalboainn.com 🌐 www.thebalboainn.com/lanier

Casa Las Americas
866-573-8588 +507-3997-783
Ron Griffith

60 – 105 $US BB
6 rooms, 4 pb
Visa, MC, *Rated*
C-yes/S-ltd/P-no/H-ltd
English, Spanish

Full breakfast
A/C, cable TV, WiFi, free phone
calls to US/Canada, TWO customer
computer areas available, common
room with cable TV/DVD, safe, child
care services, laundry, free parking

*Gorgeous large home in a quiet and peaceful setting, tropical plants surround a large swimming pool,
short distance from restaurants, and business districts, our inn is economical but ideal for tourists,
business travelers and retirees*

✉ mail@casalasamericas.com 🌐 www.casalasamericas.com

Cerrito Tropical
+507-6489-0074
Cynthia Mulder

75 – 130 $US BB
7 rooms, 7 pb
Visa, MC, *Rated*, •
C-yes/S-ltd/P-ltd/H-no
Spanish, English, Dutch
(not onsite)

Full breakfast
Chef & full menu: local, seafood &
international
A/C, ceiling fans, fridge, beach & bath
towels, WiFi, DVD's, books, tropical
garden, patio, gazebo, ocean view
balcony, bath amenities, special
events, small weddings

*B&B Inn Cerrito Tropical is a small hotel on Taboga Island near Panama City. A natural place to
spend your tropical beach holiday. Perched on a quiet hillside, ocean view backed by rain forest &
mango trees, walk to the beach, or relax in the hammock.*

✉ info@cerritotropicalpanama.com 🌐 www.cerritotropicalpanama.com

Peru
LIMA

D'osma Bed & Breakfast	42 – 50 $US BB	Full breakfast
Lima	5 rooms, 4 pb	Hot drinks available 24/7
646-340-3830 +511-251-4178	C-yes/S-ltd/P-no/H-ltd	Internet WiFi available in all the
Francisco Gonzalez	English, Spanish	house.

D'osma B&B is located in Lima Peru, in the artistic area of Barranco, one of the best areas near the ocean. We offer 5 rooms for our guests, giving a personal touch that you can't find elsewhere. Here you can find all you need, with the best quality.

✉ reservas@deosma.com 🌐 www.deosma.com

Portugal
VIANA DO CASTELO

Casa Santa Filomena	50 – 60 € BB	Continental breakfast
+351-25-898-1619	5 rooms, 4 pb	Beverages & snacks
+351-22-617-4161	*Rated*	Sitting room, lounge, Sat-TV, A/C, bar,
Mary Kendall	C-yes/S-ltd/P-no/H-no	gardens, parking
	Portuguese	

Casa Santa Filomena, a solid stonewalled building, a renovated farmhouse that was built in the 1920s, tucked away into a quiet corner of an already quiet village between the hills and seaside.

✉ soc.com.smiths@mail.telepac.pt

St. Lucia
MARIGOT BAY

Mango Beach Inn	120 – 160 $US BB	Continental breakfast
758-458-3188	4 rooms, 4 pb	Drinks, snacks, kid's meals, coffee &
Judith Verity	Visa, MC, *Rated*, •	tea in room
	C-yes/S-ltd/P-no/H-no	Pool & sundeck, WiFi, books & board
	English, French, (some)	games, babysitting service, highchair,
	German	beach toys & towels, wedding service.

Historic waterfront B&B in tranquil tropical gardens, pool, sundeck, private dock, 1 minute to sandy, swimming & watersport beach, nearby marina, restaurants, bars, bakery, live music, shopping, hiking, sailing on the most beautiful bay in the Caribbean.

✉ judithverity@yahoo.co.uk 🌐 www.mangobeachmarigot.com/default.html

SOUFRIERE

La Haut Resort	100 – 250 $US BB	Full breakfast
758-459-7008	15 rooms, 15 pb	Tea, coffee & fresh fruit in season in
Stephanie Allain	Visa, MC, *Rated*, •	room daily
	C-yes/S-yes/P-no/H-yes	2 outdoor pools (including an Infinity),
	English, Patois, Danish,	gardens, lounge with snooker table &
	Italian, Spanish	piano, library w/ books & magazines,
		shuttle to town & beach at fixed times,
		beach towels

Magical views; warm & friendly staff; tours arranged; tasty, healthy and well priced food; two swimming pools; near island's main nature activities; take a step back in time; relax, unwind, enjoy the peace and serenity of the Caribbean country.

✉ lahaut@candw.lc 🌐 www.lahaut.com

Scotland, U.K.

ARGYLL

Taychreggan Hotel	118 – 283 £ BB	Full breakfast
+44-186-683-3211	18 rooms, 18 pb	Five course table d'hotel dinner £45.00
Fiona Sutherland	Visa, MC, AmEx,	per person
	Rated, •	Games room, lounge, loch fishing, bar,
	C-yes/S-no/P-ltd/H-no	free parking
	English,	
	February to December	

Top Scottish country house hotel. Beautifully situated amid the mountains and forests of Argyll on the shores of Loch Awe. Stylish and comfortable accommodations with hospitality including fine dining and a superb wine list.

✉ info@taychregganhotel.co.uk ◐ www.taychregganhotel.co.uk

EDINBURGH

Bouviere Bed and	80 – 120 £ BB	Full breakfast
Breakfast	4 rooms, 4 pb	Private garden, small groups, families,
+44-131-556-5080	Visa, MC	convenient to city centre, luggage
Cassie & Archie	C-yes/S-ltd/P-ltd/H-no	storage

The house is homely, but stylish, with a touch of class and the owners, Archie and Cassie Bouverie and Sam their housekeeper, will do everything they can to be helpful and informative. It is run in as relaxed a way as possible.

✉ bouverie@ednet.co.uk ◐ www.edinburghbedandbreakfast.co.uk

South Africa

BAKOVEN

Ocean View House	670 – 3800 RAD BB	Breakfast Buffet
+27 (0) 21-438-1982	16 rooms, 16 pb	Coffee & tea, in-room minibar
General Manager	Visa, MC, AmEx	Air-conditioning, minibar, safe, satellite
	C-yes/S-no/P-no/H-no	TV, hairdryer & robes, kettle for tea
		& coffee, broadband WiFi Internet,
		beach towels, cradles/cots, parking
		lots

Revel in the calm and peace of Ocean View House. Assimilate with the unique African sunset and unobstructed views of the Atlantic Ocean from your very own balcony. Prepare yourself for an exceptional bed and breakfast experience.

✉ info@oceanview-house.com ◐ www.oceanview-house.com

SOMERSET WEST

Remus House	95 – 120 $US BB	Full breakfast
+27 (0) 21-851-9938	3 rooms, 3 pb	Tea, coffee, cold drinks from mini-
Viktoria Dietrich	Disc, •	fridge
	C-yes/S-no/P-no/H-no	Twin beds, air conditioning, en-suite
	German, English	bathroom with shower, German and
		South African Sat-TV, CD & DVD
		Player, wireless Internet, kitchen w/
		stove, fridge, cutlery for 8

Located on a hill of the Hottentots Holland mountains, Remus House lies in a calm, safe residential area in Somerset West, near Cape Town close to beach and winelands from the terrace a fantastic view is offered of False Bay, Table Mountain and Cape Town

✉ info@remushouse.co.za ◐ www.remushouse.co.za

Spain

BARCELONA

Aparthotel Silver Barcelona +34-932-189100 Ignasi Junyent	69- 99 € EP 49 rooms, 49 pb Visa, MC, AmEx, *Rated*, • C-yes/S-no/P-no/H-yes Spanish, English, Italian, French	Wide range of restaurants of all types nearby Heating, A/C, direct phone, TV, safe, Café & Bar, private garden, room service, laundry service, parking, Free WiFi , 24hr reception, some rooms with balcony

Aparthotel Silver is one of the most highly recommended Barcelona hotels, with 49 well appointed rooms. Guests enjoy a pleasant stay thanks to constant improvements and the fact that we offer a range of hospitality, comforts and services.

✉ reservations@hotelsilver.com   🌐 www.hotelsilver.com

Barcelona Las Ramblas Apartments +34-695-097612 Paul & Raquel	25 – 35 € EP 10 rooms, 10 pb Most CC, *Rated*, • C-yes/S-ltd/P-no/H-no English, Svenska	Breakfast is available, not included in price Living room, private balcony, free use of kitchen, bed linens & towels, VAT included

Cozy apartment located in the center of Barcelona near Rambla Catalunya and Passeig de Gracia.

✉ barcelonaguesthouse@yahoo.com

Barcino 147 Bed and Breakfast +34-607-379101 Ferran	85 – 160 € BB 12 rooms, 4 pb Visa, MC, *Rated*, • C-yes/S-no/P-no/H-no English, Spanish, Catalan	Continental breakfast TV, DVD, iPod audio system, laundry, secure building with porter, use of kitchen, coffee, Espresso, tours, hair dryer, iron, wireless Internet, air conditioning

Come and enjoy Barcelona in the comfort of our classically stylish bed and breakfast. Located in the heart of the city, our spacious apartment has been beautifully renovated and furnished with local art and antiques.

✉ barcino147@yahoo.com   🌐 www.barcino147.com/index.php

COIN

Hotel Restaurant Santa Fe +34-952-452916 Marije Veugen & Jaap Schaafsma	60 – 70 € BB 3 rooms, 3 pb Visa, MC, *Rated* C-yes/S-ltd/P-no/H-no Spanish, English, Dutch	Continental breakfast A/C, en suite baths, shower rooms, mellow terracotta floors, authentic beamed ceilings, stunning views, fine dining, fragrant gardens, terrace, relaxed style, comfortable

Santa Fe is one of Andalusia's hidden gems; a boutique hotel and restaurant set in a magical restored nineteenth century finial, conveniently situated on the outskirts of the town of Coin.

✉ info@santafe-hotel.com   🌐 www.santafe-hotel.com

CUENCA

Posada De San Jose +34-969-211300 Antonio & Jennifer Cortinas	28 – 157 € EP 31 rooms, 22 pb Most CC, *Rated*, • C-yes/S-yes/P-yes/H-no English, French, Spanish	Continental buffet breakfast 9 € Home made tapas and regional dishes in the evening Bar service, sitting room, terrace & garden, Afternoon Coffee, regional tapas, light suppers available, TV in all rooms with full bath

The Posada de San Jose is situated in the heart of the old historic quarter of Cuenca, in a 17th Century Building. Its old portal invites you to admire the views. Enjoy the advantage of being within a stone's throw of all major monuments, galleries, etc.

✉ info@posadasanjose.com   🌐 www.posadasanjose.com

Tell your hosts Pamela Lanier sent you.

GRANADA

Bed & Breakfast Granada Homestay +34-655-029867 Victor Ovies	40 & Up € BB 4 rooms, 2 pb Visa, MC, *Rated* C-ltd/S-no/P-no/H-no Spanish, French, Portuguese, Italian, English	Self service, any time, no schedule Free WiFi in rooms, fridge & tea & coffee making facilities in rooms, Granada guides in up to 7 languages, free exclusive customized map of Granada

A welcoming B&B right in the center of Granada, Spain. Close to everything and connected by direct bus to the Airport and Bus Station. 10 minute walk from the Railway Station. Your hosts will provide you with local information on sights and eating.

✉ victorovies@hotmail.com   🌐 www.granadahomestay.com

El Numero 8 – Traveler House +34-958-220682 Rafael Kotcherha-Campora	50 – 65 € EP 4 rooms, 4 pb Visa, MC, *Rated* C-ltd/S-ltd/P-ltd/H-no Spanish, English	Honesty bar in patio area Laundry facilities, private kitchens, rooftop terrace, honesty bar, self-catered units

Individual apartments in the historical Albayzin neighborhood of Granada. Great prices for the quality. This area of Granada has narrow winding cobblestone streets and is very peaceful as no cars are allowed.

✉ casaocho@gmail.com   🌐 www.elnumero8.com

MADRID

Camino de Soto +34-667-441351 Juan Carlos & Ian	60 – 110 € BB 3 rooms, 1 pb • C-ltd/S-ltd/P-ltd/H-yes English, Spanish	Full breakfast Dinner available upon request Pool, garden, sitting room, stunning views, surrounded by natural beauty

Whether you choose to relax by the pool and take in the spectacular views of the Madrid mountains, or explore the surrounding countryside and famous cultural and historic sites, Camino de Soto is your home away from home.

✉ reservations@caminodesoto.com   🌐 www.caminodesoto.com

Casa de Madrid +34-915-595791 Marta Medina	199 – 399 € BB 7 rooms, 7 pb Most CC, • C-ltd/S-yes/P-yes/H-ltd English, Spanish, Italian, French, Portuguese	Continental breakfast Full healthy breakfast, private lunch or dinner Wifi, Library, Sitting Room, Airport transfers, Private and tailor made tours, Restaurant bookings, Opera tickets

Casa de Madrid is a luxury boutique guesthouse that offers a unique and special experience. Located in front of Madrid's Royal opera house, it's a perfect option for a honeymoon, a romantic gift or to simply spend a few days enjoying the best of Madrid.

✉ infomadrid@casademadrid.com   🌐 www.casademadrid.com

PINOS DEL VALLE

Casa Aire de Lecrin +34-958-793937 Ane-Muriel Bazin	55 – 60 € BB 6 rooms, 6 pb Most CC, *Rated* C-yes/S-no/P-yes/H-yes Spanish, French, English	Continental breakfast Dinners & picnic baskets by prior arrangement Daily room cleaning, fireplaces, wood stove, balconies, TV, games, roof terrace, pool

In the heart of the wonderful Lecrin Valley in the picturesque village of Pinos del Valle, we have now opened a rare old house which offers accommodation and breakfast.

✉ contact@casa-aire-de-lecrin.com   🌐 www.casa-aire-de-lecrin.com

PRIEGO DE CORDOBA

Casa Olea	79 – 99 € BB	Continental plus breakfast
+34-696-748209	6 rooms, 6 pb	Fresh, seasonal, home-cooked evening
Claire & Tim Murray-Walker	Visa, MC	meals
	C-yes/S-no/P-no/H-yes	Egyptian cotton bedding, super-
	Spanish, English	king beds, cozy lounge with log fire,
		swimming pool, sun terrace, mountain
		bike rental, helpful advice for day trips
		to Granada & Cordoba

Casa Olea is an idyllic luxury B&B in the heart of Andalucia. Half-way between Granada and Cordoba it is ideal for visits to the Alhambra and Mezquita. A traditional Andalucian farmhouse with indulgent touches, 100% renewable energy and hot water.

 info@casaolea.com 🌎 www.casaolea.com

SIURANA D'EMPORDA

El Moli	80 – 100 € BB	Full breakfast
+34-972-525139	6 rooms, 6 pb	Evening meal offered for added cost
Maria Pages	Visa, MC, *Rated*	Private baths, balconies, living area,
	C-ltd/S-no/P-ltd/H-no	terrace, dinner served nightly, farm
	Spanish, English,	stay, spacious with comfortable king
	French	beds, new massage services.

This Catalan B&B is situated in the center of Alt Empordà, in the Girona province, (Spain) set in a rural atmosphere and close to Costa Brava and Cap de Creus. The house is surrounded by a large garden, full of trees, on the banks of the Siurana Brook.

✉ casaelmoli@hotmail.com 🌎 www.elmolidesiurana.com

Switzerland

ADELBODEN

Boutique Hotel Beau-Site	85 – 180 CHF BB	Breakfast Buffet
Fitness & Spa	36 rooms, 36 pb	Two restaurants offering snacks or fine
+41-33-673-8282	Visa, MC, *Rated*, •	dining
Markus Luder	C-yes/S-ltd/P-ltd/H-ltd	Bath or shower, most with balcony
	German, English,	and/or safe, hairdryer, cable TV,
	French, Italian	phone, mini bar, tea & coffee-maker,
		spa with sauna/steam bath, garden
		sauna, fitness studio

Located just 40 minutes from Interlaken. The Hotel Beau-Site in the Bernese Highlands provides a rare opportunity to enjoy life to the fullest. A special hotel in a special setting which is breath taking and beautiful all year round.

✉ info@hotelbeausite.ch 🌎 www.hotelbeausite.ch

INTERLAKEN

Hotel Rugenpark-B&B	52 – 200 CHF BB	Hearty Swiss breakfast buffet
Interlaken	21 rooms, 10 pb	Free coffee & tea, self-service guest
+41-33-822-3661	Visa, MC, *Rated*	kitchen
Ursula Grossniklaus & Chris	C-yes/S-no/P-yes/H-no	Free wireless, Internet station, booking
Ewald	German, French,	office for excursions and adventure
	Spanish, English	activities, guest kitchen, English book
		exchange, lovely garden, free parking,
		guest laundry

Interlaken Switzerland's top rated B&B accommodation with free Internet, free wireless LAN, guest kitchen, laundry facilities, excellent personal service, clean and cozy rooms, lovely garden, a huge breakfast buffet and all at low budget hostel rates.

 info@rugenpark.ch 🌎 www.rugenpark.ch

INTERLAKEN

Swiss-Inn Apartments +41-33-822-3626 J. P. & Veronica Mueller	85 – 160 $US EP 9 rooms, 9 pb Visa, MC, AmEx, *Rated* C-yes/S-ltd/P-no/H-no English	Complimentary coffee & tea in room TV, balconies, wireless Internet, laundromat, A/C in Apartments, fireplace, free parking, relaxing garden, childrens' playground

Located in a quiet residential area, owned and operated by the Family Müller-Lohner, just a three minute walk to the train station, and the center of town. The Swiss Inn has been renovated several times and now offers five apartments and four rooms

✉ info@swiss-inn.ch 🌐 www.swiss-inn.ch

LES PLEIADES

Les Sapins Hotel **Restaurant** +41-21-943-1395 Mirek & Agnès Mazur	100 -220 CHF BB 15 rooms, 5 pb Visa, MC, *Rated*, • C-yes/S-no/P-ltd/H-yes French, English, German, Spanish, Polish	Buffet Breakfast Halfboard or a la carte dinner and/or lunch Jacuzzi, sauna, snowshoe & mountain bike rentals, safe, TV, WiFi, bathrobes, cheese fondues, cooking with wild plants (May-Sep), Agnes has recipes on request

Les Sapins at Lally offers wonderful views from its beautiful setting nestled on a mountainside. High up in the alpine meadowlands above Lake Geneva, this hotel and restaurant offers the best of Swiss hospitality and cuisine at reasonable prices.

✉ info@les-sapins.ch 🌐 www.les-sapins.ch

MONTREUX-VEYTAUX

Hotel Masson +41-21-966-0044 Mrs. Anne-Marie Sevegrand	200 – 280 CHF BB 31 rooms, 31 pb MostCC, Cash, *Rated*, • C-yes/S-ltd/P-yes/H-no French, German, English March through end of October	Continental breakfast Restaurant, dinner, afternoon tea, bar service Sitting room, Jacuzzi, sauna, garden, mini bar, safe, lounge, direct dial phone, cable TV, radio alarm clock, two romantic lounges, alps & lake view terrace, parking, WiFi

This pleasant hotel, 31 rooms (60 beds) is the oldest in Montreux, dating from 1829. Hotel Masson is situated near famous Chillon Castle, close to the lake, the woods, just 20 minutes walk from the center of Montreux along the lakeside promenade.

✉ hotelmasson@bluewin.ch 🌐 www.hotelmasson.ch

REGENSBERG

Rote Rose +41-44-853-1013 Christina Schaefer	220 – 410 CHF BB 8 rooms, 8 pb MC, *Rated*, • C-ltd/S-no/P-no/H-no English, German, French, Italian	Continental breakfast Afternoon tea, snacks Kitchens & sitting rooms, en-suites, rose gardens, art gallery, swimming pool

The Rote Rose is an elegant country inn set in a fully restored ancient building. The spacious, antique-filled suites with superb views and a beautiful rose garden are located in the unspoiled medieval village of Regensberg. ✉ info@rote-rose.com 🌐 www.rote-rose.com

RICHTERSWIL

B&B Villa Magnolia **Richterswil** +41-44-784-3964 Lonny Jeszenszky	150 – 250 CHF BB 4 rooms, 4 pb Visa, MC, AmEx, *Rated*, • C-yes/S-no/P-yes/H-no German, English, French, Italian Closed mid-Feb-mid- Aug, mid-Sept-mid-Dec	Rich Continental Breakfast Buffet On advance order: Five O'Clock Tea Credit cards via PayPal only – living room, tea kitchen, non-smoking house, quiet rooms, garden/gazebo, high- speed Internet, bathrobes, hairdryer, sauna, radio, TV/DVD

Romantic "Hotel de Charme" en miniature near downtown Zurich, a cozy hideaway and small luxury world designed with love. Calm garden with Mediterranean flair, 3 min. walk from the lake and train station. ✉ villa-magnolia-richterswil@bluewin.ch 🌐 villa-magnolia.ch/index

ZURICH

Claridge Hotel Zurich	220 – 450 CHF EP	Breakfast buffet 29 CHF
+41-44-267-8787	31 rooms, 31 pb	Market fresh local & Mediterranean
Mr. Beat R. Blumer	Visa, MC, AmEx,	cuisine
	Rated, •	Trendy Lounge & Bar, terrace, parking,
	C-yes/S-ltd/P-yes/H-no	computer workstation in every room
	English, French,	with free high-speed Internet, TV,
	German, Spanish,	radio, coffee & tea facilities, WLan
	Italian, Chinese	
	Closed Christmas &	
	New Year	

The Claridge Hotel Zurich is perfectly located right in the city center, yet very quiet, near theaters & the museum of fine art. Within walking distance to Lake Zurich and all of the city's main attractions, shopping, business districts, and hospitals.

✉ info@claridge.ch 🌐 www.claridge.ch

Dakini's Bed & Breakfast	75 – 80 $US BB	Continental breakfast
+41-44-291-4220	7 rooms	Digital TV, wireless Internet, laundry
Susanne G. Seiler	*Rated*	facilities, communal kitchen,
	C-yes/S-no/P-ltd/H-no	hairdryer, towels & sheets, all rooms
	German, English,	are non-smoking
	French, Italian, Dutch	

Dakini's B&B is located 7 minutes from Zurich Main Station in a young, green and trendy neighborhood with lovely old houses. The inner city and the lake are within walking distance.

✉ sleep@dakini.ch 🌐 www.dakini.ch

Palais Kraft	330 – 490 CHF BB	Continental breakfast buffet
+41-44-388- 8485	3 rooms, 3 pb	Complimentary veggie snacks & soft
Martin Frank	MostCC, Cash,	drinks
	Rated, •	Coffee maker, express checkout, local
	C-yes/S-no/P-yes/H-yes	calls, parking, hairdryers, laundry/
	German, English,	valet services, mini bar, room service,
	French, Italian, Thai	safe deposit box, sauna, Internet, voice
		mail

The Palais Kraft is a neo-classical mansion in Zurich's prime residential area "Zurichberg" (tram stop "Toblerplatz").

✉ welcome@palaiskraft.com 🌐 www.palaiskraft.com

Tortola BVI

ROAD TOWN

Fort Recovery Beachfront	210 – 5200 $US BB	Coffee, tea, breads, jams
Villa & Suites Hotel	32 rooms, 32 pb	Full American breakfast offered &
800-367-8455 284-495-4467	Visa, MC, AmEx,	dinner daily
Anita Macshane Cottoy	*Rated*, •	Sitting room, library, swimming pool,
	C-yes/S-ltd/P-no/H-yes	private beach, mini spa, WiFi, historic
	English, Spanish	Fort, restaurant

Fort Recovery Resort is located on the calm, Caribbean side of the island where cooling trade winds give us constant breezes. This unique, villa hotel provides an intimate and fantastic Caribbean vacation experience, with resort conveniences.

✉ ftrhotel@surfbvi.com 🌐 www.fortrecovery.com/tortola

Trinidad / Tobago

MARAVAL

Monique's Guest House 868-628-2351 868-628-3334 Monica Charbonne	90 – 108 $US EP 20 rooms, 20 pb Visa, MC, *Rated*, • C-yes/S-yes/P-no/H-yes English	Restaurant has breakfast daily (lunch by request) Pink Anthurium Restaurant & Bar, I-Net, daily maid service, laundry, iron/board, microwave w/kitchenette rooms, coffee & tea facilities w/ standard rooms

Though small, our accommodation compares with multinational hotels, combined with personalized attention, and a homey atmosphere.

✉ info@moniquestrinidad.com   🌐 www.moniquestrinidad.com

Turkey

ISTANBUL

Almina Hotel Istanbul +90-212-638-3800 Sinan Koksal	50 – 150 € BB 29 rooms, 29 pb Visa, MC, AmEx, *Rated*, • C-yes/S-no/P-no/H-no Turkish, English	Buffet Breakfast Ararat Restaurant A/C, direct dial phones, LCD SAT-TV, hairdryer, WiFi, minibar, concierge services, health club, room safe, Turkish Bath (Hamam), sauna, steamroom & lounge, bar/lounge

Almina Hotel is located in the most ancient part of central Istanbul with 29 rooms as a four star luxury boutique hotel. The Hotel has started to serve high quality service and accommodation comfort and familiar environment in 2009 again.

✉ info@alminahotel.com.tr   🌐 www.alminahotel.com.tr

Terrace Guesthouse +90-212-638-9733 Dogan Yildirim	69 – 88 € BB 8 rooms, 8 pb MostCC, Cash, *Rated* C-yes/S-no/P-yes/H-no English, Turkish	Full breakfast Wake-up calls & air transport available, A/C, sea views, direct phone, mini-bar, colorful Turkish carpets

The Terrace Guest House in the Old City section of Istanbul, offers a home-away-from-home feeling. Many changes since my family started welcoming guests many years ago, but one thing hasn't changed – our legendary Turkish hospitality. Come join us!

✉ support@terracehotelistanbul.com   🌐 www.terracehotelistanbul.com

SULTANAHMET

Deniz Houses Hotel +90-212-518-9595 Mr. Kerem Benligil	35 – 80 € BB 27 rooms, 27 pb Visa, MC C-yes/S-no/P-no/H-ltd German, English	Open Buffet Breakfast A/C, double glazed windows, mini bar, hairdryer, LCD SAT-TV, phone

Deniz Houses -The Sea Mansion- An elegant & traditional Bed and Breakfast with panoramic views over the sea and Blue Mosque & only 10 minutes walk to Sultanahmet imperial city center. 27 comfortable en-suite rooms decorated with traditional fabrics.

✉ info@denizhouses.com   🌐 www.denizhouses.com

Naz Wooden House Inn +90-212-516-7130 Aslý DurmuÞ	40 – 100 € BB 7 rooms, 7 pb Visa, MC C-yes/S-no/P-no/H-ltd English	Continental breakfast Tea, coffee & orange juice Private bathroom Free WiFi Minibar Airport transfers Phone in rooms

An important detail distinguishing NAZ from other wooden houses is that it also contains the remains of an older building made of stone which dates back to the 8th century. Naz Wooden House is a small attractive hotel in the heart of old Istanbul.

✉ reservation@nazwoodenhouseinn.com   🌐 www.nazwoodenhouseinn.com